Economics

Principles for a Changing World

4th edition

Economics
Principles for a Changing World

Eric P. Chiang
Florida Atlantic University

worth publishers
Macmillan Learning
New York

Vice President, Social Sciences: CHARLES LINSMEIER
Publisher: SHANI FISHER
Acquisitions Editor: TOM DIGIANO
Editorial Assistant: COURTNEY LINDWALL
Marketing Assistant: MORGAN RATNER
Senior Development Editor: BRUCE KAPLAN
Director, Content Management Enhancement: TRACEY KUEHN
Managing Editor: LISA KINNE
Media Editor: LINDSAY NEFF
Media Producer: ANDREW VACCARO
Photo Editor: CHRISTINE BUESE
Photo Researcher: DONNA RANIERI
Director of Design, Content Management: DIANA BLUME
Senior Design Manager: VICKI TOMASELLI
Cover Designer: PAULA JO SMITH
Interior Text Designer: AMANDA KAVANAGH
Senior Project Editor: JODI ISMAN
Art Manager: MATTHEW MCADAMS
Illustrations: ELI ENSOR
Production Manager: STACEY B. ALEXANDER
Composition: MPS LIMITED
Printing and Binding: LSC COMMUNICATIONS
Cover Photos: TSHOOTER/SHUTTERSTOCK (AIRPLANE WINDOW); ANTON BALAZH/SHUTTERSTOCK (EARTH IMAGE)
Back Cover Photo: IZABELA HABUR/ISTOCKPHOTO

Library of Congress Control Number: 2016931970

ISBN-13: 978-1-4641-8666-0
ISBN-10: 1-4641-8666-9

First printing

Printed in the United States of America

Worth Publishers
One New York Plaza
Suite 4500
New York, NY 10004-1562
www.macmillanlearning.com

To John and Tina Chiang:
my parents, who instilled in me a work
ethic that allowed me to pursue endless
opportunities

Tribute to Jerry Stone

Jerry Stone long-believed that the best principles of economics textbooks are authored by people invested in their students' classroom experience. The decisions made in the shaping of the first several editions of *CoreEconomics* were educated by Jerry's thirty-plus years in the classroom. The foundation of this edition is a testament to Jerry's accomplishment: a book envisioned, designed, and executed to be the principles of economics book that teaches better than any other textbook on the market.

Jerry had a remarkable career as a longtime teacher at Metropolitan State University of Denver and as an author of two successful principles of economics textbooks. Those who knew Jerry miss his steadfast commitment to the teaching of economics, a legacy that lives on in each new edition of *Economics: Principles for a Changing World*. Jerry Stone passed away after a difficult battle with cancer in August of 2010.

about the author

Eric P. Chiang received his bachelor's degree in economics from the University of Nevada Las Vegas, and his master's and doctorate in economics from the University of Florida. His first academic position was at New Mexico State University. Currently, Eric is an associate professor and graduate director of the Department of Economics at Florida Atlantic University. Eric also serves as the director of instructional technology for the College of Business.

In 2009 Eric was the recipient of Florida Atlantic University's highest teaching honor, the Distinguished Teacher of the Year Award. Among numerous other teaching awards, he also was named the Stewart Distinguished Professor at the College of Business. He has written approximately thirty articles in peer-reviewed journals on a range of subjects, including technology spillovers, intellectual property rights, telecommunications, and health care. His research has appeared in leading journals, including the *Review of Economics and Statistics, Journal of Technology Transfer*, and *Southern Economic Journal*. He is a frequent presenter at major economics conferences and at universities across the country and around the world.

As an instructor who teaches both face-to-face and online courses, Eric uses a variety of technological tools, including clickers, Web-based polling, lecture capture, and homework management systems to complement his active-learning-style lectures. As an administrator in the College of Business, Eric's role as director of instructional technology involves assisting instructors with effectively implementing classroom technologies. In this position, Eric also ensures that the quality of online courses meets accreditation standards, including those set by the Association to Advance Collegiate Schools of Business (AACSB).

In addition to his dedication to teaching economic principles and his administrative duties, Eric devotes time to new research in economic education. His current research focuses on student learning outcomes in economics education based on the different methods of instruction in use today.

The fourth edition of *Economics: Principles for a Changing World* embodies Eric's devotion to economics education and the benefits of adapting to the new, often creative ways in which students learn and instructors teach.

In his spare time, Eric enjoys studying cultures and languages, and travels frequently. He has visited all fifty U.S. states, many of them to run half-marathons, and over eighty countries, and enjoys long jogs and walks when he travels in order to experience local life to the fullest.

Vision and Story of Economics

Economics is a way of looking at the world and understanding how and why it's changing.

Every time I teach principles of economics, I keep in mind that many of my students are learning about economics for the first time, and how they perceive my course may influence their perceptions of economics for a long time. This was a guiding notion in the first edition of *CoreEconomics* and continues with this fourth edition, renamed *Economics: Principles for a Changing World*. Why the change in title?

The fourth edition still represents the "core" of economic principles. But it also provides students with a global perspective on how economic problems are addressed, an appreciation of data and how data are used, and the application of technology. I believe that such an approach is best suited to the changing world we live in.

Instructors and students face two sets of problems with each principles of economics class. Instructors ask, "How many students can we reach today? Can we reach each one?" Students constantly ask, "How does this affect *my* life?"

I have taught over 15,000 students since 2001—in small classrooms, large auditoriums, online classes, day classes, evening classes, and even overseas. The diversity of my students has provided abundant examples of learning by experience. Each setting provides a laboratory for using innovative teaching techniques and technologies to motivate students to appreciate the endless possibilities that thinking like an economist can provide.

The challenge, of course, is reaching each and every student. This challenge is made especially difficult by the sheer amount of information now available to students and subsequently by the increasing number of ways in which students learn.

Part of the work on this edition and the last one actually led me to consider active learning methodologies. Instructors often encourage or even require students to read their textbook prior to the related lecture. If students do, class time can be used more effectively to refine the knowledge. The problem is that students often don't read the book ahead of class.

When I started doing research on this, I eventually came to the conclusion that using a textbook in such a way may not be all that effective, and I instead was inspired to create FlipItEcon along with my co-author José Vázquez. The textbook and its technology obviously still play a critical role in learning, but they may be better suited to providing deeper understanding *after* the lecture. This edition was created with that active learning objective in mind. Each chapter contains a wealth of vivid examples, intuitive explanations, and visuals to help build a more comprehensive understanding of concepts.

It's no longer enough to write a good or even great textbook. The book is just one avenue for delivering information when students are accustomed to consuming information from so many different sources. To reach students, it's now essential to deliver information in a variety of formats beyond the textbook or even the lecture itself. I've thus worked with Worth Publishers to develop each of the elements of technology for *Economics: Principles for a Changing World*, so it is much more of an effective teaching tool for instructors.

—Eric P. Chiang

Principles for a Changing World

Developed by Eric Chiang's experiences teaching thousands of students around the world.

Today's students are bombarded by information from many sources. To apply economic thinking to this constant flow of data, students must recognize differences in perspective. The most effective instructors are flexible, using different channels and methods to present information from different economic perspectives. *Economics: Principles for a Changing World* is designed to give you the tools to do so.

Technology as a Tool for Success

Students are accustomed to using technology to learn, just as modern economists use technology for research. It stands to reason that the technology portion of this fourth edition should be just as integral as the textbook itself.

- **FlipItEcon** The only system designed for pre-lecture and ideal for active learning. **Eric Chiang** is the only principles author to have also authored an online learning system.

- **LaunchPad** Groundbreaking homework system created as part of the fourth edition, with content from the author and used in his own classes.

- **CourseTutor** The most comprehensive study guide in economics, now in a digital format within LaunchPad and tied to Chiang's signature author videos.

Data Literacy

Data can be used to support any number of stories. *By the Numbers* features and their accompanying exercises focus on helping students to read and understand data, instilling a critical eye to the data presented in daily life.

Global Perspective

Most principles texts simply seek to provide an international context for economic principles. The *Around the World* features help students recognize that people all over the world are faced with many of the same economic problems, yet seek to solve these challenges in different ways.

WHAT'S NEW IN THE FOURTH EDITION?

Three themes integrated in every chapter with By the Numbers infographics, Around the World features, and LaunchPad activity callouts.

Expanded video program with an author video for every chapter, including new coverage of **health care** and the Affordable Care Act.

A complete revision of sustainability coverage in Chapter 13, "Externalities and Public Goods."

New coverage of the central importance of economic growth in Chapter 18, "Economic Growth."

Rethinking the Connection Between Author, Text, and Technology

FlipItEcon FlipItEcon.com

Throughout his academic career, Eric Chiang has conducted a great deal of research on pedagogy in economic education. Much of this research has focused on increasing student retention and engagement, which inspired him to create FlipItEcon along with co-author José Vázquez. Although FlipItEcon can be used with any combination of textbook and resources, it's an ideal solution for *Economics,* Fourth Edition, instructors simply looking to better prepare their students for class time and "flip" their level of engagement.

Ordinarily, textbooks are developed by first writing chapters, then making decisions about art and images, and finally assembling a test bank and ancillaries. Eric Chiang writes the text, develops the visual program, and assembles the resources for the homework system at the same time. These threads come together for a complete learning program, with every element integrated by the author himself.

1. Animated **prelecture** tutorials provide a base-level understanding of core economic topics before students ever "set foot" in a class.

   - Straightforward animations provide information in an engaging format without distraction.
   - Information is "chunked" into short, easily remembered segments.
   - Embedded questions and a pacing system put learning in the students' hands.

2. **Bridge** questions are designed to inform an instructor of students' level of understanding before lecture as well as lead to discussion, review, use of iClickers, or another activity during lecture. They "bridge" prelecture time to lecture time.

   - Students first answer a question designed to either be open-ended, address a typical misconception, or otherwise lead to further discussion in the lecture.
   - Students then must explain the rationale behind their answer, allowing the instructor a deep level of insight into their understanding.

Once students have completed the Prelectures and Bridges, an instructor can assign Problems as either practice or post-class homework.

   - Each unit has between 30–50 Problems, and all non-definitional problems include video feedback provided by the author himself.

LaunchPad features the most author-driven and text-specific content of any integrated homework system available. In this edition, you will find exciting changes to **LaunchPad**, including a collection of new activities designed to augment in-chapter content and features to support student learning.

LaunchPad for *Economics: Principles for a Changing World*, Fourth Edition, includes:

- **Complete e-Book**

- **Pre-built Units** Offer instructors and students ready-made units for study with **LearningCurve** quizzes, e-Book pages, tutorials, and graded homework for every chapter. Units are flexible and easy to adapt or expand to suit individual preferences.

- NEW! **Expanded Author Videos** This hugely popular feature now provides concise and engaging explanations for nearly every chapter along with assessment, including new coverage of health care and the Affordable Care Act.

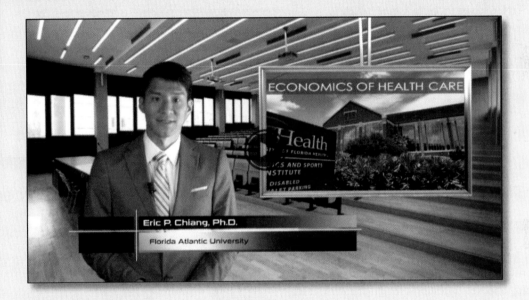

Eric P. Chiang, Ph.D.
Florida Atlantic University

- NEW! **Digitized CourseTutor** One of the most notable features of *CoreEconomics* from its first edition, the CourseTutor study guide has now been brought into **LaunchPad** as part of the course units.

LearningCurve: Adaptive, formative quizzing, **LearningCurve**'s game-like quizzing motivates each student to engage with the course, and reporting tools help teachers get a handle on what their class needs. Just as apps are continuously updated and improved,

LearningCurve now features the first in a series of updates to continually improve the user experience.

- *Customizable format* allows instructors to tailor quizzes to the exact content they are teaching.

- *Accessible format* was redone in compliance with WCAG2.0 AA standards for users with disabilities.

- *New design* emphasizes useful study tools, like the personalized study plan, links to the e-Book, and hints to structure student reading.

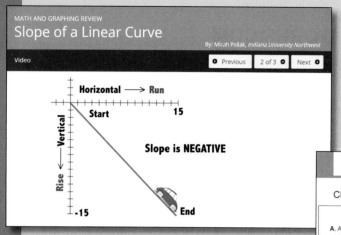

◀ NEW! **Math and Graphing Review** is a critically important new **LaunchPad** resource created by a team of instructors for students who would benefit from a review of basic math and graphing—skills needed to do well in an introductory economics course. It is organized as a series of activities, each with a pretest question, an animation with clear explanations, and five concluding questions to test comprehension.

▶ NEW! **Work It Out** activities are skill-building tutorials that walk students through each step of solving an end-of-chapter problem using choice-specific feedback and video explanations for each step. The new activity is a useful extension of the end-of-chapter Solved Problem feature, which provide detailed text feedback while leading students through a stepped-out problem.

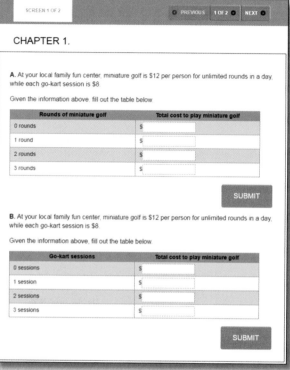

LaunchPad provides instructors with the following resources:

FOR ASSESSMENT

Test Bank contains more than 8,000 carefully constructed, thoroughly edited and revised, and comprehensively accuracy-checked questions. Each chapter's test bank contains "anchor" questions written by the author himself.

End-of-Chapter Problems have been converted to a multiple-choice format accompanied by answer-specific feedback.

Graded Homework Assignments Each **LaunchPad** unit concludes with a pre-built assignment, providing instructors with a curated set of multiple-choice and graphing questions that are easily assigned for graded assessment.

ADDITIONAL RESOURCES

Gradebook offers clear feedback to students and instructors on individual assignments and on performance in the course as a whole.

LMS Integration ensures that **LaunchPad** is easily integrated into a school's learning management system and that an instructor's gradebook and roster are always in sync.

Instructor's Teaching Manual is the ideal resource for many classroom teaching styles. The Teaching Manual focuses on expanding and enlivening classroom lectures by highlighting varied ways to bring real-world examples into the classroom.

Lecture Slides are designed with visual learning in mind. This set of slides contains fully animated graphs, visual learning images, and additional examples and created links. *Economics,* Fourth Edition, is the only principles of economics textbook with slides created by the author.

Also available for instructors and students:

saplinglearning.com Online homework system that helps students get better grades with targeted instructional feedback tailored to each individual's responses. It also helps instructors spend less time preparing for and managing a course by providing personalized classroom support from a doctorate- or master's-level colleague fully trained in Sapling's system.

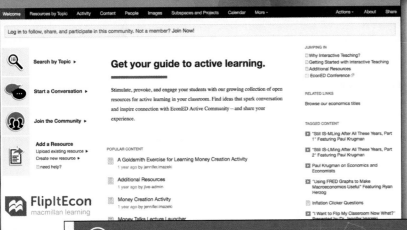

econedactive.com EconED Active is a community focused on curating the best open source active learning content aligned to key topics in principles of economics. Find everything from classroom activities to experiments, to new ways of presenting topics. Rate and share ideas and connect with other instructors passionate about teaching.

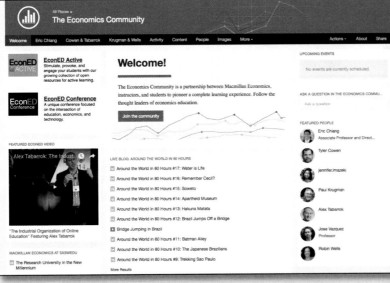

community.macmillan.com Worth Economics partners with authors, instructors, and students to pioneer a complete learning experience. Our Economics Community is an outlet for you to interact with some of the thought leaders of economics education, follow their latest work, and share your own experiences in teaching and learning.

Thinking About Data Literacy

Students who continue on from principles to intermediate economics will be asked to use data to solve economics problems. Before they can get to that point, they must learn to interpret and understand various formats of data presented to them. With the abundance of data in our daily lives and its growing importance in all manner of professions, developing this skill is just as important to students who will never take an economics course beyond principles as it is to future economists.

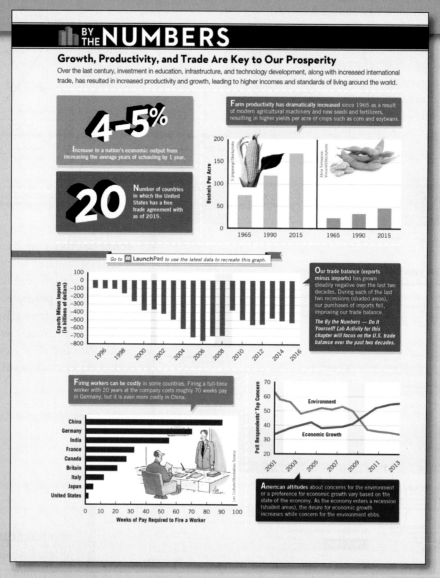

The **By the Numbers** feature in every chapter helps students visualize data from real life and offers an easy way to see how they link to concepts in the chapter. In addition to online **LaunchPad** exercises in interpreting data, two end-of-chapter problems test students on how well they understand the data presented.

Thinking About What Global Means

One of the unique things about Eric Chiang is his philosophy on travel. Essentially, get in, get out, and try to gain as many impressions of world locales as you can. Years ago, he started his "Around the World in 80 Hours" trips where he would circumnavigate the globe, briefly stopping off in international spots, and film himself talking about the local economy. Why? People around the world are faced with many of the same economic problems and yet they solve them in surprisingly different ways.

AROUND THE WORLD Q

Tokyo Disneyland: Is THAT the Line for Space Mountain?!

What are some factors that cause Tokyo Disneyland to be so crowded even during the middle of winter?

A 200-minute wait for a ride at Tokyo Disneyland.

How long are you willing to wait to experience your favorite ride at a theme park? 20 minutes? 60 minutes? How about 3 hours? On an ordinary day at Tokyo Disneyland, one of the most popular theme parks in the world, the line for its famous attractions such as Space Mountain, Splash Mountain, and Tower of Terror can reach 200 minutes. . . . That's over a 3-hour wait to enjoy a 3-minute ride! What causes lines to form at theme parks?

Theme park rides have lines because the quantity of rides demanded exceeds the quantity supplied. Why is that? Because most theme parks charge a fixed admission fee for unlimited rides, visitors typically demand more rides than the theme park is able to supply, even if a ride is operating at full capacity. The extent of the shortage, and consequently the length of wait time, are influenced largely by market factors.

First, consider the role of preferences. Disneyland has a worldwide following, and for those living in Japan, visiting Tokyo Disneyland is certainly easier than visiting Disney parks in California or Florida. Second, consider the number of potential buyers. Tokyo Disneyland is located in a metropolitan area with over 30 million people. The sheer number of potential visitors will lead to higher demand. And third, consider the role of pricing. Given its popularity, Tokyo Disneyland could charge higher prices to reduce the quantity demanded. Yet, in 2016 a one-day adult admission to Tokyo Disneyland cost only $58, while its counterparts in California and Florida charged nearly $120.

The combination of preferences, proximity to potential buyers, and relatively low prices cause demand for Tokyo Disneyland rides to far exceed the park's reasonable capacity (at least by U.S. standards), creating massive lines. Yet for enthusiastic Disney fans, smiling faces abound. Despite the crowds, it's still the "Happiest Place on Earth!"

GO TO **LaunchPad** TO PRACTICE THE ECONOMIC CONCEPTS IN THIS STORY

Eric started these journeys on his own accord to help illustrate this concept to his students. His experiences have been developed into the new **Around the World** feature in every chapter. Students read a synopsis of an international issue faced around the world, view media to further their understanding (some featuring Eric himself), and answer a question on how that issue is resolved in different places throughout the world.

AROUND THE WORLD Q

Nunavut: Land of Abundance and Scarcity

How does the condition of scarcity determine the economic tradeoffs observed in Canada's newest and largest province?

What products is Canada known for? Canada is a northern country known for its lakes and forests. And what are forests made of? Trees, of course. How important are trees? Just ask the 32,000 residents in the newest Canadian province of Nunavut. They know, because they have no trees!

Larger in area than Alaska and California combined, Nunavut has many natural resources, but lacks the one resource most often associated with Canada: trees. With much of Nunavut's land mass situated above the tree line, it must rely on goods supplied by other provinces and imported from other countries for its building materials and agricultural products. A visit to Nunavut highlights the prevalence of scarcity and the necessity of specialization and trade.

For example, nearly all of Nunavut's food, household goods, and building materials must be flown in to its sparsely populated communities accessible only by air or snowmobile, resulting in extremely high prices for most goods. However, Nunavut has many gold mines and fisheries that allow it to specialize and export precious metals and its famous Arctic char fish, a close relative to the salmon.

Residents of even the most remote places of the world can solve the challenge of scarcity and gain access to many goods and services by engaging in specialization and trade.

GO TO **LaunchPad** TO PRACTICE THE ECONOMIC CONCEPTS IN THIS STORY

THOROUGH UPDATING

BY THE NUMBERS feature updated and now presented as an infographic

WORK IT OUT problem in every chapter

New **END-OF-CHAPTER PROBLEMS** in every chapter

AROUND THE WORLD feature added to every chapter

CHAPTER 1

NEW ISSUE: Would a city change its name for a game show?

NEW PRINCIPLE: Economic growth, low unemployment, and low inflation are three economic goals that do not always coincide.

AROUND THE WORLD: Nunavut, abundance and scarcity

CHAPTER 2

AROUND THE WORLD: Ironbridge and the start of the Industrial Revolution

NEW ISSUE: the ocean and land reclamation

CHAPTER 3

AROUND THE WORLD: Tokyo Disneyland and how people deal with long lines

CHAPTER 4

AROUND THE WORLD: Singapore's attempt to control traffic by using peak-pricing tolls

CHAPTER 5

NEW CHAPTER OPENING EXAMPLE: gasoline

CONTENT REVISION: completely rewritten section on taxes and elasticity

AROUND THE WORLD: Norway and the incentive not to drive

CHAPTER 6

AROUND THE WORLD: the economic influence of superstitions

CHAPTER 7

CONTENT REVISION: expanded discussion of sunk costs

AROUND THE WORLD: living like royalty

CHAPTER 8

AROUND THE WORLD: Colombian coffee and perfect competition

CHAPTER 9

CONTENT REVISION: rewritten section on the future of antitrust

AROUND THE WORLD: when a monopoly may not set a monopoly price (contestable markets)

CHAPTER 10

AROUND THE WORLD: the ways in which McDonald's has modified the Big Mac in different global markets

CONTENT REVISIONS: game theory sections focusing on sequential-move games, and expanded discussion of the main applications of game theory

CHAPTER 11

CONTENT REVISION: updated discussion of unions

NEW ISSUE: public pensions

AROUND THE WORLD: sherpas

CHAPTER 12

NEW ISSUE: class with 10,000 students (MOOC)

AROUND THE WORLD: ski resort in the desert of Dubai

CHAPTER 13

CONTENT REVISION: completely rewritten section on climate change and sustainable development

NEW SECTION: health care as a public good

NEW ISSUE: resurgence of nearly eradicated diseases

AROUND THE WORLD: the Barbary macaques in Gibraltar

CHAPTER 14

NEW ISSUE: credit card offers that are too good to be true

AROUND THE WORLD: drones that make deliveries to rural Rwanda

CHAPTER 15

NEW INTRODUCTION: poverty in America

NEW ISSUE: the 1%

AROUND THE WORLD: South Africa and income inequality

CHAPTER 16

NEW CHAPTER OPENER: covers a broad range of issues, including the introduction of classical vs. Keynesian economics

CONTENT REVISIONS: fewer subcategories in section on income approach to GDP; clearer breakdown of national income in Table 3; differences between nominal GDP, real GDP, and GDP-PPP clarified

AROUND THE WORLD: Costa Rica, happiness, and GDP

CHAPTER 17

CONTENT REVISION: rewritten section on underemployment and discouraged workers, with key data better linked to Department of Labor definitions

AROUND THE WORLD: boom and bust in Dickinson, North Dakota

CHAPTER 18

NEW INTRODUCTION: China's current growth problems

NEW ISSUE: the argument that dramatic growth in the United States in the 20th century is a thing of the past, and will not be so transformative in the future

AROUND THE WORLD: growth champion Kazakhstan

CHAPTER 19

Thoroughly updated introduction

CONTENT REVISION: more prominent multiplier section

AROUND THE WORLD: how the Beco do Batman area in Brazil turned graffiti into an engine for economic growth

CHAPTER 20

CONTENT REVISIONS: clarification of the effect of "business expectations"; how interest rates affect AD through consumption and investment

AROUND THE WORLD: Myanmar and what it takes to open up a military regime to democracy

CHAPTER 21

CONTENT REVISIONS: shortened discussion of taxes and fewer equations; examination of the concepts of injections and withdrawals; clarification of national and public debt

AROUND THE WORLD: fiscal policy as an engine of growth in Qatar

CHAPTER 22

CONTENT REVISIONS: downplay of traveler's checks as part of M1; expanded discussion of government deficits on the market for loanable funds includes an explanation of how government borrowing actually reduces private saving

AROUND THE WORLD: use of plastic money (literally) in Australia

CHAPTER 23

AROUND THE WORLD: the rise and fall of the Swiss Bank account

CHAPTER 24

CONTENT REVISIONS: updated sections on the Eurozone crisis and monetary theories

AROUND THE WORLD: why a South American country would use the U.S. dollar as its own currency

CHAPTER 25

AROUND THE WORLD: post-unification Germany

CHAPTER 26

AROUND THE WORLD: how China's New Year's festival disrupts international trade

CHAPTER 27

AROUND THE WORLD: Hyder, Alaska, a town in the United States that uses Canadian currency and Canadian public services

acknowledgments

No project of this scope is accomplished alone. *Economics: Principles for a Changing World* and its suite of learning resources came together as a result of the dedication of many individuals who devoted incredible amounts of time to the project. These include reviewers of manuscript chapters, workshop participants, accuracy reviewers, supplements contributors, project specialists, and the production and editorial staff at Worth Publishers.

I want to thank those reviewers of the fourth edition who read through chapters in manuscript form and offered many important suggestions that have been incorporated into this project. They include:

Steve Abid, *Grand Rapids Community College*

Gian Aryani, *Collin College*

Mohammad Bajwa, *Northampton Community College*

Mihajlo Balic, *Harrisburg Area Community College*

Yoram Bauman, *Stand-Up Economist*

Dixie Button, *Trident Technical College*

Jennifer Bryant, *Lamar State College*

Joe Cahill, *Lonestar College Tomball*

Michael Dale, *Trident Technical College*

Lisa Gloege, *Grand Rapids Community College*

Clark Goodlett, *Trident Technical College*

Daniel Kuester, *Kansas State University*

James Latham, *Collin College*

Eric Levy, *Florida Atlantic University*

Ting Levy, *Florida Atlantic University*

Ishuan Li, *Minnesota State University Mankato*

Grace O, *Georgia State University*

Erick Perez, *Broward College*

Chirinjev Peterson, *Greenville Technical College*

Dennis Petruska, *Youngstown State University*

Olga Shemyakina, *Georgia Institute of Technology*

Robert Simonson, *Minnesota State University, Mankato*

One of my most enjoyable activities as an author and professor is to travel to campuses to present guest lectures to students or to facilitate workshops for instructors. The questions and feedback received during these visits contributed immensely to the development of this edition. I would like to thank those who have invited me to their campuses, including:

Vicky Chiu-Irion, *Honolulu Community College*

Debbie Evercloud, *University of Colorado at Denver*

Paul Fisher, *Henry Ford College*

Jolien Helsel, *Youngstown State University*

Linda Hooks, *Washington and Lee University*

Jennifer Imazeki, *San Diego State University*

Venoo Kakar, *San Francisco State University*

Gerard Klonarides, *Broward College*

Jackie Lindo, *Kapiolani Community College*

Daniel Murgo, *Miami Dade College*

Max Nagiel, *Daytona State College*

Tomi Ovaska, *Youngstown State College*

Erick Perez, *Broward College*

Larry Rowland, *Hawaii Pacific University*

Martin Sabo, *University of Colorado at Denver*

Ravi Samitamana, *Daytona State College*

Sue Stockly, *Eastern New Mexico University*

A. J. Sumell, *Youngstown State University*

Andrew Tucker, *Tallahassee Community College*

Enrique Valdes, *Miami Dade College*

I would like to thank my current and former student assistants who helped with data collection and shared ideas for examples that would click with college students today. These students include Jonathan Lu, Alan Jagessar, Eileen Schneider, Yoko Uyehara, Kevin Brady, Craig Haberstumpf, Felicia Lu, and Thomas Thornton. I also thank all the students who have taken my principles courses. Their comments, body language, and facial expressions provided cues to whether my concept explanations and applications were clear and provided guidance on how to approach these topics in the book.

I am thankful to have a friend and colleague in Vicky Chiu-Irion of Honolulu Community College, who has contributed to the new edition in more ways than I can adequately describe. In addition to her eagle eye for detail, she provided many new examples used in this edition and class-tested new features in LaunchPad. Vicky's support on this edition was indispensable.

I am very grateful to Debbie Evercloud of University of Colorado at Denver and Varun Gupta of Wharton County Junior College for inspiring me to introduce the Around the World feature in this edition and for providing excellent reviews on drafts. I also thank Venoo Kakar of San Francisco State University for her valuable reviews.

I also want to thank Thomas Dunn for his tireless examination of every set of page proofs and various LaunchPad resources. Despite dozens of eyes that have read through manuscript and proofs, Thomas still managed to catch errors that none of us want to see in the final product.

A huge debt of gratitude is owed to Lindsay Neff and the supplements authors. Lindsay did a remarkable job to get the best people to author the supplements. They include Jane Himarios of the University of Texas at Arlington who managed the revision of the Test Bank, Albert J. Sumell of Youngstown State University and Dixie Button of Trident Technical College who revised and adapted the former CourseTutor into a new digital feature within LaunchPad, and Solina Lindahl of California Polytechnic University–San Luis Obispo for coordinating the pedagogical resources available to instructors. I would also like to thank Ting Levy, Tamika Steward, Enrique Valdes, Heather Luea, Brian Lynch, Katie Lotz, Mary Lesser, Winnie Lee, Kevin Beckwith, Beth Haynes, Karl Geisler, Greg Gilpin, Jan Wolcutt, Jackie Lindo, Scott Hegerty, Jesse Liebman, Kristen Zaborski, Varun Gupta, Sue Stockly, and Venoo Kakar for the development of materials for LaunchPad for this new edition. The fourth edition came together into a cohesive set of instructor and student resources because of their efforts.

I owe a significant debt to the team of technology specialists who created many fascinating digital resources for *Economics*, Fourth Edition. I thank Tom Acox for his instrumental role in the development and management of the online resources, especially LaunchPad. There has been more than one occasion when a situation with my class required immediate attention, and Tom was always available, day and night, to resolve the problem. He truly exemplifies his title as director of customer experience.

I am truly indebted to Jeremy Brown, who over the years has taught me the tools and tricks of digital technology that have become indispensable in today's media-driven world. These tools include video editing, animation, and other visual effects, creating a professional Web site, and maximizing the effectiveness of social media. Whenever I have a technology-related question, I can count on Jeremy for an answer. His influence has given me the confidence to use cutting-edge technology to its maximum potential to the benefit of the *Economics*, Fourth Edition, suite of resources.

The production team at Worth is truly the best in the industry. My heartfelt thanks go to the entire team, including Vicki Tomaselli, senior designer, for creating a fantastic set of interior and cover designs; Jodi Isman, senior project editor, for skillfully managing the copyediting and proofing of the book; Stacey Alexander, production manager; Matthew McAdams, art manager, for creating beautiful figures and graphs; Patti Brecht for her superb copyediting; photo editors Christine Buese and Donna Ranieri for their immense efforts at finding and obtaining rights to the hundreds of photos used in the book; Tracey Kuehn, director, content management enhancement; and Lisa Kinne, managing editor. Each of these individuals made sure each part of the production process went smoothly. Thank you very much for a job well done.

I am very thankful to Charles Linsmeier, vice president, social sciences of Macmillan Learning, who signed me as an author in 2010 and has provided continuous support with each edition. I thank Shani Fisher, publisher, for her determination to broaden the appeal of the textbook to the wider market. I also thank Carlise Stembridge, editor, for her tireless efforts in ensuring that the textbook meets the needs of today's instructors and students. She is always interested in hearing feedback from the book's users in order to enhance its ability to improve the learning experience. And I thank Paul Shensa, who has provided valuable advice for many years; his steadfast commitment to the book's success is truly evident.

There is no one person I can thank more than Bruce Kaplan, senior development editor, who has guided me on the revision of *Economics*, Fourth Edition, from start to finish. Bruce had a long working relationship with Jerry Stone on his first two editions and was able to provide continuity into the third edition without Jerry's presence. In fact, in my last conversation with Jerry Stone, he told me to "stick with Bruce; he's the best and will take you far." Jerry's words ring true each time I work with Bruce, who is the best editor and mentor an author can have. My working relationship with Bruce has continued to be productive and efficient through the fourth edition. As a night owl, I would send Bruce drafts of chapters in the wee hours of the morning, only to have him (as an early riser) read them almost immediately!

You couldn't ask for a better marketing team than that at Worth. I thoroughly enjoy working with Tom Digiano, marketing manager, who possesses remarkable talent and enthusiasm when developing innovative experiences to current and prospective users. These efforts resulted in many unique conference events, including the annual EconED teaching conference, regional focus group events, campus visits, webinars, and new social media campaigns such as econedactive.com and the Macmillan Community. In early 2016 Tom became an editor of this book, providing a seamless transition from marketing to editorial. I also enjoyed traveling with Tom in the fifth annual Around the World in 80 Hours economics documentary (viewable on YouTube).

Finally, I thank Jerry Stone, a true friend and colleague who put his full trust in me when he offered me the opportunity to take over authorship of *CoreEconomics* in 2010 and carry the book forward to a new generation of students and instructors with new needs. I wish Jerry were still here to collaborate on the textbook he created so successfully in the first two editions. I will never cease my efforts to make this book a long-lasting legacy of Jerry's brilliance and dedication to students and instructors.

—*Eric P. Chiang*

brief contents

1 Exploring Economics 1

2 Production, Economic Growth, and Trade 29

3 Supply and Demand 53

4 Markets and Government 83

5 Elasticity 105

6 Consumer Choice and Demand 135

7 Production and Costs 167

8 Perfect Competition 193

9 Monopoly 219

10 Monopolistic Competition, Oligopoly, and Game Theory 249

11 The Labor Market 279

12 Land, Capital Markets, and Innovation 313

13 Externalities and Public Goods 339

14 Network Goods 371

15 Poverty and Income Distribution 395

16 Introduction to Macroeconomics 423

17 Measuring Inflation and Unemployment 449

18 Economic Growth 477

19 Aggregate Expenditures 501

20 Aggregate Demand and Supply 529

21 Fiscal Policy and Debt 555

22 Saving, Investment, and the Financial System 585

23 Money Creation and the Federal Reserve 611

24 Monetary Policy 637

25 Macroeconomic Policy: Challenges in a Global Economy 667

26 International Trade 695

27 Open Economy Macroeconomics 721

Sources for By the Numbers / S-1

Glossary / G-1

Index / I-1

contents

BRIEF CONTENTS xxi

1 Exploring Economics • 1

BY THE NUMBERS Economics as a Career 3

What Is Economics About? 4

Why Should One Study Economics? 4

Microeconomics Versus Macroeconomics 5

Economic Theories and Reality 6

  Model Building 6

  Ceteris Paribus: All Else Held Constant 6

Efficiency Versus Equity 6

ISSUE Do Economists Ever Agree on Anything? 7

Positive Versus Normative Questions 7

Key Principles of Economics 8

Principle 1: Economics Is Concerned With Making Choices With Limited Resources 8

Principle 2: When Making Decisions, One Must Take into Account Tradeoffs and Opportunity Costs 9

Principle 3: Specialization Leads to Gains for All Involved 10

Principle 4: People Respond to Incentives, Both Good and Bad 10

ISSUE Would a City Change Its Name for a Game Show? 10

Principle 5: Rational Behavior Requires Thinking on the Margin 11

Principle 6: Markets Are Generally Efficient; When They Aren't, Government Can Sometimes Correct the Failure 12

Principle 7: Economic Growth, Low Unemployment, and Low Inflation Are Economic Goals That Do Not Always Coincide 13

Principle 8: Institutions and Human Creativity Help Explain the Wealth of Nations 14

AROUND THE WORLD Nunavut: Land of Abundance and Scarcity 14

Summing It All Up: Economics Is All Around Us 15

ADAM SMITH (1723–1790) 13

Chapter Summary 16

KEY CONCEPTS 18

QUESTIONS AND PROBLEMS 18

ANSWERS TO QUESTIONS IN CHECKPOINTS 19

APPENDIX
Working With Graphs and Formulas 20

Graphs and Data 20

Time Series 20

Scatter Plots 20

Pie Charts 21

Bar Charts 22

  Simple Graphs Can Pack In a Lot of Information 22

  A Few Simple Rules for Reading Graphs 23

Graphs and Models 23

Linear Relationships 24

Computing the Slope of a Linear Line 24

Nonlinear Relationships 25

Computing the Slope of a Nonlinear Curve 26

Ceteris Paribus, Simple Equations, and Shifting Curves 26

Ceteris Paribus: All Else Equal 26

Simple Linear Equations 27

Shifting Curves 27

Correlation Is Not Causation 28

2 Production, Economic Growth, and Trade • 29

BY THE NUMBERS Growth, Productivity, and Trade Are Key to Our Prosperity 31

Basic Economic Questions and Production 32

Basic Economic Questions 32

  Economic Systems 32

  Resources and Production 33

Land 33

Labor 33

Capital 33

Entrepreneurial Ability 33

Production and Efficiency 33

AROUND THE WORLD Ironbridge: The Beginnings of the Industrial Revolution 34

Production Possibilities and Economic Growth 35

Production Possibilities 35

Opportunity Cost 36

Increasing Opportunity Costs 37

Economic Growth 38

Expanding Resources 39

Technological Change 40

Summarizing the Sources of Economic Growth 41

ISSUE Is the Ocean the Next Frontier? Land Reclamation and Underwater Cities 41

Specialization, Comparative Advantage, and Trade 42

Absolute and Comparative Advantage 43

The Gains from Trade 45

Practical Constraints on Trade 46

ISSUE Do We Really Specialize in That? Comparative Advantage in the United States and China 47

DAVID RICARDO (1772–1823) 43

Chapter Summary 48

KEY CONCEPTS 50

QUESTIONS AND PROBLEMS 50

ANSWERS TO QUESTIONS IN CHECKPOINTS 52

3 Supply and Demand • 53

BY THE NUMBERS The World of Markets 55

Markets 56

ISSUE Do Markets Exist for Everyone, Including Dogs and Cats? 56

The Price System 57

Demand 57

Willingness-to-Pay: The Building Block of Market Demand 57

The Law of Demand: The Relationship Between Quantity Demanded and Price 58

The Demand Curve 59

Determinants of Demand 60

Tastes and Preferences 61

Income 61

Prices of Related Goods 61

The Number of Buyers 62

Expectations About Future Prices, Incomes, and Product Availability 62

Changes in Demand Versus Changes in Quantity Demanded 62

Supply 64

The Law of Supply: The Relationship Between Quantity Supplied and Price 64

The Supply Curve 64

Market Supply Curves 65

Determinants of Supply 65

Production Technology 65

Costs of Resources 66

Prices of Related Commodities 66

Expectations 66

Number of Sellers 67

Taxes and Subsidies 67

Changes in Supply Versus Changes in Quantity Supplied 67

Market Equilibrium 69

Moving to a New Equilibrium: Changes in Supply and Demand 71

Predicting the New Equilibrium When One Curve Shifts 71

ISSUE Two-Buck Chuck: Will People Drink $2-a-Bottle Wine? 73

Predicting the New Equilibrium When Both Curves Shift 73

AROUND THE WORLD Tokyo Disneyland: Is THAT the Line for Space Mountain?! 75

ALFRED MARSHALL (1842–1924) 71

Chapter Summary 76

KEY CONCEPTS 78

QUESTIONS AND PROBLEMS 78

ANSWERS TO QUESTIONS IN CHECKPOINTS 81

4 Markets and Government • 83

BY THE NUMBERS Price Controls and Supports in the Economy Today 85

Consumer and Producer Surplus: A Tool for Measuring Economic Efficiency 86

Using Consumer and Producer Surplus: The Gains from Trade 89

The Consequences of Deviating from Market Equilibrium 89
   When Prices Exceed Equilibrium 89
   When Prices Fall Below Equilibrium 90
Market Failure 92
   Lack of Competition 92
   Information Is Not Shared by All Parties 92

AROUND THE WORLD Singapore: Resolving Traffic Jams and Reducing Pollution Using Price Controls 92
   The Existence of External Benefits or Costs 93
   The Existence of Public Goods 93
Market Efficiency Versus Equity 93

Price Ceilings and Price Floors 94

Price Ceilings 94
Price Floors 96

ISSUE Are Price Gouging Laws Good for Consumers? 97

NOBEL PRIZE: PAUL A. SAMUELSON (1915–2009) 91

Chapter Summary 99

KEY CONCEPTS 101
QUESTIONS AND PROBLEMS 101
ANSWERS TO QUESTIONS IN CHECKPOINTS 104

5 Elasticity • 105

BY THE NUMBERS Elasticity: How Markets React to Price Changes 107

Elasticity of Demand 108

Price Elasticity of Demand as an Absolute Value 108
Measuring Elasticity With Percentages 109
Elastic and Inelastic Demand 109
   Elastic 109
   Inelastic 109
   Unitary Elastic 110
Determinants of Elasticity 110
   Substitutability 111
   Proportion of Income Spent on a Product 111
   Luxuries Versus Necessities 111
   Time Period 111
Computing Price Elasticities 112
   Using Midpoints to Compute Elasticity 112

Total Revenue and Other Measures of Elasticity 114

Elasticity and Total Revenue 114
   Inelastic Demand 114
   Elastic Demand 114
   Unitary Elasticity 114
   Elasticity and Total Revenue Along a Straight-Line (Linear) Demand Curve 115
Other Elasticities of Demand 116
   Cross Elasticity of Demand 117
   Income Elasticity of Demand 117

ISSUE Using Loss Leaders to Generate Higher Total Revenue 118

Elasticity of Supply 119

Time and Price Elasticity of Supply 120
   The Market Period 120
   The Short Run 121
   The Long Run 121

Taxes and Elasticity 122

Taxes on Income Sources and Their Economic Burden 123
Taxes on Spending and the Incidence of Taxation 123
Analyzing the Effects of Taxes on a Market 124
When Elasticity Puts a Greater Burden of a Tax on Consumers 125
When Elasticity Puts a Greater Burden of a Tax on Producers 125

AROUND THE WORLD Norway: An Oil Producing Nation With an Incentive *NOT* to Drive 126

ISSUE Are Sales Taxes Fair to Low-Income Households? 127

Chapter Summary 129

KEY CONCEPTS 131
QUESTIONS AND PROBLEMS 131
ANSWERS TO QUESTIONS IN CHECKPOINTS 133

6 Consumer Choice and Demand • 135

BY THE NUMBERS How Do We Decide What to Buy? 137

The Budget Line and Choices 138

The Budget Line 138

Changes to the Budget Line 139

    Changes to the Price of a Good 139

    Changes to Income 140

Marginal Utility Analysis 141

Preferences and Utility 142

    Total and Marginal Utility 142

    The Law of Diminishing Marginal Utility 143

    Maximizing Utility 143

Deriving Demand Curves 145

Limitations of Marginal Utility Analysis 146

Behavioral Economics 148

Sunk Cost Fallacy 148

Framing Bias 149

Overconfidence 149

Overvaluing the Present Relative to the Future 150

Altruism 150

ISSUE Tipping and Consumer Behavior 151

AROUND THE WORLD What's Wrong With the 4th Floor? The Economic Influence of Superstitions 152

JEREMY BENTHAM (1748–1832) 141

Chapter Summary 154

KEY CONCEPTS 156

QUESTIONS AND PROBLEMS 156

ANSWERS TO QUESTIONS IN CHECKPOINTS 158

APPENDIX
Indifference Curve Analysis 159

Indifference Curves and Consumer Preferences 159

Properties of Indifference Curves 160

Indifference (or Preference) Maps 160

Optimal Consumer Choice 161

Using Indifference Curves 162

Deriving Demand Curves 162

Income and Substitution Effects 163

APPENDIX KEY CONCEPTS 165

APPENDIX QUESTIONS AND PROBLEMS 165

ANSWER TO QUESTION IN APPENDIX CHECKPOINT 166

7 Production and Costs • 167

BY THE NUMBERS Innovation, Productivity, and Costs Rule Business 169

Firms, Profits, and Economic Costs 170

Firms 170

Entrepreneurs 170

    Sole Proprietors 170

    Partnerships 171

    Corporations 171

Profits 171

ISSUE The Vast World of Corporate Offshoring and Profits 172

Economic Costs 172

Economic and Normal Profits 173

Short Run Versus Long Run 174

Production in the Short Run 175

Total Product 175

Marginal and Average Product 177

Increasing and Diminishing Returns 177

Costs of Production 178

Short-Run Costs 178

    Fixed and Variable Costs 179

Sunk Costs 179

    Marginal Cost 180

    Average Costs 181

Short-Run Cost Curves for Profit-Maximizing Decisions 182

    Average Variable Cost (AVC) 182

    Average Total Cost (ATC) 183

    Marginal Cost (MC) 183

Long-Run Costs 183

    Long-Run Average Total Cost 184

    Economies and Diseconomies of Scale 184

    Economies of Scope 185

    Role of Technology 186

AROUND THE WORLD Live Like a Royal: Castles Turning into Hotels 186

Chapter Summary 188

KEY CONCEPTS 190

QUESTIONS AND PROBLEMS 190

ANSWERS TO QUESTIONS IN CHECKPOINTS 192

8 Perfect Competition • 193

BY THE NUMBERS Perfect Competition and Efficiency 195

Market Structure Analysis 196

Primary Market Structures 197

    Perfect Competition 197

    Monopolistic Competition 197

    Oligopoly 197

    Monopoly 197

Defining Perfectly Competitive Markets 197

The Short Run and the Long Run (A Reminder) 199

Perfect Competition: Short-Run Decisions 199

Marginal Revenue 199

Profit-Maximizing Output 200

Economic Profits 201

Five Steps to Maximizing Profit 201

Normal Profits 202

Loss Minimization and Plant Shutdown 203

The Short-Run Supply Curve 205

Perfect Competition: Long-Run Adjustments 206

Adjusting to Profits and Losses in the Short Run 206

Competition and the Public Interest 208

AROUND THE WORLD Colombian Coffee: The Perils of Existing in a Perfectly Competitive Industry 209

Long-Run Industry Supply 210

ISSUE Globalization and "The Box" 210

Summing Up 212

NOBEL PRIZE: HERBERT SIMON (1916–2001) 205

Chapter Summary 213

KEY CONCEPTS 215

QUESTIONS AND PROBLEMS 215

ANSWERS TO QUESTIONS IN CHECKPOINTS 217

9 Monopoly • 219

BY THE NUMBERS Monopoly and Market Power 221

Monopoly Markets 222

Sources of Market Power 222

    Control Over a Significant Factor of Production 222

    Economies of Scale 223

    Government Franchises, Patents, and Copyrights 223

Monopoly Pricing and Output Decisions 224

    $MR < P$ for Monopoly 224

    Equilibrium Price and Output 225

    Using the Five Steps to Maximizing Profit 225

    Monopoly Does Not Guarantee Economic Profits 227

ISSUE "But Wait . . . There's More!" The Success and Failure of Infomercials 227

Comparing Monopoly and Competition 228

Higher Prices and Lower Output From Monopoly 229

Rent Seeking and X-Inefficiency 230

Monopolies and Innovation 230

Benefits Versus Costs of Monopolies 231

AROUND THE WORLD A Convenience Store on Every Corner, as Far as the Eye Can See 231

Price Discrimination 232

Perfect (First-Degree) Price Discrimination 233

Second-Degree Price Discrimination 233

Third-Degree Price Discrimination 234

ISSUE Is Flexible Ticket Pricing the New Form of Price Discrimination? 236

Regulation and Antitrust 236

Regulating the Natural Monopolist 237

    Marginal Cost Pricing Rule 237

    Average Cost Pricing Rule 237

    Regulation in Practice 238

Antitrust Policy 238

The Major Antitrust Laws 239

Defining the Relevant Market and Market Power 239

    Concentration Ratios 240

    Herfindahl–Hirschman Index 240

Applying the HHI   241

Contestable Markets   241

The Future of Antitrust Policy   241

NOBEL PRIZE: GEORGE STIGLER (1911–1991)   238

Chapter Summary   243

KEY CONCEPTS   245

QUESTIONS AND PROBLEMS   245

ANSWERS TO QUESTIONS IN CHECKPOINTS   247

10 Monopolistic Competition, Oligopoly, and Game Theory • 249

BY THE NUMBERS   Product Differentiation and Market Share   251

Monopolistic Competition   252

Product Differentiation and the Firm's Demand Curve   252

The Role of Advertising   253

ISSUE   Do Brands Really Represent Pricing Power?   254

Price and Output Under Monopolistic Competition   254

Comparing Monopolistic Competition to Perfect Competition   256

AROUND THE WORLD   A McDonald's Big Mac Without Beef?   256

Oligopoly   257

Defining Oligopoly   257

Cartels: Joint Profit Maximization and the Instability of Oligopolies   258

The Kinked Demand Curve Model and the Stability of Oligopolies   259

Game Theory   261

Basic Game Setup and Assumptions   262

Simultaneous Versus Sequential-Move Games   262

Sequential-Move Games   263

Simultaneous-Move Games   263

Nash Equilibrium   265

Nash Equilibrium: A Personal Example   265

ISSUE   Mission Impossible: The Power of Focal Points in a Simulated Mission   266

Applications of Game Theory   267

The Prisoner's Dilemma   267

The Classic Prisoner's Dilemma   268

Other Examples of Prisoner's Dilemma Outcomes   269

Resolving the Prisoner's Dilemma   269

Repeated Games   270

Grim Trigger   270

Trembling Hand Trigger   270

Tit-for-Tat   270

Using Sequential-Move Analysis to Model Repeated Games   271

Leadership Games   271

Chicken Games   271

Summary of Market Structures   272

NOBEL PRIZE: JOHN NASH (1928–2015)   262

Chapter Summary   274

KEY CONCEPTS   276

QUESTIONS AND PROBLEMS   276

ANSWERS TO QUESTIONS IN CHECKPOINTS   278

11 The Labor Market • 279

BY THE NUMBERS   The Changing Economic Landscape on the Labor Force   281

Competitive Labor Supply   282

Individual Labor Supply   282

Substitution Effect   282

Income Effect   282

Market Labor Supply Curves   283

Factors That Change Labor Supply   283

Demographic Changes   284

Nonwage Aspects of Jobs   284

Wages in Alternative Jobs   284

Nonwage Income   284

Competitive Labor Demand   285

Marginal Revenue Product   285

Factors That Change Labor Demand   287

Changes in Product Demand   287

Changes in Productivity   287

Changes in the Prices of Other Inputs   287

Elasticity of Demand for Labor   288

Factors That Affect the Elasticity of Demand for Labor   288

Elasticity of Demand for the Product   288

Ease of Input Substitutability   288

Labor's Share of Total Production Costs   288

Competitive Labor Market Equilibrium   289

AROUND THE WORLD   Life as a Sherpa: Risking One's Life in Exchange for Financial Security   290

Economic Discrimination   291

Becker's Theory of Economic Discrimination   291

Segmented Labor Markets   292

Public Policy to Combat Discrimination   294

The Equal Pay Act of 1963   294

Civil Rights Act of 1964   294

Executive Order 11246—Affirmative Action   294

Age, Disabilities, and Sexual Orientation   295

Labor Unions and Collective Bargaining   295

Types of Unions   296

Benefits and Costs of Union Membership   296

Brief History of American Unionism   296

ISSUE   The End of the Road for Pensions: Unions Fight to Preserve Promises Made to Retirees   297

Union Versus Nonunion Wage Differentials   298

The Changing World of Work   299

Jobs of the Past Versus the Present   299

Future Jobs in the U.S. Economy   300

NOBEL PRIZE: GARY BECKER (1930–2014)   291

Chapter Summary   301

KEY CONCEPTS   303

QUESTIONS AND PROBLEMS   303

ANSWERS TO QUESTIONS IN CHECKPOINTS   305

APPENDIX
Imperfect Labor Markets   306

Monopoly Power in Product Markets   306

Monopsony   307

KARL MARX (1818–1883)   309

APPENDIX KEY CONCEPTS   310

APPENDIX SUMMARY   310

APPENDIX QUESTIONS AND PROBLEMS   310

ANSWERS TO QUESTIONS IN APPENDIX CHECKPOINT   311

12   Land, Capital Markets, and Innovation • 313

BY THE NUMBERS   Innovation Is the Cornerstone of Growth   315

Land and Physical Capital   316

Land   316

Physical Capital   317

Present Value Approach   319

Rate of Return Approach   320

Financial Capital   321

Banks and Borrowing   321

Bonds (Debt Capital)   322

Stocks (Equity Capital)   323

Venture Capital and Private Equity   324

ISSUE   Venture Capital: A Few Success Stories and One Big Missed Opportunity   325

Investment in Human Capital   326

Education and Earnings   326

Education as Investment   327

Equilibrium Levels of Human Capital   328

Implications of Human Capital Theory   329

Human Capital as Screening or Signaling   330

ISSUE   A Class With 10,000 Students? MOOCs and Human Capital   330

On-the-Job Training   331

Entrepreneurship and Innovation   331

Entrepreneurship   332

Innovation and the Global Economy   332

AROUND THE WORLD   Ski Dubai: A Ski Resort in the Desert   333

Chapter Summary   334

KEY CONCEPTS   336

QUESTIONS AND PROBLEMS   336

ANSWERS TO QUESTIONS IN CHECKPOINTS   337

13   Externalities and Public Goods • 339

BY THE NUMBERS   The Environment and Sustainability   341

Externalities 342

Negative Externalities 343

The Coase Theorem 344

Positive Externalities 346

Limitations 346

Public Goods 347

What Are Public Goods? 347

The Demand for Public Goods 348

Optimal Provision of Public Goods 349

Common Property Resources 349

AROUND THE WORLD Life at the Top of the Rock:
Protecting the Barbary Macaques 350

Health Care as a Public Good 351

ISSUE The Resurgence of Nearly Eradicated Diseases—A
Free Rider Problem 352

Environmental Policy 353

Intergenerational Questions 353

Socially Efficient Levels of Pollution 354

Overview of Environmental Policies 355

Command and Control Policies 356

Market-Based Policies 357

Emissions Taxes 357

Marketable or Tradable Permits 357

Other Market-Based Policies 358

ISSUE Cap-and-Trade: The Day Liberal Environmentalists
and Free-Market Conservatives Agreed 359

The Economics of Climate Change and
Sustainable Development 360

Understanding Climate Change 360

The Causes of Climate Change 360

The Consequences of Climate Change Today and in the
Future 361

The Challenges of Addressing Climate Change 362

Promoting Sustainable Development 363

Corporate Social Responsibility 363

Individual Social Responsibility 363

NOBEL PRIZE: RONALD COASE (1910–2013) 345

NOBEL PRIZE: ELINOR OSTROM (1933–2012) 362

Chapter Summary 365

KEY CONCEPTS 367

QUESTIONS AND PROBLEMS 367

ANSWERS TO QUESTIONS IN CHECKPOINTS 369

14 Network Goods • 371

BY THE NUMBERS How We Are Connected Today 373

What Is a Network Good? 374

Types of Network Goods 374

Network Effects 374

AROUND THE WORLD The Drone Highway: A Lifeline
for Rural Rwandans 375

Demand Curve for a Network
Good 376

Demand for a Fixed Capacity Network Good 376

Deriving the Full Network Demand Curve 377

Examples of Network Demand Curve Pricing in Our
Daily Lives 378

Market Equilibrium for a Network
Good 379

Economies of Scale and Marginal Cost 379

Finding an Equilibrium in the Market for Network
Goods 379

Network Goods Can Face a Virtuous Cycle or a
Vicious Cycle Very Quickly 380

ISSUE The Broadband Effect: Virtuous and Vicious
Cycles in Network Goods 381

Competition and Market Structure for
Network Goods 382

Competition and Pricing Strategies 383

Capturing New Customers Using Teaser Strategies 383

Retaining Existing Customers Using Lock-In
Strategies 383

Using Market Segmentation to Maximize
Profits 383

ISSUE A 0% Credit Card Offer: Is It Too Good to
Be True? 384

Should Network Goods Be
Regulated? 386

Promoting Network Competition with
Interconnection 386

Industry Standards and Network Compatibility 387

Does Interconnection Improve Efficiency in Network
Industries? 387

Can Poor Regulation Be Worse Than No
Regulation? 388

Chapter Summary 389

KEY CONCEPTS 391

QUESTIONS AND PROBLEMS 391

ANSWERS TO QUESTIONS IN CHECKPOINTS 393

15 Poverty and Income Distribution • 395

BY THE NUMBERS Poverty and the Economy 397

The Distribution of Income and Wealth 398

Life Cycle Effects 398

The Distribution of Income 398

Personal or Family Distribution of Income 399

Lorenz Curves 400

Gini Coefficient 402

The Impact of Redistribution 402

Causes of Income Inequality 404

Human Capital 405

Other Factors 405

ISSUE How Much Do You Need to Earn to Be In the Top 1%? 407

Poverty 408

Measuring Poverty 408

The Incidence of Poverty 409

Depth of Poverty 410

Alternative Measures of Poverty 411

AROUND THE WORLD South Africa: A Nation of Rich Treasures and Income Inequality 412

Causes of Poverty 413

Eliminating Poverty 413

Reducing Income Inequality 413

ISSUE What Is Considered "Poor" Around the World? 414

Increasing Economic Growth 414

Rawls and Nozick 415

Mobility: Are Poor Families Poor Forever? 416

Chapter Summary 418

KEY CONCEPTS 420

QUESTIONS AND PROBLEMS 420

ANSWERS TO QUESTIONS IN CHECKPOINTS 422

16 Introduction to Macroeconomics • 423

BY THE NUMBERS A Slow and Steady Macroeconomic Recovery 425

Business Cycles 426

Defining Business Cycles 427

Dating Business Cycles 428

Alternative Measures of the Business Cycle 429

National Activity Index 429

Leading Economic Index 429

Yield Curve 430

ISSUE The End of the Recession . . . It Does Not Feel Like It 431

National Income Accounting 432

The Core of the NIPA 433

The Circular Flow Diagram 433

Spending and Income: Looking at GDP in Two Ways 433

Gross Domestic Product 434

The Expenditures (Spending) Approach to Calculating GDP 435

Personal Consumption Expenditures 435

Gross Private Domestic Investment 435

Government Purchases 436

Net Exports of Goods and Services 436

Summing Aggregate Expenditures 437

The Income Approach to Calculating GDP 437

Compensation of Employees 437

Proprietors' Income 438

Corporate Profits 438

Rental Income 438

Net Interest 438

Miscellaneous Adjustments 438

Summing Up Income Measures 438

GDP and Our Standard of Living 439

Different Ways of Comparing GDP Across Countries 440

Population and GDP per Capita 440

Environmental Quality 440

AROUND THE WORLD Costa Rica: *Pura Vida* and Happiness Without a High Level of GDP 441

Nonmarket Activities and the Informal Economy 442

NOBEL PRIZE: SIMON KUZNETS (1901–1985) 433

Chapter Summary 444

KEY CONCEPTS 446

QUESTIONS AND PROBLEMS 446

ANSWERS TO QUESTIONS IN CHECKPOINTS 448

17 Measuring Inflation and Unemployment • 449

BY THE NUMBERS The Twin Evils of Inflation and Unemployment 451

Inflation 452

What Causes Inflation? 453

Measuring Inflation: Consumer Price Index, Producer Price Index, and GDP Deflator 453

The Consumer Price Index 454

The Producer Price Index 455

The GDP Deflator 456

Adjusting for Inflation: Escalating and Deflating Series (Nominal Versus Real Values) 456

Escalator Clauses 457

Deflating Series: Nominal Versus Real Values 457

The Effect of Overstating Inflation 457

The Consequences of Inflation 457

Hyperinflation 458

ISSUE The Consequences of Counterfeit Money on Inflation 459

Unemployment 460

The Historical Record 460

Defining and Measuring Unemployment 461

Employed 461

Unemployed 462

Labor Force 463

Monthly Employment Surveys 463

The Household Survey 463

The Payroll Survey 463

Employment Trends 464

Weekly Jobs Report 464

Relationship Between Employment and the Unemployment Rate 464

Problems with Unemployment Statistics 464

Underemployment and Marginally Attached Workers 465

AROUND THE WORLD The Boom and Bust of Dickinson, North Dakota 466

Unemployment and the Economy 467

Types of Unemployment 467

Frictional Unemployment 467

Structural Unemployment 468

Cyclical Unemployment 468

Defining Full Employment 468

The Natural Rate of Unemployment 468

Changes in the Unemployment Rate Around the Natural Rate 469

Jobless Recoveries Prolong Unemployment Above the Natural Rate 470

ISSUE Why Do Unemployment Rates Differ So Much Within the United States? 470

Chapter Summary 472

KEY CONCEPTS 474

QUESTIONS AND PROBLEMS 474

ANSWERS TO QUESTIONS IN CHECKPOINTS 476

18 Economic Growth • 477

BY THE NUMBERS Why Should We Care About Economic Growth? 479

Why Is Economic Growth Important? 480

How Is Economic Growth Measured? 480

Small Differences in Growth Lead to Large Differences in Income Over Time 481

Power of Compounding Growth Rates 482

Rule of 70 482

ISSUE Can Economic Growth Bring a Billion People Out of Poverty? 483

Thinking About Short-Run and Long-Run Economic Growth 484

Short-Run Versus Long-Run Growth 484

Short-Run Growth Involves a Fixed Capacity 484

Long-Run Growth Involves Expanding Capacity 484

Factors of Production 485

Production Function 486

Applying the Production Function: Achieving Economic Growth 488

Achieving More Land or Natural Resources 488

Growth of the Labor Force 488

Increasing the Quality of the Labor Force 488

Increasing the Capital-to-Labor Ratio 489

Improvements in Technology and Ideas 490

Including Everything Else: Total Factor Productivity 490

AROUND THE WORLD Kazakhstan: The Next Destination of Growth and Trade 491

The Role of Government in Promoting Economic Growth 492

Government as a Contributor to Physical Capital, Human Capital, and Technology 492

Physical Capital: Public Capital and Private Investment 492

Human Capital: Public Education and Financial Aid 493

Technology: Government R&D Centers and Federal Grants 493

Government as a Facilitator of Economic Growth 493

Enforcement of Contracts 493

Protection of Property Rights 493

Stable Financial System 494

Government as a Promoter of Free and Competitive Markets 494

Competitive Markets and Free Trade 494

Economic Freedom 494

ISSUE Did Economic Growth Peak a Century Ago? Prospects for Future Growth 495

THOMAS MALTHUS (1766–1834) 490

Chapter Summary 497

KEY CONCEPTS 499

QUESTIONS AND PROBLEMS 499

ANSWERS TO QUESTIONS IN CHECKPOINTS 500

19 Aggregate Expenditures • 501

BY THE NUMBERS The Role of Spending in the Economy 503

Aggregate Expenditures 504

Some Simplifying Assumptions 504

Consumption and Saving 504

Average Propensities to Consume and Save 506

Marginal Propensities to Consume and Save 506

Other Determinants of Consumption and Saving 508

Investment 508

Investment Demand 509

Aggregate Investment Schedule 510

The Simple Aggregate Expenditures Model 511

Macroeconomic Equilibrium in the Simple Model 512

The Multiplier 514

The Multiplier Works in Both Directions 515

Paradox of Thrift 516

ISSUE Do High Savings Rates Increase the Risk of a Long Recession? 517

AROUND THE WORLD Brazil's Beco Do Batman: How Graffiti Revived a Neighborhood 518

The Full Aggregate Expenditures Model 519

Adding Government Spending and Taxes 519

Tax Changes and Equilibrium 519

The Balanced Budget Multiplier 520

Adding Net Exports 521

Recessionary and Inflationary Gaps 522

Recessionary Gap 522

Inflationary Gap 522

ISSUE Was Keynes Right About the Great Depression? 523

JOHN MAYNARD KEYNES (1883–1946) 513

Chapter Summary 524

KEY CONCEPTS 526

QUESTIONS AND PROBLEMS 526

ANSWERS TO QUESTIONS IN CHECKPOINTS 528

20 Aggregate Demand and Supply • 529

BY THE NUMBERS The Sheer Size of Aggregate Demand and Aggregate Supply 531

Aggregate Demand 532

Why Is the Aggregate Demand Curve Negatively Sloped? 532

The Wealth Effect 533

Export Price Effect 533

Interest Rate Effect 533

Determinants of Aggregate Demand 533

Consumer Spending 533

Investment 534

Government Spending and Net Exports 535

AROUND THE WORLD Myanmar: Opening a Country to a Boom in Aggregate Demand 536

Aggregate Supply 537

Long Run 537

Determinants of Long-Run Aggregate Supply 538

Short Run 538

Determinants of Short-Run Aggregate Supply 538

Input Prices 539

Productivity 539

Taxes and Regulation 540

Market Power of Firms 540

Inflationary Expectations 540

Macroeconomic Equilibrium 541

The Spending Multiplier 542

The Great Depression 543

Demand-Pull Inflation 544

Cost-Push Inflation 545

ISSUE Why Didn't Stimulus Measures Over the Past Decade Lead to Inflation? 546

Chapter Summary 548

KEY CONCEPTS 550

QUESTIONS AND PROBLEMS 550

ANSWERS TO QUESTIONS IN CHECKPOINTS 552

APPENDIX
Deriving the Aggregate Demand Curve 553

21 Fiscal Policy and Debt • 555

BY THE NUMBERS Your Government and Its Financial Operation 557

Fiscal Policy and Aggregate Demand 558

Discretionary and Mandatory Spending 558

Discretionary Fiscal Policy 558

Government Spending 559

Taxes 559

Transfers 560

Expansionary and Contractionary Fiscal Policy 561

Fiscal Policy and Aggregate Supply 563

Infrastructure Spending 564

Reducing Tax Rates 564

Expanding Investment and Reducing Regulations 565

AROUND THE WORLD Qatar: A Nation Built for the Future 566

Implementing Fiscal Policy 567

Automatic Stabilizers 567

Fiscal Policy Timing Lags 568

The Government's Bias Toward Borrowing and Away from Taxation 568

Financing the Federal Government 569

Defining Deficits and the National Debt 570

Balanced Budget Amendments 571

ISSUE How Big Is the Economic Burden of Interest Rates on the National Debt? 572

Financing Debt and Deficits 573

Why Is the Public Debt So Important? 574

Is the Size of the Public Debt a Problem? 575

Does It Matter If Foreigners Hold a Significant Portion of the Public Debt? 575

Does Government Debt Crowd Out Consumption and Investment? 576

How Will the National Debt Affect Our Future? Are We Doomed? 577

Chapter Summary 579

KEY CONCEPTS 581

QUESTIONS AND PROBLEMS 581

ANSWERS TO QUESTIONS IN CHECKPOINTS 583

22 Saving, Investment, and the Financial System • 585

BY THE NUMBERS The Financial System and Its Sheer Size and Scope 587

What Is Money? 588

The Functions of Money 588
  Medium of Exchange 588
  Unit of Account 589
  Store of Value 589
Defining the Money Supply 589

AROUND THE WORLD Using Plastic Money (Literally) in Australia 590

  Narrowly Defined Money: M1 591
  A Broader Definition: M2 591

The Market for Loanable Funds 592

Supply and Demand for Loanable Funds 592
Shifts in the Supply of Loanable Funds 593
  Economic Outlook 593
  Incentives to Save 593
  Income or Asset Prices 594
  Government Deficits 594
Shifts in the Demand for Loanable Funds 594
  Investment Tax Incentives 594
  Technological Advances 594
  Regulations 594
  Product Demand 594
  Business Expectations 594

The Financial System 595

The Bridge Between Savers and Borrowers 595
The Roles of Financial Institutions 596
  Reducing Information Costs 596
  Reducing Transaction Costs 596
  Diversifying Assets to Reduce Risk 596
Types of Financial Assets 596
Bond Prices and Interest Rates 597
Stocks and Investment Returns 598

Financial Tools for a Better Future 599

Short-Term Borrowing 599
The Power (or Danger) of Compounding Interest 600
Risk Assessment and Asset Allocation 601

Saving for the Future: Employer-Based Programs 601
  To Contribute or Not to Contribute? 601
  In What Assets Should One Invest? 602
Other Retirement Savings Tools: Social Security, Pensions, and IRAs 602
  Social Security 602
  Pension Plans 602

ISSUE Can a Stock Market Crash Increase Long-Term Savings? 603

  Individual Retirement Arrangements (IRAs) 603

Chapter Summary 605

KEY CONCEPTS 607
QUESTIONS AND PROBLEMS 607
ANSWERS TO QUESTIONS IN CHECKPOINTS 609

23 Money Creation and the Federal Reserve • 611

BY THE NUMBERS Banks and the Federal Reserve 613

How Banks Create Money 614

Creating Money as If Out of Thin Air 614
Fractional Reserve Banking System 616
  The Money Creation Process 616

The Money Multiplier and Its Leakages 618

Bank Reserves and the Money Multiplier 619
Money Leakages 619
  Bank Leakages 619
  Leakages by Individuals and Businesses 620
  The Effect of Foreign Currency Holdings 621
What Is the Actual Money Multiplier in the Economy? 621

AROUND THE WORLD The Rise and Fall of the Famous (and Infamous) Swiss Bank Account 621

The Federal Reserve System 623

The Structure of the Federal Reserve 623
  The Board of Governors 623
  Federal Reserve Banks 624
  Federal Open Market Committee 625

The Fed as Lender of Last Resort   625

The Federal Reserve at Work: Tools, Targets, and Policy Lags   626

Reserve Requirements   626

Discount Rate   627

Open Market Operations   627

   The Federal Funds Target   627

Monetary Policy Lags   628

   Information Lags   628

   Recognition Lags   628

   Decision Lags   628

ISSUE   What Can the Fed Do When Interest Rates Reach 0%?   629

   Implementation Lags   629

Chapter Summary   631

KEY CONCEPTS   633

QUESTIONS AND PROBLEMS   633

ANSWERS TO QUESTIONS IN CHECKPOINTS   635

24 Monetary Policy • 637

BY THE NUMBERS   Monetary Policy in Action   639

What Is Monetary Policy?   640

The Twin Goals of Monetary Policy   640

Examples of Monetary Policy in Action   640

Why Is the Interest Rate So Important to the Economy?   641

When Is It Optimal to Loosen or Tighten Monetary Policy?   641

   Expansionary Monetary Policy   641

   Contractionary Monetary Policy   642

Monetary Theories   643

The Short Run Versus the Long Run: What's the Difference?   643

The Long Run: The Classical Theory   644

Short-Run Effects of Monetary Policy   645

   Money Illusion and Sticky Wages and Prices   645

   Keynesian Model   646

   Monetarist Model   646

Summary of the Effectiveness of Monetary Policy   647

Monetary Policy and Economic Shocks   648

   Demand Shocks   648

Supply Shocks   649

Implications for Short-Run Monetary Policy   650

Modern Monetary Policy   650

Rules Versus Discretion   651

The Federal Funds Target and the Taylor Rule   651

A Recap of the Fed's Policy Tools   653

Transparency and the Federal Reserve   653

ISSUE   The Record of the Fed's Performance   654

New Monetary Policy Challenges   655

The Fed: Dealing with an Economic Crisis Not Seen in 80 Years   655

The Eurozone Crisis and the Role of the European Central Bank   656

ISSUE   The Challenges of Monetary Policy with Regional Differences in Economic Performance   658

AROUND THE WORLD   Why Would a Country Give Up Its Monetary Policy?   659

IRVING FISHER (1867–1947)   644

NOBEL PRIZE: MILTON FRIEDMAN (1912–2006)   646

Chapter Summary   661

KEY CONCEPTS   663

QUESTIONS AND PROBLEMS   663

ANSWERS TO QUESTIONS IN CHECKPOINTS   665

25 Macroeconomic Policy: Challenges in a Global Economy • 667

BY THE NUMBERS   The Long Road Back: The Great Recession and the Jobless Recovery   669

The Great Recession and Macroeconomic Policy   670

From the Housing Bubble to the Financial Crisis   670

   Subprime Mortgages and Collateralized Debt Obligations   670

   Collapsing Financial Markets   672

The Government's Policy Response   672

The Financial Crisis and Its Effects   673

Effectiveness of Macroeconomic Policy: Phillips Curves and Rational Expectations   674

Unemployment and Inflation: Phillips
Curves 674

Productivity, Prices, and Wages 675

The Importance of Inflationary Expectations 676

Inflationary Expectations and the Phillips
Curve 677

The Long-Run Phillips Curve 677

Accelerating Inflation 678

Returning Inflation to Normal Levels 679

Rational Expectations and Policy Formation 679

Policy Implications of Rational Expectations 680

A Critique of Rational Expectations 681

Macroeconomic Issues That Confront
Our Future 682

Are Recoveries Becoming "Jobless Recoveries"? 683

Will Rising Debt and Future Debt Obligations Lead to
Inflation? 685

Rising Future Debt Obligations: Health Care and Social
Security 685

The Cost of Financing Debt 685

The Effects of Debt on Inflation 686

ISSUE Inflating Our Way Out of Debt: Is This an Effective
Approach? 686

Will Globalization Lead to Increased Obstacles to
Economic Growth? 687

AROUND THE WORLD Life on the Autobahn:
Germany's Role in European Growth and Stability 688

NOBEL PRIZE: ROBERT LUCAS 679

Chapter Summary 689

KEY CONCEPTS 691

QUESTIONS AND PROBLEMS 691

ANSWERS TO QUESTIONS IN CHECKPOINTS 693

26 International Trade • 695

BY THE NUMBERS International Trade 697

The Gains from Trade 698

Absolute and Comparative Advantage 699

Gains from Trade 700

Practical Constraints on Trade 700

ISSUE The Challenge of Measuring Imports and Exports
in a Global Economy 702

The Terms of Trade 703

Determining the Terms of Trade 703

The Impact of Trade 704

How Trade Is Restricted 705

Effects of Tariffs and Quotas 705

ISSUE Do Foreign Trade Zones Help or Hurt American
Consumers and Workers? 707

Arguments Against Free Trade 708

Traditional Economic Arguments 708

Infant Industry Argument 709

Antidumping 709

Low Foreign Wages 709

National Defense Argument 710

Recent Globalization Concerns 710

Trade and Domestic Employment 710

Trade and the Environment 711

Trade and Its Effect on Working Conditions in
Developing Nations 711

AROUND THE WORLD Can One Country's Festival
Disrupt World Trade? 712

Chapter Summary 714

KEY CONCEPTS 716

QUESTIONS AND PROBLEMS 716

ANSWERS TO QUESTIONS IN CHECKPOINTS 719

27 Open Economy
Macroeconomics • 721

BY THE NUMBERS The Foreign Exchange
Market 723

The Balance of Payments 724

The Current Account 724

Imports and Exports 724

Income 725

Transfers 725

The Capital Account 725

Exchange Rates 726

Defining Exchange Rates 726

Nominal Exchange Rates 726

Real Exchange Rates 726

Purchasing Power Parity 727

Exchange Rate Determination 728

A Market for Foreign Exchange 728

Flexible Exchange Rates 729

Currency Appreciation and Depreciation 729

Determinants of Exchange Rates 730

Exchange Rates and the Current Account 731

Changes in Inflation Rates 731

Changes in Domestic Disposable Income 731

Exchange Rates and the Capital Account 731

Interest Rate Changes 731

Expected Exchange Rate Changes 732

Exchange Rates and Aggregate Supply and
Demand 732

ISSUE Would a Stronger Chinese Yuan Be Good for
Americans? 733

Monetary and Fiscal Policy in an Open
Economy 734

Fixed and Flexible Exchange Rate Systems 734

Pegging Exchange Rates Under a Flexible Exchange
Rate System 735

Policies Under Fixed Exchange Rates 736

Policies Under Flexible Exchange Rates 737

AROUND THE WORLD Hyder, Alaska: An American
Town That Uses the Canadian Dollar 738

NOBEL PRIZE: ROBERT MUNDELL 737

Chapter Summary 740

KEY CONCEPTS 742

QUESTIONS AND PROBLEMS 742

ANSWERS TO QUESTIONS IN CHECKPOINTS 744

Sources for By the Numbers S-1

Glossary G-1

Index I-1

Economics

Principles for a Changing World

1

Exploring Economics

Understanding how economics explains everyday decisions made by individuals, businesses, and governments

Bruce Bennett/Getty Images

Learning Objectives

1.1 Explain how economic analysis can be used in decision making.

1.2 Differentiate between microeconomics and macroeconomics.

1.3 Describe how economists use models.

1.4 Describe the *ceteris paribus* assumption.

1.5 Discuss the difference between efficiency and equity.

1.6 Describe the key principles in economics.

1.7 Apply the key principles to situations faced in everyday life.

Imagine jumping over open pits of fire, being chased by crazed people with sticks, diving through muddy pools of water under barbed wire, and climbing over a series of rocky walls. This does not describe a war zone or a military boot camp. Instead, these are typical challenges found in the increasingly popular sport of obstacle course racing. Also known as Warrior Dash, Tough Mudder, and Spartan Runs, obstacle course racing incorporates demanding physical and mental obstacles to challenge individuals over the standard 3- to 5-mile (or longer) length of the course.

Does this sound thrilling? Or perhaps crazy? These are common thoughts that come to mind when people talk about the increasing popularity of new adventure sports. Would you imagine that whether or not to participate in such an activity is an economic question? Most people probably would not. But this example resembles an economic problem in many ways. Obstacle course racing involves a challenge, one with a *benefit* (a sense of accomplishment) and a *cost* (including monetary costs, physical demands on the body, and a risk of injury). It involves *tradeoffs* such as the countless hours spent practicing and training in order to be successful. And it involves societal beliefs about whether such activities should be regulated or restricted to persons of a minimum age and well-being. Benefits, costs, tradeoffs, and regulation: These are the foundations for making an economic decision. Nearly all decisions made by individuals, firms, and governments in pursuit of an objective or goal can be understood using these economic concepts.

By the end of this course, you will come to understand that economics involves all types of decisions, from small everyday decisions on how to manage one's time to world-changing decisions made by the president of the United States. Consumers make decisions about what clothes to buy and what foods to eat. Businesses must decide what products to make and how much of each product to stock on store shelves. Indeed, one cannot escape making decisions, and the outcomes of these decisions affect not only our own lives but also those of entire societies and countries.

You still might be asking yourself: Why should I study economics? First, you will spend roughly the next 40 years working in an economic environment: paying taxes, experiencing ups and downs in the overall economy, investing money, and voting on various economic issues. It will benefit you to know how the economy works. More important, economic analysis gives you a structure from which you can make decisions in a more rational manner. Economics teaches you how to make better and wiser decisions given your limited resources. This course may well change the way you look at the world. It can open your eyes to how you make everyday decisions, from what to buy to where you choose to live.

Like our opening example, economic analysis involves decisions that are not just "economic" in the general sense of the term. Certainly, economic thinking may change your views on spending and saving, on how you feel about government debt, and on your opinion of environmental policies or globalization. But you also may develop a different perspective on how much time to study for each of your courses this term, or where you might go for spring break this year. Such is the wide scope of economic analysis.

Economics as a Career

Economics is one of the most popular college majors in the country. This is because so much of what we do, the decisions we face, and the issues we confront involve economics.

Each chapter in this book includes a By the Numbers box. It has two purposes. First, items in the feature preview some of the topics covered in the chapter. We hope these topics motivate you to read on. Second, the data explosion affecting our understanding of the world will only continue to accelerate. Numerical literacy will grow in importance. This By the Numbers box seeks to encourage a nonthreatening familiarity with data and numbers. At the end of each chapter, there are two Using the Numbers questions to test how well you understood the numbers.

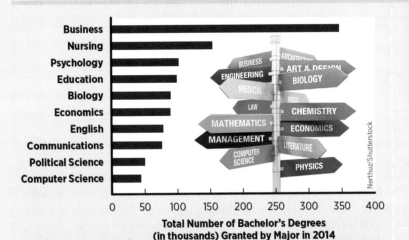

Total Number of Bachelor's Degrees (in thousands) Granted by Major in 2014

Business majors represented the largest number of college graduates in terms of the total number of bachelor's degrees granted in 2014. Economics majors represented the sixth most popular degree granted.

Technology Company CEO Majors:
1. Economics (22%)
2. Computer Science (20%)
3. Engineering (17%)

Fortune 100 Company CEO Majors:
1. Engineering (17%)
2. Economics (12%)
3. Business Administration (12%)

41% **P**ercent of Fortune 500 Companies (America's largest companies by revenue) founded by immigrants or their children.

$94,700

The median salary of workers with economics degrees after 15 years of work experience.

Go to **LaunchPad** *to use the latest data to recreate this graph.*

■ Early Career Pay
■ Mid-Career Pay

Average Pay (in thousands of dollars)

The average pay by major as reported on payscale.com in March 2016, provides an indication of the demand and prospects for economics majors.

The By the Numbers—Do It Yourself! Lab Activity gives you the opportunity to explore this data in greater depth.

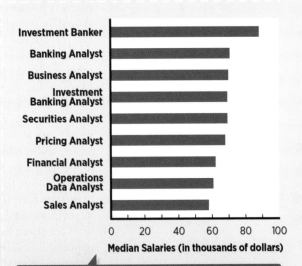

Median Salaries (in thousands of dollars)

What do economists do? Common jobs held by economists with bachelor's degrees and their median salaries.

This introductory chapter takes a broad look at economics. First, we study a key method of economic analysis: model building. Economists use stylized facts and the technique of holding some variables constant to develop testable theories about how consumers, businesses, and governments make decisions. Then we turn to a short discussion of some key principles of economics to give you a sense of the guiding concepts you will encounter in this book.

This chapter will give you a sense of what economics is, what concepts it uses, and what it finds to be important. Do not go into this chapter thinking you have to memorize these concepts. Rather, use this chapter to get a sense of the broad scope of economics. You will be given many opportunities to understand and use these concepts throughout this course. Return to this chapter at the end of the course and see if everything has now become crystal clear.

WHAT IS ECONOMICS ABOUT?

economics The study of how individuals, firms, and society make decisions to allocate limited resources to many competing wants.

Economics is a very broad subject. It often seems that economics has something important to say about almost everything.

To boil it down to a simple definition, **economics** is about making choices. Economics studies how individuals, firms, and societies make decisions to maximize their well-being given limitations. In other words, economics attempts to address the problem of having too many wants but too few resources to achieve them all, an important concept called **scarcity.** Note that scarcity is not the same thing as something being *scarce.* Although all resources are scarce, certain goods are less scarce than others. For example, cars are not very scarce— there are car dealerships around the country chock-full of cars ready to be sold, but that doesn't mean you can go out tonight and buy three. Scarcity refers to the fact that one must make choices given the resource limitations she or he faces.

scarcity Our unlimited wants clash with limited resources, leading to scarcity. Everyone (rich and poor) faces scarcity because, at a minimum, our time on earth is limited. Economics focuses on the allocation of scarce resources to satisfy unlimited wants as fully as possible.

What kind of limitations are we referring to here? It could be money, but money is not the only resource that allows us to achieve the life we want. It's also our time, our knowledge, our work ethic, and anything else that can be used to achieve our goals. It is this broad notion of economics being the study of how people make decisions to allocate scarce resources to competing wants that allows the subject to be applied to so many topics and applications.

Why Should One Study Economics?

The first answer that might come to mind as to why you are taking this course is "because I have to." Although economics is a required course for many college students, economics should be thought of as something much, much more. For example, studying economics can prepare you for many types of careers in major industries and government. Studying economics also is a great launching pad for pursuing a graduate degree in law, business, or other fields. More practically speaking, economics helps you to think more clearly about the decisions you make every day and to understand better how the economy functions and why certain things happen the way they do.

For example, economics has some important things to say about the environment. Most people care about the environment to some degree, and do their part by recycling, not littering, and turning off the lights when leaving a room. But not all people make decisions in the same way: Some might do much more to conserve resources, such as driving less or driving a more fuel-efficient car, joining a local organization to plant trees, or even writing to policymakers to support sustainability legislation. The extent to which people participate in environmental activities depends on the benefit they perceive when pursuing such actions compared to the costs, which can include monetary costs, time and effort, and forgone opportunities such as driving a larger, more comfortable car. Economics looks at all of these factors to determine how people make decisions that affect the environment, which affects us all. Economics is a way of thinking about an issue, not just a discipline that has money as its chief focus.

Economists tend to have a rational take on nearly everything. Now all of this "analysis/speculation" may bring only limited insight in some cases, but it gives you some idea of how economists think. We look for rational responses to **incentives.** Incentives are the factors, both good and bad, that influence how people make decisions. For example, tough admissions requirements for graduate school provide an incentive for students to study harder in college, while lucrative commissions push car salespeople to sell even the ugliest or most unreliable car. Economics is all about how people respond to incentives. We begin most questions by considering how rational people would respond to the incentives that specific situations provide. Sometimes (maybe even often) this analysis leads us down an unexpected path.

incentives The factors that motivate individuals and firms to make decisions in their best interest.

Microeconomics Versus Macroeconomics

Economics is split into two broad categories: microeconomics and macroeconomics. **Microeconomics** deals with decision making by individuals, businesses, and industries. It is concerned with issues such as which orange juice to buy, which job to take, and where to go on vacation, as well as which items a business should produce and what price it should charge, and whether a market should be left on its own or be regulated.

microeconomics The study of the decision making by individuals, businesses, and industries.

Microeconomics looks at how markets are structured. Some markets are very competitive, and where many firms offer similar products. Other markets have only one or two large firms, offering little choice. What decisions do businesses make under different market structures? Microeconomics also extends to such topics as labor laws, environmental policy, and health care policy. How can we use the tools of microeconomics to analyze the costs and benefits of differing policies?

Macroeconomics, on the other hand, focuses on the broader issues we face as a nation. Most of us don't care whether an individual buys Brooks or Sperry shoes. We *do* care whether prices of *all* goods and services rise. Inflation—a general increase in prices economy-wide—affects all of us. So does unemployment (virtually every person will at some point in their life be unemployed, even if it's just for a short time when switching from one job to another) and economic growth. What decisions do governments make to deal with macroeconomic problems such as inflation and recessions?

macroeconomics The study of the broader issues in the economy such as inflation, unemployment, and national output of goods and services.

Macroeconomics uses microeconomic tools to answer some questions, but its main focus is on the broad aggregate variables of the economy. Macroeconomics has its own terms and topics, such as business cycles, recession, and unemployment. Macroeconomics looks at policies that increase economic growth, the impact of government spending and taxation, the effect of monetary policy on the economy, and inflation. It also looks closely at theories of international trade and international finance. All of these topics have broad impacts on our economy and our standard of living.

Still not clear? Here's an easy way to remember the difference between microeconomics and macroeconomics. Only one letter separates the two terms, so just remember that the "i" in microeconomics refers to "individual" entities (such as a person or a firm), while the "a" in macroeconomics refers to "aggregate" entities (such as cities or a nation as a whole).

Although we break economics into microeconomics and macroeconomics, there is considerable overlap in the analysis. Both involve the analysis of how individuals, firms, and governments make decisions that affect the lives of people. We use simple supply and demand analysis to understand *both* individual markets and the general economy as a whole. You will find yourself using concepts from microeconomics to understand fluctuations in the macroeconomy.

Economics is a social science that uses many facts and figures to develop and express ideas. This inevitably involves numbers. For macroeconomics, this means getting used to talking and thinking in huge numbers: billions (nine zeros) and trillions (twelve zeros). Today, we are talking about a federal government budget of about $4 trillion. To wrap your mind around such a huge number, consider how long it would take to spend a trillion dollars if you spent a dollar every second, or $86,400 per day. To spend $1 trillion would require over 31,000 years. And the federal government now spends about 4 times this much in one year.

Economic Theories and Reality

If you flip through any economics text, you'll likely see a multitude of graphs, charts, and equations. This book is no exception. The good news is that all of the graphs and charts become relatively easy to understand, since they all basically read the same way. The few equations in this book stem from elementary algebra. Once you get through one equation, the rest are similar.

Graphs, charts, and equations are often the simplest and most efficient ways to express data and ideas. Equations are used to express relationships between two variables. Complex and wordy discussions can often be reduced to a simple graph or figure. These are efficient techniques for expressing economic ideas.

Model Building As you study economics this term, you will encounter stylized approaches to a number of issues. By *stylized,* we mean that economists boil down facts to their basic relevant elements and use assumptions to develop a stylized (simple) model to analyze the issue. There are always situations that lie outside these models, but they are exceptions. Economists generalize about economic behavior and reach broadly applicable results.

We begin with relatively simple models, then gradually build to more difficult ones. For example, in the next chapter, we introduce one of the simplest models in economics, the production possibilities frontier which illustrates the limits of economic activity. This model has profound implications for the issue of economic growth. We can add in more dimensions and make the model more complex, but often this complexity does not provide any greater insight than the simple model.

ceteris paribus Assumption used in economics (and other disciplines as well), that other relevant factors or variables are held constant.

Ceteris Paribus:* All Else Held Constant** To aid in our model building, economists use the ***ceteris paribus assumption: "Holding all other things equal." That means we will hold some important variables constant. For example, to determine how many songs you might be willing to download from iTunes in any given month, we would hold your monthly income constant. We then would change song prices to see the impact on the number purchased (again holding your monthly income constant).

Though model building can lead to surprising insights into how economic actors and economies behave, it is not the end of the story. Economic insights lead to economic theories, but these theories must then be tested. In some cases, such as the extent to which a housing bubble could lead to a financial crisis, economic predictions turned out to be false. Thus, model building is a *process*—models are created and then tested. If models fail to explain reality, new models are constructed.

Efficiency Versus Equity

efficiency How well resources are used and allocated. Do people get the goods and services they want at the lowest possible resource cost? This is the chief focus of efficiency.

Efficiency deals with how well resources are used and allocated. No one likes waste. Much of economic analysis is directed toward ensuring that the most efficient outcomes result from public policy. *Production efficiency* occurs when goods are produced at the lowest possible cost, and *allocative efficiency* occurs when individuals who desire a product the most get those goods and services. As an example, it would not make sense for society to allocate a large amount of cranberry sauce to someone who wouldn't eat it. Efficient policies are generally good policies.

equity The fairness of various issues and policies.

The other side of the coin is **equity,** or fairness. Is it fair that the CEOs of large companies make hundreds of times more money than rank-and-file workers? Is it fair that some have so much and others have so little? Should society take care of the homeless and disabled? There are many divergent views about fairness until we get to extreme cases. When just a few people earn nearly all of the income and control nearly all of a society's wealth, most people agree that this is unfair.

Throughout this course, you will see instances where efficiency and equity collide. You may agree that a specific policy is efficient, but think it is unfair to some group of people. This will be especially evident when you consider tax policy and its impact

ISSUE

Do Economists Ever Agree on Anything?

> Give me a one-handed economist! All my economists say, "on one hand . . . on the other."
>
> —Harry S. Truman

President Truman once exclaimed that the country needed more *one-handed economists*. What did he mean by that? He was saying that anytime an economist talks about a solution to an economic problem, the economist will often follow that statement by saying, "on the other hand. . . ."

Economics is about making choices with scarce resources and the tradeoffs that result. Because individuals place different values on the benefits and costs within these tradeoffs, nearly every economic issue can be viewed from different perspectives, so much so that economists seemingly disagree with one another on everything.

For example, suppose we debate whether gasoline taxes are too high. *On the one hand*, higher gasoline taxes will reduce oil consumption, reduce pollution, reduce traffic congestion, and generate money to promote public transportation such as buses, subways, and high-speed trains. *On the other hand,* higher gasoline taxes raise the cost of commuting to work and school, make travel more expensive, and result in higher prices for many consumer goods due to higher shipping costs.

Different opinions about the relative weights of benefits and costs make economic policymaking challenging. Economic conditions are always changing. This is why economists rely so much on models and assumptions in order to prescribe a solution based on the conditions facing the economy.

John Lund/Getty Images

But despite differences and frequent disagreements in economic policy, economists do agree on many things, such as the value of specialization, the efficiency of markets, and the role of incentives. These areas of consensus are grounded in the key economic principles described in the next section of this chapter.

---

on income distribution. Fairness, or equity, is a subjective concept, and each of us has different ideas about what is just and fair. When it comes to public policy issues, economics will help you see the tradeoffs between equity and efficiency, but you will ultimately have to make up your own mind about the wisdom of the policy given these tradeoffs.

Positive Versus Normative Questions

Returning to the example in the chapter opener, we ask ourselves many questions whenever a decision needs to be made or an issue is debated. Some questions involve the understanding of basic facts, such as how risky a particular sport is, or how much enjoyment one receives from participating in the sport. Economists call these types of questions **positive questions.** Positive questions (which need not be positive or upbeat in the literal sense) are questions that can be answered one way or another as long as the information is available. This does not mean that people will always agree on an answer, because presentation of facts and information can differ.

Another type of question that arises is how something ought to be, such as whether extreme sports should be banned or whether additional safety measures should be required. Economists call these types of questions **normative questions.** Normative questions involve societal beliefs on what should or should not be done; differing opinions on an issue can sometimes make normative questions difficult to resolve.

Throughout this book, positive and normative questions will arise, which will play an important role in how individuals and firms make decisions, and how governments form policy proposals that may or may not become law. Indeed, economics encompasses many ideas and questions that affect everyone.

positive question A question that can be answered using available information or facts.

normative question A question whose answer is based on societal beliefs on what should or should not take place.

CHECKPOINT

WHAT IS ECONOMICS ABOUT?

- Economics is about making decisions under scarcity, in which wants are unlimited but resources are limited.
- Economics is separated into two broad categories: microeconomics and macroeconomics.
- *Microeconomics* deals with individuals, firms, and industries and how they make decisions.
- *Macroeconomics* focuses on broader economic issues such as inflation, employment and unemployment, and economic growth.
- Economics uses a stylized approach, creating simple models that hold all other relevant factors constant (*ceteris paribus*).
- Economists and policymakers often face a tradeoff between efficiency and equity.
- Positive questions can be answered with facts and information, while normative questions ask how something should or ought to be.

QUESTION: In each of the following situations, determine whether it is a microeconomic or macroeconomic issue.

1. Hewlett-Packard announces that it is lowering the price of its printers by 15%.
2. The president proposes a tax cut.
3. You decide to look for a new job.
4. The economy is in a recession, and the job market is bad.
5. The Federal Reserve announces that it is raising interest rates because it fears inflation.
6. You get a nice raise.
7. Average wages grew by 2% last year.

Answers to the Checkpoint questions can be found at the end of this chapter.

KEY PRINCIPLES OF ECONOMICS

Economics has a set of key principles that show up continually in economic analysis. Some are more restricted to specific issues, but most apply universally. These principles should give you a sense of what you will learn in this course. In the following, we summarize eight key principles that will be applied throughout the entire book. By the end of this course, these principles should be crystal clear and you will likely find yourself using these principles throughout your life, even if you never take another economics course.

Principle 1: Economics Is Concerned With Making Choices With Limited Resources

Economics deals with nearly every type of decision we face each day. But when a typical person is asked what economics is about, the most common answer is "money." Why is economics commonly misconceived as dealing only with money? This may be due in part to how economics is portrayed in the news—dealing with financial issues, jobs and wages, and the cost of living, among other money matters. While money matters are indeed an important issue studied in economics, you now know that economics involves much, much more.

Economics is about making decisions on allocating limited resources to maximize an individual or society's well-being. Money is just one source of well-being, assuming that more money makes a person happier, all else equal. But other factors also improve a person's well-being, such as receiving a day off from work with pay. Even if one does not have a lot of money or free time, satisfaction can come from other activities or events, such as participating in a fun activity with friends or family, or watching one's favorite team win.

In sum, many aspects of life contribute to the well-being of individuals and of society. Unfortunately, often these are limited by various resource constraints. Therefore, one must think of economics in a broad sense of determining how best to manage all of society's resources (not just money) in order to maximize well-being. This involves tradeoffs and opportunity costs, which we consider next.

Principle 2: When Making Decisions, One Must Take Into Account Tradeoffs and Opportunity Costs

Wouldn't it be great if we all had the resources of Mark Zuckerberg (the founder of Facebook) and could buy just about any material possession one could possibly want? Most likely we won't, so back to reality.

We all have limited resources. Some of us are more limited than others, but each of us, even Mark Zuckerberg, faces limitations (and not because Mark chooses to wear a $30 shirt instead of a $3,000 Brioni suit). For example, we all face time limitations: There are only 24 hours in a day, and some of that must be spent sleeping. The fact that we have many wants but limited resources (scarcity) means that we must make tradeoffs in nearly everything we do. In other words, we have to decide between alternatives, which always exist whenever we make a decision.

How is this accomplished? What factors determine whether you buy a nicer car or use the extra money to pay down debt? Or whether you should spend the weekend at a local music festival or use the time to study for an exam? Economists use an important term to help weigh the benefits and costs of every decision we make, and that term is **opportunity cost.** In fact, economics is often categorized as the discipline that always weighs benefits against costs.

At its very core, opportunity cost is determined by asking yourself, in any situation, "What could I be doing right now if I weren't _____ (fill in the activity)?" or "What could I have bought if I hadn't bought this _____ (fill in the last good or service you bought)?" In other words, opportunity cost measures the value of the next best alternative use of your time or money, or what you *give up* when you make an economic decision. And since there are always alternatives, one cannot avoid opportunity costs.

A common mistake that people make is that they sometimes do not fully take their opportunity costs into account. Have you ever camped out overnight in order to get tickets for a concert? Was it even worth going to the concert? Opportunity cost includes the value of everything you give up in order to attend the concert, including the cost of the tickets and transportation, and the time spent buying tickets, traveling to and from the venue, and of course attending the concert. The sum of all opportunity costs can sometimes outweigh the benefits.

Another example of miscalculating opportunity costs occurs when a student spends a copious amount of time to dispute a $15 parking ticket. Like the previous example, the opportunity cost (time and effort disputing the ticket that can be used for some other activity) may exceed the $15 savings if successful and certainly if the attempt to dispute the ticket fails.

In other cases, individuals do respond to opportunity costs. Why do many people choose a paper towel over a hand dryer in a public restroom when given the choice? It's because the opportunity cost of using the hand dryer is higher than using a paper towel.

Every activity involves opportunity costs. Sleeping, eating, studying, partying, running, hiking, and so on, all require that we spend resources that could be used on another activity. Opportunity cost varies from person to person. A company president rushing from meeting to meeting has a higher opportunity cost than a retired senior citizen, and therefore is more likely to choose the quickest option to accomplish day-to-day activities.

Opportunity costs apply to us as individuals and to societies as a whole. For example, if a country chooses to spend more on environmental conservation, it must use resources that could be used to promote other objectives, such as education and health care.

Bloomberg/Getty Images

opportunity cost The value of the next best alternative; what you give up to do something or purchase something.

Principle 3: Specialization Leads to Gains for All Involved

Whenever we pursue an activity or a task, we use time that could be used for other activities or tasks. However, sometimes these other tasks are best left to others to perform. Life would be much more difficult if we all had to grow our own food. This highlights the idea that tradeoffs (especially with one's time) can lead to better outcomes if one is able to specialize in activities in which she or he is more proficient.

Suppose you and your roommate can each cook your own dinner and clean your own rooms. Alternatively, you might have your roommate clean both rooms (he's better at it than you) in exchange for you preparing dinner for two (you're a better cook). Using this arrangement, both tasks are completed in less time since each of you is specializing in the activity you're better at, plus both of you will benefit from a cleaner apartment and a tastier dinner.

Therefore, specialization in tasks in which one is more proficient can lead to gains for all parties as long as exchange is possible and those involved trade in a mutually beneficial manner. Each person is acting on the opportunity to improve his or her well-being, an example of how incentives affect people's lives.

Principle 4: People Respond to Incentives, Both Good and Bad

Each time an individual or a firm makes a decision, that person or firm is acting on an incentive that drives the individual or firm to choose an action. These incentives often occur naturally. For example, we choose to eat every day because we face an incentive to survive, and we study and work hard because we face an incentive to be successful in our careers. However, incentives also can be formed by policies set by government to encourage individuals and firms to act in certain ways, and by businesses to encourage consumers to change their consumption habits.

For example, tax policy rests on the idea that people respond to incentives. Do we want to encourage people to save for their retirement? Then let them deduct a certain amount that they can put into a tax-deferred retirement account. Do we want businesses to spend more to stimulate the economy? Then give them tax credits for new investment. Do we

---

 ISSUE

Would a City Change Its Name for a Game Show?

Driving along Interstate 25 in central New Mexico, one encounters a city with a very peculiar name, one that required the state's Department of Transportation to order extra-long road signs: Truth or Consequences. Originally named Hot Springs, the small city is popular for its natural hot springs and small quaint lodges that dot the landscape in this remote part of the desert. How did the city of Hot Springs end up changing its name?

In 1950 a popular radio game show called *Truth or Consequences*, hosted by Ralph Edwards, offered a challenge. If any city was willing to rename itself Truth or Consequences, Mr. Edwards would host his show from that location. Hot Springs saw this as an opportunity to raise its city profile, and therefore acted on the incentive to be the first and only city to accept the challenge. It subsequently changed its official name to Truth or Consequences, New Mexico, a name that remains in use.

Truth or Consequences has benefited from its name change long after it. The city continues to host an annual fiesta that welcomed Mr. Edwards in person every year for the 50 years that followed the name change. Today, Truth or Consequences remains a small city of 6,500 residents and is still popular for its natural springs. But on the hori-

zon is another famous person, Richard Branson, the founder of Virgin Galactic, who plans to develop a commercial space flight industry in New Mexico. The location, Spaceport America, is just 30 miles from Truth or Consequences, another attraction that will add to the city's unique character.

want people to go to college? Then give them tax advantages for setting up education savings accounts.

Tax policy is an obvious example in which people follow incentives. But this principle can be seen in action wherever you look. Want to encourage people to fly during the slow travel season? Offer price discounts or bonus frequent flyer miles for flying during that time. Want to increase business at restaurants? Give early-bird discounts to those willing to eat at 5:00 P.M., before peak dining time.

Note that in saying that people follow incentives, economists do not claim that everyone follows each incentive every time. Though you may not want to eat dinner at 5:00 P.M., there might be other people who are willing to eat earlier in return for a price discount.

If not properly constructed, incentives might lead to harmful outcomes. During the 2008 financial crisis, it became clear that the way incentives for traders and executives were set up by Wall Street investment banks was misguided. Traders and executives were paid bonuses based on short-term profits. This encouraged them to take extreme risks to generate quick profits and high bonuses with little regard for the long-term viability of the bank. The bank might have been gone the next day, but these people still had those huge bonuses.

Responding to badly designed incentives is often described as greed, but they are not always the same. If you found a $20 bill on the sidewalk, would you pick it up? Of course, but would that make you a greedy person? The stranger who accidentally dropped the bill an hour ago might think so, but you are just responding to an incentive to pick up the money before the next lucky person does. Could incentives ever be designed to prevent people from picking up money they find? It may surprise you that one industry has: In many casinos, it is prohibited to keep chips or money you find on the floor.

The natural tendency for society to respond to incentives leads individuals and firms to work hard and generate ideas that increase productivity, a measure of a society's capacity to produce that determines our standard of living. A worker who can do twice as much as another is likely to earn a higher salary, because productivity and pay tend to go together. The same is true for nations. Countries with the highest standards of living are also the most productive.

Principle 5: Rational Behavior Requires Thinking on the Margin

Have you ever noticed that when you eat at an all-you-can-eat buffet, you always go away fuller than when you order and eat at a nonbuffet restaurant? Is this phenomenon unique to you, or is there something more fundamental? Remember, economists look at facts to find incentives to economic behavior.

In this case, people are just rationally responding to the price of *additional* food. They are thinking on the margin. In a nonbuffet restaurant, dessert costs extra, and you make a decision as to whether the enjoyment you receive from the dessert (the marginal benefit) is worth the extra cost (the marginal cost). At the buffet, dessert is included, which means the marginal cost is zero. Even so, you still must ask yourself if dessert will give you satisfaction. If the dessert tastes terrible or adds unwanted calories to your diet, then you might pass on dessert even if it is free. But the fact that one is more likely to have dessert at a buffet than at a menu-based restaurant highlights the notion that people tend to think on the margin.

The idea of thinking on the margin applies to a society as well. Like asking ourselves whether we want another serving of dessert, a society must ask itself whether it wants a little bit more or a little bit less of something, and policymakers and/or citizens vote on such policy proposals. An example of society thinking on the margin is whether taxes should be raised a little to pay for other projects, or whether a country should send up another space exploration craft to study other planets.

Throughout this book, we will see examples of thinking on the margin. A business uses marginal analysis to determine how much of its products it is willing to supply to the market. Individuals use marginal analysis to determine how many hours to exercise or study. And governments use marginal analysis to determine how much pollution should be permitted.

Principle 6: Markets Are Generally Efficient; When They Aren't, Government Can Sometimes Correct the Failure

Individuals and firms make decisions that maximize their well-being, and markets bring buyers and sellers together. Private markets and the incentives they provide are the best mechanisms known today for providing products and services. There is no government food board that makes sure that bread, cereal, coffee, and all the other food products you demand are on your plate during the day. The vast majority of products we consume are privately provided.

Competition for the consumer dollar forces firms to provide products at the lowest possible price, or some other firm will undercut their high price. New products enter the market and old products die out. Such is the dynamic characteristic of markets.

What drives and disciplines markets? Prices and profits are the keys. Profits drive entrepreneurs to provide new products (think of Apple) or existing products at lower prices (think of Walmart). When prices and profits get too high in any market, new firms jump in with lower prices to grab away customers. This competition, or sometimes even the threat of competition, keeps markets from exploiting consumers.

Individuals and firms respond to prices in markets by altering the choices and quantities of goods they purchase and sell, respectively. These actions highlight the ability of markets to provide an efficient outcome for all. Markets can achieve this efficiency without a central planner telling what people should buy or what firms should sell. This phenomenon that markets promote efficiency through the incentives faced by individuals and firms (as if they were guided by an omnipotent force) is referred to as the *invisible hand*, a term coined by Adam Smith, considered the father of modern economics.

As efficient as markets usually are, society does not desire a market for everything. For example, markets for hard drugs or child pornography are largely deemed undesirable. In other cases, a market does not provide enough of a good or service, such as public parks or public education. For these products and services, markets can fail to provide an optimal outcome.

But when markets do fail, they tend to do so in predictable ways. Where consumers have no choice but to buy from one firm (such as a local water company), the market will fail to provide the best solution, and government regulation is often used to protect consumers. Another example is pollution: Left unregulated, companies often will pollute the air and water. Governments then intervene to deal with this market failure. Finally, people rely on information to make rational decisions. When information is not readily available

Markets can be crowded and chaotic, but they generally promote an efficient outcome by bringing buyers and sellers together.

Oriental Touch/Robert Harding

or is known only to one side of the market, markets again can fail to produce the socially desirable outcome.

We also can extend the idea of market efficiency to the greater economy. The market forces of supply and demand generally keep the economy in equilibrium. But occasionally, fluctuations in the macroeconomy will occur, and markets take time to readjust on their own. In some cases, the economy becomes stuck in a severe downturn. In these instances, government can smooth the fluctuations in the overall economy by using policies such as government spending or tax cuts. But remember, just because the government *can* successfully intervene does not mean it *always* successfully intervenes. The macroeconomy is not a simple machine. Successful policymaking is a tough task.

Principle 7: Economic Growth, Low Unemployment, and Low Inflation Are Economic Goals That Do Not Always Coincide

The reliance on private markets and reasonable government intervention aims to maximize societal gains in terms of higher incomes and standards of living. The key to higher standards of living is economic growth, which can be measured a number of ways, most commonly by estimating the change in a country's real gross domestic income per capita. Yet, other measures of economic growth include average household income, quality of education, infrastructure development, improvement in technology and innovation, environmental sustainability, and poverty reduction.

The goal of economic growth is fostered by policies set by government, including fiscal

policy and monetary policy. But things are not always so simple, given the two persistent economic obstacles that naturally occur in the economy: unemployment and inflation. Unemployment and inflation often run opposite to one another; for example, when unemployment is high, inflation is generally low, and vice versa. When either unemployment or inflation is too high, economic growth can be inhibited. Government policy is therefore used to correct one problem at the potential expense of exacerbating the other.

In 2015 the U.S. Federal Reserve faced an important decision: whether to raise interest rates, which had been kept very low for almost a decade, to address unemployment stemming from the financial crisis of 2007-2009. Although raising interest rates would help keep inflation from rising, doing so may cause unemployment to rise. Determining policy to boost economic growth is like walking a tightrope: One must stay balanced to prevent toppling over to one side.

ADAM SMITH (1723–1790)

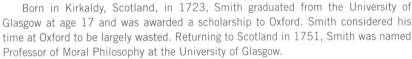

When Adam Smith was 4 years old, he was kidnapped and held for ransom. Had his captors not taken fright and returned the boy unharmed, the history of economics might well have turned out differently.

Born in Kirkaldy, Scotland, in 1723, Smith graduated from the University of Glasgow at age 17 and was awarded a scholarship to Oxford. Smith considered his time at Oxford to be largely wasted. Returning to Scotland in 1751, Smith was named Professor of Moral Philosophy at the University of Glasgow.

After 12 years at Glasgow, Smith began tutoring the son of a wealthy Scottish nobleman. This job provided him with the opportunity to spend several years touring the European continent with his young charge. In Paris, Smith met some of the leading French economists of the day, which helped stoke his own interest in political economy. While there, he wrote a friend, "I have begun to write a book in order to pass the time."

Returning to Kirkaldy in 1766, Smith spent the next decade finishing *An Inquiry Into the Nature and Causes of the Wealth of Nations.* Before publication in 1776, he read sections of the text to Benjamin Franklin. Smith's genius was in taking the existing forms of economic analysis available at the time and putting them together in a systematic fashion to make sense of the national economy as a whole. Smith demonstrated how individuals left free to pursue their own economic interests end up acting in ways that enhance the welfare of all. This is Smith's famous "invisible hand." In Smith's words: "By directing that industry in such a manner as its produce may be of the greatest value, he intends only his own gain, and he is in this, as in many other cases, led by an invisible hand to promote an end which was no part of his intention."

How important was Adam Smith? He has been called the "father of political economy." Many of the foundations of economic analysis we still use today are based on Adam Smith's writings of several centuries ago.

Information from Howard Marshall, *The Great Economists: A History of Economic Thought* (New York: Pitman Publishing), 1967; Paul Strathern, *A Brief History of Economic Genius* (New York: Texere), 2002; Ian Ross, *The Life of Adam Smith* (Oxford: Clarendon Press), 1995.

Principle 8: Institutions and Human Creativity Help Explain the Wealth of Nations

We have seen how individuals and firms make decisions to maximize their well-being, and how tradeoffs, specialization, incentives, and marginal analysis play an important role. We then saw how markets bring buyers and sellers together to promote better outcomes, and that governments sometimes step in when markets fail to produce the best outcome. But how does all of this affect the overall wealth of a nation? Two important factors influencing the wealth of nations are good institutions and human creativity.

Institutions include a legal system to enforce contracts and laws and to protect the rights of citizens and the ideas they create, a legislative process to develop laws and policies that provide incentives to individuals and firms to work hard, a government free of corruption, and a strong monetary system.

AROUND THE WORLD

Nunavut: Land of Abundance and Scarcity

How does the condition of scarcity determine the economic tradeoffs observed in Canada's newest and largest province?

What products is Canada known for? Canada is a northern country known for its lakes and forests. And what are forests made of? Trees, of course. How important are trees? Just ask the 32,000 residents in the newest Canadian province of Nunavut. They know, because they have no trees!

Larger in area than Alaska and California combined, Nunavut has many natural resources, but lacks the

Eric Chiang

one resource most often associated with Canada: trees. With much of Nunavut's land mass situated above the tree line, it must rely on goods supplied by other provinces and imported from other countries for its building materials and agricultural products. A

visit to Nunavut highlights the prevalence of scarcity and the necessity of specialization and trade.

For example, nearly all of Nunavut's food, household goods, and building materials must be flown in to its sparsely populated communities accessible only by air or snowmobile, resulting in extremely high prices for most goods. However, Nunavut has many gold mines and fisheries that allow it to specialize and export precious metals and its famous Arctic char fish, a close relative to the salmon.

Residents of even the most remote places of the world can solve the challenge of scarcity and gain access to many goods and services by engaging in specialization and trade.

GO TO **LaunchPad** TO PRACTICE THE ECONOMIC CONCEPTS IN THIS STORY

Equally as important as institutions is the ability of societies to create ideas. Ideas change civilizations. Ideas are the basis for creating new products and finding new ways to improve existing goods and services. Human creativity starts with a strong educational system, and builds with proper incentives that allow innovation and creativity to flourish into marketable outcomes to improve the lives of all.

Summing It All Up: Economics Is All Around Us

The examples presented in these key principles should have convinced you that economic decisions are a part of our everyday lives. Anytime we make a decision involving a purchase, or decide what we plan to eat, study, or do with our day, we are making economic decisions. Just keep in mind that economics is broader than an exclusive concern with money, despite the great emphasis placed on money in our everyday economic discussions.

Instead, economics is about making decisions when we can't have everything we want, and how we interact with others to maximize our well-being given limitations. The existence of well-functioning markets allows individuals and firms to come together to achieve good outcomes, and government institutions and policies provide incentives that can lead to a better standard of living for all residents.

The key principles discussed in this chapter will be repeated throughout this book, and you will learn more about these important principles as the term progresses. For now, realize that economics rests on the foundation of a limited number of important principles. Once you fully grasp these basic ideas, the study of economics will be both rewarding and exciting, because after this course you will discover and appreciate how much more you understand the world around you.

 CHECKPOINT

KEY PRINCIPLES OF ECONOMICS

- Economics is concerned with making choices with limited resources.
- When making decisions, one must take into account tradeoffs and opportunity costs.
- Specialization leads to gains for all involved.
- People respond to incentives, both good and bad.
- Rational behavior requires thinking on the margin.
- Markets are generally efficient; when they aren't, government can sometimes correct the failure.
- Economic growth, low unemployment, and low inflation are economic goals that do not always coincide.
- Institutions and human creativity help explain the wealth of nations.

QUESTION: McDonald's introduced a premium blend of coffee that sells for more than its standard coffee. How does this represent thinking at the margin?

Answers to the Checkpoint questions can be found at the end of this chapter.

chapter summary

Section 1
What Is Economics About?

Wallace Garrison/Getty Images

AP Images/YVES LOGGHE

1.1 **Economics** is the study of how individuals, firms, and societies make decisions to improve their well-being given limitations.

Scarcity is the idea that people have unlimited wants but limited resources. Resources can be money, time, ability, work ethic, or anything that can be used to generate productive outcomes.

Scarce versus scarcity: Large uncut diamonds are scarce—only a few are found in the world each year—and are sold for millions of dollars each. A car, on the other hand, is less scarce, as car dealerships around the country have lots full of them. But both large diamonds and cars are subject to scarcity—many people want them, but can only buy what they can afford.

1.2 **What Is the Difference Between Microeconomics and Macroeconomics?**

- M"i"croeconomics deals with individual entities, such as individuals, firms, and industries. (Remember "i" = "individual".)

- M"a"croeconomics deals with aggregate entities, such as cities or the nation. (Remember "a" = "aggregate" or "all".)

1.3 Economic analysis uses a stylized approach: models boil issues and facts down to their basic relevant elements.

1.4 To build models means that we make use of the *ceteris paribus* assumption and hold some important variables constant. This useful device often provides surprising insights about economic behavior.

1.5 Economists and policymakers often confront the tradeoff between efficiency and equity. Efficiency reflects how well resources are used and allocated. Equity (or fairness) of an outcome is a subjective matter, where differences of opinion exist.

age fotostock/SuperStock

How governments deal with pollution is an important problem that can be addressed using economic analysis.

Efficiency   Equity

Fernando Jose Vascocelos Soares/Dreamstime.com

Section 2 Key Principles of Economics

1.6
1.7

1. Economics Is Concerned With Making Choices With Limited Resources

Economics involves making decisions to maximize one's well-being, which can come from many sources, including money, time, happiness, or a fortuitous event.

"We should have done something different this weekend. . . ."

2. When Making Decisions, One Must Take Into Account Tradeoffs and Opportunity Costs

Choice and scarcity force tradeoffs because we face unlimited wants but limited resources. We must make tradeoffs in nearly everything we do. Opportunity costs are resources (e.g., time and money) that could be used in another activity. Everything we do involves opportunity costs, the value of the next best alternative use of our resources.

3. Specialization Leads to Gains for All Involved

Specializing in tasks in which one is comparatively better at doing than another allows individuals to achieve productivity gains as long as the work is shared in a mutually beneficial manner.

4. People Respond to Incentives, Both Good and Bad

Incentives encourage people to work hard and be more productive.

Rewarding the top salesperson in the company creates a valuable incentive to work hard.

Maximizing your food intake at a buffet is not thinking at the margin if you end up bloated from overeating.

5. Rational Behavior Requires Thinking on the Margin

When making a decision involving benefits and costs, one should continue to consume or produce as long as the marginal (additional) benefit exceeds the marginal (additional) cost.

6. Markets Are Generally Efficient; When They Aren't, Government Can Sometimes Correct the Failure

Markets bring buyers and sellers together. Competition forces firms to provide products at the lowest possible price. New products are introduced to the market and old products disappear. This dynamism makes markets efficient. In some instances, though, markets might fail, such as in dealing with pollution, leading governments to intervene to correct the failure.

7. Economic Growth, Low Unemployment, and Low Inflation Are Economic Goals That Do Not Always Coincide

Economic growth is an important factor in improving the standard of living in a country. A government uses various policies to promote economic growth by keeping unemployment and inflation low. However, addressing one goal (unemployment) often comes at the expense of the other (inflation).

Market equilibrium often is achieved by letting market participants make decisions freely.

8. Institutions and Human Creativity Help Explain the Wealth of Nations

Institutions include the legal system, laws and policies, a government free of corruption, and a strong monetary system. Ideas and innovation lead to new products and improve on existing ones, raising the standard of living of all residents.

economics, p. 4
scarcity, p. 4
incentives, p. 5
microeconomics, p. 5

macroeconomics, p. 5
ceteris paribus, p. 6
efficiency, p. 6
equity, p. 6

positive questions, p. 7
normative questions, p. 7
opportunity cost, p. 9

QUESTIONS AND PROBLEMS

Check Your Understanding

1. What is wrong with the statement "Economics is everything to do with money"?

2. Does your going to college have anything to do with expanding choices or reducing scarcity? Explain.

3. What is the difference between a positive question and a normative question?

4. You normally stay at home on Wednesday nights and study. Next Wednesday night, your best friend is having his big 21st birthday party. What is the opportunity cost of going to the party?

5. What is the incentive to spend four years of one's life and tens of thousands of dollars to earn a college degree?

6. Why do markets typically lead to an efficient outcome for buyers and sellers?

Apply the Concepts

7. In contrasting equity and efficiency, why do high-tech firms seem to treat their employees better (better wages, benefits, working environments, vacations, etc.) compared to how landscaping or fast-food franchises treat their employees? Is this fair? Is it efficient?

8. Stores depend on feedback from their customers as a way to improve their business practices and to market their products. To encourage customers to offer feedback, stores will sometimes offer an incentive, such as a discount on a future purchase or additional reward points in a frequent shopper program. Why do some customers, but not all, take advantage of the incentive to leave feedback? Does the actual shopping experience of the customer affect his or her willingness to do so?

9. The black rhinoceros is extremely endangered. Its horn is considered a powerful aphrodisiac in many Asian countries, and a single horn fetches many thousands of dollars on the black market, creating a great incentive for poachers. Unlike other stories of endangered species, this one might have a simple solution. Conservationists could capture as many rhinos as possible and remove their horns, reducing the incentive to poach. Do you think this will help reduce poaching? Why or why not?

10. Most amusement parks in the United States charge a fixed price for admission, which includes unlimited roller coaster rides for the day. Some people attempt to ride the roller coasters as often as possible in order to maximize the value of their admission. Why is riding a roller coaster at an amusement park over and over to "get your money's worth" not considered *thinking on the margin*?

11. Because the U.S. government wants to reduce the nation's reliance on fossil fuels, greater use of solar panels has been encouraged among households and businesses. However, the cost of installing solar panels can be prohibitively expensive for most people. Because people follow incentives, what can the government do to encourage more households and businesses to install solar panels?

12. Some colleges and universities charge tuition by the credit hour, while others charge tuition by the term, allowing students to take as many classes as they desire. How do these tuition structures affect the incentives students face when deciding how many classes to take? Provide an example of a beneficial effect and an example of a potentially harmful effect resulting from the incentives created with each system. How does marginal analysis affect the incentives with each system?

In the News

13. The *New York Times* reported on January 18, 2012, in an article titled "What the Top 1% of Earners Majored In," that 8.2% of Americans who majored in economics for their undergraduate degree are in the top 1% of salary earners. Only those who majored in pre-med had a higher percentage in the top 1%. What might be some reasons why economics majors have done well in the job market?

14. According to the U.S. Department of Transportation, U.S. commercial airlines collected over $3.8 billion in baggage fees in 2015. Some airlines even charge passengers to bring carry-on bags onto the plane. How do baggage fees affect travelers' behavior? What is a potential cost to the airline from this policy that might offset the benefit from the bag revenues?

Solving Problems

15. Suppose your favorite band is on tour and coming to your area. Tickets are $100, and you take a day off from work for which you could have earned $60. What is your opportunity cost of going to the concert?

WORK IT OUT   **LaunchPad** | interactive activity

16. At your local family fun center, miniature golf is $12 per person for unlimited rounds in a day, while each go-kart session is $8. If you played 3 rounds of miniature golf and rode the go-karts 3 times, what was the marginal cost of the third round of miniature golf? What was the marginal cost of the third go-kart session?

USING THE NUMBERS

17. According to By the Numbers, what is the average salary for a recent graduate who majored in economics? About how much does this average salary increase by one's mid-career?

18. According to By the Numbers, about how many economics degrees were awarded to college graduates in 2014? How does this number compare to the number of nursing degrees? Communications degrees?

ANSWERS TO QUESTIONS IN CHECKPOINTS

Checkpoint: What Is Economics About? 8
(1) microeconomics, (2) macroeconomics, (3) microeconomics, (4) macroeconomics, (5) macroeconomics, (6) microeconomics, (7) macroeconomics.

Checkpoint: Key Principles of Economics 15
McDonald's is adding one more product (premium coffee) to its line. Thinking at the margin entails thinking about how you can improve an operation (or increase profits) by adding to your existing product line or reducing costs.

Appendix
Working With Graphs and Formulas

You can't watch the news on television or read a newspaper without seeing a graph of some sort. If you have flipped through this book, you have seen a large number of graphs, charts, and tables, and a few simple equations. This is the language of economics. Economists deal with data for all types of issues. Just looking at data in tables often doesn't help you discern the trends or relationships in the data.

Economists develop theories and models to explain economic behavior and levels of economic activity. These theories or models are simplified representations of real-world activity. Models are designed to distill the most important relationships between variables, and then these relationships are used to predict future behavior of individuals, firms, and industries, or to predict the future course of the overall economy.

In this short section, we will explore the different types of graphs you are likely to see in this course (and in the media) and then turn to an examination of how graphs are used to develop and illustrate models. This second topic leads us into a discussion of modeling relationships between data and how to represent these relationships with simple graphs and equations.

Graphs and Data

The main forms of data graphs are time series, scatter plots, pie charts, and bar charts. Time series, as the name suggests, plot data over time. Most of the figures you will encounter in publications are time series graphs.

Time Series

Time series graphs involve plotting time (minutes, hours, days, months, quarters, or years) on the horizontal axis and the value of some variable on the vertical axis. Figure APX-1 illustrates a time series plot for civilian employment of those 16 years and older. Notice that since the early 1990s, employment has grown by almost 25 million for this group. The vertical strips in the figure designate the last three recessions. Notice that in each case when the recession hit, employment fell, then rebounded after the recession ended.

Scatter Plots

Scatter plots are graphs in which two variables (neither variable being time) are plotted against each other. Scatter plots often give us a hint if the two variables are related to each other in some consistent way. Figure APX-2 plots one variable, median household income, against another variable, percentage of Americans holding a college degree.

Two things can be seen in this figure. First, these two variables appear to be related to each other in a positive way. A rising percentage of college graduates leads to a higher median household income. It is not surprising that college degrees and earnings are related, because increased education leads to a more productive workforce, which translates into more income. Second, given that the years for the data are listed next to the dots, we can see that the percentage of the population with college degrees has risen significantly over the last half-century. From this simple scatter plot, we can see a lot of information and ideas about how the two variables are related.

FIGURE APX-1 **CIVILIAN EMPLOYMENT, 16 YEARS AND OLDER**

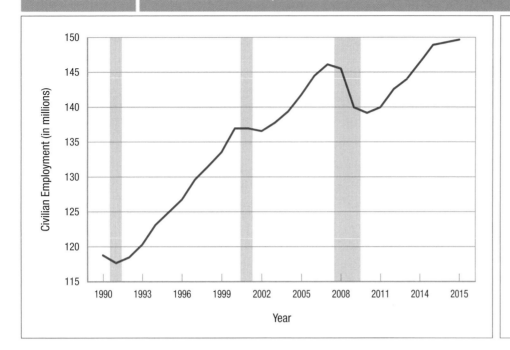

This time series graph shows the number of civilians 16 years and older employed in the United States since 1990. Employment has grown steadily over this period, except in times of recession, indicated by the vertical strips. Note that employment fell during the recession, and then bounced back after each recession ended.

FIGURE APX-2 **THE RELATIONSHIP BETWEEN THE MEDIAN HOUSEHOLD INCOME AND THE PERCENTAGE OF AMERICANS HOLDING A COLLEGE DEGREE**

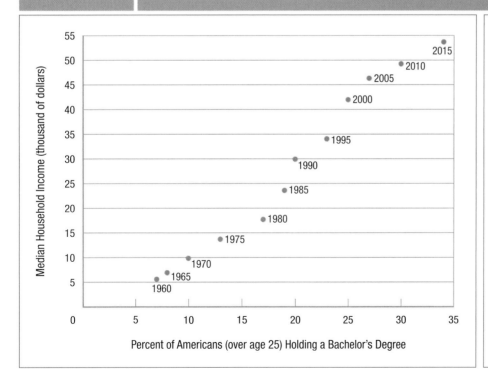

This scatter diagram plots the relationship between median household income and the percentage of Americans holding a college degree. Median household income increased as a greater proportion of Americans earn college degrees. Note that the percentage of Americans earning college degrees has increased significantly in the last half-century.

Pie Charts

Pie charts are simple graphs showing data that can be split into percentage parts that combined make up the whole. A simple pie chart for the relative importance of components in the consumer price index (CPI) is shown in Figure APX-3. It reveals how the typical urban household budget is allocated. By looking at each slice of the pie, we see a picture of how typical families spend their income.

FIGURE APX-3	RELATIVE IMPORTANCE OF CONSUMER PRICE INDEX (CPI) COMPONENTS (2015)

This pie chart shows the relative importance of the components of the consumer price index, showing how typical urban households spend their income.

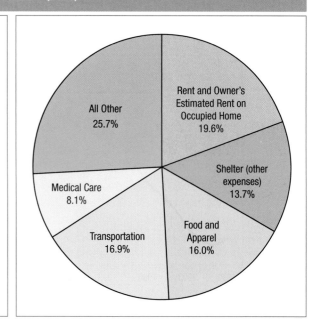

Bar Charts

Bar charts use bars to show the value of specific data points. Figure APX-4 is a bar chart showing the annual changes in real (adjusted for inflation) gross domestic product (GDP). Notice that over the last 50 years, the United States has had only 7 years when GDP declined.

Simple Graphs Can Pack In a Lot of Information   It is not unusual for graphs and figures to have several things going on at once. Look at Figure APX-5, illustrating the number of social media users as a percent of each age group. On the horizontal axis are

FIGURE APX-4	PERCENT CHANGE IN REAL (INFLATION ADJUSTED) GDP

This bar chart shows the annual percent change in real (adjusted for inflation) gross domestic product (GDP) over the last 50 years. Over this period, GDP declined only 7 times.

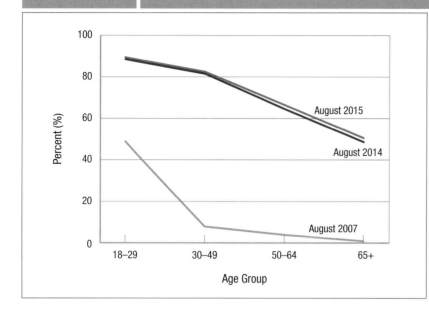

FIGURE APX-5 **SOCIAL MEDIA USAGE ACROSS AGE GROUPS**

These curves show the percentage of Americans using a social media site by age. The curves slope downward because older Americans are less likely to use social media than younger Americans. However, over time, more Americans in all age groups are using social media, as evidenced by each point on the August 2014 curve being higher than the corresponding point on the August 2007 curve, and each point on the August 2015 curve being higher than the corresponding point on the August 2014 curve.

the age groups in years. On the vertical axis is the percent of each age group that regularly used social media. Figure APX-5 shows the relationship between age and social media penetration for different periods. They include the most recent period shown (August 2015), a year previous (August 2014), and eight years ago (August 2007).

You should notice two things in this figure. First, the relationship between the variables slopes downward. This means that older Americans are less likely to use social media than younger Americans. Second, use of social media has increased across all ages over the three periods studied (from August 2007 to August 2014 to August 2015) as shown by the position of the curves. Each point on the August 2015 curve is above the corresponding point on the August 2014 curve, which is subsequently above each point on the August 2007 curve.

A Few Simple Rules for Reading Graphs Looking at graphs of data is relatively easy if you follow a few simple rules. First, read the title of the figure to get a sense of what is being presented. Second, look at the label for the horizontal axis (*x* axis) to see how the data are being presented. Make sure you know how the data are being measured. Is it months or years, hours worked or hundreds of hours worked? Third, examine the label for the vertical axis (*y* axis). This is the value of the variable being plotted on that axis; make sure you know what it is. Fourth, look at the graph itself to see if it makes logical sense. Are the curves (bars, dots) going in the right direction?

Look the graph over and see if you notice something interesting going on. This is really the fun part of looking closely at figures both in this text and in other books, magazines, and newspapers. Often, simple data graphs can reveal surprising relationships between variables. Keep this in mind as you examine graphs throughout this course.

One more thing. Graphs in this book are always accompanied by explanatory captions. Examine the graph first, making your preliminary assessment of what is going on. Then carefully read the caption, making sure it accurately reflects what is shown in the graph. If the caption refers to movement between points, follow this movement in the graph. If you think there is a discrepancy between the caption and the graph, reexamine the graph to make sure you have not missed anything.

Graphs and Models

Let's now take a brief look at how economists use graphs and models, also looking at how they are constructed. Economists use what are called "stylized graphs" to represent

This figure shows a hypothetical linear relationship between average study hours and GPA. Without studying, a D average results, and with 10 hours of studying, a C average is obtained, and so on.

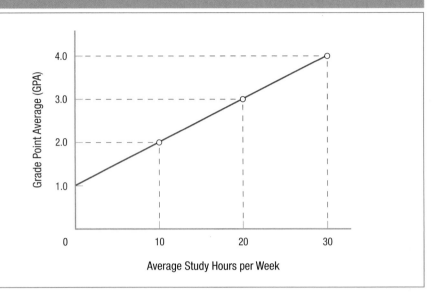

relationships between variables. These graphs are a form of modeling to help us simplify our analysis and focus on those relationships that matter. Figure APX-6 is one such model.

Linear Relationships

Figure APX-6 shows a linear relationship between average study hours and grade point average (GPA), indicating a higher GPA the more you study. By a linear relationship, we mean that the "curve" is a straight line. In this case, if you don't study at all, we assume you are capable of making D's and your GPA will equal 1.0, not enough to keep you in school for long. If you hit the books for an average of 10 hours a week, your GPA rises to 2.0, a C average. Studying for additional hours raises your GPA up to its maximum of 4.0.

The important point here is that the curve is linear; any hour of studying yields the same increase in GPA. All hours of studying provide equal yields from beginning to end. This is what makes linear relationships unique.

Computing the Slope of a Linear Line

Looking at the line in Figure APX-6, we can see two things: The line is straight, so the slope is constant, and the slope is positive. As average hours of studying increase, GPA increases. Computing the slope of the line tells us how much GPA increases for every hour of additional studying. Computing the slope of a linear line is relatively easy and is shown in Figure APX-7.

The simple rule for computing slope is: Slope is equal to rise over run (or rise ÷ run). Since the slope is constant along a linear line, we can select any two points and determine the slope for the entire curve. In Figure APX-7, we have selected points a and b, where GPA moves from 2.0 to 3.0 when studying increases from 10 to 20 hours per week.

Your GPA increases by 1.0 for an additional 10 hours of study. This means that the slope is equal to 0.1 (1.0 ÷ 10 = 0.1). So for every additional hour of studying you add each week, your GPA will rise by 0.1. Thus, if you would like to improve your grade point average from 3.0 to 3.5, you would have to study five more hours per week.

Computing slope for negative relations that are linear is done exactly the same way, except that when computing the changes from one point to another, one of the values will be negative, making the relationship negative.

| **FIGURE APX-7** | **COMPUTING SLOPE FOR A LINEAR LINE** |

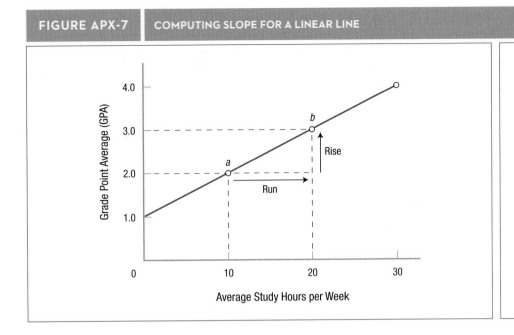

Computing the slope is based on a simple rule: rise over run (rise divided by run). In the case of this straight line, the slope is equal to 0.1 because every 10 additional hours of studying yield a 1.0 increase in GPA.

Nonlinear Relationships

It would be nice for model builders if all relationships were linear, but that is not the case. It is probably not really the case with the amount of studying and GPA either. Figure APX-8 depicts a more realistic nonlinear and positive relationship between studying and GPA. Again, we assume that one can get a D average (1.0) without studying and reach a maximum of straight A's (4.0) with 30 hours of studying per week.

Figure APX-8 suggests that the first few hours of study per week are more important to raising GPA than are the others. The first 10 hours of studying yield more than the last 10 hours. The first 10 hours of study raise one's GPA from 1.0 to 3.3 (a gain of 2.3), while the 20th to the 30th hours raise GPA from 3.8 to 4.0 (a gain of only 0.2). This curve exhibits

| **FIGURE APX-8** | **STUDYING AND YOUR GPA (NONLINEAR)** |

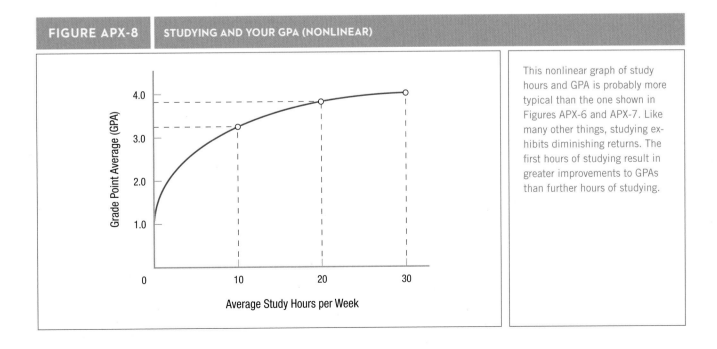

This nonlinear graph of study hours and GPA is probably more typical than the one shown in Figures APX-6 and APX-7. Like many other things, studying exhibits diminishing returns. The first hours of studying result in greater improvements to GPAs than further hours of studying.

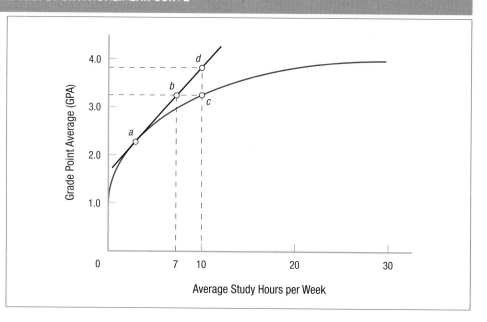

FIGURE APX-9 | **COMPUTING SLOPE FOR A NONLINEAR CURVE**

Computing the slope of a nonlinear curve requires that you compute the slope of each point on the curve. This is done by computing the slope of a tangent to each point.

what economists call diminishing returns. Just as the first bite of pizza tastes better than the 100th, so the first 5 hours of studying bring a bigger jump in GPA than the 25th to 30th hours.

Computing the Slope of a Nonlinear Curve

As you might suspect, computing the slope of a nonlinear curve is a little more complex than for a linear line. But it is not that much more difficult. In fact, we use essentially the same rise over run approach that is used for linear lines.

Looking at the curve in Figure APX-8, it should be clear that the slope varies for each point on the curve. It starts out very steep, then begins to level out above 20 hours of studying. Figure APX-9 shows how to compute the slope at any point on the curve.

Computing the slope at point *a* requires drawing a line tangent to that point, then computing the slope of that line. For point *a*, the slope of the line tangent to it is found by computing rise over run again. In this case, it is length *dc* ÷ *bc* or [(3.8 − 3.3) ÷ (10 − 7)] = 0.5 ÷ 3 = 0.167. Notice that this slope is significantly larger than the original linear relationship of 0.1. If we were to compute the slope near 30 hours of studying, it would approach zero (the slope of a horizontal line is zero).

Ceteris Paribus, Simple Equations, and Shifting Curves

Hold on while we beat this GPA and studying example into the ground. Inevitably, when we simplify analysis to develop a graph or model, important factors or influences must be controlled. We do not ignore them, we hold them constant. These are known as *ceteris paribus* assumptions.

Ceteris Paribus: All Else Equal

By *ceteris paribus*, we mean other things being equal or all other relevant factors, elements, or influences are held constant. When economists define your demand for a product, they want to know how much or how many units you will buy at different prices. For example, to determine how many swimsuits you will buy at various prices (your demand for swimsuits), we hold your income and the price of shoes and shirts

FIGURE APX-10 | STUDYING AND YOUR GPA: A SIMPLE EQUATION

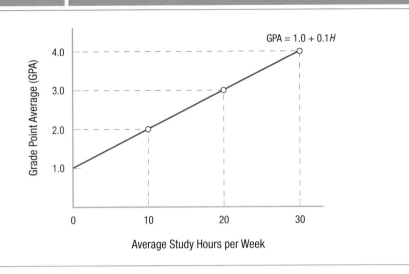

The formula for a linear relationship is $Y = a + bX$, where Y is the y axis variable, X is the x axis variable, and a and b are constants. For the original relationship between study hours and GPA, this equation is $GPA = 1.0 + 0.1H$.

constant. If your income suddenly jumped, you would be willing to buy more swimsuits at all prices, but this is a whole new demand curve. *Ceteris paribus* assumptions are a way to simplify analysis; then the analysis can be extended to include those factors held constant, as we will see next.

Simple Linear Equations

Simple linear equations can be expressed as: $Y = a + bX$. This is read as, Y equals a plus b times X, where Y is the variable plotted on the y axis and a is a constant (unchanging), and b is a different constant that is multiplied by X, the value on the x axis. The formula for our studying and GPA example introduced in Figure APX-6 is shown in Figure APX-10.

The constant a is known as the vertical intercept because it is the value of GPA when study hours (X) is zero, and therefore it cuts (intercepts) the vertical axis at the value of 1.0 (D average). Now each time you study another hour on average, your GPA rises by 0.1, so the constant b (the slope of the line) is equal to 0.1. Letting H represent hours of studying, the final equation is $GPA = 1.0 + 0.1H$. You start with a D average without studying, and as your hours of studying increase, your GPA goes up by 0.1 times the hours of studying. If we plug 20 hours of studying into the equation, the answer is a GPA of 3.0 $[1.0 + (0.1 \times 20) = 1.0 + 2.0 = 3.0]$.

Shifting Curves

Now let's introduce a couple of factors that we have been holding constant (the *ceteris paribus* assumption). These two elements are tutoring and partying. So, our new equation now becomes $GPA = 1.0 + 0.1H + Z$, where Z is our variable indicating whether you have a tutor or whether you are excessively partying. When you have a tutor, $Z = 1$, and when you party too much, $Z = -1$. Tutoring adds to the productivity of your studying (hence $Z = 1$), while excessive late-night partying reduces the effectiveness of studying because you are always tired (hence $Z = -1$). Figure APX-11 shows the impact of adding these factors to the original relationship.

With tutoring, your GPA-studying curve has moved upward and to the left. Now, because $Z = 1$, you begin with a C average (2.0), and with just 20 hours of studying (because of tutoring), you can reach a 4.0 GPA (point a). Alternatively, when you don't have tutoring and you party every night, your GPA–studying relationship has worsened (shifted downward and to the right). Now you must study 40 hours (point c) to accomplish a 4.0 GPA. Note that you begin with failing grades.

The effects of tutoring and partying on our simple model of studying and GPA is shown. Partying harms your academic efforts and shifts the relationship to the right, making it harder to maintain your previous average (you now have to study more hours). Tutoring, on the other hand, improves the relationship (shifts the curve to the left).

The important point here is that we can simplify relationships between different variables and use a simple graph or equation to represent a model of behavior. In doing so, we often have to hold some things constant. When we allow those factors to change, the original relationship is now changed and often results in a shift in the curves. You will see this technique applied over and over as you study economics this term.

Correlation Is Not Causation

Just because two variables seem related or appear related on a scatter plot does not mean that one causes another. Economists 100 years ago correlated business cycles (the ups and downs of the entire economy) with sunspots. Because they appeared related, some suggested that sunspots caused business cycles. The only rational argument was that agriculture was the dominant industry and sunspots affected the weather; therefore, sunspots caused the economy to fluctuate.

Other examples of erroneously assuming that correlation implies causality abound, some of which can be preposterous or humorous. For example, did Facebook cause the Greek debt crisis? Both the number of Facebook users and the total Greek debt skyrocketed between the years of 2005 and 2015. Just because two variables appear to be related does not mean that one causes the other to change.

Understanding graphs and using simple equations are a key part of learning economics. Practice helps.

2

Production, Economic Growth, and Trade

Understanding how economies grow based on the goods and services they choose to produce

Learning Objectives

2.1 Describe the three basic questions that must be answered by any economy.

2.2 Describe production and the factors that go into producing various goods and services.

2.3 Describe the opportunity cost an economy incurs to increase the production of one product.

2.4 Use a production possibilities frontier (PPF) to analyze the limits of production.

2.5 Describe economic growth and how it is stimulated by education and training, capital accumulation, and technological improvements.

2.6 Describe the concepts of absolute and comparative advantage.

2.7 Explain how specialization and trade can lead to gains for all countries involved.

Can a speck of sand be the most significant driver of economic growth of the last generation? Just about every piece of electronic and computing equipment contains a microchip, a tiny piece of circuitry that allows devices to function and to store immense amounts of data and multimedia. Most chips are made of silicon, which is nothing more than a basic element found in sand, and aside from oxygen is the most abundant element in the Earth's crust.

Extracting silicon from sand, melting it, and creating silicon wafers on which transistors are produced to create a functioning microchip is a complex process. More impressive is how efficient the process has become. A single chip smaller than the size of a dime can hold billions of transistors, enough to store and display all of the music, videos, and photos you could ever want on a single device.

Arguably, no invention has transformed the economy more in the past 30 years than the development and advancement of the silicon chip. Technological change has made production methods more efficient, allowing countries to produce more goods and services using fewer physical and natural resources. And as we emphasized in the previous chapter on the importance of scarcity, determining how to achieve more using less—fewer resources—is one of the important goals of economics.

An industry that has experienced significant technological change is telecommunications. In 1950 long-distance phone calls were placed with the assistance of live operators, every minute on the line costing the average consumer the equivalent of several hours' pay. Today, with Internet communications technology allowing one to call virtually anyone in the world for pennies or less, the globe is shrinking as communications brings us closer together and contributes to greater productivity.

Another driver of economic growth is trade. Several centuries ago, individuals produced most of what they consumed. Today, most of us produce little of what we consume. Instead, we work at specialized jobs, then use our wages to purchase the goods we need.

Nearly every country engages in commercial trade with other countries to expand the opportunities for consumption and production by its people. As products are consumed, new products must be produced, allowing increased consumption in one country to spur economic growth in another. Given the ability of global trade to open economic doors and raise incomes, trade is vital for economic growth in all nations.

This chapter gives you a framework for understanding economic growth. It provides a simple model for thinking about production, then applies this model to economies at large so you will know how to think about economic growth and its determinants. It then goes on to analyze international trade as a special case of economic growth. By the time you finish this chapter, you should understand the importance of economic growth and what drives it.

Growth, Productivity, and Trade Are Key to Our Prosperity

Over the last century, investment in education, infrastructure, and technology development, along with increased international trade, has resulted in increased productivity and growth, leading to higher incomes and standards of living around the world.

4-5%

Increase in a nation's economic output from increasing the average years of schooling by 1 year.

20

Number of countries in which the United States has a free trade agreement with as of 2015.

Farm productivity has dramatically increased since 1965 as a result of modern agricultural machinery and new seeds and fertilizers, resulting in higher yields per acre of crops such as corn and soybeans.

Bushels Per Acre — Ii jingwang/iStockphoto — Alina Solowyova-Vincent/iStockphoto

Go to **LaunchPad** *to use the latest data to recreate this graph.*

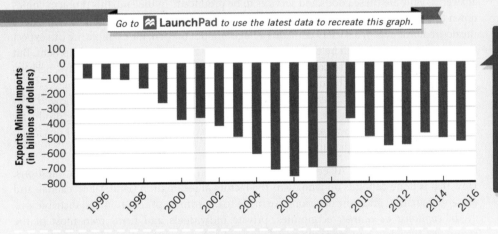

Exports Minus Imports (in billions of dollars) — 1996 1998 2000 2002 2004 2006 2008 2010 2012 2014 2016

Our trade balance (exports minus imports) has grown steadily negative over the last two decades. During each of the last two recessions (shaded areas), our purchases of imports fell, improving our trade balance.

The By the Numbers — Do It Yourself! Lab Activity for this chapter will focus on the U.S. trade balance over the past two decades.

Firing workers can be costly in some countries. Firing a full-time worker with 20 years at the company costs roughly 70 weeks pay in Germany, but it is even more costly in China.

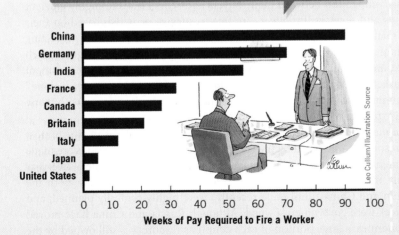

China
Germany
India
France
Canada
Britain
Italy
Japan
United States

0   10   20   30   40   50   60   70   80   90   100
Weeks of Pay Required to Fire a Worker

Leo Cullum/Illustration Source

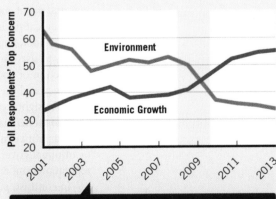

Poll Respondents' Top Concern — Environment — Economic Growth — 2001 2003 2005 2007 2009 2011 2013

American attitudes about concerns for the environment or a preference for economic growth vary based on the state of the economy. As the economy enters a recession (shaded areas), the desire for economic growth increases while concern for the environment ebbs.

BASIC ECONOMIC QUESTIONS AND PRODUCTION

Regardless of the country, its circumstances, or its precise economic structure, every economy must answer three basic questions.

Basic Economic Questions

The three basic economic questions that each society must answer are:

- What goods and services are to be produced?
- How are these goods and services to be produced?
- Who will receive these goods and services?

The response an economy makes to the first question—What goods and services should it produce?—depends on the goods and services a society wants. In a communist state, the government decides what a society wants, but in a capitalist economy, consumers signal what products they want by way of their demands for specific commodities. In the next chapter, we investigate how consumer demand for individual products is determined and how markets meet these demands. For now, we assume that consumers, individually and as a society, are able to decide on the mix of goods and services they most want, and that producers supply these items at acceptable prices.

Once we know what goods a society wants, the next question its economic system must answer is, How are these goods and services to be produced? In the end, this problem comes down to the simple question of how land, labor, and capital should be combined to produce the desired products. If a society demands a huge amount of corn, for example, we can expect the use of its resources will be different from a society that demands digital equipment. But even an economy devoted to corn production could be organized in different ways, perhaps relying on extensive use of human labor, or perhaps relying on automated equipment.

Once an economy has determined what goods and services to produce and how to produce them, it is faced with the distribution question: Who will get the resulting products? *Distribution* refers to the way an economy allocates to consumers the goods and services it produces. How this is done depends on how the economy is organized.

Economic Systems   All economies have to answer the three basic economic questions. How that is done depends on who owns the factors of production (land, labor, capital, and entrepreneurship) and how decisions are made to coordinate production and distribution.

In *capitalist* or *market* economies, private individuals and firms own most of the resources. The what, how, and who decisions are determined by individual desires for products and profit-making decisions by firms. Product prices are the principal mechanism for communicating information in the system. Based on prices, consumers decide whether to buy or not, and firms decide how to employ their resources and what production technology to use. This competition between many buyers and sellers leads to highly efficient production of goods and services. Producers are free to survive or perish based on their efficiency and the quality of their products. The government's primary roles are protecting property rights, enforcing contracts between private parties, providing public goods such as national defense, and establishing and ensuring the appropriate operating environment for competitive markets. Today, the U.S. economy is not a pure *laissez-faire* ("leave it alone," or minimal government role) market economy but more of a mixed economy with many regulations and an extended role for government.

In contrast, *planned* economies (socialist and communist) are systems in which most of the productive resources are owned by the state and most economic decisions are made by central governments. Big sweeping decisions for the economy, often called "five-year plans," are centrally made and focus productive resources on these priorities. Both the former Soviet Union and China (until quite recently) were highly centrally planned, and virtually all resources were government owned. Although Russia and China have moved toward market economies, a large portion of each country's resources is still owned by the state. Socialist countries (e.g., the Scandinavian nations of Europe) enjoy a high degree of freedom, but government plays a big role in providing services paid for by high taxes, and in regulating private businesses.

Resources and Production

Having examined the three basic economic questions, let's take a look at the production process. **Production** involves turning **resources** into products and services that people want. Let's begin our discussion of this process by examining the scarce resources used to produce goods and services.

Land For economists, the term **land** includes both land in the usual sense as well as all other natural resources that are used in production. Natural resources such as mineral deposits, oil and natural gas, and water are all included by economists in the definition of land. Economists refer to the payment to land as *rent*.

Labor Labor as a factor of production includes both the mental and physical talents of people. Few goods and services can be produced without labor resources. Improvement to labor capabilities from training, education, and apprenticeship programs—typically called "human capital"—all add to labor's productivity and ultimately to a higher standard of living. Labor is paid *wages*.

Capital Capital includes all manufactured products that are used to produce other goods and services. This includes equipment such as drill presses, blast furnaces for making steel, and other tools used in the production process. It also includes trucks and automobiles used by businesses, as well as office equipment such as copiers, computers, and telephones. Any manufactured product that is used to produce other products is included in the category of capital. Capital earns *interest*.

Note that the term "capital" as used by economists refers to real (or physical) capital—actual manufactured products used in the production process—not money or financial capital. Money and financial capital are important in that they are used to purchase the real capital that is used to produce products.

Entrepreneurial Ability Entrepreneurs *combine* land, labor, and capital to produce goods and services, and they assume the *risks* associated with running a business. Entrepreneurs combine and manage the inputs of production, and manage the day-to-day marketing, finance, and production decisions. Today, the risks of running a business are huge, as the many bankruptcies and failures testify. Globalization has opened many opportunities as well as risks. For undertaking these activities and assuming the risks associated with business, entrepreneurs earn *profits*.

Production and Efficiency

Production turns *resources*—land, labor, capital, and entrepreneurial ability—into products and services. The necessary production factors vary for different products. To produce corn, for instance, one needs arable land, seed, fertilizer, water, farm equipment, and the workers to operate that equipment. Farmers looking to produce corn would need to devote hundreds of acres of open land to this crop, plow the land, plant and nurture the corn, and finally harvest the crop. Producing digital equipment, in contrast, requires less land but more capital and more highly skilled labor.

As we have seen, every country has to decide what to produce, how to produce it, and who receives the output. Countries desire to do the first two as efficiently as possible by choosing the production method that results in the greatest output using the least amount of resources. Figure 1 shows how factors of production enter into a production method to generate goods and services. Determining the production method is the role of a manager, who must decide how factors of production are best used. Economists refer to this actual choice as the production function, a concept that will be discussed in greater detail in a later chapter. For now, just understand that *how* resources are used is as important as the amount of resources available.

production The process of converting resources (factors of production)—land, labor, capital, and entrepreneurial ability—into goods and services.

resources Productive resources include land (land and natural resources), labor (mental and physical talents of people), capital (manufactured products used to produce other products), and entrepreneurial ability (the combining of the other factors to produce products and assume the risk of the business).

land Includes natural resources such as mineral deposits, oil, natural gas, water, and land in the usual sense of the word. The payment for land used as a resource is rent.

labor Includes the mental and physical talents of individuals who produce products and services. The payment to labor is wages.

capital Includes manufactured products such as tractors, welding equipment, and computers that are used to produce other goods and services. The payment for capital is interest.

entrepreneurs Entrepreneurs combine land, labor, and capital to produce goods and services. They absorb the risk of being in business, including the risk of bankruptcy and other liabilities associated with doing business. Entrepreneurs receive profits for their effort.

Ironbridge:
The Beginnings of the
Industrial Revolution

How did the city of Ironbridge solve a logistical problem using factors of production, and how did it lead to enhanced production and economic growth?

Eric Chiang

What is arguably the most important building material in modern societies? It's steel, which is made primarily from iron ore. Prior to the Industrial Revolution, the use of iron was mostly limited to producing coins and other small trinkets. The Industrial Revolution began with the mass production of iron, and the town of Ironbridge, England, claims to be one of the birthplaces of the Industrial Revolution. Why Ironbridge?

Abraham Darby was an 18th-century British entrepreneur. He developed innovative ways to power machinery using water. In the mid-18th century, Darby built a large aqueduct to harness the natural flow of the river to power his iron furnace. In 1779, when iron began to be produced on a large scale, Darby began building an iron bridge, which was completed in 1781.

How was this bridge revolutionary in design? Made of cast iron, the iron bridge was sturdier than any other bridge built before it. A single span allowed large boats to easily pass underneath its high arch. In fact, the original bridge remains open today, setting the standard for constructing bridges and buildings for centuries to come. The iron bridge represents a feat of engineering that led to the development of physical capital as a key factor of production.

Today, it's difficult to imagine production without the use of machines and other modern tools, and the creative ideas that employ these resources to produce goods efficiently. Physical capital and entrepreneurship are two key factors of production that greatly enhance the other factors of production, land and labor. Combining all of the factors of production has allowed economic growth to flourish over the past two centuries, and this can be traced back to a small Victorian town that bears the name of its most famous landmark.

GO TO **LaunchPad** TO PRACTICE THE ECONOMIC CONCEPTS IN THIS STORY

FIGURE 1 — FROM FACTORS OF PRODUCTION TO OUTPUT

Each of the four factors of production is employed in a production method in order to generate goods and services. The ability to use factors of production efficiently within a production method increases the amount of output given an amount of inputs used.

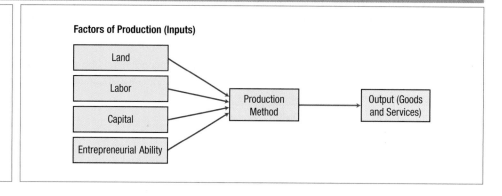

Productivity is a measure of efficiency determined by the amount of output produced given the amount of inputs used. But economists also use specific concepts to describe two different aspects of efficiency: production efficiency and allocative efficiency.

Production efficiency occurs when the mix of goods is produced at the lowest possible resource or opportunity cost. Alternatively, production efficiency occurs when as much output as possible is produced with a given amount of resources. Firms use the best technology available and combine the other resources to create products at the lowest cost to society.

Allocative efficiency occurs when the mix of goods and services produced is the most desired by society. In capitalist countries, this is determined by consumers and businesses and their interaction through markets. The next chapter explores this interaction in some detail. Needless to say, it would be inefficient (a waste of resources) to be producing cassette tapes in the age of digital music players. Allocative efficiency requires that the right mix of goods be produced at the lowest cost.

production efficiency Goods and services are produced at their lowest resource (opportunity) cost.

allocative efficiency The mix of goods and services produced is just what the society desires.

Every economy faces constraints or limitations. Land, labor, capital, and entrepreneurship are all limited. No country has an infinite supply of available workers or the space and machinery that would be needed to put them all to work efficiently. No country can break free of these natural restraints. Such limits are known as production possibilities frontiers, and they are the focus of the next section.

 CHECKPOINT

BASIC ECONOMIC QUESTIONS AND PRODUCTION

- Every economy must decide what to produce, how to produce it, and who will get what is produced.

- Production is the process of converting factors of production (resources)—land, labor, capital, and entrepreneurial ability—into goods and services.

- To the economist, land includes both land and natural resources. Labor includes the mental and physical resources of humans. Capital includes all manufactured products used to produce other goods and services. Entrepreneurs combine resources to manufacture products, and they assume the risk of doing business.

- Production efficiency requires that products be produced at the lowest cost. Allocative efficiency occurs when the mix of goods and services produced is just what society wants.

QUESTION: The one element that really seems to differentiate entrepreneurship from the other resources is the fact that entrepreneurs shoulder the *risk* of the failure of the enterprise. Is this important? Explain.

Answers to the Checkpoint questions can be found at the end of this chapter.

PRODUCTION POSSIBILITIES AND ECONOMIC GROWTH

As we discovered in the previous section, all countries and all economies face constraints on their production capabilities. Production can be limited by the quantity of the various factors of production in the country and its current technology. Technology includes such considerations as the country's infrastructure, its transportation and education systems, and the economic freedom it allows. Although perhaps going beyond the everyday meaning of the word "technology," for simplicity, we will assume that all of these factors help determine the state of a country's technology.

To further simplify matters, production possibilities analysis assumes that the quantity of resources available and the technology of the economy remain constant, and that the economy produces only two products. Although a two-product world sounds far-fetched, this simplification allows us to analyze many important concepts regarding production and tradeoffs. Further, the conclusions drawn from this simple model will not differ fundamentally from a more complex model of the real world.

Production Possibilities

Assume that our simple economy produces backpacks and tablet computers. Figure 2 with its accompanying table shows the production possibilities frontier for this economy. The table shows seven possible production levels (*a–g*). These seven combinations, which range from 12,000 backpacks and zero tablets to zero backpacks and 6,000 tablets, are graphed in Figure 2.

When we connect the seven production possibilities, we delineate the **production possibilities frontier (PPF)** for this economy (some economists refer to this curve as the production possibilities curve). All points on the PPF are considered *attainable* by our economy. Everything to the left of the PPF is also attainable, but is an inefficient use of

production possibilities frontier (PPF) Shows the combinations of two goods that are possible for a society to produce at full employment. Points on or inside the PPF are attainable, and those outside of the frontier are unattainable.

| FIGURE 2 | PRODUCTION POSSIBILITIES FRONTIER |

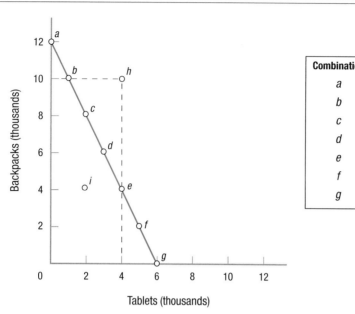

Combination	Backpacks	Tablets
a	12,000	0
b	10,000	1,000
c	8,000	2,000
d	6,000	3,000
e	4,000	4,000
f	2,000	5,000
g	0	6,000

Using all of its resources, this stylized economy can produce many combinations of backpacks and tablets. Production levels on, or to the left of, the resulting PPF are attainable for this economy. Production levels to the right of the PPF are unattainable.

resources—the economy can always do better. Everything to the right of the curve is considered *unattainable.* Therefore, the PPF maps out the economy's limits; it is impossible for the economy to produce at levels beyond the PPF without an increase in resources or technology, or both.

What the PPF in Figure 2 shows is that, given an efficient use of limited resources and taking technology into account, this economy can produce any of the seven combinations of tablets and backpacks listed, each of which represents a combination where the economy cannot produce another unit without giving up something. If society wants to produce 1,000 tablets, it will only be able to produce 10,000 backpacks, as shown by point *b* on the PPF. Should the society decide that mobile Internet access is important, it might decide to produce 4,000 tablets, which would force it to cut backpack production to 4,000, shown by point *e*. At each of these points, resources are fully employed in the economy, and therefore increasing production of one good requires giving up some production of the other. Also, the economy can produce any combination of the two products on or within the PPF, but not any combination beyond it.

Contrast points *c* and *e* with production at point *i.* At point *i,* the economy is only producing 2,000 tablets and 4,000 backpacks. Clearly, some resources are not being used. When fully employed, the economy's resources could produce more of both goods (point *d*).

Because the PPF represents combinations of goods using resources fully, the economy could not produce 4,000 tablets and still produce 10,000 backpacks. This situation, shown by point *h,* lies to the right of the PPF and hence outside the realm of possibility. Anything to the right of the PPF is impossible for our economy to attain.

Opportunity Cost Whenever a country reallocates resources to change production patterns, it does so at a price. This price is called **opportunity cost.** Recall from Chapter 1 that opportunity cost is what you *give up* when making an economic decision. Here, society is deciding how many backpacks and tablets to produce. If society decides to produce more tablets, it gives up the ability to produce more backpacks. Shown through the PPF, the opportunity cost of producing more of one good is determined by the amount of the other good that is given up. In moving from point *b* to point *e* in Figure 2, tablet production increases by 3,000 units, from 1,000 units to 4,000 units. However, the country must forgo

opportunity cost The cost paid for one product in terms of the output (or consumption) of another product that must be forgone.

producing 6,000 backpacks because production falls from 10,000 backpacks to 4,000 backpacks. Giving up 6,000 backpacks for 3,000 more tablets represents an opportunity cost of 6,000 backpacks for these 3,000 tablets, or two backpacks for each tablet.

Opportunity cost thus represents the tradeoff required when an economy wants to increase its production of any single product. Governments must choose between infrastructure and national parks, or between military spending and social spending. Since there are limits to what taxpayers are willing to pay, spending choices are necessary. Think of opportunity costs as what you or the economy must give up to have more of a product or service.

Increasing Opportunity Costs   In most cases, land, labor, and capital cannot easily be shifted from producing one good or service to another. You cannot take a semitrailer and use it to plow a field, even though the semi and a top-of-the-line tractor cost about the same. The fact is that some resources are suited to specific sorts of production, just as some people seem to be better suited to performing one activity over another. Some people have a talent for music or art, and they would be miserable—and inefficient—working as accountants or computer programmers. Some people find they are more comfortable working outside, while others require the amenities of an environmentally controlled, ergonomically designed office.

Thus, a more realistic production possibilities frontier is shown in Figure 3. This PPF is concave to (or bowed away from) the origin, because opportunity costs rise as more factors are used to produce increasing quantities of one product. Another way of saying this is that resources are subject to diminishing returns as more resources are devoted to the production of one product. Let's consider why this is so.

Let's begin at a point at which the economy's resources are strictly devoted to backpack production (point *a*). Now assume that society decides to produce 3,200 tablets. This will require a move from point *a* to point *b*. As we can see, 2,000 backpacks must be given up to obtain the added 3,200 tablets. This means the opportunity cost of 1 tablet is 0.625 backpacks (2,000 ÷ 3,200 = 0.625). This is a low opportunity cost, because those resources that are better suited to producing tablets will be the first ones shifted into this industry.

But what happens when this society decides to produce an additional 2,000 tablets, or moves from point *b* to point *c* on the graph? As Figure 3 illustrates, each additional tablet

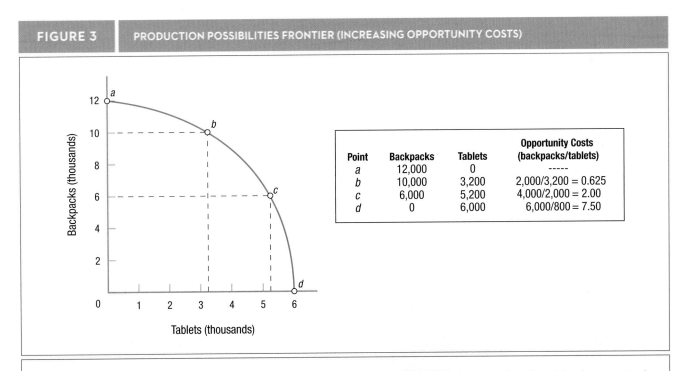

FIGURE 3   **PRODUCTION POSSIBILITIES FRONTIER (INCREASING OPPORTUNITY COSTS)**

Point	Backpacks	Tablets	Opportunity Costs (backpacks/tablets)
			-----
a	12,000	0	-----
b	10,000	3,200	2,000/3,200 = 0.625
c	6,000	5,200	4,000/2,000 = 2.00
d	0	6,000	6,000/800 = 7.50

This figure shows a more realistic production possibilities frontier for an economy. This PPF is bowed out from the origin, since opportunity costs rise as more factors are used to produce increasing quantities of one product or the other.

costs 2 backpacks because producing 2,000 more tablets requires the society to sacrifice 4,000 backpacks. Thus, the opportunity cost of tablets has more than tripled due to diminishing returns on the tablet side, which arise because added resources are not as well suited to the production of tablets.

To describe what has happened in plain terms, when the economy was producing 12,000 backpacks, all its resources went into backpack production. Those members of the labor force who are engineers and electronic assemblers were probably not well suited to producing backpacks. As the economy reduces backpack production to start producing tablets, the opportunity cost of tablets was low, because the resources first shifted, including workers, were likely to be the ones most suited to tablet production and least suited to backpack manufacture. Eventually, however, as tablets became the dominant product, manufacturing more tablets required shifting workers skilled in backpack production to the tablet industry. Employing these less suitable resources drives up the opportunity costs of tablets.

You may be wondering which point along the PPF is the best for society. Economists have no grounds for stating unequivocally which mixture of goods and services would be ideal. The perfect mixture of goods depends on the tastes and preferences of the members of society. In a capitalist economy, resource allocation is determined largely by individual choices and the workings of private markets. We consider these markets and their operations in the next chapter.

Economic Growth

We have seen that PPFs map out the maximum that an economy can produce: Points to the right of the PPF are unattainable. But what if the PPF can be shifted to the right? This shift would give economies new maximum frontiers. In fact, we will see that economic growth can be viewed as a shift in the PPF outward. In this section, we use the production possibilities model to determine some of the major reasons for economic growth. Understanding these reasons for growth will enable us to suggest some broad economic policies that could lead to expanded growth.

The production possibilities model holds resources and technology constant to derive the PPF. These assumptions suggest that economic growth has two basic determinants: expanding resources and improving technologies. The expansion of resources allows producers to increase production of all goods and services in an economy. Specific technological improvements, however, often affect only one industry directly. The development of a new color printing process, for instance, will directly affect only the printing industry.

Nevertheless, ripples from technological improvements can spread out through an entire economy, just like ripples in a pond. Specifically, improvements in technology can lead to new products, improved goods and services, and increased productivity.

Sometimes technological improvements in one industry allow other industries to increase their production with existing resources. This means producers can increase output without using added labor or other resources. Alternatively, they can get the same production levels as before by using fewer resources than before. This frees up resources in the economy for use in other industries.

When the electric lightbulb was invented, it not only created a new industry (someone had to produce lightbulbs), but it also revolutionized other industries. Factories could stay open longer since they no longer had to rely on the sun for light. Workers could see better, thus improving the quality of their work. The result was that resources operated more efficiently throughout the entire economy.

The modern-day equivalent of the lightbulb might be the smartphone. Widespread use of these mobile devices enables people all across the world to produce goods and services more efficiently. Insurance agents can file claims instantly from disaster sites, deals can be closed while one is stuck in traffic, and communications have been revolutionized. Thus, this new technology has ultimately expanded time, the most finite of our resources. A similar argument could be made for the Internet. It has profoundly changed how many products are bought, sold, and delivered, and has expanded communications and the flow of information.

"Beaming" objects might not be restricted to *Star Trek* fantasy with the development of 3D printers capable of reproducing objects. Could this be the next big technological advancement in printing?

Monty Rakusen/Getty Images

| FIGURE 4 | ECONOMIC GROWTH BY EXPANDING RESOURCES |

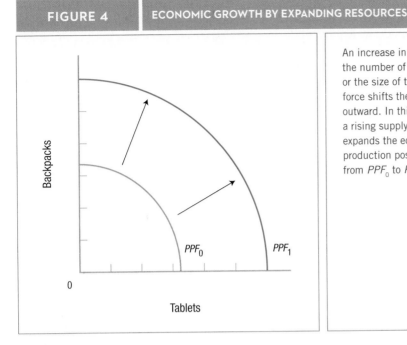

An increase in population, the number of households, or the size of the labor force shifts the PPF outward. In this figure, a rising supply of labor expands the economy's production possibilities from PPF_0 to PPF_1.

Expanding Resources The PPF represents the possible output of an economy at a specific time. But economies are constantly changing, and so are PPFs. Capital and labor are the principal resources that can be changed through government action. Land and entrepreneurial talent are important factors of production, but neither is easy to change by government policies. The government can make owning a business easier or more profitable by reducing regulations, or by offering low-interest loans or favorable tax treatment to small businesses. However, it is difficult to turn people into risk takers through government policy.

Increasing Labor and Human Capital A clear increase in population, the number of households, or the size of the labor force shifts the PPF outward, as shown in Figure 4. With added labor, the production possibilities available to the economy expand from PPF_0 to PPF_1. Such a labor increase can be caused by higher birthrates, increased immigration, or an increased willingness of people to enter the labor force. This last type of increase has occurred over the past several decades as more women have entered the labor force on a permanent basis. America's high level of immigration (both legal and illegal) fuels a strong rate of economic growth.

Rather than simply increasing the number of people working, however, the labor factor can also be increased by improving workers' skills. Economists refer to this as *investment in human capital*. Education, on-the-job training, and other professional training fit into this category. Improving human capital means people are more productive, resulting in higher wages, a higher standard of living, and an expanded PPF for society.

Capital Accumulation Increasing the capital used throughout the economy, usually brought about by investment, similarly shifts the PPF outward, as shown in Figure 4. Additional capital makes each unit of labor more productive and thus results in higher possible production throughout the economy. Adding robotics and computer-controlled machines to production lines, for example, means each unit of labor produces many more units of output.

The production possibilities model and the economic growth associated with capital accumulation suggest a tradeoff. Figure 5 illustrates the tradeoff all nations face between current consumption and capital accumulation.

Let's first assume that a nation selects a product mix in which the bulk of goods produced are consumption goods—that is, goods that are immediately consumable and have short life spans, such as food and entertainment. This product mix is represented by point *b* in Figure 5. Consuming most of what it produces, a decade later the economy is at PPF_b. Little growth has occurred, because the economy has done little to improve its productive capacity—the present generation has essentially decided to consume rather than to invest in the economy's future.

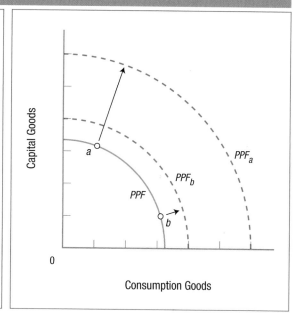

| FIGURE 5 | CONSUMPTION GOODS, CAPITAL GOODS, AND THE EXPANSION OF THE PRODUCTION POSSIBILITIES FRONTIER |

If a nation selects a product mix in which the bulk of goods produced are consumption goods, it will initially produce at point *b*. The small investment made in capital goods has the effect of expanding the nation's productive capacity only to PPF_b over the following decade. If the country decides to produce at point *a*, however, devoting more resources to producing capital goods, its productive capacity will expand much more rapidly, pushing the *PPF* out to PPF_a over the following decade.

Contrast this decision with one in which the country at first decides to produce at point *a*. In this case, more capital goods such as machinery and tools are produced, while fewer consumption goods are used to satisfy current needs. Selecting this product mix results in the much larger PPF a decade later (PPF_a), because the economy steadily built up its productive capacity during those 10 years.

Technological Change   Figure 6 illustrates what happens when an economy experiences a technological change in one of its industries, in this case, the tablet industry. As the figure shows, the economy's potential output of tablets expands greatly, although its maximum production of backpacks remains unchanged. The area between the two curves represents an improvement in the society's standard of living. People can produce and consume more of both goods than before: more tablets because of the technological advancement, and more backpacks because some of the resources once devoted to tablet production can be shifted to backpack production, even as the economy is turning out more tablets than before.

This example reflects the United States today, where the computer industry is exploding with new technologies. Companies such as Apple and Intel lead the way by relentlessly developing newer, faster, and more powerful products. Consequently, consumers have seen home computers go from clunky conversation pieces to powerful, fast, indispensable machines. Today's computers are more powerful than the mainframe supercomputers of just a few decades ago. And the latest developments in smartphones allow them to do much more than what powerful computers did a decade ago.

Besides new products, technology has dramatically reduced the cost of producing tablets and other high-tech items, allowing countries to produce and consume more of other products, expanding the entire PPF outward. However, the effect of technology on an economy also depends on how well its important trade centers are linked together. If a country has mostly dirt paths rather than paved highways, you can imagine how this deficiency would affect its economy: Distribution will be slow, and industries will be slow to react to changes in demand. In such a case, improving the roads might be the best way to stimulate economic growth.

As you can see, there are many ways to stimulate economic growth. A society can expand its output by using more resources, perhaps by encouraging more people to enter the workforce or raising educational levels of workers. The government can encourage people to invest more, as opposed to devoting their earnings to immediate consumption. The public sector can spur technological advances by providing incentives to private firms to do research and development or underwrite research investments of its own.

FIGURE 6	TECHNOLOGICAL CHANGE AND EXPANSION OF THE PRODUCTION POSSIBILITIES FRONTIER

In this figure, an economy's potential output of tablets has expanded greatly, while its maximum production of backpacks has remained unchanged. The area between the two curves represents an improvement in the society's standard of living, since more of both goods can be produced and consumed than before. Some of the resources once used for tablet production can be diverted to backpack production, even as the number of tablets produced increases.

Summarizing the Sources of Economic Growth Economic growth is driven by many factors, as we have seen. A study by the Organisation for Economic Co-operation and Development (OECD)[1] focused on what has been driving economic growth in twenty-one nations over the last several decades. The study first looked at contributions to economic growth from the macroeconomic perspective of added resources and technological

ISSUE

Is the Ocean the Next Frontier? Land Reclamation and Underwater Cities

Can a city exist underneath the ocean surface? A team of engineers in Japan say that such cities can become a reality by 2030. They created a proposal for an underwater city that is powered by a process called *ocean thermal energy conversion,* in which power is generated from the differences in seawater temperatures at different depths. Can a self-sustained underwater city be a reality? If so, it could generate a vast amount of new territory around the world, since the majority of the Earth is covered by oceans that could become the next frontier.

In fact, using the vast expanse of the ocean has already become a reality in some countries. Japan, Hong Kong, Singapore, and the United Arab Emirates have built islands off of their coastlines using a process called *land reclamation,* in which sand is moved from other parts of the ocean to create new land above the ocean's surface. More recently, China made headlines by building islands *far* from its coastline, which brings into question the role of property rights.

One of the concerns with underwater cities or land reclamation is who actually owns the right to live in the ocean. Because international waters begin 12 nautical miles beyond a country's coastline, some have questioned whether creating underwater cities or new islands in the ocean is merely a way

for a country to acquire new territory, and subsequently the resources deriving from that territory, such as fish, natural resources, or a strategic geographic location for military purposes.

[1] *The Sources of Economic Growth in the OECD Countries* (Paris: Organisation for Economic Co-operation and Development), 2003.

improvements as we have been discussing in this chapter. It then looked at some benefits from good government policies that stimulate growth, and finally examined the industry and individual firm level for clues to the microeconomic sources of growth. The study showed that some of the policies that have led to growth and subsequently higher standards of living in these countries include:

- Increasing business investment (physical capital).
- Increasing average education levels (human capital).
- Increasing research and development.
- Reducing both the level and variability of inflation.
- Reducing the tax burden.
- Increasing the level of international trade.

One important point to take away from this discussion is that our simple stylized model of the economy using only two goods gives a good first framework upon which to judge proposed policies for the economy. While not overly complex, this simple analysis is still quite powerful.

 CHECKPOINT

PRODUCTION POSSIBILITIES AND ECONOMIC GROWTH

- A production possibilities frontier (PPF) depicts the different combinations of goods that a fully employed economy can produce, given its available resources and current technology (both assumed fixed in the short run).
- Production levels inside and on the frontier are possible, but those outside the curve are unattainable.
- Because production on the frontier represents the maximum output attainable when all resources are fully employed, reallocating production from one product to another involves *opportunity costs*: The output of one product must be reduced to get the added output of the other. The more of one product that is desired, the higher its opportunity cost because of diminishing returns and the unsuitability of some resources for producing some products.
- The PPF model suggests that economic growth can arise from an expansion in resources or improvements in technology. Economic growth is an outward shift of the PPF.

QUESTION: Taiwan is a small mountainous island with 23 million inhabitants, little arable land, and few natural resources, while Nigeria is a much larger country with 7 times the population, 40 times more arable land, and tremendous deposits of oil. Given Nigeria's sizable resource advantage, why is Nigeria's total annual production less than that of Taiwan's?

Answers to the Checkpoint questions can be found at the end of this chapter.

SPECIALIZATION, COMPARATIVE ADVANTAGE, AND TRADE

As we have seen, economics is all about voluntary production and exchange. People and nations do business with one another because all expect to gain from the transactions. Centuries ago, European merchants ventured to the Far East to ply the lucrative spice trade. These days, American consumers buy wines from Italy, cars from Japan, electronics from Korea, and millions of other products from countries around the world.

Many people assume that trade between nations is a zero-sum game—a game in which, for one party to gain, another party must lose. This is how poker works. If one player walks away from the table a winner, someone else must have lost. But this is not how voluntary trade works. Voluntary trade is a positive-sum game: Both parties to a transaction score positive gains. After all, who would voluntarily enter into an exchange if he or she did not believe there was some gain from it? To understand how all parties to an exchange (whether individuals or nations) can gain from it, we need to consider the concept of comparative advantage developed by David Ricardo roughly 200 years ago, and how this concept differs from the concept of absolute advantage.

Absolute and Comparative Advantage

Figure 7 shows hypothetical production possibilities frontiers for the United States and Mexico. To simplify the analysis, we assume that opportunity costs are constant (PPFs are straight lines); however, the same analysis applies to PPFs with increasing opportunity costs. Both countries are assumed to produce only crude oil and silicon chips. Given the PPFs in Figure 7, the United States has an **absolute advantage** over Mexico in producing both products. An absolute advantage exists when one country can produce more of a good than another country. In this instance, the United States can produce 2 times more oil (40 million versus 20 million barrels) and 5 times as many silicon chips (40 million versus 8 million chips) as Mexico.

At first glance, you might wonder why the United States would even consider trad-

DAVID RICARDO (1772-1823)

David Ricardo's rigorous, dispassionate evaluation of economic principles influenced generations of theorists, including such vastly different thinkers as John Stuart Mill and Karl Marx. Ricardo was born in London as the third of 17 children. At age 14, he joined his father's trading business on the London Stock Exchange. At 21, he started his own brokerage and within five years had amassed a small fortune.

While vacationing in Bath, England, he chanced upon a copy of Adam Smith's *The Wealth of Nations,* and decided to devote his energies to studying economics and writing. He once wrote to his lifelong friend Thomas Malthus (another prominent economist of the time) that he was "thankful for the miserable English climate because it kept him at his desk writing." Ricardo and Malthus corresponded on a regular basis, and their exchanges led to the development of many economic concepts still used today.

Later, as a member of the British Parliament, Ricardo was an outspoken critic of the 1815 Corn Laws, which placed high tariffs on imported grain to protect British landowners. Ricardo was a strong advocate of free trade, and his writings reflected this view. His theory of "comparative advantage" suggested that countries would mutually benefit from trade by specializing in export goods they could produce at a lower opportunity cost than another country. His classic example was trade in cloth and wine between Britain and Portugal.

Ricardo died in 1823 of an ear infection, leaving an enduring legacy of classical (pre-1930s) economic analysis.

Information from E. Ray Canterbery, *A Brief History of Economics* (New Jersey: World Scientific), 2001; Howard Marshall, *The Great Economists: A History of Economic Thought* (New York: Pitman Publishing), 1967; Steven Pressman, *Fifty Major Economists,* 2nd ed. (New York: Routledge), 2006.

ing with Mexico. The United States has so much more production capacity than Mexico, so why wouldn't it just produce all of its own crude oil and silicon chips? The answer lies in comparative advantage.

One country has a **comparative advantage** in producing a good if its opportunity cost to produce that good is lower than the other country's. We can calculate each country's opportunity cost for each good using the production possibility frontiers in Figure 7.

If the United States uses all of its resources efficiently, it can produce a maximum of 40 million barrels of oil *or* 40 million silicon chips. It can also produce some of both goods, though clearly not 40 million of each, because in order to produce more of one good, it must reduce production of another (its opportunity cost). Because the PPF is linear, the tradeoff between oil and chips is constant. For the United States, it can substitute 1 million barrels of oil for 1 million silicon chips, which means it can produce 20 million barrels of oil and 20 million silicon chips. The opportunity cost for each good is summarized as follows:

- For every barrel of oil the United States produces, it must give up producing one silicon chip.

- For every silicon chip the United States produces, it must give up producing one barrel of oil.

Now let's look at Mexico. If it uses its resources efficiently, it can produce a maximum of 20 million barrels of oil *or* 8 million silicon chips. For Mexico, although the tradeoff between

absolute advantage One country can produce more of a good than another country.

comparative advantage One country has a lower opportunity cost of producing a good than another country.

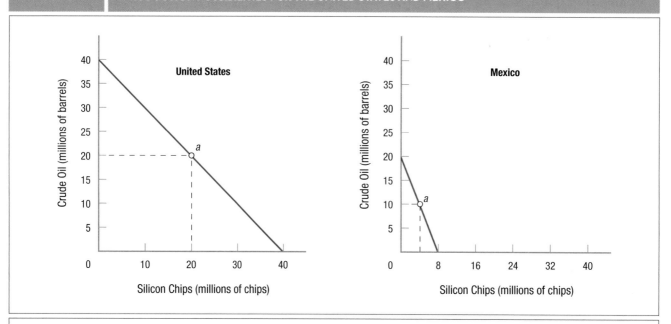

FIGURE 7 PRODUCTION POSSIBILITIES FOR THE UNITED STATES AND MEXICO

One country has an absolute advantage if it can produce more of a good than another country. In this case, the United States has an absolute advantage over Mexico in producing both silicon chips and crude oil—it can produce more of both goods than Mexico can. Even so, Mexico has a comparative advantage over the United States in producing oil, since it can increase its output of oil at a lower opportunity cost than can the United States. This comparative advantage leads to gains for both countries from specialization and trade.

goods also is constant, the tradeoff is not one-for-one as in the United States. Because Mexico is better at producing oil than silicon chips, its opportunity cost for each good is as follows:

- For every barrel of oil Mexico produces, it must give up producing 0.4 silicon chips.
- For every silicon chip Mexico produces, it must give up producing 2.5 barrels of oil.

Note that the values of 0.4 and 2.5 are reciprocals of one another. In other words, $1/0.4 = 2.5$, and $1/2.5 = 0.4$. This relationship exists when calculating opportunity costs in a two-product economy.

Now that we have determined the opportunity cost of each good in both countries, we can conclude that Mexico has a comparative advantage over the United States in producing oil. This is because Mexico gives up only 0.4 chips for every barrel of oil it produces, while the United States must give up 1 chip. Thus, Mexico's opportunity cost of producing oil is less than that of the United States, giving Mexico a comparative advantage.

Conversely, the United States has a comparative advantage over Mexico in producing silicon chips: Producing a silicon chip in the United States costs one barrel of oil, whereas the same chip in Mexico costs two-and-a-half barrels of oil. Table 1 summarizes the opportunity costs of each good and which country has the comparative advantage.

TABLE 1	COMPARING OPPORTUNITY COSTS FOR OIL AND CHIP PRODUCTION		
	United States Opportunity Cost	Mexico Opportunity Cost	Comparative Advantage
Oil Production	1 chip	0.4 chips	Mexico
Chip Production	1 barrel of oil	2.5 barrels of oil	United States

Note that each country has a comparative advantage in one good, even though the United States has an absolute advantage in both goods. However, it is comparative advantage that generates gains from trade. These relative costs suggest that the United States should pour its resources into producing silicon chips, while Mexico specializes in crude oil. The two countries can then engage in trade to their mutual benefit. As long as opportunity costs differ between countries, specialization and trade can be mutually beneficial, allowing all countries to consume more.

The same idea applies to individuals. Although we have focused on trade between countries, the concept of comparative advantage explains why individuals specialize in a few tasks and then trade with one another. For example, if you are relatively better at understanding economics than your roommate who is on the golf team, you might offer to tutor him in economics in exchange for golf lessons. Comparative advantage explains all trade: between individuals as well as between countries.

The Gains From Trade

To see how specialization and trade can benefit all trading partners, let's return to our example in which the United States has the ability to produce more of both goods than Mexico. Assume that each country is at first (before trade) operating at point *a* in Figure 7. At this point, both countries are producing and consuming only their own output; the United States produces and consumes 20 million barrels of oil and 20 million silicon chips; Mexico, 10 million barrels of oil and 4 million chips. Table 2 summarizes these initial conditions.

Now assume that Mexico focuses on oil, producing the maximum it can: 20 million barrels. We also assume both countries want to continue consuming 30 million barrels of oil between them. Therefore, the United States only needs to produce 10 million barrels of oil because Mexico is now producing 20 million barrels. For the United States, this frees up some resources that can be diverted to producing silicon chips. Because each barrel of oil in the United States costs one chip, reducing oil output by 10 million barrels means that 10 million more chips can be produced.

Table 3 shows each country's production after Mexico has begun specializing in oil production.

Notice that the combined production of crude oil has remained constant, but the total output of silicon chips has risen by 6 million chips. Assuming that the two countries agree to share the added 6 million chips between them equally, Mexico will now ship 10 million

TABLE 2	INITIAL CONSUMPTION-PRODUCTION PATTERN		
	United States	Mexico	Total
Oil	20	10	30
Chips	20	4	24

TABLE 3	PRODUCTION AFTER MEXICO SPECIALIZES IN PRODUCING CRUDE OIL		
	United States	Mexico	Total
Oil	10	20	30
Chips	30	0	30

TABLE 4	FINAL CONSUMPTION PATTERNS AFTER TRADE		
	United States	**Mexico**	**Total**
Oil	20	10	30
Chips	23	7	30

barrels of oil to the United States in exchange for 7 million chips. From the 10 million additional chips the United States produces, Mexico will receive 4 million (its original production) plus 3 million for a total of 7 million, leaving 3 million additional chips for U.S. consumption. The resulting mix of products consumed in each country is shown in Table 4. Clearly, both countries are better off, having engaged in specialized production and trade.

The important point to remember here is that even when one country has an absolute advantage over another, both countries still benefit from trading with one another. In our example, the gains were small, but such gains can grow. As two economies become more equal in size, the benefits of their comparative advantages grow.

Practical Constraints on Trade

Before leaving the subject of international trade and how it contributes to growth in both countries, we should take a moment to note some practical constraints on trade. First, every transaction involves costs, including transportation, communications, and the general costs of doing business. Even so, over the last several decades, transportation and communication costs have been declining all over the world, resulting in growing global trade.

Second, the production possibilities curves for nations are not linear, but rather governed by increasing costs and diminishing returns. Therefore, it is difficult for countries to specialize in producing one product. Complete specialization would be risky, moreover, because the market for a product can always decline, perhaps because the product becomes technologically obsolete. Alternatively, changing weather patterns can wreak havoc on specialized agricultural products, adding further instability to incomes and exports in developing countries.

Finally, although two countries may benefit from trading with one another, expanding this trade may well hurt some industries and individuals within each country. Notably, industries finding themselves at a comparative disadvantage may be forced to scale back production and lay off workers. In such instances, government may need to provide workers with retraining, relocation, and other help to ensure a smooth transition to the new production mix.

When the United States signed the North American Free Trade Agreement (NAFTA) with Canada and Mexico, many people experienced what we have just been discussing. Some U.S. jobs went south to Mexico because of low production costs. By opening up more markets for U.S. products, however, NAFTA did stimulate economic growth, such that retrained workers ended up with new and better jobs.

ISSUE

Do We Really Specialize in That? Comparative Advantage in the United States and China

What do tofu, edamame, ink, soy sauce, livestock feed, and soy milk have in common? They are all important products commonly made from soybeans. Although direct human consumption of soybeans in the United States is often confined to health food products and food in Asian restaurants, soybeans are much more important to the U.S. economy than most people think. The United States has a comparative advantage in soybean production. It produces and sells more soybeans than any other country, with much of it being sold to China.

How can a rich, technologically advanced country like the United States end up with a comparative advantage in an agricultural good like soybeans? Several factors play a role. First, the United States has an abundance of farmland ideal in climate and soil for soybean production. Second, modern fertilizers and seed technologies have made soybean production a much more innovative industry than in the past, allowing farms to increase soybean yields per acre of land. And third, a strong appetite for soy-based products, particularly in China, has made soybeans a very lucrative industry.

China is the second largest trading partner to the United States after Canada, trading $610 billion worth of goods between the countries in 2014. Yet, the top five U.S. export goods (items sold) and import goods (items bought) with China, listed below, may be surprising.

Dušan Kostić/iStockphoto

Top Five Exports to China (2014)

1. Soybeans ($15.3 billion)
2. Aircraft ($13.9 billion)
3. Automobiles ($13.2 billion)
4. Machinery ($12.5 billion)
5. Electrical goods ($12.0 billion)

Top Five Imports from China (2014)

1. Electrical goods ($129.8 billion)
2. Machinery ($108.1 billion)
3. Furniture ($28.0 billion)
4. Toys/sporting goods ($23.7 billion)
5. Footwear ($17.8 billion)

Although the United States sells a lot of machines and electrical goods to China (mostly specialized machinery and electronics used in factories and research labs), it buys significantly greater amounts of these products *from* China. In other words, the United States is a net buyer of machinery and electrical goods, industries that include many consumer technology goods we use, such as smartphones, computers, and digital equipment. Besides soybeans, wood pulp, copper, and wood are three other resource industries (not listed here but in the top 10) that constitute a large portion of U.S. sales *to* China.

In sum, specialization and trade are not as simple as they used to be. Products such as computers and electronics that once were the purview of "rich" countries like the United States are now being manufactured in China and other countries, while improved technology in the agricultural and natural resource industries has given the United States a form of specialization that would have been unheard of 50 years ago.

 CHECKPOINT

SPECIALIZATION, COMPARATIVE ADVANTAGE, AND TRADE

- An absolute advantage exists when one country can produce more of some good than another.
- A comparative advantage exists if one country has lower opportunity costs of producing a good than another country. Both countries gain from trade if each focuses on producing those goods with which it has a comparative advantage.
- Voluntary trade is a positive-sum game, because both countries benefit from it.

QUESTION: Why do Hollywood stars (and many other rich individuals)—unlike most people—have full-time personal assistants who manage their personal affairs?

Answers to the Checkpoint questions can be found at the end of this chapter.

chapter summary

Section 1

Basic Economic Questions and Production

2.1 Every economy must decide:

1. What to produce.
2. How to produce it.
3. Who will get the goods produced.

Bloomberg/Getty Images

Using scarce resources productively leads to:

Production efficiency: Goods and services are produced at their lowest possible resource cost.

Allocative efficiency: Goods are produced according to what society desires.

2.2 Factors of Production (Inputs)

Section 2

Production Possibilities and Economic Growth

2.3 The **production possibilities frontier (PPF)** shows the different combinations of goods that a fully employed economy can produce, given its available resources and current technology.

2.4 Production possibilities frontiers (PPFs) illustrate tradeoffs—if an economy operates at full employment (on the PPF), producing more of one good requires producing less of the other. A concave PPF shows how opportunity costs rise due to diminishing returns.

Tony Bock/Toronto Star/ZUMA Press

Some pizza makers were never meant to produce computers and some computer workers were never meant to produce pizza, which increases the opportunity cost of production as more of one good is produced.

Corbis News/Corbis

The production possibilities model shows how economic growth can arise from an expansion in resources or from improvements in technology, or both.

2.5 **Changes in the *PPF*:**
From *PPF_A* to *PPF_B*: An increase in productivity in the production of one good (e.g., an increase in the number of students studying computer engineering).

From *PPF_A* to *PPF_C*: An increase in productive capacity of both goods (e.g., an increase in overall technology, or an increase in labor or capital resources).

Increase in Production Capacity of One Good — Pizza vs Tablets, PPF_A to PPF_B

Increase in Production Capacity of All Goods — Pizza vs Tablets, PPF_A to PPF_C

Section 3
Specialization, Comparative Advantage, and Trade

2.6 An **absolute advantage** exists when one country can produce more of some good than another.

A **comparative advantage** exists when one country can produce a good at a lower opportunity cost than another.

Gains from trade result when a country specializes in the production of goods in which it has a comparative advantage, and trades these goods with another country. Trade is a positive-sum game. Both countries can benefit even if one country has an absolute advantage in both goods.

Calculating Opportunity Costs Using Production Numbers
(units produced per day per worker)

	Australia	New Zealand
Boomerangs	20	8
Kiwi	12	16

- Opportunity cost of 1 boomerang:
  Australia: 12 kiwi/20 boomerangs = 0.6 kiwi per boomerang.
  New Zealand: 16 kiwi/8 boomerangs = 2 kiwi per boomerang.
  Australia has a lower opportunity cost of producing boomerangs.

- Opportunity cost of 1 kiwi:
  Australia: 20 boomerangs/12 kiwi = 1.7 boomerangs per kiwi.
  New Zealand: 8 boomerangs/16 kiwi = 0.5 boomerangs per kiwi.
  New Zealand has a lower opportunity cost of producing kiwi.

Ocean/Corbis

StockFood GmbH/Alamy

2.7 Countries export goods for which they have a comparative advantage, and import goods for which they do not, leading to gains from trade to both countries.

KEY CONCEPTS

production, p. 33
resources, p. 33
land, p. 33
labor, p. 33
capital, p. 33

entrepreneurs, p. 33
production efficiency, p. 34
allocative efficiency, p. 34
production possibilities frontier
(PPF), p. 35

opportunity cost, p. 36
absolute advantage, p. 43
comparative advantage, p. 43

QUESTIONS AND PROBLEMS

Check Your Understanding

1. When can an economy increase the production of one good without reducing the output of another?

2. In which of the three basic questions facing any society does technology play the greatest role?

3. Explain the important difference between a straight-line PPF and the PPF that is concave to (bowed away from) the origin.

4. How would unemployment be shown on the PPF?

5. List three factors that can contribute to an economy's growth.

6. How can a country that does not have an absolute advantage in producing goods still benefit from trade?

Apply the Concepts

7. China's tremendous growth rate over the past two decades has allowed its economic output to nearly catch up to that of the United States. If China continued to grow much faster than the United States, would this eventually lead to the elimination of scarcity in China?

8. Describe how a country producing more capital goods than consumption goods ends up in the future with a PPF that is larger than that of a country that produces more consumption goods and fewer capital goods.

9. The United States has an absolute advantage in making many goods, such as short-sleeved cotton golf shirts. Why do Indonesia and Bangladesh make these shirts and export them to the United States?

10. Why is it that the United States uses heavy street-cleaning machines driven by one person to clean the streets, while China and India use many people with brooms to do the same job?

11. If specialization and trade as discussed in this chapter lead to a win-win situation in which both countries gain, why is there often opposition to trade agreements and globalization?

12. The issue of climate change has risen to the forefront of economic discussion, especially among industrialized countries such as the United States and those in Europe. Critics, however, argue that greater environmental regulations restrict economic growth. Explain how relatively wealthy countries might react differently to this tradeoff compared to poor countries.

In the News

13. According to an April 4, 2015, *New York Times* report, California experienced the most severe drought in over a millennium from 2011 to 2015, when reservoirs and underground aquifers that farmers, households, and businesses depend on dried up. As a result, California's governor ordered a major cut in water usage statewide that made

it harder to live and work in the Golden State. If the drought forces some households and businesses to move out of California, what might happen to California's ability to achieve economic growth? Illustrate your answer using a PPF.

14. At the 2015 White House Science Fair, a $240 million private-public initiative was announced for the purpose of boosting STEM (science, technology, engineering, and math) education, as the United States continues to fall behind other industrialized nations in student achievement in these fields. How would spending on STEM initiatives today, which leads to higher costs in the near term, pay off in future benefits to the economy?

Solving Problems

15. Iceland and Denmark both produce skis and sleds. Iceland can produce 3 skis or 6 sleds using one day of labor, while Denmark can produce 4 skis or 12 sleds using one day of labor. Which country has an absolute advantage in producing skis? Sleds? Which country has a comparative advantage in producing skis? Sleds? Are gains from trade possible between Iceland and Denmark? If yes, which good should each country specialize in producing?

16. The table below shows the potential output combinations of oranges and jars of prickly pear jelly (from the flower of the prickly pear cactus) for Florida and Arizona.

   a. Compute the opportunity cost of oranges in Florida in terms of jars of prickly pear jelly. Do the same for prickly pear jelly in terms of oranges.

   b. Compute the opportunity cost of oranges in Arizona in terms of jars of prickly pear jelly. Do the same for prickly pear jelly in terms of oranges.

   c. Would it make sense for Florida to specialize in producing oranges and for Arizona to specialize in producing prickly pear jelly and then trade? Why or why not?

Florida		Arizona	
Oranges	**Prickly Pear Jelly**	**Oranges**	**Prickly Pear Jelly**
0	10	0	500
50	8	20	400
100	6	40	300
150	4	60	200
200	2	80	100
250	0	100	0

USING THE NUMBERS

17. According to By the Numbers, in which period (1965–1990 or 1990–2015) did corn and soybean production increase more in terms of yield per acre?

18. According to By the Numbers, during the period between 1997 and 2015, in how many years did the U.S. trade balance improve from the previous year and in how many years did the trade balance deteriorate? (Assume the trade balance deteriorated from 1996 [not shown in the figure] to 1997.)

Checkpoint: Basic Economic Questions and Production 35

Typically, entrepreneurs put not only their time and effort into a business but also their money, often pledging private assets as collateral for loans. Should the business fail, they stand to lose more than their jobs, rent from the land, or interest on capital loaned to the firm. Workers can get other jobs, landowners can rent to others, and capital can be used in other enterprises. The entrepreneur must suffer the loss of personal assets and move on.

Checkpoint: Production Possibilities and Economic Growth 42

Although Nigeria has significantly more natural resources and labor (two important factors of production) than Taiwan, these resources alone do not guarantee a higher ability to produce goods and services. Factors of production also include physical capital (machinery), human capital (education), and technology (research and development), all of which Taiwan has in great abundance. Thus, despite the lack of land, labor, and natural resources, Taiwan is able to use its resources efficiently and expand its production possibilities well beyond those of Nigeria.

Checkpoint: Specialization, Comparative Advantage, and Trade 47

For Hollywood stars and other rich people, the opportunity cost of their time is high. As a result, they hire people at lower cost to do the mundane chores that each of us is accustomed to doing because our time is relatively less valuable.

3 Supply and Demand

Using the basic tools of supply and demand to determine how prices and quantities are set in a market economy

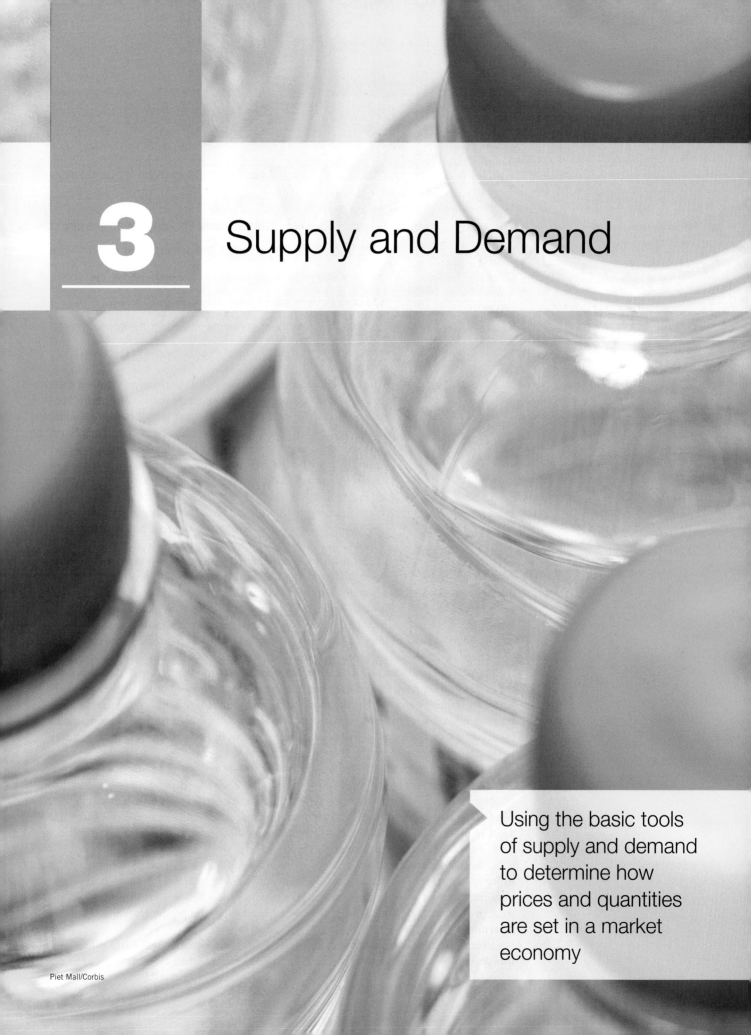

Learning Objectives

3.1 Describe the characteristics and purposes of markets.

3.2 Describe the nature of demand, demand curves, and the law of demand.

3.3 Describe the determinants of demand and be able to forecast how a change in one or more of these determinants will change demand.

3.4 Explain the difference between a change in demand and a change in quantity demanded.

3.5 Describe the nature of supply, supply curves, and the law of supply.

3.6 Describe the determinants of supply and be able to forecast how a change in one or more of these determinants will change supply.

3.7 Determine market equilibrium price and output.

3.8 Determine and predict how price and output will change given changes to supply and demand in the market.

What $100+ billion global industry sells a product that many people typically can obtain easily from another source free of charge? The bottled water industry! This industry began its meteoric rise in the early 1990s, and today, the ubiquitous bottle of water has changed the way we live. It also has created new concerns regarding the environmental impact of the billions of plastic bottles used and discarded.

The bottled water industry took off as consumers changed their hydration habits, spurred by greater awareness of the health benefits of drinking water, including weight loss, illness prevention, and overall health maintenance. As water consumption increased, people started wanting something more than just ordinary water from the tap. They desired water that was purer, more consistent in taste, or infused with flavor or minerals. Plus, consumers wanted water that was easy to carry. Bottled water was the product consumers wanted, and the market was willing to provide it.

Bottled water comes from many sources, both domestic and foreign, and consists of either spring water (from natural springs underneath the Earth's surface) or purified water (ordinary tap water that undergoes a complex purification process). As the industry grew, new varieties of water were made available. Water from exotic faraway springs, vitamin-infused water, flavored water, and carbonated water were some of the choices consumers were given. The total amount of water produced for the bottled water industry continued to increase as long as there were customers willing to pay for it in the market.

In the late 2000s, falling incomes from a deteriorating global economy, concerns about the harmful effects of discarded plastic bottles on the environment, increased use of home water purification devices, and even some laws against the use of bottled water eventually halted the market's growth. The economy has since improved, and the bottled water industry responded to the environmental concerns by using bottles made from recycled plastic or by using new technologies to reduce the plastic content in water bottles, again responding to the desires of consumers. As a result, sales increased again.

Consumers have many choices of what water to buy and where to buy it. Even so, the bottled water market is one in which prices vary considerably depending on the location of purchase. A single bottle of water of the same brand might cost $0.69 at a grocery store, $0.99 at a convenience store, $1.25 from a vending machine, $1.49 at a local coffee shop, and $3.00 or more at a theme park, sports stadium, or movie theater. How can the same product be sold in different places at so many different prices?

This chapter analyzes the various factors influencing how consumers value goods in different settings and circumstances. We also study how producers take costs and incentives into account in determining what products to produce, how much to produce, and what prices to charge. The interaction between consumers and producers within a market determines the prices we pay.

In any given market, prices are determined by "what the market will bear." Which factors determine what the market will bear, and what happens when events that occur in the

The World of Markets

Markets form the foundation of all economic transactions. As various factors affect the supply and demand for goods and services, prices adjust upward or downward correspondingly to reach equilibrium.

The dramatic growth of Uber drivers between 2012 and 2015 has come as a result of partnerships between the company and participating cities.

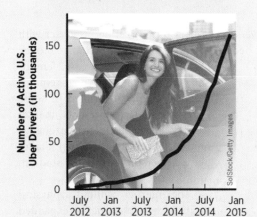

SolStock/Getty Images

Number of Active U.S. Uber Drivers (in thousands)

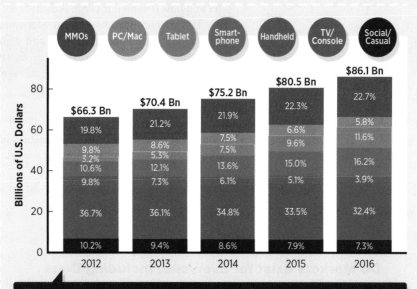

MMOs · PC/Mac · Tablet · Smartphone · Handheld · TV/Console · Social/Casual

	2012 $66.3 Bn	2013 $70.4 Bn	2014 $75.2 Bn	2015 $80.5 Bn	2016 $86.1 Bn
Social/Casual	19.8%	21.2%	21.9%	22.3%	22.7%
TV/Console	9.8%	8.6%	7.5%	6.6%	5.8%
Handheld	3.2%	5.3%	7.5%	9.6%	11.6%
Smartphone	10.6%	12.1%	13.6%	15.0%	16.2%
Tablet	9.8%	7.3%	6.1%	5.1%	3.9%
PC/Mac	36.7%	36.1%	34.8%	33.5%	32.4%
MMOs	10.2%	9.4%	8.6%	7.9%	7.3%

Billions of U.S. Dollars

The proportion of the global video game revenues captured by each platform (such as smartphones, tablets, and computers) has changed over the past few years.

Estimated total value (in U.S. dollars) of the worldwide online gaming market in 2016.

$86,100,000,000

Total number of half-liter water bottles consumed in the United States in 2014 (over 250 bottles or 34.2 gallons per person).

82,100,000,000

Billions of U.S. Dollars

1984 · 1994 · 2004 · 2014

Total sales of bottled water in the United States took off in the 1990s and continued to grow steadily since.

Bloomberg/Getty Images

University of Pheonix is the largest for-profit university with around 300,000 students.

Go to 🗂 **LaunchPad** to use the latest data to recreate this graph.

Percent of Total Enrollment

- Public 2-year
- Public 4-year
- Private Not-For-Profit
- For Profit

1997 · 2001 · 2005 · 2009 · 2013

Enrollment at for-profit universities grew significantly from 1997 to 2009 but has since fallen slightly. Still, it was the fastest growing segment over the past two decades.

The By the Numbers — Do It Yourself! Lab Activity for this chapter will focus on enrollment levels in different higher education institutions.

marketplace cause prices to change? For answers to these questions, economists turn to supply and demand analysis. The basic model of supply and demand presented in this chapter will let you determine why product sales rise and fall, in what direction prices move, and how many goods will be offered for sale when certain events happen in the marketplace. Later chapters use this same model to explain complex phenomena such as how wages are set and how personal income is distributed.

This chapter introduces some of the basic economic concepts you need to know to understand how the forces of supply and demand work. These concepts include markets, the law of demand, demand curves, the determinants of demand, the law of supply, supply curves, the determinants of supply, and market equilibrium.

markets Institutions that bring buyers and sellers together, so they can interact and transact with each other.

MARKETS

A **market** is an institution that enables buyers and sellers to interact and transact with one another. A lemonade stand is a market because it allows people to exchange money for a product, in this case, lemonade. Ticket scalping, which remains illegal or highly restricted in some states, similarly represents market activity, since it leads to the exchange of money for tickets, whether it takes place in person outside the stadium or online.

The Internet, without a physical location, has dramatically expanded the notion of markets. Online market sites such as eBay permit firms and individuals to sell a large number of low-volume products, ranging from rare collectible items to an extra box of unused diapers, and still make money. This includes students who resell their textbooks on Amazon.com and Half.com. The Internet also has launched markets for virtual goods. For example, buying virtual tools, cash, and animals in online games has become an important part of social media sites.

Even though all markets have the same basic component—the transaction—they can differ in a number of ways. Some markets are quite limited because of their geographical location, or because they offer only a few different products for sale. The New York Stock Exchange serves as a market for just a single type of financial instrument, stocks, but it facilitates exchanges worth billions of dollars daily. Compare this to the neighborhood flea market, which is much smaller and may operate only on weekends, but offers everything from food and crafts to T-shirts and electronics.

💬 ISSUE

Do Markets Exist for Everyone, Including Dogs and Cats?

Over 78 million dogs and 86 million cats call the United States home, with many times more finding homes around the world. Over four in ten U.S. households include at least one pet, which is often treated as a beloved member of the family. The expenses associated with pet ownership often extend beyond the basic necessities of food and vet checkups.

Jefferson Graham

Total spending on pet-related products in the United States has increased every year since 2001, surpassing $60 billion in 2015. Even during the depths of the economic downturn of 2007 to 2009, spending on pets continued to increase. The seeming immunity of the pet goods market to economic hardships raises an interesting question of to whom the market is geared: the pets or their sometimes fanatical owners?

Manufacturers of pet goods have increased the types of "consumer" goods and services for pets. These include a greater selection of pet foods and toys, but increasingly sellers are being more creative in their offerings. For example, the number of pet spas, pet hotels, and even pet airlines, allowing pets to bathe in luxury as they or their owners travel, has boomed over the past decade.

Pet consumerism has even gone high-tech. Since the introduction of tablets, programmers have introduced new tablet apps designed for cats, including games that are played feline versus human. Such apps highlight the ability of businesses to turn pets into consumers, whose desires (even if imagined by their owners) turn into actual purchases.

The power of consumer decisions extending beyond the wants of humans demonstrates the broad reach of markets. Because humans share a deep connection with their furry loved ones, they will often incorporate their pets' desires into real consumption choices. And based on the growth of this market, it's likely that dogs and cats will continue to be avid consumers.

Cement manufacturers are typically restricted to local markets due to high transportation costs, whereas Internet firms can easily do business with customers around the world.

The Price System

When buyers and sellers exchange money for goods and services, accepting some offers and rejecting others, they are also doing something else: They are communicating their individual desires. Much of this communication is accomplished through the prices of items. If buyers value a particular item sufficiently, they will quickly pay its asking price. If they do not buy it, they are indicating they do not believe the item to be worth its asking price.

Prices also give buyers an easy means of comparing goods that can substitute for each other. If the price of margarine falls to half the price of butter, this will suggest to many consumers that margarine is a better deal. Similarly, sellers can determine what goods to sell by comparing their prices. When prices rise for tennis rackets, this tells sporting goods store operators that the public wants more tennis rackets, leading the store operators to order more. Prices, therefore, contain a considerable amount of useful information for both consumers and sellers. For this reason, economists often call our market economy the **price system.**

price system A name given to the market economy because prices provide considerable information to both buyers and sellers.

 CHECKPOINT

MARKETS

- Markets are institutions that enable buyers and sellers to interact and transact business.
- Markets differ in geographical location, products offered, and size.
- Prices contain a wealth of information for both buyers and sellers.
- Through their purchases, consumers signal their willingness to exchange money for particular products at particular prices. These signals help businesses decide what to produce, and how much of it to produce.
- The market economy is also called the price system.

QUESTION: What are the important differences between the markets for financial securities such as the New York Stock Exchange and your local farmer's market?

Answers to the Checkpoint questions can be found at the end of this chapter.

DEMAND

Whenever you purchase a product, you are voting with your money. You are selecting one product out of many and supporting one firm out of many, both of which signal to the business community what sorts of products satisfy your wants as a consumer.

Economists typically focus on wants rather than needs because it is so difficult to determine what we truly need. Theoretically, you could survive on tofu and vitamin pills, living in a lean-to made of cardboard and buying all your clothes from thrift stores. Most people in our society, however, choose not to live in such austere fashion. Rather, they want something more, and in most cases they are willing and able to pay for more.

Willingness-to-Pay: The Building Block of Market Demand

Imagine sitting in your economics class around mealtime. In your rush to class, you did not have a chance to make a sandwich at home or to stop at the cafeteria on your way to class. You think about foods that sound appealing to you (just about anything at this point), and plan to go to the cafeteria immediately after class and buy a sandwich. Given your growling stomach, you think more about what you want on your sandwich and less about how much the sandwich will cost. In your mind, your **willingness-to-pay (WTP)** for that sandwich can be quite high, say, $10 or even more.

willingness-to-pay An individual's valuation of a good or service, equal to the most an individual is willing and able to pay.

| FIGURE 1 | FROM INDIVIDUAL WILLINGNESS-TO-PAY TO MARKET DEMAND |

In panel A, you would be willing to pay up to $10 for your first sandwich and $4 for the second. Jane, however, is only willing to pay up to $6 for her first sandwich and $2 for a second (panel B). Placing the WTP for sandwiches by you and Jane in order from the highest to lowest value, we generate a market with two consumers shown in panel C. As more and more individuals are added to the market, the demand for sandwiches becomes a smooth downward-sloping line, shown in panel D.

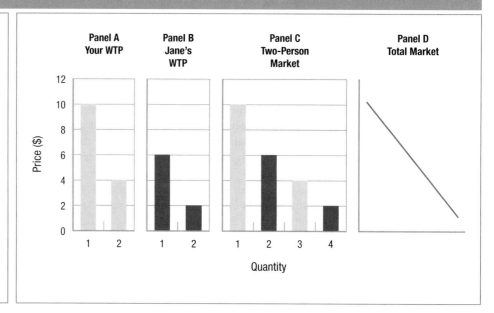

Economists refer to WTP as the maximum amount one would be willing to pay for a good or service, which represents the highest value that a consumer believes the good or service is worth. Of course, one always hopes that the actual price would be much lower. In your case, WTP is the cutoff between buying a sandwich and not buying a sandwich.

WTP varies from person to person, from the circumstances each person is in to the number of sandwiches one chooses to buy. Suppose your classmate ate a full meal before she came to class. Her WTP for a sandwich would be much lower than yours because she isn't hungry at that moment. Similarly, after you buy and consume your first sandwich, your WTP for a second sandwich would decrease because you would be less hungry. The desires consumers have for goods and services are expressed through their purchases in the market.

Figure 1 illustrates how individuals' WTP is used to derive market demand curves. Suppose you are willing to pay up to $10 for the first sandwich and $4 for the second sandwich (shown in panel A), while Jane, your less-hungry classmate, would pay up to $6 for her first sandwich and only $2 for her second sandwich (shown in panel B). If we take the WTP for your two sandwiches and the WTP of Jane's two sandwiches and place all four values in order from highest to lowest, a two-person market for sandwiches is created as shown in panel C. Notice how the distance between steps becomes smaller in the two-person market. Now suppose we combine the WTPs for everybody in the class (or for an entire city or country) into a single market. What would that diagram look like? In large markets, the difference in WTP between each unit of a good becomes so small that it becomes a straight line, as shown in panel D.

These illustrations show how ordinary demand curves, which we will discuss in detail in the remainder of this section, are developed from the perceptions of what individual consumers believe a good or service is worth to them (their WTP). Let's now discuss an important characteristic of market demand.

The Law of Demand: The Relationship Between Quantity Demanded and Price

Demand refers to the goods and services people are willing and able to buy during a certain period of time at various prices, holding all other relevant factors constant (the *ceteris paribus* condition). Typically, when the price of a good or service increases (say your favorite

demand The maximum amount of a product that buyers are willing and able to purchase over some time period at various prices, holding all other relevant factors constant (the *ceteris paribus* condition).

café raises its prices), the quantity demanded will decrease because fewer and fewer people will be willing and able to spend their money on such things. However, when prices of goods or services decrease (think of sales offered the day after Thanksgiving), the quantity demanded increases.

In a market economy, there is a negative relationship between price and quantity demanded. This relationship, in its most basic form, states that as price increases, the quantity demanded falls, and conversely, as price falls, the quantity demanded increases.

This principle, when all other factors are held constant, is known as the **law of demand.** The law of demand states that the lower a product's price, the more of that product consumers will purchase during a given time period. This straightforward, commonsense notion happens because, as a product's price drops, consumers will substitute the now cheaper product for other, more expensive products. Conversely, if the product's price rises, consumers will find other, less expensive products to substitute for it.

To illustrate, when videocassette recorders first came on the market 35 years ago, they cost $3,000, and few homes had one. As VCRs became less and less expensive, however, more people bought them, and others found more uses for them. Two decades later, VCRs became obsolete as DVD players became the standard means of watching movies at home. Today, DVD players are becoming obsolete as digital movie streaming surpassed DVD sales. Similarly, digital music players have altered the structure of the music business, and digital cameras have essentially replaced cameras that use film.

Time is an important component in the demand for many products. Consuming many products—watching a movie, eating a pizza, playing tennis—takes some time. Thus, the price of these goods includes not only their monetary cost but also the opportunity cost of the time needed to consume them. It follows that, all other things being equal, including the cost of a ticket, we would expect more consumers to attend a two-hour movie than a four-hour movie. The shorter movie simply requires less of a time investment.

The day after Thanksgiving, dubbed "Black Friday," is when stores offer steep discounts to jumpstart the holiday shopping season. This leads to massive quantities of goods sold, in an example of the law of demand.

law of demand Holding all other relevant factors constant, as price increases, quantity demanded falls, and as price decreases, quantity demanded rises.

The Demand Curve

The law of demand states that as price decreases, quantity demanded increases. When we translate demand information into a graph, we create a **demand curve.** This demand curve, which slopes down and to the right, graphically illustrates the law of demand. A demand curve shows both the willingness-to-pay for any given quantity and what the quantity demanded will be at any given price. In Figure 1, we saw how individual demands (measured by willingness-to-pay) can be combined to represent market demand, which can consist of many consumers. For simplicity, from this point we will assume that all demand curves, including those for individuals, are linear (straight lines).

Consider the market for gaming apps, games that can be downloaded onto one's smartphone or tablet. The mobile gaming industry is a $25 billion industry. Although each gaming app costs no more than a few dollars to download, sales of gaming apps have surpassed sales of PC and console games. Gaming apps such as *Candy Crush Saga, Angry Birds,* and *Words with Friends* have each been downloaded hundreds of millions of times. Let's examine the relationship between the price of gaming apps and the quantity demanded by individual consumers and the market. For simplicity, assume that all gaming apps are the same price.

Suppose Abe and Betty are the only two consumers in the market for gaming apps. Figure 2 shows each of their annual demands using a demand schedule and a demand curve. A **demand schedule** is a table indicating the quantities consumers are willing to purchase at each price. Looking at the demand schedule, we can see that both Abe and Betty are willing to buy more gaming apps as the price decreases. When the price is $10, Abe is willing to buy 10 games, while Betty buys none. When the price falls to $8, Abe is willing to buy 15 games and Betty would buy 5.

We can take the values from the demand schedule in the table and graph them in a figure, with price shown on the vertical axis and quantity of gaming apps on the horizontal

demand curve A graphical illustration of the law of demand, which shows the relationship between the price of a good and the quantity demanded.

demand schedule A table that shows the quantity of a good a consumer purchases at each price.

FIGURE 2	MARKET DEMAND: HORIZONTAL SUMMATION OF INDIVIDUAL DEMAND CURVES

Abe and Betty's demand schedules (the table) and their individual demand curves (the graph) for gaming apps are shown. Abe will purchase 15 gaming apps when the price is $8, buy 25 apps when the price falls to $4, and buy more as prices continue to fall. Betty will purchase 5 gaming apps when the price is $8 and buy 15 when the price falls to $4. The individual demand curves for Abe and Betty are shown as D_a and D_b, respectively, and are horizontally summed to get market demand, D_{Mkt}. Horizontal summation involves adding together the quantities demanded by each individual at each possible price.

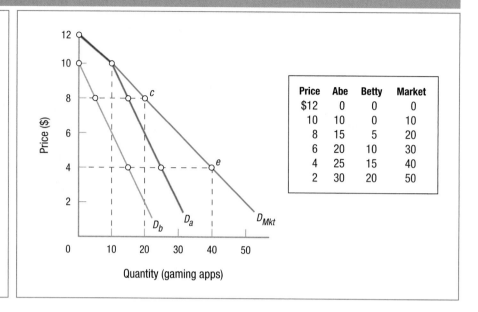

Price	Abe	Betty	Market
$12	0	0	0
10	10	0	10
8	15	5	20
6	20	10	30
4	25	15	40
2	30	20	50

axis, following the convention in economics of always placing price on the vertical axis and quantity on the horizontal axis. By doing so, we can create a demand curve for both Abe and Betty. Both the table and the graph convey the same information. They also both portray the law of demand. As the price decreases, Abe and Betty demand more gaming apps.

Although individual demand curves are interesting, market demand curves are far more important to economists, as they can be used to predict changes in product price and quantity. Further, one can observe what happens to a product's price and quantity and infer what changes have occurred in the market. Market demand is the sum of individual demands. To calculate market demand, economists simply add the number of units of a product all consumers will purchase at each price. This process is known as **horizontal summation.**

Turning to the demand curves in Figure 2, the individual demand curves for Abe and Betty, D_a and D_b, are shown. For simplicity, let's assume they represent the entire market, but recognize that this process would work for any larger number of people. Note that at a price of $10 a game, Betty will not buy any, although Abe is willing to buy 10 apps at $10 each. Above $10, therefore, the market demand is equal to Abe's demand. At $10 and below, however, we add both Abe's and Betty's demands at each price to obtain market demand. Thus, at $8, individual demand is 15 for Abe and 5 for Betty; therefore, the market demand is equal to 20 (point c). When the price is $4 an app, Abe buys 25 and Betty buys 15, for a total of 40 apps (point e). The heavier curve, labeled D_{Mkt}, represents this market demand; it is a horizontal summation of the two individual demand curves.

This all sounds simple in theory, but in the real world estimating market demand curves is tricky, given that many markets contain millions of consumers. Economic analysts and marketing professionals use sophisticated statistical techniques to estimate the market demand for particular goods and services in the industries they represent.

The market demand curve shows the maximum amount of a product consumers are willing and able to purchase during a given time period at various prices, all other relevant factors being held constant. Economists use the term *determinants of demand* to refer to these other, nonprice factors that are held constant. This is another example of the use of *ceteris paribus:* holding all other relevant factors constant.

horizontal summation The process of adding the number of units of the product purchased or supplied at each price to determine market demand or supply.

Determinants of Demand

Up to this point, we have discussed only how price affects the quantity demanded. When prices fall, consumers purchase more of a product; thus quantity demanded rises. When prices rise, consumers purchase less of a product; thus, quantity demanded falls. But several other factors besides price also affect demand, including what people like, what their income is, and how much related products cost. More specifically, there are five key **determinants of demand:** (1) tastes and preferences; (2) income; (3) prices of related goods; (4) the number of buyers; and (5) expectations regarding future prices, income, and product availability. When one of these determinants changes, the *entire* demand curve changes. Let's see why.

Tastes and Preferences We all have preferences for certain products over others, easily perceiving subtle differences in styling and quality. Automobiles, fashions, phones, and music are just a few of the products that are subject to the whims of the consumer.

Remember Crocs, those brightly colored rubber sandals with the little air holes that moms, kids, waitresses, and many others favored? They were an instant hit. Initially, demand was D_0 in Figure 3. They then became such a fad that demand jumped to D_1 and for a short while Crocs were hard to find. Eventually, Crocs were everywhere. Fads come and go, and now the demand for them settled back to something like D_2, less than the original level. Notice an important distinction here: More Crocs weren't sold because the *price* was lowered; the entire demand curve shifted rightward when they were hot and more Crocs could be sold at *all* prices. Now that the fad has subsided, fewer will be sold at all prices. It is important to keep in mind that when one of the determinants changes, such as tastes and preferences, the *entire* demand curve shifts.

Income Income is another important factor influencing consumer demand. Generally speaking, as income rises, demand for most goods will likewise increase. Get a raise, and you are more likely to buy more clothes and acquire the latest technology gadgets. Your demand curve for these goods will shift to the right (such as from D_0 to D_1 in Figure 3). Products for which demand is positively linked to income—when income rises, demand for the product also rises—are called **normal goods.**

There are also some products for which demand declines as income rises, and the demand curve shifts to the left. Economists call these products **inferior goods.** As income grows, for instance, the consumption of discount clothing and cheap motel stays will likely fall as individuals upgrade their wardrobes and stay in more comfortable hotels when traveling. Similarly, when you graduate from college and your income rises, your consumption of ramen noodles will fall as you begin to cook tastier dinners and eat out more frequently.

Prices of Related Goods The prices of related commodities also affect consumer decisions. You may be an avid concertgoer, but with concert ticket prices often topping $100, further rises in the price of concert tickets may entice you to see more movies and

determinants of demand
Nonprice factors that affect demand, including tastes and preferences, income, prices of related goods, number of buyers, and expectations.

normal good A good for which an increase in income results in rising demand.

inferior good A good for which an increase in income results in declining demand.

FIGURE 3	SHIFTS IN THE DEMAND CURVE

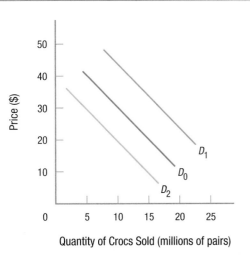

The demand for Crocs originally was D_0. When they became a fad, demand shifted to D_1 as consumers were willing and able to purchase more at *all* prices. Once the fad cooled off, demand fell (shifted leftward) to D_2 as consumers wanted less at each price. When a determinant such as tastes and preferences changes, the *entire* demand curve shifts.

fewer concerts. Movies, concerts, plays, and sporting events are good examples of **substitute goods,** because consumers can substitute one for another depending on their respective prices. When the *price* of concerts rises, your *demand* for movies increases, and vice versa. These are substitute goods.

Movies and popcorn, on the other hand, are examples of **complementary goods.** These are goods that are generally consumed together, such that an increase or decrease in the consumption of one will similarly result in an increase or decrease in the consumption of the other—see fewer movies, and your consumption of popcorn will decline. Other complementary goods include cars and gasoline, hot dogs and hot dog buns, and ski lift tickets and ski rentals. Thus, when the *price* of lift tickets increases, the quantity of lift tickets demanded falls, which causes your *demand* for ski rentals to fall as well (shifts to the left), and vice versa.

The Number of Buyers Another factor influencing market demand for a product is the number of potential buyers in the market. Clearly, the more consumers there are who would be likely to buy a particular product, the higher its market demand will be (the demand curve will shift rightward). As our average life span steadily rises, the demands for medical services and retirement communities likewise increases. As more people than ever enter universities and graduate schools, demand for textbooks and backpacks increases.

Expectations About Future Prices, Incomes, and Product Availability
The final factor influencing demand involves consumer expectations. If consumers expect shortages of certain products or increases in their prices in the near future, they tend to rush out and buy these products immediately, thereby increasing the present demand for the products. The demand curve shifts to the right. During the Florida hurricane season, when a large storm forms and begins moving toward the coast, the demand for plywood, nails, bottled water, and batteries quickly rises.

The expectation of a rise in income, meanwhile, can lead consumers to take advantage of credit in order to increase their present consumption. Department stores and furniture stores, for example, often run "no payments until next year" sales designed to attract consumers who want to "buy now, pay later." These consumers expect to have more money later, when they can pay, so they go ahead and buy what they want now, thereby increasing the present demand for the promoted items. Again, the demand curve shifts to the right.

The key point to remember from this section is that when one of the determinants of demand changes, the *entire* demand curve shifts rightward (an increase in demand) or leftward (a decline in demand). A quick look back at Figure 3 shows that when demand increases, consumers are willing to buy more at all prices, and when demand decreases, they will buy less at each and every price.

Changes in Demand Versus Changes in Quantity Demanded

When the price of a product rises, consumers buy fewer units of that product. This is a movement along an existing demand curve. However, when one or more of the determinants changes, the entire demand curve is altered. Now at any given price, consumers are willing to purchase more or less depending on the nature of the change. This section focuses on this important distinction between *changes in demand* versus *changes in quantity demanded*.

A **change in demand** occurs whenever one or more of the determinants of demand change and demand curves shift. When demand changes, the demand curve shifts either to the right or to the left. Let's look at each shift in turn.

Demand increases when the entire demand curve shifts to the right. At all prices, consumers are willing to purchase more of the product in question. Figure 4 shows an increase in demand for gaming apps; the demand curve shifts from D_0 to D_1. Notice that more gaming apps are purchased at all prices along D_1 as compared to D_0.

Now look at a decrease in demand, when the entire demand curve shifts to the left. At all prices, consumers are willing to purchase less of the product in question. A drop in consumer income is normally associated with a decrease in demand (the demand curve shifts to the left, as from D_0 to D_2 in Figure 4).

FIGURE 4	CHANGES IN DEMAND VERSUS CHANGES IN QUANTITY DEMANDED

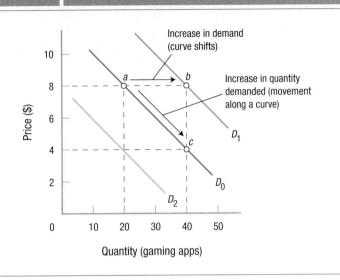

A shift in the demand curve from D_0 to D_1 represents an *increase in demand,* and consumers will buy more of the product at each price. A shift from D_0 to D_2 reflects a *decrease in demand.* A movement along D_0 from point *a* to point *c* indicates an *increase in quantity demanded;* this type of movement can only be caused by a change in the price of the product.

Whereas a change in demand can be brought about by many different factors, a **change in quantity demanded** can be caused by only one thing: *a change in product price.* This is shown in Figure 4 as a reduction in price from $8 to $4, resulting in sales (quantity demanded) increasing from 20 (point *a*) to 40 (point *c*) apps. This distinction between a change in demand and a change in quantity demanded is important. Reducing price to increase sales is different from spending a few million dollars on Super Bowl advertising to increase sales at all prices.

These concepts are so important that a quick summary is in order. As Figure 4 illustrates, given the initial demand D_0, increasing sales from 20 to 40 apps can occur in either of two ways. First, changing a determinant (say, increasing advertising) could shift the demand curve to D_1 so that 40 apps would be sold at $8 (point *b*). Alternatively, 40 apps could be sold by reducing the price to $4 (point *c*). Selling more by increasing advertising causes an increase in demand, or a shift in the entire demand curve. Simply reducing the price, on the other hand, causes an increase in quantity demanded, or a movement along the existing demand curve, D_0, from point *a* to point *c*.

change in quantity demanded
Occurs when the price of the product changes, shown as a movement along an existing demand curve.

 CHECKPOINT

DEMAND

- A person's willingness-to-pay is the maximum amount she or he values a good to be worth at a particular moment in time and is the building block for demand.

- Demand refers to the quantity of products people are willing and able to purchase at various prices during some specific time period, all other relevant factors being held constant.

- The law of demand states that price and quantity demanded have an inverse (negative) relation. As price rises, consumers buy fewer units; as price falls, consumers buy more units. It is depicted as a downward-sloping demand curve.

- Demand curves shift when one or more of the determinants of demand change.

- The determinants of demand are consumer tastes and preferences, income, prices of substitutes and complements, the number of buyers in a market, and expectations about future prices, incomes, and product availability.

- A shift of a demand curve is a *change in demand*, and occurs when a determinant of demand changes.

- A *change in quantity demanded* occurs only when the price of a product changes, leading consumers to adjust their purchases along the existing demand curve.

QUESTIONS: Sales of electric plug-in cars, such as the Tesla, have risen in recent years. Despite their relatively high price compared to gasoline-powered cars and the limited distance the cars can travel before requiring a recharge, other manufacturers are adding new models of plug-ins to their lines. What has led to the rising popularity of plug-in cars? Is this an increase in demand or an increase in quantity demanded?

Answers to the Checkpoint questions can be found at the end of this chapter.

SUPPLY

The analysis of a market economy rests on two foundations: supply and demand. So far, we've covered the demand side of the market. Let's focus now on the decisions businesses make regarding production numbers and sales. These decisions cause variations in product supply.

The Law of Supply: The Relationship Between Quantity Supplied and Price

supply The maximum amount of a product that sellers are willing and able to provide for sale over some time period at various prices, holding all other relevant factors constant (the *ceteris paribus* condition).

Supply is the maximum amount of a product that producers are willing and able to offer for sale at various prices, all other relevant factors being held constant. The quantity supplied will vary according to the price of the product.

What explains this relationship? As we saw in the previous chapter, businesses inevitably encounter rising opportunity costs as they attempt to produce more and more of a product. This is due in part to diminishing returns from available resources, and in part to the fact that when producers increase production, they must either have existing workers put in overtime (at a higher hourly pay rate) or hire additional workers away from other industries (again at premium pay).

Producing more units, therefore, makes it more expensive to produce each individual unit. These increasing costs give rise to the positive relationship between product price and quantity supplied to the market.

law of supply Holding all other relevant factors constant, as price increases, quantity supplied rises, and as price declines, quantity supplied falls.

Unfortunately for producers, they can rarely charge whatever they would like for their products; they must charge whatever the market will permit. But producers can decide how much of their product to produce and offer for sale. The **law of supply** states that higher prices will lead producers to offer more of their products for sale during a given period. Conversely, if prices fall, producers will offer fewer products to the market. The explanation is simple: The higher the price, the greater the potential for higher profits and thus the greater the incentive for businesses to produce and sell more products. Also, given the rising opportunity costs associated with increasing production, producers need to charge these higher prices to increase the quantity supplied profitably.

Let's return to our market for gaming apps. Why do programmers spend countless hours developing new gaming apps? Because they have an incentive to do so. Much like how consumers download more gaming apps when the price goes down, the opposite is true for suppliers. As the price rises, programmers are more willing to create new games, enhance existing games, and provide more server capacity (to ensure games operate smoothly) and technical support, all to increase the quantity of gaming apps supplied. Although gaming apps are not a physical good, the law of supply still applies. This is no different than an oil producer drilling for more oil when the price rises. In each case, producers respond to changes in price.

The Supply Curve

supply curve A graphical illustration of the law of supply, which shows the relationship between the price of a good and the quantity supplied.

Just as demand curves graphically display the law of demand, **supply curves** provide a graphical representation of the law of supply. The supply curve shows the maximum

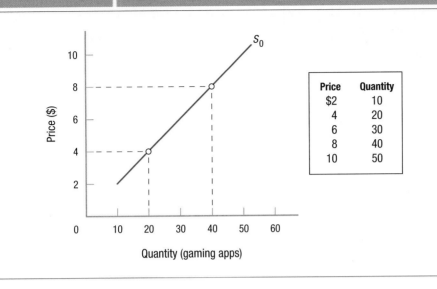

FIGURE 5	SUPPLY OF GAMING APPS

Price	Quantity
$2	10
4	20
6	30
8	40
10	50

This supply curve graphs the supply schedule and shows the maximum quantity of gaming apps that producers will offer for sale over some defined period of time. The supply curve is positively sloped, reflecting the law of supply. In other words, as prices rise, quantity supplied increases; as prices fall, quantity supplied falls.

amounts of a product a producer will furnish at various prices during a given period of time. While the demand curve slopes *down* and to the right, the supply curve slopes *up* and to the right.[1] This illustrates the positive relationship between price and quantity supplied: The higher the price, the greater the quantity supplied.

Market Supply Curves

As with demand, economists are more interested in market supply than in the supplies offered by individual firms. To compute market supply, use the same method used to calculate market demand, horizontally summing the supplies of individual producers. A hypothetical market supply curve for gaming apps is depicted in Figure 5. The quantity of gaming apps that producers will offer for sale increases as the price of gaming apps rises. The opposite would happen if the price of gaming apps falls.

Determinants of Supply

Like demand, several nonprice factors help to determine the supply of a product. Specifically, there are six **determinants of supply:** (1) production technology, (2) costs of resources, (3) prices of related commodities, (4) expectations, (5) the number of sellers (producers) in the market, and (6) taxes and subsidies.

determinants of supply
Nonprice factors that affect supply, including production technology, costs of resources, prices of related commodities, expectations, number of sellers, and taxes and subsidies.

Production Technology Technology determines how much output can be produced from given quantities of resources. If a factory's equipment is old and can produce only 50 units of output per hour, then no matter how many other resources are employed, those 50 units are the most the factory can produce in an hour. If the factory is outfitted with newer, more advanced equipment capable of turning out 100 units per hour, the firm can supply more of its product at the same price as before, or even at a lower price. In Figure 6, this would be represented by a shift in the supply curve from S_0 to S_1. At every single price, more would be supplied.

Technology further determines the nature of products that can be supplied to the market. A hundred years ago, the supply of computers on the market was zero because computers did not yet exist. More recent advances in microprocessing and miniaturization brought a wide array of products to the market that were not available just a few years

---

[1] There are some exceptions to positively sloping supply curves. But for our purposes, we will ignore them for now.

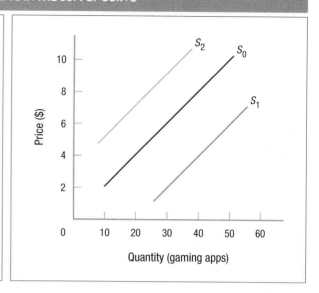

| FIGURE 6 | SHIFTS IN THE SUPPLY CURVE |

The supply of gaming apps originally is S_0. If supply shifts to S_1, producers are willing to sell more at *all* prices. If supply falls, supply shifts leftward to S_2. Now firms are willing to sell less at each price. When a determinant of supply changes, the *entire* supply curve shifts.

ago, including mini-tablets, auto engines that go 100,000 miles between tune-ups, and constant-monitoring insulin pumps that automatically keep a diabetic patient's glucose levels under control.

Costs of Resources   Resource costs clearly affect production costs and supply. If resources such as raw materials or labor become more expensive, production costs will rise and supply will be reduced (the supply curve shifts to the left, from S_0 to S_2 in Figure 6). The reverse is true if resource costs drop (the supply curve shifts to the right, from S_0 to S_1). The growing power of microchips along with their falling cost has resulted in cheap and plentiful electronics and computers. Nanotechnology—manufacturing processes that fashion new products through the combination of individual atoms—may soon usher in a whole new generation of inexpensive products.

However, when the cost of resources (such as oil and farm products) rise, the cost of products using those resources in their manufacture will go up, leading to the supply being reduced (the supply curve shifts leftward). If labor costs rise because immigration is restricted, this drives up production costs of California vegetables (fewer farmworkers) and software in Silicon Valley (fewer software engineers from abroad) and leads to a shift in the supply curve to the left in Figure 6.

Prices of Related Commodities   Most firms have some flexibility in the portfolio of goods they produce. A vegetable farmer, for example, might be able to grow celery or radishes, or some combination of the two. Given this flexibility, a change in the price of one item may influence the quantity of other items brought to market. If the price of celery should rise, for instance, most farmers will start growing more celery. And since they all have a limited amount of land on which to grow vegetables, this reduces the quantity of radishes they can produce. Hence, in this case, the rise in the price of celery may well cause a reduction in the supply of radishes (the supply curve for radishes shifts leftward).

Expectations   The effects of future expectations on market supplies can be confusing, but it need not be. When sellers expect prices of a good to rise in the future, they are likely to restrict their supply in the current period in anticipation of receiving higher prices in some future period. Examples include homes and stocks—if you believe prices are going up, you'd be less likely to sell today, which decreases the supply of such goods (supply shifts to the left). Similarly, expectations of price reductions can increase supply as sellers try to sell off their inventories before prices drop (supply shifts to the right).

Eventually, if prices do rise in the next period, producers would increase the quantity supplied of the good; however, this would be due to the law of supply, not due to a shift of the supply curve. In other words, rising prices result in a movement along the supply curve. Only when producers anticipate a change in a future price, causing a reaction now, does supply shift.

Number of Sellers Everything else being held constant, if the number of sellers in a particular market increases, the market supply of their product increases. It is no great mystery why: Ten dim sum chefs can produce more dumplings in a given period than five dim sum chefs.

Taxes and Subsidies For businesses, taxes and subsidies affect costs. An increase in taxes (property, excise, or other fees) will shift supply to the left and reduce it. Subsidies are the opposite of taxes. If the government subsidizes the production of a product, supply will shift to the right and rise. A proposed new tax on expensive health care insurance plans may reduce supply (the tax is equivalent to an increase in production costs), while today's subsidies to ethanol producers expand ethanol production.

Changes in Supply Versus Changes in Quantity Supplied

A **change in supply** results from a change in one or more of the determinants of supply; it causes the entire supply curve to shift. An increase in supply of a product, perhaps because advancing technology has made it cheaper to produce, means that more of the commodity will be offered for sale at every price. This causes the supply curve to shift to the right, as illustrated in Figure 7 by the shift from S_0 to S_1. A decrease in supply, conversely, shifts the supply curve to the left, since fewer units of the product are offered at every price. Such a decrease in supply is represented by the shift from S_0 to S_2.

A change in supply involves a shift of the entire supply curve. In contrast, the supply curve does not move when there is a **change in quantity supplied.** Only a change in the price of a product can cause a change in the quantity supplied; hence, it involves a movement along an existing supply curve rather than a shift to an entirely different curve. In Figure 7, for example, an increase in price from $4 to $8 results in an increase in quantity supplied from 20 to 40 apps, represented by the movement from point a to point c along S_0.

In summary, a change in supply is represented in Figure 7 by the shift from S_0 to S_1 or S_2, which involves a shift in the entire supply curve. For example, an increase in supply from S_0

change in supply Occurs when one or more of the determinants of supply change, shown as a shift in the entire supply curve.

change in quantity supplied Occurs when the price of the product changes, shown as a movement along an existing supply curve.

FIGURE 7	CHANGES IN SUPPLY VERSUS CHANGES IN QUANTITY SUPPLIED

A shift in the supply curve from S_0 to S_1 represents an *increase in supply,* because businesses are willing to offer more of the product to consumers at *all* prices. A shift from S_0 to S_2 reflects a decrease in supply. A movement along S_0 from point a to point c represents an *increase in quantity supplied;* this type of movement can only be caused by a change in the price of the product.

to S_1 results in an increase in supply from 20 gaming apps (point *a*) to 40 (point *b*) provided at a price of $4. More apps are provided at the same price. In contrast, a change in quantity supplied is shown in Figure 7 as a movement along an existing supply curve, S_0, from point *a* to point *c* caused by an increase in the price of the product from $4 to $8.

As on the demand side, this distinction between changes in supply and changes in quantity supplied is crucial. It means that when a product's price changes, only quantity supplied changes—the supply curve does not move. A summary of the determinants for both supply and demand is shown in Figure 8.

FIGURE 8	SUMMARY OF CHANGES IN DEMAND AND SUPPLY AND THEIR DETERMINANTS

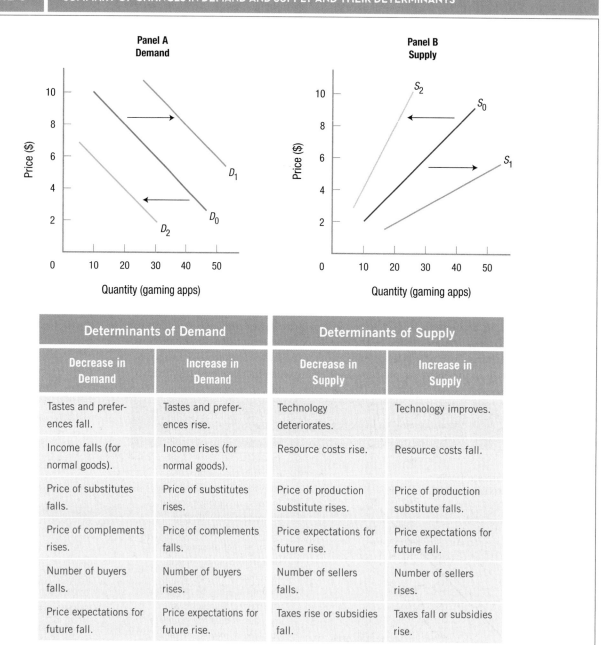

Determinants of Demand		Determinants of Supply	
Decrease in Demand	**Increase in Demand**	**Decrease in Supply**	**Increase in Supply**
Tastes and preferences fall.	Tastes and preferences rise.	Technology deteriorates.	Technology improves.
Income falls (for normal goods).	Income rises (for normal goods).	Resource costs rise.	Resource costs fall.
Price of substitutes falls.	Price of substitutes rises.	Price of production substitute rises.	Price of production substitute falls.
Price of complements rises.	Price of complements falls.	Price expectations for future rise.	Price expectations for future fall.
Number of buyers falls.	Number of buyers rises.	Number of sellers falls.	Number of sellers rises.
Price expectations for future fall.	Price expectations for future rise.	Taxes rise or subsidies fall.	Taxes fall or subsidies rise.

Various factors cause a market demand curve to shift to the left (decrease in demand) or shift to the right (increase in demand) in panel A. Similarly, various factors cause a market supply curve to shift to the left (decrease in supply) or shift to the right (increase in supply) in panel B. The table summarizes the factors influencing demand and supply shifts.

CHECKPOINT

SUPPLY

- Supply is the quantity of a product producers are willing and able to put on the market at various prices, all other relevant factors being held constant.

- The law of supply reflects the positive relationship between price and quantity supplied: The higher the market price, the more goods supplied, and the lower the market price, the fewer goods supplied.

- As with demand, market supply is derived by horizontally summing the individual supplies of all of the firms in the market.

- A change in supply occurs when one or more of the determinants of supply change.

- The determinants of supply are production technology, the cost of resources, prices of related commodities, expectations about future prices, the number of sellers or producers in the market, and taxes and subsidies.

- A *change in supply* is a shift in the supply curve. A shift to the right reflects an increase in supply, while a shift to the left represents a decrease in supply.

- A *change in quantity supplied* is only caused by a change in the price of the product; it results in a movement along the existing supply curve.

QUESTIONS: At the end of the term, bookstores often increase the prices offered to students for their used textbooks in order to stock their shelves for the following term. Would an increase in the buyback price affect the supply or the quantity supplied of used textbooks? Suppose an unusually difficult professor leads to many students having to retake the course the next term. How might this affect the supply for used textbooks?

Answers to the Checkpoint questions can be found at the end of this chapter.

MARKET EQUILIBRIUM

Supply and demand together determine the prices and quantities of goods bought and sold. Neither factor alone is sufficient to determine price and quantity. It is through their interaction that supply and demand do their work, just as two blades of a scissors are required to cut paper.

A market will determine the price at which the quantity of a product demanded is equal to the quantity supplied. At this price, the market is said to be cleared or to be in **equilibrium,** meaning that the amount of the product that consumers are willing and able to purchase is matched exactly by the amount that producers are willing and able to sell. This is the **equilibrium price** and the **equilibrium quantity.** The equilibrium price is also called the market-clearing price.

Figure 9 puts together Figures 2 and 5, showing the market supply and demand for gaming apps. It illustrates how supply and demand interact to determine equilibrium price and quantity. Clearly, the quantities demanded and supplied equal one another only where the supply and demand curves cross, at point *e.* From the table in Figure 9, you can see that quantity demanded and quantity supplied are the same at only one price. At $6 per app, sellers are willing to provide exactly the same quantity as consumers would like to purchase. Hence, at this price, the market clears, since buyers and sellers both want to transact the same number of units.

The beauty of a market is that it automatically works to establish the equilibrium price and quantity, without any guidance from anyone. To see how this happens, let us assume that gaming apps are initially priced at $8, a price above their equilibrium price. As we can see by comparing points *a* and *b,* sellers are willing to supply more apps at this price than consumers are willing to buy. Economists characterize such a situation as one of excess supply, or **surplus.** In this case, at $8, sellers supply 40 apps to the market (point *b*), yet buyers want to purchase only 20 (point *a*). This leaves an excess of 20 apps overhanging the market; these unsold apps ultimately become surplus inventories.

equilibrium Market forces are in balance when the quantities demanded by consumers just equal the quantities supplied by producers.

equilibrium price The price at which the quantity demanded is just equal to quantity supplied.

equilibrium quantity The output that results when quantity demanded is just equal to quantity supplied.

surplus Occurs when the price is above market equilibrium, and quantity supplied exceeds quantity demanded.

Market equilibrium is achieved when quantity demanded and quantity supplied are equal at the market price. In this graph, that equilibrium occurs at point *e*, at an equilibrium price of $6 and an equilibrium output of 30. If the market price is above equilibrium ($8), a surplus of 20 computer apps will result (*b* − *a*), and market forces would drive the price back down to $6. When the market price is too low ($4), a shortage of 20 computer apps will result (*d* − *c*), and businesses will raise the offering prices until equilibrium is again restored.

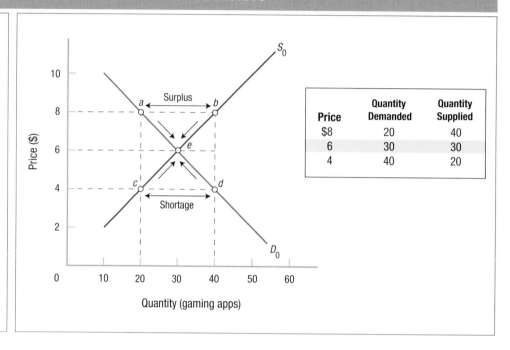

Price	Quantity Demanded	Quantity Supplied
$8	20	40
6	30	30
4	40	20

shortage Occurs when the price is below market equilibrium, and quantity demanded exceeds quantity supplied.

Here is where the market kicks in to restore equilibrium. As inventories rise, most firms cut production. Some firms, moreover, start reducing their prices to increase sales. Other firms must then cut their own prices to remain competitive. This process continues, with firms cutting their prices and production, until most firms have managed to exhaust their surplus inventories. This happens when prices reach $6 and quantity supplied equals 30, because consumers are once again willing to buy up the entire quantity supplied at this price, and the market is restored to equilibrium.

In general, therefore, when prices are set too high, surpluses result, which drive prices back down to their equilibrium levels. If, conversely, a price is initially set too low, say, at $4, a **shortage** results. In this case, buyers want to purchase 40 apps (point *d*), but sellers are only providing 20 (point *c*), creating a shortage of 20 apps. Because consumers are willing to pay more than $4 to obtain the few apps available on the market, they will start bidding up the price of gaming apps. Sensing an opportunity to make some money, firms will start raising their prices and increasing production once again until equilibrium is restored. Hence, in general, excess demand causes firms to raise prices and increase production.

When there is a shortage in a market, economists speak of a tight market or a seller's market. Under these conditions, producers have no difficulty selling off all their output. On the other hand, when a surplus of goods floods the market, this gives rise to a buyer's market, because buyers can buy all the goods they want at attractive prices.

We have now seen how changing prices naturally works to clear up shortages and surpluses, thereby returning markets to equilibrium. Some markets, once disturbed, will return to equilibrium quickly. Examples include the stock, bond, and money markets, where trading is nearly instantaneous and extensive information abounds. Other markets react very slowly. Consider the labor market, for instance. When workers lose their jobs due to a plant closing, most will search for new jobs that pay at least as much as the salary at their previous jobs. Some will be successful, while others might struggle, having to settle for a lower-paying position after a long job search. Similarly, real estate markets can be slow to adjust because sellers will often refuse to accept a price below what they are asking, until the lack of sales over time convinces sellers to adjust the price downward.

These automatic market adjustments can make some buyers and sellers feel uncomfortable: It seems as if prices and quantities are being set by forces beyond anyone's control. In fact, this phenomenon is precisely what makes market economies function so efficiently.

Without anyone needing to be in control, prices and quantities naturally gravitate toward equilibrium levels. Adam Smith was so impressed by the workings of the market that he suggested that it is almost as if an "invisible hand" guides the market to equilibrium.

Given the self-correcting nature of the market, long-term shortages or surpluses are almost always the result of government intervention, as we will see in the next chapter. First, however, we turn to a discussion of how the market responds to changes in supply and demand, or to shifts of the supply and demand curves.

Moving to a New Equilibrium: Changes in Supply and Demand

Once a market is in equilibrium and the forces of supply and demand balance one another out, the market will remain there unless an external factor changes. But when the supply curve or demand curve shifts (some determinant changes), equilibrium also shifts, resulting in a new equilibrium price and/or output. The ability to predict new equilibrium points is one of the most useful aspects of supply and demand analysis.

Predicting the New Equilibrium When One Curve Shifts When only supply or only demand changes, the change in equilibrium price and equilibrium output can be predicted. We begin with changes in supply.

ALFRED MARSHALL (1842–1924)

British economist Alfred Marshall is considered the father of the modern theory of supply and demand—that price and output are determined by both supply *and* demand. He noted that the two go together like the blades of a scissors that cross at equilibrium. He assumed that changes in quantity demanded were only affected by changes in price, and that all other factors remained constant. Marshall also is credited with developing the ideas of the laws of demand and supply, and the concepts of consumer surplus and producer surplus—concepts we will study in the next chapter.

With financial help from his uncle, Marshall attended St. John's College, Cambridge, to study mathematics and physics. However after long walks through the poorest sections of several European cities and seeing their horrible conditions, he decided to focus his attention on political economy.

In 1890 he published *Principles of Economics*. In it he introduced many new ideas, though he would never boast about them as being novel. In hopes of appealing to the general public, Marshall buried his diagrams in footnotes. And, although he is credited with many economic theories, he would always clarify them with various exceptions and qualifications. He expected future economists to flesh out his ideas.

Above all, Marshall loved teaching and his students. His lectures were known to never be orderly or systematic because he tried to get students to think *with* him and ultimately think for themselves. At one point near the turn of the 20th century, essentially all of the leading economists in England had been his students. More than anyone else, Marshall is given credit for establishing economics as a discipline of study. He died in 1924.

Information from E. Ray Canterbery, *A Brief History of Economics: Artful Approaches to the Dismal Science* (Hackensack, NJ: World Scientific), 2001; Robert Skidelsky, *John Maynard Keynes: Volume 2, The Economist as Saviour 1920–1937* (New York: Penguin Press), 1992; and John Maynard Keynes, *Essays in Biography* (New York: Norton), 1951.

Changes in Supply Figure 10 shows what happens when supply changes. Equilibrium initially is at point *e*, with equilibrium price and quantity at $9 and 30, respectively. But let us assume that a rise in wages or the bankruptcy of a key business in the market (the number of sellers falls) causes a decrease in supply. When supply declines (the supply curve shifts from S_0 to S_2), equilibrium price rises to $12, while equilibrium output falls to 20 (point *a*).

If, on the other hand, supply increases (the supply curve shifts from S_0 to S_1), equilibrium price falls to

Eric Chiang

When Universal Studios in Florida expanded its popular Wizarding World of Harry Potter attraction in 2014 with the opening of Diagon Alley and Hogwarts Express, demand for Universal Studios tickets increased. A one-day ticket (allowing entry to both parks) now exceeds $160. And that doesn't include the wand (another $30 to $40) needed to operate many of the Harry Potter experiences!

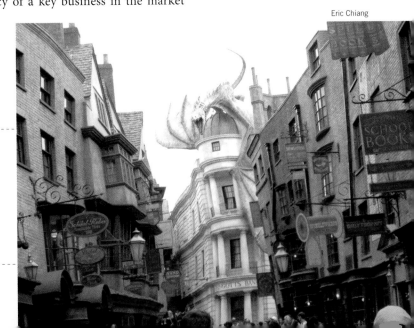

FIGURE 10 — EQUILIBRIUM PRICE, OUTPUT, AND SHIFTS IN SUPPLY

When supply alone shifts, the effects on both equilibrium price and output can be predicted. When supply increases (S_0 to S_1), equilibrium price will fall and output will rise. When supply declines (S_0 to S_2), the opposite happens: Equilibrium price will rise and output will fall.

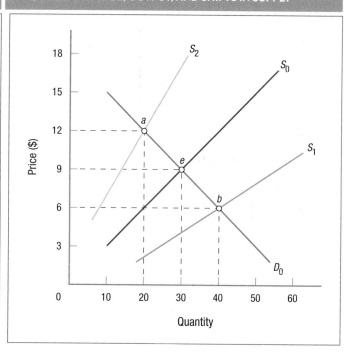

$6, while equilibrium output rises to 40 (point *b*). This is what has happened in the electronics industry: Falling production costs have resulted in more electronic products being sold at lower prices.

We have seen how equilibrium price and quantity will change when supply changes. When supply increases, equilibrium price will fall and output will rise; when supply decreases, equilibrium price will rise and output will fall.

Changes in Demand The effects of demand changes are shown in Figure 11. Again, equilibrium is initially at point *e*, with equilibrium price and quantity at $9 and 30, respectively.

FIGURE 11 — EQUILIBRIUM PRICE, OUTPUT, AND SHIFTS IN DEMAND

When demand alone changes, the effects on both equilibrium price and output can again be determined. When demand grows (D_0 to D_1), both price and output rise. Conversely, when demand falls (D_0 to D_2), both price and output fall.

ISSUE

Two-Buck Chuck: Will People Drink $2-a-Bottle Wine?

The great California wines of the 1990s put California vineyards on the map. Demand, prices, and exports grew rapidly. Overplanting of new grapevines was a result. When driving along Interstate 5 or Highway 101 north of Los Angeles, one can see vineyards extending for miles, and most were planted in the mid- to late 1990s. The 2001 recession reduced the demand for California wine, and a rising dollar made imported wine relatively cheaper. The result was a sharp drop in demand for California wine and a huge surplus of grapes.

Bronco Wine Company president Fred Franzia made an exclusive deal with Trader Joe's, an unusual supermarket that features innovative food and wine products. He bought the excess grapes at distressed prices, and in his company's modern plant produced inexpensive wines—chardonnay, merlot, cabernet sauvignon, shiraz, and sauvignon blanc—under the Charles Shaw label. Consumers flocked to Trader Joe's for wine costing $1.99 a bottle and literally hauled cases of wine out by the carload. In less than a decade, 400 million bottles of Two-Buck Chuck, as

joel zatz/Alamy

it is known, have been sold. This is not rotgut: The 2002 shiraz beat out 2,300 other wines to win a double gold medal at the 28th Annual International Eastern Wine Competition in 2004. Still, to many Napa Valley vintners, it is known as Two-Buck Upchuck.

Two-Buck Chuck was such a hit that other supermarkets were forced to offer their own discount wines. This good, low-priced wine has had the effect of opening up markets. People

who previously avoided wine because of the cost have begun drinking more. However, the influence of Two-Buck Chuck, which sold 60 million bottles in 2012, may be waning. Because of the rising costs of producing the wine in recent years, largely due to the severe California drought, Two-Buck Chuck is now sold between $2.99 and $3.99 per bottle. Although the price is still a bargain, the product that changed the wine industry may need a new nickname.

But let us assume that the economy then enters a recession and incomes sink, or perhaps the price of some complementary good soars; in either case, demand falls. As demand decreases (the demand curve shifts from D_0 to D_2), equilibrium price falls to $6, while equilibrium output falls to 20 (point a).

During the same recession just described, the demand for inferior goods (beans and bologna) will rise, as falling incomes force people to switch to less expensive substitutes. For these products, as demand increases (shifting the demand curve from D_0 to D_1), equilibrium price rises to $12, and equilibrium output grows to 40 (point b).

Like changes in supply, we can predict how equilibrium price and quantity will change when demand changes. When demand increases, both equilibrium price and output will rise; when demand decreases, both equilibrium price and output will fall.

Predicting the New Equilibrium When Both Curves Shift When both supply and demand change, things get tricky. We can predict what will happen with price in some cases and output in other cases, but not what will happen with both.

Figure 12 portrays an increase in both demand and supply. Consider the market for corn. Suppose that an increase in corn-based ethanol production causes demand for corn to increase. Meanwhile, suppose that bioengineering results in a new corn hybrid that uses less fertilizer and generates 50% higher yields, causing supply to also increase. When demand increases from D_0 to D_1 and supply increases from S_0 to S_1, output grows to Q_1 as shown in the left panel.

FIGURE 12   INCREASE IN SUPPLY, INCREASE IN DEMAND, AND EQUILIBRIUM

When both demand and supply increase, output will clearly rise, but what happens to the new equilibrium price is uncertain. If demand grows relatively more than supply, price will rise, but if supply grows relatively more than demand, price will fall.

Price increases because the increase in demand exceeds the increase in supply.

Price remains the same because the increase in demand is the same as the increase in supply.

Price decreases because the increase in demand is less than the increase in supply.

But what happens to the price of corn is not so clear. If demand and supply grow the same, output increases, but price remains at P_0 (also captured in the middle panel to the right). If demand grows relatively more than supply, the new equilibrium price will be higher (top panel on the right). Conversely, if demand grows relatively less than supply, the new equilibrium price will be lower (bottom panel on the right). Figure 12 is just one of the four possibilities when both supply and demand change. The other three possibilities are shown in Table 1 along with the four possibilities when just one curve shifts. When only one curve shifts, the direction of change in equilibrium price and quantity is certain. But when both curves shift, the direction of change in either the equilibrium price or quantity will be indeterminate.

TABLE 1   THE EFFECT OF CHANGES IN DEMAND OR SUPPLY ON EQUILIBRIUM PRICES AND QUANTITIES

	Change in Demand	Change in Supply	Change in Equilibrium Price	Change in Equilibrium Quantity
One Curve Shifting	No change	Increase	Decrease	Increase
	No change	Decrease	Increase	Decrease
	Increase	No change	Increase	Increase
	Decrease	No change	Decrease	Decrease
Both Curves Shifting	Increase	Increase	Indeterminate	Increase
	Decrease	Decrease	Indeterminate	Decrease
	Increase	Decrease	Increase	Indeterminate
	Decrease	Increase	Decrease	Indeterminate

Tokyo Disneyland: Is THAT the Line for Space Mountain?!

What are some factors that cause Tokyo Disneyland to be so crowded even during the middle of winter?

How long are you willing to wait to experience your favorite ride at a theme park? 20 minutes? 60 minutes? How about 3 hours? On an ordinary day at Tokyo Disneyland, one of the most popular theme parks in the world, the line for its famous attractions such as Space Mountain, Splash Mountain, and Tower of Terror can reach 200 minutes. . . . That's over a 3-hour wait to enjoy a 3-minute ride! What causes lines to form at theme parks?

Theme park rides have lines because the quantity of rides demanded exceeds the quantity supplied. Why is that? Because most theme parks

A 200-minute wait for a ride at Tokyo Disneyland.

charge a fixed admission fee for unlimited rides, visitors typically demand more rides than the theme park is able to supply, even if a ride is operating at full capacity. The extent of the shortage, and consequently the length of wait time, are influenced largely by market factors.

First, consider the role of preferences. Disneyland has a worldwide following, and for those living in Japan, visiting Tokyo Disneyland is certainly

easier than visiting Disney parks in California or Florida. Second, consider the number of potential buyers. Tokyo Disneyland is located in a metropolitan area with over 30 million people. The sheer number of potential visitors will lead to higher demand. And third, consider the role of pricing. Given its popularity, Tokyo Disneyland could charge higher prices to reduce the quantity demanded. Yet, in 2016 a one-day adult admission to Tokyo Disneyland cost only $58, while its counterparts in California and Florida charged nearly $120.

The combination of preferences, proximity to potential buyers, and relatively low prices cause demand for Tokyo Disneyland rides to far exceed the park's reasonable capacity (at least by U.S. standards), creating massive lines. Yet for enthusiastic Disney fans, smiling faces abound. Despite the crowds, it's still the "Happiest Place on Earth!"

GO TO **LaunchPad** TO PRACTICE THE ECONOMIC CONCEPTS IN THIS STORY

✔ CHECKPOINT

MARKET EQUILIBRIUM

- Together, supply and demand determine market equilibrium, which occurs when the quantity supplied exactly equals quantity demanded.
- The equilibrium price is also called the market-clearing price.
- When quantity demanded exceeds quantity supplied, a shortage occurs and prices are bid up toward equilibrium. When quantity supplied exceeds quantity demanded, a surplus occurs and prices are pushed down toward equilibrium.
- When supply and demand change, equilibrium price and output change.
- When only one curve shifts, the resulting changes in equilibrium price and quantity can be predicted.
- When both curves shift, we can predict the change in equilibrium price in some cases or the change in equilibrium quantity in others, but never both. We have to determine the relative magnitudes of the shifts before we can predict both equilibrium price and quantity.

QUESTIONS: In China, where lines are a routine part of everyday life, a growing industry of professional line waiters has developed. Exactly as it sounds, these people are paid an average of $3 an hour to wait in line for others, a wage that is higher than what a typical factory worker in China earns. Today, the professional line waiter has popped up in cities around the world, including New York, though at significantly higher prices than in China. Given that one can pay someone to wait, what might happen in the market for goods and services most prone to long waiting lines, such as prime concert tickets or the latest technology gadget?

Answers to the Checkpoint questions can be found at the end of this chapter.

chapter summary

Section 1 Markets

3.1 A **market** is an institution that enables buyers and sellers to interact and transact with one another.

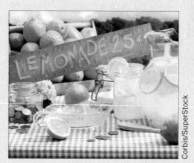

Buyers and sellers communicate their desires in a market through the prices at which goods and services are bought and sold. Hence, a market economy is called a **price system.**

Markets can be as simple as a lemonade stand, as large as an automobile lot, as valuable as the stock market, as virtual as an Internet shopping site, or as illegal as a ticket scalping operation.

Corbis/SuperStock

Stars and Stripes/Alamy

robertharding/Corbis

Section 2 Demand

3.2 **Demand** refers to the goods and services people are willing and able to buy during a period of time. It is a horizontal summation of individual demand curves in a defined market.

The **law of demand** states that as prices increase, quantity demanded falls, and vice versa, resulting in a downward-sloping demand curve.

Roller coasters are a lot of fun, but riding the same one over and over gives less satisfaction with each ride; therefore, willingness-to-pay falls with each ride.

Flint/Corbis

3.3 Determinants of Demand: How Demand Curves Shift

- ↑ Tastes and preferences: Demand shifts right.
- ↑ Income: Demand for normal goods shifts right, while demand for inferior goods shifts left.
- ↑ Price of substitutes: Demand shifts right.
- ↑ Price of complements: Demand shifts left.
- ↑ Number of buyers: Demand shifts right.
- ↑ Price expectations: Demand shifts right.

When investors expect stock prices to increase, demand for stock increases.

Bryan Smith/ZUMA Press

3.4 A Common Confusion in Terminology

A "change in demand" is a shift of the entire demand curve and is caused by a change in a nonprice demand factor.

A "change in quantity demanded" is a movement from one point to another on the same demand curve, and is caused only by a change in price of that good.

Section 3 Supply

3.5 Supply analysis works the same way as demand, but looking at the market from the firm's point of view.

Philip Gostelow/Aurora Photos/Corbis

The **law of supply** states that as price increases, firms want to supply more, and vice versa. It leads to an upward-sloping supply curve.

3.6 Determinants of Supply: How Supply Curves Shift

- ↑ Production technology: Supply shifts right.
- ↑ Cost of resources: Supply shifts left.
- ↑ Price of related commodities: Supply shifts left.
- ↑ Price expectations: Supply shifts left.
- ↑ Number of sellers: Supply shifts right.
- ↑ Taxes: Supply shifts left.
- ↑ Subsidies: Supply shifts right.

Section 4 Market Equilibrium

3.7 **Market equilibrium** occurs at the price at which the quantity supplied is equal to quantity demanded, and where the demand and supply curves intersect.

How does equilibrium change?

Which curve slopes up and which slopes down? Two tricks to aid in memory:

- S"up"ply contains the word "up" for upward-sloping.
- Only the fingers on your right hand can make a "d" for demand. Hold that hand up in front of you!

3.8 A shift in demand or supply will change equilibrium price and quantity.

robertharding premium/Corbis

Higher oil prices raise the cost of resins used to produce surfboards.

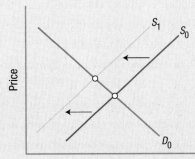

Supply of surfboards shifts left, raising equilibrium price and lowering equilibrium quantity.

Summary of Demand and Supply Shifts on Equilibrium Price and Quantity:		
D shifts right:	P↑	Q↑
D shifts left:	P↓	Q↓
S shifts right:	P↓	Q↑
S shifts left:	P↑	Q↓

markets, p. 56
price system, p. 57
willingness-to-pay, p. 57
demand, p. 58
law of demand, p. 59
demand curve, p. 59
demand schedule, p. 59
horizontal summation, p. 60
determinants of demand, p. 61

normal good, p. 61
inferior good, p. 61
substitute goods, p. 62
complementary goods, p. 62
change in demand, p. 62
change in quantity demanded, p. 63
supply, p. 64
law of supply, p. 64
supply curve, p. 64

determinants of supply, p. 65
change in supply, p. 67
change in quantity supplied, p. 67
equilibrium, p. 69
equilibrium price, p. 69
equilibrium quantity, p. 69
surplus, p. 69
shortage, p. 70

QUESTIONS AND PROBLEMS

Check Your Understanding

1. Product prices give consumers and businesses a lot of information besides just the price. What kinds of information?

2. Name and explain the determinants of demand. Why are they important?

3. Assume there is a positive relationship between aging and cholesterol levels. As the world population ages, will the demand for cholesterol drugs increase, decrease, or remain the same? Would this cause a change in demand or a change in quantity demanded?

4. Describe some of the reasons why supply changes. Improved technology typically results in lower prices for most products. Why do you think this is true? Describe the difference between a change in supply and a change in quantity supplied.

5. If a strong economic recovery boosts average incomes, what would happen to the equilibrium price and quantity for a normal good? How about for an inferior good?

6. Suppose the market for tomatoes is in equilibrium, and events occur that simultaneously shift both the demand and supply curves to the right. Is it possible to determine how the equilibrium price and/or quantity would change? Explain.

Apply the Concepts

7. Demand for tickets to sporting events such as the Super Bowl has increased. Has supply increased? What does the answer to this tell you about the price of these tickets compared to prices a few years ago?

8. Suppose the price of monthly data plans required to access the Internet anywhere using a tablet computer falls. How would this affect the market for tablet computers?

9. Using the accompanying figures, answer the following questions:
   a. On the Demand panel:
      - Show an increase in demand and label it D_1.
      - Show a decrease in demand and label it D_2.
      - Show an increase in quantity demanded.
      - Show a decrease in quantity demanded.
      - What causes demand to change?
      - What causes quantity demanded to change?
   b. On the Supply panel:
      - Show an increase in supply and label it S_1.
      - Show a decrease in supply and label it S_2.

- Show an increase in quantity supplied.
- Show a decrease in quantity supplied.
- What causes supply to change?
- What causes quantity supplied to change?

10. Several medical studies have shown that drinking red wine in moderation is good for the heart. How would such a study affect the public's demand for wine? Would it have an impact on the type of grapes planted in new vineyards?

11. Assume initially that the demand and supply for premium coffees (one-pound bags) are in equilibrium. Now assume Starbucks introduces the world to premium blends, and so demand rises substantially. Describe what will happen in this market as it moves to a new equilibrium. If a hard freeze eliminates Brazil's premium coffee crop, what will happen to the price of premium coffee?

12. Over the past decade, cruise ship companies have dramatically increased the number of mega-ships (those that carry 3,000 passengers or more), increasing the supply of cruises. At the same time, the popularity of cruising has increased among consumers, increasing demand. Explain how these two effects can coincide with a decrease in the average price of cruise travel.

In the News

13. In 2015 Google's Self-Driving Cars had driven over 1 million miles on public roads and were involved in only twelve minor accidents, all of which were caused by the non-self-driving car. In response to the early success of self-driving cars, nearly every major auto manufacturer in the world is developing its own version of a driverless car (*CBS News*, "Driverless Cars Prepare to Hit the Road," October 4, 2015), potentially increasing the supply of such cars in the market. What factors might cause demand for driverless cars to take off and become the new standard? What factors might cause demand to falter, leading the industry to fail?

14. When the Segway was unveiled in 2001, many believed it would become the future of transportation, replacing bicycles and even cars. Yet this expensive, bulky device never quite took off other than those used in Segway tours offered in many cities and by security officers in malls and airports. A decade later, other companies began developing newer, lighter, and less expensive motorized transportation devices such as the IO Hawk. A February 23, 2015, online article by Oxy.com, "This Motorized Skateboard Might Kick Segway to the Curb," suggests that Segways may become obsolete. Using a demand and supply diagram for Segways, show the effect of the introduction of the IO Hawk on the market for Segways. Based on the article, are Segways and IO Hawks substitutes or complements?

Solving Problems

WORK IT OUT **LaunchPad** | interactive activity

15. A popular tradition when traveling to Hawaii is to receive a *lei*, a wreath of flowers to welcome guests. Although a lei can be made of flowers, leaves, nuts, or even candy and money, orchids remain the most popular flower used to create them. Suppose that supply and demand in the orchid lei market in Hawaii are as represented in the table below:

Price ($/unit)	Quantity Demanded (thousands)	Quantity Supplied (thousands)
5	24	8
10	20	12
15	16	16
20	12	20
25	8	24

a. Graph both the supply (S_0) and demand (D_0) curves. What is the current equilibrium price? Label that point *a*.

b. Assume that the Hawaiian lei industry increases its use of orchids from Thailand (where they are grown at a lower price), allowing orchid lei supply to increase by 8,000 units at every price. Illustrate the increase in the supply in your graph. Label the new supply curve (S_1). What will the new equilibrium price in the market be? Label that point *b*.

c. Now assume that luxury hotels in Hawaii begin cost-cutting measures by no longer presenting guests with a lei upon check-in, reducing orchid lei demand by 8,000 units at every price. Label the new demand curve (D_1). What will the new equilibrium price be? Label this new equilibrium point *c*.

d. Subsequently assume that severe monsoons and civil unrest in Thailand lead to a reduction in orchid production, reducing supply back to the original curve (S_0). What will the new equilibrium price be? Label this new equilibrium point *d*.

16. The following figure shows the supply and demand for strawberries. Answer the questions that follow.

Supply and Demand of Strawberries

a. Indicate the equilibrium price and equilibrium quantity.

b. Suppose sellers try to sell strawberries at $4. How much of a shortage or a surplus of strawberries would result?

c. Now suppose that the demand for strawberries falls by 10 units at every price. Draw the new demand curve in the figure, and estimate what the new equilibrium price and equilibrium quantity would be.

d. If sellers still try to sell strawberries at $4, would the shortage or the surplus increase or decrease?

⊕ USING THE NUMBERS

17. According to By the Numbers, about how many times larger is the bottled water market in the United States in the year 2014 compared to 1984?

18. According to By the Numbers, in which 6-month period between July 2012 and January 2015 did Uber experience the greatest increase in terms of number of drivers? Would you describe the growth of Uber drivers over this 2.5-year period as linear (constant growth) or exponential (rising growth)?

ANSWERS TO QUESTIONS IN CHECKPOINTS

Checkpoint: Markets 57

The market for financial securities is a huge, well-organized, and regulated market compared to local farmer's markets. Trillions of dollars change hands each week in the financial markets, and products are standardized.

Checkpoint: Demand 63

The ability to avoid high gasoline prices, a general rise in environmental consciousness, incentives such as preferred parking and reduced tolls offered by some states, an increase in the availability of charging stations (reducing opportunity cost), and improvements in quality have all led to an increase in demand for plug-in electric cars. These factors led to a change in demand, because factors other than the price of the car itself have led to an increase in demand for these cars. However, as the costs of production eventually fall, prices will decrease, which will result in an increase in quantity demanded.

Checkpoint: Supply 69

A higher textbook buyback price would entice more students to sell their textbooks instead of keeping them. Because the price of the offer has increased, it results in an increase in the quantity supplied of used textbooks. If, however, many students are forced to retake a class, they would likely not sell their textbooks; hence, the supply of used textbooks would shift to the left.

Checkpoint: Market Equilibrium 75

Waiting in line for a new product or a good deal adds to the cost of acquiring a good. For those with higher opportunity costs of time, hiring a professional line waiter reduces this cost, making the product more affordable. Therefore, professional line waiters would cause an increase in demand for goods and services more prone to lines, causing even greater lines and shortages if prices do not adjust upward.

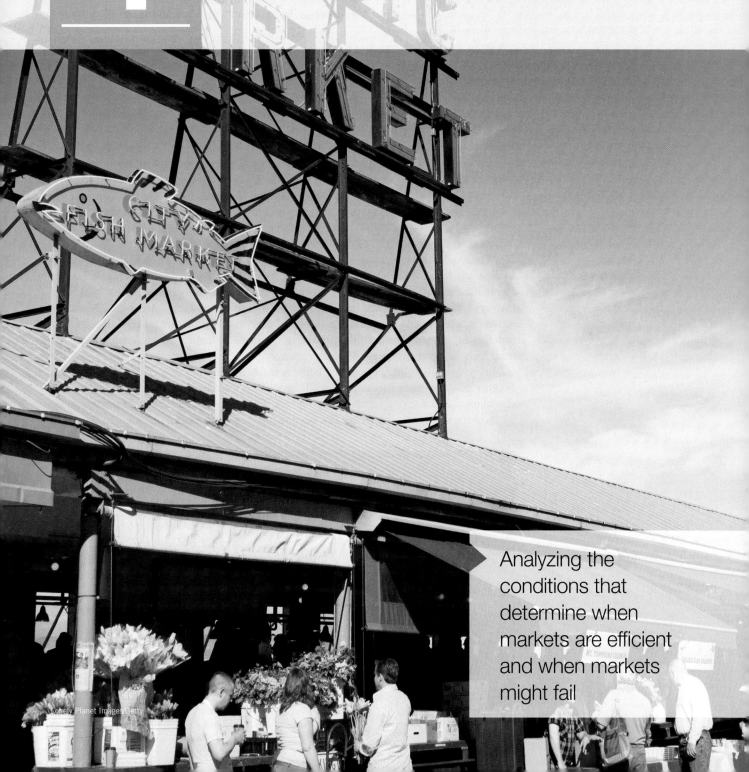

4 Markets and Government

Analyzing the conditions that determine when markets are efficient and when markets might fail

Learning Objectives

4.1 Define the concepts of consumer surplus and producer surplus, and explain how they are used to measure the benefits and costs of market transactions.

4.2 Use consumer surplus and producer surplus to describe the gains from trade.

4.3 Explain the causes of deadweight loss and how markets can mitigate them.

4.4 Understand why markets sometimes fail to provide an optimal outcome.

4.5 Describe what an effective price ceiling or price floor does to a market and how it creates shortages or surpluses.

4.6 Identify the winners and losers when price ceilings and price floors are implemented.

Once an exotic food from the Orient eaten by few outside Asia, sushi has become part of the U.S. diet in all parts of the country, available in sushi bars, cafés, buffets, and even grocery stores. The popularity of sushi stems largely from the known health benefits of eating fish, providing omega-3-rich, low-fat, and low-calorie meals. But to have sushi, one must have access to fresh fish, not easy for those not living near a coastline. Or is it?

To provide fresh sushi to inland consumers, fish must be caught, flash frozen (to kill bacteria), then flown to destinations in a short period of time in order to maintain the fish's freshness. In some cases, fish is flown around the world to meet the demand. At the Tsukiji fish market in Tokyo, Japan, the largest fish market in the world, over 5 million pounds of fish are auctioned off *each morning* and then flown to wholesalers and restaurants around the globe.

Why would fishermen, fish markets, wholesalers, and restaurants go through so much trouble just to provide fresh sushi to customers in faraway places whom they will never meet? Because the market provides incentives for each person to do so. Every person in the supply chain for sushi acts in his or her own best interest by supplying what the market wants (as determined by the prices received for their goods), and that leads to an efficiently functioning market. Adam Smith's notion of the *invisible hand* works to ensure that, in a market society, consumers get what they want.

Everywhere we look in the world there are markets, and not just the big markets for fish or other major industries. Countless smaller markets dot our local landscapes, and many new virtual markets are springing up on the Internet. All play a similar role in terms of providing what consumers want, using prices as a way to signal the values placed on goods and services.

Hamachi, Unagi, Ikura, Maguro, Toro. . . . Fish from an ocean halfway around the world to a dinner plate in a rural inland town highlights the ability of efficient markets to provide what consumers want.

Rita Jayaraman/Dreamstime.com

Price Controls and Supports in the Economy Today

Efficient markets are an essential part of modern societies. However, sometimes governments intervene in markets to address equity concerns. The use of price controls and price supports is a common way of intervening in markets, as the following illustrates.

The average tuition at public universities in the United States (for in-state residents attending a public university in that state) is $8,983. However, there is wide variation in average tuition rates across states, from $4,646 in Wyoming to $14,712 in New Hampshire. But even the most expensive in-state tuition is still lower than the market rate, and therefore represents a price ceiling. Unlike traditional price ceilings, which create a shortage, states provide subsidies to public universities to offset the difference between the market rate and price ceiling.

The use of renewable energy has increased in recent years as the government provides subsidies to offset the higher initial costs compared to fossil fuels. However, as more consumers use renewable energy over time, costs should fall, allowing the industry to become less dependent on government subsidies.

Average In-State Tuition at Public Universities by State

State	Average Tuition	State	Average Tuition	State	Average Tuition
NH	$14,712	CO	$9,487	DC	$7,516
VT	$14,419	AL	$9,470	ND	$7,513
PA	$13,246	ME	$9,422	NE	$7,404
NJ	$13,002	KY	$9,188	LA	$7,314
IL	$12,770	CA	$9,173	NY	$7,292
MI	$11,909	IN	$9,023	OK	$6,895
SC	$11,449	OR	$8,932	MS	$6,861
DE	$11,448	TX	$8,830	NC	$6,677
MA	$10,951	WI	$8,781	WV	$6,661
RI	$10,934	MD	$8,724	ID	$6,602
VA	$10,899	TN	$8,541	NV	$6,418
WA	$10,846	MO	$8,383	FL	$6,351
CT	$10,620	GA	$8,094	MT	$6,279
MN	$10,527	KS	$8,086	NM	$6,190
AZ	$10,398	IA	$7,857	UT	$6,177
OH	$10,100	SD	$7,653	AK	$6,138
HI	$9,740	AR	$7,567	WY	$4,646

Government Subsidies (in millions) for Renewable Energy by Type (2013)

3% $345
3% $395
4% $594
5% $629
40% ▶ $5,328
$5,936 ◀ 45%

- ■ Wind
- ■ Solar
- ■ Biomass
- ■ Other
- ■ Hydro
- ■ Geothermal

$7.25 The U.S. federal minimum wage (price floor) for workers over age 16 in 2016.

$20,000,000,000,000 Spending by the U.S. government in 2015 to maintain agricultural price floors.

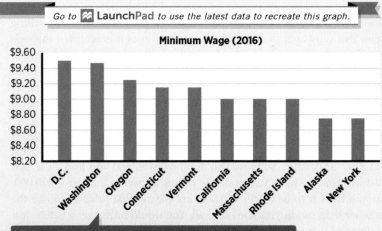

Go to ⧉ LaunchPad to use the latest data to recreate this graph.

Minimum Wage (2016)

(Bar chart, values from $8.20 to $9.60: D.C., Washington, Oregon, Connecticut, Vermont, California, Massachusetts, Rhode Island, Alaska, New York)

Over half of U.S. states have a statewide minimum wage higher than the federal minimum wage of $7.25 per hour.

The By the Numbers — Do It Yourself! Lab Activity will explore state-mandated minimum wages.

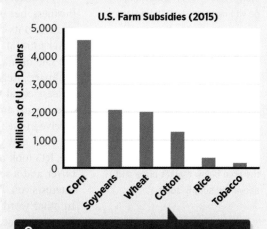

U.S. Farm Subsidies (2015)

Millions of U.S. Dollars (0 to 5,000)

(Bar chart: Corn, Soybeans, Wheat, Cotton, Rice, Tobacco)

Certain agricultural crops are protected by price supports (price floors), with the difference from their market prices paid by the U.S. government.

The previous chapter considered how supply and demand work together to determine the quantities of various products sold and the equilibrium prices consumers must pay for them in a market economy. The markets we have studied thus far have been stylized versions of competitive markets: They have featured many buyers and sellers, a uniform product, consumers and sellers who have complete information about the market, and few barriers to market entry or exit.

In this chapter, we start with this stylized competitive market and introduce tools for measuring the efficiency of competitive markets. We then apply these tools to reveal the gains from trade. We briefly consider some of the complexities inherent to most markets. The typical market does not meet all the criteria of a truly competitive market. That does not mean that the supply and demand analysis you just absorbed will not be useful in analyzing economic events. Often, however, you will need to temper your analysis to fit the specific conditions of the markets you study. Finally, we will look at what happens when government intervenes in markets.

CONSUMER AND PRODUCER SURPLUS: A TOOL FOR MEASURING ECONOMIC EFFICIENCY

Suppose you find a rare comic book on eBay that you believe is worth $100, and start putting in bids hoping to buy it. After a week, you get the comic book with the winning bid of $80. You are happy because not only will you get the comic book you've been looking for, but you have also paid a price lower than what you were willing to pay. However, you're likely not the only one who is happy. The person who sold you that comic book found it in her granddad's old trunk that she inherited, and had hoped to get at least $60 for it. In fact, she ended up receiving more money than the minimum amount she had hoped to receive. In this situation, the transaction took place, and both the buyer and seller are better off.

When consumers go about their everyday shopping or when they seek out their next major purchase, their objective typically is to find the lowest price relative to the perceived value of the product. It is the reason why consumers compare prices, shop online, or bargain with sellers. In other words, the general goal of consumers is to find the product at a price no greater than their willingness-to-pay (perceived value); if the price is less, consumers benefit more. These "savings," so to speak, are referred to as **consumer surplus,** and are a measure of the net benefits consumers receive in the market.

Producers also have a corresponding objective. When an entrepreneur opens up a new business, her intention is to maximize its success by getting the highest price for a product relative to its cost for as large a quantity as possible. Sometimes this is achieved by selling fewer units at a higher markup (such as rare art), while other times it is achieved through the sale of mass quantities of products at relatively small markups (such as goods sold at Walmart). Regardless of the strategy used, the general goal of producers is to obtain a price at least equal to their willingness-to-sell; if the price is higher, producers benefit more. These gains are called **producer surplus,** and are a measure of the net benefits producers receive in the market.

Now that you have an intuitive sense of what consumer surplus and producer surplus are, let's look more carefully into how they are measured. We begin with a single case of a buyer and a seller at a car dealership. Suppose you are the buyer, and you find a car that interests you. Let's assume that the most you would be willing to pay for that car is $20,000. In other words, you find the car to be worth $20,000, but paying that price would be the worst-case scenario other than not buying the car at all. You would rather get a better deal by negotiating with the sales manager. But now let's look at the other side: Assume that the sales manager has a minimum price of $15,000 at which he is willing to sell the car. Selling the car at this price would be his worst-case scenario other than not selling the car.

consumer surplus The difference between what consumers (as individuals or the market) would be willing to pay and the market price. It is equal to the area above market price and below the demand curve.

producer surplus The difference between the market price and the price at which firms are willing to supply the product. It is equal to the area below market price and above the supply curve.

FIGURE 1

FIGURE 1	WILLINGNESS-TO-PAY AND WILLINGNESS-TO-SELL

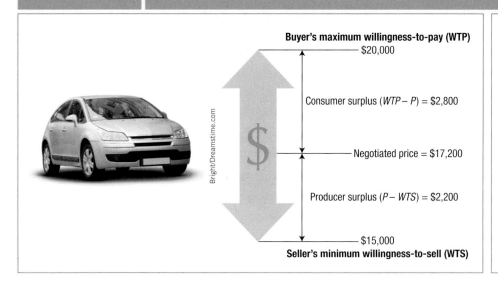

Buyer's maximum willingness-to-pay (WTP)
$20,000

Consumer surplus ($WTP - P$) = $2,800

Negotiated price = $17,200

Producer surplus ($P - WTS$) = $2,200

$15,000
Seller's minimum willingness-to-sell (WTS)

In a transaction with a single buyer and a single seller, consumer surplus ($2,800) is the difference between the maximum amount the buyer was willing to pay ($20,000) and the actual price paid ($17,200). Producer surplus ($2,200) is the difference between the actual price received ($17,200) and the minimum amount the seller was willing to accept ($15,000).

We have now determined a potential "gain" of $5,000 that can be shared by the buyer and seller depending on the final negotiated price for this car. Figure 1 shows this gain as the difference between the buyer's willingness-to-pay (WTP) and the seller's willingness-to-sell (WTS). Assume that the final negotiated price of the car is $17,200. We can now use this information to calculate consumer surplus ($WTP - P = \$20,000 - \$17,200 = \$2,800$) and producer surplus ($P - WTS = \$17,200 - \$15,000 = \$2,200$).

This example is unique in that the price of the car is negotiated between the buyer and seller. In most of our daily transactions, however, the prices of goods and services are not negotiated. When you go to the grocery store, all of the prices are fixed. You don't negotiate over the price of milk, bread, or chicken. Nonetheless, the measurements of consumer surplus and producer surplus remain the same when prices are fixed.

Suppose that instead of just one buyer and one seller, the market contains dozens or even thousands of buyers and sellers. What would change? Let's look at the market for Frisbees used in the popular intramural sport of Ultimate. First, each of the many buyers would have a different WTP, which would be represented as a downward-sloping demand curve (by definition, demand is just a collection of WTPs of all consumers in a market). Second, each of the many sellers would have a different WTS, which would be represented as an upward-sloping supply curve. But the definition of consumer surplus ($WTP - P$) and producer surplus ($P - WTS$) remains the same, except that now we apply it to the entire market. Figure 2 illustrates how consumer and producer surplus is determined in a small market for Frisbees with specific consumers and firms and for the overall market.

Panel A in Figure 2 represents a small market with 6 individual buyers and 6 individual sellers, with an equilibrium price of $6 (from equilibrium point e) at which 6 units of output are sold. In this market, Alanna has the highest willingness to pay, because she values a Frisbee to be worth $11. Because the market determines that $6 is the price everyone pays, Alanna clearly gets a bargain by purchasing the unit and receiving a consumer surplus equal to $5 ($11 − $6). Ben, however, values a Frisbee a little less at $10, but still receives a consumer surplus of $4 ($10 − $6). And so on for Christine, David, and Erika, who receive a consumer surplus of $3, $2, and $1, respectively. Only Francis, who values a Frisbee to be worth exactly the same amount as the market price, earns no consumer surplus. Total consumer surplus for the 6 consumers in panel A is found by adding all of the individual consumer surpluses for each unit purchased. Thus, total consumer surplus in panel A is equal to $5 + $4 + $3 + $2 + $1 + $0 = $15.

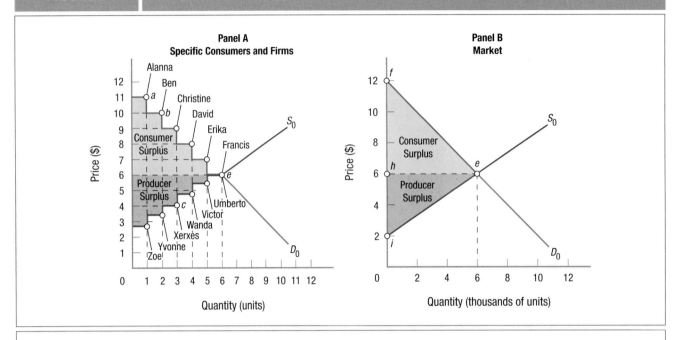

Panel B shows a market consisting of many more of the specific consumers and firms shown in panel A. This market determines equilibrium price to be $6 (point e), and total sales for the market are 6,000 units. Consumer surplus is equal to the area under the demand curve but above the equilibrium price of $6. Producer surplus is the area under the equilibrium price but above the supply curve.

In a similar way, assume that each point on the supply curve represents a specific seller, each with a Frisbee to sell but each with a different willingness to sell. Equilibrium price is still $6; therefore, Zoe, who is willing to sell her Frisbee for just $2.67, receives a producer surplus of $3.33 ($6 − $2.67). Yvonne, Xerxes, Wanda, and Victor, who each have a higher willingness-to-sell, receive a correspondingly smaller producer surplus equal to $2.67, $2.00, $1.33, and $0.67, respectively. And Umberto, who had a willingness-to-sell of $6, receives no producer surplus for his sale. Total producer surplus in panel A is equal to $3.33 + $2.67 + $2.00 + $1.33 + $0.67 + $0 = $10.

Panel B illustrates consumer and producer surplus for an entire market. For convenience, we have assumed that the market is 1,000 times larger than that shown in panel A, so the x axis is output in thousands. Whereas in panel A we had discrete buyers and sellers, we now have one big market; therefore, consumer surplus is equal to the area under the demand curve and above equilibrium price, or the area of the shaded triangle labeled "consumer surplus."

To put a number to the consumer surplus triangle (*feh*) in panel B, we can compute the area of the triangle using the formula 1/2(base × height). Thus, total market consumer surplus in panel B is [1/2 × (6,000) × ($12 − $6)] = $18,000. The shaded triangle labeled "producer surplus" (area *hei*) is found in the same way by computing the value of the triangle. Producer surplus is equal to [1/2 × (6,000) × ($6 − $2)] = $12,000.

Although we simplify the calculation of consumer and producer surplus using the area of the triangle, remember that it is still the sum of many individual consumer and producer surpluses. It is merely because of the fact that markets have thousands of buyers and sellers that the steps in panel A of Figure 2 become very small, thus resulting in smooth demand and supply curves in panel B.

We have now defined consumer surplus and producer surplus for individuals and for markets. But how do we know whether the market leads to an ideal outcome for consumers and producers? The next section goes on to reveal the efficiency of markets.

CHECKPOINT

CONSUMER AND PRODUCER SURPLUS: A TOOL FOR MEASURING ECONOMIC EFFICIENCY

- Consumers and producers attempt to maximize their well-being by achieving the greatest gains in their market transactions.
- Consumer surplus occurs when consumers would have been willing to pay more for a good or service than the actual price paid. It represents a form of savings to consumers.
- Producer surplus occurs when businesses would have been willing to provide a good or service at prices lower than the market price. It represents a form of earnings to producers.

QUESTION: At the end of the semester, four college students list their economics textbooks for sale on the bulletin board in the student union. The minimum price Alex is willing to accept is $20, Caroline wants at least $25, Kira wants at least $30, and Will wants at least $35. Now assume that four college students taking an economics class next semester are searching for a deal on the textbook. Cole wishes to pay no more than $50, Jacqueline no more than $55, Sienna no more than $60, and Tessa no more than $65. Suppose that the actual sales price for each of the four textbooks is $40. What is the total consumer surplus received by the four buyers and the total producer surplus received by the four sellers?

Answers to the Checkpoint questions can be found at the end of the chapter.

USING CONSUMER AND PRODUCER SURPLUS: THE GAINS FROM TRADE

Markets are efficient when they generate the largest possible amount of net benefits to all parties involved. When transactions between a buyer and a seller take place, each party is better off than before the transaction, leading to gains from trade. We had previously looked at gains from trade in an earlier chapter from the perspectives of individuals, firms, and countries specializing in activities and engaging in mutually beneficial transactions. This is no different than our present market examples, in which buyers and sellers mutually gain from transacting with one another.

At the equilibrium price, shortages and surpluses are nonexistent, and all consumers wanting to buy a good at that price are able to find a seller willing to sell at that price. The market efficiency that results maximizes the sum of consumer surplus and producer surplus, referred to as **total surplus.** Total surplus is a measure of the total net benefits a society achieves when both consumers and producers are valued components of an economy.

To see why markets are efficient at equilibrium, we need to analyze what happens to total surplus when markets deviate from equilibrium.

total surplus The sum of consumer surplus and producer surplus, and a measure of the overall net benefit gained from a market transaction.

The Consequences of Deviating From Market Equilibrium

The market mechanism ensures that goods and services get to where they are most needed, because consumers desiring them bid up the price, while suppliers eager to make money supply them. Adam Smith termed this process the *invisible hand* to describe how resources are allocated efficiently through individual decisions made in markets.

But not all markets end up in equilibrium, especially if buyers or sellers hold inadequate information about products, or if buyers or sellers hold unrealistic or inaccurate expectations about market prices and behavior. Let's examine two scenarios in the market for treadmills in which prices deviate from the equilibrium price.

When Prices Exceed Equilibrium Figure 3 illustrates a market for treadmills with an equilibrium price of $300. Suppose that due to unrealistic expectations of demand, prices for treadmills are set at $400, above the equilibrium price. We know from the previous chapter that a price above equilibrium leads to excess supply, because consumers only demand 10,000 units

Compared to the equilibrium price, a price of $400 would prevent some consumers from purchasing the product. A loss of consumer surplus equal to the blue area occurs. Further, consumers who still purchase the product pay $100 more than the equilibrium price, causing an additional loss of consumer surplus equal to the pink area. Producers, meanwhile, lose producer surplus equal to the yellow area resulting from the units that consumers no longer buy, but earn additional producer surplus equal to the pink area as a result of the higher price. Total lost surplus, called deadweight loss, is represented by the blue and yellow areas (no one gets this because some trades are not made now). The pink area is surplus transferred from consumers to producers because of the higher price.

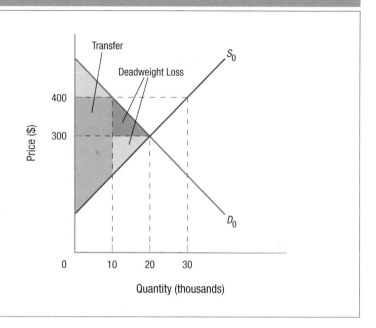

while producers desire to sell 30,000. Our tools of consumer surplus and producer surplus allow us to evaluate the effects on buyers and sellers in this market.

When prices are above equilibrium, consumer surplus shrinks due to two effects. First, a price of $400 causes some consumers to not make a purchase, because these consumers were only willing to pay between $300 and $400. The area shown in blue represents the lost consumer surplus from these forgone purchases. Second, the consumers who still are willing and able to purchase a unit pay $100 more, which represents a loss in consumer surplus equal to the pink area. In sum, the pink and blue regions represent the total reduction in consumer surplus from the higher price.

Producers, on the other hand, will likely benefit from the higher price but face two opposing effects. First, the fact that the higher price causes some consumers to not purchase a unit causes a loss in producer surplus equal to the yellow area. However, this is offset by the additional money earned from the consumers who buy the unit at the higher price, which is represented by the pink area.

Therefore, the pink area represents a transfer of surplus from consumers to producers. The blue and yellow areas represent **deadweight loss,** the loss of consumer surplus and producer surplus caused by the inefficiency of a market not operating at equilibrium. Nobody gets the blue and yellow areas. Deadweight loss represents a loss in total surplus, because both buyers and sellers would have benefited from these transactions.

deadweight loss The reduction in total surplus that results from the inefficiency of a market not in equilibrium.

When Prices Fall Below Equilibrium When prices are below equilibrium, the opposite effects happen as a result of a shortage. Figure 4 shows the market for treadmills in which the price of $200 is below the equilibrium price. At that price, sellers provide 10,000 units for sale, while buyers demand 30,000 units, causing a shortage.

At a price of $200, producers are clearly worse off. Some producers are unable to sell at that low price, causing a loss of producer surplus equal to the yellow area, while those who still sell the product earn $100 less per unit, resulting in a loss of producer surplus equal to the pink area.

At first, you might believe consumers are better off with the lower price, and some in fact are. But these gains, shown by the pink area, are limited to consumers lucky enough to purchase the good. The rest of the consumers who are affected by the shortage are worse off, because consumer surplus equal to the blue area is lost because of trades never made. In sum, deadweight loss equal to the blue and yellow areas results.

FIGURE 4   CONSUMER AND PRODUCER SURPLUS WHEN PRICES ARE BELOW EQUILIBRIUM

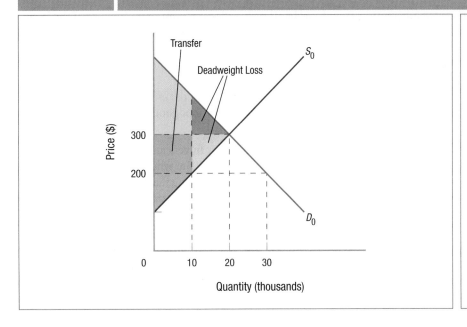

Compared to the equilibrium price, a price of $200 causes some producers to not sell the product. A loss of producer surplus equal to the yellow area occurs. Further, producers who still sell the product earn $100 less than before, causing an additional loss of producer surplus equal to the pink area. Consumers, meanwhile, lose consumer surplus equal to the blue area resulting from the shortage of units, but receive additional consumer surplus equal to the pink area as a result of the lower price for those lucky enough to find units for sale. Once again, deadweight loss is the blue and yellow areas, and the pink area is surplus transferred.

The two scenarios shown in Figures 3 and 4 demonstrate that whenever prices deviate from equilibrium, total surplus as measured by the sum of consumer surplus and producer surplus falls, resulting in a deadweight loss from mutually beneficial transactions between buyers and sellers not taking place. But why would markets not achieve equilibrium? Sometimes a market will fail to achieve equilibrium because it is prevented from doing so on its own.

PAUL A. SAMUELSON (1915–2009)

NOBEL PRIZE

In 1970 Paul Samuelson became the first American to win the Nobel Prize in Economics. One could say that Paul Samuelson literally wrote the book on economics. In 1948, when he was a young professor at the Massachusetts Institute of Technology, the university asked him to write a text for the junior-year course in economics. Seventy years later, more than 4 million copies of his textbook *Economics* have been sold.

Samuelson's interests were wide ranging, and his contributions include everything from the highly technical and mathematical to a popular column for *Newsweek* magazine. He made breakthrough contributions to virtually all areas of economics.

Born in Gary, Indiana, in 1915, Samuelson attended the University of Chicago. He received the university's Social Science Medal and was awarded a graduate fellowship, which he used at Harvard, where he published eleven papers while in the graduate program.

He wanted to remain at Harvard, but was only offered an instructor's position. However, MIT soon made a better offer and, as he describes it, "On a fine October day in 1940 an *enfant terrible emeritus* packed up his pencil and moved three miles down the Charles River, where he lived happily ever after." He often remarked that a pencil was all he needed to theorize. Seven years later, he published his Ph.D. dissertation *Foundations of Economic Analysis,* a major contribution to the area of mathematical economics.

Harvard made several attempts to lure him back, but he spent his entire career at MIT and is often credited with developing a department as good as or better than Harvard's. Samuelson was an informal adviser to President John F. Kennedy. A prolific writer, his *Collected Works* takes up five volumes and includes more than 350 articles. He was an active economist until his death in 2009 at the age of 94. As you read through this book, keep in mind that in virtually every chapter, Paul Samuelson created or added to the analysis in substantial ways.

Information from David Warsh, *Knowledge and the Wealth of Nations: A Story of Economic Discovery* (New York: Norton), 2006; Paul Samuelson, "Economics in My Time," in William Breit and Roger Spencer, *Lives of the Laureates: Seven Nobel Economists* (Cambridge, MA: MIT Press), 1986.

Market Failure

Markets are inherently efficient mechanisms for allocating resources because of the incentives that drive consumers and firms to act in their own best interests. But like all things, exceptions occur when circumstances prevent the market from achieving the socially desirable outcome. When freely functioning markets fail to provide an optimal amount of goods and services, a **market failure** occurs.

market failure Occurs when a free market does not lead to a socially desirable outcome.

There are four major reasons why markets fail: a lack of competition, a mismatch of information, external benefits or costs, and the existence of public goods. Each causes total surplus to fall, and deadweight loss to appear.

Lack of Competition When a market has many buyers and sellers, no one seller has the ability to raise its price above that of its competitors. But when a market lacks competition, a firm can raise its price in the market without worrying that other firms will undercut its price. For example, in most communities the local water provider is a firm that lacks competition. This can lead to inefficient production and higher prices unless the market failure is corrected using government regulation.

Information Is Not Shared by All Parties An important condition for efficient markets is that buyers and sellers must possess adequate information about products. Sometimes, one party knows more about a product than the other, a situation known as **asymmetric information.** For example, a seller of a used car knows more about the true condition of the car than a potential buyer. Conversely, an art or antiques buyer may know

asymmetric information Occurs when one party to a transaction has significantly better information than another party.

Singapore: Resolving Traffic Jams and Reducing Pollution Using Price Controls

> **How did Singapore use economic tools to intervene in the market to improve traffic flow and to correct a potential market failure?**

Eric Chiang

How much time is spent waiting in gridlock traffic in major cities? According to a study by the transportation analytics firm INRIX, in 2015, American drivers spent 8 billion hours stuck in traffic. Traffic creates an opportunity cost that leads to reduced productivity. Moreover, traffic jams reduce fuel efficiency and generate more air pollution. Is there an economic solution to these problems? Singapore may have the answer.

Singapore uses an electronic road-pricing system that charges drivers a toll on dozens of its major roads and

highways. Unlike traditional toll roads, Singapore's road charges vary throughout the day. During times when roads are less subject to congestion, the fee is very minimal or even zero, while during times of the day when roads are likely to be congested, the fee is higher. As it becomes more expensive to drive during certain periods of the day, drivers are incentivized to drive less, to drive during off-peak times, or to find alternative means of transportation. The outcome is a road system that is less prone to congestion, reducing an inefficiency.

Singapore is not the only city that uses congestion charges. It costs approximately $15 to drive in Central

London between the hours of 7 A.M. and 6 P.M. Even in the United States, the introduction of express lanes in Los Angeles, Atlanta, Miami, and other cities has allowed motorists to pay a toll to bypass traffic. Similar to Singapore, these tolls vary throughout the day, with prices rising as roads become more congested.

Not only do congestion charges incentivize people to drive less; they also encourage companies to change the way they operate. Companies that do not need to operate during traditional business hours might encourage their employees to arrive at work later and return home later, avoiding times when congestion charges are at their peak. By reducing traffic congestion, less time is wasted, productivity rises, and pollution is reduced. Furthermore, the fees collected are a valuable source of government revenue.

Many economists believe that market-based pricing mechanisms such as congestion charges can lead to increased efficiency and equity.

GO TO **LaunchPad** TO PRACTICE THE ECONOMIC CONCEPTS IN THIS STORY

more about the value of items than the seller at an estate sale. In these cases, a mismatch of information may lead to prices being set too high or too low.

The Existence of External Benefits or Costs When you drive your car on a crowded highway, you inflict external costs on other drivers by adding to congestion. When you receive a flu shot, you confer external benefits on the rest of us by reducing the chances of spreading an illness. Markets rarely produce the socially optimal output when external costs or benefits are present. When deciding whether to drive or obtain a flu shot, you tend not to think of the costs and benefits you impose on others. As a result, more people drive and fewer people receive flu shots than would be ideal to achieve the socially optimal outcome.

The Existence of Public Goods Most goods we buy are private goods, such as meals and concert tickets; once we buy them, no one else can benefit from them. Public goods, however, are goods that one person can consume without diminishing what is left for others. Public television, for example, is a public good that illustrates nonrivalry (my watching of PBS does not mean there is less PBS for you to watch) and nonexclusivity (once a good is provided, others cannot be excluded from enjoying it). Because of these characteristics, public goods are difficult to provide in the private market.

Market Efficiency Versus Equity

Reducing the effects of market failure is an important goal of government, which can enact policies to address markets in which private transactions do not lead to the optimal outcome. But the role of government extends beyond that of achieving social efficiency. It is also tasked with the goal of achieving equity in markets. For example, is it fair when teachers or firefighters who earn modest salaries are unable to afford market rents for apartments, or when a single parent working full time is unable to earn enough to avoid poverty? If a policy creates considerable unfairness, while spurring only a small gain in efficiency, some other policy might be better. One tool used by government to balance efficiency with equity is price controls, which we turn to next.

 CHECKPOINT

USING CONSUMER AND PRODUCER SURPLUS: THE GAINS FROM TRADE

- The sum of consumer surplus and producer surplus is total surplus, a measure of the overall net benefit for an economy.
- Markets are efficient when all buyers and all sellers willing to buy and sell at the market price are able to do so.
- When buyers and sellers engage in a market transaction, gains from trade are created from consumer surplus and producer surplus.
- Total surplus is maximized at a market equilibrium.
- Deadweight loss is created when markets deviate from equilibrium.
- Markets are typically efficient, although sometimes they can fail by not providing the socially optimal amount of goods and services.
- Market failure is caused by a lack of competition, mismatched information, external costs and external benefits, or the existence of public goods.

QUESTION: Waiting for an organ transplant is an ordeal for patients. Some wait years for a compatible donor organ to become available. Some economists have suggested that offering monetary compensation to organ donors would increase the supply of available organs. Would such a system lead to gains from trade? Why are such incentives difficult to implement?

Answers to the Checkpoint questions can be found at the end of this chapter.

PRICE CEILINGS AND PRICE FLOORS

To this point, we have assumed that competitive markets are allowed to operate freely, without any government intervention. Economists refer to freely functioning markets as **laissez-faire,** a French term meaning "let it be." The justification for this type of economic policy is that when competitive markets are left to determine equilibrium price and output, they clear. This means that businesses provide consumers with the quantity of goods they want to purchase at the established prices; there are no shortages or surpluses. Consumer and producer surplus together, or total surplus, is maximized.

However, as we saw at the end of the previous section, sometimes freely functioning markets fail to achieve the optimal quantity of goods and services. An example of this is when many people consider the equilibrium price to be unfair. Because of these economic (*efficiency*) or political (*equity*) reasons, governments will sometimes intervene in the market by setting limits on the prices of various goods and services. Governments use price ceilings and price floors to keep prices below or above market equilibrium. What really happens when government sets prices below or above market equilibrium? The previous section hinted at the answer. Let's look at price ceilings and floors more closely.

Price Ceilings

When the government sets a **price ceiling,** it is legally mandating the maximum price that can be charged for a product or service. This is a legal maximum; regardless of market forces, price cannot exceed this level. An historical example of a price ceiling is the establishment of rent-controlled apartments in New York City during World War II, some of which still exist today. However, more common examples of price ceilings include limits on what insurance companies can charge customers, price caps on telecommunications and electric services to customers in rural or remote locations, and limits on tuition hikes at public universities.

Panel A in Figure 5 shows an *effective* price ceiling, or one in which the ceiling price is set below the equilibrium price. In this case, equilibrium price is P_e, but the government has set a price ceiling at P_c. Quantity supplied at the ceiling price is Q_1, whereas consumers want Q_2; therefore, the result is a shortage of $Q_2 - Q_1$ units of the product. As we saw in the

laissez-faire A market that is allowed to function without any government intervention.

price ceiling A maximum price established by government for a product or service. When the price ceiling is set below equilibrium, a shortage results.

FIGURE 5	A PRICE CEILING BELOW EQUILIBRIUM CREATES SHORTAGES

When the government enacts a price ceiling below equilibrium (panel A), consumers will demand Q_2 and businesses will supply only Q_1, creating a shortage equal to Q_2-Q_1, and causing deadweight loss equal to the shaded area. If the price ceiling is set above equilibrium (panel B), the price ceiling has no effect, and the market price and quantity prevail with no deadweight loss created.

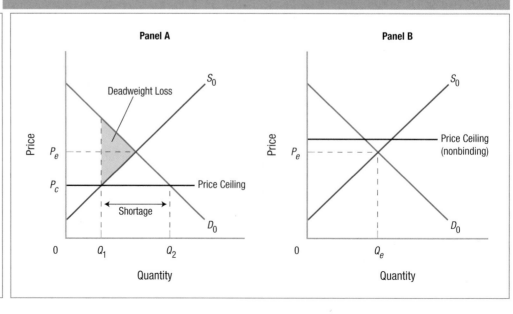

previous section, setting a price below equilibrium alters consumer and producer surplus and results in a deadweight loss indicated by the shaded area. If the price ceiling is raised toward equilibrium, the shortage is reduced along with the deadweight loss. If the price ceiling is set above P_e (as shown in panel B), the market simply settles at P_e, and the price ceiling has no impact; it is nonbinding, and no deadweight loss occurs. A price ceiling can also *become* nonbinding if market factors cause supply to increase or demand to fall, pushing the equilibrium price below the ceiling.

A common mistake when analyzing the effect of price ceilings is assuming that effective price ceilings appear above the market equilibrium, because the word "ceiling" refers to something *above you*. Instead, think of ceilings as something that keep you from moving higher. Suppose you build a makeshift skateboarding ramp in your apartment hallway, and tempt your friends to test it out. If the ceiling is too low, some of your friends might end up with a severe headache. In other words, an effective (binding) ceiling is one that is kept lower than normal. If the ceiling can be raised by 5 feet, then all of your friends would achieve their jumps without bumping their heads. In sum, price ceilings have their strongest effects when kept very low; as the ceiling is raised, the effect of the policy diminishes, and the ceiling becomes nonbinding once the equilibrium price is reached.

Given the price ceiling, one might argue that although shortages might exist, at least prices will be kept lower and therefore more "fair." The question is, fairer to whom? Suppose your university places a new price ceiling on the rents of all existing apartments located on campus, one that is below the rents of similar apartments off campus. This might sound like a great idea, but often what sounds like a great idea comes with costs.

A price ceiling increases the quantity demanded for on-campus apartments, and without an increase in supply, a shortage results. Those lucky enough to obtain an on-campus apartment benefit from the lower rents. But what about those who couldn't? Because some students who really could have benefited from lower rents (those with lower incomes or without cars) cannot find an on-campus apartment, while other students who could have easily afforded a higher-priced off-campus apartment managed to snatch one up, a **misallocation of resources** is created. Further, when on-campus apartments do open up, students eager to obtain one might spend a lot of time and resources trying. These resources (an opportunity cost) end up offsetting some or all of the savings from finding an on-campus apartment.

misallocation of resources Occurs when a good or service is not consumed by the person who values it the most, and typically results when a price ceiling creates an artificial shortage in the market.

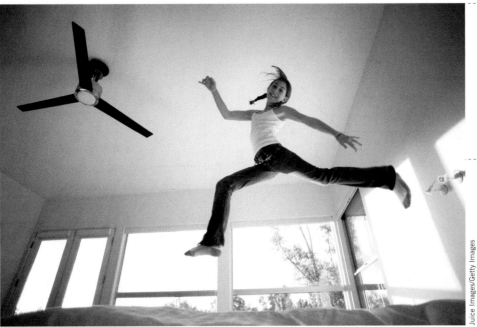

The ability to jump on one's bed depends on the height of the ceiling. The lower the ceiling, the more it restricts this fun activity. Similarly, price ceilings below equilibrium (rather than above equilibrium) restrict the market and lead to shortages.

Juice Images/Getty Images

Besides the misallocation of resources and potential opportunity costs of long waits and search costs, price ceilings also lead to some unintended long-term consequences. For example, if a landlord owns some apartments on campus (where rents are controlled) and some apartments off campus (where rents are higher), on which apartments is she likely to spend more money for upgrades and/or maintenance? The quality of goods and services subjected to price ceilings tends to deteriorate over time, as the incentives shift toward products with higher prices. Further, when it comes time to invest in new apartments, where do you think they are likely to be built—on campus or off?

The key point to remember here is that price ceilings are intended to keep the price of a product below its market or equilibrium level. When this happens, consumer surplus increases for those able to purchase the good, while producer surplus falls. The ultimate effect of a price ceiling, however, is that the quantity of the product demanded exceeds the quantity supplied, thereby producing a shortage of the product in the market. When shortages occur, deadweight losses are created because some mutually beneficial transactions do not take place, causing a reduction in total surplus.

Price Floors

price floor A minimum price established by government for a product or service. When the price floor is set above equilibrium, a surplus results.

A **price floor** is a government-mandated minimum price that can be charged for a product or service. Regardless of market forces, product price cannot legally fall below this level.

Figure 6 shows the economic impact of a price floor. In panel A, the price floor, P_f, is set above equilibrium, P_e, resulting in a surplus of $Q_2 - Q_1$ units. At price P_f, businesses want to supply more of the product (Q_2) than consumers are willing to buy (Q_1), thus generating a surplus. Depending on the government policy in place with the price floor, producers may end up having to store the excess supply if only Q_1 is transacted in the market, or in some cases the government may buy the surplus goods. Either way, inefficiency is created in the market. However, if the price floor is set below equilibrium (as shown in panel B), the equilibrium price, P_e, will prevail in the market. Therefore, a price floor set below P_e has no impact on the market and no deadweight loss occurs. Likewise, a price floor can *become* nonbinding if market factors push the equilibrium price above the price floor.

Throughout much of the past century, the U.S. government has used agricultural price supports (price floors) in order to smooth out the income of farmers, which often fluctuates

FIGURE 6	A PRICE FLOOR ABOVE EQUILIBRIUM CREATES SURPLUSES

When the government sets a price floor above equilibrium (panel A), businesses try to sell Q_2 at a price of P_f, but consumers are willing to purchase only Q_1 at that price. This results in a surplus equal to $Q_2 - Q_1$, causing either producers to store the excess supply or the government to buy the surplus units.

ISSUE

Are Price Gouging Laws Good for Consumers?

During the summer hurricane season, residents along the Atlantic and Gulf Coasts brace for hurricanes that can wreak havoc on the unprepared. The routine is well known: Buy plywood and shutters to protect windows; fill up gas tanks in cars and buy extra gas for generators; and stock up on batteries, bottled water, and nonperishable foods. Because of the huge spike in demand, numerous states have introduced price gouging laws, which prevent stores from raising prices above the average price of the past 30 days. Penalties for violating such laws are severe.

Price gouging laws generally pass with huge majority votes from both major political parties. The logic seems clear—to prevent businesses from exploiting a bad situation to their benefit by raising prices. Passing such laws always appears to be a victory for the consumer. But is it really?

Price gouging laws are price ceilings placed at the price last existing when times were normal. But during a natural disaster, the market is far from normal—demand is higher, and supplies are often restricted due to plant closures. The figure shows what happens when these two effects come together—the market price spikes upward. But price gouging laws require that prices remain at the *original* level, resulting in

The inside of a jumbo jet cargo plane can carry a tremendous amount of supplies to address supply shortages, as long as an incentive exists to use that plane for this purpose.

a shortage when demand increases to D_1 and supply falls to S_1.

What happens during a shortage? Huge lines form at home improvement stores, gas stations, and grocery stores. Time spent waiting in line is time that could be spent completing other tasks in preparation for the storm. What might be a better solution?

Instead of capping prices and causing a shortage, efforts can be made to provide incentives to businesses to generate more supply. If supply shifts enough to the right to compensate for the increase in demand, then prices need not increase, regardless of the price ceiling. But the question is, How do we incentivize supply? Subsidies to offset increased transportation costs might be an example. Imagine how many supplies could be flown in on a single jumbo jet cargo plane from a non–hurricane-prone area. Quite a bit, but firms aren't willing to spend that money. If the incentive is provided, supply will increase, reducing shortages and costs to everyone.

Prices cannot exceed the old market price.

due to wide annual variations in crop prices. This approach is not limited to the United States. Many developed countries, including members of the European Union and Japan, have long protected their agriculture industries by ensuring a minimum price level for many types of crops.

These price supports act very much as they are intended. By ensuring a minimum price for a crop, farmers have an incentive to grow more of these crops relative to crops that aren't protected by price supports. Further, because the price supports typically are above market equilibrium prices, resulting in higher prices for consumers, demand for such crops is less than what it would be without the supports.

Thus, with greater supply and smaller demand, price supports lead to surpluses of crops. What happens to these surpluses? Because the government guarantees the price

Surplus foods resulting from government price floors are often given to public schools to be used in school lunches.

Kelly Cline/iStockphoto

levels of the crops, it must purchase the excess supply, which is typically stored for use in the event of future shortages. But agricultural surpluses eventually rot, which means government must find other ways to use the surplus before it goes bad. One common use of surplus foods is in public school lunches, leading to some criticism that the types of foods being provided (wheat, grains, and corn) are not the most nutritious foods for children to eat.

Another criticism of agricultural price supports comes from developing countries that depend on agricultural exports for their economic output. These countries claim that price supports hamper their economic development by preventing them from selling goods in which they have a comparative advantage. In other words, agricultural price supports restrict gains from trade.

Despite their questionable economic justification, political pressures have ensured that agricultural price supports and related programs still command a sizable amount of the discretionary domestic federal budget.

Price floors are also used to analyze minimum wage policy. To the extent that the minimum wage is set above the equilibrium wage, unemployment—a surplus of labor—may result if jobs go uncreated when employers are forced to pay the higher minimum wage. However, the minimum wage offers a potential positive effect of reducing income inequality by raising earnings among low-wage workers. This effect is stronger if increasing the minimum wage subsequently leads to higher wages for workers who are already earning slightly more than the minimum wage.

In sum, price ceilings and price floors often are policies aimed at promoting equity or fairness in a society, such as preventing rapid price increases for consumers or ensuring fair wages for workers. Still, governments must be careful when setting price ceilings and price floors to avoid meddling with markets.

 CHECKPOINT

PRICE CEILINGS AND PRICE FLOORS

- Governments use price floors and price ceilings to intervene in markets.
- A price ceiling is a maximum legal price that can be charged for a product. Price ceilings set below equilibrium result in shortages.
- A price floor is the minimum legal price that can be charged for a product. Price floors set above market equilibrium result in surpluses.

QUESTION: The day after Thanksgiving, also known as *Black Friday*, is a day on which retailers advertise very steep discounts on selected items such as televisions or laptops. Assuming the number of units available at the discounted price is limited, in what ways are the effects of this pricing strategy similar to a price ceiling set by the government? In what ways do they differ?

Answers to the Checkpoint questions can be found at the end of the chapter.

chapter summary

Section 1 Consumer and Producer Surplus: A Tool for Measuring Economic Efficiency

Paul Bradbury/Getty Images

4.1 Economic efficiency is measured by the gains that consumers and producers achieve when engaging in an economic transaction.

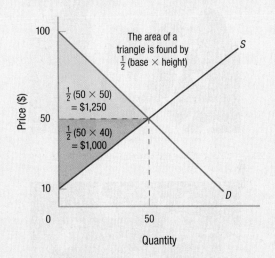

Consumer surplus is the difference between a person's willingness-to-pay and the price paid. For a market, consumer surplus is the area between the demand curve and the market price. In the figure, consumer surplus equals $1,250.

Producer surplus is the difference between the price a seller receives and its willingness-to-sell. For a market, producer surplus is the area between the market price and the supply curve. In the figure, producer surplus equals $1,000.

Section 2 Using Consumer and Producer Surplus: The Gains From Trade

Markets exhibit efficiency when every buyer and every seller eager to buy or sell goods are able to do so, resulting in **gains from trade.** Gains from trade are measured by the **total surplus,** or the sum of consumer and producer surplus in a market. Total surplus is maximized when a market is at equilibrium.

4.2 Suppose the price of a good rises above equilibrium to $75. The higher price causes two effects on consumer surplus and two effects on producer surplus:

1. Consumers who are priced out of the market lose consumer surplus equal to the blue area.

2. Consumers who continue to buy the good pay more, and lose consumer surplus equal to the pink area.

3. Producers who want to sell more at $75, but cannot, lose producer surplus equal to the yellow area.

4. Producers who do sell units earn $25 more per unit, equal to the pink area.

4.3 **Deadweight loss** occurs when prices deviate from equilibrium. In the preceding example, deadweight loss is shown by the blue and yellow areas.

Markets can sometimes fail to produce the socially optimal output. Reasons for **market failure** include:

4.4 **Lack of competition**

When a firm faces little to no competition, it has an incentive to raise prices.

Existence of external benefits or costs

Markets tend to provide too little of products that have external benefits, and too much of products with external costs.

A mismatch of information

Asymmetric information occurs when either a buyer or a seller knows more about a product than the other.

Existence of public goods

Public goods are nonrival and nonexclusive. This means:

- My consumption does not diminish your ability to consume.
- Once a good is provided for one person, others cannot be excluded from enjoying it.

Planting trees creates external benefits.

Ecological conservation is a public good. Once people devote time and resources to saving the environment, everybody benefits from it, even if one does not contribute to the costs of maintaining it.

Talking loudly on your phone creates external costs.

Section 3 Price Ceilings and Price Floors

4.5 A **price floor** is a minimum price for a good. A binding price floor appears above equilibrium and causes a surplus.

A **price ceiling** is a maximum price for a good. A binding price ceiling appears below equilibrium and causes a shortage.

Prices cannot go below the floor

S

Price Floor

Price

Price Ceiling

Prices cannot go above the ceiling

D

Quantity

4.6 A literal mountain of surplus corn caused by agricultural price floors.

KEY CONCEPTS

consumer surplus, p. 86
producer surplus, p. 86
total surplus, p. 89
deadweight loss, p. 90

market failure, p. 92
asymmetric information, p. 92
laissez-faire, p. 94
price ceiling, p. 94

misallocation of resources, p. 95
price floor, p. 96

QUESTIONS AND PROBLEMS

Check Your Understanding

1. Describe how consumer surplus and producer surplus are measured.

2. Using the following graph, show what happens to consumer surplus when a new technology reduces the cost of production.

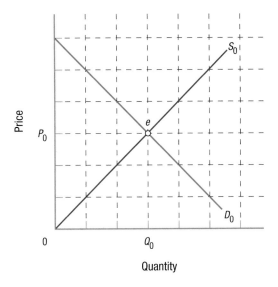

3. Explain why deadweight loss can occur with a price below equilibrium even when some consumers benefit from it.

4. Provide three examples of activities that generate external benefits and three activities that generate external costs.

5. Why does an effective price ceiling appear below the equilibrium rather than above it?

6. If a price floor is reduced toward equilibrium but not below it, explain what happens to the total surplus and deadweight loss in this market.

Apply the Concepts

7. An increasing number of charities have turned to online auctions as a way to raise money by selling unique experiences donated by celebrities (such as a *meet-and-greet* with a celebrity before a concert or a walk-on role on a television show). Why would the use of auctions lead to a better outcome for the charity as opposed to just setting a fixed price? Explain using the concepts of consumer surplus and producer surplus.

8. Luigi's is the only pizzeria in a small town in northern Alaska. It is constantly busy, but there is never a wait for a table. One of Luigi's friends suggests that he would earn much more money if he raises his menu prices by 25%, because no one is likely to open a new pizzeria in the near future. If Luigi follows his friend's advice, what would happen to consumer and producer surplus, and efficiency, in this market?

9. Over the past decade, many American candy companies, including Hershey Company, Brach's Confections, and Ferrara Pan Candy, opened factories in Mexico and Canada to produce candy that is then shipped back to the United States for sale. Although lower wages in Mexico might explain part of this move, wages in Canada are comparable to U.S. wages. Explain how U.S. price supports (price floors) for the sugar industry may have encouraged these moves.

10. Academic studies suggest that the amount people tip in restaurants is only slightly related to the quality of service, and that tips are poor measures of how happy people are with the service. Is this another example of market failure? What might account for this situation?

11. In cities around the country, the government provides assistance to families with low incomes to rent apartments at prices capped by the U.S. Department of Housing and Urban Development (HUD), essentially setting a price ceiling on apartments. These designated apartments tend to rent quickly, and tenants are less likely to move once they find an apartment. Explain how rent controls affect market prices for non-rent-controlled apartments. How are incentives by landlords affected in terms of maintaining rent-controlled and non-rent-controlled apartments? Would your answer change if the government provided a subsidy payment to landlords to offset the difference between the price ceiling and the market price?

12. The U.S. Department of Labor reports that of the roughly 150 million people employed, just over half are paid by the hour, but fewer than 5% earn the minimum wage or less; 95% of wage earners earn more. And of those earning the minimum wage or less, 25% are teenagers living at home. If so few people are affected by the minimum wage, why does it often seem to be such a contentious political issue?

In the News

13. Over the past few years, several U.S. states have either legalized recreational marijuana or at least decriminalized its use ("Would Legalizing Marijuana Help the Economy?," Debate.org). Proponents argue that legalizing the use of marijuana would help the economy by boosting economic activity and reducing costs. Do you agree? Why or why not? Use the concepts of supply and demand, and consumer and producer surplus to support your answer.

14. In 2015 Governor Cuomo of New York approved a measure to raise the minimum wage for all fast-food workers to $15 per hour by 2018 ("New York Oks $15 Minimum Wage for Fast-Food Workers," *USA Today*, September 11, 2015). Proponents argue that this policy helps the working poor who hold full-time jobs yet are not able to pull their families out of poverty. Meanwhile, opponents argue that the policy would cause harm in the labor market. Provide an example of a situation that would support each side's argument.

Solving Problems

15. Consider the market shown in the following graph.

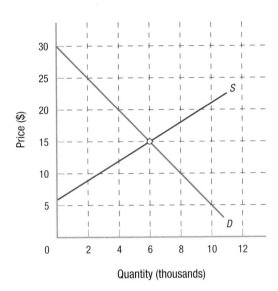

Quantity (thousands)

a.   Compute the consumer surplus.

b.   Compute the producer surplus.

Now assume that government puts a price floor on this product at $20 a unit.

c.   Compute the new consumer surplus.

d.   Compute the new producer surplus.

e.   Would consumers or producers be more likely to have their advocates or lobbyists support price floors? Explain.

WORK IT OUT   📖 **LaunchPad** | interactive activity

---

16. Suppose the U.S. government places a price ceiling on the sale of gasoline at $2 per gallon in the accompanying figure.

   a.   How much of a shortage or surplus of gasoline would result?

   b.   Calculate the effects of this policy in terms of the changes in consumer surplus and producer surplus.

   c.   How much deadweight loss is created?

   d.   What would happen if the price ceiling is raised to $5 per gallon?

Quantity (in millions of gallons)

USING THE NUMBERS

17. According to By the Numbers, how much would you earn in one year if you worked 2,000 hours (50 weeks × 40 hours) at the federal minimum wage? How much more would you earn per year if you worked at the minimum wage rate in Washington state?

18. According to By the Numbers, which state has the highest average in-state tuition in the country, and which state has the lowest average in-state tuition? How do universities deal with shortages when in-state tuition prices are below the equilibrium price?

ANSWERS TO QUESTIONS IN CHECKPOINTS

Checkpoint: Consumer and Producer Surplus: A Tool for Measuring Economic Efficiency 89

Cole's consumer surplus is ($50 − $40) = $10, Jacqueline's is ($55 − $40) = $15, Sienna's is ($60 − $40) = $20, and Tessa's is ($65 − $40) = $25. Total consumer surplus is $10 + $15 + $20 + $25 = $70. Alex's producer surplus is ($40 − $20) = $20, Caroline's is ($40 − $25) = $15, Kira's is ($40 − $30) = $10, and Will's is ($40 − $35) = $5. Total producer surplus is $20 + $15 + $10 + $5 = $50.

Checkpoint: Using Consumer and Producer Surplus: The Gains From Trade 93

Although many people voluntarily become organ donors because of the goodwill they feel knowing that their actions can potentially save a life, still many others choose not to become organ donors because they do not see any monetary benefit from doing so. Compensating individuals for becoming organ donors, thereby raising the "price" of organs, would be a way to increase the supply of organs, allowing the shortage to dissipate until equilibrium is reached. In doing so, organ donors and recipients both benefit, resulting in gains from trade. However, moral objections to selling body parts have led to many laws preventing organ donors from being compensated. As a result, shortages continue to be a problem.

Checkpoint: Price Ceilings and Price Floors 98

Black Friday specials are typically deeply discounted in order to attract customers into the store, which is why such specials are prominently shown on the first page of sales circulars. Like a price ceiling that is set below the equilibrium price, the quantity demanded for the discounted good increases, while stores limit the number of units available for sale, creating a shortage. Some buyers will be fortunate to find units available to purchase, while subsequent shoppers will find that the product has sold out. Deadweight loss is generated because some customers who would have been willing to pay a little more are unable to purchase the good. However, unlike with a price ceiling, stores strategically choose to advertise goods with many alternatives, such as different brands of televisions and laptops, so that when the discounted product sells out, customers may consider buying a nondiscounted product. Therefore, the pricing strategy leads to a strategic shortage that is designed to attract customers into the store to buy goods in addition to those that are advertised.

5 Elasticity

Measuring the extent to which consumers and producers react to changes in prices in a market

iStock/Getty Images

Learning Objectives

5.1 Understand the concept of elasticity and why percentages are used to measure it.

5.2 Describe the difference between elastic and inelastic demand.

5.3 Describe the determinants of price elasticity of demand.

5.4 Compute the price elasticity of demand using the base and midpoint methods.

5.5 Describe the relationship between total revenue and price elasticity of demand.

5.6 Describe cross elasticity of demand and use this concept to define substitutes and complements.

5.7 Use income elasticity of demand to define normal, inferior, and luxury goods.

5.8 Use the concept of price elasticity of supply to measure the relationship between changes in product price and quantity supplied.

5.9 Describe the time periods economists use to study elasticity, and the variables that can be changed in each period.

5.10 Describe the relationship between elasticity and the burden and incidence of taxes.

A t the start of the new millennium, the price of gasoline hovered around $1.50 per gallon. Encouraged by low gas prices, consumer appetites for large vehicles rose, leading to an increase in sales in sport utility vehicles (SUVs) and trucks. Over the next ten years, however, increased tensions in the Middle East and a large spike in oil demand from emerging markets such as China and India pushed the price of a gallon of gas to over double what it was in 2000. How did consumers respond to the 100% increase in the average price of gasoline? They reduced consumption by driving less, buying more fuel-efficient cars, and using public transportation. But by *how much* did the quantity of gasoline demanded fall?

When global oil prices rose significantly, not only did consumers respond by reducing the amount of gasoline demanded but producers also reacted by increasing oil drilling in previously untapped oil fields. As a result, the United States and countries in Africa and Northern Europe became major oil producers, adding to the supply of gasoline on the market. But by *how much* did the quantity of gasoline supplied increase?

Not only did higher prices change the quantity demanded and supplied for gasoline. It also affected the demand and supply for related goods. For example, rising gasoline prices led to an increase in demand for fuel-efficient vehicles, such as hybrid and plug-in electric cars. It also led to an increase in the use of renewable fuels, such as ethanol and biodiesel. Finally, it spurred government to increase investment in public transportation. But by *how much* have these other industries been affected?

We learned in a previous chapter that consumers respond to higher prices by buying less, while producers respond to higher prices by producing more. We also know that as prices rise, demand for complements falls while demand for substitutes rises. However, we have not yet measured the extent of such responses. In other words, how responsive are consumers and producers to changes in prices in terms of what and how much are purchased and produced?

We answer the important "how responsive" question in this chapter by studying how consumers and producers respond to changes in the price of goods and services.

"Elasticity"—the responsiveness of one variable to changes in another—is the term economists use to measure this change. In the preceding example, we know that the price of gasoline is one variable and the quantity of gasoline demanded or supplied is the other variable. The concept of elasticity lets us measure the relative change in the quantity demanded or quantity supplied corresponding to a change in the price of gasoline.

Yet, as our example shows, elasticity can be measured for many other related goods that are affected by the change in price. If the price of gasoline changes, how will this affect sales

BY THE NUMBERS

Elasticity: How Markets React to Price Changes

Elasticity varies across goods and services, largely due to factors involving the price of the good, availability of substitutes, and whether a good is a necessity. Elasticity also varies across consumer groups and by country.

Salt (0.1)
Roel Smart/iStockphoto

Movies (0.9)
Fancy/Alamy

Foreign Travel (4.0)
photo360/Dreamstime.com

Inelastic   **Unitary Inelastic**   **Elastic**

Prescription Medicine (0.3)

Note: The numbers in parentheses refer to the price elasticity of demand.

Hong Chan/Dreamstime.com

Fast Food (1.3)
Johnfoto/Dreamstime.com

Diamonds (4.2)
Daniel Gilbey/Dreamstime.com

Food is necessary for survival, and thus an inelastic good. Yet, elasticity varies by country; when the price of food rises, poorer countries reduce consumption more than rich countries.

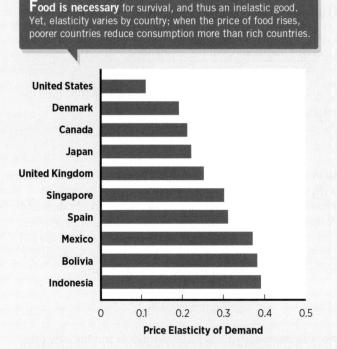

Price Elasticity of Demand

(Bar chart showing countries from top to bottom: United States, Denmark, Canada, Japan, United Kingdom, Singapore, Spain, Mexico, Bolivia, Indonesia — x-axis from 0 to 0.5)

 Go to LaunchPad to use the latest data to recreate this graph.

Number of Vehicles in Use

- ■ Liquefied Petroleum Gas
- ■ Compressed Natural Gas
- ■ Liquefied Natural Gas
- ■ E85 Ethanol
- ■ Electric

67,295
139,477
118,214
862,837
3,436

Alternative fuel vehicles have grown in popularity. The most popular type is E85 (ethanol) vehicles, though electric cars have been increasing in sales.

The By the Numbers — Do It Yourself! Lab Activity will look more closely at alternative fuel vehicles in the United States.

Don't like paying for parking? You're not alone. When the price of downtown parking in major cities increased 10%, people on average:

- Used that parking lot 5.4% less.
- Used farther parking lots 8.3% more.
- Used park & ride 3.6% more.
- Rode public transit 2.9% more.
- Reduced the number of trips downtown 4.6%.

Jennifer Pitiquen/Dreamstime.com

42% **A**verage rise in public university tuition (a highly inelastic good) from 2005–2015.

56% **A**verage fall in international calling rates (a highly elastic good) from 2005–2015.

of SUVs? Plug-in electric cars? How would demand for train and bus tickets change? And we need not limit our analysis to prices either. For example, income elasticity measures changes in consumer demand in response to changes in income. As incomes rise with a growing economy, by how much will demand for cars increase? This is information auto-makers want to know.

Elasticity is a simple economic concept that nonetheless contains a tremendous amount of information about demand for specific products. If a restaurant raises its menu prices by 10%, will it end up with more revenue, or will the increase in price lead to a drop in quantity demanded that more than offsets the price increase? Knowing a product's price elasticity allows economists to predict the amount by which quantity demanded will drop in response to a price increase, or grow in response to a price decrease. The concept of elasticity helps you to put supply and demand concepts to work.

ELASTICITY OF DEMAND

We know by the law of demand that as prices rise, quantity demanded falls. The important question is, *How much* will quantity demanded fall? Each year, prices for certain items such as college tuition, textbooks, and insurance premiums seem to keep rising, yet very few people stop buying these items. Meanwhile, prices for cable TV and movie theater tickets have also increased, though in these cases many consumers have responded by forgoing these items and looking for alternatives. The concept of elasticity is important in understanding why consumers react more to certain price changes than others.

price elasticity of demand A measure of the responsiveness of quantity demanded to a change in price, equal to the percentage change in quantity demanded divided by the percentage change in price.

Price elasticity of demand (E_d) is a measure of how responsive quantity demanded is to a change in price and is defined as

$$E_d = \frac{\text{Percentage Change in Quantity Demanded}}{\text{Percentage Change in Price}}$$

For example, if the price of strawberries increases by 5% and sales fall by 10%, then the price elasticity of demand for strawberries is

$$E_d = \frac{-10\%}{+5\%} = -2$$

Alternatively, if a 5% reduction in strawberry prices results in a 10% gain in sales, the price elasticity of demand also is −2 ($E_d = 10 \div [-5] = -2$).

Often, we are not given percentage changes. Rather, we are given numerical values and have to convert them into percentage changes. For example, to compute a change in price, take the new price (P_{new}) and subtract the old price (P_{old}), then divide this result by the old price (P_{old}). This approach to calculating percentage changes is known as the *base method*. Finally, to put this ratio in percentage terms, multiply by 100. In equation form,

$$\text{Percentage Change} = \frac{(P_{new} - P_{old})}{P_{old}} \times 100$$

For example, if the old price of gasoline (P_{old}) was $2.00 per gallon and the new price goes up by $1.00 to $3.00 per gallon, then the percentage change is

$$\text{Percentage Change} = \frac{\$3.00 - \$2.00}{\$2.00} = \frac{\$1.00}{\$2.00} = 0.50 \times 100 = 50\%$$

Price Elasticity of Demand as an Absolute Value

The price elasticity of demand is always a negative number. This reflects the fact that the demand curve's slope is negative: As price increases, quantity demanded falls. Price and quantity demanded stand in an inverse relationship to one another, resulting in a negative value for price elasticity. Economists nevertheless frequently refer to price elasticity of demand in positive terms. They simply use the *absolute value* of the computed price elasticity of demand. Recalling our examples, where $E_d = -2$, we can take the absolute value of

−2, written as |−2|, and refer to E_d as 2. For price elasticity of demand, we use the absolute value of elasticity and ignore the minus sign.

What does this elasticity value of 2 tell us? Quite simply, that for every 1% increase in price, quantity demanded will decline by 2%. Conversely, for every 1% decline in price, quantity demanded will increase by 2%.

Measuring Elasticity With Percentages

Measuring elasticity in percentage terms rather than specific units enables economists to compare the characteristics of various unrelated products. Comparing price and sales changes for houses, cars, and hamburgers in dollar amounts would be so complex as to be meaningless. Because a dollar increase in the price of gasoline is different from a dollar increase in the price of a BMW, by using percentage change, we can compare the sensitivity of demand curves of different products. Percentages allow us to compare changes in prices and sales for any two products, no matter how dissimilar they are; a 100% increase is the same percentage change for any product.

We have seen how to compute the price elasticity of demand, and we have seen why working with percentage changes is so important. Elasticity is a measure giving us a way to compare products with widely different prices and output measures.

Elastic and Inelastic Demand

All products have some price elasticity of demand. When prices go up, quantity demanded will fall. That is the basis of the negative slope of the demand curve. But people are more responsive to changes in the prices of some products than others. Economists label the demand for goods as being *elastic, inelastic,* or *unitary elastic.*

Elastic   When the absolute value of the computed price elasticity of demand is greater than 1, economists refer to this as **elastic demand.** An elastic demand curve is one that is responsive to price changes. At the extreme is the *perfectly elastic* demand curve shown in panel A of Figure 1. Notice that it is horizontal, showing that the slightest increase in price will result in zero output being sold.

In reality, no branded product—Coca-Cola, Apple iPhone, or Toyota Prius—ever has a perfectly elastic demand curve. Still, products with many close substitutes face highly elastic demand curves. For example, the market for bath tissue is very elastic because nearly all brands—Kleenex, Charmin, Quilted Northern, and others—sell a nearly identical product. If the price of Charmin is raised, sales would quickly fall as people switch to Quilted Northern or Scott. Canned peaches, nuts and bolts, cereal, and bottled water are all examples of products facing highly elastic demands. If one bottled water company were to raise its price, many consumers would switch to other brands, because all bottled water tastes pretty much the same. Demand curves for elastic goods are relatively flat, as shown in panel B in Figure 1.

Inelastic   At the other extreme, what about products that see little change in sales even when prices change dramatically? The opposite of the perfectly elastic demand curve is the curve showing no response to changes in price. Economists call this a *perfectly inelastic* demand curve. An example appears in panel E of Figure 1. This curve is vertical, not horizontal as in panel A. For products with perfectly inelastic demands, quantity demanded does not change when price changes.

What products might have inelastic demand? Consider products that are immensely important to our lives but have

elastic demand   The percentage change in quantity demanded is greater than the percentage change in price. This results in the absolute value of the price elasticity of demand to be greater than 1. Goods with elastic demands are very responsive to changes in price.

If your furry friend needed some medicine to stay healthy, would you still buy it if the price doubled? Most pet owners wouldn't hesitate, making pet medicines a very inelastic good.

Charles Mann/Getty Images

FIGURE 1   THE SHAPE AND ELASTICITY OF DEMAND CURVES

The horizontal demand curve in panel A represents perfectly elastic demand because when price increases, quantity demanded drops to zero. Panel E, on the other hand, illustrates a perfectly inelastic demand curve where quantity demanded does not change when the price changes. Panel B shows an elastic demand curve, which is relatively flat, and panel D shows an inelastic demand curve, which is relatively steep. Panel C shows that if elasticity of demand is unitary, then a 1% increase in price will result in a 1% decrease in quantity demanded. Note that the unitary elastic demand curve is not a straight line.

few substitutes—for example, drugs that treat life-threatening illnesses such as heart disease or stroke, and insulin for diabetics. If people who need these products have the money, they will buy them, no matter how high the price. Some products that are relatively, though not perfectly, inelastic include gasoline, tobacco, and most spices. If gasoline prices rise too sharply, some consumers will curtail their driving. Still, it takes a fairly drastic rise in gasoline prices before most people cut back their driving significantly. Doubling the price of cinnamon will probably not reduce our demand because it is such a small fraction of our overall food budget. Economists define **inelastic demand** as demand curves with elasticity coefficients that are less than 1. These demand curves are relatively steep, as shown in panel D in Figure 1.

inelastic demand The percentage change in quantity demanded is less than the percentage change in price. This results in the absolute value of the price elasticity of demand to be less than 1. Goods with inelastic demands are not very responsive to changes in price.

Note that the demand for gasoline is inelastic, but the demand for specific brands of gasoline is elastic. Brand preferences for commodities that are nearly identical to one another, such as gasoline, are weak, and many different outlets exist for buying gas. If your local Shell station raises gasoline prices by a significant amount, you will probably go to the Exxon station down the street. Giving up using gasoline altogether, on the other hand, is much harder. Over time, public transportation or electric cars may be possible substitutes for gas-powered cars, but few people will be able to adopt these substitutes in the short run. On the contrary, many people are highly dependent on their gas-powered cars; therefore, gas purchases do not drop substantially when prices rise. Thus, demand for a particular brand of gas (Exxon, Shell) is elastic, while the demand for gasoline as a commodity is inelastic.

Unitary Elastic Elastic demand curves have an elasticity coefficient that is greater than 1, while inelastic demand curves have a coefficient of less than 1. That leaves those products with an elasticity coefficient just equal to 1. Products that meet this condition have **unitary elastic demand.** This means the percentage change in quantity demanded is precisely equal to the percentage change in price. Panel C of Figure 1 shows a demand curve where price elasticity of demand equals 1. Note that this demand curve is not a straight line. The reasons for this will become clear in our discussion later in the chapter.

unitary elastic demand The percentage change in quantity demanded is just equal to the percentage change in price. This results in the absolute value of the price elasticity of demand to be equal to 1.

Determinants of Elasticity

Price elasticity of demand measures how sensitive sales are to price changes. But what determines elasticity itself? The four basic determinants of a product's elasticity of demand are (1) the availability of substitute products, (2) the percentage of income or household budget spent on the product, (3) the difference between luxuries and necessities, and (4) the time period being examined.

Substitutability The more close substitutes, or possible alternatives, a product has, the easier it is for consumers to switch to a competing product and the more elastic the demand. For many people, beef and chicken are substitutes, as are competing brands of cola, such as Coke and Pepsi. All have relatively elastic demands. Conversely, if a product has few close substitutes, such as insulin for diabetics or tobacco for heavy smokers, its elasticity of demand tends to be lower.

Proportion of Income Spent on a Product A second determinant of elasticity is the proportion (percentage) of household income spent on a product. In general, the smaller the percent of household income spent on a product, the lower the elasticity of demand. For example, you probably spend little of your income on salt, or on cinnamon or other spices. As a result, a hefty increase in the price of salt, say, 25%, would not affect your salt consumption because the impact on your budget would be tiny. But if a product represents a significant part of household spending, elasticity of demand tends to be greater, or more elastic. A 10% increase in your rent upon renewing your lease, for example, would put a large dent in your budget, significantly reducing your purchasing power for many other products. Such a rent increase would likely lead you to look around for a less expensive apartment.

Luxuries Versus Necessities The third determinant of elasticity is whether the good is considered a luxury or a necessity. Luxuries tend to have demands that are more elastic than those of necessities. Necessities such as food, electricity, and health care are more important to everyday living, and quantity demanded does not change significantly when prices rise. Luxuries such as African safaris, yachts, and designer watches, on the other hand, can be given up when prices rise.

Time Period The fourth determinant of elasticity is the time period under consideration. When consumers have some time to adjust their consumption patterns, demand becomes more elastic. When they have little time to adjust, demand tends to become more inelastic. Thus, as we saw earlier, when gasoline prices rise, most consumers cannot immediately change their transportation patterns; therefore, gasoline sales do not drop significantly. Over time, however, consumers are more likely to make changes, such as buying more fuel-efficient cars.

Table 1 provides a sampling of estimates of elasticities for specific products. As we might expect, medical prescriptions and taxi service have relatively inelastic price elasticities of demand, while foreign travel and restaurant meals have relatively elastic demands.

TABLE 1		SELECTED ESTIMATES OF PRICE ELASTICITIES OF DEMAND			
Inelastic		**Roughly Unitary Elastic**		**Elastic**	
Salt	0.1	Movies	0.9	Shrimp	1.3
Gasoline (short run)	0.2	Shoes	0.9	Furniture	1.5
Cigarettes	0.2	Tires	1.0	Commuter rail service (long run)	1.6
Medical care	0.3	Private education	1.1	Restaurant meals	2.3
Medical prescriptions	0.3	Automobiles	1.2	Air travel	2.4
Pesticides	0.4			Fresh vegetables	2.5
Taxi service	0.6			Foreign travel	4.0

Data compiled from numerous studies reporting estimates for price elasticity of demand.

| FIGURE 2 | COMPUTING ELASTICITY OF DEMAND USING MIDPOINTS |

A problem can occur when calculating elasticity over a range of prices. The calculated value can vary depending on whether price is increasing or decreasing. To avoid getting different results when approaching the same analysis from different directions, economists use midpoint price and midpoint quantity.

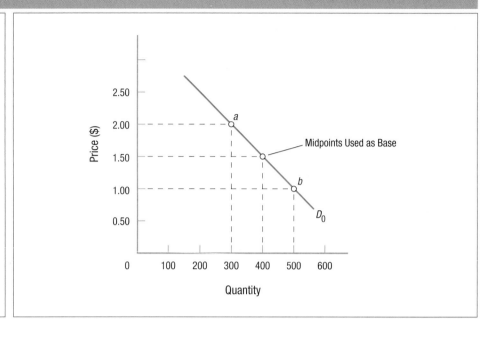

Computing Price Elasticities

When elasticity is computed between two points, the calculated value will differ depending on whether price is increasing or decreasing. For example, in Figure 2, if the price *increases* from $1.00 to $2.00, elasticity is equal to

$$E_d = \frac{300 - 500}{500} \div \frac{2.00 - 1.00}{1.00}$$

$$= \frac{-200}{500} \div \frac{1.00}{1.00}$$

$$= -0.4 \div 1$$

$$= |-0.4|$$

$$= 0.4$$

But when price *decreases* from $2.00 to $1.00, elasticity is equal to

$$E_d = \frac{500 - 300}{300} \div \frac{1.00 - 2.00}{2.00}$$

$$= \frac{200}{300} \div \frac{-1.00}{2.00}$$

$$= 0.67 \div -0.5$$

$$= |-1.33|$$

$$= 1.33$$

Using Midpoints to Compute Elasticity To avoid getting different results computing elasticity from different directions, economists compute price elasticity using the midpoints of price $[(P_0 + P_1)/2]$ and the midpoints of quantity demanded $[(Q_0 + Q_1)/2]$

as the base. This approach to calculating percentage changes is referred to as the *midpoint method*.

Therefore, the *price elasticity of demand* formula (assuming price falls from P_0 to P_1 and quantity demanded rises from Q_0 to Q_1) is

$$E_d = \frac{Q_1 - Q_0}{(Q_0 + Q_1)/2} \div \frac{P_1 - P_0}{(P_0 + P_1)/2}$$

Using the midpoints of price and quantity to compute the relevant percentage changes essentially gives us the average elasticity between point *a* and point *b*. Price elasticity of demand is the difference in quantity over the sum of the two quantities divided by 2, divided by the difference in price over the sum of the two prices divided by 2. In Figure 2, the price elasticity of demand between points *a* and *b* would equal

$$E_d = \frac{500 - 300}{(300 + 500)/2} \div \frac{1.00 - 2.00}{(2.00 + 1.00)/2}$$

$$= \frac{200}{400} \div \frac{-1.00}{1.50}$$

$$= 0.50 \div -0.67$$

$$= |-0.75|$$

$$= 0.75$$

Check for yourself to see that this elasticity formula yields the same results whether you compute elasticity for a price increase from $1.00 to $2.00 or for a price decrease from $2.00 to $1.00.

Now that we have seen what price elasticity of demand is and how to calculate it, let's put this knowledge to work by looking at how elasticity affects total revenue.

 CHECKPOINT

ELASTICITY OF DEMAND

- Elasticity summarizes how responsive one variable is to a change in another variable.
- Price elasticity of demand summarizes how responsive quantity demanded is to changes in price.
- Price elasticity of demand is defined as the percentage change in quantity demanded divided by the percentage change in price.
- Inelastic demands are relatively unresponsive to changes in price, while elastic demands are more responsive to changes in price.
- Elasticity is determined by a product's substitutability, its proportion of the budget, whether it is a luxury or a necessity, and the time period considered.
- Economists use midpoints to derive consistent estimates whether price rises or falls.

QUESTION: Using your knowledge of the determinants of elasticity, why is gasoline inelastic in the short term but elastic in the long term? Explain why automobiles tend to have the opposite effect, being elastic in the short term but inelastic in the long term?

Answers to the Checkpoint questions can be found at the end of this chapter.

TOTAL REVENUE AND OTHER MEASURES OF ELASTICITY

Elasticity is important to firms because elasticity measures the responsiveness of quantity sold to changes in price, which provides valuable information to firms in deciding whether to increase or decrease prices. Owners of a restaurant that is completely full each evening might ponder raising its prices, but only if it can retain most of its customers. Another restaurant, which has few customers, might wish to lower its prices to generate more business, but only if it generates enough business to offset the lower prices it charges.

Elasticity is also important because it allows firms to determine how a change in the price of one product might affect the demand for other items, or how changes in economic conditions might affect the market for their goods. If a supermarket discounts the price of sirloin steaks, how would this affect the demand for other cuts of beef, or other meats? Would it increase sales of steak sauce and potatoes? These are questions we address in this section using other measures of elasticity.

Elasticity and Total Revenue

total revenue Price × quantity demanded (sold). If demand is elastic and price rises, quantity demanded falls off significantly and total revenue declines, and vice versa. If demand is inelastic and price rises, quantity demanded does not decline much and total revenue rises, and vice versa.

The elasticity of demand, which we learned about in the previous section, has an important effect on the total revenues of the firm. **Total revenue** (*TR*) is equal to the number of units sold (*Q*) times the price of each unit (*P*), or

$$TR = Q \times P$$

The sensitivity of output sold to price changes greatly influences how much total revenue changes when price changes.

Inelastic Demand When consumers are so loyal to a product or so few substitutes exist that consumers continue to buy the product even when its price goes up, the demand for that product is inelastic. Panel A of Figure 3 shows the impact of a price increase on total revenue when the demand for a product is inelastic. Price rises from $2.00 to $4.00, and sales decline from 600 to 500 units. In this case, total revenue *rises*. We know this because the revenue gained from the price hike [($4.00 − $2.00) × 500 = $1,000] is greater than the revenue lost [($2.00 × (600 − 500) = $200]. We can see this by comparing the size of the area labeled "Revenue Gained" with the area labeled "Revenue Lost" in the figure. What has happened here? The price hike has driven off only a few customers, but the firm's many remaining customers are paying a much higher price, thus driving up the firm's total revenue.

This may suggest that firms would always want the demand for their products to be inelastic. Unfortunately for them, inelastic demand has a flip side. Specifically, if supply increases (due to a technical advance, say), sales will rise only moderately, even as prices fall dramatically. This leads to a drop in total revenue: Consumers indeed buy more of the product at its new lower price, but not enough to offset the lower price per unit received by firms.

Elastic Demand Elastic demand is the opposite of inelastic demand. Firms with elastically demanded products will see their sales change dramatically in response to small price changes. Panel B of Figure 3 shows what happens to total revenue when a firm increases the price of a product with elastic demand. Although price does not increase much, sales fall significantly. Revenue lost greatly exceeds the revenue gained from the price increase; thus, total revenue falls.

The opposite occurs when prices fall and demand is elastic. The high elasticity of demand faced by restaurants helps explain why so many of them offer "Happy Hour" specials and other discounts. As prices fall, sales have the potential to expand rapidly, thus increasing revenue.

Unitary Elasticity We have looked at the impact of changing prices on revenue when demand is elastic and inelastic. When the elasticity of demand is unitary ($E_d = 1$), a 10%

FIGURE 3 | TOTAL REVENUE AND ELASTICITY OF DEMAND

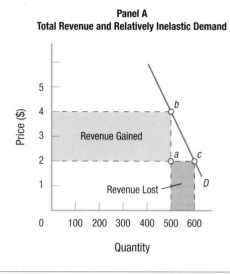

Panel A
Total Revenue and Relatively Inelastic Demand

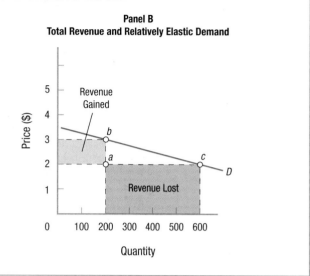

Panel B
Total Revenue and Relatively Elastic Demand

Given inelastic demand in panel A, when price rises from $2 to $4, revenue rises because the revenue gained from the price hike ($1,000) is greater than the revenue lost from fewer sales ($200). The price hike may have driven off a few customers, but the firm's many remaining customers are paying a much higher price, thus increasing the firm's revenue. When products have elastic demand as shown in panel B, usually because many substitutes are available, firms feel a greater impact from changes in price. A small rise in price causes sales to fall off dramatically.

increase in price results in a 10% reduction in quantity demanded. As a result, total revenue is unaffected.

Table 2 summarizes the effects price changes have on total revenue for different price elasticities of demand.

TABLE 2 | TOTAL REVENUE, PRICE CHANGES, AND PRICE ELASTICITY OF DEMAND

	Elasticity		
Price Change	**Inelastic**	**Elastic**	**Unitary Elastic**
Price increases	*TR* increases	*TR* decreases	No change in *TR*
Price decreases	*TR* decreases	*TR* increases	No change in *TR*

Elasticity and Total Revenue Along a Straight-Line (Linear) Demand Curve

Elasticity varies along a straight-line demand curve. Figure 4 shows a linear demand curve in panel A and the corresponding total revenue graph in panel B. In panel A, the elastic part of the curve is that portion above point *e*. Notice that when price falls from $11 to $10, the revenue gained ($100) is much larger than the revenue lost ($10), and thus total revenue rises. This is shown in panel B, where total revenue rises when output grows from 10 to 20 units.

As we move down the demand curve, elasticity will eventually equal 1 (at point *e*), where elasticity is unitary elastic. Price was falling up to this point, while total revenue kept rising until the last price reduction just before $6, where revenue did not change. Revenue is at its maximum at point *e* or a price of $6.

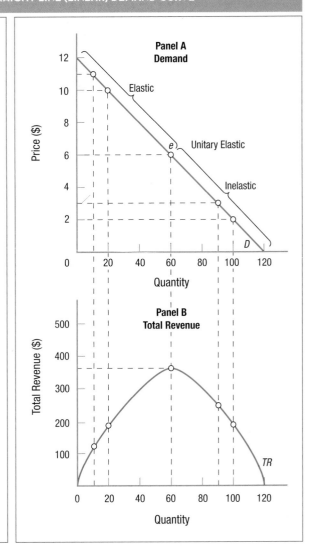

FIGURE 4 — PRICE ELASTICITY AND TOTAL REVENUE ALONG A STRAIGHT-LINE (LINEAR) DEMAND CURVE

Price elasticity varies along a straight-line demand curve. In panel A, the elastic part of the curve lies above point e. Thus, when price falls from $11 to $10, revenue rises, as shown in panel B. As we move down the demand curve, elasticity equals 1 (at point e), where elasticity is unitary. Revenue is maximized at this point. As price continues to fall below $6, demand moves into an inelastic range. When price falls from $3 to $2, revenue declines, as shown in panel B.

As price continues to fall below $6, the demand curve moves into an inelastic range because the percentage change in quantity demanded is less than the percentage change in price. Therefore, when price falls from $3 to $2, revenue declines. The revenue gained ($20) is less than the revenue lost ($90). This decline in revenue is shown in panel B, as total revenue falls as output rises from 90 to 100 units sold.

To summarize, elasticity changes along a negatively sloped linear demand curve because the *percentage* change in price and quantity varies along the curve. When the price of a product is low, a 1-unit change in price is a large percentage change, while the percentage change in quantity demanded is small. When the price is high, a 1-unit change in price is a small percentage change, but the percentage change in quantity is large.

Other Elasticities of Demand

Besides the price elasticity of demand, two other elasticities of demand are important. The first, *cross elasticity of demand*, measures how changes in the price of one good affect the demand for other related goods. If Toyota is planning a price reduction, what impact will this have on the sale of Fords? Ford will want to estimate this to decide whether to ignore Toyota or lower its own automobile prices.

Another type of elasticity measures how responsive quantity demanded is to changes in income. This is called *income elasticity of demand.* Incomes vary as the economy expands or contracts. To plan their future employment and production, many industries want to know how the demand for their products will be affected when the economy changes. How much will airline travel be affected if the economy moves into a recession? What will happen to sales of lattes at Starbucks? Each business faces a different situation.

Let's consider these two elasticities of demand more closely, beginning with cross elasticity of demand.

Cross Elasticity of Demand Cross elasticity of demand (E_{ab}) measures how responsive the quantity demanded of one good (product a) is to changes in the price of another (product b):

$$E_{ab} = \frac{\text{Percentage Change in Quantity Demanded of Product a}}{\text{Percentage Change in Price of Product b}}$$

Using cross elasticity of demand, we can classify goods in two ways. Products a and b are **substitutes** if their cross elasticity of demand is positive ($E_{ab} > 0$). Common sense tells us that chicken and turkey are substitutes. Therefore, if the price of turkey rises, people will substitute away from turkey and toward chicken; thus, the quantity demanded for chicken will grow. This illustrates a positive cross elasticity. Similar relationships exist between Toyota and Honda cars, wireless services provided by AT&T and Verizon, and the price of gas and public transportation.

Second, products a and b are **complements** if their cross elasticity of demand is negative ($E_{ab} < 0$). This is an instance in which the minus sign conveys important information. Complementary products are those goods and services that are consumed together, such as lift tickets and snowboard rentals. When the price of lift tickets rises, the result is that the demand for snowboard rentals falls as fewer people head to the mountains. Other complementary goods include coffee and cream, hamburgers and french fries, and hot dogs and hot dog buns. Finally, two goods are *not related* if a cross elasticity of demand is zero, or near zero.

Income Elasticity of Demand The **income elasticity of demand** (E_Y) measures how responsive quantity demanded is to changes in consumer income. We define the income elasticity of demand as

$$E_Y = \frac{\text{Percentage Change in Quantity Demanded}}{\text{Percentage Change in Income}}$$

Depending on the value of the income elasticity of demand, we can classify goods in three ways. First, a **normal good** is one whose income elasticity is positive, but less than 1 ($0 < E_Y < 1$). As income rises, quantity demanded at any given price rises as well, but not as fast as the rise in income. Most products are normal goods. If your income doubles, you will probably buy more sporting equipment and restaurant meals, but not twice as many.

A second category, *income superior goods* or **luxury goods,** includes products with an income elasticity greater than 1 ($E_Y > 1$). As income rises, quantity demanded at any given price grows faster than income. Goods and services such as Mercedes automobiles, caviar, fine wine, and visits to European spas are examples of luxury or income superior goods.

Finally, **inferior goods** are those goods for which income elasticity is negative ($E_Y < 0$). When income rises, the quantity demanded at any given price falls. Inferior goods include

cross elasticity of demand A measure of how responsive the quantity demanded of one good is to changes in the price of another good.

substitutes Goods consumers substitute for one another depending on their relative prices, such as coffee and tea. Substitutes have a positive cross elasticity of demand.

complements Goods that are typically consumed together, such as coffee and sugar. Complements have a negative cross elasticity of demand.

income elasticity of demand A measure of how responsive quantity demanded is to changes in consumer income.

normal goods Goods that have positive income elasticities less than 1. When consumer income grows, demand for normal goods rises, but less than the rise in income.

luxury goods Goods that have income elasticities greater than 1. When consumer income grows, demand for luxury goods rises more than the rise in income.

inferior goods Goods that have income elasticities that are negative. When consumer income grows, demand for inferior goods falls.

ISSUE

Using Loss Leaders to Generate Higher Total Revenue

At the start of each school year, office supply stores will often advertise items for as low as 1 cent. These items typically are essential school supplies such as paper, pencils, and folders that parents need to buy for their children. Because school supplies are necessities and generally low-priced, they are relatively inelastic goods. Why, then, would stores choose to reduce their prices, knowing that such actions would lead to a fall in total revenue?

The answer lies not in how prices for school supplies affect total revenue, but instead the effect that those remarkably low prices, known as *loss leaders*, have on the cross elasticity of demand for pricier items, such as laptops, color printers, and office furniture, sold at the store. In other words, the practically free school supplies are

used as an incentive to attract parents into the store.

Wouldn't some parents just buy the school supplies on sale and nothing else? Some actually do. But the potential gain from just one customer choosing to buy a high-priced computer or printer would offset the lost revenue from the loss leaders many times over. And because the start of the school year is when many high-priced school items are purchased, few parents end up buying just the advertised items.

Loss leaders are an effective advertising tool to increase total revenues from the sale of higher-priced related goods. And loss leaders are not limited to office supply stores. Other examples of loss leaders include convenience stores advertising a free soda or coffee on large banners visible to potential

customers at the gas pump, fast-food restaurants featuring a 99 cent sandwich special on their marquee, or a campus sporting goods store offering a free T-shirt just for stopping by. In each case, stores are betting on consumers making decisions beyond that of the loss leader, thus illustrating the importance of cross elasticity of demand in business decisions.

Barbara Helgason/Dreamstime.com

---

potatoes, beans, cheap motels, and nosebleed section concert tickets. Get yourself a nice raise, and you will probably buy concert tickets that let you see the band up close and personal.

Keep in mind that inferior goods are not necessarily poor in quality; they simply describe goods that one buys fewer of as income increases, and vice versa. Therefore, inferior goods can vary from person to person. Nosebleed seats might be an inferior good for an avid concertgoer, but can be a normal good to a person who rarely goes to concerts.

Understanding how product sales are affected by changing incomes and economic conditions can help firms diversify their product lines so that sales and employment can be stabilized to some extent over time. For example, firms that produce all three types of goods can try to switch production toward the good that current economic conditions favor: In boom times, production is shifted more toward the making of luxury goods. Chevrolet will produce more Corvettes in boom times, and more Chevy Sparks during economic slowdowns.

This is a good place to stop and reflect on what we have discovered so far. We have seen that elasticity measures the responsiveness of one variable to changes in another. Elasticity measures changes in percentage terms so that products of different magnitudes—a bottle of soda and an airplane—can be compared. Products that have a price elasticity of demand greater than 1 are elastic; products with price elasticity of demand less than 1 are inelastic; and products with a price elasticity of demand equal to 1 are unitary elastic. We saw how total revenue increases when price rises for an inelastic good, but decreases when price rises for an elastic good. Finally, we saw that elasticity can be used to measure the effects of related goods using cross elasticity of demand, as well as changes in income using income elasticity of demand.

After college, incomes rise, which means fewer packed lunches on the lawn and more fancy lunches at the local bistro.

Ocean/Corbis

CHECKPOINT

TOTAL REVENUE AND OTHER MEASURES OF ELASTICITY

- When demand is inelastic and prices rise, total revenue rises. When demand is inelastic and prices fall, total revenue falls.
- When demand is elastic and prices rise, total revenue falls. When demand is elastic and prices fall, total revenue rises.
- Straight-line demand curves show three regions: elastic demand (at higher prices), unitary elastic demand, and inelastic demand (at lower prices).
- Cross elasticity of demand measures how responsive the demand of one product is to price changes of another. Substitutes have positive cross elasticities, while complements have negative cross elasticities.
- Income elasticity of demand measures how responsive demand is to changes in income. This determines whether a good is a luxury, normal, or inferior good.

QUESTION: Two clothing stores located in the same shopping center have a big sale: 20% off on everything in the store. After the sale, Store 1 finds that its total revenue has increased, while Store 2 finds that total revenue has decreased. What does this tell you about the price elasticity of demand for the clothes in each store?

Answers to the Checkpoint questions can be found at the end of this chapter.

ELASTICITY OF SUPPLY

So far, we have looked at the consumer when we studied the elasticity of demand. Now let us turn our attention to the producer, and analyze elasticity of supply.

Price elasticity of supply (E_s) measures the responsiveness of quantity supplied to changes in the price of the product. Price elasticity of supply is defined as

$$E_s = \frac{\text{Percentage Change in Quantity Supplied}}{\text{Percentage Change in Price}}$$

Note that because the slope of the supply curve is positive, the price elasticity of supply will always be a positive number. Economists classify price elasticity of supply in the same way that they classify price elasticity of demand. Classification is based on whether the percentage change in quantity supplied is greater than, less than, or equal to the percentage change in price. When price rises just a little and quantity increases by much more, supply is elastic, and vice versa. The output of many commodities such as gold and seasonal vegetables cannot be quickly increased if their price increases, so they are inelastic. In summary,

Elastic supply: $E_s > 1$
Inelastic supply: $E_s < 1$
Unitary elastic supply: $E_s = 1$

Looking at the three supply curves in Figure 5, we can easily determine which curve is inelastic, which is elastic, and which is unitary elastic. First, note that all three curves go through point a. As we increase the price from P_0 to P_1, we see that the response in quantity supplied is different for all three curves. Consider supply curve S_1 first. When price changes to P_1 (point b), the change in output (Q_0 to Q_1) is the smallest for the three curves. Most important, the percentage change in quantity supplied is smaller than the percentage change in price; therefore, S_1 is an inelastic supply curve.

Contrast this with S_3. In this case, when price rises to P_1 (point d), output climbs from Q_0 all the way to Q_3. Because the percentage change in output is larger than the percentage change in price, S_3 is elastic. And finally, curve S_2 is a unitary elastic curve because the percentage change in output is the same as the percentage change in price.

price elasticity of supply A measure of the responsiveness of quantity supplied to changes in price. Elastic supply has elasticity greater than 1, whereas inelastic supply has elasticity less than 1.

elastic supply Price elasticity of supply is greater than 1. The percentage change in quantity supplied is greater than the percentage change in price.

inelastic supply Price elasticity of supply is less than 1. The percentage change in quantity supplied is less than the percentage change in price.

unitary elastic supply Price elasticity of supply is equal to 1. The percentage change in quantity supplied is equal to the percentage change in price.

FIGURE 5	PRICE ELASTICITY OF SUPPLY

All three supply curves in this figure run through point a, but they respond differently when price changes from P_0 to P_1. Considering supply curve S_1 first, when price changes, the percentage change in quantity supplied is smaller than the percentage change in price; thus, S_1 is an inelastic supply curve. Curve S_2 is a unitary elastic supply curve, because the percentage change in output is the same as the percentage change in price. For supply curve S_3, the percentage change in output is greater than the percentage change in price, so S_3 is elastic. Elastic linear supply curves cross the price axis, inelastic linear supply curves cross the quantity axis, and unitary elastic linear supply curves go through the origin.

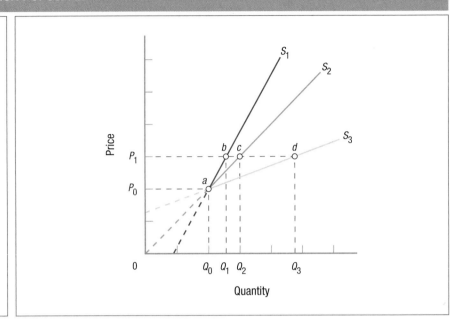

Here is a simple rule of thumb. When the supply curve is linear, like those shown in Figure 5, you can always determine if the supply curve is elastic, inelastic, or unitary elastic by extending the curve to the axis and applying the following rules:

- Elastic supply curves always cross the price axis, as does curve S_3.
- Inelastic supply curves always cross the quantity axis, as does curve S_1.
- Unitary elastic supply curves always cross through the origin, as does curve S_2.

Time and Price Elasticity of Supply

The primary determinant of price elasticity of supply is time. To adjust output in response to changes in market prices, firms require time. Firms have both variable inputs, such as labor, and fixed inputs, such as plant capacity. To increase their labor force, firms must recruit, interview, and hire more workers. This can take as little time as a few hours—a call to a temp agency—or as long as a few months. On the other hand, building another plant or expanding the existing plant to increase output involves considerably more time and resources. In some instances, such as building a new oil refinery or computer chip plant, it can take as long as a decade, with environmental clearance alone often requiring years of study and costing millions of dollars. Finally, in some markets, such as that for original Rembrandt paintings, new supply will never be created (assuming that the dead cannot return). Economists typically distinguish among three types of time periods: the market period, the short run, and the long run.

The Market Period The **market period** is so short that the output and the number of firms in an industry are fixed; firms have no time to change their production levels in response to changes in product price. Consider a raspberry market in the summer. Even if consumers flock to the market, their tastes having shifted in favor of fresh raspberries, farmers can do little to increase the supply of raspberries until two years later. Figure 6 shows a market period supply curve (S_{MP}) for agricultural products such as raspberries. During the market period, the quantity of product available to the market is fixed at Q_0. If demand changes (shifting from D_0 to D_1), the only impact is on the price of the product. In Figure 6, price moves from P_0 (point e) to P_1 (point a). In summary, if demand grows over the market period, price will rise, and vice versa.

market period The time period so short that the output and the number of firms are fixed. Agricultural products at harvest time face market periods. Products that unexpectedly become instant hits face market periods (there is a lag between when the firm realizes it has a hit on its hands and when inventory can be replaced).

FIGURE 6   TIME AND PRICE ELASTICITY OF SUPPLY

During the market period, the quantity of output available to the market is fixed and the only impact will be on the price of the product, which will rise from P_0 to P_1 if demand increases. Over the short run, firms can change the amount of inputs they employ to adjust their output to market changes. Thus, the short-run supply curve (S_{SR}) is more elastic than the market period curve, and price increases are more moderate. In the long run, firms can change their plant capacity and enter or exit an industry. Long-run supply curve S_{LR} is elastic, and a rise in demand leads to a small increase in price.

Changes in demand over the market period can be devastating for firms selling perishable goods. If demand falls, cantaloupes cannot be kept until demand grows; they must either be sold at a discount or trashed.

The Short Run The **short run** is defined as a period of time during which plant capacity and the number of firms in the industry cannot change. Firms can, however, change the amount of labor, raw materials, and other variable inputs they employ in the short run to adjust their output to changes in the market. Note that the short run does not imply a specific number of weeks, months, or years. It simply means a period short enough that firms cannot adjust their plant capacity, but long enough for them to hire more labor to increase their production. A restaurant with an outdoor seating area can hire additional staff and open this area in a relatively short timeframe when the weather gets warm, but manufacturing firms usually need more time to hire and train new people for their production lines. Clearly, the time associated with the short run differs depending on the industry.

This also is illustrated in Figure 6. The short-run supply curve, S_{SR}, is more elastic than the market period curve. If demand grows from D_0 to D_1, output expands from Q_0 to Q_2 and price increases to P_2 as equilibrium moves from point e to point b. Because output can expand in the short run in response to rising demand, the price increase is not as drastic as it was in the market period.

The Long Run Economists define the **long run** as a period of time long enough for firms to alter their plant capacity and for the number of firms in the industry to change. In the long run, some firms may decide to leave the industry if they think the market will be unfavorable. Alternatively, new firms may enter the market, or existing firms can alter their production capacity. Because all these conceivable changes are possible in the long run, the long-run supply curve is more elastic, as illustrated in Figure 6 by supply curve S_{LR}. In this case, a rise in demand from D_0 to D_1 gives rise to a small increase in the price of the product, while generating a major increase in output, from Q_0 to Q_3 (point c).

In giving the long-run supply curve S_{LR} a small but positive slope, we are assuming that an industry's costs will increase slightly as it increases its output. Firms must compete with other industries to expand production. Wages and other input prices rise in the industry

short run The time period when plant capacity and the number of firms in the industry cannot change. Firms can employ more people, have existing employees work overtime, or hire part-time employees to produce more, but this is done in an existing plant.

long run The time period long enough for firms to alter their plant capacities and for the number of firms in the industry to change. Existing firms can expand or build new plants, or firms can enter or exit the industry.

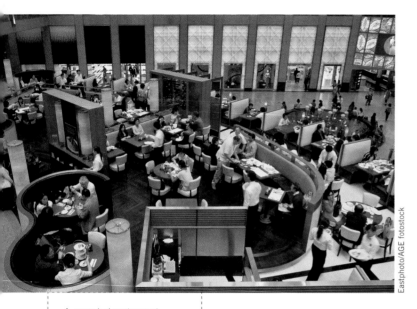

as firms attempt to draw resources away from their immediate competitors and other industries.

Some industries may not face added costs as they expand. Fast-food chains, copy centers, and coffee shops seem to be able to reproduce at will without incurring increasing costs. Therefore, their long-run supply curves may be nearly horizontal.

At this point, we have seen how elasticity measures the responsiveness of demand to a change in price and how total revenue is affected by different demand elasticities. We have also seen that supply elasticities are mainly a function of the time needed to adjust to price changes. Next, let's apply our findings about elasticity to a subject that concerns all of us: taxes.

A crowded restaurant might encourage its owner to expand. In the market period (i.e., same day), little can be done to accommodate more diners. In the short run, the restaurant can rearrange tables and hire more waitstaff. In the long run, it can expand the restaurant or open a second location.

 CHECKPOINT

ELASTICITY OF SUPPLY

- Elasticity of supply measures the responsiveness of quantity supplied to changes in price.
- Elastic supply is very responsive to price changes. With inelastic supply, quantity supplied is not very responsive to changing prices.
- Supply is highly inelastic in the market period, but can expand (become more elastic) in the short run because firms can hire additional resources to raise output levels.
- In the long run, supply is relatively elastic because firms can enter or exit the industry, and existing firms can expand their plant capacity.

QUESTION: A number of products are made in preparation for the annual flu season, although the types of goods vary in terms of their elasticity of supply. Rank the following goods from most elastic to least elastic: (a) over-the-counter flu remedies, (b) flu shots, (c) chicken soup, and (d) boxes of tissue.

Answers to the Checkpoint questions can be found at the end of this chapter.

TAXES AND ELASTICITY

On average, families pay more than 40% of their income in taxes, including income, property, estate, sales, and excise taxes. (An excise tax is a sales tax applied to a specific product, such as gasoline or tobacco.) Add to this the taxes that are embedded into the goods and services we buy, such as tariffs (taxes) on imports, tourism taxes, and airport security taxes, and it's no wonder that taxes are a perennial issue of debate among policymakers and their constituents.

Nobody likes paying taxes, but they are necessary to provide many of the public goods and services (such as roads, national defense, police protection, public education, clean air, and parks) from which everybody receives some benefit. The questions economists deal with are how to determine the efficient level of taxation and what is the most efficient way to reach that level.

Taxes can be separated into two general categories: taxes on income sources and taxes on spending. We now study how the economic burden of both categories of taxes can vary depending on how the tax policy is designed (in the case of income) and on the elasticity of the good or service being purchased (in the case of spending).

We begin by studying the various ways taxes are collected on income.

TABLE 3	TYPES OF TAXES AND THEIR ECONOMIC BURDEN	
Type of Tax	**Example**	**Description of Tax Burden**
Progressive	Individual income tax	As income rises, income is taxed at a higher percentage rate when a higher tax bracket is reached.
Flat	Medicare tax	Medicare tax is 2.9% of all income earned (half of which is paid by employees and half paid by employers).
Regressive	FICA tax	The FICA tax is a flat tax of 6.2% paid by both employees and employers up to an income cap and is used to fund Social Security. Those earning above the cap will pay a lower overall percentage of income in payroll taxes.

Taxes on Income Sources and Their Economic Burden

Taxes on income sources constitute the largest source of revenues for the federal government and many state governments. The most common types of taxes include individual income tax, payroll tax (such as FICA, also known as the Social Security tax), corporate income tax, dividend tax (taxes on earnings from financial assets), and capital gains tax (taxes on the rising values of assets such as property and financial instruments when sold).

Much of the debate on the economic burden of income taxes focuses on whether taxes are progressive, flat, or regressive with respect to income earned. **Progressive taxes** are those that rise in burden as income increases. **Flat taxes** take a constant percentage of one's income. **Regressive taxes** fall in burden as income increases, which means that individuals with lower incomes pay a greater percentage of their income in taxes than individuals with higher incomes. A type of regressive tax is called a **lump-sum tax**, which takes a fixed amount of tax regardless of income earned, and therefore falls in percentage as income rises. Table 3 lists the three categories of taxes and provides an example of an actual tax that falls within each category.

Taxes on Spending and the Incidence of Taxation

The typical household pays a substantial amount of taxes on goods and services. Almost everybody pays taxes on goods and services purchased, homeowners pay property taxes each year on the value of their homes, and all sorts of excise taxes exist on everything from car rentals and hotel stays to gasoline and wireless service plan purchases.

Although income taxes typically represent the largest burden on most households, taxes on spending are sometimes larger for certain groups of people. For example, households with very low incomes often pay little to no income taxes, but pay a sizeable portion of their income in sales and excise taxes. Similarly, wealthy households often receive most of their income by way of investment earnings, which are taxed at a lower rate than traditional income earnings. For these households, taxes paid on property (often on multiple homes) and luxury taxes (on yachts and other expensive toys) may constitute a larger portion of their tax burden.

In sum, taxes on spending are not trivial, and elasticity plays an important role in determining the impact of these various taxes on individuals and businesses. Economists studying taxes are interested in the **incidence of taxation**, which refers to who bears the economic burden of a tax. Although statutes determine what is taxed and who must pay various taxes, the individuals or businesses paying a tax may not be the ones bearing its economic burden. This burden can be *shifted* onto others.

Let's analyze how the elasticity of a good or service can affect the incidence of taxation. To simplify the analysis, we will focus on excise taxes.

progressive tax A tax that rises in percentage of income as income increases.

flat tax A tax that is a constant proportion of one's income.

regressive tax A tax that falls in percentage of income as income increases.

lump-sum tax A fixed amount of tax regardless of income. It is a type of regressive tax.

incidence of taxation Refers to who bears the economic burden of a tax. The economic entity bearing the burden of a particular tax will depend on the price elasticities of demand and supply.

FIGURE 7   EFFECT OF AN EXCISE TAX ON AIRLINE TICKETS

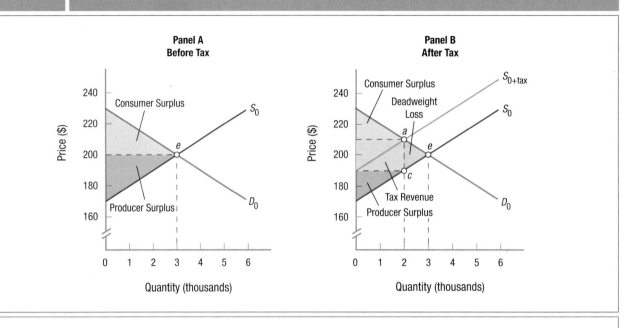

The market for airline tickets shown in panel A is in equilibrium at point e. When a $20 excise tax is placed on each airline ticket, the supply curve shifts upward by the amount of the tax, from S_0 to S_{0+tax} (panel B). With demand remaining constant at D_0, equilibrium moves to point a (2,000 units). When a tax is imposed, output falls because prices are pushed higher, and a deadweight loss is created. In this case, consumers and producers share the burden of the tax equally.

Analyzing the Effect of Taxes on a Market

Let us consider what happens when an excise tax is levied on a product such as airline tickets. Panel A of Figure 7 shows the market before an excise tax is imposed. The initial supply curve S_0 is supply before the tax and demand curve D_0 reflects demand. The market is in equilibrium at point e, at which 3,000 tickets are sold for $200 each. At equilibrium, consumer and producer surplus are substantial, with no deadweight loss because the market is operating efficiently.

In panel B, we now add a per unit tax of $20 paid by the airline. This, in effect, adds $20 to the cost of each airline ticket and adds a wedge between what consumers pay and what airlines receive. Supply curve S_0 therefore shifts upward by this amount, to S_0 + tax. The new supply curve runs parallel to S_0, with the distance the curve has shifted (ac) equaling the $20 tax per ticket collected by the government.

Assuming demand remains constant at D_0, the new equilibrium is at point a, with 2,000 tickets sold for a price of $210. The airline receives $210 per ticket, of which it must send $20 to the government, keeping $190 for itself. In this case, the airline shifted half of the tax burden ($10 of the $20 tax) onto consumers. Meanwhile, the government collects the $20 tax on the 2,000 tickets. This amount ($20 × 2,000 = $40,000) is represented by the blue area. Consumer surplus now equals the area above the blue section, and producer surplus equals the area below it. Note that consumers and producers lose surplus equal not only to the revenue gained by the government but also to area cae, which represents a deadweight loss. Although this area is lost to society as a result of the tax, how the tax revenues are used to benefit society determines whether society is better or worse off with the tax.

In this example, consumers and producers share the tax burden equally, but that is not always the case, as we'll see next.

FIGURE 8   TAX BURDEN WITH INELASTIC DEMAND AND ELASTIC SUPPLY

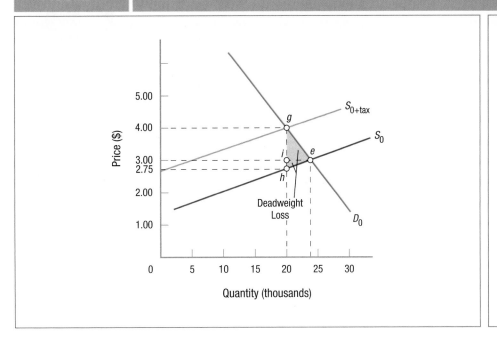

S_0 is the initial supply curve for a product with inelastic demand. When a $1.25 excise tax is placed on the product, the supply curve shifts upward by the amount of the tax, to S_{0+tax}. Assuming demand remains constant at D_0, the new equilibrium will be at point g. Because this demand is inelastic, consumers are less responsive to the rise in price, and therefore bear a larger burden of the tax. And because the supply curve is elastic, producers are more responsive to changes in price, which also contributes to the tax burden shifting more toward consumers.

When Elasticity Puts a Greater Burden of a Tax on Consumers

Earlier in the chapter, we learned that inelastic demand means that consumers react less strongly to price changes, while elastic demand means that consumers react strongly to price changes. The same is true of how producers react when supply is inelastic or elastic. Using this knowledge, we can examine how consumers and producers react when prices of goods and services change due to a tax.

Figure 8 shows a market for sparklers, one in which consumer demand is inelastic, while supply is relatively elastic. In this situation, how would a tax affect the equilibrium price in this market? Like our previous analysis, the supply curve S_0 shifts to S_{0+tax}, moving the equilibrium point from e to g at a new equilibrium price of $4.00.

Compared to the equilibrium prior to the tax, consumers pay an additional $1.00 for each unit, but producers end up bearing a much smaller burden of 25 cents. Because consumers were less sensitive to changes in prices than producers, producers were able to shift a greater portion of the tax forward to consumers.

Therefore, we can generalize about the effects of elasticity on the tax burden as follows: For a given supply of some products, the lower the price elasticity of demand, the greater the share of the total tax burden shifted to consumers. Likewise, for a given demand of some products, the higher the price elasticity of supply, the greater the share of the total tax burden shifted to consumers. In sum, when demand for a good is inelastic while the supply of a good is elastic, consumers will end up bearing most of the burden of a tax.

When Elasticity Puts a Greater Burden of a Tax on Producers

Naturally, if inelastic demand and elastic supply shift the tax burden toward consumers, the opposite would be true when demand is elastic and supply is inelastic. Figure 9 again shows the market for sparklers, but this time demand is relatively elastic (flat) while supply is relatively inelastic (steep). When an excise tax of $1.25 per unit is levied, the equilibrium moves from point e to g. At the new equilibrium, consumers pay $3.25 per unit (or 25 cents per unit more than before the tax), while producers receive $2.00 per unit (or $1 per unit less than before the tax). In this case, because consumers are more sensitive to price

Norway: An Oil Producing Nation With an Incentive *NOT* to Drive

How are the preferred modes of transportation in Norway and Saudi Arabia affected by the way that each country has influenced retail gas prices?

Gasoline prices vary around the world, but not necessarily for the same reasons. Oil-rich nations such as Saudi Arabia and Venezuela offer their citizens very low fuel prices, well below international market prices, which has led to large cars and SUVs clogging the streets of Riyadh and Caracas. In the United States, increased domestic oil production and low taxes have reduced gas prices in recent years, leading to more auto purchases and congestion on U.S. roads. Meanwhile, European nations have raised gas taxes in order to curtail driving and traffic. But because the demand for gasoline is inelastic, higher gas prices might not immedi-

Luxury cars and SUVs clog the streets of Riyadh, Saudi Arabia, where only men can legally drive, while the streets in Oslo, Norway, remain tranquil despite the nation being oil-rich.

ately eliminate traffic congestion. How high must fuel prices rise before drivers give up their cars? An answer may be found in one oil-rich nation: Norway.

Norway is one of the world's largest oil producers, with its rich oil fields in the Baltic Sea. But unlike Saudi Arabia, where a gallon of gas costs around 45 cents, the Norwegian government taxes gasoline heavily. In Norway, a gallon of gasoline costs about $10! The consequence of high gas prices is that the streets of Oslo, the capital and largest city, are mostly

free of traffic as many of its citizens use its efficient public transportation or choose to ride bicycles, even in the cold Norwegian winters.

Elasticity plays an important role in how consumers respond to changes in gasoline prices. Although changes in prices may not lead to immediate changes in how people use their cars, over time, elasticities will rise as more alternatives become available. In the case of Norway, the alternatives were developed more quickly due to the rapid increase in prices.

GO TO **LaunchPad** TO PRACTICE THE ECONOMIC CONCEPTS IN THIS STORY

FIGURE 9	TAX BURDEN WITH ELASTIC DEMAND AND INELASTIC SUPPLY

S_0 is the initial supply curve for a product with elastic demand. When a $1.25 excise tax is placed on the product, the supply curve shifts upward by the amount of the tax, to S_{0+tax}. Assuming demand remains constant at D_0, the new equilibrium will be at point g. Because demand is elastic, consumers are more responsive to the rise in price, and therefore producers are less able to shift the tax to consumers. And because supply is inelastic, producers are less responsive to changes in price, which forces them to bear more of the tax burden.

changes, producers are less able to shift the tax to consumers, resulting in producers bearing the majority of the tax burden.

Just like the previous example, we can generalize about the effects of elasticity when it causes a larger tax burden on producers. The higher the price elasticity of demand and the lower the price elasticity of supply, the lower the share of the total tax burden shifted to consumers. Therefore, when demand for a good is elastic while the supply is inelastic, producers will end up bearing most of the burden of a tax.

Note what happens in all of the tax cases described. Figures 7 to 9 show that whenever a tax is added, the tax moves the market away from its equilibrium point, regardless

 ISSUE

Are Sales Taxes Fair to Low-Income Households?

With few exceptions, sales taxes are added to the price of nearly everything we buy. Sales taxes vary by state, and can also vary by cities or counties within states. Unlike income taxes, for which the tax rate changes as income rises, sales taxes are a fixed percentage of one's total purchase. For example, in the state of New Jersey, with a sales tax rate of 7%, you would pay $3.50 in sales tax if you bought a watch that sells for $50. Because of this fixed percentage, sales taxes are often referred to as a flat (or proportional) tax, because the tax rate remains constant regardless of the amount purchased. But is this an accurate depiction of the economic burden of sales taxes?

Many economists argue that sales taxes are *regressive* in nature, meaning that households with lower incomes pay a greater share of their income in sales taxes than households with higher incomes. Such claims have led some economists to vehemently oppose legislation that proposes higher sales taxes as a way to increase state tax revenues.

To measure the burden of sales taxes, one must first analyze how households spend their money. For example, a household earning $25,000 a year spends approximately $5,500 on items subject to the sales tax. These expenditures include most goods (except groceries in many states), auto lease payments, and many services. Major items not subject to sales taxes include rent and mortgage payments, tuition payments, and most financial instruments. Using an average sales tax rate of 7%, this household would spend

$385 a year on sales taxes, or 1.54% of total income. A household earning $100,000 a year, however, spends approximately $18,000 on taxable items. This amounts to $1,260 a year in sales tax, or 1.26% of total income. Therefore, sales taxes *are* regressive.

How do states compare in terms of the average sales tax rate? The following table shows the ten states with the highest average sales tax rate and the ten states with the lowest. Surprisingly, the four states with the highest sales tax rates, Tennessee, Arkansas, Louisiana, and Alabama, are those with lower average incomes. This creates a double whammy—income tends to be lower in these states, and being poor takes an even greater toll with high sales taxes.

In sum, when municipalities and states need to raise revenue, the sales tax is the type of tax that hurts the poor the most. Therefore, a few states have opted not to use sales taxes at all, and instead rely on state income taxes, corporate taxes, or property taxes that are *progressive*, meaning that those with higher incomes pay a greater percentage in taxes. But for most states, sales taxes remain an important source of revenues.

Highest Average Sales Tax Rate	Lowest Average Sales Tax Rate
1. Tennessee (9.46%)	41. Virginia (5.63%)
2. Arkansas (9.30%)	42. Maine (5.50%)
3. Louisiana (9.00%)	43. Wyoming (5.42%)
4. Alabama (8.97%)	44. Wisconsin (5.41%)
5. Washington (8.89%)	45. Hawaii (4.35%)
6. Oklahoma (8.82%)	46. Alaska (1.78%)
7. Illinois (8.64%)	47. (tied) Delaware (0.00%)
8. Kansas (8.60%)	47. (tied) Montana (0.00%)
9. New York (8.49%)	47. (tied) New Hampshire (0.00%)
10. California (8.48%)	47. (tied) Oregon (0.00%)

Data from Tax Foundation, 2016. (Percentages are state sales tax rate + average local sales tax rate.)

of whether the tax is borne by consumers, producers, or both. All taxes generate a tax wedge, resulting in a deadweight loss to society. Does deadweight loss vary based on elasticity?

Generally, the more elastic the demand or supply, the greater is the total deadweight loss to society. Why is that? We can deduce this intuitively by understanding that higher elasticities indicate a larger response by both consumers and producers in terms of the quantity demanded and supplied, respectively. Therefore, larger responses to price changes tend to move the equilibrium quantity farther from the pre-tax equilibrium, generating a larger deadweight loss.

The last three chapters have given us the powerful tools of supply and demand analysis. Elasticity is important because it captures the complex relationships among prices, quantity demanded, and total revenues in just two words: "elastic" and "inelastic". When demand is inelastic and some incident marginally reduces supply, policymakers (and now you) know that price will go up substantially, although consumers will continue to purchase the product. Again, this is what happens when any inelastic product rises in price. When tuition increases, students continue to purchase roughly the same number of credits as before; thus, revenues collected by universities rise substantially in the short run.

If, however, demand is elastic and the same incident reduces supply, prices will rise, but by a smaller amount, and output and employment will fall a lot more. If weather conditions in California and Florida ruin the orange crop, reducing the supply and increasing the price of orange juice, consumers will readily substitute other juices. As a result, output, employment, and revenues will decline in the orange industry.

 CHECKPOINT

TAXES AND ELASTICITY

- Taxes on income can be progressive, flat, or regressive based on the percentage of income that is paid in taxes. Most income taxes are progressive, but certain forms of flat and regressive taxes exist.

- When price elasticity of demand is elastic, consumers bear a smaller burden of taxes while more is borne by sellers. When demand is inelastic, a higher share of the total tax burden is shifted to consumers.

- When the price elasticity of supply is elastic, buyers bear a larger burden of taxes. Elastic supply also leads to a larger deadweight loss. When supply is inelastic, more of the tax burden is shifted to sellers, but the deadweight loss is lower.

QUESTION: Excise taxes were the principal taxes levied in the United States for the first 100 years or so after the Revolutionary War. Today, excise taxes fall mainly on cigarettes, liquor, luxury cars and boats, telephones, gasoline, diesel fuel, aviation fuel, gas-guzzling vehicles, and vaccines. What do all of these products seem to have in common?

Answers to the Checkpoint questions can be found at the end of this chapter.

chapter summary

Section 1 Elasticity of Demand

5.1 The **price elasticity of demand** measures how sensitive consumers are to changes in price.

What Do the E_d Numbers Mean?

5.2 $E_d > 1$: Elastic Demand (many substitutes, high-priced goods, longer time horizon, luxury goods)
$E_d < 1$: Inelastic Demand (few substitutes, low-priced goods, shorter time horizon, necessities)
$E_d = 1$: Unitary Elastic Demand (a change in price results in an equal percentage change in quantity demanded)

Determinants of Elasticity of Demand

5.3
- Substitutability
- Proportion of income spent
- Luxuries versus necessities
- Time period

5.4 The formula for price elasticity of demand is

E_d = % Change in Quantity Demanded / % Change in Price

Since all E_d must be negative according to the law of demand, the convention is to drop the negative sign.

Calculating percentage changes:

Base method: % Change in P = Change in P/old P
The base method is simple because it is how one normally calculates percentages in everyday life, such as for store discounts or restaurant tips. For example, adding a 15% tip to a $20 bill is $3, or taking 25% off of a $40 shirt makes the shirt $30.

Midpoint method: % Change in P = Change in P/[(old P + new P)/2]
The midpoint method is slightly more difficult to calculate; however, the advantage is that the percentage change stays the same whether a value increases or decreases. For example, using the midpoint method, going from 10 to 20 or from 20 to 10 is a 66.7% change in either direction.

Tshooter/Shutterstock;
Anton Balazh/Shutterstock

Your textbook is an **inelastic** good because few alternatives to it exist for your class and it may be required (a necessity).

Fancy/Alamy

A spring break trip is **elastic** because many choices of destinations exist, it is expensive, and it is not really a necessity.

How Do You Remember Which Diagram Is Elastic?

Think of a pair of shorts: You can easily pull them **side-to-side** because the waistband is very elastic!

John Lund/Paula Zacharias/Getty Images

Panel A	Panel B	Panel C	Panel D	Panel E
Perfectly Elastic	Elastic	Unitary Elastic	Inelastic	Perfectly Inelastic
$E_d = \infty$	$1 < E_d < \infty$	$E_d = 1$	$0 < E_d < 1$	$E_d = 0$

The flatter the demand curve, the more elastic the demand for the good or service; the steeper the demand curve, the more inelastic the demand for the good or service. Because elasticity changes along a linear demand curve, unitary elastic demand has a curved shape.

Section 2
Total Revenue and Other Measures of Elasticity

Terra/Corbis

5.5 **Total revenue** is calculated as Price × Quantity Demanded.

Total revenue increases when price rises on an inelastic good or is lowered on an elastic good.

Total revenue decreases when price rises on an elastic good or is lowered on an inelastic good.

Elasticity and total revenue vary along a straight-line demand curve. Total revenue is maximized at the point where demand is unitary elastic.

When competition is nearly nonexistent, sellers can raise prices and increase total revenue because the good is inelastic.

5.6 **Cross elasticity of demand** measures how responsive demand for one good is to a change in the price of another good:

E_{ab} = % Change in Q_a/% Change in P_b

$E_{ab} > 0$: Goods a and b are substitutes.

$E_{ab} < 0$: Goods a and b are complements.

$E_{ab} = 0$: Goods a and b are unrelated.

5.7 **Income elasticity of demand** measures how demand responds to changes in income:

E_Y = % Change in Q/% Change in Income.

$0 < E_Y < 1$: normal good

$E_Y > 1$: luxury good

$E_Y < 0$: inferior good

Section 3 Elasticity of Supply

5.8 The **elasticity of supply** measures the extent to which businesses react to price changes, and its formula is virtually identical to that of demand:

E_s = **% Change in Quantity Supplied / % Change in Price**

The base and midpoint methods are both still used to calculate percentage changes.

5.9 The **time horizon** affects the elasticity of supply: The longer the period, the more a firm is able to adjust to changing prices, and therefore the more elastic the good.

Short run: a time period in which plant capacity is fixed and the number of firms in an industry does not change.

Long run: a time period long enough for firms to alter their plant capacity or for firms to enter or leave the industry.

Section 4
Taxes and Elasticity

5.10 The **incidence of taxation** refers to who bears the economic burden of a tax.

The more elastic the demand or inelastic the supply, the greater the incidence of a tax on sellers. The more inelastic the demand or elastic the supply, the greater the incidence of a tax on consumers.

A new tax collected on sellers shifts the supply curve to the left. The intersection of S_{0+tax} and D_0 determines the price consumers pay, P_C. P_S is the price sellers receive. The difference between P_C and P_S is the tax per unit.

The tax created a deadweight loss shown in gray, along with a reduction in consumer surplus (*CS*) and producer surplus (*PS*). The government collects tax revenue shown as the area in blue.

price elasticity of demand, p. 108
elastic demand, p. 109
inelastic demand, p. 110
unitary elastic demand, p. 110
total revenue, p. 114
cross elasticity of demand, p. 117
substitutes, p. 117
complements, p. 117

income elasticity of demand, p. 117
normal goods, p. 117
luxury goods, p. 117
inferior goods, p. 117
price elasticity of supply, p. 119
elastic supply, p. 119
inelastic supply, p. 119
unitary elastic supply, p. 119

market period, p. 120
short run, p. 121
long run, p. 121
progressive tax, p. 123
flat tax, p. 123
regressive tax, p. 123
lump-sum tax, p. 123
incidence of taxation, p. 123

QUESTIONS AND PROBLEMS

Check Your Understanding

1. When the demand curve is relatively inelastic and the price falls, what happens to total revenue? If the demand is relatively elastic and price rises, what happens to total revenue?

2. Why is the demand for gasoline relatively inelastic, while the demand for Exxon's gasoline is relatively elastic?

3. Describe cross elasticity of demand. Why do substitutes have positive cross elasticities? Describe income elasticity of demand. What is the difference between normal and inferior goods?

4. Describe the impact of time on the price elasticity of supply.

5. Why would the demand for business airline travel be less elastic than the demand for vacation airline travel by retirees?

6. Would an excise tax placed on cereal be more likely or less likely to be passed on to consumers than an excise tax on wireless phone and data services? Why or why not?

Apply the Concepts

7. One major rationale for farm price supports is that rapidly improving technology, better crop strains, improved fertilizer, and better farming methods increased supply so significantly that farm incomes were severely depressed. Explain how the elasticity of demand for these crops influences this rationale.

8. If the price of chicken rises by 15% and the sales of turkey breasts expand by 10%, what is the cross elasticity of demand for these two products? Are they complements or substitutes?

9. For which of the following pairs of goods or services would the cross elasticity of demand be negative? (a) Uber and Yellow Cab, (b) movie streaming subscriptions and tablets, (c) camping tents and camping permits, (d) bowling and co-ed softball, (e) textbooks and study guides.

10. Consider chip plants: potato and computer. Assume there is a large rise in the demand for computer chips and potato chips.

    a. How responsive to demand is each in the market period?

    b. Describe what a manufacturer of each product might do in the short run to increase production.

    c. How does the long run differ for these products?

11. If one automobile brand has an income elasticity of demand of 1.5 and another has an income elasticity equal to −0.3, what would account for the difference? Give an example of a specific brand for each type of car.

12. Suppose you estimated the cross elasticities of demand for three pairs of products and came up with the following three values: 2.3, 0.1, −1.7. What could you conclude

about these three pairs of products? If you wanted to know if two products from two different firms competed with each other in the marketplace, what would you look for?

In The News

13. In September 2015 Turing Pharmaceuticals decided to increase the price of the drug Daraprim, which is used to treat a life-threatening parasitic infection. Unlike typical price increases that never make the evening news, Turing raised the price from $13.50 per dose to $750 per dose, representing an increase of over 50 times the price. Turing's CEO Martin Shkreli argued that the extreme price increase was justified based on market demand and the fact that the drug does save lives. How would you describe the elasticity of Daraprim? For practically any other business that chooses to raise its price by 50 times, the business would surely lose most if not all of its customers. Why is Turing still in business? How would the elasticity of Daraprim change if there were generic versions of the drug offered by other companies?

14. The market for organic and locally sourced foods has skyrocketed over the past decade as consumers focus on improving their eating habits. However, severe droughts have caused organic food prices to rise significantly, forcing many consumers to shop at conventional supermarkets (which are increasingly adding organic food options) instead of organic food markets such as Whole Foods. In response, companies such as Whole Foods have begun offering more nonorganic options on their store shelves in order to provide their consumers with more affordable options. Based on this response, what did companies such as Whole Foods realize about the elasticity of demand for organic foods that caused them to lower their prices by changing the type of foods they sell?

Solving Problems

WORK IT OUT **LaunchPad** | interactive activity

15. Rising peanut prices have forced peanut butter makers to raise the price of peanut butter from $2 to $3 per jar, causing quantity demanded to fall. In addition, sales of jelly also dropped by 15%. Soon thereafter, makers of chocolate spread dropped its price from $4 to $3 per jar. This resulted in a further decline in peanut butter sales by 20%.

a. What is the cross elasticity of demand between peanut butter and jelly (use the midpoint method)? Are these two products complements or substitutes?

b. What is the cross elasticity of demand between peanut butter and chocolate spread (use the midpoint method)? Are these two products complements or substitutes?

16. Suppose the demand and supply for imported *wagyu* beef is as shown in the figure. Now assume that the U.S. government imposes an import tax of $10 per pound on *wagyu* beef.

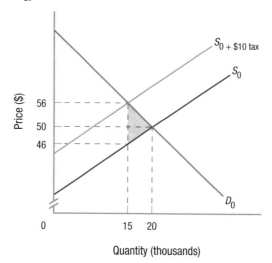

a. How does the market price change with the imposition of the $10 per pound tax?

b. Do the buyers or sellers of *wagyu* beef bear the greater burden of the tax?

c. How much tax revenue does the government collect from this market?

d. Calculate the approximate value of deadweight loss created in this market from the tax.

USING THE NUMBERS

17. According to By the Numbers, how much greater is the elasticity of demand for food in Canada than in the United States? How about Mexico compared to the United States?

18. According to By the Numbers, rank the types of alternative fuel vehicles in use from the most popular to the least popular.

ANSWERS TO QUESTIONS IN CHECKPOINTS

Checkpoint: Elasticity of Demand 113

Gasoline is inelastic in the short-term because it is difficult to switch quickly to more fuel-efficient options. In the long-term, one can buy a more fuel-efficient car or move closer to work or to public transportation, allowing one to be more responsive to prices. Automobiles, however, tend to have the opposite effect. When prices of cars increase, consumers might keep their existing cars longer (an elastic response). In the long-term, however, older cars become more costly to maintain, and consumers would more likely buy a new car despite the higher prices (an inelastic response).

Checkpoint: Total Revenue and Other Measures of Elasticity 119

Store 1 has an elastic demand for its clothes, while store 2 faces an inelastic demand. Look back at Table 2.

Checkpoint: Elasticity of Supply 122

Although these rankings can be subjective, the most likely rank from most elastic to least elastic is: chicken soup, boxes of tissue, over-the-counter flu remedies, flu shots (generally requires over six months to produce, giving it the least flexibility in response to a price change for the current flu season).

Checkpoint: Taxes and Elasticity 128

They all appear to have relatively inelastic demands. This reduces the impact of taxes on the industries and leads to higher tax revenues.

6

Consumer Choice and Demand

Understanding how consumers make choices to maximize their well-being given the resource constraints they face

Learning Objectives

6.1 Use a budget line to determine the constraints on consumer choices.

6.2 Determine how budget lines change when prices or income changes.

6.3 Describe the difference between total and marginal utility.

6.4 Explain the law of diminishing marginal utility.

6.5 Define the utility maximization rule and explain how it optimizes consumption given a budget.

6.6 Equate the marginal utility per dollar between two or more goods.

6.7 Explain why individuals sometimes make irrational decisions in predictable ways.

6.8 Describe five psychological factors that influence economic decision making.

Each day, virtually every person makes consumption choices, whether that means going to the mall to buy a new outfit, to a restaurant to dine with friends, or to the supermarket to stock up on groceries. The consumption choices that people make form what we have described as demand. But how do consumers make these choices? One of the important lessons from prior chapters is that individuals aim to maximize their well-being given a limited amount of resources.

In order to make consumption choices, individuals must first determine what choices of goods and services are affordable given their budget. Although we naturally think of income as the primary determinant of what can be afforded, prices also play a key role. Think of how a sale at a department store increases the amount of goods we can buy, or how higher energy prices restrict what we can spend on other goods. Once we know what we can afford, the next question is then how to allocate budgets to maximize our well-being.

The process by which individuals choose goods and services to maximize their overall happiness can be tricky to analyze. The main reason is that demand analysis rests on an important assumption: People are rational decision makers. Do people always act rationally? Of course not. You might spend more money eating out than you had wanted because your friends convinced you to go, which then caused you to give up buying a new shirt that would have given you more satisfaction. In these situations, individuals often come to realize that money is not always spent in the optimal manner; if it were, we would never regret the spontaneous purchases we make.

The fact that individuals sometimes make irrational decisions makes the analysis of consumer choice difficult to predict. However, a number of economists, called behavioralists, have been studying certain situations in which people make irrational decisions. What these economists have found is that although the decisions we make may sometimes appear irrational, they are irrational in *predictable* ways. For example, after paying $100 to enter a theme park only to find it crowded and unbearably hot, would you be reluctant to leave right away? Or, a person attempting to start a diet program may purchase a long-term plan given an optimistic anticipation of completing the program, only to give up after a few months. These examples illustrate how psychological factors influence our consumption choices in ways that lead to decisions economists would view as irrational.

Although this work on the irrational is important, it does not discredit the assumption that people choose rationally. If there were a preponderance of irrationality, society would come to a halt because we could not predict anything. What pedestrian would cross the street even if the light said "walk" if there was a modicum of fear that drivers would act irrationally and ignore a red light? People *do* miss or ignore red lights, but not often.

So we are left with an underlying assumption of rational decision making that is not bedrock, but is reasonable and powerful nonetheless. In this chapter, we are going to see what lies behind demand curves by looking at how consumers choose. In the next chapter, we will examine what lies behind supply curves by looking at how producers choose to produce what they do.

How Do We Decide What to Buy?

Each day, we make economic decisions on what to buy, what to eat, and how to allocate our limited time. Although marginal utility analysis can guide us into making rational decisions, behavioral economic factors play an important role as well.

The average distribution of U.S. household budgets on various expenditure components in 2014, along with trends in selected components from 2012 to 2014.

The By the Numbers — Do It Yourself! Lab Activity will explore expenditures of U.S. households.

Go to **LaunchPad** *to use the latest data to recreate this graph.*

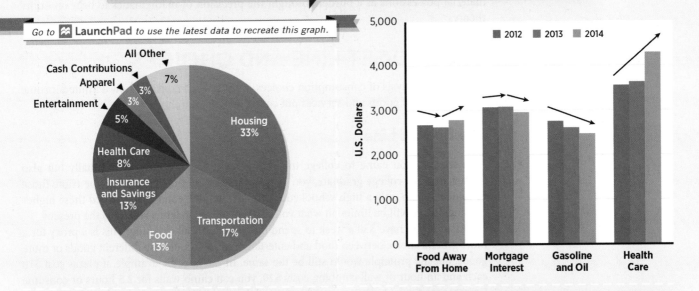

Pie chart: Household budget distribution
- Housing 33%
- Transportation 17%
- Food 13%
- Insurance and Savings 13%
- Health Care 8%
- Entertainment 5%
- Apparel 3%
- Cash Contributions 3%
- All Other 7%

Bar chart (2012, 2013, 2014), U.S. Dollars:
- Food Away From Home
- Mortgage Interest
- Gasoline and Oil
- Health Care

Total number of passenger vehicles registered in the United States in 2013 (1 car for every 1.2 persons).

255,876,822

Total amount of charitable giving by Americans in 2014 (over $1,100 per person).

$358,380,000,000

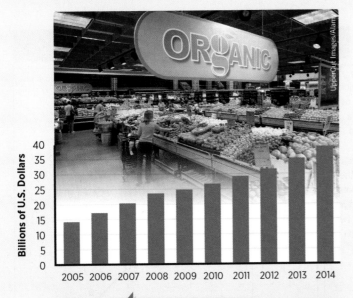

As preferences for organic foods increase, more supermarket chains respond, leading to rising sales of organic foods.

Player jerseys represent the largest component of the $3 billion annual NBA product market. The top selling jerseys in the 2014–2015 season were:

1. **LeBron James**, Cleveland Cavaliers
2. **Stephen Curry**, Golden State Warriors
3. **Kobe Bryant**, Los Angeles Lakers
4. **Kevin Durant**, Oklahoma City Thunder
5. **Derrick Rose**, Chicago Bulls

There are two major ways to approach consumer choice. The first theory explaining what people choose to buy, given their limited incomes, is known as *utility theory* or *utilitarianism,* and owes its roots to the work of 18th-century philosopher Jeremy Bentham. This theory holds that rational consumers will allocate their limited incomes so as to maximize their happiness or satisfaction.

The second approach, *indifference curve analysis,* is covered in the Appendix. Developed by Francis Ysidro Edgeworth in the late 19th century, it added analytical rigor to utility analysis by developing *indifference curves,* which portray combinations of two goods of equal total utility. Edgeworth, a shy man who studied in public libraries because he saw material possessions as a burden, brought the precision of mathematics to bear on utility theory.

THE BUDGET LINE AND CHOICES

To begin an analysis of consumption choices, we first must consider how a limited income and the prices of goods and services put constraints on our choices.

The Budget Line

As a student, you came to college to improve your life not only intellectually but also financially. As a college graduate, you can expect your lifetime earnings to be triple those of someone with only a high school education. Even once you have achieved these higher earnings, there will be limits on what you can buy. But first, let us return to the present.

Assume you have $50 a week to spend on pizza and wall climbing. This is a proxy for a more general choice between food and entertainment. We could use different goods or more goods, but the principle would still be the same. In our specific example, if pizzas cost $10 each and an hour of wall climbing costs $20, you can climb walls for 2.5 hours or consume 5 pizzas each week, or do some combination of these two. Your options are plotted in Figure 1.

This **budget line** (constraint) is a lot like the production possibilities frontier (PPF) discussed in Chapter 2. Although you might prefer to have more of both goods, you are limited to consumption choices lying on the budget line, or inside the budget line if you want to save any part of your $50 weekly budget. As with the PPF, however, any points to the right of the line are unattainable for you—they exceed your available income.

budget line A line that graphically illustrates the possible combinations of two goods that can be purchased with a given income, given the prices of both goods.

FIGURE 1	THE BUDGET CONSTRAINT OR LINE

When pizzas cost $10 each, wall climbing costs $20 per hour, and you have $50 a week to spend, you could buy 5 pizzas per week, 2.5 hours of wall climbing, or some combination of the two. The budget line makes clear all of the possible purchasing combinations of two products given a particular budget.

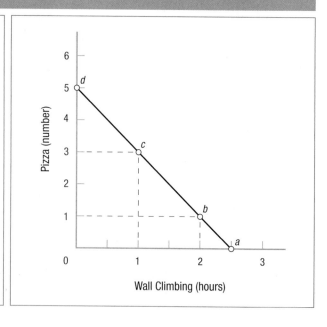

In this example, the budget line makes clear that many different combinations of wall climbing and pizzas will exhaust your $50 budget. But which of these possible combinations will you select? That depends on your personal preferences. If you love pizza, you will probably make different choices than if you are a fitness fanatic who rarely consumes fatty foods. Your own preferences determine how much pleasure you can expect to get from the various possible options. We study how optimal choices are made in the next section of this chapter.

Changes to the Budget Line

The budget line, like most money matters, is subject to changes in the prices of goods or changes in income. When the price of a good or income changes, the combinations of goods that become affordable change as well. Let's look at how the budget line changes.

Changes to the Price of a Good Suppose the wall-climbing establishment offers a half-price discount to college students, reducing the price of wall climbing from $20 to $10 per hour. Figure 2 illustrates what happens when the price of wall climbing changes as the price of pizza stays the same. Notice that the vertical intercept remains at 5 pizzas; because the price of pizza did not change, the total number of pizzas that can be purchased for $50 is still 5. However, the reduction in the price of wall climbing allows the total number of hours that can be purchased to increase from 2.5 to 5. In Figure 2, the budget line pivots outward to budget line *b*, which opens up many more combinations of pizza and wall climbing that previously were unaffordable.

Notice that in this case it is possible for a person to actually consume *more* of both pizza and wall climbing, even though the price of pizza did not change, nor did the income of $50. Suppose that originally you would spend the entire $50 on wall climbing, purchasing 2.5 hours. Because the price is now $10, the new cost of maintaining the same purchase of 2.5 hours is $25, leaving $25 to use on *either* more wall climbing or pizza, or both. Even though your actual income did not change, you can now purchase more than you could before, as if you had a higher income. This is true for any point along the original budget line except for the one point at which the entire budget was spent on pizza. Only in this case does the fall in price of wall climbing not increase the number of pizzas that can be purchased.

Now suppose that instead of a discount on wall climbing, the gym decides to raise the price to $25. How would this affect the budget line? It pivots inward. In Figure 2, budget

FIGURE 2	CHANGES IN PRICE ON A BUDGET LINE

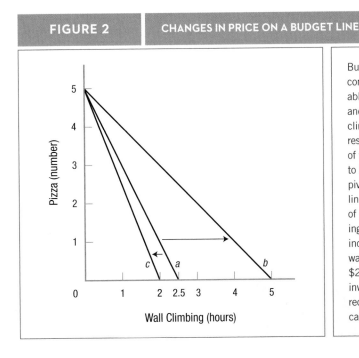

Budget line *a* shows the consumption choices available with a budget of $50 and prices of pizza and wall climbing at $10 and $20, respectively. When the price of wall climbing decreases to $10, the budget line pivots outward to budget line *b*. The combinations of pizza and wall climbing that can be purchased increase. When the price of wall climbing increases to $25, the budget line pivots inward to budget line *c*, reducing the amounts that can be purchased.

| FIGURE 3 | CHANGES IN INCOME ON A BUDGET LINE |

Budget line *a* shows the consumption choices available with a budget of $50 and prices of pizza and wall climbing at $10 and $20, respectively. When the budget increases to $100, the budget line shifts parallel outward to budget line *b*, doubling the quantities that can be purchased. When the budget falls to $20, the budget line shifts inward to budget line *c*, reducing the amounts that can be purchased.

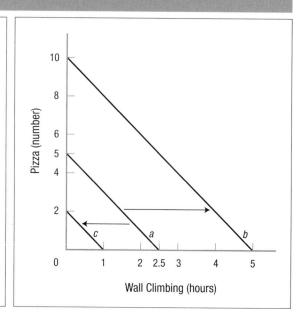

line *c* shows the maximum quantity of wall climbing decreasing to two hours. The increase in price reduces the combinations of both pizza and wall climbing that can be purchased with $50.

Changes to Income We now know that changes in the price of a good will pivot the budget line inward or outward along the axis for that good. But what if income itself changes? Suppose that prices of pizza and wall climbing remain at $10 and $20, respectively, but you are given extra money by your parents, allowing you to increase your food and entertainment budget to $100 per week. Figure 3 illustrates how an increase in income shifts your budget line outward to budget line *b* in a parallel fashion. Because $100 is double the original income, you can now afford twice as many pizzas and wall climbing hours as before as long as prices do not change. Budget line *b* shows that the maximum quantity of pizza that can be purchased increases to 10 and the maximum quantity of climbing hours increases to 5.

Similar to price changes, we can analyze the effect of a decrease in income on the budget line as well. Suppose increased expenses elsewhere force you to cut back on entertainment spending from $50 to $20 per week. Figure 3 shows how the reduced income shifts the budget line parallel inward to budget line *c*.

Now that we have analyzed how budget lines determine what we can afford, we must answer the important question of what combination of goods and services results in the highest satisfaction. One approach is to use marginal utility analysis, which we turn to next.

> A decrease in the price of a good that you typically buy has the same effect as an increase in income. In both cases, your budget line expands outward, allowing for more consumption choices.

Ron Zmiri/AGE fotostock

CHECKPOINT

THE BUDGET LINE AND CHOICES

- The budget line graphically illustrates the limits on purchases for a given income (budget).
- Changes in the price of a good cause the budget line to pivot inward or outward, affecting the combinations of goods that can be afforded.
- When the price of one good decreases, perceived income increases, allowing one to purchase more of both goods.
- Changes in income (budget) cause a parallel shift of the budget line.

QUESTION: Suppose that each week you eat ten meals on campus at $7.50 each and five meals off campus at $15 each. What is your total spending on meals? Suppose the price of off-campus meals decreases to $10. Explain how you can eat more meals in both locations (on campus and off campus), even though the price of on-campus meals stayed the same.

Answers to the Checkpoint questions can be found at the end of this chapter.

MARGINAL UTILITY ANALYSIS

The previous section showed how our choices of goods and services are limited to what we can afford given a budget. Similar to how PPFs showed the maximum output an economy can produce, budget lines show the maximum quantity of goods (in various combinations) that can be purchased. And like PPF analysis, an individual is able to select a point on the budget line that would maximize one's satisfaction. But which point would accomplish this goal?

To answer this question, we need to determine which combination of goods and services results in the highest level of satisfaction. Solving this riddle of consumer behavior can be accomplished using **marginal utility analysis.** Let's begin by defining preferences and utility, and then discuss how marginal utility analysis allows a person to maximize his or her well-being.

marginal utility analysis A theoretical framework underlying consumer decision making. This approach assumes that satisfaction can be measured and that consumers maximize satisfaction when the marginal utilities per dollar are equal for all products and services.

JEREMY BENTHAM (1748–1832)

Jeremy Bentham was a social philosopher, legal reformer, and writer who founded the philosophy known as utilitarianism. As an economic theorist, his most valuable contribution was the idea of *utility,* which explained consumer choices in terms of maximizing pleasure and minimizing pain.

Born in 1748, Bentham was the son of a wealthy lawyer. At age 12, he entered Oxford University, then studied for the bar although he decided not to practice law. Instead, he pursued a life of writing and thinking, with his primary contribution analyzing the notion of utility as a driving force in social and economic behavior. Bentham believed that the aim of society and government should be to maximize utility, or to promote the "greatest happiness for the greatest number." In 1789 he published his most famous work, *Introduction to the Principles of Morals,* which laid out his utilitarian philosophy. Bentham believed it was possible to derive a "Felicific Calculus" to compare the various pleasures or pains.

Although modern economists have cast doubt on the notion that utility could be measured or calculated, Bentham had many ideas that were ahead of his time, including the notion of cost-benefit analysis, which logically followed from his utilitarian views on government policies. Bentham also formulated the contemporary notion of marginal utility. After reading this chapter, it will be hard for you to avoid thinking in Bentham's terms about your own consumption choices, and you'll find yourself asking questions such as, "Do I really get $12 worth of satisfaction out of a Coke and popcorn at the movies, or do I have better alternatives for that money?"

Preferences and Utility

utility A hypothetical measure of consumer satisfaction.

Utility is a hypothetical measure of consumer satisfaction. It was introduced by early economists attempting to explain how consumers make decisions. The utilitarian theory of consumer behavior assumes, first of all, that utility is something that *can* be measured. Returning to our example from the previous section, the theory assumes that we can quantify the utility (satisfaction) you derive from consuming one or more pizzas, and how much utility you derive from spending one or more hours on the climbing wall. Table 1 provides estimates of the utility you derive from both pizzas and wall climbing, measured in *utils,* hypothetical units of satisfaction or utility. Compare columns (1) and (2) with columns (4) and (5).

At first glance, it might seem that if you wanted to maximize your utility given your $50 budget, you would simply go wall climbing for 2.5 hours, thereby maximizing your total utility at 270 utils. If you spent a little time analyzing the table, you would notice that combinations give you more total utility. If you went wall climbing for 2 hours and had 1 pizza (again spending your entire $50 budget), your total utility would be 330 utils (260 + 70 = 330), much more than concentrating on one item alone.

Other than trial and error, how do we determine the best combination? Before we can see just which combination of these two goods would actually bring you the most happiness, we need to distinguish between *total utility* and *marginal utility.*

Total and Marginal Utility

Total utility is the total satisfaction that a person receives from consuming a given quantity of goods and services. In Table 1, the total utility received from consuming 3 pizzas is 180 utils, whereas the total utility from 4 pizzas is 220 utils. Marginal utility is something different.

total utility The total satisfaction that a person receives from consuming a given amount of goods and services.

marginal utility The additional satisfaction received from consuming one more unit of a given product or service.

Marginal utility is the additional satisfaction derived from consuming *one more unit* of a given product or service. It is determined by taking the difference between the total utility derived from, say, consuming 4 pizzas and consuming 3 pizzas. The total utility derived from 4 pizzas is 220 utils, and that from 3 pizzas is 180 utils. Therefore, consuming the fourth pizza yields only an additional 40 utils of satisfaction (220 − 180 = 40 utils).

The marginal utility for both pizza eating and wall climbing is listed in Table 1. Notice that as we move from one quantity of pizza to the next, total utility rises by an amount exactly equal to marginal utility. This is no coincidence. Marginal utility is nothing but the change in total utility obtained from consuming one more pizza (the marginal pizza); therefore, as pizza eating increases by 1 pizza, total utility will rise by the amount of additional satisfaction derived from consuming that additional pizza. Also note that, for both pizzas and wall climbing, marginal utility declines as more of a particular product or activity is consumed.

TABLE 1	TOTAL AND MARGINAL UTILITY FROM PIZZAS AND WALL CLIMBING				
	Pizza			**Wall Climbing**	
(1) Quantity	(2) Total Utility	(3) Marginal Utility	(4) Quantity	(5) Total Utility	(6) Marginal Utility
0	0	—	0.0	0	—
1	70	70	0.5	90	90
2	130	60	1.0	170	80
3	180	50	1.5	230	60
4	220	40	2.0	260	30
5	250	30	2.5	270	10

The Law of Diminishing Marginal Utility Why does marginal utility decline as the consumption of one product or activity increases? No matter our personal tastes and preferences, we eventually become sated once we have consumed a certain amount of any given commodity. Most of us love ice cream. As youngsters, some of us imagined a world in which meals consisted of nothing but ice cream—no casseroles, no vegetables, just ice cream. To children this might sound heavenly, but as adults, we recognize that we would quickly grow sick of ice cream. Human beings simply crave diversity; we quickly tire of the same product or service if we consume it day after day.

This fact of human nature led early economists to formulate the **law of diminishing marginal utility.** This law states that as we consume more of a product, the rate at which our total satisfaction increases with the consumption of each additional unit will decline. And if we continue to consume still more of the product after that, our total satisfaction will eventually begin to decline.

This principle is illustrated by Figure 4, which graphs the total utility and marginal utility for pizza eating, as listed in Table 1. Notice that total utility, graphed in panel A, rises continually as we move from 1 pizza per week to 5 pizzas. Nevertheless, the rate of this increase declines as more pizzas are consumed. Accordingly, panel B shows that marginal utility declines with more pizzas eaten. On your student budget, you could not afford any more than 5 pizzas a week, but we can imagine that if you were to keep eating pizzas—20 pizzas in a week—your total utility would actually start to drop with each additional pizza. At some point, it simply hurts to stuff down any more pizzas.

It is one thing to grasp the obvious fact that consumers have limited budgets and that the products they can choose among provide them increasing satisfaction but are subject to diminishing marginal utility. It is another thing to figure out exactly how consumers allocate their limited funds so as to maximize their total level of satisfaction or utility. We now turn our attention to how early economists solved the problem of maximizing utility and the analytic methods that resulted from their work.

Maximizing Utility Let's take a moment to review everything we need to know to plot the budget line in Figure 1: your total income and the prices of all the products you could purchase. In our example, the weekly budget is $50, pizzas cost $10 apiece, and wall climbing is $20 per hour or $10 per half-hour. This is enough information to plot all of the options available to you.

Given these options, how do individuals maximize their total utility from consuming various combinations of goods? Knowing the marginal utility of each unit of a good consumed is not enough. Surely, the marginal utility of a new car is greater than the marginal utility of a cup of coffee. But the price of the car is also much greater than the price of coffee. The ability to maximize utility given a fixed budget requires us to compare the marginal utilities *per dollar* spent on each good.

Take a look at columns (4) and (8) of Table 2. These two columns express the marginal utilities of pizzas and wall climbing, respectively, in terms of marginal utility per dollar; these amounts are computed by dividing the marginal utility of each product by the product's price.

To see the importance of computing marginal utility per dollar, consider the following. Given the figures in columns (4) and (8), and assuming you want to get the most for your money, on which activity would you spend the first $10 of your weekly budget? You can spend the first $10 on a pizza or on a half-hour of wall climbing. A pizza returns 70 utils of satisfaction, whereas a half-hour of wall climbing yields 90 utils. Since 90 is greater than 70, clearly the first $10 would be better spent on wall climbing.

Now, for the sake of simplicity, let's keep your spending increments constant. On what will you spend your next $10—pizza or climbing? Look again at the table. Your first pizza still gives you 70 utils, while the second half-hour of wall climbing returns 80 utils. Wall climbing again is the obvious choice. If your total budget had only been $20 per week, you would have been inclined to give up pizzas completely.

Mega buffets in Las Vegas draw millions of diners each year. Diminishing marginal utility from each additional plate of food keeps the amount of food consumed by each diner at a reasonable level.

Eric Chiang

law of diminishing marginal utility
As we consume more of a given product, the added satisfaction we get from consuming an additional unit declines.

FIGURE 4   TOTAL AND MARGINAL UTILITY FOR PIZZA

Total utility, graphed in panel A, rises continually as we move from 1 pizza per week to 5. Nevertheless, the rate of this increase declines as more pizzas are consumed. Accordingly, panel B shows that marginal utility declines with more pizzas eaten.

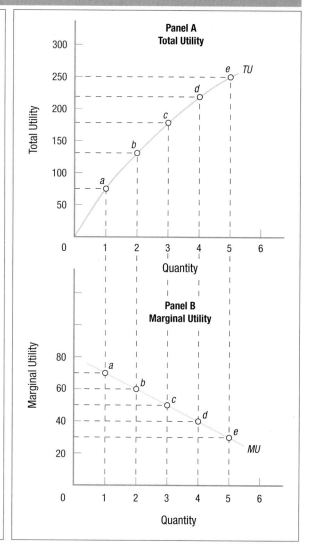

TABLE 2   TOTAL AND MARGINAL UTILITY PER DOLLAR FROM PIZZAS AND WALL CLIMBING

Pizza				Wall Climbing			
(1) Quantity (units of pizza)	(2) Total Utility	(3) Marginal Utility	(4) Marginal Utility per Dollar (price = $10)	(5) Quantity (hours of wall climbing)	(6) Total Utility	(7) Marginal Utility	(8) Marginal Utility per Dollar (price = $10 per half-hour)
0	0	—	—	0.0	0	—	—
1	70	70	7	0.5	90	90	9
2	130	60	6	1.0	170	80	8
3	180	50	5	1.5	230	60	6
4	220	40	4	2.0	260	30	3
5	250	30	3	2.5	270	10	1

Proceeding in the same way, using your third $10 to buy your first pizza will yield an additional 70 utils of satisfaction, whereas using this money to purchase a third half-hour of wall climbing will bring only 60 utils. (Wall climbing is starting to get a bit boring.) Thus, because 70 is greater than 60, with your third $10 you buy your first pizza.

The next $10 provides the same amount of utility (60 utils) regardless of whether you buy another pizza or another half-hour of wall climbing. Therefore, you split the remaining $20 of your budget evenly between these two activities. When the consumption of additional units of two products provides equal satisfaction, economists say consumers are *indifferent* to which product they consume first.

By following this incremental process, we have determined that you will spend your $50 on 2 pizzas ($20) and 1.5 hours of wall climbing ($30). This results in a total utility of 360 utils (130 for pizza and 230 for wall climbing). This level is shown as the shaded row of Table 2. *No other combination of pizzas and wall climbing will result in total satisfaction this high,* as you can prove to yourself by trying to spend the $50 differently.

Note also that for the last 2 units of each product consumed, the marginal utilities per dollar were equal at 6. This result is to be expected. Simple logic tells us that if one activity yields more satisfaction per dollar than some other, you will continue to pursue the activity with the higher satisfaction per dollar until some other activity starts yielding more satisfaction. This observation leads to a simple rule for maximizing utility: You should allocate your budget so that the marginal utility per last dollar spent on each of your purchases is the same. This **utility-maximizing rule,** in turn, leads to the following equation, where MU = marginal utility and P = price.

utility-maximizing rule Total utility is maximized where the marginal utility per dollar is equal for all products, or $MU_a/P_a = MU_b/P_b = \cdots = MU_n/P_n$.

$$\frac{MU_{\text{Pizza}}}{P_{\text{Pizza}}} = \frac{MU_{\text{Wall Climbing}}}{P_{\text{Wall Climbing}}}$$

This equation and the analyses described earlier can be generalized to cover numerous goods and services. For all goods and services $a, b, \ldots n$:

$$\frac{MU_a}{P_a} = \frac{MU_b}{P_b} = \cdots = \frac{MU_n}{P_n}$$

The important point to remember is that, according to this theory of consumer behavior, consumers approach every purchase by asking themselves which of all possible additional acts of consumption would bring them the most satisfaction per dollar.

You have seen how the marginal utility analysis of consumer behavior works when we assume that satisfaction or well-being can be measured directly (in utils). We can now use this theory of consumer behavior to derive the demand curve for wall climbing.

Deriving Demand Curves

We know that consumers will maximize their utility by spending each dollar of their limited budgets on the goods and services yielding the highest marginal utility per dollar. In our previous example, with pizzas costing $10 each and an hour of wall climbing costing $20, this meant you bought 2 pizzas and 1.5 hours of wall climbing. Would your consumption choices change if these prices changed? Let us consider what happens when the cost of wall climbing increases to $30 per hour.

Now that wall climbing costs $30 per hour or $15 per half-hour, column (8) of Table 3 has been altered to reflect this new rate for wall climbing. The first half-hour of climbing yields 90 utils and now costs $15, so each dollar yields 6 utils. Now your first $10 will be spent on a pizza ($MU/P = 7$ for pizza versus $MU/P = 6$ for wall climbing).

The next $25 is split between another pizza ($10) and a half-hour of wall climbing ($15) because $MU/P = 6$ for both. Your final $15 is spent on wall climbing because its marginal utility per dollar (5.33) is higher than for a third pizza (5).

Thus, your final allocation is 2 pizzas and 1 hour of wall climbing. Clearly, consumer choices respond to changes in product prices. With wall climbing at $20 per hour, you consumed 1.5 hours of climbing and 2 pizzas. When the price of wall climbing rose to

TABLE 3	TOTAL AND MARGINAL UTILITY PER DOLLAR FROM PIZZAS AND WALL CLIMBING (PRICE OF WALL CLIMBING INCREASES TO $30 PER HOUR OR $15 PER HALF-HOUR)						
Pizza				**Wall Climbing**			
(1) Quantity (units of pizza)	(2) Total Utility	(3) Marginal Utility	(4) Marginal Utility per Dollar (price = $10)	(5) Quantity (hours of wall climbing)	(6) Total Utility	(7) Marginal Utility	(8) Marginal Utility per Dollar (price = $15 per half-hour)
0	0	—	—	0.0	0	—	—
1	70	70	7	0.5	90	90	6.00
2	130	60	6	1.0	170	80	5.33
3	180	50	5	1.5	230	60	4.00
4	220	40	4	2.0	260	30	2.00
5	250	30	3	2.5	270	10	0.67

$30 per hour, you altered your consumption. Now, instead of 1.5 hours and 2 pizzas, you consume 1 hour and 2 pizzas. This new level is shown in the shaded row of Table 3.

Figure 5 plots both your budget constraint and your demand for wall climbing based on the results of Tables 2 and 3. Panel A shows the effect of increasing the price of wall climbing from $20 to $30 per hour. At the increased price of wall climbing, if you were to spend your entire budget on this activity, you could only climb for 1.67 hours ($50/$30 = 1.67). This price increase rotates the budget line leftward, reducing your consumption opportunities, as the figure illustrates.

When the price of wall climbing was $20 per hour, you climbed for 1.5 hours (point *a* in both panels of Figure 5). When the price was increased to $30 per hour, marginal utility analysis led you to reduce your consumption of wall climbing to 1 hour (point *b* in both panels). Connecting these points in panel B of Figure 5 yields the demand curve for wall climbing.

Thus, the marginal utility theory of consumer behavior helps explain both how consumers allocate their income according to their personal preferences and the law of demand. Remember that the law of demand posited an inverse (negative) relationship between price and quantity demanded. This negative relationship is shown in panel B.

Limitations of Marginal Utility Analysis

Marginal utility analysis explains not only how consumers purchase goods and services but also how all household choices are made. We can analyze the decision of whether or not to get a job, for example, by comparing the marginal utility of work versus the marginal utility of leisure. As a college student, you are familiar with having many demands made on your time. More work means more money but less time for leisure, and vice versa. Marginal utility theory helps us to identify that point at which work and leisure (and hopefully study) balance out.

Although marginal utility theory is an elegant and logically consistent theory that helps us to understand how consumers behave, it does have some limitations. First, it assumes that consumers are able to measure the utility they derive from various sorts of consumption. Yet, this is virtually impossible in everyday life—how many utils do you get out of eating a bowl of ice cream? This is not to suggest that marginal utility theory is invalid. It

FIGURE 5

FIGURE 5 | **DERIVING THE DEMAND FOR WALL CLIMBING USING MARGINAL UTILITY ANALYSIS**

Panel A
Budget Lines

$wc = \$20/hour$

$wc = \$30/hour$

Panel B
The Demand for Wall Climbing

D_{wc}

With the price of wall climbing at $20 per hour, you climb for 1.5 hours (point *a* in both panels). When the price increases to $30 per hour, you reduce your consumption of wall climbing to 1 hour (point *b* in both panels). Connecting these points in panel B yields the demand curve for wall climbing.

simply requires one very restrictive assumption, that people are able to measure their satisfaction for every purchase.

Others have argued that it is absurd to think that we could carry out the mental calculus required to compare the ratios of marginal utility to price for all possible goods and services. This is no doubt true, but even if we do not compare all possible goods and services in this way, we do draw some comparisons. After all, we somehow need to be able to distinguish between the desirability of going to a movie or going to a concert, because we cannot do both at the same time. Marginal utility theory is still a good way of approaching this choice, in a general way.

Lastly, marginal utility analysis has been criticized for not fully explaining why individuals sometimes act irrationally, at least according to what economic models predict. Indeed, human psychology often plays games with rational thinking, leading individuals to make decisions that would seem to go against the goal of maximizing utility. This topic of behavioral economics, which studies how human psychology enters into economic behavior, is one that has become increasingly popular among economists in recent decades, and is the focus of the next section.

CHECKPOINT

MARGINAL UTILITY ANALYSIS

- Utility is a hypothetical measure of consumer satisfaction.
- Total utility is the total satisfaction a person obtains from consuming a specific amount of goods.
- Marginal utility is the additional satisfaction a consumer obtains from consuming one more unit of a good or service.
- The law of diminishing marginal utility states that as consumption of a specific good increases, the increase in total satisfaction will decline.
- Consumers maximize satisfaction by purchasing goods up to the point at which the marginal utility per dollar is equal for all goods.
- Demand curves for products can be derived from marginal utility analysis by changing the price of one good and plotting the resulting changes in consumption.

QUESTIONS: Even though convenience stores have significantly higher prices than normal grocery stores such as Safeway, they seem to do well, judging by their numbers. Why are people willing to pay these higher prices? If a Safeway began to operate 24/7, how would this affect the sales of a nearby convenience store?

Answers to the Checkpoint questions can be found at the end of this chapter.

BEHAVIORAL ECONOMICS

Up to this point, we generally have assumed that individuals make rational decisions that maximize their well-being. Yet, an increasing number of economists have devoted their attention to studying situations in which individuals *do not* appear to follow rational economic thinking, at least the behavior that economic models predict will result. This section turns our attention to the study of behavioral economics. **Behavioral economics** is the study of how human psychology enters into economic behavior as a way to explain why individuals sometimes act counter to how economic models predict.

All individuals from time to time make irrational decisions; that is part of human nature. An important point to keep in mind is that we are not analyzing random behavior. Instead, behavioral economics looks at situations in which people act irrationally in *predictable* ways. This could be a big deal because it challenges the notion of economic rationality that we have assumed in our models. The fact that irrational behavior can occur in predictable ways means that clever people try to take advantage of this behavior. What psychological factors influence irrational behavior, and how do these factors translate into clever opportunism?

This section presents five important psychological factors influencing economic behavior: (1) sunk cost fallacy, (2) framing bias, (3) overconfidence, (4) overvaluing the present relative to the future, and (5) altruism. Each of these factors influences decisions we make every day. In fact, marketers of goods and services often exploit these factors in order to attract consumers to make purchases they otherwise might not make. Let's look at each factor and some common examples illustrating each concept.

Sunk Cost Fallacy

Suppose a few months ago you paid a registration fee of $200 to attend the Comic-Con to be held this weekend. The fee is not refundable or transferable to another person. Therefore, the $200 fee you paid is a **sunk cost,** a cost that has been paid and cannot be recovered. As the weekend approaches, you realize that you are extremely behind in your studies, so much so that going to the convention would likely take away the last bit of time to prepare for upcoming midterm exams.

You think to yourself, "If I would have known I'd be so busy with school, I wouldn't have paid $200 to register for the convention. But since I've already paid it, I'm certainly

behavioral economics The study of how human psychology enters into economic behavior as a way to explain why individuals sometimes act in predictable ways counter to economic models.

sunk cost A cost that has been paid and cannot be recovered; therefore, it should not enter into decision making affecting the present or future.

not going to let my money go to waste, so I'm going to go despite the potential consequences to my grades." Does this seem logical?

According to economic theory, it does not. Sunk costs are costs that cannot be undone. Therefore, the decision whether to attend should not hinge upon past payments, because the registration fee has already been paid. By incorporating sunk costs into present and future decisions, a **sunk cost fallacy** occurs as people make decisions based on how much was already spent rather than how the decision might affect their current well-being. In this case, because going to the convention may have consequences on your grades, the wise decision would be to forgo the convention. Either way, the money is already gone.

The sunk cost fallacy often appears in situations in which people feel that they have invested too much time or money into a project to quit. Another common example is the tuition paid for school, a sunk cost. Often, students who fail the midterm and have little hope of raising their grades are reluctant to withdraw from a class because they are unwilling to give up a class that is already paid for, instead hoping for a miracle (or a sympathetic professor) that the final grade will be a passing one. But often the result is a failing grade, which means not only do they need to retake the class (and pay for it once more), but worse, a failing grade appears on their transcript.

sunk cost fallacy Occurs when people make decisions based on how much was already spent, rather than how the decision might affect their current well-being.

Framing Bias

Does a price of $9.99 seem a lot different from $10.00? It really shouldn't, given the difference is one-tenth of 1%. Even more startling are prices displayed at most gas stations, which often show prices in tenths of a cent, such as 2.99^9 (the next time you pass by a gas station, notice the extra nine-tenths of a cent). Compared to $3.00, 2.99^9 is a difference of just one-thirtieth of 1%. Finally, does "Buy One Get One Half-Off" sound like a better deal than "25% off"? It might; however, if you buy two items with the same price, the total cost is the same under each deal.

In each of the preceding examples, the percentage difference between the two prices is zero or virtually zero. Yet, consumers tend to react differently to these prices, with the former being interpreted as a lower price than the latter, enough to influence buying decisions. This ability to influence consumer decisions by how prices are displayed is an example of a **framing bias,** which occurs when individuals are steered toward one choice over another by how those choices are portrayed. Framing techniques are used by marketers to increase sales of products without actually lowering the price.

Framing biases are not limited to pricing strategies. Much in the same way that firms steer consumers toward buying products using prices, a broad range of framing effects can be used to steer individuals toward one political candidate or one political issue over another, toward one product over another in advertising campaigns, and toward one policy over another in legislative debates.

Framing biases also occur when firms convince buyers that what they purchased is worth much more than what they paid. This type of strategy attempts to alter the perceptions of buyers into believing they are always receiving a great deal. Ever notice that some stores perpetually have sales of 10% to 20% off everything, or give money back in the form of gift cards for future visits? Wouldn't it be the same if a store just marks down the sticker prices of everything? Perhaps, but consumers tend to respond more positively to sales and other seemingly good offers.

framing bias Describes when individuals are steered into making one decision over another or are convinced they are receiving a higher value for a product than what was paid for it.

Getty Images News/Getty Images

The not-so-noticeable nine-tenths of a cent added to the price of a gallon of gasoline adds up to over $1 billion in revenue for gas stations each year.

Overconfidence

Feeling confident about one's abilities, attractiveness, or intellectual capacity is a trait often instilled from one's childhood. No doubt, self-esteem plays an important role in the success of many people. But overconfidence in one's abilities can have the opposite effect.

Watch the auditions of any reality talent show, and notice the pitchy, off-key singers who belt their hearts out as if they were on stage at the Grammy Awards, only to be brought back to reality by the harsh criticism of the judges. Being overconfident can lead to decisions that have consequences, such as picking the wrong stock in which to invest, spending too much time and effort applying to only the very top graduate school or law school, or turning down potential respectable boyfriends or girlfriends in hopes of a dream mate.

Wanting to feel confident about one's abilities and choices sometimes leads to decisions that run counter to economic theory, and marketers often take advantage of this factor. One- and two-year gym memberships offered for an attractive upfront prepaid price is a great deal for someone eager to lose weight and get in shape. But often such ambitions fall short, leading many gym memberships to go unused (with the money comfortably in the gym's bank account).

Overvaluing the Present Relative to the Future

It is often difficult to plan for the future. Money saved today can earn interest, and money invested in financial instruments and assets can increase in value over time. Despite the higher value of money in the future, it is still money one must give up using *today*. Therefore, people sometimes are reluctant to save for the future despite lucrative incentives such as retirement fund matching programs offered by employers.

The same is true for paying off debt. Paying the minimum payment on credit card balances seems easy, but accruing finance charges of 15% or more can put a severe crunch on finances in the future. Although differences in time preferences themselves are not irrational per se, because the future often appears so distant, it can blur the reasoning behind sound economic decisions. For example, a society's unwillingness to fully tackle climate change results from overvaluing present benefits relative to future costs.

Altruism

altruism Actions undertaken merely out of goodwill or generosity.

The last factor to be discussed is **altruism,** or actions undertaken merely out of goodwill or generosity. Buying a sandwich for a homeless person you will likely not see again, donating money to a charitable organization, or helping a tourist find his or her way to a hotel all are friendly gestures that do not provide any reward except for the positive feeling one receives from helping others.

Helping the community by volunteering one's time provides satisfaction that is not measured by monetary gains.

WireImage/Getty Images

ISSUE

Tipping and Consumer Behavior

If consumers maximize their utility with a given (limited) budget, why would they ever tip? Consider that tips come at the end of a meal. How can tips affect the quality of service already given?

Many reasons might explain tipping. First, if it is a restaurant you frequent, tips might assure better service in the future. Second, you might consider tips to be rewards for higher-quality service. Third, tipping is a custom and is part of the income for several dozen occupations.

What would happen if many people refused or neglected to tip? Would people in various occupations seek to make tipping legally binding? It is likely this

would be the result, if a recent case in New York is any guide. If you have ever gone to a restaurant with a large party, you will notice that menus and bills often state that a set tip will be added for large parties. One large party gave

a very small tip after what they considered to be inadequate service. The restaurant sued, claiming that an 18% tip was mandatory. The court's decision for the tipper turned on the phrasing in the menu. This could be viewed as a first shot: If too many people refuse to tip or tip poorly, we can expect legal redress.

We can establish, then, that tipping is a custom that leads to better service, and so is followed even though the tip comes after the service is performed. In this way, it seems to run counter to the idea of people tipping based on a calculation of marginal utility. And how much we tip raises questions about how we calculate marginal utility.

Economists have found only a weak statistical link between quality of service and size of the tip. Tipping also appears to be unrelated to the number of courses in the meal, and whether or not people intend to return to the restaurant. The accompanying table shows some of the things that do affect the size of the tip.

Obviously, a waiter or waitress cannot do all of these things and expect to see tips increase by the sum of all the percentages, but we all have experienced many of these techniques in restaurants. Interestingly, if a waitress draws a smiley face on the bill, her tips go up, but if a waiter does the same, his tips go down. Suggestive selling raises the tip because people tend to tip based on the size of the bill. After having read about this study, you probably will find yourself being a little cynical when some of these techniques are used the next time you dine out.

PERCENTAGE INCREASE IN TIPS FROM SPECIFIC BEHAVIOR BY WAITSTAFF

Tip-Enhancing Action	Change in Tip
Wearing a flower in hair	17%
Introducing yourself by name	53%
Squatting down next to the table	20%–25%
Repeating order back to customers	69%–100%
Suggestive selling	23%
Touching customer	22%–42%
Using tip trays with credit card insignia	22%–25%
Waitress drawing a smiley face on check	18%
Writing "thank you" on the check	13%

See Michael Lynn, *Mega Tips 2: Twenty Tested Techniques to Increase Your Tips*, 2011, p. 18.

Thus, altruistic behavior provides utility in the sense of feeling good about one's actions, even though the actions require resources (such as money, time, and effort) that will reduce one's ability to consume other items. Although altruism is generally not viewed as a *mistake,* it nonetheless represents a limitation of the rational choice model. And because altruistic behavior is so commonplace (such as the generosity of individuals in times of natural disasters, both within the country and abroad), economic models need to account for the utility gained from being generous. Yet, such feelings of goodwill are difficult to measure in economic models, which makes it a factor left to behavioral economists to take into account.

Each of the five factors described in this section adds to the discussion in the previous section that marginal utility analysis does not capture all circumstances of individual economic behavior. But it is important to note that these limitations and the behavioral factors are the exceptions to the rule; marginal utility analysis still plays an important role in how we live our daily lives.

Recognizing the validity of these criticisms, economists have tried to limit themselves to working with the sorts of data they can collect, in this case, purchases by individuals. By formulating hypotheses about what consumers purchase and what this says about their preferences, economists have managed to develop a theory of consumer behavior that does not require that utility be measured. This more modern approach to analyzing consumer behavior that reaches the same conclusions as marginal utility theory is known as *indifference curve analysis*. Because indifference curve analysis extends the discussion of consumer behavior beyond the principles of consumer choice, it is discussed in the Appendix.

What's Wrong With the 4th Floor? The Economic Influence of Superstitions

How do number superstitions vary across cultures and how do these affect the way consumers and businesses make economic decisions?

This elevator in Taipei, Taiwan (left), has a button for the 13th floor but not the 4th floor, while in Las Vegas (right), this elevator skips floors 40 to 49, which do not exist.

When entering an elevator in China or Japan, it's unlikely you will see a button for the 4th floor, while in the United States, it's rare to see a button for the 13th floor. International flight numbers to and from Beijing, Shanghai, and Tokyo often contain the number 8 and rarely a 4, while many flight numbers to and from Las Vegas contain the number 7. Is this all a coincidence? Hardly!

Number superstitions occur in nearly every society. In many Western countries, the number 7 is considered lucky, while the number 13 is considered unlucky. In many Eastern societies, however, 8 is a lucky number, while 4 is a very unlucky number. Why? When the number 4 is spoken in Chinese, Japanese, Korean, and Vietnamese, it sounds like the word "death" translated in each language.

In Eastern societies, number superstitions can be seen affecting everyday economic decisions. For example,

landlords often discount apartments located on the 4th floor even if that floor isn't called the 4th floor (after all, renters do know how to count floors), and some consumers will request a new phone number if assigned one containing the number 4. In some countries, it is possible to auction a lucky phone number containing many 8's and no 4's for a substantial profit.

The power of superstition in economic decisions can especially be seen in cities that thrive on "good fortune," such as Las Vegas. Why else

would the number 7 appear on many slot machines? And because Las Vegas gaming establishments serve a large Asian clientele, one might take notice of Eastern number superstitions as well. Steve Wynn, of Wynn Resorts, was the first major CEO in Las Vegas to address Asian superstitions by removing nearly all 4's from room numbers at the Bellagio Hotel (where he previously was CEO) and at all of his current hotels. An understanding of number superstitions can explain economic outcomes that might otherwise seem puzzling.

GO TO **LaunchPad** TO PRACTICE THE ECONOMIC CONCEPTS IN THIS STORY

✔ CHECKPOINT

BEHAVIORAL ECONOMICS

■ Behavioral economics involves incorporating human psychology into economic decision making to explain why individuals sometimes do not act according to what economic models predict.

■ Behavioral economics studies *predictable* deviations from rational behavior.

■ The sunk cost fallacy is a common mistake when individuals feel obligated to take sunk cost expenditures into account when making present and future decisions.

■ Framing biases occur when marketers present prices in a way that makes them appear lower than what they actually are.

■ Overconfidence, overvaluing the present relative to the future, and altruistic actions are other factors influencing economic behavior.

QUESTIONS: A practice in some supermarkets is to hang signs in the soup section that read "limit 12 per customer." Would our previous economic models predict that consumer behavior would change at all? How about behavioral economics? If it did, what deviation would this be?

Answers to the Checkpoint questions can be found at the end of this chapter.

chapter summary

Section 1
The Budget Line and Choices

6.1 A **budget line** shows all the combinations of two goods that can be purchased with a given income and given the prices of each good.

Example: Monthly workout budget = $100; price per wall climbing session = $20; price per racquetball session = $10.

6.2 Changes in Prices and Income (initial budget = $30; initial price of movie ticket and cover charge = $10 each)

If the cover charge falls by 50% and the price of movie tickets stays the same, the budget line pivots outward.

If the prices stay the same, but the budget doubles, the budget line shifts outward, expanding consumption choices.

Section 2 Marginal Utility Analysis

6.3 **Utility** is a hypothetical measure of satisfaction.

Total utility is the satisfaction a person receives from consuming a quantity of a good, while **marginal utility** is the additional satisfaction received from consuming *one more unit* of a good.

6.4 Wall climbing is fun, but climbing the same rock wall every time might make the experience less exciting over time due to the **law of diminishing marginal utility.**

6.5 **Where should one consume on the budget line?** The budget line shows what combinations are affordable, but not which point maximizes utility. The **utility maximization rule,** which says that utility is maximized when the marginal utility per dollar is equal across all goods, is used to determine the "best" combination.

Section 2 Marginal Utility Analysis (continued)

6.6 The **utility maximization rule** states that total utility is maximized when the marginal utility per dollar is equal for all products purchased:

$$\frac{MU_a}{P_a} = \frac{MU_b}{P_b} = \dots = \frac{MU_n}{P_n}$$

When this rule is not met, one should consume fewer goods providing smaller marginal utility per dollar and more goods providing larger marginal utility per dollar.

Lucas Tange/Corbis

Watching a boring movie is likely to provide very little utility, resulting in even smaller marginal utility per dollar spent at the cinema. Money in this case ought to have been spent on an activity providing greater marginal utility per dollar in order to maximize total utility.

Section 3 Behavioral Economics

6.7 **Behavioral economics** is the incorporation of human psychology into economic decision making to explain why individuals sometimes act differently from what economic models predict.

6.8 Psychological Factors Influencing Economic Decisions

- **Sunk cost fallacy:** occurs when individuals take sunk costs into account when making decisions about the present or future.

- **Framing bias:** occurs when individuals are steered toward making one decision over another, or when individuals are led to believe that they are getting a better deal than they actually are.

- **Overconfidence:** occurs when strong feelings of one's abilities lead to irrational decisions.

- **Overvaluing the present relative to the future:** occurs when future decisions appear too distant to be concerned about in the present, leading to irrational decisions.

- **Altruism:** occurs when feelings of goodwill lead individuals to make decisions that benefit others at the expense of their own consumption.

Corbis

Overconfidence in one's ability to select stocks may cause some to lose significant sums of money. Further, once losses in the stock market occur, traders are often reluctant to sell, and instead hold onto stocks as they potentially fall further in price, an example of the sunk cost fallacy.

budget line, p. 138
marginal utility analysis, p. 141
utility, p. 142
total utility, p. 142
marginal utility, p. 142

law of diminishing marginal
utility, p. 143
utility-maximizing rule, p. 145
behavioral economics, p. 148
sunk cost, p. 148

sunk cost fallacy, p. 149
framing bias, p. 149
altruism, p. 150

QUESTIONS AND PROBLEMS

Check Your Understanding

1. Using a budget line, why does a decrease in the price of a good allow one to potentially consume more of both goods?

2. Why do price changes cause a budget line to pivot, while income changes cause a budget line to shift in a parallel manner?

3. Describe the utility-maximizing rule. Explain why it makes sense.

4. What conditions are necessary for total utility to be positive, while marginal utility is negative?

5. Why should sunk costs not be taken into consideration when making decisions about the present or the future?

6. Why do the prices of many goods and services end in 99 cents? Why don't businesses just round to the nearest whole dollar?

Apply the Concepts

7. Scruffie the cat has $15 to spend each month on cat toys, which cost $3 each, and cat treats, which cost $1.50 each. Draw a budget line to show the combinations of each good that Scruffie can afford if she spends her entire budget. Now suppose that cat treats go on sale for $1 each. How does this change in price affect the budget line (describe and show on a graph)?

8. Eric enjoys having sushi and sashimi for lunch every day. Suppose the marginal utility of the last sushi roll Eric eats is 40 and the marginal utility of the last piece of sashimi Eric eats is 20. If the price of a roll of sushi is $8 and the price per piece of sashimi is $2, did Eric maximize his utility? Explain.

9. For most consumers, maximizing utility through consumption generally means finding good deals in order to maximize the utility received for each dollar spent. However, some makers of luxury goods believe that their customers actually achieve utility by paying high prices, such that lowering prices may lead to reduced sales. How is this counterintuitive view rationalized in our analysis of consumer behavior and the utility-maximizing rule?

10. Advertisements on television both inform consumers and persuade them to purchase products in differing proportions, depending on the ad. But today, because digital video recorders can be found in virtually all households, much of what these households watch is recorded, and the vast bulk of the ads are skipped. If this trend continues, where will consumers find out about new products?

11. An organization holding a charity event sold raffle tickets for 50% off last week. This week, it changed the offer: Instead of discounting tickets, it offered buyers a 60% bonus (e.g., for every 10 tickets purchased, buyers get 6 more tickets free). If raffle tickets normally sell for $10 each and a person wishes to buy $100 in raffle tickets, is the 60% bonus offer better? Why or why not?

12. A common practice at many supermarkets is to show the customer's total "savings" on their purchase at the bottom of the receipt. Such savings include the total discounts from goods purchased along with savings from coupons used. How would listing the

total savings on a receipt influence an individual's consumption habits? Of what type of behavioral factor does this strategy take advantage?

In the News

13. In today's technology-driven society, individuals are often multitasking with the help of mobile devices, with the objective of increasing productivity by always being "connected." However, countering this belief is a growing interest in the role of *mindfulness*, which is defined as being attentive to one's experiences in the present moment (*Time*, "The Mindful Revolution," January 23, 2014). Adherents of mindfulness believe that one should limit activities (such as the constant checking of messages) that may appear productive but actually are counterproductive. In fact, Google has taken this one step further by promoting one of its lead engineers, Chade-Meng Tan, to the official title of "Jolly Good Fellow (which nobody can deny)." Mr. Tan's well-paid job is to help Google's employees be more mindful. Discuss how Google's decision to have a Jolly Good Fellow on its payroll might affect consumers of Google's products despite not directly producing any goods or services.

14. In a *New York Times* article by economist Richard Thaler ("The Power of Nudges, for Good and Bad," October 31, 2015), nudging is described as strategies that encourage consumers to buy products that they might otherwise not consider. It points to a common practice among online newspapers to restrict access to articles without an online subscription, but then offering a free one-month trial to facilitate access. This free trial then turns into an automatic renewal at the regular price that consumers must then call to cancel. How might the practice of nudging be harmful to consumers attempting to maximize utility? Provide an example of how nudging by a corporation or other organization might lead to a good outcome for society.

Solving Problems

15. Assume a consumer has $40 to spend and for both products the marginal utilities are shown in the following table:

Quantity	MU_A	MU_B
1	35	80
2	20	40
3	12	18

Assume that each product sells for $10 per unit.

a. How many units of each product will the consumer purchase?

b. Assume the price of product B rises to $20 per unit. How will this consumer allocate her budget now?

c. If the prices of both products rise to $20 per unit, what will be the budget allocation?

WORK IT OUT ━━ LaunchPad | interactive activity

16. Answer the questions following the table.

	First-Run Movies			Bottles of Wine	
Quantity	Total Utility	Marginal Utility	Quantity	Total Utility	Marginal Utility
0	0	—	0	0	—
1	140	_____	1	180	_____
2	260	_____	2	340	_____
3	360	_____	3	460	_____
4	440	_____	4	510	_____
5	500	_____	5	540	_____

a. Complete the table.

b. Assume that you have $50 a month to devote to entertainment (column labeled First-Run Movies) and wine with dinner (column labeled Bottles of Wine). What will be your utility maximizing combination if the price to see a movie is $10 and a bottle of wine costs $10 as well?

c. A grape glut in California results in Napa Valley wine dropping in price to $5 per bottle, and you view this wine as a perfect substitute for what you were drinking earlier. Now what will be your equilibrium allocation between movies and wine?

d. Given these data, calculate your elasticity of demand for wine when the price fell from $10 to $5 (see the midpoint method in Chapter 5).

USING THE NUMBERS

17. Using By the Numbers, list the top five categories on which the average U.S. household spent their incomes in the year 2014 (start with the largest expenditure and proceed downward in terms of percentage of household budget).

18. According to By the Numbers, what category or categories of goods and services have increased in price (on average) every year from 2012 to 2014? What category or categories have fallen in price every year from 2012 to 2014?

ANSWERS TO QUESTIONS IN CHECKPOINTS

Checkpoint: The Budget Line and Choices 141

The total amount spent on meals each week is $(10 \times \$7.50) + (5 \times \$15) = \$150$. If the price of off-campus meals decreases to $10, the cost of maintaining the same routine as before (10 meals on campus and 5 meals off campus) falls to $125, leaving $25 left over. This extra money (savings from the price decrease) can be used to purchase more meals at either location, including more meals on campus.

Checkpoint: Marginal Utility Analysis 148

Convenience stores offer a small set of products at high prices nearer to home and have extended hours of operation. They also provide quicker service in that customers are in and out of the store quickly with their purchase. The marginal utility of convenience overcomes the higher prices; thus, people shop there because time is money. A 24/7 Safeway would have an impact on convenience store sales. At off-hours, supermarkets might be as fast as convenience stores, but cheaper.

Checkpoint: Behavioral Economics 153

According to marginal utility analysis, displaying a sign indicating a limit of 12 cans of soup per customer should not affect buying behavior, unless the shopper actually planned to buy more than 12 cans, in which case the sign puts a restriction on the purchase. However, in behavioral economics, putting up this sign represents a framing technique: By putting a limit of 12 cans, the supermarket is implying that the soup is so good that customers have a habit of buying large quantities (which may not be likely at all). By suggesting the soup is "popular," it draws customers into buying the soup that they otherwise might overlook, creating a framing bias.

Appendix
Indifference Curve Analysis

Learning Objectives

A6.1 Understand the properties of indifference curves and preference maps.

A6.2 Use indifference curves to derive demand curves and measure income and substitution effects.

Marginal utility analysis provides a good theoretical glimpse into the consumer decision-making process, yet it requires that utility be measured and that marginal utility per dollar be computed for innumerable possible consumption choices. In reality, measuring utility is impossible, as is mentally computing the marginal utility of thousands of products. To get around these difficulties, economists have developed a modern explanation of consumer decisions that does not require measuring utility. The foundation of this analysis is the indifference curve.

Indifference Curves and Consumer Preferences

If consumers cannot precisely measure the exact satisfaction they receive from specific products, economists reason that people can distinguish between different bundles of goods and decide whether they prefer one bundle over another. This analysis eliminates the idea of measuring consumer satisfaction. It instead assumes that consumers will either be able to choose between any two bundles, or else be *indifferent* to which bundle is chosen. An **indifference curve** shows all points at which consumers' choices are indifferent—points at which consumers express no preference between combinations of two products.

To illustrate how an indifference curve works, let us return to our original example of pizzas and wall climbing, now graphed in Figure APX-1. Compare the combination represented by point *b* (2 pizzas and 1.5 hours of climbing) and the combination at point *e* (2 pizzas and 0.5 hour of wall climbing). Which would you prefer, assuming you enjoy both of these? Clearly, the combination at point *b* is preferable to the combination at point *e* because you get the same amount of pizza but more wall climbing. By the same logic, bundle *f* is preferable to bundle *b* because you get the same amount of climbing, but 3 more pizzas.

indifference curve A curve that shows the combinations of two goods from which the consumer is indifferent (receives the same level of satisfaction).

FIGURE APX-1	AN INDIFFERENCE CURVE

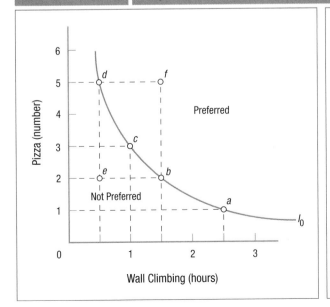

All of the different possible combinations lying on the indifference curve I_0 represent bundles of goods to which you are indifferent—each of these combinations is equally satisfying to you. But compare the combination represented by point *b* and the combination at point *f*. Which would you prefer? Point *f*, of course, because you get more. All points upward and to the right are preferred to all points on indifference curve I_0.

These choices have all been easy enough to make. But now assume you are offered bundles *d* and *b*. Bundle *d* contains more pizzas than bundle *b*, but bundle *b* has more climbing time. Given this choice, you may well conclude that you do not care which bundle you get—you are indifferent. In fact, all of the different possible combinations lying on the indifference curve I_0 represent bundles to which you are indifferent, such that you would just as soon have any one of these combinations as any other. And this tells us what an indifference curve is: It identifies all possible combinations of two products that offer consumers the same level of satisfaction or utility. Notice that this mode of analysis does not require us to consider the precise quantity of utility that various bundles yield, but only whether one bundle would be preferable to another.

Properties of Indifference Curves

Indifference curves have negative slopes and are convex to the origin; they bow inward, that is. They have negative slopes because we assume consumers will generally prefer to have more, rather than less, of each product. Yet, to obtain more of one product and maintain the same level of satisfaction, consumers must give up some quantity of the other product. Hence, the negative slope.

Indifference curves are bowed inward toward the origin because of the law of diminishing marginal utility discussed earlier. When you have a lot of pizzas (point *d* in Figure APX-1), you are willing to give up 2 pizzas to obtain another half-hour of climbing (moving from point *d* to point *c*). But once you have plenty of wall time, yet few pizzas (point *b*), you are unwilling to give up as many pizzas to get more climbing time. This is the law of diminishing marginal utility at work: As we consume more of any particular product, the satisfaction we derive from consuming additional units of this product falls.

Indifference (or Preference) Maps

An indifference curve is a curve that represents a set of product bundles to which a consumer is indifferent. An **indifference map,** or *preference map,* is an infinite set of indifference curves, each representing a different level of satisfaction. Three possible indifference curves, forming part of a preference map, are shown in Figure APX-2.

Indifference curve I_0 is the same curve shown in Figure APX-1. Indifference curve I_1 provides consumers with greater satisfaction than I_0 because it is located farther from the origin. In general, utility rises as curves move outward from the origin, because these curves represent larger quantities of both goods. Conversely, indifference curve I_2 offers

indifference map An infinite set of indifference curves in which each curve represents a different level of utility or satisfaction.

FIGURE APX-2	THREE INDIFFERENCE CURVES FOR PIZZA AND WALL CLIMBING (AN INDIFFERENCE MAP)

An indifference map, or preference map, contains an infinite set of indifference curves, each representing a different level of satisfaction. Three possible indifference curves for pizzas and wall climbing, forming part of a preference map, are shown here.

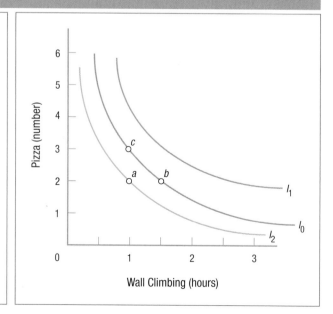

consumers less total satisfaction because it is located closer to the origin and represents smaller amounts of both products than I_0.

To confirm the observations just made, compare point a on indifference curve I_2 with point b on indifference curve I_0. Points a and b contain the same amount of pizza, but point b contains more climbing time. Hence, point b offers a higher level of satisfaction than point a. An analysis of points a and c yields a similar conclusion. Because both points c and b on indifference curve I_0 are preferred to point a on I_2, indifference curve I_0 must generally offer higher levels of satisfaction than the points on indifference curve I_2.

This result leads us to one final property of indifference curves: They do not intersect. Because all of the points on any indifference curve represent bundles of goods to which consumers are indifferent, if two indifference curves were to cross, this would mean that some of the bundles they represent offered the same level of satisfaction (where the curves meet), but others did not (where the curves do not touch). Yet, this is a logical impossibility, because each indifference curve is defined as a set of bundles offering exactly the same level of satisfaction.

We now turn to the question of how consumers use such preference maps to optimize their satisfaction within their budget constraints.

Optimal Consumer Choice

Figure APX-3 superimposes a budget line of $50 per week onto a preference map that assumes pizzas cost $10 each and wall climbing costs $20 per hour. Maximizing your satisfaction on your limited income requires that you purchase some bundle of goods on the highest possible indifference curve. In this example, the best you can do is indicated by point b: 2 pizzas and 1.5 hours of wall climbing. Clearly, if you were to pick any other point on the budget line, your satisfaction would be diminished because you would end up on a lower indifference curve (such as points a or c on I_2 in Figure APX-3). It follows that the indifference curve running tangent to the budget line identifies your best option—in this case, the indifference curve that just touches the budget line at point b.

Of course, this is the same result we reached earlier using marginal utility analysis, specifically in Table 2. Notice, however, that using indifference curve analysis, we did not have to assume that utility can be measured. We were able to understand how you would allocate your budget between two goods so as to achieve the highest possible level of satisfaction, even without knowing exactly how high that level might be.

FIGURE APX-3   OPTIMAL CONSUMER CHOICE

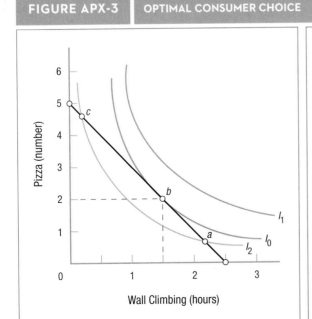

Maximizing your satisfaction on your limited income requires purchasing some bundle of goods on the highest possible indifference curve. The best you can do in this situation is indicated by point b: 2 pizzas and 1.5 hours of wall climbing. Indifference curve I_0 is the highest indifference curve that can be reached with the budget line shown.

Using Indifference Curves

Indifference curves are a useful device to help us understand consumer demand. Economists use indifference curves, for instance, to shed light on the impact of changes in consumer income and product substitution resulting from a change in product price. Indifference curve analysis, moreover, provides some insight into how households determine their supply of labor (this analysis, however, is left to a later chapter). Before we move on to applications of indifference curve analysis, though, we first need to derive a demand curve from an indifference map.

Deriving Demand Curves

We derive the demand curve using indifference curve analysis in much the same way we did using marginal utility analysis. Panel A of Figure APX-4 restates the results of Figure APX-3: When you have a budget of $50 per week, the price of pizza is $10, and climbing is $20 per hour, your optimal choice is found at point *a*. In panel B, we want to plot the demand curve for wall climbing. We know that when wall climbing costs $20 per hour, you will climb for 1.5 hours, so let us indicate this on panel B by marking point *a*.

FIGURE APX-4	DERIVING THE DEMAND FOR WALL CLIMBING USING INDIFFERENCE CURVE ANALYSIS

In panel A, when wall climbing costs $20 per hour, your optimal choice is found at point *a*. When the price of wall climbing rises to $30 per hour, this produces a new budget line, *cd*, shifting the optimal choice to point *b*. Transferring points *a* and *b* down to panel B and connecting the points generate the demand curve for wall climbing.

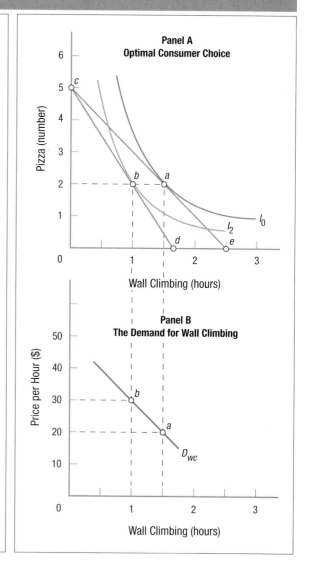

To fill out the demand curve, let us now increase the price of wall climbing to $30 per hour. This produces a new budget line, *cd*. (Point *d* is located at 1.67 hours because $50/$30 = 1.67 hours of possible wall climbing.) This shift in the budget line yields a new optimal choice at point *b* on indifference curve I_2, now indicating the highest level of satisfaction you can attain. As panel A shows, the ultimate result of this hike in the price of wall climbing to $30 an hour is a reduction in your climbing to 1 hour per week. Transferring this result to panel B, we mark point *b*, where price = $30 and climbing hours = 1. Now connecting points *a* and *b* in panel B, we are left with the demand curve for wall climbing.

Once again, therefore, we arrive at the same conclusion using indifference curve analysis as we did earlier using marginal utility analysis. Both approaches are logical and elegant, and both approaches tell us something about the thought processes consumers must use as they make their spending decisions. Indifference curve analysis, however, arrives at its conclusion without requiring that utility be measurable or that consumers perform complex arithmetic computations.

Income and Substitution Effects

Another way economists use indifference curves is to separate income and substitution effects when product prices change. First, we need to distinguish between these two effects.

When the price of some product you regularly purchase goes up, your spendable income is thereby essentially reduced. If you always buy a latte a day, for instance, and you continue to do so even when the price of lattes goes up, you must then reduce your consumption of other goods. This essentially amounts to a reduction in your income. And we know that when income falls, the consumption of normal goods likewise declines. Hence, when higher prices essentially reduce consumer incomes, the quantity demanded for normal goods generally falls. Economists call this the **income effect.**

When the price of a particular good rises, meanwhile, the quantity demanded of that good will fall simply because consumers substitute lower-priced goods for it. This is called the **substitution effect.** Thus, when the price of wall climbing rises from $20 to $30, you cut back on your climbing, in part because you decide to dedicate more of your money to pizza eating. The challenge for us now is to determine just how much of this reduction in your climbing is due to the substitution effect (more pizzas mean less climbing) and how much is due to the income effect (the rise in price effectively leaves you with less money to spend).

Figure APX-5 reproduces panel A of Figure APX-4, adding one line (*gh*) to divide the total change in purchases into the income and substitution effects. To see how this line is derived, let us begin by reviewing what has happened thus far. At point *a*, you split your $50 budget into 2 pizzas at $10 each and 1.5 hours of wall climbing at $20 per hour. When the price of wall climbing rose to $30 per hour, you reduced your climbing time to 1 hour.

Consider now what happens when we evaluate what you are getting for your *current* allocation of money, but using the *old* price of wall climbing ($20 per hour). You are now getting 2 pizzas, worth $10 apiece, plus 1 hour of wall climbing, formerly valued at $20. This means that your budget has effectively been cut to $40. The ultimate effect of the rise in the price of climbing, in other words, has been to reduce your income by $10. In Figure APX-5, the hypothetical budget line *gh* represents this new budget of $40, though again reflecting the old price of climbing.

Compare the original equilibrium point *a* on budget line *ce* with the new equilibrium point *f* on budget line *gh*. This new budget line *gh* reflects a budget of $40 with the old price of climbing ($20 per hour). Had your income previously been $40, you would have reduced your climbing by 15 minutes (to point *f*). This is the *income effect* associated with the rise in the price of wall climbing from $20 to $30 per hour. The rising price essentially reduced your income, causing you to consume 15 minutes less of wall climbing and 0.5 fewer pizzas due to this income reduction alone.

The change in price is the only thing that differentiates equilibrium point *b* from point *f*, income having been held constant. This difference of 15 minutes between point *f* and point *b* therefore represents a *substitution effect*. By changing the price of climbing while holding income constant, you consume 0.5 more pizza and 15 minutes less wall climbing.

income effect When higher prices essentially reduce consumer income, the quantity demanded for normal goods falls.

substitution effect When the price of one good rises, consumers will substitute other goods for that good; therefore, the quantity demanded for the higher-priced good falls.

FIGURE APX-5 | INCOME AND SUBSTITUTION EFFECTS

Panel A of Figure APX-4 is reproduced in this figure. The price of climbing having risen to $30 per hour, this effectively reduces your budget to $40 per week, assuming you continue climbing as much as you did before. Line *gh* represents a new budget of $40, though reflecting the old price of climbing. This new budget line *gh* allows us to divide the total change in purchases into the income and substitution effects. Increasing the price of wall climbing from $20 to $30 an hour would mean a reduction in wall climbing (holding income constant at $40) from point *f* to point *b*. This is the substitution effect. The income effect is thus the reduction in consumption from point *a* to point *f*. Adding both effects together yields the total reduction.

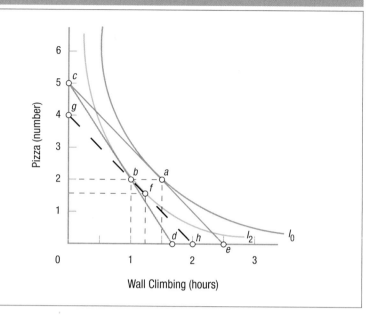

Combined, the substitution and income effects constitute the entire change in quantity demanded when the price of wall climbing rises by $10 per hour. The income effect (movement from point *a* to point *f*) is a movement from one budget line to another. The substitution effect (movement from point *f* to point *b*) is a movement along the new budget line. Together, they represent the total change in quantity demanded. In this case, the income and substitution effects were the same, 15 minutes, but this will not always be the case.

This chapter examined how consumers and households make decisions. Households attempt to maximize their well-being or satisfaction within the constraints of limited incomes. We have seen that the analysis of consumer decisions can be approached in two different ways, using marginal utility analysis or indifference curve analysis.

Marginal utility analysis assumes that consumers can readily measure utility and make complex calculations regarding the utility of various possible consumption choices. Both of these assumptions are empirically rather dubious. This does not, however, invalidate marginal utility analysis; it just makes it difficult to use and test in an empirical context. Indifference curve analysis gives us a more powerful set of analytical tools without these restrictive assumptions.

 CHECKPOINT

INDIFFERENCE CURVE ANALYSIS

- Indifference curve analysis does not require utility measurement. All it requires is that consumers can choose between different bundles of goods.
- An indifference curve shows all the combinations of two goods where the consumer has the same level of satisfaction.
- Indifference curves have negative slopes, are convex to the origin due to the law of diminishing marginal utility, and do not intersect with one another.
- An indifference map is an infinite set of indifference curves.
- Consumer equilibrium occurs where the budget line is tangent to the highest indifference curve.
- When the price of one product rises, not only will your consumption of that product fall (the substitution effect), but also your relative income will be reduced as well, and for normal goods you will consume less (the income effect). The opposite occurs when price falls.

QUESTION: Consumers face a set of goods called "credence goods." Consumers of such goods must "take it on faith that the supplier has given them what they need and no more."[1] Examples include surgeons, auto mechanics, and taxi drivers. These experts tell us what medical procedures, repairs, and routes we require to satisfy our needs, and very often we don't know the price until the work is done. If we do not know the price and cannot establish whether we actually need some of these goods, how does this square with our indifference curve analysis?

Answer to the Checkpoint question can be found at the end of this appendix.

[1] "Economic Focus: Sawbones, Cowboys and Cheats," *Economist*, April 15, 2006.

APPENDIX KEY CONCEPTS

indifference curve, p. 159
indifference map, p. 160

income effect, p. 163

substitution effect, p. 163

APPENDIX QUESTIONS AND PROBLEMS

1. Indifference curves cannot intersect. Why not?

2. Explain why the following bundles of apples (A) and bananas (B) cannot be on the same indifference curve: (4A, 2B); (1A, 5B); (4A, 3B).

3. Answer the following questions using the figure below:

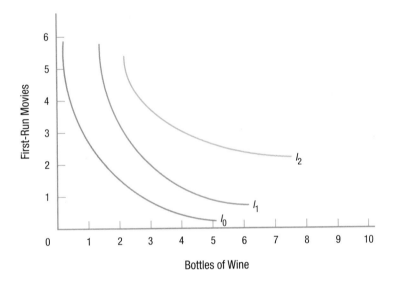

   a. Assume that you have $50 a month to devote to entertainment (First-Run Movies) and wine with dinner (Bottles of Wine). What will be your equilibrium allocation if the price to see a movie or buy a bottle of wine is $10? Graph the equilibrium on the figure and label it point *a*.

   b. A grape glut in California results in Napa Valley wine dropping in price to $5 a bottle, and you view this wine as a perfect substitute for what you were drinking. Now what will be your equilibrium allocation between movies and wine? Graph that on the figure and label the new equilibrium as point *b*.

4. Some economists have suggested that terrorists are not spurred by poverty, but rather are educated individuals who live in countries with a lack of civil liberties. As such, terrorists are rational actors who maximize a set of goals subject to constrained resources.

   Assume that terrorists can choose between nonviolent acts and violent acts. Draw a budget line and indifference curves that show where a utility-maximizing combination of these activities would occur. Now suppose that the U.S. government can choose between two types of antiterrorism policies: (1) a defensive approach such as increased airport screenings, and (2) a proactive approach, which includes activities such as infiltrating terrorist cells and freezing bank assets. Analyze how these policies affect the budget line of terrorists and how it affects the utility-maximizing combination of terrorist activities.

Checkpoint: Indifference Curve Analysis 164

Not very well. They are largely a problem of incomplete information and a challenging problem for consumers. If doctors make more money performing complex operations, they will be inclined to prescribe them more often. One study found that doctors elect surgery for themselves less often than nondoctors. As long as consumers are aware of the incentive structure of these transactions, they can build this into the decision calculus, but ultimately, information asymmetries are not adequately represented in this model.

Production and Costs

Understanding how various costs affect the ability of firms to earn profits

Learning Objectives

7.1 Describe the nature of firms and markets.

7.2 Explain the difference between accounting and economic costs and how they affect the determination of profits.

7.3 Differentiate between the short run and long run.

7.4 Describe the nature of short-run production, total product, marginal product, and average product.

7.5 Differentiate among increasing, decreasing, and negative marginal returns.

7.6 Describe and compare the differences among fixed costs, variable costs, marginal costs, and average costs.

7.7 Explain the importance of marginal costs in a firm's production decision.

7.8 Use a graph to show the relationship between the short-run average total cost and marginal cost curves.

7.9 Describe long-run costs.

7.10 Describe the reasons for economies and diseconomies of scale.

Thirty years ago, most people did not think much about what they could do to conserve fossil fuels. Energy and gas prices were low, and the problem of climate change was not very prominent in everyday discussions and news reports. This has changed, and many people today do think about the impact their consumption habits have on the environment. This has led to a rise in demand for energy-efficient products to address not only climate change issues but also wallet issues as energy costs take a larger share of a household's budget.

In the automobile industry, the use of sustainable energy resources such as ethanol remains expensive. However, in the mid-1990s, manufacturers foresaw an opportunity to satisfy consumer demand for cars that achieve much greater fuel efficiency, resulting in a similar effect as using sustainable energy. In 1997 Toyota unveiled the Prius, the first well-selling car to use hybrid electric technology. Then in 2008, Tesla unveiled its powerful electric plug-in cars that started a movement toward electric cars that nearly every auto manufacturer has since followed.

Creating a new type of car, especially one that runs on a new source of energy, is not like creating a new type of pizza. It costs much more to develop, design, and produce the very first car. Toyota invested over $1 billion to develop the Prius, a great deal of money for a new compact car in an untested market. Tesla also invested heavily to develop its plug-in cars, to a point that it nearly went bankrupt in its early years. What motivated Toyota and Tesla to undertake such expensive investments? The answer is profits.

Profits are one of the most important goals of firms. To determine profits, a firm must calculate its revenues from sales and subtract all of its costs. How does a firm measure these costs, and what do these costs include?

In this chapter, we look at what motivates firms to do what they do—profits. We then look at the production and cost part of the profit equation. We discuss the concept of profit as properly understood by economists. Unlike an accountant or agents of the Internal Revenue Service, economists use a different measure of profit, one that takes into account explicit (out-of-pocket) costs and then adds the opportunity costs (the value of forgone opportunities) of a business decision. We then go on to discuss the production process and how output is determined based on the amount of inputs used. Finally, we take a look at the measurement of costs. Specifically, economists break down costs into different categories in order to create decision rules that firms follow to maximize profits. In subsequent chapters, we add in the revenue part to the production part. In this way, we will discover what lies behind supply curves.

BY THE NUMBERS

Innovation, Productivity, and Costs Rule Business

To remain in business, firms must innovate not only by improving the products they make but also by controlling their costs. Controlling costs is done by introducing new technologies in production and increasing productivity. This holds for the service sector as well.

The cost of industrial robots has fallen over 60% since 1994.

Index of Industrial Robot Prices (1994 = 100)

Ikon Images/Getty Images

Science Photo Library/Getty Images

Go to **LaunchPad** to use the latest data to recreate this graph.

Labor productivity has doubled since 1994.

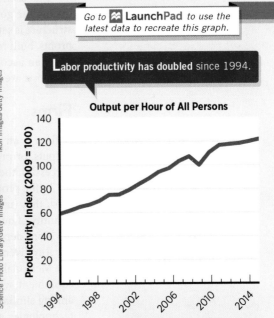

Output per Hour of All Persons

Productivity Index (2009 = 100)

1,260,000 Square Feet

Size of Amazon's largest warehouse (equivalent to 28 football fields).

150

Average number of flights into and out of Memphis Airport by FedEx, nearly all during the night between 10pm and 6am.

"We've found the key to productivity. It's Fred, down in the shop. He makes the stuff."

From The Wall Street Journal, permission Cartoon Features Syndicate

Cost breakdown for an iPad

Retail price: $399

Costs:

Touch display screen	$85
Hard drive	$52
Battery	$22
App processor	$14
Misc. components	$56
Assembly	$10
Distribution costs	$70
Profit for Apple	$90

Businesses face a relentless need to lower costs, which has changed the way we live and travel. The percentage of travelers purchasing airline tickets and checking in online highlights this trend.

Online Flight Bookings

Percent

9% (2000), 38% (2005), 75% (2010), 91% (2015)

Ricardo Infante Alvarez/Getty Images

Online Flight Check-ins

Percent

1% (2000), 5% (2005), 27% (2010), 71% (2015)

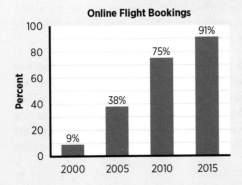

FIRMS, PROFITS, AND ECONOMIC COSTS

In the opening story, Toyota and Tesla had to make a decision about producing a product. Who makes such decisions? It's the firms and entrepreneurs who choose to take on the risk and effort to launch a new product. They are motivated by the profits that can be earned if the investment proves successful. But how do we measure profits?

This section highlights the important role that firms and entrepreneurs play in producing the goods and services we enjoy as consumers. No matter how the organizational structure is set up, firms and entrepreneurs hold profits as their motivating force. To achieve profits, both revenues and costs must be considered. As we will see, profits can be measured using an accounting approach or an economics approach. These approaches differ in the way costs are measured.

Firms

firm An economic institution that transforms resources (factors of production) into outputs.

A **firm** is an economic institution that transforms inputs, or factors of production, into outputs, or products. Most firms begin as family enterprises or small partnerships. When successful, these firms can evolve into corporations of considerable size.

In the process of producing goods and services, firms must make numerous decisions. First, they have to determine a market need. Then, most broadly, firms must decide what quantity of output to produce, how to produce it, and what inputs to employ. The latter two decisions depend on the production technology that the firm selects.

Any given product can typically be produced in a wide variety of ways. Some businesses, like McDonald's franchises and Dunkin' Donuts shops, use considerable amounts of capital equipment, whereas others, such as T-shirt shops and small eateries, require very little. Even among similar firms, the quality and quantity of resources available often determine what technologies are used. Firms located in areas with an abundance of low-cost labor tend to use basic technology, labor-intensive production methods. In areas in which high-skill, high-wage labor is the norm, production is more often done using advanced technology, capital-intensive processes.

Entrepreneurs

If a product or service is to be provided to the market, someone must first assume the risk of raising the required capital, assembling workers and raw materials, producing the product, and, finally, offering it for sale. Markets provide incentives and signals, but it is entrepreneurs who provide products and services by taking risks in the hopes of earning profits.

In the United States, 9.7% of people ages 18 to 64 classify themselves as entrepreneurs. This means they are running start-up businesses or businesses less than 42 months old. Entrepreneurial rates in Europe are about half (4.8%) the U.S. rate, while Japanese entrepreneurship is only 2.7%.[1]

Entrepreneurs can be divided into three basic business structures: sole proprietorships (one owner), partnerships (two or more owners), and corporations (many stockholders). The United States has more than 25 million businesses, over 70% of them sole proprietorships or small businesses. Only 20% of U.S. businesses are corporations. Nevertheless, corporations sell nearly 90% of all products and services in the United States. Likewise, around the world, the corporate form of business has become the dominant form. To see why, we must first take a brief look at the advantages and disadvantages of each business structure.

sole proprietorship A type of business structure composed of a single owner who supervises and manages the business and is subject to unlimited liability.

Sole Proprietors The **sole proprietorship** represents the most basic form of business organization. A sole proprietorship is composed of one owner, who usually supervises the business operation. Local restaurants, dry cleaning businesses, and auto repair shops are often sole proprietorships. A sole proprietorship is easy to establish and manage, having much less paperwork associated with it than other forms of business organization. But the sole proprietorship has disadvantages. Single owners are often limited in their ability to raise

---

[1] *Global Entrepreneurship Monitor,* "2014 Global Report," 2015.

capital. In many instances, all management responsibilities fall on this single individual. And most important, the personal assets of the owner are subject to unlimited liability. If you own a pizza shop as a sole proprietor and someone slips on the floor, he or she can sue you and you could lose your house and your life savings if you do not have sufficient insurance coverage.

Partnerships **Partnerships** are similar to sole proprietorships except that they have more than one owner. Establishing a partnership usually requires signing a legal partnership document. Partnerships find it easier to raise capital and spread around the management responsibilities. Like sole proprietors, however, partners are subject to unlimited liability, not only for their share of the business, but for the entire business. If your partner takes off for Bermuda, you are left to pay all the bills, even those your partner incurred. The death of one partner dissolves a partnership, unless other arrangements have been made ahead of time. In any case, the death of a partner often creates problems for the continuity of the business.

Corporations The **corporation** is the premier form of business organization in most of the world. In 2015 roughly 6 million U.S. corporations sold over $29 trillion worth of goods and services worldwide. This is a remarkable statistic when you consider that the country's 20 million sole proprietorships had sales totaling just over $1.5 trillion. Clearly, corporations are structured in a way that enhances growth and efficiency.

Corporations have most of the legal rights of individuals; in addition, they are able to issue stock to raise capital, and most significant, the liability of individual owners (i.e., stockholders) is limited to the amount they have invested in (or paid for) the stock. This is what distinguishes corporations from the other forms of business organization: the ability to raise large amounts of capital because of limited liability.

Some scholars argue that corporations are the greatest engines of economic prosperity ever known.[2] Daniel Akst writes:

> When I worked for a big company, there was a miracle in the office every couple of weeks, just like clockwork. It happened every payday, when sizable checks were distributed to a small army of employees who also enjoyed health and retirement benefits. Few of us could have made as much on our own, and somehow there was always money left over for the shareholders as well.[3]

Without the corporate umbrella, most of the jobs we hold would not exist; most of the products we use would not have been invented; and our standard of living would be a fraction of what it is today.

What is it that motivates business owners of all types to take on the risks of creating a product? Profits.

Profits

Entrepreneurs and firms employ resources and turn out products with the goal of making profits. This is not to say that firms put profit above all else (i.e., that they would do something immoral or socially irresponsible to increase profits), but instead that firms do not intentionally make decisions that would knowingly result in lower profit. **Profit** is the difference between total revenue and total cost.

Total revenue is the amount of money a firm receives from the sales of its products. It is equal to the price per unit times the number of units sold ($TR = p \times q$). Note that we use lowercase p and q when we are dealing with an individual firm and uppercase letters when describing a market. **Total cost** includes both out-of-pocket expenses and opportunity costs; we will discuss this concept shortly.

Steve Wozniak (right) and the late Steve Jobs began their computer business in the Jobs family garage as a partnership before turning it into a public company, Apple, in 1980. As of 2016, Apple is the largest company in the world by market value.

partnership Similar to a sole proprietorship, but involves more than one owner who share the management of the business. Partnerships are also subject to unlimited liability.

corporation A business structure that has most of the legal rights of individuals, and in addition, can issue stock to raise capital. Stockholders' liability is limited to the value of their stock.

profit Equal to the difference between total revenue and total cost.

total revenue Equal to price per unit times quantity sold.

total cost The sum of all costs to run a business. To an economist, this includes out-of-pocket expenses and opportunity costs.

[2] John Micklethwait and Adrian Wooldridge, *The Company: A Short History of a Revolutionary Idea* (New York: Modern Library), 2003.
[3] Daniel Akst, "Where Those Paychecks Come From," *Wall Street Journal*, February 3, 2004.

ISSUE

The Vast World of Corporate Offshoring and Profits

Most Americans are aware of the fact that corporations, particularly in manufacturing industries, often relocate factories to developing countries to take advantage of lower costs for labor and raw materials (in a process called offshoring) and to gain access to emerging markets for their products. Yet, another incentive exists for why companies choose to place important offices, even headquarters, abroad, and that is to avoid U.S. regulations and taxes.

One common example of corporate offshoring occurs in the cruise ship industry. Despite many cruise ships starting and ending trips at U.S. ports, virtually all large cruise vessels are registered outside of the United States, allowing cruise lines to circumvent, for example, U.S. labor laws (ever wonder how a room steward is able to legally work seven days a week, day and night, at less than minimum wage?).

The more egregious examples of offshoring occur when companies relocate headquarters to certain countries to take advantage of lower tax rates. And by relocating, this often does not mean moving to a shiny new skyscraper in a major European or Asian capital. On the contrary, it sometimes involves merely having a mailbox in an obscure town or island serving as the headquarters for a multimillion dollar enterprise.

Recent media attention exposing the abuse of corporate offshoring has led to new reforms being proposed in the United States and the European Union. Various proposed legislation, such as the Stop Tax Haven Abuse Act, aimed at curbing the use of corporate offshoring when the sole purpose is to avoid taxes (as opposed to traditional offshoring to take advantage of less expensive inputs of production). But like all new policies, tradeoffs exist, as com-

Zug, Switzerland, is home to roughly 30,000 corporate headquarters from around the world. Impressive for a quiet lakeside town with just 28,000 residents.

panies affected by the new legislation claim such rules would reduce competition and raise consumer prices. The costs and benefits of any new policy are likely to be debated extensively before becoming law.

Economists explicitly assume that firms proceed rationally and have the maximization of profits as their primary objective. Alternative behavioral assumptions for firms have been tested, including sales maximization, various goals for market share, and customer satisfaction. Although these more complex assumptions for firm behavior often predict different outcomes, economists have not been persuaded that any of them yield results superior to those of the profit maximization approach. Profit maximization has stood the test of time, and thus we will assume it is the primary economic goal of firms.

Economic Costs

When economists talk about "profit," they take into account business costs from the opportunity cost perspective. They separate costs into explicit costs, or out-of-pocket expenses, and implicit costs, or opportunity costs. **Economic costs** are the sum of explicit and implicit costs.

Explicit costs are those expenses paid directly to some other economic entity. These costs include wages, lease payments, expenditures for raw materials, taxes, utilities, and so on. A company can easily determine its explicit costs by summing all of the payments it has made during the normal course of doing business.

Implicit costs refer to all of the opportunity costs of using resources that belong to the firm. Recall that opportunity cost measures the value of the next best alternative use of resources, including that of time and capital. Implicit costs include depreciation, the depletion of business assets, and the opportunity cost of a firm's capital.

In any business, some assets are depleted over time. Machines, cars, and office equipment depreciate with use and time. Finite oil or mineral deposits are depleted as they are mined or pumped. Even though firms do not actually pay any cash as these assets are worn down or used up, these costs nonetheless represent real expenses to the firm.

economic costs The sum of explicit (out-of-pocket) and implicit (opportunity) costs.

explicit costs Those expenses paid directly to another economic entity, including wages, lease payments, taxes, and utilities.

implicit costs The opportunity costs of using resources that belong to the firm, including depreciation, depletion of business assets, and the opportunity cost of the firm's capital employed in the business.

Another major component of implicit costs is the capital firms have invested. Even small firms incur large implicit costs from their capital investment. Small entrepreneurs, for example, must invest both their own capital and labor into their businesses. Such people could normally be working for someone else, so their "lost salary" must be treated as an implicit cost when determining the true profitability of their businesses. Similarly, any capital invested in a business enterprise could just as well be earning interest in a bank account or returning dividends and capital gains through the purchase and sale of stock in other enterprises. Though not directly paid out as expenses, these forgone earnings nonetheless represent implicit costs for the firm.

Economic and Normal Profits

The primary goal of any firm is to earn a profit. However, how the Internal Revenue Service (IRS) measures profit for tax purposes is different from how an economist determines profit. Suppose that after graduating, you decide to open a new billiards hall on campus. After a year, counting all the revenues and subtracting all explicit costs (costs that you actually pay out), you end up with a profit of $20,000. Is your business a success? The IRS certainly thinks so, as it will collect taxes on these profits. And you might brag to friends that you turned a profit in your first year. But then you start thinking of all the time you spent on the business and the missed opportunities, such as the $40,000 a year job offer you turned down, and the money you could have earned had you invested your savings in stocks or bonds rather than in your business. Now, your business doesn't feel successful.

Economists include both explicit and implicit costs in their analysis of business profits. An **accounting profit** is calculated by including only explicit costs, while an **economic profit** is calculated using both explicit and implicit costs. Therefore, when a firm is earning economic profits, it is generating profits in excess of zero once implicit costs are factored in. This brings us to an important benchmark called **normal profits,** which occurs when economic profit equals zero. Economists refer to this level of profit as a *normal rate of return* on capital, a return just sufficient to keep investors satisfied and to keep capital in the business over the long run. If a firm's rate of return on capital falls below this rate, investors will put their capital to use elsewhere.

Although earning zero economic profit might sound dismal, this simply means that the firm is earning the same profit it would have earned had it chosen its next best alternative use of its capital, which can be quite substantial in terms of accounting profit. For example, if Mark Zuckerberg left Facebook and opened a new business, his new business (assuming he uses the same amount of capital and labor) would have to earn billions of dollars a year just to achieve normal profits. Not bad for *zero* economic profit. In other words, any profit less than what would be earned at Facebook under his leadership would be considered an *economic loss*. A firm earning normal profits means that it is earning just enough to cover the opportunity cost of its capital. Therefore, a firm may be earning *accounting profits* as defined by the IRS for tax purposes, yet still be suffering economic losses, because taxable income does not reflect all implicit costs.

Let's look at the difference between accounting profits and economic profits further in Table 1, using our example of the billiards hall. Suppose your annual total revenue is $120,000. After subtracting out-of-pocket (explicit) costs of $100,000, you end up with an accounting profit of $20,000. However, if you could have earned $40,000 working elsewhere and $10,000 more by putting your savings into a stock or bond investment rather than into your business, you would incur a $30,000 economic loss.

Economists designate normal profits as economic profits equal to zero. To achieve normal profits, you would need to be just as well off operating the billiard hall as you would if you instead took another job and invested your savings elsewhere, which means earning $50,000 in accounting profits. Because you earned only $20,000 (or $30,000 less than the alternative), this results in an economic loss of $30,000. Normal profits are the profits necessary to keep a firm in business over the long run. This brings us to an important economic distinction, between the short run and the long run.

accounting profit The difference between total revenue and explicit costs. These are the profits that are taxed by the government.

economic profit Profit in excess of normal profits. These are profits in excess of both explicit and implicit costs.

normal profits The return on capital necessary to keep investors satisfied and keep capital in the business over the long run.

TABLE 1	COMPARING ACCOUNTING VERSUS ECONOMIC PROFITS FROM OPERATING A BUSINESS

Fancy Collection/SuperStock

Item	Accountant	Economist
Annual revenue	$120,000	$120,000
Less **explicit costs**		
Wages	−$50,000	−$50,000
Lease payments	−$20,000	−$20,000
Cost of goods sold	−$15,000	−$15,000
Utilities	−$5,000	−$5,000
Insurance	−$5,000	−$5,000
Office supplies	−$5,000	−$5,000
Accounting Profit	+$20,000	
Less **implicit costs**		
Forgone earnings from job offer	—	−$40,000
Forgone earnings from money invested	—	−$10,000
Economic Profit		−$30,000

Short Run Versus Long Run

Although the short and the long run generally differ in their temporal spans, they are *not* defined in terms of time. Rather, economists define these periods by the ability of firms to adjust the quantities of various resources that they are employing.

The **short run** is a period of time over which at least one factor of production is fixed, or cannot be changed. For the sake of simplicity, economists typically assume that plant capacity is fixed in the short run. Output from a fixed plant can still vary depending on how much labor the firm employs. Firms can, for instance, hire more people, have existing employees work overtime, or run additional shifts. For discussion purposes, we focus here on labor as the variable factor, but changes in the raw materials used can also result in output changes.

The **long run,** conversely, is a period of time sufficient for a firm to adjust all factors of production, including plant capacity. Since all factors can be altered in the long run, existing firms can even close and leave the industry, and new firms can build new plants and enter the market.

In the short run, therefore, with plant capacity and the number of firms in an industry being fixed, output varies only as a result of changes in employment. In the long run, as plant capacity and other factors are made variable, the industry may grow or shrink as firms enter or leave the business, or some firms alter their plant capacity.

Because all industries are unique, the time required for long-run adjustment varies by industry. Family-owned restaurants, lawn-mowing services, and roofing firms can come and go fairly rapidly. High-capital industries, on the other hand, such as the chemical, petroleum, and semiconductor industries, face obstacles to change that require a long time to overcome, whether these be strenuous environmental regulation, immense research and development requirements, or huge capital costs for plant construction. Adding plant capacity in one of these industries can take a decade or more and cost billions of dollars.

The important point to note from this section is that firms seek economic profits and determine profits by first calculating their costs. These costs may differ over the short run versus the long run. Therefore, we look first at production basics, then consider costs in both the short run and the long run.

short run A period of time over which at least one factor of production (resource) is fixed, or cannot be changed.

long run A period of time sufficient for firms to adjust all factors of production, including plant capacity.

CHECKPOINT

FIRMS, PROFITS, AND ECONOMIC COSTS

■ Firms are economic institutions that convert inputs (factors of production) into products and services.

■ Entrepreneurs provide goods and services to markets. Entrepreneurs can be organized into three basic business structures: sole proprietorships, partnerships, and corporations.

■ Corporations are the premier form of business organization because they give owners (shareholders) limited liability, unlike sole proprietorships and partnerships.

■ Profit is the difference between total revenues and total costs.

■ Explicit costs are those expenses, such as rent and the cost of raw materials, paid directly to some other economic entity. Implicit costs represent the opportunity costs of doing business, including depreciation and the firm's capital costs.

■ Normal profits (or normal rates of return) are equal to zero economic profit. The firm is earning just enough to keep capital in the firm over the long run. Economic profits are those in *excess* of normal profits.

■ The short run is a period of time during which one factor of production (usually plant capacity) is fixed. In the long run, all factors can vary and the firm can enter or exit the industry.

QUESTION: Assume for a moment that you want to go into business for yourself and that you have a good idea. What are the pros and cons of setting up your company as a corporation as opposed to keeping it as a sole proprietorship?

Answers to the Checkpoint questions can be found at the end of this chapter.

PRODUCTION IN THE SHORT RUN

Production is the process of turning inputs into outputs. Most products can be made using a variety of different technologies. As discussed earlier, these can be either capital-intensive or labor-intensive. The type of technology a firm chooses will depend on many things, including ease of implementation and the relative cost of each input into the process.

production The process of turning inputs into outputs.

Again, in the simplified model we are working with, firms can vary their output in the short run only by altering the amount of labor they employ, because plant capacity is fixed in the short run. The extent to which output will change from adding labor depends on the ability to specialize in tasks and use other resources efficiently. But like all resources, labor is eventually subject to diminishing returns. Therefore, an individual firm's production possibilities will follow the same general pattern as the production function for the entire economy. In the short run, output for an existing plant will vary by the amount of labor employed. This output is referred to as *total product*.

Total Product

Let's examine some production basics by assuming that you start your own firm. Imagine that you decide to begin manufacturing windsurfing sails in an old warehouse that you rent. Your physical plant is constrained in the short run by the size of the manufacturing facility. Table 2 lists your firm's total output (total product) as you hire more workers.

Panel A of Figure 1 displays your total product curve for windsurfing equipment, based on the data in columns (1) and (2) of Table 2. Output of sails varies with the number of people you employ. Output rises from 0 to 16 when 3 people are working to a maximum of 28 when 6 people are employed (point *b*). As you continue to hire employees beyond 6, you encounter *negative returns*. Total output actually begins to fall, possibly because the workplace has become overly crowded, confusing, hazardous, or noisy. Clearly, hiring any more than 6 employees would be counterproductive, because output falls but costs (such as the total wages of all the employees) rise.

TABLE 2	PRODUCTION DATA FOR WINDSURFING SAIL FIRM

(1) L (labor)	(2) Q (total product)	(3) MP (marginal product)	(4) AP (average product)
0	0		—
1	3	3	3.00
2	8	5	4.00
3	16	8	5.33
4	22	6	5.50
5	26	4	5.20
6	28	2	4.67
7	26	−2	3.71
8	23	−3	2.88

FIGURE 1	TOTAL PRODUCT CURVE, MARGINAL PRODUCT, AND AVERAGE PRODUCT

These two panels show the relationship between additional labor and productivity. Panel A shows how increasing labor increases productivity, up to a point. Panel B shows marginal and average product. Marginal product reaches its maximum as the third worker is hired, after which marginal product starts decreasing. Total product keeps increasing, however, until you reach 6 employees. At that point, marginal product becomes negative, meaning that each additional employee actually reduces production.

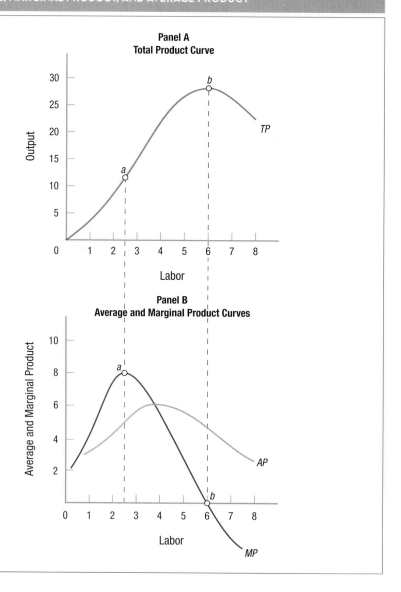

Panel A
Total Product Curve

Panel B
Average and Marginal Product Curves

Marginal and Average Product

Marginal product [column (3) in Table 2] is the change in output that results from a change in labor input. Marginal product is computed by dividing the change in output (ΔQ) by the change in labor (ΔL). The delta (Δ) symbol is used to denote "change in." Thus, marginal product (MP) is equal to $\Delta Q/\Delta L$; it is the change in output that results from adding additional workers.

Notice that when employment rises from 2 workers to 3 workers, output grows from 8 to 16 sails. Marginal product is therefore 8 sails at this point (point a in panel B of Figure 1). This is shown graphically with a point placed between the second and third worker, because this represents the change in output going from 2 workers to 3 workers. Contrast this with a change in employment when 6 people are already employed. Adding another employee actually reduces the total output of windsurfing sails from 28 to 26; therefore, marginal product is −2 from the sixth to the seventh worker.

Average product (AP) or output per worker is found by dividing total output by the number of workers employed to produce that output (Q/L). Average product is shown in panel B of Figure 1. When employment is 3 people and output is 16, for instance, average product is 5.33.

marginal product The change in output that results from a change in labor ($\Delta Q/\Delta L$).

average product Output per worker, found by dividing total output by the number of workers employed to produce that output (Q/L).

Increasing and Diminishing Returns

In our example, each of the first 3 workers adds more to output than the previous worker hired. Therefore, the marginal product going from 0 to 1 worker, 1 to 2 workers, and 2 to 3 workers increases. This is called the **increasing marginal returns** portion of the curve. In this range, output grows faster as you employ additional labor.

However, after you have employed 3 people, *marginal productivity* begins to trail off. Between 3 and 6 workers, you face **diminishing marginal returns** because each additional worker adds to total output, but at a diminishing rate.

Finally, once you have hired 6 employees, if you hire any more, this will result in negative marginal returns. Therefore, the marginal product curve crosses the horizontal axis at the sixth worker, which corresponds to the highest point on the total product curve (point b in Figure 1). Hiring additional people will actually reduce output; therefore, rational firms never operate in this range.

Meanwhile, the average product curve follows a similar path as the marginal product curve, although there isn't as dramatic a change as each worker is added. Average product gives you a sense of the overall productivity of a firm. The relationship between marginal product and average product is an important one. When marginal product exceeds average product—when a new worker adds more to output than the average of the previous workers—hiring an additional worker increases average productivity. This might be because hiring more people allows you to establish more of a production line, thereby increasing specialization and raising productivity. The marginal product curve always crosses the average product curve at its highest point, because once marginal product falls below the average product, the average product must fall as well.

Firms hire workers to produce output based on available resources, many of which are fixed in the short run. By adding more workers, firms can increase productivity by allowing workers to specialize in tasks for which they are more suited. As more workers are hired, diminishing or even negative returns can set in. The typical production curves shown in Figure 1 embody the *law of diminishing returns*. All firms eventually face diminishing marginal returns, but this does not mean production should be avoided as long as the value of the additional output produced exceeds the additional costs.

This analysis is important because it shows how much output is generated based on the number of workers hired, which will eventually translate into revenues for the firm once the output is sold. Therefore, production is an important component of profits, but not enough to determine the optimal production output. To maximize profits, we must also evaluate the costs of production, to which we turn next.

increasing marginal returns A new worker hired adds more to total output than the previous worker hired, so that both average and marginal products are rising.

diminishing marginal returns An additional worker adds to total output, but at a diminishing rate.

✅ CHECKPOINT

PRODUCTION IN THE SHORT RUN

- Production is the process of turning inputs into outputs.
- Total product is the total output produced by the production process.
- Marginal product (*MP*) is the change in output that results from a change in labor input and is equal to $\Delta Q/\Delta L$.
- Average product (*AP*) is output per worker and is equal to Q/L.
- Increasing marginal returns occur when adding a worker adds *more* to output than the previous worker hired.
- Diminishing marginal returns occur when adding a worker adds *less* to output than the previous worker hired.
- Negative marginal returns occur when adding a worker actually leads to less *total* output than with the previous worker hired.
- In most production processes, firms experience first increasing and then diminishing marginal returns to labor as workers are added.

QUESTION: Suppose a company has a policy to hire workers only when each additional worker hired is more productive than the previous worker hired. Using what you know about labor productivity, would this be a good policy?

Answers to the Checkpoint questions can be found at the end of this chapter.

COSTS OF PRODUCTION

Production tells only part of the story. We have to calculate how much it costs to produce this output in order to figure out if it is profitable to do so. Let's now bring resource prices, including labor costs, into our analysis to develop the typical cost curves for the firm, both in the short run and the long run.

Short-Run Costs

In a very straightforward way, production costs are determined by the productivity of workers. Ignoring all costs except wages, if you, by yourself, were to produce ten pizzas an hour and you were paid $8 an hour, then each pizza would cost an average of 80 cents to produce—the cost of your labor. Yet, to ignore any other cost would be to neglect a significant portion of business expenses known as *overhead,* or fixed costs.

A cruise ship can cost hundreds of millions of dollars, a fixed cost that is spent regardless of how many passengers cruise. Food for meals, however, is a variable cost because it varies based on how many passengers are on board.

To understand production costs more generally, we split the production period into the short run and the long run. In the short run, as least one factor is fixed, whereas in the long run, all factors are variable. This has led economists to define costs as fixed and variable.

Fixed and Variable Costs **Fixed costs** are costs that do not change as a firm's output expands or contracts. Lease or rental payments, administrative overhead, and insurance premiums are examples of fixed costs—they do not rise or fall as a firm alters production to meet market demands. **Variable costs,** on the other hand, do fluctuate as output changes. Labor and material costs are examples of variable costs because making more products requires hiring more workers and purchasing more raw materials.

Certain costs don't always fall so neatly into these two categories. For example, a new wireless communications tower can serve thousands of customers at the same time (and resembles a fixed cost), but once capacity is reached, a new tower is needed (and resembles a variable cost). These types of costs are known as *incremental costs*. To keep things simple, however, we will assume that all costs fit into either the fixed of variable cost categories, such that total cost (*TC*) is equal to total fixed cost (*FC*) plus total variable cost (*VC*), or

$$TC = FC + VC$$

The measurement of total cost is an important part of determining profits. However, in doing so, sometimes businesses incur costs that are not recoverable should production need to be changed. These irrecoverable costs, which can be both fixed and variable, are called **sunk costs**, and are incurred by individuals and businesses when making decisions.

Sunk Costs

The previous chapter introduced the concept of sunk costs and how they sometimes lead to imprudent decision making. For example, should you leave in the middle of a movie because it stinks? The cost of the movie ticket has already been paid, and staying until the end might add to the anguish of an already bad situation. Similarly, tuition is a sunk cost. Most colleges and universities do not provide refunds for dropped courses beyond the first week or two of the term.

But what does a "sunk" cost really mean, exactly? Because these costs are not recoverable, future decisions by individuals and businesses should not consider them. For example, the tuition that's already been paid (the sunk cost) should not influence the decision to drop a course one is failing. Similarly, a business's decision to air an advertisement on television should not depend on how much it spent producing the ad (the sunk cost), but instead whether the additional cost of airing the ad is justified.

The concept of sunk cost is often difficult to grasp because it goes against what we are often told—"Never quit!" or "Always finish what you start!" Sound familiar? Although these words of encouragement are appropriate in most cases, there are situations as described earlier when it might not be the best course of action, when it's best to just cut one's losses.

And finally, although most sunk costs are fixed costs, they can also be variable. If one prints 100 party invitations only to find out the party needs to be cancelled, that is an example of a variable sunk cost. The decision to cancel the party shouldn't depend on the fact that the invitations were already printed.

Now that we have introduced the concepts of fixed, variable, and total cost, let's discuss how total cost changes when the level of output changes.

fixed costs Costs that do not change as a firm's output expands or contracts, often called overhead.

variable costs Costs that vary with output fluctuations, including expenses such as labor and material costs.

sunk costs Costs that have been incurred and cannot be recovered.

Participating in the Chicago Marathon requires an entry fee of approximately $200, a fee that is nonrefundable and therefore a sunk cost. If one is not fully prepared to run 26.2 miles on race day, it may be wiser to withdraw from the race than to risk injury.

Getty Images Sport/Getty Images

Marginal Cost Although measuring total cost is important in determining the overall profitability of a business, the decision of whether to increase or decrease production largely depends on how total costs change when one increases or decreases the quantity produced. If the additional cost of producing one more unit of a good is greater than the additional revenue earned from that unit, then this unit would not be worth producing. Therefore, it is important to measure the change in costs with each additional unit of output produced.

Let's return to the windsurfing sail business example. Suppose your firm has orders for 10 windsurfing sails this month, and you get an order for 1 more sail at the last minute. Just how much would this additional windsurfing sail cost to produce? Or, in the language of economics, what is the *marginal cost* of the next sail produced?

Marginal cost is the change in total cost arising from the production of additional units of output. Marginal cost (MC) is equal to the change in total cost (ΔTC) divided by the change in output (ΔQ), or

$$MC = \Delta TC/\Delta Q = \Delta FC/\Delta Q + \Delta VC/\Delta Q$$

Note that, for simplicity, we have been discussing changes of 1 unit of output, but we can calculate MC for a change in output of any amount by plugging in the appropriate value for ΔQ. And because fixed costs do not vary with changes in output, $\Delta FC/\Delta Q = 0$, and thus marginal cost is also equal to $\Delta VC/\Delta Q$.

Table 3 provides us with more complete cost data for your windsurfing sail business. Assuming that you pay $1,000 per month in rent for the warehouse, fixed costs equal $1,000 [column (2)]. Your variable costs (the wages you pay your employees plus the price of raw materials) vary depending on the number of sails produced, and are shown in column (3). The total cost, therefore, is the sum of fixed and variable costs and is shown in column (4). Marginal cost measures the change in total (or variable) cost with each additional sail produced, and is given in column (5).

Let's go through one row so that you can be sure of how we arrived at the numbers in columns (2) to (5). Looking at the row showing 4 sails, the fixed cost is $1,000 because this does not change based on the number of sails produced. Variable cost does change because more work hours are needed to produce more sails; to produce 4 sails, the variable cost is $1,400. Total cost is simply fixed cost plus variable cost, or $2,400 for 4 sails. Finally, the marginal cost of the fourth sail is the change in total cost from producing 3 sails ($2,000) to producing 4 sails ($2,400). Therefore, the marginal cost of the fourth sail is the change from $2,000 to $2,400, or $400, and is shown in column (5) between the third and fourth units. It is common for marginal costs to first fall and then rise, which gives the marginal cost curve its distinct shape, which we will see later.

marginal cost The change in total costs arising from the production of additional units of output ($\Delta TC/\Delta Q$). Because fixed costs do not change with output, marginal costs are the change in variable costs associated with additional production ($\Delta VC/\Delta Q$).

| TABLE 3 | COST DATA FOR WINDSURFING SAIL FIRM |

(1) Q	(2) FC	(3) VC	(4) TC	(5) MC	(6) AFC	(7) AVC	(8) ATC
0	$1,000	$0	$1,000		—	—	—
				$500			
1	$1,000	$500	$1,500		$1,000.00	$500.00	$1,500.00
				$300			
2	$1,000	$800	$1,800		$500.00	$400.00	$900.00
				$200			
3	$1,000	$1,000	$2,000		$333.33	$333.33	$666.67
				$400			
4	$1,000	$1,400	$2,400		$250.00	$350.00	$600.00
				$500			
5	$1,000	$1,900	$2,900		$200.00	$380.00	$580.00
				$700			
6	$1,000	$2,600	$3,600		$166.67	$433.33	$600.00
				$1,000			
7	$1,000	$3,600	$4,600		$142.86	$514.29	$657.14

Senai Aksoy/Dreamstime.com

Average Costs When a firm produces a product or service, it typically wants a breakdown of how much labor, raw material, plant overhead, and sales costs are embedded in each unit of the product. Modern accounting systems permit a detailed breakdown of costs for each unit of production. For our purposes, however, that level of detail is not necessary. For us, cost per unit of output (or *average cost*), average fixed cost, and average variable cost are sufficient.

If we divide the total cost equation (*TC*) by total output *Q*, we get

$$TC/Q = FC/Q + VC/Q$$

Economists refer to total fixed costs divided by output (*FC/Q*) as **average fixed cost** (*AFC*). This represents the average amount of overhead for each unit of output. Total variable costs divided by output is known as **average variable cost** (*AVC*). It represents the labor and raw materials expenses that go into each unit of output. Adding *AFC* and *AVC* together results in **average total cost** (*ATC*), and thus the preceding equation can be rewritten as

$$ATC = AFC + AVC$$

Hence, average cost per unit (*ATC*) is the sum of average fixed cost (*AFC*) and average variable cost (*AVC*).

Average total cost is an important piece of information for firms. Specifically, it provides a general measurement of productivity—how cost-efficient a firm is in producing a specified number of units. Further, it provides the firm guidance as to whether it is earning a profit or whether it should shut down the business and leave the industry altogether.

Returning to Table 3, columns (6), (7), and (8) provide the average fixed cost, average variable cost, and average total cost, respectively, for each quantity of windsurfing sails produced. Let's calculate the average costs of producing 4 sails. The average fixed cost is calculated by taking the fixed cost of $1,000 and dividing it by 4 to equal $250. Average variable cost takes the variable cost of $1,400 and divides by 4 to equal $350 in *AVC*. We can calculate average total cost in two ways. First, we can take total cost of $2,400 and divide by 4 sails to equal $600 in *ATC*. Second, we know that *ATC = AFC + AVC*, so if we know that *AFC* is $250 and *AVC* is $350, then $250 + $350 = $600.

Notice a few trends in the average cost data. First, the average fixed cost falls continuously as more output is produced; this is because your overhead expenses are getting spread out over more and more units of output (this is known as the *spreading effect*). Figure 2

average fixed cost Equal to total fixed cost divided by output (*FC/Q*).

average variable cost Equal to total variable cost divided by output (*VC/Q*).

average total cost Equal to total cost divided by output (*TC/Q*). Average total cost is also equal to *AFC + AVC*.

FIGURE 2	THE AVERAGE FIXED COST CURVE

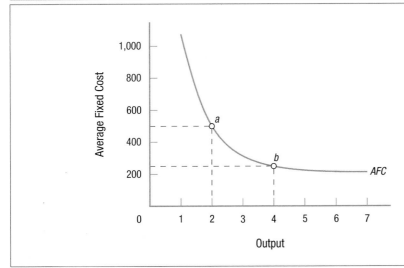

The average fixed cost (*AFC*) curve always decreases as production increases. This is because, in the short run, total fixed costs do not change so that increasing production spreads the fixed costs over more units of output (the *spreading effect*).

shows the average fixed cost curve using the data from Table 3. If 2 sails are produced, the average fixed cost is $1,000/2 = $500 (point *a* on the *AFC* curve); if 4 sails are produced, the average fixed cost is $1,000/4 = $250 (point *b* on the *AFC* curve). Average fixed costs are important to entrepreneurs, who often seek out new businesses with low fixed costs, allowing them to recover these expenses quickly.

Second, average variable costs and average total costs typically fall initially before rising, just like marginal costs. In the short run, these costs initially fall as the costs of procuring variable inputs fall and due to the *spreading effect* (which affects the average total cost curve), but these costs eventually rise with greater output as access to available resources dries up, leading to diminishing returns (resulting in a *diminishing returns effect*). Finally, average variable cost will always be smaller than the average total cost according to the *ATC* = *AFC* + *AVC* equation. These trends will be important as we make greater use of average cost in the next three chapters.

Short-Run Cost Curves for Profit-Maximizing Decisions

Table 3 provides the numerical values for costs. Although all of the costs are important in their own way, we focus on three costs that will provide guidance to firms in their need to maximize profits. These are average variable cost, average total cost, and marginal cost. Let us now translate these costs into figures to make their analysis simpler. Figure 3 shows the three cost measures in graphical form, drawn using the data from Table 3.

Average Variable Cost (AVC) The *AVC* and *ATC* curves are U-shaped. At relatively low levels of output, the curves slope downward, reflecting an increase in returns as average costs drop. As production levels rise, however, diminishing returns set in, and average costs start to climb back up. We get some sense of this by examining Table 3, in which the numbers for *AVC* and *ATC* fall and then rise, but the figure makes it far easier to see.

In Figure 3, the average variable cost curve reaches its minimum where 3 sails are produced (point *c*). Since *AVC* = *VC/Q*, then *VC* = *AVC* × *Q*. Thus, at point *c*, *VC* is equal to the rectangular area 0*ace*, or $1,000 ($333.33 × 3).

FIGURE 3	AVERAGE TOTAL COST, AVERAGE VARIABLE COST, AND MARGINAL COST

The average variable cost (*AVC*), average total cost (*ATC*), and marginal cost (*MC*) curves are shown. The bowl shape of the *AVC* and *ATC* curves demonstrates the law of diminishing returns: Beyond a certain level of output, average costs increase. Marginal costs represent the added cost of producing one more unit of output. Note that the marginal cost curve passes through the minimum points on both the *AVC* and *ATC* curves.

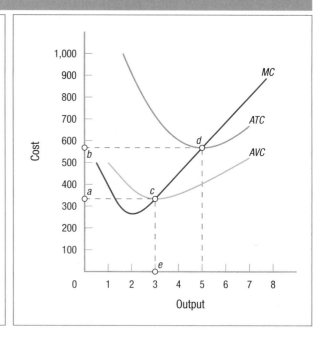

Average Total Cost (ATC) Average total cost equals total costs divided by output ($ATC = TC/Q$), or average fixed costs plus average variable cost ($ATC = AFC + AVC$). In Figure 3, the average total cost reaches its minimum where 5 sails are produced (point d). At this point, the average total cost is $580. As in the previous example, we can calculate the total cost of the firm at any point along the average total cost curve by multiplying the average total cost by the output produced. For example, the total cost of 5 sails would be $580 × 5 = $2,900, exactly as shown in Table 3.

Therefore, the use of cost curves allows us to determine both the total and average costs for a firm, which again are important components in determining profits. Still, we cannot proceed until we examine marginal costs, a key determinant in whether firms should produce more or less output.

Marginal Cost (MC) Drawing our discussion of short-run costs to a close, Figure 3 plots the marginal cost curve, adding it to the AVC and ATC curves we have plotted already.

Notice that the marginal cost curve intersects the minimum points of both the AVC and ATC curves. This is not a coincidence. Marginal cost is the cost necessary to produce another unit of a given product. When the cost to produce another unit is *less* than the average of the previous units produced, average costs will *fall*. For the AVC curve in Figure 3, this happens at all output levels less than 3 units (point c); for the ATC curve, it happens at all output levels less than 5 units (point d). But when the cost to produce another unit *exceeds* the average cost for all previous output, average costs will *rise*.

In Figure 3, this happens at output levels greater than 3 units (point c) for AVC and greater than 5 units (point d) for ATC. Over these ranges, marginal cost exceeds AVC and ATC, respectively, and thus the two curves rise. At points c and d, marginal cost is precisely equal to average variable cost and average total cost, respectively, and thus the AVC and ATC curves are at their minimum values (where the slopes are zero).

The average variable cost, average total cost, and marginal cost curves will help us analyze the profit-maximizing equilibrium for each market structure in the next three chapters. We will see how marginal cost provides guidance to firms on the quantity of output to produce, and how average variable cost and average total cost inform firms whether to maintain or expand operations, shut down, or leave the industry.

We have now examined short-run costs for firms when one factor, in this case, plant size, is fixed. When this occurs, firms face decisions about whether to operate or shut down given that the fixed costs are paid up front. As we analyze different types of markets in the next three chapters, we will examine how firms make short-run decisions when fixed and variable costs are taken into consideration. Let us now turn to costs in the long run, when all factors, including plant size, are variable. This means that fixed costs do not exist in the long run, because given enough time, a firm can expand or close its plant, and enter or leave an industry.

Long-Run Costs

In the long run, firms can adjust all factor inputs (such as labor and capital) to meet the needs of the market. Here, we focus on variations in plant size, while recognizing that all other factors, including technology, can vary.

Figure 4 shows the short-run average total costs curves using three different production functions for three different plant sizes. Plant 1 (ATC_1) has fewer machines than either plant 2 or plant 3. With a smaller fixed cost, plant 1 can produce smaller quantities at lower cost than plant 2 or plant 3, which have higher fixed costs. However, if plant 1 tries to increase output, its limited machinery will cause average costs to rise very quickly. For a small output, say, Q_0, plant 1 produces at an average cost of AC_0 (point b). Plant 2, with its additional overhead, can produce Q_0 output, but only for a higher average cost of AC_2 (point a). And plant 3's average cost of producing Q_0 would be even higher.

This figure shows the average total cost curve for three plants of different sizes. The larger plants have relatively high average total costs at lower levels of output, but much lower average total costs at higher output levels. Firms are free to adjust plant size in the long run; therefore, they can switch from one plant type to the next to minimize their costs at each production level. The green envelope curve represents the firm's lowest cost to produce any given output in the long run and represents the *LRATC* curve.

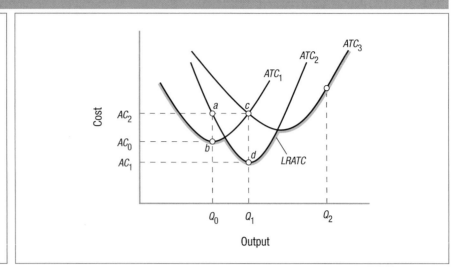

Therefore, at lower levels of production, plant 1 is able to achieve the lowest average cost. However, plant 2 and plant 3 achieve greater cost savings at higher levels of production. Once output rises to Q_1, plant 2 begins to enjoy the benefits of a lower average cost of production. The additional machines mean that plant 2 can produce Q_1 for AC_1 (point *d*), whereas the machines in plant 1 become overwhelmed at this level of output, resulting in an average cost of AC_2 (point *c*). Similarly, if a firm expects market demand eventually to reach Q_2, it would want to build plant 3 because plant 1 and plant 2 are too small to accommodate that level of production efficiently.

long-run average total cost In the long run, firms can adjust their plant sizes so that *LRATC* is the lowest unit cost at which any particular output can be produced in the long run.

Long-Run Average Total Cost The **long-run average total cost** (*LRATC*) curve represents the lowest unit cost at which any specific output can be produced in the long run, when a firm is able to adjust the size of its plant. In Figure 4, the *LRATC* curve is indicated by the green segments of the various short-run cost curves; these are the segments of each curve at which output can be produced at the lowest per unit cost (also known as the *envelope* curve, named after its telltale shape). In short, the *LRATC* assumes that, in the long run, firms will build plants of the size best fitting the levels of output they wish to produce.

Although the *LRATC* curve in Figure 4 is relatively bumpy, it will tend to smooth out as more plant size options are considered. In some industries, such as agriculture and food service, the options for plant size and production methods are virtually unlimited. In other industries, such as semiconductors, however, sophisticated plants may cost several billion dollars to build and require being run at near capacity to be cost-effective.

These huge, sophisticated plants are so complex that Intel Corporation has dedicated teams of engineers that build new plants and operate them exactly as all others. These teams ensure that any new plant is a virtual clone of the firm's other operating facilities. Even small deviations from this standard have proven disastrous to cost control in the past.

economies of scale As a firm's output increases, its *LRATC* tends to decline. This results from specialization of labor and management, and potentially a better use of capital and complementary production techniques.

Economies and Diseconomies of Scale As a firm's output increases, its *LRATC* tends to decrease. This is because, as the firm grows in size, **economies of scale** result from such items as specialization of labor and management, better use of capital, and increased possibilities for making several products that utilize complementary production techniques.

A larger firm's ability to have workers specialize in particular tasks reduces the costs associated with shifting workers from one task to another. Similarly, management in larger

FIGURE 5   ECONOMIES, DISECONOMIES, AND CONSTANT RETURNS TO SCALE

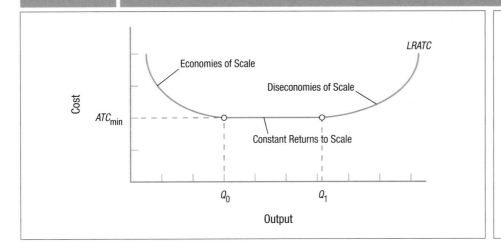

The curve in this figure shows how increasing production affects long-run average total cost (*LRATC*). Up to Q_0, economies of scale reduce *LRATC* as production increases. Over the range Q_0 to Q_1, the firm enjoys constant returns to scale, meaning that it can expand without affecting *LRATC*. Past Q_1, however, diseconomies of scale kick in, such that any further expansion causes an increase in *LRATC*.

operations can use technologies and specialized capital equipment that smaller firms cannot afford because of their smaller production volumes. Therefore, larger firms are better able to engage in complementary production and use by-products more effectively.

The area for *economies of scale* is shown in Figure 5 at levels of output below Q_0 (average costs are falling).

In many industries, there is a wide range of output wherein average total costs are relatively constant. Examples include fast-food restaurants, family restaurants, and automotive service shops. Such businesses tend to have steady average costs because the cost to replicate their business in any community is relatively constant. Constructing and running a Subway franchise, for example, cost roughly the same no matter where it is operated. In Figure 5, this area of **constant returns to scale** is represented by output levels between Q_0 and Q_1.

As firms continue to grow, they eventually encounter **diseconomies of scale.** At some point, the firm gets so big that management is unable to control its operations efficiently. Some firms become so big that they get bogged down in bureaucracy and cannot make decisions quickly. In the late 1980s, Apple fell into this trap—slow to react to changing market conditions for computers and software, the company was left behind by sleeker competition from Dell and Microsoft. Only through downsizing, reorganizing, refocusing, and a management change did Apple get back on track in the late 1990s. Diseconomies of scale—where increased output increases costs disproportionately—are shown at outputs above Q_1 in Figure 5.

Economies of Scope   When firms produce a number of products, it is often cheaper for them to produce another product when the production processes are interdependent. These economies are called **economies of scope.** For example, once a company has established a marketing department, it can take on the campaign of a new product at a lower cost. It has already developed the expertise and contacts necessary to sell the product. Book publishers can introduce a new book into the market more quickly and cheaply, and with more success than can a new firm starting in the business.

Some firms generate ideas for products, then send the production overseas. After they have been through this process, they become more efficient at it. Economists refer to this as *learning by doing*. Economies of scope often play a role in mergers as firms look for other firms with complementary products and skills.

Procter & Gamble makes hundreds of household products, taking advantage of large economies of scope by producing many products that use the same inputs and equipment. For example, some of the chemicals used to produce Tide detergent are also used to produce Cascade dishwasher tablets.

constant returns to scale A range of output where average total costs are relatively constant. The expansion of fast-food restaurant franchises and movie theaters, which are essentially replications of existing franchises and theaters, reflects this.

diseconomies of scale A range of output where average total costs tend to increase. Firms often become so big that management becomes bureaucratic and unable to control its operations efficiently.

economies of scope By producing a number of products that are interdependent, firms are able to produce and market these goods at lower costs.

Eric Chiang

Procter & Gamble makes hundreds of household products, taking advantage of large economies of scope by producing many products that use the same inputs and equipment.

Role of Technology We know that technology creates products that were the domain of science fiction writers of the past. Dick Tracy's wrist radio, first introduced in the comics of 1940s, has now morphed into the many wireless products we see today.

But we should mention in passing the role technology plays in altering the shape of the *LRATC* curve. The output level at which diseconomies of scale are reached has significantly and continuously expanded since the beginning of the Industrial Revolution.

Enhanced production techniques, instantaneous global communication, and the use of computers in accounting and cost control are just a few recent examples of ways in which technology has permitted firms to increase their scale beyond what anyone had imagined possible 50 years earlier. Who would have imagined a century ago that one firm could have millions of employees and billions of dollars in annual sales? Today, Walmart has more than 2 million employees and annual sales of over $500 billion.

What spurs firms and entrepreneurs to develop new technologies and bring new products to market? Three things: profits, profits, and profits. In this chapter, we analyzed where profits come from by looking at what firms do, how they measure profits, and how they determine production and costs. In the next chapter, we will look at revenues, as well as examine how firms can maximize their profits by adjusting output to market demand.

AROUND THE WORLD

Live Like a Royal: Castles Turning into Hotels

Why did investors in Ireland spend enormous sums of money to convert historic castles and homes into hotels?

As global demand for tourism rises, travelers are increasingly seeking unique experiences that they cannot have at home. For example, with the popularity of shows such as *Downton Abbey,* who wouldn't want to live the life of nobility, even if just for a day? One industry that has been eager to provide such experiences to travelers is the hospitality industry. Hotels have long attempted to offer unique amenities to their guests. But can hotels go one step further by offering a history lesson and a chance for an ordinary person to ape nobility?

Eric Chiang

Dromoland is a 16th-century castle turned luxury hotel in Ireland.

In Ireland, a country with many historical landmarks and castles, hoteliers have transformed historical homes and even centuries-old castles into hotels and bed-and-breakfasts for all budgets, from rustic hotels to five-star luxury resorts. Such efforts at restoring historical estates require

significant fixed costs, often funded by well-heeled investors and investment firms. Once restored, the variable costs are similar to those of other hotels.

At Dromoland Castle near Shannon, Ireland, guests enter the grounds of a refurbished 16th-century castle that looks every bit like it might have 500 years ago. With drawing rooms, old gateways, secret entrances and passageways, and walled gardens, this castle allows the guest to experience life as a noble or royal, even if only for a few days. Dromoland is just one of hundreds of refurbished castles and historical homes now welcoming guests from around the world. For the owners of these unique hotels, the draw of earning profits makes the substantial fixed costs a worthwhile investment. For the hotel guest, it's a rare opportunity to live like a king or queen in a real castle.

GO TO LaunchPad TO PRACTICE THE ECONOMIC CONCEPTS IN THIS STORY

✅ CHECKPOINT

COSTS OF PRODUCTION

- Fixed costs (overhead) are those costs that do not vary with output, including lease payments and insurance. Fixed costs occur in the short run—in the long run, firms can change plant size or even exit an industry.

- Variable costs rise and fall as a firm produces more or less output. These variable costs include raw materials, labor, and utilities.

- Total cost equals fixed cost plus variable cost ($TC = FC + VC$).

- Average fixed cost, average variable cost, and average total cost provide a general measure of efficiency when looking at the total amount of output produced.

- Marginal cost is the change in total cost divided by the change in output ($MC = \Delta TC/\Delta Q$). Marginal cost provides important information to firms deciding whether to produce more or less output.

- The long-run average total cost curve ($LRATC$) represents the lowest unit cost at which specific output can be produced in the long run.

- As a firm grows in size, economies of scale result from specialization of labor and better use of capital, while diseconomies of scale occur because a firm gets so big that management loses control of its operations and the firm becomes bogged down in bureaucracy.

- Economies of scope result when firms produce a number of interdependent products, so it is cheaper for them to add another product to the line.

- Modern communications and computers have permitted firms to become huge before diseconomies of scale are reached.

QUESTION: In the late 1990s, Boeing reported that it took roughly 12 years and $15 billion to bring a new aircraft from the design stage to a test flight. Boeing signed a 20-year exclusive agreement to supply aircraft to Delta, American, and Continental (now United) Airlines. The rationale for the agreement was that every time production of the plane doubled, the average production cost per plane would fall by about 20%. Why would doubling production cut costs per unit by 20%?

Answers to the Checkpoint questions can be found at the end of this chapter.

chapter summary

Section 1 Firms, Profits, and Economic Costs

7.1 **Firms** are economic institutions that transform inputs (factors of production) into outputs (products and services).

Nearly half of all businesses in the United States close within five years as new businesses take their place.

Types of Businesses

Sole proprietorship: unlimited liability, full control

Partnership: unlimited liability, shared control

Corporation: limited liability, ability to issue stock

Profit = Total Revenue – Total Cost

7.2 Accounting Costs   vs.   Economic Costs
Include only   Include explicit
explicit (out-of-pocket) and implicit
costs   (opportunity) costs

Economic Profit = Total Revenue – Economic Costs
Normal profit is an economic profit of $0.

7.3 **Short run:** period of time during which at least one factor of production is fixed
Long run: a period long enough that firms can vary all factors, as well as leave and enter industries

Section 2 Production in the Short Run

7.4 **Total product** is the quantity of output produced using a certain amount of labor inputs.
Marginal product is the change in output associated with hiring one additional worker, or $\Delta Q/\Delta L$.

7.5

Increasing Versus Decreasing Returns to Labor

When *increasing returns* are present, each additional worker adds more to total output than previous workers. Eventually, all production is subject to the *law of diminishing returns*, causing decreasing returns from adding more workers.

Having extra workers is very productive at first, but eventually everyone gets in each other's way, leading to decreasing returns to labor.

Section 3 Costs of Production

7.6 Short-Run Costs

In the short run, firms have **fixed costs** (*FC*) that do not vary with output and **variable costs** (*VC*) that do vary.

Total Cost (*TC*) = Fixed Cost + Variable Cost
Marginal Cost (*MC*) = Change in Total Cost From Producing One More Unit

Average Fixed Cost (*AFC*) = Fixed Cost/Quantity
Average Variable Cost (*AVC*) = Variable Cost/Quantity
Average Total Cost (*ATC*) = Total Cost/Quantity

Sunk Costs

Sunk costs are the costs that are not recoverable once spent. Future decisions should not depend on sunk costs already incurred.

Abbreviated Cost Table for a Firm in the Short Run

Q	FC	VC	TC	MC	ATC
0	20	0	20		—
				25	
1	20	25	45		45
				15	
2	20	40	60		30
				45	
3	20	85	105		35

Opening a personal training business involves fixed costs (equipment or gym membership) and variable costs (time spent with each client).

7.7 Why Does *MC* Cross *ATC* at Its Minimum Point?

When the next unit costs less than the average (*MC* < *ATC*), *ATC* falls. When the next unit costs more than the average (*MC* > *ATC*), *ATC* rises. For example, suppose your current course grade is 85%. If your grade on your next exam is 90%, your marginal exam score is greater than your average score; therefore, your average rises. However, if your next exam grade (marginal score) is 70%, your average falls.

7.8

7.9 Long-Run Average Total Cost

In the long run, all factors of production are variable, and firms can enter or leave the industry. The **long-run average total cost** (*LRATC*) curve is the lowest unit cost for any specific output level in the long run.

7.10 **Economies of scale** occur when the average cost of production falls as a firm grows and cost savings from specialization in labor and management occur.
Eventually, **diseconomies of scale** occur when a firm's size becomes so large that efficient management becomes impossible. **Economies of scope** are cost savings resulting from the ability of firms to produce many interdependent products.

Advanced computer and communications technologies have radically increased the size of firms that can be efficiently managed. IKEA, for example, operates over 350 gigantic stores in 40 countries.

firm, p. 170
sole proprietorship, p. 170
partnership, p. 171
corporation, p. 171
profit, p. 171
total revenue, p. 171
total cost, p. 171
economic costs, p. 172
explicit costs, p. 172
implicit costs, p. 172
accounting profit, p. 173

economic profit, p. 173
normal profits, p. 173
short run, p. 174
long run, p. 174
production, p. 175
marginal product, p. 177
average product, p. 177
increasing marginal returns, p. 177
diminishing marginal returns, p. 177
fixed costs, p. 179
variable costs, p. 179

sunk costs, p. 179
marginal cost, p. 180
average fixed cost, p. 181
average variable cost, p. 181
average total cost, p. 181
long-run average total cost, p. 184
economies of scale, p. 184
constant returns to scale, p. 185
diseconomies of scale, p. 185
economies of scope, p. 185

QUESTIONS AND PROBLEMS

Check Your Understanding

1. What is the difference between explicit and implicit costs? What is the difference between economic and accounting profits? Are these four concepts related? How?

2. Why should sunk costs be ignored for decision making?

3. How does the short run differ from the long run? Is the long run the same for all industries? Why or why not?

4. Why should a firm never hire a worker when negative marginal returns set in?

5. Why is the average fixed cost curve not U-shaped? Why does it not turn up as the average variable cost and average total cost curves do?

6. What is the difference between marginal cost and average total cost?

Apply the Concepts

7. If you work hard building your business and end up earning zero economic profit for the year, would this be considered a failed business to an economist? Why or why not?

8. In order to take this class, you had to pay tuition, buy the textbook, and buy a new laptop. Which of these items (if any) would be considered a sunk cost? Explain your reasoning.

9. The movie industry earns a substantial portion of its total revenues through Internet streaming and downloads. Although producing a movie can costs tens of millions of dollars, the marginal cost of producing another copy or download is practically nothing. For this industry, would short-run *ATC* and *MC* still be U-shaped? If not, what would these curves look like?

10. List some of the reasons why the long-run average total cost curve has sort of a flat bowl shape. It declines early on, then is rather flat over a portion, and finally slopes upward.

11. The Finger Lakes region in New York State produces wine. The climate favors white wines, but reds have been produced successfully in the past 15 years. Categorize the following costs incurred by one winery as either fixed or variable:

    a. the capital used to buy 60 acres of land on Lake Seneca

    b. the machine used to pick some varieties of grapes at the end of August and the beginning of September

    c. the salary of the chief vintner, who is employed year-round

    d. the wages paid to workers who bind the grape plants, usually in April, and usually over a period of 3 to 4 days

    e. the wages paid to the same workers who pick the grapes at the end of August or early September

    f.   the costs of the chemicals sprayed on the grapes in July

    g.   the wages of the wine expert who blends the wine in August and September, after the grapes have been picked

    h.   the cost of the building where wine tastings take place from April to October

    i.   the cost of the wine used in the wine tasting

12. If marginal cost is less than average total cost, are average total costs rising or falling? Alternatively, if marginal cost is more than average total cost, are average total costs rising or falling? Explain how this example might apply to a basketball player attempting to achieve a high average *points per game.*

In The News

13. Fracking is the process by which oil is extracted from underground using a high-pressure water mixture. This procedure has led to accusations that it causes earthquakes as a result of the wastewater that is injected back underground. As a result, several cities and states have banned fracking operations, while others have proposed regulations on how fracking should be conducted. How do new regulations affect the costs of doing business? Do regulations represent a fixed or variable cost, or can they be both? Explain.

14. Colorado was the first state to legalize recreational marijuana in 2012. Since then, several states have followed, leading to a boom in the number of growers and shops selling marijuana. A problem, however, is that federal law still prohibits the sale of marijuana, though in practice state laws have been respected. Still, many shop owners choose to conduct transactions only in cash to avoid leaving an evidence trail from credit card transactions, which reduces the risk of prosecution but raises the risk of theft or loss. With so much retail competition along with added risk, why do many choose to venture into this business?

Solving Problems

15. Suppose you pay $10 to watch a movie at the local cineplex, and afterward you sneak into the next theater to watch a second movie without paying. What is your marginal cost of watching the second movie? What is the average cost of watching the two movies? After the movies, you go to the batting cages and stand in for two rounds of pitches, each round costing $2. What is your marginal cost of batting the second round? What is the average cost of batting two rounds?

■■■ WORK IT OUT ■■■■■■■■■■■ ☒ LaunchPad | interactive activity ■■■

16. Using the following table, answer the following questions.

Labor	Output	Marginal Product	Average Product
0	0		—
1	7	_____	_____
2	15	_____	_____
3	25	_____	_____
4	33	_____	_____
5	40	_____	_____
6	45	_____	_____

    a.   Complete the table, filling in the answers for marginal and average products.

    b.   Over how many workers is the firm enjoying increasing returns?

    c.   At what number of workers do diminishing returns set in?

    d.   Are negative returns shown in the table?

USING THE NUMBERS

17. According to By the Numbers, explain why a correlation exists between the costs of industrial robots and the productivity rate over the last 20 years.

18. According to By the Numbers, between which 5 years from 2000 to 2015 did Internet flight bookings increase the most (by percentage of overall sales)? Between which 5 years from 2000 to 2015 did Internet flight check-ins increase the most (by percentage of overall check-ins)?

ANSWERS TO QUESTIONS IN CHECKPOINTS

Checkpoint: Firms, Profits, and Economic Costs 175

Setting up your firm as a corporation has its benefits and its costs. One benefit of a corporation is limited liability, which means that if your company fails, the company can declare bankruptcy without it affecting your personal assets or credit. Another benefit is the ability to raise capital by issuing bonds or stocks. The downside of setting up a corporation is that profits are potentially shared by many shareholders. Also, corporations involve much more paperwork (such as setting up the firm and filing tax returns) than a sole proprietorship, which is much easier to set up and manage.

Checkpoint: Production in the Short Run 178

Hiring a worker only when she or he is more productive than the last worker hired means that a company insists on maintaining increasing marginal returns to labor. However, this generally occurs only for a limited number of workers. Eventually, all firms face diminishing marginal returns. This doesn't mean a firm should stop hiring, because the additional workers may still provide valuable productivity relative to their cost.

Checkpoint: Costs of Production 187

This immense $15 billion development cost is a fixed cost that is spread over more planes as production rises. Therefore, Boeing has an incentive to enter into contracts with airlines to ensure that both economies of scale and economies of scope can be achieved.

8 Perfect Competition

Understanding how firms stay in business when they have no control over the price of the goods they sell

Radius Images / Alamy

Learning Objectives

8.1 Name the primary market structures and describe their characteristics.

8.2 Define a perfectly competitive market and the assumptions that underlie it.

8.3 Determine a competitive firm's profit-maximizing quantity and price.

8.4 Analyze the conditions for profit maximization, loss minimization, and plant shutdown for a firm.

8.5 Derive the firm's short-run supply curve.

8.6 Use the short-run competitive model to determine market entry and exit in achieving long-run equilibrium.

8.7 Describe why competition is in the public interest.

Visit your local farmer's market on a weekend morning, and you'll find dozens of individual stands offering the freshest fruits and vegetables, many of which are grown locally and delivered to the market directly by the grower. As you meander through the market, you notice that the prices for any one type of fruit or vegetable are virtually the same from one stand to another. Further, the prices at the farmer's market often aren't much different from those that you might find in your grocery store's produce section.

With prices being nearly identical, shoppers are then left with the challenge of selecting the fruits and vegetables that look, feel, smell—and sometimes taste, if samples are available—the best, which for a food connoisseur is one of the pleasures of visiting a farmer's market. The rest of us, who do not have the skill to select the juiciest watermelon or peach, are often left to rely on our instincts. Even so, the difference in quality of the fruit across the various sellers is likely to be so small (because all are grown in the same area with the same climate) that typically one need not worry about making a bad choice.

This is the essence of a purely competitive market—the quality of a product is mostly indistinguishable, and hence the prices tend to be the same across sellers. In fact, each individual seller, being just one among thousands of sellers of fruit and vegetables, has little control over prices, another characteristic of a highly competitive market that forces sellers to be efficient. It's an example of the classic "survival of the fittest" problem—either produce high-quality produce at the lowest prices, or be sent packing.

The nature of intense competition extends well beyond farming, of course. Many of the goods we consume each day are produced in massive factories, often in Asia, where thousands of workers toil diligently in an often dreary environment to provide what we desire at the lowest cost. Before we debate the merits of whether this is good or bad for the factory workers, let's look at why many companies are using this form of production to stay competitive.

A firm's production function describes the manner in which inputs (resources such as labor and capital) are turned into outputs (goods). Since the cost of a set amount of inputs is fixed, being able to manufacture *more* with those inputs reduces the cost of production and increases productivity.

How does a firm increase productivity? First, it can hire better workers or offer training to make each worker more productive. Second, it can utilize better machinery (capital). And third, it can design the factory in a way to maximize the production given the workers and capital available. Choosing the production method by which inputs such as labor and capital are used is critical to productivity and the success of a firm. This is the role of the manager. If a firm uses inputs inefficiently, more efficient firms will drive it out of business.

The goal of any firm is to maximize profits given the market structure in which it exists. This is easier in some markets than in others. For example, if a company is the industry

BY THE NUMBERS

Perfect Competition and Efficiency

Cost efficiency plays an important role in the survival of firms in perfectly competitive industries. Because each firm represents just one of many firms in the market, the actions of one firm do not affect any other firm.

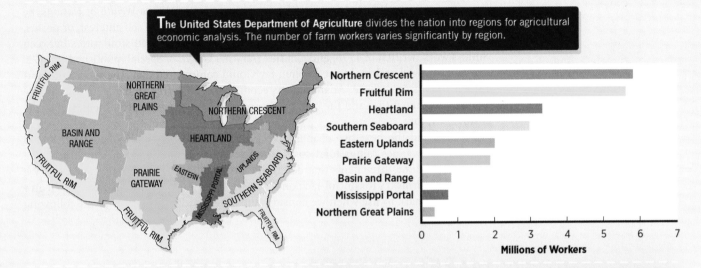

The United States Department of Agriculture divides the nation into regions for agricultural economic analysis. The number of farm workers varies significantly by region.

Map regions: FRUITFUL RIM, NORTHERN GREAT PLAINS, NORTHERN CRESCENT, BASIN AND RANGE, HEARTLAND, EASTERN UPLANDS, PRAIRIE GATEWAY, MISSISSIPPI PORTAL, SOUTHERN SEABOARD

Bar chart — Millions of Workers (0 to 7):
- Northern Crescent
- Fruitful Rim
- Heartland
- Southern Seaboard
- Eastern Uplands
- Prairie Gateway
- Basin and Range
- Mississippi Portal
- Northern Great Plains

Millions of Workers

The World's Top Tea Producers

Pie chart:
- China 25.1%
- India 22.6%
- Kenya 7.6%
- Sri Lanka 7.4%
- Turkey 4.4%
- Indonesia 4.0%
- Rest of World 28.9%

11,163,975,220   **T**otal world production of tea (in pounds) in 2015.

21,895,360,880   **T**otal world production of coffee (in pounds) in 2015.

epa European Pressphoto Agency creative account/Alamy

The legalization of **marijuana** in certain states has dramatically increased the number of growers in a highly competitive market, despite risk of federal prosecution.

AP Images/Jeff Barnard

Go to **LaunchPad** *to use the latest data to recreate this graph.*

The average price per bushel of soybeans, wheat, and corn increased significantly from 2006 to 2012 and then decreased in recent years.

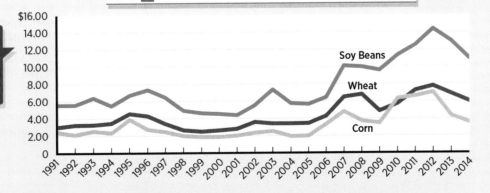

Line graph ($0 to $16.00), years 1991–2014: Soy Beans, Wheat, Corn leader and has few competitors, earning profits is easier than it is for a struggling company facing intense competition.

This chapter focuses on market structure and the purest form of competition, which we call perfect competition. We explore some of the implications competition has for markets and consider why the competitive market structure is so central to the thinking of economists. When Adam Smith wrote his classic book *The Wealth of Nations,* he wrote of a "hidden hand" that guides businesses in their pursuit of self-interest, or profits, allowing only the efficient to survive. Some observers have noted similarities between Smith's work, written in 1776, and Charles Darwin's *Origin of Species,* published in 1872. The late biologist and zoologist Stephen Jay Gould commented that "the theory of natural selection is, in essence, Adam Smith's economics transferred to nature."[1] Clearly, the notions of competition and the competitive market have played a prominent role in the history of ideas.

In this and the next two chapters, keep in mind the profitability equation. Profits equal total revenues minus total costs. Total revenues equal price times quantity sold. Keep in mind the three items that determine profitability: price, quantity, and cost. We will see how firms try to control each one of these. What you learn in this chapter will give you a benchmark to use when we consider the other market structures in the following chapters.

MARKET STRUCTURE ANALYSIS

market structure analysis By observing a few industry characteristics such as number of firms in the industry or the level of barriers to entry, economists can use this information to predict pricing and output behavior of the firm in the industry.

To appreciate competitive markets, we need to look at competition within the full range of possible market structures. Economists use **market structure analysis** to categorize industries based on a few key characteristics. By knowing simple industry facts, economists can predict the behavior of firms in that industry in such areas as pricing and sales.

The following four factors help to define the intensity of competition in an industry and to provide some sense of the issues behind each one.

- **Number of firms in the industry:** Does the industry comprise many firms, each with limited or no ability to set the market price, such as local strawberry farms, or is it dominated by a large firm such as Apple that can influence price regardless of the number of other firms?

- **Nature of the industry's product:** Are we talking about a homogeneous product such as plain table salt, for which no consumer will pay a premium or are we considering leather handbags, which consumers may think vary greatly, in that some firms (Coach, Gucci) produce better goods than others?

- **Barriers to entry:** Does the industry require low start-up and maintenance costs such as found at a roadside fruit and vegetable stand, or is it a computer-chip business that may require $1 billion to build a new chip plant?

- **Extent to which individual firms can control prices:** Pharmaceutical companies can set prices for new medicines, at least for a period of time, because of patent protection. Farmers and copper producers have virtually no control and get their prices from world markets.

Possible market structures range from perfect competition, characterized by many firms, to monopoly, where an industry is made up of only one firm. These market structures will make more sense to you as we consider each one in the chapters ahead. Right now, use this list and the descriptions as reference points. You can always return here and put the discussion in context.

---

[1] Stephen Jay Gould, *The Structure of Evolutionary Theory* (Cambridge, MA: Belknap Press of Harvard University Press), 2002, pp. 121–125.

Primary Market Structures

The primary market structures economists have identified, along with their key characteristics, are as follows:

Perfect Competition

- Many buyers and sellers
- Homogeneous (standardized) products
- No barriers to market entry or exit
- No long-run economic profit
- No control over price (no market power)

Monopolistic Competition

- Many buyers and sellers
- Differentiated products
- Little to no barriers to market entry or exit
- No long-run economic profit
- Some control over price (limited market power)

Oligopoly

- Fewer firms (such as the auto industry)
- Mutually interdependent decisions
- Substantial barriers to market entry
- Potential for long-run economic profit
- Shared market power and considerable control over price

Perfectly competitive fruit stands in New York City operate in the shadows of large oligopoly financial institutions, adjacent to a city-run bus system (a monopoly), and in front of monopolistically competitive restaurants and shops.

Monopoly

- One firm
- No close substitutes for product
- Nearly insuperable barriers to entry
- Potential for long-run economic profit
- Substantial market power and control over price

Putting off discussion of the other market structures for later chapters, we turn to an extended examination of the requirements for a perfectly competitive market. In the remainder of this chapter, we explore short-run pricing and output decisions, and also the importance of entry and exit in the long run. Moreover, we use the conditions of perfect competition to establish a benchmark for efficiency as we turn to evaluate other market structures in the following chapters.

Defining Perfectly Competitive Markets

The theory of **perfect competition** rests on the following assumptions:

1. Perfectly competitive markets have many buyers and sellers, each of them so small that none can individually influence product price.

2. Firms in the industry produce a homogeneous or standardized product.

3. Buyers and sellers have all the information about prices and product quality they need to make informed decisions.

perfect competition A market structure with many relatively small buyers and sellers who take the price as given, a standardized product, full information to both buyers and sellers, and no barriers to entry or exit.

4. Barriers to entry or exit are nonexistent; in the long run, new firms are free to enter the industry if doing so appears profitable, while firms are free to exit if they anticipate losses.

One implication of these assumptions is that perfectly competitive firms are **price takers.** Market prices are determined by market forces beyond the control of individual firms. That is, firms must take what they can get for their products. Paper for copy machines, most agricultural products, basic computer memory chips, and many other goods are produced in highly competitive markets. The buyers or sellers in these markets are so small that their ability to influence market price is nonexistent. These firms must accept whatever price the market determines, leaving them to decide only how much of the product to produce or buy.

Panel A of Figure 1 portrays the supply and demand for windsurfing sails in a perfectly competitive market; the market is in equilibrium at a price of $200 per sail and industry output Q_e. Remember that this product is a standardized sail (similar to 2×4 lumber, corn, or crude oil) and that the market contains many buyers and sellers, who collectively set the product price at $200.

Panel B shows the demand for a seller's products in this market. The firm can sell all it wants at $200 or below. Yet, what firm would set its price below $200 when it can sell everything it produces at $200? Were the firm to set its price above $200, however, it would sell nothing. What consumer, after all, would purchase a standardized sail at a higher price when it can be obtained elsewhere for $200? The individual firm's demand curve is horizontal at $200. The firm can still determine how much of its product to produce and sell, but this is the only choice it has. The firm cannot set its own price; therefore, it is a *price taker.*

Recall the profitability equation. Profit equals total revenue minus total cost. Total revenue equals price times quantity sold. In perfectly competitive markets, a firm's profitability is based on a given market price, quantity sold, and its costs. So how does it determine how much to sell?

price taker Individual firms in perfectly competitive markets determine their prices from the market because they are so small they cannot influence market price. For this reason, perfectly competitive firms can sell all the output they produce at market-determined prices.

| **FIGURE 1** | THE MARKET FOR COMPETITIVE PRODUCTS WITH AN EQUILIBRIUM PRICE OF $200 |

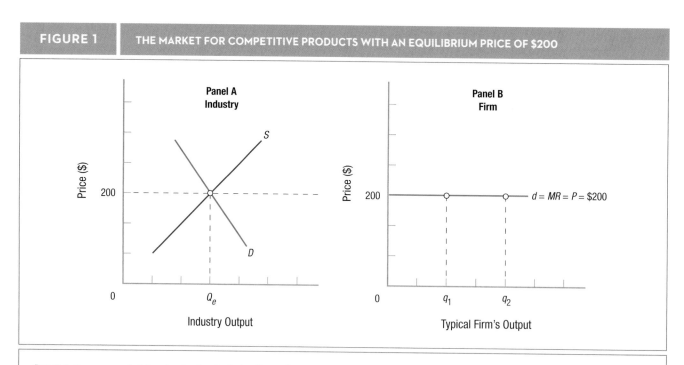

Panel A shows a market for standardized windsurfing sails in equilibrium at a price of $200 and industry output Q_e. This price is determined by the market's many buyers and sellers. Panel B illustrates product demand for an individual seller. The individual firm can sell all it wants to at $200 and has no reason to set its price below that. If it tries to sell at prices higher than $200, it sells nothing. The demand curve for the individual firm is horizontal at $200.

The Short Run and the Long Run (A Reminder)

Before turning to a more detailed examination of how firms decide how much output to produce in a perfectly competitive market, we need to recall a distinction introduced in the last chapter between the *short run* and the *long run*.

In the *short run,* one factor of production is fixed, usually the firm's plant size, and firms cannot enter or leave an industry. Thus, in the short run, the number of firms in a market is fixed. Firms may earn economic profits, break even, or suffer losses, but still they cannot exit the industry, nor can new firms enter.

In the *long run,* all factors are variable, and thus the level of profits induces entry or exit. When losses prevail, some firms will leave the industry and invest their capital elsewhere. When economic profits are positive, new firms will enter the industry. The long run is far more dynamic than the short run.

 CHECKPOINT

MARKET STRUCTURE ANALYSIS

- Market structure analysis allows economists to categorize industries based on a few characteristics and use this analysis to predict pricing and output behavior.

- The intensity of competition is defined by the number of firms in the industry, the nature of the industry's product, the level of barriers to entry, and how much firms can control prices.

- Market structures range from perfect competition (many buyers and sellers), to monopolistic competition (differentiated product), to oligopoly (only a few firms that are interdependent), to monopoly (a one-firm industry).

- Perfect competition is defined by four attributes: Many buyers and sellers who are so small that none individually can influence price, firms that produce and sell a homogeneous (standardized) product, buyers and sellers who have all the information necessary to make informed decisions, and barriers to entry and exit that are nonexistent.

- Firms in perfectly competitive markets get the product price from national or global markets. In other words, firms are price takers.

- In the short run, one factor (usually plant size) is fixed. In the long run, all factors are variable, and firms can enter or leave the industry.

QUESTION: For the following firms, explain where in our market structure approach each firm best fits: Verizon (a wireless communications service provider), NFL (a professional football organization), Grandma's Southern Kitchen (a small café), Jack's Lumber (an independent lumber mill).

Answers to the Checkpoint questions can be found at the end of this chapter.

PERFECT COMPETITION: SHORT-RUN DECISIONS

Figure 1 in the previous section presented a perfectly competitive market with an equilibrium price of $200. This translates into a horizontal demand curve for individual firms at that price. Individual firms are price takers in this competitive situation: They can sell as many units of their product as they wish at $200 each.

Marginal Revenue

Economists define **marginal revenue** as the change in total revenue that results from the sale of one additional unit of a product. Marginal revenue (*MR*) is equal to the change in total revenue (ΔTR) divided by the change in quantity sold (Δq); thus,

$$MR = \Delta TR / \Delta q$$

marginal revenue The change in total revenue from selling an additional unit of output. Because competitive firms are price takers, $P = MR$ for competitive firms.

Total revenue (*TR*), meanwhile, is equal to price per unit (*p*) times quantity sold (*q*); thus,

$$TR = p \times q$$

In a perfectly competitive market, we know that price will not change based on the output of any one firm. And because marginal revenue is defined as the change in revenue that comes from selling 1 more unit, marginal revenue is simply equal to price. To verify, suppose a firm sells 10 units of a good at $200 each, earning a total revenue of $2,000. If the firm sells 11 units at $200 each, total revenue becomes $2,200. Using our marginal revenue equation, the added revenue a firm receives from selling the 11th unit is $200, which is equal to the product price. Thus, determining marginal revenue in a perfectly competitive market is easy. As we will see in later chapters, this gets more complicated in market structures in which firms have some control over price.

Profit-Maximizing Output

Suppose that you own a windsurfing sail manufacturing firm in a perfectly competitive market. Figure 2 shows the price and marginal cost curve that your firm faces while it seeks to maximize profits. As the price and cost curve show, you can sell all you want at $200 a sail. Our first instinct might be to conclude that you will produce all that you can, but this is not the case. Given the marginal cost curve shown in Figure 2, if you produce 85 units, profit will be less than the maximum possible. This is because revenue from the sale is $200, but the 85th sail costs $210 to produce (point *b*). This means producing this last sail reduces profits by $10.

Suppose instead that you produce 84 sails. The revenue from selling the 84th unit (*MR*) is $200. This is precisely equal to the added cost (*MC*) of producing this unit, $200 (point *e*). Therefore, your firm earns zero economic profit by producing and selling the 84th sail. Zero economic profit, or normal profits, mean that your firm is earning a normal return on its capital by selling this 84th sail. If you produce only 83 sails, however, the additional cost (point *a*) will be less than the price, and you will have to relinquish the normal return associated with the 84th sail. Profits from selling 83 sails will therefore be lower than if 84 sails are sold because the normal return on the 84th sail is lost.

FIGURE 2	PROFIT MAXIMIZATION IN THE SHORT RUN IN PERFECTLY COMPETITIVE MARKETS

If the firm produces 85 standardized windsurfing sails, the marginal cost to produce the last sail exceeds the revenue from its sale, thus reducing the firm's profits. For the 84th unit produced, marginal cost and price are both equal to $200; therefore, the firm earns a normal return from producing this unit. Producing only 83 units means relinquishing the normal return that could have been earned from the 84th sail. Hence, the firm maximizes profits at an output of 84 (point *e*), where *MC* = *MR* = *P* = $200.

These observations lead us to a **profit-maximizing rule:** *A firm maximizes profit by continuing to produce and sell output until marginal revenue equals marginal cost (MR = MC).* As we will see in subsequent chapters, this rule applies to all firms, regardless of market structure.

Economic Profits

Continuing with the example of your windsurfing sail manufacturing firm, assume that the market has established a price of $200 for each sail. Your marginal revenue and cost curves are shown in Figure 3 (the *MR* and *MC* curves are the same as those shown in Figure 2).

Earlier, we found that profits are maximized when your firm is producing output such that *MR = MC*, in this case, 84 sails. Looking at Figure 3, we see that profits are maximized at point *a,* because this is where *MR = MC* at $200. We can compute the profit in this scenario by multiplying average profit (profit per unit) by output. Average profit equals price minus average total cost (*P − ATC*). In the figure, the average total cost of producing 84 sails is $180 (point *b*). Thus, when 84 sails are produced, average profit is the distance *ab* in Figure 3, or $200 − $180 = $20. Total profit, or average profit times output [(*P − ATC*) × *Q*], is $20 × 84 = $1,680; this is represented in the figure by area *cfab*. This area also is equivalent to total revenue minus total cost (*TR − TC*).

Note that there *is* a profit-maximizing point. The competitive firm cannot produce and produce—it has to take into consideration its costs. Therefore, for the price-taking competitive firm, its cost structure is crucial.

Five Steps to Maximizing Profit

Profit maximization is an important goal of any firm in any market structure. Yet, understanding revenue and cost curves can be frustrating given the many market structures

profit-maximizing rule Firms maximize profit by producing output where *MR = MC*. No other level of output produces higher profits.

| FIGURE 3 | A PERFECTLY COMPETITIVE FIRM EARNING ECONOMIC PROFITS |

Profits are maximized where marginal revenue equals marginal cost (*MR = MC*), or at an output of 84 and a price of $200. Price minus average total cost equals average profit per unit, represented by the distance *ab*. Average profit per unit times the number of units produced equals total profit; this is represented by area *cfab*.

FIGURE 4 | **FIVE-STEP PROCESS TO DETERMINE MAXIMUM PROFIT**

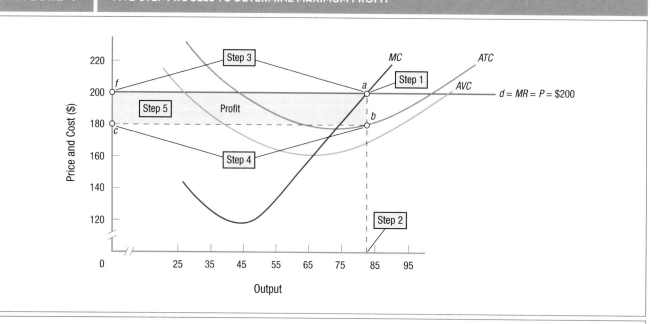

The five steps shown provide a consistent approach to determining the profit-maximizing output and price and the area representing profit using revenue and cost curves in any market structure.

and the different types of curves facing each market. Wouldn't it be useful to have a single approach when solving for a profit-maximizing outcome?

Let's review how we solved for the profit-maximizing equilibrium in the previous section, but this time using five simple steps that are illustrated in Figure 4.

Step 1: Find the point at which marginal revenue (MR) equals marginal cost (MC). Remember that in a perfectly competitive market, MR equals price.

Step 2: At the point at which $MR = MC$, find the corresponding point on the horizontal axis; this is the profit-maximizing output.

Step 3: At the profit-maximizing output, draw a line straight up to the demand curve (which is equal to MR in a perfectly competitive market) and then to the vertical axis. This is the profit-maximizing price.

Step 4: Again using the profit-maximizing output, draw a line straight up to the average total cost curve, and then to the vertical axis. This is the average total cost per unit.

Step 5: Find the profit, which is the rectangle formed between the profit-maximizing price and average total cost on the vertical axis, and the profit-maximizing output on the horizontal axis.

Some of these steps might seem redundant. However, using this approach will help you to identify the profit-maximizing price, output, and profit in any type of market structure, as we'll see in the next two chapters. It is therefore useful to remember these steps now when the diagrams are easier to follow.

Normal Profits

When the price of a windsurfing sail is $200, your firm earns economic profits. Consider what happens, however, when the market price falls to $175 a sail. This price happens

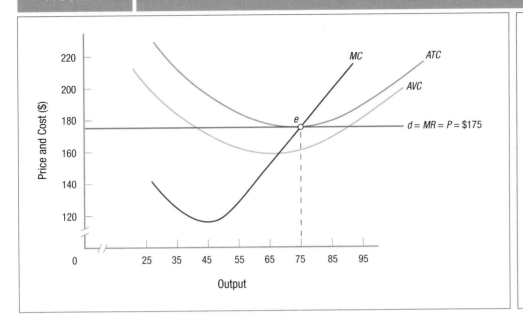

FIGURE 5 | A PERFECTLY COMPETITIVE FIRM EARNING NORMAL PROFITS (ZERO ECONOMIC PROFIT)

If the market sets a price of $175, the firm's demand curve is tangent to the minimum point on the ATC curve (point e). The best the firm can do under these circumstances is to earn normal profits on the sale of 75 windsurfing sails.

to be the minimum point on the average total cost curve, corresponding to an output of 75 sails. Figure 5 shows that at the price of $175, the firm's demand curve is just tangent to the minimum point on the ATC curve (point e), which means that the distance between points a and b in Figure 3 has shrunk to zero. By producing 75 sails, your firm earns normal profits, or zero economic profit.

Remember that when a firm earns zero economic profit, it is generating just enough income to keep investor capital in the business. When the typical firm in an industry is earning **normal profits,** there are no pressures for firms to enter or leave the industry. As we will see in the next section, this is an important outcome in the long run.

normal profits Equal to zero economic profits; where P = ATC

Loss Minimization and Plant Shutdown

Assume for a moment that an especially calm summer with little wind leads to a decline in the demand for windsurfing sails. Assume also that, as a consequence, the price of windsurfing sails falls to $170. Figure 6 illustrates the impact on your firm. Market price has fallen below your average total cost of production (which takes into account the fixed cost, which in this case is $1,000, an amount determined in the previous chapter), but remains above your average variable cost. Profit maximization—or, in this case, *loss minimization*—requires that you produce output at the level at which MR = MC. That occurs at point e, where output falls to 65 units.

Using Figure 6, at 65 units, the average total cost at this production level is $178; thus, with a market price of $170, loss per unit is $8. The total loss on 65 units is $8 × 65 = $520, corresponding to area *abce*.

These results may look grim, but consider your alternatives. If you were to produce more or fewer sails, your losses would just mount. You could, for instance, furlough your employees. But you will still have to pay your fixed costs of $1,000. Without revenue, your losses would be $1,000. Therefore, it is better to produce and sell 65 sails, taking a loss of $520, thereby cutting your losses nearly in half.

But what happens if the price of windsurfing sails falls to $160? Such a scenario is shown in Figure 7. Your revenue from the sale of sails has fallen to a level just equal to variable costs. If you produce and sell 60 units of output (where MR = MC), you will be able to pay your employees their wages, but have nothing left over to pay your

FIGURE 6   A PERFECTLY COMPETITIVE FIRM MINIMIZING LOSSES

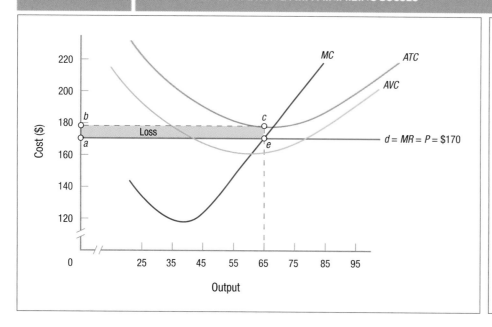

Assume that the price of wind-surfing sails falls to $170 a sail. Loss minimization requires an output at which $MR = MC$, in this case, at 65 units (point e). Average total cost is $178 (point c); therefore, loss per unit is equal to $8. Total loss is equal to $8 \times 65 = $520. Notice that this is less than the fixed costs ($1,000) that would have to be paid even if the plant was closed.

shutdown point When price in the short run falls below the minimum point on the *AVC* curve, the firm will minimize losses by closing its doors and stopping production. Because $P < AVC$, the firm's variable costs are not covered; therefore, by shutting the plant, losses are reduced to fixed costs only.

overhead; thus, your loss will be $1,000. Point e in Figure 7 represents a **shutdown point,** because your firm will be indifferent to whether it operates or shuts down—you lose $1,000 either way.

If prices continue to fall below $160 a sail, your losses will grow still further, because revenue will not even cover wages and other variable expenses. Once prices drop below the minimum point on the *AVC* curve (point e in Figure 7), losses will exceed total fixed costs and your loss-minimizing strategy must be to close the plant. It follows that the greatest loss a firm is willing to suffer in the short term is equal to its total fixed costs. Remember that the firm cannot leave the industry at this point, because market participation is fixed in the short run, but it can shut down its plant and stop production.

FIGURE 7   PLANT SHUTDOWN IN A PERFECTLY COMPETITIVE INDUSTRY

When prices fall below $160, or below the minimum point of the *AVC* curve, losses begin to exceed fixed costs. The firm will close if price falls below this minimum point (point e); this is the firm's shutdown point.

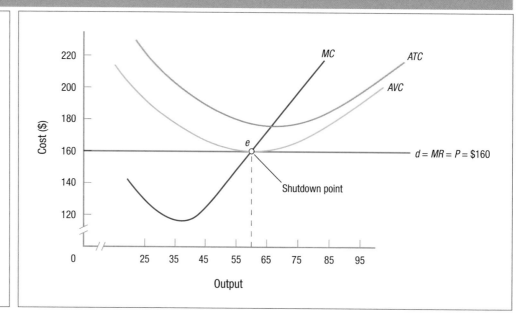

How practical is it to shut down production? That depends on the size of the firm and whether short-run losses are temporary or indicative of a permanent trend. The owner of a small kiosk selling decorative baskets might shut down and lay off the staff if losses mount and prospects for future profits are grim, while the owner of a fishing boat might furlough her employees during the off-season, with the expectation of resuming operations later on when prices recover and profits return.

The Short-Run Supply Curve

A glance at Figure 8 will help to summarize what we have learned so far. As we have seen, when a competitive firm is presented with a market price of P_0, corresponding to the minimum point on the AVC curve, the firm will produce output of q_0. If prices should fall below P_0, the firm will shut its doors and produce nothing. If, on the other hand, prices should rise to P_1, the firm will sell q_1 and earn normal profits (zero economic profits). And if prices continue climbing above P_1, say, to P_2, the firm will earn economic profits by selling q_2. In each instance, the firm produces and sells output where $MR = MC$.

HERBERT SIMON (1916–2001)

NOBEL PRIZE

When he was awarded the Nobel Prize for Economics in 1978, Herbert Simon (1916–2001) was an unusual choice on two fronts. First, he wasn't an economist by trade; he was a professor of computer science and psychology at the time of his award. Second, Simon's major contribution to economics was a direct challenge to one of the basic tenets of economics: Firms, in fact, do not always act to maximize profits.

In his book *Administrative Behavior,* Simon approached economics and the behavior of firms from his outsider's perspective. Simon thought real-world experience showed that firms are not always perfectly rational, in possession of perfect information, or striving to maximize profits. Rather, he proposed, as firms grow larger and larger, the access to perfect information becomes a fiction and that firms are run by individuals whose decisions are altered by their inability to remain perfectly and completely rational.

To Simon, the reality is not that firms tilt at the mythical windmill of maximizing profits, but that, as he said in his Nobel Prize acceptance speech, they recognize their limitations and instead try to come up with an "acceptable solution to acute problems" by setting realistic goals and making reasonable assessments of their successes or failures.

Simon's views provided a new approach to analyzing market structure models. Simon brought data, theories, and knowledge from other disciplines and paved the way for behavioral economics (discussed in Chapter 6) to eventually become a prominent field of economics by broadening its scope and applying more realistic conditions found in the marketplace.

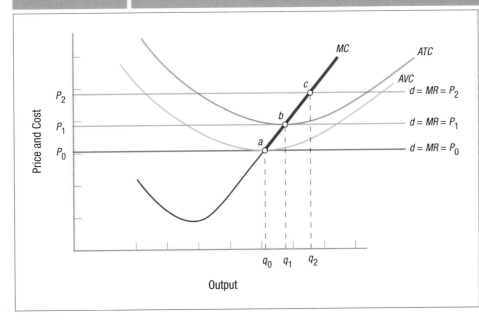

| FIGURE 8 | THE SHORT-RUN SUPPLY CURVE FOR A PERFECTLY COMPETITIVE FIRM |

If prices fall below P_0, the firm will shut its doors and produce nothing. For prices between P_0 and P_1, the firm will incur losses, but these losses will be less than fixed costs; thus, the firm will remain in operation and produce where $MR = MC$. At a price of P_1, the firm earns a normal return. If price should rise above P_1 (e.g., to P_2), the firm will earn economic profits by selling an output of q_2. The portion of the MC curve above the minimum point on the AVC curve, here thickened, is the firm's short-run supply curve.

short-run supply curve The marginal cost curve above the minimum point on the average variable cost curve.

From this quick summary, we can see that a firm's **short-run supply curve** is equivalent to the *MC* curve above the minimum point on the *AVC* curve. This curve, shown as the thickened portion of the *MC* curve in Figure 8, shows how much the firm will supply to the market at various prices, keeping in mind that it will supply no output at prices below the shutdown point.

Keep in mind also that the short-run supply curve for an industry is the horizontal summation of the supply curves of the industry's individual firms. To obtain industry supply, in other words, we add together the output of every firm at various price levels.

 CHECKPOINT

PERFECT COMPETITION: SHORT-RUN DECISIONS

- Marginal revenue is the change in total revenue from selling an additional unit of a product.
- Perfectly competitive firms are price takers, getting their price from markets, enabling them to sell all they want at the going market price. As a result, their marginal revenue is equal to product price and the demand curve facing the perfectly competitive firm is a horizontal straight line at market price.
- Perfectly competitive firms maximize profit by producing that output where marginal revenue equals marginal cost (*MR = MC*).
- When price is greater than the minimum point of the average total cost curve, firms earn economic profits.
- When price is just equal to the minimum point of the average total cost curve, firms earn normal profits.
- When price is below the minimum point of the average total cost curve, but above the minimum point of the average variable cost curve, the firm continues to operate, but earns an economic loss.
- When price falls below the minimum point on the average variable cost curve, the firm will shut down and incur a loss equal to total fixed costs.
- The short-run supply curve of the firm is the marginal cost curve above the minimum point on the average variable cost curve.

QUESTION: Describe why profit-maximizing output occurs where *MR = MC*. Does this explain why perfectly competitive firms do not sell "all they can produce"?

Answers to the Checkpoint questions can be found at the end of this chapter.

PERFECT COMPETITION: LONG-RUN ADJUSTMENTS

We have seen that perfectly competitive firms can earn economic profits, normal profits, or losses in the short run because their plant size is fixed, and they cannot exit the industry. We now turn our attention to the long run. In the long run, firms can adjust all factors, even to the point of leaving an industry. And if the industry looks attractive, other firms can enter it in the long run. Why are some industries (such as medical marijuana) thriving, while others (such as photo developing) are declining? The answer is tied to economic profits and losses.

Adjusting to Profits and Losses in the Short Run

If firms in the industry are earning short-run economic profits, new firms can be expected to enter the industry in the long run, or existing firms may increase the scale of their operations. Figure 9 illustrates one such possible adjustment path when the firms in an industry are earning short-run economic profits. To simplify the discussion, we will assume there are no economies of scale in the long run.

FIGURE 9 — LONG-RUN ADJUSTMENT WITH SHORT-RUN ECONOMIC PROFITS

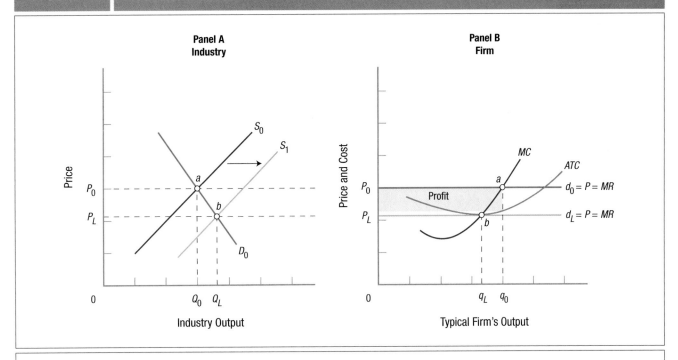

Panel A
Industry

Panel B
Firm

Industry Output

Typical Firm's Output

Panel A shows a market initially in equilibrium at point *a*. Industry supply and demand equal S_0 and D_0, and equilibrium price is P_0. This equilibrium leads to the short-run economic profits shown in the shaded area in panel B. Short-run economic profits lead other firms to enter the industry, thus raising industry output to Q_L in panel A, while forcing prices down to P_L. The output for individual firms declines as the industry moves to long-run equilibrium at point *b*. In the long run, firms in perfectly competitive markets can earn only normal profits, as shown by point *b* in panel B.

In panel A, the market is initially in equilibrium at point *a*, with industry supply and demand equal to S_0 and D_0, and equilibrium price equal to P_0. For the typical firm shown in panel B, this translates into a short-run equilibrium at point *a*. Notice that, at this price, the firm produces output exceeding the minimum point of the *ATC* curve. The shaded area represents economic profits.

These economic profits (sometimes called supernormal profits) will attract other firms into the industry. Remember that in a perfectly competitive market, entry and exit are easy in the long run; therefore, many firms decide to get in on the action when they see these profits. As a result, industry supply will shift to the right, to S_1, where equilibrium is at point *b*, resulting in a new long-run industry price of P_L. For each firm in the industry, output declines to q_L and is just tangent to the minimum point on the *ATC* curve. Thus, all firms are now earning normal profits and keeping their investors satisfied. There are no pressures at this point for more firms to enter or exit the industry.

Consider the opposite situation—that is, firms in an industry that are incurring economic losses. Figure 10 depicts such a scenario. In panel A, market supply and demand are S_0 and D_0, with equilibrium price at P_0. In panel B, firms suffer economic losses equal to the shaded area. These losses cause some firms to reevaluate their situations and some decide to leave the industry, thus shifting the industry supply curve to S_1 in panel A, generating a new equilibrium price of P_L. This new price is just tangent to the minimum point of the *ATC* curve in panel B, expanding output for those individual firms remaining in the industry. Firms in the industry are now earning normal profits; therefore, the pressures to leave the industry dissipate.

Notice that in Figures 9 and 10, the final equilibrium in the long run is the point at which industry price is just tangent to the minimum point on the *ATC* curve. At this point, there are no net incentives for firms to enter or leave the industry.

FIGURE 10 | LONG-RUN ADJUSTMENT WITH SHORT-RUN LOSSES

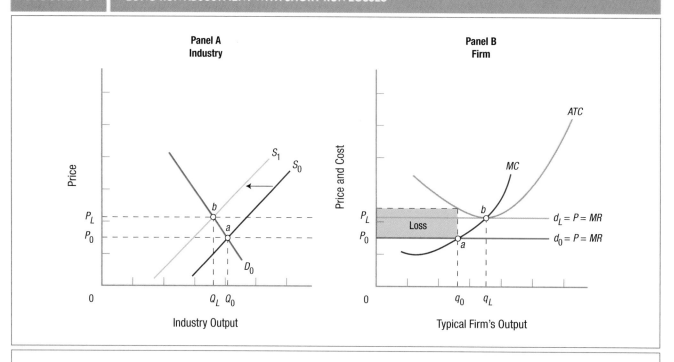

Panel A shows a market initially in equilibrium at point *a*. Industry supply and demand equal S_0 and D_0, and equilibrium price is P_0. This equilibrium leads to the short-run economic losses shown in the shaded area in panel B, thus inducing some firms to exit the industry. Industry output contracts to Q_L in panel A, raising prices to P_L and expanding output for the individual firms remaining in the industry, as the industry moves to long-run equilibrium at point *b*. Again, in the long run, firms in perfectly competitive markets will earn normal profits, as shown by point *b* in panel B.

If industry price rises above this point, the economic profits being earned will induce other firms to enter the industry; the opposite is true if price falls below this point. A simple way to remember this is with the *elimination principle*: In a competitive industry in the long run with easy entry and exit, profits are eliminated by firm entry, and losses are eliminated by firm exit.

Competition and the Public Interest

Competitive processes dominate modern life. You and your friends compete for grades, concert tickets, spouses, jobs, and many other benefits. Competitive markets are simply an extension of the competition inherent in daily life. Figure 11 illustrates the long-run equilibrium for a firm in a competitive market. Market price in the long run is P_{LR}; it is equal to the minimum point on both the short-run average total cost (*SRATC*) curve and the long-run average total cost (*LRATC*) curve. At point *e*, the following is true:

$$P = MR = MC = SRATC_{min} = LRATC_{min}$$

This equation illustrates why competitive markets are the standard (benchmark) by which all other market structures are evaluated. First, competitive markets exhibit *productive efficiency*. Products are produced and sold to consumers at their lowest possible opportunity cost. For consumers, this is an excellent situation: They pay no more than minimum production costs plus a profit (a normal profit, to be precise) sufficient to keep producers in business, and consumer surplus shown in panel A is maximized. When we look at monopoly firms in the next chapter, consumers do not get such a good deal.

Second, competitive markets demonstrate *allocative efficiency*. The price that consumers pay for a given product is equal to marginal cost. Because price represents the value consumers place on a product, and marginal cost represents the opportunity cost to society to

Colombian Coffee: The Perils of Existing in a Perfectly Competitive Industry

> What aspects of the coffee market make it difficult for Colombian coffee growers to maintain a consistent income every year?

Each day, over 2 billion cups of coffee are consumed globally. Although coffee baristas around the world use their talents to produce the best cup of latte or espresso, the most crucial input remains the coffee bean, which can be produced only in tropical climates with volcanic soil and with the right amount of rain. With an ideal climate, a country can produce billions of pounds of coffee beans, providing income to millions of workers. But what

happens when the weather doesn't cooperate? Farmers in one country, Colombia, can share that experience.

Colombia has long been one of the largest coffee producers in the world. Although it's never been the top coffee producer (that award goes to Brazil), Colombian coffee is famous due in large part to Colombia's ideal climate suited for growing high-quality Arabica beans, along with the marketing of Colombian coffee by the National Federation of Coffee Growers and their famous fictional spokesperson Juan Valdez. Although this may sound like market power, Colom-

bia's coffee industry faces competition from many countries whose coffee is nearly identical to Colombia's, making the industry perfectly competitive. Moreover, much like other coffee-producing countries, Colombia's coffee industry comprises hundreds of thousands of individually owned coffee farms that sell their output to the national federation.

Because the price that individual farmers receive for their coffee is determined by the market, fluctuations in coffee prices can result in a large windfall or a devastating drop in a coffee producer's household income. Moreover, unpredictable weather patterns and crop diseases, as experienced in recent years, can destroy a harvest altogether. The income risk involved with producing in a perfectly competitive industry such as coffee means that farmers need to prepare for a rainy day, both figuratively and literally.

GO TO 🔷 **LaunchPad** TO PRACTICE THE ECONOMIC CONCEPTS IN THIS STORY

| **FIGURE 11** | **LONG-RUN EQUILIBRIUM FOR THE PERFECTLY COMPETITIVE FIRM** |

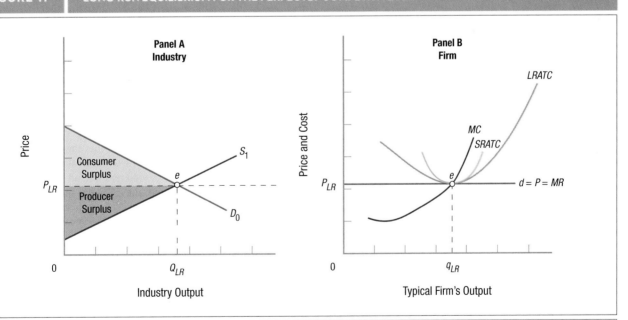

Market price in the long run is P_{LR}, corresponding to the minimum point on the $SRATC$ and $LRATC$ curves. At point e, $P = MR = MC = SRATC_{min} = LRATC_{min}$. This is why economists use perfectly competitive markets as the benchmark when comparing the performance of other market structures. With competition, consumers get just what they want because price reflects their desires, and they get these products at the lowest possible price ($LRATC_{min}$). Further, as panel A illustrates, the sum of consumer and producer surplus is maximized. Any reduction in output reduces the sum of consumer and producer surplus.

produce that product, when these two values are equal, the market is allocating the production of various goods according to consumer wants.

The flip side of these observations is that if a market falls out of equilibrium, the public interest will suffer. If, for instance, output falls below equilibrium, marginal cost will be less than price. Therefore, consumers place a higher value on that product than it is costing firms to produce. Society would be better off if more of the product were put on the market. Conversely, if output rises above the equilibrium level, marginal cost will exceed price. This excess output costs firms more to produce than the value placed on it by consumers. We would be better off if those resources were used to produce another commodity more highly valued by society.

Long-Run Industry Supply

Recall from an earlier chapter that supply curves tend to be more elastic (flat) over time as businesses have time to adjust their output to changing prices. In addition to responding to market prices, firms also respond to changes in production costs as output changes. Economies or diseconomies of scale determine the shape of the long-run average total cost (*LRATC*) curve for individual firms. A firm that enjoys significant economies of scale will see its *LRATC* curve slope down for a wide range of output. Firms facing diseconomies of

ISSUE

Globalization and "The Box"

When we think of disruptive technologies that radically changed an entire market, we typically think of computers, the Internet, and smartphones. Competitors must adapt to the change or wither away. One disruptive technology we take for granted today, but one that changed our world, is "the box"—the standardized shipping container. Today the vast majority of the world's deep-sea general cargo is transported in containers.

Before containers, shipping costs added about 25% to the cost of some goods and represented over 10% of U.S. exports. The process was cumbersome; hundreds of longshoremen would remove boxes of all sizes, dimensions, and weight from a ship and load them individually onto trucks (or from trucks to a ship if they were going the other way). This process took a lot of time, was subject to damage and theft, and was costly and inconvenient for business.

In 1955 Malcom McLean, a North Carolina trucking entrepreneur, got the idea to standardize shipping containers. He originally thought he would drive a truck right onto a ship, drop a trailer, and drive off. Realizing that the wheels would consume a lot of space, he soon settled on standard containers that would stack together, but would also

load directly onto a truck trailer. Containers are 20 or 40 feet long, 8 feet wide, and 8 or 8½ feet tall. This standardization greatly reduced the costs of handling cargo. McLean bought a small shipping company, called it Sea-Land, and converted some ships to handle the containers. In 1956 he converted an oil tanker and shipped fifty-eight containers from Newark, New Jersey, to Houston, Texas. It took roughly a decade of union bargaining and capital investment by firms for containers to catch on, but the rest is history.

Longshoremen and other port operators thought he was nuts, but as the idea took hold, the West Coast longshoremen went on strike to prevent the introduction of containers. They received some concessions, but containerization was inevitable. Containerization was so cost-effective that it could not be stopped. It set in motion the long-run adjustments we see in competitive markets. Ports that didn't adjust went out of business, and trucking firms that failed to add containers couldn't compete. The same was true for oceanic shipping companies.

Much of what we call globalization today can be traced to "the box." Firms producing products in foreign countries can fill a container, deliver it to a

Youssouf Cader/Dreamstime.com

port, and send it directly to the customer or wholesaler in the United States. The efficiency, originally seen by McLean, was that the manufacturer and the customer would be the only ones to load and unload the container, keeping the product safer, more secure, and cutting huge chunks off the cost of shipping. Today, a 40-foot container with 32 tons of cargo shipped from China to the United States costs roughly $5,000 to ship, or 7 cents a pound! This efficient technology has facilitated the expansion of trade worldwide and increased the competitiveness of many industries.

Information from Mark Levinson, *The Box* (Princeton, NJ: Princeton University Press), 2006.

FIGURE 12 | LONG-RUN INDUSTRY SUPPLY CURVES

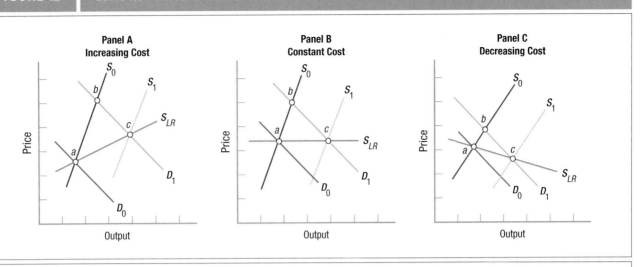

Panel A shows an increasing cost industry. Demand and supply are initially D_0 and S_0, with equilibrium at point a. When demand increases, price and output rise in the short run to point b. As new firms enter the industry, they drive up the cost of resources. Supply increases in the long run to S_1 and the new equilibrium point c reflects these higher resource costs. In constant cost industries (panel B), firms can expand in the long run without economies or diseconomies; therefore, costs remain constant in the long run. In decreasing cost industries (panel C), expansion leads to external economies and thus to a long-run equilibrium at point c, with lower prices and a higher output than before.

scale will see their average costs rise as output rises. The nature of these economies and diseconomies of scale determines the size of the competitive firm.

Long-run industry supply is related to the degree to which increases and decreases in industry output influence the prices firms must pay for resources. For example, when all firms in an industry expand or new firms enter the market, this new demand for raw materials and labor may push up the price of some inputs. When this happens, it gives rise to an **increasing cost industry** in the long run.

To illustrate, panel A of Figure 12 shows two sets of short-run supply and demand curves. Initially, demand and supply are D_0 and S_0, and equilibrium is at point a. Assume demand increases, shifting to D_1. In the short run, price and output will rise to point b. As we have seen earlier, economic profits will result and existing firms will expand or new firms will enter the industry, causing product supply to shift to S_1 in the long run. Note that at the new equilibrium (point c), prices are higher than at the initial equilibrium (point a). This is caused by the upward pressure on the prices of industry inputs, notably raw materials and labor that resulted from industry expansion. Industry output has expanded, but prices and costs are higher. This is an *increasing cost industry*.

Alternatively, an industry might enjoy economies of scale as it expands, as suggested by panel C of Figure 12. In this case, price and output initially rise as the short-run equilibrium moves to point b. Eventually, however, this industry expansion leads to lower prices; perhaps suppliers enjoy economies of scale as this industry's demand for their product increases. The semiconductor industry seems to fit this profile: As the demand for semiconductors has risen over the past few decades, their price has fallen dramatically. In the long run, therefore, a new equilibrium is established at point c, where prices are lower and output is higher than was initially the case. This illustrates what happens in a **decreasing cost industry.**

Finally, some industries seem to expand in the long run without significant change in average cost. These are known as **constant cost industries** and are shown in panel B in Figure 12. Some fast-food restaurants and retail stores, such as Walmart, seem to be able to clone their operations from market to market without a noticeable rise in costs.

increasing cost industry An industry that, in the long run, faces higher prices and costs as industry output expands. Industry expansion puts upward pressure on resources (inputs), causing higher costs in the long run.

decreasing cost industry An industry that, in the long run, faces lower prices and costs as industry output expands. Some industries enjoy economies of scale as they expand in the long run, typically the result of technological advances.

constant cost industry An industry that, in the long run, faces roughly the same prices and costs as industry output expands. Some industries can virtually clone their operations in other areas without putting undue pressure on resource prices, resulting in constant operating costs as they expand in the long run.

Summing Up

This chapter has focused on markets in which there is perfect competition—that is, in which industries contain many sellers and buyers, each so small that they ignore the others' behavior and sell a homogeneous product. Sellers are assumed to maximize the profits they earn through the sale of their products, and buyers are assumed to maximize the satisfaction they receive from the products they buy. Further, we assume that buyers and sellers have all the information necessary for informed transactions, and that sellers can sell as much of their products as they want at market equilibrium prices.

These assumptions allow us to reach some clear conclusions about how firms operate in competitive markets. In the long run, firms will produce the efficient level of output at which *LRATC* is minimized, and profits are enough to keep capital in the industry. This output level is efficient because it gives consumers just the goods they want and provides these goods at the lowest possible opportunity costs. Competitive market efficiency represents the benchmark for comparing other market structures.

Competitive markets as we have described them might seem to have such restrictive assumptions that this model only applies to a few industries, such as agriculture, minerals, and lumber. Most businesses you deal with don't look like the assumptions of these competitive markets. This is true, but most businesses you encounter, such as bars, restaurants, coffee shops, fast-food franchises, cleaners, grocery stores, and shoe and clothing stores, do share some of the characteristics of perfectly competitive markets such as earning normal profits over the long run. In the chapter after next, we examine those markets where consumers see products as differentiated and see how that industry's behavior is different from a perfectly competitive market.

Because perfect competition is so clearly in the public interest and is the benchmark for comparing other market structures, we can ponder the answer to the following question: Do firms seek the competitive market structure? The answer is: Generally, no. Why? Recall the profit equation. In perfectly competitive markets, firms are price takers. They can achieve economic profits in the short run, but find it almost impossible to have long-run economic profits. Most firms instead want to achieve long-run economic profits. To do so, they must have some ability to control price. In the next chapter, we will see what firms do to achieve this market power.

 CHECKPOINT

PERFECT COMPETITION: LONG-RUN ADJUSTMENTS

- When perfectly competitive firms are earning short-run economic profits, these profits attract firms into the industry. Supply increases and market price falls until firms are just earning normal profits.

- The opposite occurs when firms are making losses in the short run. Losses mean some firms will leave the industry. This reduces supply, thus increasing prices until profits return to normal.

- Competitive markets are efficient because products are produced at their lowest possible opportunity cost, and the sum of consumer and producer surplus is at a maximum.

- An industry in which prices rise as the industry grows is an increasing cost industry, and increased costs may be caused by rising prices of raw materials or labor as the industry expands.

- Decreasing cost industries see their prices fall as the industry expands, possibly due to large economies of scale or rapidly improving technology.

- Constant cost industries seem to be able to expand without facing higher or lower costs.

QUESTION: Most of the markets and industries in the world are highly competitive, and presumably most CEOs of businesses know that competition will mean that they will only earn normal profits in the long run. Given this analysis, why do they bother to stay in business, when any economic profits will vanish in the long run?

Answers to the Checkpoint questions can be found at the end of this chapter.

chapter summary

Section 1 Market Structure Analysis

A **market structure** describes an industry based on several characteristics, including the number of firms, nature of the industry's product, barriers to entry, and the extent to which individual firms can control prices.

Design Pics Inc / Alamy

8.1 Types of Market Structure

Perfect competition: Many price-taking firms producing a nearly identical product

Monopolistic competition: Many firms producing a differentiated product

Oligopoly: A few large firms producing a standardized product

Monopoly: One firm producing a unique product protected by barriers to entry

8.2 Soybeans are produced in a perfectly competitive market. Because each soybean farmer produces a small portion of total soybean production, each farmer has no influence on price and is therefore a **price taker.**

In a perfectly competitive market, the price of a good is determined by ordinary industry supply and demand curves, and that price becomes the horizontal demand curve for the price-taking firm. Any shift in demand or supply (such as the demand shift from D_0 to D_1) causes price to change for the firm.

Section 2 Perfect Competition: Short-Run Decisions

Marginal revenue is the change in total revenue from producing 1 more unit, or $\Delta TR/\Delta Q$. In a perfectly competitive market, price does not change; therefore, $P = MR$.

The **profit-maximizing rule** says that firms maximize profit at an output where marginal revenue equals marginal cost.

When price (MR) > MC, the firm should increase production.
When price (MR) < MC, the firm should decrease production.

Economic Versus Normal Profits

Economic profits take into account all explicit costs AND implicit costs such as the value of the next best use of time and money (opportunity cost).
Normal profits occur when economic profits are zero. But remember, zero economic profits can still represent substantial normal profits on paper.

Many shops in ski villages shut down during the summer when AVC cannot be covered due to fewer tourists.

8.3 Five Steps to Maximizing Profits in a Competitive Market

1. Find $MR = MC$.
2. Find optimal quantity where $MR = MC$.
3. Find optimal price. (*Hint:* It's already given!)
4. Find the average total cost at the optimal Q.
5. Find the profit = $(P - ATC) \times Q$.

In the graph below, this competitive firm is earning economic profits equal to the blue shaded area.

Output

The Short-Run Supply Curve for a Competitive Firm

8.4 When $P < AVC$: The firm shuts down immediately.
When $AVC < P < ATC$: The firm operates in the short run to minimize losses, but exits the industry in the long run.
When $P > ATC$: The firm is earning economic profits.

8.5 The MC curve above AVC equals the firm's short-run supply curve.

Section 3
Perfect Competition: Long-Run Adjustments

8.6 Firm Entry and Exit

Because perfectly competitive markets have no barriers to entry, short-run profits and losses are eliminated in the long run.

Short-run profits encourage new firms to enter, shifting supply right, lowering price until profits return to zero.

Short-run losses encourage inefficient firms to exit, shifting supply left, raising price until losses are eliminated.

8.7 Productive and Allocative Efficiency

In the long run, the price of goods in a perfectly competitive market equals the minimum point on the *LRATC* curve. This demonstrates productive efficiency (goods are produced at their lowest possible cost) and allocative efficiency (goods are produced according to what society desires).

A **long-run industry supply curve** is flatter than a short-run industry supply curve, and can slope upward (increasing cost industry), downward (decreasing cost industry), or can be horizontal (constant cost industry). Costs are determined by industry structure, technology, and economies of scale.

Technology goods are a decreasing cost industry. Over time, the cost of production falls due to economies of scale. Further, costs fall as new technologies enable firms to produce the product at a much lower cost.

KEY CONCEPTS

market structure analysis, p. 196
perfect competition, p. 197
price taker, p. 198
marginal revenue, p. 199

profit-maximizing rule, p. 201
normal profits, p. 203
shutdown point, p. 204
short-run supply curve, p. 206

increasing cost industry, p. 211
decreasing cost industry, p. 211
constant cost industry, p. 211

QUESTIONS AND PROBLEMS

Check Your Understanding

1. Why must price cover average variable costs if the firm is to continue operating?

2. Why do perfectly competitive firms sell their products only at the market price? Why not try to raise prices to make more profit or lower them to garner more sales?

3. Describe the role that easy entry and exit play in competitive markets over the long run.

4. Why are marginal revenue and price equal for the perfectly competitive firm?

5. Why, if competitive firms are earning economic profits in the short run, are they unable to earn them in the long run?

6. Describe the reasons why an industry's costs might increase in the long run. Why might they decrease over the long run?

Apply the Concepts

7. When a sports team consistently struggles, one strategy is to replace the coach. But when this happens, the new coach initially has the same players (its primary input). How can a new coach improve the team's record when the players are mostly the same?

8. Why isn't a short-run supply curve for a perfectly competitive firm equivalent to the entire marginal cost curve?

9. Suppose you master the art of growing herbs in your garden and selling them for profit at the local farmer's market. Your neighbor sees your profitable business and decides to do the same; however, with less experience he faces a much higher marginal cost curve. How is it possible for both you and your neighbor to sell herbs at the same price?

10. Assume a competitive industry is in long-run equilibrium and firms in the industry are earning normal profits. Now assume that production technology improves such that average total cost declines by $5 per unit. Describe the process this industry will go through as it moves to a new long-run equilibrium.

11. When a competitive firm is earning economic profits, is it also maximizing profit per unit? Why or why not?

12. In this chapter, we suggested that whenever market price fell below average variable costs, the firm would shut down. At that point, revenue is not covering its variable costs and the firm is losing more money than if it just shut down and lost fixed costs. Clearly, shutting the firm is more complicated than that. Under what circumstances might the firm continue to operate even though prices are below its average variable cost?

In The News

13. The growth of ride-sharing services such as Uber and Lyft has generated much discussion in the news. Drivers operate as independent businesses, working as many hours as they choose and earning a portion of the fares set by the company. However, during periods of high demand, the market price increases (such as "surge" pricing by Uber). Provide a few reasons why ride-sharing companies share the characteristics of a perfectly competitive industry.

14. The opening of formal Cuban relations with the United States has led to greater trade between the two countries, especially in perfectly competitive products such as sugar, tobacco, and oranges. Explain what is likely to happen in the market for these agricultural products under increased trade with Cuba, and how that might affect individual farmers in the United States. What are the potential benefits to consumers and other producers?

Solving Problems

 WORK IT OUT LaunchPad | interactive activity

15. Use the following figure for a firm in a perfectly competitive market.

    a. What is the output that maximizes the firm's profit?

    b. At the profit-maximizing output, calculate total revenue and total cost.

    c. If the firm maximizes profit, how much profit does it earn?

    d. What will likely happen to market demand or market supply in the long run?

    e. What will likely happen to the market price in the long run?

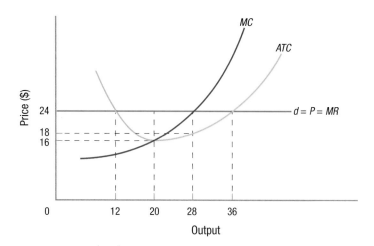

16. Use the figure below to answer the following true/false questions:

    a. If market price is $25, the firm earns economic profits.

    b. If market price is $20, the firm earns economic profit equal to roughly $100.

    c. If market price is $9, the firm produces roughly 55 units.

    d. If market price is $12.50, the firm produces roughly 70 units and makes an economic loss equal to roughly $210.

    e. Total fixed costs for this firm are roughly $100.

    f. If market price is $15, the firm sells 80 units and makes a normal profit.

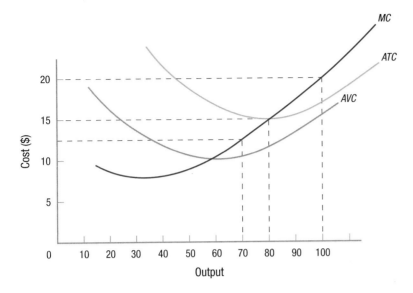

USING THE NUMBERS

17. According to By the Numbers, which two regions employ the highest number of people in the farm and farm-related industries? Approximately how many total persons are employed in the farm and farm-related industries in these two regions combined?

18. According to By the Numbers, in which year (since 1991) did the following crops reach their highest and lowest prices per bushel: corn, wheat, soybeans?

ANSWERS TO QUESTIONS IN CHECKPOINTS

Checkpoint: Market Structure Analysis 199

Verizon is one of a few major wireless providers in the U.S. market (others include AT&T, T-Mobile, and Sprint). The industry has considerable barriers to entry (e.g., the costs of cellular towers) and is therefore an oligopoly. The NFL is the only major organization for professional football teams, having complete control over all NFL teams nationwide. It also has exclusive contracts with advertisers and television networks. The NFL is best described as a monopoly. Grandma's Southern Kitchen is one of many restaurants serving southern food, and is differentiated by its location, menu, and quality of food. It is therefore a monopolistically competitive firm. Finally, Jack's Lumber is one of thousands of lumber mills across the country, each producing a standardized product. It is therefore in a perfectly competitive industry.

Checkpoint: Perfect Competition: Short-Run Decisions 206

Keep in mind that marginal cost is the additional cost to produce another unit of output, and price equals marginal revenue and is the additional revenue from selling one more unit of the product. If *MR* is greater than *MC*, the firm earns more revenue than cost by selling that next unit; therefore, the firm will sell up to the point at which *MR* = *MC*. At that last unit at which *MR* = *MC*, the firm is earning a normal profit on that unit (a positive accounting profit). When *MC* > *MR*, the firm is spending more to produce that unit than it receives in revenue and is losing money on that last unit, lowering overall profits. Thus, firms will not produce and sell all they can produce: They will produce and sell up to the point at which *MR* = *MC*.

Checkpoint: Perfect Competition: Long-Run Adjustments 212

All businesses are looking for the "next new thing" that will generate economic profits and propel them to monopoly status. Even normal profits are not trivial. Remember, normal profits are sufficient to keep investors happy in the long run. When firms do find the right innovation, such as the iPad, Windows operating system, or a blockbuster drug, the short-run returns can be tremendous.

9 Monopoly

Understanding the effects of market power on consumers and producers

Learning Objectives

9.1 Describe the characteristics of a monopoly and market power.

9.2 Describe the ways in which firms maximize market power using barriers to entry.

9.3 Use monopoly market analysis to determine the equilibrium level of output and price for a monopoly.

9.4 Describe the differences between monopoly and competition.

9.5 Describe the different forms of price discrimination.

9.6 Describe the different approaches to regulating a natural monopoly.

9.7 Relate the history and purpose of antitrust legislation to monopoly analysis.

9.8 Apply concentration ratios and the Herfindahl–Hirschman index to analyze the likelihood of regulation in a given market.

9.9 Describe the conditions of a contestable market and its significance.

When was the last time you used Google to search for information? How about YouTube, Gmail, Google+, Google Docs, Chrome, Google Maps, Waze, or any Android app? If you have used any of these services within the past 24 hours, you're in the majority of Americans who rely on at least one of over one hundred Web-based services offered by Google. And the best part is . . . it's all free. Or is it?

Although Google users rarely pay to use any of its Web services, the market value of the company in 2016 was over $500 billion, or about the same total market value of Walmart (with its 12,000 stores), McDonald's (with its 35,000 restaurants), and Coca-Cola (which sells 1.7 billion servings each day)—combined. How can Google be worth so much if it doesn't *sell* any physical products?

The answer is that Google sells advertising services, and lots of them (over $75 billion in sales in 2016), to companies worldwide that pay to have their Web sites show up more prominently on Web search results, or along the top and sides of Google's "free" services. Incredibly, Google charges some companies over $50 every time someone clicks on their ad links, although the average price is closer to $1. But with over 2 billion Google users worldwide, it doesn't take much to bring in a significant amount of revenue.

How is Google so profitable? In the previous chapter, we constructed a model of perfectly competitive markets in which many sellers compete against one another for the business of many buyers. This model assumed that different firms sell almost identical products, produce at the point where price equals marginal cost, and face no barriers to entry, entering or exiting industries as profit opportunities rise and fall. Keep in mind that firms in perfectly competitive markets have no pricing power. They are price takers, accepting the market price as given—they have no ability to change prices.

Although Google has competitors, such as Yahoo!, Bing, and others, Google commands a dominant share (over 70%) of the search engine market. Unlike perfectly competitive firms, Google has a lot of market power. By market power, we mean the ability to have some control over price.

In reality, most firms have some market power. You see this every day. The cleaners located at the train station is more convenient than the cleaners located in town, at least for those taking the train, and therefore can get away with charging a little more for cleaning and pressing shirts or skirts. A gas station located near a highway can charge a little more than a gas station a mile away.

As we move down the market structure spectrum from perfectly competitive firms on one end to monopolistically competitive firms, and then to oligopolies, finally ending up with monopolies at the other end, we will see that firms obtain more and more market power. We will see why firms want to be monopolies.

What is a monopoly? When a single company is the only firm in the industry, the company is a pure monopoly. Google is not a pure monopoly because it has some competitors, but it is so dominant that it comes close. In both situations, the economic analysis is similar, and for simplicity we refer to these firms as monopolies, even if they are not in the purest sense.

Monopoly and Market Power

Monopolies achieve market power by establishing barriers to entry preventing competition. These barriers include prohibitive fixed costs, control of a key resource, and government protection.

Professional sports leagues exhibit market power by establishing exclusive relationships with players, teams, and television networks.

Facebook maintains a dominant market share in social media despite attempts by competitors to wrestle this power away.

U.S. Television Viewers By Championship Series

Series	Viewers
NFL 2015 Super Bowl (1 game)	114,400,000
NBA 2015 (6 games)	112,640,000
MLB 2015 World Series (5 games)	73,500,000
NHL 2015 Stanley Cup (6 games)	33,600,000

Viewers (in millions)

AP Images/Paul Sakuma

$250,000

Published price (in 2016) for one ride on Virgin Galactic into space.

84.6%

Global desktop market share of Microsoft Windows in 2016.

Pharmaceutical companies spend billions of dollars developing successful drugs. Government patents allow companies to recoup their investment by preventing competition for a fixed period of time, allowing drugs to be priced high when they cost pennies to reproduce (marginal cost is very low).

The World's Most Expensive Drugs by Annual Cost of Treatment

Drug	Cost
1. **Glybera** (to treat an extremely rare pancreas disease)	$1,210,000
2. **Soliris** (to treat a rare immune system disease)	$700,000
3. **Naglazyme** (to treat a rare metabolic disease)	$485,747
4. **Vimizim** (to treat Morquio A syndrome, a metabolic disease)	$380,000
5. **Elaprase** (to treat Hunter syndrome)	$375,000

Pictac/Dreamstime.com

Many electric companies are natural monopolies protected from competition by the government. However, electricity demand per capita has leveled off in recent years as competition from renewable energy increases.

John Kroetch/Dreamstime.com

Go to **LaunchPad** *to use the latest data to recreate this graph.*

Electricity Demand per Capita

Kilowatt Hours

1955 1960 1965 1970 1975 1980 1985 1990 1995 2000 2005 2010 2015

This chapter studies the theory of monopoly, which is at the other market structure extreme from the competitive model. Whereas the competitive model is in the public interest, we can guess at the outset that monopolies generally are not. We will see why monopolies exist and how they act. Then we will see what it means to have market power, the ability to set price, and why monopolies have maximum market power. After that, we will see what can be done to mitigate the powers of monopolies that must exist, and how the government tries to prevent monopolies from arising in the first place.

We also study how monopolies can be beneficial. Some monopolies create economies of scale or provide product innovation and creativity. Many of today's new technologies and pharmaceuticals would never have been created if firms with complete market power did not exist. These products create benefits to users that offset some of the inefficiencies firms with market power pass on to consumers through higher prices. As with all economic analysis, costs and benefits must be weighed to determine the effect on consumers and producers, and the study of monopoly is no different.

MONOPOLY MARKETS

The very word "monopoly" almost defines the subject matter: a market in which there is only one seller. For example, when you want to watch professional basketball, you will probably watch an NBA or WNBA game. If you pay a monthly water bill, it's likely that you do not have a choice of which company services your apartment or house. Economists define a **monopoly** as a market sharing the following characteristics:

monopoly A one-firm industry with no close product substitutes and with substantial barriers to entry.

- The market has just one seller—one firm *is* the industry. This contrasts sharply with the competitive market, where many sellers comprise the industry.

- No close substitutes exist for the monopolist's product. Consequently, buyers cannot easily substitute other products for that sold by the monopolist. In communities with only one electricity provider, one could install solar panels, but such options are often prohibitively expensive.

- A monopolistic industry has significant barriers to entry. Though competitive firms can enter or leave industries in the long run, monopoly markets are considered nearly impossible to enter. Thus, monopolists face no competition, even in the long run.

market power A firm's ability to set prices for goods and services in a market.

This gives pure monopolists what economists call **market power.** Unlike competitive firms, which are price takers, monopolists are *price makers.* Their market power allows monopolists to adjust their output in ways that give them significant control over product price.

As we noted already, nearly every firm has some market power, or some control over price. Your neighborhood dry cleaner, for instance, has some control over price because it is located close to you, and you are probably not going to want to drive 5 miles just to save a few cents. This control over price reaches its maximum in the case of monopolies, and becomes minor as markets approach more competitive conditions at the other end of the market structure spectrum.

Sources of Market Power

Monopoly is defined as one firm serving a market in which there are no close substitutes and entry is nearly impossible. Market power means that a firm has some control over price. As a market structure approaches monopoly, one firm gains the maximum market power possible for that industry. The key to the market power of monopolies is significant **barriers to entry.** These barriers can be of several forms.

barriers to entry Any obstacle that makes it more difficult for a firm to enter an industry, and includes control of a key resource, prohibitive fixed costs, and government protection.

Control Over a Significant Factor of Production
If a firm owns or has control over an important input in the production process, that firm can keep potential rivals out of the market. This was the case with Alcoa Aluminum 75 years ago. Alcoa owned nearly all the world's bauxite ore, a key ingredient in aluminum production, before the company was eventually broken up by the government.

A contemporary example would be the National Football League (NFL), which has negotiated exclusive rights with colleges to draft top players (the most important input), along with exclusive rights with television networks and sponsors to broadcast games. Such control over key components of football entertainment makes entry into the industry very difficult.

Economies of Scale The **economies of scale** in an industry (when average total cost declines with increased production) give an existing firm a competitive advantage over potential entrants. By establishing economies of scale early, an existing firm has the ability to underprice new competitors, thereby discouraging their entry into the market. By doing so, a firm increases its market power.

In some industries, economies of scale can be so large that demand supports only one firm. Figure 1 illustrates this case. Here the long-run average total cost curve ($LRATC$) shows extremely large economies of scale. With industry demand at D_0, one firm can earn economic profits by producing between Q_0 and Q_1. If the industry were to contain two firms, however, demand for each would be D_1, and neither firm could remain in business without suffering losses. Economists refer to such cases as *natural monopolies*.

Utility industries have traditionally been considered natural monopolists because of the high fixed costs associated with power plants and the inefficiency of several different electric companies stringing their wires throughout a city. Recent technology, however, is slowly changing the utilities industry, as smaller plants, solar units, and wind generators permit a smaller efficient scale of operation. Smaller plants can be quickly turned on and off, and the energy from the sun and wind is beginning to be stored and transported to where it is needed in the system.

Government Franchises, Patents, and Copyrights The government is the source of some barriers to market entry. A government franchise grants a firm permission to provide specific goods or services, while prohibiting others from doing so, thereby eliminating potential competition. The United States Postal Service, for example, has an exclusive franchise for the delivery of mail to your mailbox. Similarly, water companies typically are granted special franchises by state or local governments.

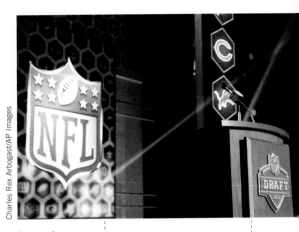

Charles Rex Arbogast/AP Images

The NFL draft is an annual event at which the best players are offered multi-million dollar contracts. The exclusivity of the event gives the NFL maximum market power.

economies of scale As the firm expands in size, average total cost declines.

FIGURE 1	ECONOMIES OF SCALE LEADING TO MONOPOLY

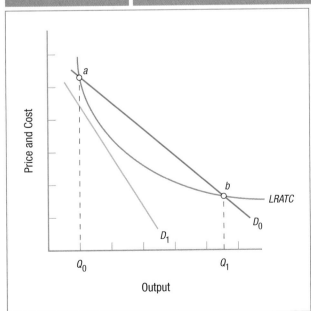

The economies of scale in an industry can be so large that demand supports only one firm. In the industry portrayed here, one firm could earn economic profits (by producing output between Q_0 and Q_1 when faced with demand curve D_0). If the industry consisted of two firms, however, demand for each would be D_1, and neither firm could remain in business without suffering losses.

Patents provide legal protection to individuals who invent new products and processes, allowing the patent holder to reap the benefits from the creation for a limited period, usually 20 years. Patents are immensely important to many industries, including pharmaceuticals, technology, and automobile manufacturing. Many firms in these industries spend huge sums of money each year on research and development—money they might not spend if they could not protect their investments through patenting. Similarly, a copyright protects ideas created by individuals or firms in the form of books, music, art, or software code, allowing these innovators to benefit from their creativity.

Some firms guard trade secrets to protect their assets for even longer periods than the limited timeframes provided by patents and copyrights. Only a handful of the top executives at Coca-Cola, for instance, know the secret to blending Coke.

Copyrights allow Matt Stone and Trey Parker, creators of *South Park*, to earn royalties on every episode (new and repeated) shown on television.

Monopoly Pricing and Output Decisions

Monopolies gain market power because of their barriers to entry. Shortly we will discuss some ways in which this power is maintained. First, however, let us consider the basics of monopoly pricing and output decisions. In the previous chapter, we saw that competitive firms maximize profits by producing at a level of output where $MR = MC$, selling this output at the established market price. The monopolist, however, *is* the market. It has the ability to set the price by adjusting output.

***MR < P* for Monopoly**   A monopolist faces a demand curve, just like a perfectly competitive firm. But there is a big difference. For the monopolist, marginal revenue is less than price ($MR < P$). To see why, look at Figure 2. Panel A shows the demand curve for a perfectly

FIGURE 2	MARGINAL REVENUE FOR MONOPOLIES AND PERFECTLY COMPETITIVE FIRMS

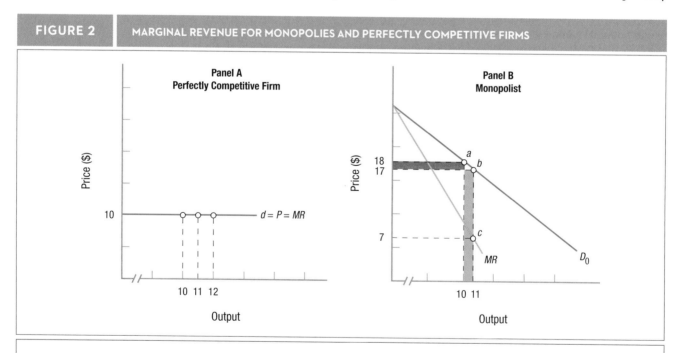

Panel A shows the demand curve for a perfectly competitive firm. At a price of $10, the competitive firm can sell all it wants. For each unit sold, revenue rises by $10; hence, marginal revenue is $10. Panel B shows the demand curve for a monopolist. Because the monopolist constitutes the entire industry, it faces a downward-sloping demand curve (D_0). If the monopolist decides to sell 10 units at $18 each (point *a*), total revenue is $180. Alternatively, if the monopolist wants to sell 11 units, the price must be dropped to $17 (point *b*). This raises total revenue to $187 (11 × $17), but marginal revenue falls to $7 ($187 − $180, point *c*). Gaining the added $17 in revenue from the sale of the 11th unit requires the monopolist to give up $10 in additional revenue that would have come from selling the previous 10 units for an extra $1, or $18 each.

competitive firm. At a price of $10, the competitive firm can sell all it wants. For each unit sold, total revenue rises by $10. Recalling that marginal revenue is equal to the change in total revenue from selling an added unit of the product, marginal revenue is also $10.

Contrast this with the situation of the monopolist in panel B. Because the monopolist constitutes the entire industry, it faces the downward-sloping demand curve (D_0). If the monopolist decides to produce and sell 10 units, they can be sold in the market for the highest price the market would pay for 10 units (based on the demand curve), which is $18 each (point *a*), generating total revenue of $180. Alternatively, if the monopolist wants to sell 11 units, the price must be dropped to $17 (point *b*). This raises total revenue to $187 ($11 \times $17). Notice, however, that marginal revenue, or the revenue gained from selling this added unit, is only $7 ($187 − $180). In other words, the $17 in revenue (shown in green) gained from the sale of the 11th unit requires that the monopolist give up $10 in revenue (shown in red) that would have come from selling the previous 10 units for $1 more, or $18 each. Marginal revenue for the 11th unit is shown as $7 (point *c*) in panel B, which is also the difference between the green and red areas.

Notice that we are assuming the monopolist cannot sell the 10th unit for $18 and then sell the 11th unit for $17; rather, the monopolist must offer to sell a given quantity to the market at a single price per unit. We are assuming, in other words, that there is no way for the monopolist to separate the market by specific individuals who are willing to pay different prices for the product. Later in this chapter, we will relax this assumption and discuss *price discrimination.*

In summary, we can see from panel B of Figure 2 that $MR < P$, and the marginal revenue curve is always plotted below the demand curve for the monopolist. This contrasts with the situation of the perfectly competitive firm, for which price and marginal revenue are always the same. We should also note that marginal revenue can be negative. In such an instance, total revenue falls as the monopolist tries to sell more output. However, no profit-maximizing monopolist would knowingly produce in this range because costs are rising even as total revenue is declining, thus reducing profits.

Equilibrium Price and Output As noted earlier, product price is determined in a monopoly by how much the monopolist wishes to produce. This contrasts with the perfectly competitive firm that can sell all it wishes, but only at the market-determined price. Both types of firms wish to make profits. Finding the monopolist's profit-maximizing price and output is a little more complicated, however, because competitive firms have only output to consider.

Like competitive firms, the profit-maximizing output for the monopolist is found where $MR = MC$. Turning to Figure 3, we find that marginal revenue equals marginal cost at point *e,* where output is 120 units. Now we must determine how much the monopolist will charge for this output. This is done by looking to the demand curve. An output of 120 units can be sold for a price of $30 (point *a*).

Profit for each unit is equal to $8, the difference between price ($30) and average total cost ($22). Profit per unit times output equals total profit ($8 \times 120 = $960), as indicated by the shaded area in Figure 3. Following the $MR = MC$ rule, profits are maximized by selling 120 units of the product at $30 each.

Using the Five Steps to Maximizing Profit We can use the same five-step approach to analyzing equilibrium for a profit-maximizing monopolist as we used for a perfectly competitive firm in the previous chapter. The main difference is that for a monopolist, the demand and marginal revenue curves are downward-sloping, but that does not change the procedure, as shown in Figure 4.

Step 1: Find the point at which $MR = MC$.

Step 2: At that point, look down and determine the profit-maximizing output on the horizontal axis.

Step 3: At this output, extend a vertical line upward to the demand curve and follow it to the left to determine the equilibrium price on the vertical axis.

FIGURE 3 | MONOPOLIST EARNING ECONOMIC PROFITS

Profit-maximizing output is found for monopolists, as for competitive firms, at the point where $MR = MC$. In this figure, marginal revenue equals marginal cost at point e, where output is 120 units. These 120 units are sold for $30 each (point a). Profit is equal to average profit per unit times units sold: Profit $= (P - ATC) \times Q = (\$30 - \$22) \times 120 = \$8 \times 120 = \$960$. The shaded area represents profit.

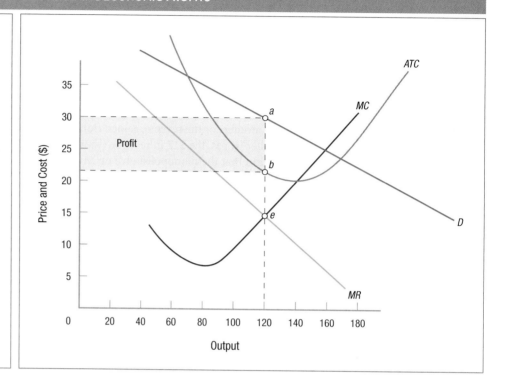

The same five steps that were used to determine the profit-maximizing output, price, and profit in a perfectly competitive market can be used in a monopoly market. The process begins by finding $MR = MC$, and then locating the optimal output and price, average total cost, and finally profit.

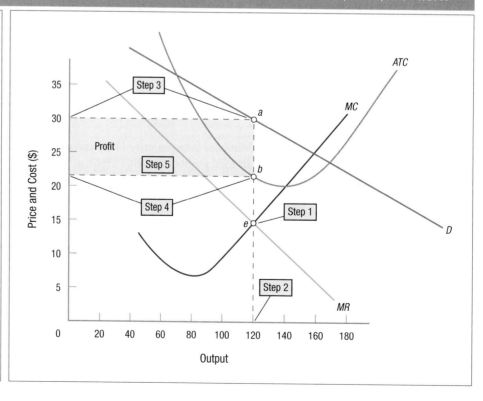

Step 4: Using the same vertical line, find the point on the *ATC* curve to determine the average total cost per unit on the vertical axis.

Step 5: Find total profit by taking $P - ATC$, and multiply by output.

Using the five-step process to determine a monopolist's optimal output, price, and profit is a useful way to avoid making mistakes when analyzing revenue and cost curves. The same five steps can be used to analyze a perfectly competitive market, as shown in the previous chapter, and a monopolistically competitive market, as will be seen in the next chapter.

Monopoly Does Not Guarantee Economic Profits We have seen that competitive firms may or may not be profitable in the short run, but in the long run, they must earn at least normal profits to remain in business. Is the same true for monopolists? Yes. Consider the monopolist in Figure 5. This firm maximizes profits by producing where $MR = MC$ (point *e*) and selling 80 units of output for a price of $25.

In this case, however, price ($25) is lower than average total cost ($28), and thus the monopolist suffers the loss of $240 ($-\$3 \times 80 = -\$240$) indicated by the shaded area. Because price nonetheless exceeds average variable costs, the monopolist will minimize its losses in the short run by continuing to produce. But if price should fall below *AVC*, the monopolist, just like any competitive firm, will minimize its losses at its fixed costs by shutting down its plant. If these losses persist, the monopolist will exit the industry in the long run.

This is an important point to remember. Being a monopolist does not automatically mean that there will be monopoly profits to haul in. Even monopolies face *some* cost and price pressures, and they face a demand curve, which ultimately limits their price making.

 ISSUE

"But Wait . . . There's More!" The Success and Failure of Infomercials

"But wait . . . there's more!" is a familiar phrase to anyone who has watched an infomercial selling unique products that generally are not sold in retail stores. The size of the infomercial industry is significant and growing. In 2015 infomercials generated about $250 billion in sales. What do infomercials sell? Why are they successful and why do many infomercial products fail?

Unlike regular television commercials, which air for 30 seconds or 1 minute during daytime and primetime shows, infomercials typically are longer, ranging from 1 minute to 30 minutes or longer. The longest infomercials typically air in the middle of the night when television advertising rates are much lower.

Infomercials typically sell newly invented products that are not well known. Most infomercial products fit the monopoly market structure because although the product may have similarities to other products, infomercials advertise them as one-of-a-kind products. Examples include new types of knives, towels, beauty products, and workout equipment. However, because not all infomercials are able to convince prospective buyers of the distinction from existing products, many infomercial products fail.

Infomercials focus on the product characteristics that make the product completely different from anything on the market. Because the target market of infomercials is consumers who buy on impulse, even in the middle of the night, they use various techniques to increase sales. First, many infomercials show a high "retail" price (such as $100) and then reduce it rapidly until it becomes $19.99. Second, infomercials will offer something extra with the tag line "But wait . . . there's more!" Third, many infomercials show a fixed time period in which to buy, often within hours,

Eric Chiang

even if the deadline is not actually enforced. And last, infomercials tend to offer return policies and often lifetime warranties (which is attractive but not that valuable if the company fails).

Some infomercials have become remarkably successful, with the product even sold in stores. One example of a successful product that started from an infomercial is the Ped Egg, a cheese-grater-like device that removes dead skin from one's feet, which has sold over 50 million units and is now available through retailers such as Walgreens and Amazon.com.

FIGURE 5 | MONOPOLIST FIRM MAKING ECONOMIC LOSSES

Like perfectly competitive firms, monopolists may or may not be profitable in the short run, but in the long run, they must at least earn normal profits to remain in business. The monopolist shown here maximizes profits (minimizes losses) by producing at point *e*, selling 80 units of output at $25 each. Price is lower than average total cost, so the monopolist suffers the loss indicated by the shaded area. Because price still exceeds average variable cost (*AVC*), in the short run, the monopolist will minimize its losses by continuing to produce.

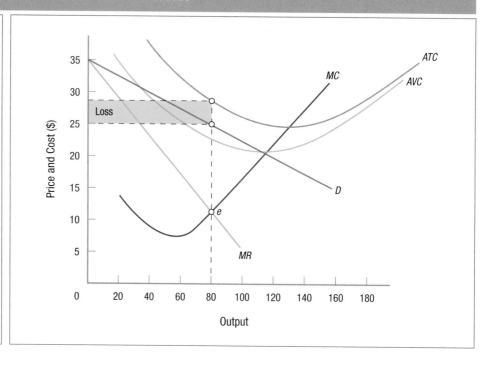

✅ CHECKPOINT

MONOPOLY MARKETS

- Monopoly is a market with no close substitutes, high barriers to entry, and one seller; the firm is the industry. Hence, monopolists are price makers.

- Monopolies gain maximum market power from control over an important input, economies of scale, or from government franchises, patents, and copyrights.

- For the monopolist, $MR < P$ because the industry's demand is the monopolist's demand.

- Profit is maximized by producing that output where $MR = MC$ and setting the price from the demand curve.

- Being a monopolist does not guarantee economic profits if demand is insufficient to cover costs.

QUESTIONS: When legendary country singer Dolly Parton goes on tour, sometimes she will perform in a relatively small (<1,500 seats) venue when she could easily fill much larger arenas. Why would music artists intentionally choose a smaller venue? Wouldn't they make more money if they performed in a larger arena?

Answers to the Checkpoint questions can be found at the end of this chapter.

COMPARING MONOPOLY AND COMPETITION

We have seen that perfectly competitive firms are price takers and produce as much as they can where $MR = MC$. In contrast, monopolies are price makers: They have the market power to set price and quantity, constrained only by their demand curve.

Would our economy be better off with more or fewer monopolies? This question almost answers itself. Who would want more monopolies—except the few lucky monopolists? The answer is, consumers are better off when competition is strong and monopolies are limited to certain industries. The reasons for this have to do with the losses associated with monopoly markets and market power. Losses directly attributed to monopolies include reduced output at higher prices, deadweight losses, rent-seeking behavior of monopolists, and x-inefficiency losses. But as we'll see later in this section, part (but not all) of these losses can be at least partially offset by some benefits that monopolies provide.

Higher Prices and Lower Output From Monopoly

Imagine for a moment that a competitive industry is monopolized, and the monopolist's marginal cost curve happens to be the same as the competitive industry's supply curve. Figure 6 illustrates such a scenario. In panel A, the competitive industry produces where supply equals demand, and thus where price and output are P_C and Q_C (point a). In panel B, monopoly price and output, as previously determined, are P_M and Q_M (point b).

Clearly, monopoly output is lower, and monopoly price is higher, than the corresponding values for competitive industries. How does this translate into the welfare of consumers and producers? Recall that we measure consumer surplus as the difference between market demand and price, as shown by the green areas in each panel. Producer surplus is the difference between price and market supply (marginal cost), as shown by the orange areas in each panel. The higher price charged by a monopolist results in part of the consumer surplus from panel A being transferred into producer surplus in panel B. Panel B shows a smaller consumer surplus and a larger producer surplus under a monopoly compared to a competitive market in panel A. But this is not the end of the story.

Notice that at monopoly output Q_M, consumers value the Q_Mth unit of the product at P_M (point b), even though the cost to produce this last unit of output is considerably less (point c). This difference creates inefficiency because additional beneficial transactions

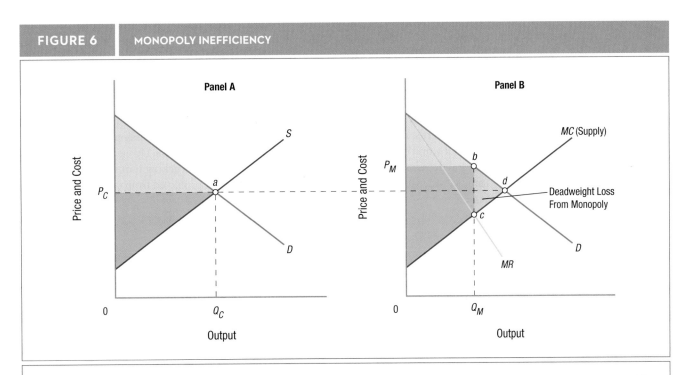

FIGURE 6	MONOPOLY INEFFICIENCY

This figure shows what would happen if a competitive industry were monopolized and the new monopolist's marginal cost curve was the same as the competitive industry's supply curve. When the industry was competitive, it produced where $S = D$, and thus where price and output are P_C and Q_C (point a in panel A). Monopoly price and output, however, are P_M and Q_M (point b in panel B); output is lower and price is higher than the corresponding values for competitive firms. As a result, part of consumer surplus (shown in green) is transferred into producer surplus (shown in orange) in a monopoly, and in the process, inefficiency is created in the form of deadweight loss (shaded area bcd).

could take place if output were expanded. This inefficiency, known as *deadweight loss,* is made up of consumer surplus and producer surplus that are lost from producing less than the efficient output. In panel B, deadweight loss from monopoly is shown as the shaded area *bcd.* This area represents the deadweight loss to society from a monopoly market.

Even though deadweight loss derives partly from lost producer surplus, monopoly firms willingly forgo this portion of producer surplus in order to transfer a larger portion of consumer surplus into producer surplus (the orange rectangular area above the P_c line in panel B). Therefore, monopoly firms use their market power to gain producer surplus at the expense of consumers and create inefficiency in the form of deadweight loss. But this is not the only source of inefficiency caused by firms with complete market power.

Rent Seeking and X-Inefficiency

Monopolies earn economic profits by producing less and charging more than competitive firms. Although these actions generate deadweight loss, monopolists are protective of the profits they earn. If barriers to entry to the market were eased, economic profit would evaporate as price falls, as it does in competitive markets. How, then, can a monopolist protect itself from potential competition? One way is to spend resources that could have been used to expand its production on efforts to protect its monopoly position.

rent seeking Resources expended to protect a monopoly position. These are used for such activities as lobbying, extending patents, and restricting the number of licenses permitted.

Economists call this behavior **rent seeking**—behavior directed toward avoiding competition. Firms hire lawyers and other professionals to lobby governments, extend patents, and engage in a host of other activities intended solely to protect their monopoly position. For example, in order to pick up passengers on the street, taxis in New York City require a medallion registered with the Taxi and Limousine Commission. Because restricting the number of medallions drives up their price, taxi drivers have an incentive to lobby for restrictions against companies such as Uber whose drivers do not require medallions but compete for the same customers. Many industries spend significant resources lobbying Congress for tariff protection to reduce foreign competition. All these activities are inefficient, in that they use resources and shift income from one group to another without producing a useful good or service. Rent seeking thus represents an added loss to society from monopoly.

x-inefficiency Protected from competitive pressures, monopolies do not have to act efficiently. Examples include spending on luxury corporate jets, lavish travel, and other nonessential perks.

Another area in which society might lose from monopolies is called **x-inefficiency.** Some economists suggest that because monopolies are protected from competitive pressures, they do not have to operate efficiently. Management can offer itself and their employees perks, such as elaborate corporate retreats or suites at professional sports stadiums, without worrying about whether costs are kept at efficient levels. Deregulation over the last several decades, particularly in the communications and trucking industries, has provided ample evidence of inefficiencies arising when firms are protected from competition by government regulations. Many firms in these industries had to cut back on lavish expenses when competitive pressures were reintroduced into their industries.

Monopolies and Innovation

Much of our analysis of monopolies has focused on the inefficiencies created and the detrimental effects on consumers. However, monopolies do create some benefits that are shared among all of society. For example, monopolies provide new products, technologies, and medical breakthroughs that benefit many consumers. The incentives to earn monopoly profits created by patents and copyrights encourage firms to invest in developing these new products. Otherwise, what firm would be willing to spend hundreds of millions of dollars inventing a product only to have it copied and sold by other firms?

Similarly, much of the entertainment industry, including music, television shows, books, and movies, would not exist to such a great extent if copyrights did not provide singers, authors, and other media creators the monetary incentive to create such products for our enjoyment. Therefore, the ability to achieve market power through innovation provides an incentive to individuals and firms to invest time and money to create new products and other creative works that could generate substantial profits over time.

Benefits Versus Costs of Monopolies

Are there any other benefits to monopolies aside from innovation? The answer to this question is, "Possibly yes, though generally no." If the economies of scale associated with an industry are so large that many small competitors would face substantially higher marginal costs than a monopolist, a monopolist would produce and sell more output at a lower price than could competitive firms.

This is the case of natural monopolies, and the justification for why monopolies are allowed to exist in industries such as the provision of water or electricity in many communities. Imagine what might happen if a storm knocks out power to your neighborhood, and instead of one electric company restoring power to your street, each household needed to wait for its specific electricity provider to show up.

Larger firms, moreover, can allocate more resources to research and development than smaller firms, and the possibility of economic profits may be the incentive monopolists require to invest.

Still, economists tend to doubt that monopolies are beneficial enough to outweigh their disadvantages.

In actuality, pure monopolies are rare, in part because of public policy and anti-trust laws—more about this later in this chapter—and in part because rapidly changing technologies limit most monopolies to short-run economic profits—witness the battle between Instagram and Snapchat for domination in social networking, and Apple, Microsoft, Samsung, and several other firms to dominate the tablet market. Even so, firms seek to increase their market power by trying to become monopolies and gain the ability to influence price.

We have seen what monopolies are and how they arise. We also saw why a monopolist produces less than the socially optimal quantity at a higher than socially

Although often criticized for inefficient operations, the U.S. Postal Service still offers the ability to send a letter to any address in the country, including far-away places such as Hawaii, Alaska, or Guam, for the price of a single stamp.

Rachel Epstein/The Image Works

AROUND THE WORLD

A Convenience Store on Every Corner, as Far as the Eye Can See

Why don't ABC stores in Hawaii use their market power to raise prices?

When traveling to Hawaii, one typically enjoys the beautiful beaches, mountains, and unique Polynesian culture. In Waikiki, the center of the tourist area, another ubiquitous sight can be seen: the ABC store. Founded in 1964, the ABC chain has stores throughout Hawaii. In fact, approximately thirty-eight nearly identical stores are located within a 1-mile radius in Waikiki. From one street corner, one can see multiple ABC stores.

What made these stores so prominent in Waikiki, and how is this chain of convenience stores able to maintain its market power? The products sold in an ABC store are not unique. However,

Eric Chiang

unlike a typical convenience store that sells snacks and other basic necessities, ABC stores are stocked with souvenirs, gifts, and other products catering specifically to tourists. Essentially, it's a one-stop shop for tourists, substituting for the souvenir shop, grocery store, and everyday discount store.

Why does ABC have market power?

Because it was able to achieve economies of scale. Although each ABC shop is relatively small, the combined size of the thirty-eight stores within close proximity to one another makes it comparable in size to a giant retail store. By easily stocking its stores, it can source large quantities at favorable prices, giving ABC an advantage that a competitor might not achieve.

Why don't they then use their market power to raise prices?

Because it is a contestable market. This means that the threat of new competition keeps ABC's prices low, preventing it from exploiting its market power as fully as a true monopoly would. Therefore, although the sheer concentration of store locations has allowed ABC to achieve some market power, to survive and prosper, it serves its customers by offering convenient locations and a wide selection of items at reasonable prices.

GO TO **LaunchPad** TO PRACTICE THE ECONOMIC CONCEPTS IN THIS STORY

desirable price, and witnessed how monopoly compares unfavorably to the competitive model. Furthermore, we looked at an expensive drawback of monopolies: the amount of resources wasted in maintaining a monopolist's position. In the next section, we relax the assumption of one price, revealing strategies monopolies use to increase profits.

 CHECKPOINT

COMPARING MONOPOLY AND COMPETITION

- Monopoly output is lower and price is higher when compared to competition, resulting in deadweight loss.

- Monopolies are subject to rent-seeking behavior directed toward avoiding competition (lobbying and other activities to extend the monopoly).

- Because monopolies are protected from competitive pressures, they often engage in x-inefficiency behavior—extending perks to management and other inefficient activities.

- Monopolies can provide benefits in the form of economies of scale and incentives to innovate. However, these benefits are outweighed by the costs resulting from the lack of competition.

QUESTIONS: About 25 years ago, nearly every household that wanted a wide selection of television channels subscribed to cable, which was essentially a monopoly with 98% of market share, facing only a tiny level of competition from expensive, behemoth satellite dishes. Today, cable companies control less than half of the market share. What has changed in the industry that led to increased competition? How has competition affected the efficiency and reliability of cable services?

Answers to the Checkpoint questions can be found at the end of this chapter.

PRICE DISCRIMINATION

When firms have some market power, they will try to charge different customers different prices for the same product. For example, senior citizens might pay less for a movie ticket than you do. This is called **price discrimination** and it is used to increase the firm's profits by converting part or all of consumer surplus into producer surplus. If a product sells for $100 in a competitive market but you are willing to pay $150, a monopolist wants to grab as much of your $50 consumer surplus as possible.

Remember that unlike monopolies, competitive firms cannot price discriminate because they get their prices from the market (they are price takers). Several conditions are required for successful price discrimination:

- Sellers must have some market power.
- Sellers must be able to separate the market into different consumer groups based on their elasticities of demand.
- Sellers must be able to prevent arbitrage; that is, they must be able to keep low-price buyers from reselling to higher-price buyers.

There are three major types of price discrimination. The first is known as **perfect (first-degree) price discrimination.** It involves charging each customer the *maximum price* each is willing to pay. Because firms cannot always determine individual willingness-to-pay, other forms of price discrimination exist. **Second-degree price discrimination** involves charging different customers different prices based on the *quantities* of the product they purchase. The final and most common form of price discrimination is **third-degree price discrimination,** which occurs when firms *charge different groups of people different prices.* This is an everyday occurrence with airline, bus, and movie theater tickets.

price discrimination Charging different consumer groups different prices for the same product.

perfect (first-degree) price discrimination Charging each customer the maximum price each is willing to pay, thereby expropriating all consumer surplus.

second-degree price discrimination Charging different customers different prices based on the quantities of the product they purchase.

third-degree price discrimination Charging different groups of people different prices based on varying elasticities of demand.

Perfect (First-Degree) Price Discrimination

When perfect price discrimination can be employed, a firm will charge each customer the maximum price each is willing to pay. This type of price discrimination is perhaps best exemplified by an online auction, where buyers often bid up the price of a good to their maximum willingness to pay. Figure 7 portrays such a scenario for a market with constant cost conditions (assumed for simplicity) and where 1 unit of the good is offered to the highest bidder each day. Every point on the demand curve represents a price. The first customer, who values the product the most, is charged the highest price. The next customer is charged a slightly lower price. The Q_Mth customer is charged P_M (point a), and so on, until the last unit is sold to the Q_Cth customer for P_C (point b). As a result, a monopolist using perfect price discrimination sets prices equal to each consumer's marginal benefit and earns profits equal to the shaded area $P_C P_T b$.

Figure 7 shows why firms would want to price discriminate. Typical monopoly profits in this case, assuming the monopolist sells Q_M units at price P_M, would be the rectangular area $P_C P_M ac$ (the lighter shaded area). This area is considerably smaller than the triangle $P_C P_T b$, earned by the perfectly price-discriminating monopolist. That is why price discrimination exists—it is profitable. Note also that the *last* unit of the product sold by this monopolist is priced at P_C, the competitive price. In this limited sense, then, the monopolist who can perfectly price discriminate is as efficient as a competitive firm. Notice that perfectly price-discriminating monopolists manage to expropriate the entire consumer surplus.

Second-Degree Price Discrimination

Second-degree price discrimination involves charging consumers different prices for different blocks of consumption. For example, by purchasing items in bulk (such as a pack of six tubes of toothpaste) at Costco or Sam's Club, the cost per unit is typically less than buying just one tube at the local store. Similarly, producers of electric, gas, and water utilities often incorporate block pricing. You pay one rate for the first so many kilowatt-hours of electricity and a lower rate for more, and so on.

| **FIGURE 7** | **PERFECT PRICE DISCRIMINATION** |

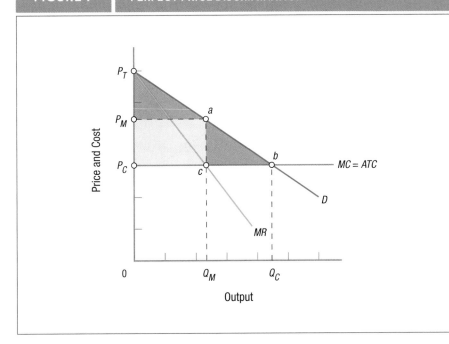

With perfect price discrimination, firms charge each customer the maximum price each is willing to pay in order to extract all consumer surplus. Thus, every point on the demand curve in this figure represents a price. The first few customers—those who value the product most—are charged the highest price. The next customers are charged slightly lower prices, and so on, until the last unit is sold for P_C (point b). As a result, a perfectly discriminating monopolist earns profits represented by the shaded area $P_C P_T b$. This is considerably more profit than the monopolist would earn by selling Q_M units at price P_M, represented by area $P_C P_M ac$.

The rationale for second-degree price discrimination is twofold. First, the cost of selling many units of a good to one customer is often less than that of selling a single unit to many customers due to overhead costs such as cashiers and accounting expenses. Second, if stores convince consumers to buy more than they had intended by offering discounts, profits can be earned as long as the discounted price exceeds marginal cost.

An illustration of second-degree price discrimination is shown in Figure 8 using the block pricing scheme example.

For the first Q_0 units of the product, consumers are charged P_0; between Q_0 and Q_1, the price falls to P_1; and after that, the price is reduced to P_C. This results in profit to the firm equal to the shaded area. The shaded profit area for the price-discriminating monopolist is greater than that of the monopolist charging just one price P_M (area $P_C P_M ac$). The most common price discrimination scheme, however, is third-degree, in which *groups* of consumers are charged different prices.

Third-Degree Price Discrimination

Third-degree, or imperfect, price discrimination involves charging different groups of people different prices. An obvious example would be the various fares charged for airline flights. Business travelers have much lower elasticities of demand for flights than do vacationers; therefore, airlines place all sorts of restrictions on their tickets to separate people into distinct categories. Purchasing a ticket several weeks in advance, for instance—which vacationers can usually do, but businesspeople may not be able to—often results in a significantly lower fare. Arbitrage (the ability of low-price buyers to sell to higher-price buyers) is prevented, meanwhile, by rules stipulating that passengers can only travel on tickets purchased in their name. Other examples of third-degree price discrimination include different ticket prices for children, adults, and seniors at movie theaters; student discounts for many services; and even ladies' night at clubs, where female customers receive free admission.

Firms engage in third-degree price discrimination in order to increase their producer surplus by serving more customers. For example, if a software firm is restricted to offering their product at one price, it would choose the profit-maximizing monopoly price, which means customers with lower willingness-to-pay would be priced out of a purchase. However, by offering a discounted price to these customers (and only these customers who otherwise would not have made a purchase), firms can gain more producer surplus as long as the discounted price exceeds the marginal cost of providing the extra units.

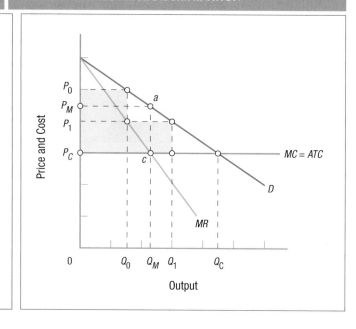

| FIGURE 8 | SECOND-DEGREE PRICE DISCRIMINATION |

Second-degree price discrimination involves charging different customers different prices based on the quantities of the product they purchase. A single-price monopolist would earn economic profits equal to $P_C P_M ac$, but by charging three different prices—P_0, P_1, and P_C—profits increase, as shown by comparing the shaded area with area $P_C P_M ac$.

Third-degree price discrimination is illustrated in Figure 9. The two demand curves, D_0 and D_1, represent two segments of a market with different demand elasticities. The less elastic market, D_1, is offered price P_1. This is higher than price P_0 offered to the more elastic market, D_0. Profits are maximized for both markets. For market D_0, profits are $P_C P_0 bc$, and for less elastic market D_1, they are $P_C P_1 ad$. Like the previous examples of price discriminating firms, the third-degree price-discriminating monopolist earns profits that exceed those that would come from a normal one-price policy.

We can look at price discrimination in an intuitive way by focusing on a restaurant. Most dinner customers frequent the restaurant after 6:30 P.M. However, the restaurant is still open from 4:30 to 6:30 P.M. and incurs costs (if workers start their shifts before the 6:30 rush). It is in the restaurant's interest to offer early bird specials, discounting dinners purchased before 6:30, as long as this policy attracts new customers and does not pull in too many of its later-appearing regular diners. In this way, the restaurant generates profits from two separate groups, while charging two separate prices. As long as the restaurant has some market power—it can offer these two prices without driving its regular customers from higher-priced meals to lower-priced meals—it makes sense for it to act this way. Therefore, we can conclude that firms with market power will always try to price discriminate.

In all three types of price discrimination, monopoly firms use their market power to increase their producer surplus. Although part of this increase in producer surplus comes from consumers in the form of higher prices, the rest comes from the reduction in deadweight loss. Unlike a single-price monopolist, efficiency is improved in multiple-price scenarios because more output is being produced, allowing more consumers to purchase the good. Still, all forms of monopoly pricing (single-price or multiple-price through price discrimination) create concerns about the welfare of consumers. Therefore, regulations and rules are sometimes used to reduce the market power firms exert. We turn to these topics in the next section.

Eric Chiang

Theme park pricing shows both second-degree price discrimination (the more days you buy, the lower the average price per day) and third-degree price discrimination (lower prices for guests under age 10).

FIGURE 9   THIRD-DEGREE PRICE DISCRIMINATION

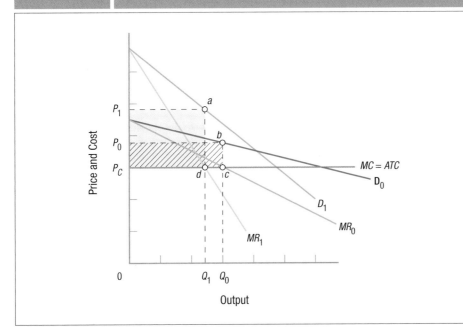

This figure illustrates third-degree price discrimination, in which firms segment markets based on consumers' willingness-to-pay in order to maximize producer surplus. The two demand curves, D_0 and D_1, represent two segments of a market with different demand elasticities. The less elastic market, D_1, is offered price P_1, which is higher than price P_0, offered to the more elastic market, D_0, thus maximizing the profits in both markets.

ISSUE

Is Flexible Ticket Pricing the New Form of Price Discrimination?

Ticketmaster (also known as Live Nation) has long held market power in the entertainment and sports ticket-selling industry. Although Ticketmaster faces competition from other ticket sellers, its market power stems from the exclusive contracts it establishes with concert promoters, artists, and sports teams.

When an agreement is made with Ticketmaster, it becomes the only site through which consumers can purchase tickets other than the ticket resale market. This gives ticket sellers and the entertainers and shows they represent considerable market power to set prices.

Ticketmaster's traditional pricing model is to offer several ticket tiers with different fixed prices based on seating location. However, setting prices too

low results in a quick sellout, leading to a resale market in which tickets initially sold at one price are resold at much higher prices, with the profits going to the reseller instead of Ticketmaster. Setting prices too high, on the other hand, leaves many tickets unsold and results in many tickets being given away in radio promotions and other deals.

A few years ago, Ticketmaster began experimenting with a new flexible pricing model that has been successfully used in the airline industry. With flexible pricing, concert tickets do not have a fixed price. Instead, ticket prices are set and changed based on demand—if tickets sell too fast, prices would rise; if tickets sell too slowly, prices would fall. This form of price discrimination allows ticket sellers to reap more consumer

ANDREW GOMBERT/Corbis

surplus that otherwise might go to the resale market. This new approach to ticket sales is another example of how firms use strategies to maximize their market power.

 ## CHECKPOINT

PRICE DISCRIMINATION

- Firms with market power price discriminate to increase profits.
- To price discriminate, firms must have some market power (control over price) and must be able to separate the market into different consumer groups based on their elasticity of demand, and firms (sellers) must be able to prevent arbitrage.
- With perfect price discrimination, the firm can charge each customer a different price and expropriate the entire consumer surplus for itself.
- Second-degree price discrimination involves charging customers different prices for different quantities of the product.
- Third-degree price discrimination (the most common) involves charging different groups of people different prices.
- Price discrimination may lead to higher prices for some consumers, but it also improves efficiency by allowing more consumers to purchase the good, reducing deadweight loss.

QUESTIONS: Researchers at Yale University and the University of California, Berkeley, found that minorities and women pay about $500 more, on average, for a car than white men when bargaining directly with car dealers. However, when minorities and women used online auto retailers such as Autobytel.com to purchase a car, the price discrimination disappeared. Is this price discrimination the same as that discussed in this section? Why or why not?

Answers to the Checkpoint questions can be found at the end of this chapter.

REGULATION AND ANTITRUST

We have seen that monopolies have the ability to raise prices and restrict quantities, putting them at the other end of the spectrum from the competitive market price-taker ideal. Thus, monopolies are price makers. Also, we have just seen that firms use their market power to price discriminate, attempting to achieve as much producer surplus as they can even if it comes by way of reducing consumer surplus. In an attempt to mitigate the maximum market power of monopolies, government has used two approaches: regulation and antitrust.

Regulating the Natural Monopolist

As we saw when we discussed barriers to entry, there are some instances when natural monopolies occur. A **natural monopoly** exists when economies of scale are so large that the minimum efficient scale of operation is roughly equal to market demand. In this case, efficient production can only be accomplished if the industry lies in the hands of one firm—a monopolist. Public utilities and water departments are examples.

How can policymakers prevent natural monopolists from abusing their positions of market dominance? There are various approaches to dealing with natural monopolies: (1) They can be publicly owned, (2) they can be privately owned but subjected to price and quantity constraints, or (3) their right to operate could be auctioned to the firm agreeing to the most competitive price and quantity conditions.

A market representing a natural monopoly is shown in Figure 10. Notice that the average cost and marginal cost curves decline continually because of large economies of scale.

If the monopolist were a purely private firm, it would produce only output Q_M and sell this for price P_M (point a). Accordingly, the monopolist would earn economic or monopoly profits, and consumers would be harmed, receiving a lower output at a higher price. This is the major argument for regulation.

Marginal Cost Pricing Rule Ideally, regulators would like to invoke the $P = MC$ rule of competitive markets and force the firm to sell Q_C units for a price of P_C. This is the **marginal cost pricing rule** and would be the optimal resource allocation solution. Yet, because price P_C is below the average total cost of production for output Q_C, this would force the firm to sustain losses of cd per unit, ultimately driving it out of business. The public sector could subsidize the firm by an amount equal to area $P_C C_C dc$; this subsidy allows the firm to supply the socially optimal output at the socially optimal price, while earning a normal return. This approach has not been used often in the United States. Amtrak, with its history of heavy subsidies for maintaining rail service, may be the one major exception.

Average Cost Pricing Rule The more common approach to regulation in the United States has been to insist on an **average cost pricing rule.** Such a rule requires that the monopolist produce and sell output where price equals average total cost. This is illustrated by point b in Figure 10, where the demand curve intersects the ATC curve and the firm

natural monopoly An industry exhibiting large economies of scale such that the minimum efficient scale of operations is roughly equal to market demand.

marginal cost pricing rule Regulators would prefer to have natural monopolists price where $P = MC$, but this would result in losses (long term) because $ATC > MC$.

average cost pricing rule Requires a regulated monopolist to produce and sell output where price equals average total cost. This permits the regulated monopolist to earn a normal return on investment over the long term and therefore remain in business.

| FIGURE 10 | REGULATING A NATURAL MONOPOLY |

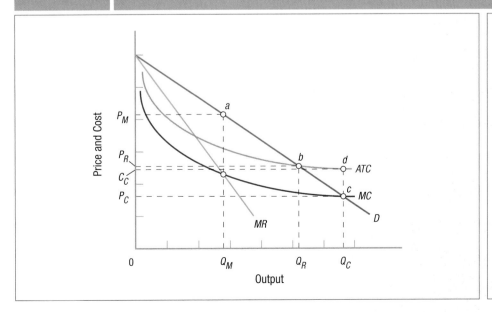

A natural monopoly exists when economies of scale are so large that the minimum efficient scale of operation is roughly equal to market demand. In this case, efficient production can only be accomplished if the industry lies in the hands of one firm—a monopolist. Yet, if the monopolist is a purely private firm, it will produce only output Q_M, selling it for price P_M (point a). This is the principal rationale for regulating natural monopolies to produce output Q_R for a price of P_R (point b).

GEORGE STIGLER (1911–1991)

NOBEL PRIZE

Few modern economists have broken ground in so many different areas as George Stigler, described by some admirers as the "ultimate empirical economist." His 1982 Nobel Prize cited seminal work in industrial structure, the functioning of markets, and the causes and effects of public regulation.

Born in 1911 in the Seattle suburb of Renton, Washington, Stigler attended graduate school at the University of Chicago with fellow students and eventual Nobel Prize winners Milton Friedman and Paul Samuelson. Stigler later became a professor at the University of Chicago, where he remained until his death in 1991.

Exploring the relationship between size and efficiency led him to the "Darwinian" conclusion that by observing competition in an industry, he could determine the most efficient sizes for firms, a method he called "the survivor technique." In the 1960s, Stigler studied the impacts of government regulation on the economy with skepticism, arguing that government interventions were often designed to optimize market conditions for producers instead of protecting the public interest. This work opened up a new field known as "regulation economics" and kindled greater interest in the relationship between law and economics.

produces output Q_R and sells it for price P_R. The result is that the firm earns a normal return. Consumers do lose something, in that they must pay a higher price for less output than they would under ideal competitive conditions. Still, the normal profits keep the firm in business, and the losses to consumers are significantly less than if the firm were left unregulated.

Regulation in Practice The United States has a long history of public utility regulation. For most of this history, regulation has been accepted as the lesser of two evils. Monopolists have long been viewed with distrust, but regulators have just as often been portrayed as incompetent and ineffectual, if not lapdogs of the industries they regulate.[1] Although this characterization is probably unfair, a number of economists, including Nobel Prize–laureate George Stigler, viewed regulation with skepticism and proposed changes on improving the efficiency of regulation.

Regulating a large enterprise always presents immense difficulties and tradeoffs. For one thing, finding a point like *b* in Figure 10 is difficult in practice, given that estimating demand and cost curves is an inexact science, at best, and markets are always changing. In practice, regulators must often turn to *rate of return* or *price cap* regulation.

rate of return regulation Permits product pricing that allows the firm to earn a normal return on capital invested in the firm.

Rate of return regulation allows a firm to price its product in such a way that it can earn a normal return on capital invested. This leads to added regulations about the acceptable items that can be included in costs and capital expenditures. Can the country club memberships of top executives be counted as capital investments? Predictably, firms always want to include more expenses as legitimate business expenses, and regulators want to include fewer. Regulatory commissions and regulated firms often have large staffs to deal with such issues, and protracted court battles are not uncommon.

price caps Maximum price at which a regulated firm can sell its product. They are often flexible enough to allow for changing cost conditions.

Alternatively, regulators can impose **price caps** on regulated firms, which place maximum limits on the prices firms can charge for products. These caps can be adjusted in response to changing cost conditions, including changes in labor costs, productivity, technology, and raw material prices.

Today, the pace of technological change is so rapid that regulation has lost some of its earlier luster and is not used as often. In fact, many utilities such as telephone services and cable television are so competitive that regulation is not as necessary compared to when they were once monopolies. Therefore, rather than regulate natural monopolies, government has sought to prevent monopolies and monopolistic practices from arising at all—what is called antitrust policy.

Antitrust Policy

antitrust law Laws designed to maintain competition and prevent monopolies from developing.

Rather than regulatory tinkering, governments have tried a broader approach to deal with monopolies and their market power. The goal of **antitrust law** is to preserve competition and prevent monopolies with their maximum market power from arising in the first place.

The origin of antitrust policy came in the late 1800s, when many large trusts were established, which brought many firms under one organizational structure allowing them to act

[1] See George Stigler, "The Theory of Economic Regulation," *Bell Journal of Economics,* 1971, pp. 3–21.

as monopolists. Massive wealth accumulations by such "robber barons" as John D. Rockefeller (Standard Oil) and Jay Gould (railroads and stock manipulation) sparked resentment and fear against trusts and the growing inequity of income and wealth. Trusts had become so powerful—and so hated—that Congress passed the first antitrust act, the Sherman Act, in 1890. Antitrust laws and policies thus had their origins in trust-busting activity. Many of these laws still are in existence today with their primary role of preventing the inefficiencies associated with monopoly behavior.

The Major Antitrust Laws

Several major statutes form the core of the country's antitrust laws. The most important provisions of these laws (as amended) are described in Table 1.

The intensity of antitrust enforcement has varied over the past century, from an early focus on monopolies, then on mergers, and more recently on price fixing—conspiracies by firms to agree on industry prices to suppress or eliminate competition. Although price-fixing cases have been prominent, it is merger policy developed in the 1950s that has really stood the test of time. Mergers occur for many reasons, such as to eliminate competition from a former rival, to enlarge the size of a company, to achieve more market power, or to merge with a foreign company to pay lower taxes abroad. Regardless, economists and judges generally agree that the reason for antitrust enforcement is to prevent the inefficiencies associated with significant market power. Premerger notification for approval or challenge by the Department of Justice is designed to prevent mergers that have a reasonable likelihood of inhibiting market competition. This is easier said than done.

Defining the Relevant Market and Market Power

The first problem involves defining market power. What is the relevant product market? Some markets can be severely limited geographically, such as concrete, with its extremely high transport costs, and dry cleaning, limited by the unwillingness of consumers to travel far for this service. Other markets are national in scope, like airlines, breakfast cereals, and electronics. Still others extend beyond the borders of a country, with the forces of global competition increasingly reducing domestic market power.

TABLE 1	MAJOR ANTITRUST LAWS

I. The Sherman Act (1890)

   A. Activity in "restraint of trade" is made a felony.

   B. Monopolization or attempt to monopolize is made a felony.

   C. Conviction in either carries a fine of up to $10 million for corporations and $350,000 for individuals, and/or a prison sentence of up to 3 years.

   D. Congress purposefully left "restraint of trade" and "monopolization" undefined, thus requiring the courts to flesh them out.

II. The Clayton Act (1914)

   A. Unlawful to price discriminate if such discrimination substantially lessens competition. This rule was strengthened by the Robinson-Patman Act in 1936, although today the federal government rarely enforces its provisions, viewing them as outdated.

   B. Companies cannot acquire all or part of another where the effect may be to substantially lessen competition or create a monopoly. This rule was strengthened by the 1950 Celler-Kefauver Act by preventing mergers via asset acquisition and setting up elaborate premerger notification requirements for mergers exceeding a certain size.

III. The Federal Trade Commission Act (1914)

   A. Unfair methods of competition and deceptive acts are made illegal.

   B. Established an independent regulatory body, the Federal Trade Commission (FTC).

   This Act is the centerpiece of federal consumer protection. The Supreme Court has given the FTC the power to enforce antitrust laws, except the Sherman Act.

The second problem is determining the proper measuring device of market power. As an industry moves from competition to monopoly, pricing power rises from zero to total. One of the challenges economists have faced is developing one measure that accurately reflects market power or concentration for all these market structures.

Industries that become more concentrated generally increase the losses to society. Therefore, any measure of concentration should accurately reflect the ability of firms to increase prices above that point which would prevail under competitive conditions.

concentration ratio The share of industry shipments or sales accounted for by the top four or eight firms.

Concentration Ratios A widely used measure of industry concentration is the **concentration ratio.** The *n*-firm concentration ratio is the share of industry sales accounted for by the industry's *n* largest firms. Typically, four- and eight-firm concentration ratios (CR-4 and CR-8) are reported.

Although useful in giving a quick snapshot of an industry, concentration ratios express only one piece of the market power distribution picture: the market share enjoyed by the industry's four or eight largest firms. Table 2 shows the market shares of the four largest firms in two different industries. Industry 1 contains a dominant firm with 65% of the market, followed by a bunch of smaller firms. Industry 2 consists of four fairly equal-sized firms, followed by a bunch of smaller firms. In both industries, however, the four-firm concentration ratio is 85; that is, the top four firms control 85% of industry sales. But do the two industries exhibit the same level of monopoly power? Hardly! The second industry, whose top four firms are roughly equal in size, would be expected to be more competitive than the first, in which 65% of the market is controlled by one firm.

Without more information about each industry, concentration ratios are not overly informative, except to point out extreme contrasts. If one industry's four-firm concentration ratio is 85, for instance, and another's is 15, the first industry has considerably more monopoly power than the second.

Economists and antitrust enforcers, however, need finer distinctions than concentration ratios permit. For this reason, the profession has developed the Herfindahl–Hirschman index.

Herfindahl–Hirschman index (HHI) A way of measuring industry concentration, equal to the sum of the squares of market shares for all firms in the industry.

Herfindahl–Hirschman Index The **Herfindahl–Hirschman index (HHI)** is the principal measure of concentration used by the Department of Justice to evaluate mergers and judge monopoly power. The HHI is defined by the equation

$$\text{HHI} = (S_1)^2 + (S_2)^2 + (S_3)^2 + \cdots + (S_n)^2$$

where $S_1, S_2, \ldots S_n$ are the percentage market shares of each firm in the industry. Thus, the HHI is the sum of the squares of each market share. In a five-firm industry, for instance, in which each firm enjoys a 20% market share, the HHI is

$$\begin{aligned}\text{HHI} &= 20^2 + 20^2 + 20^2 + 20^2 + 20^2 \\ &= 400 + 400 + 400 + 400 + 400 \\ &= 2{,}000\end{aligned}$$

TABLE 2	FOUR-FIRM CONCENTRATION RATIO		
		Industry 1	Industry 2
Firm 1's market share		65%	25%
Firm 2's market share		10%	20%
Firm 3's market share		5%	20%
Firm 4's market share		5%	20%
All other firms' market share combined		15%	15%
Four-firm concentration ratio		**85**	**85**

Industry 1 is dominated by a large firm with 65% of market share, whereas Industry 2 contains four fairly equal-sized firms, with smaller firms making up the rest of both industries. The CR-4 is the same in both industries, although Industry 2 would be expected to be much more competitive.

The HHI ranges from roughly zero (a huge number of small firms) to 10,000 (a one-firm monopoly: $100^2 = 10,000$). By squaring market shares, the HHI gives greater weight to those firms with large market shares. Thus, a five-firm industry with market shares equal to 65, 15, 10, 5, and 5 would have an HHI equal to

$$
\begin{aligned}
\text{HHI} &= 65^2 + 15^2 + 10^2 + 5^2 + 5^2 \\
&= 4{,}225 + 225 + 100 + 25 + 25 \\
&= 4{,}600
\end{aligned}
$$

The HHI is consistent with our intuitive notion of market power. It seems clear that an industry with several competitors of roughly equal size will be more competitive than an industry in which one firm controls a substantial share of the market.

Applying the HHI The Hart-Scott-Rodino Act (1976) requires prenotification of large proposed mergers to the FTC and the antitrust division of the Department of Justice. Prenotification gives federal agencies a chance to review proposed mergers for anticompetitive impacts. This approach prevents some mergers from taking place that would ultimately have to be challenged by Sherman Act litigation, a far more costly alternative for the government and for the firms involved.

The Department of Justice and the FTC in 2010 issued revised merger guidelines based on the HHI. These guidelines classify industries as follows:

- HHI < 1,500: Industry is not concentrated.
- 1,500 < HHI < 2,500: Industry is moderately concentrated.
- HHI > 2,500: Industry is highly concentrated.

Mergers where the resulting HHI is below 1,500 will often be approved. Mergers with postmerger HHIs between 1,500 and 2,500 will be closely evaluated; they are often challenged if the proposed merger raises the HHI by 200 points or more. When the HHI for the industry exceeds 2,500, a postmerger rise in the HHI of 100 points is enough to spark a challenge.

These guidelines have worked well, giving businesses a good idea of when the government will challenge mergers. Most mergers are rapidly approved; the remainder often require only minor adjustments or more information to satisfy government agencies. In the end, only a few proposed mergers are seriously challenged.

Contestable Markets

Sometimes what looks like a monopolist does not act like a monopolist. Markets that are contestable fit this description. **Contestable markets** are those markets with entry costs low enough that the sheer threat of entry keeps prices low. Potential competition constrains firm behavior. For example, Microsoft might charge more for its latest version of Windows if Linux were not nipping at its heels. Similarly, the Around the World from earlier in this chapter showed how ABC stores in Hawaii keep prices low due to the threat of market entry.

contestable markets Markets that look monopolistic, but where entry costs are low and the sheer threat of entry keeps prices low.

Another common example of a contestable market is the airline industry. Small regional carriers often fly unique routes from small airports to major tourist destinations such as Las Vegas and several spots in Florida. Although many of these routes are unique (in that only one airline serves the route), airlines tend to keep fares reasonable rather than exploit their market power for that route. Airlines realize that if fares are priced at the monopoly level, another airline might enter and compete. The ability to change airline service routes quickly forces airlines to keep prices at a competitive level, even if they are the only airline providing service between two cities.

The Future of Antitrust Policy

Today's economy differs from the old economy in many ways. The old economy was grounded in manufacturing and selling physical goods such as steel, automobiles, appliances, and shoes, which involved significant production and distribution costs. Much of the new economy involves intellectual property, or the use of innovation to provide valuable services such as mobile apps, streaming services, and online education. When distribution costs for services are nearly zero, monopolies can be vulnerable when new ideas are created.

Antitrust laws and policy therefore need to be adjusted to new market realities. Rather than regulate traditional natural monopolies such as electricity or taxi services, opening these services to competition is seen as a more efficient solution that reduces the need for bureaucratic rules. One federal judge and economist, Richard Posner, argues that all antitrust laws should be repealed and replaced with a simple statute that prohibits "unreasonably anti-competitive practices."[2]

This and the last chapter looked at the polar opposite market structures, competition and monopoly, with the characteristics of each shown in Table 3. The next chapter examines the market structures in the middle and also a more modern approach to analyzing firm behavior, game theory.

TABLE 3	COMPARISON BETWEEN PERFECT COMPETITION AND MONOPOLY	

Perfectly competitive firms and monopoly firms differ in the number of firms in the industry, the ability to set prices, the barriers to enter the industry, the ability to earn long-run economic profits, and the likelihood of achieving a socially efficient output.

Perfect Competition	Monopoly
Many firms	One firm
Price taking	Price making
No barriers to entry	Significant barriers to entry
Marginal Revenue = Price	Marginal Revenue < Price
Zero economic profit in the long run	Potential economic profits in the long run
No deadweight loss (efficiency)	Deadweight loss (inefficiency)

 CHECKPOINT

REGULATION AND ANTITRUST

- Regulating monopolies may involve a marginal cost pricing rule (have the monopolist set price equal to marginal cost) or an average cost pricing rule (have the monopolist set price equal to average total cost).
- In practice, regulation often involves setting an acceptable rate of return on capital or setting price caps on charges.
- The Sherman Act (1890), Clayton Act (1914), and Federal Trade Commission Act (1914) each prohibited various forms of business practices that inhibit competition.
- Concentration ratios measure market concentration by looking at the share of industry sales accounted for by the top *n* firms.
- The Herfindahl–Hirschman index (HHI) measures concentration by computing the sum of the squares of market shares for all firms in the industry.
- The Department of Justice uses the HHI to set premerger guidelines.
- Contestable markets are markets with low entry costs such that the potential threat of entry keeps prices low.

QUESTION: In September 2011 AT&T attempted to buy one of its major competitors, T-Mobile, in a $39 billion acquisition that the U.S. Department of Justice eventually blocked. Explain why the Department of Justice would block such a merger from taking place. Assume that the wireless communications industry contains four equal-sized firms (AT&T, Verizon, Sprint, and T-Mobile). How would the HHI be used to justify the government's decision?

Answers to the Checkpoint questions can be found at the end of this chapter.

---

[2]Richard A. Posner, *Antitrust Law*, 2nd ed. (Chicago: University of Chicago Press), 2001, p. 260.

chapter summary

Section 1 Monopoly Markets

9.1 A **monopoly** is a one-firm industry with no close product substitutes and with substantial barriers to entry.

9.2 Types of Barriers to Entry

Control over a significant factor of production: Occurs when a company owns a significant share of its key ingredient or input in production
Economies of scale: Occur when firms must incur large fixed costs before production can begin
Government protection: Patents and copyrights that provide an exclusive right to sell a product

9.3 Five Steps to Maximizing Profits for a Monopolist

1. Find $MR = MC$.
2. Find optimal quantity where $MR = MC$.
3. Find optimal price where quantity meets the demand curve.
4. Find average total cost at the optimal Q.
5. Find the profit $= (P - ATC) \times Q$.

The firm's demand and supply curve is the same as the industry's demand and supply curve.

Marginal revenue is less than price for a monopoly: If a firm can sell 4 units at $10 but must drop price to $9 to sell 5 units, marginal revenue equals $5 because the seller loses a dollar from each of the previous 4 units (red area) but gains $9 from the sale (green area).

Just because a monopolist has no competitors doesn't mean it always earns profits. Think of late-night infomercials selling, at times, bizarre products. Some are successful but others fail.

Mop slippers were a unique invention that really never took off. Not all monopolies are profitable.

Section 2 Comparing Monopoly and Competition

In a monopoly market, output is lower and price is higher compared to a competitive market due to the lack of competitors to the monopoly firm.

9.4 A firm with market power is more likely to engage in **rent-seeking** behavior (spending resources to protect market power) and **x-inefficiency** (wasting resources because competition doesn't exist).

Without competition from another football league, the NFL likely produces fewer games and charges higher prices than it would in a competitive market.

Section 3 Price Discrimination

Price discrimination is charging different prices for the same product in an attempt to grab more surplus from consumers.

Conditions for Price Discrimination to Work Best

1. Firm must have market power (i.e., cannot be a price taker).
2. Market can be segmented into different consumer groups.
3. Seller must be able to prevent arbitrage.

9.5 Three Forms of Price Discrimination

Perfect (first-degree) price discrimination: Seller charges exactly what consumers are willing to pay, and extracts all consumer surplus.

Second-degree price discrimination: Prices differ based on the quantity being purchased.

Third-degree price discrimination: Prices differ based on consumer characteristics, such as age (e.g., kids and senior discounts), status (e.g., student or military discounts), or flexibility (e.g., airline pricing).

Francis Dean/Corbis

Shopping at Costco might save you money, but you often need to buy in bulk, an example of second-degree price discrimination.

Section 4 Regulation and Antitrust

9.6 A **natural monopoly** has large economies of scale such that one firm is more efficient than multiple firms. The profit-maximizing point occurs where *MC* (and *ATC*) is falling. To prevent exploitation of market power, natural monopolies are often regulated.

mood/board/Corbis

Besides economies of scale, most people prefer just one electric company as a monopolist, rather than multiple electric companies, each with its own power lines.

Antitrust laws are designed to promote competition and prevent monopolies from developing.

Two Major Antitrust Laws

9.7 **Sherman Act of 1890:** Outlawed trusts and cartels—restraint of trade and monopolization.
Clayton Act of 1914: Outlawed some forms of price discrimination and mergers that would significantly reduce competition.

9.8 Ways to Measure Market Power

Concentration ratios: Adding up the market shares of the 4 or 8 largest firms in an industry, and ranges from 0 to 100.

HHI index: Sum of the square of market shares of all firms in an industry, and ranges from 0 (perfect competition) to 10,000 (monopoly). HHI values over 2,500 are concentrated industries where mergers are likely to be challenged.

Getty Images News/Getty Images

9.9 A **contestable market** looks like a monopoly but does not act like one because the threat of entry keeps prices low. Small airlines that serve unique routes still offer low prices if they fear entry by larger airlines.

monopoly, p. 222
market power, p. 222
barriers to entry, p. 222
economies of scale, p. 223
rent seeking, p. 230
x-inefficiency, p. 230
price discrimination, p. 232
perfect (first-degree) price
  discrimination, p. 232

second-degree price discrimination,
  p. 232
third-degree price discrimination,
  p. 232
natural monopoly, p. 237
marginal cost pricing rule, p. 237
average cost pricing rule, p. 237
rate of return regulation, p. 238
price caps, p. 238

antitrust law, p. 238
concentration ratio, p. 240
Herfindahl–Hirschman index
  (HHI), p. 240
contestable markets, p. 241

QUESTIONS AND PROBLEMS

Check Your Understanding

1. Are McDonald's and Starbucks monopolies? Why or why not?

2. Explain why $MR < P$ for the monopolist, but $MR = P$ for perfectly competitive firms.

3. What do economists mean when they call monopolies inefficient? What is the dead-weight loss of monopoly?

4. Why are monopoly firms able to earn long-run economic profits while perfectly competitive firms cannot?

5. Under what market conditions would a firm find it easier to engage in price discrimination?

6. What is a natural monopoly and why is such a monopoly often regulated by government?

Apply the Concepts

7. How important is the existence of a significant barrier to entry to maintaining a monopoly? What would be the result if a monopoly market could easily be entered? Why might a monopoly in a high-tech field such as computers, the Internet, and consumer electronics be rather short-lived?

8. One can typically find a high-quality color laser printer for $300, which comes pre-installed with four color-toner cartridges that are about half-filled. However, the cost of replacing all four toner cartridges is usually over $400. Why would companies charge more to replace the toner than to buy the printer itself?

9. The taxi industry in many large cities spends millions of dollars lobbying local policy-makers not to build rail links connecting airports to the city center, even if such mass transportation infrastructure would benefit many consumers traveling to and from the airport. Explain why such actions by the taxi industry are taken. Then, explain why taxi owners in cities without airport rail links are less likely to invest in fuel-efficient cars and in-taxi technologies such as televisions and Internet access.

10. If the Miami Heat can sell five courtside seats for $2,000 each or six courtside seats if it reduces the price to $1,600 each, what is the marginal revenue of the sixth seat? Should the owner make this sixth seat available? If all six seats can be sold for $1,800 each, would this make the sixth seat worth selling? (*Hint:* What costs are involved with selling the sixth seat?)

11. Sally owns the only cake shop in town (she is a monopolist). At a quantity of five, the marginal cost of producing one more cake is $12, while the marginal revenue from selling one more cake is $10. In order for Sally to maximize profits, should she increase or decrease output? Should she increase or decrease prices? Explain.

12. Airlines that compete against one another have at times merged with each other to create a larger airline. What are some factors that would determine whether such a merger would constitute an uncompetitive environment according to antitrust law?

In the News

13. In December 2014 United Airlines and Orbitz Travel sued a 22-year-old person who had created a Web site helping travelers save money using a technique called "hidden-city ticketing" (*CNN Money*, December 29, 2014). Hidden-city ticketing works when one desires to travel non-stop between an airline's major hubs (such as Houston to Denver on United), but can find a less expensive fare by booking a connecting flight from Houston to, say, Colorado Springs via Denver, and then simply not taking the connecting flight. Why would an airline charge more for a single flight than one that continues onward to another destination? Because courts have ruled against the airlines, what can they do to prevent customers from resorting to this technique?

14. In November 2015 Marriott Hotels announced that it would acquire its rival, Starwood Hotels, creating the world's largest hotel chain. Look at each hotel chain's Web site and list all of the specific hotel brands operated by Marriott and Starwood that would now be managed by this merged company. Given that so many hotel brands are involved, why would this merger be allowed? Wouldn't it create a near monopoly in the hotel market? What other types of lodging compete against hotels?

Solving Problems

WORK IT OUT   **LaunchPad** | interactive activity

15. Using the accompanying figure for a monopoly firm, answer the following questions.

    a. What will be the monopoly price, output, and profit for this firm?

    b. If this monopolist could perfectly price discriminate, what would profit equal?

    c. If this industry were competitive, what would be the price, output, and profit?

    d. How large (in dollars) is the deadweight loss from this monopolist?

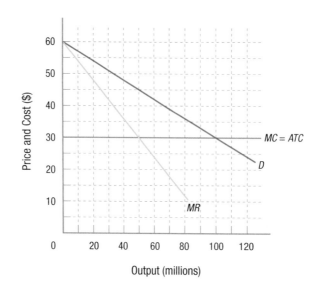

16. The following table represents the sales figures for the eight largest firms in the auto industry in the United States in 2014:

Company	Sales (billions of dollars)
General Motors	84.1
Ford	67.0
Toyota	66.1
Fiat Chrysler	59.2
Honda	42.0
Nissan	35.9
Hyundai	33.7
Volkswagen	17.6
Total	**405.6**

a. Compute the four-firm concentration ratio for the industry.

b. Compute the HHI for the industry (assuming the industry contains just these eight firms).

c. Assuming the industry is represented by these eight firms, if Ford and Toyota wanted to merge, and you were the head of the Department of Justice, would you permit the merger? Why or why not? (*Hint:* Calculate the new values from parts a and b assuming the merger takes place.) How about if Nissan and Hyundai wanted to merge?

#️ USING THE NUMBERS

17. According to By the Numbers, assuming that the number of viewers for each of the five games in the 2015 NBA Finals were the same, approximately how many more people watched the 2015 Super Bowl than the final game of the 2015 NBA Finals?

18. According to By the Numbers, per capita demand for electricity has risen since 1955. Between which 5 year periods did demand for electricity fall?

ANSWERS TO QUESTIONS IN CHECKPOINTS

Checkpoint: Monopoly Markets 228

By performing in a smaller venue (such as a performing arts hall with 1,500 seats instead of an arena with 10,000 or more seats), the artist can target the core fans willing to pay high prices for tickets. With market power in pricing (there is only one Dolly Parton), nearly all seats would be sold at the high price, as opposed to having to offer much lower prices to fill a larger arena. If the costs of performing at a larger arena are significant, artists can do better by producing less (selling fewer tickets), charging a much higher price, and reducing the costs of putting on the concert.

Checkpoint: Comparing Monopoly and Competition 232

Competition against cable began when satellite technologies improved, allowing satellite companies such as Dish Network and DIRECTV to offer television services using satellite dishes that were affordable and much more compact in design. Then, competition intensified with improved broadband access, allowing consumers to watch television using their computers and tablets with subscriptions to various streaming services. As cable's market share fell, it had to improve the quality of service it offers. No more waiting all day for the notorious "cable guy." Today, cable companies must provide precise service appointments and friendly customer service in order to stay in business.

Checkpoint: Price Discrimination 236

No, this is not the same type of price discrimination discussed in this section. This type of discrimination occurs because of information problems, gender discrimination, racism, or other factors. The authors conclude that a large part of the price differences between buying online and bargaining in the showroom comes from the fact that online consumers have better information. Price discrimination in this section of the chapter is based on consumers with different elasticities of demand, not information problems or racism. Examples include student, senior, and adult pricing in movie theaters.

Checkpoint: Regulation and Antitrust 242

The government aims to prevent powerful monopolies, which can restrict competition and lead to fewer choices and higher prices, from forming. The Sherman Antitrust Act of 1890 and the Clayton Act of 1914 provide the legal basis for such action. The government uses concentration ratios or the HHI as a gauge to determine whether a pending merger would harm competition. If each of four firms controls 25% of the market, the HHI is 2,500, already a very concentrated industry. By allowing AT&T and T-Mobile to merge, the HHI would increase from 2,500 to 3,750, making the industry even more concentrated.

10 Monopolistic Competition, Oligopoly, and Game Theory

Comparing the many ways in which producers compete for their customers

Learning Objectives

10.1 Describe product differentiation and its impact on the firm's demand curve, and how it determines the market power that a monopolistically competitive firm can exercise.

10.2 Compare pricing and output decisions for monopolistically competitive firms in the short run and long run, and explain why firms earn only normal profits in the long run.

10.3 Describe the characteristics of oligopolies and why cartels sometimes form.

10.4 Explain the kinked demand curve model and why prices can be relatively stable in oligopoly industries.

10.5 Describe the basic components of a game and explain the difference between simultaneous-move and sequential-move games.

10.6 Solve for Nash equilibria using a best-response analysis and understand their importance to economists.

10.7 Recognize why Prisoner's Dilemma outcomes occur and provide real-life examples of such situations.

10.8 Explain how firms can overcome the Prisoner's Dilemma using cooperative strategies and repeated actions.

Gareth Byrne/Alamy

A scientific calculator in the early 1970s was an expensive investment, about $400 at the time, which is over $2,000 in today's dollars.

Home computing made its debut in the early 1980s. At that time, a basic computer with a single-color monitor and disk drive (not for DVDs, but rather for 5¼-inch floppy disks—do you know what those are?) with less computing power than a basic cell phone today cost several thousand dollars. What changed over the past three decades? A combination of technology and innovation, driven by competition, spurred better products that could be produced at lower cost.

The previous two chapters studied perfect competition and monopoly, which are at the opposing extremes of market structures we typically see. Perfect competition assumes a homogeneous (identical) good produced by many firms, while a monopoly assumes a unique good produced by just one firm. In reality, over 90% of the goods and services we consume do not fall into either category. Most of the goods and services we consume are competitive in nature but are also differentiated (or branded) in some way.

Suppose you want a quick burger for lunch. Your choices include McDonald's, Wendy's, Burger King, Five Guys, and many other burger joints located in your town. The market for burgers is clearly not a monopoly. Yet, given the variety of burgers from which to choose, it's not pure competition either, unless you think that all burgers are the same—but most people do not. This chapter looks at two market structures, monopolistic competition and oligopoly, in which firms face intense competition for market share. Important differences exist between these markets in terms of the number of firms and the types of pricing strategies used. But in both market structures, pressures to remain competitive and to gain market share are important factors in a firm's success.

These pressures limit the market power that can be exercised by monopolistically competitive and oligopolistic firms. We saw in the previous chapter that monopolies have the most market power, which is the ability to set price (and get away with it). We contrasted this with perfectly competitive firms, which are price takers: They have no ability to set price. In this chapter, we will see that monopolistically competitive firms have a very limited amount of market power. Oligopolies have more market power, but less than monopolies.

While market power is a downside of monopolistic competition and oligopoly, competitive pressures on them can result in benefits to all. Firms are constantly looking for ways to make their products better (to increase their value) or less expensive to produce. In doing so, a number of important changes in the competitive global market have appeared:

1. Increase in technological development
2. Increase in variety of goods and services
3. Reduction in the price of inputs and resources (with economies of scale or offshoring production)
4. Reduction in transportation costs
5. Reduction in trade barriers

Product Differentiation and Market Share

For nearly all goods and services we buy, we are faced with numerous choices: brands, features, quality, style, and more. Product differentiation is a signature characteristic of monopolistically competitive markets, and to a lesser extent oligopoly markets.

Go to 🔊 **LaunchPad** *to use the latest data to recreate this graph.*

The largest fast-food chains in the United States (numbers of stores as of April 2016).

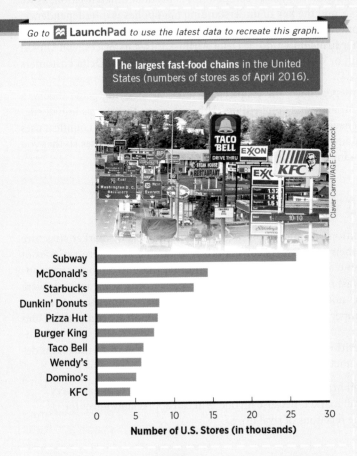

Claver Carroll/AGE Fotostock

Number of U.S. Stores (in thousands)
- Subway
- McDonald's
- Starbucks
- Dunkin' Donuts
- Pizza Hut
- Burger King
- Taco Bell
- Wendy's
- Domino's
- KFC

(0, 5, 10, 15, 20, 25, 30)

The wireless communications market is an oligopoly dominated by four large firms, controlling 86% of total market share. Of the remaining market share, 11% is controlled by mobile virtual network operators (MVNO), which are smaller companies (such as prepaid wireless service providers) that lease wireless service from the four major carriers.

PSL Images/Alamy

Pie chart:
- Other 3%
- MVNO 11%
- Verizon 33%
- Sprint 13%
- T-Mobile 14%
- AT&T 26%

Colleges and universities are differentiated by size, location, athletic prowess and academic reputation. They also vary considerably in cost, especially between public and private schools.

john norman/Alamy

Most Expensive Private College Tuition Per Year in the United States in 2016

1. **Vassar College**; Poughkeepsie, NY	$51,300
2. **Sarah Lawrence College**; Bronxville, NY	$51,034
3. **Trinity College**; Hartford, CT	$50,776
4. **Tufts University**; Medford, MA	$50,604
5. **Oberlin College**; Oberlin, OH	$50,586

Most Expensive Public College Tuition Per Year (state residents) in the United States in 2016

1. **University of Pittsburgh**; Pittsburgh, PA	$17,772
2. **College of William & Mary**; Williamsburg, VA	$17,656
3. **Pennsylvania State University**; State College, PA	$17,502
4. **Maine Maritime Academy**; Castine, ME	$17,120
5. **Colorado School of Mines**; Golden, CO	$16,918

Erick W. Rasco/Sports Illustrated/Getty Images

980

Total marathons in the United States in 2016 (differentiated by location, size, elevation change, and scenery).

1,500+

Total number of shoe models produced by Nike Corporation since 1972.

Recall that when supply increases (shifts to the right), the market price falls and the market quantity rises. For each of the factors listed previously, a corresponding increase in supply results, helping to explain why this year's computers and smartphones cost less than in previous years—even if the suppliers of computers and smartphones are oligopolies with some degree of market power.

The key to understanding monopolistic competition is product differentiation, as we saw in the burger example, and the key to understanding oligopolies is interdependence. By interdependence, economists mean that pricing and other decisions have to be made by considering what other firms might do. If Delta Airlines raises its prices, will United and American follow suit, or will they freeze their prices hoping to lure Delta customers away?

To best explain interdependence, the chapter concludes by studying game theory, a modern way to examine strategy and competition. Although game theory was initially developed to analyze the behavior of interdependent oligopolistic firms, it has countless uses and applications in our daily lives. We will touch on a few of these many uses so that you can see the richness of taking a game theory approach.

MONOPOLISTIC COMPETITION

Until the 1920s, competition and monopoly were the only models of market structure that economists had in their toolbox. As consumerism expanded and more varieties of goods and services became available, economists found that these two models were inadequate to explain the vast markets for many goods. In other words, some markets were considered imperfect, or not fitting the mold of the traditional competitive structure. This led to the study of imperfect markets, which included monopolistic competition and oligopoly.

Monopolistic competition is nearer to the competitive end of the spectrum and is defined by the following characteristics:

- A large number of small firms. Similar to perfect competition, each firm has a very small share of the overall market. Because no one firm can appreciably affect the market, most ignore the reactions of rival firms.

- Entry and exit are easy.

- Unlike perfect competition, products are different. Each firm produces a product that is different from its competitors or is perceived to be different by consumers. What distinguishes monopolistic competition from perfectly competitive markets is product differentiation.

Product Differentiation and the Firm's Demand Curve

Most firms sell products that are in some way differentiated from their competitors. For example, this differentiation can take the form of a superior location. Your local dry cleaner, restaurant, grocery, and gas station can have slightly higher prices, but you will not abandon them altogether. Other companies have branded products that give them some ability to increase price without losing all of their customers, as would happen under perfect competition.

Product differentiation gives the firm some (however modest) control over price (market power). This is illustrated in Figure 1. Curve d_c is the competitive demand curve, and d_{mc} is the demand curve faced by a monopolistic competitor. This is similar to the monopolist's demand, but the demand curve is considerably more elastic. Because a monopolistic competitor is small relative to the market, there are still a lot of substitutes. Thus, any increase in price is accompanied by a substantial decrease in output demanded. But unlike the perfectly competitive firm that faces a horizontal demand curve with no power to raise price, a monopolistically competitive firm has some market power.

---

monopolistic competition A market structure with a large number of firms producing differentiated products. This differentiation is either real or imagined by consumers and involves innovations, advertising, location, or other ways of making one firm's product different from that of its competitors.

FIGURE 1	PRODUCT DIFFERENTIATION AND DEMAND

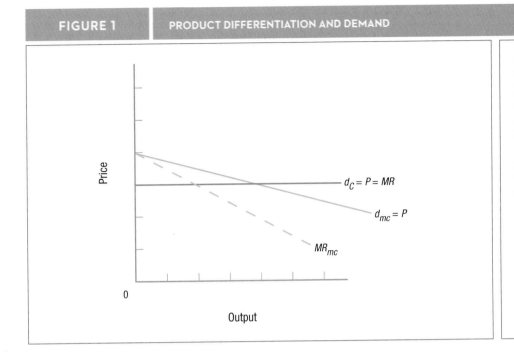

Product differentiation gives the firm some market power to raise prices. Demand curve d_{mc} is the demand curve for a monopolistically competitive firm with modest price-making ability. Marginal revenue curve MR_{mc} also slopes downward, reflecting the weak negative slope of the demand curve.

Like a monopolist, the monopolistically competitive firm faces a downward-sloping marginal revenue curve, shown in Figure 1 as MR_{mc}.

Product differentiation can be the result of a superior product, a better location, superior service, clever packaging, or advertising. All of these factors are intended to increase demand or reduce the elasticity of demand and generate loyalty to the product or service. Therefore, the demand curve for monopolistically competitive firms can vary. Although demand curves tend to be elastic (flat), firms that are able to successfully differentiate their products can achieve greater market power, which makes their demand curves steeper, allowing them to charge higher prices.

product differentiation One firm's product is distinguished from another's through advertising, innovation, location, and so on.

The Role of Advertising An important way to differentiate products is through advertising. Economists generally classify advertising in two ways: informational and persuasive. The informational aspects of advertising let consumers know about products and reduce search costs. Advertising is a relatively inexpensive way to let customers know about the quality and price of a company's products. It can also enhance competition by making consumers aware of substitute products. Advertising also has the potential to reduce average costs by increasing sales, bringing about economies of scale.

But advertising does have a negative side as well. Because so much of advertising is persuasive (ads containing little informational content, but designed to shift buyers to competitors producing similar products), the result is that the cost of advertising drives up the price of many products. With all the advertising we see, a significant portion probably cancels each other out.

Advertising is another area in which technology has transformed the medium: Digital video recorders permit ad-skipping and have significantly reduced the impact of TV ads. A lot of advertising dollars are shifting away from conventional media (newspapers, magazines, and television) and moving to the Internet, where consumers can be targeted more inexpensively and efficiently.

All of these ways to differentiate their products give monopolistically competitive firms some control over price. This market power means that their profit-maximizing decisions will be a little different from those of perfectly competitive firms.

Product differentiation counts. Although hundreds of brands of blue jeans compete in the same general market, product differentiation in style and comfort allows some brands to achieve substantial market power, resulting in higher prices.

ISSUE

Do Brands Really Represent Pricing Power?

What is a brand? All of us know brands through their names and logos. Nike has the swoosh, Intel has a logo and the four-note jingle that sounds whenever its processors are advertised, Coca-Cola has a distinctive way of spelling its name. Names and logos are communication devices, but brands are more than this. They are a promise of performance. A branded product or service raises expectations in a consumer's mind. If these expectations are met, consumers pay a price premium. If expectations are not met, the value of the brand falls as consumers seek alternatives.

Brand names start with the company that makes the product or provides the service. In the past, this meant that brand names came from a limited number of sources. Some companies were named after their founders, such as Walt Disney; some companies were named after what they supplied, such as IBM (International Business Machines); and some have also been named by their main product, such as

the Coca-Cola Company. Sometimes the company name has a tenuous link with the product but is strong nevertheless, such as the Starbucks name for coffee products: Master Starbuck was first mate to Captain Ahab in *Moby-Dick* and did drink coffee in the book, but who remembers that?

Whatever their origins, these brands have recognizable brand names, and they command price premiums. According to the annual BrandZ study by Millward Brown, Apple was the most valuable brand in 2015, valued at nearly $247 billion, followed by Google, Microsoft, IBM, and Visa. The top ten brands were all American, though Chinese brands Tencent, Alibaba, and China Mobile came in at 11th, 13th, and 15th, respectively. In fact, Chinese brands are the fastest growing in the world, as China's economy continues to transform to include major high-tech companies. Brands this valuable must convey some considerable pricing power, or what we called market power.

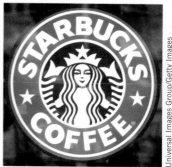

Market power is what companies want. It allows companies to charge more for goods that are similar to those of lesser-known brands. In some cases, a product can be identical (such as over-the-counter medications), but the brand-name version is priced much higher because of the power of the brand and the confidence that it provides to customers.

Information from BrandZ Top 100 Most Valuable Global Brands 2015, Millward Brown, WPP Companies.

Price and Output Under Monopolistic Competition

Profit maximization in the short run for the monopolistically competitive firm is a lot like that for a monopolist, but given the competition against firms with similar products, profit will tend to be less. Short-run profit-maximizing behavior is shown in Figure 2. The firm maximizes profit where $MR = MC$ (point c) by selling output q_0 at a price of P_0. Total profit is the shaded area $C_0 P_0 ab$. All of this should look very familiar from the last chapter (review the five-step approach to maximizing profit). The difference is that the monopolistically competitive demand curve is quite elastic, and economic profits are diminished. The level of profit is dependent on the strength of demand, but in any event will be considerably lower than that of a monopolist.

This does not mean that profits are trivial. Many huge global firms sell their products in even larger global markets, and their profits are significant. They are large firms, but do not have significant market power. Many companies—such as Gap, Nike, and Samsung—are all quite large, but relative to their markets face daunting competition.

If firms in the industry are earning economic profits like those of the firm shown in Figure 2, new firms will want to enter. Since there are no restrictions to entry or exit, new firms will enter, soaking up some industry demand and reducing the demand to each firm in the market. Demand will continue to decline as long as economic profits exist. At equilibrium in the long run, the typical firm in the industry will look like the one shown in Figure 3.

Notice that the demand curve is just tangent to the long-run average total cost (*LRATC*) curve, resulting in the firm earning normal profits in the long run. The firm produces and

FIGURE 2	SHORT-RUN EQUILIBRIUM FOR MONOPOLISTIC COMPETITION

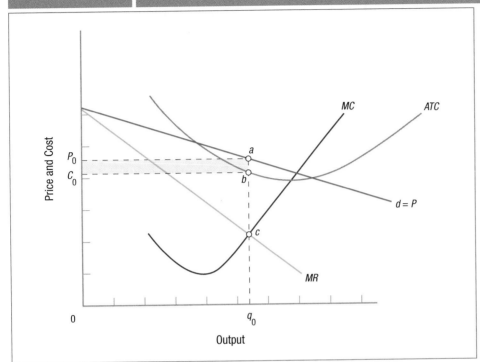

This monopolistically competitive firm will maximize profits in the short run by producing where $MR = MC$ (point c). Profits are equal to the shaded area.

sells q_L output at a price of P_L (point a). Note that price P_L is not at the minimum point of the *LRATC*, which shows that prices in monopolistically competitive markets are higher than prices in perfectly competitive markets. Once the typical firm reaches this point, there is no longer any incentive for other firms to enter the industry. Like perfectly competitive firms, monopolistically competitive firms earn normal profits in the long run.

FIGURE 3	LONG-RUN EQUILIBRIUM FOR MONOPOLISTIC COMPETITION

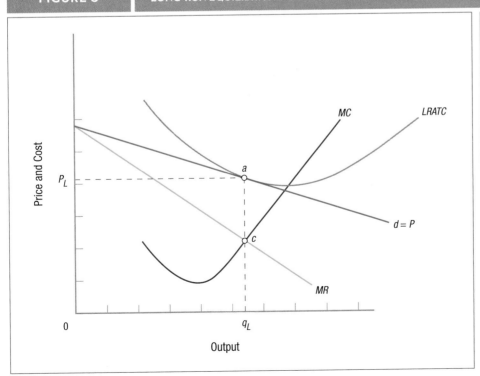

In the long run, easy entry and exit will adjust the demand each firm faces so that the demand curve will be tangent (at point a in this case) to the long-run average total cost curve. This is the long-run equilibrium because existing firms are earning normal profits and there is no incentive for further entry or exit. Compared to perfect competition, this long-run output does not minimize *LRATC*, which means prices are higher in a monopolistically competitive industry.

Comparing Monopolistic Competition to Perfect Competition

Are firms in monopolistically competitive industries as efficient as those in perfectly competitive industries? Because firms in both earn normal profits, one might think that both market structures are equally efficient. But they are not. Differentiated products create mini-markets within each industry. For example, Wrangler and True Religion are both brands of blue jeans, but each caters to a different set of customers, allowing True Religion to charge almost 10 times more per pair. And because differentiating products reduces economies of scale, the prices will be slightly higher.

The relatively small differences in price and output represent the cost we pay for greater variety and innovation. For example, dozens of flavors of sodas exist so that we need not drink the same brand every time. And watches offer everything from basic time and date to GPS capabilities and Internet service to cater to each customer's intended use of the product. Product differentiation is important and for most of us valuable, but not free.

From this discussion, you might get some sense of the pressures firms face to differentiate their products. The more they can move away from the competitive model, the better chance they have of using their market power to make more profit. But because market power evaporates over the long run for monopolistically competitive firms, these firms have to try to sustain the value in the differentiated product. This is hard to do. The price premium charged by Hollister will not be paid when the Hollister brand is no longer as popular, or becomes more like everyone else. Yet, it is in the firm's interest to product differentiate as long as it can. When you see firms trying to differentiate their products, ask yourself if the products are really so different after all.

A McDonald's Big Mac Without Beef?

Why do U.S. fast-food chains choose to alter their menus and business practices in nearly every country in which they operate?

There are few places left in the world that are not exposed to American fast-food. American staples such as McDonald's, Domino's, and KFC can be found in places from Paris to the most remote parts of China, whose residents have developed a taste for American food. But just as popular ethnic cuisine in the United States is often tailored (or "Americanized") to American tastes, American fast-food is tailored to local tastes everywhere it is sold. Can you imagine the iconic Big Mac without the two all-beef patties tucked within three layers of buns? For most McDonald's customers in India, they've never seen such a combination of ingredients.

Because beef is rarely eaten in India due to the sacred nature of cows

Because beef is rarely eaten in India, burgers at McDonald's consist of chicken or fish, an example of companies adjusting their product to cater to local tastes and customs.

david pearson/Alamy

in the Hindu religion, restaurants in India cater to local tastes and customs by using other meats such as chicken, lamb, or fish. When one visits a McDonald's restaurant in Mumbai, the signature sandwich will resemble a Big Mac, but is called the Maharaja Mac, consisting of two chicken patties within three layers of buns. Of course, in major cities in India, you can still find real beef in select restaurants; these are the *authentic* foreign restaurants that cater to foreigners or Indian

foodies seeking out a unique culinary experience. This is no different than American foodies seeking out authentic restaurants in the United States serving exotic dishes such as snake stew or chicken feet. It's all about preferences.

Examples of fast-food chains altering menu items or business practices to local tastes and customs can be seen throughout the world. In France, alcoholic beverages are commonly sold in fast-food restaurants. In Israel, many McDonald's restaurants are kosher, which eliminates the cheeseburger—no dairy and meat together. And when ordering a soda to go in Japan, it will likely be placed inside of a bag because Japanese etiquette frowns upon eating and drinking in public spaces.

Part of the success of multinational companies such as McDonald's lies in knowing the preferences of their customers and the nature of their competition. Therefore, although product differentiation is necessary to gain market share, being *too* different, especially when a product goes against cultural norms, can hurt a company's profits.

GO TO **LaunchPad** TO PRACTICE THE ECONOMIC CONCEPTS IN THIS STORY

✓ CHECKPOINT

MONOPOLISTIC COMPETITION

- Monopolistically competitive firms look like perfectly competitive firms (a large number of firms in a market in which entry and exit are unrestricted), but have differentiated products.

- Monopolistically competitive firms have elastic downward-sloping demand curves.

- Similar to a monopolist, the short-run equilibrium for a monopolistically competitive firm is the output level where $MR = MC$, and can result in positive, zero, or negative profits.

- In the long run, easy entry and exit result in monopolistically competitive firms earning only normal profits.

- Monopolistically competitive firms have some market power. Therefore, output is lower and price is higher for monopolistically competitive firms when compared to price and output for perfectly competitive firms.

QUESTION: At Disney World in Florida, you can stay at the Disney Grand Floridian Resort for $350/night or at the Disney All-Star Resort for $125/night. Both hotels are located within the park boundaries and are owned by Disney. How does product differentiation explain the significant price difference? Search and browse the hotels' Web sites to provide examples of product differentiation between the hotels.

Answers to the Checkpoint questions can be found at the end of this chapter.

OLIGOPOLY

Oligopoly markets are those in which a large market share is controlled by just a few firms. What constitutes a few firms controlling a large market share is not rigidly defined. Further, these firms can sell either a homogeneous product (e.g., gasoline, sugar) or a differentiated product (e.g., automobiles, pharmaceuticals).

Industries can be composed of a dominant firm with a few smaller firms making up the rest of the industry (e.g., computer operating systems), or the industry can be composed of a few similarly sized firms (e.g., automobiles, tobacco). The point of this discussion is that oligopoly models are numerous and varied, and we will explore only a few. Oligopoly models do, however, have several common characteristics.

oligopoly A market with just a few firms dominating the industry, where (1) each firm recognizes that it must consider its competitors' reactions when making its own decisions (mutual interdependence), and (2) there are significant barriers to entry into the market.

Defining Oligopoly

All oligopoly models share several common assumptions:

- There are only a few large firms in the industry.
- Each firm recognizes that it must take into account the behavior of its competitors when it makes decisions. Economists refer to this as **mutual interdependence.**
- There are significant barriers to entry into the market.

Because there are only a few firms, each firm possesses substantial market power. However, because the products sold by oligopolists are similar to each other, the actions of one will affect the ability of the others to sell or price their output successfully. If one firm changes the specifications of its product or increases its advertising budget, this will have an impact on its rivals, and they can be expected to respond in kind. Thus, one firm cannot forecast its change in sales for a new promotion without first making some assumptions about the reaction of its rivals.

In an industry composed of just a few firms, entry scale is often huge. Plus, with just a few firms, typically brand preferences are quite strong on the part of consumers, and a new firm may need a substantial marketing program just to get a foot in the door.

mutual interdependence When only a few firms constitute an industry, each firm must consider the reactions of its competitors to its decisions.

Cartels: Joint Profit Maximization and the Instability of Oligopolies

Cartels are theft—usually by well-dressed thieves.
GRAEME SAMUEL, HEAD OF AUSTRALIA'S ANTITRUST OFFICE

cartel An agreement between firms (or countries) in an industry to formally collude on price and output, then agree on the distribution of production.

The first oligopoly model we examine is *collusive* joint profit maximization, or a **cartel** model. Here, we assume that a few firms collude (combine secretly) to operate like a monopoly, using maximum market power to set the monopoly price and output and share the monopoly profits. Cartels are illegal in the United States and in the European Union, although international laws do not ban them.

Cartels are not as common today as they were two or three decades ago. The most famous cartel is OPEC, the Organization of Petroleum Exporting Countries, which consists of twelve countries that set production quotas in order to limit overall oil production to drive up prices. Although OPEC was powerful from the 1970s up until the last decade, today, competition from non-OPEC countries in Africa, Europe, and North America has made OPEC considerably less influential. Perhaps more influential in today's economy are underground cartels, such as those that distribute narcotics and hold substantial market power.

Figure 4 illustrates a hypothetical cartel consisting of five firms. By forming a cartel, these five firms agree to fix their overall output equal to the profit-maximizing output of a monopolist, which is 100. At this restricted output, each cartel member produces its fixed quota of output (20 units per firm, assuming the cartel divides total output equally), and shares the resulting profit. Under this scenario, the cartel exhibits maximum market power equal to a single-firm monopolist.

However, cartels are inherently unstable because of the incentive to cheat by individual members. Although the cartel as a whole is maximizing profits, each individual member can potentially earn more profits by producing more than its output quota. As illustrated in Figure 4, if one firm exceeds its quota by doubling output from 20 to 40, the overall output of the cartel increases from 100 to 120 units. By expanding production, the market price falls from $10 to $8, causing revenues to fall by $200 ($2 × 100 units), shown as the yellow area. This reduction in revenues is *shared* by all five firms, with each firm losing $40 (or one share of the yellow area). Despite this loss, the cheating firm benefits because the extra 20 units it produces earn the firm $160 in additional revenue ($8 × 20 units), shown as the

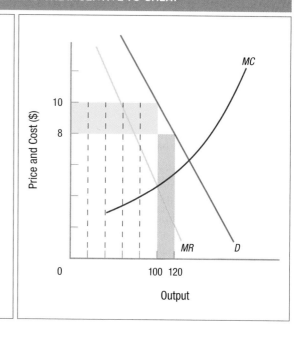

| FIGURE 4 | CARTELS AND THE INCENTIVE TO CHEAT |

A cartel consisting of five firms collectively agrees to restrict total output to the monopoly output of 100 units and charges $10 per unit. If one firm chooses to cheat by increasing its output by an additional 20 units, total output increases to 120 units and price falls to $8. This results in a loss of revenue of $200, which is shared equally among the five cartel members ($40 loss per member, equal to one share of the yellow area). However, the cheating member gains $160 from the additional 20 units sold at $8 each (green area). The marginal revenue for the cheating member is therefore $160 − $40 = $120.

green area. The marginal revenue from cheating is therefore $160 – $40 = $120. As long as the marginal cost of producing the extra 20 units is less than $120, the firm benefits from cheating on the cartel agreement.

However, when one firm cheats, this often leads to other firms cheating. As more and more cartel members cheat, the price continues to fall toward the competitive price, greatly hurting the noncheating members. The instability of cartels is enhanced when a member can increase its output relatively undetected, and when the cost of production is low, making cheating more profitable. Over time, the cartel falls apart when all members increase their output, resulting in a competitive outcome. Therefore, market power in a cartel can range from the monopoly case (if all members adhere to their quotas) to the competitive case when cartels completely break down.

Although cartels are inherently unstable, certain factors can enhance the likelihood of the cartel's survival. First, cartel stability is enhanced with fewer members with similar goals. With fewer members, any action that breaches the cartel agreement is more easily noticed and punishable. Second, stability is improved if the cartel is maintained with legal provisions (such as government protection). Third, stability is improved if firms are unable to differentiate their products (such as providing enhanced service or some other product as an inducement to purchase). Fourth, stability is improved when each firm's cost structure is similar, thereby not giving any firm a cost advantage over another. Finally, a cartel is more stable when there are significant barriers to entry preventing new firms from competing against existing cartel members.

These factors do not bode well for the future of the twelve member countries of OPEC. Although OPEC members produce a uniform product (crude oil) and have similar cost structures, enforcement of the quotas has at times been shaky with politically unstable countries. Further, OPEC's total share of world oil production has been surpassed by non-OPEC countries, led by the United States, Russia, China, Canada, Mexico, and Brazil. Maintaining an effective oil cartel will become more difficult as more countries enter the industry and as new alternative fuels are developed.

The Kinked Demand Curve Model and the Stability of Oligopolies

Oligopoly industries share a characteristic that prices tend to be stable for extended periods of time. For example, prices for wireless data plans are similar across all major wireless providers and rarely fluctuate. Why do these prices tend to stay the same when the underlying costs of providing the services change?

Figure 5 provides an explanation for the price stability in oligopoly industries by showing two demand curves. Demand curve d is relatively elastic, and represents demand for one firm when competing firms choose not to follow its price changes. Therefore, any change in price is generally met with significant changes in quantity demanded. On the other hand, demand curve D is relatively inelastic, and represents the demand for one firm when competing firms do match price changes. As a result, any change in price will not lead to much change in quantity demanded.

The **kinked demand curve** model assumes the following:

- If a firm raises the price for its product, its competitors will not react in hopes of capturing more market share.

- If a firm lowers its price, its competitors will react with lower prices of their own to avoid losing market share.

As a result, the relevant demand curve facing the firm is the darkened portion of demand curves d and D that is kinked at point e. The relevant portion of the marginal revenue curve is the darkened dashed curve MR with the discontinuity between points a and b. Notice, we are just using the relevant portions of MR_d and MR_D. The graph shows MC_1 and MC_0 intersecting the MR curve at points a and b, respectively. However, the equilibrium price and output remain at P_0 and Q_0. In fact, any marginal cost curve located between MC_1 and MC_0 will result in the same equilibrium price and output.

kinked demand curve An oligopoly model that assumes that if a firm raises its price, competitors will not raise theirs. However, if the firm lowers its price, its competitors will lower their price to match the reduction. This leads to a kink in the demand curve and relatively stable market prices.

FIGURE 5 | THE KINKED DEMAND CURVE MODEL OF OLIGOPOLY

The kinked demand curve model of oligopoly shows why oligopoly prices appear stable. The model assumes that if the firm raises its price, competitors will not follow the price increase. But if the firm lowers its price, other firms will follow. These reactions create a "kink" in the firm's demand curve at point e, and a discontinuity in the MR curve equal to the distance between points a and b. This discontinuity permits any marginal cost curve located between points a and b to produce the same output level, Q_0.

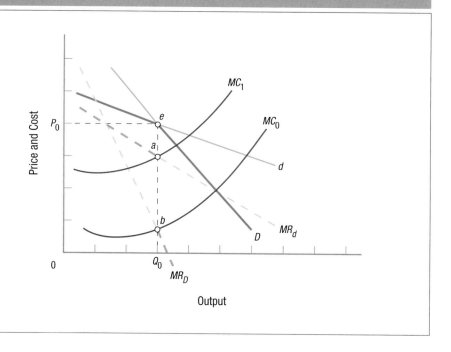

The analysis of unstable and stable oligopoly models underscores the importance of the mutual interdependence of firms. How one firm reacts to a competitor's market strategy determines the nature of competition in the industry. These ideas led to game theory, which we consider in the next section.

 CHECKPOINT

OLIGOPOLY

- Oligopolies are markets (a) with only a few firms, (b) where each firm takes into account the reaction of rivals to its policies, and (c) where there are significant barriers to entry.

- The market power for an oligopoly can be substantial, although the ability of a firm to utilize its market power fully depends on its interdependence with competing firms.

- Cartels result when several firms collude to set market price and output. Cartels typically use their market power to act like monopolists and share the economic profits that result.

- Cartels are inherently unstable because individual firms can earn higher profits by selling more than their allotted quota. As more firms in the cartel cheat, prices fall, defeating the agreement.

- The observation that prices are stable in oligopoly industries (other than in cartels) gave rise to the kinked demand curve model. The model assumes that competitors will follow price reductions but not price increases. This leads to a discontinuity in MR, permitting cost to vary substantially before prices are changed.

QUESTION: The major drug cartels operating along the U.S.–Mexico border have at times become very violent as cartels try to protect their trafficking routes to the U.S. market from competitors. But in addition to conflicts with external competition, cartel members have been murdered for exceeding their distribution quotas. Given the nature of how cartels function, explain why cartel leaders have become increasingly violent as a result of these events.

Answers to the Checkpoint questions can be found at the end of this chapter.

GAME THEORY

Technology is constantly changing. Compare your current smartphone with your previous one and notice the features that have become standard, such as voice recognition typing and advanced GPS applications. Behind the scenes, technology firms such as Apple and Samsung engage in fierce competition in the development of the next technological feature. But developing a new feature itself is not enough; to become the industry standard, all firms must adopt compatible features. Meanwhile, competing firms strive to improve upon existing features to avoid becoming obsolete and losing market power. The study of how oligopoly firms use strategies to gain market power and their effects on both competing firms and consumers form the foundation of game theory.

Game theory is the study of how individuals and firms make strategic decisions to achieve their goals when other parties or factors can influence that outcome. In short, it is the study of strategy and strategic behavior and is used in any situation in which one must consider the possible actions of others and respond by choosing among more than one strategy, each resulting in a potentially different outcome. Although game theory was first developed from the analysis of imperfect competition, particularly in explaining the actions of firms that are oligopolies, today it is used to study situations that extend well beyond the typical economic problems we have seen thus far in this book.

Real-life applications of game theory are abundant, and include situations common in sports coaching, business pricing, management, politics and elections, law and courtroom proceedings, military strategy, and even games such as poker. In 1995 Johnnie Cochran successfully defended O. J. Simpson against a murder charge when the evidence seemed to be stacked against him. In 2008 Barack Obama surpassed favorite Hillary Clinton to become his party's presidential nominee and eventually the president. In 2011 Google launched its Google+ social media service to challenge Facebook, but ultimately Mark Zuckerberg of Facebook prevailed in maintaining a dominant market share over Google+. As these events suggest, the importance of strategic thinking is a reason why game theory is an interdisciplinary topic that extends well beyond economics.

This section highlights key concepts of game theory, beginning with the important concept of a Nash equilibrium, named after famous mathematician-turned-economist and eventual Nobel Prize winner John Nash. In the next section, we extend this analysis to realistic cases and applications to illustrate how game theory is a part of our lives. We will see how game theory helps explain the actions of oligopolies.

game theory The study of how individuals and firms make strategic decisions to achieve their goals when other parties or factors can influence that outcome.

What do Mark Zuckerberg, Vanessa Selbst, and Bill Belichick have in common? They are all experts in strategic thinking.

JOHN NASH (1928–2015)
NOBEL PRIZE

No person arguably has had more influence on strategic economic analysis than John Nash, a mathematician-turned-economist whose theories led to the development of modern game theory. Born in 1928 to well-educated parents in Bluefield, West Virginia, John Nash was encouraged to pursue educational interests at a young age. As his aptitude for math developed, he enrolled in advanced mathematics classes at a local college while still in high school.

At age 16, he attended the Carnegie Institute of Technology (now Carnegie Mellon University), where by age 19 he earned both his bachelor's and master's degrees in mathematics. His adviser wrote a one-line letter of recommendation for his graduate school applications: "He is a mathematical genius." Nash continued his education at Princeton University, where he earned his Ph.D. at age 22, completing what remains one of the shortest yet most influential dissertations: a 28-page study of noncooperative games whose conclusion would eventually be called the Nash equilibrium.

John Nash worked as a professor at the Massachusetts Institute of Technology and also for the U.S. government as an expert code breaker. It was during these early adult years when mental illness began to set in, and he eventually was diagnosed with paranoid schizophrenia. His battles with severe disillusions consumed much of his life, and he was often seen talking to imaginary figures. Yet, his ability to make new contributions to game theory, a relatively new topic at the time, earned him a permanent faculty position at Princeton.

In 1994 John Nash was recognized with the Nobel Prize in Economics for his contributions to game theory. His life would be the subject of several books, including Sylvia Nasar's *A Beautiful Mind*, published in 1998. The book was adapted into the 2001 blockbuster movie by the same name, starring Russell Crowe, that would go on to win four Academy Awards, including Best Picture. John Nash died tragically in a taxi crash in 2015 while returning home from Norway, where he had just accepted the prestigious Abel Prize in Mathematics.

Basic Game Setup and Assumptions

The basic setup of a "game" requires players, information, strategies, outcomes, and payoffs. This game setup applies to virtually all situations in which strategy (game theory) is used to analyze a real-life scenario. Let's look at each component.

- **Players:** Players can be firms competing for customers, a plaintiff and a defendant in a courtroom, two or more countries at war, or actual players in a sporting match or card game.

- **Information:** Each player holds information that is either known to others or is private. Having private information changes the way in which a game is played and the outcomes it produces.

- **Strategies:** Players make choices based on strategies devised from the information they have and the information they suspect other players hold. Players use strategies to improve the likelihood of achieving their best outcome.

- **Outcomes:** Outcomes refer to all possibilities, good or bad, that can occur given the strategies employed by players. In zero-sum games, outcomes are a "win" or a "loss." In any given hand in poker, for example, one person wins the pot of money while everyone else loses. In other games, there may be no losers per se, but firms compete for market share, or job applicants compete for various types of jobs.

- **Payoffs:** The payoff is the value players attach to each outcome. Each player has his or her own perception of each outcome, because rarely do players in a game have exactly the same objective. Payoffs are what players ultimately try to maximize.

In addition to identifying the setup described above, analyses of situations involving game theory typically make two general assumptions:

1. *Preferences are clearly defined.* The objectives of each player must be known. For example, a firm's objective might be to maximize its profits, while a golfer's objective is to achieve a low score.

2. *Players rationally choose strategies to achieve objectives.* Players make consistent decisions that improve their chances of achieving their goals. Sometimes, however, people make decisions that seem irrational. Game theory does have something to say about irrational behavior, but this is beyond the scope of this section.

Simultaneous Versus Sequential-Move Games

simultaneous-move games Games in which players' actions occur at the same time, forcing players to make decisions without knowing how the other players will act. These games are analyzed using diagrams called game tables.

Game theory moves can be simultaneous or sequential. **Simultaneous-move games** involve actions by players that occur at the same time. Examples include sporting matches such as a soccer game with offensive and defensive players, and business pricing where firms must decide on prices to be placed in ads without knowing what prices their competitors will choose. **Sequential-move games** are situations in which one player at a time makes a move. Examples include games such as chess or tic-tac-toe, but also extend to examples such as negotiations (where offers are made back and forth), golf, or reality show competitions.

The analysis of simultaneous-move and sequential-move games differs. We'll begin by briefly discussing how sequential-move games are analyzed, and then proceed to a more in-depth analysis of simultaneous-move games, which are more common in everyday decision making. The next section will then provide additional applications of game theory using both sequential-move and simultaneous-move game analysis.

sequential-move games Games in which players make moves one at a time, allowing players to view the progression of the game and to make decisions based on previous moves.

Sequential-Move Games

Sequential-move games are analyzed using a game tree (also known as a decision tree or extensive form analysis). Figure 6 illustrates a game tree with two players, Virgin Galactic and SpaceX, deciding whether or not to continue pursuing a commercial space flight program. Because Virgin is closer to commercial space flight than SpaceX, it would make the first move, illustrated in the first node with two branches, each specifying a strategy choice. After Virgin makes its choice, SpaceX will then decide whether to pursue its program, knowing what Virgin has decided. The four possible outcomes each correspond to a set of payoffs in parentheses, where the first number is Virgin's payoff and the second number is SpaceX's payoff.

The solution to the game tree is found by analyzing how SpaceX responds to Virgin's strategies and then working *backward*. If Virgin chooses to pursue, SpaceX's best response is to pull back (because $60 > 30$); but if Virgin pulls back, SpaceX's best response is to pursue (because $90 > 10$). Being able to predict how SpaceX will respond to each of Virgin's moves, Virgin then chooses its best outcome, which is to pursue (because $100 > 40$). Therefore, the equilibrium in this sequential-move game would be Virgin pursuing the commercial space program with SpaceX pulling back. Although the resulting payoff of 100 for Virgin and 60 for SpaceX is not the best payoff for SpaceX, it is the best it can do given Virgin's decision. In this game, Virgin has an advantage by moving first. Not all games have a first-mover advantage. For example, in a game of golf, it's often better to move last, because one can gain valuable information from observing the other players' shots.

Simultaneous-Move Games

Figure 7 illustrates a two-player simultaneous-move game in a diagram called a game table (also known as a payoff matrix or normal form analysis). In our example, Lowe's and Home Depot must choose one of two policies: advertise in the local paper or don't advertise. Lowe's strategies are listed in rows, while Home Depot's strategies are listed in columns. Because players (firms) move at the same time, outcomes are determined by the interaction of strategies chosen by each player. In this case, four potential outcomes exist, with Lowe's

| FIGURE 6 | SEQUENTIAL-MOVE GAME ILLUSTRATED IN A GAME TREE |

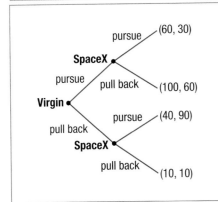

A sequential-move game is illustrated between Virgin and SpaceX. Virgin makes the first move to either pursue or pull back. After seeing Virgin's decision, SpaceX responds by choosing to pursue or pull back. For each possible outcome, a payoff results for each firm. The first number in each outcome is Virgin's payoff, and the second number is SpaceX's payoff. Because Virgin can anticipate SpaceX's response to each of its two strategies, Virgin's best action is to pursue, and SpaceX's best response to this move is to pull back.

FIGURE 7	SIMULTANEOUS-MOVE GAME ILLUSTRATED IN A GAME TABLE

A simultaneous-move game between Lowe's and Home Depot is shown in which both firms must choose whether to advertise in the local paper or not, without knowing what the other will do. The choice made by each firm results in a different payoff for each.

		Home Depot			
		Advertise		Don't advertise	
Lowe's	Advertise	$100,000	$100,000	$300,000	$50,000
	Don't advertise	$50,000	$300,000	$200,000	$200,000

payoff shown before Home Depot's payoff in each outcome box. The final outcome depends on which strategy each player actually chooses.

Let's go through each outcome, to show you how to read the figure. If Lowe's and Home Depot both advertise, each will earn a profit of $100,000. The advertising will induce some customers to buy now, but won't much affect whether they will buy at Lowe's or at Home Depot. There is a cost to advertising, which is why profits are lower when both firms advertise than when both do not. When both do not advertise, each earns a profit of $200,000. Customers continue to go to Lowe's and Home Depot about equally, and both firms do not bear the cost of the advertising.

What happens if one advertises while the other does not? The one that advertises increases profits. If Lowe's advertises while Home Depot does not, it earns a profit of $300,000 compared to Home Depot's payoff of $50,000. Why this result? Lowe's has to pay the cost of advertising, but more than makes up for it by taking customers away from Home Depot. By not advertising, Home Depot saves on this cost, but it does not make up for the loss of customers. This result is the same, but reversed, if Lowe's does not advertise while Home Depot does: Home Depot sees $300,000 in profit while Lowe's profit is only $50,000.

Strategically, what is each firm's best strategy: Advertise or not advertise? Let's first look at the best possible outcome for Lowe's. Its best outcome would be to advertise when Home Depot does not, allowing Lowe's to earn $300,000 while Home Depot ends up at its worse outcome, earning only $50,000. Alternatively, the best collective outcome for Lowe's and Home Depot occurs when both do not advertise and each earns $200,000. Is either of these outcomes likely?

Let's approach this question by looking at the best response of one firm to the other's action. Suppose Home Depot strives for its highest possible outcome of $300,000 by advertising. What would be Lowe's best response? Clearly, Lowe's does not want to bear the minuscule profits of $50,000 if it does not advertise when Home Depot does advertise; therefore, it advertises and earns $100,000. Thus, choosing to advertise is a best response if competitors advertise. In Figure 7, this payoff is underlined.

Looking at this game from Home Depot's point of view, it also advertises in response to Lowe's advertising, because it too would not want Lowe's to grab too many of its customers. Advertising is a best response for Home Depot because it results in a payoff of $100,000 (underlined) instead of $50,000. If both Lowe's and Home Depot act strategically by advertising to avoid the worst possible outcome, then the best-case scenario of earning $300,000 is not possible.

If the best outcome is not possible, then how about the best collective outcome in which both firms choose not to advertise and each earns $200,000? Clearly, this outcome is better than if both firms advertise. But they cannot call each other up and say, "I will not advertise if you do not advertise." This is collusion, prevented by law in many countries. Each firm has to make a decision without knowing what the other will do.

Again using the best-response approach, if Home Depot chooses not to advertise, Lowe's would still be better off advertising, because (1) it eliminates the worst-case outcome if Home Depot does, in fact, advertise, and (2) if Home Depot does not advertise, advertising would allow Lowe's to achieve its highest payoff of $300,000. Therefore, Lowe's best response to Home Depot not advertising is still to advertise (the corresponding payoff is underlined in Figure 7). From Home Depot's perspective, its best response if Lowe's does not advertise would be to advertise as well.

In sum, the best action each firm can take, *considering each of the possible actions the other might take*, is to advertise. This outcome is what economists call a Nash equilibrium.

Nash Equilibrium

A **Nash equilibrium** occurs when all players in a game use an optimal strategy in response to all other players' strategies. It is the outcome that maximizes all players' expected payoffs (the value of each potential outcome times the probability of that outcome occurring) given the information they have. In other words, aiming for the outcome with the highest payoff is not always prudent if the likelihood of achieving that outcome is small. Solving for Nash equilibrium is therefore valuable because it represents a player's best payoff taking into account the self-interested actions of all other players affecting the outcome. Once a Nash equilibrium is achieved, no individual player can do better by changing his or her mind.

For example, it is possible that Lowe's or Home Depot could see higher profits if it chose not to advertise, but there's a higher probability of it leading to lower profits. Nash equilibrium guides players to choose strategies that result in the best expected payoff. In the Lowe's–Home Depot example, the Nash equilibrium is for each to advertise when neither knows what the other will do.

An outcome is a Nash equilibrium if it results from all players acting strategically (using a best response) to each other's actions. In some cases, players choose the same action regardless of what others do, while in other cases, players choose different actions in response to other players' actions. In the Home Depot–Lowe's example, each firm's best response is to advertise regardless of what the other firm does, and is known as a dominant strategy. A **dominant strategy** occurs when one player chooses the same action regardless of what the other player chooses. When both players have a dominant strategy, a single Nash equilibrium will result. For Lowe's and Home Depot, both advertising is the Nash equilibrium. But not all Nash equilibria are the result of dominant strategies. In fact, games need not be limited to one Nash equilibrium. When dominant strategies do not exist, games can have no Nash equilibrium while others might have more than one, as we'll soon see.

Also, a Nash equilibrium outcome is not always obvious. In Figure 7, it might seem that Lowe's and Home Depot not advertising would be a Nash equilibrium; besides, the profits for both are higher than the profits with advertising. But such a quick conclusion does not take into account the fact that one firm could do even better by advertising if the other does not. And because neither firm wishes to risk the worst-case scenario, they both engage in advertising as their best-response action. Fortunately, not all Nash equilibrium outcomes are so pessimistic. In many cases, acting in response to another player's actions can lead to a good outcome for all players, as we'll see next.

Nash Equilibrium: A Personal Example Let's look at a personal example to make sure that the idea of a Nash equilibrium is clear. Suppose you are meeting a classmate to study for an upcoming exam. You didn't exchange phone numbers, but plan to meet at the local Starbucks tonight. As you head out, you realize that there are two Starbucks near campus: one north of campus and one south. And your classmate also came to the same realization. Without the ability to communicate with your classmate, which location do you choose?

In this scenario, assuming both you and your classmate are making strategic decisions to achieve the same objective, there are four potential outcomes, illustrated in Figure 8. Two of the four outcomes result in a successful meeting, while two result in a missed encounter. In this example, two outcomes meet the criteria for a Nash equilibrium, which is common for coordination-type games when players are attempting to achieve a mutually beneficial outcome. In each Nash equilibrium, both players used strategic thinking to achieve a good outcome. But not so fast! There are actually two Nash equilibria. How would you know which one is the "correct" outcome? Here lies the challenge of this game. Although "Nash equilibrium" describes the outcomes when both players use a best-response strategy,

Nash equilibrium An outcome that occurs when all players choose their optimal strategy in response to all other players' potential moves. At a Nash equilibrium, no player can be better off by unilaterally deviating from the noncooperative outcome.

dominant strategy Occurs when a player chooses the same strategy regardless of what his or her opponent chooses.

FIGURE 8

| FIGURE 8 | STUDY SESSION COORDINATION PROBLEM: WHICH LOCATION TO MEET? |

The two outcomes in which both players choose the same location both represent a Nash equilibrium.

		Classmate	
		North	South
You	North	Successful meet-up	Missed opportunity
	South	Missed opportunity	Successful meet-up

Cultura/Getty Images

it doesn't say anything about how to narrow it down to just one outcome. Therefore, players need to use focal points, which are clues that point to a greater likelihood of a successful meeting. The following Issue describes focal points in greater detail.

To review, a Nash equilibrium describes any outcome when all players respond optimally to all possible actions by other players. At that outcome, no player would choose to deviate unilaterally from that outcome; this doesn't mean that a better outcome might prevail with some cooperation, but rather that no player would change her position by herself. Finding a Nash equilibrium is therefore useful because it represents the best outcome given the self-interested actions of all other players.

 ISSUE

Mission ~~Impossible~~: The Power of Focal Points in a Simulated Mission

Barry Nalebuff is a respected economist who has published several books on game theory, and is known for constructing unorthodox methods of using game theory to solve life's problems. A few years ago, Barry Nalebuff teamed up with the show *PrimeTime* to create a unique game theory experiment dealing with Nash equilibria and focal points. They took six pairs of people who did not know one another and placed them in different locations in New York City's Manhattan. The objective of this game was to have at least one pair find one of the other five pairs within a day, not knowing where they would be or what they looked like. Trying to locate an unfamiliar person among millions in Manhattan is a true needle-in-a-haystack problem. Sound impossible? Perhaps. But game theory teaches us to use clues effectively to solve such problems. In this case, when players have the same goal, strategies can be employed to maximize the chances of achieving it.

Recall the concepts of Nash equilibrium in the study session coordination problem described previously. Unlike that situation, which contained four potential outcomes and two Nash equilibria, the present example contains infinite outcomes and infinite Nash equilibria (since pairs could meet at any of millions of locations at any time of the day). When many possible solutions exist, players must use focal points to reach an equilibrium solution. Focal points are solutions that seem more obvious based on clues and past experience.

In the present example, focal points rely on three dimensions: where, when, and who. Where would pairs go to facilitate spotting others? Common answers might include Times Square, the Empire State Building, the Statue of Liberty, and Grand Central Terminal, among others. By listing these likely locations, we reduce the number of likely outcomes from millions of locations to fewer than a dozen. Next is the timing

issue. Two pairs could be at the same location but at different times. Thus, a focal point in time is necessary; obvious times might be noon (the strongest focal point), 9 A.M., 3 P.M., or 5 P.M. Lastly, two pairs could be at the same location at the same time, but still not recognize one another. Thus, a focal point on recognizing another pair is necessary, and can be achieved through costumes, posters and signs, and noisemaking devices. Would the combination of each of the dimensions of focal points turn a seemingly impossible task into a successful one?

On the show, the six teams had resounding success. Three teams found each other at the top of the Empire State Building at noon wearing signs, while another three teams found each other in Times Square at noon also holding signs and using whistles and other noisemakers. Clearly, the use of game theory is a powerful and effective tool when confronted with some of life's biggest challenges.

We have seen two situations with different Nash equilibrium outcomes. For Lowe's and Home Depot, the Nash equilibrium was an outcome that neither firm truly desired. In the next section, we will classify these outcomes as a Prisoner's Dilemma and show what can be done to overcome such outcomes. For the study session coordination problem, we found more than one Nash equilibrium in which both players would be happy. But we need not stop here. The next section will highlight other Nash equilibrium outcomes that can result depending on the circumstances facing each player. Because the Nash equilibrium in each situation is not automatically obvious, it's important to use the best-response method to solve for the Nash equilibrium to ensure that each player's expected payoff is maximized.

 CHECKPOINT

GAME THEORY

- Game theory uses sophisticated mathematical analysis to explain the actions of oligopolies, as well as develop optimal strategies for life's everyday situations.
- Game theory characteristics include the number of players and strategies, information completeness, and the value of potential outcomes (payoffs).
- Simultaneous-move games occur when players make decisions without knowing what other players will choose, and are analyzed using diagrams called game tables.
- Nash equilibrium analysis describes outcomes in which all players respond optimally to all possible actions by other players to achieve the highest expected payoff.
- It is possible to have zero, one, two, or more Nash equilibria in a game.

QUESTION: A common scenario when talking with a friend on a phone occurs when the call is dropped, forcing one person to call back the other in order to resume the conversation. As long as one person calls back and the other person waits, a Nash equilibrium will result. However, achieving this equilibrium is not always easily accomplished. Using your own personal experiences, what strategies (or focal points) do you use with your friends in these circumstances to determine who would call back and who would wait, assuming that you do not communicate using any other method such as texting?

Answers to the Checkpoint questions can be found at the end of this chapter.

APPLICATIONS OF GAME THEORY

This section focuses on four common categories of games: Prisoner's Dilemma, repeated games, leadership games, and chicken games. In each of the examples within each category, we solve for a Nash equilibrium using the best-response method introduced in the previous section, and discuss the characteristics of these outcomes that are found in real-life examples. In doing this, you should get a sense of how game theory helps explain many oligopoly behaviors.

The Prisoner's Dilemma

Ever notice how competing stores pay very close attention to what their competitors do? When Office Depot offers back-to-school specials, Staples is sure to do the same. When one airline offers a summer fare sale, other airlines tend to follow. In our example of Lowe's and Home Depot in the previous section, each firm chooses to advertise even if it results in lower profits than if neither advertises. If you were a manager of one of these firms, shouldn't you immediately cease advertising? Not necessarily. Game theory helps to explain this seemingly counterintuitive outcome. In each of these situations, the Nash equilibrium that results is an outcome that is inferior to another outcome that can be achieved through cooperation, and is referred to as a **Prisoner's Dilemma.**

Given the similarities of products sold by monopolistically competitive and oligopoly firms, Prisoner's Dilemma outcomes occur frequently as firms compete for market share,

Prisoner's Dilemma A noncooperative game in which players cannot communicate or collaborate in making their decisions, which results in inferior outcomes for both players. Many oligopoly decisions can be framed as a Prisoner's Dilemma.

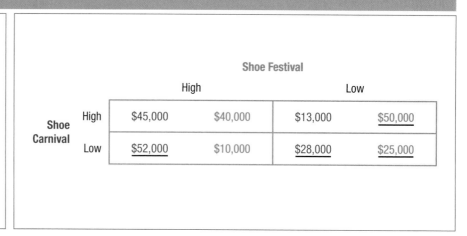

FIGURE 9 | **PRISONER'S DILEMMA GAME BETWEEN TWO FIRMS**

Intense competition between Shoe Carnival and Shoe Festival results in both stores pricing their products low, resulting in a Nash equilibrium payoff of $28,000 for Shoe Carnival and $25,000 for Shoe Festival. However, another outcome provides a greater profit for *both* stores, that is, if both stores price high. But because the two stores cannot openly collude, and neither trusts the other to maintain high prices, both stores end up pricing their products low, resulting in lower profits.

such as AT&T and Verizon in wireless communications, Carnival and Royal Caribbean in cruise vacations, and Target and Walmart in discount retailing.

For consumers, however, Prisoner's Dilemma outcomes are beneficial because they result in lower prices for goods. As competing firms lower their prices to gain market share, they earn a smaller profit from each customer. In some cases, competition becomes so intense that a competitor is forced out of business. Just ask Circuit City, Borders, Sharper Image, and Linens-N-Things, just to name a few. Why would firms compete to the point of nearly zero profit margins? Wouldn't it make sense for competing firms to utilize their collective market power by all raising their prices to make more money?

Alas, here's the dilemma: Firms cannot openly collude to raise prices (that is illegal under antitrust laws). However, firms *can* silently collude by raising prices unilaterally and hoping that others will follow. But will the others follow?

Suppose two shoe stores operate near campus, Shoe Carnival and Shoe Festival. Assume, for simplicity, that each has two pricing strategies: a high markup and a low markup. If both stores choose the same strategy, they each attract the same number of customers. But if one store is less expensive than the other, it takes most of the customers and profits (despite earning less profit per customer at the lower price). Figure 9 shows a game table with presumed profits under the four outcomes.

Using the best-response method to solve for Nash equilibrium, Shoe Carnival's best response to a high price by Shoe Festival is to price low ($52,000 > $45,000), thereby stealing most of Shoe Festival's customers and earning a higher profit. And to prevent the same from happening if Shoe Festival prices low, Shoe Carnival's best response is also to price low ($28,000 > $13,000). Therefore, Shoe Carnival has a dominant strategy to keep its prices low regardless of what Shoe Festival does. In Figure 9, the strategies selected by Shoe Carnival in response to each strategy by Shoe Festival are underlined. If we conduct the same analysis for Shoe Festival, we also find that Shoe Festival has a dominant strategy to price low, resulting in a Nash equilibrium when both stores price low, resulting in a payoff of $28,000 for Shoe Carnival and $25,000 for Shoe Festival.

Does this equilibrium seem odd? It might because another outcome (where both stores price high) provides greater profit to *both* stores. Yet, that outcome is *not* a Nash equilibrium. A Prisoner's Dilemma therefore results because players are unable to cooperate effectively with one another. Why don't the stores just agree to price their products high? They can't do it by colluding; that is illegal. And if one store raises its prices unilaterally, there is no guarantee the other store will follow, thus risking a loss of customers and profit.

The Classic Prisoner's Dilemma How did the Prisoner's Dilemma get its name? Two criminal suspects (say, Matthew and Chris) are apprehended on a charge of robbery. They are separated, put in solitary confinement, are unable to speak to each other, and are not expected to meet each other even after the prison term is finished. Each prisoner is

FIGURE 10 | THE CLASSIC PRISONER'S DILEMMA

		Chris			
		Do not confess		Confess	
Matthew	Do not confess	1 year	1 year	3 years	0 years
	Confess	0 years	3 years	2 years	2 years

Matthew and Chris are two suspects held in separate cells. Each is given an opportunity to confess to the crime, with the resulting jail sentences shown for each outcome. Under this payoff structure, the optimal response by each player is to confess, resulting in a single Nash equilibrium where each receives two years of jail time. This Nash equilibrium is a Prisoner's Dilemma because a better outcome (not confessing) exists for both players.

offered the same bargain: Confess that you and your partner both committed the crime and you will go free while your non-confessing partner will go to prison for three years. If neither confesses, the state likely will convict them both on lesser charges, resulting in a one-year sentence for each. Finally, if both confess, they each will go to prison for two years.

Figure 10 illustrates this game in which payoffs represent the number of years in prison. The prisoners must make a decision without knowing what the other chose, and decisions are irrevocable. Each prisoner is only concerned with his own welfare—minimizing his time in prison. Is there a unique solution?

Using the best-response method, Matthew and Chris both have a dominant strategy to confess! This outcome results despite the fact that both would be better off by not confessing: one year served in prison versus two. The Prisoner's Dilemma results because neither player trusts the other not to confess given the structure of the payoffs.

Other Examples of Prisoner's Dilemma Outcomes Now that you have an idea of what a Prisoner's Dilemma entails, particularly when oligopoly firms compete, let's mention a few other examples in which a Prisoner's Dilemma might occur.

- **Political Campaigns:** Politicians spend immense amounts of time, effort, and money to win elections. Some members of Congress in swing districts spend half of their two-year terms in office campaigning, leaving little time to get anything else done, like passing laws. If competing candidates have roughly equal amounts of time and money, the result is likely to be similar if the candidates agree not to campaign at all; but that requires each candidate to trust the other not to break that promise, which is not an easy proposition.

- **Legal Disputes:** When individuals or firms end up in litigation, plaintiffs and defendants often will spend large amounts of money in legal fees and for consultants merely to offset what the other side spends. For high-profile cases, add the costs of media coverage and the costs incurred by family, friends, and curious onlookers, and the outcome often is more costly for all parties involved.

- **Trade Disputes:** When one country restricts imported goods to protect domestic producers from foreign competition, other countries have an incentive to do the same, making it difficult for domestic producers to sell their goods abroad. When countries restrict trade against each other, a Prisoner's Dilemma outcome occurs because trade barriers cause a reduction in the gains from specialization and trade, harming all countries.

Resolving the Prisoner's Dilemma Prisoner's Dilemma type of situations are difficult to resolve in a noncooperative framework when the players are not able to coordinate their strategies, whether as a result of antitrust laws or an inability to retaliate against other players if the cooperative action is not played. Although Prisoner's Dilemma outcomes might be bad for firms in a pricing game or for litigants in a trial, they surely are beneficial for consumers who enjoy lower prices and for lawyers who might earn a lot of money in a high-profile case.

Let's consider a case of trade protection in which a Prisoner's Dilemma might be resolved successfully. A Prisoner's Dilemma occurs when countries enact trade barriers, causing the gains from trade to be restricted. Free trade agreements are a way for countries to overcome the Prisoner's Dilemma by agreeing to promote free trade among members. And unlike collusive agreements between firms, free trade agreements are legal and have been implemented extensively in recent decades.

Another way to overcome the Prisoner's Dilemma is by ensuring that the game is repeated over time. When games are played just once, players have an incentive to maximize their payoffs in the game without worrying about long-term consequences. However, when a game is repeated indefinitely, incentives change, and players worry about retaliation.

Repeated Games

Sunday ads: an example of a repeated game by retailers.

Pick up a Sunday newspaper and notice the large selection of circulars included. Many retailers advertise their products using a Sunday ad without knowing what their competitors' ads look like. But because this game is repeated every Sunday, no firm would risk retaliation by advertising prices that are *too* low relative to other firms. Thus, repeated games provide a way for competing players to check how other players are behaving, and to provide a way of punishing unfair players.

Games can be endlessly (infinitely) repeated or repeated for a specific number of rounds. In either case, repeating opens the game to different types of strategies that are unavailable for a game played only once. These strategies can take into account the past behavior of rivals. This section briefly explores such strategies and some of their implications for understanding oligopoly behavior.

One possibility is simply to cooperate or defect from the beginning. These strategies, however, leave you at the mercy of your opponent, or lead to unfavorable outcomes where both firms earn less or suffer losses. A more robust set of strategies are **trigger strategies,** where action is taken contingent on your opponent's past decisions. Here are a few of them.

trigger strategies Action is taken contingent on your opponent's past decisions.

Grim Trigger Let's start by considering an industry that is earning oligopoly profits. Suppose that all of a sudden, one firm lowers its price, maybe because it is in financial trouble and wants to increase sales right away. Under the grim trigger rule, the other firms lower their prices—but they do not stop there. They permanently lower their prices, making the financial condition of the original firm that reduced prices even more severe.

Any decision by your opponent to defect (choose an unfavorable outcome) is met by a permanent retaliatory decision forever. This grim trigger is a harsh decision rule. Moreover, misinterpretation of a player's actions can result. For example, has your competition lowered its price in an attempt to gain market share at your expense, or has the market softened for the product in general? This strategy can quickly lead to the unfavorable Prisoner's Dilemma result. To avoid this problem, oligopoly firms might use other trigger strategies.

Trembling Hand Trigger A trembling hand trigger strategy allows for a mistake by your opponent before you retaliate. This gives your opponent a chance to make a mistake and reduces misreads that are a problem for the grim trigger strategy. This approach can be extended to accept two nonsequential defects, and so on, but they can be exploited by clever opponents who figure out that they can get away with a few "mistakes" before their opponent retaliates.

tit-for-tat strategies A trigger strategy that rewards cooperation and punishes defections. If your opponent lowers its price, you do the same. If your opponent returns to a cooperative strategy, you do the same.

Tit-for-Tat A tit-for-tat strategy is one that repeats the prior move of competitors. If one firm lowers its price, its rivals follow suit one time. If the same firm offers discounts or special offers, rivals do exactly the same in the next time period. This strategy has efficient qualities in that it rewards cooperation and punishes defection.

This short list of strategies illustrates the richness of repeated games. Strategies tend to be more successful if they are relatively simple and easy to understand by competitors, tend

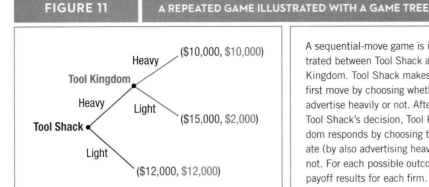

| FIGURE 11 | A REPEATED GAME ILLUSTRATED WITH A GAME TREE |

A sequential-move game is illustrated between Tool Shack and Tool Kingdom. Tool Shack makes the first move by choosing whether to advertise heavily or not. After seeing Tool Shack's decision, Tool Kingdom responds by choosing to retaliate (by also advertising heavily) or not. For each possible outcome, a payoff results for each firm.

to foster cooperation, have some credible punishment to reduce defections, and provide for forgiveness to avoid the costly mistakes associated with misreading opponents.[1]

Using Sequential-Move Analysis to Model Repeated Games Because repeated games involve multiple iterations of the same game, it can be shown in the sequential-move game tree described in the previous section. In Figure 11, a game tree is shown between two hardware firms that advertise each week in the Sunday ads. To avoid the Prisoner's Dilemma, both firms must choose to advertise lightly. They continue to do so unless one firm chooses to advertise heavily, which would lead to a trigger strategy in the next stage. Suppose Tool Shack contemplates advertising heavily this week: Tool Kingdom can respond to this action by advertising heavily next week, or choose not to. In the figure, Tool Shack makes the first decision whether to advertise lightly or heavily. If Tool Shack chooses to advertise heavily, Tool Kingdom then chooses whether to respond.

Looking at Tool Kingdom's payoffs, it is in its best interest to advertise heavily if Tool Shack chooses to advertise heavily. Tool Shack, knowing that advertising heavily would be Tool Kingdom's best response in the next stage, would likely choose to maintain its light advertising to avoid the Prisoner's Dilemma outcome. The sequential nature of game trees allows players to see the progression of moves across time from start to finish.

Resolving the Prisoner's Dilemma is an important outcome of cooperative strategies. But not all competitive games lead to a Prisoner's Dilemma. One example is called a leadership game, where an industry is dominated by a market leader.

Leadership Games

Facebook is the world's largest social media provider, which earns its revenues primarily through advertising and sets prices to maximize its profits. Yet, other smaller social networks also compete for revenues. Unlike earlier examples, in which competing firms are of similar size, Facebook's market dominance allows it to ignore the pricing actions of its smaller competitors. In other words, if Facebook loses a few advertisers due to lower prices on other networks, the loss in revenues is smaller than what it would lose if Facebook lowered its prices.

Another example of a leadership game occurs when a small low-fare airline competes against a larger airline. Frontier Airlines is a relatively small airline based in Denver; it competes on many routes that United Airlines serves. But because United is a significantly larger airline with greater market power, it does not always match Frontier's lower fares because United believes it would not lose many customers.

Chicken Games

Another category of game that does not result in a Prisoner's Dilemma can be seen where collective bargaining (organized labor) is powerful, such as labor unions and unions for

[1] Nick Wilkinson, *Managerial Economics: A Problem Solving Approach* (Cambridge, U.K.: Cambridge University Press), 2005, p. 373.

FIGURE 12	A CHICKEN GAME BETWEEN NHL PLAYERS AND NHL OWNERS

NHL Owners

		Tough		Loose	
NHL Players	Tough	0	0	4	1
	Loose	1	4	2	2

Neither side wishes to give in to the other side in a labor dispute, but if neither gives in, the worst outcome of 0, 0 results (i.e., a lockout or strike). In chicken games, two Nash equilibria exist, each with one player achieving his ideal result while the other side settles.

professional sports. Every once in a while, a labor dispute reaches a point where a strike is either threatened or sometimes carried out. Although we discuss labor disputes in the next chapter, this is an example of an important class of games called chicken.

A chicken game is portrayed in the classic movie *Rebel Without a Cause*, in which James Dean's character is challenged by a rival to a stunt challenge. Both players race their cars toward a cliff, and the first person to jump out is the "chicken." The winner is the person who stays in the car longer. Of course, if neither player leaves his car, they both plunge to their deaths.

Chicken games describe games of holdouts or brinkmanship. Players involved in chicken games want to hold out as long as they can to win, trying to get the other side to give in. If neither side does, the worst outcome occurs. Examples of brinkmanship occur regularly in Congress. Neither Democrats nor Republicans wish to concede anything up to the very end, when some catastrophic consequence threatens the economy such as a government default (from failing to raise the debt ceiling) or a *fiscal cliff* of higher taxes and severe spending cuts (from failing to agree on a budget). Brinkmanship often ties one's hands.

Figure 12 illustrates a chicken game using the 2012 NHL labor dispute as an example. The players union and the team owners were in a dispute over salaries. Each side can remain tough, or loosen their position. The worst outcome occurs when both sides refuse to give in, resulting in a lockout or strike that is devastating to both sides, not to mention all the fans, who are not able to watch their favorite teams play.

Using the best-response method, we find that chicken games have two Nash equilibria, where one side ultimately *gives in* to the other. Specifically, if NHL owners choose the tough strategy by refusing to compromise, the best response of players would be to loosen their position and earn a payoff of 1 instead of 0. If NHL owners are willing to compromise, the best response of players would be to maintain a tough position and earn a payoff of 4 instead of 2. The same best-response strategies can be determined by the NHL owners in response to the NHL players' strategies.

Thus, in a chicken game, one party is much happier with a Nash equilibrium result than the other. Yet, the *loser* still would not have wanted to change its strategy, for doing so unilaterally would result in an even worse outcome. Unfortunately for the NHL, a Nash equilibrium did not occur as both sides refused to give in, resulting in a lockout and a severely compromised 2012–2013 season. This is an outcome that occasionally occurs in chicken games, one that had clear consequences for both players and owners, not to mention many disappointed fans.

As seen in the many applications in this and the last section, game theory is a powerful tool to analyze market competition when firms each have the ability to influence price and the market share of their competitors. The ability to anticipate another player's actions and respond optimally is the key to achieving a Nash equilibrium. Nash equilibrium is the outcome that maximizes all players' expected payoffs. Recognizing such outcomes allows all players to achieve the best outcome given the self-interested motives of all other players involved. Game theory has applications that extend beyond oligopoly competition and economics in general.

Summary of Market Structures

In this and the previous two chapters, we have studied the four major market structures: perfect competition, monopolistic competition, oligopoly, and monopoly. As we move through

TABLE 1	SUMMARY OF MARKET STRUCTURES			
	Perfect Competition	Monopolistic Competition	Oligopoly	Monopoly
Number of Firms	Many	Many	Few	One
Product	Homogeneous	Differentiated	Homogeneous or differentiated	Unique
Barriers to Entry or Exit?	None	Little to none	Substantial	Impenetrable
Strategic Interdependence?	No	No	Yes	Not applicable
Ability to Set Price (Market Power)	None	Limited	Some	Absolute
Long-Run Price Decision	$P = ATC$	$P = ATC$	$P > ATC$	$P > ATC$
Long-Run Profits	Zero	Zero	Usually economic	Economic
Key Summary Characteristic	Price taker	Product differentiation	Mutual interdependence	One-firm industry

this list, market power becomes greater, and the ability of the firm to earn economic profits in the long run grows.

Table 1 summarizes the important distinctions among these four market structures. Keep in mind that market structure analysis allows you to look at the overall characteristics of the market and predict the pricing and profit behavior of the firms. The outcomes for perfect competition and monopolistic competition are particularly attractive for consumers because firms price their products equal to average total costs and earn just enough to keep them in business over the long haul.

In contrast, the outcomes for oligopoly and monopoly industries are not as favorable to consumers. Concentrated markets have considerable market power, which shows up in pricing and output decisions. However, keep in mind that markets with market power (oligopolies) often involve giants competing with giants. Even though there is a mutual interdependence in their decisions and they may not always compete vigorously over prices, they often are innovative because of some competitive pressures. We see this today especially in the electronics and automobile markets.

 CHECKPOINT

APPLICATIONS OF GAME THEORY

- The Prisoner's Dilemma is a noncooperative game in which players minimize their maximum prison time by both confessing, a strategy that neither would have taken had they been able to communicate with one another.

- Applications of Prisoner's Dilemma games extend well beyond criminal cases, and can involve firm pricing strategies, legal disputes, international trade protection, and political campaigns.

- Resolving the Prisoner's Dilemma is not easy because of antitrust laws preventing firms from colluding. However, when games are repeated, the threat of retaliation encourages players to use a cooperative strategy.

- Games that are repeated lead to more nuanced trigger strategies, including grim trigger, trembling hand trigger, and tit-for-tat.

- Leadership games describe competitive games in which one player is dominant in size relative to the rest of the players.

- Chicken games involve players who try to hold out for the optimal outcome; however, if neither side gives in, the worst outcome occurs. Labor disputes that often end in strikes or lockouts are examples of chicken games.

QUESTIONS: Suppose your economics professor grades the class on a curve, such that exactly 25% of the class receives an A, 25% receives a B, 25% receives a C, and 25% receives a D, regardless of how the class actually performs. One of your classmates comes up with an idea: Instead of having the entire class study for hours and hours for each exam, everyone in the class agrees *not* to study, with the presumption that everyone would likely receive the same grade as if they did study given the grade distribution. Would this strategy work? Why or why not? What type of game does this best represent, a chicken game or a Prisoner's Dilemma? Explain.

Answers to the Checkpoint questions can be found at the end of this chapter.

chapter summary

Section 1 Monopolistic Competition

10.1 A **monopolistically competitive** industry has the following characteristics:

- Large number of firms, each with insignificant market share.
- Little to no barriers to entry and exit.
- Products sold by firms are similar but differentiated (has a brand name).
- Limited market power and ability to set prices.

10.2 Short-run profit maximization for a firm in a monopolistically competitive industry looks identical to a monopoly. In the long run, however, the demand curve is tangent to the average total cost curve, signaling zero economic profit.

Because of product differentiation, a firm's demand curve is downward sloping. However, it is highly elastic due to the competitive nature of the industry.

Types of Product Differentiation

Location

Quality

Style, Design, and Features

Advertising

A shopping mall offers dozens of stores at which to buy clothing, each of which is differentiated.

Section 2 Oligopoly

10.3 **Oligopoly** industries are controlled by a few large firms. Barriers to entry are significant, products are less differentiated than in monopolistically competitive industries, and pricing decisions by one firm directly impact other firms (mutual interdependence). Oligopoly firms possess market power, but not as much as a monopoly.

Cartels are agreements to restrict output to push prices higher, but are inherently unstable because cheating is profitable.

10.4 A **kinked demand curve** occurs because firms are reluctant to match price increases but not price decreases. The kink creates a discontinuity in the marginal revenue curve, allowing the marginal cost curve to vary (from MC_0 to MC_1) while output and prices remain stable.

Nearby competing gas stations keep their prices similar.

Section 3 Game Theory

10.5 **Game theory** is the study of strategic decision making when multiple players each act in their own interests.

Components of a Game

Players	Information	Strategy Choices	Outcomes	Payoffs

Sequential-move games: Games in which players move one at a time, and are analyzed using game trees.

Simultaneous-move games: Games in which players move at the same time, and are analyzed using game tables.

Golf is a sequential-move game, in which players take their shots one at a time.

Nash equilibrium is an outcome that results from all players responding optimally to all other players' actions to maximize their expected payoffs. In a Nash equilibrium, no player wishes to deviate unilaterally from that outcome.

10.6 Solving for a Nash equilibrium requires analyzing a game table for best responses to the other player's possible actions.

Player 2

		Left		Right	
	Top	_8_	4	2	_6_
Players 1	Down	6	3	_7_	_5_

Player 1's best response to "Left" is "Top" = 8.

Player 1's best response to "Right" is "Down" = 7.

Player 2's best response to "Top" is "Right" = 6.

Player 2's best response to "Down" is "Right" = 5.

One Nash equilibrium is "Down", "Right" = (7, 5).

Section 4 Applications of Game Theory

10.7 A **Prisoner's Dilemma** occurs when optimal noncooperative play results in an outcome that is inferior to another outcome for both players.

10.8 Ways to Overcome the Prisoner's Dilemma

Collusion: This is illegal in most cases, although international cartels exist, such as the OPEC oil cartel and various drug cartels. Also, free trade agreements are a legal form of cooperation between countries.

Repeated games: Games that are repeated by the same players, and often results in one player taking the lead on a cooperate strategy, and others follow. The possibility of retaliation in a repeated game increases the likelihood of cooperation.

American Airlines was the first major airline to charge for checked baggage. Almost all other airlines followed, allowing the airlines to achieve a mutually beneficial outcome.

Trigger Strategies Used in Repeated Games

Grim trigger: When one player defects, the other refuses to cooperate again (no forgiveness).

Trembling hand trigger: Players forgive certain instances of defection as "mistakes" before retaliation is taken.

Tit-for-tat trigger: Essentially an eye for an eye: If one player defects, the other player punishes this player until cooperation resumes.

Leadership games: Describes situations that occur when a small firm competes against a large firm, and where the market share captured by the small firm is not large enough to warrant a reaction by the large firm.

Chicken games: Describes situations that occur when opposing players have an incentive to maintain a tough stance; however, if neither player refuses to back down, the worst outcome for both players occurs.

monopolistic competition, p. 252
product differentiation, p. 253
oligopoly, p. 257
mutual interdependence, p. 257
cartel, p. 258

kinked demand curve, p. 259
game theory, p. 261
simultaneous-move games, p. 262
sequential-move games, p. 263
Nash equilibrium, p. 265

dominant strategy, p. 265
Prisoner's Dilemma, p. 267
trigger strategies, p. 270
tit-for-tat strategies, p. 270

QUESTIONS AND PROBLEMS

Check Your Understanding

1. How do monopolistically competitive markets differ from perfectly competitive markets? If monopolistically competitive firms are making economic profits in the short run, what happens in the long run?

2. How do monopolistically competitive firms exhibit market power? In what ways can a firm increase market power?

3. Explain what strategic interdependence means and how it applies to oligopoly markets.

4. Why is it difficult for cartels to maintain high prices effectively over the longer term?

5. Why would the use of repeated games make overcoming the Prisoner's Dilemma easier compared to a game that is played only once?

6. What is the difference between a tit-for-tat trigger strategy and a grim trigger strategy?

Apply the Concepts

7. "Monopolistic competition has a little of monopoly and a little of competition, hence its name." Do you agree? Why or why not?

8. Many product markets exhibit characteristics of both monopolistic competition and oligopoly, such as video game consoles and movie theater chains. What characteristics in each of these markets make it more monopolistically competitive? Which characteristics make it more like an oligopoly?

9. In both perfectly competitive and monopolistically competitive markets, firms earn normal profits in the long run. What enables oligopoly firms to have the opportunity to earn economic profits in the long run?

10. Poker players are known to *bluff* once in a while, meaning that they will make a large bet despite holding bad cards in an effort to pressure other players to *fold* their hands. Would bluffing be considered a dominant strategy to be used in poker?

11. Suppose you choose to pledge for your top choice of sorority or fraternity at your university. Despite the tiny odds of getting accepted into your top choice, that does not deter you from spending all of rush week focusing on your top choice. Would this strategy coincide with a best-response strategy in a Nash equilibrium?

12. Suppose two competing stores each announce a "low price guarantee," meaning that each store would match the prices of the other store if they were lower. Does providing this guarantee make it easier or more difficult to overcome the Prisoner's Dilemma facing the two firms?

In the News

13. In recent years, the expansion of the *Open Skies Agreement* has dramatically increased nonstop international flights to cities around the world. For example, U.S. airlines now fly nonstop to many cities in the Middle East, Africa, and China, providing a potential benefit to U.S. cities from the increased flow of foreign tourists and investors. However, an unexpected consequence of the agreement that resulted in a major dispute in 2015

is that foreign airlines also can fly direct to many U.S. cities, increasing competition against U.S. airlines. U.S. airlines alleged that foreign airlines, especially those from the Middle East, received government subsidies that allowed them to underprice U.S. airlines on competing routes. Discuss how the expansion of Open Skies affects the market structure and concentration of the airline industry. If the allegations of unfair competition are true, who is potentially hurt and who potentially benefits?

14. "Bank of America Faces Outrage over Debit Card Charge" was the headline in the *Washington Post* on September 30, 2011. Bank of America attempted to institute a new fee on debit card accounts by charging its debit card users $5 per month, in hopes that other banks would follow its lead. However, no other major bank did, and Bank of America was pummeled in the media and by customers who closed their accounts until Bank of America relented and dropped the new fee. Explain how Bank of America was attempting to overcome the Prisoner's Dilemma. Provide reasons why this attempt was unsuccessful.

Solving Problems

15. Suppose each member of a diamond cartel consisting of five producers agrees to sell 100 carats of diamonds a day. With 500 total carats being sold, the market price is $1,000/carat, and each firm earns $100,000. Now assume that one producer cheats by producing 110 carats, causing the market price for 510 total carats to drop to $980/carat. How does this action affect the revenues of the cheating firm and the noncheating firms? Suppose the four noncheating firms change course and all produce 110 carats, and the market price for 550 total carats drops to $850/carat. How much does each firm earn now? How important is loyalty to maintaining an effective cartel?

▰▰ WORK IT OUT ▰▰   ⮭ LaunchPad | interactive activity ▰▰

16. The following shows a pricing game between Allegiant and Delta. Each airline has a choice between offering a fare sale and not offering a fare sale. The resulting profits of each airline are provided, where the first number in each payoff box equals Allegiant's profit and the second number is Delta's profit.

		Delta			
		Fare sale		**No fare sale**	
Allegiant	Fare sale	80	500	200	800
	No fare sale	50	700	100	1200

a. Indicate the best-response strategy by Delta if:

   Allegiant chooses Fare sale: _____
   Allegiant chooses No fare sale: _____

b. Indicate the best-response strategy by Allegiant if:

   Delta chooses Fare sale: _____
   Delta chooses No fare sale: _____

c. Does either airline have a dominant strategy?

d. What is the Nash equilibrium of this game?

e. Does this game resemble a Prisoner's Dilemma? Explain why or why not.

＃ USING THE NUMBERS

17. According to By the Numbers, in terms of number of restaurants, what percentage of all restaurants among the top ten chains is a Subway, McDonald's, or a Starbucks? (*Hint:* First calculate the total number of Subways, McDonald's, and Starbucks combined and compare with the total restaurants among all top ten chains.)

18. According to By the Numbers, if the third and fourth largest wireless providers merged into one new company, would the combined company surpass the market share of either of the largest two firms prior to the merge?

Checkpoint: Monopolistic Competition 257

Although both hotels are located on Disney property, the Grand Floridian Resort is much closer to the theme parks, and is located on the Monorail for easy transportation throughout the park. Also, the Grand Floridian is an upscale hotel with many fine restaurants and shops, and offers luxurious room amenities. The All-Star Resort, on the other hand, caters to budget-conscious families that are willing to forgo some convenience and amenities in exchange for significant savings. Disney differentiates its hotels to cater to different groups of customers with varying willingness-to-pay. The result is a significant price difference between the two hotels.

Checkpoint: Oligopoly 260

A cartel functions best when its members adhere to the established quotas (which keep prices for drugs high) and also when no external competition exists (allowing the cartel to operate as if it were a monopoly). Competition from noncartel drug traffickers as well as cartel members exceeding their production quotas poses a threat to the cartel's existence, and hence cartels will often use violence to prevent those activities from occurring. When the drug trade is dominated by several large and powerful organizations, the actions of one organization have a significant effect on the others, an example of the mutual interdependence of firms in an oligopoly.

Checkpoint: Game Theory 267

This is a situation in which each player must develop a coordination strategy to achieve a Nash equilibrium (a connected call). No rule exists for coordination strategies. Instead, such strategies often are formed by experience. For example, the person who calls back might be the one who made the initial call, or the one who typically calls. Or, it might be the one who has more at stake in the call (such as a pesky friend asking to borrow money). With more experience, coordination strategies become easier to implement.

Checkpoint: Applications of Game Theory 273

This strategy might work in theory if everybody in the class is committed to it. Practically speaking, it's highly unlikely that everyone would stick to the agreement. For example, if you were someone destined to receive a C or a D, and you know that the A and B students promised not to study if you don't study, you would have a strong incentive to break your promise and study hard knowing that an A or a B is now within easier reach. At the same time, those destined for an A or a B might want to insure themselves against the plan by studying to secure the high grade. In the end, the cooperative agreement does not hold, because each player has a dominant strategy to study. This represents a Prisoner's Dilemma because, in the end, everyone studies and the scheme falls apart. One caveat: Unlike other Prisoner's Dilemma games that result in a true loss of resources, the extra time spent studying could be interpreted as a good outcome.

11 The Labor Market

Understanding how wages are determined in various labor markets

Digital Vision/Getty Images

Learning Objectives

11.1 Discuss the tradeoffs between work and leisure according to the substitution and income effects.

11.2 Explain why an individual labor supply curve is backward-bending.

11.3 Describe the factors that can change labor supply.

11.4 Describe the factors that can change labor demand.

11.5 Determine the competitive market equilibrium for labor.

11.6 Identify the ways in which economic discrimination can occur.

11.7 Describe the concept of segmented labor markets and how they affect wage levels.

11.8 Identify the federal laws and policies aimed at combating discrimination.

11.9 Describe the history, costs, and benefits of trade unions.

11.10 Discuss how the labor market has adapted to changing economic conditions over the last few decades.

Did you see where some baseball player just signed a contract for $50,000 a year just to play ball? It wouldn't surprise me if someday they'll be making more than the President.

QUOTE FROM 1955

Some professions, such as baseball, try to maintain their traditions, but salaries for Major League Baseball players certainly have not remained the same. The average professional athlete was not formerly a multimillionaire. In 1964 the average salary in Major League Baseball was a mere $14,000 (about $100,000 in current inflation-adjusted dollars), suggesting that professional athletes back then chose their careers for the love of the game rather than as a way to become rich. Today, the labor market for professional athletes has changed. With lucrative advertising revenue and broadcasting rights, professional sport has become big business. In 2015, companies spent $52.2 billion for advertising in all U.S. sports.

Because the labor market demand for athletes is so great, professional sports leagues need to pay much higher salaries than they did 50 years ago in order to encourage the very best athletes to seek a career in sports. In 2015 the average salary for a Major League Baseball player was $4.25 million, with the top earning player, Clayton Kershaw, earning $32.6 million. Even relatively unknown players, such as Chris Withrow and Luis Jimenez, made over $507,500, the minimum salary in Major League Baseball in 2015. The president of the United States makes $400,000 a year. Indeed, the prediction from 1955 came true . . . for every player in the major leagues!

This chapter and the next begin our analysis of input markets, also called factor markets. Behind the production of all goods and services are inputs: workers, machinery, and manufacturing plants. Input markets are similar to product markets in that both rely on demand and supply analysis. The main difference, however, is that in input markets, firms demand inputs, whereas in product markets, firms supply goods and services.

This chapter focuses on the analysis of labor markets. The first two sections look at competitive labor markets, where the participants—firms and employees—are price takers. We then take a closer look at several situations in which wages are not set by competitive markets: instances of economic discrimination, and the economic effects of labor unions.

Competitive labor markets are similar to competitive product markets. We make several key assumptions. First, we assume that firms operate in competitive industries with many buyers and sellers, a homogeneous product, and easy entry and exit. A second assumption of competitive labor markets is that workers are regarded as equally productive, such that firms have no preference for one employee over another. Inhumane as it sounds, labor is treated as a homogeneous commodity. Third, a competitive labor market assumes that information in the industry is widely available and accurate. Everyone knows what the going wage rate is; therefore, well-informed decisions about how much labor to supply are made by workers, and firms can wisely decide how many workers to hire.

A firm's demand for labor is a derived demand; it is derived from consumer demand for the firm's product and the productivity of labor. The labor supply, on the other hand, is determined by the individual preferences of potential workers for work or leisure. Like

BY THE NUMBERS

The Changing Economic Landscape on the Labor Force

The labor force is constantly changing as certain industries thrive, while others fade due to changes in consumer preferences and global competition. The ten fastest growing occupations are in the areas of health care, renewable energy, and transportation.

*Go to **LaunchPad** to use the latest data to recreate this graph.*

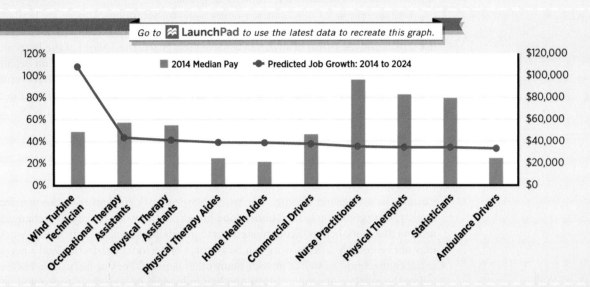

82.5% Average salary for women as a percent of men's salaries for the same occupation in 2015

45.8% Average cost of full-time employee benefits (paid vacation, sick leave, health insurance, retirement benefits, and employer tax contributions) as a percent of wages

Careers with flexible working hours ("flextime") increased in the 1980s and 1990s and have since leveled off. Today, 3 in 10 full-time workers in the United States have flexible work schedules.

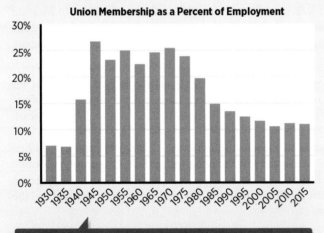

Union membership has declined since the 1970s. Recent state laws banning collective bargaining among public workers may further reduce union membership.

Globalization has altered the labor market as companies seek lower wages in other countries. Countries such as Bangladesh and Mexico have seen significant foreign investment.

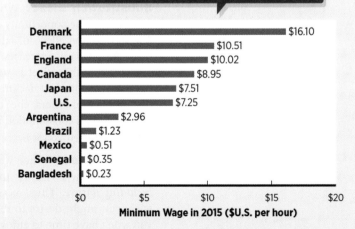

all competitive markets, supply and demand interact to determine equilibrium wages and employment.

Following the analysis of the competitive labor market, we then ask why some people make more than others. Although differences in occupation and skill levels play a dominant role in determining wages, how often are wage differences the result of discrimination against people of a certain race, ethnicity, or gender?

Another reason for differences in wages is the role of unions. Unions are legal associations of employees that bargain with employers over terms and conditions of work. Unions use strikes and the threat of strikes to achieve their goals. The Major League Baseball Players Association is a powerful union, which negotiates salaries and benefits on behalf of its members. Sometimes disputes between the players union and team owners have resulted in strikes. In 1994–1995, a long strike led to a very short baseball season. Without the union, today's baseball players might not all be making more than the president of the United States.

COMPETITIVE LABOR SUPPLY

Economists divide your activities into two categories: work and leisure. When you decide to work, you are giving up leisure, understood broadly as nonwork activity, in exchange for the income that work brings. Economists assume people prefer leisure activities to work. This may not be entirely true, as work can be a source of personal satisfaction and a network of social connections, as well as provide many other benefits. For our discussion, however, we follow the practice of economists in dividing individual or household time into just work and leisure. Note that the term *leisure* encompasses all activities that do not involve paid work, including caring for children, doing household chores, and activities that are truly leisurely.

Individual Labor Supply

supply of labor The amount of time an individual is willing to work at various wage rates.

The **supply of labor** represents the time an individual is willing to work—the labor the individual is willing to supply—at various wage rates. On a given day, the most a person can work is 24 hours, although clearly such a schedule could not be sustained for long, given that we all need rest and sleep. For high wages, you would probably be willing to work horrendous hours for a short time, whereas if wages were low enough, you might not be willing to work at all. Between these two extremes lies the normal supply of labor curve for most people.

Figure 1 shows a typical labor supply curve for individuals. This individual is willing to supply l_1 hours of work per day when the wage is W_1. What happens if the wage rate increases? Assume that wages increase to W_2: This individual now is willing to increase hours spent working from l_1 to l_2 (point b). But if the wage rate increases further to W_3, this individual reduces the hours spent working back to l_1 (point c). What determines how many hours a person is willing to work at each wage rate?

substitution effect Higher wages mean that the value of work has increased, and the opportunity costs of leisure are higher; hence, work is substituted in place of leisure.

Substitution Effect   When wages rise, people tend to substitute work in place of leisure because the opportunity cost of leisure grows. This is known as the **substitution effect.** The substitution effect for labor supply is always positive; it leads to more hours of work when the wage rate increases.

Note that this effect is similar to the substitution effect consumers experience when the price of a product declines. When the price of one product falls, consumers substitute that product for others. The substitution effect for consumer products, however, is negative (price falls and consumption rises), while it is always positive for labor (wages rise and the supply of labor increases).

Income Effect   When wages rise, if you continue to work the same hours as before, your income will rise. As income rises, you have an ability to purchase more goods, *including leisure.* Thus, as wages rise to a level high enough to live the lifestyle you wish, you might desire to reduce the hours you work (besides, if you work too much, you won't have time to enjoy spending the money you earned). This notion of working

FIGURE 1	INDIVIDUAL SUPPLY OF LABOR

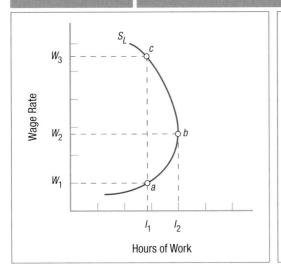

When wages are W_1, this individual will work l_1 hours, but when the wage rate rises to W_2, her willingness to work rises to l_2. Over these two wage rates, she is substituting work for leisure. Once the wage rises above W_2, the income effect begins to dominate, since she now has sufficient income that leisure is more important, and her labor supply curve is backward-bending.

less (and consuming more leisure) as wages rise is known as the **income effect.** The income effect on labor supply is normally negative—higher wages and income lead to fewer hours worked as individuals desire more leisure. This effect counteracts the substitution effect, which encourages individuals to work more as wages rise.

Both the substitution and income effects are present for all individuals, but at varying levels. The individual supply of labor, therefore, depends on which effect is stronger at each wage rate, and the individual labor supply curve is *backward-bending,* as shown in Figure 1.

When the labor supply curve is positively sloped, as it is below W_2 in Figure 1, the substitution effect is stronger than the income effect; income is more important than leisure at these wage levels; thus, higher wages lead to more hours worked. Conversely, when the supply of labor curve bends backward, as it does above W_2, the income effect overpowers the substitution effect. In this case, higher wages mean fewer hours worked.

Backward-bending labor supply curves have been observed empirically in developed and developing countries. Still, it takes rather high income levels before the income effect begins to overpower the substitution effect. People like to have incomes well beyond what is required to satisfy their basic needs before they select more leisure over work as wages rise.

income effect Higher wages mean that you can maintain the same standard of living by working fewer hours. The impact on labor supply is generally negative.

Market Labor Supply Curves

The labor supply for any occupation or industry is upward-sloping; higher wages for a job mean more inquiries and job applications. Thus, although an individual's labor supply curve may be backward-bending, market labor supply curves are normally positively sloped, as shown in Figure 2. Note that this is true for all other inputs to the production process, including raw materials such as copper, steel, and silicon, as well as for capital and land: Higher prices mean higher quantities supplied.

Changes in wage rates change the quantity of labor supplied. For example, increasing wages in one industry attract labor from other industries. This is a movement along the market labor supply curve, shown as a movement along S_0 from points d to e as wages (input prices) rise from W_1 to W_2.

Factors That Change Labor Supply

What factors will cause the entire market labor supply curve to shift from, say, S_0 to S_1 in Figure 2 so that L_2 workers are willing to work for a wage of W_1 (point f)? These include

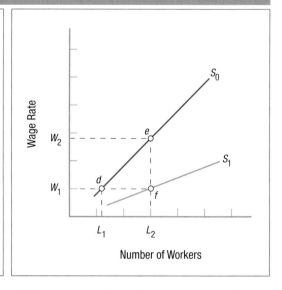

| FIGURE 2 | MARKET LABOR SUPPLY |

Market labor supply is positively related to the wage rate. Increasing wages in one industry attract labor from other industries (a movement from point *d* to point *e* as the wage rises from W_1 to W_2). In contrast, market labor supply curves *shift* in response to demographic changes, changes in the nonwage benefits of jobs, wages paid in other occupations, and nonwage income.

demographic changes, nonwage aspects of jobs, wages paid in other occupations, and nonwage income.

Demographic Changes Changes in population, immigration patterns, and labor force participation rates (the percentage of individuals in a group who enter the labor force) all change labor supplies by altering the number of qualified people available for work.

Over the past three decades, labor force participation rates among women have steadily risen, continually adding workers to the expanding U.S. labor force; dual-earner households are increasingly the norm. Today, both parents work in about 60% of all married-couple households with children.

Another demographic change is the increasing portion of population growth in the United States resulting from immigration (both legal and illegal). An estimated 88% of net population growth over the next five decades will result from immigrants and their U.S.-born descendants.[1] This will have a significant effect on the labor supply.

Finally, other demographic changes have shifted the labor supply curve by modifying the labor–leisure preferences among workers. Health improvements, for example, have lengthened the typical working life, thereby increasing the supply of labor.

Nonwage Aspects of Jobs Changes in the nonwage aspects of an occupation will similarly shift the supply of labor in that market. If employers can manage to increase the pleasantness, safety, or status of a job, labor supply will increase. Other nonmoney perks also help. The airline industry, for example, has greatly increased the number of people willing to work in mundane positions by allowing employees to fly anywhere free.

Wages in Alternative Jobs When worker skills in one industry are readily transferable to other jobs or industries, the wages paid in those other markets will affect wage rates and the labor supply in the first industry. For example, Web site designers and computer technicians are useful in all industries, and their wages in one industry affect all industries. Because at least some of the skills that all workers possess will benefit other employers, all labor markets have some influence over each other. Rising wages in growth industries will shrink the supply of labor available to firms in other industries.

Nonwage Income Changes in income from sources other than working (such as income from a trust) will change the supply of labor. As nonwage income rises, hours of work supplied declines. If you have enough income from nonwork sources, after all, the retirement urge will set in no matter what your age.

[1] Pew Research Center, "Modern Immigration Wave Brings 59 Million to U.S., Driving Population Growth and Change Through 2065," September 28, 2015.

The key thing to remember here is that market labor supply curves are normally positively sloped, even though an individual's labor supply curve may be backward-bending. In the next section, we put this together with the other blade of the scissors: the demand for labor in competitive labor markets.

CHECKPOINT

COMPETITIVE LABOR SUPPLY

- Competitive labor markets assume that firms operate in competitive product markets and purchase homogeneous labor, and that information is widely available and accurate.

- The supply of labor represents the time an individual is willing to work.

- The substitution effect occurs when wages rise, as people tend to substitute work in place of leisure because the opportunity cost of leisure is higher, or vice versa when wages fall.

- When wages rise and you continue to work the same number of hours, your income rises. When wages rise high enough, an income effect occurs in which additional income is given up for leisure, and the supply of labor curve for individuals is backward-bending.

- Industry or occupation labor supply curves are upward-sloping.

- The labor supply curve shifts with demographic changes, changes in the nonwage aspects of an occupation, changes in the wages of alternative jobs, and changes in nonwage income.

QUESTIONS: Assume that you take a job with flexible hours, but initially your salary is based on a 40-hour week. Your salary begins at $15 an hour, or $30,000 a year. Assuming your salary rises, at what salary (hourly wage) would you begin to work fewer than 40 hours a week (remember, the job permits flexible hours)? If your rich aunt dies and leaves you $500,000, would this alter the wage rate at which you cut your work hours? Would this wage rate change if you have children?

Answers to the Checkpoint questions can be found at the end of this chapter.

COMPETITIVE LABOR DEMAND

The competitive firm's **demand for labor** is derived from the demand for the firm's product and the productive capabilities of a unit of labor.

demand for labor Demand for labor is derived from the demand for the firm's product and the productivity of labor.

Marginal Revenue Product

Assume that a firm wants to hire an additional worker, and that worker is able to produce 15 units of the firm's product. This additional output a firm receives from employing an added unit of labor is the **marginal physical product of labor** (MPP_L), calculated as the change in output divided by the change in labor, or $\Delta Q \div \Delta L$. Further, assume that the product sells in a competitive market for $10 a unit, and labor is the only input cost (such as blackberry picking in Oregon). The last worker hired is therefore worth $150 to the firm ($15 \times \$10 = \$150$). The value of another worker to the firm is referred to as the **marginal revenue product** (MRP_L), and is equal to the marginal physical product of labor times marginal revenue:

$$MRP_L = MPP_L \times MR$$

marginal physical product of labor The additional output a firm receives from employing an added unit of labor ($MPP_L = \Delta Q \div \Delta L$).

marginal revenue product The value of another worker to the firm is equal to the marginal physical product of labor (MPP_L) times marginal revenue (MR).

If the cost of hiring this worker is $150 or less (assuming that a normal profit is included in the cost of labor), then the firm will hire this person. If the wage rate for labor exceeds $150, a competitive firm will not hire this marginal worker.

MRP_L differs from worker to worker. As we saw in a previous chapter, production is subject to diminishing marginal returns. In the example of blackberry picking, the first

TABLE 1	COMPETITIVE LABOR MARKET			
(1) L	(2) Q	(3) MPP_L	(4) MRP_L ($P = \$10$)	(5) W
0	0	—	—	—
1	7	7	$70	$100
2	15	8	$80	$100
3	25	10	$100	$100
4	40	15	$150	$100
5	54	14	$140	$100
6	65	11	$110	$100
7	75	10	$100	$100
8	84	9	$90	$100
9	90	6	$60	$100
10	95	5	$50	$100

blackberry picker takes the nearest low-hanging fruit. The next picker takes low-hanging fruit farther away. The third has to do a little more work to harvest the same amount of fruit. Because each additional worker is able to pick less fruit per day, the MRP_L of each additional worker will correspondingly fall. This decrease in MRP_L represents the same diminishing marginal returns concept introduced in the product market.

To see how this works in greater detail, look at Table 1. The production function here is similar to the one used earlier in the chapter on production. Column (1) is labor input (L), column (2) is total output (Q), and column (3) is the MPP_L.

In this example, the firm is operating in a competitive market; therefore, it can sell all the output it produces at the prevailing market price of $10. When a fourth worker is added, output is increased from 25 to 40, resulting in a marginal physical product of labor of 15 units. Multiplying 15 units times the marginal revenue—or price in this competitive market—of $10 per unit results in a marginal revenue product of $150.

value of the marginal product

The value of the marginal product of labor (VMP_L) is equal to marginal physical product of labor times price, or $MPP_L \times P$.

A related term to marginal revenue product is the **value of the marginal product,** defined as $VMP_L = MPP_L \times P$. Because competitive firms are price takers for whom marginal revenue is equal to the price of the product ($MR = P$), $VMP_L = MRP_L$ in the competitive case.

Column (4) contains the firm's MRP_L. Additional workers add this value to the firm. Thus, the marginal revenue product curve is the firm's demand for labor, which is graphed in Figure 3. Note how the marginal revenue product reaches a maximum at 4 workers, as shown in column (4) of the table and in the figure.

Competitive firms hire labor from competitive labor markets. Because each firm is too small to affect the larger market, it can hire all the labor it wants at the market-determined wage.

Table 1 and Figure 3 assume that the going wage for labor (W) is $100. For our firm, this results in 7 workers being hired at $100 (point e), because this is the employment level at which $W = MRP_L$. Note that $W = MRP_L$ at 3 workers as well, but because the marginal revenue product is greater than the wage rate for workers 4 to 6, the firm would hire 7 workers, not 3, to maximize its gains. The value to the firm of hiring the seventh worker is just equal to what the firm must pay this worker. Profits are maximized for the competitive firm when workers are hired out to the point at which $MRP_L = W$.

However, if market wages were to fall to $90, the firm would hire an eighth worker to maximize profits, because with 8 employees, MRP_L is also equal to $90.

In a competitive labor market, the prevailing wage ($90 in this case) would be paid to each worker regardless of the actual MRP_L. Thus, firms maximize gains from hiring workers

FIGURE 3	THE COMPETITIVE FIRM'S DEMAND FOR LABOR

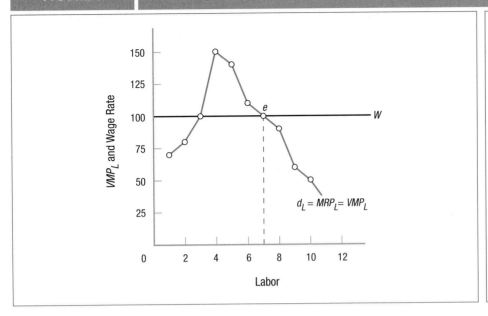

This figure reflects the data from columns (4) and (5) of Table 1. In this example, the firm is operating in a competitive market; therefore, it can sell all the output it produces at the prevailing market price. The value of the additional worker to the firm, the marginal revenue product (MRP_L), is equal to the marginal physical product of labor times marginal revenue (or price in this case). MRP_L is the competitive firm's demand for labor. If wages are equal to $100, the firm will hire 7 workers (point e).

in the labor market similarly to how consumers maximize consumer surplus when buying goods and services in the product market.

Factors That Change Labor Demand

The demand for labor is derived from product demand and labor productivity—how much people will pay for the product and how much each unit of labor can produce. It follows that changes in labor demand can arise from changes in either product demand or labor productivity. Because most production also requires other inputs, changes in the price of these other inputs also change the demand for labor.

Changes in Product Demand A decline in the demand for a firm's product will lead to lower market prices, reducing MRP_L, and vice versa. As MRP_L for all workers declines, labor demand will shift to the left. Anything that changes the price of the product in competitive markets will shift the firm's demand for labor.

Over the past 5 years, the movie industry has changed as people now primarily download movies directly to their tablets instead of purchasing or renting DVDs. This has decreased demand for movies on DVDs, and subsequently led to a reduction in prices. As a result, labor demand by DVD movie manufacturers has shifted to the left.

Changes in Productivity Changes in worker productivity (usually increases) can come about from improving technology or because a firm uses more capital or land along with its workforce. For example, some supermarkets have introduced digital price tags on their store shelves, allowing prices to be changed remotely instead of having a store clerk physically replace each tag on the shelf as prices change. Such improvements in productivity raise MPP_L. The demand for the marginal worker rises, shifting the demand for labor to the right as firms are willing to pay higher wages. To be sure, the number of workers hired may fall due to digitalization, but the workers programming the price codes, as in any capital-intensive industry, are generally more highly skilled and hence earn higher wages.

Changes in the Prices of Other Inputs Changes in input prices can affect the demand for labor through their effect on capital prices. For example, rising steel and glass

Digital price tags, such as the one found in this European supermarket, make workers more productive.

prices can dramatically raise the costs of equipment such that firms are unable to replace aging equipment. Without the ability to afford the rising costs of new capital equipment, firms are forced to use more labor in place of capital, thus increasing the demand for labor. Relative costs of capital and labor will therefore affect the capital and labor mix firms choose for their production.

At this point, we know that more labor will be hired when wages fall, but how much more? The answer depends on the elasticity of demand for labor.

Elasticity of Demand for Labor

elasticity of demand for labor The percentage change in the quantity of labor demanded divided by the percentage change in the wage rate.

The **elasticity of demand for labor** (E_L) is the percentage change in the quantity of labor demanded (Q_L) divided by the percentage change in the wage rate (W). This elasticity is found the same way we calculated the price elasticity of demand for products, except that the wage rate instead of the price of the product is used in the denominator.

$$E_L = \frac{\%\Delta Q_L}{\%\Delta W}$$

The elasticity of demand for labor measures how responsive the quantity of labor demanded is to changes in wages. An inelastic demand for labor is one in which the absolute value of the elasticity is less than 1. Conversely, an elastic curve's computed elasticity is greater than 1.

The time firms have to adjust to changing wages will affect elasticity. In the short run, when labor is the only truly variable factor of production, elasticity of demand for labor is more inelastic. In the long run, when all production factors can be adjusted, elasticity of demand for labor tends to be more elastic.

Factors That Affect the Elasticity of Demand for Labor

Although time affects elasticity, three other factors also affect the elasticity of demand for labor: elasticity of product demand, ease of substituting other inputs, and labor's share of the production costs. Let's briefly consider each of these.

Elasticity of Demand for the Product The more price elastic the demand for a product, the greater the elasticity of demand for labor. Higher wages result in higher product prices, and the more easily consumers can substitute away from the firm's product, the greater the number of workers who will become unemployed. An elastic demand for labor means that employment is more responsive to wage rates. The opposite is true for products with inelastic demands.

Ease of Input Substitutability The more difficult it is to substitute capital for labor, the more inelastic the demand for labor will be. At this point, computers cannot yet substitute for pilots in commercial airplanes, which results in an inelastic demand for pilots. As a result, pilots have been able to secure high wages from airlines. The easier it is to substitute capital for labor, the less bargaining power workers have, and labor demand tends to be more elastic.

Labor's Share of Total Production Costs The share of total costs associated with labor is another factor determining the elasticity of demand for labor. If labor's share of total costs is small, the demand for labor will tend to be rather inelastic. In the example of airline pilots, the percentage of costs going to pilot wages is small, perhaps 10%. Thus, a large increase in pilot wages would have a relatively small effect on ticket prices and demand, resulting in little change in demand for pilot labor. The opposite is true when labor's share of costs is large.

Competitive Labor Market Equilibrium

Generalized market equilibrium in competitive labor markets requires that we take into account the industry supply and demand for labor. The market supply for labor (S_L) is the horizontal sum of the individual labor supply curves in the market.

The market demand for labor, however, is not simply a summation of the demand for labor by all the firms in the market. When wages fall, for instance, this affects all firms—all want to hire more labor and produce more output. This added production reduces market prices for their output and negatively affects the demand for labor. For our purposes, it is enough to be aware that market demands for labor are not the horizontal summation of individual firm demands.

Turning to Figure 4, we have put both sides of the market together. In panel A, the competitive labor market determines equilibrium wage ($100 per day) and employment (300 workers) based on market supply and demand. Individual firms, in light of their own situation, hire 6 workers at the point where this equilibrium wage is equal to marginal revenue product (MRP_L), point e in panel B. Much like the product markets we discussed in earlier chapters, the invisible hand of the marketplace sets wages and in the end determines employment.

To this point, we have assumed that labor markets are competitive and that firms are able to hire as many workers as they desire at the prevailing wage rate. This analysis of competitive labor markets goes a long way, but just as with product markets, it does not tell the whole story. We are going to look at two familiar cases in which the competitive model is clearly not the case. The first case is economic discrimination in the labor market in which the personal preferences of employers, employees, or consumers cause some workers to be preferred over others, creating wage differentials. The second case involves unions, which restrict labor supply in certain industries to raise wages relative to nonunion industries. When wage differentials exist for workers performing the same tasks, we say that labor markets are imperfect. There are other, more technical instances of imperfect labor markets—we hold these until the Appendix.

FIGURE 4	COMPETITIVE LABOR MARKETS

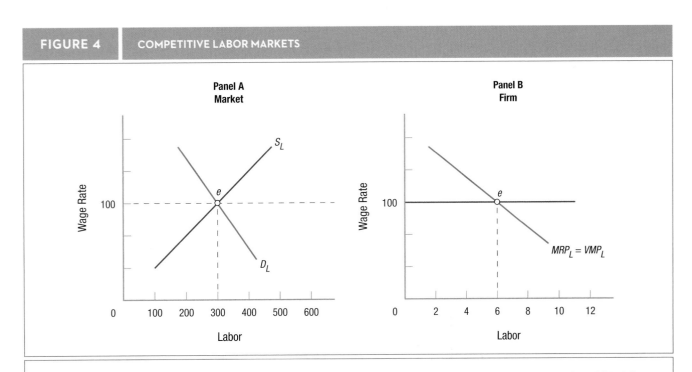

In panel A, the competitive labor market determines equilibrium wages ($100 per day) and employment (300 workers). Individual firms hire 6 workers, where this equilibrium wage is equal to marginal revenue product (MRP_L), point e in panel B.

Life as a Sherpa: Risking One's Life in Exchange for Financial Security

Why do the Sherpa people of Nepal risk their lives performing hard manual labor for tourists at very meager pay?

A Sherpa in Nepal carries supplies for foreign mountaineers aiming to conquer the world's tallest peaks.

In the Himalayas, home to nine of the ten tallest mountains on the planet, mountaineers come from around the world to conquer one of the peaks that dot the landscape. Kathmandu, the capital of Nepal, is the starting point for many of these mountaineers who range from seasoned climbers seeking to conquer the tallest peak on every continent, to the "leisure" climber allured to the Himalayas in search of a life story. But behind the scenes of these great expeditions is an ethnic group critical to the mountaineering industry: Sherpas.

How essential are Sherpas to the existence of this industry?

Sherpas are a Nepalese ethnic group who for generations have served as porters, guides, and technical specialists to foreign climbers. Sherpas have lived in the Himalayas for centuries, developing an ability to handle high-altitude environments. For most humans, even surviving at Mount Everest's base camp at over 17,000 feet is a challenge without having to exert valuable energy carrying loads of equipment and supplies farther up the mountain, risking their lives in the process. Why do Sherpas endure such hardship for the sake of tourism?

The labor market for mountaineering support has high derived demand. Most climbers spend $50,000 or more on a 2-month expedition and require the services of several porters and guides. Although there is no shortage of Sherpas willing to work, the fact that the job requires an enormous amount of agility and risk limits the quantity of labor supplied. The equilibrium wage for a Sherpa is $2,000 to $3,000 per expedition. This may sound cheap by Western standards (especially for a job with a high fatality rate—would you risk your life for $3,000?), but by Nepalese standards, that amount of money can support a family for an entire year. Landing a job in an expedition is an opportunity that could mean life or death in a different sense for the Sherpa's family, which is why the mountaineering industry continues to thrive.

As long as wages can adjust for risks such as those Sherpas face every day, one person's nightmare job might be another person's dream job.

GO TO **LaunchPad** TO PRACTICE THE ECONOMIC CONCEPTS IN THIS STORY

CHECKPOINT

COMPETITIVE LABOR DEMAND

- The firm's demand for labor is a derived demand—derived from consumer demand for the product and the productivity of labor.
- Marginal revenue product is equal to the marginal physical product of labor times marginal revenue.
- The demand for labor is equal to the marginal revenue product of labor for competitive firms.
- The demand for labor curve will change if there is a change in the demand for the product, if there is a change in labor productivity, or if there is a change in the price of other inputs.
- The elasticity of demand for labor is equal to the percentage change in quantity of labor demanded divided by the percentage change in the wage rate.
- The elasticity of demand for labor will be *more* elastic the greater the elasticity of demand for the product, the easier it is to substitute other factors for labor, and the larger the share of total production costs attributed to labor.
- Market equilibrium occurs at the point at which the labor demand and supply curves intersect.

QUESTIONS: Individuals are different in terms of ability, attitude, and willingness to work. Given this fact, does it make sense to assume labor is homogeneous? Does this model better fit firms such as Walmart that hire 800+ employees at each store at roughly standardized wages than, say, firms such as Google, which look for highly skilled computer geeks?

Answers to the Checkpoint questions can be found at the end of this chapter.

ECONOMIC DISCRIMINATION

We have seen that all workers are paid the same wage in competitive labor markets. This is seen in real life in low-skilled industries (such as fast-food restaurants) in which workers earn close to the minimum wage, or even in some occupations that require high-skilled workers whose wages are determined by contract based on market conditions. For example, public elementary school teachers in a district might all earn a starting salary set by a county school board. However, in industries in which managers are given discretion to set the wages of their employees, different wages may be given to employees doing the same work. Although these wage differentials may be due to differences in training or work experience, some differentials may be due to economic discrimination.

Economic discrimination takes place whenever workers of equal ability and productivity are paid different wages or are otherwise discriminated against in the workplace because of their race, color, religion, gender, age, national origin, sexual orientation, or disability. This can mean that one group is paid lower wages than another for doing the same job, or that members of different groups are segregated into occupations that pay different wages.

The U.S. Bureau of Labor Statistics (BLS) measures wages for persons of various races and ethnicities as well as by gender in the labor force. Each year, it collects data on the gender wage gap, the salary that women make as a percentage of what men earn in the same occupation. The trend has represented a narrowing of the wage gap, indicating that gender discrimination has diminished over time. Less certain based on the data is whether discrimination based on race or ethnicity has seen similar improvements. Data from the BLS continue to show that African Americans and Latinos earn substantially less than Caucasians and Asians; however, these data are not separated by occupation. Thus, it is uncertain the extent to which these differences in earnings are due to discrimination as opposed to occupational choices.

Economic theories of discrimination generally take one of two approaches. The first, developed by Gary Becker, rests on the notion that bias is articulated in the *discriminatory tastes* of employers, workers, and consumers. The second approach, the *segmented markets approach,* maintains that labor markets are divided into segments based on race, gender, or some other category. This approach is often referred to as the *job crowding hypothesis,* or the *dual labor market hypothesis.*

economic discrimination When workers of equal ability are paid different wages or in any other way discriminated against because of race, color, religion, gender, age, national origin, sexual orientation, or disability.

Becker's Theory of Economic Discrimination

Gary Becker's main contribution to economics is that he vastly broadened the issues that economists study. This was no small feat. Before Becker's influence, economists focused almost exclusively on the production and exchange of material goods and services. One early example shows the difficulties Becker faced in broadening this focus.

In 1955 Becker was asked to speak at Harvard about his dissertation on the economics of discrimination. Becker noted that his audience was perplexed. "They thought I would discuss price discrimination"—that is, the analysis of why businesses charge

GARY BECKER (1930–2014)

NOBEL PRIZE

The 1992 winner of the Nobel Prize in Economic Sciences, Gary Becker, applied the theory of "rational choice" to areas of human behavior not ordinarily associated with economic analysis and research. He offered provocative insights on a broad array of subjects, including family relations, racial discrimination, and the criminal justice system.

Born in Pottsville, Pennsylvania, in 1930, Becker completed his undergraduate degree at Princeton before entering the University of Chicago, where he studied under economist Milton Friedman. In 1957 he published his dissertation *The Economics of Discrimination*, an analysis of the effects of racial prejudice on earnings and employment among minorities.

In 1981 he published his book *A Treatise on the Family.* According to his theory, rising wages led to changes in the family, including more women working outside the home instead of "specializing" in child care and housework. On questions of crime and punishment, Becker suggested that most criminals react in predictable ways to the costs and benefits of illegal activity; namely, that the probability of being caught and punished was a greater deterrent than the harsh nature of the punishment. On the question of race, Becker viewed discrimination as a "tax wedge" between social and private returns, concluding that prejudice tends to be economically detrimental to all parties concerned.

different prices for the same goods. "No one conceived that an economist would talk about race discrimination in those days."[2]

Published in 1957, *The Economics of Discrimination* was not warmly received by the profession. Not until the mid-1960s, when the civil rights movement gained momentum, did the book receive the recognition it deserved. Surprisingly enough, Becker challenged the conventional view that discrimination benefits the person who discriminates. Let's see why he thought the conventional wisdom was wrong.

Becker argued that employers who discriminate against women will lose market share and profit opportunities, both because they do not always hire the best employees available, and because they must pay mostly high-wage male employees. Nondiscriminating firms, in contrast, will have lower labor costs, having more women earning lower wages on the payroll. Nondiscriminating firms will attract the most productive managers and employees, many of whom will be women. Profits for the nondiscriminating firm should therefore be higher. Becker concluded that the cost of wage differentials and the pressures of the market-place should drive discrimination down to zero in the long run.

In practice, we know that wage discrimination still exists. According to the Bureau of Labor Statistics, women in 2015 earned 82.5% of what men earned in the same occupation. Why might competition fail to erase wage differentials? For one thing, the adjustment costs of firing unproductive workers, giving them severance pay, then recruiting and training new workers can be extremely high, especially considering the protections unions and the legal system offer workers. Second, women may be less mobile than men when it comes to work. They may be less willing to move to accommodate employer preferences, and thus be forced to accept lower-wage positions. Third, if women continue to choose occupations with more flexible career paths that do not heavily penalize extended absences from the labor market, wage differentials between men and women may always exist. Note, however, that such differentials could also be caused by discrimination that precedes labor market entry, as when social norms direct girls toward lower-wage occupations such as elementary education or social work.

Segmented Labor Markets

segmented labor markets Labor markets split into separate parts. This leads to different wages paid to different sectors even though both markets are highly competitive.

Economists who advocate **segmented labor market** theories argue that discrimination does not arise due to a lack of competitive labor markets, but rather because these markets, although competitive, are segmented into a variety of constituent parts. And these different parts, while interacting, are noncompeting sectors. Segmented labor market theories have been developed along several different lines.

- The *dual labor market hypothesis* splits the labor market into primary and secondary sectors. The primary market consists of jobs that offer high wages, good working conditions, job stability, and advancement opportunities, while jobs in the secondary market tend to have low wages and benefits, poor working conditions, high labor turnover, and little chance of advancement.

- The *job crowding hypothesis* breaks occupations into predominately male and female jobs. In 1922 Edgeworth recognized this problem when he wrote, "The pressure of male trade unions appears to be largely responsible for that crowding of women into a comparatively few occupations, which is universally recognized as a main factor in the depression of their wages."[3]

- The *insider–outsider theory* maintains that workers are segregated into those who belong to unions and those who are unemployed or are nonunion workers. Alternatively, economists have recognized that large firms use internal promotion and job security to inspire loyalty to the firm; however, such practices can also become an indirect method of segregating the labor market.

---

[2] Peter Passell, "New Nobel Laureate Takes Economics Far Afield," *The New York Times,* October 14, 1992, p. D1.
[3] F. Y. Edgeworth, "Equal Pay to Men and Women for Equal Work" (1922), p. 439, cited in Stephen Smith, *Labour Economics* (New York: Routledge), 1994, p. 102.

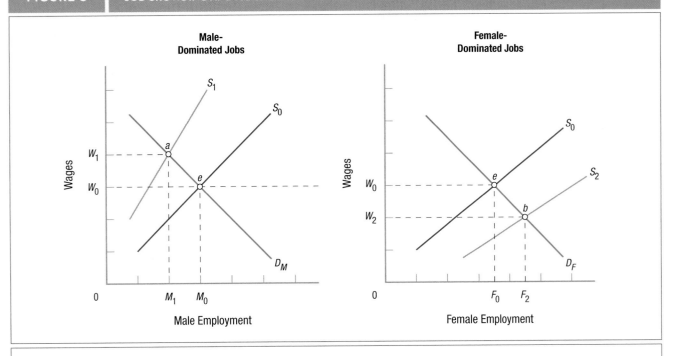

| FIGURE 5 | JOB CROWDING AND A DUAL LABOR MARKET |

Segregated markets can lead to significant wage differentials between men and women. Without discrimination, equilibrium wages will be W_0 for everyone, with total employment at $M_0 + F_0$. If, however, there is some form of discrimination in male-dominated jobs, the supply of labor to that segment will decline to S_1, wages will rise to W_1, and employment will fall to M_1 (point a). Those women who are excluded from jobs in this sector will have to move to available jobs in the female-dominated sector, thus increasing the labor supplied for these jobs to S_2, raising employment to F_2, but reducing wages to W_2 (point b). The result is a wage differential equal to $W_1 - W_2$.

These hypotheses all predict that separate job markets will emerge for different groups. Figure 5 shows how segregated markets can lead to significant wage differentials, such as those we see for men and women.

In a world without discrimination, equilibrium wages for everyone would be W_0, with total employment at $M_0 + F_0$. If some form of discrimination in male-dominated jobs is present, labor supply to that segment will decline to S_1, wages will rise to W_1, and hiring will fall to M_1 (point a). Those women who are excluded from jobs in this sector will have to move to jobs available in the female-dominated sector, thus increasing the supply of labor there to S_2, reducing wages to W_2, and increasing employment to F_2 (point b). The result is a wage differential equal to $W_1 - W_2$.

Notice that once such a wage differential is established, the firms in competitive markets have no real incentive to eliminate the gap. Men and women are both being paid their marginal revenue products; therefore, no profits are gained by substituting workers.

Wage differentials can arise for a variety of reasons. Some people may simply prefer one occupation to another. If such preferences have their roots in specific social groups, group-wide wage differentials can be expected to arise. Wages will vary between occupations, moreover, because of differences in their attractiveness, difficulty, riskiness, social status, and the human capital investments required. Still, lingering wage differentials today may be the result of past discriminatory practices that barred women from entering some occupations or professional schools.

Do wage differentials necessarily mean that discrimination exists in the market? Job crowding and wage differentials could just reflect different levels of human capital investment or different professional choices. Many women, for instance, may truly prefer occupations that are complementary to parenting. Further, female labor force participation is often interrupted when women take a break from working to have children. Therefore, jobs such

Traditional female-dominated and male-dominated professions are becoming less prevalent as gender discrimination and the gender wage gap continue to narrow.

as nursing, teaching, and administrative work may look attractive as women can leave their jobs, later returning or finding a new employer, with little loss in salary or benefits.

Public Policy to Combat Discrimination

For the first half of the last century, the inequities associated with various forms of discrimination were mostly accepted as a part of life in the United States. Gradually, however, a groundswell developed to end racial segregation and other forms of discrimination, culminating in passage of the Civil Rights Act in 1964. In what follows, we briefly outline the major acts and public policies that have been implemented with the goal of ending discrimination. Because of these policies, discrimination, wage differentials, and segmented labor markets have declined markedly over the past five decades.

The Equal Pay Act of 1963 The Equal Pay Act of 1963 amended the Fair Labor Standards Act of 1938. It requires that men and women receive equal pay for equal work. Equal work is defined as work performed under similar circumstances requiring equal effort, skill, and responsibility. Some argue that the Equal Pay Act was a hollow victory because occupational segregation forced women into specific occupations, causing them to earn less than men for essentially comparable work. Further, the law provided a limited time during which a worker must file a case against an employer for wage discrimination. This prevented many women from filing cases out of fear that they would lose their jobs.

In 2009 the Lily Ledbetter Fair Pay Act was signed into law, providing employees more flexibility to file cases asserting that they have been discriminated against with respect to pay. Specifically, it allowed the 180-day statute of limitations for filing a case to be reset with each discriminating paycheck received. Thus, a worker could file a case long after the discriminatory action began, as long as the worker had worked at the company within the last 180 days.

Civil Rights Act of 1964 Title VII of the Civil Rights Act of 1964 makes it unlawful to

refuse to hire or to discharge any individual, or otherwise to discriminate against any individual with respect to his [her] compensation, terms, conditions, or privileges of employment, because of such individual's race, color, religion, sex, or national origin.

To date, most of the litigation brought under this statute has focused on the meaning of the phrase *to discriminate*, requiring a plaintiff to show that an employment practice inflicts a "disparate" or unequal impact on members of a minority group, as compared to its impact on others. Once this has been demonstrated, the burden shifts to the defendant (the employer) to show that its employment practices are related to employee performance or are otherwise a matter of "business necessity." Plaintiffs may sue for a full range of remedies, including back pay, reinstatement, court costs, attorney's fees, and punitive damages.

Executive Order 11246—Affirmative Action In 1965 President Lyndon Johnson issued Executive Order 11246. A key provision of this order required that firms doing at least $50,000 in business with the federal government submit an affirmative action program that includes a detailed analysis of their labor force.

Affirmative action programs have been controversial from the outset. Critics see such programs as "enforced quotas," whereas supporters see them as a way of breaking down discriminatory hiring barriers. Further, affirmative action has extended to other selection criteria such as college admissions.

In the summer of 2003, the U.S. Supreme Court ruled in the University of Michigan case (*Gratz v. Bollinger*) that adding a large specific numerical adjustment for minority group status to university admission criteria was unacceptable. The Law School at Michigan, on the other hand, simply took race into account in a nuanced approach to improving diversity of the class. The Supreme Court found this approach acceptable (*Grutter v. Bollinger*).

Age, Disabilities, and Sexual Orientation Two other acts were designed to reduce discrimination based on age and physical or mental disabilities. The Age Discrimination in Employment Act of 1967 protects workers over age 40 from discrimination based on age. The Americans with Disabilities Act of 1990 prohibits discrimination against people with a physical or mental disability who could still perform a job with reasonable accommodation by an employer. What constitutes "reasonable accommodation" has been a point of contention in many recent court cases. Lastly, the proposed Employment Non-Discrimination Act would prohibit discrimination against employees on the basis of sexual orientation or gender identity by civilian, nonreligious employers with at least 15 employees.

 CHECKPOINT

ECONOMIC DISCRIMINATION

- Economic discrimination occurs whenever workers of equal ability and productivity are paid different wages or otherwise discriminated against because of their race, color, religion, gender, age, national origin, sexual orientation, or disability.

- Becker's analysis of discrimination assumed that employers had a taste for discrimination, and he showed that both parties were harmed by discrimination.

- Segmented labor markets assume that separate markets lead to wage differentials that represent discrimination.

- Public policy to eliminate discrimination has included the Equal Pay Act of 1963, Civil Rights Act of 1964, Executive Order 11246 (Affirmative Action), Age Discrimination in Employment Act of 1967, Americans with Disabilities Act of 1990, and the Lily Ledbetter Fair Pay Act of 2009.

QUESTION: Some types of labor discrimination are more likely to be eroded by market forces than others. Provide an example of a type of discrimination that is likely to dissipate through the labor market and one that is likely to persist over time.

Answers to the Checkpoint questions can be found at the end of this chapter.

LABOR UNIONS AND COLLECTIVE BARGAINING

Suppose Max, an engineer and project coordinator, has worked at a large construction company for eight years. He had been training new employees on various aspects of cost estimating and job specification, and he noticed that these new people were being hired at salaries approaching his own. He requested a raise several times, but was essentially ignored. Exasperated, he refused to go to work one day, informing his boss that he would not return without a raise. He did not quit; he simply staged a walkout and refused to return until given a raise. In other words, Max staged a one-man strike. He was out for two weeks before his supervisor called and asked him how much he wanted. They settled on a raise of over 20%.

This story is unique in that one-person strikes are rarely successful; more often they are career busters. In most instances, individual employees have little control over wages or job conditions, essentially being at the mercy of employers and the market. This is the primary reason that unions exist: Collective action is more powerful than the action of one individual. As individuals, we can easily be replaced (except in rare occasions as for Max in the story above). To replace an entire workforce, on the other hand, imposes serious costs to an employer.

This section looks at the role unions play in our economy, their history, and their effects on the labor market. We show how unions create wage differentials that work against the assumptions of the competitive labor market in which all workers earn the same wage. We will see that although unions have been successful in some industries, their influence has faded in other industries.

Types of Unions

Labor unions are legal associations of employees that bargain with employers over terms and conditions of work, including wages, benefits, and working conditions. They use strikes and threats of strikes, as well as other tactics, to try to achieve their goals.

Unions are usually defined by industry, or by craft or occupation. A *craft* union represents members of a specific craft or occupation, such as air traffic controllers (PATCO), truck drivers (Teamsters), and teachers (AFT). An *industrial* union represents all workers employed in a specific industry. Examples include auto workers (UAW) and public employees (AFSCME).

Benefits and Costs of Union Membership

Without a union, each individual employee would have to bargain with management over his or her own wages, benefits, and working conditions. Unions bring collective power to this bargaining arrangement. The source of this power is ultimately the willingness of the union to strike if no agreement is reached during negotiations. Collective bargaining often leads to a more equitable pay schedule than individual negotiation. It also provides workers with greater job security by protecting them against arbitrary or vindictive decisions by management.

Union membership, like everything else, has its price. First, union members must pay monthly dues. Then, if negotiations break down and a strike is called, wages are lost and the possibility exists, however remote, that management will refuse to settle with the union and replace the entire workforce. Finally, union workers must give up some individual flexibility because their work rules are more rigid.

Brief History of American Unionism

Labor unions date to the late 18th century in England. In the United States, public attitudes toward unions were highly unfavorable until the Great Depression. In the early part of the 20th century, employers could easily secure legal injunctions against union organization by arguing that unions behaved like monopolies, in violation of antitrust laws. Employers often required employees to sign enforceable *yellow dog contracts,* in which they agreed not to join a union as a condition of employment. As a result, unions represented only 7% of workers in 1930.

With the onset of the Great Depression, attitudes about collective bargaining changed. In 1932 Congress passed the Norris-LaGuardia Act, which outlawed yellow dog contracts and prohibited injunctions against union organizing. Then, in 1935, Congress enacted the Wagner Act, or the National Labor Relations Act (NLRA). It prohibited employers from firing employees for engaging in union activities and required employers to "bargain in good faith," among other rules. The act also established the National Labor Relations Board (NLRB) to oversee the process of union elections and certifications. These acts, along with improved attitudes toward unions, increased union membership dramatically until the late

1940s, when unions represented over one-quarter of American workers, mostly in large manufacturing industries.

The consequence of higher union participation is the increased likelihood of work stoppages, or strikes, which became more common. This resulted in some pushback, however, as many people believed unions had become too powerful. Because of this swing in public opinion, in 1947, Congress passed the Taft-Hartley Act, which prohibited unions from coercing or discriminating against workers who chose not to join the union, and required unions to bargain in good faith, just like employers. Specifically, the act prohibited **closed shops**, workplaces in which workers are required to be union members before being hired. It also placed restrictions on **union shops**, which required nonunion hires to join the union within a specified period, usually 30 days, and **agency shops**, in which employees are not required to join the union but must still pay union dues to compensate the union for its services. The Taft-Hartley Act essentially balanced the pro-labor aspects of the 1935 Wagner Act.

From the 1950s to the 1970s, union membership was steady. The right to collective bargaining was extended to federal workers in 1962, though public employees are not permitted to strike, but rather must submit to binding arbitration to resolve disputes. Since the 1970s, however, union membership has declined, partly due to political reasons but also due to changes in the economic landscape. Another aspect of the Taft-Hartley Act was to allow states to pass **right-to-work laws** that prohibit union shops. Today, about half

closed shop Workers must belong to the union before they can be hired.

union shop Nonunion hires must join the union within a specified period of time.

agency shop Employees are not required to join the union, but must pay dues to compensate the union for its services.

right-to-work laws Laws resulting from the Taft-Hartley Act that permitted states to outlaw union shops.

 ISSUE

The End of the Road for Pensions: Unions Fight to Preserve Promises Made to Retirees

Pensions were once one of the most valuable benefits of working for a company or the government. The longer an employee stays with a company or government agency, the greater the monthly pension one would expect to receive upon retirement (usually at age 55 or 65) for the rest of one's life. For employees who devoted decades of their life to a company, it was common to receive a monthly pension close to or even equal to what they earned while working. Unions played an important role in preserving pension plans for their members.

Times have changed. As the average life expectancy of retirees increased, so has the cost of funding pensions. Moreover, the cost of pensions is an unpredictable expense, because it depends on an unknown period of payments until the recipient passes away. Therefore, as union membership declined in the private sector, many companies switched from offering pension plans to defined contribution plans, such as a 401K in which a company deposits funds into an employee's retirement

account throughout his or her working career. The benefit of 401K plans to companies is that once an employee retires, they are no longer liable for any additional expense. The downside, as unions are quick to point out, is that this reduces the financial security of retirees because the money they save can run out.

Today, the fight over pensions largely deals with public sector employees, including government agency workers and public school teachers, who until recently still had the ability to choose generous state-sponsored pension plans. In the last economic recession, many state and local government budgets ran dry, making it difficult to meet their long-term pension obligations. For example, California's state pension program had a $130 billion shortfall as of 2015 to cover all future pension obligations. Some cities, such as Detroit and Stockton, California, even declared bankruptcy, forcing unions to fight especially hard to force those cities to honor their pen-

Cultura/Getty Images

sion commitments. Although courts have mostly sided with pension recipients, it hasn't prevented cities and states from using loopholes to reduce the size of pension payments.

The challenge faced by unions to protect the pension plans earned by workers who have devoted their lives to a company or the government will likely be difficult for another generation until all existing pension recipients' obligations are fulfilled. For those entering the workforce today, pensions are a relic of a past era. Workers today must proactively plan and save to ensure a comfortable retirement.

The International Brotherhood of Teamsters, founded
in 1903, is one of the oldest and largest labor unions
in the United States. Its
most famous leader, Jimmy
Hoffa, served as president
of the Teamsters from
1958 to 1971.

of U.S. states have right-to-work laws in place, and some
states have passed even tougher legislation to ban collective bargaining for public employees. But equally as important as the changes in labor laws is the fact that the
service sector, which does not have a strong history of
unionism, has expanded while manufacturing has fallen.
As a result, union membership represents less than 10%
of workers today and continues to shrink.

Union Versus Nonunion Wage Differentials

Why join a union? The primary benefit to unionization
should be higher wages, given the union's collective bargaining power. The general theoretical argument for union–
nonunion wage differentials is illustrated in Figure 6.

This figure shows how unions are able to increase the wages in their sectors by restricting entry into union jobs. The markets for both unionized and nonunion labor begin
at equilibrium, at point e in both panels of Figure 6. Thus, union and nonunion wages are
initially equal, at W_0. If the union successfully restricts supply to S_1 in panel A, union wages will rise to W_1, but employment will fall to L_1 (point a). The remaining workers, however, have no choice but to move over to the nonunion sector represented in panel B, thus
shifting its supply to S_2. Equilibrium in the nonunion sector moves to point b, where more
workers (L_2) are employed at lower wages (W_2). The resulting wage differential, $W_1 - W_2$,
is caused by successful collective bargaining in the union sector. Notice that this analysis

FIGURE 6   UNION VERSUS NONUNION WAGE DIFFERENTIALS

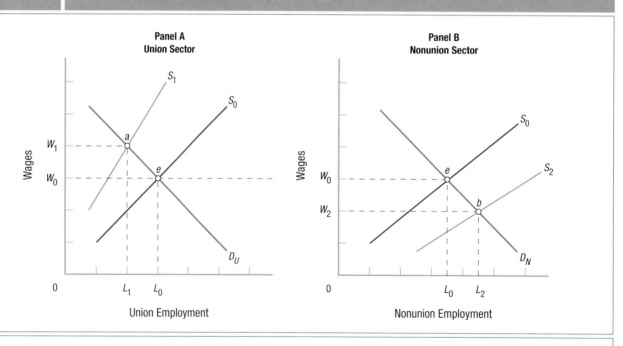

This figure illustrates the analysis of union–nonunion wage differentials. Unions increase wages in their sectors by restricting entry
into union jobs. Assuming the markets for unionized and nonunion-
ized jobs begin at equilibrium, at point e in both panels, union and
nonunion wages are initially W_0. If the union successfully restricts
supply to S_1 in panel A, union wages will rise to W_1, but employment will fall to L_1 (point a). Those workers released will have no
choice but to move to the nonunion sector represented in panel B,
thus increasing its supply to S_2. Equilibrium in the nonunion sector
thus moves to point b, where more workers (L_2) are employed at a
lower wage (W_2). The result is a wage differential equal to $W_1 - W_2$.

is substantially the same as that for discrimination in the segmented labor force described in Figure 5 earlier.

Union–nonunion wage differentials vary by the union, occupation, industry, and historical period. In general, average union wages are 10% to 20% higher than the average nonunion wage. Union wage effects are most pronounced among blue-collar workers and service employees. These differentials suggest that unionization may tend to reduce the inequities inherent in labor markets.

 CHECKPOINT

LABOR UNIONS AND COLLECTIVE BARGAINING

- Unions are typically organized around a craft or an industry.
- Unions and the managers of firms must bargain "in good faith."
- In a closed shop, only union members are hired. This was outlawed by the Taft-Hartley Act. In a union shop, nonunion workers can be hired, but they must join the union within a specified period. An agency shop permits both union and nonunion workers, but the nonunion workers must pay union dues.
- Union wage differentials are between 10% and 20% higher.

QUESTION: Union negotiations always seem to run up against a "strike deadline." Are there incentives for both sides to put off a settlement until the very last moment?

Answers to the Checkpoint questions can be found at the end of this chapter.

THE CHANGING WORLD OF WORK

Labor markets, like all other markets, change with time and the wishes of their participants. Over the last three decades, the entry of women into the labor force has been a major factor spurring economic growth. Over this same period, two-earner families increased so that today about 60% of all families with children are two-earner households.

These demographic changes have shifted the focus of labor politics from union bargaining to issues such as telecommuting, family leave policies, affirmative action, and the question of how much employers should pay for medical benefits. As Social Security begins to look more fragile and the baby boomers begin flooding the retirement ranks, employer retirement packages will undoubtedly receive even more attention.

Immigration, legal and illegal, has caught the attention of labor economists. The United States has relatively open borders. Some argue that we need new immigrants to do the work that most Americans are unwilling to do. Other economists suggest that, in the absence of such inflows, salaries in these low-skill occupations would be high enough to attract the needed labor. This tide of immigrants into lower-wage jobs, together with the growth of high-skilled, high-wage jobs and the rise in dual-earner households, has resulted in a significant change in the types of jobs available today.

Jobs of the Past Versus the Present

Ask your parents or grandparents about the job opportunities they had when they completed school and you're likely to receive a description much different from the opportunities you have today. Prior to the Internet revolution and the globalization of manufacturing, the United States produced many of its own goods, including clothing, electronics, and household goods. As a result, work in factory plants was plentiful, and an individual with a high school diploma could find a well-paying job that led to a comfortable standard of living. What has changed over the past 25 to 50 years?

First, a shift from manufacturing to service industries occurred. Rather than producing physical products, considerable growth in the health care, computer programming, transportation, telecommunications, and technology industries led to greater production of services than goods. Service industries generally require a higher level of training as well as interpersonal and communications skills that one generally acquires with greater education.

Second, significant growth in international trade and foreign direct investment, components of globalization, changed labor demand. In addition to trading goods between countries, which reduces the need to produce certain goods in our own country, many industries have outsourced labor-intensive jobs to other countries, where wages are much lower. At the same time, significant growth in high-skilled jobs in the United States has resulted from globalization, as the world demands better wireless connectivity, health care services, and technology goods, which the United States is a leader in providing.

Third, the Internet has transformed the manufacturing process. With the ability to manage production in real time, many companies have moved away from producing and storing goods and now can source goods quickly from a variety of companies. For example, Amazon.com is a company that sells just about everything one can think of through its Web site, yet it hardly produces anything that it sells, but rather relies on thousands of individual manufacturers to provide ordered goods on demand. Similarly, for a small manufacturer, there are now thousands of Internet sites through which it can sell its goods. These changes have made the labor needs of firms much more flexible. Firms need not always rely on their own production to fill their customers' orders, and thus do not require an abundance of labor on their payrolls.

Future Jobs in the U.S. Economy

The future growth of jobs in the United States will likely continue to focus on those requiring increasingly higher levels of education and training, which we refer to as human capital and will be discussed in the next chapter. Growing professions such as health care professionals, financial analysts, Internet security investigators, renewable energy specialists, telecommunications technicians, and others will continue to exert increasing pressure to achieve greater levels of education. Projections from the Bureau of Labor Statistics *Occupational Outlook Handbook* show that the industries that are expected to generate the most new jobs over the next 10 years are health care, scientific and technical services, and education.

chapter summary

Section 1

Competitive Labor Supply

11.1 **Work Versus Leisure:** The Relationship Between Wages and Hours Worked

- **Substitution effect:** Higher wages lead to more hours worked, and vice versa.
- **Income effect:** Higher wages lead to fewer hours worked, and vice versa.

11.2 A strong **income effect** means that a worker chooses to work fewer hours as wages increase to pursue other activities (such as studying). This leads to a backward-bending *individual* labor supply curve.

11.3 Factors That Change Labor Supply

- Demographic changes (population growth, immigration, labor force participation)
- Nonwage aspects of jobs
- Wages in alternative jobs
- Nonwage income

Market labor supply curves are upward-sloping and can shift due to the factors listed previously.

Stefanie Grewel/Corbis

Section 2 Competitive Labor Demand

A firm's demand for labor is a derived demand: It depends on the productivity of labor and the demand for the good or service workers produce.

11.4 Factors That Change Labor Demand

- Change in product demand (affecting MR)
- Changes in productivity (affecting MPP_L)
- Changes in prices of other inputs

In a competitive labor market, wages are determined by the intersection of labor supply and labor demand. For an individual firm, they take wages as given (firms are price takers) and hire workers until its MRP_L equals the wage.

11.5 Marginal Revenue Product $(MRP_L) = MPP_L \times MR$

- MPP_L is the marginal physical product.
- MR is the marginal revenue from the product.
- MRP_L is the value provided by the last worker.
- Firms hire workers until MRP_L = wage.

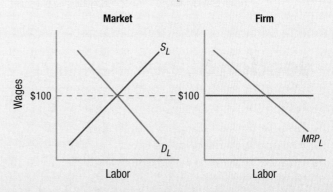

Section 3 Economic Discrimination

11.6 **Economic discrimination** occurs whenever workers of equal ability and productivity are paid different wages or otherwise discriminated against because of their:

- race or color
- religion
- gender
- age
- national origin
- sexual orientation
- disability

11.8 **Laws Banning Labor Discrimination**

- On gender: Equal Pay Act of 1963
- On race/ethnicity: Civil Rights Act of 1964
- On age: Age Discrimination in Employment Act of 1967
- On disabilities: Americans with Disabilities Act of 1990

11.7 **Firms That Discriminate Must Pay More for Labor**

- The supply of "preferred" workers decreases in a segmented market, increasing their wage.
- "Nonpreferred" workers enter a different market, increasing the labor supply and decreasing their wage.
- Firms that hire "nonpreferred" workers enjoy greater profits from a lower cost of labor.

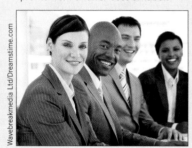

Employers choosing not to discriminate have access to a greater pool of talented labor.

Wavebreakmedia Ltd/Dreamstime.com

Section 4 Labor Unions and Collective Bargaining

11.9 **Labor unions** are legal associations of employees formed to bargain collectively with employers over the terms and conditions of employment. They use:

- strikes
- threats of strikes
- other tactics

Unions restrict labor supply, shifting the labor supply to the left, raising wages. Those not in the union are forced to find nonunion jobs, increasing the labor supply in those markets and lowering wages, creating a wage gap of $W_1 - W_2$.

Major Laws Affecting Unions in the United States

- Wagner Act (National Labor Relations Act): protected union workers and their rights
- Taft-Hartley Act: Placed rules on unions to prevent them from becoming too powerful

Union Employment   Nonunion Employment

Because pilots are not easily replaced and also are in high demand as airline travel increases, the pilots union remains very powerful today.

Getty Images News/Getty Images

Section 5 The Changing World of Work

11.10 Changes in the U.S. Labor Force

- Two-earner families: More women in labor force
- Immigration growth filling low-wage jobs
- Increase in flex-time workers: Workers who are able to set their own work hours

Significant Changes in Careers in the Past 50 Years

- Shift from manufacturing to service industries
- Significant growth in international trade and foreign direct investment
- The introduction of the Internet, which has transformed the manufacturing process

KEY CONCEPTS

supply of labor, p. 282
substitution effect, p. 282
income effect, p. 283
demand for labor, p. 285
marginal physical product of labor,
   p. 285

marginal revenue product, p. 285
value of the marginal product, p. 286
elasticity of demand for labor, p. 288
economic discrimination, p. 291
segmented labor markets, p. 292

closed shop, p. 297
union shop, p. 297
agency shop, p. 297
right-to-work laws, p. 297

QUESTIONS AND PROBLEMS

Check Your Understanding

1. Why are individual supply curves of labor potentially backward-bending, but market and industry supply curves are always positively sloped?

2. What factors will increase the demand for labor?

3. When there is discrimination in the labor market, who loses? Why? Why is it harder to discriminate when both labor and product markets are competitive?

4. What are the important laws in place in the United States to prevent discrimination in the workplace based on race or gender?

5. How do unions exert their influence in the labor market?

6. What are some changes in the types of jobs available in the United States over the past 50 years and what are some trends for future labor employment?

Apply the Concepts

7. Prior to health care reform that made it illegal for insurance companies to deny health insurance to those with preexisting conditions such as heart problems, some employees felt locked into their jobs because their employer-provided health insurance was not transferable to other companies. This "job lock" phenomenon was especially severe when someone in a family had a preexisting condition that would otherwise prevent him or her from obtaining private health insurance at reasonable rates. What were the effects of this type of inflexibility on labor markets? What has the impact been given the health care reforms that eliminate the potential loss of insurance?

8. Why do college professors who usually spend five to seven years in graduate school and play such an important role in shaping our society make so much less than a Hollywood producer such as Jerry Bruckheimer, who is unknown to most people (he has produced over 45 films and a dozen TV shows)?

9. Why do we permit price discrimination with different ticket prices at movies based on age, or ladies' nights at bars (when women get in free or pay less for drinks), or insurance coverage, for which women sometimes pay more (health) or less (automobile), but we do not permit discrimination in wage rates?

10. Has globalization made it more difficult for unions to negotiate higher wages? Why or why not?

11. The airline pilots union has been very successful in negotiating six-figure salaries for pilots. The unions representing flight attendants have not been nearly as successful. What probably accounts for the difference?

12. Reality television has altered the labor market for entertainment over the past two decades. No longer does an aspiring actor or actress need to find an agent and wait years for an opportunity to audition for a specific role. Today, aspiring "TV stars" can freely audition (often by submitting a self-produced video online) at one of many auditions for reality shows such as *Big Brother, The Voice,* and *America's Got Talent.*

From the reality show's perspective, producers are constantly looking to cast new people each season. Using the tools of labor supply and demand, explain how reality television has changed the labor market for entertainers.

In the News

13. The rise of terrorist attacks around the world has intensified the debate on immigration, with some legislators eager to pass laws making it harder for foreign citizens to work or study in this country. Many of these would-be immigrants are high-skilled workers who have studied math, science, and technology, subjects that contribute significantly to economic growth and higher wages for all citizens. Using the tools of labor supply and demand, evaluate the effects of a tighter immigration policy on the labor market and on the overall economy.

14. A commonly cited statistic from the U.S. Bureau of Labor Statistics is that women earn between 77% and 82% of what men earn for full-time work, which subsequently leads some to conclude that gender discrimination is the cause of this wage gap. However, most economists acknowledge that not all of this wage gap can be attributed to gender discrimination. Some studies have estimated that over half of the wage gap is explained by occupational choices, experience levels, and the amount of leave time taken. Briefly discuss how these three factors might cause women to earn less than men.

Solving Problems

15. Rocco's Studio offers lessons in Latin dance styles for $50 per session. Currently, Rocco has three dance instructors who were able to teach a total of 40 classes last week. This week, he hired a fourth dance instructor specializing in samba, and the four instructors together gave a total of 52 sessions. What is the marginal revenue product of the fourth dance instructor?

WORK IT OUT ■■■ 🅜 LaunchPad | interactive activity

16. In the following table, suppose the price of output is $10 per unit. What are the marginal physical product and the marginal revenue product of the sixth worker? If the wage of each worker is $150, should the sixth worker be hired?

Number of Workers	Units of Output
1	50
2	110
3	170
4	220
5	250
6	270

USING THE NUMBERS

17. According to By the Numbers, during which eight-year period did the percentage of Americans with flexible work schedules increase the most?

18. According to By the Numbers, between which five-year period did union membership increase the most as a percentage of the labor force? Between which five-year period did union membership decrease the most?

Checkpoint: Competitive Labor Supply 285

Each person will have a different wage where his or her supply of labor curve bends backward. Getting a large inheritance will generate substantial nonwage income and typically lead to fewer hours worked. Having a family will probably raise the income required before you will cut your hours.

Checkpoint: Competitive Labor Demand 290

For many jobs, firms have standardized procedures that each employee follows. Therefore, the difference in productivity between individuals is relatively narrow. While homogeneous labor is a simplification, taking in everyone's difference would make analysis impractical. No, the model explains both since markets exist for each broad category of workers.

Checkpoint: Economic Discrimination 295

Discrimination in the workplace can be caused by preferences of employers, employees, or customers. If the discriminatory tastes are strictly due to employer preferences, then employers who discriminate will be forced to pay a higher wage for the "preferred" worker. Because employers who do not discriminate are able to hire an equally talented but less preferred worker at a lower wage, these employers will have a cost advantage in production. Over time, discriminating employers may need to reduce their discriminatory tastes or be forced out of business by lower-cost competitors. Therefore, market forces tend to dissipate the extent of discrimination.

If the discriminatory tastes lie with the employees or customers, however, firms may be less able to reduce labor discrimination. For example, if employees refuse to work with a certain type of worker, or if customers refuse to buy goods and services from a particular type of worker, hiring these workers may negatively affect the firm's profit. Therefore, firms may choose to maintain segmented markets because the higher cost of labor is needed to prevent a potentially larger loss of revenues if their employees or customers act on their discriminatory tastes by refusing to work for or buy from the firm.

Checkpoint: Labor Unions and Collective Bargaining 299

Both sides work hard to get the best bargain for their constituents. There are incentives to continue negotiations up to the last moment to obtain the best deal and to appear to be driving a hard bargain. Strikes involve costs, and both sides use the threat of imposing these costs as a bargaining chip.

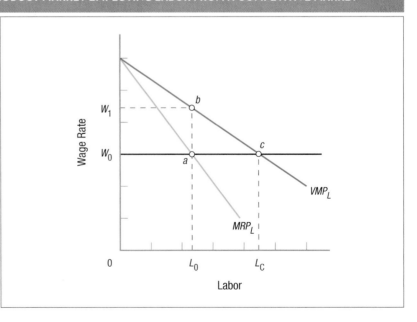

Learning Objectives

A11.1 Explain why market power allows a firm to benefit from the labor market.

A11.2 Define a monopsony and explain how it affects wages in the labor market.

A11.3 Explain why imperfect labor markets are less efficient than competitive input (labor) markets.

Appendix
Imperfect Labor Markets

In the world as we know it, markets are not perfectly competitive. Product markets and labor markets contain *monopolistic* and *oligopolistic* elements. In many product markets, a few firms control the bulk of market share. They may not be monopolies, but they do have some market power, through brand loyalty if nothing else.

Similarly, in most communities, there is only one government hiring firefighters and police officers. When the market contains only one buyer of a resource, economists refer to this lone buyer as a *monopsonist. Monopsony power,* meanwhile, is the control over input supply that the monopsonist enjoys. Before we look at the impact of **monopsony** on the labor market, let us first consider monopoly power in the product market.

monopsony A labor market with one employer.

Monopoly Power in Product Markets

As we know, firms that enjoy monopoly power in product markets are price makers, not price takers. Because $P > MR$, it follows that $VMP_L > MRP_L$. Figure APX-1 shows why. The firm depicted has monopoly power in the product market, but buys inputs in a competitive environment.

As Figure APX-1 shows, a competitive firm would equate the wage and the value of the marginal product (VMP_L), hiring L_C workers and paying the going wage of W_0 (point c). The firm with monopoly power, however, will equate the wage and marginal revenue product (MRP_L), thus hiring L_0 workers, though again paying the prevailing wage W_0 (point a). Therefore, although both firms hire workers at the same wage, the firm with monopoly power hires fewer workers.

FIGURE APX-1 | **MONOPOLY FIRM IN PRODUCT MARKET EMPLOYING LABOR FROM A COMPETITIVE MARKET**

Firms with monopoly power in product markets are price makers. Because $P > MR$, it follows that $VMP_L > MRP_L$. A competitive firm would equate wages and value of the marginal product (VMP_L), hiring L_C workers and paying the going wage of W_0 (point c). A firm with monopoly power, however, will equate wages and marginal revenue product (MRP_L), thus hiring L_0 workers, although again paying the prevailing wage W_0 (point a). Hence, although both firms hire workers at the same wage, the firm with monopoly power hires fewer workers. Also, the value of the marginal product (VMP_L) of workers in the monopolistic firm is much higher than what they are paid; their value to the firm is W_1 (point b), although they are only paid W_0 (point a). This difference is called monopolistic exploitation of labor.

This means that the value of the marginal product (VMP_L) of workers in the monopolistic firm is much higher than what they are paid. Their value to the firm (point b) is W_1, even though they are only paid W_0. This difference is referred to as **monopolistic exploitation of labor.** The term is loaded, but what economists mean by it is that workers get paid less than the value of their marginal product when working for a monopolist. This is, as you might expect, a source of monopoly profits.

Monopsony

A monopsony is a market with one buyer or employer. The United States Postal Service, for instance, is the sole employer of mail carriers in this country, just as the armed forces are the only employers of military personnel. Single-employer towns once dotted the American landscape, and some occupations still face monopsony power regularly. Nurses and teachers, for example, often have only a few hospitals or local school districts for which they can work.

Because a monopsonist is the only buyer of some input, it will face a positively sloped supply curve for that input, such as supply curve S_L in Figure APX-2. This firm could hire 14 workers for $10 (point a), or it could increase wages to $11 and hire 15 workers (point b). Because the supply of labor is no longer flat, however, as it was in the competitive market, adding one more worker will cost the firm more than the new worker's higher wage. But just how much more?

The **marginal factor cost** (MFC) is the added cost associated with hiring 1 more unit of labor. In Figure APX-2, assume that 14 workers earn $10 an hour (point a), and hiring the 15th worker requires paying $11 an hour (point b). Assume that you decide to go ahead and hire a 15th worker. When you employed 14 workers, total hourly wages were $140 ($10 × 14). But when 15 workers are employed at $11 an hour, all workers must be paid the higher hourly wage, and thus the total wage bill rises to $165 ($11 × 15). The total wage bill has risen by $25 an hour, not just the $11 hourly wage the 15th worker demanded. The marginal factor cost of hiring the 15th worker, in other words, is $25 per hour. This is shown as point c. Because the supply of labor curve is positively sloped, the MFC curve will always lie above the S_L curve.

How does being a monopsonist in the labor market affect the hiring of a firm that is competitive in the product market? The monopsonist shown in Figure APX-3 is a competitor in the product market and has a demand for labor equal to its VMP_L. This firm faces the supply of labor, S_L. It will hire at the level where $MFC = VMP_L$ (point a),

monopolistic exploitation of labor Occurs when workers are paid less than the value of their marginal product because the firm has monopoly power in the product market.

marginal factor cost The added cost associated with hiring 1 more unit of labor. For competitive firms, it is equal to the wage; but for monopsonists, it is higher than the new wage (W) because all existing workers must be paid this higher new wage, making $MFC > W$.

FIGURE APX-2	MARGINAL FACTOR COST

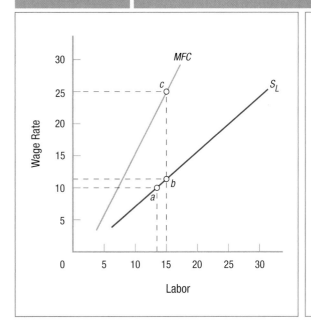

This monopsonistic firm faces a positively sloped supply curve, S_L. The firm could hire 14 workers for $10 an hour (point a), or it could increase wages to $11 an hour and hire 15 workers (point b). Since the supply curve is positively sloped, however, adding one more worker will cost the firm more than the cost of a new worker. To hire an added worker requires a higher wage, and all current employees also must be paid the higher wage. Therefore, the total wage bill rises by more than just the added wages of the last worker hired. The marginal factor cost curve reflects these rising costs.

FIGURE APX-3   COMPETITIVE FIRM IN THE PRODUCT MARKET THAT IS A MONOPSONIST IN THE INPUT MARKET

The monopsonist in this figure is a competitor in the product market and has a demand for labor equal to its VMP_L, while facing supply of labor, S_L. The firm will hire at the level where $MFC = VMP_L$ (point *a*), hiring L_0 workers at wage W_0 (point *b*). Note that these L_0 workers, although paid W_0, are worth W_1. This is called the monopsonistic exploitation of labor. Note also that the wages paid in this monopsony situation (W_0) are less than those paid under competitive conditions (W_c), and that monopsony employment (L_0) is lower than competitive employment (L_c).

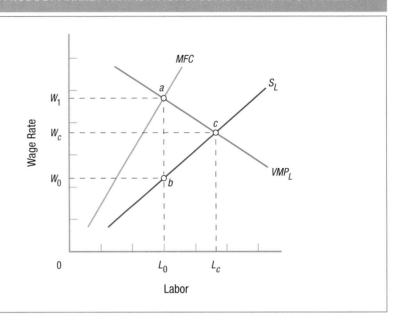

monopsonistic exploitation of labor Occurs when workers are paid less than the value of their marginal product because the firm is a monopsonist in the labor market.

thus hiring L_0 workers at wage W_0 (point *b*). Note that these L_0 workers, although paid W_0, are actually worth W_1. Economists refer to this disparity as the **monopsonistic exploitation of labor.** Again, the term is loaded, but to economists it describes a situation in which labor is paid less than the value of its marginal product.

Note that the wages paid in the monopsony situation (W_0) are less than those paid under competitive conditions (W_C), and that monopsony employment (L_0) is similarly lower than competitive hiring (L_C). As was the case with monopoly power, monopsony power leads to results that are less than ideal when compared to competitive markets.

To draw together what we have just discussed, Figure APX-4 portrays a firm with both monopoly and monopsony power. The firm's equilibrium hiring will occur at the point where $MFC = MRP_L$ (point *a*), and thus the firm will hire L_0 workers, although

FIGURE APX-4   MONOPOLIST FIRM IN THE PRODUCT MARKET THAT IS A MONOPSONIST IN THE INPUT MARKET

This firm has both monopoly and monopsony power. The firm's equilibrium hiring will be at the point at which $MFC = MRP_L$ (point *a*), and thus the firm will hire L_0 workers, although at wage W_0. Note that this is the lowest wage and employment level shown in the graph. If the firm only had monopsony power, it would hire L_1 workers (point *b*) at a wage of W_1. If the firm only had monopoly power, it would also hire L_1 workers for wage W_1 (point *c*). Both of these employment levels and wage rates are less than the competitive outcome of L_c and W_c (point *d*).

KARL MARX (1818–1883)

Working men of all countries unite!" With this exhortation, Karl Marx ended his seminal *Communist Manifesto*, neatly summing up both his philosophy and his view of the world.

Karl Marx was born in Germany in 1818, but spent much of his adult life in England. By the time of his death in 1883, Marx and Friedrich Engels had crafted the essence of communism—the last ideology to seriously challenge capitalism in the 20th century. In their two major works, *The Communist Manifesto* (1848) and *Das Kapital* (1867), Marx and Engels offered a severe critique of capitalism and extolled the virtues of proletariat rebellion.

To preserve their privileges, the ruling class had always striven to oppress the underclasses. Marx saw a struggle between the bourgeoisie (or property owners) and the proletariat (the working class). This exploitation—the essence of capitalism—not only kept the bourgeoisie in power, but it also alienated the proletariat from its own labor, which to Marx was the true essence of all economic value. The only prescription to cure the monopolistic and monopsonistic exploitation of labor was proletariat revolution.

at wage W_0. Note that this is the lowest wage and employment level shown in the graph. If the firm only had monopsony power, it would hire L_1 workers (point *b*) at a wage of W_1, which is higher than W_0. If the firm only had monopoly power, it would also hire L_1 workers for wage W_1 (point *c*). Both of these employment levels and wage rates are less than the competitive outcome of L_C and W_C (point *d*).

The key lesson to remember here is that competitive input (factor) markets are the most efficient, because inputs in these markets are paid precisely the value of their marginal products, and the highest employment results. This translates into the lowest prices for consumers at the highest output, assuming efficient production. Thus, just as competition is good for product markets, so too is it good for labor and other input markets.

✅ CHECKPOINT

IMPERFECT LABOR MARKETS

- When a firm is a monopolist in the product market and hires labor from competitive markets, the firm will hire labor at the point where the marginal revenue product is equal to the competitive wage.
- Monopolistic exploitation results because the monopolist pays less than the value of the marginal product of labor.
- Monopsony is a market with one employer. A monopsonist that sells its product in a competitive market hires labor at the point where the value of the marginal product is equal to the marginal factor cost.
- Monopsonistic exploitation occurs when the monopsonist pays labor less than the value of its marginal product.

QUESTIONS: Are public schools in rural areas a monopsony? Do they set wages in a way that is different from how wages are set in large urban areas?

Answers to the Checkpoint questions can be found at the end of this appendix.

monopsony, p. 306
monopolistic exploitation of
    labor, p. 307

marginal factor cost, p. 307

monopsonistic exploitation of
    labor, p. 308

APPENDIX SUMMARY

Imperfect Labor Markets

If wages are determined in a competitive market, a firm will hire labor until $MRP_L = W$. But if the firm enjoys some market power in the product market, marginal revenue product will be less than the value of the marginal product because $MR < P$. The resulting difference in wages is known as monopolistic exploitation of labor.

A monopsony is a market with a single buyer or employer. Marginal factor cost (MFC) is the added cost associated with hiring 1 more unit of labor. For the monopsonist, the MFC curve lies above the supply of labor curve because the firm must increase the wages of all workers to attract added labor. A monopsonist, which is a competitor in the product market, hires labor up to the point at which $VMP_L = MFC > W$. At this point, the value of labor's marginal product exceeds the wage rate; economists refer to this as monopsonistic exploitation of labor.

APPENDIX QUESTIONS AND PROBLEMS

1. This figure shows the supply of labor, marginal factor costs, and the demand for labor for a firm that is large enough that it is essentially a monopsonist in the community in which it operates. Assume that all workers are paid the same wage and that they work 2,000 hours per year (40 hours a week for 50 weeks).

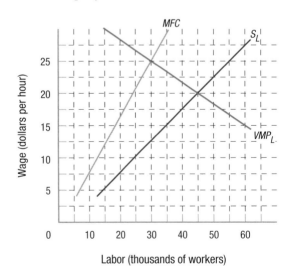

a. What is the total wage bill (total wages paid by the firm) for this monopsonistic firm?

b. If the firm was actually hiring from a competitive labor market, what would be the total wage bill for the firm?

c. What is the total value of the monopsonistic exploitation of labor by this firm?

d. Is the firm a competitor or a monopolist in the product market?

2. Would unions be more likely to organize successfully in highly competitive markets or in markets with monopsony power? Explain.

ANSWERS TO QUESTIONS IN APPENDIX CHECKPOINT

Checkpoint: Imperfect Labor Markets 309

Yes, they are monopsonists when it comes to hiring teachers. Generally, there is only one school district in rural areas. They probably act more like monopsonists when setting wages when compared to their urban counterparts, which have competition for teachers from other districts and private schools.

12 Land, Capital Markets, and Innovation

Understanding how input markets and innovation drive the production process

Richard Kail/Science Source

Learning Objectives

12.1 Describe the impact of the supply of land on markets.

12.2 Determine the present value of an investment.

12.3 Compute the rate of return of an investment.

12.4 Describe how businesses acquire financial capital.

12.5 Describe the relationship between education and earnings.

12.6 Understand how market equilibrium levels for human capital are determined.

12.7 Describe the impact of economic profits on entrepreneurs and markets.

12.8 Explain the role of innovation in improving standards of living.

Have you ever dreamed of venturing into space without having to undergo years of astronaut training? Richard Branson, the CEO of Virgin Group, wants to make that dream a reality with the launch of Virgin Galactic. Already an innovator in the aerospace industry, Branson's new space travel service will take six passengers at a time on a 3.5-hour suborbital flight 65 miles above Earth's surface, allowing passengers to experience several minutes of weightlessness before the spacecraft returns to Earth. How does a business like Virgin Galactic go about creating its service and what resources would it need?

In the previous chapter, we studied how businesses rely on labor markets to acquire the workers needed to produce their products. To build a technologically advanced product such as a space plane, much more than labor is needed. First, the firm must buy abundant amounts of capital inputs, such as aluminum, glass, and engines, in addition to the massive machinery required to put the plane together. Second, the firm must obtain the financial resources to fund the operation until the planes are built, placed into service, and generate revenue. Third, the firm must find labor that has the knowledge to build airplanes. For Virgin Galactic, it would seek workers who studied aerospace engineering in college or those who have acquired skills from previous jobs, such as serving in the Air Force. Last, the firm must have the overall vision to provide the market with what it wants—or what it thinks the market will want in the immediate future.

Although space travel might be just a dream for those unable to afford the expensive ride, examples of innovation abound in the aerospace industry. If you have recently flown on a commercial airliner, you may have noticed the technological innovations that are becoming more prevalent on airplanes. In some aircraft, you can now watch live TV, view movies on demand, and browse the Internet. Such features are just some of the amenities airlines are offering to make airline travel more enjoyable. Further, innovations in aircraft operation, such as lighter composite materials used in new aircraft, result in significant savings in fuel, the largest cost component of airlines. Developing a plane that provides customers with new amenities while cutting operating costs is a major goal of the aerospace industry.

The necessary inputs (also called factors) for the production of commercial spaceships and airplanes require firms to use other resource markets, such as those for land and capital, in addition to the labor market. Land markets are used to obtain actual land along with natural resources. Capital markets are used to obtain physical capital, financial capital, and human capital.

This chapter begins with an analysis of the land market, followed by a study of the three capital markets and the role that each plays in the economy. The chapter concludes with a discussion of entrepreneurship, the factor of production that brings together all physical inputs to generate profits and leads to innovation that increases economic growth.

Innovations in airplanes have made traveling more enjoyable. Many airlines offer economy class passengers a personal video screen, Internet access, USB charge port, and other amenities.

Siwabud Veerapaisarn/Shutterstock

Innovation Is the Cornerstone of Growth

Innovation is the use of ideas and knowledge to produce new goods and services that raise a country's standard of living. Human capital and financial capital are important drivers of innovation that lead to economic growth.

Go to **LaunchPad** *to use the latest data to recreate this graph.*

Human capital investment has grown over the past 40 years as the percent of high school graduates enrolling in college continues to increase. The percent of college graduates pursuing postgraduate degrees increased in the late 2000s but then fell in recent years as an improved economy encouraged more college graduates to seek jobs instead.

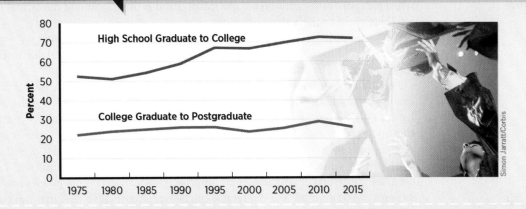

High School Graduate to College

College Graduate to Postgraduate

Simon Jarratt/Corbis

300,678 — Total number of patents granted in 2015 by the U.S. Patent and Trade Office

61,819 — Total number of patents granted in 1980 by the U.S. Patent and Trade Office

Venture capital firms provide financial capital to entrepreneurs to produce new products that lead to economic growth. The 2007–2009 recession dramatically reduced the amount of venture capital funds available.

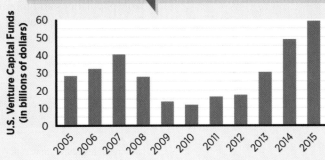

U.S. Venture Capital Funds (in billions of dollars): 2005, 2006, 2007, 2008, 2009, 2010, 2011, 2012, 2013, 2014, 2015

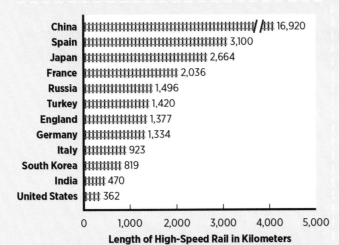

Country	Length of High-Speed Rail in Kilometers
China	16,920
Spain	3,100
Japan	2,664
France	2,036
Russia	1,496
Turkey	1,420
England	1,377
Germany	1,334
Italy	923
South Korea	819
India	470
United States	362

Length of High-Speed Rail in Kilometers

The Acela from Washington, D.C., to Boston is the only high-speed rail service currently in operation in the United States, with a top speed of 150 mph.

The development of high-speed rail travel (defined as rail travel over 150 mph) is an innovation that saves time and costs in transporting passengers and freight. As of January 2016, China led the world in total length (in kilometers) of high-speed rail in operation.

Corbis

LAND AND PHYSICAL CAPITAL

In the previous chapter, we discussed the importance of labor in the production process. But certainly more is required than just workers to run a business and produce products. A business also needs land and physical capital.

Land

rent The return to land as a factor of production. Sometimes called economic rent.

For economists, the term *land* includes both land in the usual sense and other natural resources that are inelastically supplied. **Rent,** sometimes called *economic rent,* is any return or income that flows to land as a factor of production. This is a different meaning from when we speak of the rent on an apartment. Land is unique among the factors of production because of its inelasticity of supply.

In some instances, the supply of land is perfectly inelastic. Finding an empty lot on which to build in San Francisco is virtually impossible. The land available is fixed by the terrain; it cannot be added to nor moved from one place to another.

Figure 1 shows how rent is determined when the available supply of land is fixed. In this example, the number of acres of usable land is fixed at L_0 (or supply S_0). If the demand for land is D_0, the economic rent will be r_0 (point *a*). When demand rises to D_1, rent increases to r_1 (point *b*). Notice that because the supply of land in this example is perfectly inelastic, rent depends entirely on demand. If demand were to fall, rent would fall as well.

In a strict sense, land is not perfectly fixed in supply. Land can be improved. Land that is arid, like the deserts of Arizona, can be improved through irrigation. Jungles can be cleared, swamps can be drained, and mountains can be terraced, making land that was once worthless productive.

Even more ambitious are cities that have reclaimed land in the ocean by extending out from the coastline or creating new islands using large amounts of sand. Balboa Island off Newport Beach, California, and Star Island off Miami Beach, Florida, are examples of artificially made islands. Much larger projects are seen in Asia, where land is limited due to large populations and mountainous terrain. Still, even if the supply of land is not perfectly inelastic, it is quite inelastic when compared to other production inputs.

The price of land varies based on many factors, such as its terrain, its view, but most importantly, its location. Why are land prices so much higher in Manhattan and San Francisco

FIGURE 1	**DETERMINATION OF RENT**

This figure shows how rent is determined when the available supply of land is fixed. The acres of usable land are fixed at L_0 (supply S_0). If the demand for land is D_0, the economic rent is r_0 (point *a*). When demand rises to D_1, rent increases to r_1 (point *b*). Notice that because the supply of land in this example is perfectly inelastic, rent depends entirely on demand. If demand were to fall, rent would fall as well.

Reclaimed land was used to build Hong Kong Disneyland in 2005 in an area that once was ocean. Although such methods have been used in coastal cities throughout the world, these expensive projects to increase the availability of land constitute a tiny portion of total land.

than in Iowa? Land prices are driven by demand from households and firms choosing to build a home or a business. Because the supply of land in any single location is fixed (or the least inflexible), changes in demand will cause large variations in land prices between more desirable and less desirable locations. But what determines a household or a firm's desire to locate in a particular place? The cost of land is an obvious factor, but other factors also influence a firm's potential profitability. For example, a business generally prefers to be close to its product market or its input suppliers.

Industrial agglomeration describes the geographical clusters of firms within an industry that choose to locate in close proximity with one another, such as Silicon Valley for the computer industry, Detroit for the auto industry, Dalton, Georgia, for the carpet industry, and Hollywood for the entertainment industry. By doing so, these firms benefit from external economies of scale. In a similar way, people of similar cultures sometimes choose to live near one another as well, leading to Chinatowns, Koreatowns, and Brazilian communities in various metropolitan areas throughout the country. Any time people choose a particular location for their home or business, demand for the land in that area increases, which will affect prices.

Physical Capital

Capital is the other important physical input in production. **Physical capital** includes all manufactured products that are used to produce goods and services. Examples of physical capital range from the massive cranes used to construct new skyscrapers to the espresso machine Starbucks uses to make your daily latte. Firms must determine what capital inputs are needed, and then calculate the value of adding additional capital to their production. When firms purchase capital inputs, it is called investment. The investment decisions by firms involve calculating the marginal benefits and costs of each capital input.

In the previous chapter, we introduced the concept of the marginal revenue product of labor (MRP_L) and showed how firms choose to add additional units of labor if the cost of labor, or wage (W), is less than the MRP_L. In the capital market, we study a similar concept called the marginal revenue product of capital (MRP_K). Like MRP_L, MRP_K is downward-sloping, showing that the returns a firm earns on its investments diminish as more capital is invested.

When firms choose which capital inputs in which to invest, they clearly would make their most productive investments first. For a fast-food burger joint, for example, a working

physical capital All manufactured products that are used to produce goods and services.

deep-fryer would be more valuable than an automatic soda dispenser. Firms continue to invest until the cost of capital is equal to the MRP_K.

The cost of capital is the price of an additional unit of capital. Because the price of actual capital inputs varies significantly, we simplify things by measuring the cost of capital by its opportunity cost, or interest rate (i). In other words, to buy another capital input, firms must either borrow money and pay interest, or use savings and forgo interest. Thus, the interest rate can be used to measure the cost of capital.

Financial resources to pay for capital inputs come from the savings of households and other firms. Suppliers of funds and the demanders of these funds interact through what is called the *loanable funds market.* As with competitive labor markets, in which the market determines wages and each individual firm determines how many workers to employ, the loanable funds market determines interest rates, leaving individual firms to calculate how much they should borrow.

Through their interactions in the loanable funds market, suppliers and demanders determine the interest rates to be charged for funds. Individual firms then evaluate their investment opportunities to determine their own investment levels. Figure 2 shows how this process works. The demand and supply of loanable funds are shown in panel A, where equilibrium interest rates equal i_0. Note that the demand for loanable funds looks just like a normal demand curve. Its downward slope shows that, as the price of funds declines—as interest rates go down—the quantity of funds demanded rises. The supply of funds is positively sloped because individuals will be willing to supply more funds to the market when their price (interest rate) is higher.

Once the market has determined an equilibrium rate of interest, an individual firm like the one shown in panel B will take this rate of interest, or cost of capital, and determine how much to invest.

This admittedly simplifies the investment process, but it is a good general model of investment decisions. Next, we turn to two more precise ways in which investment is determined, the present value approach and the rate of return approach.

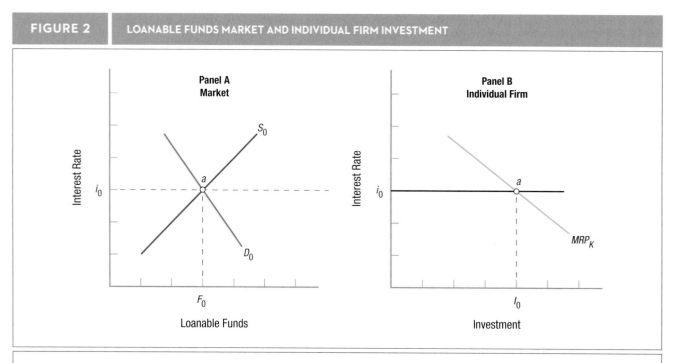

FIGURE 2   LOANABLE FUNDS MARKET AND INDIVIDUAL FIRM INVESTMENT

Panel A shows the market demand and supply of loanable funds, with equilibrium interest rates equal to i_0. Individual firms such as the one shown in panel B will take this rate of interest, or cost of capital, and determine how much to invest. Firms make their best investments first, and then continue investing (to I_0) until the cost of capital (i_0) is equal to the MRP_K.

Present Value Approach

When a firm considers upgrading its information system or purchasing a new piece of equipment, a building, or a manufacturing plant, it must evaluate the returns it can expect over time. Firms invest money today, but earn returns over years. To compare investments having different income streams and different levels of required investment, firms look at the *net* **present value** of the investment.

The sum of $100 *a year from now* is worth *less* than $100 *today*. This is illustrated by the fact that you could put less than $100 in the bank today, earn interest on this money over the next year, and still end up with $100 at year's end. Yet, exactly how much less than $100 would you be willing to give up today for $100 received a year from today? To answer this question, let us begin by looking at a simple form of financial assets, annuities.

An annuity is a financial instrument that pays the bearer a certain dollar amount in perpetuity, or generally for the life of the annuity holder. Assume that the market rate of interest is 5%, and you are offered an annuity that pays you or the holder of the annuity $1,000 a year indefinitely. How much would you be willing to pay for this annuity? If you want to follow the market in earning 5% a year, then the question you must ask is this: On what amount of money does $1,000 a year in income represent a 5% return? The answer is found through the formula:

$$PV = X/i$$

where PV is the present value of the investment (what you are willing to pay for the annuity today), X is the annual income ($1,000 in this case), and i is the market interest rate. In this case, you would be willing to pay $20,000 for this annuity, since $20,000 = $1,000/0.05. We have thus reduced an infinite stream of income to the finite amount you would pay today. You would pay $20,000, and the annuity would give you $1,000 a year, for an annual return on your investment of 5%.

What happens to the value of this annuity if the market interest rate should rise to 10%? You will still receive $1,000 a year, but if you want to sell the annuity to someone else, the buyer will only be willing to pay $10,000 for it ($10,000 = $1,000/0.10). Interest rates doubled, and the value of your annuity has been halved. Higher interest rates mean that income in future years is not worth as much today.

Valuing future income today by this process is known as *discounting*. This principle applies not only to annuities, but computing for years less than perpetuity requires a more complex formula. For example, assume that someone agrees to pay you $500 in two years as a gift upon your graduation, and that the going interest rate is 5%. What would you be willing to accept today instead of having to wait two years (assuming that you still will graduate)? The answer is found using the following formula:

$$PV = X/(1 + i)^n$$

Again, PV is the present value of the future payment, X is the future payment of $500, i is the interest rate (5%), and n is the number of years into the future before the payment is made. In this case, the calculations are

$$PV = \$500/(1 + 0.05)^2$$
$$= \$500/[(1.05)(1.05)]$$
$$= \$500/1.1025$$
$$= \$453.51$$

Hence, you would be willing to accept only $453.51 for this $500 payment coming two years in the future. Again, the higher the interest or discount rate, the lower the present value.

present value The value of an investment (future stream of income) today. The higher the discount rate, the lower the present value today, and vice versa.

When only one future payment is at stake, computing the present value of that payment is fairly simple. When future streams of income are involved, however, things get more complicated. We must compute the present value of each individual future payment. The general formula looks nearly the same as before:

$$PV = \Sigma X_n/(1 + i)^n$$

Here, the Greek letter Σ (sigma) stands for "sum of," and X_n is the individual payment received at year n. Assume, then, that you are going to receive $500, $800, and $1,200 over the next three years, and that the interest rate is still 5%. The present value of this income stream is therefore

$$
\begin{aligned}
PV &= \$500/(1.05)^1 + \$800/(1.05)^2 + \$1,200/(1.05)^3 \\
&= \$500/(1.05) + \$800/(1.1025) + \$1,200/(1.1576) \\
&= \$476.19 + \$725.62 + \$1,036.63 \\
&= \$2,238.44
\end{aligned}
$$

Given the complexity of such computations, economists often use computers to solve for present value, especially when the annual income stream is complicated. When the annual income is constant, tables of discount factors are also available. In any case, the point to note is that payments to be made in the future are worth a lower dollar amount today.

Firms often use present value analysis to determine if potential investments are worthwhile. Turning back to our chapter opener, suppose that an airline is considering installing broadband Internet access in all of its planes. Assume that the service will yield a stream of income (from charging users a fee) exceeding operating costs over a given period. The present value of this income is then compared to the cost of installing the Internet service. The service's *net present value* (NPV) is equal to the difference between the present value of the income stream and the cost of installing the service. If NPV is positive, the firm will invest; if it is negative, the firm will choose not to invest.

When interest rates are high, firms will find fewer investment opportunities where NPV is positive because the higher discount rate reduces the value of the income streams for investments. As interest rates fall, more investment is undertaken by firms.

Rate of Return Approach

An alternative approach to determining whether an investment is worthwhile involves computing the investment's rate of return. This rate of return is also known as a firm's *marginal efficiency of capital,* or its *internal* **rate of return.**

rate of return Uses the present value formula, but subtracts costs, then finds the interest rate (discount rate) at which this investment would break even.

Computing an investment's rate of return requires using essentially the same present value formula for income streams introduced previously with a slight modification: You have to explicitly consider the cost of capital in the calculation. This new formula is

$$PV = [\Sigma X_n/(1 + i)^n] - C$$

where C represents the cost of capital. The question we must ask is: At what rate of interest (i) will the investment just break even? You would compute the present value of the income streams, then subtract the cost of the capital investment, and finally find the rate of interest (i) where the present value equals zero. This discount rate is the rate of return on the investment.

Suppose you find a rare vintage car for sale at $20,000 that you believe will be worth $25,000 next year. If you buy this car with the intention of selling it next year, the rate of return that would allow your investment to break even would be calculated as

$$0 = [\$25,000/(1 + i)^1] - \$20,000$$

Solving for i yields a rate of return of 25%.

The calculated rate of return can be compared to the firm's required rate of return on investments to determine whether the investment is worthwhile. The firm might require, say, a 20% yield on all projects based on the opportunity cost of the investment, in which case investments yielding returns of less than 20% are deemed not worthwhile. Risk in investment projects is usually managed by adding a risk premium to the required rate of return for risky projects. This risk premium can vary by project type or with the business cycle. Some investments, such as drilling for oil or researching innovative new drugs, are risky and require high rates of return if they are to be undertaken.

 CHECKPOINT

LAND AND PHYSICAL CAPITAL

- Land includes both land and natural resources and is inelastically supplied. Returns on land are called rents (or economic rent).

- Because land is inelastically supplied, the rent on land is determined by demand.

- Firms weigh the benefits of investing in physical capital such as new buildings or machinery versus their costs.

- To compare investments with different investment streams over time, firms will use either the present value approach or the rate of return approach.

QUESTION: Suppose a good friend asks you to invest in some new equipment for her smoothie shop on campus in exchange for a share of the income earned at the end of the year. It will cost $10,000 to lease the new equipment for one year. What type of data and information would you be interested in estimating before you decide whether to pursue this investment?

Answers to the Checkpoint questions can be found at the end of this chapter.

FINANCIAL CAPITAL

To this point, we have introduced various physical inputs needed to produce a product, including labor, land, and physical capital. But how does a firm pay for these inputs? Most new businesses start out small, using personal savings or help from family to come up with the money to lease business space and rent or buy equipment. In fact, the founders of Apple, Steve Wozniak and Steve Jobs, started out in the Jobs family garage, and Mark Zuckerberg started Facebook out of his college dorm room. How does a relatively new business expand? Sometimes a business can expand using the profits earned and saved from its initial operation. But eventually, most if not all businesses require larger sources of **financial capital,** which is money required to purchase inputs for production. Firms use capital markets to acquire financial capital.

In the previous section, we described generally how firms calculate the cost of capital using the interest rate determined in the *loanable funds market*. Firms use the cost of capital to determine how many inputs to employ in their production process. But the loanable funds market is a general description of all sources of capital funding, whether that be borrowing from banks, or using more complex instruments such as bonds, stocks, or venture capital. In this section, we describe the specific mechanisms that firms can use to acquire financial capital to build, operate, and expand their businesses.

financial capital The money required by businesses to purchase inputs for production and to run their operations.

Banks and Borrowing

Let's start with the simplest means of acquiring financial capital other than self-financing. Suppose you wish to open a new sporting goods store and estimate that you will need $100,000 in financial capital. One way to obtain this money is through your local bank. Banks and other financial institutions offer small business loans (called commercial and

collateral An asset used to secure a loan; the asset can be sold if the borrower fails to repay a loan.

industrial loans) based on your credit history, the potential success of the business, and the ability to resell collateral used to secure the loan. **Collateral** is an asset, such as a home or building, that a bank can sell if a borrower is unable to repay a loan. If you buy a car and take out a loan to pay for it, the car is the collateral for the loan.

The ability to run a business with a bank loan is restricted to what the bank is willing to lend. This amount may not be enough to build a business and sustain its operation until a consistent cash flow is established to pay back the loan. Further, banks are more likely to address the inherent information problem between lenders and borrowers by scrutinizing the business plan and auditing files to ensure that a business is capable of paying back its loan. When bank borrowing is not feasible, the bond market may offer a more plentiful source of financial capital.

Bonds (Debt Capital)

Because bank loans are subject to credit restrictions and are usually limited in amount, it often is necessary for firms to borrow money by issuing bonds. A bond is an IOU certificate that promises to pay back a certain amount over time. The bond market offers firms an opportunity to acquire financial capital. The bond market is made up of firms that issue bonds and bondholders willing to invest by loaning money in exchange for an interest rate commensurate with the risk of that loan. Would you be willing to buy a bond issued by Intel or Coca-Cola? How about one issued by the Pep Boys—Manny, Moe, and Jack? This is an indication of what is meant by risk.

face value The value of a bond that is paid upon maturity. This value is fixed, and therefore not the same as the market value of a bond, which is influenced by changes in interest rates and risk.

There are three main components to a bond: its face value, its coupon rate, and its maturity date. The **face value** of a bond is the amount that must be repaid to the bondholder upon its maturity. A **coupon rate** is a periodic fixed payment made to a bondholder expressed as a percent of the face value; some bonds do not have coupon payments, and instead are repaid in a single payment (these bonds are called zero-coupon bonds or, more generally, discount bonds). A **maturity** date is the date when the face value of a bond must be paid to the bondholder. Maturity dates vary, and the length of time to maturity can range from a few months to up to 30 years. Some bonds even have no maturity dates (called perpetuity bonds).

coupon rate A periodic fixed payment to the bondholder measured as an annual percent of the bond's face value.

Many types of bonds exist, including corporate bonds, Treasury bonds, and municipal bonds, in addition to the many bond choices within each category. Corporate bonds are most likely to be used by firms to purchase productive inputs. In most cases, corporate bonds can be bought and resold in a bond market between investors. Because the price of a bond will vary based on the coupon rate, current market interest rates, and risk factors at the time of the transaction, a bond's yield is an important value for investors. The **yield** is the current annual return to a bond measured as the coupon payment as a percentage of the current price of a bond.

maturity The date on which the face value of the bond must be repaid.

A bond's yield is positively related to its risk. In other words, the greater the risk that the company issuing the bond might default on its bond payments, the greater return an investor would demand for holding that bond. A bond's risk is measured by various bond agencies, including Moody's, Standard & Poor's (S&P), and Fitch. These agencies provide bond ratings that range from AAA (the safest bonds) to C (the riskiest rating by Moody's) or D (the riskiest by S&P and Fitch).

yield The annual return to a bond measured as the coupon payment as a percentage of the current price of a bond.

Figure 3 shows a corporate bond listing on January 4, 2016, showing the coupon rate, maturity date, bond ratings, the last price, and the yield. Looking at the first row, for Bank of America, this bond pays a coupon rate of 5.0% per year. However, because the bond's risk rating has improved since its initial issuance, the price has risen from its base price of 100 to 109.03. Because the face value of most corporate bonds is $1,000, this means one must pay $1,090.30 for this bond. Because the price exceeds the face value to earn the bond's fixed coupon payment, the yield falls to 3.157%, reflecting the reduced risk perceived by investors.

Looking at the last row, the Chesapeake Energy bond offers a coupon rate of 5.75%. In addition, you could have bought the bond for $305 in January 2016, and cash this bond

FIGURE 3	CORPORATE BOND LISTING ON JANUARY 4, 2016				
Issuer Name	Coupon	Maturity	Rating: Moody's/S&P/Fitch	Last Price	Yield
Bank of America	5.000%	May 2021	Baa1/BBB+/A	109.03	3.157
Microsoft	4.500%	Oct 2040	Aaa/AAA/AA+	107.61	4.012
Intel	2.700%	Dec 2022	A1/A+/A+	100.05	2.692
ADT	3.500%	Jul 2022	Ba2/BB−/BBB−	90.25	5.283
Sprint	7.125%	Jun 2024	Caa1/B+/B+	72.50	12.480
Chesapeake Energy	5.750%	Mar 2023	B3/CCC+/B	30.53	29.499

Corporate bond listings are shown with their current price in the "Last Price" column. Bond prices are standardized such that each bond is worth "100" percent of the $1,000 face value upon maturity. Bond prices higher than 100 mean that the yield rate is lower than the coupon rate, which indicates that the bond is viewed as less risky relative to that suggested by the coupon rate. Conversely, bond prices lower than 100 suggest riskier bonds.

Information from FINRA.

in for $1,000 at maturity in March 2023. The yield for this bond is significantly higher at 29.49%. Sounds like a great investment, but notice its risk rating of B3/CCC+/B, indicating a high likelihood of default. If Chesapeake Energy files for bankruptcy at any time until March 2023, the expected 29.49% annual return will turn into a negative return after the bankruptcy filing. Indeed, high yields equal high risk.

Bonds provide advantages and disadvantages to acquiring financial capital compared to borrowing money from a bank. The benefits of bonds are that other investors share the risk of the business, and a business can generally raise more money through bonds by offering higher interest rates. The drawbacks are that bonds are a claim against a business, and the ability to issue future bonds depends on the ratings issued by ratings agencies and the overall demand and supply for its bonds in the market.

Although differences exist between bonds and bank loans, they still share similar characteristics. Both are IOUs to a lender, whether that be a bank or a bondholder. In both cases, the business maintains control over the management of the business. There is no risk of an outside investor or firm forcefully taking over the business, because the entire ownership is maintained by the company's owners. The disadvantage of relying on bonds and banks, however, is that the ability to raise large sums of capital may be difficult or expensive, and the burden of making debt payments may limit the performance of the business. An alternative approach is for a firm to acquire financial capital from the public in exchange for a share of ownership in the company. This involves stocks, which we discuss next.

share of stock A unit of ownership in a business that entitles the shareholder to one vote at shareholder meetings and one share of any dividends paid.

This stock certificate represents partial ownership in the Walt Disney Company, entitling the shareholder to dividends as well as voting rights.

Stocks (Equity Capital)

An alternative to using debt instruments such as a bank loan or the issuing of bonds to acquire financial capital is to offer partial ownership (also known as equity) in the company. The most common approach is to issue stock shares. Each **share of stock** issued represents one fraction (of the total shares issued) of ownership in the company, and subsequently one vote in shareholder meetings and one share of any dividends (periodic payments to shareholders).

When a firm issues stock, it receives money in exchange for ownership in the company. This is handled in what is

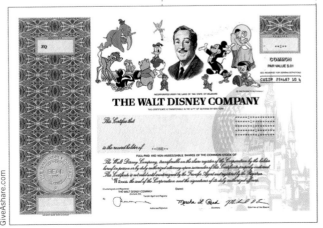

THE WALT DISNEY COMPANY

GiveAshare.com

market cap The market value of a firm determined by the current price per share of its stock multiplied by the total number of shares outstanding.

known as an initial public offering, or IPO. Typically, the founders of the company will retain a significant portion of the shares for themselves. However, the more shares that are issued, the smaller the value that each share will be. Therefore, when firms increase the number of shares issued without justifying their value to existing shareholders through actual or potential earnings, it is likely that the price per share will fall.

The **market cap** of a firm is what a firm is estimated to be worth based on its stock value, calculated as the current price per share multiplied by the total number of shares outstanding. The price of a share of stock is determined by supply and demand just as in any other market, and for every buyer of a share of stock there must be a seller. Shares of stock generally are traded in stock exchanges (such as the New York Stock Exchange or NASDAQ).

An important point here is that firms receive money only once from issuing a share of stock. Once a share of stock is issued, the trading of that share among investors and the corresponding price fluctuations of that share do not provide any additional funds to the company, although company executives who hold a significant number of shares clearly would benefit from a higher share price of their stock.

Apple Campus
One Infinite Loop

INFINITE LOOP

Kristoffer Tripplaar / Alamy

Like bonds, there are advantages and disadvantages to firms that raise financial capital from issuing stock. Advantages of issuing stock relative to bonds include the ability to raise substantial amounts of financial capital by sharing ownership in the business and its profits. In addition, businesses are not required to make repayments to stockholders, allowing them to reinvest their earnings as opposed to repaying lenders. Lastly, should the business fail, the losses are spread among all shareholders, not just to the business's founder, a concept known as *limited liability*. The main disadvantage of issuing stock is that partial ownership in the business is given up. This means that full disclosure of company data must be made public, providing valuable information to competitors. Furthermore, with enough shareholder votes, an external investor can vote to replace a firm's management and/or board of directors, or even take over the company outright by buying all or a majority of the shares in the company.

Suppose that for your fifth birthday in 2001, instead of a shiny new bike, your parents bought you 10 shares of Apple Computer Inc. stock for $216 (each share of Apple stock was worth $21.60 on January 1, 2001). Those 10 shares, adjusted for two stock splits that would turn the 10 shares into 140 shares, would be worth over $15,000 today. Would you rather have that bike or a brand new car today?

From an investor's point of view, why would people find stocks an attractive investment given the real risks of businesses failing? Some companies do fail, and stockholders in these cases often lose their entire investment as opposed to bondholders, who are able to make claims on a firm's remaining assets before shareholders. However, historical data have shown that investing in stocks, despite the higher risk, generates a much higher return over the long run than investing in bonds, buying certificates of deposit (CDs), or keeping money in a savings account. In other words, by owning a share of stock, one is entitled to a share of the company's future value. For many businesses that do succeed, this can result in a very profitable return. In some cases, owning shares in certain businesses over time has made investors very wealthy.

Venture Capital and Private Equity

An alternative approach to raising financial capital using equity instruments is to secure venture capital or private equity, both of which are large sums of money offered by financial investment firms eager to earn potentially large profits by investing a significant amount of money in a company.

The difference between venture capital firms and private equity firms lies primarily in the type of firms targeted. Venture capital firms typically invest in new start-up companies, providing seed money to entrepreneurs with potentially profitable ideas in exchange for a share of company ownership. Private equity firms typically target mature firms that are struggling to maximize profits or are on the verge of bankruptcy. By providing a substantial capital investment to a struggling firm in exchange for a

ISSUE

Venture Capital: A Few Success Stories and One Big Missed Opportunity

Hardly a day goes by without most of us performing an Internet search using Google. Google has become one of the most successful Internet companies in history. How did Google get its start, and how did it find the financial capital to begin its remarkable climb to success? The story begins in 1996 with Larry Page and Sergey Brin.

Larry Page and Sergey Brin were Ph.D. candidates at Stanford University when in March 1996 they started a project called the Stanford Digital Library Project. It then became known as BackRub. Their first source of funding came in August 1998, when Andreas (Andy) von Bechtolsheim, co-founder of Sun Microsystems, and Professor David Cheriton of Stanford, provided $100,000 each in start-up capital in exchange for partial ownership of the still unincorporated company. The company was officially named Google as a play on the word "googol," which is a number representing a 1 with 100 zeros after it.

The following year, in June 1999, Google secured $25 million in venture capital from two venture capital firms (Sequoia Capital and Kleiner Perkins Caufield & Byers), which each received 10% ownership in the company. In the year prior to securing these funds, Page and Brin had made an offer to sell the entire company (albeit a much smaller company at the time) for as little as $750,000!

In 2004 Google made an initial public offering of stock shares, generating a huge infusion of cash, while Page, Brin, Bechtolsheim, Cheriton, the original venture capital firms, and Google's employees collectively retained nearly 90% of the shares for themselves. As of April 2016, Google was worth over $500 billion based on its stock value. For the venture capitalists who turned $12.5 million into $50 billion (10% ownership), that is a 400,000% return over 17 years. For Bechtolsheim and Cheriton, who each turned $100,000 into $5.0 billion, that is a 5,000,000% return over 18 years. Unfortunately, not all venture capitalists became billionaires. It was quite a missed opportunity for those who turned down Page and Brin's original offers.

large (often majority) share of company ownership, private equity firms can replace a firm's board of directors as well as management in an effort to turn around a company's performance.

How do venture capital and equity capital differ from financial capital acquired through the stock market? The key factors are timing, volume, and risk. A venture capital firm seeks out the next Fortune 500 company in its earliest stages, hoping to turn a relatively small amount of money into a huge return. Similarly, a private equity firm seeks large returns by reorganizing existing firms. In both cases, individual stock investors may be hesitant to invest, either because the company is too young (or has not established a product to generate revenues), or the company is nearing bankruptcy. By purchasing a large share of a company, venture capital and private equity firms take substantial risks in exchange for potential large returns to their own shareholders.

According to the National Venture Capital Association (NVCA), the largest trade association for venture capital firms, over 800 venture capital firms in the United States invested a total of $58.8 billion in new businesses in many industries in 2015. According to the Private Equity Growth Capital Council, there were over 4,100 private equity firms in the United States in 2015. The amount of private equity investment is more difficult to measure, given the frequent buying and selling of shares in existing firms as opposed to the providing of start-up capital by venture capital firms, which is easier to measure.

Despite the year-to-year fluctuations in venture capital and private equity investments, these investments represent a large source of financial capital in the United States. While some investments have gone sour, some have turned into moneymaking machines. The Issue feature describes one of the most successful venture capital stories: Google. Yet, even today there are new firms that may potentially provide even bigger success stories, and investors are actively seeking out these firms.

✔ **CHECKPOINT**

FINANCIAL CAPITAL

- Firms require financial capital to purchase inputs needed in their production.
- Financial capital can be obtained from bank loans, from the issuing of bonds or stock shares, or from venture capital or private equity firms.
- Bonds are IOU notes that provide a return based on their level of risk.
- Owning a share of stock entitles an investor to one share of ownership in a business, and can lead to substantial gains if the business is successful.
- Venture capital and private equity firms take on risk in exchange for potential large returns by investing in new or underperforming companies, respectively.

QUESTIONS: What is the difference between a bond and a share of stock? What are some advantages and disadvantages of acquiring financial capital by issuing bonds in the bond market instead of issuing shares in the stock market?

Answers to the Checkpoint questions can be found at the end of this chapter.

INVESTMENT IN HUMAN CAPITAL

In the previous chapter, we discussed reasons why some people are paid more than others, including discrimination in the labor market and the role of unions. But even if we put these important considerations aside, other factors may lead to wage differences, such as how much education one has. Previously, we had treated labor as a homogeneous input to simplify our analysis. In this section, we look at labor that has been enriched by training or education and how it affects the productivity of firms.

Is there a relationship between your earnings and your education? Let us first consider the role education and on-the-job-training (OJT) play in determining wage levels in labor markets. Workers, students, and firms all invest in themselves or their employees to increase productivity. This is called **investment in human capital.** Workers invest by accepting lower wages while they undertake apprenticeships. Students invest by paying for tuition and books, and by forgoing job opportunities, to learn new skills. Firms invest in their workers through OJT and in-house training programs that involve workers being paid to attend classes. These investments entail costs in the current period that are borne in the interest of raising future productivity.

investment in human capital
Investments such as education and on-the-job training that improve the productivity of labor.

Education and Earnings

One of the surest ways to advance in the job world and increase your income is by investing in education. The old saying "To get ahead, get an education" still holds true. Figure 4 shows the median earnings and unemployment rates by highest degree earned for persons age 25 and over in 2014. It provides strong evidence that education and earnings are related.

Median earnings for those without a high school diploma were $25,376, while earnings for those completing high school were $34,736, a 37% increase. Getting a bachelor's degree bumped median earnings up to $57,252, a 65% rise over those with only a high school diploma. Going on to get a professional degree moved median earnings all the way up to $85,228, almost 50% more than what a worker made with a bachelor's degree alone. It's also very evident that unemployment rates fall as one obtains more education. The unemployment rate for those without a high school diploma was 9%, while for those with a professional or doctoral degree, it was only about 2%. Clearly, acquiring more human capital makes a person more valuable to an employer, which results in more employment opportunities and higher earnings.

Figure 4 suggests that education is a good investment. But like any investment, future earnings must be balanced against the cost of obtaining that education. The costs of education must be borne today, but the earnings benefits do not arrive until later. Making optimal educational decisions therefore requires some tools to help evaluate investments in human capital markets.

FIGURE 4 | AVERAGE UNEMPLOYMENT RATES AND MEDIAN EARNINGS BY HIGHEST DEGREE EARNED, 2014

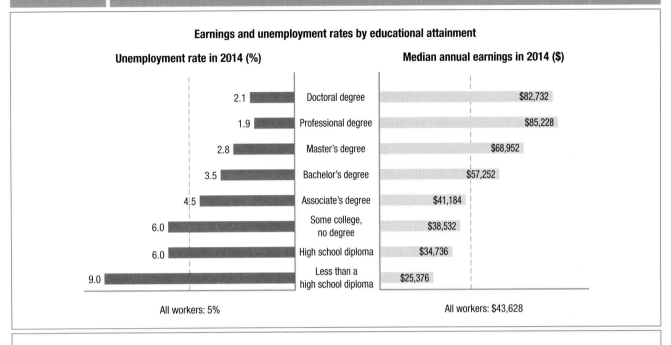

Earnings and unemployment rates by educational attainment

Unemployment rate in 2014 (%)		Median annual earnings in 2014 ($)
2.1	Doctoral degree	$82,732
1.9	Professional degree	$85,228
2.8	Master's degree	$68,952
3.5	Bachelor's degree	$57,252
4.5	Associate's degree	$41,184
6.0	Some college, no degree	$38,532
6.0	High school diploma	$34,736
9.0	Less than a high school diploma	$25,376

All workers: 5%   All workers: $43,628

Data from U.S. Bureau of Labor Statistics, http://www.bls.gov/emp/ep_chart_001.htm.

Education as Investment

To keep our analysis simple, we will focus on the decision to attend college for four years. The basic approach outlined in this section will nonetheless apply to other investments in education or training.

Figure 5 presents a stylized graph showing the benefits and costs of a college education. For simplicity, we will assume students go to college at age 18. If an individual chooses not to go to college, the high school earnings path applies: On leaving high school, the

FIGURE 5 | BENEFITS AND COSTS OF A COLLEGE EDUCATION

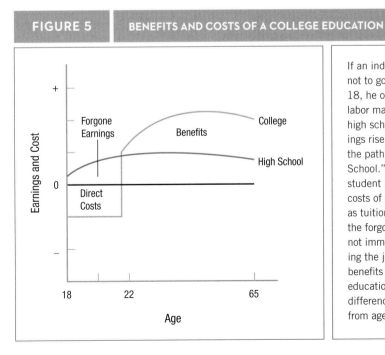

If an individual chooses not to go to college at age 18, he or she enters the labor market on leaving high school, and earnings rise and fall along the path labeled "High School." The college student incurs the direct costs of education, such as tuition and books, and the forgone earnings of not immediately entering the job market. The benefits of the college education show up as the difference in earnings from ages 22 to 65.

person enters the labor market immediately, and earnings begin rising along the path labeled "High School." Note that the earnings are positive throughout the individual's working life.

A college student immediately incurs costs in two forms. First, tuition, books, and other fees must be paid. These direct costs exclude living expenses, such as food and rent, because these must be paid whether one works or goes to college. Tuition varies substantially depending on whether one attends a private or public university.

Second, students give up earnings as they devote most or all of their time to their studies (and to the occasional party). These costs can be substantial when compared to the direct costs of an education at a state-supported institution, because the average earnings for high school graduates range between $17,000 and $22,000 a year.

The benefits from a college degree show up as the difference in earnings from ages 22 to 65. If the return on a college degree is to be positive, this area must offset the direct costs of college and the forgone earnings. We must also keep in mind that a large part of the income high school and college graduates earn will not come until well into the future. For college graduates, this is especially important, because they will not see income for at least four years. How can we tell if this sacrifice is worth it? The fact that the median earnings of college graduates exceeded those of high school graduates by about 65% suggests a college education is worth it.

An alternative way to decide which of the two career paths is best is to compute the rate of return on a college degree. If the annual return on a college education over the course of one's working life is 10% a year, the earnings of the college graduate in middle age will exceed those of the high school graduate by enough to generate a 10% return. A lower return would mean that the difference in earnings is smaller, while a higher return suggests the difference in earnings is greater. An extensive study[1] of rates of return to higher education in nearly 100 countries put the average return at nearly 20%. That is, college graduates around the world earn, on average, nearly 20% more per year over the course of their working lifetime than high school graduates, taking into consideration all of the costs of going to college.

Equilibrium Levels of Human Capital

Each of us must decide how much to invest in ourselves. This decision, like so many in economics, ultimately depends on supply and demand, in this case, the supply of, and demand for, funds to be used for human capital investment. A hypothetical market for human capital is shown in Figure 6. In this scenario, "price" is the percentage rate of return on human capital investments and the interest cost of borrowing funds.

The demand for human capital investment slopes down and to the right, reflecting the diminishing returns of more education and that more time in school leaves you less time to earn back its costs. Students pursuing a Ph.D. or a medical degree are often into their thirties before they can begin paying back their student loans. As a result, they require higher salaries to bring up their rates of return above those of college-educated workers.

The supply of investable funds, meanwhile, is positively sloped, because students will use the lowest-cost funds first—mom and dad paying for college—then turn to government-subsidized funds, and finally use private market funds, if needed.

With demand (D_0) and supply (S_0), equilibrium in this market occurs at point e. Human capital investment is equal to H_e, with the rate of return equaling the interest rate (i_e). Notice that reducing the supply of funds, or shifting the supply curve to S_1, will increase interest rates and the cost of investment. This results in lower investments in education. Similarly, anything reducing the demand for funds, or shifting the demand curve to D_1, will result in reduced human capital investment. Let us briefly consider some of the factors that might cause these curves to shift.

---

[1] G. Psacharopoulos and H. Patrinos, "Returns to Investment in Education: A Further Update," *Education Economics,* 2004.

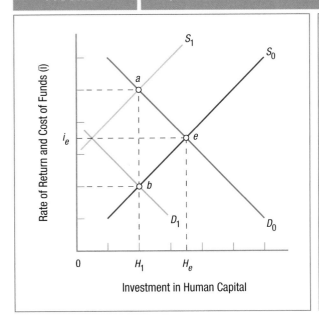

FIGURE 6 | EQUILIBRIUM LEVELS OF INVESTMENT IN HUMAN CAPITAL

This graph portrays a hypothetical market for human capital; the percentage rates of return and the interest costs of borrowing funds are shown on the vertical axis. With demand D_0 and supply S_0, equilibrium will be at point e. If the supply of funds is reduced (S_1), interest rates and the cost of investment increase, resulting in less investment. Reduced demand for education (D_1) similarly reduces human capital investment.

The most important factor determining the supply of investable funds for students consists of family resources. Students from well-off families can draw on a pool of inexpensive funds, but students from poorer families must scratch together funds that are often expensive. At the aggregate level, reductions in federally subsidized low-interest student loans will result in a shift in the supply curve to S_1, meaning lower investments in human capital (H_1). Conversely, the GI bills enacted after World War II and the Vietnam War, along with tax policies that allow certain individuals to deduct a portion of their tuition payments from their taxes, have made a college education easier to afford. These policies have shifted the supply curve to the right and increased college enrollments and the stock of human capital.

Another factor influencing human capital investment is discrimination. Assume D_0 represents the demand for human capital investment for individuals facing no discrimination in the labor market. If these same people were to face a reduced wage in the market from wage discrimination, their demand for education would fall to D_1, reflecting the reduced return on investment in human capital. A similar decline in demand would result if the choice of jobs is limited by occupational discrimination.

The demand for human capital is also influenced by an individual's abilities and learning capacity: The more able the person, the larger the expected benefits of human capital investment.

Implications of Human Capital Theory

Individuals are more productive because of their investment in human capital, and thus they are capable of earning more during their working lives. Because younger people have longer earning horizons, they are more likely to invest in human capital and education. As workers become older and gain labor market experience and higher wages, their opportunity costs for attending college grow larger, while their potential post-college earning period shrinks. This explains why most students in college classrooms are young.

The greater the market earnings differential between high school and college graduates, the more people will attend college, because a higher earnings differential raises the return on a college education. Similarly, reductions in the cost of education lead to greater educational investment.

Further, the more an individual discounts the future—the more she or he values present earnings over future earnings—the less investment in human capital we would expect.

People with high discount rates often are not willing to pursue doctoral or medical degrees because the time between the beginning of the training process and the point when earnings begin is simply too long.

Human Capital as Screening or Signaling

screening or **signaling** The use of higher education as a way to let employers know that the prospective employee is intelligent and trainable and potentially has the discipline to be a good employee.

Human capital theorists see investments in human capital as improving the productivity of individuals. This higher productivity then translates into higher wages. There is another view of why higher educational levels lead to higher wages: Higher education acts as a **screening** or **signaling** device for employers.

Economists who advocate this view concede that some education will undoubtedly lead to higher productivity. But these economists argue that higher education is largely an indicator to employers that the college graduate is trainable, has discipline, and is intelligent. In their view, the job market is one big competition in which entry-level workers compete for on-the-job training. As a result, earning a college degree does little more than give the college graduate a leg up in this competition.

Most economists, however, doubt the theory that screening is the only purpose served by higher education. If it were, the high costs of college education and the higher wages employers must pay college graduates would create tremendous incentives for workers and employers to develop an alternative, less expensive screening device.

ISSUE

A Class With 10,000 Students? MOOCs and Human Capital

The format by which college education is delivered has changed significantly over the past decade. Traditionally, attending a class required physically going to a classroom and interacting with a professor and fellow students. The Internet has changed that, as nearly every institution of higher learning now offers online education in some form. And even the way online courses are delivered has changed. Technologies such as lecture capture and live chat rooms permit professors to deliver content online much like one would in a classroom, allowing students to interact with each other virtually.

Innovation in online education has made a college degree attainable for those whose circumstances do not allow for a traditional on-campus education. These include those who work full-time, have young children, or serve in the military.

One of the benefits of online education is that classroom capacities no longer exist. As a result, some colleges have created super-sized classes taught by star professors who are the most innovative, and sometimes entertaining, in their teaching methods. This also has led to the development of massive open

The global reach of MOOCs can be seen in just one economics class with students from over 50 nations.

online courses, or MOOCs, which are courses taught by one professor but offered (usually for free) to anyone in the world who wishes to take the class. José Vazquez, a professor at the University of Illinois at Urbana-Champaign, teaches one of the largest online courses in the country, with over 10,000 students studying economics each term.

The ability to take online courses for free has allowed persons from around

the world to create human capital that otherwise might not be possible, especially in the most rural and poor areas of the world. All that is required is a computer with Internet service, which are becoming increasingly available in even the poorest nations. Over time, opportunities such as these will allow aspiring students from anywhere in the world to achieve a college education without ever needing to leave home.

On-the-Job Training

On-the-job training (OJT) is the investment by firms to increase the human capital of their workers, and can take many different forms. First, training can be as simple as receiving instructions from a supervisor on how to help customers, operate a machine, or retrieve items from inventory. Second, training can take place in a more formal setting away from the job, almost like a college course. Last, training can consist of a firm providing tuition reimbursement for college courses, professional certificates, or MBA degrees.

College internship programs are a good example of OJT that offers firms an extended look at potential employees while providing students with a look at several different firms and industries before graduating and entering the job market.

Today, spending on OJT exceeds $100 billion a year, including training costs and the wages paid to employees during training. The costs of OJT are usually borne by employers, but workers may bear some of the costs through reduced wages during the training period. Firms benefit from OJT by gaining more productive workers, and workers gain by becoming more versatile, and thus more competitive, in labor markets. Because all OJT entails present costs meant to yield future benefits, firms choose to provide OJT if the returns from this investment compare favorably to other investment alternatives.

Investments in human capital go a long way toward explaining why people are paid different wages. Education and earnings are closely related. Human capital theorists believe that this is because education and productivity are closely related. For this reason, firms are willing to pay higher wages to individuals with greater amounts of human capital. For industries that require advanced skills, such as in computer programming, aerospace, and biotechnology (just to name a few), human capital is difficult if not impossible to replace with ordinary labor. Therefore, human capital is considered a capital input in the factors of production.

on-the-job training Training typically offered by employers, ranging from suggestions at work to intensive workshops and seminars.

 ## CHECKPOINT

INVESTMENT IN HUMAN CAPITAL

- Investment in human capital includes all investments in human beings such as education and on-the-job training.
- There is a positive relationship between education and earnings.
- The rate of return to education is computed by comparing the streams of income from two different levels of education.
- The greater the wage differential between two levels of education, the more people will pursue that next level of education.
- Higher education may just be a screening or signaling device telling potential employers that this individual is trainable, has discipline, and is intelligent.
- Firms are willing to provide on-the-job training when the future returns to human capital investment in terms of increased productivity to the firm exceed the costs of that training.

QUESTIONS: If a country decided, as part of an immigration reform package, to restrict immigration only to those with college degrees, and thus decided to allow only 500,000 foreigners a year to enter, what would happen to the rate of return on college education? Alternatively, if, as part of a reform package, 500,000 low-skilled workers were permitted to enter the country, what would happen to the rate of return on college education?

Answers to the Checkpoint questions can be found at the end of this chapter.

ENTREPRENEURSHIP AND INNOVATION

We have now addressed the basic requirements of production—acquiring land, labor, physical and human capital, and finding financial capital to pay for it. Is that all that is required to operate a business? Not quite. Recall that the four factors of production are land, labor, capital, and entrepreneurship.

What is entrepreneurship? Entrepreneurship is the willingness to take risks and to use ideas to convert physical inputs into final products that are appealing to consumers. Entrepreneurship is an essential factor of production—without a great idea on how to use resources, the final products will likely be of little value or may not even be produced.

Entrepreneurship

Profits are the rewards entrepreneurs receive for (1) combining land, labor, and capital to produce goods and services, and (2) assuming the risks associated with producing these goods and services. Entrepreneurs must combine and manage all the inputs of production; make day-to-day production, finance, and marketing decisions; innovate constantly if they hope to remain in business over the long run; and simultaneously bear the risks of failure and bankruptcy.

As we have seen over the past decade, large firms that have become household names can implode quickly. Circuit City, Blockbuster, and Borders are a few companies that have closed after filing for bankruptcy.

Even for large firms, business is risky. Bankruptcy or business failure, meanwhile, can be exceedingly painful for business owners, stockholders, employees, and communities. Still, a free economy requires such failures. If firms were guaranteed never to fail, perhaps through government subsidies, they would have little incentive to be efficient or to innovate, or to worry about what consumers want from them.

When a firm earns economic profits—profits exceeding normal profits—this is a signal to other firms and entrepreneurs that consumers want more of the good or service the profitable firm provides, and that they are willing to pay for it. Profit signals shift resources from areas of lower demand to the products and services consumers desire more highly.

Innovation and the Global Economy

Innovation describes both entrepreneurship, when individuals and firms develop something new, and the constant retooling of existing products. Innovation arguably is the most productive input in the production process. Many countries, such as those in sub-Saharan Africa, have abundant natural resources and labor, yet have not been able to convert those inputs into substantial outputs. Meanwhile, countries such as Japan, Germany, and Sweden, have compensated for their more limited natural resources by generating high levels of human capital and innovation, and consequently generate a very high standard of living for their citizens.

An important issue is that to encourage innovation, those who innovate must be provided with incentives to make the money and effort invested worthwhile. For example, an individual's or a firm's innovations can be protected using **intellectual property rights,** including patents, copyrights, trademarks, and industrial designs, allowing innovators an exclusive right to earn profits from their investments for a fixed amount of time.

The importance of innovation as a driver of economic growth will continue to increase as the economy becomes more globalized. Specifically, deficiencies in physical capital can easily be resolved through trade and foreign direct investment. But deficiencies in human capital and innovation are a much more difficult obstacle to overcome.

Therefore, the future of a country's economic growth will depend on its ability to generate new ideas and find more productive uses of its limited resources. At the start of this chapter, we discussed the aerospace industry and its goals of developing planes that provide more comfort to passengers, and reduce operating costs. Both objectives increase the productive use of limited resources, which will allow the industry to grow as people demand more travel.

intellectual property rights A set of exclusive rights granted to a creator of an invention or creative work, allowing the owner to earn profits over a fixed period of time. The types of protection include patents, copyrights, trademarks, and industrial designs.

Investment in wind and solar energy technology has increased as more countries emphasize innovations in renewable energy.

Visdia/Dreamstime.com

Ski Dubai:
A Ski Resort in the Desert

How does Dubai use capital and innovation to provide a ski destination in the middle of the desert?

The ability to enjoy skiing and other winter sports on a regular basis usually requires one to live near a ski resort that receives ample amounts of snow during the winter. Those who live in Colorado, Switzerland, or Norway have no shortage of places to hit the slopes. But what if one lives somewhere without mountains and where it never snows? Are winter sports simply a mirage? One could obviously travel to a ski destination, but the city of Dubai in the United Arab Emirates devised a different solution: It built a massive

An indoor ski resort in Dubai allows for winter sports every day of the year.

indoor ski resort, Ski Dubai, in the desert.

Indoor skiing is not new. Since the late 1980s, indoor ski resorts have opened in Japan, Germany, the Netherlands, and other countries where the demand for winter sports extends beyond the winter months. Ski Dubai opened in 2005 inside of a large shopping mall, making winter sports readily available to

persons of all ages and abilities. It features a four-person chair lift, two main ski runs, a terrain park, tobogganing and sledding, and even a café midway up the "mountain." And to a skier's delight, the ski resort is open every day of the year and the temperature is kept cool but comfortable all day long.

Ski Dubai is an example of using capital and innovation to bring land (mountains and snow) to the desert. Having either mountains or natural snow would have helped, but having neither posed a significant but not insurmountable challenge. Around $400 million was needed. This significant amount of financial capital was readily available at the time, the height of the oil boom. With enough innovation and financial capital, just about anything one can dream of, including a ski slope in the desert, is possible.

Eric Chiang

GO TO **LaunchPad** TO PRACTICE THE ECONOMIC CONCEPTS IN THIS STORY

But advances in innovative technology cannot be limited to just a few industries. All industries must avoid falling behind the trend of increasing productivity throughout the world. Emerging countries have begun to invest significant sums to improve physical infrastructure and human capital. This had led to innovations in all industries and an improvement in the standards of living in these countries. In order for rich nations to continue increasing their standard of living, they must continue to innovate; otherwise, emerging countries such as China or India will be quick to catch up.

 CHECKPOINT

ENTREPRENEURSHIP AND INNOVATION

- Entrepreneurs earn profits for combining other inputs to create products and for assuming the risks of producing goods and services.
- Innovation includes the efforts by entrepreneurs to produce new products as well as efforts by firms to make existing products better.
- Entrepreneurship and innovation are arguably the most productive factors of production, allowing countries to use limited resources to produce valuable outputs that lead to a higher standard of living.

QUESTIONS: Why is entrepreneurship considered a factor of production despite the fact that it does not exist in physical form? Suppose a country has abundant amounts of natural resources and labor. Would this automatically translate into a highly productive economy?

Answers to the Checkpoint questions can be found at the end of this chapter.

chapter summary

Section 1 Land and Physical Capital

12.1 Land prices are driven by a fixed supply and by demand factors such as the terrain, attributes, view, and location.

Kuosumo/Dreamstime.com

Timiskim/Dreamstime.com

MRP_K is the additional value that a unit of capital brings to the firm. It represents the maximum a firm is willing to pay for capital.

MRP_K slopes downward; where it crosses i is the amount a firm will invest.

Rent is the return or income that flows to land or physical capital as a factor of production.

Present Value Versus Rate of Return

12.2
- Present value measures the value today of money collected in the future.
- $PV = X/(1 + i)^n$, where i = discount rate and n = years.

12.3
- Rate of return is the interest rate that is required for a project to break even in the long run.
- Calculating the rate of return requires solving for the interest rate that makes the present value of all future income from a project equal to its cost of capital.

Section 2 Financial Capital

12.4 **Banks:** Banks offer loans based on credit history and ability to produce collateral in case of default; the amount borrowed is usually limited.

Najlah Feanny-Hicks/Corbis

Four Sources of Financial Capital

Perry Toone/Dreamstime.com

Bond market: Bonds are claims on a company's assets. A bond pays a fixed payment called a coupon rate and a face value upon maturity.

Stock market: Stocks give partial ownership in a company, entitling owners (shareholders) to a vote in company matters and a share of dividends.

Rudy Sulgan/Corbis

David Sailors/Corbis

Venture capital: Venture capital firms provide seed money to new businesses in exchange for partial ownership in the company.

Section 3 Investment in Human Capital

12.5 Investment in human capital can come from

- education.
- on-the-job-training

12.6 The greater the wage differential between two levels of human capital investment, the more people will pursue that next level.

Is education just a signal or does it provide inherent productive value? Most economists believe education does both.

Median Earnings by Highest Degree Earned

Categories (left to right): No HS Diploma, HS Diploma, Some College, Bachelor's Degree, Professional Degree. Y-axis from $0 to $100,000.

Education is a good investment in terms of human capital accumulation, which translates to higher average salaries.

Section 4 Entrepreneurship and Innovation

12.7 **Entrepreneurs** assume the risk of using capital and labor markets to create new goods and services and to make existing products better.

Failure is a part of free markets, as some innovations do not make it, such as Toshiba's HD DVD format.

Entrepreneurship is an important factor of production. It allows countries to turn limited resources into productive outputs and higher standards of living.

Success brings great rewards to entrepreneurs, many of whom have become rich, such as the inventor of the popular self-balancing scooters.

12.8 **Intellectual property rights** are needed to protect innovation and provide rewards for entrepreneurs. These include

- patents: to protect ideas and inventions.
- copyrights: to protect writings and artistic impression.
- trademarks: to protect names and symbols.
- industrial designs: to protect product designs.

rent, p. 316
physical capital, p. 317
present value, p. 319
rate of return, p. 320
financial capital, p. 321
collateral, p. 322

face value, p. 322
coupon rate, p. 322
maturity, p. 322
yield, p. 322
share of stock, p. 323
market cap, p. 324

investment in human capital, p. 326
screening or signaling, p. 330
on-the-job training, p. 331
intellectual property rights, p. 332

QUESTIONS AND PROBLEMS

Check Your Understanding

1. What does the term "land" refer to in economics and why is it very inelastic in supply?

2. If the interest rate is 4% and you are offered a bond that will pay you $1,000 in two years, but no interest between now and then, what would you be willing to pay for this bond today?

3. What are the different ways in which businesses can acquire financial capital?

4. Why are colleges filled with young people rather than middle-aged individuals? If interest rates rose to over 10%, would this have any impact on the number of people attending college or its composition?

5. What is the difference between physical capital and human capital?

6. What do intellectual property rights protect and why are they important to entrepreneurship?

Apply the Concepts

7. How do times of growth in the general economy encourage capital investments? How do recessions discourage capital investments? What happens to the cost of capital in boom times when the economy is growing? What happens in recessionary times?

8. Brazil spent billions in capital expenditures building new stadiums, roads, and public transportation to host the 2014 World Cup, and billions more in Rio de Janeiro to host the 2016 Summer Olympics. Brazil hoped that the major investment and global exposure from these events would generate future tourism and business investment. Explain how Brazil would use a rate of return approach to determine whether the effort and cost to host these events were worthwhile.

9. Suppose you wish to purchase a corporate bond that offers a coupon rate of 10% in the bond market. On a particular day, you notice the price of the bond listed as greater than "100." Given this price, would the yield on this bond be greater than or less than 10%? List some possible reasons that would cause the price of the bond to exceed "100."

10. When a company uses resources to train staff or subsidize tuition for employees, it is clearly investing in human capital. However, this investment is treated as current spending (cost of selling or producing goods) rather than investment. Should these activities be treated as investments and be reflected in the investment statistics of the economy?

11. Does it seem reasonable that a certain portion of the benefits of a college education is essentially a way to show prospective employers that you are reasonably intelligent, trainable, and have a certain degree of discipline?

12. The installation of solar panels is an expensive cost that provides savings over time. If the government passes higher tax deductions to individuals and firms who install solar panels, what will this do to the rate of return on solar panels?

In the News

13. Food trucks have become a billion dollar industry, serving creative and often healthy food options in places where traditional food options might be limited. For example, a food truck might stop at a local college campus during lunchtime, then go to an under-privileged district in the afternoon, and finally park near a local club in the evening. What are some advantages that food trucks have over traditional restaurants in terms of their land and capital costs?

14. A growing number of politicians are proposing to eliminate college tuition at public colleges and universities to every admitted student. Some have proposed this policy for two-year institutions, while others support the policy for all public institutions. Discuss the benefits and costs of this proposal in terms of human capital and financial capital.

Solving Problems

15. Suppose you win the lottery and are given a choice to collect either the grand prize of $5 million in 10 annual installments of $500,000, or collect an immediate one-time payment of $4 million today. If the interest rate is 5% and that is what you use to discount future earnings, which option should you select to maximize the present value of the winnings?

WORK IT OUT   LaunchPad | interactive activity

16. The mayor of your city is considering building a new toll road to reduce congestion. The cost of the toll road is $10 million and is estimated to generate a profit (from tolls collected less expenses collecting the tolls and maintaining the road) of $2 million per year. If the discount rate is 8%, how many years would it take before the road is paid for if future income is discounted? (*Hint:* Calculate the present value of the annual profit—for year 1, discount $2 million by 8%.)

USING THE NUMBERS

17. According to By the Numbers, in the year 2015 (the last year for which data are reported), approximately what percentage of high school graduates attended college? Approximately what percentage of college graduates attended a graduate program?

18. According to By the Numbers, by approximately what percentage did venture capital funding rise from its lowest point in 2010 to its peak in 2015?

ANSWERS TO QUESTIONS IN CHECKPOINTS

Checkpoint: Land and Physical Capital 321

To determine whether this investment is worthwhile, you would want to know how much income the store expects to generate over the year, as well as the current market interest rate. Using this information, you can estimate the net present value of the investment to determine whether it is a good idea or not. The higher the market interest rate, the greater the income stream you would require to invest.

Checkpoint: Financial Capital 326

Bonds are promises to pay back a lender (bondholder) a specific amount on a specific date, while stocks represent actual ownership (to the extent of the number of shares held) in a business. A bondholder does not own any part of the business, and therefore does not influence the day-to-day management of the firm.

An advantage of issuing bonds is that it allows a business to maintain control of its management. Another advantage is that the business is unlikely to be subjected to a forceful takeover by a large investor. A disadvantage of bonds is that a business must pay an interest rate that is sometimes high depending on how investors perceive their risk. Another disadvantage of bonds is that a business must make periodic coupon payments to bondholders, as well as pay back the bonds as they mature. This may restrict a business's ability to use available cash funds to invest in additional capital inputs.

Checkpoint: Investment in Human Capital 331

Letting in a large number of college-educated immigrants would drive down the rate of return on college as the wages of college graduates would not grow very rapidly. The opposite would occur when unskilled immigrants enter, holding down the wages of those without college educations, leading to a growing gap between those with college degrees, increasing the rate of return to a college degree.

Checkpoint: Entrepreneurship and Innovation 333

Entrepreneurship is the idea and vision to turn physical inputs such as land, labor, and capital into valuable outputs that people demand. An economy cannot produce goods without someone willing and able to determine what the market wants. Therefore, entrepreneurship is a vital factor of production.

Although having abundant amounts of natural resources and labor may provide a country with an advantage in production, a country still must innovate to turn those physical inputs into valuable products people desire. Thus, having abundant physical inputs does not automatically result in a productive economy. The reverse is also true—having few physical inputs does not preclude a country from being productive if it is able to use its limited resources effectively.

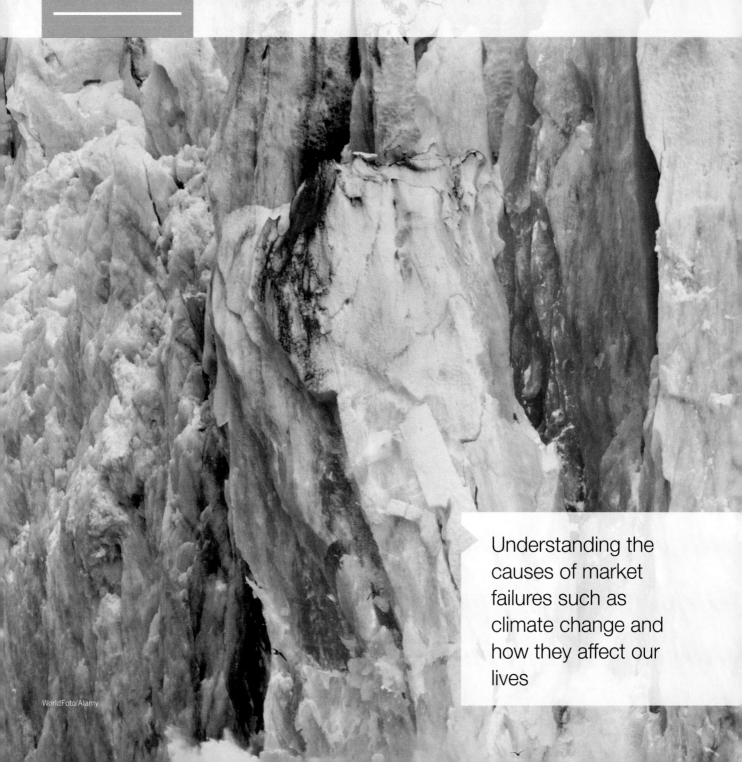

13 Externalities and Public Goods

Understanding the causes of market failures such as climate change and how they affect our lives

Learning Objectives

13.1 Describe the impact of negative and positive externalities on society.

13.2 Describe the Coase theorem on social costs and the role transaction costs play in the optimal allocation of resources.

13.3 Explain the nature of public goods and why private markets will usually not provide them.

13.4 Explain how common property resources can lead to resource degradation.

13.5 Discuss how health care exhibits characteristics of public goods and why it is prone to the free rider problem.

13.6 Recognize the importance of the discount rate in assessing the costs and benefits of environmental policies.

13.7 Use marginal analysis to determine the optimal level of pollution.

13.8 Describe the differences between command and control policies and market-based approaches to environmental regulation.

13.9 Understand the economic issues surrounding global climate change.

13.10 Discuss strategies that minimize greenhouse gases and promote sustainable development.

E ach day, thousands of spectacular explosions occur in a process called calving, when ice breaks off from mountains of glaciers and falls into the ocean as icebergs, eventually melting away. The withering ice shelves and frozen tundra that constitute the vast wilderness of the arctic (and the Antarctic) have affected the landscape that hundreds of wildlife species, including the polar bear, call home.

According to a recent NASA study, the volume and area of the Arctic ice caps fluctuate from year to year based on atmospheric cycles, but the overall trend has been declining as average surface temperatures rise. Estimates show that the overall area covered by the thickest ice, known as multiyear ice, has been shrinking between 12% and 17% per decade over the last 30 years. Other ice caps and glaciers around the world are also melting, and the consequences extend beyond the wildlife affected. Human lives also are affected as ocean levels rise. Despite widely varying estimates that ocean levels will rise between 7 inches and 63 inches by the end of the century, these statistics highlight the important idea that actions taken today, both positive and negative, will affect future generations.

The impact of human actions that contribute to global climate change is one that economic policy tries to address, although not without significant challenges and obstacles. An important issue is that the Earth's climate is shared. One country's efforts are not enough, while achieving consensus on environmental policy is difficult, if not impossible.

How environmental policies are set depends largely on the priorities placed by individual countries. For example, during much of the 20th century, the United States was a highly industrialized country; standards of living increased dramatically, but at the cost of greater pollution. However, many Americans now place a higher priority on maintaining a cleaner environment for future generations. This transformation from a polluting industrial society to a cleaner, energy-efficient society can

1980   2012

NASA/Goddard Scientific Visualization Studio

A computerized visualization of the Arctic ice caps shows the extent to which the area covered by the thickest ice, known as *multiyear ice*, has diminished from 1980 to 2012.

BY THE NUMBERS

The Environment and Sustainability

Having a sustainable economy will likely require a focus on energy other than fossil fuels, finding better methods to recycle waste, and developing methods to manage the natural environment.

Hybrid sales grew quickly from 2000 to 2007, then declined from 2008 to 2011 due to the last recession and slow economic recovery, before picking up again in 2012.

Millions of tons of solid waste fill landfills, while some is recovered and recycled. To be sustainable, the United States must recover more in the future.

49¢
Average gasoline tax per gallon in the United States

$4.52
Average gasoline tax per gallon in Britain

Go to **LaunchPad** to use the latest data to recreate this graph.

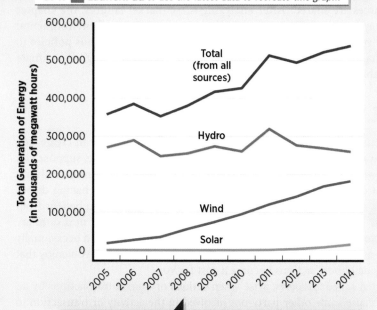

$49
Annual savings from replacing five 60-watt incandescent bulbs with LED bulbs

Actions to prevent climate change create external benefits to all of the planet's inhabitants. One of the most effective actions to mitigate climate change is the reduction in fossil fuel usage.

Top 10 States in Wind Power Generation Capacity (megawatts)

1.	Texas	16,406
2.	California	6,022
3.	Iowa	5,710
4.	Oklahoma	4,330
5.	Illinois	3,842
6.	Kansas	3,168
7.	Oregon	3,153
8.	Washington	3,075
9.	Minnesota	3,035
10.	Colorado	2,593

be seen in many developed nations, such as the United States, the countries of the European Union, Japan, and Australia.

In contrast, much of the world remains very poor. In these developing countries, efforts to improve basic living conditions often take precedence over environmental concerns. In countries that have grown significantly in recent years, such as China and India, polluting factories are churning out goods as fast as they can, and consumers are buying more cars and air travel. China is now the largest market in the world for new cars. The ability of previously impoverished nations to experience economic prosperity often comes at the expense of the environment.

Because of differing environmental priorities among nations, it is difficult to achieve a consensus. In addition, any one country's efforts to improve the environment benefit the entire world, yet that country bears the full costs of these efforts. Meanwhile, other countries may exploit the environment for their economic gain, offsetting the environmental efforts made by others.

At a microeconomic level, individuals and firms make decisions that affect the environment, such as the type of cars we buy and the production methods companies use. Each of these decisions affects not only the individual or company, but also others who share the environment that is being affected.

On a brighter note, economic growth has led to increasing efficiencies in resource use. The growing popularity of hybrid and plug-in electric cars has improved fuel efficiency. Even new technologies in cow feed (such as the infusion of garlic) have reduced the level of harmful methane gases emitted by cows. Yet, clearly we still have many environmental problems that must be addressed, including global climate change, species extinction, overharvesting of fisheries, and overcrowding of highways and parks.

Still, global climate change seems to be an almost intractable problem. Beyond the obvious scientific issues of how to reduce our environmental footprints stands market failure. Market failure describes how markets fail in specific ways to provide the socially optimal amount of goods and services. In the particular case of global climate change, what makes it so hard to deal with is that several specific market failures come together to make a solution tough to reach.

This chapter starts by examining market failures caused when actions taken by consumers or producers have effects on third parties (externalities), when certain types of goods called public goods provide little or no incentives to market participants, and when specific resources are shared. After analyzing these market failures, the chapter then looks at the ways policy tries to mitigate them in the context of environmental issues. Finally, after you get your hands around market failures and various policies to resolve them, the chapter takes what you have learned and applies it to global climate change and sustainable development.

EXTERNALITIES

Actions by individuals and firms affect not only those involved, but also can create side effects for others in ways that can be either beneficial or costly. For example, suppose you share an apartment with a neat and organized person. Because your roommate always keeps the apartment clean and uncluttered, you reap the benefits of not having dishes piling up in the sink or potato chip crumbs all over the sofa. Clearly, you benefit from this situation. On the other hand, suppose the occupants of the apartment next door are members of an aspiring heavy metal band. They blast loud music all day, and occasionally have a jam session—and you're forced to hear everything they play. Unless you enjoy that music yourself, your neighbors' actions become a cost for you.

Externalities, often called *spillovers,* arise when actions or market transactions by an individual or a firm cause some other party not involved in the activity or transaction to benefit or be harmed. If the activity imposes costs on others, it is called a *negative externality* and it creates an *external cost.* If the activity creates benefits to others, this is a *positive externality* and it creates an *external benefit.* Negative externalities include air and water pollution, littering, and chemical runoff that affect fish stocks. Examples of activities that

externalities The impact on third parties of some transaction between others in which the third parties are not involved. An external cost (or negative externality) harms the third parties, whereas external benefits (positive externalities) result in gains to them.

TABLE 1	EXTERNALITIES BY ORIGIN AND IMPACT				
	Impact **Victims and Beneficiaries of an Externality**				
	Consumers		**Producers**		
Origin of Externality	**Positive**	**Negative**	**Positive**	**Negative**	
Consumers	• Private schools • Immunizations • Landscaping	• Auto pollution • Littering • Smoking	• Flu shot reducing sick days	• Private auto use that adds to road congestion, slowing down commercial traffic	
	Positive	**Negative**	**Positive**	**Negative**	
Producers	• New factory leading to new shops and restaurants in town	• Factory air pollution on wilderness hikers • Pesticide runoff affecting trout fishing	• Honey bees improving apple orchards	• Pollution that harms commercial fishing	

generate positive externalities include getting a flu shot, acquiring more education, landscaping, and maintaining beehives next to apple orchards.

The presence of externalities leads to a misallocation of resources, causing a **market failure** to occur, when markets fail to provide a socially optimal level of goods and services. Both producers and consumers can create externalities and can feel the effects of them. Table 1 identifies the origin and impact of some common external effects.

market failure When markets fail to provide a socially optimal level of output, and will provide output at too high or low a price.

Negative Externalities

When a market transaction harms people not involved in the transaction, negative externalities exist. Pollution of all sorts is the classic example. Firms and consumers rarely consider the impact their production or consumption will have on others. For simplicity, we focus on the pollution caused by production. Figure 1 shows a typical market.

Supply curve S_p represents the manufacturer's marginal private cost (MPC) of production. This supply curve ignores the external costs imposed on others from the pollution generated during production. These external costs might include toxic wastes dumped into lakes or streams, smokestack soot, or the clear-cutting associated with timber harvests. Ignoring these costs, market equilibrium is at point e, at which the product is priced at $6 and 30 units are sold.

One way to measure the well-being of consumers and producers in a market is to measure the consumer surplus and producer surplus. Consumer surplus is the difference between what consumers are willing to pay for a good (shown by the demand curve) and the market price (equal to $6 in Figure 1). Therefore, consumer surplus is equal to $45 [(($9 − $6) × 30) / 2]. Producer surplus is the difference between the market price and the minimum amount at which sellers are willing to sell a product (shown by the supply curve), and is equal to $45 as well [(($6 − $3) × 30) / 2]. Summing up consumer surplus and producer surplus equals $90, which is shown as area *ace* in the figure.

Now let's assume that for every unit of the product produced, pollution costs (or effluent) equal to $2 are generated. Thus, at an output level of 30 units (point e), $60 in pollution costs (or negative externalities) is generated. Subtracting this $60 in pollution from total consumer and producer surplus results in $30 of real social benefit from this output.

This means that the true marginal cost of producing the product, including pollution costs, is equal to supply curve S_s, representing the marginal social cost (MSC) of production. This new supply curve incorporates both the private and social costs of production,

FIGURE 1 | **THE NEGATIVE EXTERNALITY CASE**

Supply curve S_p represents the manufacturer's supply when only its private costs are considered, ignoring the external costs imposed on others through pollution. Market equilibrium is 30 units sold at $6 each (point e). If each unit of production results in $2 in pollution costs, then supply curve S_s represents the marginal social costs (MSC) to manufacture the product. Socially optimal output is 20 units sold at $7 each (point g).

thus shifting supply upward by an amount equal to ef, or $2. Equilibrium moves to point g, at which 20 units of the product are sold at $7. This is the socially optimal production for this product given the pollution it creates.

So why is it better for society than when 30 units were produced? First, notice that when output is 20, the cost of the last unit produced—including the cost of pollution—is $7 (point g). This is just equal to the value society attributes to the product. Hence, consumers get just what they want when all costs are considered. Second, notice that consumer and producer surplus at an output of 20 units is $40 [(($9 − $5) × 20) / 2]. More important, it is now higher than the $30 of consumer and producer surplus minus the pollution costs when output was 30 units (point e).

Each unit of output produced beyond 20 costs more—taking both private and social costs into account—than its value to consumers.

Imagine a situation in which external costs exceed the consumer and producer surplus from consuming the good. Such a situation might arise when an extremely toxic substance is a by-product of production. Society is better off not permitting production of this good.

What has this analysis shown? First, when negative externalities are present, an unregulated market will produce too much of a good at too low a price. Second, optimal pollution levels are not zero, except in the case just mentioned of extremely toxic agents. In Figure 1, the socially optimal production is 20 units with total pollution costs of $40 ($2 × 20). Pollution reduction as a good has no price. Even so, we can infer a price, known as a shadow price, equal to the marginal damages—$2 per unit in this case. As we will see later, prices for the "right to pollute" will provide us with better approximations of the costs of pollution.

The Coase Theorem

Ronald Coase was awarded the Nobel Prize in Economics for his seminal paper "The Problem of Social Cost." Coase has written few articles—about a dozen—but, as economist Robert Cooter noted, although "most economists maximize the amount they write, Coase maximized the amount others wrote about his work."[1] Indeed, Coase's paper on social cost is one of the most cited works in economics.

Reducing output to an optimal level results in gains to "victims" because pollution is reduced. The reduction in output, however, causes losses to producers. The presence of losses

[1] Peter Passell, "Economics Nobel to a Basic Thinker," *New York Times*, October 16, 1991, p. D6.

and gains to two distinct parties, Coase argued, introduces the possibility of bargaining, provided that the parties are awarded the property rights necessary for negotiation.

The **Coase theorem** states that if transaction costs are minimal (near zero), the resulting bargain or allocation of resources will be efficient—output will decline to an optimal level—regardless of the initial allocation of property rights. A socially optimal level of production will be reached, that is, no matter whether polluters are given the right to pollute or victims are given the right to be free of pollution.

Even so, the distribution of benefits or income will be different in these two cases. If victims, for example, are assigned the property rights, their income will grow, but if polluters are assigned these rights, the income of victims will decline.

As Coase noted, for these efficient results to be achieved, transaction costs must approach zero. This means it must be possible for polluters and victims to determine their collective interests accurately, then negotiate and enforce an agreement. In many situations, however, this is simply not feasible. In cases involving air pollution, for instance, polluters and victims are so widely dispersed that negotiating is not practical. In other cases, individuals may be both victims and polluters, making it difficult for an agreement to be reached and enforced.

Another problem associated with assigning rights to one party or another might be called *environmental mugging*. Polluters might at first threaten to pollute more than they anticipate, for instance, to increase their bargaining leverage and, ultimately, their income. Victims, in like manner, might assert exaggerated environmental concerns, again to bid up their compensation. Alternatively, if negotiations should prove to be unfruitful, polluters might start lobbying for legal relief, thus devoting their money to rent-seeking behaviors rather than buying pollution-abatement equipment.

Although the private negotiations Coase proposed have their limitations, his insights proved to be a turning point in environmental policy. Coase challenged the prevailing practice of assuming that victims had a right to be pollution-free. His analysis stressed that it does not matter to whom the rights are assigned (e.g., the polluter or the pollution victim). No matter how property rights were assigned, if information was good and transaction costs were low, efficiency would result. Given the costs of pollution, affected parties have an incentive to work out efficient agreements.

This idea was so radical when Coase published "The Problem of Social Cost" in 1960 that another Nobel Prize winner, George Stigler, wondered "how so fine an economist could make such an obvious mistake." Coase was later invited to the University of Chicago to discuss his ideas; Stigler described what transpired[2]:

> *We strongly objected to this heresy. Milton Friedman did most of the talking, as usual. He also did much of the thinking, as usual. In the course of two hours of argument the vote went from twenty against and one for Coase to twenty-one for Coase. What an exhilarating event! I lamented afterward that we had not had the clairvoyance to tape it.*

Coase theorem If transaction costs are minimal (near zero), a bargain struck between beneficiaries and victims of externalities will be efficient from a resource allocation perspective. As a result, a socially optimal level of production will be reached.

RONALD COASE (1910–2013)
NOBEL PRIZE

University of Chicago Professor Ronald Coase won the Nobel Prize in Economic Sciences in 1991 for "his discovery and clarification of the significance of transaction costs and property rights for the institutional structure and functioning of the economy." According to his analysis, traditional microeconomic theory was incomplete because it neglected the costs of executing contracts and managing firms. To Coase, these "transaction costs" were the principal reason that firms existed. Coase also introduced the concept of property rights as an important element of economic analysis.

Born in 1910 in Willesden, a suburb of London, Coase attended the London School of Economics (LSE), where he earned a Bachelor of Commerce degree in 1932, and returned 15 years later and earned a Doctor of Science degree in economics in 1951. Having "a liking for life in America," he migrated to the United States in 1951 and taught at the University of Buffalo. Coase's 1960 article "The Problem of Social Cost" questioned whether governments could efficiently allocate resources for social purposes through taxes and subsidies. He argued that arbitrarily assigning property rights and using markets to reach a solution was usually better than costly government regulation. This was instantly controversial and led to a lengthy exchange of papers in economics journals. In 1964 Coase joined the faculty at the University of Chicago and became editor of the *Journal of Law and Economics*. The journal was an important catalyst in developing the economic interpretation of legal issues. Coase died in 2013 at the age of 102.

[2] George Stigler, *Memoirs of an Unregulated Economist* (New York: Basic Books, 1988), p. 76.

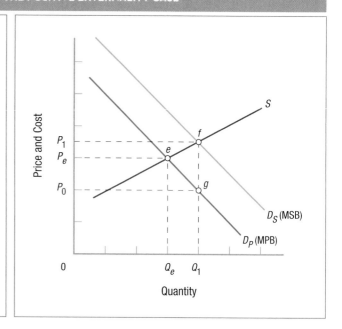

| FIGURE 2 | THE POSITIVE EXTERNALITY CASE |

Market supply curve *S* and private demand curve *D_P* represent the market for college education. Equilibrium is at point *e*, and the number of students enrolled is Q_e. Society would benefit, however, if more people would go to college. Demand curve D_S represents the marginal social benefit (MSB), which includes the private demand for college education plus the external benefits that flow from it. Socially optimal enrollment would be Q_1 (point *f*).

The Coase theorem has changed the way economists look at many issues, not just environmental problems. In cases in which the costs of negotiation are negligible and the number of parties involved is small, economists and jurists have begun to look more closely at legal rules assigning liability.

Positive Externalities

When private market transactions generate benefits for others, a situation opposite to that just described results. Figure 2 illustrates a positive externality. Market supply curve *S* and private demand curve D_P (equal to the marginal private benefit, MPB, of consumption) represent the market for college education. Equilibrium occurs at point *e*, with Q_e students enrolling. Society would clearly benefit, however, if more people received a college education. Tax revenues would rise, crime rates would fall, and a better-informed electorate might produce a better-operating democracy.

Taking these considerations into account, social demand curve D_S is the private demand for college education plus the external benefits that flow from it. Socially optimal enrollment would be Q_1 (point *f*). How can society tweak the market so that more students will attend college? Students will demand Q_1 levels of enrollment only if its price is P_0 (point *g*). The public must therefore subsidize college education by *fg* to draw its price down to P_0.

The U.S. government recognizes that college education benefits society at large when it provides low-interest student loans, grants, and scholarships to students attending colleges and universities.

Limitations

The analysis of externalities is important when determining public policy. However, some caveats need to be noted. For example, consumer surplus and producer surplus are good measures of a society's welfare if incomes are distributed in an equitable manner. When they are not, efforts to increase efficiency can be unconvincing for public policy. Because it is difficult to reach consensus on issues of income distribution, economists generally focus on efficiency. Also, our analysis of externalities with respect to pollution does not fully take into account important aspects such as the cumulative long-term effects of pollution, the difficulty of valuing damages resulting from pollution, and the fact that there are ways to reduce pollution other than reducing output. Despite these limitations, the analysis presented here helps us focus our attention on ways of reducing the harm done to society by negative externalities.

We now turn our attention to another type of market failure that occurs when resources are not privately owned.

 CHECKPOINT

EXTERNALITIES

- Externalities arise when the production of one good generates benefits (positive externalities) or costs (negative externalities) for others not involved in the transaction.
- When negative externalities exist, overproduction results. When positive externalities are generated, underproduction of the good is the norm.
- The Coase theorem states that if transaction costs are minimal (near zero), no matter which party is provided the property rights to pollution (polluter or victim), the resulting bargain will result in a socially optimal level of pollution.

QUESTION: A major problem facing many cities today is traffic congestion. One policy proposal to ease traffic congestion is to make all public transportation free, paid for either by a higher local gasoline tax or higher auto registration fees. What would be an external benefit and an external cost of implementing such a proposal to alleviate traffic congestion?

Answers to the Checkpoint questions can be found at the end of this chapter.

PUBLIC GOODS

We saw in the previous section that externalities can lead to markets not providing the socially optimal amount of a good at the optimal price. Either too much or too little of the good is produced, or it is offered at too high or too low a price, leading to a market failure. The presence of externalities is one cause of market failure. This section looks at two other causes of market failure that arise when no individual or firm is able to claim ownership of a product. These goods and services are called *public goods* and *common property resources.*

What Are Public Goods?

Pure **public goods** are nonrival in consumption, and exhibit nonexcludability. **Nonrivalry** means that the consumption of a good or service by one person does not reduce the utility of that good or service to others. **Nonexcludability** means that it is not possible to exclude some consumers from using the good or service once it has been provided.

By way of contrast, a can of Coke is a rival product. When you drink a can of Coke, no one else can drink that same can. Airline flights exhibit excludability—one must either buy a ticket or obtain an award ticket to board the plane, even if empty seats are available. But consider a lighthouse. Once it is built and in operation, all ships can see the lighthouse and use the light to avoid obstacles. One captain's use of the lighthouse does not prevent another from using it, nor can a ship realistically be excluded from using the lighthouse's services. Hence, the lighthouse is a public good. Other examples of public goods include national defense, accumulated knowledge, standards such as a national currency, protection of property rights, vaccinations, mosquito spraying, and clean air. Table 2 provides a taxonomy of private and public goods.

Consumers cannot be excluded from a public good once it is provided; therefore, they have little incentive to pay for the good in question. Instead, most will essentially be **free riders.** Think of the lighthouse again. If you have a ship and cannot be excluded from the benefits the lighthouse provides, why should you contribute anything to the lighthouse's upkeep? But if everyone took this position, there would be no support for the lighthouse, and it would

public goods Goods whose consumption by one person cannot diminish the benefit to others of consuming the good (i.e., nonrivalry), and once they are provided, no one person can be excluded from consuming (i.e., nonexcludability).

nonrivalry The consumption of a good or service by one person does not reduce the utility of that good or service to others.

nonexcludability Once a good or service is provided, it is not possible to exclude others from enjoying that good or service.

free rider An individual who avoids paying for a good because he or she cannot be excluded from enjoying the good once provided.

TABLE 2	TAXONOMY OF PRIVATE AND PUBLIC GOODS	
Property Rights		
Characteristics of Goods	Exclusive	Nonexclusive
Rival	Pure private good • Airline seat • Ice cream bar	Common property resource • Ocean fishery • Highways
Nonrival	Public good with exclusion • Cable TV • Satellite radio	Pure public good • National defense • Public broadcasting

go into decline. With free riders, private producers cannot hope to sell many units of a good, and thus they have no incentive to produce it. Private markets will therefore fail to provide public goods, even if the goods are things everyone would like to see produced. This is why the government or special interest groups must get involved in the provision of products and services that have significant public good characteristics.

The Demand for Public Goods

Assessing the public's demand for public goods is clearly different from that of private goods where we found market demand by horizontally summing private demands. But the fact that once a public good is supplied, no one can be excluded from consuming it, and one person's consumption does not affect another's, plays a crucial role. Figure 3 provides a solution to finding the demand for public goods.

Figure 3 shows demand for a public good by two different consumers. Individual A wants none when the price is $40 and is willing and able to buy 40 units when the price approaches zero. Individual B wants none when the price is $60 and only is willing to buy 30 units when the price nears zero. Because each consumer can consume any given amount of a public good at the same time, the total demand for a public good is found by summing

FIGURE 3	DEMAND FOR PUBLIC GOODS: VERTICAL SUMMATION OF INDIVIDUAL DEMAND CURVES

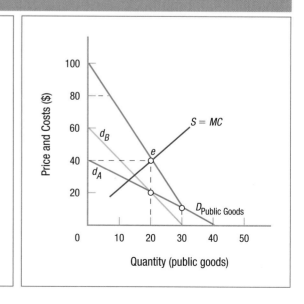

For public goods, exclusion is not possible, individuals can consume the good simultaneously, and market demand is found by summing vertically. Market demand for public goods is really a willingness-to-pay curve because the government will have to provide the good and levy taxes to pay the cost. The total demand for the public good is shown by the heavy line labeled $D_{\text{Public Goods}}$ and is the vertical summation of individual demands.

the individual demands *vertically.* To see why, consider when both individuals demand 20 units. This is the point at which the two demand curves cross, and both are willing to pay $20 for 20 units. Thus, total willingness-to-pay for 20 units is $40. The total demand for the public good in Figure 3 is shown by the heavy line labeled $D_{\text{Public Goods}}$ and is the vertical summation of individual demands.

Notice how this differs from our discussion of market demand curves for private goods. For private goods, others could be excluded from consuming any good we bought; therefore, demands were horizontally summed. In contrast, with public goods, exclusion is not possible; therefore, both individuals can consume the good simultaneously, and market demand is found by summing vertically. Market demand for public goods is really a *willingness-to-pay curve,* because the government will have to provide the good and levy taxes to pay the cost.

Optimal Provision of Public Goods

Providing the optimal amount of public goods is easy in theory and is illustrated in Figure 3. The supply of public goods is equal to the marginal cost curve ($S = MC$) shown in the figure. Just like the competitive market equilibrium we covered earlier, optimal allocation is where $MC = P$, and in this instance, it is 20 units of the good at a total price of $40 (point *e*). In this example, the taxes are split equally between individuals A and B. Determining how much tax each person should (or would be willing to) pay is hampered by the fact that once the public good is provided, no one can be excluded; therefore, individuals will be unwilling to reveal their true preferences for the good because it might mean that they would have to pay a higher tax.

In reality, providing public goods such as national defense involves the political process. This means that politicians, bureaucrats, special interest groups, and many others generate the decisions on how much of any particular public good to provide. Since the demand for a public good represents the benefits to society and the supply curve represents society's costs, equating marginal benefits and marginal costs yields the optimal amount. But estimating the demand (benefits) from public goods and their costs can be a complex process. Most people desire the benefits of a strong military, but few enjoy paying the taxes required to pay the cost. Because people cannot be excluded from the good once provided, they have little incentive to reveal their true preferences, making this type of market failure difficult to overcome.

Common Property Resources

Commonly held resources are subject to nonexclusion but are rival in consumption. The market failure associated with such resources is often referred to as the **"tragedy of the commons."**[3] The tragedy here is the tendency for commonly held resources to be overused and overexploited. Because the resource is held in common, individuals race to "get theirs" before others can grab it all.

One example of commonly held resources giving rise to problems involves oil fields. Oil reservoirs often span the subsurface property of many landowners. Because oil reservoirs are regarded as common property, each landowner has an incentive to drill as many wells as possible and to pump out oil as rapidly as possible. Having too many wells pumping too quickly, however, reduces the oil field's water and gas pressure, thus reducing the total recoverable oil from the reservoir. Each owner's decision to drill a well therefore imposes an external cost on the other owners of land over the reservoir. At one point, this problem grew so severe that it resulted in passage of the 1935 Connally "Hot Oil" Act. This act restricted drilling, regulated the number and location of oil wells, and capped pumping rates.[4]

"tragedy of the commons"
Resources that are owned by the community at large (e.g., parks, ocean fish, and the atmosphere) therefore tend to be overexploited because individuals have little incentive to use them in a sustainable fashion.

[3] Garrett Hardin, "The Tragedy of the Commons," *Science* 162, 1968, pp. 1243–1248.

[4] Daniel Yergin, *The Prize* (New York: Simon & Schuster), 1991.

Life at the Top of the Rock: Protecting the Barbary Macaques

How are Barbary macaques able to roam freely in the tiny British territory of Gibraltar when they have been completely driven away everywhere else in Europe?

The Barbary macaque is a tailless monkey with origins in the Atlas Mountains of Morocco and Algeria, and in Southern Europe. Decades of logging, however, have decimated the natural habitat to a point that the macaques have become an endangered species. Today, Barbary macaques no longer roam freely in Europe—with the exception of one small place where they still call home: Gibraltar.

Gibraltar is a tiny English enclave at the southern tip of Spain, across the Strait of Gibraltar from Morocco. At barely 2 square miles, Gibraltar is so tiny that its airport runway crosses the main highway, halting auto traffic every time an airplane lands or takes off.

Why would this tiny tourist destination be home to hundreds of freely roaming Barbary macaques?

An ideal natural habitat for Barbary macaques has been bolstered by Gibraltar's laws that have protected the species as a public good. Gibraltar is home to the Rock, a towering monolith of limestone that serves as a nature preserve where Barbary macaques have thrived because of its popularity as a tourist attraction. The macaques have adapted to life on the Rock, allowing tourists to approach them with remarkable ease. It is the only population of wild monkeys that remains in Europe, and the citizens of Gibraltar have taken great effort to ensure their well-being.

The protection of Barbary macaques in Gibraltar is a public good because the ability to see and appreciate these monkeys in the wild is a benefit that can be experienced by everyone without exclusion or rivalry. The cost of maintaining the population had long been paid for by the government and managed by the British military stationed in Gibraltar. More recently, their care has been transferred to a nonprofit organization called the Gibraltar Ornithological & Natural History Society.

As long as people are willing to contribute to their upkeep, Barbary macaques will remain a unique attraction to locals and tourists for years to come.

GO TO **LaunchPad** TO PRACTICE THE ECONOMIC CONCEPTS IN THIS STORY

Road congestion is another illustration of the "tragedy of the commons." Figure 4 shows a market for usage of a road that is fully used and is right at the tipping point before becoming congested. In Figure 4, demand for driving on this road is D_0, and the

FIGURE 4   ROAD CONGESTION

Assume that this road is fully used and is right at the tipping point before becoming congested. Demand for driving on this road is D_0, and the marginal cost of using the road—gas, time, and auto expenses—is MC_0. Equilibrium is at point e, with Q_0 miles a day being driven. Consumer surplus is area P_0ae for the typical driver. When a new driver begins using the road, this increases the marginal cost of driving to MC_1 for everyone, because the tipping point has been passed, and the road is now congested. Consumer surplus shrinks because of overuse of this common good.

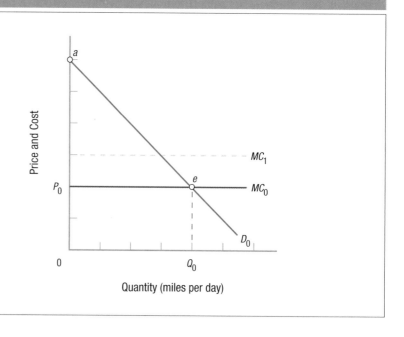

marginal cost to use the road—gas, time, and auto expenses—is initially MC_0. Equilibrium is at point e, with Q_0 miles per day driven. Consumer surplus is area P_0ae for the typical driver.

Now assume that a new driver begins using the road. This increases the marginal cost of driving to MC_1 for everyone, because the tipping point has been passed, and the road is now congested. Consumer surplus shrinks because of overuse of the commons. Note that the new driver did not take these external costs into consideration; the driver assumed that the marginal cost would be equal to MC_0, not MC_1.

Possible solutions to common property resource problems involve establishing private property rights, using government policy to restrict access to the resource, or informal organizations that restrict each user's benefits from the resource. Reduced congestion, for example, could be achieved by raising the tax on gasoline, subsidizing bus or rapid transit travel, or privatizing roads and allowing the owners to charge tolls.

A crowded public beach makes the experience less enjoyable.

The optimal provision of public goods, whether pure public goods or common property resources with significant public goods characteristics, is a significant challenge faced by society. Individuals tend to act in their self-interest when using public goods without contributing to their provision (free riding) or overusing a resource without considering the impact of such use on others. Other examples of public goods that have risen to the forefront of policy debate include health care and environmental policy, which we turn to next.

Health Care as a Public Good

Among the most contentious recent issues has been the expansion of health care access with the Affordable Care Act (ACA) in 2010. Although health care services are guaranteed by the government to those serving in the military along with veterans, those over the age of 65 with Medicare, and those who fall below certain income limits that qualify for Medicaid, most Americans rely on the private insurance market for their health care services. Much of this insurance is paid for by employers of full-time workers. But part-time workers, self-employed workers, and unemployed persons must find health care coverage on their own, often at high prices, especially when individuals are deemed by insurance companies to be high-risk. Consequently, in 2010, about 1 in 6 Americans did not have health care insurance.

One problem with private health care provision and private insurance markets is **asymmetric information,** when one party knows more about a situation than another. For example, individuals know more about their daily health habits than private insurers, and might try to hide unhealthy habits. Doctors know more about medical conditions than their patients, leading some to order excessive medical tests or prescribe more expensive treatment options than what might be necessary. A consequence of asymmetric information is an increase in the cost of health care resulting from inefficiencies in delivering health care, which leads to higher insurance prices that become unaffordable to many. Addressing the problem of asymmetric information requires greater transparency in medical records to prevent patients and doctors from exploiting information to their advantage. Otherwise, it may lead to greater escalation in the cost of health care, as the following example shows.

Suppose that consumers with bad habits (such as poor eating habits, lack of exercise, aggressive driving, or a penchant for high-impact sports) fail to disclose this information. This leads to insurance companies underestimating risk and setting premiums too low, causing losses. Because insurance companies do not always know who is failing to disclose

asymmetric information Occurs when one party to a transaction has significantly better information than another party.

information, premiums are raised on all customers who share the characteristics of those with risky behaviors. The rise in premiums causes some to drop coverage (especially young healthy people), making the insurance pool even weaker. Because asymmetric information exacerbates the problem of less healthy people seeking health insurance and healthy people forgoing it, the private insurance market becomes less sustainable, leading insurance providers to take more drastic actions, such as restricting coverage to anyone who might be deemed high-risk.

Because of the growing number of Americans who either did not qualify for insurance or chose not to purchase it, the ACA was passed in 2010, though not without tremendous controversy and subsequent attempts by Congress to eliminate it. The aim of the ACA is to reduce the percentage of Americans without health care coverage. This is accomplished through many rules, such as preventing insurance companies from refusing customers due to preexisting conditions (such as a previous bout of cancer that would have previously disqualified a person from obtaining affordable insurance), removing lifetime limits on coverage, providing subsidies to make insurance more affordable, and requiring all Americans to buy insurance or face a tax penalty at the end of the year (commonly known as the *individual mandate*). From 2010 to 2016, the uninsured rate fell from 16% to 11%.

The ACA remains controversial because of the individual mandate that forces all consumers to buy insurance, even if they do not want it. Mandated health care has many characteristics of public goods, something that all persons have access to and a service that one cannot opt out of.

Why would a government force its citizens to buy health insurance? First, like other public goods, it is subject to the free rider problem. Those without health insurance often use hospital emergency rooms for illnesses and accidents because many laws prevent caregivers such as hospitals from denying emergency care, regardless of ability to pay. The cost is borne by caregivers, who pass this on in the form of higher prices for everyone else. Second, much like other public goods such as clean air, fire department services, or

ISSUE

The Resurgence of Nearly Eradicated Diseases—A Free Rider Problem

Prior to the 1960s, cases of whooping cough and measles were common among children, with up to 200,000 cases of whooping cough and more than a million cases of measles in the United States (and likely much more due to underreporting), resulting in hundreds of deaths each year.

By the 1970s, advances in childhood vaccinations led to a dramatic reduction in cases of measles, whooping cough, polio, and other illnesses, and the eradication of smallpox. Such progress in public health research led to decades of progress in ensuring that all children receive access to affordable immunizations.

Over time, however, complacency has arisen. Some parents began to worry that the perceived risks of vaccines outweighed their benefits. Fears of vaccines rose when a 1998 study

Blend Images/Getty Images

published in *The Lancet* claimed a link between vaccines and autism. Although this study was eventually determined to be fraudulent, leading *The Lancet* to retract the study and the doctor behind the study to be stripped of his medical license, that did not slow down a growing number of parents choosing not to vaccinate their children. This led to grave outcomes, as cases of whooping cough and measles surged in recent

years, with 667 confirmed cases of measles and 32,971 cases of whooping cough in the United States in 2014.

The effect of immunizations is one that highlights the importance of health care as a public good. When the entire population is free of a disease, choosing to forgo vaccinations means one will likely not be exposed to an illness. However, once enough people choose not to vaccinate, the immunity of the population (called *herd immunity*) fades. In other words, people who choose not to vaccinate depend on others not to spread diseases. They free ride on the willingness of others to get vaccinated. But like all public goods, when the number of free riders increases, an optimal provision of the public good fails. The resurgence of nearly eradicated diseases is an example of the consequences that can result.

elementary education, health care provides societal benefits such as improved productivity and earlier diagnosis of severe illnesses, which allows for greater treatment options and lower costs.

The ACA is likely to remain unpopular among many for some time. This is common whenever a debate ensues on the best approach to providing public goods. In the long run, however, once consumers become accustomed to the benefits created by the ACA, they will be less likely to accept those same benefits being taken away.

 CHECKPOINT

PUBLIC GOODS

■ Pure public goods are nonrival in consumption, and once the good is provided, no one can be excluded from using it.

■ The demand for public goods is found by vertically summing individual demand curves.

■ Optimal provision of public goods is found where the marginal benefit of public goods (demand) is equal to the marginal cost of provision.

■ Common property resources have the characteristics of nonexcludability but are rival. This typically leads to overuse and overexploitation.

■ Health care is an example of an industry with public good characteristics in which asymmetric information and free ridership are common.

QUESTIONS: On most college campuses, the use of the recreation center is open to all registered students without an additional fee. The cost of running the recreation center typically is paid for by an activity fee paid by all students, regardless of whether they use the facilities or not. In what ways does your campus recreation center resemble a public good? In what ways does it not?

Answers to the Checkpoint questions can be found at the end of this chapter.

ENVIRONMENTAL POLICY

We have seen that market failure can lead to excessive amounts of products that pollute or generate other negative externalities, or to overuse of commonly owned resources that result in environmental degradation. This section puts these market failures together by looking at environmental policy.

Market failure is one reason why unregulated markets may produce inequitable or inefficient results. Government policies, however, do not always make things better. **Government failure** occurs when (1) public policies do not bring about an optimal allocation of resources, and/or (2) the incentives of politicians and government bureaucrats are not in line with the public interest.

Government failure may result from the practical inability of policymakers to gather enough information to set good policies. Water pollution, for instance, is well understood, resulting in fairly obvious regulatory policies, but the same is not true for issues such as global climate change. Even if we all agree that the Earth is getting warmer and humans are partly to blame, controversy remains about the adequacy of public policy to address this problem.

Despite the challenges of creating and implementing environmental policy, it is still an issue that must be tackled. We now discuss various questions that arise when setting goals for environmental policy and the many choices that are available to policymakers.

government failure The result when the incentives of politicians and government bureaucrats do not align with the public interest.

Intergenerational Questions

Should politicians consider the interests of voters who haven't yet been born? Environmental issues raise complex questions involving how resources are to be allocated across

| FIGURE 5 | PRESENT VALUE OF $1,000 TO BE PAID IN 30 YEARS DISCOUNTED AT 1%, 5%, AND 10% |

This figure is a reminder of the effects discount rates have on the present value of a fixed payment that will come due at a future date. A higher discount rate means that the value today of a future payment will be lower. The higher the discount rate we choose, the lower the value we place on the environmental damage to be suffered by future generations. The lower our discount rate, the more we are willing to protect the health of the future environment.

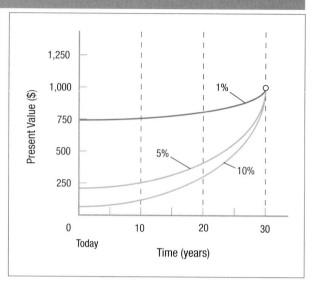

generations. Some resources, such as sunlight, are continual and renewable. Others, such as forests, fisheries, and the soil, are renewable but exhaustible if overexploited. And some resources are nonrenewable, such as oil and coal. These resources are finite and cannot be renewed, but their available stock can be expanded through exploration or the use of new technologies that allow greater extraction or more efficient use.

When we develop environmental policies, we need to consider and evaluate different possible futures. Figure 5 is a reminder of the effects that discount rates have on the present value of a fixed payment that will come due at some date in the future. For environmental policies, the discount rate we choose is crucially important.

A higher discount rate means that the value today of a future payment will be less. At a 10% discount, a payment of $1,000 in 30 years is worth only $42 today, whereas discounting the same $1,000 at 1% yields a present value of $748. The higher the discount rate we choose, the lower the value we place on the environmental damage to be suffered by future generations. The lower our discount rate, conversely, the more we are willing to protect the health of the future environment. As always, crafting good public policies requires striking a balance between the two.

Socially Efficient Levels of Pollution

We have already seen that some pollution is acceptable to society. To require that no one pollute, period, would bring most economic activity as we know it to a halt. Yet, pollution damages our environment. The harmful effects of pollution range from direct threats to our health coming from air and water pollution to reductions in species from deforestation.

The damages that come from pollution are a cost we incur for living. To be alive is to generate some pollution. Our focus is on marginal damage, which resembles the marginal cost curves we studied earlier. The marginal damage (*MD*) curve in Figure 6 shows the change in damages that comes from a given change in emission levels. Notice that as emissions levels rise, the added damages rise.

The horizontal axis of Figure 6 measures the tons of pollution emitted into the environment (tons per year). Note that E_0 represents the maximum pollution (no environmental cleanup at all). The vertical axis measures the environmental costs in dollars. These costs represent a dollar value for various environmental losses, including the physical costs of pollution (asthma attacks and other lung diseases), the aesthetic losses (visual impact of clear-cutting), and the losses associated with species reduction.

FIGURE 6	MARGINAL DAMAGES AND MARGINAL ABATEMENT COSTS

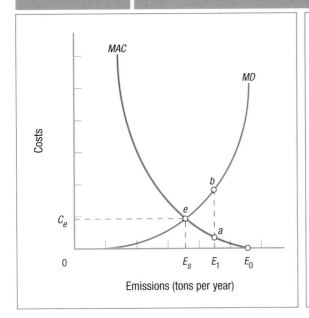

The marginal damage curve (*MD*) shows the *change* in damages that come from a given *change* in emission levels. The horizontal axis measures pollution. Note that E_0 is the maximum pollution that can occur without environmental cleanup. The vertical axis measures the environmental costs of this pollution. Marginal abatement costs curve (*MAC*) begins at zero at E_0, then rises as emission levels are reduced (moving leftward from E_0). Socially optimal pollution is E_S, at a cost to society of C_e (point *e*).

Abatement costs are the costs associated with reducing emissions. A utility plant dumping effluent into a river can treat the effluent before discharge, but this costs money. In Figure 6, marginal abatement costs (*MAC*) begin at zero at E_0, then rise as emission levels are reduced (moving leftward from E_0). The *MAC* curve in Figure 6 is a generalized abatement cost function, but in practice, the costs vary for different sources of pollution and the technologies available for reducing them. Chemical plants face different problems than utilities that release hot water into rivers. Cooling the water before release clearly requires a different technology—and is much easier—than eliminating toxic chemicals from effluent flow.

The socially optimal level of pollution in Figure 6 is E_S, at a cost to society of C_e (point *e*). To see why this is so, assume that we are at pollution level E_1. The cost to reduce another unit of emissions is found at point *a* (measuring on the vertical axis), while the damage that would result from this pollution is found at point *b*. Since $b > a$, society is better off if emissions are reduced. Once we begin reducing emissions below E_S, however, abatement costs overtake marginal damages, or the costs of cleanup begin to outweigh the benefits.

The total damage from pollution in Figure 6 is represented by the area beneath the marginal damages curve and to the left of E_S. Total abatement costs, meanwhile, are equal to the area beneath the marginal abatement costs curve and to the right of E_S. Combined, these two costs represent the total social costs from emissions. We turn now to consider how environmental policy can ensure that emissions approach this optimal level.

Overview of Environmental Policies

Over the years, many types of environmental policies have been developed in response to different problems, covering the spectrum from centralized control to decentralized economic incentives. To be effective, all environmental policies must be efficient, fair, and enforceable, and they must provide incentives for improvement in the environment.

As a general rule, the more centralized an environmental policy, the more likely it represents a **command and control** philosophy. This means that a centralized agency sets the rules for emissions, including levels of effluents allowed, usable technologies, and enforcement procedures. Command and control policies usually set standards of conduct that are enforced by the legal and regulatory system. Abatement costs at this point become compliance costs of meeting the standards. Standards are popular because they are simple, they treat all firms in an industry the same way, and they prevent competing firms from polluting.

command and control policies
Environmental policies that set standards and issue regulations, which are then enforced by the legal and regulatory system.

At the other end of the spectrum are **market-based policies,** which use charges, taxes, subsidies, deposit-refund systems, or tradable emission permits to achieve the same ends. Examples of this approach include water effluent charges, user charges for water and wastewater management, glass and plastic bottle refund systems, and tradable permits for ozone reduction. We begin with a brief look at command and control policies, contrasting them with abatement taxes, then look at the case for tradable emission permits.

Command and Control Policies

Policymakers determine the pollution control or abatement that is best, then introduce the most efficient policies to achieve those ends. Figure 7 shows the supply and demand for pollution abatement. Demand curve $D_A = MB_A$ represents society's demand for abatement; it is a reflection of the marginal damage curve we looked at earlier. Note that the demand curve for abatement is negatively sloped because the *marginal benefit* from abatement declines as the environment becomes cleaner. The gains from an ever cleaner environment eventually become smaller and smaller because of the law of diminishing returns.

The marginal costs of abatement are the costs of cleaning up pollution. These costs rise with abatement efforts and become high as zero pollution, A_0, is approached. Optimal abatement comes at A_e, costing c_e. This means that optimal pollution, $A_0 - A_e$, is greater than zero. Command and control policies could set A_e as the abatement requirement and then set the right standards to meet this requirement. Aiming for abatement higher than A_e would be inefficient, because marginal costs would exceed marginal benefits.

Setting abatement requirements (or standards) equal to A_e in Figure 7 is a classic example of a command and control policy. Again, command and control policies that set rigid standards for polluters have long been a favorite of policymakers. Yet, this approach can lead to inefficiencies, because different industries may emit the same (or equivalently dangerous) substances, but face different technical problems and costs in reducing their pollution. To minimize the cost of reducing pollution, each source of pollution needs to be reduced to the point at which the marginal cost of abatement is equal for all sources. This can be achieved through market-based policies.

| **FIGURE 7** | **MARGINAL COST OF ABATEMENT AND ABATEMENT DEMAND** |

Demand curve D_A represents society's demand for abatement. The marginal benefit from abatement (MB_A) declines as the environment becomes cleaner, because the gains from an ever cleaner environment become smaller and smaller (diminishing returns). The marginal costs of abatement are the costs of reducing pollution. These costs rise with abatement efforts and become high as zero pollution A_0 is approached (again, because of the law of diminishing returns, or increasing costs). Optimal abatement is A_e, costing c_e. This means optimal pollution, $A_0 - A_e$, is greater than zero.

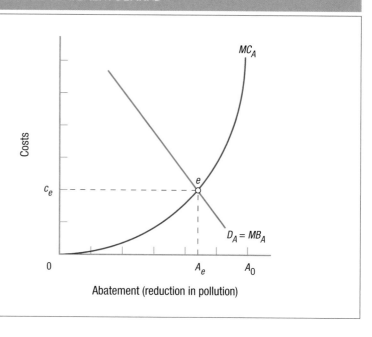

Market-Based Policies

Economists argue that market-oriented, or indirect, approaches to environmental policy are more efficient than command and control policies. Two of the most popular and effective of these indirect approaches are the use of emissions taxes and marketable or tradable permits.

Emissions Taxes An alternative to command and control policies is an emissions tax on every unit of pollution produced to achieve the socially efficient outcome. Taxes of this sort are known as **Pigouvian taxes** (named after Arthur Pigou who developed the idea in 1920). Unlike command and control policies, polluting firms are not limited to a fixed amount of pollution. Instead, by forcing firms to pay for every unit of pollution created, firms would invest in pollution reduction measures up to the point at which the cost of abatement measures is no longer less than the tax. Such policies take into account the fact that some firms are able to reduce pollution at less cost than others. Therefore, it creates efficiencies by allowing firms with higher costs of pollution abatement to pollute more by paying more taxes, while encouraging firms with lower costs of pollution abatement to utilize such measures to reduce their tax burden.

> **Pigouvian tax** A tax that is placed on an activity generating negative externalities in order to achieve a socially efficient outcome.

Returning to Figure 7, achieving the optimal level of pollution abatement, A_e, could be achieved by charging a tax equal to c_e per unit of pollution. Firms would adopt pollution controls up to A_e, because the costs to reduce pollution to this point are less than the tax. Firms would emit only $A_0 - A_e$ pollution. As a result, the same level of abatement is achieved using taxes as with using command and control policies; however, allowing the market to achieve this outcome through taxes allows for a more efficient outcome for the firms involved.

Marketable or Tradable Permits Another way that markets are used to limit pollution is through the use of marketable or tradable permits. Economists initially proposed marketable or tradable permits when environmental laws were first being debated and enacted in the 1960s and 1970s. Environmental regulators essentially ignored this suggestion until the 1990s.

Today, tradable permits are used to reduce water effluents in the Fox River in Wisconsin, Tar-Pamlico River in North Carolina, and Dillon Reservoir in Colorado. One of the most successful uses of marketable permits for air pollution, described in the Issue in this section, has reduced the sulfur dioxide (SO_2) emissions in the Midwest that create acid rain in the East. Originally, the cost of this cleanup was expected to be significant, but technical advances steadily reduced abatement costs, causing the price of the permits to decline sharply.

Marketable permits require that a regulatory body set a maximum allowable quantity of effluents allowed, typically called the "cap," and issue permits granting the "right" to pollute a certain amount. These permits can be bought and sold, thus creating the property rights that permit transactions of the sort Coase advocated. Sales are normally between two polluters, with one polluter buying a permit from a more efficient operator. Polluters do not have to be the only purchasers. Victims or environmental groups could conceivably purchase pollution rights and hold them off the market, thereby reducing pollution below the established cap.

Figure 8 illustrates how such a market works. We assume that there are two firms in the market, each producing 10 tons of pollution, and that the government wishes to limit pollution to a total of 10 tons. Without restrictions, firms do zero abatement and total pollution is 20 tons. Setting a goal of 10 tons amounts to cutting pollution in half.

Assume, for simplicity, that the government at first gives the permits to firm X. (Remember that the Coase theorem suggests efficiency is not affected by who owns the rights to pollute.) Demand curve D_Y represents firm Y's demand for these permits, while supply curve S_X represents firm X's willingness to sell some of the permits it was granted. Assume that the market for permits is competitive; thus, equilibrium will be at point e with a permit price equal to $300. Firm Y buys 7 permits and pollutes that amount, and firm X pollutes 3 tons.

Firm X pollutes less and sells 7 permits to firm Y because it can reduce more of its pollution before its marginal abatement costs reach $300. In this case, firm Y faces high cleanup costs that reach $300 a ton at 3 tons. Thus, it buys 7 tons of pollution rights from firm X.

FIGURE 8 ☰ TRADABLE PERMITS

This figure illustrates how a market for tradable pollution permits works. Assume there are only two firms (X and Y) in the market and the government wishes to limit total pollution to 10 tons. Without restrictions, both firms do zero abatement and pollution is 20 tons. Setting a goal of 10 tons therefore amounts to cutting pollution in half. Assume that the government gives the permits to firm X. Demand curve D_Y represents firm Y's demand for these permits. Given a competitive market for permits, equilibrium will be at point e with a permit price equal to $300. Firm Y buys 7 permits and pollutes that amount, and firm X emits 3 tons of pollution.

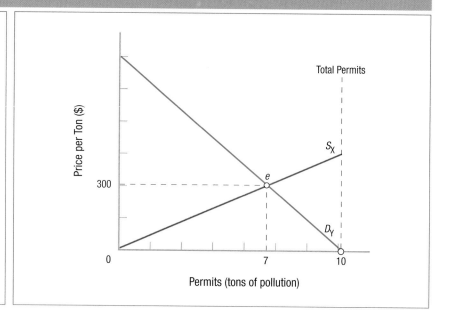

Firm X in this example ends up with the revenue from permit sales, while firm Y's income declines by the same amount ($2,100). Auctioning off the permits produces the same result, but the government receives the revenue.

Keep in mind that regulators could have set a $300 per ton tax on effluents and achieved the same result. One advantage of permits over taxes is that no knowledge of marginal abatement costs is needed to ensure that the permit price is optimal. The market price of permits will adjust to variances in abatement costs. All the regulator must determine is how much to reduce pollution levels. If reducing pollution by a certain amount, regardless of the cost, is the goal, permits will achieve this goal.

Other Market-Based Policies We have looked at two of the most frequently used market-based policies, taxes and marketable permits. Emission taxes and charges have been used for water effluents, waste management, pesticide packaging, batteries, tires, and other products and processes. User charges are the most common way to finance wastewater treatment facilities.

Federal subsidies, the flip side of taxes or charges, are used when local communities do not have the resources for pollution control. Marketable permits have been most successful in programs to reduce air pollution, as well as those targeting acid rain and ozone reduction. Deposit-refund systems have been used mainly for recyclable products such as cans, bottles, tires, and batteries.

Over the years, most environmental policies have been of the command and control variety. The 1970 Clean Air Act focused on specific forms of air pollution—particulates, carbon monoxide, and so forth—and established air quality standards. Today, economic or market-based approaches to environmental policy are considered more efficient than command and control policies. Most environmental agencies, however, in this country and abroad have not used these tools until recently.

One reason for this is probably that many people in the regulatory and environmental communities resist viewing environmental resources as commodities to be subjected to market forces of supply and demand. It is market failures, after all, that led to environmental decay in the first place. Why would we want to put the environment on the market? Many pollutants, moreover, are frequently mixed together and their individual impacts are difficult to determine. Consequently, setting the right tax rate or issuing the right number of allowable permits is difficult. Finally, some policymakers balk at giving corporations the right to pollute, even a limited amount.

ISSUE

Cap-and-Trade: The Day Liberal Environmentalists and Free-Market Conservatives Agreed

Environmental policies in recent decades have epitomized the battle between liberal environmentalists and free-market conservatives, with the former arguing for more limits on pollution, while the latter want more market freedom. How then, could the two sides come to an agreement that would satisfy both of their primary objectives?

In the late 1980s, the problem of acid rain reached a boiling point, with heavy pollution from sulfur dioxide emissions causing health issues, polluted lakes and rivers, and reduced visibility. Further, it heightened tensions with Canada, which suffered negative externalities from the pollution from American power plants. With the environmental damage reaching front-page news and a fierce political battle on how to fix it, it looked like a lost cause.

Then came a very unlikely alliance between Dan Dukek of the Environmental Defense Fund and Boyden Gray, a multimillionaire conservative who was appointed President Bush's White House counsel in 1988. Gray, a strong

proponent of free-market principles, had long supported a method of allowing individuals and firms to buy and sell permits to pollute. The acid rain crisis allowed Dudek and Gray to propose an emissions permit trading program that placed significant caps on sulfur dioxide (placating environmentalists), while eliminating regulations and allowing the marketplace to determine permit prices (placating free-market proponents).

The program became law with the *Clean Air Act of 1990.* When the law, which became known as "cap-and-trade," took effect in 1995, emissions fell and led to significant external cost savings in what has been considered a resounding success in solving a major environmental problem using a market-based approach as opposed to a command and control approach.

Today, much discussion centers on the proposed use of cap-and-trade to reduce carbon dioxide emissions. Such programs are law in the European Union and elsewhere, but proposals to pass cap-and-trade legislation in the

Westend61/superstock

United States since 2008 have been held up, ironically by the same market-based proponents who created the strategy that worked in the past. Opponents of cap-and-trade today argue that cap-and-trade still imposes harsh limits on the broader market. Yet, without cap-and-trade, resolutions to reduce global warming become less likely. It may take another unlikely alliance before the problem of global warming is solved.

Information from Richard Conniff, "The Political History of Cap and Trade," Smithsonian, August 2009.

✓ CHECKPOINT

ENVIRONMENTAL POLICY

- Government failure can occur when politicians and government do not have the right incentives to bring about an optimal allocation of resources.

- The discount rate chosen for environmental policies determines the intergenerational impact of policy.

- The socially optimal level of pollution occurs where the marginal damage is equal to the marginal abatement costs.

- Policymakers determine the optimal pollution levels and then often use command and control policies to set the most efficient regulations or levels of abatement.

- Tradable permits use market forces to bring pollution within limits set by regulators.

QUESTIONS: If a cap-and-trade program for carbon dioxide emissions is implemented in the United States, with the overall limit slowly reduced each year, what would happen to the price of permits if all production activity stays the same and the cost of pollution abatement remains unchanged? What would need to happen in order for the price of permits to fall over time?

Answers to the Checkpoint questions can be found at the end of this chapter.

THE ECONOMICS OF CLIMATE CHANGE AND SUSTAINABLE DEVELOPMENT

Among the most significant economic issues facing the world today is the effect of human actions on the environment. There is scientific consensus that without a significant reduction in the production of greenhouse gases, which engulf the atmosphere and lead to global warming, irreversible damage to the climate, ecosystems, and coastlines will result. However, the course of action needed to address climate change deals with equity issues that are difficult to achieve consensus on.

Many individuals and corporations understand that natural resources are scarce and many do their parts by conserving water and energy resources, and recycling. Those who are more dedicated might choose public transportation over cars, install solar panels and other energy-saving technologies in homes and businesses, and plant trees or donate to one of many organizations that will do so on one's behalf. The choice to engage in actions to minimize climate change by individuals, businesses, and governments is one that involves a **cost-benefit analysis**. A cost-benefit analysis provides a formal, rational model for policy decisions, by focusing on the choices that are available, the preferences of individuals, and the present value of benefits and costs that will be incurred by today's and future generations.

The challenge with using cost-benefit analysis for environmental policies is that many of the benefits and costs are difficult to quantify. For example, what is the cost of living in a polluted city? What is the benefit of preventing a species from going extinct? The answers require a more thorough understanding of the causes and effects of climate change. Moreover, climate change has an intergenerational effect, as actions today will affect future generations. This has led many corporations and countries to adopt **sustainable development** goals, which refers to the ability to meet the needs of the present without compromising the ability of future generations to meet their own needs. Through greater knowledge of the issues at stake, individuals are more likely to make informed decisions about their impact on the environment.

cost-benefit analysis A methodology for decision making that looks at the discounted value of the costs and benefits of a given project.

sustainable development The ability to meet the needs of the present without compromising the ability of future generations to meet their own needs.

Understanding Climate Change

Climate change refers to the gradual change in the Earth's climate due to an increase in average temperatures resulting from both natural and human actions. It is largely irreversible, particularly in its effect on rising sea levels and on ecosystems. According to the Intergovernmental Panel on Climate Change (IPCC), the average temperature "from 1983 to 2012 was *likely* the warmest 30-year period of the last 1400 years in the Northern Hemisphere."[5] And the trend has not ebbed, as average temperatures in the year 2015 reached the highest ever recorded in modern times. Understanding the causes and effects of climate change is necessary to adopt appropriate actions to address the problem.

The Causes of Climate Change   The primary causes of climate change are related to actions that emit greenhouse gases. Greenhouse gases created largely by human activities include carbon dioxide (CO_2) from fossil fuel and industrial processes, carbon dioxide (CO_2) from forestry and other land use (FOLU), methane (CH_4), nitrous oxide (N_2O), and fluorinated gases (F). Figure 9 shows both the global nominal rise in each of these greenhouse gases from 1970 to 2010, along with the percentage of overall greenhouse gases that each source represents.

The largest portion of greenhouse gases is carbon dioxide, which is created by fossil fuel usage, industrial production, and deforestation. Fossil fuel usage includes the use of automobiles and airplanes, electricity and home heating fuels, and the production of products such as plastics and tires, and even everyday items such as ink pens, cosmetics, and toothpaste.

[5] *IPCC, 2014: Climate Change 2014: Synthesis Report. Contribution of Working Groups I, II and III to the Fifth Assessment Report of the Intergovernmental Panel on Climate Change* [Core Writing Team, R.K. Pachauri and L.A. Meyer (eds.)]. IPCC, Geneva, Switzerland, 151 pp.

FIGURE 9   ANNUAL GREENHOUSE GAS EMISSIONS, 1970–2010

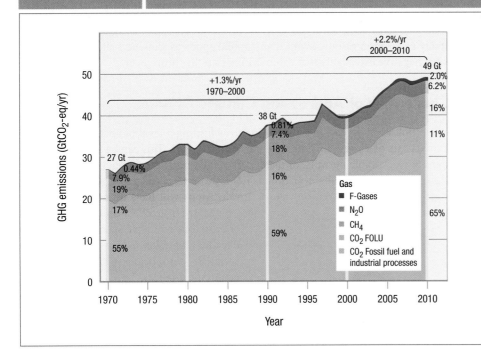

FIGURE 9   ANNUAL GREENHOUSE GAS EMISSIONS, 1970–2010

Greenhouse gases from human activities include carbon dioxide from fossil fuel and industrial processes, carbon dioxide from forestry and other land use (FOLU), methane, nitrous oxide, and fluorinated gases. From 1970 to 2010, the nominal amount of all greenhouse gases increased. As a percentage of all greenhouse gases, carbon dioxide from fossil fuel and industrial processes increased from 55% to 65%, while fluorinated gases increased from 0.44% to 2%.

Information obtained from the IPCC's 2014 Climate Change Synthesis Report.

Deforestation contributes to greenhouse gases because trees absorb carbon dioxide, and when they are cut down, the stored carbon dioxide is released into the atmosphere.

Other forms of greenhouse gases include methane, nitrous oxide, and fluorinated gases. Methane is generated largely from livestock farming, landfills, and the production and use of fossil fuels. Nitrous oxide is produced on farms from the use of synthetic fertilizers along with fossil fuel usage. Finally, fluorinated gases are created in products such as modern refrigerators, air conditioners, and aerosol cans. Because fluorinated gases do not harm the ozone layer and are energy efficient, products that emit these gases have grown in popularity over the past decade, though they still contribute significantly to global warming.

The Consequences of Climate Change Today and in the Future
A sense of urgency surrounds climate change because the state of climate change science has advanced to the point where scientists are able to put probability estimates on certain impacts of warming, some of which are catastrophic. The major impacts of climate change are in the areas of food security, water resources, ecosystems, extreme weather events, and rising sea levels. The IPCC summarizes the consequences of climate change by listing five key "reasons for concern," as follows:

1. **Unique and threatened systems:** Many ecosystems are at risk, such as the diminishing Arctic sea ice and coral reefs, which leads to the extinction of species.

2. **Extreme weather events:** An increase in heat waves, heavy precipitation, and coastal flooding leads to major economic costs due to natural disasters and reductions in agricultural yields.

3. **Distribution of impacts:** The risks of climate change on disadvantaged people and communities are greater, especially those that depend on agricultural production.

4. **Global aggregate impacts:** Extensive biodiversity loss affects the global economy.

5. **Large-scale singular events:** Melting ice sheets will lead to rising sea levels, causing significant loss of coastal lands.

The difficulty with addressing these effects is that unlike air or water pollution that can be seen today, climate change has a cumulative effect. In other words, this year's CO_2 adds to that from the past to raise concentrations in the future. Once CO_2 levels reach a certain level, it may lead to extreme consequences that cannot be reversed. The global environment is essentially a common resource with many public goods aspects, and climate change is a huge global negative externality that extends long into the future.

The Challenges of Addressing Climate Change

Cleaning up pollution problems typically involves finding a level of abatement at which the marginal costs of abatement equal the marginal benefits. This can be achieved by taxing, assigning marketable permits, or using command and control policies to limit emissions. However, reducing global warming is not a short-term objective, but a cumulative process across many years. Yet, our short-run decisions will have immense impacts in the long run. Small changes in emissions today may have little effect on the current generation, but will have sizable effects many decades out. This aspect of the problem seriously complicates policymaking and economic analysis.

To further compound the problem, global climate change is a public good. Nobody can have less of it when someone has more (nonrivalry), and nobody can be excluded from its negative effects (nonexcludability). Technical innovations that help reduce CO_2 emissions are costly to develop and are difficult to profit from due to the free rider problem, which means that efforts to combat climate change need to involve governments or organizations wishing to fix the problem for the greater good.

Even so, issues of equity arise when combating global warming. Why would one country invest in expensive clean energy processes when its neighbor continues to spew out emissions unhindered? Currently, nearly half of the world's greenhouse gases are produced by China and the United States, which are the world's two largest countries economically. Does that mean the United States and China should spend at least a proportionate amount reducing emissions? How well will that appeal to the citizens in each country? Such issues of equity will continue to be raised as increased global cooperation to combat climate change takes on increased urgency in the near future. For some corporations and countries, waiting is not an option, and efforts to promote sustainable development have increasingly become part of corporate sustainability missions and political platforms, respectively.

ELINOR OSTROM (1933–2012)

NOBEL PRIZE

When economists talk about common property resources, they typically discuss the "tragedy of the commons" and suggest a solution that involves privatization or central government takeover and management of the resource. Elinor Ostrom was awarded the 2009 Nobel Prize in Economic Sciences for challenging this conventional wisdom by showing how *user-managed* resources, where people cooperate to solve a resource issue, can be effective.

Born in 1933 during the depths of the Great Depression and completing her doctorate in political science in 1965, her dissertation looked at a case in which saltwater was seeping into western Los Angeles's water basin. A group of individuals formed a water association to solve the problem by creating rules and injected water along the coast. Their efforts saved the basin. This experience led her to look at other common resource problems from a new perspective.

She used field studies and thousands of case studies by other social scientists along with game theory to determine how these informal organizations evolved and what conditions make them successful.

Her work has determined the requirements for sustainable user-managed common resource property, including (a) rules must clearly define entitlement to the resource, (b) adequate conflict resolution measures must exist, (c) an individual's duty to maintain the resource must be in proportion to his or her benefits, (d) monitoring and sanctioning must be by users or accountable to users, (e) sanctions should be graduated—mild for a first violation and stricter as violations are repeated, (f) governance and decision processes must be democratic, and (g) self-organization is recognized by outside authorities. When these institutional conditions are met, user management of common pool resources typically is successful.

Ostrom's insights and research have opened up an alternative to prevent the "tragedy of the commons." Her work will be particularly important as nations work together to reduce the potential harm from global climate change, maybe our biggest common resource problem to date.

Promoting Sustainable Development

As the world's population continues to grow and countries become wealthier, there is an enhanced effort to improve sustainable development to prevent future generations from suffering the consequences of actions taken today. Sustainable development involves a concerted effort by individuals, businesses, and governments to recognize the causes and impacts of climate change, and to take appropriate actions. Much of the technology needed to reduce greenhouse gas emissions is already available today, and corporations and individuals play as much of a role as governments to keep global warming from worsening.

Corporate Social Responsibility

Nearly every company's primary responsibility to shareholders is to maximize profits. However, promoting the image of the company as socially responsible has also become common. Take a glance at most major corporations' Web sites and one will see a link to the company's page on corporate social responsibility, highlighting its efforts to improve sustainable development and to provide educational opportunities and other economic programs for local communities.

But much like equity issues faced by countries, corporations face equity issues, too. Those in competitive industries must balance what they spend on their social responsibilities with their ability to generate sufficient monetary returns. Some companies have used social responsibility as a marketing strategy to promote market share. For example, both PepsiCo and Coca-Cola have extensive corporate social responsibility teams that spend tens of millions of dollars each year to improve the efficiency of their operations and to operate programs helping the environment and local communities. Today, it has become a necessity for corporations to promote sustainability, though large differences in commitment still exist.

Individual Social Responsibility

One of the most common methods of reducing greenhouse gases by individuals is through recycling, with some communities even requiring households and businesses to recycle or face fines. Yet, the process of recycling itself uses energy, in addition to labor and other resources. A more effective means of promoting sustainability is to conserve resources. Examples of ways to improve conservation include the following actions:

- Forgo paper financial statements and printed newspapers, magazines, and books—for example, the use of online homework systems and digital textbooks has significantly reduced the use of paper.
- Use LED or compact fluorescent bulbs that use up to 90% less energy than traditional incandescent bulbs (many countries including the United States have passed laws phasing out incandescent bulbs).
- Install smart temperature controls in homes that automatically reduce air conditioning and heating when the home is empty.
- Plant trees or purchase carbon offsets to fund efforts to plant trees.
- Drive less or drive fuel-efficient or alternative fuel cars.
- Insulate walls and modernize windows.
- Install solar panels.

Clearly, undertaking efforts to reduce our carbon footprint as a nation represents an insurance policy on the future. As new climate change information and technology becomes available, policies can be adjusted to reduce the potential costs in the future.

To that end, carbon dioxide emissions are frequently placed on political agendas. However, a slow economic recovery makes it harder to focus people's attention on this issue. Moreover, environmental policies such as cap-and-trade remain largely unfamiliar to everyday citizens, allowing politicians to portray policies in a manner that helps to promote their own goals rather than the goals of society. Political issues combined with economic issues will continue to make climate change a thorny problem for the future.

Globally, there has been increased effort in recent years to combat climate change, especially in the United States and China, the two biggest emitters of greenhouse gases. In 2015 the United States implemented the Clean Power Plan, setting new standards for reducing carbon emissions in power plants. Then in late 2015 the United Nations Climate Change Conference held in Paris led to the most comprehensive global accord passed to date. Signed by nearly 200 countries including the United States and China, the accord requires every country to enact a plan to reduce emissions, without mandating a specific level of reductions, which could conceivably cause political opposition within some countries. However, the agreement requires signing nations to reconvene every five years to report their progress, essentially creating global peer pressure to achieve its goals.

As with climate change, each of the examples described in this chapter dealt with market failure in which externalities, public goods, or shared resources lead the market away from a socially desirable output. Resolving a market failure generally requires some policy tool, such as the assignment of property rights, regulation, or the creation of market incentives to achieve the ideal outcome. However, determining which policy tool to use often leads to intense debate, making issues of market failure a challenge that societies and their policymakers will continue to face.

 CHECKPOINT

THE ECONOMICS OF CLIMATE CHANGE AND SUSTAINABLE DEVELOPMENT

- Global climate change is a huge negative externality with an extremely long time horizon.
- The public goods aspects of climate change make it a truly global problem.
- Balancing the current generation's costs and benefits against the potential harm to future generations raises difficult economic issues.
- Actions taken today to reduce a potential future calamity are a form of insurance.

QUESTION: One of the most difficult aspects of climate change policy is determining how much individuals are willing to sacrifice today for a better environment in the future. What are some factors that may influence whether a person holds a high or low discount rate on the future with regard to environmental policy?

Answers to the Checkpoint questions can be found at the end of this chapter.

chapter summary

Section 1 Externalities

13.1 **Externalities**, or spillovers, arise when a transaction benefits or harms parties not involved in the transaction. Externalities lead to **market failure** when external benefits or external costs push markets away from the socially optimal output.

Taking care of the front lawn creates an external benefit to the neighbors.

Factories spewing dirty smoke create an external cost to the area residents.

13.2 The **Coase theorem** suggests that when transaction costs are near zero, bargaining between parties will lead to an efficient allocation of resources no matter how property rights are allocated.

Example: If students have the right to party, the neighbors can pay the students to stay quiet. If neighbors have the right to a quiet environment, students can pay the neighbors for the right to party. Either way, those with the property rights can exercise their rights or accept payment to forgo the rights.

Section 2 Public Goods

13.3 **Public goods** exhibit two characteristics:

Nonrivalry: One person's consumption of a good does not reduce the availability of that good to others.

Nonexcludability: Once a good has been provided, no consumer can be excluded from consuming the product.

Public goods lead to market failure when individuals lack the incentive to pay for them, leading to such goods being underprovided.

13.5 The health care industry exhibits characteristics of public goods because of the **free-rider problem,** when consumers choose to forgo paying for insurance or obtaining vaccines but still rely on others to do so.

13.4 **Common property resources** are owned by the community, and therefore individuals tend to overuse and overexploit them.

Section 3 Environmental Policy

13.6 **Environmental policies** depend on the discount rate chosen for how society values events in the future. A high discount rate places a significant burden on future generations, while a low discount rate places a greater burden on the current generation.

13.7 **The optimal pollution level** in any society is rarely zero. Instead, some pollution is acceptable if the cost of abatement exceeds its benefit. Therefore, optimal pollution levels are found where marginal abatement costs (*MAC*) equal the marginal damage (*MD*) caused by pollution. As long as the cleanup costs exceed damage, it would be optimal to allow pollution until *MAC* equals *MD* at E_s.

A surprising source of pollution is the methane and ammonia gases produced by cows through belching and flatulence, contributing approximately 14% of the world's greenhouse gases.

Eric Chiang

13.8 Environmental policy aimed at addressing market failure takes on several forms:

- **Command and control:** Fixed standards for polluters that are enforced through inspections and legal action (does not always lead to optimal pollution levels).

- **Emissions taxes:** A fee that is paid to the government per unit of pollution emitted (can lead to optimal pollution levels if the fee is set appropriately).

- **Pollution permits:** Also known as cap-and-trade, allows firms to buy, sell, and trade permits to pollute (can lead to optimal pollution levels).

Section 4 The Economics of Climate Change and Sustainable Development

13.9 Global climate change is a huge global negative externality accompanied by public goods aspects and extremely long time horizons, making the inherent market failure difficult to address.

Equity issues arise when some countries (often developed) pay significantly more to reduce global climate change than developing countries.

13.10 Solutions to global climate change require countries and corporations to engage in **sustainable development**. Individuals can do their part by taking actions to reduce fossil fuel usage through conservation efforts in everyday life.

Randy Olson/Corbis

Crowded streets filled with polluting vehicles are a common scene in India, contributing to global pollution as the nation develops.

KEY CONCEPTS

externalities, p. 342
market failure, p. 343
Coase theorem, p. 345
public goods, p. 347
nonrivalry, p. 347

nonexcludability, p. 347
free rider, p. 347
"tragedy of the commons," p. 349
asymmetric information, p. 351
government failure, p. 353

command and control policies, p. 355
market-based policies, p. 356
Pigouvian tax, p. 357
cost-benefit analysis, p. 360
sustainable development, 360

QUESTIONS AND PROBLEMS

Check Your Understanding

1. When trying to estimate the external benefits of a college education, what kinds of specific benefits would you include?

2. How might the government use market forces to encourage recycling?

3. What makes public goods different from private goods?

4. Why wouldn't a rural highway in Montana, Freeway 405 in Los Angeles, and the New Jersey Turnpike (toll) all be classified as public goods? Which would be most like a public good and which would be least?

5. Assume that you are convinced that if something isn't done now, global warming is going to create extensive problems and damage by the end of this century. If you were preparing a cost-benefit analysis of the impacts and had a 100-year horizon for your projections, would you use a 3% or an 8% discount rate?

6. What is the "tragedy of the commons"? How can it be mitigated?

Applying the Concepts

7. "Internalizing" the cost of negative externalities means that we try to set policies that require each product to include the full costs of its negative spillovers in its price. How do such policies affect product price and industry output and employment? Are these kinds of policies easy to implement in practice? How has globalization of production affected our ability to control pollution?

8. As a way to increase the funds for wildlife conservation, why don't we just auction off (say, on eBay) the right to name a new species when it is discovered? Why not do the same for existing species?

9. Anecdotal studies have shown that when given a choice between paper towels and an air dryer in a public restroom, more people choose paper towels to dry their hands. Why would people rationally choose paper towels, a method that is potentially more harmful to the environment? Are there some disadvantages to providing air dryers as the only option, as in many countries throughout Europe?

10. Garbage dumps are a particular source of a potent global-warming gas, the methane that bubbles up as the garbage decomposes. Why does it make sense for companies in the European Union to help Brazilian garbage dumps reduce their releases of methane as a way of meeting their Kyoto Protocol obligations?

11. The Presidio, previously a military base in San Francisco, is now a national park. It sits in the middle of San Francisco on some of the most valuable real estate in the United States. Congress, when it created the park, required that it rehabilitate the aging buildings and be self-sufficient within a decade or so, or the land would be sold off to developers. To achieve self-sufficiency, land was leased to private firms—Lucasfilm has built a large digital animation studio, and other firms have undertaken similar projects. These projects all must maintain the general character of the park and generate

rent that will cover the park's expenses in the future. Would this privatization approach work with most of America's other national parks? Why or why not?

12. The expansion of health care coverage to include more uninsured persons creates both external costs and external benefits. List two such costs and benefits from expanding health care coverage. Then, provide two reasons why health care can be viewed as a public good.

In the News

13. In the Canadian province of Northern Territories in the Arctic, ice roads (pathways for cars and trucks made on frozen lakes) are an important means of transportation during the winter months, when trucks are able to reach remote mines that generate many jobs. However, in 2015, the 248-mile Tibbitt to Contwoyto Winter Road faced a shorter season due to warmer weather that delayed the freezing of the lakes. Moreover, the thawing permafrost surrounding the area releases carbondioxide and methane trapped underneath, adding greenhouse gases to the atmosphere. What are some external costs that residents in the Northern Territories face from global warming?

14. Over a two-year period from January 2014 to January 2016, global oil prices fell from over $100 per barrel to $25 per barrel. The world supply of oil (aided by many more countries including the United States drilling for oil) dramatically outpaced demand as economic growth in oil-thirsty countries such as China slowed. Meanwhile, fuel prices dropped to 10-year lows, resulting in a spike in car and truck sales and an increase in airline travel. Analyze the effects of rising and falling oil prices on consumer behavior and how they affect the environment. Explain how oil prices and fuel consumption create a catch-22 for the environment.

Solving Problems

WORK IT OUT   📖 **LaunchPad** | interactive activity

15. Suppose the market supply and demand for flu shots are shown in the figure. Not taking into account the external benefits from flu shots, what are the equilibrium price and quantity of flu shots? Now suppose that every flu shot generates $10 in external benefits (from others being less likely to get sick). Show how this positive externality affects the graph (draw in a new curve). Taking into account external benefits, what would be the new equilibrium price and quantity of flu shots?

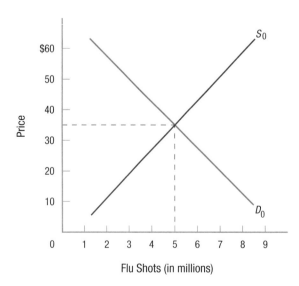

16. Suppose that the individual demand schedules for Al and Jane, the only two residents on a quiet city street, are shown in the table for speed bumps aimed at slowing cars

passing through. In a single diagram, plot Al and Jane's individual demand curve, and then plot the total demand curve for each unit of the public good.

Al		Jane	
Quantity	Marginal benefit	Quantity	Marginal benefit
1	$50	1	$100
2	$25	2	$50
3	$10	3	$25
4	$5	4	$10

#️⃣ USING THE NUMBERS

17. According to By the Numbers, rank the generation of the three most common forms of renewable energy from the least to the greatest in the year 2014.

18. According to By the Numbers, which two waste products are most recovered (recycled) by percentage, and which two waste products are least recovered?

ANSWERS TO QUESTIONS IN CHECKPOINTS

Checkpoint: Externalities 347

An external benefit of the policy would be reduced commuting times, which may contribute to improved standards of living and increased work productivity. Removing cars from the road and reducing cars idling in slow traffic would also reduce greenhouse gases. And income inequality can be reduced by providing low-income households (who are more likely to use public transportation) with free transportation. External costs might include higher costs for companies that depend on driving, such as delivery companies and ride-sharing companies, which may translate to higher prices for consumers.

Checkpoint: Public Goods 353

If the recreation center on campus allows all students to use it without an additional fee, it resembles some of the characteristics of a public good. Although it can exclude nonstudents from the facility, it is open to all students. Therefore, it is partially nonexcludable. However, if too many students use it, it can become crowded, resembling more of a common property resource.

Checkpoint: Environmental Policy 359

If the cap on total carbon dioxide emissions is reduced each year while economic activity stays the same, permit prices would rise to encourage firms to produce less to meet the cap. In order for permit prices to fall, the costs of pollution abatement must fall due to technological advances, or new production methods (using clean energy) must be introduced to emit less carbon dioxide.

Checkpoint: The Economics of Climate Change and Sustainable Development 364

Many answers are valid. But any factor that causes one to place greater emphasis on the future would result in a lower discount rate. Such factors might include having children or grandchildren, a greater desire to preserve Earth's natural beauty, having higher income or a business that relies on the availability of natural resources, or having empathy for future residents. Factors that might result in a high discount rate may include poverty, where emphasis is on improving one's current economic well-being in the future, or other difficult situations (wars and civil strife) that focus more attention on the present than on the future.

14 Network Goods

Understanding the extent to which networks influence our everyday lives

Learning Objectives

14.1 Describe the similarities and differences among the three main types of networks.

14.2 Explain what a network good is and how consuming a network good generates an external benefit.

14.3 Describe the steps in deriving a demand curve for a network good.

14.4 Discuss how the opposing forces of the network effect and price effect determine who are core users and casual users of network goods.

14.5 Describe how networks can rapidly expand or decline due to network effects.

14.6 Describe the strategies firms use to compete in the market for network goods.

14.7 Discuss the role of regulation in promoting network efficiency and competition.

14.8 Explain how interconnection promotes competition in industries with essential facilities.

When you use your AT&T cell phone to call your mother on her Verizon cell phone, do you ever consider what would happen if Verizon refused to connect your call from the AT&T network? Of course not—this just does not happen in the United States. But this is not always the case in other parts of the world. In Nigeria, for example, it is common for cell-phone providers to ignore calls placed by callers using competing networks. The result? If you want to call your mom using a different network than hers, it might not work. In countries where customers using different networks are unable to place calls to one another reliably, people often carry multiple phones to make sure they can connect with their families and friends.

As this example illustrates, networks are an important part of our daily lives. In most developed nations, people often take networks for granted, failing to appreciate that without the efficient functioning of networks, we would be forced to endure a great deal of inconvenience and frustration. Where would you be without the word processing software you use to work collaboratively with others on group projects, or without the social networking site you use to stay in touch with friends?

This chapter studies the role of networks and network goods. Companies that provide network goods engage in competitive strategies to maintain the strength of their networks. Network industries tend to be volatile, and a market leader can quickly evaporate in this type of industry. Do you remember Friendster, AltaVista, Netscape, WordPerfect, and Sega Genesis? Each of these networks was once the market leader in its respective industry, but quickly lost its dominance when an opposing network became stronger.

Network goods are unique in economic analysis. Network goods have a different type of demand curve than we have previously seen, which makes them interesting to economists. More important, because of the nature of network industries, firms that provide network goods often become monopolies in their industries and devise strategies to maintain their monopoly status. However, these seemingly unbeatable monopolies are often short-lived, as was the case with the social networking company Myspace, which had gone from the world's most popular social network to one that is now struggling to reinvent itself as a niche social network. The fleeting nature of some network monopolies raises the question of where network goods fall in market structure analysis. Are they monopolies, oligopolies, fierce competitors, or somehow a mixture of these market structures? Also, the market for network goods exhibits externalities, a concept studied in the previous chapter, which influence how firms allocate their resources to maximize profits.

This chapter begins by defining three types of networks and discussing the importance of network effects, a concept related to externalities. We then describe how a network demand curve is derived based on network capacity. We go on to analyze equilibrium in the network industry, and explain how networks can expand or decline quickly due to

Networks have changed the way we learn, from elementary schools to college.

How We Are Connected Today

The importance of networks in the global economy has led to dramatic growth in network goods over the past decade, especially those that use the Internet. As network capabilities continue to expand, industries and markets will transform and people everywhere will adjust to the new way of life.

The popularity of ridesharing services such as Uber and Lyft has skyrocketed since 2014. Ridesharing surpassed taxi services as the most popular form of local transportation as a result of a strong network effect as more drivers and passengers enter the market.

Go to 🔲 **LaunchPad** to use the latest data to recreate this graph.

The percentage of people using the Internet as of 2016 varied significantly around the world. However, developing regions are rapidly catching up. In the past 5 years, the number of Internet users in Africa has more than doubled.

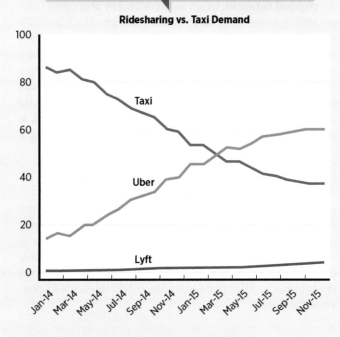

Ridesharing vs. Taxi Demand

Taxi
Uber
Lyft

Jan-14, Mar-14, May-14, Jul-14, Sep-14, Nov-14, Jan-15, Mar-15, May-15, Jul-15, Sep-15, Nov-15

Percent of Population Using Internet

Africa 28.6
Asia 40.2
World Average 46.4
Middle East 52.2
Latin America/Caribbean 55.9
Oceania/Australia 73.2
Europe 73.5
North America 87.9

900 million

Number of Whatsapp users worldwide in 2016

1.55 billion

Number of Facebook users worldwide in 2016

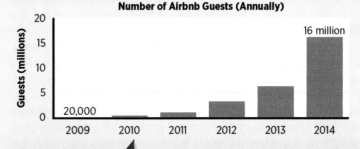

Number of Airbnb Guests (Annually)

Guests (millions)

20,000
16 million

2009, 2010, 2011, 2012, 2013, 2014

% of Revenues in 2012

Online 12%
DVD/Blu-ray 88%

% of Revenues in 2015

DVD/Blu-ray 45%
Online 55%

Staying in someone else's spare room or house while traveling provides comforts not found in hotels, such as private pools, full kitchens, and washer and dryers. Airbnb achieved a virtuous cycle as bookings increased as a result of network effects. As more homeowners around the world offer rooms or homes for rent, Airbnb's popularity will continue to rise.

Revenues from online streaming of movies surpassed revenues from DVD and Blu-ray movie unit sales in 2015. The change in the medium by which consumers view movies in recent years was dramatic.

network A structure that connects various entities with one another. A network can be physical, virtual, or social.

physical network A network connected by a physical structure such as fiber optics, transportation routes, or satellites.

virtual network A network connected by groups of people using the same type or brand of good.

Popular Science/Getty Images

Physical networks include telecommunications cables that connect the world. Physical networks are more expensive and less fluid than virtual or social networks.

social network A network that combines elements of physical and virtual networks.

network good A good or service that requires the existence of a physical, virtual, or social network to exist.

network externality An external benefit generated from the consumption of a network good.

network effect Describes how individuals and firms incorporate the external benefit generated from network goods into their decision making, which increases the value of the good further.

network effects, which can lead to a successful or failed network. Because of the speed with which networks can expand or decline, firms engage in a variety of competitive strategies to promote and sustain their network. Finally, we look at the role of government regulation in network industries. One example of such regulation is the requirement that networks interconnect, which allows multiple networks, no matter the size, to coexist in a competitive market. But regulation also creates costs, and the tradeoff between the benefits and costs of a regulatory policy helps to determine whether such regulations are necessary.

WHAT IS A NETWORK GOOD?

A **network** is a type of structure that connects various entities with one another. There are three kinds of networks. First, there are **physical networks,** which are connected by fiber optics (such as a telephone network), transportation routes (such as an airline), satellites (such as a GPS network), or other physical connections. Second, there are **virtual networks,** which describe a network connected by groups of people using the same type or brand of good (such as mobile phone service, video game console, search engine, or software). Third, there are **social networks,** which combine elements of physical and virtual networks and describe groups of people using the same product or service who also are connected more directly (for business or entertainment purposes) within the network, such as through the use of "friends" on social networking sites and face-to-face networking in traditional business clubs, country clubs, or health clubs.

Types of Network Goods

A **network good** describes a type of good or service that depends on the existence of a physical network, virtual network, or social network to exist. Although network goods have existed for centuries, the Internet created an immense rise in their importance, given the increased interaction between people and the information they share with one another. Today, network goods are ubiquitous and include but are not limited to smartphones, the Internet, satellite radio, software, digital music, MP3 players, 3D printers, and social networking sites.

Network Effects

An important characteristic of a network good, whether connected physically or virtually, is that the production or consumption of that good creates a positive external benefit to others. For example, owning the newest Microsoft Xbox console capable of network play is not very useful if no one else owns the same system. As more people purchase the system, there are more people to play games with online, which encourages companies to develop more games. As a result, the value rises to those who already own the console and to those considering whether to purchase one. This rise in value is referred to as a **network externality.** When this benefit is taken into account in an individual's or firm's decision making, it is known as a **network effect.**

Suppose you start a new social networking site for economics majors around the country to interact with one another. Initially, the value of such a network is limited to you and a few classmates who sign up. However, with each additional user, the potential benefit expands and generates spillovers to all users. Similarly, by subscribing to Facebook, you gain access to more than 1.5 billion potential "friends" (a clear benefit to you), while you provide an external benefit (albeit quite small unless you're famous) to all 1.5 billion existing users.

These examples highlight an important difference between a network externality and a positive externality described in earlier chapters. With a positive externality, a person generating an external benefit does not directly benefit from the externality he or she is creating. However, a network externality benefits all users, including the initial user and even potential users, because the external benefit increases the value of the overall network. This, in turn, generates even more demand for the network good.

Figure 1 illustrates the network effect described previously. The consumer generates an external benefit equal to the vertical distance between the private demand curve, D_p, and

FIGURE 1 | EXTERNAL BENEFIT OF CONSUMPTION PULLS PRIVATE DEMAND FARTHER TO THE RIGHT

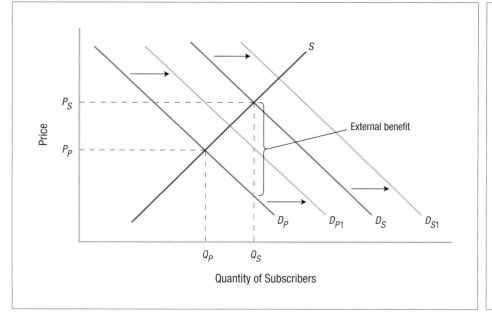

Each consumer who joins a network generates an external benefit (the vertical distance between the private demand curve, D_P, and the social demand curve, D_S) enjoyed by all other people within the network. This, in turn, generates even more demand, shifting D_P and D_S farther to the right, to D_{P1} and D_{S1}, respectively. This effect on demand becomes smaller as more people join the network; a smaller effect is due to diminishing returns to the network externality. The same dynamic effect can work in reverse if a consumer chooses to leave the network.

The Drone Highway: A Lifeline for Rural Rwandans

How did Rwanda use networking to overcome a lack of physical infrastructure?

Rwanda is a country known for its natural beauty and indigenous population of gorillas. But traveling across this landlocked mountainous country of 12 million people is not easy due to limited paved roads, no railroad system, and no major waterways. Although Rwanda has made some progress in improving its roads since its devastating civil war and genocide two decades ago, access to remote villages remains difficult. When a country such as Rwanda lacks physical networks to transport goods and services to consumers, it must seek solutions using new technologies. What strategy did Rwanda use to help connect its remote communities?

A drone in Rwanda carries valuable supplies to remote villages that are difficult to reach using the nation's limited infrastructure.

Rwanda built the world's first commercialized drone highway, including an operational drone port. Designed by European architects and supported by various world organizations, Rwanda's drone highway is an example of using modern innovation and technology to overcome network deficiencies. In fact, the lack of traditional networks (such as commercial flights or extensive power lines

that obstruct the airspace) in Rwanda makes drones easier to operate.

Because drones have grown significantly in popularity, not only for leisure activities but also for weather prediction, security (such as anti-poaching initiatives), and medical supply transport, the cost of producing drones has fallen due to economies of scale, making commerce using drones more viable. When connecting remote villages with traditional infrastructure is prohibitively expensive, drones are an efficient way of using 21st-century technology to overcome obstacles.

The use of modern technology such as drones to overcome deficient infrastructure is not new. Many developing nations in recent decades installed mobile phone networks instead of costly landlines. As network technology becomes more efficient and less costly, developing nations such as Rwanda will benefit from their ability to leapfrog old technologies, allowing for greater growth and improved standards of living.

GO TO ⊠ **LaunchPad** TO PRACTICE THE ECONOMIC CONCEPTS IN THIS STORY the social demand curve, D_S. This external benefit increases the value of the overall network to its existing and potential users. The rise in the value of the network generates even more demand, as shown by the rightward shift of D_P and D_S to D_{P1} and D_{S1}, respectively. Although marginal benefit is not shown, it is important to note that external benefits are subject to diminishing returns. As a network becomes larger, an increase in demand generates fewer additional benefits to others. The benefit added by the 100th user in a new network is greater than the benefit added by the 100-millionth user.

Network effects also can work in reverse. When a consumer leaves a network, the value of the network is reduced to all remaining users, which may lead to a larger leftward shift in demand than is warranted by the loss of only one user. Note that this is not the same as a negative externality, which *imposes a cost* on others and causes the supply curve to shift to the left. In the present case, leaving a network *removes the external benefit* that had been provided to others. The dynamic nature of how network effects influence the demand for network goods affects how a network demand curve is derived.

 CHECKPOINT

WHAT IS A NETWORK GOOD?

- Networks can be categorized into physical networks, virtual networks, and social networks.

- A network good is a good whose demand depends on the existence of a physical, virtual, or social network.

- Network externalities are generated when the consumption and/or production of a good leads to additional benefits to all existing users of a good. Taking away these externalities leads to diminished benefits but does not add a cost.

- When network externalities are taken into account in an individual's or firm's decision making, they are referred to as network effects. Network effects can lead to a larger rise or a larger decline in demand than would occur in a non-network industry.

QUESTION: Suppose your best friend purchases a new high-tech laptop that allows users to work simultaneously on the same software file. How might your friend's purchase lead to a network effect that generates additional demand?

Answers to the Checkpoint questions can be found at the end of this chapter.

DEMAND CURVE FOR A NETWORK GOOD

network demand curve A demand curve for a good or service that produces a network effect, causing it to slope upward at lower quantities before sloping downward once the market matures.

Because the value of network goods is influenced by external benefits, a demand curve for a network good does not look like a typical downward-sloping demand curve. A **network demand curve** reflects the fact that the value of the good initially rises as more people purchase or subscribe to the good, which means that the demand curve has an upward-sloping portion at lower quantities. A general model of demand for network goods is described next.[1]

Demand for a Fixed Capacity Network Good

The model for a network demand curve makes two important assumptions. First, the model assumes that the short-run supply curve is limited to the capacity of the firm's fixed investment, and therefore is vertical. For example, a new entrant in the airline industry starts off with just a few planes, and therefore the number of customers it can serve is fixed until it expands by purchasing more planes. Further, an airline must expand in large increments (i.e., it must buy a new airplane that can serve hundreds of passengers a day), rather than by small increments, such as when a baker decides whether to make one more cake. Second, the model assumes that there is a short-run demand curve corresponding to each vertical

[1] This model is discussed in greater detail in Nicholas Economides, "The Economics of Networks," *International Journal of Industrial Organization,* 1996.

FIGURE 2	A SMALL NETWORK WITH FIXED CAPACITY

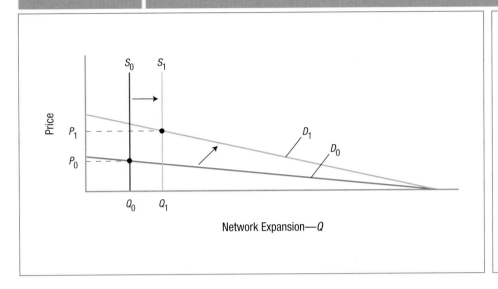

A small network has a fixed capacity of Q_0, resulting in a vertical supply curve, S_0. The intersection of S_0 and D_0 results in an equilibrium price of P_0. As the network expands to S_1, the value to existing and new users increases due to network effects, causing the demand curve to pivot to D_1. The intersection of S_1 and D_1 leads to a higher equilibrium price of P_1. This differs from a market for a non-network good, in which an increase in supply leads to a lower price.

supply curve that reflects the higher value of a larger network due to network externalities. These assumptions make the analysis easier, but do not change the conclusions.

Figure 2 shows how a network market demand curve is developed. We start with a small network with a capacity of Q_0, where demand is small and price (P_0) is determined by the intersection of a vertical supply curve S_0 at Q_0 and demand D_0 for that capacity. As the network expands (supply shifts to the right by an increment to S_1), demand increases because the value to existing and new users increases. This is shown by the demand curve pivoting higher to D_1 (while intersecting the horizontal axis at the same point as D_0 to indicate a maximum demand for the network good) and reflecting a higher value to initial users and a higher market price at P_1. This differs from a market for a non-network good, in which an increase in supply would not result in an increase in demand. For a non-network good, the increase in supply would lead to a lower price on the demand curve.

Deriving the Full Network Demand Curve

Network effects are strongest in the early stages of a network good's development, as each additional consumer increases the marginal benefit to all consumers of the good. However, this network effect is always opposed by the law of demand. As price rises, quantity demanded falls. Which effect predominates?

When the quantity of a good provided on the market increases (without any change in demand), the price must fall in order for the market to clear. But the existence of network externalities causes demand to increase when a network expands, allowing prices to rise. Because the price effect and the network effect work in opposition to one another, the market price for a network good depends on which effect is stronger. For most network goods, the network effect dominates the price effect for small quantities, resulting in an upward-sloping portion of the network demand curve, as shown in Figure 3.

As the network expands along the upward-sloping portion of the network demand curve, the price increases as more **core users**—those who benefit most from consuming the good—purchase the good. The demand curve slopes upward as the network effect (which shifts demand to the right as quantity increases, increasing the price) dominates the price effect of an increase in quantity (which reduces the price).

As the market for a network good grows and reaches a critical number of consumers to support the network, additional consumers add fewer external benefits due to diminishing returns. These consumers who purchase the network good after it matures are called **casual users** (think of your grandmother buying the newest tablet only after everyone else in the

core user A consumer who has a very high willingness to pay for a new product or service and is among the first to purchase it.

casual user A consumer who purchases a good only after the good has matured in the market and is more sensitive to price.

FIGURE 3	A NETWORK MARKET DEMAND CURVE

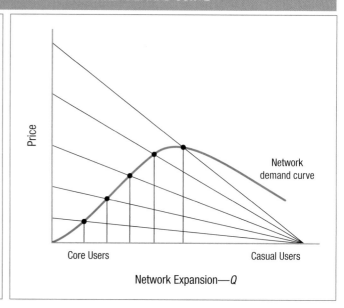

Network goods initially have an upward-sloping demand curve as core users build the network by attracting others to buy the good. Once the market matures, a network demand curve becomes downward-sloping as casual users buy the good when the price drops.

Justin Timberlake allowed his album *The 20/20 Experience* to be previewed in its entirety on music streaming sites such as Spotify and iTunes at no charge. The album generated a tremendous network effect that helped it sell nearly 1 million *paid* album downloads in its first week of official release in 2013.

family has one). Once a network good reaches this stage, the network demand curve slopes downward as the price effect (from the increase in supply due to lower production costs) dominates the network effect.

By connecting all of the intersections of supply and demand, a network demand curve is generated, which slopes upward from the origin as core users increase the value of the good and then slopes downward once the product matures and casual users buy the good.

Examples of Network Demand Curve Pricing in Our Daily Lives

What does the presence of a network demand curve mean for prices? It suggests that as a new network good is introduced, the price is kept low to attract new users. As the number of users increases, prices rise because people are willing to pay more for a network good used by more people. Prices continue to rise until the good matures, at which point prices must fall in order to sell a greater quantity.

Consider the following example: When Google launched in 1998, the search engine results displayed were quite bare—no ads, no preferred listings; the cost to use Google was essentially zero. However, as the number of users increased, Google began "charging" people to use the service by placing ads and suggested links alongside the search results. Although not a monetary cost, users pay an opportunity cost when viewing ads.

Another example of network demand curve pricing is a new rock band attempting to gain recognition by initially playing for nothing at local clubs, and/or offering their music free online. Once the band becomes more well known, it begins charging for shows and for music downloads. Eventually, a downward-sloping demand curve will return, in which case lower prices are needed to increase quantity demanded. A similar effect can occur when an established musical artist prepares to release a new album. These examples demonstrate the upward- and downward-sloping nature of network demand curves.

CHECKPOINT

DEMAND CURVE FOR A NETWORK GOOD

- The production of network goods is typically carried out in large increments due to high fixed capital costs.
- The short-run equilibrium for a network good occurs at the intersection of a fixed capacity vertical supply curve and the demand curve for that quantity.
- As a network expands, the effect of network externalities is reduced due to diminishing returns as the price effect becomes stronger.
- A network demand curve is upward-sloping for smaller quantities (when network effects are strong) and downward-sloping for larger quantities (when the network good matures and network effects weaken).
- A network demand curve reflects the role that core users (represented on the upward-sloping portion of the curve) have in building the value of the network.

QUESTION: Why does a network demand curve slope upward for small quantities of a good, then slope downward for higher quantities?

Answers to the Checkpoint questions can be found at the end of this chapter.

MARKET EQUILIBRIUM FOR A NETWORK GOOD

Now that we have learned how a network demand curve is developed, we can study how market equilibrium is reached in this type of industry. The market equilibrium for a network good occurs once most network effects are realized. Therefore, equilibrium generally is found on the downward-sloping portion of the network demand curve. However, not all network goods reach market equilibrium. As we will soon see, network goods can thrive or fail over a short period of time, making market equilibrium difficult both to achieve and to sustain.

Economies of Scale and Marginal Cost

An important characteristic of network goods is that they generally require a very large fixed cost to produce. Fixed costs can include the cost of writing and producing a new hit song, or the huge cost of building cell-phone towers across the country. In earlier chapters, we saw how monopolies and oligopolies can form when industries exhibit high fixed costs and low marginal costs. Network goods are an excellent example of goods produced in such industries, for once a song is produced or a cell-phone tower is built, the cost to serve customers (a firm's marginal cost) is minimal. An outcome from this type of industry is large economies of scale.

Finding an Equilibrium in the Market for Network Goods

Let's assume that the marginal cost of a network good is fixed at P_1, as shown in Figure 4. The equilibrium is point *d*, the intersection of the downward-sloping portion of the network demand curve and the marginal cost curve. To achieve equilibrium, the network for that good must expand from the origin to point *b*, which is called the **tipping point** (or **critical mass**), the quantity from which network effects are strong enough to continue building the network.

Once a network reaches point *b*, the existence of network effects will continue to generate more demand, allowing the network to expand on its own until it reaches equilibrium at point *d*. This is referred to as a **virtuous cycle,** in which network effects push demand farther to the right, creating even more value for the network.

tipping point (or **critical mass**) The quantity from which network effects are strong enough to support the network.

virtuous cycle The point at which a network good reaches its tipping point, when network effects cause demand for the good to increase on its own. As more people buy or subscribe to a good or service, it generates even more external benefits and more demand.

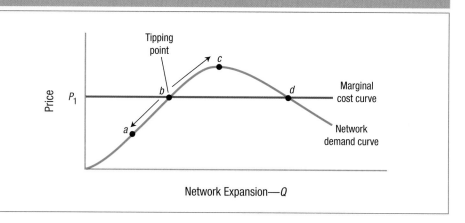

| FIGURE 4 | EQUILIBRIUM IN A MARKET FOR NETWORK GOODS |

Point *b* represents the tipping point—the point at which the network has achieved enough momentum to continue expanding until it reaches point *d* (an equilibrium created by a virtuous cycle). However, if a market fails to reach point *b*, a vicious cycle may result, leading to a collapse in market share.

vicious cycle When a network good does not reach its tipping point, and therefore does not increase in value enough to retain its customers, customers leave the network, thereby further diminishing the value of the good until all customers leave the network.

A long line of core users waiting to buy a new product can propel a network good into a virtuous cycle.

However, if a network good fails to reach point *b*, or if a new competing network good causes demand to move to a point left of point *b*, a **vicious cycle** can result. In a vicious cycle, people stop consuming a product or service, thereby reducing the value of the product to others, which causes even more people to avoid consuming the good. The result is typically a failed product, shown as a good at point *a* in Figure 4.

An example of a product entering a vicious cycle was the HD DVD format introduced by Toshiba in 2006. Toshiba competed vigorously for market share against Sony's Blu-ray format, but because Toshiba did not reach a critical mass, studios stopped offering their movies in HD DVD format, leading to a vicious cycle and the discontinuation of the format in 2008. Interestingly, several years later, Blu-ray entered its own vicious cycle as online streaming of movies made physical media less relevant, leading to fewer movie offerings in Blu-ray format and a steep drop in sales.

Note how the network demand curve slopes upward to point *c*, then downward. What explains this change in slope? Point *c* represents the point of product maturity, when the network effect no longer dominates the price effect. Remember that a demand curve slopes downward due to a price effect—it requires a lower price for people to consume more. However, network effects counter the price effect by raising the value of the good as consumers buy more. At point *c*, the network effect and price effect are equal in magnitude. Thus, the upward-sloping segment represents core users who are less price sensitive, and the downward-sloping segment represents casual users who are more price sensitive.

Network Goods Can Face a Virtuous Cycle or a Vicious Cycle Very Quickly

The speed at which network effects can influence the success or failure of a product or service can be remarkably fast. As shown in Figure 4, once a firm enters a vicious cycle by moving down the network demand curve to the left of point *b*, it is often difficult to stop the cycle. Meanwhile, firms entering virtuous cycles enjoy what seems to be limitless growth over a very short period.

Table 1 provides examples of network goods that experienced a change in market leader at some point over the last two decades. In some cases the change was gradual (such as the transition from film to digital, because ardent film photographers took many years to make the switch to digital), whereas in other cases the change was almost instantaneous (such as when the HP Mini netbook was quickly made obsolete by the Apple iPad).

Interestingly, the quality of a network good is not always the most important factor in determining the market leader in a network industry. Because network effects are so powerful, consumers sometimes choose an inferior product that many people use over

TABLE 1	EXAMPLES OF NETWORK GOODS FACING VIRTUOUS AND VICIOUS CYCLES	
Industry	**Previous Market Leaders**	**Current Market Leader**
Social networking	Friendster (2002–2004)	Facebook (2009–)
	Myspace (2005–2008)	
Internet search engines	AltaVista (1997–2000)	Google (2001–)
Word processing software	WordPerfect (1980–1996)	Microsoft Word (1997–)
Video game consoles	PlayStation 1 and 2 (1995–2007)	Sony PS4 (2014–)
	Nintendo Wii (2008–2011)	
	Microsoft Xbox 360 (2012–2013)	
Internet browsers	Netscape (1995–1998)	Google Chrome (2012–)
	Internet Explorer (1999–2008)	
	Mozilla Firefox (2009–2011)	
Internet service providers	Prodigy (1991–1994)	Comcast Xfinity (2013–)
	America Online (1995–2003)	
	AT&T DSL (2004–2012)	
Photography	Kodak (film) (1936–2004)	Canon (digital) (2005–)
Smartphones	Blackberry (2003–2010)	Apple iPhone (2011–)
Tablets/netbooks	HP Mini (2008–2009)	Apple iPad (2010–)

 ISSUE

The Broadband Effect: Virtuous and Vicious Cycles in Network Goods

Most Americans rely on broadband Internet connections for work, school, or entertainment. Over 73% of U.S. households in 2016 had a broadband connection, up from just 11% in 2002. Part of this dramatic rise in broadband connectivity has been the result of government efforts to promote broadband usage in all areas of the country, especially in rural areas where it is costly to establish broadband connections.

In 2015, the U.S. Federal Communications Commission (FCC) implemented the second phase of its Connect America Fund to promote the goal of ensuring that every household has access to broadband capability. This fund consists of fees collected from all broadband users nationwide and is used to subsidize service in high-cost areas such as rural and mountainous communities. The FCC lists the social benefits of such an effort as including improved education, health care, public safety, and civic engagement in rural areas. These ultimately benefit the entire nation.

No doubt, the nearly universal use of broadband has resulted in significant changes to network industries. For example, network services such as movie and live television streaming, online conferencing, worldwide telecommunications via Skype and other online providers, and instant music and software downloads were all either previously unavailable or excruciatingly time-consuming to use prior to broadband. These services experienced a virtuous cycle as more and more consumers gain access to faster Internet connections, leading to a validation of Metcalfe's law, which states that the value of a telecommunications network increases exponentially with the number of users.

But not all industries fared well with the rise in broadband usage. Some markets faced a vicious cycle as consumers moved away from certain network goods. These include traditional

Daniel Draghici/Dreamstime.com

international calling, calling cards, and prepaid phones. Beyond telecommunications, broadband also contributed to the demise of most physical DVD and game rental stores, CD music stores, and software stores, as all of these services can now be obtained online.

Like all industries, goods come and go, and network goods are no different. What is remarkable is how quickly this transformation took place over the last decade. How today's network goods fare in the future will be an interesting question to examine as technological improvements continue to change the way we live.

a superior product that fewer people use. For example, some video game enthusiasts claimed that Sony's PlayStation 3 was superior in graphics and capabilities to Nintendo's Wii. Yet, the Wii system held its position as market leader for four years, partly due to its lower price but also due to a virtuous cycle it had enjoyed until Microsoft's Xbox 360 took over as the market leader in 2012, and then subsequently by Sony's improved PS4 system in 2014.

Because of the speed at which market demand for network goods can occur, no firm is ever "safe" with its market share. Aware of this, businesses often engage in various competitive strategies to increase or secure their market shares. The next section describes some of these strategies.

 CHECKPOINT

MARKET EQUILIBRIUM FOR A NETWORK GOOD

- Network goods generally exhibit large economies of scale due to their high fixed costs and low marginal costs of production.

- A network good must reach its tipping point (or critical mass) to enter a virtuous cycle in which network effects generate additional demand until equilibrium is reached.

- Network goods that do not reach their tipping point enter into a vicious cycle, leading to a sharp decline in market share and likely failure of the good.

- Network goods can enter virtuous or vicious cycles in a very short period, such that no good is ever safe from rapid decline.

QUESTION: Mobile apps are a multibillion dollar industry that is constantly changing. Today, over 1 million apps are available for smartphone users to download, though the vast majority of these apps never become popular. Even apps that do become popular can be quickly replaced by new apps just months after reaching their peak number of downloads. Gaming apps have the shortest average lifespan among all categories of apps. How does the network demand curve explain the speed by which gaming apps rise in popularity and then fall to obscurity?

Answers to the Checkpoint questions can be found at the end of this chapter.

COMPETITION AND MARKET STRUCTURE FOR NETWORK GOODS

The network goods industry provides opportunities for firms to gain substantial market power. Such opportunities often lead to intense competition. A recent example of competition in network goods was the market for high-speed home Internet service between DSL providers (such as AT&T) and cable Internet providers (such as Comcast). With a majority of U.S. households having switched from dial-up Internet services to high-speed providers in the past decade, the race to become the dominant provider was critical to AT&T and Comcast.

AT&T focused on bundling strategies with their U-verse program that incorporates home phone, digital television, and high-speed Internet for one price. Comcast, in addition to their Xfinity program that bundles television, home phone, and Internet, invested heavily in television advertising featuring the Slowskys, a turtle couple that had an aversion to anything fast and was used as a metaphor for DSL-service speed.

This section describes some of the common strategies used to protect network goods from entering a vicious cycle or to increase the likelihood of entering a virtuous cycle. Undoubtedly, as a consumer, you encounter many of these marketing strategies when making decisions about which network goods to purchase. The goal of firms using these strategies is to attract you to their product and to keep you as a customer for a long time.

Competition and Pricing Strategies

Network goods are characterized as having high fixed costs with low marginal costs. Further, network effects can cause some firms to flourish while causing others to fail, even when little or no quality differences exist between the firms' products. The determinant of market success is not always dependent on the quality of the good, but rather on competitive strategies to capture market share. Low marginal costs means it does not cost much to serve customers once they are committed to a product. Therefore, firms spend significant sums of money to gain new customers and use various strategies to keep existing customers. These strategies include teaser strategies, lock-in strategies, and market segmentation (such as product differentiation and price discrimination).

Capturing New Customers Using Teaser Strategies
Teaser strategies are used by firms to gain new customers by offering various sign-up incentives and/or low prices for a short introductory period. Examples of teaser deals include wireless companies offering a free or highly discounted phone when you purchase a two-year wireless plan, cable companies offering six months of free cable or Internet service, banks offering 0% finance charges for a limited time when you open a new credit card account, online music companies offering new customers 50 free music downloads, and software companies allowing new users to sample their products with a 30-day free trial.

Why do companies offer such great deals to new customers? Unlike decisions for non-network goods, such as which brand of cereal to buy—a decision that is relatively easy to switch back and forth—purchasing a network good typically requires a long-term commitment. This can be due to a legal commitment, such as a one- or two-year contract, or it can be due to the nonmonetary costs of switching from one product to another.

Have you ever had to switch from a software program that you have used for many years? Once you learn how to use a particular software program or once you are accustomed to a certain email program, it can be a hassle to switch to another. These **switching costs,** which include monetary and nonmonetary costs of switching from one good to another, often are substantial for network goods. Therefore, to provide incentives for consumers to incur these costs to switch, firms must offer attractive up-front deals.

Retaining Existing Customers Using Lock-In Strategies
In addition to offering teaser deals to entice new customers, firms also employ strategies to keep existing customers from leaving. **Lock-in strategies** occur after a customer adopts a product, and typically involve the firm engaging in strategies that raise the switching costs of consumers, thereby increasing the likelihood of retaining the customer.

Switching costs include the hassle of learning a new format and its features, dealing with the loss of other features one has become accustomed to, and so forth. In some cases, switching costs may be minimal or offset by benefits; for example, the excitement of purchasing the latest smartphone or computer may outweigh the switching costs of learning how to use it. But consumers generally do not like changing network goods once they are accustomed to one brand.

Common examples of lock-in strategies include the offering of loyalty programs, which reward consumers the more they use or the longer they stay with a company's products. Lock-in strategies also include preventing certain features from being transferred to another product, such as a phone's contact list or saved text messages.

Using Market Segmentation to Maximize Profits
In an earlier chapter, we saw how market power can reduce the elasticity of demand for a firm's product and increase potential profits of monopolies and monopolistically competitive firms. We draw from those analyses by studying how **market segmentation** strategies can be used to increase market share and profits in the market for network goods. Market segmentation is achieved when firms can differentiate their products in a way that allows similar goods to be priced differently to different groups of consumers. In other words, it allows firms to price discriminate, which increases producer surplus.

Because network goods generally have a low marginal cost of production, firms have greater flexibility in segmenting their products to allow for a greater range of prices, each

teaser strategies Attractive up-front deals used as an incentive to entice new customers into a network.

switching cost A cost imposed on consumers when they change products or subscribe to a new network.

lock-in strategies Techniques used by firms to raise the switching costs for their customers, making it less attractive to leave the network.

market segmentation A strategy of making a single good in different versions to target different consumer markets with varying prices.

Wd2007/Dreamstime.com

ISSUE

A 0% Credit Card Offer: Is It Too Good to Be True?

Credit card debt is one of the most common forms of consumer debt in the United States. The average American carries over $5,000 in credit card debt, often at interest rates higher than what is paid on home mortgages, car loans, or student loans. However, many credit card companies offer new credit card subscribers 0% financing for a limited period of time. These offers are attractive for individuals with debt, many of whom might transfer debt from another credit card. Do credit card companies profit by giving customers such a great deal? Yes, more than you might think.

Nearly all 0% financing offers are teaser strategies, and not all are created equal. They vary in terms of the length of the offer, the initial transfer fees, and whether finance charges are accrued. Zero percent interest offers generally vary from 6 to 18 months from the opening of a new credit card, and

most are *balance transfer* offers that pay off another credit card balance but require an initial transfer fee of 3% to 5%. Therefore, if one pays a 5% fee to enjoy a 0% interest rate for 6 months, that is the equivalent of a 10% annual interest rate. Finally, some credit card companies *accrue* finance charges over the promotional period if the balance is not paid off. For example, if one has a $1,000 balance at 0% for 12 months, which then increases to 15% after 12 months, an accrued finance charge means that if the $1,000 balance is not paid off in 12 months, the 15% rate is charged from day 1, eliminating any benefit from the 0% offer. One should always read the terms of a 0% offer to avoid unexpected fees.

Finally, there is an income effect. When a consumer can buy goods at a 0% interest rate, a consumer *feels* wealthier, which may lead to greater spending.

Zero percent interest lending rate deals abound to attract new customers, but beware, they do not last for long!

Because credit card companies charge businesses 2% to 3% on every purchase for processing the transaction, they will still earn money on every purchase, even if you never pay a penny in finance charges.

---

versioning A pricing strategy that involves differentiating a good by way of packaging into multiple products for people with different demands.

intertemporal pricing A type of versioning in which goods are differentiated by the level of patience of consumers. Less patient consumers pay a higher price than more patient consumers.

peak-load pricing A versioning strategy of pricing a product higher during periods of higher demand, and lower during periods of lower demand.

targeting a different subset of the market. Market segmentation strategies in network goods include versioning, intertemporal pricing, peak-load pricing, and bundling strategies.

Versioning refers to pricing strategies that involve differentiating a good by way of packaging it into multiple products for people with different needs. A common example is the choice of a wireless plan. Do you choose an unlimited monthly plan, a fixed-minute monthly plan, or a prepaid plan? A single firm can offer each of these plans and price each plan to attract the appropriate subset of customers.

A similar but slightly different strategy is **intertemporal pricing.** Like versioning, a firm uses intertemporal pricing strategies to target different groups of consumers by differentiating their product, but in this case, by time. Specifically, they use the fact that some consumers are more impatient than others to buy a product. For example, new books often first appear in bookstores as expensive hardcover editions, then as less expensive paperbacks or eBook versions a couple of months later, followed by the availability of the book for loan from public libraries at no cost for the most patient consumers.

Another example of intertemporal pricing, shown in Table 2, is the release of a new movie. A new movie first appears in theaters, followed by on-demand or pay-per-view, then via paid online streaming or DVD rental, then on premium movie channels, and lastly on network TV. With each step, the price to view the movie generally decreases.

Firms that successfully use versioning and intertemporal pricing can price discriminate among consumers by charging less patient consumers, who have lower elasticities of demand, higher prices than those consumers with more patience and higher elasticities of demand. Once consumers with less elastic demand are served, the price is dropped to serve those with more elastic demand. The firm earns more profit by versioning products using time as the differentiating factor.

Peak-load pricing focuses less on differentiating a product than it does on charging higher prices when there is greater demand for the product. For example, ticket prices for evening movies and Broadway shows typically are higher than prices for matinees. Most

TABLE 2	INTERTEMPORAL PRICING OF A NEW MOVIE	
Movie Format	**Average Wait Time from Movie Release**	**Approximate Cost to View**
Movie theater	Immediate	$10 per person
On-demand/pay-per-view	2 to 3 months	$10 per group of viewers
Paid streaming/DVD rental	3 to 6 months	$5 per group of viewers
Premium channels	6 months to 1 year	Cost of channel subscription
Network TV/free streaming	1 year or longer	Free (basic TV or Internet access)

wireless plans come with free or highly discounted evening and weekend usage. And airlines typically charge less for tickets on the nonpeak travel days of Tuesday, Wednesday, and Saturday. Similar to versioning and intertemporal pricing, the use of peak-load pricing attempts to segment the market into consumers with less flexible demand and those with more flexible demand.

Figure 5 illustrates a market with peak-load pricing, where P_P represents the higher prices charged during peak times when demand D_P is greater, whereas P_0 is the lower price charged during off-peak times when demand D_0 is lower.

Finally, network industries engage in **bundling** strategies to increase demand for related products. Because network goods generally have low marginal costs to produce, it does not cost the firm much to package several products together. Customers who purchase one product are then more likely to use other products from the same company, thus supporting the firm's network and the value of all its goods. One example is Apple's strategy of bundling many types of software into its iOS operating system. Bundled programs such as Safari, iMovie, iTunes, and GarageBand provide users with convenient "free" options, thereby reducing the need to use other network providers (such as Adobe and Real), which sell competing media products.

bundling A strategy of packaging several products into a single product with a single price. Bundling allows firms to capture customers of related products by making it more attractive to use the same firm's products.

FIGURE 5	PEAK-LOAD PRICING

Demand curve D_P represents a greater demand during peak periods, leading to an optimal price of P_P. During off-peak times, demand D_0 is much lower, leading to a lower price of P_0. Peak-load pricing can occur by time of day (telephone calls, live shows, movies), by day of the week (airline tickets), or by season (ski lift tickets).

CHECKPOINT

COMPETITION AND MARKET STRUCTURE FOR NETWORK GOODS

- Competition for market share in network goods is often intense as firms attempt to avoid the vicious cycle of a failed network good.
- Teaser strategies include attractive up-front savings to customers willing to switch to another network good provider, while lock-in strategies are used to make it more costly to leave a network good provider.
- Market segmentation involves separating consumers based on their elasticity of demand, with less patient consumers (those with inelastic demands) paying more than patient consumers with elastic demands.
- Versioning is the practice of differentiating a good into multiple products from which consumers can choose. Versioning also can be done by time (intertemporal pricing) or by peak usage (peak-load pricing).
- Firms bundle their goods because the marginal cost of adding additional products is minimal and the benefit from network effects is high if consumers use the included products instead of purchasing them separately from competing firms.

QUESTIONS: Why would a firm selling a network good choose to segment its customers by charging different prices? Wouldn't it make more money by just charging everyone a high price?

Answers to the Checkpoint questions can be found at the end of this chapter.

SHOULD NETWORK GOODS BE REGULATED?

In a market where firms compete to become the dominant provider, whether as a monopolist or an oligopolist, firms use strategies to strengthen and maintain their market power. In such a market, governments must assess the effects of these strategies on consumers. Unlike other firms with market power, those producing network goods face the continuing threat that a new network good might lead them into a vicious cycle. Therefore, competition can exist even when a network good is dominated by a single firm. This brings about the important question of whether or not governments should regulate these firms.

Microsoft's market dominance with its Windows operating system, office-suite products (Office), and email and Internet programs (Outlook and Explorer) led the U.S. Department of Justice, along with governments in the European Union, to investigate whether this dominance was achieved fairly. Specifically, some question Microsoft's bundling tactics, which make it convenient (perhaps too convenient) to adopt its related products once one product is purchased.

The government generally aims to ensure that competition for network goods leads to low prices for consumers, ample choices, and improvements in quality. However, governments also must ensure that regulations do not impede productivity or create burdensome costs to firms. Just because a firm is a monopoly does not mean it doesn't face the threat of competition, which can keep firms from exploiting their market power.

One way to promote a competitive environment for network goods is not to break up monopolies, but rather to ensure that firms are prevented from securing exclusive access to a set of consumers. One such regulatory policy is to require interconnection.

Promoting Network Competition with Interconnection

Many types of network goods include industry standards or essential facilities. An **industry standard** is a common format that is used, for example, in televisions, in digital recorders, and in software programs. **Essential facilities** are inputs that are needed to produce a product or to allow a person to consume a product. **Interconnection,** the physical linking of a

---

industry standard A common format that is used, for example, in televisions, in digital recorders, or in software programs.

essential facility An input that is needed to produce a product or to allow a person to consume a product.

interconnection The physical linking of a network to another network's essential facilities. Interconnection promotes competition by ensuring that no firm has exclusive access to a set of customers.

network to another network's essential facilities, helps to promote competition in situations in which firms are able to use their market power to block competitors from entering the industry. When interconnection is required, firms must allow competing providers access to their networks. As discussed in the chapter opener, a Verizon customer, for example, must be able to make a call to an AT&T customer in order for multiple networks to operate efficiently in the same market. For such calls to be possible, they must travel across networks owned by different firms.

Consider the incredible arrangement of networks required to make a telephone call to a friend in another country. To complete this call, parties must work together, starting with a wireless provider or local telephone provider (called a local exchange carrier), connecting to the distance call provider, then the network provider interconnecting to the foreign network operator, and finally connecting to the friend's local exchange carrier. Even more amazing is how the cost of this service has fallen dramatically over the years. How is this possible? We looked at the role of network effects, network competition, and interconnection to explain how competing networks are able to provide efficient and seamless service that in the past could only be possible via large natural monopolies. What is more important is the degree to which global markets are dependent on network technologies that did not exist 15 years ago—technologies that we often take for granted today.

An important role of regulation in network goods is to ensure that providers of essential facilities allow access to competing firms. The most common example of an essential facility is the phone line in your house. Prior to 1984, AT&T owned about 80% of all of these phone lines, and could effectively prevent any competitor from offering phone service because rival firms would not be able to complete a call without access to your (i.e., AT&T's) phone line. In 1984 the U.S. government forced AT&T to break up into smaller firms, and eventually forced these firms to open their networks to competition, paving the way for both land-based and wireless providers to enter the market. The effect on prices was substantial. If you watch an old TV show from the 1970s or early 1980s, you may catch some interesting scenes in which characters make a big deal about calling long distance. Today, we don't think twice about calling long distance, or even making international calls. In fact, long-distance calling has lost its identity as a market, leading to the demise of many long-distance companies.

Industry Standards and Network Compatibility

A common issue with network goods is that firms tend to compete vigorously (leading to standards wars) to become the industry standard, thereby "owning" the network. A consequence of this competition is that firms spend large sums of money on marketing strategies to dominate the market (to become a monopoly), rather than to achieve productivity gains and cost reductions typical of more competitive markets. Network compatibility allows competing standards to coexist in a market by ensuring that media can be used on competing formats. For example, a spreadsheet can be shared by a person using a Windows computer and someone using a Mac computer. And the spreadsheet itself can be edited using either Microsoft Excel or Google Docs.

Does Interconnection Improve Efficiency in Network Industries?

A common theme throughout the discussions of market structure in earlier chapters is that competitive markets generate more consumer surplus than monopoly markets. Further, firms with market power generate deadweight loss. In network industries where monopolies can be created if network effects are strong, interconnection can bring about gains to society by facilitating competition and reducing deadweight loss.

In the long run, interconnection creates a more competitive environment that forces firms to be more efficient, leading to reduced costs. Yet, a more competitive market might limit the network effects and economies of scale that exist with fewer firms. Therefore, implementing regulation to promote competition involves a tradeoff between benefits and costs. In fact, the potential costs of regulation can even exceed the benefits.

Can Poor Regulation Be Worse Than No Regulation?

Throughout this section, it was argued that regulation can promote competition by preventing firms from exploiting their access to essential facilities. However, the benefits of network effects most likely contributed to a firm's dominance in the market. For example, although we enjoy having our choice of wireless carriers, which is a benefit from regulation, such choices do not come without cost.

Competition for exclusive contracts with phone makers has made it difficult to use certain providers with certain phones. A similar situation arises in sports broadcasting, in which television networks sign contracts with sports organizations to be the sole broadcaster of games to viewers (such as ESPN's exclusive right to broadcast *Monday Night Football*). Although these cases create minor burdens, other forms of regulation intended to protect consumers have led to major disasters.

The California electricity crisis of 2000–2001 is one such example of poor regulation of a network good. Although the initial objective of placing a price cap (a price ceiling) on electricity prices was to keep prices from rising too rapidly for consumers, it quickly led to strategic responses by producers. Because producers could not raise prices in California to compensate for rising input prices, many firms instead chose to reduce the quantity of electricity provided, creating a huge shortage of electricity. Ultimately, the price ceiling led to massive blackouts and much inconvenience to individuals and businesses for several months.

When determining whether network goods should be regulated or not, the benefits and costs of each policy must be evaluated to determine whether it would be best to implement the policy or to just leave the market alone. In many situations, such as with the California electricity price cap, life might have been brighter (pun intended) without regulation.

 CHECKPOINT

SHOULD NETWORK GOODS BE REGULATED?

- The purpose of regulatory policy is to promote a competitive market that will lead to more consumer choices and lower prices.

- One common form of regulation is requiring network providers to allow interconnection with their competitors—that is, allowing access to each other's network and essential facilities.

- Industry standards can lead to intense competition when competing firms attempt to become the dominant standard; however, network compatibility allows competing industry standards to coexist in a market.

- Interconnection facilitates competition and generally improves efficiency by forcing firms to be more productive and cost-effective.

- The costs of regulation, especially poor regulation, can be substantial and can exceed its potential benefits. Any regulatory policy should be evaluated based on the tradeoff between its benefits and costs.

QUESTIONS: The Apple iPod, iPhone, and iPad all serve as MP3 devices that allow individuals to play music that can be downloaded using Apple's iTunes music store and many other music providers. Why is an MP3 player considered an essential facility for playing music? Would regulatory policy ever be needed to prevent Apple from exploiting its essential facility?

Answers to the Checkpoint questions can be found at the end of this chapter.

chapter summary

Section 1 What Is a Network Good?

14.1 **Networks** connect various entities with one another. They can include:

1. **Physical networks:** Structures connected by fiber optics, satellites, or other physical connections.
2. **Virtual networks:** Connect groups of people using the same type or brand of good.
3. **Social networks:** Connect people within a virtual network, such as Facebook or LinkedIn.

Network goods are either produced within a network, or depend on a network for their existence.

© Stephen Frost/Alamy Stock Photo

14.2 Every new user of a social media app increases the value of the network to every existing user and potential user, generating a **network externality.** When these external benefits are taken into account in the decision making by individuals and firms, they are referred to as **network effects.**

Section 2 Demand Curve for a Network Good

14.3 Networks typically involve high fixed costs and therefore are produced in large increments, such as adding a new wireless tower that can serve many customers. This leads to a **network demand curve.**

Deriving a Network Demand Curve

A network begins with a vertical short-run supply curve that represents a fixed capacity (a maximum number of customers it can serve), and a corresponding demand curve. As the network expands, the vertical supply curve shifts to the right, and the corresponding demand curve increases due to a network effect.

14.4 Two Opposing Effects on Prices in a Network

- **Network effect:** Puts upward pressure on prices as output increases.
- **Price effect:** Puts downward pressure on prices as output increases.

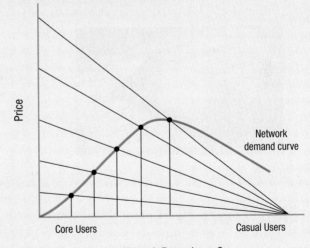

A network demand curve has upward-sloping and downward-sloping segments:

- **Upward-sloping segment:** Shown where the network effect exceeds the price effect, and typically occurs when a network is relatively new. **Core users** of network goods are the target in this part of the network demand curve.

- **Downward-sloping segment:** Shown where the price effect exceeds the network effect, and typically occurs once a network matures. In this part of the network demand curve, **casual users** join the network.

Lisa F. Young/Dreamstime.com

Even grandma and grandpa eventually fall in love with the newest technology gadget. However, older consumers are more likely to be casual users who buy network goods, such as tablet computers, after the goods have become common in society.

Section 3 Market Equilibrium for a Network Good

14.5 A network demand curve contains a **tipping point** (or **critical mass**), defined as the level of output that allows a network to expand further without significant effort by producers. When a tipping point is reached, the power of network effects propels the demand for a network good to a higher equilibrium point. This is referred to as a **virtuous cycle.** If a network good fails to reach its tipping point or falls below its tipping point, a **vicious cycle** can result as customers leave the network, further decreasing the value of the network to other users.

Goods can enter a virtuous cycle or a vicious cycle very quickly, especially if there is a competing network in the market.

Dropbox enjoyed a virtuous cycle in 2012 when over 50 million people signed up for this service that allows users to access and share files on any computer or mobile device.

Section 4 Competition and Market Structure for Network Goods

14.6 Firms engage in a variety of marketing strategies to increase the likelihood of entering a virtuous cycle or to avoid entering a vicious cycle. The pressure to gain and retain customers is enhanced by the low marginal cost of production, which makes customers more valuable the longer they use a firm's product.

Common strategies used by firms include:

- Teaser strategies
- Lock-in strategies
- Market segmentation by versioning (intertemporal pricing, peak-load pricing, and bundling)

Section 5 Should Network Goods Be Regulated?

14.7 Network effects allow successful firms to achieve significant market power, sometimes even a monopoly. To prevent firms from exploiting their market power, governments turn to regulation as a way to limit the abuse of market power.

Poor regulation can sometimes be worse than no regulation. Regulation is not always necessary when the costs of regulation exceed its benefits. The potential of competition itself can prevent monopolies from exploiting their market power.

14.8 **Interconnection** is a common requirement in the regulation of network industries, in which firms are required to give competitors access to each other's **essential facilities,** such as telephone wires that allow for DSL broadband service.

KEY CONCEPTS

network, p. 374
physical network, p. 374
virtual network, p. 374
social network, p. 374
network good, p. 374
network externality, p. 374
network effect, p. 374
network demand curve, p. 376

core user, p. 377
casual user, p. 377
tipping point (critical mass), p. 379
virtuous cycle, p. 379
vicious cycle, p. 380
teaser strategies, p. 383
switching cost, p. 383
lock-in strategies, p. 383

market segmentation, p. 383
versioning, p. 384
intertemporal pricing, p. 384
peak-load pricing, p. 384
bundling, p. 385
industry standard, p. 386
essential facility, p. 386
interconnection, p. 386

QUESTIONS AND PROBLEMS

Check Your Understanding

1. What is a network externality and how does it differ from a typical externality?

2. Explain why a network demand curve slopes upward for small quantities.

3. List three strategies a firm can use to segment its market for a network good.

4. True or false: Once a firm's network good becomes the market leader, it is extremely unlikely for the firm to lose that position within a five-year period. Explain.

5. Why does the 3D printer industry exhibit large economies of scale? Would there also be network externalities in the consumption of 3D printers? Explain.

6. When one mails a letter to a foreign destination, what are the essential facilities involved and why is interconnection needed?

Apply the Concepts

7. Suppose that two community organizations each plan their own public beach volleyball tournament on the same day at the same beach. Each organization wishes to have as many participants as possible. Further, a larger tournament is more fun for the participants. Suppose that a team consists of four players and at least four teams are required to hold a tournament. Explain what the tipping point would be and why a vicious cycle can develop if that number fails to be achieved.

8. If a person decides to unsubscribe from a popular social network, it decreases the value of the network to everyone else. Why wouldn't this action be considered a negative externality?

9. Suppose that expansion of the productive capacity of a firm producing a network good reduces the average cost due to economies of scale, but generates a very large increase in demand due to the network effect. Is this good likely to be on the upward-sloping or downward-sloping portion of the network demand curve? Explain.

10. Suppose that a new Harry Potter book called *The Untold Stories of Harry Potter* is released for sale, and fans line up for days to be the first to buy it. Are these fans core users or casual users in their demand for the new book? How could the book publisher maximize its profit using intertemporal pricing?

11. Suppose that your bank opens up a dozen more automatic teller machines (ATMs) throughout the city, making it much easier to find one. What happens to the demand and supply curves for this network as it expands?

12. Whenever a new car with satellite radio capability is purchased, the buyer is typically offered a free 90-day subscription to a satellite radio service such as SiriusXM. Explain why this offer would be considered a teaser strategy. Why wouldn't SiriusXM just charge a monthly subscription fee from the start?

In the News

13. When Google Apps launched almost a decade ago, it revolutionized the software in-dustry. No longer was software confined to a single computer. Instead, apps are stored online allowing users to access documents and spreadsheets wherever they go. Google's market dominance did not last forever, as Microsoft's Office 365's market share sur-passed Google's in 2015. What were some advantages of Office 365 that allowed it to gain market share so quickly against a market leader? When Google responded by eliminating fees by Office 365 users to switch to Google Apps, what strategy was Google employing?

14. Internet interconnection has become an important issue as countries improve their network infrastructure. According to the International Charging Arrangements for Internet Services (ICAIS) agreement, countries wishing to access U.S. Web sites or use U.S. backbones (Internet networks) must pay the full cost of interconnection (as op-posed to, say, telephone interconnection, where each side shares the cost). Why would a country agree to this type of arrangement in the first place (in the 1990s), and what developments have taken place since then that would cause them to now oppose this arrangement?

Solving Problems

WORK IT OUT   **LaunchPad** | interactive activity

15. Suppose Caroline values video game X at $70 and video game Y at $30, whereas Jacqueline values video game X at $30 and video game Y at $60. The marginal cost to produce each game is $0. If a firm that produces both games decides to bundle X and Y, what price should it charge, and why is this bundling strategy more profit-able than selling each game separately at a single price (assuming price discrimination is not possible)?

16. The accompanying figure shows two demand curves for ski lift tickets, one representing demand during February (peak season) and the other for April (low season). If the ski resort wishes to maximize its profit using peak-load pricing, what price should the ski resort set for lift tickets in February and what price should it set in April?

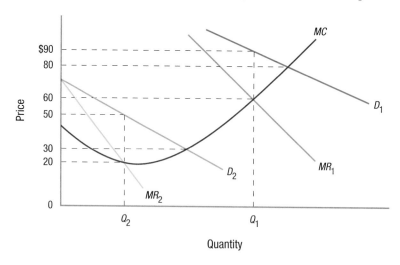

USING THE NUMBERS

17. According to By the Numbers, in what month and year did Uber surpass taxi services as the most popular form of local transportation? How much did Uber's market share increase from the beginning of 2014 to the end of 2015?

18. Compare the growth in Airbnb home-sharing guests from 2012 to 2014 with Uber's growth in users from 2014 to 2015. What are the similarities in how these different industries achieved such dramatic increases in market share in such a short period of time?

ANSWERS TO QUESTIONS IN CHECKPOINTS

Checkpoint: What Is a Network Good? 376

When your friend purchases a laptop capable of using newer, more elaborate software, it generates a benefit to anyone else (especially you) who would find it useful to collaborate on projects. As a result, your friend's laptop purchase increases the value of the laptop to you (a network effect), increasing the likelihood that you will purchase a similar laptop. And once you purchase the laptop, this will generate additional benefits to your other friends, potentially generating even more demand.

Checkpoint: Demand Curve for a Network Good 379

A network demand curve gains value based on the number of people who use it. For example, a network good with one consumer is virtually worthless. As more consumers buy the network good, its value rises and the network good becomes attractive to even more consumers. Once a good matures, the network effect weakens and additional consumers will buy the good only after the price drops. Hence, the demand curve slopes downward for higher quantities of the good.

Checkpoint: Market Equilibrium for a Network Good 382

Most apps depend on a network effect for their existence. As more people use an app, a virtuous cycle may result as word-of-mouth marketing from existing users leads to even greater demand. But because newer apps are frequently introduced in the gaming industry, users tend to lose interest in older apps over time. According to the network demand curve, once users begin to drop, a network effect occurs that reduces the value of the app to all other users. Because gaming apps tend to be interactive, in which users play against one another, the speed of the network effect is stronger than other apps such as news apps that are less interactive. Even the gaming apps that have survived the longest, such as *Angry Birds* or *Candy Crush,* have seen downloads fall dramatically from their peak as new games are created.

Checkpoint: Competition and Market Structure for Network Goods 386

A network good generally has a low marginal cost of production; therefore, any revenue a firm collects, even at low prices, typically increases its profit. By segmenting the market, the firm is separating customers based on their elasticity of demand. Customers with lower elasticities of demand are willing to pay a higher price than customers with higher elasticities of demand. Firms can segment the market by versioning their products. Products can be differentiated by time, peak usage, or bundling to create different versions of the same good at different prices.

Checkpoint: Should Network Goods Be Regulated? 388

An MP3 player is needed to play digital music, and therefore is considered an essential facility. Because Apple produces its own MP3 player, it could potentially restrict its products to play only music downloaded from its iTunes music store. Doing so would prevent its customers from playing music downloaded from other music providers, restricting competition in the digital music market. If that were the case, then regulatory policy could be implemented to prevent producers of MP3 players from restricting sources from which music can be downloaded. But Apple is unlikely to make this restriction, because it benefits from the ability of people to play music downloaded from iTunes on non-Apple devices.

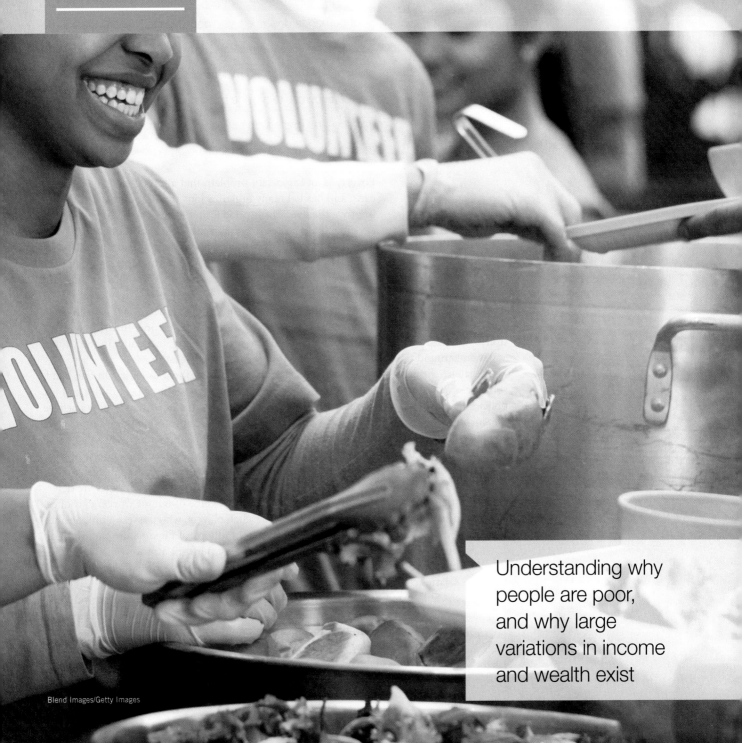

15

Poverty and Income Distribution

Understanding why people are poor, and why large variations in income and wealth exist

Learning Objectives

15.1 Describe the difference between wealth and income.

15.2 Analyze functional, personal, and family income distributions.

15.3 Use a Lorenz curve and Gini coefficient to measure and describe the distribution of wealth and income.

15.4 Describe the impact of income redistribution efforts.

15.5 Describe the causes of income inequality.

15.6 Describe how poverty thresholds are determined.

15.7 Describe the two measures for determining depth of poverty for families.

15.8 Discuss alternative methods of measuring poverty.

15.9 Describe the prevailing theories on how to deal with poverty and income inequality.

O n any given day, millions of families visit a food pantry to acquire basic groceries to get through the week; millions of children eat a free or reduced-price lunch at school, which may be their only nutritious meal of the day; and millions live in neighborhoods described as "food deserts," where there is no easy access to a supermarket to buy fresh fruits, vegetables, and other healthy foods. And millions simply go hungry because of a lack of resources to provide basic necessities for living. Although this scenario exists in many parts of the world, the facts above describe the everyday life of those living in poverty in *America*.

Poverty is an important problem that affects over 1 in 7 Americans, and has led many organizations to call for greater action to improve the lives of the poor. One such call is to ensure that every citizen has access to basic health care, education, and a living wage. Many who are concerned about poverty point to the problem of rising income inequality, which characterizes an economy that has prospered since recovering from the Great Recession of 2007–2009 but has not meaningfully improved the lives of the poor.

The issue of income inequality rose to the forefront in the United States as data show that the richest 1% of the population earned nearly 20% of total income in 2015 and controlled about 90% of all wealth. This is a trend that is not slowing; inequality in the United States and around the world has expanded over the last three decades.

What are the causes of income inequality? Two opposing theories exist. On one hand, some believe that income inequality is the direct result of economic opportunities and tax policies that favor the wealthy few over the vast majority. On the other hand, others believe that income inequality is the direct result of robust market incentives that reward innovative ability and success. These people do not believe income inequality is a result of some social injustice. Instead, they feel that wealth is the reward that comes from the opportunity for anyone to work hard, become successful, and be paid what they are worth to the economy.

Earlier, we saw that when input and product markets are competitive, wages are determined by worker productivity and the market value of output workers produce. This explains why some professional baseball players, who possess a unique ability to throw a 95-mph fastball and attract millions of fans, secure multimillion dollar contracts, while teachers, who arguably perform a more valuable service but do so in a profession shared by millions of others with similar skills, earn salaries closer to the average.

Still, many people have trouble accepting that baseball pitchers earn millions, while teachers earn only thousands, and many others eke out subsistence wages. Income inequality is among the most contentious issues facing economists and other social scientists today.

Questions of fairness are normative. They can only be answered through individual value judgments. Economics has no right or wrong answers to offer in this area, but economists frequently contribute to these discussions.

The San Francisco and Marin Food Bank's *Canstruction* competition brings together design and construction teams to build sculptures from canned goods, which are then donated to those in need.

Will Chiang

Poverty and the Economy

Poverty is a problem facing people in virtually all countries, both rich and poor. Each country uses different methods to address poverty, including assistance for food, housing, health care, and education.

Go to **LaunchPad** to use the latest data to recreate this graph.

The U.S. federal minimum wage is an example of government policy aimed at curbing poverty. In the 1960s and 1970s, one person working a full-time job at the minimum wage was roughly able to keep a family of three out of poverty. Since the 1980s, the minimum wage has not kept up.

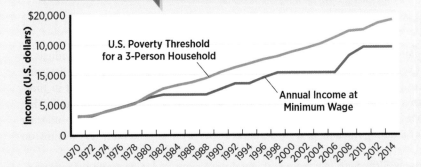

Income (U.S. dollars)

$20,000 — 10,000 — 15,000 — 5,000 — 0

U.S. Poverty Threshold for a 3-Person Household

Annual Income at Minimum Wage

1970 1972 1974 1976 1978 1980 1982 1984 1986 1988 1990 1992 1994 1996 1998 2000 2002 2004 2006 2008 2010 2012 2014

A single-parent working full-time at the minimum wage is unable to keep a family out of poverty.

Richard B. Levine/Newscom

Every country has its own measure of poverty, making a comparison of countries and their official poverty rate misleading. For example, Switzerland and China both have an official poverty rate of less than 8%. In China, this means a family of four living on less than $1,500 a year; in Switzerland, it means living on less than $48,000 a year plus having generous health care, education, and retirement benefits.

68,900,000

Number of Medicaid (health care for low-income persons) recipients in 2015

$583

Average monthly U.S. government housing subsidy for a qualified household in 2015

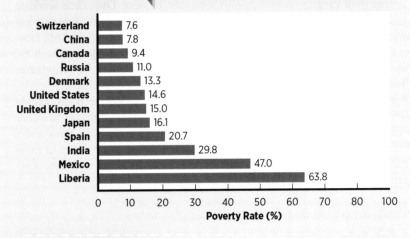

Country	Poverty Rate (%)
Switzerland	7.6
China	7.8
Canada	9.4
Russia	11.0
Denmark	13.3
United States	14.6
United Kingdom	15.0
Japan	16.1
Spain	20.7
India	29.8
Mexico	47.0
Liberia	63.8

0 10 20 30 40 50 60 70 80 90 100
Poverty Rate (%)

The percentage of Americans receiving food stamps fluctuates with the economy. The last recession and slow recovery caused food stamp usage to rise.

Percent (%)

16 14 12 10 8 6 4 2 0

1984 1986 1988 1990 1992 1994 1996 1998 2000 2002 2004 2006 2008 2010 2012 2014

Unlike food stamps of the past, food stamps today work like a debit card.

Melanie Stetson Freeman/Christian Science Monitor/The Image Works

Economic analysis gives us some insight into why income inequality exists. We have already seen how market power, unions, and discrimination can potentially skew income distribution. Even when public policy focuses on reducing these market imperfections, inequalities persist. Regardless of the causes of income inequality, addressing its effects requires special attention to the bottom of the income distribution: those who live in poverty.

This chapter looks at income inequality, its trends, its causes, and how it is measured. We then turn our attention to poverty, focusing on how poverty is traditionally measured, and the U.S. Census Bureau's new approach to measuring poverty. Finally, we look at current poverty trends and the causes of poverty. Throughout this chapter, we use economic analysis to provide a framework for analyzing income distribution, poverty, and the public policies used to combat poverty.

THE DISTRIBUTION OF INCOME AND WEALTH

income A flow measure reflecting the funds received by individuals or households over a period of time, usually a week, month, or year.

Income is a *flow*, **wealth** is a *stock*. Income measures the receipt of funds by individuals or households over time, usually a week, month, or year. Income is a *flow of funds* measure. Wealth, in contrast, measures a family's assets net of liabilities, at a given point in time. You may earn a certain income in 2017, but your net wealth is measured on a specific day, say, December 31, 2017. Many people were wealthy on January 1, 2007, but after suffering the ravages of a falling housing and stock market, they were considerably less wealthy on July 1, 2009.

wealth A stock measure of an individual's or family's assets, net of liabilities, at a given point in time.

You can be wealthy with low income if you do not work and your assets are in homes, stocks, and bonds that earn little to no interest or dividends. Alternatively, you can have little wealth, yet a high income, if you are like a rookie professional ballplayer who earns a seven-figure salary but has not yet accumulated assets.

Life Cycle Effects

Family and individual incomes vary significantly over the course of people's lives. Young people just starting their careers often earn only a modest income. Over their working careers, they become more experienced and their salaries increase, with income peaking roughly between the ages of 45 and 55. At some point between ages 45 and 60, family size begins to decline as the kids grow up and leave home. As people approach 60, income begins declining, while household saving rises as they prepare for retirement. Incomes decline with retirement, but then again, so do family responsibilities.

One result of this economic life cycle is that an aging society can expect to see changes in income distribution as a greater number of households falls into lower income brackets. The life cycle also has implications for the economic effects of immigration. Newcomers to the United States often possess limited skills; therefore, when the country admits more immigrants, it can expect more low-income households. The children of immigrants, however, move up the income distribution ladder.

The Distribution of Income

functional distribution of income The distribution of income for resources or factors of production (land, labor, capital, and entrepreneurial ability).

Income distribution can be considered from several different perspectives. First, we can look at the **functional distribution of income,** which splits income among the inputs (factors) of production. The functional distribution for the United States between 1929 and 2015 is shown in Table 1.

Labor's share of national income rose from 1929 to the 1970s but fell each decade after. The share of income going to small businesses, called "proprietor's income," has declined over this period, but has stabilized at slightly under 10%. Rental income's share fell from 1960 to 1990, but has since grown back to over 4%. The share accruing to corporate profits has increased in recent years to over 14%.

As Table 1 illustrates, the biggest fluctuations in income share have been associated with income from interest earned by individuals and firms, and are caused largely by

TABLE 1	FUNCTIONAL DISTRIBUTION OF INCOME (ABSOLUTE DOLLARS IN BILLIONS, NUMBERS IN PARENTHESES ARE PERCENTAGES OF TOTAL INCOME)				
Year	Wages	Proprietor's Income	Rent	Corporate Profits	Net Interest
1929	51.1 (60.3)	14.9 (17.6)	4.9 (5.8)	9.2 (10.8)	4.7 (5.5)
1940	52.1 (65.4)	12.9 (16.2)	2.7 (3.4)	8.7 (10.9)	3.3 (4.1)
1950	154.8 (65.5)	38.4 (16.3)	7.1 (3.0)	33.7 (14.3)	2.3 (1.0)
1960	296.4 (69.4)	51.9 (12.1)	16.2 (3.8)	52.3 (12.2)	10.7 (2.5)
1970	617.2 (73.7)	79.8 (9.5)	20.3 (2.4)	81.6 (9.7)	38.4 (4.6)
1980	1651.7 (73.6)	177.6 (7.9)	31.3 (1.4)	198.5 (8.8)	183.9 (8.2)
1990	3351.7 (72.2)	381.0 (8.2)	49.1 (1.1)	408.6 (8.8)	452.4 (9.7)
2000	5715.2 (71.6)	715.0 (9.0)	141.6 (1.8)	876.4 (11.0)	532.7 (6.7)
2010	8093.9 (69.3)	1059.3 (9.1)	425.0 (3.6)	1435.1 (12.3)	661.9 (5.7)
2015	9737.1 (67.8)	1400.1 (9.8)	663.6 (4.6)	2049.9 (14.3)	508.3 (3.5)

Data from Bureau of Economic Analysis.

changes in interest rates. It declined until 1960, then rose until the 1990s, before falling again in the last two decades.

Personal or Family Distribution of Income

When most people use the expression "the distribution of income," they typically mean **personal or family distribution of income.** This distributional measure is concerned with how much income, in percentage terms, goes to specific segments of the population.

To analyze personal and family income distribution, the Census Bureau essentially arrays households from the lowest incomes to the highest. It then splits these households into quintiles, or fifths, from the lowest 20% of households to the highest 20%. After totaling and averaging household incomes for each quintile, the Census Bureau computes the percentage of income flowing to each quintile.

Today, the United States contains approximately 125 million households. Therefore, the 25 million households with the lowest incomes compose the bottom quintile, and the 25 million households with the highest incomes compose the top quintile. Because much of the country's income is concentrated at the top, the Census Bureau breaks down the highest quintile further, showing the percentage of income flowing to the richest 5% and 1% of the population.

Table 2 shows the official income distribution estimates for the United States since 1970. These estimates are based on money income before taxes and do not include the value of noncash benefits, such as food stamps, public housing, Medicaid, or employer-provided benefits.

Note that if the income distribution were perfectly equal, all quintiles would receive 20% of aggregate income. A quick look at these income distributions over the past four decades suggests that our distribution of income has been growing more unequal. Specifically, the share of income received by the highest quintile has steadily risen since 1970, while the share of income received by each of the four other quintiles has steadily fallen since 1970. Even more notable is how the income flowing to the top 1% has increased the most, with that share of income more than doubling since 1970. Keep in mind that these numbers ignore taxes and transfers (direct payment to households such as welfare and food stamps) that temper income inequality somewhat.

personal or family distribution of income The distribution of income to individuals or family groups (typically quintiles, or fifths, of the population).

TABLE 2	SHARE OF AGGREGATE INCOME RECEIVED BY EACH HOUSEHOLD QUINTILE: 1970–2014 AND THE GINI COEFFICIENT							
Year	Lowest	Second	Third	Fourth	Highest	Top 5%	Top 1%	Gini Coefficient
1970	4.1	10.8	17.4	24.5	43.3	19.9	8.5	0.394
1975	4.4	10.5	17.1	24.8	43.2	20.1	8.2	0.397
1980	4.3	10.3	16.9	24.9	43.7	20.2	8.8	0.403
1985	4.0	9.7	16.3	24.6	45.3	23.0	11.2	0.419
1990	3.9	9.6	15.9	24.0	46.6	23.9	11.9	0.428
1995	3.7	9.1	15.2	23.3	48.7	25.5	12.2	0.450
2000	3.6	8.9	14.9	23.0	49.6	26.5	17.3	0.462
2005	3.4	8.6	14.6	23.0	50.4	27.1	17.4	0.469
2010	3.3	8.5	14.6	23.4	50.3	27.8	18.5	0.470
2014	3.1	8.2	14.3	23.2	51.2	29.2	19.3	0.480

Data from U.S. Census Bureau, *Current Population Survey*, Annual Social and Economic Supplement (Washington, D.C.: U.S. Government Printing Office), 2015.

Still, incomes of the richest Americans have fared best over the last generation, and one piece of evidence has been the meteoric rise in CEO salaries. Adjusting for inflation, the average salary of a CEO increased 8-fold since 1978, while real wages for workers have barely changed. Such stark differences in worker compensation contributed to the growth of the Occupy movement in recent years and its claims against the power held by the richest 1%.

Compressing distribution data into quintiles allows us to see how distribution has evolved. Economists have developed two primary measures that allow comparisons to be drawn with ease across time and between countries. These measures are Lorenz curves and the Gini coefficient.

Lorenz Curves

Lorenz curve A graph showing the cumulative distribution of income or wealth. Households are measured on the horizontal axis while income or wealth is measured on the vertical axis.

A **Lorenz curve** cumulates households of various income levels on the horizontal axis, and relates this to their cumulated share of total income on the vertical axis. Figure 1, for simplicity, shows a two-person economy. Assume that each person earns 50% of the total income, or that income is divided evenly. Point *a* in Figure 1 marks this point, resulting in the equal distribution curve 0*ac*.

The second curve in Figure 1 shows a two-person economy where the low-income person earns 25% of the total income and the upper-income person receives 75% (point *b*). This graph is skewed to the right (curve 0*bc*), indicating an unequal distribution. If this two-person income distribution were as unequal as possible (0% and 100%), the Lorenz curve would be equal to curve 0*dc*.

Figure 2 and its accompanying table offer more realistic Lorenz curves for income and wealth data for the United States in the year 2014. The quintile income distribution in the second column of the table is cumulated in the third column and plotted in Figure 2. (To *cumulate* a quintile means to add its percentage of income to the percentages earned by all lower quintiles.)

In Figure 2, for instance, the share of income received by the lowest fifth is 3.1%; it is plotted as point *a*. Next, the lowest two quintiles are summed (3.1 + 8.2 = 11.3) and

FIGURE 1 | LORENZ CURVES (TWO-PERSON ECONOMY)

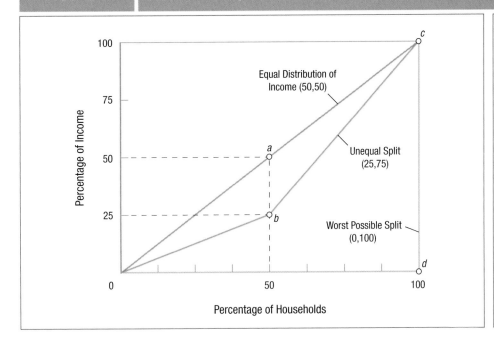

If both people in this two-person economy earn 50% of the total income, income will be distributed perfectly equally, shown by the equal distribution curve O*ac*. Curve O*bc* represents the same economy in which the low-income person earns 25% of the total income and the upper-income person earns 75%. This curve is skewed to the right, indicating an unequal distribution. The most extreme distribution between these two individuals (0% and 100%) is represented by the Lorenz curve O*dc*.

FIGURE 2 | LORENZ CURVES

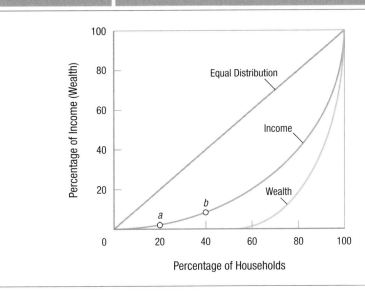

	Income		Wealth	
Quintile	Income	Cum.	Wealth	Cum.
Lowest	3.1	3.1	0.1	0.1
Second	8.2	11.3	0.2	0.3
Third	14.3	25.6	3.2	3.5
Fourth	23.2	48.8	7.6	11.1
Highest	51.2	100.0	88.9	100.0

The graph shows the most recent Lorenz curves for income and wealth in the United States. The quintile distribution of income, found in the second column of the accompanying table, is cumulated in the third column and then plotted as a Lorenz curve. Notice how wealth is much more unequally distributed than income.

Data from U.S. Census Bureau.

plotted as point *b*. The process continues until all quintiles have been plotted to create the Lorenz curve.

Figure 2 also plots the Lorenz curve for wealth; it shows how wealth is much more unequally distributed than income. The wealthiest 20% of Americans control nearly 90% of wealth, even though they earn only half of all income.

FIGURE 3   THE GINI COEFFICIENT

The Gini coefficient is a measure of income inequality, defined as the ratio of the area between the Lorenz curve and the equal distribution line, and the total area below the equal distribution line. Thus, the Gini coefficient is equal to the ratio between area *A* and area (*A* + *B*). If distribution were equal, area A would be zero, and the Gini coefficient would equal zero. If distribution were as unequal as possible, area *B* would disappear; thus, the Gini coefficient would be 1.

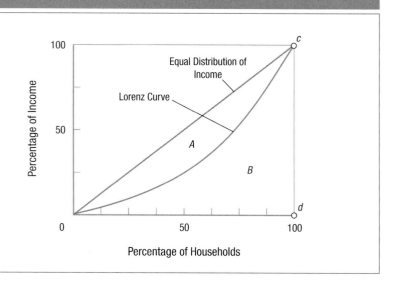

Gini Coefficient

Gini coefficient A measure of income inequality defined as the area between the Lorenz curve and the equal distribution line divided by the total area below the equal distribution line.

Lorenz curves provide a good graphical summation of income (or wealth) distributions, but they can be inconvenient to use when comparing distributions between different countries or across time. Economists prefer to use one number to represent the inequality of an economy's income (or wealth) distribution: the **Gini coefficient**.

The Gini coefficient provides a measure of the position of the Lorenz curve. It is calculated by dividing the area between the Lorenz curve and the equal distribution line by the area below the equal distribution line. In Figure 3, the Gini coefficient is the ratio of area *A* to area (*A* + *B*).

If the distribution were equal, area *A* would disappear (equal zero); thus, the Gini coefficient would be zero. If the distribution were as unequal as possible, with one individual or household earning all national income, area *B* would disappear; thus, the Gini coefficient would be 1.

As a rule, the lower the coefficient, the more equal the distribution; the higher the coefficient, the more unequal. Looking back at the last column in Table 2, the Gini coefficient confirms that the basic income distribution has become more unequal since 1970. The Gini coefficient has risen from 0.394 in 1970 to 0.480 in 2014.

The Impact of Redistribution

In the United States, there is a vast array of income redistribution policies, including the progressive income tax (where those with higher incomes pay a higher rate than those with lower incomes), housing subsidies, and other transfer payments and in-kind benefits such as Medicaid and Medicare, Social Security, and traditional welfare programs. Remember that the income distribution data in Table 2 *excluded* such government-provided cash and noncash benefits, and the effects of taxation.

Figure 4 provides an estimate of the impact progressive taxes and transfer payments (cash and in-kind) had on the income distribution in the United States. As we would expect, distribution became more equal: The Gini coefficient declined from 0.480, according to the official measure using gross income, to 0.391 after adjusting for taxes and transfer payments.

FIGURE 4	LORENZ CURVES FOR THE UNITED STATES: MONEY INCOME AND INCOME ADJUSTED FOR TAXES AND TRANSFER PAYMENTS

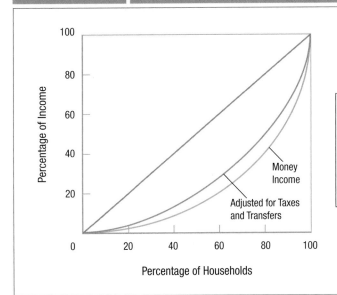

Quintile	Money Income Percent	Cum.	Adjusted Income Percent	Cum.	Taxes Percent	Cum.
Lowest	3.1	3.1	5.3	5.3	0.6	0.6
Second	8.2	11.3	9.6	14.9	3.9	4.5
Third	14.3	25.6	14.1	29.0	8.9	13.4
Fourth	23.2	48.8	20.4	49.4	17.9	31.3
Highest	51.2	100.0	50.6	100.0	68.7	100.0

These Lorenz curves provide an estimate of the impact progressive taxes and transfer payments (cash and in-kind) had on income distribution in the United States. As one would expect, distribution becomes more equal once taxes and transfer payments are taken into account. In this case, the Gini coefficient declined from 0.480 to 0.391.

Data from U.S. Census Bureau.

Table 3 provides some examples of how income distribution varies around the world. Income in European countries is generally more equally distributed than in the United States, while many South American countries have more unequal distributions.

TABLE 3	GINI COEFFICIENTS FOR VARIOUS COUNTRIES, 2014

Country	Gini Coefficient	Country	Gini Coefficient
Australia	0.349	Italy	0.352
Bolivia	0.481	Japan	0.321
Brazil	0.529	Mexico	0.481
Canada	0.337	New Zealand	0.362
Chile	0.505	South Africa	0.634
China	0.421	Spain	0.359
Denmark	0.291	Sweden	0.273
France	0.331	United Kingdom	0.326
Israel	0.428	United States	0.480

Data from World Bank, *World Development Indicators* (Washington, D.C.: World Bank), 2015.

Rio de Janeiro, Brazil, is one of the most beautiful cities in the world, but it also has some of the largest slums in the world.

Redistribution policies are the subject of intense debates. Those on the political right argue that differences in income are the natural result of a market system in which different individuals possess different personal endowments, schooling, and ambition. They believe, moreover, that the incentives of the marketplace are needed to encourage people to work and produce. The opportunities that markets provide mean that some people will be winners and others will lose. These analysts are unconcerned about the distribution of income unless it becomes so unequal that it discourages incentives and reduces efficiency.

Those on the political left argue that public policy should ultimately be guided by human needs. They see personal wealth as being the product of community effort as much as individual effort, and therefore they favor greater government taxation of income and wealth. By and large, European nations have found this argument more compelling than has the United States. This is reflected in the breadth of European social welfare policies. Because there is no correct answer (except possibly keeping distribution away from the extremes), this debate continues.

Causes of Income Inequality

Many factors contribute to income inequality in our society. First, as just mentioned, people are born into different circumstances with differing natural abilities. Families take varying interest in the well-being of their children, with some kids receiving immense inputs of family time and capital, while others receive little. These family choices largely fall outside the realm of public policy.

TABLE 4	MEAN EARNINGS BY HIGHEST DEGREE EARNED, 2014			
	Mean Earnings by Highest Degree			
	No High School Diploma	High School Graduate	College Graduate	Advanced Degree
All Persons	$25,376	$34,736	$57,252	$72,072
Male	26,884	39,052	64,948	84,760
Female	21,268	30,056	50,180	61,620
White	25,636	36,192	58,864	72,280
Black	22,880	30,108	46,540	59,748
Asian	24,804	31,408	59,748	81,224
Hispanic	24,232	30,940	48,724	64,220

Data from U.S. Census Bureau and Bureau of Labor Statistics.

Human Capital The guarantee of a free public education through high school and huge subsidies to public colleges and universities for all Americans are designed to even out some of the economic differences among families. Still, public education does not eliminate the disparities. Some parents plan their children's education long before they are born, while other parents ignore education altogether.

Table 4 provides evidence of the impact investments in education have on earnings. Those without high school diplomas earned the least, roughly a third less than high school graduates. A college degree resulted in mean earnings about 2.5 times higher than what individuals without high school diplomas earned.

The U.S. economy has become more technologically complex. Manufacturing jobs have dwindled, reducing the demand for these workers, reducing their real wages. Several decades ago, people with low education levels could find highly productive work in manufacturing, with good wages and benefits. Globalization and increased capital mobility, however, have caused many of these jobs to migrate to lower-wage countries. The result is that real wages have declined for Americans in many manufacturing occupations.

Our economy is increasingly oriented toward service industries, making investments in human capital more important than ever. The service industry spans more than just burger flipping, maid service, and landscaping. The United States is still the world leader in the design and development of new products, basic scientific research and development, and other professional services. All these industries and occupations have one thing in common: the need for highly skilled and highly educated employees.

Other Factors In an earlier chapter, we saw that economic discrimination leads to an income distribution skewed against those subject to discrimination. Reduced wages then reduce an individual's incentive to invest in human capital because the returns are lower, perpetuating a vicious cycle.

Table 5 outlines some characteristics of households occupying two different income quintiles. By comparing the lowest quintile with the highest, we can see some of the reasons for income inequality. As the Census Bureau summarizes these differences, "High-income households tended to be family households that included two or more earners, lived in the suburbs of a large city, and had a working householder between 35 and 54 years old. In contrast, low-income households tended to be in a city with an elderly householder who lived alone and did not work."

TABLE 5	DISTRIBUTION OF HOUSEHOLDS BY SELECTED CHARACTERISTICS WITHIN INCOME QUINTILES, 2014	
Characteristic	**Lowest Quintile**	**Highest Quintile**
Type of Residence		
Inside metropolitan area	81.4%	90.7%
Inside principal city	39.8	30.4
Outside principal city	41.6	60.3
Outside metropolitan area	18.6	9.3
Type of Household		
Family households	39.0	86.0
Married-couple families	16.6	77.0
Nonfamily households	61.0	14.0
Householder living alone	57.0	6.8
Age of Householder		
15 to 34 years	22.0	15.6
35 to 54 years	26.1	49.7
55 to 64 years	18.1	22.2
65 years or older	33.8	12.5
Number of Earners		
No earners	61.5	3.1
One earner	34.2	20.9
Two or more earners	4.4	76.0

Data from U.S. Census Bureau, *Current Population Survey,* Annual Social and Economic Supplement (Washington, D.C.: U.S. Government Printing Office), 2015.

The rise in two-earner households over the last two decades accounts for a large part of the growing inequality in income. Note in Table 5 that only 4.4% of the lowest quintile households had two earners, while 76.0% of the highest quintile did. Also, only 3.1% of top quintile householders did not work, but 61.5% of those in the bottom quintile were not working.

It is hardly surprising that households with two people working tend to have higher incomes than households with only one person or none working. In most households, whether one or two people work represents a choice. Today, clearly more couples are opting for two incomes. This is significant, given that rising income inequality is often cited as evidence that the United States needs to change its public policies to reduce inequalities. Yet, if the rise in inequality is due largely to changes in household attitudes toward work and income, with more couples choosing dual-career households, changes in public policy may not be needed. Rising inequality may simply be a reflection of the changing personal choices of many households.

This overview of income distribution and inequality provides a broad foundation for the remainder of the chapter, which focuses on poverty, its causes, and possible cures.

ISSUE

How Much Do You Need to Earn to Be in the Top 1%?

Among the most contentious issues of the past decade has been the rising income and wealth of the richest Americans. Even during the depths of the Great Recession, average incomes of the richest 1% continued to rise, much to the angst of the rest of the population, many of whom had lost jobs or seen stagnant wages.

Still, the ability to work hard and achieve great wealth is engrained in the hopes of millions who dream to become part of the 1%. And each year, thousands of Americans reach this exclusive group for the first time. How much does one need to earn in order to be included among the top 1%? In 2015 the minimum annual income was approximately $500,000. Although this is a tremendous amount of money, remember that it's the *minimum* income required to be in the top 1%. The *average* income of the top 1% is over $1.3 million per year!

The minimum income to be in the top 1% also varies by state, as shown in the table. In Connecticut, one must earn at least $677,608 to be among the top

DigitalVision Vectors/Getty Images

MINIMUM INCOME FOR THE TOP 1% (TOP 5 AND BOTTOM 5 STATES, INCLUDING THE DISTRICT OF COLUMBIA)			
1. Connecticut	$677,608	47. Mississippi	$262,809
2. District of Columbia	555,341	48. Kentucky	262,653
3. New Jersey	538,666	49. West Virginia	242,774
4. Massachusetts	532,328	50. New Mexico	240,847
5. New York	506,051	51. Arkansas	228,298

Data from CNN Money, January 27, 2015.

1% of income earners, while in Arkansas, it *only* requires $228,298. Do you think these amounts are unattainable without a rich uncle leaving you millions to jumpstart a lucrative business? Not quite. Only 2 in 5 members of the 1% inherited wealth. The vast majority of those in the 1% are highly educated, motivated individuals who pursue lucrative careers or take chances to build successful businesses. Pursuing a college degree is certainly an important step along the way.

 CHECKPOINT

THE DISTRIBUTION OF INCOME AND WEALTH

- The functional distribution of income splits income among factors of production.
- The family or personal distribution of income typically splits income into quintiles.
- A Lorenz curve cumulates households of various income levels on the horizontal axis and their cumulative share of income on the vertical axis.
- The Gini coefficient is the ratio of the area between the Lorenz curve and the equal distribution line to the total area below the equal distribution line. It is used to compare income distribution across time and between countries.
- Income redistribution activities such as progressive taxes, Medicare, Medicaid, and other transfer and welfare programs reduce the Gini coefficient and reduce the inequality in the distribution of income.
- Income inequality is caused by a number of factors, including individual investment in human capital, natural abilities, and discrimination.

QUESTION: Suppose that a proposal is made to streamline the role of government by reducing the bureaucracy of social income programs. For example, the government would eliminate Social Security, Medicare, Medicaid, and other welfare programs, and instead simply give $10,000 a year to every citizen over the age of 18. Would this improve the income distribution in the United States? Why or why not?

Answers to the Checkpoint questions can be found at the end of this chapter.

POVERTY

Thus far, we have examined income distribution in general terms, looking at the spectrum from the top to the bottom. This section focuses on the bottom of the income spectrum—those who live in poverty. First, we look at poverty thresholds and how they are defined. Then we turn to the incidence of poverty and its trends. We then take a brief look at some experimental measures of poverty, considering their impact on measured rates of poverty. Lastly, we discuss the causes of poverty and how poverty can be reduced.

How difficult is life in poverty? A household of four in the United States that lived on less than $24,259 in the year 2015 was considered in poverty. That is equivalent to one wage earner working full-time as a maintenance worker at an apartment complex earning $12 per hour, or about $2,000 per month before taxes. And this is a household living right at the poverty line; many households earn even less. Can a family get by on such meager income? In the United States, nearly 15% of all households do.

A household of four living on $2,000 per month can expect to have $1,750 after payroll and other taxes are deducted. Subtracting the rent on a modest subsidized apartment or a public housing apartment of $700 per month, $250 per month in utilities (electricity, gas, water, trash pickup, telephone, and basic Internet and cable), $250 per month toward

> About 1 in 7 persons in the United States lives in poverty. For a family of four, this means living on less than $24,259 a year.

Lucidwaters/Dreamstime.com

a car payment, and $150 per month for fuel and auto insurance, this household has $400 left, or about $100 per week for everything else: food, clothing, school expenses, health insurance, child care, and entertainment. Not to mention the occasional car repair, doctor and dentist co-payment, or parking ticket. And it certainly does not leave much to buy a $5 cup of coffee.

Living in poverty means that tough choices must be made to make ends meet. Some choose to give up their car and instead rely on public transportation. Others give up cable or the landline telephone. In more severe cases, some households are forced to cut back on food or health care. These choices are faced by 1 out of 7 persons in the United States. Why does the world's richest nation have so many poor citizens? Let's start to answer this by looking at how poverty is measured.

Measuring Poverty

poverty thresholds Income levels for various household sizes, below which people are considered to be living in poverty.

Poverty thresholds were developed by Mollie Orshansky in the 1960s. They were based on the Department of Agriculture's Economy Food Plan, the least expensive plan by which a family could feed itself. The Department of Agriculture first surveyed the food-buying patterns of low-income households, using these data to determine the cost of a nutritionally balanced food plan on a low-income budget. Orshansky then extrapolated these costs to determine the cost of maintaining such a food plan for households of various compositions. Finally, to determine the official poverty threshold, Orshansky multiplied the cost of the food plan, adjusted for family size, by 3. This multiplier assumes that an average household spends about a third of its income on food.[1]

Poverty thresholds are updated each year to account for inflation using the consumer price index (CPI). Table 6 shows the poverty thresholds for 2015. If a household earns less than the threshold, every person in that household is considered poor. Poverty thresholds do not vary geographically. Also, "income" includes income before taxes, including cash benefits, but not capital gains or noncash benefits such as food stamps, public housing, or Medicaid benefits. Poverty thresholds are updated by the Census Bureau and are used primarily for statistical purposes.

In practice, to qualify for certain federal programs, a slightly modified measure called the poverty guidelines is used. These guidelines are issued by the Department of Health and Human Services, and are very similar to the poverty thresholds from the Census Bureau. The exception is that there are separate poverty guidelines for Alaska and Hawaii due to the

[1] See Constance F. Citro and Robert T. Michael, *Measuring Poverty: A New Approach* (Washington, D.C.: National Academy Press), 1995, p. 13 and Chapter 2, for more detail on how thresholds are measured.

TABLE 6	U.S. POVERTY THRESHOLDS, 2015
One person	$12,085
Two people	15,397
Three people	18,872
Four people	24,259
Five people	28,729
Six people	32,512
Seven people	36,971
Eight people	41,017
Nine people	49,079

Information from U.S. Census Bureau.

higher cost of living in these states. For the purposes of our analysis, we will use the poverty thresholds from the Census Bureau.

The Incidence of Poverty

The **poverty rate** is the percentage of the population living in poverty. Poverty rates for the United States since 1960 are shown in Figure 5. Poverty fell rapidly between 1960 and 1975, but has remained roughly stable ever since, fluctuating with the business cycle: rising around recessions (the shaded vertical bars) and falling when times are good.

poverty rate The percentage of the population living in poverty.

FIGURE 5	POVERTY RATES IN THE UNITED STATES, 1960–2014

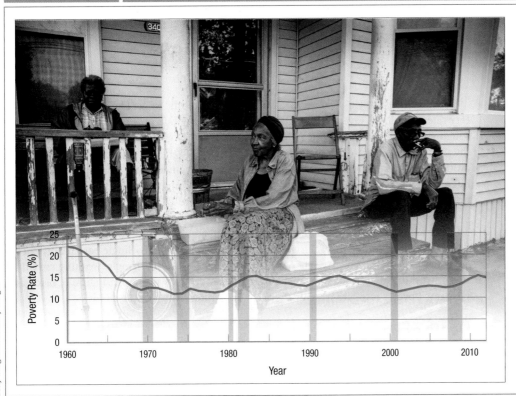

Poverty fell rapidly between 1960 and 1975, but has remained roughly stable ever since.

Data from U.S. Census Bureau, Current Population Reports, P60-252, *Income and Poverty in the United States: 2014* (Washington, D.C.: U.S. Government Printing Office), 2015.

Getty Images News/Getty Images

Poverty rates for whites, blacks, and Hispanics are shown for the years 1970, 1990, and 2014. The poverty rates for blacks and Hispanics have fallen since the 1990s to around 25% today, but remain well above the poverty rate for whites.

Data from U.S. Census Bureau, *Current Population Reports*, P60-252, *Income and Poverty in the United States: 2014* (Washington, D.C.: U.S. Government Printing Office), 2015.

Poverty rates vary considerably along racial and ethnic lines. Figure 6 charts the poverty rate since 1970. Over most of this time, the poverty rate for blacks and Hispanics was roughly twice the rate for whites. Both of these minority groups benefited, however, from the strong economic growth of the 1990s and early 2000s, their poverty rates dropping from around 30% to around 25% today. White poverty remained fairly steady over the 1990s, fluctuating between 10% and 11%. However, the recession in 2007–2009 and the slow economic recovery pushed the poverty rate for whites above 12%.

These data suggest that robust economic growth is a major force for reducing poverty. The expression "a rising tide floats all boats" would appear to have something to it.

Table 7 shows other characteristics that contribute to poverty. Single parent households have 2 to 5 times the poverty rate of married couples. Not surprisingly, working part-time or not working at all leads to higher poverty rates. And, as we saw in Figure 6, black and Hispanic poverty rates are roughly twice that of whites.

Depth of Poverty

It is one thing to say that a certain percentage of the population is poor. It is another to determine just how poor they are. The poverty threshold for a family of four today is a little over $24,000. If most poor families have incomes approaching this threshold, we could be

TABLE 7	PEOPLE AND FAMILIES IN POVERTY BY SELECTED CHARACTERISTICS, 2014

Characteristic	Poverty Rate
Type of Household	
Married-couple households	6.2%
Female households (no husband)	30.6
Male households (no wife)	15.7
Work Experience	
Worked full-time, year round	3.0
Worked part-time, year round	15.9
Did not work	33.7
Race	
White	10.1
Black	26.2
Asian	12.0
Hispanic	23.6

Data from U.S. Census Bureau, *Current Population Reports,* P60-252, *Income and Poverty in the United States: 2014* (Washington, D.C.: U.S. Government Printing Office), 2015.

confident that poverty was just a transitory stage—one phase of the life cycle—and that many people who are poor today would have higher incomes tomorrow.

But if, conversely, many poor families have incomes below $10,000, our view of poverty would be different, and our public policies aimed at reducing poverty would need to be considerably more robust.

To gain a view of the broad spectrum of poverty, economists have developed two *depth of poverty* measures that describe the economic well-being of lower-income families. One measure, the **income deficit,** tells us how far below the poverty threshold a family's income lies. In 2014, the income deficit for families living in poverty averaged $10,137. Using the poverty threshold for a family of four, the average income for a family living in poverty was $14,122.

income deficit The difference between the poverty threshold and a family's income.

The second measure of poverty, the one we will focus on, is the **ratio of income to poverty.** It compares family income to the poverty threshold and expresses this comparison as a ratio. Thus, the ratio for families with incomes equal to the poverty threshold equals 1.0; the ratio for those living at half the threshold income is 0.5. The Census Bureau considers people who live in families with ratios below 0.5 to be "severely or desperately poor." Those with ratios between 0.5 and 1.0 are "poor," and people with ratios above 1.0 but less than 1.25 (less than 25% above the poverty threshold) are considered to be "near poor."

ratio of income to poverty The ratio of family income to the poverty threshold. Families with ratios below 0.5 are considered severely poor, families with ratios between 0.5 and 1.0 are considered poor, and those families with ratios between 1.0 and 1.25 are considered near poor.

Of the 47 million poor people in 2014, over 20 million of them were desperately poor, and an additional 15 million were categorized as near poor. These measures (income deficit and the ratio of income to poverty) provide us with a more nuanced picture of poverty.

Alternative Measures of Poverty Many researchers have questioned the relevance of the current method for determining poverty thresholds. The National Academy of Sciences studied the official approach to poverty thresholds and concluded that the measure is flawed because "[it]counts taxes as income, [and] is flawed in the adjustments to the thresholds for different family circumstances."[2]

[2] Citro and Michael, *Measuring Poverty,* pp. 97–98.

South Africa: A Nation of Rich Treasures and Income Inequality

How is South Africa, one of the richest countries in Africa, trying to reduce income inequality and poverty?

AfriPics.com/Alamy

South Africa is known for its many beautiful beaches and wildlife parks, which attract tourists from around the world desiring to venture on a safari or other adventures without sacrificing the modern conveniences that many other African countries lack. And although the average income in South Africa is among the highest in Africa, this statistic does not tell the entire story of the typical life of South Africans, of whom nearly half live in poverty.

How severe is income inequality in one of the wealthiest countries in Africa?

A common measure of income inequality is the Gini coefficient, in which higher values represent greater income inequality. According to the World Bank, South Africa has one of the highest Gini coefficients in the world at 0.63. In comparison, the Gini coefficient in the United States is 0.48, while in Norway, which has one of the lowest Gini coefficients in the world, it is 0.25. South Africa's income inequality can be seen most dramatically in the major cities of Cape Town

and Johannesburg, where glittering condos and luxury shops are found not too far from decrepit homes and neighborhoods that one would expect to see in an impoverished country.

Part of the problem can be traced to its history, in which the well-connected have had access to better schools and opportunities to work in one of many major corporations or the government. Yet, much of South Africa's economy relies on the informal market, small makeshift shops and cafés where millions of South Africans make meager incomes.

Efforts to reduce income inequality and poverty have centered on government efforts to attract foreign investment and promote small businesses that help drive economic activity, especially in the poorest parts of the country. Moreover, since the end of apartheid, the government has pumped

significant amounts of money to build infrastructure such as modern utilities and new schools in places like Soweto, a historically poor township near Johannesburg that today is buzzing with trendy new shops and restaurants. The home of Soweto's most famous former resident, the late Nelson Mandela, is now a museum attracting thousands of tourists whose spending further boosts the local economy.

Although the problems of poverty and income inequality still persist in South Africa, increased foreign investment and a more favorable economic environment have resulted in a fast-growing middle class, leading to better lives for many people. With the right policies and incentives in place, unequal income distributions can be overcome, allowing all citizens to enjoy the fruits of economic growth.

GO TO **LaunchPad** TO PRACTICE THE ECONOMIC CONCEPTS IN THIS STORY

The main argument that the study puts forth is that poverty thresholds should not be "one-size-fits-all," and should be adjusted for geographic differences and other circumstances such as health care needs. Moreover, given how much our standard of living has changed over the last 50 years, using a definition of poverty based on 1963 data adjusted for inflation is no longer relevant.

Given the Academy's findings, the Census Bureau developed some new ways of measuring poverty. These alternative measures of poverty differ from the old in basing their estimates on after-tax income plus capital gains and counting as income such noncash benefits as food stamps and housing subsidies plus imputed return on home equity (i.e., the savings from owning a home versus paying rent each month).

The Census Bureau derived its new estimates of income thresholds from a survey of expenditures on food, clothing, housing, utilities, and other necessities for the typical family of four (two adults and two kids). These figures were then adjusted to reflect differences in family composition and size, given that children consume less than adults, some household economies are associated with larger families, and the first child in a one-adult family costs more to support than the first child in a two-adult family. Under these measures, poverty rates fell by roughly a quarter.

Causes of Poverty

The reasons why poverty persists are wide-ranging. Traditional causes of poverty include a lack of human capital, mental or physical disabilities, and drug addictions that inhibit persons from achieving gainful employment. Reasons also include an unwillingness to work or an apathy toward work that leads to frequent terminations. Another reason for poverty is that some people refuse to relocate for work, despite having the skills and work ethic to escape poverty. This last reason explains why many rural communities in Appalachian states continue to experience high poverty rates. As industries moved out and jobs disappeared, residents chose to remain, seeking jobs that pay meager wages.

As economic and social change took place in recent decades, new factors have contributed to the rise in poverty. First, wages generally have not kept up with rising costs; specifically, a single parent working at the minimum wage cannot escape poverty today, whereas 40 years ago it was possible. Second, technological changes and globalization have changed employment opportunities and led to unemployment in certain industries that forced people into poverty. Third, rising health costs have led some to give up work to care for an ill family member, forgoing earnings. And finally, changes in family structure, particularly an increase in single parenthood, have made it more difficult to avoid a life of poverty. These reasons and others have encouraged policymakers to rethink approaches to eliminating poverty.

Eliminating Poverty

Poverty can be a relative or an absolute measure. As we saw earlier, the official measure of poverty in the United States is based on an absolute number, the poverty threshold. Some researchers, however, think a relative measure would be more useful, such as labeling the bottom 20% of American households as "poor."

If we decide to use such a measure, poverty will never be eliminated, no matter how wealthy our country might become. A relative measure obscures the fact that poverty in the United States means something different than it does in the developing world. In the United States, being poor might mean scraping by paycheck to paycheck and having to give up such things as cable television or eating out. In some developing countries, being poor might mean literally starving.

The official U.S. poverty threshold for an individual is an income of roughly $32 a day. In the developing world, by contrast, the World Bank and other agencies define poverty as incomes of less than $2 a day. By World Bank standards, poverty has already been eradicated in the United States.

Reducing Income Inequality Regardless of how poverty is defined, the question of how to reduce it remains controversial. The political left views income and wealth redistribution as the chief means to reduce poverty. Social justice, they argue, requires that the government provide an extensive safety net for the poor. In their view, services that the government already provides, including public education, housing subsidies, Medicaid, and unemployment compensation, should be greatly expanded.

Moreover, they claim these policies should be supplemented by increasing the progressivity of the tax system. This would reduce the inequalities in wealth and income. By increasing the tax burden on the well-to-do, people of modest incomes could lead more meaningful and just lives. It may also reduce acts of desperation,

ISSUE

What Is Considered "Poor" Around the World?

Every country uses its own definition of what constitutes being poor. In the United States, the official poverty threshold is calculated as an absolute measure. This means a family of four making $24,259 or less in the year 2015 was considered poor. However, a family of four making $24,259 a year in China or India would be considered quite wealthy in their countries. Compared to many developing countries, being poor in America still allows for a relatively comfortable life.

Many countries in the European Union, however, use a relative measure of poverty. In Denmark, a family is considered poor if it earns less than 60% of the median income. With the median household income being over $75,000 a year, this means a family earning less than $45,000 a year is considered poor. In addition, Denmark offers full health care coverage to every citizen and free college tuition. Certainly, an American family earning $45,000 a year and receiving free health care and college education for its children would not be considered poor.

The main culprits for the difficulty in defining and comparing poverty rates between countries involve differences in the cost of living, the role of government, and overall economic devel-

What is considered poor in America, such as living in a small old house in a rural community, might be considered rich elsewhere, such as in undeveloped areas of Africa where residents do not have access to running water or electricity.

opment. In rich countries, the cost of living is higher, governments often provide more services, and citizens have a higher expectation of what is considered necessary for survival. In poor countries, the cost of living is low, governments often cannot provide much assistance, and citizens are merely surviving.

To provide a better comparison of poverty across the world, various organizations have devised methods to compare living standards and poverty rates across countries. The United Nations publishes the *Human Development Index* each year, which provides an overall picture of a country's living standard based on factors such as access to education, running water and sanitation, health care, and communications. How-

ever, it does not provide a percentage of the country being poor. The World Bank uses an absolute measure with thresholds ranging from $1.25 a day (extreme poverty) to $2 a day, adjusted to the cost of living, to estimate the number of poor in mostly developing countries. Finally, the Organisation for Economic Co-operation and Development (OECD) publishes comparisons of poverty rates among mostly developed countries based on a fixed percentage of median incomes.

The availability of these statistics allows us to compare poverty rates around the world better. Still, difficulties remain when cultural differences influence what is considered vital for survival in each country.

such as shoplifting and home burglaries, representing an external benefit from reducing poverty.

Increasing Economic Growth The opposite side of the political spectrum argues that such programs, when allowed to become too expansive, can be disastrous. Welfare significantly reduces the incentive to work and produce, thereby reducing the economy's output. A vibrant market economy accommodates the wishes of those who want full-time, upwardly mobile careers as well as those who want to work a minimal amount so that they can pursue other interests.

Because wages provide nearly 70% of all income, those on the political right note that there inevitably will be some inequality in a market system. Some people, after all, make bad choices and fail to invest enough in their education or job skills. Yet, the possibility of failure itself provides an incentive to work hard and invest, and the political right sees this sort of efficiency in the economy as being more important than equity or fairness. The best way to cure poverty, they argue, is by implementing policies that increase the economic pie shared by all, not just by splitting up the pie more evenly.

This political dispute has fueled a controversy in economics. One group of economists argues that economic growth raises low incomes at a rate similar to that of average incomes, such that the poor benefit from growth just as much as anyone else. Other economists reply that the shift toward freer markets around the world, combined with the resulting economic growth, has widened inequalities, causing the poor to fall further behind.

Who is right? Jagdish Bhagwati, a well-known development economist, argued that economic growth creates gainful employment, lifting people out of poverty. Further, economic growth increases government revenue, allowing for greater spending on health and education for the poor. He argues that

in economic terms, growth [is] an instrument, not a target—the means by which the true targets, like poverty reduction and the social advancement of the masses, would be achieved.

He adds a caveat, however, that

the political sustainability of the growth-first model requires both symbolic and material efforts. While growth does benefit the poor, the rich often benefit disproportionately. So to keep the poor committed to the system as their economic aspirations are aroused, the wealthy would be well advised to indulge less in conspicuous consumption.[3]

In sum, Bhagwati states that economic growth raises all incomes in absolute terms, including the poor, which reduces poverty. However, relative incomes may continue to suffer, as income inequality can widen with economic growth.

Rawls and Nozick   Unfortunately, there is no unified theory of income distribution that takes the various issues we have discussed into account. Earlier chapters suggested that income depends on productivity—in competitive markets, each input (factor) is paid the value of its marginal product.

Human capital analysis adds that as people invest in themselves, their productivity and income rise. Analysis of imperfect input markets, however, shows that income distribution advantages accrue more to those with market power.

Our analysis of economic discrimination suggested several more reasons why incomes may be skewed in favor of some groups rather than others. The bargaining strength of labor unions is yet another factor that can skew income distribution, in this case in favor of union members.

These analyses have focused, in one way or another, on whether certain patterns of income distribution are economically efficient. Yet, how do we know whether various income distributions are equitable or fair? Is there anywhere to turn for theoretical help in addressing this question? The answer is a qualified "yes." Two philosophers, John Rawls and Robert Nozick, published competing views on this subject in the early 1970s.[4]

John Rawls proposed the "maximin principle," in which he argued that society should maximize the welfare of the least well-off individual. He asks us to conduct a thought experiment: Assume that you must decide on the income distribution for your society, without knowing where in the distribution you will end up. Because chance could lead to you being the least well-off individual in the society, Rawls suggests people would favor significant income redistribution under these circumstances.

Robert Nozick argued that it is "illegitimate to use the coercive power of the state to make some better off at the expense of others." To Nozick, justice requires protecting property rights "legitimately acquired or legitimately transferred."[5] Using Nozick's argument, gaming app developers who succeeded in creating fun and highly addictive games such

[3] Jagdish Bhagwati, "Does Redistributing Income Reduce Poverty?" Project Syndicate, October 27, 2011.

[4] John Rawls, *A Theory of Justice* (Oxford: Clarendon), 1972; Robert Nozick, *Anarchy, State and Utopia* (Oxford: Blackwell), 1974.

[5] John Kay, *The Truth about Markets: Their Genius, Their Limits, Their Follies* (London: Penguin Books), 2003, p. 187.

as *Candy Crush Saga* and *Angry Birds* and subsequently became very wealthy because millions willingly bought premium game subscriptions, cannot be considered unjust. Instead, Nozick would argue it would be unjust if the creators were not rewarded for their innovation that has provided countless hours of fun for so many people.

This debate highlights the perennial tradeoff in economic policy between equity and efficiency, a tradeoff that serves as a bone of contention in nearly every discussion of economic and public policy. Although microeconomics is sometimes beset by controversy, at its best it provides us with a dispassionate framework for analyzing and discussing many issues.

Mobility: Are Poor Families Poor Forever? The poverty rates and income distribution data provide a snapshot in time. How about over time? What is the human side to this? Do people start in poverty or fall into poverty and then stay there, or is there movement out of poverty?

A study by the U.S. Census Bureau tracking over 42,000 American households from 2009 to 2011 provides an answer. The study found that of the households that were living in poverty at the start of 2009, 35% were no longer living in poverty by the end of 2011.[6] Of these households, about half were living just above the poverty line, while the other half did much better and were earning incomes well above the poverty line. The results indicate that mobility between income groups is possible, and that not all who are in poverty stay there forever.

However, additional data from the Census Bureau tell the other side of the story. Although millions of households pull themselves out of poverty each year, millions more find themselves falling into poverty. During the last economic recession and the slow economic recovery that followed, millions of households fell into poverty for the first time, causing the poverty rate to rise above 15% in 2010. The fortunate news is that many of these households remained in poverty only temporarily as new jobs were created with continued economic growth.

The movements of households in and out of poverty mirror the findings of the University of Michigan's Panel Study of Income Dynamics, which has followed 18,000 individuals since 1968. It shows how fluid the income distribution really is. Data from this study show that within a 10-year period, over half of individuals in the poorest income quintile moved up the income distribution ladder. Surprisingly, the same pattern of mobility appears in the richest quintile: Roughly half were replaced by households from other quintiles. Overall, only one-third to one-half of all households remained in the original quintile after a decade.

Chris Tilly, director of UCLA's Institute for Research on Labor and Employment, states that "poverty is dynamic; not everybody stays in poverty long term. We've always known that people move in and out of poverty, [but] there are people who tend to get stuck."[7] Households that remain in poverty over time, although a relatively small percentage of the population, are the most worrisome. Research by Richard B. Freeman of Harvard tells us that there is a core of poor people who stay poor. This core has physical disabilities, suffers from substance abuse, or is unable to work for a host of other reasons.

These findings suggest that poverty will never be totally eradicated. They also suggest that policies to deal with core poverty should be different from policies that deal with people who start or who have fallen into poverty but are highly likely to escape.

---

[6] U.S. Census Bureau, *Current Population Reports*, P70-137, *Dynamics of Economic Well-Being: Poverty, 2009–2011* (Washington, D.C.: U.S. Government Printing Office), 2014.

[7] Ari Bloomekatz, "Poverty Often a Temporary State, U.S. Census Study Finds," *The Los Angeles Times*, March 28, 2011.

✅ CHECKPOINT

POVERTY

- Poverty thresholds were developed in the 1960s based on a food budget, adjusted for family size, then multiplied by 3.
- Economic growth has been a major force in reducing poverty in the United States.
- The income deficit measures how far below the poverty threshold a family's income lies.
- The other depth of poverty measure is the ratio of income to poverty. If the ratio is below 0.5, the family is considered "severely or desperately poor." A ratio greater than 1.0 but less than 1.25 indicates the family is "near poor."
- The Census Bureau has introduced new measures of poverty that consider health care costs, transportation needs, and child care costs.
- The controversy surrounding reducing poverty focuses on whether reducing income inequality or increasing economic growth is the best approach.
- Philosopher John Rawls proposed a "maximin principle" that suggests society should maximize the welfare of the least well-off individual.
- Robert Nozick argued that the state should not use its coercive power to make some people better off at the expense of others.
- Income mobility is quite robust in the United States, with more than half of all families moving up and down the income distribution ladder in any decade.

QUESTION: Suppose that the United States adopts a relative measure of poverty based on a threshold determined by 60% of the median household income. If the median household income for a family of four is $55,000, how would this new measure affect the poverty rate using the existing absolute thresholds?

Answers to the Checkpoint questions can be found at the end of this chapter.

chapter summary

Section 1 The Distribution of Income and Wealth

15.1 **Income:** A flow of funds by individuals or households over time

Wealth: A stock of assets less liabilities at a given point in time

A household can have considerable wealth without much income, such as this retired couple who saved over their working years.

Spotmatik/Dreamstime.com

15.2 Types of Income Distribution

Functional distribution of income: The distribution of income according to inputs (factors) of production. Wages constitute nearly 70% of income using this approach.

Personal or family distribution of income: The percentage of income flowing to specific segments of the population. Quintiles (20% of the population) are used by the U.S. Census Bureau to measure income distribution.

Income inequality is measured either by constructing a Lorenz curve or by calculating a Gini coefficient for a specific population.

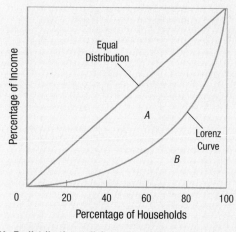

15.3 A **Lorenz curve** shows the cumulative income earned by each segment of the population. The farther the curve is from the 45 degree line, the more unequal the distribution of income.

A **Gini coefficient** is calculated as the ratio between A (area of income inequity) and $A + B$ (total area below equal distribution line). The larger the Gini coefficient, the more unequal the distribution of income.

15.4 **Redistribution policies** are designed to reduce income inequality. Three common policies are:

1. **Progressive taxation:** Higher tax rates as income increases
2. **In-kind transfers:** Unemployment benefits, welfare, Pell Grants (for college)
3. **Noncash benefits:** Subsidized or public housing, Medicaid, food stamps

Stephen Finn/Alamy

15.5 Since the 1970s, income distribution in the United States has become more unequal. Causes include:

- Differences in education (human capital)
- Economic discrimination
- Increase in the number of two-earner households

Section 2 Poverty

15.6 **Poverty** is defined differently by each country and by various international organizations.

The **poverty rate** according to the U.S. Census Bureau is the percentage of the population with income below the poverty threshold. The poverty threshold includes all money income (before taxes are deducted) and cash benefits but excludes capital gains and noncash benefits.

The poverty rate in the United States dropped in the 1960s and 1970s, and has stabilized since, with minor drops during economic expansions and minor rises during recessions (shaded vertical bars).

15.8 Alternative Methods of Measuring Poverty

- Includes after-tax money income
- Includes noncash benefits (such as food stamps and housing subsidies)
- Deducts work-related expenditures (such as transportation and child care) and out-of-pocket medical expenditures

Hongqi Zhang (aka Michael Zhang)/Dreamstime.com

15.7 **The depth (or severity) of poverty** can be measured in two ways:

Income deficit: The dollar difference between the poverty threshold and a family's income.

Ratio of income to poverty: The ratio of family income to the poverty threshold.

0.00–0.50: severely poor

0.51–1.00: poor

1.01–1.25: near poor

15.9 Two Solutions to Reduce Poverty

1. Reduce income inequality by expanding welfare and redistribution programs and making taxes more progressive.

2. Increase incentives to promote economic growth, which benefits all people, including the poor.

Stuart Key/Dreamstime.com

Joel Stettenheim/Corbis

Considerable movement occurs between income groups (quintiles). About half of all households in a quintile move to a different quintile each decade.

Rawls: Rawlsian theory states that a society's well-being is only as good as its least fortunate citizen. Therefore, to reduce poverty, it advocates for the least amount of income inequality.

versus

Nozick: This theory is based on the argument that property rights (including income) must be protected to provide incentives for growth, which will reduce poverty.

KEY CONCEPTS

income, p. 398
wealth, p. 398
functional distribution of income,
    p. 398

personal or family distribution of
    income, p. 399
Lorenz curve, p. 400
Gini coefficient, p. 402

poverty thresholds, p. 408
poverty rate, p. 409
income deficit, p. 411
ratio of income to poverty, p. 411

QUESTIONS AND PROBLEMS

Check Your Understanding

1. If you look at income distribution over the life cycle of a family, would it be more equally distributed than for one specific year?

2. List some of the reasons why household incomes differ.

3. How does the Gini coefficient differ from the Lorenz curve?

4. Currently, the poverty threshold for a family of four is just over $24,000 a year. What does this amount take into account and not take into account?

5. Are the poor in year 2017 just as poor as the poor in 1957? What has changed in 60 years to make poverty different today?

6. What are the primary factors that lead to poverty?

Apply the Concepts

7. Is there an efficiency–equity tradeoff when income is redistributed from the rich to the poor? Explain.

8. What do you think has been the impact on the distribution of income in the United States from the combined impact of the large number of unskilled illegal immigrants and the growing number of dual-earner households?

9. It is probably fair to say that when we classify people as rich or poor at any given moment in time, we are simply describing similar people at different stages in life. Does this life cycle of income and wealth make the income distribution concerns a little less relevant? Why or why not?

10. What would be the change in the distribution of income (Gini coefficient) if the United States decided to permit 10 million new immigrants into the United States who were highly skilled doctors, engineers, executives of large foreign firms, and wealthy foreigners who just want to migrate to the United States? How would the Gini coefficient change if, instead, the United States decided to permit 10 million unskilled foreign workers to enter?

11. Roughly half of all marriages in the United States end in divorce. What is the impact of this divorce rate on the distribution of income and poverty?

12. Poverty rates have declined for blacks and have been relatively stable for everyone else over the last 40 years. But the poverty rate still hovers near 15%. What makes it so difficult to reduce poverty below 10% to 15% of the population?

In the News

13. In 2014, the Nobel Peace Prize went to Malala Yousafzai for her courage and action to expand educational opportunities for girls who were barred from going to school in their countries. She faced grave dangers in her activist role, including nearly being killed by the Taliban in her own nation of Pakistan. Her efforts led to countless children enjoying the freedom to go to school. Explain how her efforts to increase the number of young girls attending school will reduce poverty and result in a more peaceful planet.

14. According to the U.S. Department of the Treasury, people in the top income quintile (20%) pay roughly 70% of all federal income taxes, with the remaining 80% paying less than 30%. Further, the bottom half of the population pays less than 10% of all taxes. Many politicians often assert that they want to bring tax relief (presumably with the idea of redistributing income) to "middle- and lower-income" families. Given this distribution of income tax payments, what would middle- and lower-income tax relief look like?

Solving Problems

WORK IT OUT   ⚏ **LaunchPad** | interactive activity

15. Use the two different distributions of income in the table below to answer the questions that follow.

Quintile	A	B
Poorest	10.5	2.5
Second	13.2	6.8
Middle	21.6	13.9
Fourth	26.4	24.2
Richest	28.3	52.6

a. Use the grid below and graph the two Lorenz curves.

b. Which curve has a more equal distribution?

c. Are these distributions more or less equal than that for the United States today?

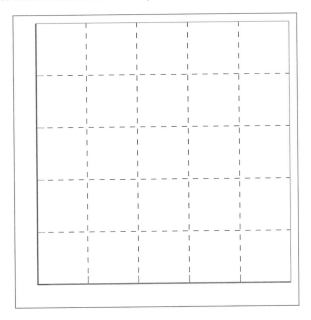

16. The following households each have four persons. Their annual incomes are as follows:

The Adams:	$22,100
The Bensons:	$27,600
The Camachos:	$30,800
The Davidsons:	$11,800

Assume that the poverty threshold for a household of four is $24,000. Calculate the income deficit, if any, and the income-to-poverty ratio for each family. Classify each family as either not poor, near poor, poor, or severely poor.

#️⃣ USING THE NUMBERS

17. According to By the Numbers, over what period of time did the gap between the full-time minimum wage earnings and the poverty threshold expand the most?

18. According to By the Numbers, about how many Americans used food stamps (now known as SNAP benefits) in the year 2000? How about in the year 2014? (*Hint:* Use the approximate U.S. population of 280 million in the year 2000 and 320 million in the year 2014.)

ANSWERS TO QUESTIONS IN CHECKPOINTS

Checkpoint: The Distribution of Income and Wealth 407

Because $10,000 a year per person represents a substantial amount of money to those in the lowest income brackets, it would clearly improve (make more equal) the before-tax and benefits distribution of income. However, many social income programs benefit those with low incomes; for example, those who depend on Social Security and Medicare may be worse off under the proposal, which could make the after-tax and benefits distribution of income worse.

Checkpoint: Poverty 417

If a relative measure is used to measure poverty, those earning less than 60% of the median household income of $55,000, or $0.60 \times \$55,000 = \$33,000$, would be considered living in poverty. This amount is higher than the current absolute threshold of about $24,000, which means the poverty rate would rise under this new measure.

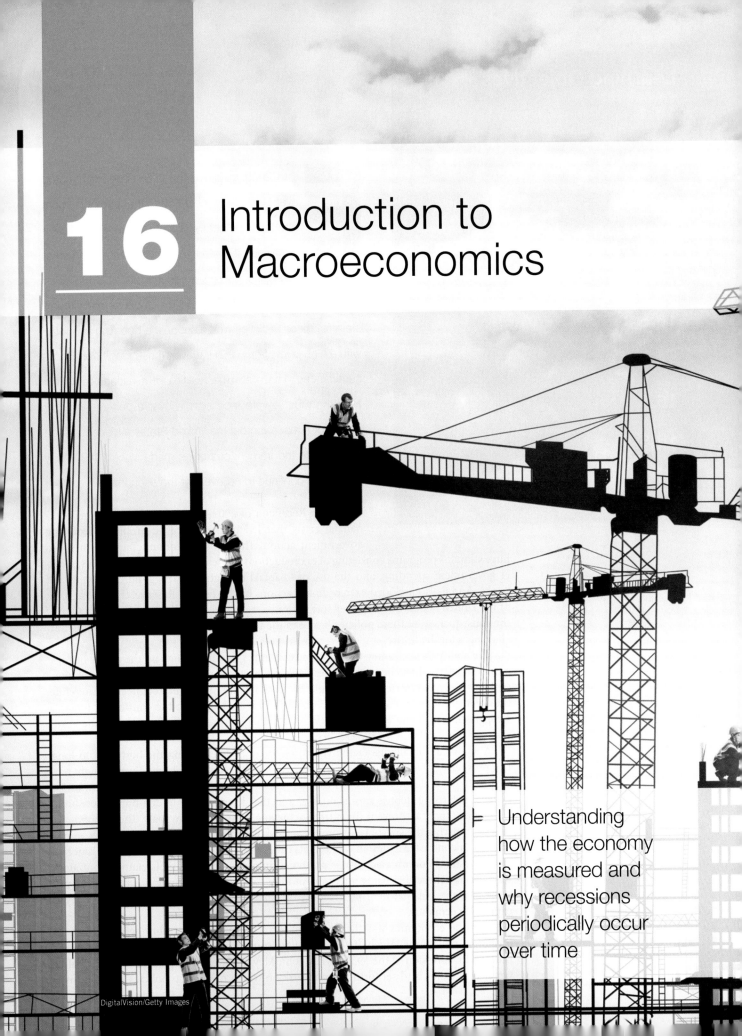

16 Introduction to Macroeconomics

Understanding how the economy is measured and why recessions periodically occur over time

Learning Objectives

16.1 Describe the four phases of the business cycle and how they are dated by the NBER.

16.2 Describe other methods used to measure the business cycle.

16.3 Describe the national income and product accounts (NIPA).

16.4 Describe the circular flow of income and discuss why GDP can be computed using either income or expenditure data.

16.5 List the four major expenditure components of GDP.

16.6 List the major income components of GDP.

16.7 Describe the shortcomings of GDP as a measure of our standard of living.

16.8 Describe how nonmarket activities and the informal economy create both positive and negative effects on society.

From 2009 to 2016, the U.S. economy created over 10 million new jobs, the unemployment rate fell from nearly 10% to below 5%, inflation remained at historic lows, the housing market soared in many cities, and cheap energy prices led to lower costs of transportation and production. Under normal circumstances, these statistics would suggest a booming economy with a high level of growth. However, these aren't normal circumstances. These are the realities of a nation recovering from the most severe recession in over a generation. How severe of a recession did the United States experience such that despite the tremendous gains made since 2009, many Americans continue to believe that the economy is weak?

The Great Recession of 2007–2009 resulted from a major financial crisis that led to many drastic problems requiring government action. These macroeconomic actions included huge stimulus programs consisting of tax reductions, increased government benefits, greater government spending, and the use of financial bailouts for struggling companies and banks. And it also included extraordinary actions by the Federal Reserve, the central bank of the United States, that kept key interest rates at or near 0% for nearly a decade. One of the consequences of these policies has been the buildup of the national debt, creating new challenges for the future.

The ability for a country to maintain economic growth depends on the ability of companies to sell products not only domestically but also to foreign consumers as part of international trade. Countries in today's global economy are highly interconnected. Therefore, the recent economic slowdown in China and Brazil, along with the continuing financial struggles facing many European nations in managing their unified currency (the euro), makes it more difficult for the U.S. economy to expand.

A significant challenge facing countries today is determining the best path to long-run prosperity. Over the course of the past century, two dominant schools of thought have frequently been debated: the classical view and the Keynesian view. Classical economists believe that rising debt is unsustainable, and that it creates an undue burden on future generations that can prevent them from achieving their economic goals. These economists believe in paring the size of government and relying more on markets to dictate economic actions. In contrast, Keynesian economists believe that an active government role is needed to ensure that economic activity is promoted in areas where markets cannot do it alone. Keynesians believe that using government tools to manage economic downturns will promote growth, and that debt incurred in the short run will eventually be reduced by an expanding economy.

Classical economics was the dominant form of thinking a century ago when macroeconomic policy was largely based on microeconomic analysis. That all changed during the Great Depression of the 1930s, when John Maynard Keynes explained the causes of the Great Depression and set forth a framework on which to develop policies to avoid future

A Slow and Steady Macroeconomic Recovery

The 2007–2009 recession was the most severe economic downturn to face the United States in over 70 years. Although this recession officially lasted only 18 months, it took about 60 months of recovery before the economy returned to the level of employment and growth seen prior to the recession.

Go to **LaunchPad** *to use the latest data to recreate this graph.*

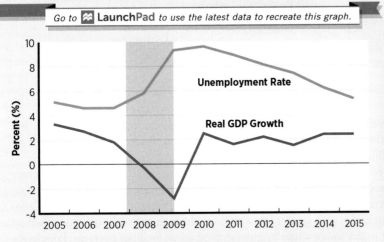

Unemployment Rate

Real GDP Growth

Savings rates have steadily fallen over the last three decades. However, high unemployment and income anxiety, especially during economic downturns, led consumers to tighten their belts and increase savings.

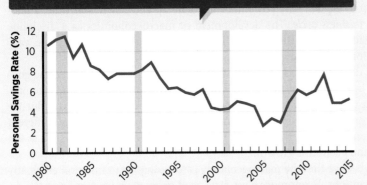

$18,128,200,000,000

United States gross domestic product (GDP) in 2016

$76,321,320,000,000

Gross world product (sum of GDP from every country in the world) in 2016

Regional Impact is Uneven: States with the highest and lowest unemployment in December, 2015

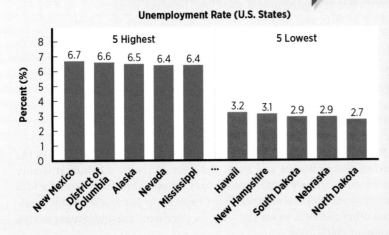

Unemployment Rate (U.S. States)

5 Highest — New Mexico 6.7, District of Columbia 6.6, Alaska 6.5, Nevada 6.4, Mississippi 6.4

5 Lowest — Hawaii 3.2, New Hampshire 3.1, South Dakota 2.9, Nebraska 2.9, North Dakota 2.7

Jobs
Employment Opportunities

Artem Vorobiev/Getty Images

Pixsooz/Getty Images

| FIGURE 1 | MARKETS AND INSTITUTIONS IN THE MACROECONOMY |

Labor, capital, and product markets, along with financial and government institutions, come together to influence macroeconomic outcomes such as the unemployment rate.

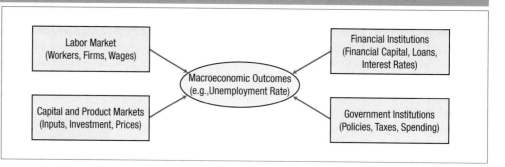

severe macroeconomic downturns. This led to the development of macroeconomics as a discipline. Today, the use of Keynesian policy is common, as evidenced by government actions taken to minimize the effects of past recessions.

Managing the economy is not an easy task. Changes in the macroeconomy occur every day, and many changes are beyond the control of government. Because the world has become more connected, recessions in one country have an effect on other countries. Competition for jobs intensifies with greater labor mobility through immigration and with more companies seeking to pay lower wages by moving production facilities overseas. Population growth means more jobs are needed for a country just to remain at its same employment level. And pressures to earn profits in a competitive global economy force businesses to find more efficient means of production, including the use of automation, leading to some job loss as workers are replaced by machines.

These factors help to explain why economies fluctuate up and down over time, a phenomenon called the *business cycle*. The development of macroeconomics as a discipline came after the realization that business cycles occurred and the fact that they can vary significantly in duration and severity.

Macroeconomics describes how individuals, businesses, financial institutions, and government institutions interact to achieve the goals of job growth, low inflation, and economic growth. It is not just the conditions of one industry or group of workers that influence macroeconomic outcomes, but rather the conditions of all. Figure 1 illustrates how different markets and institutions come together to influence macroeconomic outcomes such as the unemployment rate and economic growth.

Most economists believe that the macroeconomy is too complex to function efficiently without policy interventions. Economists have developed many tools for managing the severity of business cycles. This chapter deals with how the macroeconomy is analyzed and measured. The first section considers how business cycles are defined. The second section looks at the system of national income accounts. These accounts give us our primary measures of income, consumer and government spending, business investment, and foreign transactions including exports and imports. The last section raises the question of how well the national income accounts measure our standard of living. We look at alternative measures of standard of living, nonmarket transactions, and the effect of environmental degradation and conservation. The foundation established in this chapter will apply to topics covered throughout the course.

BUSINESS CYCLES

business cycles Alternating increases and decreases in economic activity that are typically punctuated by periods of recession and recovery.

Macroeconomics is concerned with **business cycles,** those short-run fluctuations in the macroeconomy known also as booms and busts. Business cycles are a common feature of industrialized economies, and are important to study because they emphasize the idea that markets are intertwined with one another. What happens in one market is not usually independent from other markets, as we saw with the persistent unemployment during and after the recession of 2007–2009.

Defining Business Cycles

Business cycles are defined as alternating increases and decreases in economic activity. As economists Arthur Burns and Wesley Mitchell wrote,

> *Business cycles are a type of fluctuation found in the aggregate economic activity of nations that organize their work mainly in business enterprises: a cycle consists of expansions occurring at about the same time in many economic activities, followed by similarly general recession, contractions and revivals which merge into the expansion phase of the next cycle.*[1]

Figure 2 shows the four phases of the business cycle. These phases, around an upward trend, include the peak (sometimes called a boom), followed by a recession (often referred to as a downturn or contraction), leading to the trough or bottom of the cycle, finally followed by a recovery or an expansion to another peak.

A peak in the business cycle usually means that the economy is operating at its capacity. Peaks are followed by downturns or recessions. This change can happen simply because the boom runs out of steam and business investment begins to decline, causing economic growth to slow or turn negative.

Once a recession is under way, businesses react by curtailing hiring and perhaps even laying off workers, thus adding to the recession's depth. Eventually, however, a trough is reached, and economic activity begins to pick up as businesses and consumers become more optimistic about the economy. Often, the federal government or the Federal Reserve Bank institutes fiscal or monetary policies to help reverse the recession. We will look at government actions in future chapters.

Figure 2 suggests that business cycles are fairly regular, but in fact the various phases of the cycle can vary dramatically in duration and intensity. As Table 1 shows, the recessions of the last 65 years have lasted anywhere from 6 months to 18 months. Expansions or recoveries have varied even more, lasting from 1 year to as many as 10 years. Some recessions, moreover, have been truly intense, bringing about major declines in income, while others have been little more than potholes in the road, causing no declines in real income.

A good metaphor for the wide variation in business cycles is a roller coaster. Some roller coasters rise higher than others, fall faster than others, or climb slower than others.

FIGURE 2	TYPICAL BUSINESS CYCLE

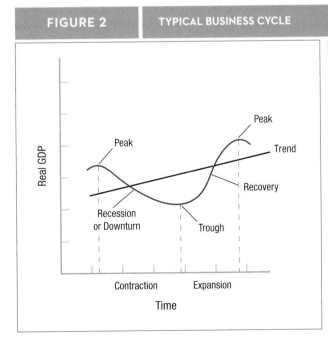

The four phases of the business cycle are the peak or boom, followed by a recession (often called a downturn or contraction), leading to the trough or bottom of the cycle, followed by a recovery or an expansion leading to another peak. Note that although this diagram suggests business cycles have regular movements, in reality the various phases of the cycle vary widely in duration and intensity.

[1] Arthur Burns and Wesley Mitchell, *Measuring Business Cycles* (New York: National Bureau of Economic Research), 1946, p. 3.

TABLE 1	SELECTED DATA FOR U.S. BUSINESS CYCLES SINCE 1950					
Years	Peak	Trough	Recession Length (months)	Expansion Length (months)	Percentage Change in Real GDP	Maximum Unemployment Rate (%)
1953–1954	July 1953	May 1954	10	39	−2.2	5.9
1957–1958	Aug. 1957	April 1958	8	24	−3.6	7.4
1960–1961	April 1960	Feb. 1961	10	106	−0.6	7.1
1969–1970	Dec. 1969	Nov. 1970	11	36	+0.2	6.1
1973–1975	Nov. 1973	March 1975	16	58	−1.8	9.0
1980	Jan. 1980	July 1980	6	12	−2.3	7.8
1981–1982	July 1981	Nov. 1982	16	92	−2.2	10.8
1990–1991	July 1990	March 1991	8	120	−1.0	6.9
2001	March 2001	Nov. 2001	8	73	+0.5	5.8
2007–2009	Dec. 2007	June 2009	18	—	−4.1	10.0

Eric Chiang

Business cycles resemble roller coasters—some are higher, faster, or longer than others, but all are similar in terms of the up-and-down nature of the ride.

double-dip recession A recession that begins after only a short period of economic recovery from the previous recession.

Some roller coasters have one large dip followed by a series of smaller ups and downs, while others may have a large dip followed by another large dip. This is true with business cycles—some business cycles are higher, faster, or longer than others, but all have the same four phases described earlier. An important difference between a business cycle and a roller coaster, however, is that a roller coaster typically ends at the same level as it starts, while business cycles tend to have an upward long-run trend in most countries, indicating a growing economy over time.

Unemployment has shown a similar variability: The more severe the recession, the higher the unemployment rate goes. In the recessions of 1990–1991 and 2001, the economy as a whole showed remarkable resiliency, but the recoveries were termed *jobless recoveries* because the economic growth following the recessions did not coincide with strong levels of job growth. In fact, sometimes an economy's recovery falls short and enters another recession before it fully recovers; this is referred to as a **double-dip recession.** The last double-dip recession occurred in the early 1980s. However, the slow recovery following the 2007–2009 recession caused many economists to worry that another double-dip recession would occur. Fortunately, it did not.

Dating Business Cycles

Business cycles are officially dated by the National Bureau of Economic Research (NBER), a nonprofit research organization founded in 1920. The NBER assigns a committee of economists the task of dating "turning points"—times at which the economy switches from peak to downturn or from trough to recovery. The committee looks for clusters of aggregate data pointing either up or down. Committee members date turning points when they reach a consensus that the economy has switched directions.

The committee's work has met with some criticism because the decisions rest on the consensus of six eminent economists, who often bring different methodologies to the table. The committee's deliberations, moreover, are not public; the committee announces only its final decision. Finally, the NBER dates peaks and troughs only after the fact: Their decisions appear several months after the turning points have been reached.[2] By waiting, the panel

---

[2] Marcelle Chauvet and Jeremy Piger, "Identifying Business Cycle Turning Points in Real Time," *Review* (St. Louis: The Federal Reserve Bank of St. Louis), March/April 2003, pp. 47–61.

can use updated or revised data to avoid premature judgments. But some argue that the long lag renders the NBER's decisions less useful to policymakers.

Nonetheless, the work of the NBER in dating the turning points is important for investors and businesses alike, as they help form expectations of how the economy might perform based on the phase of the business cycle it has reached. Businesses are more likely to invest during a time of expansion, and they don't want to be investing in greater production capacity at a time of recession when sales might fall.

Alternative Measures of the Business Cycle

Because the NBER focuses on historical data to date phases of the business cycle *after* they occur, economists have developed tools to analyze trends in an effort to predict phases of the business cycle *before* they occur. The following are three examples of methods used to predict business cycle movements.

National Activity Index The National Activity Index, developed by the Federal Reserve Bank of Chicago, is a weighted average of 85 indicators of national economic activity. These indicators are drawn from a huge swath of economic activity including production, income, employment, unemployment, hours worked, personal consumption, housing, sales, orders, and inventories.

Figure 3 shows the index since 1985. When the index has a zero value, the economy is growing at its historical trend rate of growth. Negative values mean that the economy is growing slower and positive rates imply it's growing faster than its long-term trend. When the index moves below −0.70 following a period of expansion, this suggests a high likelihood that the economy has moved into a recession. The index has done a remarkable job in pinpointing the signs of recessions in a reasonably current time frame.

Leading Economic Index The Leading Economic Index (or LEI) established by The Conference Board, an independent business and research association, is another index that economists look to when predicting movements in the business cycle. The LEI uses ten important leading indicators to produce a weighted index. Because each indicator is

| FIGURE 3 | THE FEDERAL RESERVE BANK OF CHICAGO'S NATIONAL ACTIVITY INDEX |

The National Activity Index is a weighted average of 85 indicators of economic activity in the economy. When the index moves below −0.70 (dashed line), the economy is probably moving into a recession. This index appears to track the official NBER peak turning points.

a predictor of how the economy should perform in the near future, any change in the LEI today is supposed to reflect how the economy will change tomorrow.

Indicators in the LEI

Average weekly hours, manufacturing
Average weekly initial claims for unemployment insurance
Manufacturers' new orders, consumer goods and materials
Index of supplier deliveries—vendor performance
Manufacturers' new orders, nondefense capital goods
Building permits, new private housing units
Stock prices, 500 common stocks
Money supply, M2
Interest rate spread, ten-year Treasury bonds less federal funds
Index of consumer expectations

The LEI predicts a recession whenever the index falls for three months in a row (compared to the same month the previous year). In fact, it has successfully predicted the last seven recessions since 1969, although critics point to the fact that it has also provided some false warnings of recessions (a funny adage shared among economists is that forecasters have predicted ten of the last seven recessions).

Yield Curve Perhaps the simplest, and surprisingly accurate, predictor of changes in the business cycle is the yield curve. A **yield curve** shows the interest rates for bonds (shown on the vertical axis) with different maturity rates (shown on the horizontal axis). For example, it would show the difference in interest rates between a three-month Treasury bill and a thirty-year Treasury bond (a "bill" is a type of bond with a maturity of less than one year).

One approach economists have used to predict recessions, shown in Figure 4, is to take the interest rate of a long-term ten-year bond and subtract the interest rate on a short-term three-month bill. Whenever this value turns negative (in other words, interest rates on short-term bills exceed those on long-term bonds), a recession is likely to occur. Why? When investors believe an economic slowdown may occur, they buy long-term bonds to lock in interest rates, pushing interest rates on long-term bonds lower. This has been true for seven of the last eight recessions. However, some economists remain skeptical, pointing to several false warnings that the yield curve has given which did not result in actual recessions.

yield curve Shows the relationship between the interest rate earned on a bond (measured on the vertical axis) and the length of time until the bond's maturity date (shown on the horizontal axis).

| **FIGURE 4** | **TREASURY SPREAD** |

The 10-year bond rate minus 3-month bill rate (monthly average). Shaded bars indicate recessions. In all but one recession since 1960, the difference in rates turned negative prior to the recession.

Data from New York Federal Reserve: https://www.newyorkfed.org/medialibrary/media/research/capital_markets/Prob_Rec.pdf.

ISSUE

The End of the Recession . . . It Does Not Feel Like It

According to the National Bureau of Economic Research, the last U.S. recession officially ended in June 2009. But ask most people (besides economists) at the time or even a year later whether they thought the recession was over and you would have likely been laughed at. Indeed, in June 2009, the economy was not in good shape: The unemployment rate was 9.5%, GDP was over 4% below its peak, and the stock market was nearly 40% below its high two years prior. Why would such dismal economic conditions signal the end of the recession?

Part of the explanation is how economists date the business cycle. The NBER looks at "turning points" when the economy goes from a peak to a downturn or from a trough to a recovery. A recession officially ends when the economy is at the trough, which occurs when the economy is at its worst (or near worst) condition. In fact, the NBER generally waits until evidence of two quarters of GDP growth is found before declaring the recession over. Therefore, some recovery may already have occurred when a recession ends.

Looking at the lives of everyday people, the beginning of a recovery is sometimes a more difficult time to live through than the recession itself. This brings about the other part of the explanation—how economists define each phase of the business cycle. A recession describes a decrease in the growth of the economy from its peak, while a recovery describes an increase in the growth of the economy from its trough. Therefore, although a recession may have officially begun, life is still good (for the time being), and people subsequently believe that the economy is still strong. Contrast this with the start of a recovery, in which life is dismal (for the time being) and people subsequently believe the economy is still in recession. The following tables provide a comparison.

To many people, life at the start of a recession was much better than life at the start of the recovery. In fact, the 2007–2009 recession had such a slow recovery period that even after two years from the official end of the recession, the unemployment rate stood at 9.1%, much higher than the 6.2% unemployment rate during the middle of the re-

For some communities, the recession did not seem to have ended in 2009.

cession in 2008. It would take another four years (in 2015) until the unemployment rate returned to 5%.

In sum, how economists date recessions and recoveries is based largely on the turning points of the business cycle, which may not always reflect what everyday people experience.

Start of Recession (December 2007)	Start of Recovery (June 2009)
Unemployment Rate = 5.0%	Unemployment Rate = 9.5%
GDP (2005 dollars) = $13.4 trillion	GDP (2005 dollars) = $12.8 trillion
Stock Market (Dow) = 13,500	Stock Market (Dow) = 8,800

Middle of Recession (September 2008)	Two Years of Recovery (June 2011)
Unemployment Rate = 6.2%	Unemployment Rate = 9.1%
GDP (2005 dollars) = $13.2 trillion	GDP (2005 dollars) = $13.4 trillion
Stock Market (Dow) = 11,200	Stock Market (Dow) = 12,000

Each of the three indices is one of many methods economists use to predict the movements of the business cycle. Although a perfect predictor of booms and busts is not possible, many people follow these indices because of the importance of the business cycle in the macroeconomy.

The duration and intensity of business cycles are measured using data collected by the Bureau of Economic Analysis and U.S. Department of Labor. These data for aggregate income and output come from the national income and product accounts. We turn in a moment to see how these data are collected and analyzed and consider how well they measure our standard of living. Keep in mind that these data are the key ingredients economists use to determine the state of the macroeconomy.

CHECKPOINT

BUSINESS CYCLES

- Business cycles are alternating increases and decreases in economic activity.
- The four phases of the business cycle include the peak, recession (or contraction), trough, and recovery (or expansion).
- Business cycles vary in intensity, duration, and speed.
- Business cycles are dated by the National Bureau of Economic Research (NBER). Business cycles are usually dated some time after the trough and peak have been reached.
- Economists have developed different methods to predict movements in the business cycle, including the use of the National Activity Index, the Leading Economic Index, and the yield curve.

QUESTION: Do you think that the business cycle has a bigger impact on automobile and capital goods manufacturers or on grocery stores?

Answers to the Checkpoint questions can be found at the end of this chapter.

NATIONAL INCOME ACCOUNTING

The national income and product accounts (NIPA) let economists judge our nation's economic performance, compare U.S. income and output to that of other nations, and track the economy's condition over the course of the business cycle. Many economists would say that these accounts represent one of the greatest inventions of the 20th century.[3]

Before World War I, estimating the output of various sectors of the economy—and to some extent the output of the economy as a whole—was a task left to individual scholars. Government agencies tried to measure various sorts of economic activity, but little came of these efforts. When the Great Depression struck, the lack of reliable economic data made it difficult for the administration and Congress to design timely and appropriate policy responses. Much of the information that was available at the time was anecdotal: newspaper reports of plant shutdowns, stories of home and farm foreclosures, and observations of the rapid meltdown of the stock market.

In 1933 Congress directed the Department of Commerce (DOC) to develop estimates of "total national income for the United States for each of the calendar years 1929, 1930, and 1931, including estimates of the portions of national income originating from [different sectors] and estimates of the distribution of the national income in the form of wages, rents, royalties, dividends, profits and other types of payments." This directive was the beginning of the NIPA.

In 1934 a small group of economists working under the leadership of Simon Kuznets and in collaboration with the NBER produced a report for the Senate. The report defined many standard economic aggregates still in use today, including gross national product, gross domestic product, consumer spending, and investment spending. Kuznets was later awarded a Nobel Prize for his lifetime of work in this area.

Work continued on the NIPA through World War II, and by 1947 the basic components of the present day income and product accounts were in place. Over the years, the DOC has modified, improved, and updated the data it collects. These data are released on a quarterly basis, with preliminary data being put out in the middle of the month following a given quarter. By the end of a given quarter, the DOC will have collected about two-thirds of the survey data it needs, allowing it to estimate the remaining data to generate preliminary figures.

---

[3] William Nordhaus and Edward Kokkelenberg (eds.), *Nature's Numbers: Expanding the National Economic Accounts to Include the Environment* (Washington, D.C. National Academy Press), 1999, p. 12.

The Core of the NIPA

The major components of the NIPA can be found in either of two ways: by adding up the income in the economy or by adding up spending. A simple circular flow diagram of the economy shows why either approach can be used to determine the level of economic activity.

The Circular Flow Diagram Figure 5 is a simple **circular flow diagram** that shows how businesses and households interact through the product and resource markets.

Let us first follow the arrows that point in a clockwise direction. Begin at the bottom of the diagram with households. Households supply labor (and other inputs or factors of production) to the resource market; that is, they become employees of businesses. Businesses use this labor (and other inputs) to produce goods and services that are supplied to the product markets. Such products in the end find their way back into households through consumer purchases. The arrows pointing clockwise show the flow of real items: hours worked, goods and services produced and purchased.

The arrows pointing counterclockwise, in contrast, represent flows of money. Businesses pay for inputs (factors) of production: land, labor, capital, and entrepreneurship. Factors are paid rents, wages, interest, and profits. These payments become income for the economy's households, which use these funds to purchase goods and services in the product market. This spending for goods and services becomes sales revenues for the business sector.

Spending and Income: Looking at GDP in Two Ways The circular flow diagram illustrates why economic aggregates in our economy can be determined in either of two ways. The spending in the economy accrues on the right side of the diagram. In this simple diagram, all spending is assumed to be consumer spending for goods and services.

SIMON KUZNETS (1901–1985)

NOBEL PRIZE

Simon Kuznets was awarded the Nobel Prize in 1971 for devising systematic approaches to the compilation and analysis of national economic data. Kuznets is credited with developing gross national product as a measurement of economic output.

Kuznets developed methods for calculating the size and changes in national income known as the national income and product accounts (NIPA). Caring little for abstract models, he sought to define concepts that could be observed empirically and measured statistically. Thanks to Kuznets, economists have had a large amount of data with which to test their economic theories.

circular flow diagram Illustrates how households and firms interact through product and resource markets and shows that economic aggregates can be determined by examining either spending flows or income flows to households.

| FIGURE 5 | A SIMPLE CIRCULAR FLOW DIAGRAM |

This circular flow diagram illustrates why the economic aggregates in our economy can be determined in either of two ways. Spending flows through the right side of the diagram, while the left side of the diagram shows incomes flowing to households. Note that one person's spending is another person's income.

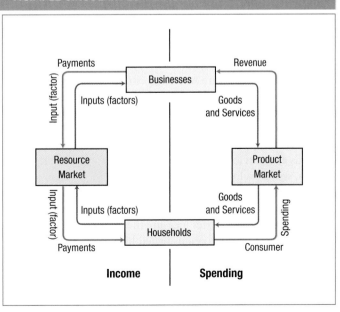

We know, however, that businesses spend money on investment goods such as equipment, plants, factories, and specialized vehicles to increase their productivity. Also, government buys goods and services, as do foreigners. This spending shows up in the NIPA, although it is not included in our simple circular flow diagram.

Second, similar income is generated equal to the spending in the product market. This is shown on the left side of the diagram. Wages and salaries constitute the bulk of income in our economy (roughly two-thirds of it), with rents, interest, and profits comprising the rest. Everything that is spent on the right side represents income on the left side; all spending must equal input (factor) incomes.

The main idea of a circular flow diagram is that every dollar spent in an economy becomes a dollar of income to someone else. For example, suppose you spend $5 on a smoothie, and suppose this $5 goes to the following:

$1 to rent and equipment = income to landlord and equipment makers
$1 to fruits and juices = income to farmers
$1 to wages for store workers and managers = income to labor
$1 to taxes = income to government
$1 to profit = income to investors

Therefore, regardless of whether economic activity is measured by the $5 in spending by the consumer or the $5 in income generated to various parties, the resulting measurement is the same.

Gross Domestic Product

Eric Chiang

gross domestic product (GDP) A measure of the economy's total output; it is the most widely reported value in the national income and product accounts (NIPA) and is equal to the total market value of all final goods and services produced by resources in a given year.

Gross domestic product (GDP) is a measure of the economy's total output; it is the most widely reported value in the NIPA. Technically, the nation's *GDP is equal to the total market value of all final goods and services produced by resources in the United States in a given year.* A few points about this definition need to be noted.

First, GDP reflects the *final* value of goods and services produced. Therefore, measurements of GDP do not include the value of intermediate goods used to produce other products. This distinction helps prevent what economists call "double counting," because a good's final value includes the intermediate values going into its production.

To illustrate, consider a box of toothpicks. The firm producing these toothpicks must first purchase a supply of cottonwood, let's say for $0.22 a box. The firm then mills this wood into toothpicks, which it puts into a small box purchased from another company at $0.08 apiece. The completed box is sold to a grocery store wholesale for $0.65. After a markup, the grocery store sells the box of toothpicks for $0.89. The sale raises GDP by $0.89, *not* by $1.84 (0.22 + 0.08 + 0.65 + 0.89), because the values of the cottonwood, the box, and the grocery store's services are already included in the final sales price of a box of toothpicks. Thus, by including only final prices in GDP, double counting is avoided.

A second point to note is that, as the term gross *domestic* product implies, GDP is a measure of the output produced by resources in the United States. It does not matter whether the producers are American citizens or foreign nationals as long as the production takes place within the country's borders. GDP does not include goods or services produced abroad, even if the producers are American citizens or companies.

In contrast to GDP is *gross national product* (GNP), the standard measure of output the Department of Commerce used until the early 1990s. GNP reflects the market value of all goods and services produced domestically and abroad using resources supplied by U.S. citizens, while excluding the value of goods and services produced in the United States by foreign-owned businesses. The difference between GDP and GNP is small. The main reason the DOC switched its measurements was to ensure that its data were more directly comparable to how other countries measure the size of their economic output. Also, in an increasingly globalized world, foreign-owned businesses contribute significantly to our economy in terms of jobs and domestic investment; GDP takes these contributions into account.

Third, whenever possible, the NIPA uses market values, or the prices paid for products, to compute GDP. Therefore, even if a firm must sell its product at a loss, the product's final sales price is what figures into GDP, not the firm's production cost or the original retail price.

Fourth, the NIPA accounts focus on market-produced goods and services. The major exceptions to this approach include substituting payroll costs for the value of government services and estimating (imputing) the rental value of owner-occupied housing. This focus on market values has been criticized on the grounds that child care services, for instance, when provided by a nanny, are figured into GDP, while the values for these same services when performed by parents are not.

The Expenditures (Spending) Approach to Calculating GDP

Again, GDP can be measured using either spending or income. With the expenditures approach, all spending on final goods and services is added together. The four major categories of spending are personal consumption expenditures, gross private domestic investment (GPDI), government spending, and net exports (exports minus imports).

Personal Consumption Expenditures **Personal consumption expenditures** are goods and services purchased by residents and businesses of the United States. Goods and services are divided into three main categories: durable goods, nondurable goods, and services. Durable goods are products that have an average useful life of at least three years. Automobiles, major appliances, books, and musical instruments are all examples of durable goods. Nondurable goods include all other tangible goods, such as canned soft drinks, frozen pizza, toothbrushes, and underwear (all of which should be thrown out before they are three years old). Services are commodities that cannot be stored and are consumed at the time and place of purchase, for example, legal, barber, and repair services. Table 2 gives a detailed account of U.S. personal consumption spending in 2016. Notice that personal consumption is almost 70% of GDP, by far the most important part of GDP, and services constitute the largest portion of personal consumption.

personal consumption expenditures Goods and services purchased by residents of the United States, whether individuals or businesses; they include durable goods, nondurable goods, and services.

Gross Private Domestic Investment The second major aggregate listed in Table 2 is **gross private domestic investment (GPDI),** which, at 16.7% of GDP, refers to *fixed investments,* or investments in such things as structures (residential and nonresidential), equipment, and software. It also includes changes in private inventories.

gross private domestic investment (GPDI) Investments in such things as structures (residential and nonresidential), equipment, and software, and changes in private inventories.

TABLE 2	THE EXPENDITURES APPROACH TO GDP (2016)	
Category	**Billions of $**	**% of GDP**
Personal Consumption Expenditures	**12,429.0**	**68.5**
Durable goods	1,347.6	7.4
Nondurable goods	2,663.3	14.7
Services	8,418.1	46.4
Gross Private Domestic Investment	**3,019.2**	**16.7**
Fixed nonresidential	2,311.6	12.8
Fixed residential	631.8	3.5
Change in inventories	75.8	0.4
Government Purchases of Goods and Services	**3,206.5**	**17.7**
Federal	1,235.6	6.8
State and local	1,970.9	10.9
Net Exports	**−526.5**	**−2.9**
Exports	2,214.7	12.2
Imports	2,741.2	15.1
Gross Domestic Product	**18,128.20**	**100.0**

Data from U.S. Department of Commerce, Bureau of Economic Analysis, www.bea.gov.

Residential housing represents about one-fifth of GPDI, and nonresidential structures make up most of the rest because inventory changes are small. Nonresidential structures include such diverse structures as hotels and motels, manufacturing plants, mine shafts, oil wells, and fast-food restaurants. Improvements to existing business structures and new construction are counted as fixed investments.

A "change in inventories" refers to a change in the physical volume of the inventory a private business owns, valued at the average prices over the period. If a business increases its inventories (whether intentionally or unintentionally due to weak sales volumes), this change is treated as an investment because the business is adding to the stock of products it has ready for sale. This type of investment is generally the least desirable, because excess inventory does not increase productivity and could fall in value if the goods become outdated or if the market price falls.

Private investment is a key factor driving economic growth and an important determinant of swings in the business cycle. Figure 6 tracks GPDI as a percentage of GDP since 1980. Recessions are represented by the vertical shaded columns. Notice that during each recession, GPDI turns down, and when the recession ends, GPDI turns up. Investment is, therefore, an important factor shaping the turning points of the business cycle, especially at the troughs, and an important determinant of how severe recessions will be.

Government Purchases The government component of GDP measures the impact that **government spending** has on final demand in the economy. As Figure 7 illustrates, at 17.7% of GDP, government spending is a relatively large component of GDP. It includes the wages and salaries of government employees (federal, state, and local) and the purchase of products and services from private businesses and the rest of the world. Government spending also includes the purchase of new structures and equipment.

Net Exports of Goods and Services **Net exports** of goods and services are equal to exports minus imports for the current period. Exports include all the items we sell overseas, such as agricultural products, movies, pharmaceutical drugs, and military equipment. Our imports are all those items we bring into the country, including vegetables from Mexico, clothing from India, and cars from Japan. Most years our imports exceed our exports, and therefore net exports are a negative percentage of GDP.

government spending Includes the wages and salaries of government employees (federal, state, and local); the purchase of products and services from private businesses and the rest of the world; and government purchases of new structures and equipment.

net exports Exports minus imports for the current period. Exports include all goods and services we sell abroad, while imports include all goods and services we buy from other countries.

FIGURE 6   GROSS PRIVATE DOMESTIC INVESTMENT (GPDI) AS A PERCENT OF GDP

Private investment is a key factor driving economic growth and an important determinant of swings in the business cycle. This graph tracks GPDI as a percentage of GDP since 1980.

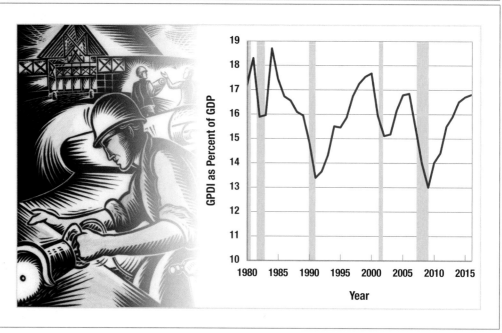

Illustration Works/Alamy

FIGURE 7	GOVERNMENT SPENDING AS A PERCENT OF GDP

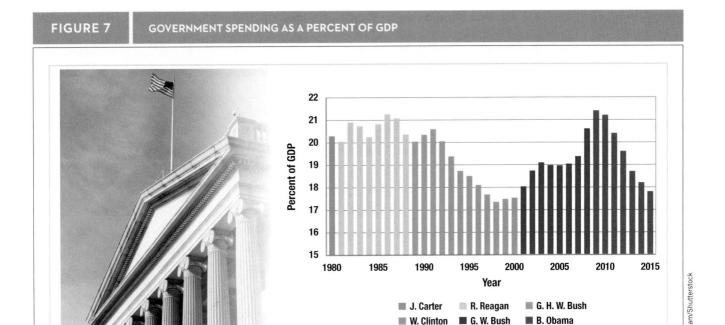

Government spending as a percent of GDP fell in the 1990s, rose in the 2000s until peaking in 2009, and has since fallen every year.

Summing Aggregate Expenditures The four categories just described are commonly abbreviated as C (consumption), I (investment), G (government spending), and $X - M$ (net exports; exports minus imports). Together, these four variables constitute GDP. We summarize this by the following equation:

$$GDP = C + I + G + (X - M)$$

Using the information from Table 2, we can calculate GDP for 2016 (in billions of dollars) as

$$18,128.2 = 12,429.0 + 3,019.2 + 3,206.5 + (-526.5)$$

The Income Approach to Calculating GDP

As we have already seen, spending that contributes to GDP provides an income for one of the economy's various inputs (factors) of production. And in theory, this is how this process works. In practice, however, the national income accounts need to be adjusted to fully account for GDP when we switch from the expenditures to the income approach. Let's work our way through the income side of the NIPA, which Table 3 summarizes.

Compensation of Employees Compensation to employees refers to payments for work done, including wages, salaries, and benefits. Benefits include the social insurance payments made by employers to various government programs, such as Social Security, Medicare, and workers' compensation and unemployment insurance. Some other benefits that count as labor income are employer-provided pensions, profit-sharing plans, group health insurance, and in-kind benefits such as day care services. Employee compensation is 54% of GDP.

TABLE 3	THE INCOME APPROACH TO GDP (2016)	
Category	Billions of $	% of GDP
Compensation of Employees	9,852.6	54.3
Wages and salaries	7,994.8	44.1
Supplements to wages and salaries	1,857.8	10.2
Proprietors' Income	1,412.8	7.8
Corporate Profits	1,667.9	9.2
Rental Income	670.6	3.7
Net Interest	676.8	3.8
Miscellaneous Adjustments	1,202.7	6.6
National Income	15,483.4	85.4
Adjustments to National Income	2,644.8	14.6
Consumption of fixed capital	2,856.7	15.8
Statistical discrepancy	−211.9	−1.2
Gross Domestic Product	18,128.2	100.0

Data from U.S. Department of Commerce, Bureau of Economic Analysis, www.bea.gov.

Proprietors' Income Proprietors' income represents the current income of all sole proprietorships, partnerships, and tax-exempt cooperatives in the country. It includes the imputed (estimated) rental income of owner-occupied farmhouses. Proprietors' income is adjusted by a capital consumption allowance to account for depreciating equipment (equipment that is used up while producing goods and services). Although there are a lot of proprietorships in the United States, their combined income is less than 8% of GDP.

Corporate Profits Corporate profits are defined as the income that flows to corporations, adjusted for inventory valuation and capital consumption allowances. Most corporations are private enterprises, although this category also includes mutual financial institutions, Federal Reserve banks, and nonprofit institutions that mainly serve businesses. Despite the huge profit figures often reported in the news media, corporate profits are less than 10% of GDP.

Rental Income Rental income, at 3.7% of GDP, is the income that flows to individuals engaged in renting real property (calculated as rent collected less depreciation, property taxes, maintenance and repairs, and mortgage interest). It does not include the income of real estate agents or brokers, but it does include the imputed rental value of homes occupied by their owners (again, less depreciation, taxes, repairs, and mortgage interest), along with royalties from patents, copyrights, and rights to natural resources.

Net Interest Net interest is the interest paid by businesses less the interest they receive, from this country and abroad, and is 3.8% of GDP. Interest expense is the payment for the use of capital. Interest income includes payments from home mortgages, home improvement loans, and home equity loans.

Miscellaneous Adjustments Both indirect business taxes (sales and excise taxes) and foreign income earned in the United States are part of GDP, but must be backed out of payments to factors of production in this country. Neither is paid to U.S. factors of production, and therefore appear in a separate category for measurement purposes.

Summing Up Income Measures To this point, we have described different measures of income including wages, salaries, and benefits; profits (for sole proprietors, partnerships, and corporations); rental income; and interest. Summing each of these measures along with the miscellaneous adjustments equals the **national income.** But be careful—national income is not the same as GDP. National income is income generated from the use of a country's resources, whether at home or abroad.

In order to complete the calculation of GDP using the income approach, two additional measures need to be included. First, an allowance for the depreciation (or consumption) of fixed capital is added. This is the amount of capital or infrastructure that a country needs to undertake in order to maintain its productivity. Second, a small statistical discrepancy is included because like all macroeconomic measurements, it is difficult to be exactly precise, especially in a country as large as the United States. Once these factors are included, GDP is the same whether it is derived from spending or income.

We have now seen how the national income and product accounts determine the major macroeconomic aggregates. But what does the NIPA tell us about the economy? When GDP rises, are we better off as a nation? Do increases in GDP correlate with a rising standard of living? What impact does rising GDP have on the environment and the quality of life? We conclude this chapter with a brief look at some of these questions.

national income All income, including wages, salaries and benefits, profits (for sole proprietors, partnerships, and corporations), rental income, and interest.

 CHECKPOINT

NATIONAL INCOME ACCOUNTING

- The circular flow diagram shows how households and firms interact through product and resource markets.
- GDP can be computed as spending or as income.
- GDP is equal to the total market value of all final goods and services produced by labor and property in an economy in a given year.
- Personal consumption expenditures are goods and services purchased by individual and business residents of the United States.
- Gross private domestic investment (GPDI) refers to fixed investments such as structures, equipment, and software.
- GDP is equal to consumer expenditures, investment expenditures, government purchases, and exports minus imports. In equation form, $GDP = C + I + G + (X - M)$.
- GDP can also be computed by adding all of the payments to factors of production. This includes compensation to employees, proprietors' income, rental income, corporate profits, and net interest, along with some statistical adjustments.

QUESTIONS: Each individual has a sense of how the macroeconomy is doing based on his or her own experience. How might individual experiences lead one astray in thinking about what is happening in the overall economy? How might it help?

Answers to the Checkpoint questions can be found at the end of this chapter.

GDP AND OUR STANDARD OF LIVING

GDP data provide us with one way of comparing the productivity of different nations. But it doesn't necessarily give us an accurate picture of the standard of living in each country. For example, China, India, and Brazil each have a GDP that places them among the top ten largest economies in the world. But clearly one would not describe the average citizen in these countries as wealthy. This section describes some of the factors that make it challenging to use GDP measures to compare the standard of living of average citizens across countries.

Different Ways of Comparing GDP Across Countries

The previous section described the two ways of measuring GDP using total expenditures and total income in an economy. But once the value of GDP is determined, does that mean it can be used to compare the size of the overall economy between two countries? To some extent, yes, in that countries with larger GDP do produce more output based on the final value of goods and services *in that country* and *in a particular year*. Herein lies an important caveat regarding GDP measures: Nominal GDP statistics do not do a good job of factoring changes in the prices of goods and services over time, nor taking into account differences in the cost of living between countries.

real GDP The total value of final goods and services produced in a country in a year measured using prices in a base year.

To address the first issue of changing prices, the U.S. Bureau of Economic Analysis reports GDP statistics in both nominal terms as well as in *real* terms. **Real GDP** statistics adjust each year's data to prices in a single base year (such as 2005). Therefore, real GDP does a better job of measuring actual growth in output, rather than counting the rise in prices of goods and services over time. The next chapter on inflation discusses nominal and real values in greater detail.

To address the second issue of differences in the cost of living between countries, organizations that report GDP statistics across countries, such as the World Bank's World Development Indicators, also report GDP statistics based on *purchasing-power-parity–* adjusted measures, or GDP-PPP. For example, a haircut in India may cost $3, while that same haircut in Switzerland may cost $30. Since the service is the same, is it accurate to count a haircut ten times more in Switzerland than in India in terms of GDP? By using a GDP-PPP measure, countries in which prices of goods and services (especially nontraded items such as haircuts and restaurant meals) are lower than a representative base country will have their GDP numbers increased, while countries in which prices are higher than the base country will have their GDP statistics lowered.

The effect of using GDP-PPP can be substantial. Although the United States remains the world's largest economy in terms of nominal GDP, it falls to second place behind China when GDP-PPP is used. The reason is because the cost of living in China (on average) is still lower than the cost of living in the United States. But despite this remarkable achievement by China in terms of GDP-PPP, the average Chinese citizen is much less well off than the average American. This is because aggregate GDP measures do not take into account population.

Population and GDP per Capita

GDP per capita A country's GDP divided by its population. GDP per capita provides a useful measure of a country's relative standard of living.

How can GDP measures better reflect a country's population? The most common approach is to divide GDP by a country's population, resulting in a statistic known as **GDP per capita.** GDP per capita is a useful measure of the relative standard of living of citizens in different countries. However, by simply dividing GDP by population, GDP per capita does not take into account the differences in wealth between the rich and poor within a country, and therefore might not fully reflect the standard of living of the typical citizen. For example, U.S. GDP per capita is about $55,000, but certainly the typical American family of four does not earn $220,000 a year. Yet, GDP per capita data are fairly easy to measure, and thus are a useful measure of relative wealth between countries.

An alternative measure of the standard of living is median household income. Being the median household means that half of all households make less and the other half make more. Using this statistic reduces the effect of outliers (i.e., the very destitute or the super-rich) skewing the averages. The U.S. median household income in 2016 was about $57,000, an amount that is closer to what middle-income households make.

Environmental Quality

People around the globe have become increasingly concerned with the impact economic activity has on the natural world. These days, it is difficult to watch a nightly newscast without seeing a report about some ecological disaster or looming environmental problem. U.S. consumers, businesses, and the government spend hundreds of billions of dollars annually to protect the

AROUND THE WORLD

Costa Rica: *Pura Vida* and Happiness Without a High Level of GDP

What does GDP fail to measure in terms of how well Costa Ricans live?

When one thinks of countries in which citizens live well, rich countries often come to mind, such as Luxembourg, Denmark, and Switzerland. These countries have a high GDP per capita, allowing many of their people to live comfortable, and consequently *happy*, lives. This contrasts with countries with low GDP per capita, such as Sudan, Bangladesh, or Chad, where many people lack basic necessities and where much suffering takes place.

But does a country need to be materially rich in order to be happy? One country in Central America whose name literally translates to "rich coast" doesn't think so.

Costa Rica's GDP per capita is about $10,000 a year, or one-sixth

Eric Chiang

that of the United States. However, according to the *World Happiness Report* by the Sustainable Development Solutions Network, in 2015 Costa Rica ranked 12th in terms of happiness, higher than the United States. What factors allow Costa Ricans to live happy lives despite having modest incomes? First, life expectancy in Costa Rica is slightly higher than in the United States. Good, affordable health care and guaranteed government pension payments make retiring in Costa Rica pleasant. Second, Costa Rica's emphasis on ecotourism has helped preserve its environment and

biodiversity. And third, without an army per its constitution, Costa Rica is able to devote funds otherwise spent on military uses to provide better education to its citizens.

It's no wonder why many companies including those in the United States choose to operate production facilities in Costa Rica. With a literacy rate near 100% and a healthy, long-living populace, Costa Rica offers a productive and inexpensive labor force, with manufacturing and service wages averaging $2 to $3 per hour.

Still, low wages means that many families in Costa Rica struggle with daily finances and lack the ability to afford luxuries that richer countries take for granted. But Costa Ricans, in addition to their uplifting country name, also have an uplifting national slogan, "Pura Vida," a phrase used in ordinary everyday conversations to express optimism about life. As long as people are happy, they live productive lives, which bodes well for the future of the country.

GO TO 📖 **LaunchPad** TO PRACTICE THE ECONOMIC CONCEPTS IN THIS STORY

environment at home and abroad. Surprisingly, however, our national income and production statistics do little to account for the environmental benefits or harmful impacts of economic activity.

In 1992 the Bureau of Economic Analysis decided to develop an experimental set of economic accounts known as the Integrated Environmental and Economic Satellite Accounts. Preliminary versions of these green GDP accounts were published in 1994, and later Congress directed the DOC to set up an outside panel of experts to study this issue in greater depth. The DOC asked the National Academy of Sciences to look at green economic accounting, which it did, appointing a select panel.

The DOC panel concluded that "extending the U.S. NIPA to include assets and production activities associated with natural resources and the environment is an important goal."[4] In terms of natural resources, these include the flow of services that are produced by environmental capital such as forests, national parks, and ocean fisheries.

But from a consumer's perspective, a cleaner environment also provides value. The ability to hike in parks, to suntan on clean beaches, and to swim in lakes and rivers all depend on a level of environmental quality that does not show up in our national accounts.

Santiago, Chile, is one of the richest cities in Latin America, but also one of the most polluted. Should the negative effects of pollution be reflected in Chile's GDP?

Roberto Candia/AP Images

[4] Nordhaus and Kokkelenberg, *Nature's Numbers*, pp. 2–3.

Nonmarket Activities and the Informal Economy

In addition to addressing such concerns as environmental impacts and the value of nonmarket natural resources, the DOC panel's recommendations highlight some of the broader shortcomings of the NIPA. For example, the national accounts ignore nonmarket transactions, investments in human capital, and the use of people's time.

Nonmarket transactions are an important part of our everyday lives. If a maid cleans your apartment, GDP rises, but if you did the same job yourself, GDP is unaffected. The same is true for babysitting, lawn care, and car maintenance. There is one exception—NIPA already imputes (estimates) the rental value, less expenses, of owner-occupied homes and adds this to GDP.

Many people believe that the NIPA should be an index of the well-being found within our economy. In that case, it would ideally need to take into account the implications of economic activity the DOC panel noted and more, perhaps including data on life expectancy; business spending on research and development; the stock of human capital, including education and health; greenhouse gas emissions; income distribution; poverty rates; and unemployment rates.

informal economy Includes all transactions that are conducted but are not licensed and/or generate income that is not reported to the government (for tax collection).

The **informal economy** (the underground or black market) is a large unmeasured component of our economy. The informal economy can be as simple as the money earned from a garage sale or from items sold on eBay that are not reported to the IRS. It also includes transactions dealing with illegal goods and services, such as drugs, prostitution, or unlicensed gambling. Finally, the informal economy includes the income earned by undocumented residents—those working on farms, factories, or restaurants for cash, or workers hired for housekeeping or babysitting services who are easily paid *under the table*. The size of the informal economy in the United States is estimated at around 10% of GDP. This is relatively small compared to many developing countries that can have an informal economy valued at as much as 50% of their GDP.

The effects of the informal economy can be positive and negative. On the upside, people working in the informal economy are generating and spending income, contributing to national economic activity. Countries with large informal markets have total output that is significantly larger than what is officially reported in their GDP statistics. On the downside, those working in the informal economy do not pay much if any taxes, placing a greater tax burden on the rest of society. Also, the informal economy is less regulated, which increases the probability of corruption and crime.

Despite these shortcomings in the NIPA measurements, it is important to keep the NIPA's original purpose in mind. As the DOC panel noted,

> *The modern national income and product accounts are among the great inventions of the twentieth century. Among other things, they are used to judge economic performance over time, to compare the economies of different nations, to measure a nation's saving and investment, and to track the business cycle. Much as satellites in space can show the weather across an entire continent, the national accounts can give an overall picture of the state of the economy.*[5]

The informal market ranges from casual tutoring students do in their spare time for cash to the multimillion dollar online poker industry.

The NIPA has served us well. Still, making adjustments to account for various environmental and other nonmarket considerations might provide us with an even better picture of the health of our economy. But we must keep in mind that an aggregate measure of the economy cannot be all things to all people. As we add complexity to an already complex undertaking, the NIPA may lose some effectiveness as a measure of economic activity, as pointed out earlier in the discussion of environmental quality. This is a difficult balancing act facing policymakers.

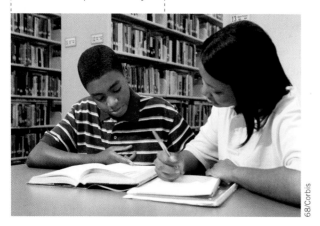

[5] Nordhaus and Kokkelenberg, *Nature's Numbers*, p. 12.

The NIPA allow us to track business cycles, compare the domestic economy with that of other nations, and take a crude measure of our standard of living. In the next chapter, we will see how two other important policy variables, unemployment and inflation, are measured.

The next several chapters will focus on developing explanations of short-term movements in the business cycle and long-term economic growth (the trend line in Figure 2). If we can understand why upturns and downturns occur, we may be able to devise policies that reduce the severity of business cycle swings while promoting economic growth. These investigations and policy objectives form the essence of modern macroeconomic analysis.

 CHECKPOINT

GDP AND OUR STANDARD OF LIVING

- Nominal GDP uses current year prices, while real GDP measures output using prices from a base year. GDP-PPP takes into account the cost of living in a country.

- GDP per capita divides GDP by population, providing a useful measure of a country's relative standard of living.

- GDP does not include most of the benefits and costs from environmental and natural resources.

- GDP does not include nonmarket activities or the informal economy.

- Despite the shortcomings of the GDP measure, GDP provides a simple and consistent way of measuring the overall economic activity in an economy.

QUESTIONS: Each summer, many of the campsites at America's favorite national parks sell out months in advance due to their limited supply, low prices, and prime locations and views. This has led entrepreneurial individuals to reserve these campsites well in advance and then sell the reservations for a high premium on sites such as Craigslist. Does the money earned by these campsite scalpers appear in GDP? Why or why not? Suppose the government attempts to minimize campsite scalping by doubling the price of campsites. Would this affect GDP? Explain.

Answers to the Checkpoint questions can be found at the end of this chapter.

chapter summary

Section 1 Business Cycles

16.1 **Business cycles** are the alternating increases and decreases in economic activity typical of market economies.

Business cycles can vary in duration and intensity, just like a roller coaster. These fluctuations take place around a long-run growth trend.

Business cycles are officially dated by the National Bureau of Economic Research, which assigns a committee of economists to determine "turning points" when the economy switches from peak to recession or from trough to recovery. They do this using past data, which means announcements take place after the turning points occur.

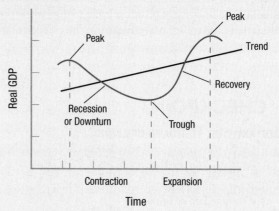

Four Phases of the Business Cycle

- **Peak:** The economy is operating at its capacity.
- **Recession:** Occurs when the economy runs out of steam and business investment falls.
- **Trough:** The economy reaches the depth of the recession.
- **Recovery:** Economic activity picks up and the economy grows.

16.2 Alternative Measures of Business Cycles

- National Activity Index
- Leading Economic Index
- Yield curve

Section 2 National Income Accounting

16.3 The national income and product accounts (NIPA) allow economists to judge our nation's economic performance, compare income and output to that of other nations, and track the economy's condition over the course of the business cycle.

Gross domestic product (GDP) is the total market value of all final goods and services produced in a year within a country's borders, regardless of a firm's nationality. *Gross national product* (GNP) measures goods produced by a country's firms, regardless of where they are produced.

Caterpillar Tractor
U.S. firm; made in USA
Part of U.S. GDP and GNP

Toyota Camry
Japanese firm; made in USA
Part of U.S. GDP, not GNP

Brooks Running Shoes
U.S. firm; made in China
Part of U.S. GNP, not GDP

16.4 **The circular flow diagram** shows how businesses and households interact through the resource and product markets. It shows spending as well as income.

The major components of the NIPA can be constructed in either of two ways: by summing the spending of the economy or by summing income. Likewise, GDP can be measured by adding together either spending or income.

16.5 **Calculating GDP Using Expenditures (% U.S. GDP)**

Personal Consumption Expenditures (*C*)	68%
Gross Private Domestic Investment (*I*)	17%
Government Purchases (*G*)	18%
Net Exports (*X* − *M*)	−3%

16.6 **Calculating GDP Using Income (% U.S. GDP)**

Compensation of Employees	54%
Proprietors' Income	8%
Corporate Profits	9%
Rental Income	4%
Net Interest	4%
Other/Adjustments	21%

Section 3 GDP and Our Standard of Living

16.7 **GDP per capita** is measured as GDP divided by the population. It provides a rough measure of a country's standard of living relative to other countries. However, it does not reflect differences in wealth within a country.

Different Measures of GDP

- **Nominal GDP:** GDP measured in current year prices
- **Real GDP:** GDP measured using prices from a base year
- **GDP-PPP:** GDP adjusted for cost of living relative to a base country

Countries are placing greater emphasis on protecting the environment. The economic benefits from a clean environment, however, are mostly unmeasured in GDP statistics. This is changing as new measures are introduced to take environmental quality and degradation into account.

Liechtenstein: small GDP but many rich citizens.

India: large GDP but many poor citizens.

16.8 The **informal economy** includes all market transactions that are not officially reported and hence are not included in GDP measures; it creates both positive and negative effects:

- **Positive:** Transactions in an informal economy create jobs and contribute to overall economic activity.
- **Negative:** Taxes are rarely paid on income in the informal economy, putting a greater tax burden on others. Also, the informal economy is less regulated, which can lead to unsafe products or risky job conditions.

business cycles, p. 426
double-dip recession, p. 428
yield curve, p. 430
circular flow diagram, p. 433
gross domestic product (GDP),
    p. 434

personal consumption
    expenditures, p. 435
gross private domestic investment
    (GPDI), p. 435
government spending, p. 436
net exports, p. 436

national income, p. 439
real GDP, p. 440
GDP per capita, p. 440
informal economy, p. 442

QUESTIONS AND PROBLEMS

Check Your Understanding

1. How are business cycles defined? Describe the four phases of business cycles.

2. What is a key problem with the way the NBER dates recessions and recoveries?

3. Describe the circular flow diagram. Why must all income equal spending in the economy?

4. Why does GDP accounting include only the final value of goods and services produced? What would be the problem if intermediate products were included?

5. Describe why GDP can be computed using either expenditures or income.

6. What does GDP per capita measure? Why is it not a precise measure of a typical person's standard of living in a country?

Apply the Concepts

7. Explain how it is possible for an economy in the recovery phase of the business cycle to have a lower GDP and a higher unemployment rate than when it was in the recession phase of the business cycle.

8. As a percentage of GDP, government spending tends to increase during recessions and decrease during times of economic expansion. Explain why government spending tends to change depending on the phase of the business cycle, and how that affects spending as a percentage of GDP.

9. Critics argue that the NIPA are outdated and fail to account for "intangibles" in our new knowledge economy. For example, many firms create copyrighted materials (movies, books, etc.) that when completed are much more valuable than just the value of the marketplace inputs that went into their production. What might be some of the problems associated with trying to include these intangibles in the NIPA?

10. Gross domestic product and its related statistics are published quarterly and are often revised in the following quarter. Do you think quarterly publication and revision in the next quarter would present problems for policymakers trying to control the business cycle? Why or why not?

11. Gross private domestic investment (GPDI) includes new residential construction as investment. Why is new housing included? Isn't this just another consumer purchase of housing services? How would the sale of an existing house be treated in the GDP accounts?

12. Suppose that a new method of calculating GDP allows for reductions in GDP as a result of the severity of environmental degradation in a country. If this method is used, which of the following countries might experience the greatest adjustment to their GDP calculation: India, Germany, or Iceland?

In the News

13. For much of the last 20 years, China's GDP has grown around 10% per year, but in recent years has fallen to around 6% per year, which is still much higher than the average U.S. growth rate in recent years of about 2% per year. Why would a slowdown in China's GDP growth be a significant concern to the U.S. macroeconomy? If prices of goods and services fall in China due to slower growth, does this help or hurt U.S. GDP?

14. According to the CIA's *World Factbook*, in 2015 the tiny country of Equatorial Guinea had the highest GDP per capita in Africa (over $20,000 per year), even higher than more developed countries such as Morocco, Egypt, or South Africa. But despite the significant overall income from the sale of its natural resources, Equatorial Guinea has extreme poverty, with half of the population lacking clean drinking water, and one of the highest infant mortality rates in the world. How can a country that looks so good on paper (in terms of GDP per capita) be one of the least desirable places to live on the planet for the average citizen?

Solving Problems

15. The table lists gross domestic product (GDP), consumption (C), gross private domestic investment (I), government spending (G), and net exports (X − M). Compute each as a percent of GDP for the six years presented.

Year	GDP	C	I	G	X − M	C (%)	I (%)	G (%)	X − M (%)
1965	719.1	443.8	118.2	151.5	5.6				
1975	1,638.3	1,034.4	230.2	357.7	16.0				
1985	4,220.3	2,720.3	736.2	879.0	115.2				
1995	7,397.7	4,975.8	1,144.0	1,369.2	−91.4				
2005	12,455.8	8,742.4	2,057.4	2,372.8	−716.7				
2015	18,128.2	12,429.0	3,019.2	3,206.5	−526.5				

a. Which category (or categories) has increased as a percent of GDP from 1965 to 2015? Which category (or categories) has decreased? And which category (or categories) has not changed much from 1965 to 2015?

b. Which category has been the most volatile in terms of changes in the percent of GDP?

c. Ignoring net exports, which component has grown the fastest as a percent of GDP since 1965?

▬▬▬ WORK IT OUT ▬▬▬   ≋ LaunchPad | interactive activity ▬▬

16. Use the following list of GDP components and data (given in millions of $U.S.) to answer the following questions.

Corporate profits	1,300 _____
Gross private domestic investment	2,800 _____
Consumption of nondurable goods	3,100 _____
Exports	1,400 _____
Proprietors' income	1,000 _____
Miscellaneous adjustments	700 _____
Consumption of services	4,300 _____
Net interest	500 _____
Compensation of employees	8,000 _____
Imports	1,900 _____
Rental income	400 _____
Government spending	2,100 _____
Consumption of durable goods	1,300 _____
Consumption of fixed capital	1,400 _____

a. Indicate whether each component is part of the expenditures approach to calculating GDP (put an "E" next to the component) or the income approach to calculating GDP (put an "I" next to the component).

b. Compute the GDP using both expenditures and income approaches. What factor explains the difference between these measures?

c. Calculate the value of national income. Which category (categories) is (are) not included in national income, but are included in the calculation of GDP using the income approach?

USING THE NUMBERS

17. According to By the Numbers, in what year since 2005 was the difference between the unemployment rate and the real GDP growth rate the largest? What phase of the business cycle would this year best represent?

18. According to By the Numbers, has the personal savings rate trended upward or downward during the last five economic recessions? Why does this trend occur?

ANSWERS TO QUESTIONS IN CHECKPOINTS

Checkpoint: Business Cycles 432

Big-ticket (high-priced, high-margin) items such as automobiles are affected by a recession more than grocery stores, where the margins are smaller and prices are lower. When the economy turns downward, investment falls; therefore, the capital goods industry is one of the first to feel the pinch.

Checkpoint: National Income Accounting 439

In general, it is probably a bad idea to interpret how the aggregate economy is doing by using your personal situation. Just because you are having trouble finding a job does not mean that everyone else is. Downsizing by Bank of America and Citigroup in recent years meant that bank workers had problems, even though the rest of the economy may have been growing steadily. There might be times when your situation (such as a layoff in an important industry) may be a leading indicator of what is coming for the economy as a whole. In general, anecdotal evidence is not particularly helpful in forecasting where the aggregate economy is going. When times are uncertain, anecdotal evidence may mislead. Even in recessions, some firms do well; therefore, anecdotal evidence is suspect. This is why the NIPA was created.

Checkpoint: GDP and Our Standard of Living 443

The money earned by the scalpers is not counted in GDP because scalpers are not likely to report this income on their tax returns, and thus this is considered part of the informal economy. The revenues earned by Craigslist, a legitimate enterprise, for the transaction would count toward GDP.

If the government doubles the price of campsites and they continue to sell out, then GDP would increase because money paid to the National Parks is part of consumption spending in GDP.

17 Measuring Inflation and Unemployment

GAS 13 $\frac{8}{10}$
TAX 4 ¢
TOTAL 17 $\frac{8}{10}$

17 8/10 Including Tax	
GALLONS	COST
1 -	.18
2 -	.36
3 -	.53
4 -	.71
5 -	.89
6 -	1.07
7 -	1.25
8 -	1.42
9 -	1.60
10 -	1.78
11 -	1.96
12 -	2.14
13 -	2.31
14 -	2.49
15 -	2.67

Understanding the effects of rising prices and unemployment on the ability of people to save and prepare for the future

Learning Objectives

17.1 Define inflation and explain how it is measured.

17.2 Use the consumer price index to estimate the effects of inflation on prices.

17.3 Describe the main causes of inflation.

17.4 Describe the economic consequences of the different forms of inflation.

17.5 Explain how "labor force," "employment," and "unemployment" are defined.

17.6 Compare alternative measures of unemployment that include marginally attached workers and underemployed workers.

17.7 Describe the different forms of unemployment and which ones can be influenced by government policies.

17.8 Explain what full employment means and how the natural rate of unemployment is measured.

Fifty years ago, a single dollar bought a lot. A gallon of gasoline cost less than 30 cents, a movie theater ticket cost about 75 cents, and a meal at a relatively new restaurant chain called McDonald's cost about 50 cents.

Today, none of these items can be purchased for a dollar. The general rise in prices in the economy is referred to as inflation. Inflation has fluctuated each year, ranging from less than 5% in the 1960s, to nearly 15% in 1980, to less than 2% in recent years. Inflation reduces the ability of consumers to purchase goods and services. Your dollar just does not go as far. Inflation is a macroeconomic issue because it reduces the purchasing power of both income and savings over time.

Another macroeconomic concern facing the economy is unemployment, which measures the number of workers without a job but who are actively seeking one. Like the inflation rate, the unemployment rate fluctuates from year to year, falling below 5% during the Internet boom of the late 1990s and the housing bubble in the early 2000s, and reaching 10% during the early 1980s and late 2000s. Unemployment is a concern because not only does it force unemployed people to cut back on consumption and to use up their savings, it influences the employed to cut back on their consumption as well. Unemployment puts considerable strain on the government when it results in lower tax revenues but higher spending on assistance programs for the unemployed.

Because inflation and unemployment can have such bad macroeconomic effects, they have been called the "twin evils" of the modern macroeconomy. Each alone is bad. Together, they amplify each other, making things worse.

In the 1960s, macroeconomists thought they had these twin evils beaten. Historical data led them to believe that inflation and unemployment were linked in an inverse fashion; when unemployment went up, inflation would go down, and vice versa. Macroeconomists thought policymakers faced a menu of choices. Pick an unemployment rate from column A and get a corresponding inflation rate from column B. Better yet, the rates at issue were thought to be relatively low: An inflation rate of 3% to 4% was thought to be needed to keep unemployment under 4%. For those unemployed in the 2007–2009 recession when unemployment reached 10%, an unemployment rate less than 4% would seem like a dream. Is a 3% to 4% inflation rate so bad?

Unfortunately, the data amassed in the 1960s gave a false reading, as the high unemployment *and* high inflation rates of the 1970s proved. According to the 1960s macroeconomic model, the macroeconomy was just not supposed to witness the twin evils together.

Jump ahead to 2016. After a long recovery since 2009 that saw persistent unemployment for several years, the silver lining was that inflation was low throughout the recovery, again confirming the trend that unemployment and inflation tend to run opposite of each other. But as the official unemployment rate fell below 5% in 2016, inflation did not rise, largely due to a steep drop in energy prices. Because both unemployment and inflation were low, the twin evils appeared seemingly defeated . . . but

McDONALD'S AMAZING MENU

100% Pure Beef Hamburger	15c
Delicious Cheeseburgers	19c
Triple-Thick Shakes (16 oz.)	20c
Golden French Fries	10c
Full-Flavored Orange Drink	10c
Delightful Root Beer	10c
Thirst-Quenching Coke	10c
Coffee As You Like It	10c
Refreshing Milk	12c

McDonald's menu in 1955.

Used with permission from McDonald's Corporation

The Twin Evils of Inflation and Unemployment

Inflation and unemployment are two variables that governments monitor carefully. Nearly every country has experienced periods of very high unemployment or inflation at some point in its past, and government policies used to correct these problems vary significantly.

Do Unemployment and Inflation Measure Our Misery?

The **Misery Index** was created by economist Arthur Okun, an adviser to President Lyndon Johnson. It is the sum of the unemployment and inflation rates. The higher the number, the more misery the economy is suffering. Running against Gerald Ford for the presidency in 1976, Jimmy Carter made an issue of the Misery Index: It was 13%. He argued that no one should be reelected as president when the Misery Index is that high. When Carter sought reelection in 1980, the Misery Index exceeded 20%; he lost to Ronald Reagan.

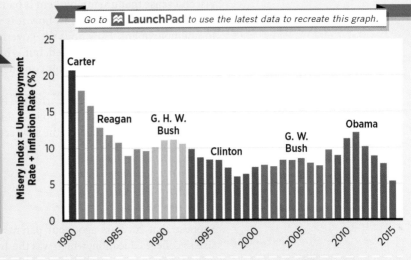

Go to LaunchPad to use the latest data to recreate this graph.

Misery Index = Unemployment Rate + Inflation Rate (%)

Carter, Reagan, G. H. W. Bush, Clinton, G. W. Bush, Obama

$70.4 billion

Total amount spent by state and federal governments on unemployment benefits in 2015

1.1%

Average yearly increase in Social Security benefits from the Cost-of-Living Adjustment from 2008 to 2016

Public Domain

The social costs of unemployment: For every 1% rise in the national unemployment rate:

- **$30 billion more is spent** by the government on unemployment benefits per year.
- **$6 billion more is spent** on food stamps (SNAP benefits) per year.
- **$12 billion less is collected** in federal and state income tax revenues.

The Zimbabwean **$100 trillion bill** was one of the largest denominations of currency ever printed. It became nearly worthless just months after it was printed.

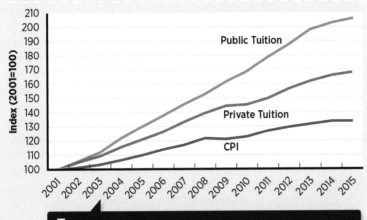

Public Tuition

Private Tuition

CPI

Index (2001=100)

The cost of tuition at public and private colleges and universities has risen faster than the consumer price index for all goods and services since 2001. (Index = 100 in year 2001.)

Index of Housing Prices

Images.com/Corbis

Housing prices rose quickly from 2001 to 2006, then fell dramatically from 2006 to 2012. Prices have since rebounded.

were they? Economists have pointed out that the extraordinary measures taken during and after the last recession resulted in growing debt and a large infusion of money into the economy, policies that could eventually lead to higher inflation. And if the slowdown in the global economy increases unemployment in the near future, we might have to confront the twin evils together again.

By now, you might be wondering: What is the big deal about inflation? You have a visceral sense that unemployment is bad. Inflation is less tangible. Thus, this chapter will start with inflation, what it is, how it is measured, and why it is bad. Then we will turn to unemployment. How does the government define the unemployment rate? An Uber driver with a Ph.D. is employed, but is he or she really underemployed? Is someone who has given up looking for a job considered unemployed? You may be surprised at the answers.

The chapter then will categorize the types of unemployment, revealing which type can be moderated by government policies and which cannot. Finally, we will return to a key concern from the last chapter: the slow economic recovery that reduced the overall number of people seeking jobs.

INFLATION

Suppose that 20 years ago, your parents put aside $18,200 each for your and your twin sister's college education, which was the average cost of four years of tuition at a public university at that time. Your money was placed into a savings account that earned 1.5% interest per year on average, and your sister's money was placed into a Treasury Inflation-Protected Security (TIPS) bond, which pays a fixed interest rate but whose value also changes with the inflation rate. Now you and your sister withdraw the money to pay for college. Big problem: The cost of tuition has more than doubled in the 20 years since your parents put the money into your accounts. Do you both still have enough to pay your tuition bill? Your sister perhaps does, but not you. Your account has $24,513 in it, and your sister's account has $38,372. Looks like your sister got the better deal.

Prices are constantly changing for the goods and services we buy. Prices for items such as concert tickets, airline tickets, and fast-food meals have risen steadily over time, making every dollar earned worth a little less in terms of how much it can buy. However, prices for some goods, such as smartphones, laptops, and other technology goods, have fallen. Overall, the prices of a typical "basket" of goods and services we buy rise each year—by 38% over the last 15 years, and 651% over the last 50 years. This gradual rise in prices each year is known as **inflation.** Over time, the effects of inflation can be substantial if one does not take action to protect against rising prices. For example, paying $4 for a gallon of milk today is much harder than paying $2.50 a gallon was back in 2002. But it would be even harder if your wages or savings have not increased over that period.

inflation A general rise in prices throughout the economy. It is a measure of changes in the cost of living.

How do individuals protect themselves against rising prices? First, workers demand higher wages to compensate for higher prices. But in a weak economy, wage increases are not always possible, especially when many people are out of work and willing to work for lower wages. Second, individuals with money saved can invest that money in assets that earn interest or can increase in value over time. Holding cash, for example, does not earn interest and therefore does not protect one against inflation.

Many forms of assets pay interest, including savings accounts, certificates of deposit (CDs), bonds, and money market accounts. But they do not pay equal amounts—safer assets, such as savings accounts, pay less than the average rise in prices, while riskier assets might pay more than the average rise in prices. One asset that pays a rate roughly equal to the rise in prices are TIPS bonds, which pay a small fixed interest rate in addition to an adjustment based on how prices change in an economy. Therefore, when prices do not rise much, a TIPS bond would pay little, but when prices rise a lot, a TIPS bond will pay a lot. Table 1 shows how $18,200 placed into different assets would have grown over 20 years. The TIPS bond better ensures that when you take money out after 20 years, you will be more able to pay for college at the higher prices.

TABLE 1	A COMPARISON OF TWO INVESTMENTS	1997	2017
Average price of 4 years of tuition at a public college or university		$18,200	$38,800
Value of $18,200 held in cash		$18,200	$18,200
Value of $18,200 held in a savings account		$18,200	$24,513
Value of $18,200 in a TIPS bond		$18,200	$38,372

What Causes Inflation?

Inflation is a measure of changes in the cost of living. In an economy like ours, prices are constantly changing. Some go up as others go down, and some prices rise and fall seasonally. Inflation is caused by many different factors, but the primary reasons can be attributed to demand factors, supply shocks, and government policy.

First, prices for goods and services are influenced by demand factors such as consumer confidence, income, or wealth. Think of a busy mall or restaurant. When there are plenty of customers, businesses are not pressured to offer discounts to attract buyers. This keeps prices higher than when consumer demand is depressed. For this reason, economic growth tends to coincide with inflation as a result of the demand for goods and services that higher incomes produce.

Second, prices are affected by supply shocks, caused by fluctuations in the price of inputs such as oil, natural resources, and farm crops. Over the last decade, the average price of a gallon of gasoline skyrocketed from less than $2 to nearly $4 a gallon due to increased demand for energy worldwide (especially in emerging countries such as China and India). But more recently, as a result of a glut in oil production and decreased global demand, gasoline prices fell back to below $2 a gallon. Farm products have seen similar fluctuations in prices as droughts and other natural disasters disrupt the supply of crops. When input prices rise, this not only raises the cost of living for individuals, but also raises the cost for businesses to produce and transport goods once produced. These higher costs of doing business typically are passed on to consumers in the form of higher prices. When input prices fall, we generally expect the opposite effect on prices to occur.

Lastly, inflation can result from specific government actions. Government has a great power that no one individual has—the power to print money. No doubt you have heard that the federal government runs a budget deficit as it spends more than it receives in tax revenues. How does the government obtain the money to overspend? It borrows by issuing Treasury bonds. When the bonds come due and the government does not have the money to buy them back, it can, in essence, run the printing presses and print up new dollars. As more new money is printed, a surplus of dollars is generated in relation to the supply of goods and services. When too much money chases a fixed quantity of goods and services, prices are bid up, which leads to inflation. Governments, like everyone else, have to obey the laws of supply and demand by limiting the growth of the money supply to prevent rampant inflation from occurring.

Now that we have described the main causes of inflation, let's discuss how inflation is measured.

Measuring Inflation: Consumer Price Index, Producer Price Index, and GDP Deflator

Each month, the U.S. Department of Labor, through its Bureau of Labor Statistics (BLS), reports several important statistics that provide us with our principal measure of inflation. It does so by reporting changes in the average

The town of Sycamore, Illinois, installed parking meters with prices reminiscent of the 1950s, when the price of parking was 1 cent per 12 minutes or 5 cents per hour. Parking citations were $1.00. The parking meters, stuck in a time long before inflation set in, became a tourist draw for the town.

AP Photo/Daily Chronicle, Eric Sumberg

price level The absolute level of a price index, whether the consumer price index (CPI; retail prices), the producer price index (PPI; wholesale prices), or the GDP deflator (average price of all items in GDP).

disinflation A reduction in the rate of inflation. An economy experiencing disinflation still faces inflation, but at a declining rate.

deflation A decline in overall prices throughout the economy. This is the opposite of inflation.

consumer price index (CPI) An index of the average prices paid by urban consumers for a typical market basket of consumer goods and services.

level of prices over the previous month in terms of the price level. The **price level** is the absolute level of a price index, whether this is the consumer price index (CPI; retail prices), the producer price index (PPI; wholesale prices), or the GDP deflator (average price of all items in GDP). The percentage increase in prices over a 12-month period is referred to as the *rate of inflation*.

Because inflation rates fluctuate up and down, the term **disinflation** is used to describe a reduction in the rate of inflation. Note that an economy going through disinflation still experiences rising prices, just at a slower pace. This was the case from the mid-1980s throughout the 1990s. However, if overall prices in an economy actually fall, this is referred to as **deflation.** Cases of deflation are rare, but did occur in the early 1930s, and briefly in 2015 as a result of a steep drop in energy prices.

Measuring consumer spending and inflation is one of the oldest data-collection functions of the BLS. The first nationwide survey was conducted in 1888–1891, which at the time emphasized the worker's role as a producer rather than as a consumer. During World War I, surveys of consumer spending were conducted to compute one of the first cost-of-living indices. During the Great Depression, extensive consumer surveys were used to study the welfare of selected groups, notably farmers, rural families, and urban families. The BLS began regular reports of the modern CPI in the late 1930s. Today, the CPI is the measure of inflation most Americans are familiar with, although the producer price index and the GDP deflator also are widely followed.

The Consumer Price Index The **consumer price index (CPI)** is an index of the average prices paid by urban consumers (CPI-U) and urban wage earners (CPI-W) for a market basket of consumer goods and services. The CPI-U covers roughly 88% of the population.

The CPI is often referred to as a "cost-of-living" index, but the current CPI differs from a true cost-of-living measure. A cost-of-living index compares the cost of maintaining the same standard of living in the current and base periods. A cost-of-goods index, in contrast, merely measures the cost of a fixed bundle of goods and services from one period to the next.

Why does CPI use a fixed bundle of goods and services? First, this avoids having to measure how consumers react to price changes; for example, if the price of beef rises, people might buy more chicken. Second, because it is difficult to follow every decision made by consumers, the government measures how prices change for a fixed basket of goods that an average consumer would buy.

The CPI is calculated by dividing the market basket's cost in the current period by its cost in the base period. The current CPI is a cost-of-goods index because it measures changes in the price of a fixed basket of goods. The reference or base period used today for the CPI is 1982–1984, but any base year would work just as well.

How the Bureau of Labor Statistics Measures Changes in Consumer Prices Measuring consumer prices requires the work of many people. Data collectors record about 83,000 prices in 87 urban areas each month from selected department stores, supermarkets, service stations, doctors' offices, rental offices, and more. Yet, the BLS does not have enough resources to price all goods and services in all retail outlets; therefore, it uses three sample groups to approximate the spending behavior of all urban consumers. These include a *Consumer Expenditure Survey* tracking the spending habits of over 30,000 families nationwide used to construct the market basket of goods and services, a *Point-of-Purchase Survey* that identifies where households purchase goods and services, and census data to select the urban areas where prices are collected.

Goods and services are divided into more than 200 categories, with each category specifying over 200 items for monthly price collection. Data from the three surveys are combined, weighted, and used to compute the cost in the current period required to purchase the fixed market basket of goods. This cost is then compared to the base period to calculate the CPI using the following formula:

$$CPI = (\text{Cost in Current Period} \div \text{Cost in Base Period}) \times 100$$

For example, assume that the market basket of goods cost \$5,000 in 2011 and that the same basket of goods now costs \$5,750. The CPI for today, using 2011 for the base year, is

$$115.0 = (\$5,750 \div \$5,000) \times 100$$

Therefore, the cost of goods has risen by 15% over this time period because the index in the base year (2011 in this case) is always 100. Again, the choice of base year does not matter as long as the CPI for each year is calculated relative to the cost in the selected base year. In fact, one can use CPI data as reported by the BLS to calculate price changes between any two years, neither of which is the base year, using the following formula:

% Change in Price = [(*CPI* in Current Year/*CPI* in Original Year) × 100] − 100

For example, if the CPI in 2016 was 238.6 and the CPI in 2011 was 224.9, the average change in prices over this five-year period was

6.1% = [(238.6/224.9) × 100] − 100

We now take a quick look at some of the problems inherent in the current approach to measuring the CPI.

Problems in Measuring Consumer Prices The CPI is a *conditional* cost-of-goods index in that it measures only private goods and services; public goods (such as national defense spending) are excluded. Other background environmental factors, meanwhile, are held constant. The current CPI, for instance, does not take into account such issues as the state of the environment, homeland security, life expectancy, crime rates, climate change, or other conditions affecting the quality of life. For these reasons alone, the CPI will probably never be a true cost-of-living index.

But even if we ignore the environmental factors and public services, the CPI still tends to overstate inflation for three key reasons: product substitution, quality improvements, and the introduction of new products.

The CPI uses a fixed market basket determined by consumer expenditure surveys that often are three to five years old. The CPI assumes that consumers continue to purchase the same basket of goods from one year to the next. We know, however, that when the price of one good rises, consumers substitute other goods that have fallen in price, or at least did not rise as much.

Also, in any given year, about 30% of the products in the market basket will disappear from store shelves. Data collectors can directly substitute other products for roughly two-thirds of these dropped products, which means that about 10% of the original market basket must be replaced by products that have been improved or modified in some important way. These quality improvements affect standards of living although they are not fully accounted for in CPI measurements.

Another problem for CPI is the introduction of new products. Not too long ago, digital streaming of books, music, and movies did not exist. Neither did iPads and other devices allowing these media to be played. Because technology is constantly changing along with the prices of technology goods, the BLS often waits until a product matures and is used by a significant number of consumers before including it in the market basket. By not measuring the benefits of new products that consumers enjoy, the actual rate of inflation will be overstated.

One final difficulty to note has to do with measuring the changing costs of health care. The CPI looks only at consumers' out-of-pocket spending on health care, and not the overall health care spending (including payments made by Medicare, Medicaid, and employer-provided insurance), which is 3 times larger. If price changes differ between out-of-pocket spending and total spending, the CPI will not reflect the true rise in costs.

One solution to these problems was the introduction of an indicator by the BLS called C-CPI-U, or chained CPI for urban consumers. The C-CPI-U uses the same data as the CPI-U, but applies a different formula to account for product substitutions made by consumers. Although the C-CPI-U does a better job of approximating a cost-of-living index, it takes longer to estimate because data must be collected over several years. The BLS reports the C-CPI-U, which has a base period of 1999, alongside CPI-U and CPI-W.

The difference in magnitudes between CPI-U and C-CPI-U varies from year to year; however, the trend has been for C-CPI-U to be lower than CPI-U by roughly 0.3% to 0.4% each year.

The Producer Price Index The **producer price index (PPI)** is an index of the average prices received by domestic producers for their output. Before 1978 this index was known as the wholesale price index (WPI). The PPI is compiled by doing extensive sampling of nearly every industry in the mining and manufacturing sectors of our economy.

producer price index (PPI) An index of the average prices received by domestic producers for their output.

The PPI contains the following:

- Price indexes for roughly 500 mining and manufacturing industries, including over 10,000 indexes for specific products and product categories

- Over 3,700 commodity price indexes organized by type of product and end use

- About 800 indexes for specific outputs of industries in the service sector, and other sectors that do not produce physical products

- Several major aggregate measures of price changes, organized by stage of processing, both commodity-based and industry-based

The PPI measures the net revenue accruing to a representative firm for specific products. Because the PPI measures net revenues received by the firm, excise taxes are excluded, but changes in sales promotion programs such as rebate offers or zero-interest loans are included. Because the products measured are the same from month to month, the PPI is plagued by the same problems discussed above for the CPI. These problems include quality changes, deleted products, and some manufacturers exiting the industry.

The GDP Deflator The **GDP deflator** shown in Figure 1 is our broadest measure of inflation. It is an index of the average prices for all goods and services in the economy, including consumer goods, investment goods, government goods and services, and exports. The prices of imports are excluded. Note that *deflation* occurred in the Great Depression. The spike in inflation occurred just after the end of World War II, when price controls were lifted. Since the mid-1980s, the economy has witnessed disinflation—inflation was present but generally at a decreasing rate.

Adjusting for Inflation: Escalating and Deflating Series (Nominal Versus Real Values)

Price indexes are used for two primary purposes: escalation and deflation. An escalator agreement modifies future payments, usually increasing them, to take the effects of inflation into

GDP deflator An index of the average prices for all goods and services in the economy, including consumer goods, investment goods, government goods and services, and exports. It is the broadest measure of inflation in the national income and product accounts (NIPA).

| FIGURE 1 | INFLATION FROM 1930 TO 2016—GDP DEFLATOR |

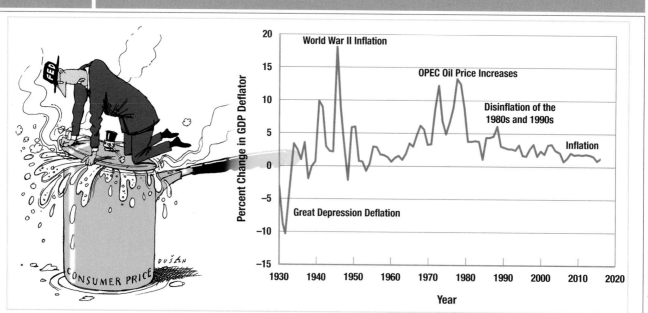

The broadest measure of inflation, the GDP deflator, is used to graph inflation from 1930 to the present. Deflation occurred during the Great Depression. The spike in inflation occurred after World War II ended, when price controls were lifted. Since then, inflation has existed in a 1%–14% range. Since the mid-1980s, the U.S. economy has generally faced disinflation (inflation, but generally at a decreasing rate).

account. Deflating a series of data with an index involves adjusting some current value (often called the nominal value) for the impact of inflation, thereby creating what economists call a *real value*. Using the GDP deflator, for instance, to deflate annual GDP involves adjusting nominal GDP to account for inflation, thereby yielding real GDP, or GDP adjusted for inflation.

Escalator Clauses Many contracts, including commercial rental agreements, labor union contracts, and Social Security payments are subject to escalator clauses. An escalator clause is designed to adjust payments or wages for changes in the price level. Social Security payments, for example, are adjusted upward (and referred to as a cost-of-living adjustment, or COLA) almost every year to account for the rate of inflation.

Escalator clauses become important in times of rising or significant inflation. These clauses protect the real value of wages as well as payments such as Social Security. In fact, voting blocs and organizations such as AARP have been formed to protect those who depend on escalator clauses to maintain their standards of living.

However, over the past decade, low inflation rates have correspondingly resulted in tiny increases in benefits. In fact, in 2009, 2010, 2015, and 2016, inflation was so low (around 0%) that no increase in Social Security benefits occurred. This caused some concern among many seniors because the lack of inflation in 2015 and 2016 was due to a large drop in energy prices, despite higher prices for food and health care, items on which seniors are more likely to spend their money. In general, though, escalator clauses are important because they do protect people from spikes in the overall price level.

Deflating Series: Nominal Versus Real Values GDP grew by 22% from 2008 to 2016, but should we be celebrating? Not really, because inflation has eroded the purchasing power of that increase. The question is, by how much did GDP really increase?

First, remember that every index is grounded on a base year, and that the value for this base year is always 100. The base year used for the GDP deflator, for instance, is 2008. The formula for converting a nominal value, or *current dollar value,* to real value, or *constant dollar* value, is

$$\text{Real} = \text{Nominal} \times (\text{Base Year Index} \div \text{Current Year Index})$$

To illustrate, nominal GDP in 2016 was $18,128.2 billion. The GDP deflator, having been 100 in 2008, was 112.3 in 2016. Real GDP for 2016 (in 2008 dollars) was therefore

$$\$16,142.6 \text{ billion} = \$18,128.2 \text{ billion} \times (100.0 \div 112.3).$$

Note that because the economy has faced some inflation—12.3% from 2008 to 2016—the nominal value of GDP has been reduced by this amount to arrive at the real value. In other words, of the 22% growth in nominal GDP, 12.3% was due to rising prices. If we subtract 12.3% from 22%, real growth of GDP from 2008 to 2016 was less than 10%, or a little over 1%, per year. The slow economic recovery following the recession of 2007–2009 played a large role in the very slow growth of real GDP over this time period.

The Effect of Overstating Inflation Many federal benefits, including Social Security payments, food stamps, and veterans' benefits, are indexed to the CPI, which means that if inflation (as measured by the CPI) goes up by 3%, these benefits are increased by 3%. If the CPI overstates inflation, federal expenditures on benefits are higher. Although individuals initially benefit from the higher payments, overstating inflation in the long run makes real earnings appear smaller than what they actually are. This leads to a different set of issues for policymakers and our economy.

Because CPI had been estimated to overstate inflation, in 1999 the Department of Labor revised its measurement tools used for estimating inflation. As a result, today's CPI is a more accurate measure of inflation.

The Consequences of Inflation

Why do so many policymakers, businesspeople, and consumers dread inflation? Your attitude toward inflation will depend in large part on whether you live on a fixed income, whether you are a creditor or debtor, and whether you have properly anticipated inflation.

Many elderly people live on fixed incomes; often, only their Social Security payments are indexed to inflation. People on fixed incomes are harmed by inflation because the purchasing power of their income declines. If people live long enough on fixed incomes, inflation can reduce them from living comfortably to living in poverty.

Creditors, meanwhile, are harmed by inflation because both the principal on loans and interest payments are usually fixed. Inflation reduces the real value of the payments they receive, while the value of the principal declines in real terms. This means that debtors benefit from inflation; the real value of their payments declines as their wages rise with inflation. Many homeowners in the 1970s and 1980s saw the value of their real estate rise from inflation. At the same time, their wages rose, again partly due to inflation, but their mortgage payment remained fixed. The result was that a smaller part of the typical household's income was needed to pay the mortgage. Inflation thus redistributes income from creditors to debtors.

This result takes place only if the inflation is unanticipated. If lenders foresee inflation, they will adjust the interest rates they offer to offset the inflation expected over the period of the loan. Suppose, for instance, that the interest rate during zero inflation periods is roughly 3%. Now suppose that a lender expects inflation to run 5% a year over the next three years, the life of a proposed loan. The lender will demand an 8% interest rate to adjust for the expected losses caused by inflation. Only when lenders fail to anticipate inflation does it harm them, to the benefit of debtors.

But the effects of unexpected inflation do not stop there. When inflation is unexpected, the incentives individuals and firms face change. For example, suppose that inflation causes prices of everyday purchases along with wages to increase by 5%. If this inflationary effect was anticipated, then consumption decisions should not change, because *real* prices stay the same when prices and wages rise by the same amount. But if the price rise was unexpected, it might cause consumers to reduce their consumption, leading to lower spending in the economy. For firms, if an increase in money due to unexpected inflation causes demand for their products to rise at their original prices, firms might react by increasing production (and their costs) rather than adjusting their prices when actual demand has not changed. Therefore, unexpected inflation leads to faulty signals, which can reduce consumer and producer welfare.

Lastly, when inflation becomes rampant, individuals and firms expend resources to protect themselves from the harmful effects of rapidly rising prices, an effect that is especially prevalent in cases of hyperinflation.

Hyperinflation

hyperinflation An extremely high rate of inflation; above 100% per year.

Hyperinflation is an extremely high rate of inflation. Today, most economists refer to an inflation rate above 100% a year as hyperinflation. But in most episodes of hyperinflation, the inflation rates dwarf 100% a year. In 2008 in Zimbabwe, prices were more than doubling *every day*, for an annual inflation rate of 231,000,000%.

Hyperinflation is not new. It has been around since paper money and debt were invented. During the American Revolutionary War, the Continental Congress issued money until the phrase "not worth a continental" became part of the language. Germany experienced

Millions, billions, and quadrillions are the types of numbers people have to deal with when using hyperinflated currencies.

ISSUE

The Consequences of Counterfeit Money on Inflation

Each day, hundreds of billions of U.S. dollars exchange hands in everyday transactions. A small fraction of these dollars are counterfeit, circulating throughout the economy as if they were genuine. When counterfeit money is created, who ends up paying for it?

Suppose you receive some money, and later realize one of the bills is fake (the ink runs, the paper is too thin, or the watermark is missing). What can you do? Many people assume they could go to a bank and exchange the fake bill for a real one. But most banks won't accept a fake bill because then the bank would lose the money. Some people pass the fake to the next unsuspecting person, but this is a punishable offense. The law states that a counterfeit bill must be reported to the nearest U.S. Secret Service field office. By doing so, you still lose the money, as there is no compensation for turning in counterfeit money.

Thus, the responsibility lies with individuals and businesses to check the authenticity of the money received, and to refuse money that appears to be counterfeit. That is not always as easy as it sounds. A low-quality counterfeit might be detected by the naked eye, by touch, or by the use of devices such as a counterfeit detector pen. But

sophisticated counterfeiters produce high-quality counterfeits that are hard to detect. For example, one counterfeiting method is to remove the ink from a lower-denomination bill and then reprint a higher denomination on the paper. The paper is real, making counterfeit detector pens ineffective, and the bill contains a watermark (however, the wrong one) and a security strip. These counterfeits are nearly indistinguishable from authentic bills, and can circulate for years without being noticed.

Restaurants and other businesses often receive counterfeits because cashiers are rushed. Consumers sometimes pass them to businesses thinking it won't hurt them. Because banks generally do not accept counterfeits, businesses with counterfeits incur a loss that acts as a tax on the business, which leads to higher prices. Therefore, even if individuals do not end up with the counterfeit in their possession, they pay for them in the form of higher prices.

What happens when a high-quality counterfeit circulates for years in the economy? In terms of its economic impact, counterfeit money acts as real money if people accept it as real money. Ultimately, the government loses. Why? The government (the U.S. Treasury to be specific) is the only institution with

the authority to print money. When another entity prints counterfeits, the amount of money in circulation rises, but the government never had the opportunity to use it first.

When more money chases a limited amount of goods and services in an economy, inflation arises. Because counterfeits produce the same effect as an increase in the money supply, inflation will occur. In sum, counterfeits hurt everyone, which is why governments invest in new technology to produce money with many security features.

Counterfeit detector pens are commonly used to monitor currency that comes into businesses. When counterfeit money doesn't get detected, businesses lose the money, which acts as a tax, which leads to higher prices.

the first modern hyperinflation after World War I. Hungary experienced the highest rate of inflation on record during World War II. By the end of the war, it took over 800 octillion (8 followed by 29 zeros) Hungarian pengos to equal 1 prewar pengo.

Hyperinflation is usually caused by an excess of government spending over tax revenues (extremely high deficits) coupled with the printing of money to finance these deficits. Post–World War I Germany faced billions of dollars in war reparations that crippled the country. The German government found it difficult to collect enough taxes to pay the reparations, and instead it simply printed more money, causing the value of the currency to fall as prices rose. Over time, financial assets in banks and pension accounts became worthless and were essentially taxed away through hyperinflation.

Stopping hyperinflation requires restoring confidence in the government's ability to bring its budget under control. It usually requires a change in government and a new currency, and most important a commitment to reduce the growth of the money supply.

Hyperinflation is an extreme case, yet it shows how inflation can have detrimental effects on an economy. This is why it is important to keep track of inflation, as it is an important measure of the health of an economy.

✓ CHECKPOINT

INFLATION

- Inflation is a measure of the change in the cost of living.
- Inflation is a general rise in prices throughout the economy.
- Disinflation is a reduction in the rate of inflation, and deflation is a decline in overall prices in the economy.
- The CPI is a price index used to measure inflation for urban consumers and is based on a survey of a fixed market basket of goods and services each month.
- The PPI is a price index used to measure price changes for the output of domestic producers.
- The GDP deflator is the broadest measure of inflation and covers all goods and services in GDP.
- Escalator clauses adjust payments (wages, rents, and other payments such as Social Security) to account for inflation.
- Real (adjusted for inflation) values are found by multiplying the nominal (current dollar) values by the ratio of the base year index to the current year index.
- Hyperinflation is an extremely high rate of inflation.

QUESTIONS: Suppose you took out $20,000 in student loans at a fixed interest rate of 5%. Assume that after you graduate, inflation rises significantly as you are paying back your loans. Does this rise in inflation benefit you in paying back your student loans? Who is hurt more from unexpected higher inflation—a borrower or a lender?

Answers to the Checkpoint questions can be found at the end of this chapter.

UNEMPLOYMENT

Unemployment is a phenomenon that affects nearly all workers at some point in their lives. When people become unemployed, the loss of wages often creates hardships on workers and their families. Moreover, the loss of income reduces consumer spending, which can lead to a ripple effect as businesses cut back production, leading to more workers losing their jobs.

A 1946 Census Bureau poster encouraging compliance with the initial unemployment survey.

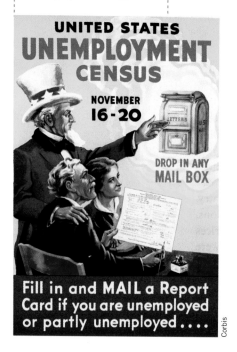

The Historical Record

The Census Bureau began collecting data on wages and earnings in the early 19th century, but it took the Great Depression to focus national attention on the need for consistent data on unemployment rather than specific instances of things such as factory closings. By the 1940s, the Department of Labor began collecting employment data using monthly surveys to get a more detailed picture of the labor force. As the Bureau of Labor Statistics has noted,

To know about unemployment—the extent and nature of the problem—requires information. How many people are unemployed? How did they become unemployed? How long have they been unemployed? Are their numbers growing or declining? Are they men or women? Are they young or old? Are they white or black or of Hispanic origin? Are they skilled or unskilled? Are they the sole support of their families, or do other family members have jobs? Are they more concentrated in one area of the country than another?[1]

Once the BLS has collected and processed the current employment statistics, policymakers use this information to craft economic policies. Before we discuss how these statistics are defined, collected, used, and made accurate, let's briefly look at the historical record of unemployment and its composition.

Figure 2 shows unemployment rates for the last century. Unemployment has varied from a high of 25% of the labor force in the middle of the Great Depression

---

[1] From the BLS Web site.

| FIGURE 2 | A CENTURY OF UNEMPLOYMENT (1916–2016) |

Over the last century, unemployment has varied from a high of 25% of the labor force in the middle of the Great Depression to a low of just over 1% during World War II. Unemployment during the past 50 years has tended to hover around the 5%–6% range.

to a low of just over 1% during World War II. Unemployment during the past 50 years has tended to hover around the 5% to 6% range, although it reached 10% during the 1981–1982 and 2007–2009 recessions.

Table 2 shows a breakdown of unemployment among various groups by gender, race, and education for 1985, 1995, 2005, and 2015. For blacks, unemployment has tended to be more than double the rate of white unemployment, and the unemployment rate for Hispanics has usually exceeded that for whites by roughly 50%. Unemployment for college graduates is consistently low. Roughly half of all unemployment is normally from job losses, but this rose to two-thirds during the 2007–2009 downturn. The next largest group involves people who have not worked in some time and are looking to reenter the labor force. Finally, those people who quit their jobs or are new entrants into the labor force constitute a small percentage of the unemployed.

Now that we have some idea of the composition of the unemployed, let us consider just how these numbers are compiled. First, we need to examine how people get categorized as employed or unemployed.

Defining and Measuring Unemployment

The three major monthly numbers the BLS reports are the size of the labor force, number of people employed, and number unemployed. The unemployment rate is the number of people unemployed divided by the labor force.

Employed People are counted as *employed* if they have done any work at all for pay or profit during the survey week. Regular full-time work, part-time work, and temporary work

TABLE 2	UNEMPLOYMENT RATES BY GENDER, RACE, EDUCATION, OCCUPATION, AND REASON FOR UNEMPLOYMENT, 1985-2015			
Industry	**1985**	**1995**	**2005**	**2015**
Total unemployment	7.2	5.6	5.1	5.3
Gender				
Men	7.0	5.6	5.1	5.4
Women	7.4	5.6	5.1	5.2
Race or Ethnicity				
White	6.2	4.9	4.4	4.6
Black	15.1	10.4	10.0	9.6
Hispanic	10.5	9.3	6.0	6.6
Education				
Less than high school diploma	8.5	9.0	7.6	8.0
High school graduate	5.2	4.8	4.7	5.4
Less than bachelor's degree	4.4	4.0	3.9	4.5
College graduate and higher	2.2	2.4	2.3	2.6
Occupation				
Managerial and professional	3.0	2.2	2.3	2.5
Office and administrative support	5.2	4.3	4.6	4.7
Production occupations	8.8	8.7	6.7	5.7
Reason Why Unemployed				
Job loser	3.6	2.6	2.5	2.6
Job leaver	0.8	0.6	0.6	0.5
Reentrant	2.0	1.9	1.6	1.6
New entrant	0.9	0.4	0.4	0.6

Data from U.S. Department of Labor, Bureau of Labor Statistics (Historical Data Series, CPS Database).

are all included. People who have a job, but are on vacation, ill, having child care problems, on family leave, on strike, prevented from working because of bad weather, or engaged in some family or personal obligation are treated as employed. These people are considered to be employed because they have jobs to return to once their temporary situations have been resolved.

One other group, called *unpaid family workers,* is considered to be employed. These are people who work 15 or more hours a week in a family enterprise; they usually show up in agriculture and retail. Unpaid family workers who work fewer than 15 hours a week are not counted as employed.

Unemployed People are counted as *unemployed* if they do not have a job, but are available for work and have been *actively* seeking work for the previous four weeks. Actively looking for work includes efforts such as responding to online job ads, sending off résumés, scheduling job interviews, visiting school placement centers, and contacting private or public employment agencies.

Note the emphasis on being active in the job search. A *passive* job search that merely involves browsing online employment openings or talking to friends about jobs is not enough to characterize someone as unemployed. One exception involves workers who have been laid off but are expecting to be recalled; they do not need to seek other work to count as being unemployed. Aside from the only other exception—namely, people suffering a temporary illness—individuals must be engaged in a job search to be counted as unemployed.

Labor Force The **labor force** is the total number of those employed and unemployed. The unemployment rate is the number of unemployed divided by the labor force, expressed as a percent.

The measurement of the labor force has important implications for the unemployment rate. To be counted in the labor force, one must either be employed or not employed, but actively seeking work. As a result, a number of groups are not included in the labor force, including full-time students who do not hold jobs, retirees, children under the age of 16, and persons who are institutionalized. If a person within these categories is not working, he or she is not counted in unemployment statistics because he or she is not in the labor force. A discussion of how changes in the labor force affect the unemployment rate appears later in this section.

labor force The total number of those employed and unemployed. The unemployment rate is the number of unemployed divided by the labor force, expressed as a percent.

Monthly Employment Surveys

The Census Bureau and the Department of Labor conduct different surveys to measure employment. The Census Bureau surveys households and the U.S. Department of Labor focuses on the payrolls of businesses and government agencies to produce their monthly reports.

The Household Survey Every month the Census Bureau, as part of the Current Population Survey (CPS), contacts roughly 60,000 households to determine the economic activity of people. The sample is drawn from over 700 geographical areas intended to represent the entire country, including urban and rural areas. The survey includes self-employed workers, unpaid family workers, agricultural workers, private household workers, and workers absent without pay.

The Census Bureau does not directly ask interviewees if they are employed. Rather, it asks a series of questions designed to elicit information that permits the Bureau to determine by its own standards whether people are employed or unemployed and whether they are in the labor force.

The Payroll Survey Officially called the Current Employment Statistics (CES) Survey, the payroll or establishment survey focuses on approximately 146,000 companies and government agencies that are asked how many employees they currently have. If jobs are cut, this survey will immediately show a decrease in the number of employees.

According to the Bureau of Labor Statistics, "Both the payroll and household surveys are needed for a complete picture of the labor market. The payroll survey provides a highly reliable gauge of monthly changes in nonfarm payroll employment. The household survey provides a broader picture of employment including agriculture and the self-employed."[2]

The household survey provides a detailed demographic picture of the labor market and captures entrepreneurial activity missed by the payroll survey. In contrast, the payroll survey provides detailed information by industry and region of the country. Because the payroll survey has a larger sample, it is generally viewed as the most accurate gauge of employment and unemployment changes, but both surveys closely track each other.

---

[2] U.S. Department of Labor, Bureau of Labor Statistics, *Employment from the BLS Household and Payroll Surveys: Summary of Recent Trends*, 2016, http://www.bls.gov.

Employment Trends

The surveys described in the previous section are important measures of employment and unemployment for the country as a whole as well as for individual states and cities included in the surveys. However, investors and economists are interested in trends in employment and how they affect the overall health of the economy. Although major companies are highlighted in the news for their decisions on hiring and laying off workers, the majority of jobs in the country are generated by small and mid-sized companies. These employment decisions fluctuate often, and therefore investors are interested in statistics that might capture these short-term trends.

Weekly Jobs Report One report that has gained increasing attention is the Unemployment Insurance Weekly Claims Report, more commonly referred to as the Weekly Jobs Report, released by the U.S. Department of Labor each Thursday. The Weekly Jobs Report contains an estimate of the number of persons filing for unemployment benefits for the first time, and is used as a way to estimate trends in layoffs and in hiring. Economists are interested in seeing how the weekly data change from week to week. These data provide a more immediate estimate of unemployment than waiting for the monthly survey report.

Relationship Between Employment and the Unemployment Rate People often generalize the negative relationship between employment and the unemployment rate. Although these terms are negatively related, the relationship is not perfect. For example, it is possible for employment to grow and the unemployment rate to increase at the same time. Recall that the unemployment rate measures the number of people unemployed and seeking work divided by the labor force. The important point to highlight here is that the labor force is constantly changing.

The labor force changes for many reasons. For example, the labor force in the United States grows by around 1.5 million persons each year just from population growth (from natural births as well as from immigration). Therefore, even without considering any other factor influencing the labor force, the United States needs to generate numerous new jobs just to keep the unemployment rate steady. Further, people enter and leave the labor force for many reasons—college, retirement, family reasons, or just frustration with the job market. As a result of these factors, the unemployment rate is not perfectly correlated with employment numbers, as we will analyze in greater detail next.

UNEMPLOYMENT INSURANCE WEEKLY CLAIMS REPORT

<u>Seasonally Adjusted Data</u>

In the week ending February 6, the advance figure for seasonally adjusted **initial claims** was 269,000, a decrease of 16,000 from the previous week's level of 285,000. The 4-week moving average was 281,250, a decrease of 3,500 from the previous

---

The Weekly Jobs Report released on February 11, 2016, shows initial unemployment claims of 269,000. Of importance to economists is that the number decreased from the previous week (along with the four-week moving average), suggesting that the employment situation for the United States was improving.

Forbes

U.S. Added 157,000 Jobs In January; Unemployment Rises To 7.9%

Only slightly emboldened by the compromise on tax increases reached in early January, American employers added 157,000 workers last month. The unemployment rate, meantime, climbed slightly to 7.9%, new Labor Department figures show.

This headline from *Forbes* (February 2, 2013) appears odd because the unemployment rate in January 2013 rose despite many jobs being created. This occurred because the labor force increased as more people began looking for work again.

Problems With Unemployment Statistics

Analyzing issues as complex and personal as employment, unemployment, and job seeking can be expected to generate its share of criticism. When the Department of Labor announces its results each month, commentators often note that these numbers understate unemployment, because they do not include chronically unemployed workers who have grown so frustrated and discouraged that they have dropped out of the labor force. Media pundits agonize over the plight of discouraged workers or the underemployed while discussing the impact of the latest numbers on the stock market.

How unemployment is measured depends on the intended use of the resulting measurements. Various uses for unemployment statistics include (1) gauging the state of the economy, (2) determining the divergence of supply and demand in labor markets, and (3) assessing the distribution of unemployment and the extent to which people are suffering from being out of work. In the United States, most unemployment statistics have been developed to gauge the state of the economy. The Bureau of Labor Statistics does, however, publish data about underemployment, discouraged workers, and other marginally attached workers.

Underemployment and Marginally Attached Workers It is not uncommon for people to take jobs that do not fully use their skills. In the early 1990s, many engineers and skilled workers who were employed in the defense industry saw their careers fall apart with the collapse of the Soviet Union. The "peace dividend" most people enjoyed generated excess supplies in defense-related labor markets. In the early 2000s, the collapse of many Internet start-ups and telecommunications firms eliminated the jobs of many highly skilled workers. The 2007–2009 recession caused by the collapse of the housing market and the subsequent financial crisis put large numbers of construction, real estate, and Wall Street workers out of work.

As a result of these shake-ups, many people were unable to find jobs that enabled them to duplicate their past standards of living. These **underemployed workers** were forced to take jobs that did not fully—or in some cases, even remotely—use their education, background, or skills. Many underemployed workers took temporary or part-time jobs to earn income to supplement their unemployment benefits (each state has different limits on how much income can be earned while receiving unemployment benefits) or gave up their unemployment benefits altogether if the temporary or part-time work paid well. For example, in recent years, many people who lost their jobs became Uber drivers or Airbnb hosts, because these are flexible jobs that allow one to earn income while searching for permanent work.

Another common situation that occurs during economic downturns is that people give up looking for work altogether. The Department of Labor categorizes those who were available for work and actively looked for it during the last 12 months, but *not* in the last 4 weeks, as **marginally attached workers.** Marginally attached workers are not counted in the official unemployment statistics, because they are not considered part of the labor force.

The reasons that people stop looking for work vary, but the most common reason is a person's belief that there simply aren't any good jobs available, and he or she consequently gives up looking for work until the labor market improves. This portion of marginally attached workers is called **discouraged workers.** The deeper the recession, the more discouraged workers there will be. Other reasons for being marginally attached include giving up the search for work due to family responsibilities or transportation problems.

Today, the Census Bureau asks other questions of respondents to determine whether they fit into the categories of a discouraged worker, other marginally attached worker, or underemployed worker. These data are then reported by the Bureau of Labor Statistics to provide a more comprehensive analysis of the employment situation. Figure 3 shows a breakdown of unemployed, discouraged, other marginally attached, and underemployed (measured by those working part-time who would prefer full-time employment) workers over the past 15 years, using the measurements defined by the Department of Labor as U-3 (the official unemployment rate), U-4, U-5, and U-6, respectively. Discouraged workers and other marginally attached workers each increase unemployment rates by a small amount, but those working part-time (underemployment) increase the overall unemployment rate the most. Adding together all these categories (U-6) nearly doubles the unemployment rate.

Other countries have different definitions of actively seeking work, classifying individuals engaged in passive job searches as unemployed. Notably, Canada and Europe have more relaxed search standards than the United States.

underemployed workers Workers who are forced to take jobs that do not fully utilize their education, background, or skills. Underemployed workers often hold part-time jobs.

marginally attached workers Workers who were available for work and actively looked for it during the last 12 months, but not in the last 4 weeks.

discouraged workers Discouraged workers are the portion of marginally attached workers who have given up actively looking for work and, as a result, are not counted as unemployed.

AROUND THE WORLD

The Boom and Bust of Dickinson, North Dakota

How did the expansion of the oil industry affect prices and employment in Dickinson, and how quickly did it unravel?

Courtesy Dickinson Convention & Visitors Bureau

From 2010 to 2013, when much of the United States was recovering from a severe recession, one town experienced a boom. High school graduates without specialized skills were earning six-figure salaries, and even fast-food workers were making double the minimum wage and receiving hiring bonuses. At the same time, prices in this small city were rising rapidly, especially for housing which couldn't keep up with the pace of new workers arriving in search of jobs and higher wages.

How did this small remote city in western North Dakota experience such a rapid rise and subsequent bust?

Dickinson is not an easy city to spot on a map, nor one that is easy to get to, being over 500 miles from the nearest major airport hub. But because of its proximity to the Bakken Formation, one of the largest oil and natural gas deposits in North America, Dickinson became a destination for workers across the country seeking lucrative job opportunities that were readily available, created by the high price of oil which kept the industry very profitable.

Although jobs were seemingly endless and unemployment practically nonexistent, the boom led to shortages of goods and services, es-

pecially housing, which couldn't keep up with demand due to the city's remote location. As a result, prices rose significantly in Dickinson and in other towns in the region. Anecdotal evidence of high inflation abounded as Dickinson residents paid rents that would be more expected in Los Angeles than in North Dakota, and where in a trip to a grocery store one might encounter prices that resemble those of a convenience store.

But alas, the boom of Dickinson would not last. As oil prices plummeted by over 60% from 2014 to 2016, oil drilling in North Dakota was no longer profitable for many companies. As a result, most drilling rigs were abandoned, resulting in rising unemployment that forced many newly arrived residents to pack up again and leave. The silver lining for residents of Dickinson is that prices fell, making living in the remote western region of North Dakota affordable once again.

GO TO **LaunchPad** TO PRACTICE THE ECONOMIC CONCEPTS IN THIS STORY

FIGURE 3 | **UNEMPLOYMENT CATEGORIES (2000–2015)**

Janusz Kapusta/Illustration Source

- Unemployment rate + discouraged + other marginally attached + part-time (U-6)
- Unemployment rate + discouraged + other marginally attached (U-5)
- Unemployment rate + discouraged workers (U-4)
- Unemployment rate (U-3)

Percent (%) — Year

The Department of Labor categorizes unemployment into those unemployed and still actively seeking work, those who are discouraged (not looked for work in the last 4 weeks), those who are marginally attached for other reasons (have looked for work in the past 12 months, but not in the last 4 weeks due to, for example, family issues or transportation problems), and those working part-time but who would prefer full-time work. The categories U-3 (the official unemployment rate), U-4, U-5, and U-6 correspond to the sum of these respective categories.

CHECKPOINT

UNEMPLOYMENT

- People are counted as employed if they are at least 16 years old, not institutionalized, and have worked for pay or profit during the survey week.

- People are unemployed if they do not have a job, but are available for work and have been actively seeking work for the previous four weeks.

- The labor force is the sum of the employed and unemployed. The unemployment rate is the number of unemployed divided by the labor force.

- The official unemployment rate statistics do not account for underemployed, discouraged, and other marginally attached workers.

QUESTIONS: Does it seem reasonable to require that to be counted as unemployed, a person must be actively seeking work? Why not just count those who do not have a job but indicate they would like to work?

Answers to the Checkpoint questions can be found at the end of this chapter.

UNEMPLOYMENT AND THE ECONOMY

Inevitably, our economy will contain some unemployment. People who are reentering the workforce or entering it for the first time will often find that landing a new job can take some time. Then they may find, moreover, that taking the first available job is not always in their best interest—that it might be better to take the time to search for another position better matching their skills and personality. Getting information and searching more extensively can extend the period people remain unemployed.

Unemployment can occur because wages are artificially set above the market clearing or equilibrium wage. Both minimum wage laws and union bargaining can have this effect, helping those workers who are employed to earn more, but shutting some potential workers out of jobs.

Employers often keep wages above market equilibrium to reduce turnover (and training costs), boost morale, and increase employee productivity. These *efficiency wages* give employees an incentive to work hard and remain with their present employers, because at other jobs they could earn only market wages. These higher wages, however, can also prevent employers from hiring additional workers, thus contributing to unemployment.

Changes in the business cycle will also generate unemployment. When the economy falls into a recession, sales decline, and employers are forced to lay off workers; therefore, unemployment grows.

Separating different types of unemployment into distinct categories will help us apply unemployment figures to our analysis of the economy.

Types of Unemployment

There are three types of unemployment: frictional, structural, and cyclical. Each type has different policy ramifications.

Frictional Unemployment Do you recall how many different part-time jobs you held during high school? How about summer jobs while in college? If you have worked several types of jobs, you're not alone, as many reasons exist why one may leave a job. You may get bored; the business may close or reduce the staff it needs; you might move to a new city; or you could have been fired. If you're enrolled in school while working part-time jobs, generally you are not considered unemployed while between jobs, because being in school generally means you're not counted in the labor force. But the reasons for changing jobs are still relevant once you graduate and work full-time.

As you pursue your career, chances are that you'll work for more than one company during your lifetime. **Frictional unemployment** describes the short-term duration of unemployment caused by workers switching jobs, often voluntarily, for a variety of reasons. Some workers quit

frictional unemployment
Unemployment resulting from workers who voluntarily quit their jobs to search for better positions, or are moving to new jobs but may still take several days or weeks before they can report to their new employers.

their jobs to search for better positions. In some cases, these people may already have other jobs, but it may still take several days or weeks before they can report to their new employers. In these cases, people moving from one job to the next are said to be frictionally unemployed.

Frictional unemployment is natural for any economy and, indeed, necessary and beneficial. People need time to search for new jobs, and employers need time to interview and evaluate potential new employees. The Internet has helped to facilitate job searches by expanding access to information; still, frictional unemployment will always exist.

Structural Unemployment Another naturally occurring phenomenon in an economy is **structural unemployment.** Whereas frictional unemployment is assumed to be of rather short duration, structural unemployment is usually associated with extended periods of unemployment.

Structural unemployment is caused by changes in the structure of consumer demands or technology. Many industries and products inevitably decline and become obsolete, and when they do, the skills honed by workers in these industries often become obsolete as well.

Declining demand for cigarettes, for instance, has changed the labor market for tobacco workers. Farm work, textile finishing, and many aspects of manufacturing have all changed drastically in the last several decades. Farms have become more productive, and many sewing and manufacturing jobs have moved overseas because of lower wages there.

People who are structurally unemployed are often unemployed for long periods and then some become discouraged workers.

To find new work, those who are structurally unemployed must often go through extended periods of retraining. But ultimately, the new skills learned make workers more productive in a changing labor market, which make production more efficient. Displaced workers with more education are more likely to retrain easily and adjust to a new occupation. For that reason, governments often provide assistance to workers seeking new skills or more education. One benefit of a growing economy is that retraining is more easily obtained when labor markets are tight.

Cyclical Unemployment Cyclical unemployment is the result of changes in the business cycle. If, for example, business investment or consumer spending declines, we would expect the rate of economic growth to slow, in which case the economy would probably enter a recession, as we will examine in later chapters. Cyclical unemployment is the difference between the current unemployment rate and what it would be at full employment, defined below.

Frictional and structural unemployment are difficult problems, and macroeconomic policies provide only limited relief. Cyclical unemployment, most economists agree, is where public policymakers can have their greatest impact. By keeping the economy on a steady, low-inflationary, solid growth path, policymakers can minimize the costs of cyclical unemployment. Admittedly, this is easier said than done given the various shocks (such as a sharp decline in consumer spending) that can affect the economy.

Defining Full Employment

Economists often describe the health of the economy by comparing its performance to *full employment.* We know full employment cannot be zero unemployment, because frictional and structural unemployment will always be present. Full employment today is generally taken to be equivalent to the natural rate of unemployment.

The Natural Rate of Unemployment The **natural rate of unemployment** has come to represent several ideas to economists. First, it is often defined as that level of unemployment at which price and wage decisions are consistent—a level at which the actual inflation rate is equal to people's inflationary expectations. The natural rate of unemployment

---

structural unemployment

Unemployment caused by changes in the structure of consumer demands or technology. It means that demand for some products declines and the skills of this industry's workers often become obsolete as well. This results in an extended bout of unemployment while new skills are developed.

Music stores selling CDs are a dying breed as consumers buy most of their music online, causing structural unemployment in CD manufacturing and in the music retail industry.

cyclical unemployment

Unemployment that results from changes in the business cycle, and where public policymakers can have their greatest impact by keeping the economy on a steady, low-inflationary, solid growth path.

natural rate of unemployment

The level of unemployment at which price and wage decisions are consistent; a level at which the actual inflation rate is equal to people's inflationary expectations and where cyclical unemployment is zero.

is also considered to be the unemployment level at which unemployment is only frictional and structural, or alternatively, when cyclical unemployment is zero.

Economists often refer to the natural rate of unemployment as the *nonaccelerating inflation rate of unemployment* (NAIRU), defined as the unemployment rate most consistent with a low rate of inflation. It is the unemployment level at which inflationary pressures in the economy are at their minimum. We will discuss these issues in greater detail throughout the remainder of the book. For now, it is enough to remember that the NAIRU is the unemployment rate consistent with low inflation and low unemployment.

Full employment, or the natural rate of unemployment, is determined by such institutional factors as the presence or absence of employment agencies and their effectiveness. Many job seekers today, for example, search online postings on sites such as Indeed or LinkedIn, reducing the time it takes to match available employees with prospective employers. Other factors might include the demographic makeup of the labor force and the incentives associated with various unemployment benefit programs and income tax rates.

Changes in the Unemployment Rate Around the Natural Rate In the previous chapter, we studied how the business cycle leads to both periods of high economic growth and periods of recessions, fluctuating around a long-term trend. The unemployment rate follows a similar pattern, rising during recessions and falling during economic booms, but fluctuating around the natural rate of unemployment. In the United States, the natural rate of unemployment is very steady and has fallen slowly over the past 30 years from about 6% to between 5 and 5.5% largely due to improvements in labor market efficiencies (such as the use of the Internet in job searches and the increase in part-time and temporary work) that has reduced the unemployment rate associated with low inflation.

Of particular importance is the length of time it takes the unemployment rate to return to the natural rate when recessions push unemployment higher. To analyze this point, Figure 4 shows the unemployment rate over the past 50 years, along with the natural rate. Periods of recession are shaded, most indicating cyclical unemployment as the unemployment rate line rises above the natural rate. It is interesting to note that the time it takes the unemployment rate to return to the natural rate varies. In most economic recoveries prior to 1990, the unemployment rate returned to the natural rate fairly quickly. The 1990–1991 and 2001 recessions did not produce much cyclical unemployment; however, the unemployment rate initially rose during the recovery, leading to a

| FIGURE 4 | UNEMPLOYMENT RATE VERSUS THE NATURAL RATE OF UNEMPLOYMENT |

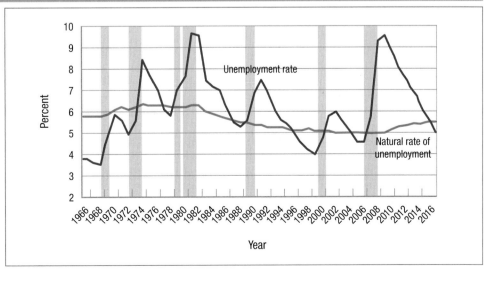

The average unemployment rate and the natural rate of unemployment are shown from 1966 to 2016. Periods of recession are shaded. The rising unemployment line and flatter downward slopes following the last three recessions indicate a longer recovery period for jobs caused by a jobless recovery.

"jobless recovery." But the longest jobless recovery occurred after the 2007–2009 recession, in which the unemployment rate stayed well above the natural rate for several years.

Jobless Recoveries Prolong Unemployment Above the Natural Rate The previous chapter discussed some of the reasons why unemployment can stay high for so long after a recession is deemed over. It highlighted the four key markets—labor, financial, capital, and output—that influence one another and affect job growth. But the fact that economic growth does not always coincide with job growth deserves an explanation.

In the labor market, recessions tend to send people looking for other options—going back to college, seeking early retirement, or just taking time off until the economy improves. Some who are out of work during these periods take temporary or part-time jobs to support their loved ones until better work can be found. Although all of these people's jobs were affected, the government does not consider them as unemployed, because they had either found temporary work or had left the labor force to pursue other options. Thus, the official unemployment rate reported during recessions tends to underestimate the actual number of people seeking work, a problem discussed in the previous section.

 ISSUE

Why Do Unemployment Rates Differ So Much Within the United States?

In December 2015, the U.S. unemployment rate was 5.0%. However, in New Mexico it was 6.7%. Meanwhile, in North Dakota, it was only 2.7%. Looking at metropolitan area unemployment rates reveals even starker differences. The unemployment rate in El Centro, California, was 19.6%, while in Ames, Iowa, it was 2.2%. Why do such large differences in unemployment exist between states and between cities?

In Europe, where citizens of the European Union are free to live and work in any other country within the union, differences in unemployment rates between member countries remain largely due to cultural reasons. People are hesitant to move to a country where people speak a different language or have a different culture. But in the United States, language and cultural differences between states are considerably less than between European countries—English is the primary language and Americans all basically watch the same types of movies and television shows.

Aside from the common language and culture, differences do arise in other areas, which helps to explain the differences in unemployment rate.

First, differences in taxes and regulations exist between states. Some states have lower taxes than others, and some

The college town of Ames, Iowa, home of Iowa State University, had virtually no unemployment in 2015.

The farming community of El Centro, California, near the southern border with Mexico, had the highest unemployment rate in the nation in 2015.

states have environmental and work rules that are more business friendly than others.

Second, many industries tend to form a cluster in order to take advantage of economies of scale and scope. For example, industrial agglomeration in the computer industry centers in greater San Jose ("Silicon Valley"). Detroit has long been the automobile capital of the country, while Gary, Indiana, was once a major steel-producing town (in addition to being the birthplace of Michael Jackson). Economic trends tend to favor some industries over others. Biotechnology, eCommerce, and health care industries have experienced much growth over the past decade, leading to employment growth in cities home to these industries. However, declines in

manufacturing and the recent collapse of the oil industry have increased unemployment in cities heavily dependent on those industries for employment.

Finally, and perhaps most obvious, people prefer certain geographic areas to others. Significant population growth has occurred in the South and Mountain West, where warm weather and scenic beauty await, respectively. Many immigrants from Mexico prefer living in states bordering Mexico for cultural reasons. And throughout much of the past century, people have moved from rural areas to urban areas. How much would you sacrifice to live in a preferred area? People ask themselves this question often.

During an economic recovery, as jobs are being created, not only do the unemployed seek these jobs, but also many of those who had left the labor force return to compete for these same jobs. When many would-be workers choose to leave the workforce during a prolonged economic downturn, competition for jobs can be more severe during an economic recovery when these workers return to the labor force.

The last few recessions saw many people temporarily leave the workforce to pursue nonwork options such as schooling, stay-at-home parenting, or volunteer work. These choices may explain why unemployment is slow to fall during economic recoveries, and one of the major reasons why jobless recoveries might remain a feature in future recessions.

Inflation, employment, unemployment, and gross domestic product (GDP) are the key macroeconomic indicators of our economic health. Our rising standards of living are closely tied to GDP growth. In the next chapter, we will investigate what causes our economy and living standards to grow over the long term.

 CHECKPOINT

UNEMPLOYMENT AND THE ECONOMY

- Frictional unemployment is inevitable and natural for any economy as people change jobs and businesses open and close.
- Structural unemployment is typically caused by changes in consumer demands or technology. It is typically of long duration and often requires that the unemployed become retrained for new jobs.
- Cyclical unemployment is the result of changes in the business cycle. When a recession hits, unemployment rises, then falls when an expansion ensues.
- Macroeconomic policies have the most effect on cyclical unemployment.
- Full employment is typically defined as that level at which cyclical unemployment is zero or that level associated with a low nonaccelerating inflation rate.

QUESTION: The financial industry experienced a rapid expansion in the middle of the last decade as a result of the housing bubble, which created jobs for millions of workers in banks, mortgage companies, financial advising companies, and insurance companies. When the bubble burst, many of these workers became unemployed as the financial industry retrenched. For many, their skills were so specialized that they were unable to find new jobs at their old salaries. Were these people frictionally, structurally, or cyclically unemployed? Explain.

Answers to the Checkpoint questions can be found at the end of this chapter.

chapter summary

Section 1 Inflation

Inflation is a general rise in prices throughout the economy. Prices for individual goods can fluctuate up or down, but the price level captures the overall trend in the movement of prices.

Market Basket

Price Level

$P_a\uparrow$ $P_e\downarrow$ $P_b\downarrow$ $P_f\uparrow$ $P_c\uparrow$ $P_g\downarrow$ $P_d\uparrow$

17.1 How Inflation Is Measured

- **Consumer price index (CPI):** An index of the average change in prices of a market basket of consumer goods and services.

- **Producer price index (PPI):** An index of the average change in prices received by producers for their output.

- **GDP deflator:** The broadest index used to measure inflation; it includes the prices of all goods and services in the economy.

17.2 Calculating Inflation Using the CPI

CPI = (Cost in current period) ÷ (Cost in base period) × 100

Example: Suppose a market basket consists of pizza and soda

Base year prices: Pizza = $6 and Soda = $2
Current year prices: Pizza = $8 and Soda = $3

CPI = ($8 + $3) ÷ ($6 + $2) × 100 = 137.5
(average prices rose 37.5% since the base year)

Yekophotostudio/ Dreamstime.com

17.3 The Main Causes of Inflation

- **Strong consumer demand:** Consumers spend more money, demand increases, and prices rise.

- **Supply shocks on key inputs:** When prices for goods with inelastic demand (such as food or oil) rise, the higher prices are passed on to other industries and to consumers.

- **Government printing money:** The government prints money to finance its borrowing, more money is chasing a relatively fixed amount of goods and services, and therefore prices rise.

Melanie Blanding/Alamy

A severe drought in the summer of 2012 pushed corn prices higher, leading to higher prices for many goods.

17.4 Disinflation Versus Deflation

Disinflation occurs when the rate of inflation falls, but is still positive.

Deflation occurs when the rate of inflation turns negative.

Hyperinflation is an extremely high rate of inflation. It typically is caused by excess government spending over tax revenues (high deficits) and the printing of money to finance deficits.

PHOTOCOPYING SERVICES PRICE LIST

A4 SINGLE SIDE	2 000 000 - 00
A4 BOTH SIDE	3 000 000 - 00
Ids/PASSPORTS	3 000 000 - 00
A3 SINGLE SIDE	6 000 000 - 00
A3 BOTH SIDE	10 000 000 - 00
Lamination	25 000 000 - 00
Spiral Binding (minimum)	45 000 000 - 00

Eric Chiang

A price list of photocopying services in Zimbabwe in 2008 during hyperinflation.

Section 2 Unemployment

The **labor force** is the total number of people employed or unemployed. **Employed** persons are individuals age 16 and over who work for pay, whether full-time, part-time, or even temporary. **Unemployed** persons are those without jobs but actively seeking work.

17.5

```
        Civilian Population (non-institutionalized)
                    ↓              ↓
              Labor Force    Not In Labor Force
                ↓       ↓
           Employed    Unemployed
```

If you work part-time at the local coffee shop after graduation while looking for a good job, you are not unemployed. Instead, you are underemployed, which still is considered employed.

17.6 Who Are NOT Considered in the Labor Force?

- **Discouraged workers** are the portion of marginally attached workers who have given up looking for work because they believe there are not enough good jobs.
- Marginally attached workers are those who have looked for work in the past 12 months but not in the last 4 weeks.
- Students who do not work are not counted in the labor force.
- Retired persons and children under 16 are not counted in the labor force.
- Institutionalized persons including persons in prison also are not counted in the labor force.

Section 3 Unemployment and the Economy

17.7 Types of Unemployment

- **Frictional unemployment:** Includes workers who voluntarily quit their jobs in search of better positions, or recent graduates seeking their first full-time job.
- **Structural unemployment:** Longer-term unemployment that is caused by changes in consumer demands or technology, and requires workers to be retrained for a career in another industry.
- **Cyclical unemployment:** Unemployment that results from the business cycle—when a recession hits, firms lay off workers until the economy recovers.

17.8 The **natural rate of unemployment** or **nonaccelerating inflation rate of unemployment (NAIRU)** is the rate of unemployment that exists when prices and wages are equal to people's expectations. At the natural rate of unemployment, the economy is at "full employment."

Natural rate of unemployment = Frictional + Structural Unemployment

The natural rate of unemployment is very stable in the United States, at around 5% to 6%.

35mm film is hardly ever used anymore, and has led to structural unemployment as workers in the 35mm film industry find new employment.

inflation, p. 452
price level, p. 454
disinflation, p. 454
deflation, p. 454
consumer price index (CPI), p. 454
producer price index (PPI), p. 455

GDP deflator, p. 456
hyperinflation, p. 458
labor force, p. 463
underemployed workers, p. 465
marginally attached workers, p. 465
discouraged workers, p. 465

frictional unemployment, p. 467
structural unemployment, p. 468
cyclical unemployment, p. 468
natural rate of unemployment,
    p. 468

QUESTIONS AND PROBLEMS

Check Your Understanding

1. Describe the three common indices used to measure inflation and the focus of each one.

2. Who loses from unanticipated inflation? Who benefits?

3. Describe the possible losses to our society and the economy when people are unemployed.

4. What is required for a person to be considered unemployed? How is the unemployment rate computed?

5. Why do teenagers and young people have high unemployment rates?

6. Describe the three types of unemployment. What types of government programs would be most effective in combating each type of unemployment?

Apply the Concepts

7. You have several student loans that have interest rates that change every year. After graduation, you can consolidate these loans into a fixed-rate single loan. You can consolidate now or one year from now. How do your expectations of the inflation rate during the next year affect your decision regarding when to consolidate?

8. Suppose you work hard at a job after graduation and after your first year, your effort is rewarded with a 3% raise when the average wage increase in your company is 2%. Then, the government releases its inflation report which states inflation is running at 5%. Given this information, did your standard of living improve? Why or why not?

9. Since 1987, the U.S. population has grown 32%, while employment has increased by 39%. Further, the number of people unemployed has risen by 3%. Are all of these indicators a sign of a strong or weak labor market over the past two decades?

10. Assume you just lost your job and have decided to take a month-long break to travel to Europe before looking for a new position. Just as you return home from your trip, you are interviewed by the Department of Labor about your employment status. How would you be classified (employed, unemployed, or not in the labor force)? Explain why.

11. The Bureau of Labor Statistics categorizes unemployed people into several groups, including job leavers, job losers, and discouraged workers. During a mild recession, which group would tend to increase the most? During a deep recession? During a boom?

12. In the beginning of a recovery after a recession, employment begins to rise and the news media report these data on job growth. Would such a report have an impact on the labor force? Would it affect the unemployment rate?

In The News

13. A debate that regularly occurs in Congress concerns raising the debt ceiling, allowing the U.S. government to continue paying its obligations. A few years ago, one politician

proposed that instead of raising the debt ceiling, the U.S. Treasury should just mint a trillion dollar coin and use it to "pay off" the federal deficit. If such a coin were to be minted, what would be its potential effects on inflation? Is this a risk-free way of paying off a fiscal deficit? Why or why not?

14. Federal unemployment benefits were extended in 2013, allowing unemployed workers to receive up to 73 weeks of benefits depending on the unemployment rate in each state. This is an extension of a program that at its peak during the last recession offered up to a maximum of 99 weeks of unemployment benefits. How does extending the federal unemployment benefit program influence the unemployment rate?

Solving Problems

15. Suppose the country of Snowland uses the following market basket of goods to determine its consumer price index, with Year 1 being the base year with a CPI of 100. Nominal GDP is also provided.

Market basket items	Year 1	Year 2	Year 3	Year 4
Loaf of bread	$2.50	$2.80	$3.00	$3.10
Movie ticket	$8.00	$8.80	$9.20	$9.50
Gallon of gasoline	$3.50	$4.20	$4.00	$3.60
Scented candle	$12.00	$13.20	$14.00	$14.30
Nominal GDP	$5 billion	$5.6 billion	$6.1 billion	$6.5 billion

a. Calculate the CPI in Snowland for each year, using Year 1 as the base year with CPI = 100.

b. Calculate the rate of inflation (based on CPI) in Year 2, Year 3, and Year 4.

c. Using the CPI, calculate the real GDP in each of the four years.

d. Between Year 1 and Year 4, what proportion of the total increase in nominal GDP was due to inflation?

16. The town of Villageton has 500 residents, of which 300 are employed, 30 are not working but actively seeking work, 80 are children in school, 40 are retirees, 30 are full-time college students, and 20 are institutionalized.

a. Calculate the unemployment rate in Villageton.

b. Suppose that 10 of the 30 college students graduate and enter the labor force actively seeking work, but only 5 find a job. How does this change the unemployment rate in Villageton?

USING THE NUMBERS

17. Using By the Numbers, describe the change in the average price of public college tuition and private college tuition relative to the overall change in prices based on CPI. Has a college education become more or less affordable in real terms?

18. By approximately what percentage did average housing prices increase from 2001 to the peak in 2006? By what percentage did average housing prices fall from the peak in 2006 to the bottom point in 2012?

Checkpoint: Inflation 460

Inflation makes the value of a dollar fall in purchasing power. Therefore, if you borrow money when inflation is low and pay back the loan when inflation is higher, the money you are paying back is worth less than what you received. You benefit by being able to pay back your loans with money that is valued at less than before. Thus, unexpected inflation hurts lenders because the money they are being paid back is worth less in purchasing power than they had planned. Alternatively, had the inflation rate unexpectedly fallen, lenders would gain, as the money being paid back would be worth more in purchasing power than was expected.

Checkpoint: Unemployment 467

The reason for the requirement that a person actively seek work is to differentiate empirically those who profess to want a job (at possibly a higher wage than they can earn in the market) from those who are actively trying to obtain work.

Checkpoint: Unemployment and the Economy 471

Many workers became structurally unemployed because the skills they had acquired for the financial industry (and in many cases, specific to the housing industry) were not as useful in other industries. Therefore, as the financial industry became smaller after the housing bubble burst, many workers needed to find work in other industries, which required learning a new skills set.

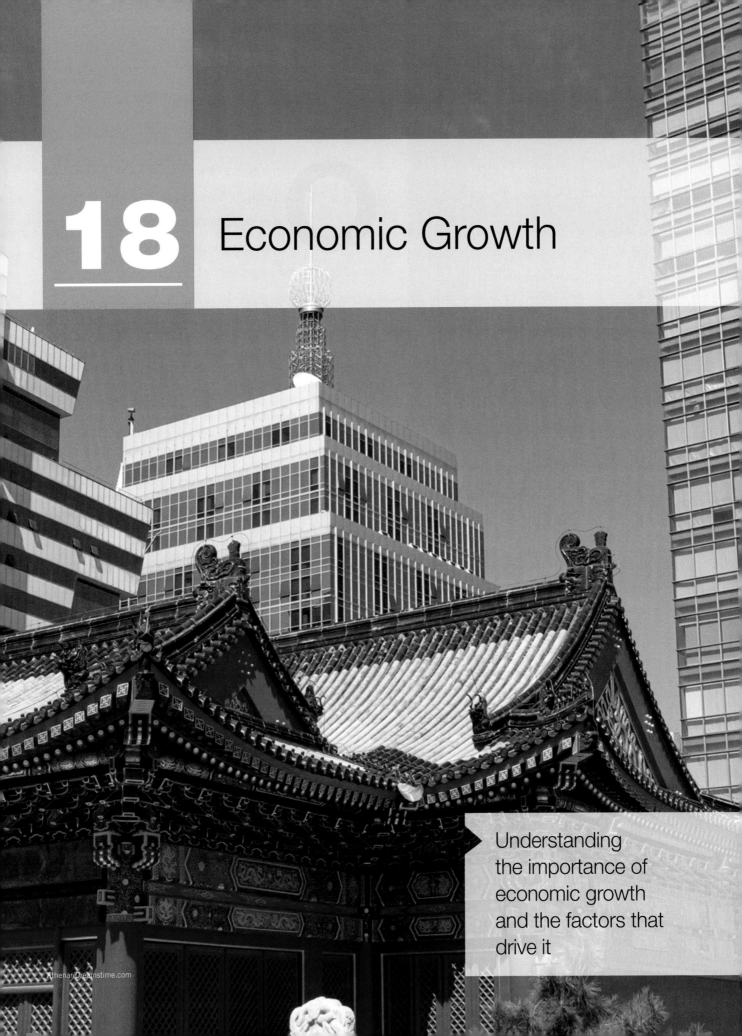

18 Economic Growth

Understanding the importance of economic growth and the factors that drive it

Learning Objectives

18.1 Describe how economic growth is measured using real GDP and real GDP per capita.

18.2 Use the Rule of 70 to approximate the number of years it takes for an economy's output to double in size.

18.3 Explain the power of compounding in making small differences much larger over time.

18.4 Explain the difference between short-run and long-run growth.

18.5 List the four factors of production and how each plays a role in the production function.

18.6 Discuss the factors that increase productivity and economic growth.

18.7 Explain total factor productivity and what it measures.

18.8 Explain how the government promotes economic growth through the provision of physical capital and the enhancement of human capital and technology.

18.9 Discuss how strong institutions and economic freedom facilitates economic growth.

O n a typical downtown street in Beijing in the 1980s, one would see thousands of bicycles and pedestrians among a trickling of cars owned by the privileged few. The skyline consisted of just a few large buildings.

How times have changed. Today, the bicycles in Beijing have largely been replaced with cars driven by millions of Chinese (now the world's largest consumers of cars) whose incomes have increased enough to afford one, the skyline is dominated by modern skyscrapers, and the pedestrians have largely moved underground, traveling on one of the world's most extensive and modern subway systems.

China's transformation from a poor, agricultural nation to an emerging world power with a growing middle and upper class has been remarkable. China's annual growth rate has averaged 9% over the past 20 years, compared to the average U.S. annual growth rate of 2% over the same period. Although a 7% difference might not seem significant, over 20 years the cumulative growth effect is staggering: China's real GDP grew 521% from 1995 to 2015, while in the United States, real GDP grew 62%.

Economic growth plays a very powerful role in how people live and how standards of living change over time. Even small differences in growth rates turn into large differences in the long run.

One generation ago, the United States, Europe, and the East Asian economies of Japan, Singapore, South Korea, Taiwan, and Hong Kong were the leaders of economic growth. These countries had consistent, strong growth, while the rest of the world lagged behind.

Today, a much different picture emerges. Some developing countries are experiencing the highest rates of growth, while those in the developed world have seen slower growth rates, especially in the aftermath of the devastating financial crisis and recession of 2007–2009.

During the 2000s, much of the world's global economic growth was concentrated in the BRIC countries: *Brazil, Russia, India,* and *China.* These countries transformed from developing economies to more advanced economies, and by doing so achieved a remarkable feat: In 2015 all four countries were among the ten largest economies in the world, measured by GDP.

Chang'an Avenue, Beijing (1981)

Dean Conger/Corbis

Chang'an Avenue, Beijing (2011)

TAO Images Limited/Alamy Stock Photo

Why Should We Care About Economic Growth?

Economic growth improves the standard of living of people through higher incomes and greater access to societal resources such as health care and clean water, which generally lead to a longer and healthier life.

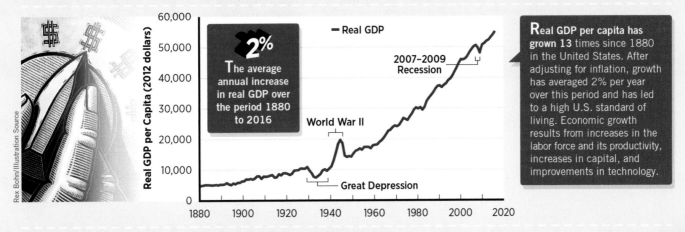

2% The average annual increase in real GDP over the period 1880 to 2016

— Real GDP

2007–2009 Recession

World War II

Great Depression

Real GDP per Capita (2012 dollars)

Real GDP per capita has grown **13** times since 1880 in the United States. After adjusting for inflation, growth has averaged 2% per year over this period and has led to a high U.S. standard of living. Economic growth results from increases in the labor force and its productivity, increases in capital, and improvements in technology.

Rex Bohn/Illustration Source

Country	GDP in 2015	Real GDP Growth (2004–14)	Real GDP Growth (2015)
United States	$17.4 trillion	+17% (1.58%/year)	+2.4%
China	$10.3 trillion	+159% (9.98%/year)	+6.9%
Japan	$4.6 trillion	+6% (0.58%/year)	+0.6%
Germany	$3.8 trillion	+13% (1.23%/year)	+1.5%
United Kingdom	$2.9 trillion	+14% (1.32%/year)	+2.2%
France	$2.8 trillion	+9% (0.87%/year)	+1.1%
Brazil	$2.3 trillion	+40% (3.42%/year)	−3.7%
Italy	$2.1 trillion	−5% (−1.58%/year)	+0.7%
India	$2.0 trillion	+109% (7.65%/year)	+7.2%
Russia	$1.8 trillion	+39% (3.35%/year)	−3.8%

Go to 🎓 **LaunchPad** *to use the latest data to recreate this graph.*

Average Life Expectancy (2015)

Japan · Switzerland · South Korea · Ireland · United States · Norway · Egypt · Brazil · Bolivia · India · Zambia · Chad

GDP per Capita (thousands of U.S. dollars)

Olivier Asselin/Alamy

Economic growth can lead to higher average life expectancies. Residents of rich countries generally live longer than residents of poor countries.

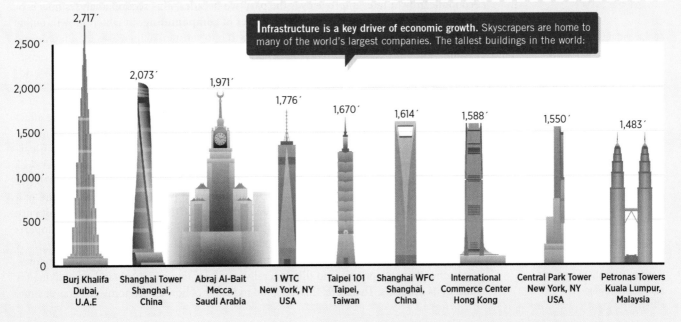

Infrastructure is a key driver of economic growth. Skyscrapers are home to many of the world's largest companies. The tallest buildings in the world:

Building	Height
Burj Khalifa, Dubai, U.A.E	2,717′
Shanghai Tower, Shanghai, China	2,073′
Abraj Al-Bait, Mecca, Saudi Arabia	1,971′
1 WTC, New York, NY, USA	1,776′
Taipei 101, Taipei, Taiwan	1,670′
Shanghai WFC, Shanghai, China	1,614′
International Commerce Center, Hong Kong	1,588′
Central Park Tower, New York, NY, USA	1,550′
Petronas Towers, Kuala Lumpur, Malaysia	1,483′

But rapid growth in any country cannot be maintained forever. Although India continued to maintain a high growth rate of over 7% in 2016, China's economy has slowed in recent years, from an average annual growth rate of nearly 10% just a few years ago to less than 7% in 2016. Even worse, Russia's and Brazil's economy both entered into recessions in 2015—Russia largely due to the significant drop in oil prices that affected the entire economy, and Brazil due to the fall in prices of other commodities such as coffee, sugar, and metals.

Meanwhile, growth in the United States continues at a slow pace, averaging around 2% per year. Where, then, are today's beacons of growth? They are concentrated in developing countries in Africa and Central/South Asia, including Ethiopia, Turkmenistan, Myanmar, and Ivory Coast, all of which are growing faster than China and India. This bodes well for bringing many more people out of poverty, just as the BRIC countries have done over the past decade.

This chapter focuses on long-term economic growth and describes the conditions needed to sustain economic growth and improve standards of living. In the long run, all variables in the economy can adjust to changing conditions. The models in this chapter provide a framework for evaluating policies meant to encourage economic growth in the long run.

WHY IS ECONOMIC GROWTH IMPORTANT?

economic growth Usually measured by the annual percentage change in real GDP, reflecting an improvement in the standard of living.

Economic growth is tied closely to how well people live. We already saw how a high growth rate in China changed the lives of much of its population—more people now can buy cars, computers, and other goods that previously were either unavailable or unaffordable. Economic growth improves the lives of people of all income levels, from the richest to the poorest citizens.

The benefits of economic growth extend beyond the goods people can buy. For example, economic growth leads to lower poverty rates and longer life expectancies as people can afford better medical care, more nutritious diets, and more leisure to reduce stress. The data speak for themselves. In 1980 the average life expectancies (females and males combined) in China and India were 67 and 54 years, respectively. In 2016 they were 75 and 68 years, respectively. Children born in China and India today can expect to live about a decade longer, on average, than their parents.

Still, according to estimates by the World Bank, over a billion people in the world live on less than $1.25 per day, and over 2 billion people live on less than $2 per day. However, the number of people living on these amounts has fallen from their peaks as many countries, such as the BRIC nations which make up over 40% of the world's population, saw economic growth rates improve over the past two decades. This section analyzes how economic growth is measured and how the power of **compounding,** in which growth builds upon prior growth, can turn small rates of growth into substantial increases in outcome and income over time, leading to better lives for all.

compounding The ability of growth to build on previous growth. It allows variables such as income and GDP (as well as debt) to increase significantly over time.

How Is Economic Growth Measured?

real GDP The total value of final goods and services produced in a country in a year measured using prices in a base year.

Small differences in growth can lead to dramatic differences in income due to the effect of compounding. To show this, we first have to measure economic growth, using the concepts of gross domestic product (GDP) and GDP per capita introduced in an earlier chapter. As we saw, GDP is a measure of the total value of final goods and services produced in a country in one year, or simply a country's total annual output. GDP per capita is a country's GDP divided by its population, and provides a rough measure of a typical person's standard of living. Also, recall that **real GDP** and **real GDP per capita** use constant dollars to remove the effects of inflation, allowing for more accurate comparisons in output from year to year.

real GDP per capita Real GDP divided by population. Provides a rough estimate of a country's standard of living.

When a country's real GDP per capita increases, the average output per person is increasing (rather than just prices), and this generally translates into a higher standard of living for most of its residents. Therefore, this is a good indicator of how an economy grows over time.

TABLE 1	COMPARING REAL GDP GROWTH DATA IN 2015	
	Annualized GDP Growth Rate	**Year-Over-Year Growth Rate**
1st quarter	+0.6%	+2.9%
2nd quarter	+3.9%	+2.7%
3rd quarter	+2.1%	+2.1%
4th quarter	+0.7%	+1.8%

Data from BEA Interactive Tables: GDP and the National Income and Product Accounts.

In the United States, real GDP is measured by the Bureau of Economic Analysis (BEA). The BEA produces quarterly reports on the changes in U.S. GDP from the previous quarter, and is reported as an annualized rate (quarterly change multiplied by 4). For example, in January 2016, the BEA reported that the U.S. economy grew 0.7% in the fourth quarter of 2015. This means that real GDP in the United States increased 0.175% from the third quarter of 2015 to the fourth quarter of 2015, which equals a rise of 0.7% when annualized.

In addition, the BEA provides GDP growth data *year-over-year*. For example, the BEA reported that the U.S. economy grew 1.8% from the fourth quarter of 2014 to the fourth quarter of 2015. Why does the BEA report year-over-year growth? Year-over-year growth allows investors and policymakers to compare how the economy has grown over an entire 12-month period, without the seasonal ups and downs most economies experience. Table 1 shows the quarterly real GDP growth rates in 2015 using the annualized and year-over-year methods. The Annualized column shows the seasonal fluctuations that influenced economic growth each quarter, while the Year-Over-Year column shows the growth rate for the preceding 12 months. Both measures are useful depending on whether one is analyzing trends in economic performance for a particular season or for the entire year.

Small Differences in Growth Lead to Large Differences in Income Over Time

When we think of a stark contrast in living standards, we need look no further than the U.S.–Mexican border. For example, driving along Interstate 10 in El Paso, Texas (which is less than 200 yards from the border at its closest point), one can see tremendous differences in the quality of housing in Mexico versus that in the United States. Yet, how did such a difference in standard of living occur? Did the U.S. economy grow that much faster? The surprising answer is that the U.S. growth rate over the past 100 years averaged just 1% higher than Mexico's growth rate. Perhaps more surprising is that Mexico's real GDP per capita is *above average* in the world. Even Mexico appears "rich" to countries such as Nicaragua and Honduras, whose real GDP per capita is only about one-fourth that of Mexico. If growth rates did not differ much between the United States and Mexico, or between Mexico and Nicaragua over the past century, why are the economies of these countries so different? The answer is the power of compounding growth.

The border between the United States and Mexico offers a glimpse at the sharp contrast between two nations with different growth paths.

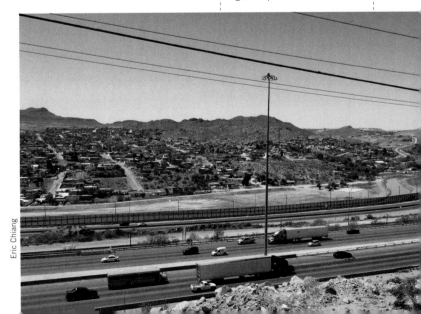

Eric Chiang

Power of Compounding Growth Rates Suppose you deposit $1,000 in a high-interest money market account that averages 10% in interest per year. If you simply let the interest accrue without adding any additional money to the account, that $1,000 would turn into $28,102 in 35 years. How is that possible? Money earns interest, in this case 10%. But interest also earns interest. In fact, jump ahead 34 years, when your $1,000 is worth $25,548. In year 35, earning 10% on $25,548 equals over $2,500 in interest, bringing your total to $28,102. In that year, you earned over 2.5 times more in interest than the $1,000 you originally put in. That is the power of compounding growth.

Suppose instead that your money grew at 5% per year. What do you think the return will be? One-half of the 10% amount of $28,102? No . . . saving $1,000 at 5% would result in a total value of $5,516 in 35 years, significantly less than half of the $28,102 had the interest rate been 10%. This example shows that small differences in interest result in big changes over time. Suppose that your money grew at 9%, just 1% less than 10%. Your $1,000 would be worth $20,414 in 35 years, a drop of almost $8,000 over this period.

These numerical examples highlight the importance of small differences in growth between the United States and Mexico over time. By growing just 1% faster over a 100-year period, two countries can end up having real GDP per capita several times apart (about 4 times in the case of the United States and Mexico and about 4 times between Mexico and Nicaragua). Over the past 100 years, the United States grew 2% a year on average, Mexico grew 1.2% a year on average, and Nicaragua grew 0.3% a year on average.

Rule of 70 Calculating compounding growth over a long period requires the use of a formula and calculator. Luckily, there is an easy way to *approximate* the number of years it takes for an amount to double in value by using the **Rule of 70**. The Rule of 70 states that the number of years required for a value (such as a nation's GDP) to double in size is equal to 70 divided by the growth rate:

Number of Years to Double Value = 70/Growth Rate

For example, if the growth rate is 10%, it would take about 70/10 = 7 years for an initial value of $1,000 to double to $2,000, another 7 years (or 14 years total) to double again to $4,000, another 7 years (or 21 years total) to double again to $8,000, and so on.

The Rule of 70 is fairly accurate for small growth rates. For larger growth rates, especially above 10%, the Rule of 70 becomes slightly less accurate over time. Table 2 provides a comparison between actual values and estimated values using the Rule of 70 for 5% and 10% growth rates. The smaller growth rate keeps the Rule of 70 estimated values closer to the actual values than the larger growth rate.

Although the Rule of 70 does not provide an exact estimate of compounded values over time, its ease of use makes it a valuable tool in understanding the power of compounding growth rates over time.

In all examples so far, we have shown how compounding growth can lead to much improved lives over time. However, it is also important to note that the reverse can be true. The compounding effect also makes debts significantly larger over time.

At 5% = $5,516   At 10% = $28,102

Doubling the interest rate on a $1,000 deposit generates over 5 times more earnings over 35 years.

Rule of 70 Provides an estimate of the number of years for a value to double, and is calculated as 70 divided by the annual growth rate.

TABLE 2	ACCURACY OF THE RULE OF 70			
	5% Growth Rate		10% Growth Rate	
	Actual	Using Rule of 70	Actual	Using Rule of 70
Initial:	$1,000	$1,000	$1,000	$1,000
14 years:	$1,979	$2,000	$3,797	$4,000
28 years:	$3,920	$4,000	$14,421	$16,000

Bryan Sikora/Shutterstock

ISSUE

Can Economic Growth Bring a Billion People Out of Poverty?

Poverty is a global concern. Although definitions of poverty vary from country to country, the World Bank defines *extreme poverty* as a person living on less than $1.90 per day (in real, inflation-adjusted dollars). According to World Bank estimates, in 1990 over 2 billion people in the world lived in extreme poverty. Twenty-five years later, that number had been cut in half. This drop in extreme poverty is even more remarkable considering that the world's population grew from 5.3 billion to 7.1 billion over this period.

How did over a billion people find themselves no longer in extreme poverty? Much of the drop can be attributed to economic growth in developing countries such as China and India, and more recently, countries in Africa. In China alone, 25 years of solid growth pulled more than 600 million people above the extreme poverty threshold. Although average wages remain low compared to those in the United States or Europe, a typical factory worker making $500 per month can live a modest life in China, where the cost of living is significantly lower, and clearly a better life than in 1990 when average monthly wages were only $20 per month.

India is another country that has seen significant reductions in extreme poverty. Although poverty rates remain much higher in India than in China, India's growth rate of over 7% led to tens of millions exiting poverty each year. And since 2005, many countries in Africa have begun seeing their poverty rates fall, as greater investment in natural resource industries has led to strong economic growth on the mineral- and oil-rich continent.

Clearly, economic growth is a powerful factor, even during times of economic downturn. Even during the 2007–2009 global economic downturn, when poverty based on higher thresholds in the United States and in Europe increased, extreme poverty as defined by the $1.90 per day threshold continued to fall. The World Bank announced in 2013 a goal of ending extreme poverty by 2030.

Economic growth is arguably the most important contributor to reducing extreme poverty worldwide. Yet, not all problems with poverty have been resolved. First, while extreme poverty has fallen precipitously, poverty as defined by higher income thresholds has dropped less than 20% since 1990. In other words, while much progress has been made to eliminate extreme poverty, nearly a third of the world's population remains very poor.

Strong economic growth in India over the past 25 years has brought hundreds of millions of people out of poverty, allowing a much more comfortable life for the next generation.

Hence, economic growth remains one of the most important, if not the most important, macroeconomic objective pursued by policymakers in order to continue the progress of reducing poverty worldwide.

Information from "World Bank Forecasts Global Poverty to Fall Below 10% for First Time; Major Hurdles Remain in Goal to End Poverty by 2030," the World Bank, October 4, 2015.

Do you keep a balance on a credit card? If so, you're not alone. The average American household carries about $16,000 in credit card balances each month. Most credit cards charge interest rates on unpaid balances between 12% and 18%, some even more. Suppose an individual has $15,000 in debt at a 17.5% interest rate. If no payments are made on this debt (let's assume a minimum monthly payment is not required), the Rule of 70 says that the debt will double about every 4 years (70/17.5). If no payments are made on this debt, that $16,000 will turn into $32,000 in 4 years, $64,000 in 8 years, $128,000 in 12 years, and $256,000 in 16 years. Paying off credit card balances can lead to significant savings over time.

In sum, the power of compounding means that policies aimed at increasing the annual rate of economic growth can have powerful long-run effects, resulting in some countries becoming rich while others that do not achieve such growth remain poor. The benefits of economic growth are highlighted through the remarkable rise in income over time that leads to a higher standard of living for all citizens. But what exactly spurs economic growth? That is a question we answer in the next section.

CHECKPOINT

WHY IS ECONOMIC GROWTH IMPORTANT?

- Economic growth is measured by the increase in real GDP and real GDP per capita. In the United States, it is measured by the BEA on a quarterly basis as an annualized percentage change as well as a year-over-year change.

- Small differences in growth rates translate into large differences in output and income over time. Just a 1% difference in growth over time can make one country appear rich and another country appear poor.

- The Rule of 70 provides an easy way to approximate the number of years required for a value to double.

QUESTIONS: In 2016 the average Chinese manufacturing worker earned about $6,000 a year, while the average U.S. manufacturing worker earned $48,000 a year. Suppose that the U.S. growth rate is 3% per year (income doubles about every 24 years using the Rule of 70), while China's growth rate is 7% per year (income doubles about every 10 years using the Rule of 70). If these growth rates do not change, in what year would the typical Chinese worker earn $48,000 a year? In what year would the typical Chinese worker catch up to the American worker if U.S. wages continue to increase by 3% per year?

Answers to the Checkpoint questions can be found at the end of this chapter.

THINKING ABOUT SHORT-RUN AND LONG-RUN ECONOMIC GROWTH

Up to this point, we have discussed why economic growth is good and how it is measured. Next, we need to discuss the differences between short-run and long-run growth and the factors that determine economic growth.

Short-Run Versus Long-Run Growth

The first step to understanding how growth occurs is to understand the difference between short-run and long-run growth.

Short-Run Growth Involves a Fixed Capacity Short-run growth occurs when an economy makes use of existing but underutilized resources. For example, abandoned shopping centers or malls could easily be reopened with new stores. Idle construction equipment and unemployed workers could quickly be put into use on a new project. In these cases, the resources to produce goods and services are available but are not being used.

Short-run growth is common when countries are recovering from an economic downturn, or when obstacles preventing resources from being fully used (such as restrictions on land use or high mandatory benefits for workers) are loosened. But to sustain growth beyond the small fluctuations common in the business cycle, efforts to expand an economy's ability to produce are necessary. This leads to long-run growth.

Long-Run Growth Involves Expanding Capacity Long-run growth occurs when an economy finds new resources or improved ways to use existing resources. In other words, the capacity to produce goods and services increases, leading to long-run growth. For example, suppose natural gas deposits that are estimated to be abundant in the United States are explored, leading to an expansion in production of natural gas–powered vehicles (NGVs). This may lead to an expansion of production capacity in the United States through the reduction of its dependence on foreign oil and through the development of more environmentally friendly cars.

In a previous chapter, we introduced production possibilities frontiers (PPF) to illustrate the maximum productive capacity of an economy if all resources are fully utilized. We now use PPF diagrams to show the difference between short-run and long-run economic growth.

| FIGURE 1 | SHORT-RUN VERSUS LONG-RUN GROWTH ILLUSTRATED ON PPF DIAGRAMS |

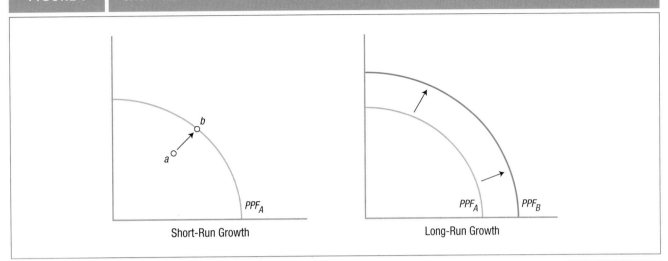

Short-Run Growth   Long-Run Growth

Short-run economic growth occurs when underutilized resources are placed into production. In a PPF diagram, this is shown as a movement from a point inside the PPF to a point closer to or on the PPF (such as from *a* to *b*). Long-run economic growth occurs when new resources are found or existing resources are used more efficiently, thus expanding an economy's capacity to produce. In this case, PPF_A expands outward to PPF_B, allowing for more production possibilities.

In Figure 1, the left panel shows an economy initially producing at point *a* inside of its PPF, indicating underutilized resources such as idle equipment or excess labor. By putting these resources to work, an economy can work toward production capacity on the PPF line at point *b*, representing short-run growth. Long-run growth, illustrated in the right panel, requires an economy to find new resources such as new natural resources or improved human capital in its workforce, or new ideas to make better use of existing resources. Such improvements in production capacity will shift PPF_A outward to PPF_B, allowing for more production possibilities.

Factors of Production

Achieving long-run growth requires an economy to acquire new resources or to find better ways to use the resources it has to generate goods and services people desire either

The United States has been called the "Saudi Arabia of Natural Gas" due to its abundance of natural gas deposits.

domestically or abroad through trade. These resources are categorized into the four factors of production, which are the building blocks for production and economic growth. Let's review these factors of production.

1. Land and natural resources (denoted as N) include land and any raw resources that come from land, such as mineral deposits, oil, natural gas, and water.

2. Labor (denoted as L) includes both the mental and physical talents of people. Human capital (denoted as H) includes the improvements to labor capabilities from training, education, and apprenticeship programs.

3. Physical capital (denoted as K) includes all manufactured products that are used to produce other goods and services. This includes machinery used in factories, cash registers in stores and restaurants, and communications networks used to track shipments.

4. Entrepreneurial ability and ideas, or technology (A) describe the ability to take resources and use them in creative ways to produce goods and services. For example, technology improves the productivity of all factors, and therefore is considered a highly valuable input in production. In other words, land, labor, and physical capital are not useful unless the idea of how to turn these resources into goods and services people want exists.

When factors of production are used to produce goods and services useful for consumption, a measurement tool is needed to calculate the extent to which inputs (resources) are turned into outputs (goods and services). The relationship between the amount of inputs used in production and the amount of output produced is called a production function.

Production Function

production function Measures the output that is produced using various combinations of inputs and a fixed level of technology.

A **production function** shows the output that is produced using different combinations of inputs combined with existing technology. Although many types of production functions exist, most are variations of the classical form: Output $= f(L, K)$, which means that output is determined by some function of available labor and capital.

Every country, industry, and even firm can have a different production function that measures how much output it can produce given the physical inputs and technology available. No two countries will produce exactly the same type or amount of products given the resources they have. Thus, a production function is a very important tool used to determine whether a country is using its limited resources efficiently and to what extent it can experience long-run growth.

Suppose $f(L, K) = L + K$ for simplicity. This means that if an economy has 10 units of labor and 10 units of capital, total output would equal $10 + 10 = 20$. Although most production functions are not this simple, the idea is that more inputs can produce more output by some function.

Because inputs are not limited to just labor and capital, a more realistic production function would look like the following:

$$\text{Output} = A \times f(L, K, H, N)$$

where total output equals technology (A) times a function of available labor (L), physical capital (K), human capital (H), and land and natural resources (N).

This equation helps to explain how an entire economy grows. For example, having a more educated labor force or having more capital will contribute to higher productive capacity of the economy (shifting the PPF outward).

But what we are truly interested in is how growth affects the lives of people living in those countries. For example, India's GDP has grown at a very fast pace, but so has its population. The important question is how economic growth affects the standard of living of the average person, or output per person. One way to achieve a close (but not exact) measure of output per person is to revise the previous production function to one that measures output per worker.

To do so, assume that the production function exhibits constant returns to scale (a reasonable assumption). This means that any proportional change in the number of inputs results in the same proportional change in output. For example, if we divide all inputs by L, we would be able to calculate the output per worker as follows:

$$\text{Output per worker} = A \times f(L/L, K/L, H/L, N/L)$$

This equation shows that output per worker equals technology times a function of physical capital per worker, human capital per worker, and land and natural resources per worker. Because we are concerned with output per worker, having more people will not automatically lead to a better standard of living (hence, $L/L = 1$). However, having more capital per person or more human capital (education) will increase the productivity of labor as each worker produces more output. Therefore, increases in capital will lead to improved standards of living.

To this point, we have discussed the importance of economic growth and defined the building blocks for economic growth using the factors of production that enter into the production function. The next section will use the production function to discuss ways in which an economy achieves growth by way of increasing productivity.

 CHECKPOINT

THINKING ABOUT SHORT-RUN AND LONG-RUN ECONOMIC GROWTH

- Short-run growth occurs from using resources that have been sitting idle or underutilized, and is represented in a PPF diagram as a movement from a point within the PPF toward the PPF.

- Long-run growth occurs when the productive capacity of an economy is expanded through more resources or better uses of existing resources (i.e., technological advancements), and is shown in a PPF diagram as an outward shift of the PPF.

- The primary factors of production are land and natural resources, labor (and human capital), physical capital, and technology (entrepreneurial ability and ideas).

- A production function measures the amount of output that can be produced using different combinations of inputs. Production functions vary by firms, industries, and countries.

- Output per person adjusts the production function for changes in population growth in a country.

QUESTION: The Ivory Coast (Côte d'Ivoire) in West Africa is a country with abundant natural resources, a long coastline, and a stable currency that is tied to the euro and managed by the French Treasury. Despite these benefits, it remains an extremely poor country with an unstable government. What does this finding suggest about the Ivory Coast's overall factors of production and its production function compared to a country, say, Iceland, with fewer physical resources but a significantly higher standard of living?

Answers to the Checkpoint questions can be found at the end of this chapter.

APPLYING THE PRODUCTION FUNCTION: ACHIEVING ECONOMIC GROWTH

productivity How effectively inputs are converted into outputs. Labor productivity is the ratio of the output of goods and services to the labor hours devoted to the production of that output. Productivity and living standards are closely related.

The production function allows us to measure how inputs are converted into outputs. The extent to which inputs are converted into outputs is referred to as **productivity**. For example, when worker productivity grows, each worker is producing more output for each hour devoted to production.

Productivity is a key driver of wages and incomes. The primary reason that the American standard of living is so high is that American workers produce more per hour than do workers in most other countries. Many people in the developing world eke out a living using tools that would remind us of an earlier century. This lower productivity is reflected in their lower standard of living.

The factors of production discussed in the previous section play an important role in increasing economic growth. As the quantity of each factor rises, output rises according to the production function for each industry. In addition, technology plays an important role in enhancing the productive output of all other resources.

A country's output is measured by the value of the goods and services it produces, which can increase based on their quantity or quality. In other words, highly productive countries are able to produce many goods that are high in value. One reason why Japan remains one of the world's richest countries is that its labor force is highly productive. Using abundant capital, human capital, and technology, Japan's labor force produces many high-priced products such as cars, robots, and advanced electronics.

Let's look at each factor of production in turn to examine what increases productivity and economic growth.

Achieving More Land or Natural Resources

Natural resources are the building blocks of production; however, they are not a significant driver of economic growth. Countries that are abundant in land and natural resources have an advantage that can translate into economic growth only if such resources are used effectively. Countries that discovered new natural resources have experienced higher rates of growth. For example, new oil deposits have been discovered in Angola and Cameroon over the past decade. These discoveries led to significant investment by oil companies from China, India, and the United States in these countries, which contributed to a higher growth rate.

Growth of the Labor Force

Many countries have experienced significant population growth, leading to an increase in the labor supply. In the United States, population growth has been spurred by a relatively open immigration policy compared to other countries. In addition to population growth, labor force participation increased over the last few decades, as more women entered the workforce and as government policies were implemented to make work more attractive. An increase in the labor force generally leads to greater output, but not necessarily more output per person. In order for economic growth to improve the standard of living of its citizens, countries must expand not only the quantity of its labor force, but also the quality of labor to ensure that economic growth exceeds population growth.

Increasing the Quality of the Labor Force

investment in human capital Improvements to the labor force from investments in skills, knowledge, and the overall quality of workers and their productivity.

One source of productivity growth comes from improvements to the labor force from **investment in human capital.** Human capital is a term economists use to describe skills, knowledge, and the quality of workers. On-the-job training and general education can improve the quality of labor. In many ways, increasing capital and a highly skilled labor force go together. Well-trained workers are needed to run the highly productive, often highly complex, machines. Unskilled workers are given the least important jobs and earn the lowest wages.

By investing in human capital, nations can ultimately raise their growth rates by improving worker productivity. Government programs that raise the literacy rate, such as universal public education, also raise the rate of economic growth.

Increasing the Capital-to-Labor Ratio

When a farmer in the small Himalayan country of Bhutan plows his field with a crude plow hitched to a couple of yaks, the amount of land he can plant and harvest is minuscule. American farmers, in contrast, use equipment that allows them to plow, plant, fertilize, water, and harvest thousands of acres; they have a high **capital-to-labor ratio.** This raises U.S. farm productivity many orders of magnitude above that of Bhutanese farmers. The ultimate result of this productivity is that American farmers earn a far higher income than their counterparts in the developing world.

Developing countries have large labor forces, but little capital. Developed nations like the United States, on the other hand, have limited labor supplies, and each worker works with a large array of capital equipment. As a rule, the more capital employed by workers, the greater their productivity and the higher their earnings.

Although a powerful contributor to productivity, capital is subject to **diminishing returns to capital.** For example, suppose that the farmer in Bhutan buys a tractor to replace his yaks. The increase in productivity would be dramatic. Now suppose that the farmer invests in an irrigation system. Surely, the irrigation system will further increase productivity, but likely not as much as the tractor did. In other words, a farmer is likely to purchase the most essential equipment first. Each subsequent piece of equipment will increase production but by a smaller amount than the previous one. For this reason, countries with abundant capital will not gain as much per additional piece of capital than countries with little capital with which to start. This is one reason why developing countries may initially grow faster than developed countries, a phenomenon called the catch-up effect.

The **catch-up effect** describes the notion that developing countries are able to achieve greater productivity for each unit of capital invested because they have the advantage of using technologies that have already been developed by other countries. This has allowed many developing countries to achieve a higher rate of growth compared to developed countries.

An example of the catch-up effect is China's expanding high-speed rail network. High-speed rail networks were largely invented and perfected by the Japanese, Germans, and French. However, large development costs required substantial government subsidies. China, on the other hand, had the advantage of building its rail network using existing technologies. As a result, China was able to expand its rail network at a lower price per mile, allowing it to catch up and to develop an even more advanced rail network than its predecessors. But because all factors face diminishing returns, the catch-up effect tends to slow over time unless new technologies are developed to keep the growth rate high.

capital-to-labor ratio The capital employed per worker. A higher ratio means higher labor productivity and, as a result, higher wages.

diminishing returns to capital Each additional unit of capital provides a smaller increase in output than the previous unit of capital.

catch-up effect Countries with smaller starting levels of capital experience larger benefits from increased capital, allowing these countries to grow faster than countries with abundant capital.

Using expensive tractors and other capital equipment, U.S. farmers are more productive than Bhutanese farmers who rely on wooden plows pulled by yaks.

THOMAS MALTHUS (1766–1834)

Thomas Malthus was raised in Surrey, England, the son of a wealthy eccentric country gentleman. Home-schooled by his father and a tutor, he had learned enough to be accepted to Cambridge University. After attending Cambridge, he spent several years as a clergyman before accepting a teaching post in political economy at the college of the East India Company, making him the first academic economist in history.

In 1793 the pamphleteer William Godwin published *Political Justice*, describing a utopian future with no war, poverty, crime, injustice, or disease. Malthus argued against the book's conclusions during a lengthy discussion with his father, who agreed with the book, but nevertheless suggested that Malthus set down his ideas in print.

The result was "An Essay on the Principle of Population As It Affects the Future Improvement of Society." Malthus argued that the origins of poverty were rooted in an unavoidable contradiction: Population, when allowed to grow without limits, increases geometrically, while the food supply could only increase arithmetically. He argued that English Poor Laws spread pauperism because any improvement in conditions of the poor would simply lead to population increases and to rising food prices and scarcities.

He even went so far as to suggest that "a proclamation should be read out at marriage ceremonies warning couples that they would have to bear the financial burden and consequences of their passion."

His dire predictions about world starvation led Thomas Carlyle a few decades later to describe the economics profession as the "Dismal Science." Although the predictions of inadequate food supply did not fully materialize due to the invention of agricultural technologies and fertilizer, the "Dismal Science" remains today as an alternative name for economics.

Information from Paul Strathern, *A Brief History of Economic Genius* (New York: Texere), 2002; Howard Marshall, *The Great Economists: A History of Economic Thought* (New York: Pitman Publishing), 1967; Donald Winch, "Malthus," in *Three Great Economists* (Oxford: Oxford University Press), 1997, pp. 105–218.

Improvements in Technology and Ideas

Technological improvements can come from various sources and play *the* major role in improving productivity, raising the standard of living, and increasing economic growth. These include enterprising individuals who discover innovative products and production methods, from Henry Ford's auto assembly line to Steve Jobs's role in developing the Apple home computer, iPod, iPhone, and iPad that have changed the way we live, work, and socialize. Technology has also improved as a result of advancements in telecommunications, the Internet, and biotechnology.

Technological progress is the primary explanation for the extraordinary economic growth the United States has enjoyed over the last century. In the production function, technology enhances the productive capacity of all other resources.

Technologies that kept our economy expanding have also helped many other countries to grow. In the developing world, growth most often comes from foreign companies building factories that employ locals at low wages. These companies often pay more than workers could have hoped to earn on their own. These higher earnings become the resources invested to ensure better education and earnings for their children.

Today, new technologies are helping many developing nations accelerate their growth. Wireless service has improved communications, inexpensive vaccinations and health education programs have reduced mortality rates, and the global movement of capital and production facilities has created new job opportunities.

Including Everything Else: Total Factor Productivity

We have shown that productivity can be measured by how well a country uses its resources to produce goods and services. However, a country's productivity is not entirely dependent on the amount of inputs it has. True, a country with more inputs such as physical and human capital will likely produce more output. However, external factors influence the ability of inputs to be used effectively. The measure of output that is not explained by the number of inputs used in production is called **total factor productivity.**

Total factor productivity captures the factors that influence the overall effectiveness of inputs. For example, suppose a major hurricane sweeps through a region, knocking out

total factor productivity The portion of output produced that is not explained by the number of inputs used in production.

Kazakhstan: The Next Destination of Growth and Trade

What policies did the government of Kazakhstan implement to promote economic growth over the past decade?

Jose Fuste Raga/Corbis

When one thinks of cities experiencing significant economic growth and trade, cities such as Hong Kong, Dubai, and Shanghai often come to mind. But in terms of rapidly growing cities, one city in Central Asia has been overlooked by many: Astana, the capital of Kazakhstan.

How did this large country relatively unknown to Americans become a beacon of growth?

Kazakhstan is a melting pot of ethnic cultures, from Russians to Kazakhs who look more like East Asians.

Once lampooned by British comedian Sasha Cohen in the movie *Borat* as an impoverished backward nation, Kazakhstan is quite the opposite today. Upon arrival in the capital of Astana, one encounters hundreds of construction cranes as new skyscrapers dot the changing city landscape. Kazakhstan is also home to the Russian Federal Space Agency, where Soyuz flights regularly take off and land in the desert steppe at Baikonur Cosmodrome, which today remains the oldest and largest space launch facility in the world.

The emphasis on growth in Kazakhstan can be attributed to several key factors. One surely is abundant natural resources, such as oil. More important are an emphasis on higher education, encouragement of international trade, and significant investment in infrastructure and technology, all backed by government policies. These government efforts attracted significant foreign investment from countries around the world, including the United States.

These efforts have resulted in strong economic growth in Kazakhstan, which today has the highest average income in Central Asia. A stroll through the modern streets of Astana and Almaty (the former capital and home to most historical sights) points to the powerful role that economic growth has on improving the lives of a country's citizens.

GO TO **LaunchPad** TO PRACTICE THE ECONOMIC CONCEPTS IN THIS STORY

power and communications for a week. Factories would likely be less productive despite having all of their workers and equipment available. Some equipment might not be able to run without electricity, and the morale of workers after a hurricane might make them less motivated to work. Such effects on output would not be captured by the number of inputs available.

Another factor affecting total factor productivity is the value of new innovations, which increases the efficiency of inputs used in production. For example, social media were originally designed to allow individuals to communicate better with one another through sites such as Facebook and Twitter. However, an external effect occurred when firms began to use these sites to market their products, which led to a dramatic change in how people learn about various products and improved the efficiency of production and consumption.

Total factor productivity also is influenced by the institutions in place within a country. For example, a country can have a very educated labor force but policies in place that prevent its human capital from being used efficiently. The country could be engaged in frequent military conflicts, preventing its resources from being used to improve the lives of its citizens. Or, a country may have a weak legal system or property rights, or a lack of economic freedom that prevents its markets from producing what people want. These institutional factors are largely influenced by the government. In the next section, we discuss government's role in fostering economic growth.

CHECKPOINT

APPLYING THE PRODUCTION FUNCTION: ACHIEVING ECONOMIC GROWTH

- Productivity is the key driver for economic growth, and rises when labor is able to produce greater quantities and higher values of output.

- Increased productivity of labor can come from increases in land and natural resources, the quality of the labor force, the capital-to-labor ratio, and technology.

- Physical capital is subjected to diminishing returns, which allows countries with less starting capital to experience a catch-up effect as they acquire more capital.

- Total factor productivity measures the portion of output that is not explained by the amount of inputs placed in use. It captures the external effects that influence the productivity of all inputs.

QUESTION: Several years ago, Warren Buffett, one of the world's richest individuals, pledged that "more than 99% of my wealth will go to philanthropy during my lifetime or at death" and noted that he would give this approximately $30 billion in installments to the Bill & Melinda Gates Foundation. The foundation focuses on grants to developing nations, helping the poorest of the poor. What suggestions would you give the foundation to help these developing nations grow?

Answers to the Checkpoint questions can be found at the end of this chapter.

THE ROLE OF GOVERNMENT IN PROMOTING ECONOMIC GROWTH

Government plays an important role in how well a country utilizes its resources in production. The policies and incentives put into place affect a country's total factor productivity. Now we discuss some of the key ways in which government plays a role in influencing productivity.

Government as a Contributor to Physical Capital, Human Capital, and Technology

The government is the single largest consumer of goods and services in the United States. Each year, the U.S. government spends over $350 billion on purchases including highways, bridges, transportation systems, public education, military equipment, and more. By investing heavily in capital goods, the government promotes a higher level of labor productivity in the country.

Physical Capital: Public Capital and Private Investment One of the reasons why some nations are rich and others are poor lies in the different levels of infrastructure development. The focus on infrastructure means that there is something important that lies behind our aggregate production: We do not just increase capital, increase labor, improve technology, and turn a crank to obtain economic growth.

infrastructure The public capital of a nation, including transportation networks, power-generating plants and transmission facilities, public education institutions, and other intangible resources such as protection of property rights and a stable monetary environment.

Infrastructure is defined as a country's public capital. It includes dams, roads, and bridges; transportation networks, such as air and rail lines; power-generating plants and power transmission lines; telecommunications networks; and public education facilities. These items are tangible public goods that can easily be measured. All are crucial for economic growth.

The government also encourages private investment in physical capital through tax incentives and other subsidies to firms willing to invest in capital projects. Industries that receive the largest tax incentives include aerospace, defense, energy, and telecommunications.

Human Capital: Public Education and Financial Aid The government plays an important role in ensuring that every person has access to a minimum level of education. In the United States, state laws mandate that children stay in school until a minimum age, typically 16. Public schools and universities are highly subsidized by local and state governments to provide affordable access to educational opportunities.

Besides providing funding directly to schools and universities, the government offers various forms of financial assistance directly to students to use toward educational expenses. These include Pell Grants and the G.I. Bill, federal subsidized loans, and various types of tax incentives that allow qualified students (or their parents) to deduct a portion of their tuition and fees from their taxable income or from their taxes directly.

The Los Alamos National Laboratory in New Mexico is one of the largest government research centers in the country. During World War II, it was a secret lab that housed the "Manhattan Project," which ultimately produced the world's first atomic bomb.

The government also allows teachers to deduct certain expenses from their taxes, and provides tax-exempt status for organizations whose mission is to provide scholarships, such as the prestigious National Merit Scholarship Program. These grants, loans, and tax incentives contribute to the government's role in promoting human capital.

Technology: Government R&D Centers and Federal Grants Some of the largest research centers in the country are government funded. These include Los Alamos National Laboratory and Sandia National Laboratories (part of the Department of Energy), the National Institutes of Health, the National Aeronautics and Space Administration (NASA), and the National Oceanic and Atmospheric Administration (NOAA), just to name a few. These government research centers employ thousands of scientists, researchers, and doctors for the purpose of advancing knowledge and inventing products that enhance the lives of all citizens and promote economic growth.

In addition to running research centers, the government provides funds directly to public and private research centers as well as to individual researchers. Among the largest grantors of funds is the National Science Foundation (NSF), founded in 1950. In 2016, the NSF provided over $7 billion in grants to around 11,000 projects, and has maintained its mission of promoting research essential for the nation's economic health and global competitiveness.

Government as a Facilitator of Economic Growth

A second major role of government in promoting economic growth is to ensure that an effective legal system is in place to enforce contracts and to protect property rights, and that the financial system is kept stable. These are the less tangible yet equally important components of a country's infrastructure.

Enforcement of Contracts The legal enforcement of contract rights is an important component of an infrastructure that promotes economic growth and well-being. Without contract enforcement, people are less likely to be willing to enter into contracts, for example, to produce and deliver goods for payment at some future date. Therefore, contract enforcement promotes economic growth by ensuring that production and purchasing commitments made by producers and consumers are honored.

Protection of Property Rights A stable legal system that protects property rights is essential for economic growth. Many developing countries do not systematically record the ownership of real property: land and buildings. Although ownership is often informally recognized, without express legal title, the capital locked up in these informal arrangements cannot be used to secure loans for entrepreneurial purposes. As a result, valuable capital sits idle; it cannot be leveraged for other productive purposes.

In addition, a legal system that recognizes and protects ideas (or intellectual property) is critical to encouraging innovation. Common legal protections for ideas include patents (for inventions), copyrights (for written works, music, and film), and trademarks (for names and symbols). Every country has its innovators; the question is whether these people are offered enough of an incentive to devote their efforts to develop the innovations that drive economic growth. The extent to which countries establish intellectual property rights varies, and even when such protections exist, enforcement of the protections varies.

Stable Financial System Another important component of a nation's infrastructure is a stable and secure financial system. Such a financial system keeps the purchasing power of the currency stable, facilitates transactions, and permits credit institutions to arise. The recent global financial turmoil is an example of the problems caused by financial instability. Further, bank runs, like those that caused major economic disruption in Uruguay and Argentina in 2001–2002, are less likely when a nation's financial environment is stable.

Unanticipated inflations or deflations are both detrimental to economic growth. Consumers and businesses rely on the monetary prices they pay for goods and services for information about the state of the market. If these price signals are constantly being distorted by inflation or deflation, the quality of business and consumer decisions suffers. Unanticipated price changes further lead to a redistribution of income between creditors and debtors. Financial instability is harmful to improving standards of living and generating economic growth.

Government as a Promoter of Free and Competitive Markets

A third role of government in promoting economic growth is maintaining competitive and efficient markets and the freedom for firms and individuals to pursue their interests.

Competitive Markets and Free Trade One of the challenges of government is choosing the right mix of policies to keep markets competitive and fair. Regulations are put into place to protect various interests, whether consumer welfare, worker rights and safety, or the environment. But government also must ensure that such regulations do not stand in the way of markets operating efficiently.

Competitive markets refer to the ability of firms to open and close businesses without unnecessary restrictions or other burdens. Also important is free trade, which refers to the ability to buy and sell products with other countries without significant barriers such as tariffs or quotas. Allowing the market to function freely within the confines of sensible regulatory laws generally creates more potential for economic growth.

Economic Freedom One of the measures used to gauge the ability of individuals and businesses to make investment and production decisions freely is the Index of Economic Freedom.

Unlike physical infrastructure such as roads and dams, which are easy to measure, attempting to measure the intangibles of doing business often requires subjective judgments. One reasonably objective measure is the 2016 Index of Economic Freedom.[1] This index incorporates information about freedoms in ten categories: business, trade, fiscal policy, government size, monetary policy, investment, finance, property rights, corruption, and labor.

Clearly, assigning some of these items a numeric value requires a bit of subjective judgment. Even so, this index is one reasonable approach to measuring the overall infrastructure of a country.

Figure 2 portrays the relationship between economic freedom and per capita GDP measured by purchasing power parity (what income will buy in each country). Those nations with the most economic freedom have the highest per capita GDP and also the highest growth rates (not shown).

In this chapter, we have seen that economic growth in the long run comes from improvements in labor productivity, increases in capital, or improvements in technology. Investments in human capital and greater economic freedom also lead to higher growth rates and higher standards of living.

---

[1] Heritage Foundation, *2016 Index of Economic Freedom* (Washington, D.C.), 2016.

ISSUE

Did Economic Growth Peak a Century Ago? Prospects for Future Growth

When one thinks of life just 15 years ago, imagine what has changed. GPS technology was nearly nonexistent, digital music was in its infancy and downloaded using very slow Internet connections, and smartphones and tablets didn't exist, at least in the way we know these products today. Certainly, life has changed from how we lived at the start of the new millennium. But was this a true transformation of our standard of living? According to one economist, the technological advances of the past few decades do not compare with the effect that inventions over a century ago had. In fact, he argues that U.S. economic growth peaked nearly a century ago. Are prospects for future growth in trouble?

Robert Gordon is a distinguished macroeconomist and economic historian who is skeptical about the technological "revolution" that has resulted from the development of the Internet and social media. In his book *The Rise and Fall of American Growth*, he argues that the true transformation of American standards of living occurred between 1870 and 1940. He argues that the tremendous period of growth a century ago may be a one-time event, and that future growth may never match it. How did Gordon come to this conclusion?

He points to the five "great inventions," which were (1) electric lights, (2) flush toilets, (3) chemicals and pharmaceuticals, (4) cars, and (5) the telephone. Each of these inventions occurred prior to 1940. Therefore, Gordon argues that life became modernized by the 1940s, and every invention since, while making life more comfortable, has not had the same effect. He makes the point that if a person today walked

Living in the 1940s was "modern" compared to the late 1800s in the sense that people today would find it mostly functional. Have changes in standards of living since the 1940s been as dramatic?

into a 1940s apartment, it would be functional, with indoor plumbing, lights, a refrigerator, and a telephone. But if a person from 1940 walked into an 1870s apartment, the same could not be said.

Is Gordon's pessimistic view on future growth accurate? Only time will tell whether recent and future inventions will measure up to those of a century ago. What would be the contenders of the new "great inventions"? The obvious choices would include personal computers, Internet, social media, biotechnology, and artificial intelligence. But have these inventions been so transformative to our lives that living without them would be as burdensome as living without lights or the modern toilet? It's a powerful thought to ponder as one considers the factors that will lead to future growth and the factors that will challenge it.

Prospects for future growth depend largely on the willingness of businesses to innovate and create new products, on the willingness of consumers to demand these new products, and on the willingness of government (and the people who elect policymakers) to foster an environ-

ment that promotes long-term economic growth. In each case, large investments and capital spending are needed, especially in research and development, infrastructure, and other ambitious projects that may not reap returns until the next generation.

Generating another strong and sustained period of growth will not be easy. First, many countries including the United States today face debt problems as populations rise and as people live longer. As a result, investing in long-term projects such as the space program or high-speed rail often gets put aside. Second, the world is affected by conflict, war, and supply shocks, making long-term investments more difficult and risky. Finally, income inequality across the world has risen, and recent economic growth has benefited the wealthy more than the poor. These obstacles make prospects for future growth more challenging. Yet, just as few predicted the five great inventions of the past century, perhaps a new set of great inventions will occur that might eliminate poverty and diseases, and lead to another period of remarkable economic growth.

In the long run, all of these factors generate growth and higher standards of living. Yet, what are we to do if the economy collapses in the short run? The Great Depression of the 1930s was to prove that for a reasonably long period (a decade), the economy could be mired in a slowdown with high unemployment rates and negative growth. A deep economy-wide downturn inflicts high costs on both today's citizens and future generations. In the next chapter, we turn to the first of our discussions on managing the economy in the short run.

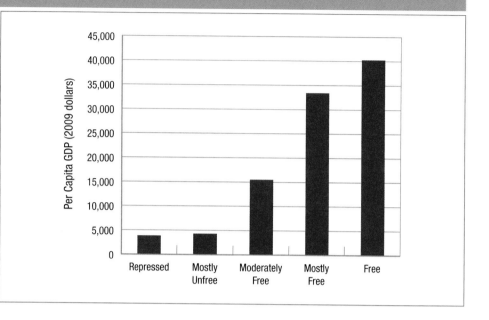

FIGURE 2   ECONOMIC FREEDOM AND PER CAPITA GDP

The relationship between economic freedom and per capita GDP is shown here. Those nations with the most economic freedom also have the highest per capita GDP.

✓ CHECKPOINT

THE ROLE OF GOVERNMENT IN PROMOTING ECONOMIC GROWTH

- Government has an important role in promoting economic growth by providing physical and human capital, ensuring a stable legal system and financial markets, and promoting free and competitive markets.

- Infrastructure is a country's public capital, including dams, roads, transportation networks, power-generating plants, and public schools.

- Governments provide capital and technology by purchasing public capital and providing incentives for private investment, supporting education through subsidies and financial aid, and supporting research with grants.

- Other less tangible infrastructure elements include protection of property rights, enforcement of contracts, and a stable financial system.

- The Index of Economic Freedom measures a country's infrastructure, which supports economic growth.

QUESTIONS: Imagine a country with a "failed government" that can no longer enforce the law. Contracts are not upheld and lawlessness is the order of the day. How well could an economy operate and grow in this environment?

Answers to the Checkpoint questions can be found at the end of this chapter.

chapter summary

Section 1 Why Is Economic Growth Important?

18.1 **Economic growth** is the most important factor influencing a country's standard of living. Economic growth is measured by a nation's ability to increase **real GDP** and **real GDP per capita.** Using *real* values instead of *nominal* values allows a country to compare growth from year to year without having to take into account the effects of inflation. Countries with high economic growth have seen rising incomes and better lives for their citizens.

Small differences in growth rates can result in large differences over time due to the power of **compounding.**

18.2 **The Rule of 70** is a simple tool used to estimate the number of years it takes for a value to double given a constant growth rate.

Number of Years = 70/Growth Rate

Examples: Number of years to double at growth rate of

1%: 70/1 = 70 years
2%: 70/2 = 35 years
5%: 70/5 = 14 years
10%: 70/10 = 7 years
20%: 70/20 = 3.5 years

18.3 Using the Rule of 70 to estimate 5% versus 10% growth:

Year	Value at 5%	Year	Value at 10%
2017	$1,000	2017	$1,000
		2024	$2,000
2031	$2,000	2031	$4,000
		2038	$8,000
2045	$4,000	2045	$16,000

In 28 years, the initial $1,000 is worth $16,000 at 10% growth versus $4,000 at 5% growth.

Section 2 Thinking About Short-Run and Long-Run Economic Growth

18.4 Short-Run Versus Long-Run Growth

Short-run growth occurs when an economy makes use of existing or underutilized resources, and is shown as a movement from inside a PPF toward the PPF (such as from point *a* to point *b*).

Long-run growth requires an expansion of production capacity through an increase in resources and/or technology, and is shown by a shift of the PPF (such as from PPF_A to PPF_B).

Short and Long Run

18.5 Factors of Production

- **Land (N):** Includes land and natural resources
- **Labor (L):** Within labor is human capital **(H),** labor improved by education or training
- **Capital (K):** Manufactured goods used in the production process
- **Entrepreneurial ability (A):** Includes ideas and the technology that is developed

A **production function** is the method by which firms turn factors of production into goods and services.

Section 3 Applying the Production Function: Achieving Economic Growth

18.6 **Productivity** is the ability to turn a fixed amount of inputs (factors of production) into more outputs (goods and services).

Ways to Increase Productivity

- Increasing access to natural resources
- Improving quality of labor (human capital)
- Increasing the capital-to-labor ratio
- Promoting innovation and technology

Rising productivity leads to growing incomes and a better standard of living.

18.7 **Total factor productivity** is a measurement of productivity taking into account all other factors beyond the quantity and quality of inputs that could influence production. Examples include natural disasters, climate, or cultural norms that influence the effectiveness of productive inputs.

Section 4 The Role of Government in Promoting Economic Growth

18.8 Government involvement in promoting economic growth occurs by way of investing in physical capital, human capital, and technology.

- **Physical capital:** The building and maintenance of the country's public capital (infrastructure), which includes roads, bridges, airports, power plants, and telecommunications networks
- **Human capital:** Providing subsidized public college education, financial aid grants, and loans
- **Technology:** Funding research via grants and the establishment of major government research labs

West Point, the United States Military Academy, is an example of government promoting physical capital (the campus and buildings), human capital (education), and technology (research by its faculty).

18.9 Government as a Guarantor of Economic Growth

- **Enforcement of contracts:** A strong legal system
- **Protection of property rights:** Ensuring that monetary rewards are provided to innovators
- **Stable financial system:** A functioning and stable monetary system ensures investment is undertaken when the opportunity arises
- **Promoting free and competitive markets:** International trade allows for specialization and gains from trade, and competitive markets ensure firms do not exploit market power, their ability to set prices for goods and services in a market

The **Index of Economic Freedom** ranks 178 nations in terms of overall environment for promoting economic growth. In 2016 Hong Kong ranked first, and the United States came in 11th.

KEY CONCEPTS

economic growth, p. 480
compounding, p. 480
real GDP, p. 480
real GDP per capita, p. 480
Rule of 70, p. 482

production function, p. 486
productivity, p. 488
investment in human capital, p. 488
capital-to-labor ratio, p. 489
diminishing returns to capital, p. 489

catch-up effect, p. 489
total factor productivity, p. 490
infrastructure, p. 492

QUESTIONS AND PROBLEMS

Check Your Understanding

1. Although having abundant natural resources can be an advantage for a country, are they necessary to ensure economic growth and a prosperous economy?
2. Why does a small difference in the economic growth rate lead to big differences over time?
3. What are some ways in which countries can improve labor productivity?
4. In what ways do governments help to build technology and ideas?
5. Why is investment in human capital good for both individuals and fostering economic growth for the economy as a whole?
6. Why is a stable financial system important to economic growth?

Apply the Concepts

7. The standard of living we enjoy today is largely due to the investments of earlier generations of Americans. Do you agree? Why or why not?
8. What role might foreign investment play in helping developing nations improve their growth rate and increase income levels?
9. Higher levels of savings and investment lead to greater rates of economic growth. What can government do to encourage more savings and investment?
10. Per capita income (or output) is the general measure used to compare the standards of living between countries. If a country's population growth is higher than its economic growth, what happens to per capita income? What are some of the limitations to using per capita income as a measure to compare the well-being of different countries?
11. Energy independence has been a goal for many decades. But only in the past decade has the increased focus on renewable energy sources, such as solar, wind, and water, taken on greater significance. How does achieving energy independence contribute to labor productivity and economic growth?
12. One of the potential negative consequences of both economic and population growth is that we will eventually exhaust Earth's natural resources, leading to our demise. What kind of activities might prevent this from happening?

In the News

13. The European Union faced many challenges in recent years, especially disparities in economic growth among member countries, to the point that citizens of the United Kingdom voted on whether they wished to remain in the EU or not. In 2015 average real GDP growth in the EU was 1.5%, while the top three fastest-growing members, the United Kingdom, Ireland, and Poland, achieved average growth of 3.3%. Is the effect of a 3.3% growth rate so different from that of 1.5%?
14. Finland consistently ranks very high in global rankings of educational achievement in science and math. This was a result of a transformation in Finland's public education system to one that focuses on small class sizes and highly trained teachers for primary and secondary education, which is considered a highly prestigious profession. At the college level, many countries fully subsidize college tuition, and in Saudi Arabia, the King Abdullah Scholarship Program offers to send its citizens to study at many of the world's prestigious universities for free. Explain how government investment in education could pay for itself in the long run.

Solving Problems

WORK IT OUT   **LaunchPad** | interactive activity

15. In 2016 U.S. GDP was approximately $18 trillion, while India's GDP was approximately $2.25 trillion. However, India is growing faster than the United States.

   a. If the U.S. economy grows at 3% per year, in what year will U.S. GDP double to $36 trillion? (*Hint:* Use the Rule of 70 to approximate the number of years needed for GDP to double.)

   b. If India's economy grows at 7% per year, in what year will its GDP double to $4.5 trillion? In what year would India's economy increase 16-fold to $36 trillion?

   c. If each country's growth rate continues at the same rate, in what year would each country's GDP reach $72 trillion?

16. Suppose a new colony is created on the moon with the following production function: Output = $A \times (L + K + H + N)$. If L, K, H, and N each equal 5, and technology (A) equals 3, how much output would this new colony produce?

USING THE NUMBERS

17. According to By the Numbers, approximately how many years did it take for real GDP per capita in the United States to double from $5,000 to $10,000? How about from $25,000 to $50,000? During which period was economic growth stronger in terms of annual growth?

18. According to By the Numbers, what is the range of life expectancies for the countries whose GDP per capita was less than $10,000 in 2015? Compare these life expectancies with those with GDP per capita greater than $35,000. Is there a strong correlation between GDP per capita and life expectancy?

ANSWERS TO QUESTIONS IN CHECKPOINTS

Checkpoint: Why Is Economic Growth Important? 484

If incomes in China double every 10 years, Chinese workers would earn $12,000 in 2026, $24,000 in 2036, and $48,000 in 2046, equaling what American workers earned in 2016. If growth continues at the same rate, Chinese workers would earn $96,000 in 2056 and $192,000 in 2066. American workers would earn $96,000 in 2040, and $192,000 in 2064. Therefore, Chinese workers would earn the same as American workers in about 50 years.

Checkpoint: Thinking About Short-Run and Long-Run Economic Growth 487

Every factor of production contributes to economic growth. Although the Ivory Coast is abundant in natural resources and labor compared to Iceland, it lacks the human capital, physical capital, and technology that are important components in the production function. In addition, the lack of stability in the country from recent civil and military strife has left many of its resources underutilized for productive purposes, further inhibiting the Ivory Coast from achieving higher long-run growth.

Checkpoint: Applying the Production Function: Achieving Economic Growth 492

An organization such as the Bill & Melinda Gates Foundation can help people improve their health through vaccinations, clean water, and sanitation, thereby enabling them to improve their productivity and earning power. Then, focus can be put on schools and improving education. All of this focus on human capital broadly can be accomplished with grants to communities or parents (by subsidizing them to send their kids to school) in developing nations.

Checkpoint: The Role of Government in Promoting Economic Growth 496

Not very well. Large-scale businesses that we are accustomed to could not exist. What's left is small individual businesses that serve small local populations. Growth is stymied, and everyone ekes out a small living. Countries such as Somalia are in this no-win situation.

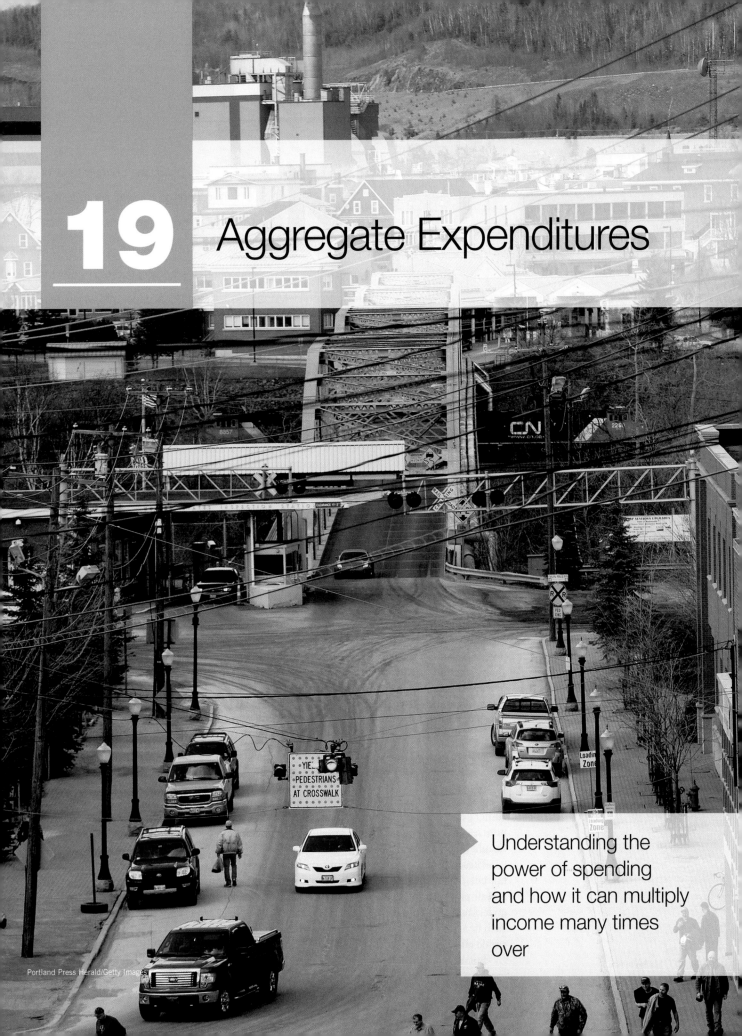

19 Aggregate Expenditures

Understanding the power of spending and how it can multiply income many times over

Portland Press Herald/Getty Images

Learning Objectives

19.1 Name the components of aggregate spending.

19.2 Analyze the relationship between consumption and income using a basic aggregate expenditures graph.

19.3 Analyze consumption and saving using marginal propensity to consume (MPC) and marginal propensity to save (MPS).

19.4 Describe the determinants of consumption, saving, and investment.

19.5 Determine macroeconomic equilibrium in the simple aggregate expenditures model of the private domestic economy.

19.6 Explain the multiplier process, how it is computed, and why it operates in both directions.

19.7 Describe macroeconomic equilibrium in the full aggregate expenditures model when government and the foreign sectors are added.

19.8 Explain why, at equilibrium, injections equal withdrawals in the economy.

19.9 Describe the differences between recessionary and inflationary gaps.

adawaska, Maine, near the northern end of U.S. 1 that extends all the way south to Key West, Florida, is like many other idyllic small towns in the United States—picturesque, friendly, and highly dependent on one industry to provide jobs for its residents. For Madawaska, it is the local paper mill, which provides jobs to 620 of its 4,100 residents. The salaries earned by its workers help to keep the rest of the town employed, including workers in restaurants and cafés, pharmacies, banks, and gas stations that serve the paper mill workers and their families.

During the depth of the 2007–2009 recession, when Madawaska's paper mill was on the brink of closure, not only did its workers face potential unemployment, but so did the rest of the community, which depends on people with jobs at the paper mill to support their businesses. Towns such as Madawaska highlight the interdependency of the economy in which the loss of one job results in a reduction in spending that affects other jobs. In 2010 the workers at the paper mill took the unusual step of accepting an 8.5% wage cut in order to keep the company (and town) from closing down. And the plan worked—the plant survived and was sold to an investment firm in 2013 that promised to keep the paper mill running in Madawaska, where it remains in operation today.

The economic crisis that Madawaska faced during the last recession was one that many cities, big and small, experienced. As unemployment rose, people had less money to spend on clothing, electronics, travel, and cars, which caused a chain reaction downward in consumption, leading to further unemployment and slow or negative economic growth. This chain reaction is what John Maynard Keynes alluded to when he published *The General Theory of Employment, Interest and Money* in 1936, which discussed the importance of aggregate spending and the government's role in stabilizing the macroeconomy.

Today, the U.S. economy (along with the majority of its cities) has recovered from the last recession. As employment opportunities grew during the recovery, more money was earned and subsequently spent, which generated more economic activity and jobs. The chain reaction in recent years has worked in a positive direction. Sometimes, however, consumers and businesses alone cannot pull an economy out of recession, and government policies are needed to speed up growth. But *how* should government act and to *what extent* should it act?

These are the more contentious questions that are debated today. Stimulus packages, tax cuts, farm subsidies, laws and regulations, and even financial aid for college students are all part of a huge arsenal of tools available to government policymakers. The goal of government stimulus programs is to put money into the hands (through jobs, tax cuts, and cash benefits) of those most likely to spend it in their communities, thus carrying a positive ripple effect through to other businesses that depend on consumer spending.

But Keynesian policies have not been without their critics as the size of government grew. Spending by government (federal, state, and local) has increased from 10% of GDP

BY THE NUMBERS

The Role of Spending in the Economy

Spending plays a vital role in spurring economic activity and creating growth and jobs. Spending occurs by consumers, investors, foreigners, and government. During economic downturns, government plays an increasingly important role in trying to influence the economy.

Go to LaunchPad to use the latest data to recreate this graph.

Government spending as a percentage of GDP rises during economic recessions (shaded).

Average government spending per person varies significantly across countries. The U.S. government spends less per person than governments of other developed countries.

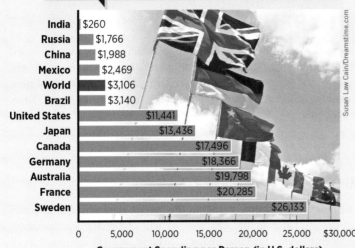

Country	Government Spending per Person (in U.S. dollars)
India	$260
Russia	$1,766
China	$1,988
Mexico	$2,469
World	$3,106
Brazil	$3,140
United States	$11,441
Japan	$13,436
Canada	$17,496
Germany	$18,366
Australia	$19,798
France	$20,285
Sweden	$26,133

Government Spending per Person (in U.S. dollars)

$3,032,500,000,000

Total U.S. private domestic investment spending in 2015

$2,223,618,000,000

Total U.S. spending by foreign consumers (exports) in 2015

The top categories of personal consumption expenditures in the United States in 2015:

Goods:
1. Food/Groceries — $899.5 billion
2. Motor Vehicles/Parts — $455.0 billion
3. Recreational Goods — $383.8 billion
4. Clothing/Footwear — $376.3 billion
5. Gasoline/Energy — $294.7 billion

Services:
1. Housing/Utilities — $2,232.0 billion
2. Health Care — $2,099.8 billion
3. Financial Services/Insurance — $931.0 billion
4. Restaurants/Hotels — $827.1 billion
5. Recreational Services — $479.3 billion

Combined spending among state and local governments roughly equals federal spending. Total spending among all governments was about $6.4 trillion in 2015. (Values in billions.)

- State $1,575.2
- Federal* $3,063.9
- Local $1,772.1

*Federal spending excludes intergovernmental transfers (money given to state and local governments).

in the 1930s to over 30% today as the size and scope of government programs expand. Although many people benefit from these programs, some believe government has overreached and they would prefer something smaller and simpler.

This sort of thinking is not new. In fact, over a century ago, government policies were rarely used to intervene in the workings of the economy, even when the economy entered a downturn. Classical economists, as they are called, viewed the role of the government as providing the necessary framework upon which the market could operate—maintaining competition, providing central banking services, providing for national defense, administering the legal system, and so forth. But government was not expected to play a role in promoting full employment, stabilizing prices, or stimulating economic growth—the economy was supposed to do this on its own. The belief at the time was that economic downturns were *self-correcting*, meaning that if the economy were left alone, the forces of supply and demand would naturally bring the economy back into equilibrium.

The classical perspective was challenged during the Great Depression by Keynes, who turned away from the classical framework with its three separate and distinct competitive markets operating through prices, wages, and interest rates. He focused instead on the economy as a whole and on aggregate spending.

In this chapter, we develop the aggregate expenditures model, which is commonly referred to as the Keynesian model. It can be used to analyze short-run macroeconomic fluctuations and how policymakers counteract the effects caused by the business cycle. Keynes's focus was on aggregate spending, and how consumption spending is a key component to explaining how the economy reaches short-term equilibrium employment, output, and income. Using this model, we will see why an economy can get stuck in an undesirable place, and why policies are useful in smoothing out the business cycle.

AGGREGATE EXPENDITURES

Recall that when we discussed measuring gross domestic product (GDP), we concluded that it could be computed by adding up either all spending or all income in the economy. We saw that the expenditures side consists of consumer spending, business investment spending, government spending, and net foreign spending (exports minus imports). Thus, **aggregate expenditures** are equal to

$$GDP = AE = C + I + G + (X - M)$$

aggregate expenditures Consist of consumer spending, business investment spending, government spending, and net foreign spending (exports minus imports): $GDP = C + I + G + (X - M)$.

Some Simplifying Assumptions

In this chapter, we first will focus on a simple model of the private economy that includes only consumers and businesses. Later in the chapter, we will incorporate government spending, taxes, and the foreign sector into our analysis. Second, we will assume that all saving is personal saving as opposed to national saving, which includes business saving and government saving. Third, because Keynes was modeling a depression economy, we follow him in assuming that there is considerable slack in the economy, much like the economy during and in the years following the 2007–2009 recession. Unemployment is high and other resources are sitting idle, which means that if demand were to rise, businesses could quickly increase output without any upward pressure on costs. We will assume therefore that the aggregate price level (the CPI, PPI, or GDP deflator) is fixed. Taking into account these assumptions, which make the analysis easier but do not affect the key points, let us begin by looking at consumption and saving.

Consumption and Saving

consumption Spending by individuals and households on both durable goods (e.g., autos, appliances, and electronic equipment) and nondurable goods (e.g., food, clothing, and entertainment).

Personal consumption expenditures (C) represent about 68% of GDP, and for this reason **consumption** is a major ingredient in our model. Figure 1 shows personal consumption expenditures for the years since 1980. Notice how closely consumption parallels disposable income.

FIGURE 1	CONSUMPTION AND DISPOSABLE INCOME

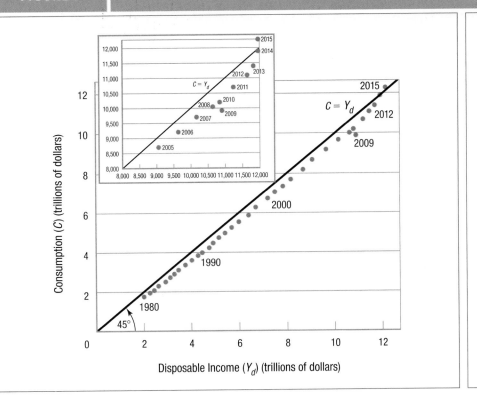

This graph shows personal consumption spending (C) for the years since 1980. The 45° line represents an economy that spends its entire income each year, resulting in no saving. Annual saving (S) is equal to the vertical difference between the 45° line and annual consumption ($S = Y_d - C$). The inset shows more clearly that consumption fell in 2009 when the economy was at the trough of the business cycle, but has since recovered.

The 45° line inserted in the figure represents all points where consumption is equal to disposable income (Y_d). If an economy spends its entire annual income, saving nothing, the 45° line would represent consumption. Consequently, annual **saving** (S) is equal to the vertical difference between the 45° reference line and annual consumption ($S = Y_d - C$). After all, what can you do with income except spend it or save it?

Notice that consumption spending increased every year since 1980 except in 2009, when disposable income rose but consumption dropped. This was an important contributor to the depth of the 2007–2009 recession. In fact, the last time annual consumption spending dropped occurred in 1933, during the depth of the Great Depression.

Keynes began his theoretical examination of consumption by noting the following:

The fundamental psychological law, upon which we are entitled to depend with great confidence both a priori from our knowledge of human nature and from the detailed facts of experience, is that men are disposed, as a rule and on the average, to increase their consumption as their income increases, but not by as much as the change in their income.[1]

Consumption spending grows, in other words, as income grows, but not as fast. Therefore, as income grows, saving will grow as a percentage of income. Notice that this approach to analyzing saving differs from the classical approach. Classical economists assumed that the *interest rate* is the principal determinant of saving and, by extension, one of the principal determinants of consumption. Keynes, in contrast, emphasized *income* as the main determinant of consumption and saving.

Table 1 portrays a hypothetical consumption function of the sort Keynes envisioned. As income grows from $4,000 to $4,200, consumption increases by $150 ($4,150 − $4,000) and saving grows from $0 to $50. Thus, the *change* in income of $200 is divided between consumption ($150) and saving ($50). Note that at income levels below $4,000, saving is negative; people are spending more than their current income either by using credit or drawing on existing savings to support consumption.

saving The difference between income and consumption; the amount of disposable income not spent.

[1] John Maynard Keynes, *The General Theory of Employment, Interest and Money* (New York: Harcourt Brace Jovanovich), 1936, p. 96.

TABLE 1	HYPOTHETICAL CONSUMPTION AND SAVING AND PROPENSITIES TO CONSUME AND SAVE					
(1) Income or Output Y (in \$)	(2) Consumption C (in \$)	(3) Saving S (in \$)	(4) APC $C \div Y$	(5) APS $S \div Y$	(6) MPC $\Delta C \div \Delta Y$	(7) MPS $\Delta S \div \Delta Y$
3,000	3,250	−250	1.08	−0.08	0.75	0.25
3,200	3,400	−200	1.06	−0.06	0.75	0.25
3,400	3,550	−150	1.04	−0.04	0.75	0.25
3,600	3,700	−100	1.03	−0.03	0.75	0.25
3,800	3,850	−50	1.01	−0.01	0.75	0.25
4,000	4,000	0	1.00	0.00	0.75	0.25
4,200	4,150	50	0.99	0.01	0.75	0.25
4,400	4,300	100	0.98	0.02	0.75	0.25
4,600	4,450	150	0.97	0.03	0.75	0.25
4,800	4,600	200	0.96	0.04	0.75	0.25
5,000	4,750	250	0.95	0.05	0.75	0.25
5,200	4,900	300	0.94	0.06	0.75	0.25
5,400	5,050	350	0.94	0.06	0.75	0.25
5,600	5,200	400	0.93	0.07	0.75	0.25

average propensity to consume
The percentage of income that is consumed ($C \div Y$).

average propensity to save The percentage of income that is saved ($S \div Y$).

Average Propensities to Consume and Save

The percentage of income that is consumed is known as the **average propensity to consume** (APC); it is listed in column (4) of Table 1. It is calculated by dividing consumption spending by income ($C \div Y$). For example, when income is \$5,000 and consumption is \$4,750, APC is 0.95, meaning that 95% of the income is spent.

The **average propensity to save** (APS) is equal to saving divided by income ($S \div Y$); it is the percentage of income saved. Again, if income is \$5,000 and saving is \$250, APS is 0.05, or 5% is saved. The APS is shown in column (5) of Table 1.

Notice that if you add columns (4) and (5) in Table 1, the answer is always 1. That is because $Y = C + S$; therefore, all income is either spent or saved. Similar logic dictates that the two percentages spent and saved must total 100%, or that $APC + APS = 1$.

marginal propensity to consume
The change in consumption associated with a given change in income ($\Delta C \div \Delta Y$).

Marginal Propensities to Consume and Save

Average propensities to consume and save represent the proportion of income that is consumed or saved. *Marginal* propensities measure what part of *additional* income will be either consumed or saved. This distinction is important because changing policies by government policymakers mean that income changes and consumers' reactions to their *changing* incomes are what we will see later drive changes in the economy.

The **marginal propensity to consume** (MPC) is equal to the change in consumption associated with a given change in income. Denoting change by the delta symbol (Δ), $MPC = \Delta C \div \Delta Y$. Thus, for example, when income grows from \$5,000 to \$5,200 (a \$200 change), and consumption rises from \$4,750 to \$4,900 (a \$150 change), MPC is equal to 0.75 (\$150 ÷ \$200).

Notice that this result is consistent with Keynes's fundamental psychological law quoted earlier, holding that people "are disposed, as a rule and on the average, to increase their consumption as their income increases, but not by as much as the change in their income." In Table 1, the MPC for all changes in income is 0.75, as shown in column (6).

marginal propensity to save The change in saving associated with a given change in income ($\Delta S \div \Delta Y$).

The **marginal propensity to save** (MPS) is equal to the change in saving associated with a given change in income; $MPS = \Delta S \div \Delta Y$. Therefore, when income grows from \$5,000 to \$5,200, and saving grows from \$250 to \$300, MPS is equal to 0.25 (\$50 ÷ \$200). Column (7) lists MPS.

Note once again that the sum of the MPC and the MPS will always equal 1, because the only thing that can be done with a change in income is to spend or save it. A small word of warning, however: Though $APC + APS = 1$ and $MPC + MPS = 1$, most of the time $APC + MPS \neq 1$ and $APS + MPC \neq 1$. Try adding a few different columns from Table 1 and you will see that this is true.

Figure 2 graphs the consumption and saving schedules from Table 1. The graph in panel A extends the consumption schedule back to zero income, where consumption is equal to $1,000 and saving is equal to −$1,000. (Remember that $Y = C + S$; therefore, if $Y = 0$ and $C = \$1,000$, then S must equal −$1,000. With no income, people in this economy would continue to spend, either borrowing money or drawing down their accumulated savings to survive.) The 45° line in panel A is a reference line where $Y = C + S$. At the point at which the consumption schedule crosses the reference line (point a, $Y = \$4,000$), saving is zero because consumption and income are equal.

The saving schedule in panel B plots the difference between the 45° reference line ($Y = C + S$) and the consumption schedule in panel A. For example, if income is $4,000, saving is zero (point f in panel B), and when income equals $5,000, saving equals $250 [line ($b − c$) in panel A, point g in panel B]. Saving is positively sloped, again reflecting Keynes's fundamental law; the more people earn, the greater percentage of income they will save (the average propensity to save rises as income rises). Make a mental note that the saving schedule shows how much people *desire* to save at various income levels.

How much people will *actually* save depends on equilibrium income, or how much income the economy is generating. We are getting a bit ahead of the story here, but planting

Suppose you receive some birthday money from your aunt. What portion of this money would you spend and what portion would you save? These portions are your marginal propensity to consume and marginal propensity to save, respectively.

FIGURE 2	**CONSUMPTION AND SAVING**

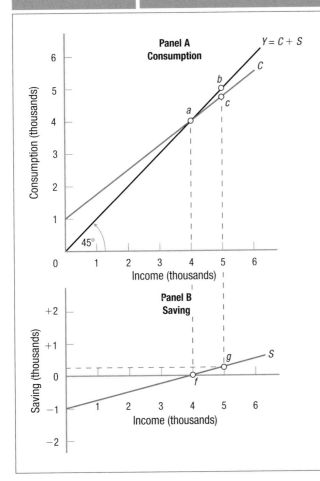

The consumption and saving schedules from Table 1 are graphed here. Panel A extends the consumption schedule back to zero income, where consumption is equal to $1,000 and saving is equal to −$1,000. At the point where the consumption schedule crosses the reference line (point a, $Y = \$4,000$), saving is zero. The saving schedule in panel B simply plots the difference between the 45° reference line and the consumption schedule in panel A. Thus, when income = $5,000, saving = $250 [line ($b − c$) in panel A, point g in panel B].

this seed will help you when we get to the section where we determine equilibrium income in the economy.

Note finally that the consumption and saving schedules in our example are straight-line functions. This need not be the case, but it simplifies some of the relationships to graph them like this at this point. When the consumption and saving schedules are linear, the MPC is the slope of the consumption function, and the MPS is the slope of the saving schedule. In this case, *MPC* = 0.75 and *MPS* = 0.25, which tells us that every time income changes by $1,000, consumption will change by $750 and saving will change by $250.

Other Determinants of Consumption and Saving
Income is the principal determinant of consumption and saving, but other factors can shift the saving and consumption schedules. These factors include the wealth of a family, their expectations about the future of prices and income, family debt, and taxation.

- *Wealth* The more wealth a family has, the higher its consumption at all levels of income. Wealth affects the consumption schedule by shifting it up or down, depending on whether wealth rises or falls. When the stock market was soaring in the late 1990s, policymakers worried about the wealth effect, that as many households saw their wealth dramatically expand, rising consumption might cause the economy's inflation rate to rise. As it turned out, the stock market collapsed in 2000, and again in 2008, and the economy moved into recession. Then, economists began worrying about the negative impact of this wealth effect as trillions of dollars of wealth evaporated from the stock market before it eventually recovered.

- *Expectations* Expectations about future prices and incomes help determine how much a person will spend today. If you anticipate that prices will rise next week, you will be more likely to purchase more products today. What are sales, after all, but temporary reductions in price designed to entice customers into the store today? Similarly, if you anticipate that your income will soon rise—perhaps you are about to graduate from medical school—you will be more inclined to incur debt today to purchase something you want, as was the case with LeBron James, who drove an expensive Hummer while in high school, knowing that when he was drafted into the NBA, he would be making a fortune. Lotto winners who receive their winnings over a 20-year span often spend much of the money early on, running up debts. Few winners spend their winnings evenly over the 20 years.

- *Household Debt* Most households carry some debt, typically in the form of credit card balances, auto loans, student loans, or a home mortgage. The more debt a household has, the less able it is to spend in the current period as it makes payments toward the debt. Although the household might want to spend more money on goods now, its debt level restricts its ability to get more credit.

- *Taxes* Taxes reduce disposable income, and therefore taxes result in reduced consumption and saving. When taxes are increased, spendable income falls; therefore, consumption is reduced by the MPC times the reduction in disposable income, and saving falls by the reduction in disposable income times the MPS. Tax reductions have the opposite effect, as we will see later in this chapter.

Investment

When the town of West Point, Georgia, received the news that South Korean automaker Kia Motors was building a $1 billion car manufacturing facility in its town, its residents couldn't have been happier. Not only was Kia creating thousands of jobs, the spending by its workers would create even more jobs throughout the region. Because Kia's manufacturing facility was new to the U.S. economy (and not simply a move from another town), it is counted as *gross private domestic investment* (the "I" in the GDP equation), an important component of the aggregate expenditures model. **Investment** can come from foreign and domestic sources, for example, when American companies expand their operations by investing in new capital such as building a new factory.

investment Spending by businesses that adds to the productive capacity of the economy. Investment depends on factors such as its rate of return, the level of technology, and business expectations about the economy.

Unlike consumer spending, which at 68% is the largest component of GDP and until recently held fairly steady from year to year, gross private domestic investment is volatile. Sure, large investment deals like Kia's new plant in West Point, Georgia, are a huge boost to the economy, but such investments tend to be sporadic. The annual percentage changes in consumption and investment spending from 1980 to 2015 are shown in Figure 3.

Notice that although consumption plodded along with annual increases between 0% and 10%, investment spending has undergone annual fluctuations ranging from −22% to +27%. Investment constitutes about 16% of GDP; therefore, its volatility often accounts for our recessions and booms.

The economic boom of the 1990s, for instance, was fueled by investments in information technology infrastructure, including massive investments in telecommunications. In the 1990s, people believed that Internet traffic would grow by 1,000% a year, doubling every three months or so. This belief led many companies to lay millions of miles of fiber optic cable. When the massive investments made in computer hardware and software over that same decade are taken into account, it is no wonder that the economy grew at a breakneck pace.

But this increase came to a halt in the early 2000s, when businesses—especially the telecoms—discovered that they had built up a massive excess capacity, and thus bandwidth prices plummeted. The resulting plunge in investment between 2000 and 2001 can be seen in Figure 3. Investment recovered by 2003, then collapsed from 2007 to 2009 as the housing and financial crises took their toll.

Investment Demand Investment levels depend mainly on the rate of return on capital. Investments earning a high rate of return are the investments undertaken first (assuming comparable risk), with those projects offering lower returns finding their way into the

Many residents in West Point, Georgia, were excited when South Korean auto manufacturer Kia Motors built a large factory in their town in 2008, saving the town's economy after decades of factory closings and job losses.

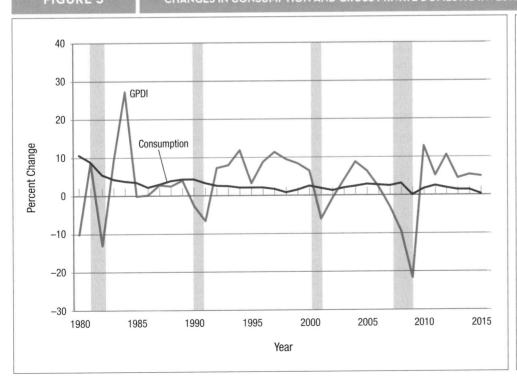

FIGURE 3 — CHANGES IN CONSUMPTION AND GROSS PRIVATE DOMESTIC INVESTMENT

The annual percentage changes in consumption and gross private domestic investment (GPDI) are shown here. Consumption is relatively stable, but investment spending is highly volatile, with annual fluctuations ranging from −22% to +27%. The shaded bars represent recessions.

Inventories	% Higher	% Same	% Lower	Index
Feb 2016	13	64	23	45.0
Jan 2016	13	61	26	43.5
Dec 2015	14	59	27	43.5
Nov 2015	13	60	27	43.0

Each month, the Institute of Supply Management provides a forecast of investment demand by asking businesses whether their inventories are higher, the same, or lower than the previous month. Investors cheer falling inventories, because it is a sign that businesses will boost factory production and investment in new facilities. Although inventories rose slightly from November 2015 to February 2016, the overall index remains low, signaling continued economic growth.

investment stream later. Interest rate levels also are important in determining how much investment occurs, because much of business investment is financed through debt. As interest rates fall, investment rises, and vice versa.

Although the rate of return on investments is the main determinant of investment spending, other factors influence investment demand, including expectations, technological change, capital goods on hand, and operating costs.

■ **Expectations** Projecting the rate of return on investment is not an easy task. Returns are forecasted over the life of a new piece of equipment or factory, yet many changes in the economic environment can alter the actual return on these investments. As business expectations improve, investment demand will increase as businesses are willing to invest more at any given interest rate.

■ **Technological Change** Technological innovations periodically spur investment. The introduction of electrification, automobiles, and phone service at the beginning of the 20th century and, most recently, mobile technology and the new products they have spawned, are examples. Producing brand-new products requires massive investments in plants, equipment, and research and development. These investments often take a long time before their full potential is realized.

■ **Operating Costs** When the costs of operating and maintaining machinery and equipment rise, the rate of return on capital equipment declines and new investment will be postponed.

■ **Capital Goods on Hand** The more capital goods a firm has on hand, including inventories of the products it sells, the less the firm will want to make new investments. Until existing capacity can be fully used, investing in more equipment and facilities will do little to help profits.

Aggregate Investment Schedule To simplify our analysis, we will assume that rates of return and interest rates fully determine investment in the short run. But once that level of investment has been determined, it remains independent of income, or *autonomous,* as economists say. Therefore, unlike consumption, which increases as income rises, we will assume that investment does not vary based on income, but instead on the rates of return that determine how potentially profitable investment will be. Figure 4 shows the resulting aggregate investment schedule that plots investment spending with respect to income.

FIGURE 4	THE INVESTMENT SCHEDULE

The aggregate investment schedule, relating investment spending to income, is shown here. Because aggregate investment is I_0 at all income levels, the curve is a horizontal straight line. This assumption simplifies the aggregate expenditures model.

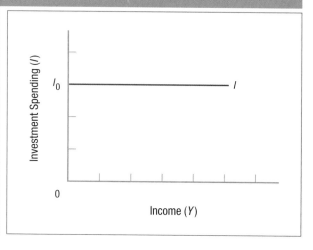

Because we have assumed that aggregate investment is I_0 at all income levels, the curve is a horizontal straight line. Investment is unaffected by different levels of income. This is a simplifying assumption that we will change in later chapters when we look at its implications.

Our emphasis in this section has been on two important components of aggregate spending: consumption and investment. Consumption is about 68% and investment is about 16% of aggregate spending. Consumption is relatively stable, but investment is volatile and especially sensitive to expectations about conditions in the economy. We have seen that, on average, some income is spent (APC) and some is saved (APS). But, it is that portion of *additional* income that is spent (MPC) and saved (MPS) that is most important for where the economy settles or where it reaches equilibrium, as we will see in the next section.

 CHECKPOINT

AGGREGATE EXPENDITURES

- Aggregate expenditures are equal to $C + I + G + (X - M)$, with consumption being about 68% of aggregate spending.
- Keynes argued that saving and consumption spending are related to income. As income grows, consumption will grow but not as fast.
- The marginal propensities to consume (MPC) and save (MPS) are equal to $\Delta C \div \Delta Y$ and $\Delta S \div \Delta Y$, respectively. They represent the change in consumption and saving associated with a change in income.
- Other factors affecting consumption and saving include wealth, expectations about future income and prices, the level of household debt, and taxes.
- Investment levels depend primarily on the rate of return on capital.
- Other determinants of investment demand include business expectations, technology change, operating costs, and the amount of capital goods on hand.
- Consumption is relatively stable. In contrast, investment is volatile.

QUESTION: Why is investment spending generally much more volatile than consumption spending?

Answers to the Checkpoint questions can be found at the end of this chapter.

THE SIMPLE AGGREGATE EXPENDITURES MODEL

Now that we have stripped the government and foreign sectors from our analysis at this point, aggregate expenditures (AE) will consist of the sum of consumer and business investment spending ($AE = C + I$). Figure 5 shows a simple aggregate expenditures model based on consumption and investment. Aggregate expenditures based on the data in Table 1 are shown in panel A of Figure 5; panel B shows the corresponding saving and investment schedules.

Let us take a moment to remind ourselves what these graphs represent. The 45° line in panel A represents the situation when income exactly equals spending, or $Y = AE$. In other words, no savings occur at any level of income. All other lines represent situations in which income does not exactly equal spending at all levels of income. Point *a* in both panels is that level of income ($4,000) at which saving is zero and all income is spent. Saving is therefore positive for income levels above $4,000 and negative at incomes below. The vertical distance *ef* in panel A represents investment (I_0) of $100; it is equal to I_0 in panel B. Note that the vertical axis of panel B has a different scale from that of panel A.

FIGURE 5 EQUILIBRIUM IN THE AGGREGATE EXPENDITURES MODEL

Ignoring government spending and net exports, aggregate expenditures (AE) consist of consumer spending and business investment ($AE = C + I$). Panel A shows AE and its relationship with income (Y); when spending equals income, the economy is on the $Y = AE$ line. Panel B shows the corresponding saving and investment schedules. Point a in both panels shows where income equals consumption and saving is zero. Therefore, saving is positive for income levels above $4,000 and negative at incomes below $4,000. The vertical distance ef in panel A represents investment ($100); it is equal to I_0 in panel B. Equilibrium income and output are $4,400 (point e), because this is the level at which businesses are producing just what other businesses and consumers want to buy.

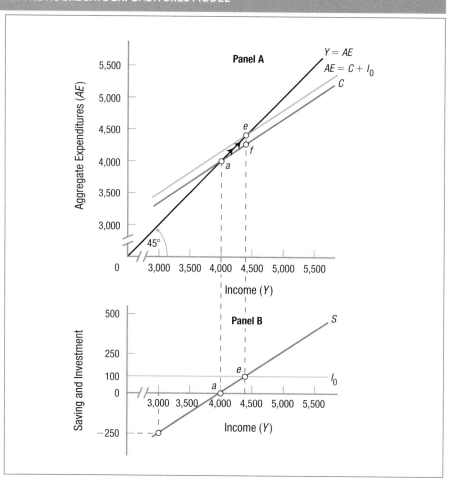

Macroeconomic Equilibrium in the Simple Model

Keynesian macroeconomic equilibrium The state of an economy at which all injections equal all withdrawals. There are no pressures pushing the economy to a higher or lower level of output.

The important question to ask is where this economy will come to rest. Or, in the language of economists, at what income will this economy reach **Keynesian macroeconomic equilibrium**? By equilibrium, economists mean that income at which there are no net pressures pushing the economy to move to a higher or lower level of output.

To find this equilibrium point, let's begin with the economy at an income level of $4,000. Are there pressures driving the economy to grow or decline? Looking at point a in panel A of Figure 5, we see that the economy is producing $4,000 worth of goods and services and $4,000 in income. At this income level, however, consumers and businesses want to spend $4,100 ($4,000 in consumption and $100 in investment). Because aggregate expenditures (AE) exceed current income and output, there are more goods being demanded ($4,100) than are being supplied at $4,000. As a result, businesses will find it in their best interests to produce more, raising employment and income and moving the economy toward income and output level $4,400 (point e).

Once the economy has moved to $4,400, what consumers and businesses want to buy is exactly equal to the income and output being produced. Businesses are producing $4,400, aggregate expenditures are equal to $4,400, and there are no pressures on the economy to move away from point e. Income of $4,400, or point e, is an equilibrium point for the economy.

Panel B shows this same equilibrium, again as point *e*. Is it a coincidence that saving and investment are equal at this point where income and output are at equilibrium? The answer is no. In this simple private sector model, saving and investment will always be equal when the economy is in equilibrium.

Remember that aggregate expenditures are equal to consumption plus business investment ($AE = C + I$). Recall also that *at equilibrium*, aggregate expenditures, income, and output are all equal; what is demanded is supplied ($AE = Y$). Finally, keep in mind that income can either be spent or saved ($Y = C + S$). By substitution, we know that, at equilibrium,

$$AE = Y = C + I$$

We also know that

$$Y = C + S$$

Substituting $C + I$ for Y yields

$$C + I = C + S$$

Canceling the *C*'s, we find that, *at equilibrium,*

$$I = S$$

Thus, the location of point *e* in panel B is not just coincidental; at equilibrium, actual saving and investment are always equal. Note that at point *a*, saving is zero, yet investment spending is $100 at I_0. This difference means businesses desire to invest more than people desire to save. With *desired* investment exceeding *desired* saving, this cannot be an equilibrium point, because saving and investment must be equal in order for the economy to be at equilibrium. Indeed, income will rise until these two values are equal at point *e*.

JOHN MAYNARD KEYNES (1883-1946)

In 1935 John Maynard Keynes boasted in a letter to playwright George Bernard Shaw of a book he was writing that would revolutionize "the way the world thinks about economic problems." This was a brash prediction to make, even to a friend, but it was not an idle boast. His *General Theory of Employment, Interest and Money* did change the way the world looked at economics.

Keynes belongs to a small class of economic earth-shakers that includes Karl Marx and Adam Smith. His one-man war on classical theory launched a new field of study known as macroeconomics. His ideas would have a profound influence on theorists and government policies for decades to come.

Keynes was once asked if there was any era comparable to the Great Depression. He replied, "It was called the Dark Ages and it lasted 400 years." His prescription to President Franklin D. Roosevelt was to increase government spending to stimulate the economy. Sundeep Reddy reports that "during a 1934 dinner . . . after one economist carefully removed a towel from a stack to dry his hands, Mr. Keynes swept the whole pile of towels on the floor and crumpled them up, explaining that his way of using towels did more to stimulate employment among restaurant workers" (*The Wall Street Journal*, January 8, 2009, p. A10).

During the world economic depression in the early 1930s, Keynes became alarmed when unemployment in England continued to rise after the first few years of the crisis. Keynes argued that *aggregate expenditures*, the sum of consumption, investment, government spending, and net exports, determined the levels of economic output and employment. When aggregate expenditures were high, the economy would foster business expansion, higher incomes, and high levels of employment. With low aggregate spending, businesses would be unable to sell their inventories and would cut back on investment and production.

The ideas formulated by Keynes dramatically changed the way government policy is used throughout the world. Today, as many countries face a slow economic recovery, governments have taken a more proactive role in their economies in hopes of avoiding another downturn of the magnitude seen in the 1930s.

What is important to take from this discussion? First, when intended (or desired) saving and investment differ, the economy will have to grow or shrink to achieve equilibrium. When desired saving exceeds desired investment—at income levels above $4,400 in panel B—income will decline. When intended saving is below intended investment—at income levels below $4,400—income will rise. Notice that we are using the words "intended" and "desired" interchangeably.

Second, at equilibrium all **injections** of spending (investment in this case) into the economy must equal all **withdrawals** (saving in this simple model). Spending injections increase aggregate income, while spending withdrawals reduce it. This fact will become important as we add government and the foreign sector to the model.

Returning to Figure 5, given an initial investment of $100 ($I_0$), equilibrium is at an output of $4,400 (point *e*). Remember that at equilibrium, what people *withdraw* from the

injections Increments of spending, including investment, government spending, and exports.

withdrawals Activities that remove spending from the economy, including saving, taxes, and imports.

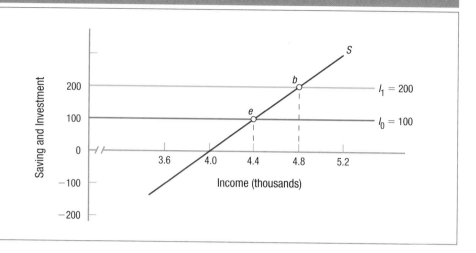

FIGURE 6 | **SAVING AND INVESTMENT**

When investment is $100, equilibrium employment occurs at an output of $4,400 (point *e*). When investment rises to $200 ($I_1$), equilibrium output climbs to $4,800 (point *b*). Thus, $100 of added investment spending causes income to grow by $400. This is the multiplier at work.

economy (saving) is equal to what others are willing to *inject* into the spending system (investment). In this case, both values equal $100. Point *e* is an equilibrium point because there are no pressures in the system to increase or decrease output; the spending desires of consumers and businesses are satisfied.

The Multiplier

Injections and withdrawals in an economy produce an effect that is greater than the initial value of the injection or withdrawal. The following example illustrates why. Assume that *full employment* occurs at output $4,800. How much would investment have to increase to move the economy out to full employment? As Figure 6 shows, investment must rise to $200 ($I_1$), an increase of $100. With this new investment, equilibrium output moves from point *e* to point *b*, and income rises from $4,400 to $4,800.

What is remarkable here is that a mere $100 of added spending (investment in this case) caused income to grow by $400. This phenomenon is known as the **multiplier** effect. Recognizing it was one of Keynes's major insights. How does it work?

In this example, we have assumed the marginal propensity to consume is 0.75. Therefore, for each added dollar received by consumers, $0.75 is spent and $0.25 is saved. Thus, when businesses invest an additional $100, the firms providing the machinery will spend $75 of this new income on more raw materials, while saving the remaining $25. The firms supplying the new raw materials have $75 of new income. These firms will spend $56.25 of this (0.75 × $75.00), while saving $18.75 ($56.25 + $18.75 = $75.00). This effect continues on until the added spending has been exhausted. As a result, income will increase by $100 + $75 + $56.25 . . . . In the end, income rises by $400. Figure 7 outlines this multiplier process.

The general formula for the spending multiplier (*k*) is

$$k = 1/(1 - MPC)$$

Alternatively, because $MPC + MPS = 1$, the $MPS = 1 - MPC$; therefore,

$$k = 1/MPS$$

multiplier Spending changes alter equilibrium income by the spending change times the multiplier. One person's spending becomes another's income, and that second person spends some (the MPC), which becomes income for another person, and so on, until income has changed by $1/(1 - MPC) = 1/MPS$. The multiplier operates in both directions.

FIGURE 7	THE MULTIPLIER PROCESS

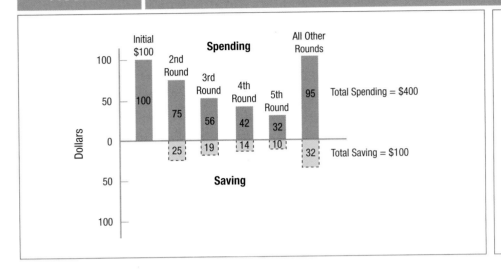

An initial $100 of spending generates more spending because of the multiplier process shown in this figure. With an $MPC = 0.75$ in the second round, $75 is spent and $25 is saved. In the third round, $56.25 of the previous $75 is spent and $18.75 is saved, and so on. Total spending is $400, and total saving is $100 when all rounds are completed.

Thus, in our simple model, the multiplier is

$$1/(1 - 0.75) = 1/0.25 = 4$$

As a result of the multiplier effect, new spending will raise equilibrium by 4 times the amount of new spending. Note that any change in spending (consumption, investment—and as we will see in the next section—government spending or changes in net exports) will also have this effect. Spending is spending. Note also—and this is important—the multiplier works in both directions.

The Multiplier Works in Both Directions

If spending increases raise equilibrium income by the increase times the multiplier, a spending decrease will reduce income in corresponding fashion. In our simple economy, for instance, a $100 decline in investment or consumer spending will reduce income by $400.

This is one reason why recession watchers are always concerned about consumer confidence. During a recession, income declines, or at least the rate of income growth falls. If consumers decide to increase their saving to guard against the possibility of job loss, they may inadvertently make the recession worse. As they pull more of their money out of the spending stream, *withdrawals* increase, and income is reduced by a multiplied amount as other agents in the economy feel the effects of this reduced spending. The result can be a more severe or longer-lasting recession.

This was the case when consumer spending peaked in the summer of 2008. After that, auto sales plummeted and housing prices and sales fell. As the recession that started in December 2007 progressed and jobs were lost, consumers reduced their spending. As their confidence in the economy deteriorated, households began to save more, consumer spending declined further, and the economy sank into a deeper recession. Figure 8 shows how consumer spending (downward arrow) fell and saving rose (upward arrow) after September 2008. Leading up to the recession, saving was less than 1% of personal income, but by mid-2009 it had grown to 7%. Before the recession, aggregate household debt had soared, and part of what we are seeing in Figure 8 may reflect households spending less in order to pay off debt and return to more sustainable levels of debt.

FIGURE 8	CONSUMPTION AND SAVING, 2007-2009

Consumption declined as the recession developed, and consumer worries about job losses and the decline in housing prices resulted in households saving more. The shaded area on the right represents the recession.

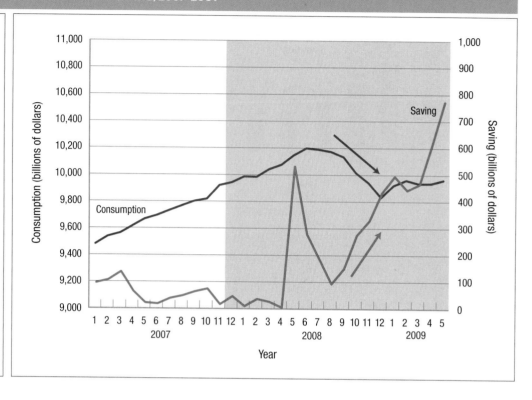

paradox of thrift When investment is positively related to income and households *intend* to save more, they reduce consumption. Consequently, income and output decrease, reducing investment such that savings actually end up decreasing.

Paradox of Thrift The implication of Keynesian analysis for actual aggregate household saving and household intentions regarding saving is called the **paradox of thrift.** As we saw in Figure 8, if households *intend* (or desire) to save more, they will reduce consumption, thereby reducing income and output, resulting in job losses and further reductions in income, consumption, business investment, and so on. The end result is an aggregate equilibrium with lower output, income, investment, and in the final analysis, lower *actual* aggregate saving.

Notice that we have modified our assumption about investment—it now varies with economic conditions and is positively related to income. When the economy improves and income (or output) rises, investment expands as well, and vice versa when the economy sours. This is shown in our simple aggregate expenditures framework in Figure 9.

FIGURE 9	PARADOX OF THRIFT

When consumers intend to save more and consume less (the saving schedule shifts from S_0 to S_1), and if investment is a rising function of income, the end result is that at equilibrium, households actually end up saving less (point *a*).

Do High Savings Rates Increase the Risk of a Long Recession?

Everyone has a frugal friend or relative who saves every penny possible, or a shopaholic friend who can't seem to save any money at all. These differences in savings rates often are influenced by economic and demographic factors.

People with higher incomes tend to save a larger portion of their incomes than those with lower incomes. Older people tend to save more than younger people. And those living in rural areas tend to save more than those in urban areas. Yet, although these factors explain savings rates *within* a country, they do not fully explain the savings rate across countries. In other words, cultural differences play an important role as well.

The following bar graph shows the average household saving rate in a sample of twelve countries in 2016. China and India rank at the top of this list, despite having a lower income per capita than any other country on the list. The United States, which has the highest income per capita among the countries shown, has a savings rate toward the bottom. And some countries have seen dramatic changes in their savings rate, such as Japan, which had one of the highest savings rates 30

years ago, but today has the lowest savings rate among the countries shown.

The savings rate plays an important role in an economy. A high savings rate, such as that in China, India, and France, gives a country's banking system a vote of confidence; people trust putting their money into financial institutions and expect the money will be available when desired. Also, savings provide opportunities for others to borrow, providing inexpensive access to loans for investment.

However, a high savings rate can also make a country vulnerable in times of recession. The adverse effects of a high savings rate are seen in China today, which has seen its growth rate fall in recent years. The natural reaction by Chinese citizens is to save even more, which may further slow economic

growth and eventually lead to a recession. In the 1990s, Japan faced a decade-long recession due to the government's inability to boost consumption and investment using incentives, largely because its citizens and businesses were too worried to consume and invest, and instead chose to save.

The ability of governments to minimize the effects of economic downturns depends on the marginal propensity to consume, which determines the multiplier. The higher the multiplier, the greater the effect government efforts to increase spending will have. Because China and India have very high savings rates, government incentives to boost consumption and investment may not be very effective, which doesn't bode well should either country enter into a recession.

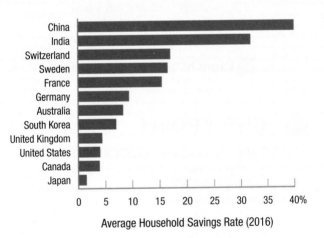

Average Household Savings Rate (2016)

Initially, the economy is in equilibrium at point *e* with saving equal to S_0. If households *desire* to save more because they feel insecure about their jobs, the savings curve will shift upward and to the left to S_1. Now at all levels of income households *intend* to save more. This sets up the chain reaction described previously, leading to a new equilibrium at point *a,* where equilibrium income has fallen to Y_1 and *actual* saving has declined to S_1. The paradox is that if everyone tries to save more (even for good reasons), in the end they may end up saving less.

Brazil's Beco Do Batman: How Graffiti Revived a Neighborhood

> **How did the Beco Do Batman neighborhood in São Paolo turn graffiti into an economic growth engine?**

Eric Chiang

In cities around the world, graffiti artists exhibit their talents on the sides of buildings, trains, and bridges, turning otherwise pristine areas into unsightly views. Graffiti is also a common tool used by gangs, which increases the perception of neighborhoods with graffiti as unsafe, leading to a reduction in their desirability as a place to live or visit. As a result, neighborhoods and cities have an incentive to clean up graffiti. But because cleanup costs can be expensive and graffiti artists often return, winning the war against graffiti becomes difficult.

In one neighborhood in São Paulo, Brazil, instead of pumping more money into a never-ending battle on graffiti, residents decided on a markedly different strategy. What did the residents of Beco Do Batman ("Batman Alley" in Portuguese) choose to do?

Instead of cleaning up the graffiti, residents *encouraged* graffiti artists to come to the area. Since the 1980s, artists from around Brazil and other countries journeyed to Beco Do Batman to paint giant murals in its alleyways. Because the lack of unpainted walls means that new artists must paint over a previous artist's work, a constantly changing art gallery is created for visitors to enjoy.

How did this strategy of welcoming graffiti affect the neighborhood?

First, overall crime *declined*. Because graffiti in Beco Do Batman was no longer a sign of gang power, criminal graffiti artists went elsewhere. This attracted wealthier residents and investors to build homes in the area, raising the property values of all homeowners and businesses.

Second, as Beco Do Batman became a unique tourist attraction, money was spent by tourists who visited the shops and restaurants in the area. The economic activity spurred by visitors created jobs and higher wages for its residents, who then had more money to spend. The cycle of increased economic activity generated a multiplier effect that allowed Beco Do Batman and its surrounding neighborhoods to thrive, pulling many of its residents out of poverty.

The graffiti art of Beco Do Batman is a unique example of how aggregate expenditures and the multiplier effect can lead to higher economic growth.

GO TO **LaunchPad** TO PRACTICE THE ECONOMIC CONCEPTS IN THIS STORY

 ## CHECKPOINT

THE SIMPLE AGGREGATE EXPENDITURES MODEL

- Ignoring both the government and the foreign sector in a simple aggregate expenditures model, macroeconomic equilibrium occurs when aggregate expenditures are just equal to what is being produced.

- At equilibrium, aggregate saving equals aggregate investment.

- The multiplier process amplifies new spending because some of the new spending is saved and some becomes additional spending. And some of that spending is saved and some is spent, and so on.

- The multiplier is equal to $1/(1 - MPC) = 1/MPS$.

- The multiplier works in both directions. Changes in spending are amplified, changing income by more than the initial change in spending.

- The paradox of thrift results when households *intend* to save more, but at equilibrium they end up saving less.

QUESTION: Business journalists, pundits, economists, and policymakers all pay attention to the results of the Conference Board's monthly survey of 5,000 households, called the Consumer Confidence Index. When the index is rising, this is good news for the economy, and when it is falling, concerns are often heard that it portends a recession. Why is this survey important as a tool in forecasting where the economy is headed in the near future?

Answers to the Checkpoint questions can be found at the end of this chapter.

THE FULL AGGREGATE EXPENDITURES MODEL

With the simple aggregate expenditures model of the domestic private sector (individual consumption and private business investment), we concluded that at equilibrium, saving would equal investment, and that changes in spending lead to a larger change in income. This multiplier effect was an important insight by Keynes. To build the full aggregate expenditures model, we now turn our attention to adding government spending and taxes and the impact of the foreign sector.

Adding Government Spending and Taxes

Although government spending and tax policy can get complex, for our purposes it involves simple changes in government spending (G) or taxes (T). As we have seen in the previous section, any change in aggregate spending causes income and output to rise or fall by the spending change times the multiplier.

Figure 10 illustrates a change in government spending. Initially, investment is $100; therefore, equilibrium income is $4,400 (point e), just as in Figure 6 earlier. Rather than investment rising by $100, let's assume that the government decides to spend another $100. As Figure 10 shows, the new equilibrium is $4,800 (point b). This result is similar to the one in Figure 6, confirming that spending is spending; the economy does not care where it comes from.

A quick summary is now in order. Equilibrium income is reached when *injections* (here, $I + G = \$200$) equal *withdrawals* (in this case, $S = \$200$). It did not matter whether these injections came from investment alone or from investment and government spending together. The key is spending.

Changes in spending modify income by an amount equal to the change in spending times the multiplier. How, then, do changes in taxes affect the economy? The answers are not as simple in that case.

Tax Changes and Equilibrium When taxes are increased, money is withdrawn from the economy's spending stream. When taxes are reduced, money is injected into the economy's spending stream because consumers and businesses have more to spend. Thus, taxes form a wedge between income and that part of income that can be spent, or disposable income. Disposable income (Y_d) is equal to income minus taxes ($Y_d = Y - T$). For simplicity, we will assume that all taxes are paid in a lump sum, thereby removing a certain fixed sum of money from the economy. This assumption does away with the need to worry now about the incentive effects of higher or lower tax rates.

FIGURE 10	SAVING, INVESTMENT, AND GOVERNMENT SPENDING

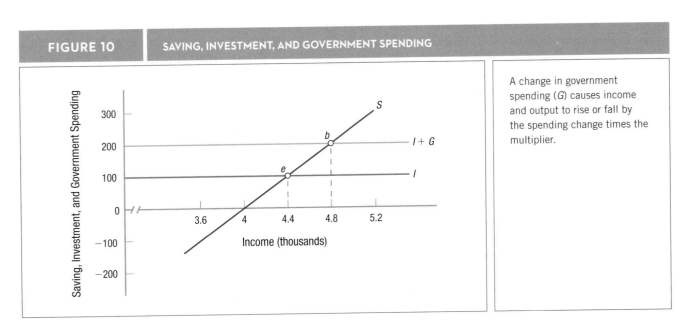

A change in government spending (G) causes income and output to rise or fall by the spending change times the multiplier.

TABLE 2	KEYNESIAN EQUILIBRIUM ANALYSIS WITH TAXES					
Income or Output (Y), in $	Taxes (T), in $	Disposable Income (Y_d), in $	Consumption (C)	Saving (S)	Investment (I)	Government Spending (G)
4,000	100	3,900	3,925	−25	100	100
4,100	100	4,000	4,000	0	100	100
4,200	100	4,100	4,075	25	100	100
4,300	100	4,200	4,150	50	100	100
4,400	100	4,300	4,225	75	100	100
4,500	100	4,400	4,300	100	100	100
4,600	100	4,500	4,375	125	100	100
4,700	100	4,600	4,450	150	100	100
4,800	100	4,700	4,525	175	100	100
4,900	100	4,800	4,600	200	100	100
5,000	100	4,900	4,675	225	100	100

Returning to the model of the economy we have been developing, consumer spending now relates to disposable income ($Y - T$), rather than just income. Table 2 reflects this change, using disposable income to determine consumption. With government spending and taxes (fiscal policy) in the model, spending *injections* into the economy include government spending plus business investment ($G + I$). *Withdrawals* from the system include saving and taxes ($S + T$).

Again, equilibrium requires that *injections* equal *withdrawals,* or in this case,

$$G + I = S + T$$

In our example, Table 2 shows that $G + I = S + T$ at income level $4,500 (the shaded row in the table). If no tax had been imposed, equilibrium would have been at the point at which $S = G + I$, and thus at an income of $4,800 (point *b* in Figure 10, not shown in Table 2). Therefore, imposing the tax reduces equilibrium income by $300. Because taxes represent a withdrawal of spending from the economy, we would expect equilibrium income to fall when a tax is imposed. Yet, why does equilibrium income fall by only $300, and not by the tax multiplied by the multiplier, which would be $400?

The answer is that consumers pay for this tax, in part, by *reducing* their saving. Specifically, with the MPC at 0.75, the $100 tax payment is split between consumption, reduced by $75, and saving, reduced by $25. When this $75 decrease in consumption is multiplied by the multiplier, this yields a decline in income of $300 ($75 × 4). The *reduction* in saving of $25 *dampens* the impact of the tax on equilibrium income because those funds were previously withdrawn from the spending stream. Changing the withdrawal category from saving to taxes does not affect income: Both are withdrawals.

Equilibrium is shown at point *g* in Figure 11. At point *g*, $I + G = S + T$, with equilibrium income equal to $4,500 and taxes and saving equal to $100 each.

The result is that a tax increase (or decrease, for that matter) will have less of a direct impact on income, employment, and output than will an equivalent change in government spending. For this reason, economists typically describe the "tax" multiplier (calculated as $MPC/(1 - MPC)$) as being smaller than the "spending" multiplier ($1/(1 - MPC)$).

The Balanced Budget Multiplier
By now you have probably noticed a curious thing. Our original equilibrium income was $4,400, with investment and saving equal at $100. When the government was introduced with a balanced budget ($G = T = $100),

FIGURE 11	SAVING, INVESTMENT, GOVERNMENT SPENDING, AND TAXES

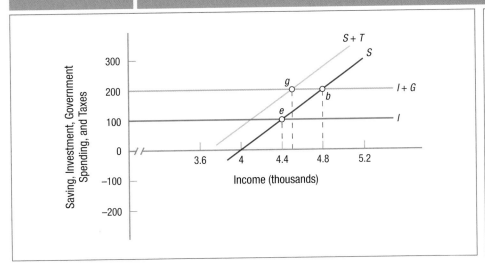

Tax increases or decreases have less of a direct impact on income, employment, and output than an equivalent change in government spending. Some of a tax increase will come from saving and some of a tax decrease will go into saving, thereby reducing the effect of these tax changes.

income rose by $100 to $4,500, while equilibrium saving and investment remained constant at $100.

This has led to what economists call the **balanced budget multiplier.** Equal changes in government spending and taxation (a balanced budget) lead to an equal change in income. Equivalently, the balanced budget multiplier is equal to 1. If spending and taxes are increased by the same amount, income grows by this amount, hence a balanced budget multiplier equal to 1. Note that the balanced budget multiplier is 1 no matter what the values of MPC and MPS.

balanced budget multiplier
Equal changes in government spending and taxation (a balanced budget) lead to an equal change in income (the balanced budget multiplier is equal to 1).

Adding Net Exports

Thus far we have essentially assumed a closed economy by avoiding adding foreign transactions: exports and imports. We now add the foreign sector to complete the aggregate expenditures model.

The impact of the foreign sector in the aggregate expenditures model is through net exports: exports minus imports $(X - M)$. Exports are *injections* of spending into the domestic economy, and imports are *withdrawals.* When Africans purchase grain from American farmers, they are injecting new spending on grain into our economy. Conversely, when we purchase French wine, we are withdrawing spending (as saving does) and injecting these funds into the French economy.

Figure 12 adds net exports to Figure 10 with investment and government spending. By adding $100 of net exports to the previous equilibrium at point *b,* equilibrium moves to $5,200 (point *c*). Again, we see the multiplier at work as the $100 in net exports leads to a $400 increase in income.

With the foreign sector included, all injections into the economy must equal all withdrawals; therefore at equilibrium,

$$I + G + X = S + T + M$$

Thus, if we import more and all other spending remains the same, equilibrium income will fall. This is one reason why many economists focus on the trade deficit or net exports $(X - M)$ figures each month.

The aggregate expenditures model illustrates the importance of spending in an economy. Investment, government spending, and exports all increase income, whereas saving, taxes, and imports reduce it. Further, the fact that consumers spend and save some of the *changes* in income (MPC and MPS) gives rise to a spending multiplier that magnifies the impact of changes in spending on the economy.

| FIGURE 12 | SAVING, INVESTMENT, GOVERNMENT SPENDING, AND NET EXPORTS |

Adding investment (*I*), government spending (*G*), and net exports (*X* − *M*) causes income and output to rise or fall by the spending change times the multiplier. In this figure, we have added net exports (*X* − *M*) of $100 to the investment and government spending in Figure 10 to get *I* + *G* + (*X* − *M*). Thus, an increase in investment spending, government spending, and net exports has the same effect on income and output.

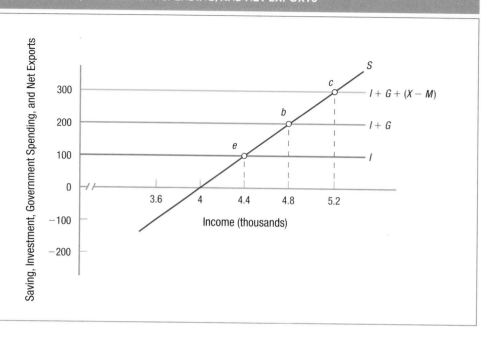

Recessionary and Inflationary Gaps

Keynesian analysis illustrated what was needed to get the economy out of the Great Depression: an increase in aggregate spending. Without an increase in spending, an economy can be stuck at a point below full employment for an extended period of time. Therefore, Keynes argued that if consumers, businesses, and foreigners were unwilling to spend (their economic expectations were clearly dismal), government should. This was also the basic rationale for the extraordinary spending measures implemented by Congress and signed by President Obama during the 2007–2009 recession. This leads to the question of just how much additional spending is needed to return the economy to full employment.

recessionary gap The increase in aggregate spending needed (when expanded by the multiplier) to bring a depressed economy back to full employment.

Recessionary Gap The **recessionary gap** is the increase in aggregate spending needed to bring a depressed economy back to full employment. Note that it is not the difference between real GDP at full employment and current real GDP, which is called the GDP gap. If full employment income is $4,400 and our current equilibrium income is $4,000, the recessionary gap is the added spending ($100) that when boosted by the multiplier (4 in this case) will close a GDP gap ($400).

inflationary gap The spending reduction necessary (when expanded by the multiplier) to bring an overheated economy back to full employment.

Inflationary Gap If aggregate spending generates income above full employment levels, the economy will eventually heat up, creating inflationary pressures. Essentially, the economy is trying to produce more output and income than it can sustain for very long. Thus, the excess aggregate spending exceeding that necessary to result in full employment is the **inflationary gap.** Using our previous example, if full employment is an income of $4,400 and our current equilibrium is $4,800, a reduction in spending is needed to close the $400 GDP gap and to prevent inflation from building. In this case, a reduction in aggregate expenditures of $100 with a multiplier of 4 would bring the economy back to full employment at $4,400. In sum, changes in aggregate expenditures expanded by the multiplier can help bring an economy facing either recessionary or inflationary pressures back into equilibrium sooner.

This Keynesian approach to analyzing aggregate spending revolutionized the way economists looked at the economy and led to the development of modern macroeconomics. In the next chapter, we extend our analysis to the aggregate demand and supply model, a modern extension of this aggregate expenditures model to account for varying price levels and the supply side of the macroeconomy.

ISSUE

Was Keynes Right About the Great Depression?

There is little disagreement that the Great Depression was one of the most important events in the United States in modern history. Good aggregate data were not yet available, but President Roosevelt and congressional leaders knew something was very wrong.

Within a couple of years, 10,000 banks collapsed, farms and businesses were lost, the stock market lost 85% of its value from the beginning of the decade, and soup kitchens fed a growing horde as unemployment soared to nearly 25%, up from 3.2% in 1929. Worse, the Great Depression persisted: It did not look to be temporary; there was no end in sight.

The aggregate expenditures model we have just studied provides some insight into the Great Depression. The figure plots hypothetical saving and investment curves over the actual data for 1929 and 1933. Both government and the foreign sector were tiny at this time; therefore, the simple aggregate expenditures model effectively illustrates why the Great Depression did not show signs of much improvement; by 1939 the unemployment rate was still over 17%.

Saving and investment were over $16 billion in 1929, or roughly a healthy 15% of GDP (point a). By 1933 investment collapsed to just over $1 billion (a 91% decline), and the economy was in equilibrium at an income of roughly half of that in 1929 (point b). Government spending remained at roughly the same levels while net exports, a small fraction of aggregate

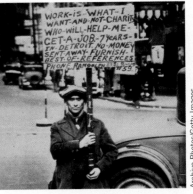

Archive Photos/Getty Images

expenditures, fell by more than half of their previous levels.

Keynes had it right: Unless something happened to increase investment or exports (not likely given that the rest of the world was suffering economically as well), the economy would remain mired in the Great Depression (point b). He suggested that government spending was needed. Ten years later (1943), the United States was in the middle of World War II, and aggregate expenditures swelled as government spending rose by a factor of 10. The Great Depression was history.

CHECKPOINT

THE FULL AGGREGATE EXPENDITURES MODEL

- Government spending affects the economy in the same way as other spending.
- Tax increases withdraw money from the spending stream but do not affect the economy as much as spending reductions, because these tax increases are partly offset by decreases in saving.
- Tax decreases inject money into the economy but do not affect the economy as much as spending increases, because tax reductions are partly offset by increases in saving.
- Equal changes in government spending and taxes (a balanced budget) result in an equal change in income (a balanced budget multiplier of 1).
- A recessionary gap is the new spending required that, when expanded by the multiplier, moves the economy to full employment.
- An inflationary gap is the spending reduction necessary (again when expanded by the multiplier) to bring the economy back to full employment.

QUESTIONS: If the government is considering reducing taxes to stimulate the economy, does it matter if the MPS is 0.25 or 0.33? What if the government reduces government spending by an equal amount to fund the tax cut?

Answers to the Checkpoint questions can be found at the end of this chapter.

chapter summary

Section 1 Aggregate Expenditures

19.1 Gross domestic product (GDP) is measured by spending or income. Using the spending approach, GDP is equal to aggregate expenditures (*AE*). Therefore,

$$GDP = AE = C + I + G + (X - M)$$

19.2

45° and Consumption Lines

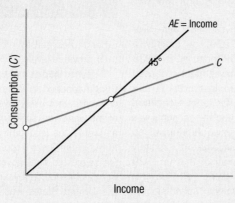

The 45° line shows where total spending (*AE*) equals income. No borrowing or saving exists.

The consumption line (*C*) starts above the origin on the vertical axis (even with no income, one still consumes by borrowing). As income increases, consumption rises, but not as fast as income (the slope of *C* depends on the MPC).

When *C* crosses *AE*, spending equals income (on the 45° line). When *C* is below the *AE* line, saving is positive.

Investment spending fluctuates much more than consumption year to year.

Disposable income, Y_D, is income after all taxes have been paid. Disposable income can either be spent (*C*) or saved (*S*). Thus, $Y_D = C + S$.

The portion that is consumed or saved is an important concept in the aggregate expenditures model:

19.3 Marginal propensity to consume (**MPC**) = $\Delta C \div \Delta Y_D$

Marginal propensity to save (**MPS**) = $\Delta S \div \Delta Y_D$

$MPC + MPS = 1$ (all money is either spent or saved)

Even with little to no income, college students still consume goods and services, often by borrowing against future income.

19.4 Determinants of Consumption and Saving

The aggregate expenditures model states that income is the main determinant of consumption and saving. But other factors also can shift the consumption schedule, such as:

- Wealth
- Expectations
- Household debt
- Taxes

Determinants of Investment Demand

Investment demand is assumed to be independent of income, but certain factors can shift investment demand, such as:

- Expectations
- Technological change
- Operating costs
- Capital goods on hand

Section 2 The Simple Aggregate Expenditures Model

Ignoring government spending and net exports, aggregate expenditures (AE) are the sum of consumer and business investment: $AE = C + I$. Because AE also equals $C + S$ at equilibrium, this means that saving equals investment.

19.5

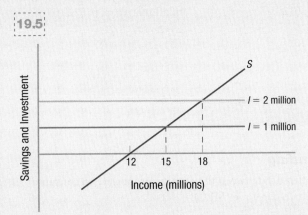

With no investment, Income = $12 million. With $1 million in investment, income rises to $15 million, an increase of $3 million. The multiplier in this example is 3.

19.6 The **multiplier effect** occurs when a dollar of spending generates many more dollars of spending in the economy.

The **multiplier** is equal to

$1/(1 - MPC)$ or $1/MPS$

Section 3 The Full Aggregate Expenditures Model

19.7 Government spending affects the economy just like any other spending, and so does spending by foreign consumers (exports). In the full aggregate expenditures model, all forms of spending are analyzed, including C, I, G, and ($X - M$).

If the multiplier for an economy is 5, a $1 million increase in investment increases income by $5 million. The same effect occurs with a $1 million increase in government spending or $1 million increase in net exports. Essentially, spending is spending, no matter where it comes from.

19.8 A general way to analyze policies that increase or decrease aggregate output is to categorize activities as either an **injection** or a **withdrawal:**

- Injections increase spending in an economy, and include investment (I), government spending (G), and exports (X).
- Withdrawals decrease spending in an economy, and include savings (S), taxes (T), and imports (M).

In equilibrium, all injections must equal all withdrawals:

$$I + G + X = S + T + M$$

19.9 Whenever the economy moves away from its full employment equilibrium, one of two gaps is created:

- **Recessionary gap:** The increase in aggregate spending (that is then multiplied) to bring a depressed economy to full employment.
- **Inflationary gap:** The reduction in aggregate spending (again expanded by the multiplier) needed to reduce income to full employment levels.

Mark Hryciw/Dreamstime.com

Purchasing an American-made car injects spending into the economy, and the economic benefits are enhanced by the multiplier.

Hupeng/Dreamstime.com

Purchasing a foreign-made car, however, results in a withdrawal because money leaves the country, and this effect is compounded by the multiplier.

aggregate expenditures, p. 504
consumption, p. 504
saving, p. 505
average propensity to consume,
   p. 506
average propensity to save, p. 506
marginal propensity to consume,
   p. 506

marginal propensity to save,
   p. 506
investment, p. 508
Keynesian macroeconomic
   equilibrium, p. 512
injections, p. 513
withdrawals, p. 513
multiplier, p. 514

paradox of thrift, p. 516
balanced budget multiplier,
   p. 521
recessionary gap, p. 522
inflationary gap, p. 522

QUESTIONS AND PROBLEMS

Check Your Understanding

1. Describe the important difference between the average propensity to consume (APC) and the marginal propensity to consume (MPC).

2. List the factors that influence an individual's marginal propensity to consume.

3. Explain why we wouldn't expect investment to grow sufficiently to pull the economy out of a depression.

4. Define the multiplier effect. Describe why a multiplier exists.

5. Explain why a $100 reduction in taxes does not have the same impact on output and employment as a $100 increase in government spending.

6. How do injections and withdrawals into an economy affect its income and output?

Apply the Concepts

7. Assume a simple Keynesian depression economy with a multiplier of 4 and an initial equilibrium income of $3,000. Saving and investment equal $400, and assume full employment income is $4,000.

   a. What is the MPC equal to? The MPS?

   b. How much would government spending have to rise to move the economy to full employment?

   c. Assume that the government plans to finance any spending by raising taxes to cover the increase in spending (it intends to run a balanced budget). How much will government spending and taxes have to rise to move the economy to full employment?

   d. From the initial equilibrium, if investment grows by $100, what will be the new equilibrium level of income and savings?

8. Other than reductions in interest rates that increase the level of investment by businesses, what factors would result in higher investment?

9. The simple aggregate expenditures model argues that one form of spending is just as good as any other; increases in all types of spending lead to equal increases in income. Is there any reason to suspect that private investment might be better for the economy than government spending?

10. Assume that the economy is in equilibrium at $5,700, and full employment is $4,800. If the MPC is 0.67, how big is the inflationary gap?

11. How does the economy today differ from that of the Great Depression, the economy Keynes used as the basis for the macroeconomic model discussed in this chapter?

12. In modern politics, the word "Keynesian" often is synonymous with "big government" spending. Does this characterization accurately reflect the role of government in spurring economic activity? How would a tax cut be characterized today versus in Keynes's time?

In the News

13. In recent years banks have encouraged their customers to save by giving incentives to join programs that automatically transfer money from checking accounts to savings accounts. For example, a bank might offer to round debit transactions to the nearest dollar, transferring the change to one's savings account, and then boost this amount with a match up to a certain amount. Although these programs were intended to encourage customers to save, some economists are not very enthusiastic about these programs. What reasons, both practical and theoretical, might cause some to be concerned?

14. The Affordable Care Act (a.k.a. Obamacare) is one of the largest government programs to be implemented in recent years, and involves the use of government subsidies to increase the percentage of Americans with health insurance. Explain how the increase in government spending may lead to a multiplier effect. How might this multiplier be affected if taxes are raised to finance the increased government spending?

Solving Problems

15. Using this aggregate expenditures table, answer the questions that follow.

Income (Y), in $	Consumption (C), in $	Saving (S), in $
2,200	2,320	−120
2,300	2,380	−80
2,400	2,440	−40
2,500	2,500	0
2,600	2,560	40
2,700	2,620	80
2,800	2,680	120
2,900	2,740	160
3,000	2,800	200

a. Compute the APC when income equals $2,300 and the APS when income equals $2,800.

b. Compute the MPC and MPS.

c. What does the multiplier equal?

d. If investment spending is equal to $120, what will be equilibrium income?

e. Using the following graph, show saving, investment, and equilibrium income.

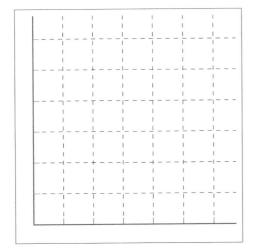

16. Use the figure to answer the following questions.

    a. What are the MPC, the MPS, and the multiplier?

    b. If the economy is currently in equilibrium at point *a*, and full employment income is $4,000, how much in *additional* expenditures is needed to move this economy to full employment? What is this level of spending called?

    c. Assume that the economy is currently in equilibrium at point *a* and full employment income is $4,000. How much of a tax decrease would be required to move the economy to full employment?

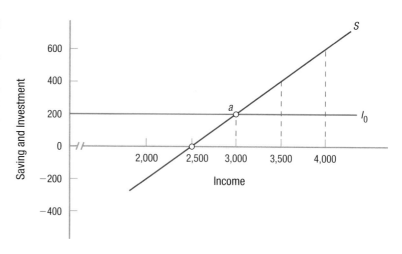

USING THE NUMBERS

17. According to By the Numbers, in the year 2015, by how much did total food and grocery consumption exceed total gasoline and energy consumption? Based on your knowledge of how food and gas prices have changed since 2015, how would this difference in spending change?

18. According to By the Numbers, the U.S. government spends less per person than any other developed country on the list. Does this mean that the overall size of the U.S. government is smaller than that of the other developed countries? Why or why not?

ANSWERS TO QUESTIONS IN CHECKPOINTS

Checkpoint: Aggregate Expenditures 511

Consumer spending, while 5 times larger in absolute size than investment spending, involves many small expenditures by households that do not vary much from month to month, such as rent (or mortgage payment), food, and utilities. Consumers change habits, but slowly. Business investment expenditures are typically on big-ticket items such as new factories and equipment, but such investments occur only when businesses have favorable expectations about the economy. When expectations sour, investment by all firms in an industry typically falls.

Checkpoint: The Simple Aggregate Expenditures Model 518

When consumer confidence is declining, this may suggest that consumers are going to spend less and save more. Because consumer spending is about 68% of aggregate spending, a small decline represents a significant reduction in aggregate spending and may well mean that a recession is on the horizon. Relatively small changes in consumer spending coupled with the multiplier can mean relatively large changes in income, and therefore forecasters and policymakers should keep a close eye on consumer confidence.

Checkpoint: The Full Aggregate Expenditures Model 523

Yes, it does matter. If the tax reduction is going to be $100, for example, and the MPS is 0.25, the multiplier is 4, and the income increase will be $75 × 4 = $300. Keep in mind that in this case, one-fourth of the tax reduction will go into saving and will not be amplified by the multiplier. However, with a MPS of 0.33, the multiplier will be 3, and one-third will not be multiplied (will go into saving); therefore, the increase in income will be $66.6 × 3 = $200. If government spending is reduced by an amount equal to the tax cut, income in the economy will fall by exactly the value of the reduction in government spending. The balanced budget multiplier is equal to 1, regardless of the value of MPS.

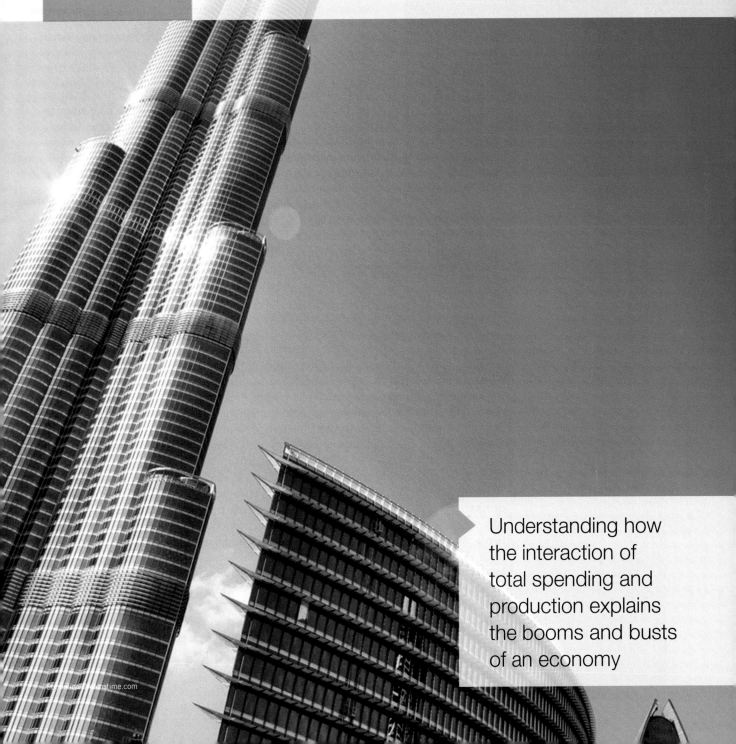

20 Aggregate Demand and Supply

Understanding how the interaction of total spending and production explains the booms and busts of an economy

Learning Objectives

20.1 Explain what an aggregate demand curve is and what it represents.

20.2 Describe why the aggregate demand curve has a negative slope due to the wealth, export, and interest rate effects.

20.3 List the determinants of aggregate demand.

20.4 Analyze the aggregate supply curve and differentiate between the short run and long run.

20.5 Describe the determinants of an aggregate supply curve.

20.6 Use AD/AS analysis to illustrate long-run and short-run macroeconomic equilibrium.

20.7 Define the multiplier and describe why it is important.

20.8 Describe demand-pull and cost-push inflation.

Among cities that have changed dramatically over the past two decades is Dubai, a large city in the Middle East that thrived on oil production. But unlike many other oil-rich cities, at the start of the new millennium, Dubai undertook a strategy of transforming its economy to one less dependent on oil, as it foresaw (correctly) a future when oil is no longer an endless source of money. What did Dubai do?

Investors and the government in Dubai invested heavily in infrastructure, building massive skyscrapers that became home to multinational corporations, luxury homes and condos (including thousands on artificial islands in the Persian Gulf) to attract wealthy foreigners seeking a vacation home, and some of the most lavish shopping malls and attractions to make Dubai a world travel destination.

By diversifying its economy, Dubai ensured that its capacity to produce goods and services that consumers desired extended beyond energy resources. The takeaway from Dubai's strategy is that the state of an economy cannot be assessed solely based on the performance of a single market, region, or time period. Likewise, government policies are often designed to meet the needs of an entire nation. It would be dangerous to look at just one region or one industry and come to conclusions or make policy recommendations for the nation as a whole.

British economist John Maynard Keynes recognized the need to develop tools to analyze the macroeconomy as a whole. He focused on aggregate expenditures by consumers, businesses, and governments as the key drivers for the economy that determined employment and output. But the model he developed during the Great Depression did not fully consider the effect that changes in the economy would have on prices. Why?

Keynes focused on the problem at hand, when resources were underutilized. For this reason, an expansion of consumption or production did not create much upward pressure on prices. For example, in times of high unemployment, more labor can be hired without raising wages because firms with job openings often are inundated with applicants.

Therefore, the initial Keynesian model was a fixed price model, one that essentially ignored the supply side because increasing production would occur without a rise in prices. The lessons from Keynes, with their focus on spending, formed the foundation of the demand side of the modern macroeconomic model. In this chapter, we add the supply side and move from a fixed price model to a flexible price model, where prices and wages adjust to macroeconomic conditions. We call this model the aggregate demand–aggregate supply (AD/AS) model. This model looks a lot like the supply and demand model for a market, but it has several important differences: It measures real output of the aggregate (overall) economy, it uses the average price level for an economy, and it focuses on short-run fluctuations around a long-run equilibrium output.

The response of prices and wages does not always change in a consistent manner. As we will see, sometimes prices and wages can be sticky in the short run, a condition that allows an economy to respond positively to economic stimulus policies. But in the long run, prices and wages tend to be very responsive to changing macroeconomic conditions.

The Sheer Size of Aggregate Demand and Aggregate Supply

Aggregate demand and aggregate supply are made up of many components in the economy. Factors that influence the extent to which consumers, businesses, and governments spend make up aggregate demand, while various short-run and long-run factors influence producers and aggregate supply.

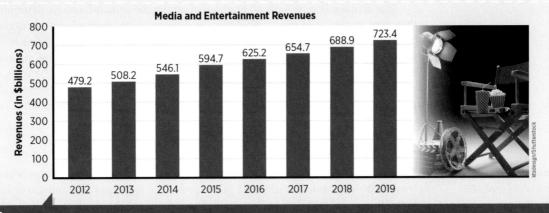

Media and Entertainment Revenues

Year	Revenues (in $billions)
2012	479.2
2013	508.2
2014	546.1
2015	594.7
2016	625.2
2017	654.7
2018	688.9
2019	723.4

The media and entertainment (M&E) industry is an important contributor to U.S. aggregate demand and supply. The industry comprises film, television, music, radio, gaming, and publishing companies. Over half of all M&E revenues are earned in foreign markets, producing a large trade surplus. Recent and projected growth of the U.S. M&E market are shown.

United States
- 1985: 5.7
- 2015: 7.0

China
- 1985: 0.7
- 2015: 4.1

Energy consumption contributes to aggregate demand and also influences aggregate supply through its effect on input prices. Oil consumption (in billions of barrels) in 1985 and 2015 in the United States and China is shown.

$74,160,000,000,000

Total World Aggregate Demand in 2015

525% Increase in NASDAQ stock index value from 1995 to 2000, creating immense wealth that increased aggregate demand

98% of all apparel and 99% of all footwear sold in the United States are imported. Imports reduce aggregate demand because money is flowing out of the country to pay for these goods.

Go to **LaunchPad** *to use the latest data to recreate this graph.*

State	Percent (%)
West Virginia	74.7
Michigan	74.3
Utah	74.3
Mississippi	72.3
Wyoming	72.2
United States	65.8
Rhode Island	58.1
Nevada	57.0
California	54.1
New York	52.9
District of Columbia	41.9

Home ownership provides a wealth effect that influences aggregate demand. States with the highest and lowest rates of home ownership in 2015.

This flexible price model expands the analysis that began with Keynes to many more modern problems facing economies. The AD/AS model builds on skills you already have: defining demand and supply curves, assessing changes in economic facts, and determining a new equilibrium. These techniques provide policymakers with a way of looking at the overall economy when many factors and differences in economic performance prevail across regions and industries.

This chapter begins with an analysis of aggregate demand and its determinants. We then turn to aggregate supply, studying the differences between a long-run aggregate supply curve and a short-run aggregate supply curve, and the determinants of each. Finally, we put the aggregate demand and aggregate supply curves together to analyze macroeconomic equilibrium. The AD/AS model gives you the tools to analyze tradeoffs between economic output and inflation. It will allow you to understand the causes of recessions and inflation, and how government policy is sometimes used to correct these problems.

AGGREGATE DEMAND

aggregate demand The output of goods and services (real GDP) demanded at different price levels.

The **aggregate demand** (AD) curve (or schedule) shows the output of goods and services (real GDP) demanded at different price levels. The aggregate demand curve in Figure 1 looks like the product demand curves we studied earlier. They both slope downward, showing how output rises as prices fall, and vice versa. However, it's important to remember that the reasons the product and aggregate demand curves slope downward are different.

Why Is the Aggregate Demand Curve Negatively Sloped?

Product demand curves slope downward due to *income* and *substitution* effects. An income effect occurs when the price of a given product falls, resulting in money being freed up, allowing consumers to afford more of all goods. A substitution effect occurs when the price of a product falls, causing consumers to purchase more of the product because they substitute it for other higher-priced goods. Income and substitution effects work the other way when the price of a given product rises. Although these explanations work for a product demand curve, they do not explain why an aggregate demand curve slopes downward, because aggregate demand does not measure the demand for just one product, but rather it measures the demand for all products. For the latter, we need to look at other factors influencing the aggregate economy.

FIGURE 1	THE AGGREGATE DEMAND CURVE

The aggregate demand curve shows the amount of real goods and services (Output = Real GDP) that will be purchased at various price levels.

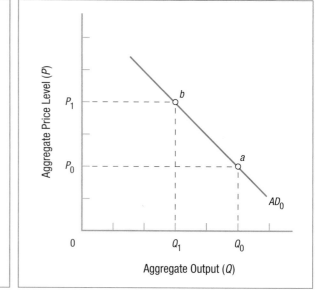

The Wealth Effect One reason that real output declines when the aggregate price level rises is the resulting reduction in household wealth, called the **wealth effect.** Households usually hold some of their wealth in financial assets such as savings accounts, bonds, and cash. A rising aggregate price level means that the purchasing power of this monetary wealth is declining. If, for example, you have $5,000 in a savings account and prices rise throughout the economy, that $5,000 will now purchase less than before. This reduction in household purchasing power means that some purchases are put on hold, thereby reducing output demanded. This is represented by a movement from point *a* to point *b* in Figure 1.

Export Price Effect When the U.S. aggregate price level rises, American goods become more expensive in the global marketplace. Higher prices mean that our goods are less competitive with the goods made in other countries. The result is that foreigners purchase fewer American products, and our exports decline. A decrease in exports means that the demand for domestically produced goods and services (the quantity purchased by foreign consumers, a component of real GDP) also declines. Therefore, higher prices result in lower real output.

Interest Rate Effect Interest rates are the prices paid for the use of money. If we assume for a moment that the quantity of money is fixed, then as aggregate prices rise, people will need more money to carry out their economic transactions. As people demand more money, the cost of borrowing money—interest rates—will go up. Rising interest rates mean reduced business investment, which results in a drop in quantity demanded for real GDP, shown in Figure 1 as a movement from point *a* to *b* and falling real output.

In summary, the aggregate demand curve is negatively sloped because of three factors. When the aggregate price level rises, this lowers household purchasing power because of the wealth effect. A rising aggregate price level also lowers the amount of exports because our goods are now more expensive. Furthermore, a rising aggregate price level increases the demand for money and therefore drives up interest rates. Rising interest rates reduce business investment and reduce the quantity demanded of real GDP. In each case, as aggregate prices rise from P_0 to P_1, quantity demanded of real GDP falls from Q_0 to Q_1.

Determinants of Aggregate Demand

We have seen that the aggregate demand curve is negatively sloped. Everything else held constant, a change in the aggregate price level will change the quantity of real GDP demanded along the aggregate demand curve. The *determinants* of aggregate demand are those factors that shift the *entire* aggregate demand curve when they change. They are the "everything else held constant." These include the components of GDP: consumption, investment, government spending, and net exports.

If one of these components of aggregate spending changes, the aggregate demand curve will shift, as shown in Figure 2. At first, aggregate demand is AD_0; therefore, a shift to AD_1 represents an increase in aggregate demand; more real output is demanded at the same price level, P_0. If, for example, businesses decide to invest more in new technology, more real output is now demanded at the current price level, P_0, and at all other price levels. For similar reasons, a decrease in aggregate demand to AD_2 means that less real output is being demanded. If consumers fear the onset of a recession and decide to reduce spending to increase their savings, then less output will be demanded at all price levels.

Let's look at these determinants of aggregate demand more closely. What might cause the various components of aggregate expenditures to change, shifting the AD curve?

Consumer Spending Consumer spending is the largest component of aggregate demand, representing about 68% of total spending in the economy. The level of spending as a percentage of overall output is relatively stable over time. Still, consumer spending is affected by several major factors: wealth, consumer confidence, household debt, interest rates, and taxes. Because consumer spending represents such a large part of the economy, even small changes in these factors can have a significant impact on the economy. And in times when consumption changes a lot, the effect on the economy can be dramatic.

| FIGURE 2 | SHIFTS IN THE AGGREGATE DEMAND CURVE |

The determinants of aggregate demand include the components of GDP and aggregate spending: consumption, investment, government spending, and net exports. A change in one will shift the aggregate demand curve, as shown here. At first, aggregate demand is AD_0; therefore, a shift to AD_1 represents an increase in aggregate demand; more real output is demanded at all price levels. A decline in aggregate demand to AD_2 means that less real output is being demanded at all price levels.

For example, when home prices skyrocketed in the mid-2000s, homeowners became wealthier, which led to more consumer spending throughout the economy. But when housing prices along with the stock market declined in 2008 and 2009, coupled with reduced consumer confidence, an unusually large drop in consumer spending resulted, which became an important factor in the depth of the recession.

Note that changes in wealth have two similar but distinct impacts on aggregate demand. First, as described earlier, when aggregate prices rise, the purchasing power of financial assets falls, reducing the *amount* of goods and services that can now be purchased with this money. This is a movement along an existing aggregate demand curve to a higher price level (point *a* to *b* in Figure 2).

Second, described here, is a decrease in wealth (e.g., caused by a stock market crash) that reduces consumption *at all price levels*. In this case, the entire aggregate demand curve shifts from AD_0 to AD_2 in Figure 2. This is the impact of changing wealth on consumer spending that is usually the focus of attention by the media and policymakers.

Consumer expectations and confidence about the economy play a significant role in determining the level of consumer spending. High confidence in the economy eases job security fears and stimulates consumer spending, shifting the aggregate demand curve to the right. High family debt ratios restrict access to future credit, reducing spending on high-ticket items often bought on credit. Higher interest rates increase the cost of borrowing (whether on loans or credit card balances), making purchases more difficult. And finally, higher taxes reduce disposable income which reduces consumer spending, shifting the aggregate demand curve to the left.

Investment Investment (spending, mostly by businesses for structures, equipment, and software) is determined mainly by interest rates and the expected rate of return on capital projects. When interest rates rise, investment will fall and the aggregate demand curve will shift to the left, and vice versa.

When business expectations become more favorable—perhaps some new technology is introduced, or excess capacity is reduced—investment will increase, and the aggregate demand curve will increase, or shift to the right. But if businesses see clouds on the horizon, such as new regulations, higher taxes, restrictions on the use of technology, or excess capacity, investment will drop, and the aggregate demand curve will shift to the left.

Because investment decisions tend to be larger in magnitude than everyday consumption purchases, investment varies much more from year to year. Therefore, although investment represents a smaller percentage of aggregate demand, its relative insta-bility can result in a significant effect on the aggregate economy.

Government Spending and Net Exports Government spend-ing and net exports have essentially the same effect on the aggregate economy as consumer and investment spending. When government spending or net exports rise, aggregate demand increases, and vice versa.

When the national income of a foreign country rises, some of this money is used to buy more American goods and services. The increase in demand for U.S. goods and services in other countries results in more exports, which increases U.S. aggregate demand. A change in foreign exchange rates will also affect aggregate demand. An appreciation, or rise, in the value of the euro, for instance, will result in Europeans buy-ing more American goods because a euro will buy more. Again, this change increases U.S. exports and U.S. aggregate demand. These effects on aggregate demand are offset by increases in imports of foreign goods, because goods are being demanded from outside of the United States.

A quick summary is now in order. The aggregate demand curve shows the quantities of real GDP demanded at different price levels. (The derivation of the AD curve using the Keynesian fixed price model is shown in the Appendix to this chapter.) The aggregate de-mand curve slopes downward because of the wealth effect (the value of monetary assets falls when the price level rises), because exports fall as domestic prices rise, and because rising prices raise interest rates, which reduce investment. On the other hand, changes in one of the determinants of aggregate demand shift the aggregate demand curve. Table 1 summarizes the determinants of aggregate demand.

Again, the determinants of aggregate demand are those "other factors held constant": consumption, investment, government spending, and net exports. If one of those deter-minants changes, the entire aggregate demand curve will shift. Keep in mind that changes in the determinants are most important for policymaking. When a policy is enacted (say,

A favorable exchange rate for the euro makes shop-ping trips to New York City for Europeans less expen-sive, providing a boost to U.S. aggregate demand.

TABLE 1	THE DETERMINANTS OF AGGREGATE DEMAND (THE AGGREGATE DEMAND CURVE SHIFTS WHEN THESE CHANGE)	
Determinant	**AD Increases**	**AD Decreases**
Consumer Spending		
• Wealth	Wealth increases	Wealth decreases
• Consumer expectations	Expectations improve	Expectations worsen
• Household debt	Debt falls	Debt rises
• Interest rates	Lower	Higher
• Taxes	Taxes are cut	Taxes increase
Investment		
• Interest rates	Lower	Higher
• Expected rate of return on investment	Higher	Lower
• Business expectations	More positive	More negative
• Taxes	Taxes are cut	Taxes increase
Government Spending	Increase	Decrease
Net Exports		
• Income in other countries	Rising	Falling
• Exchange rate changes	Depreciating dollar	Appreciating dollar

Myanmar: Opening a Country to a Boom in Aggregate Demand

How did Myanmar's transition from an authoritarian regime to a democracy lead to an increase in aggregate demand?

R.M. Nunes/Alamy Stock Photo

For many nations in Asia and Africa that had been colonized by Europeans in the 19th and 20th centuries, a cultural clash existed between the rich histories of the native inhabitants and the modern influences that were brought by the colonizers. When many of these countries (including major countries such as India and Vietnam) achieved independence in the mid-20th century, the new governments struggled to find a balance between minimizing their colonizer's cultural influences and maintaining the economic developments that were achieved. Often, this led to war and a path toward declining economic growth. For one South Asian nation whose experience under long military

rule resulted in one of the most impoverished nations in the world, the transition to a democratic nation in 2012 was a significant economic event.

What happened in Myanmar since 2012 that has resulted in a significant increase in aggregate demand?

Myanmar (formerly Burma) achieved its independence from the British in 1948, but the transition process was not smooth, as various political organizations (each supported by a segment of the military) competed for power. This culminated in 1962 with a strict authoritarian regime led by a series of political parties that ruled by force. It would take another 50 years before Myanmar held its first democratic elections.

Since 2012 foreign investment has entered the country of 53 million, welcomed by a labor force eager to work, even at low wages, for a chance at a better life. The improved employment picture led to increased consumption, and subsequently the opening of new markets and service industries.

Then, a very significant change occurred: The re-introduction of the foreign tourist, largely banned during military rule, who came by the thousands to experience Myanmar's rich 13,000-year history filled with temples and other historical treasures. These tourists brought hard currency (such as dollars, euros, and yen) into a nation seeking to connect with the world that it had long ago abandoned.

Each of these events, which led to an increase in consumption, investment, government spending, and net exports, resulted in a dramatic increase in aggregate demand, and subsequently an annual growth rate that ranks among the highest in the world. Today, Myanmar's future is as bright as its rich historical past centuries ago.

GO TO **LaunchPad** TO PRACTICE THE ECONOMIC CONCEPTS IN THIS STORY

lower tax rates), policymakers expect to stimulate consumer and investment spending, increasing aggregate demand, output, and employment.

As important as aggregate demand is in determining an economy's output, aggregate demand tells only one part of the story. The other part, aggregate supply, describes the impetus for businesses to create and produce goods and services, which we turn to next.

✓ CHECKPOINT

AGGREGATE DEMAND

- The aggregate demand curve shows the relationship between real GDP and the price level.
- The aggregate demand curve has a negative slope because of the impact of the price level on financial wealth, exports, and interest rates.
- The determinants of aggregate demand are consumer spending, investment spending, government expenditures, and net exports. Changes in any of these determinants will shift the aggregate demand curve.

QUESTION: Housing and stock market prices have risen substantially in recent years. Explain how this affects aggregate demand in an economy.

Answers to the Checkpoint questions can be found at the end of this chapter.

AGGREGATE SUPPLY

The **aggregate supply** curve shows the real GDP that firms will produce at varying price levels. Even though the definition seems similar to that for aggregate demand, note that we have now moved from the spending side of the economy to the production side. We will consider two different possibilities for aggregate supply: the short run and the long run. In the short run, aggregate supply is positively sloped and prices rise when GDP grows. In contrast, long-run aggregate supply reflects the long-run state of the economy and is represented by a vertical curve. Growth occurs in the economy by shifting this vertical aggregate supply curve to the right. Let's begin by looking at the economy from the long-run perspective.

aggregate supply The real GDP that firms will produce at varying price levels. The aggregate supply curve is positively sloped in the short run but vertical in the long run.

Long Run

The *vertical* **long-run aggregate supply (LRAS) curve** incorporates the assumptions of classical (pre-1930s) economic analysis. Classical analysis assumes that all variables are adjustable in the long run, where product prices, wages, and interest rates are flexible. As a result, the economy will gravitate to the position of full employment shown as Q_0 in Figure 3.

Full employment is often referred to as the *natural rate of output* or *the natural rate of unemployment* by economists. This long-run output is an equilibrium level at which inflationary pressures are minimal. Once the economy has reached this level, further increases in output are extremely difficult to achieve; there is no one else to operate more machines, and no more machines to operate. As we will see later, attempts to expand beyond this output level only lead to higher prices and rising inflation.

In general terms, the vertical LRAS curve represents the full employment capacity of the economy and depends on the amount of resources available for production and the available technology. Full employment is determined by the capital available, the size and quality of the labor force, and the technology employed; in effect, the productive capacity of the economy. Remember from earlier chapters that these are also the big three factors driving economic growth (shifting the $LRAS_0$ curve to the right to $LRAS_1$) once a suitable infrastructure has been put in place.

long-run aggregate supply (LRAS) curve The long-run aggregate supply curve is vertical at full employment because the economy has reached its capacity to produce.

FIGURE 3	LONG-RUN AGGREGATE SUPPLY

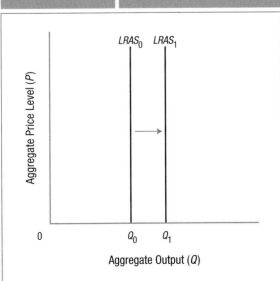

The long-run aggregate supply (LRAS) curve is vertical, reflecting the assumptions of classical economic analysis. In the long run, all variables in the economy can adjust, and the economy will settle at full employment at output Q_0. Changes in the amount of resources available, the quality of the labor force, and technology can shift the LRAS curve to the right to $LRAS_1$, at a new full employment output at Q_1.

Determinants of Long-Run Aggregate Supply

Attempts to improve technology such as automation and digitalization are clear examples of an increase in productive capacity. But so is the enhancement of labor quality. As a greater percentage of people pursue college and postgraduate degrees, productivity increases and leads to economic growth. Finally, increased trade and globalization have allowed resources to flow more freely, permitting the United States to gain access to better or cheaper inputs and more specialized labor.

Each of the shifts in the LRAS curve takes time. It's not easy to improve the human capital of an entire nation or to develop new production technologies. Therefore, although the LRAS is of concern to the long-term welfare of the country, policymakers are often more concerned about short-run outcomes. We now turn to the short-run aggregate supply (SRAS) curve.

Short Run

short-run aggregate supply (SRAS) curve The short-run aggregate supply curve is positively sloped because many input costs are slow to change (*sticky*) in the short run.

Figure 4 shows the **short-run aggregate supply (SRAS) curve,** which is positively sloped because some input costs are slow to change in the short run. When prices rise, firms do not immediately see an increase in wages or rents because these are often fixed for a specified term; in other words, input prices are *sticky*. Thus, profits will rise with the rising prices and firms will supply more output as their profits increase.

This situation, however, cannot last for long. As an entire industry or the economy as a whole increases its production, firms must start hiring more labor or paying overtime. As each firm seeks more employees, wages are driven up, increasing costs and forcing higher prices.

For the economy as a whole, a rise in real GDP results in higher employment and reduced unemployment. Lower unemployment rates mean a tightening of labor markets. This often leads to fierce collective bargaining by labor, followed by increases in wages, costs, and prices. The result is that a short-run increase in GDP is usually accompanied by a rise in the price level.

Determinants of Short-Run Aggregate Supply

We have seen that, because the aggregate supply curve is positively sloped in the short run, a change in aggregate output, other things held constant, will result in a change in

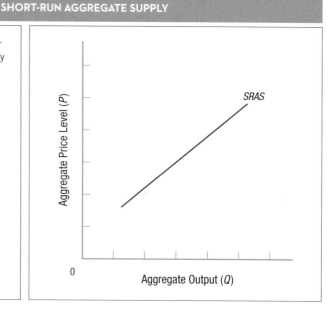

FIGURE 4	SHORT-RUN AGGREGATE SUPPLY

The short-run aggregate supply (SRAS) curve is positively sloped because many input costs are slow to change in the short run (they are *sticky*).

the aggregate price level. The determinants of short-run aggregate supply—those other things held constant—include changes in input prices, productivity, taxes, regulation, the market power of firms, or business and inflationary expectations. When any of these determinants change, the entire SRAS curve shifts, as Figure 5 illustrates.

Input Prices Changes in the cost of land, labor, or capital will change the output that firms are willing to provide to the market. When world crude oil prices rise, it is never long before prices rise at the gasoline pump. Rising input prices are quickly passed along to consumers, and the opposite is true as well. New discoveries of raw materials result in falling input prices, causing the prices for products incorporating these inputs to drop. This means that more of these products can be produced at a price of P_0 in Figure 5 as short-run aggregate supply shifts to $SRAS_1$ (point a), or now output Q_0 can be produced at a lower price on $SRAS_1$ (point b).

The dramatic rise in copper prices from 2006 to 2012 increased the cost of producing copper products, and contributed to a decrease in aggregate supply.

Productivity Changes in productivity are another major determinant of short-run aggregate supply. Rising productivity will shift the short-run aggregate supply curve to the right—from $SRAS_0$ to $SRAS_1$ in Figure 5—and vice versa. This is why changes in technology that increase productivity are so important to the economy. Technological advances, moreover, often lead to new products that expand short-run aggregate supply. The willingness of firms to invest in new capital equipment (aided by an improved business outlook) will enhance the productive capacity of an economy, which can also increase long-run aggregate supply.

An example of a technological advance is the improvement in traffic-enhanced GPS navigational devices, which allows one to select the quickest route to a destination taking into account traffic and roadblocks (such as those caused by construction projects and car crashes) in real time. Such technological enhancements let commercial vehicles reduce their time on the road, reducing transportation costs to the company. These cost

---

FIGURE 5   **SHIFTS IN SHORT-RUN AGGREGATE SUPPLY**

The determinants of short-run aggregate supply include changes in input prices, productivity, taxes, regulation, the market power of firms, and inflationary expectations. If one of these determinants changes, the entire short-run aggregate supply curve shifts. Increasing productivity, for instance, will shift the short-run aggregate supply curve to the right, from $SRAS_0$ to $SRAS_1$. Conversely, raising taxes or adding inefficient regulations can shift the short-run aggregate supply curve to the left, from $SRAS_0$ to $SRAS_2$.

reductions lead to an increase in short-run aggregate supply. If these technologies expand the overall productive capacity of the economy, they can also increase long-run aggregate supply.

Taxes and Regulation Rising taxes or increased regulation can shift the short-run aggregate supply curve to the left, from $SRAS_0$ to $SRAS_2$ in Figure 5. Excessively burdensome regulation, though it may provide some benefits, raises costs so much that the new costs exceed the benefits. This results in a decrease in short-run aggregate supply. Often, no one knows how much regulation has increased costs until some sort of deregulation is instituted.

Alternatively, tax reductions such as investment tax credits reduce the costs of production, resulting in an increase in short-run aggregate supply. Similarly, improving the process of satisfying regulations, such as reducing required paperwork, also can increase short-run aggregate supply even when the regulations themselves do not change.

Market Power of Firms Monopoly firms charge more than competitive firms. Therefore, a change in the market power of firms can increase prices for specific products, thereby reducing short-run aggregate supply. When the Organization of Petroleum Exporting Countries (OPEC) formed in 1973, it raised oil prices by over 200% within three years by reducing the global supply of oil. Because at that time there were very few substitutes for oil, higher oil prices shifted the SRAS curve to the left.

Today, with many non-OPEC nations (such as Russia, Norway, and Canada) producing large quantities of oil, OPEC's power to raise prices has fallen.

Inflationary Expectations A change in inflationary expectations by businesses, workers, or consumers can shift the short-run aggregate supply curve. If, for example, workers believe that inflation is going to increase, they will bargain for higher wages to offset the expected losses to real wages. The intensified bargaining and resulting higher wages will reduce aggregate supply.

To summarize, the short-run aggregate supply curve slopes upward because many input costs are slow to change (i.e., are *sticky*) in the short run. This SRAS curve can shift because of changes in input prices, productivity, taxes, regulation, the market power of firms, or inflationary expectations. Table 2 summarizes the determinants of short-run aggregate supply.

TABLE 2	DETERMINANTS OF SHORT-RUN AGGREGATE SUPPLY (THE SHORT-RUN AGGREGATE SUPPLY CURVE SHIFTS WHEN THESE CHANGE)	
Determinant	**SRAS Increases**	**SRAS Decreases**
Changes in Input Prices	Prices decline	Prices rise
Changes in Productivity		
• Technology	Improvements	Reductions
• Changes in human capital	Improvements	Reductions
Changes in Taxes and Regulations		
• Tax rates	Lower	Higher
• Subsidies	Higher	Lower
• Change in burdensome regulations	Reductions	Additions
Change in Market Power	Reductions	Increases
Changes in Inflationary Expectations	Lower	Higher

CHECKPOINT

AGGREGATE SUPPLY

- The aggregate supply curve shows the real GDP that firms will produce at varying price levels.
- The vertical long-run aggregate supply (LRAS) curve represents the long-run full-employment capacity of the economy.
- Increasing resources or improved technology shift the LRAS curve, which represents economic growth.
- The short-run aggregate supply (SRAS) curve is upward-sloping, reflecting rigidities in the economy because input and output prices are slow to change (sticky).
- The determinants of short-run aggregate supply include changes in input prices, productivity, taxes, regulations, the market power of firms, and inflationary expectations.

QUESTION: Because interest rates had been kept extremely low for almost a decade, many investors worried that access to cheap loans will drive prices higher as more people borrow money for purchases. How might this change in inflationary expectations affect the SRAS curve?

Answers to the Checkpoint questions can be found at the end of this chapter.

MACROECONOMIC EQUILIBRIUM

Let us now put together our aggregate demand and aggregate supply model. A *short-run* **macroeconomic equilibrium** occurs at the intersection of the short-run aggregate supply and aggregate demand curves; see point *e* in Figure 6. In this case, point *e* also represents *long-run macroeconomic equilibrium* because the economy is operating at full employment, producing output Q_f.

Output level Q_f represents full employment. The SRAS curve assumes price level expectations equal to P_e, and thus Q_f is the natural rate of unemployment or output. Remember that the natural rate of unemployment is that unemployment level at which inflation is low and consistent with inflationary expectations in the economy.

macroeconomic equilibrium
Occurs at the intersection of the short-run aggregate supply and aggregate demand curves. At this output level, there are no net pressures for the economy to expand or contract.

FIGURE 6   MACROECONOMIC EQUILIBRIUM

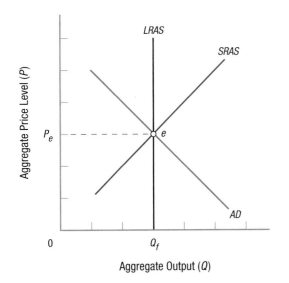

Point *e* represents a short-run macroeconomic equilibrium, the point at which the short-run aggregate supply curve and aggregate demand curve intersect. In this case, point *e* also represents a long-run macroeconomic equilibrium, because the economy is operating at full employment, producing output Q_f.

The Spending Multiplier

multiplier Spending changes alter equilibrium income by the spending change times the multiplier. One person's spending becomes another's income, and that second person spends some (the MPC), which becomes income for another person, and so on, until income has changed by $1/(1 - MPC) = 1/MPS$. The multiplier operates in both directions.

The spending **multiplier** is an important concept introduced into macroeconomics by John Maynard Keynes in 1936. The central idea is that new spending creates more spending, income, and output than just an amount equal to the new spending itself.

Let's assume, for example, that consumers tend to spend three-quarters and save one-quarter of any new income they receive. Now, assume that good weather encourages a family to spend the day at the annual county fair, spending $100 on food and rides. In other words, $100 of new spending is introduced into the economy. That $100 spent on food and rides adds $100 in income to the operator of the fair, because all spending equals income to someone else (whether that be the owner or the workers she hires). Of this additional income, suppose that $25 is saved and $75 is spent by the fair operator to fix a plumbing leak in her home. That $75 in spending becomes $75 in income to the plumber. Now that the plumber has $75 more income, suppose he saves $18.75 (25% of $75) and uses the rest ($56.25) to change the oil in his car, generating $56.25 in income to the mechanic, and so on, round-by-round.

Adding up all of the new spending (equal to the sum of $100 + $75 + $56.25 + . . .) from the initial $100 results in total spending increasing by $400. This represents an increase in output or GDP of $400. Adding up total new saving ($25 + 18.75 + . . .) equals $100, which means that the initial $100 in new spending has increased savings by the same amount through the multiplier process.

marginal propensity to consume The change in consumption associated with a given change in income.

marginal propensity to save The change in saving associated with a given change in income.

The proportion of *additional* income that consumers spend and save is known as the **marginal propensity to consume** and the **marginal propensity to save** (MPC and MPS). In our example, $MPC = 0.75$ and $MPS = 0.25$. The multiplier is equal to 4, given that $400 of new income was created with the introduction of $100 of new spending. The formula for the spending multiplier is equal to $1/(1 - MPC) = 1/MPS$, and in this case, is $1/(1 - 0.75) = 1/0.25 = 4$. This formula works as long as the aggregate price level is stable.

When the economy has many unemployed resources and excess capacity, the price level will remain constant and output will increase by the full magnitude of the multiplier. However, when the economy moves up the SRAS curve in the short run, its response to the same increase in aggregate spending is not as great. In Figure 7, aggregate demand increases the same amount as before. The new equilibrium is at point *a* with output of Q_f. But, output grows less because price increases or inflation eat up some of each spending round, resulting in less real output.

FIGURE 7	THE MULTIPLIER AND AGGREGATE DEMAND AND SUPPLY

The spending multiplier magnifies new spending into greater levels of income and output because of round-by-round spending. Your spending becomes my income, and I spend some of that income, creating further income and consumption, and so on.

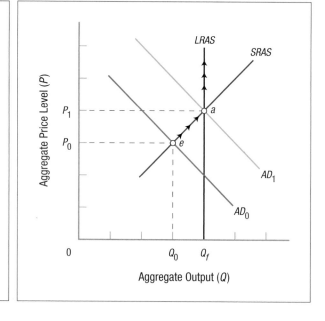

The multiplier is therefore less than the pure spending multiplier of 4 just discussed. Note that once aggregate demand is increased beyond AD_1, price increases soak up the entire increase in aggregate demand (along the LRAS curve) because real output does not change.

Let's take a moment to summarize where we are before we begin to use this model to understand some important macroeconomic events. Short-run macroeconomic equilibrium occurs at the intersection of AD and SRAS. It can also happen that this equilibrium represents long-run equilibrium, but not necessarily; equilibrium can occur at less than full employment. As we will see shortly, the Great Depression is one example of this. Increases in spending are multiplied and lead to greater changes in output than the original change in spending. For policymakers, this means that the difference between equilibrium real GDP and full-employment GDP (the GDP gap) can be closed with a smaller change in spending.

This leads us to the point where we can use the AD/AS model to analyze past macroeconomic events. By looking at these events through the AD/AS lens, we begin to see the options open to policymakers. Let's now look at what happened during the Great Depression, then examine both demand-pull and cost-push inflation. Each type of inflation presents unique challenges for policymakers.

The Great Depression

Figure 6 conveniently showed the economy in long-run equilibrium and short-run equilibrium at the same point. The Great Depression demonstrated, however, that an economy can reach short-run equilibrium at output levels substantially below full employment.

The 1930s Depression was a graphic example of just such a situation. Real GDP dropped by nearly 40% between 1929 and 1933. Unemployment peaked at 25% in 1932 and never fell below 15% throughout the 1930s.

Figure 8 shows the actual data for the Great Depression with superimposed aggregate demand and SRAS curves for 1929 and 1933. Investment is the most volatile of the GDP components, and it fell nearly 80% from 1929 to 1933. This drop in investment reduced spending, and therefore income and consumption, resulting in a deep depression. The increase in aggregate demand necessary to restore the economy back to 1929 levels was huge, and it was no wonder that a 6% increase in government spending had virtually no impact on the Depression. It wasn't until spending ramped up for World War II that the country moved beyond the Depression.

FIGURE 8	AGGREGATE DEMAND, SHORT-RUN AGGREGATE SUPPLY, AND THE DECLINE IN INVESTMENT DURING THE DEPRESSION

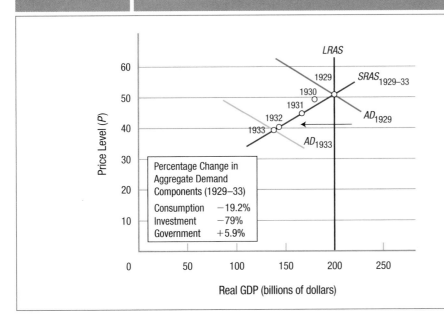

Aggregate demand and short-run aggregate supply are superimposed on the real GDP and price level data for the Great Depression. Investment dropped nearly 80% and consumption declined nearly 20%. Together, these reductions in spending created a depression that was so deep that it took the massive spending for World War II to bring the economy back to full employment.

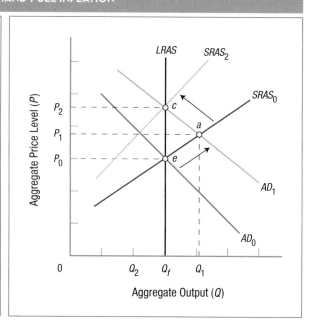

FIGURE 9 | **DEMAND-PULL INFLATION**

Demand-pull inflation occurs when aggregate demand expands and equilibrium output (point *a*) exceeds full employment output (Q_f). Because the LRAS curve has not shifted, the economy will in the end move into long-run equilibrium at point *c*. With the new aggregate demand at AD_1, prices have unexpectedly risen; therefore, short-run aggregate supply shifts to $SRAS_2$ as workers, for example, adjust their wage demands upward, leaving prices permanently higher at P_2.

Demand-Pull Inflation

demand-pull inflation Results when aggregate demand expands so much that equilibrium output exceeds full employment output and the price level rises.

Demand-pull inflation occurs when aggregate demand expands so much that equilibrium output exceeds full employment output. Turning to Figure 9, assume that the economy is initially in long-run equilibrium at point *e*. If businesses become overly exuberant and expand investments in some area (such as telecommunications in the late 1990s), this expansion will push aggregate demand out to AD_1. The economy moves to a short-run equilibrium beyond full employment (point *a*), and the price level rises to P_1.

On a temporary basis, the economy can expand beyond full employment as workers incur overtime, temporary workers are added, and more shifts are employed. Yet, these activities increase costs and prices. And because LRAS has not shifted, the economy will ultimately move to point *c* (if AD stays at AD_1), shifting short-run aggregate supply to $SRAS_2$ and leaving prices permanently higher (at P_2). In the long run, the economy will gravitate to points such as *e* and *c*. Policymakers could return the economy back to the original point *e* by instituting policies that reduce AD back to AD_0. These might include reduced government spending, higher taxes, or other policies that discourage investment, consumer spending, or exports.

Demand-pull inflation can continue for quite a while, especially if the economy begins on the SRAS curve well below full employment. Inflation often starts out slow and builds up steam.

Decade-long demand-pull inflation scenarios for the United States in the 1960s and for Japan in the last half of the 1980s and first half of the 1990s are shown in Figure 10.

For the United States, the slow escalation of the Vietnam conflict fueled a rising economy along the hypothetical short-run aggregate supply curve placed over the data in panel A. Early in the decade, the price level rose slowly as the economy expanded. But notice how the short-run aggregate supply curve began to turn nearly vertical and inflation rates rose as the economy approached full employment in 1969. Real output growth virtually halted between 1969 and 1970, but inflation was 5.3%. The economy had reached its potential.

The Japanese economy during the 1985–1995 period is a different example of demand-pull inflation. Panel B of Figure 10 shows a steadily growing economy with rising prices, throughout the 1980s and early 1990s. Japan ran huge trade surpluses and the yen appreciated (becoming more valuable). A rising yen would eventually reduce exports (Japanese products would become too expensive). To keep this from happening, the Japanese government kept interest rates artificially low, reducing the pressure on the yen and encouraging investment. But these policies fueled a huge real estate and stock bubble that began collapsing in the beginning of the 1990s and led to a decade-long recession that has been called "the lost decade."

This figure shows two examples of demand-pull inflation for the United States and Japan. Hypothetical aggregate demand and short-run aggregate supply curves are superimposed over the data for the two time periods. The Vietnam conflict expanded aggregate demand in the 1960s, and the U.S. economy experienced inflation over the entire decade and faced rising inflation rates as the economy approached full employment in 1969. Japan experienced demand-pull inflation as it enjoyed a huge trade surplus, which expanded the economy. Japanese policymakers kept interest rates artificially low, fueling a real estate and stock bubble that collapsed in the 1990s, resulting in a decade-long recession.

Demand-pull inflation can often take a while to become a problem. But once the inflation spiral gains momentum, it can pose a serious problem for policymakers.

Cost-Push Inflation

Cost-push inflation occurs when a supply shock hits the economy, shifting the short-run aggregate supply curve leftward, as from $SRAS_0$ to $SRAS_2$ in Figure 11. The 1973 oil shock is a

cost-push inflation Results when a supply shock hits the economy, reducing short-run aggregate supply, and thus reducing output and increasing the price level.

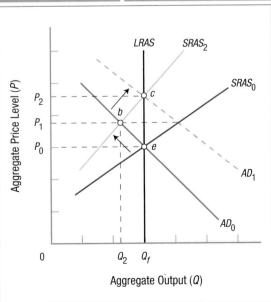

FIGURE 11   COST-PUSH INFLATION

Cost-push inflation is represented by an initial decline in short-run aggregate supply from $SRAS_0$ to $SRAS_2$. Rising resource costs or inflationary expectations will reduce short-run aggregate supply, resulting in a short-run movement from point e to point b. If policymakers wish to return the economy to full employment, they can increase aggregate demand to AD_1, but must accept higher prices as the economy moves to point c. Alternatively, they could reduce aggregate demand, but that would lead to lower output and higher unemployment.

Why Didn't Stimulus Measures Over the Past Decade Lead to Inflation?

The 2007–2009 recession and the high unemployment that persisted for years after led policymakers to implement many policies to jumpstart the economy. These included government spending (stimulus) programs, tax rebates in 2009, a reduction in payroll taxes in 2011 and 2012, extension of unemployment benefits, loan modification programs, and more. Each of these policies was designed to encourage spending by consumers and thereby increase aggregate demand. By doing so, the AD/AS model presented in this chapter predicts that rightward shifts of the AD curve would lead to a higher aggregate price level, or inflation. Yet, inflation rates in the United States have remained low. How is that possible?

First, the AD curve might not have moved at all. Much of the government spending to increase aggregate demand was offsetting corresponding decreases in aggregate demand due to high unem-

ployment, low consumer and business confidence, and low foreign demand for American goods. Thus, the role of such policies may have prevented a worsening of the economy by keeping aggregate demand in the same place as before. Using this explanation, the price level would not be affected at all.

Second, the recession created a large amount of underutilized resources. Keynes argued that during times of poor economic performance, many resources (such as labor and capital) remain underutilized. In such cases, an increase in aggregate demand, which subsequently increases demand for labor and capital, would merely be using resources that had been sitting idle. There would be little pressure on wages and prices to rise.

These reasons and others help to explain why the government was able to engage in various policies to increase the speed of economic recovery without the immediate threat of inflation. But as the

Inflation remained low despite an increase in government spending on infrastructure and tax cuts to encourage more spending by consumers.

economy recovers and idle resources are used up, any further government spending would likely lead to a higher aggregate price level, which means higher inflation can be lurking around the corner.

classic example. Because oil is a basic input in so many goods and services we purchase, skyrocketing oil prices affected all parts of the economy. After a bout of cost-push inflation, rising resource costs push the economy from point e to point b in Figure 11. Note that at point b, real output has fallen (the economy is in a recession) and the price level has risen. Policymakers can increase demand to AD_1 and move the economy back to full employment at point c. For example, they might increase government spending, reduce taxes, or introduce policies that encourage consumption, investment, or net exports. But notice that this means an even higher price level. Alternatively, policymakers could reduce inflationary pressures by reducing aggregate demand, but this leads to an even deeper recession as output and employment fall further.

Figure 12 shows the striking leftward shift in equilibrium points for 1973–1975. Output stood still, while prices rose as the economy adjusted to the new energy prices. Superimposed over the annual data are two hypothetical short-run aggregate supply curves. Notice that it took the economy roughly three years to absorb the oil shock. Only after the economy had adjusted to the new prices did it continue on a path roughly equivalent to the pre-1973 SRAS curve.

Before the Great Depression, economic analysis focused on the behavior of individuals, households, and businesses. Little attention was paid to the macroeconomic stabilization potential of government policies. The federal government had its responsibilities under the Constitution in many areas—such as national defense, the enforcement of contracts, and tax collection—but managing the economy was not among them.

The Great Depression of the 1930s and John Maynard Keynes's *The General Theory* drastically changed how economists viewed the role of the federal government. During the Depression, when unemployment reached 25% and bank failures wiped out personal savings, federal intervention in the economy became imperative. After the 1930s, the federal government's role grew to encompass

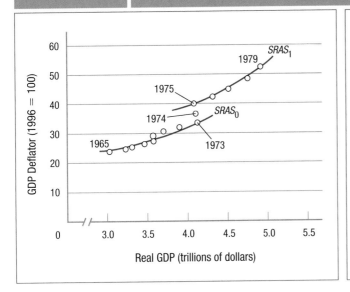

FIGURE 12   **COST-PUSH INFLATION IN THE 1970S**

The rise in equilibrium prices following the 1973 oil shocks was striking. From 1973 to 1975, prices rose, yet output stood still as the economy adjusted to the new energy prices. Superimposed over the actual annual data are two hypothetical short-run aggregate supply curves. Notice that it took the economy roughly three years to absorb the oil shock.

(1) expanded spending and taxation and the resulting exercise of fiscal policy, (2) extensive new regulation of business, and (3) expanded regulation of the banking sector, along with greater exercise of monetary policy.

The next chapter focuses on how government spending and taxation combine to expand or contract the macroeconomy. When the economy enters a recession, fiscal policy can be used to moderate the impact and prevent another depression. Later chapters will explore the monetary system and the use of monetary policy to stabilize the economy and the price level. The AD/AS model will serve as a tool to analyze both fiscal and monetary policies. As you read these chapters, keep in mind that the long-run goals of fiscal and monetary policy are economic growth, low unemployment, and modest inflationary pressures.

 CHECKPOINT

MACROECONOMIC EQUILIBRIUM

- Macroeconomic equilibrium occurs where short-run aggregate supply and aggregate demand cross.
- The spending multiplier exists because new spending generates new round-by-round spending (based on the marginal propensities to consume and save) that creates additional income.
- The formula for the spending multiplier is $1/(1 - MPC) = 1/MPS$.
- The effect of the multiplier on aggregate output is larger when the economy is in a deep recession or a depression.
- Policymakers can increase output by enacting policies that expand government spending, consumption, investment, or net exports, or reduce taxes.
- Demand-pull inflation occurs when aggregate demand expands beyond that necessary for full employment.
- Cost-push inflation occurs when short-run aggregate supply shifts to the left, causing the price level to rise along with rising unemployment.

QUESTIONS: In recent years, the price of agricultural goods, such as vegetables, fruit, and milk, rose significantly due to severe droughts in several farming regions in the United States. Describe the impact of this price increase on short-run aggregate supply. How might it affect employment, unemployment, and the price level? Would the impact depend on whether consumers and businesses thought the price increase was permanent?

Answers to the Checkpoint questions can be found at the end of this chapter.

chapter summary

Section 1 Aggregate Demand

20.1 The **aggregate demand** curve shows the quantity of goods and services (real GDP) demanded at different price levels.

Aggregate Price Level (P) / Aggregate Output (Q) — AD

20.2 The aggregate demand curve is downward-sloping for three main reasons:

- **Wealth effect:** When price levels rise, the purchasing power of money saved falls.
- **Export price effect:** Rising price levels cause domestic goods to be more expensive in the global marketplace, resulting in fewer purchases by foreign consumers.
- **Interest rate effect:** When price levels rise, people need more money to carry out transactions. The added demand for money drives up interest rates, causing investment spending to fall.

20.3 The determinants of aggregate demand include the components of aggregate spending:

1. Consumption spending
2. Investment spending
3. Government spending
4. Net exports

Changing any one of these aggregates will shift the aggregate demand curve.

The housing market recovery has resulted in a boost to aggregate demand.

Section 2 Aggregate Supply

20.4 The **aggregate supply** curve shows the real GDP firms will produce at varying price levels.

In the short run, aggregate supply is upward-sloping (SRAS).

In the long run, aggregate supply is vertical (LRAS).

In the short run, prices and wages are sticky (think of menu prices staying the same for a period of time). Therefore, firms respond by increasing output when prices rise.

In the long run, prices and wages adjust; therefore, output is not affected by the price level.

Aggregate Price Level (P) / Aggregate Output (Q) — SRAS

Aggregate Price Level (P) / Aggregate Output (Q) — LRAS

20.5 Factors that shift the SRAS curve:

- Input prices
- Productivity
- Taxes and regulation
- Market power of firms
- Inflationary expectations

Electronic toll collection booths save time and reduce transportation costs to firms, leading to an increase in short-run aggregate supply and potentially long-run aggregate supply.

Factors that shift the LRAS curve:

- Increase in technology
- Greater human capital
- Trade
- Innovation and R&D

Section 3 Macroeconomic Equilibrium

20.6 A **long-run macroeconomic equilibrium** occurs at the intersection of the LRAS and AD curves, at full employment. A **short-run macroeconomic equilibrium** occurs at the intersection of the SRAS and AD curves. Short-run equilibrium can occur below full employment (recession) or above full employment (inflationary pressure).

Long-Run Macro Equilibrium

Short-Run Equilibrium (recession)

Short-Run Equilibrium (inflation)

20.7 The spending **multiplier** exists because new spending generates income that results in more spending and income, based on the marginal propensities to consume and save.

Multiplier Example: $MPC = 0.80$ and $MPS = 0.20$

Round 1: $100 in new spending = $100 in new income.

Round 2: $80 is spent and $20 is saved ($80 in new income).

Round 3: $64 is spent and $16 is saved.

Round 4: $51.20 is spent and $12.80 is saved.

Round 5: $40.96 is spent and $10.24 is saved.

Round 6: $32.76 is spent and $8.20 is saved.

...

Round n: $0.01 is spent and $0.00 is saved.

Total Effect of $100 in Spending =
$500 in Spending and $100 in Savings

Multiplier $= 1/(1 - MPC) = 1/(1 - 0.80) = 5$

20.8 **Demand-pull inflation** occurs when aggregate demand expands so much that equilibrium output exceeds full employment output. Temporarily, the economy can expand beyond full employment as workers incur overtime and more workers are added. But as wages rise, the economy will move to a new long-run equilibrium, where prices are permanently higher.

Cost-push inflation occurs when a supply shock hits the economy, shifting the SRAS curve to the left. Cost-push inflation makes using policies to expand aggregate demand to restore full employment difficult because of the additional inflationary pressures added to the economy.

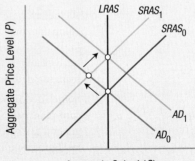

aggregate demand, p. 532
wealth effect, p. 533
aggregate supply, p. 537
long-run aggregate supply (LRAS)
   curve, p. 537

short-run aggregate supply (SRAS)
   curve, p. 538
macroeconomic equilibrium,
   p. 541
multiplier, p. 542

marginal propensity to consume,
   p. 542
marginal propensity to save, p. 542
demand-pull inflation, p. 544
cost-push inflation, p. 545

QUESTIONS AND PROBLEMS

Check Your Understanding

1. Describe the impact of rising interest rates on consumer spending.

2. When the economy is operating at full employment, why is an increase in aggregate demand not helpful to the economy?

3. When the economy is hit with a supply shock, such as rising prices for energy, food, or raw materials, why is this doubly disruptive and harmful to the economy?

4. Explain why the aggregate supply curve is positively sloped during the short run and vertical in the long run.

5. Explain how imports and exports affect aggregate demand.

6. List some examples of factors that will shift the long-run aggregate supply curve.

Apply the Concepts

7. There is little doubt that computers and the Internet have changed the economy. Information technology (IT) can boost efficiency in nearly everything: Markets are more efficient, IT is global, and IT improves the design, manufacture, and supply chain of products we produce. Use the aggregate demand and supply framework discussed in this chapter to show the impact of IT on the economy.

8. Unemployment can be caused by a reduction in aggregate demand or short-run aggregate supply. Both changes are represented by a leftward shift in the curves. Does it matter whether the shift occurs in aggregate demand or short-run aggregate supply? Use the AD/AS framework to show why or why not.

9. Why is cost-push inflation a more difficult problem for policymakers than demand-pull inflation?

10. Why is consumer confidence so important in determining the equilibrium level of output and employment?

11. As the Japanese yen appreciated in value during the 1980s and 1990s, more Japanese auto companies built manufacturing plants in other parts of Asia and in the United States. What impact did this have on net exports for the United States? Why did Japanese automakers build plants in the United States? Were the reasons similar to the reasons that American firms build plants (or establish offshore production) in China and other parts of Asia?

12. Some advocates have suggested that the United States should move to a universal health care plan paid for at the federal level, like Medicare, which would be funded out of general tax revenues. Such a plan, it is argued, would guarantee quality health care to all. Ignoring all the controversy surrounding such a plan, would the introduction of universal health care paid for from tax revenues have an impact on short-run aggregate supply? On long-run aggregate supply? Why or why not?

In the News

13. In 2016 a worldwide health scare resulted from the rapid spread of the mosquito-borne Zika virus, which was alleged to cause birth defects in infected pregnant women. Brazil was the epicenter of the epidemic, which also hosted the Summer Olympic Games that

same year. Explain how a health epidemic experienced in Brazil affected its aggregate demand and/or aggregate supply.

14. In late 2015 congressional House Speaker Paul Ryan helped pass a major budget bill signed by President Obama that eliminated many of the "sequester" provisions, or automatic spending cuts, that were implemented in 2013 after significant political gridlock. Many economists applauded the elimination of the spending cuts because they believed the cuts increased the risk of another recession when the economy was still in recovery. Using the AD/AS model and what you know about the spending multiplier, explain why economists would come to this conclusion.

Solving Problems

15. In the figure, the economy is initially in equilibrium at full employment at point e. Assume that consumption falls by 100, leading to a shift in aggregate demand from AD_0 to AD_1.

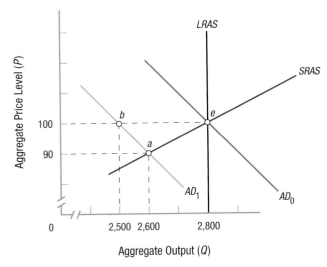

a. What is the new short-run macroeconomic equilibrium price and output?

b. How large is the simple Keynesian multiplier if there were no changes to the aggregate price level?

c. How large is the spending multiplier if the aggregate price level adjusts to the new equilibrium?

WORK IT OUT   🔖 **LaunchPad** | interactive activity

16. Use the table and grid below to answer the following questions:

Aggregate Price Level	Output (short-run aggregate supply)	Output (aggregate demand)
150	1,000	200
125	800	400
100	600	600
75	400	800
50	200	1,000

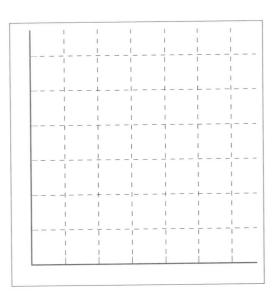

a. In the grid, graph the aggregate demand and short-run aggregate supply curves (label them AD_0 and $SRAS_0$). What are equilibrium output and the aggregate price level?

b. Assume aggregate demand grows by 200 at each price level. Graph the new aggregate demand curve and label it AD_1. What are the new equilibrium output and aggregate price level?

c. If full employment output is 600, is the economy experiencing recessionary or inflationary pressures?

d. By how much does the SRAS curve need to shift in order for the economy to return to full employment output at 600? What would the new equilibrium aggregate price level be?

USING THE NUMBERS

17. According to By the Numbers, if the average price of a barrel of oil is $50, and total aggregate demand in 2015 was $18 trillion in the United States and $11 trillion in China, what percentage of aggregate demand did oil consumption represent in each country?

18. According to By the Numbers, by what percentage did M&E revenues increase from 2012 to 2015? How does M&E growth compare to the percentage growth in overall aggregate output over this time period (which was approximately 2–3% per year)?

ANSWERS TO QUESTIONS IN CHECKPOINTS

Checkpoint: Aggregate Demand 536

An increase in home prices and stock values would increase the wealth of those who owned these assets. An increase in wealth provides greater financial security, even if income does not change. All else equal, consumption would rise, which would increase aggregate demand.

Checkpoint: Aggregate Supply 541

Low interest rates make it easier for individuals and firms to borrow for consumption and investment, which may lead to higher inflation, especially when the economy fully recovers and production resources are no longer sitting idle. As investors anticipate a rise in inflation, they will adjust production in anticipation of higher input (wage and raw materials) prices, which means SRAS will decrease.

Checkpoint: Macroeconomic Equilibrium 547

Agriculture goods are an important input in our economy. Higher crop prices increase the cost of producing food products as well as operating restaurants and cruise ships, which will reduce short-run aggregate supply. Over time, these cost increases will show up as a higher price level, reduced employment, and higher unemployment. If the economy continues to grow, these impacts will be masked, but will still reduce the level of growth. If the change is seen as permanent, consumers and businesses will begin making long-run adjustments to higher prices. For example, consumers might change their diets to include less expensive foods or plant their own crops in gardens, while businesses might consider alternative ingredients when planning menu items. If the price increases are just viewed as temporary, both groups might not adjust much at all.

Appendix

Deriving the Aggregate Demand Curve

The aggregate demand curve shows the quantities of goods and services (real GDP) demanded at different price levels, and can be derived using the aggregate expenditures model. To illustrate, panel A of Figure APX-1 shows aggregate expenditures (AE) curves at two different price levels. Remember that AE curves are drawn assuming fixed prices.

First, consider equilibrium point a on aggregate expenditures curve $AE(P_0)$. This point shows an equilibrium income of Y_0, which is equivalent to a real output of Q_0. Point a in panel B therefore represents a real output of Q_0 and a price level of P_0. However, if the aggregate price level rises to P_1, aggregate expenditures will decline to $AE(P_1)$ because at these higher prices, the same level of expenditures will not buy as much real output as before. The result is a new equilibrium at point b in both panels. Connecting points a and b in panel B, we have constructed aggregate demand curve AD, which represents the relationship between the price level and aggregate output.

FIGURE APX-1	DERIVING THE AGGREGATE DEMAND CURVE

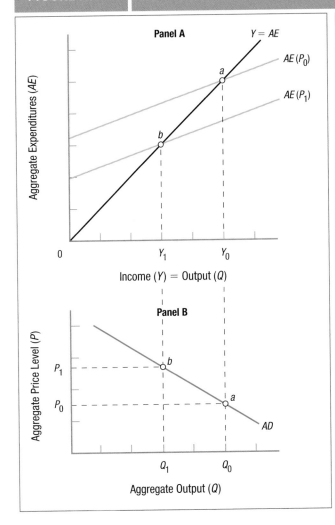

The aggregate demand curve, which shows the quantities of goods and services demanded at different price levels for the entire economy, can be derived using the aggregate spending model. Panel A shows aggregate expenditures curves at two different price levels. Point a on aggregate expenditures curve $AE(P_0)$ represents equilibrium income Y_0, equivalent to a real output of Q_0. Point a in panel B shows real output of Q_0 that is associated with equilibrium point a and its price level P_0. If the aggregate price level rises to P_1, aggregate spending will decline to $AE(P_1)$ in panel A. The result is a new equilibrium at point b in both panels. Connecting points a and b in panel B results in aggregate demand curve AD.

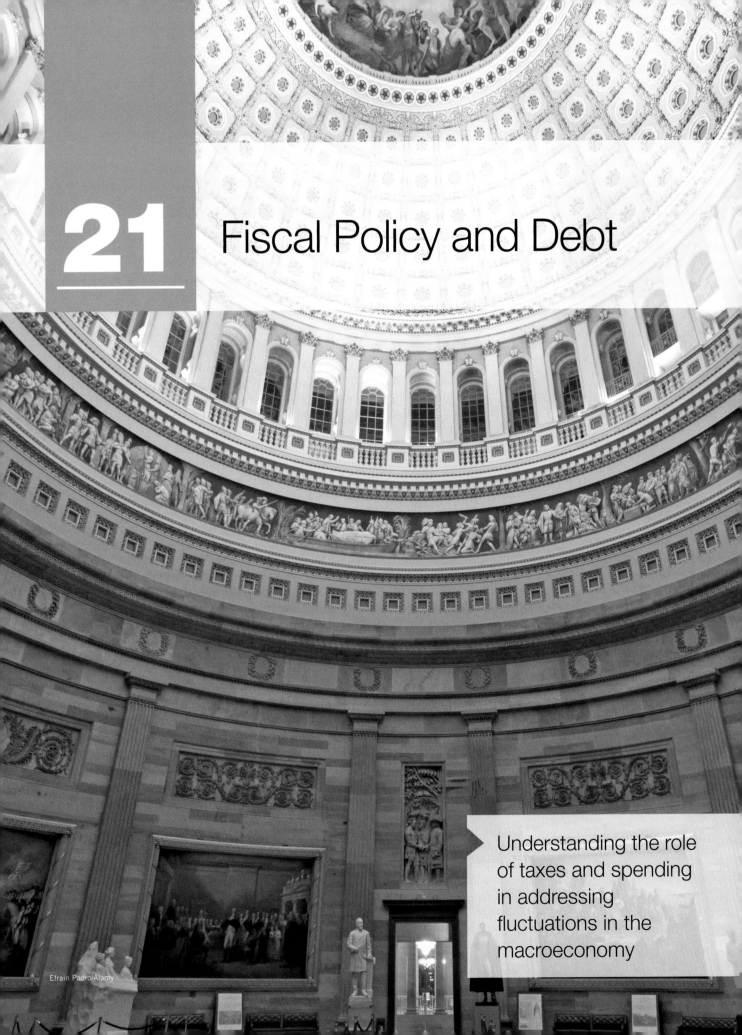

21 Fiscal Policy and Debt

Understanding the role of taxes and spending in addressing fluctuations in the macroeconomy

Efrain Padro/Alamy

Learning Objectives

21.1 Describe the tools that governments use to influence aggregate demand.

21.2 Describe expansionary and contractionary fiscal policy.

21.3 Determine the influence that the multiplier effect has on government spending and aggregate output.

21.4 Describe the fiscal policies that governments use to influence aggregate supply.

21.5 Describe the impact of automatic stabilizers, lag effects, and the propensity toward deficits from fiscal policymaking.

21.6 Identify the different lags that occur when implementing fiscal policy.

21.7 Define deficits and surpluses, and explain the difference between national debt and public debt.

21.8 Describe the potential consequences of maintaining high public debt.

When you apply for a loan to buy a car, you undoubtedly will go through a credit check and receive a credit rating, which is a number that estimates the probability of you paying back the loan. The government is also given a credit rating for the loans it takes out. This rating, like yours, estimates the probability of the government paying back its loans.

On August 5, 2011, Standard and Poor's (S&P), a credit rating agency, did something it had never done in its history: lower the debt rating of the United States government from a perfect AAA rating to a slightly less than perfect AA+ rating. Although an AA+ rating is still excellent, this change was significant, because it suggested for the first time that the United States government is not immune from all and any hardships in paying its debts.

Why did the United States government lose its perfect debt rating? One reason was its extensive use of fiscal policy in the aftermath of the 2007–2009 recession. Fiscal policy is the use of government revenue collection (mainly taxation) and spending to influence the economy. When the government taxes something, individuals and businesses have less money to spend. Therefore, taxes put the brakes on various economic activities. However, in terms of spending, think of what it means to local employment if the government decides to improve the roads and bridges in a city. By their very nature, taxation and spending affect the economy.

In extraordinary times, governments use fiscal policy to influence the macroeconomy with the express purpose of smoothing fluctuations in the business cycle. During the 2007–2009 recession, nearly $800 billion in additional government spending was added in an attempt to pull the economy out of its doldrums. If people would not spend, government would spend in their place. Spending was used to spur the economy when citizens were too scared to spend themselves. In inflationary times, government uses fiscal policy to pull money out of people's hands in an attempt to cool down spending and inflation.

Fiscal policy influences aggregate demand and aggregate supply in many ways. However, fiscal policy that is used to stimulate the economy is often accompanied by persistent budget deficits and debt. Why and to what end? This chapter will examine these issues and focus on the problem of financing deficits by accruing debt.

Most Americans are accustomed to dealing with debt. Individuals might have a home mortgage, car loan, student loan, or credit card balances, while businesses often take out loans for capital purchases and other expenses to run their operations. Most debt is managed by making periodic payments toward the balance and interest. However, when debt becomes too high to be controlled, individuals and companies face financial distress and are sometimes forced to declare bankruptcy.

As we will see, it is no surprise that governments also deal with debt. In recent years, deficits and the national debt have dominated economic headlines. The national debt grows when the government spends more than the tax revenues it collects. In 2015, the U.S. government collected about $3.25 trillion in taxes, but spent about $3.69 trillion. The difference of $440 billion represented the federal deficit that was added to the national debt.

BY THE NUMBERS

Your Government and Its Financial Operation

The U.S. government is one of the largest institutions in the world, taking in revenues of over $3 trillion each year. Still, the government in recent years has spent much more, incurring deficits that add to its public debt.

Go to **LaunchPad** to use the latest data to recreate this graph.

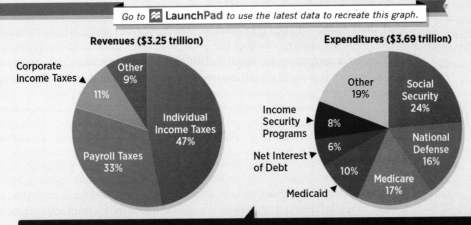

Revenues ($3.25 trillion)

- Corporate Income Taxes 11%
- Other 9%
- Individual Income Taxes 47%
- Payroll Taxes 33%

Expenditures ($3.69 trillion)

- Other 19%
- Social Security 24%
- National Defense 16%
- Medicare 17%
- Medicaid 10%
- Net Interest of Debt 6%
- Income Security Programs 8%

The government collected $3.25 trillion in 2015 primarily from individual income taxes and payroll (e.g., Social Security) taxes. It spent $3.69 trillion, over half on national defense, Social Security, and Medicare.

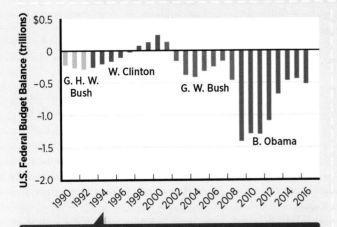

U.S. Federal Budget Balance (trillions)

G. H. W. Bush — W. Clinton — G. W. Bush — B. Obama

U.S. federal government expenditures exceeded revenues in every year since 1990 except from 1998 to 2001. The gap between spending and revenues expanded in 2008 as a result of the 2007–2009 recession, but has since become smaller.

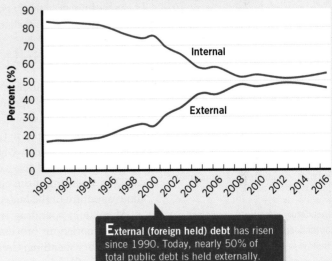

Percent (%)

Internal / External

External (foreign held) debt has risen since 1990. Today, nearly 50% of total public debt is held externally.

China, Japan, Caribbean Nations, OPEC Nations, Brazil, Ireland, Switzerland, United Kingdom, Hong Kong, Luxembourg

0 — 300 — 600 — 900 — 1,200 — $1,500

Top Ten Creditors of U.S. Treasury Debt as of January 2016 (in billions)

$19,188,228,000,000

Total U.S. national debt in March 2016

$223,400,000,000

Total interest paid on the national debt in 2015

Unlike individuals and small companies, a government has a much larger arsenal of tools to prevent it from going bankrupt, including the power to tax and the ever-powerful ability to "print" money. But even those tools can sometimes be rendered useless, causing a government to rack up sizeable debt and increasing the burden of managing the debt. Further, when a government does default on its debt, havoc in markets throughout the world may result.

In this chapter, we analyze the tools government uses to implement fiscal policy and study their effects on aggregate demand and aggregate supply, which affects income and output. We then analyze whether the amount of the federal debt is a problem, and if so, what the government can do about it. This chapter will give you a good sense of the scope of fiscal policy and the tradeoffs between relying on public debt and balancing taxes and spending.

FISCAL POLICY AND AGGREGATE DEMAND

When an economy faces underutilization of resources because it is stuck in equilibrium well below full employment, we saw that increases in aggregate demand can move the economy toward full employment without generating excessive inflation pressures. However, in normal times, influencing aggregate demand brings with it a tradeoff: Output is increased at the expense of raising the price level.

In contrast, consider decreasing aggregate demand. When the economy is in an inflationary equilibrium *above full employment*, contracting aggregate demand dampens inflation but leads to another tradeoff: unemployment. Before we examine the theory behind how government actually goes about influencing aggregate demand by using fiscal policy, let's take a brief look at what categories of spending fiscal policy typically alters.

Discretionary and Mandatory Spending

The federal budget can be split into two distinct types of spending: discretionary and mandatory. Discretionary spending is the part of the budget that works its way through the appropriations process of Congress each year. **Discretionary spending** includes such programs as national defense (primarily the military), transportation, science, environment, income security (some welfare programs and a large portion of Medicaid), education, and veterans benefits and services. As Figure 1 shows, discretionary spending has steadily declined as a percent of the budget since the 1960s, when it was over 60% of the budget, to about one-third of the budget today.

Mandatory spending is authorized by permanent laws and does not go through the same appropriations process as discretionary spending. To change one of the entitlements of mandatory spending, Congress must change the law. Mandatory spending includes such programs as Social Security, Medicare, part of Medicaid, interest on the national debt, and some means-tested income-security programs, including SNAP (Supplementary Nutrition Assistance Program, formerly known as the Food Stamp Program) and TANF (Temporary Assistance to Needy Families). This part of the budget has been growing, as Figure 1 illustrates, and now accounts for over 60% of the budget.

Even though discretionary spending is only 32% of the budget, this is still roughly $1.2 trillion, and the capacity to alter this spending is a powerful force in the economy. Therefore, we are mainly concerned with discretionary spending when we consider fiscal policy.

Discretionary Fiscal Policy

The exercise of **discretionary fiscal policy** is done with the express goal of influencing aggregate demand. It involves adjusting government spending and tax policies to move the economy toward full employment, encouraging economic growth, or controlling inflation.

Some examples of the use of discretionary fiscal policy include tax cuts enacted during the Kennedy, Reagan, and George W. Bush administrations. These tax cuts were designed

discretionary spending The part of the budget that works its way through the appropriations process of Congress each year and includes national defense, transportation, science, environment, and income security.

mandatory spending Spending authorized by permanent laws that does not go through the same appropriations process as discretionary spending. Mandatory spending includes Social Security, Medicare, and interest on the national debt.

discretionary fiscal policy Policies that involve adjusting government spending and tax policies with the express short-run goal of moving the economy toward full employment, expanding economic growth, or controlling inflation.

FIGURE 1	DISCRETIONARY AND MANDATORY FEDERAL SPENDING

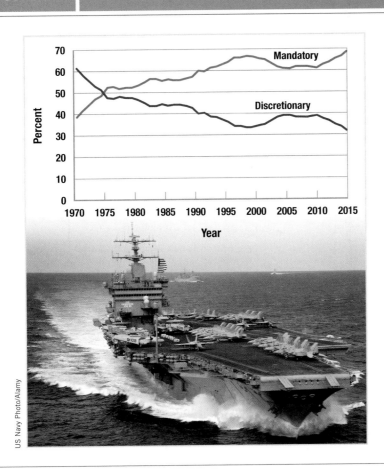

Mandatory spending includes entitlements authorized by law such as Social Security, Medicare, and the Supplemental Nutrition Assistance Program, along with interest on the national debt. Mandatory programs do not go through the normal congressional appropriations process and have been growing. Discretionary programs are authorized each year by the appropriations process of Congress and include national defense, transportation, environment, and education. Discretionary spending has been steadily declining as a percent of the budget.

to expand the economy under the belief that people would spend their tax savings, both in the near term and the long run—they were meant to influence both aggregate demand and aggregate supply. Tax increases were enacted under the George H. W. Bush and Clinton administrations in the interest of reducing the government deficit and interest rates. The Roosevelt administration used increased government spending, although small amounts by today's standards, to mitigate the impact of the Great Depression.

Government Spending Although discretionary fiscal policy can get complex, the impact of changes in government spending is relatively simple. As we know, a change in government spending or other components of GDP will cause income and output to rise or fall by the spending change *times* the multiplier.

This is illustrated in Figure 2 with the economy initially in equilibrium at point *e*, with real output at Q_0. If government spending increases, shifting aggregate demand from AD_0 to AD_1, aggregate output will increase from Q_0 to Q_f. Because the short-run aggregate supply curve is upward-sloping, some of the increase in output is absorbed by rising prices, reducing the pure spending multiplier discussed in earlier chapters.

Once the economy reaches full employment (point *a*), further spending is not multiplied as the economy moves along the LRAS curve, and only higher prices result. Finally, keep in mind that the multiplier works in both directions.

Taxes Changes in government spending modify income by an amount equal to the change in spending *times* the multiplier. How, then, do changes in taxes affect the economy? The answer is not quite as simple. Let's begin with a reminder of what constitutes spending equilibrium.

FIGURE 2	THE MULTIPLIER AND GOVERNMENT SPENDING

The economy is initially in equilibrium at point *e*. As new government spending works its way through the economy round-by-round, both income and output are multiplied, but price increases absorb some of the increase in *AD*. Once the economy reaches full employment (point *a*), price increases absorb all of the increase in *AD*.

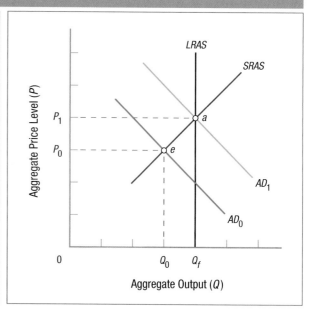

When the economy is in equilibrium,

$$GDP = C + I + G + (X - M)$$

At equilibrium, all spending *injections* into the economy equal all *withdrawals* of spending. To review, injections are activities that increase spending in an economy, such as investment (I), government spending (G), and exports (X). Withdrawals, on the other hand, are activities that remove spending from the economy, such as saving (S), taxes (T), and imports (M). Therefore, in equilibrium:

$$I + G + X = S + T + M$$

With this equation in hand, let's focus on taxes. When taxes are increased, money is withdrawn from the economy's spending stream. When taxes are reduced, consumers and businesses have more to spend. Disposable income is equal to income minus taxes ($Y - T$).

Because taxes represent a withdrawal of spending from the economy, we would expect equilibrium income to fall when a tax is imposed. Consumers pay a tax increase, in part, by *reducing* their saving. If we initially increase taxes by $100, let's assume that consumers draw on their savings for $25 of the increase in taxes. Because this $25 in savings was already withdrawn from the economy, only the $75 in reduced spending gets multiplied, reducing the change in income. The *reduction* in saving of $25 dampens the effect of the tax on equilibrium income because those funds were previously withdrawn from the spending stream. Changing the withdrawal category from saving to taxes does not affect income. A tax decrease has a similar but opposite impact because only the MPC part is spent and multiplied, and the rest is saved and thus withdrawn from the spending stream.

The result is that a tax increase (or decrease, for that matter) has less of a direct impact on income, employment, and output than an equivalent change in government spending. Another way of saying this is that the government tax multiplier is *less* than the government spending multiplier. Therefore, added government spending leads to a larger increase in GDP when compared to the same reduction in taxes.

Transfers Transfer payments are money payments paid directly to individuals. These include payments for such items as Social Security, unemployment compensation, and

FIGURE 3 — EXPANSIONARY FISCAL POLICY BELOW FULL EMPLOYMENT

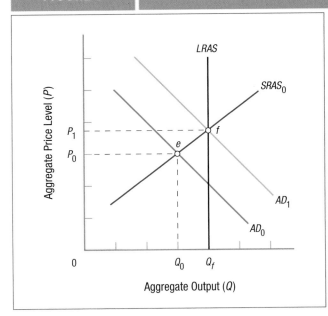

When the economy is below full employment, expansionary policies move it to full employment. Here, the economy begins at equilibrium at point *e*, below full employment. Expansionary fiscal policy increases aggregate demand from AD_0 to AD_1, raising equilibrium output to Q_f and the price level to P_1 (point *f*).

welfare. In large measure, they represent our social safety net. We will ignore them as part of the discretionary fiscal policy, because most are paid as a matter of law, but we will see later in the chapter that they are very important as a way of stabilizing the economy.

Expansionary and Contractionary Fiscal Policy

Expansionary fiscal policy involves increasing government spending (such as on highways and education), increasing transfer payments (such as unemployment benefits), and/or decreasing taxes—all to increase aggregate demand. These policies put more money into the hands of consumers and businesses. In theory, these additional funds should lead to higher spending. The precise effect expansionary fiscal policies have, however, depends on whether the economy is at or below full employment.

When the economy is below full employment, an expansionary policy will move the economy to full employment, as Figure 3 shows. The economy begins at equilibrium at point *e*, below full employment. Expansionary fiscal policy increases aggregate demand from AD_0 to AD_1, and equilibrium output rises to Q_f (point *f*) as the price level rises to P_1. In this case, one good outcome results—output rises to Q_f—though it is accompanied by one less desirable result, the price level rising to P_1.

Figure 4 shows what happens when the economy is at full employment. An expansionary policy raises prices without producing any long-run improvement in real GDP. In this figure, the initial equilibrium is already at full employment (point *e*); therefore, increasing aggregate demand moves the economy to a new output level above full employment (point *a*), thereby raising prices to P_1. This higher output is only temporary, however, as workers and suppliers adjust their expectations to the higher price level, thus shifting short-run aggregate supply upward to $SRAS_2$. Short-run aggregate supply declines because workers and other resource suppliers realize that the prices they are paying for products have risen; hence, they demand higher wages or prices for their services. Prices are then pushed up until workers adjust their inflationary expectations and the economy settles into equilibrium at point *b*. At this point, the economy is again at full employment, but at a higher price level (P_2) than before.

When an economy moves to a point beyond full employment, as just described, economists say an *inflationary spiral* has set in. The explanation for this phenomenon was suggested

expansionary fiscal policy Policies that increase aggregate demand to expand output in an economy. These include increasing government spending, increasing transfer payments, and/or decreasing taxes.

| **FIGURE 4** | EXPANSIONARY FISCAL POLICY AT FULL EMPLOYMENT |

When an economy is already at full employment, expansionary policies lead to no long-run improvement in real GDP. Beginning at full employment (point *e*), increasing aggregate demand moves the economy to output level Q_1 above full employment (point *a*). This higher output is only temporary, however, as workers and suppliers adjust their expectations to the higher price level (P_1), thus shifting short-run aggregate supply left toward $SRAS_2$. But this just pushes prices up further, until finally workers adjust their inflationary expectations, and the economy settles into a new long-run equilibrium at point *b*, where the economy is again at full employment, but at a higher price level (P_2).

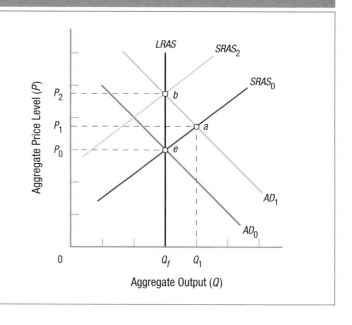

contractionary fiscal policy

Policies that decrease aggregate demand to contract output in an economy. These include reducing government spending, reducing transfer payments, and/or raising taxes.

earlier. Still, we can already see that one way to reduce such inflationary pressures is to use **contractionary fiscal policy.** These policies include reducing government spending, reducing transfer payments, and/or raising taxes (increasing withdrawals from the economy). Figure 5 shows the result of contractionary policy. The economy is initially overheating at point *e*, with output above full employment. Contractionary policy reduces aggregate demand to AD_1, bringing the economy back to full employment at price level P_1 and output Q_f.

Exercising demand-side policy requires tradeoffs between increasing output at the expense of raising the price levels, or else lowering price levels by accepting a lower output. When a recession occurs, the public is often happy to trade higher prices for greater employment and output. One would think the opposite would be true when an inflationary

| FIGURE 5 | CONTRACTIONARY FISCAL POLICY TO REDUCE INFLATION |

In this figure, the economy is overheating at point *e*, with output above full employment. Contractionary policies reduce aggregate demand to AD_1, bringing the economy back to full employment at price level P_1. These policies prevent an inflationary spiral, but the fall in aggregate output leads to an increase in unemployment.

spiral loomed on the horizon. Politicians, however, are loath to support contractionary policies that control inflation by reducing aggregate demand, because higher unemployment can cost politicians their jobs. As a result, the demand-side fiscal policy tools—government spending, transfer payments, and taxes—may remain unused. In these instances, politicians often look to the Federal Reserve to use its tools and influence to keep inflation in check. We will examine the Federal Reserve in later chapters.

 CHECKPOINT

FISCAL POLICY AND AGGREGATE DEMAND

- Demand-side fiscal policy involves using government spending, transfer payments, and taxes to influence aggregate demand and equilibrium income, output, and the price level in the economy.

- In the short run, government spending raises income and output by the amount of spending times the multiplier. Tax reductions have a smaller impact on the economy than government spending because some of the reduction in taxes is added to saving and is therefore withdrawn from the economy.

- Expansionary fiscal policy involves increasing government spending, increasing transfer payments, and/or decreasing taxes.

- Contractionary fiscal policy involves decreasing government spending, decreasing transfer payments, and/or increasing taxes.

- When an economy is at full employment, expansionary fiscal policy may lead to greater output in the short term, but will ultimately just lead to higher prices in the longer term.

- Politicians tend to favor expansionary fiscal policy because it can bring with it increases in employment although with increasing inflation. Politicians tend to shun contractionary fiscal policy because it brings unemployment.

QUESTION: During the 2007–2009 recession, the government passed a $787 billion stimulus package, which was roughly $2,500 in government spending for every person. The time required for the government to spend that sum on infrastructure projects (funding approvals, environmental clearances, and so on) meant that the spending stretched over several years. Why didn't Congress just send a $2,500 check to each woman, man, and child in America to speed up the impact on the economy?

Answers to the Checkpoint questions can be found at the end of this chapter.

FISCAL POLICY AND AGGREGATE SUPPLY

Fiscal policies that influence aggregate supply are different from policies that influence aggregate demand, as they do not always require tradeoffs between price levels and output. That is the good news. The bad news is that **supply-side fiscal policies** require more time to work than do demand-side fiscal policies. The focus of fiscal policy and aggregate supply is on long-run economic growth.

Figure 6 shows the impact that fiscal policy can have on the economy over the long run. The goal of these fiscal policies is to shift the long-run aggregate supply curve to the right, here from $LRAS_0$ to $LRAS_1$. This shift moves the economy's full employment equilibrium from point a to point b, thereby expanding full-employment output while keeping inflation in check. In Figure 6, the price level falls as output expands. In practice, this would be unusual because when the economy grows, aggregate demand typically expands and keeps prices from falling.

Figure 6 may well reflect what happens in general as the world economy embraces trade and globalization. Improvements in technology and communications increase productivity to the point that global long-run aggregate supply shifts outward. These changes, along with freer trade, help increase economic growth and keep inflation low.

supply-side fiscal policies
Policies that focus on shifting the long-run aggregate supply curve to the right, expanding the economy without increasing inflationary pressures. Unlike policies to increase aggregate demand, supply-side policies take longer to impact the economy.

FIGURE 6 | FISCAL POLICY AND AGGREGATE SUPPLY

The ultimate goal of fiscal policy directed at aggregate supply is to shift the long-run aggregate supply curve from $LRAS_0$ to $LRAS_1$. This moves the economy's full employment equilibrium from point a to point b, expanding output from Q_0 to Q_1 while keeping inflation in check. With these fiscal policies, inflationary pressures are reduced as output expands, but these policies take a longer time to have an impact.

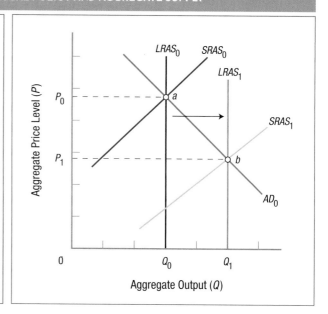

Just what fiscal policies will allow the economy to expand without generating price pressures? First, there are government policies that encourage investment in human capital (education) and policies that encourage the development and transfer of new technologies. Second, there are the fiscal policies that focus on reducing tax rates. Third, there are policies that promote investment in new capital equipment, encourage investment in research and development, and trim burdensome business regulations. These policies are intended to expand the supply curves of all businesses and industries.

Infrastructure Spending

Governments can do a great deal to create the right environment to encourage economic growth. We already have seen the benefits of building and maintaining a nation's infrastructure, including roads, bridges, dams, and communications networks, or setting up a fair and efficient legal system and stable financial system. Further, the higher the levels of human capital and the more easily technology is transferred to other firms and industries (the public good aspect of technology), the more robust economic growth. Therefore, long-run growth is enhanced through investments in higher education and research.

Reducing Tax Rates

Reducing tax rates has an impact on both aggregate demand and aggregate supply. Lower tax rates increase aggregate demand because households now have more money to spend. At the same time, lower tax rates mean that take-home wages rise and this may encourage more work effort. Also, entrepreneurial profits are taxed at lower rates, encouraging more people to take risks and start businesses. At different times, policymakers have lowered taxes to stimulate consumption: John F. Kennedy reduced tax rates in the early 1960s and George W. Bush in 2001 and 2008 provided tax rebates to taxpayers as part of economic stimulus packages. President Obama's 2009 stimulus program included tax credits along with increases in government spending.

At other times, administrations have reduced marginal tax rates, the rate paid on the next dollar earned, with the express purpose of stimulating incentives to work and for businesses to take risks. President Kennedy reduced the top marginal rate from 70% to 50%, and President Reagan reduced the top marginal rate from 50% to 28%.

FIGURE 7 — THE LAFFER CURVE

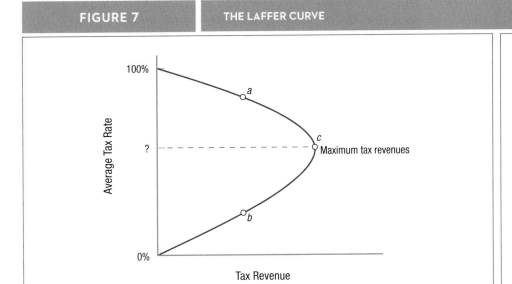

The Laffer curve shows the relationship between average tax rates and total tax revenues. As the tax rate rises from 0%, tax revenues increase. At point c, tax revenues are maximized. If tax rates continue to rise, tax revenues will decrease because higher tax rates discourage people from working and firms from producing. A government collects the same tax revenues at points a or b. The tax rates that correspond to points b and c are often debated by economists.

Clearly, high marginal income tax rates can have adverse effects on the economy. Still, there is considerable controversy regarding the benefits of the supply-side approach to macroeconomic fiscal policy. The supply-side movement that resulted in the marginal tax rate reductions in the 1980s by the Reagan administration was partially driven by reference to a simple tax revenue curve drawn by economist Arthur Laffer showing how reducing tax *rates* could increase tax *revenues*.

The **Laffer curve** in Figure 7 shows that if tax rates are 0% or 100%, tax revenues will be zero (the latter because there would be no incentive to earn income). In between these two extreme tax rates, tax revenues will be positive. Laffer argued that high tax rates (such as the one that generates revenues at point a on the Laffer curve) create disincentives to work and invest. He claimed that a lower tax rate would generate the same amount of revenue, seen as point b on the curve. Economists debate about what the tax rate corresponding to point b would be. Further, it raises a bigger debate about the tax rate at which the disincentive to work begins to reduce tax revenues. In other words, what tax rate corresponds to point c on the Laffer curve?

Laffer curve A curve that shows a hypothetical relationship between income tax rates and tax revenues. As tax rates rise from zero, revenues rise, reach a maximum, then decline until revenues reach zero again at a 100% tax rate.

Expanding Investment and Reducing Regulations

We have already seen how closely standards of living are tied to productivity. Investment increases the capital with which labor works, thereby increasing productivity. Rising productivity drives increased economic growth and raises the average standard of living, shifting the long-run aggregate supply curve to the right.

Investment can be encouraged by such policies as investment tax credits (direct reductions in taxes for new investment) and more rapid depreciation schedules for plant and equipment. When a firm can expense (depreciate) its capital equipment over a shorter period of time, it cuts its taxes now rather than later, and therefore earns a higher return on the capital now. Similarly, government grants for basic research help firms increase their budgets for research and development, which results in new products and technologies brought to market.

Nowhere is this impact more evident than in the health care field. The National Institutes of Health, part of the U.S. Department of Health and Human Services, invests over $30 billion in health care research each year, mostly in grants to medical schools, universities, and

Chromosome genetics research has led to significant advances in medical cures, and is an example of how fiscal policy can expand aggregate supply.

Florian Gaertner/Getty Images

research institutions. These investments have enabled new medicines to be developed at a much faster rate than previously. And beyond the obvious benefits this has for the people who require such medicines, investments of this sort pay dividends for the entire economy. As health care improves, workers' absentee rates are lower and productivity rises.

Another way of increasing long-run aggregate supply involves repealing unnecessarily onerous regulations that hamper business and add to costs. Clearly, some regulation of business activities is needed, as the financial industry meltdown in 2008 has shown. Still, these regulations should be subjected to rigorous cost-benefit analyses. Otherwise, excessive regulations end up adding to the costs of the products we buy, without yielding significant benefits. Examples of excessively regulated industries have included trucking and the airlines. When these industries were deregulated in the 1980s, prices fell and both industries expanded rapidly. Today, some economists argue that the Federal Drug Administration's drug approval process is too long and costly; bringing a new drug to market can cost over $1 billion.

Fiscal policies to increase aggregate supply are promoted mainly through the government's encouragement of human capital development and technology improvements, its power to tax, its ability to promote investment in infrastructure and research, and the degree and efficiency of regulation. Cutting marginal tax rates, offering investment tax credits, and offering grants for research are the favored policies. The political fervor of the 1980s supply-side movement has largely dissipated as marginal income tax rates have declined. But fiscal policies to encourage growth in long-run aggregate supply are still an important part of the government's long-term fiscal policy arsenal.

AROUND THE WORLD

Qatar: A Nation Built for the Future

How did Qatar, a tiny nation in the Middle East that has never participated in a World Cup soccer match, win its bid to host the biggest sporting event in the world?

Gavin Hellier/Getty Images

In November 2022 around 4 billion people from 200 countries will be focused on the world's most popular sports tournament, the FIFA World Cup. That year's tournament will be held in one of the smallest nations on Earth, both in size and in population. This country is still relatively unknown to most people, and its national soccer team has never qualified for the World Cup in its history. How then, did Qatar become the host of the 2022 World Cup?

Qatar is located on a peninsula off of the Persian Gulf in the Middle East, with an area smaller than the size of Connecticut and fewer than 2 million residents. But what it lacks in size and population is offset by its abundance of resources, particularly oil and natural gas. According to statistics from the World Bank, in 2015 Qatar was the richest nation on Earth in terms of GDP per capita. Its government is flush with cash from its resource exports, which has allowed it to use expansionary fiscal policy with ease.

Over the past two decades, Qatar's government invested heavily to build infrastructure, increase human capital, and attract foreign investment. These policies not only increased Qatar's aggregate demand, but also its capacity to produce through its long-run aggregate supply. While many countries struggle with debt, Qatar's commitment to infrastructure spending made it an excellent candidate to host the World Cup.

In its bid to host the World Cup in 2022, Qatar promised to build at least eight new stadiums, including five high-tech climate-controlled stadiums that are able to keep players and spectators cool even when outside temperatures exceed 100°F. In addition, the government-owned airline, Qatar Airways, will expand its operations to include direct flights to nearly all major cities around the world.

Qatar's use of expansionary fiscal policy has helped diversify its economy. This strategy is especially important given the volatility of oil prices, which will encourage oil-rich countries such as Qatar to depend on other factors such as capital and innovation to maintain economic growth.

GO TO LaunchPad TO PRACTICE THE ECONOMIC CONCEPTS IN THIS STORY

CHECKPOINT

FISCAL POLICY AND AGGREGATE SUPPLY

- The goal of fiscal policies that influence aggregate supply is to shift the long-run aggregate supply curve to the right.
- Expanding long-run aggregate supply can occur through higher investments in human capital and a focus on technological infrastructure with "public good" benefits.
- The Laffer curve suggests that reducing tax rates could lead to *higher* revenues if tax rates are high enough.
- Other fiscal policies to increase long-run aggregate supply include providing incentives for business investment and reducing burdensome regulation.
- The major limitation of fiscal policies to influence long-run aggregate supply is that they take a longer time to have an impact compared to polices aimed at influencing aggregate demand.

QUESTIONS: Some economists have suggested that an improved tax structure would entail a reduction in income taxes for individuals, corporations (corporate income tax), and investors (capital gains taxes), which is offset by an increase in consumption taxes (such as sales and excise taxes). Which part(s) of this type of proposal would be consistent with supply-side economics? Why?

Answers to the Checkpoint questions can be found at the end of this chapter.

IMPLEMENTING FISCAL POLICY

Implementing fiscal policy is often easier said than done. It is frequently a complex and time-consuming process. Three disparate entities—the Senate, House, and the president—must collectively agree on specific spending and tax policies. Ideally, these decisions are made in the open with the public fully informed. The complexities of the budgeting process and its openness (not a bad thing in itself) give rise to several inherent difficulties. We will briefly consider some problems having to do with the timing of fiscal decisions and the political pressures inherent in the process, after first looking at the automatic stabilization mechanisms contained in the federal budgeting process.

Automatic Stabilizers

There is a certain degree of stability built into the U.S. macroeconomic system. Tax revenues and transfer payments are the two principal **automatic stabilizers;** without any overt action by Congress or other policymakers, these two components of the federal budget expand or contract in ways that help counter movements of the business cycle.

When the economy is growing at a solid rate, tax receipts rise because individuals and firms are increasing their taxable incomes. At the same time, transfer payments decline, because fewer people require welfare or unemployment assistance. Rising tax revenues and declining transfer payments have contractionary effects, and act as a brake to slow the growth of GDP, helping to keep the economy from overheating, or keeping it from generating inflationary pressures. When the economic boom ends, and the economy goes into a downturn, the opposite happens: Tax revenues decline and transfer payments rise. These added funds being pumped into the economy help cushion the impact of the downturn, not just for the recipients of transfer payments, but for the economy as a whole.

The income tax is also a powerful stabilizer because of its progressivity. When incomes fall, tax revenues fall faster because people do not just pay taxes on smaller incomes, but they pay taxes at lower rates as their incomes fall. Disposable income, in other words, falls more slowly than aggregate income. But when the economy is booming, tax revenues rise

automatic stabilizers Tax revenues and transfer payments automatically expand or contract in ways that reduce the intensity of business fluctuations without any overt action by Congress or other policymakers.

faster than income, thereby withdrawing spending from the economy. This helps to slow the growth in income, thus reducing the threat of an inflationary spiral.

The key point to remember here is that automatic stabilizers reduce the intensity of business fluctuations. Automatic stabilizers do not eliminate fluctuations in the business cycle, but they render business cycles smoother and less chaotic. Automatic stabilizers act on their own, whereas discretionary fiscal policy requires overt action by policymakers, and this fact alone creates difficulties.

Fiscal Policy Timing Lags

Using discretionary fiscal policy to smooth the short-term business cycle is a challenge because of several lags associated with its implementation. First, most of the macroeconomic data that policymakers need to enact the proper fiscal policies are not available until at least one quarter (three months) after the fact. Even then, key figures often get revised for the next quarter or two. The **information lag** therefore creates a one- to six-month period before informed policymaking can even begin.

Even if the most recent data suggest that the economy is trending into a recession, it may take several quarters to confirm this fact. Short-term (month-to-month or quarter-to-quarter) variations in key indicators are common and sometimes represent nothing more than randomness in the data. This **recognition lag** is one reason why recessions and recoveries are often well under way before policymakers fully acknowledge a need for action.

Third, once policymakers recognize that the economy has trended in a certain direction, fiscal policy requires a long and often contentious legislative process, referred to as a **decision lag.** Not all legislators have the same goals for the economy; therefore, any new government spending must first survive an arduous trip through the political sausage machine. Once some new policy has become law, it often requires months of planning, budgeting, and implementation to set up a new program. This process, the **implementation lag,** rarely consumes *less* than 18 to 24 months.

The problem these lags pose is clear: By the time the fiscal stimulus meant to jumpstart a sputtering economy kicks in, the economy may already be on the mend. And if so, the exercise of fiscal policy can compound the effects of the business cycle by overstimulating a patient that is already recovering.

Some of these lags can be reduced by expediting spending already approved for existing programs rather than implementing new programs. This was the approach Congress and the administration wanted to take with the 2009 stimulus package. Congress allocated part of the increased spending to "shovel-ready" projects to reduce the time for this spending to have an impact on the economy. Also, the lags associated with tax changes are much shorter, given that new rates can go into withholding tables and take effect within weeks of enactment. Therefore, policymakers often include tax changes because of their shorter implementation lags.

The Government's Bias Toward Borrowing and Away From Taxation

Because of the uncertainties surrounding the economy, politicians often take their own interests into account when considering fiscal policy, if not for economic reasons then very likely for political ones. In times of recessions or slow economic recovery, those on the left tend to favor more government spending and transfer payments, while those on the right tend to favor reductions in taxes. Both policies are expansionary and lead to greater deficits, especially as tax receipts fall due to lower incomes and fewer jobs.

But in order to balance the budget over the long run, such policies generally need to be reversed in good times so that government spending is reduced and taxes raised, along with the generation of more tax

---

information lag The time policymakers must wait for economic data to be collected, processed, and reported. Most macroeconomic data are not available until at least one quarter (three months) after the fact.

recognition lag The time it takes for policymakers to confirm that the economy is in a recession or a recovery. Short-term variations in key economic indicators are typical and sometimes represent nothing more than randomness in the data.

decision lag The time it takes Congress and the administration to decide on a policy once a problem is recognized.

implementation lag The time required to turn fiscal policy into law and eventually have an impact on the economy.

Political gridlock can delay fiscal policy legislation for months or years.

JIM WATSON/Getty Images

receipts from higher incomes and more jobs. But politicians often are reluctant to do so. Even in good economic times, tax hikes are politically dangerous, and so are major cuts to government spending programs and transfer programs. The result is that fiscal policy is financed by deficits. Deficits persist in our system of government.

Public choice theory involves the economic analysis of public and political decision making. James Buchanan, considered the father of public choice theory, essentially fused the disciplines of economics and political science. Buchanan contrasted Adam Smith's description of social benefits that arise from private individuals acting in their own self-interest with the harm that frequently results from politicians doing the same thing. Competition among individuals and firms for jobs, customers, and profits creates wealth, and thus it benefits the entire society. Self-interested politicians, however, often instigate government interventions that are harmful to the larger economy.

Public choice economists such as Buchanan argue that deficit spending reduces the perceived cost of current government operations. The result is that taxpayers permit some programs to exist that they would oppose if required to pay the full cost today. But this situation, public choice economists charge, amounts to shifting the cost of government to the next generation, and has led to the steady expansion of the federal government.

Public choice analysis helps us to understand why deficits seem inevitable. Simply, we do not pay the full costs of today's programs. In the past 50 years, the federal government has run a deficit in 45 of these years, despite significant growth of the economy over this time. The next section focuses on the role of deficits and public debt on the economy.

public choice theory The economic analysis of public and political decision making, looking at issues such as voting, the impact of election incentives on politicians, the influence of special interest groups, and rent-seeking behaviors.

 CHECKPOINT

IMPLEMENTING FISCAL POLICY

- Automatic stabilizers reduce the intensity of business fluctuations. When the economy is booming, tax revenues rise and unemployment compensation and welfare payments fall, dampening the boom. When the economy enters a recession, tax revenues fall and transfer payments rise, cushioning the decline. This happens automatically.

- Fiscal policymakers face information lags (the time it takes to collect, process, and provide data on the economy), recognition lags (the time required to recognize trends in the data), decision lags (the time it takes for Congress and the administration to decide on a policy), and implementation lags (the time required by Congress to pass a law and see it put in place).

- These lags can often result in government policy being mistimed. For example, expansionary policy taking effect when the economy is well into a recovery or failing to take effect when a recession is under way can make stabilization worse.

- Public choice economists argue that deficit spending reduces the perceived cost of current government operations, and therefore politicians are generally more willing to enact expansionary policies that lead to deficits and a higher public debt.

QUESTION: Suppose that the president wishes to enact fiscal policies that would generate the most immediate effect on the economy, and thus improve his or her chances of re-election. What type of policies would he or she tend to favor and why?

Answers to the Checkpoint questions can be found at the end of this chapter.

FINANCING THE FEDERAL GOVERNMENT

In the late 1990s, an economic boom fueled by the expansion of the Internet and "dot com" industries resulted in tremendous economic growth and low unemployment. In 1998 an increase in tax revenues collected as a result of higher incomes and on profits earned from a rising stock market led to tax revenues exceeding government spending for the first time in nearly 30 years. This trend lasted four years until 2002, when the government again spent more than it collected in taxes, and has since never reversed course. This section begins by defining deficits and surpluses, national debt, and public debt before studying their impact on the economy.

Defining Deficits and the National Debt

deficit The amount by which annual government expenditures exceed tax revenues.

surplus The amount by which annual tax revenues exceed government expenditures.

national debt The total debt issued by the U.S. Treasury, which represents the total accumulation of past deficits less surpluses. A portion of this debt is held by other government agencies, and the rest is held by the public. It is also referred to as the gross federal debt.

A **deficit** is the amount by which annual government expenditures exceed tax revenues. A **surplus** is the amount by which annual tax revenues exceed government expenditures. In 2000 the budget surplus was $236.2 billion. By 2002 tax cuts, a recession, and new commitments for national defense and homeland security had turned the budget surpluses of 1998–2001 into deficits—a deficit of $157.8 billion for fiscal year 2002. The effects of the deep recession in 2007–2009, and the extent of fiscal policies used, changed the magnitude of the deficit picture again. Government intervention and support for the financial and automobile industries and a nearly $800 billion stimulus package to soften the recession resulted in a 2009 deficit of over $1.4 trillion. However, the economic recovery since 2009 significantly reduced the deficit to $440 billion in 2015.

The gross federal debt, or more commonly known as the **national debt**, is the total accumulation of past deficits less surpluses. The national debt is measured as the total amount of debt issued by the U.S. Treasury (including Treasury bills, notes, and bonds, and Savings bonds). The national debt in 2016 was over $19 trillion. However, a portion of this debt is held by other agencies of government, such as the Social Security Administration, the Treasury Department, and the Federal Reserve, in what is referred to as an intergovernmental transfer. What exactly does this mean?

Suppose you have a savings account with funds to be used to pay your college tuition, but due to an unexpected expensive $2,000 car repair, you temporarily borrowed from your college savings account by withdrawing $800 and borrowed the remaining $1,200 using a credit card. Although you fully intend to pay back the full $2,000 in debt (including your college savings), only $1,200 is owed to someone other than yourself. Similarly, part of the total debt that the government has incurred is owed to itself, and the rest is owed to the public.

public debt The portion of the national debt that is held by the public, including individuals, companies, pension funds, along with foreign entities and foreign governments. This debt is also referred to as net debt or federal debt held by the public.

The **public debt**, also known as the net debt or federal debt held by the public, is the portion of the national debt that is held by individuals, companies, and pension funds, along with foreign entities and foreign governments. Public debt represents a real claim on government assets, and is the debt that is more scrutinized when analyzing the health of the macroeconomy.

In sum, the national debt and public debt are distinct measures of the extent to which government spending has exceeded tax revenues over the course of time. Figure 8 shows the public debt as a percentage of gross domestic product (GDP) since 1940. During World War II, public debt exceeded GDP. It then trended downward until the early 1980s, when public debt began to climb again. Public debt as a percentage of GDP fell from the mid-1990s until 2000, first because of growing budget surpluses in the late 1990s, then because of falling interest rates (what the government has to pay on the debt), but it has risen since then. Public debt today exceeds 70% of GDP.

Public debt is held as U.S. Treasury securities, including Treasury bills, notes, bonds, and U.S. Savings Bonds. Treasury bills, or T-bills, as they are known, are short-term instruments with a maturity period of a year or less that pay a specific sum at maturity. T-bills do not pay interest. Rather, they are initially sold at a discount, and their yields are then determined by the time to maturity and the discount. T-bills are the most actively traded securities in the U.S. economy, and they are highly liquid, providing the closest thing there is to risk-free returns.

Treasury notes are financial instruments issued for periods ranging from 1 to 10 years, whereas Treasury bonds have maturity periods exceeding 10 years. Both of these instruments have stated interest rates and are traded sometimes at discounts and sometimes at premiums.

Today, interest rates on the public debt are between 1% and 4%. This relatively low rate has not always been the case. In the early 1980s, interest rates varied from 11% to nearly

FIGURE 8	PUBLIC DEBT AS A PERCENT OF GDP

The public debt as a percentage of GDP has varied considerably since 1940. During World War II, public debt exceeded GDP. It then trended downward until the early 1980s, when public debt began to climb again. In 2016 public debt held by the public (as opposed to government institutions) exceeded 70% of GDP.

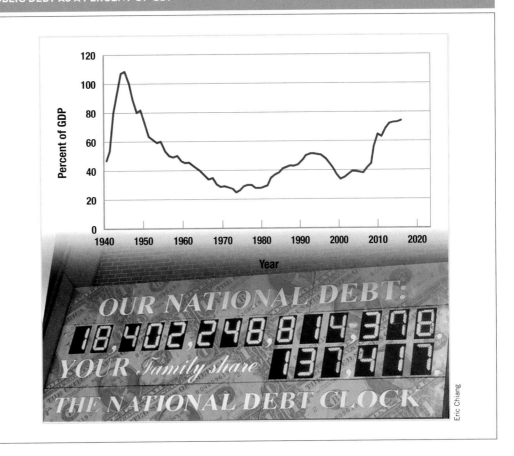

15%. Inflation was high and investors required high interest rates as compensation. When rates are high, government interest costs on the debt soar.

Balanced Budget Amendments

Although federal budget deficits have been the norm for the past 50 years, the 2007–2009 recession led to record deficits, leading many politicians to propose federal balanced budget amendments requiring the federal government to balance its budget every year. Balanced budget amendments are not new. They exist, with varying exceptions, for most state governments. At the federal level, however, such rules have not existed since the 1930s.

Most balanced budget amendments require an **annually balanced budget,** which means government would have to equate its revenues and expenditures every year. Most economists, however, believe such rules are counterproductive. For example, during times of recession, tax revenues tend to fall due to lower incomes and higher unemployment. To offset these lost revenues, an annually balanced budget would require deep spending cuts or tax hikes (in other words, contractionary fiscal policy) during a time when expansionary fiscal policies are needed. Many economists believe that balanced budget rules of the early 1930s turned what probably would have been a modest recession into the global Depression.

An alternative to balancing the budget annually would be to require a **cyclically balanced budget,** in which the budget is balanced over the course of the business cycle. The basic idea is to restrict spending or raise taxes when the economy is booming, allowing for a budget surplus. These surpluses would then be used to offset deficits accrued

annually balanced budget
Expenditures and taxes would have to be equal each year.

cyclically balanced budget
Balancing the budget over the course of the business cycle by restricting spending or raising taxes when the economy is booming and using these surpluses to offset the deficits that occur during recessions.

ISSUE

How Big Is the Economic Burden of Interest Rates on the National Debt?

The federal government paid $223 billion in interest payments on the national debt in 2016. This is money that could have been used for other public programs. In fact, interest payments on the debt were greater than the amount the government paid for education, transportation infrastructure, low-income housing, and Homeland Security combined.

Although interest payments on the debt are large, they represent a small portion of the federal budget and an even smaller portion of GDP. Interest on the debt as a percentage of GDP, as shown in the figure, was steady from 1950 to 1980, hovering around 1.5%. This percentage more than doubled during the 1980s because of high inflation and interest rates, and rising deficits. In the 1990s, interest rates dropped and deficits fell, allowing interest payments as a percentage of GDP to fall toward the level it was in the 1950s. The rising debt associated with the 2007–2009

recession increased the percentage again, but not by much due to record low interest rates. Today, interest rates remain low, allowing interest payments to remain a small percentage of GDP.

The fact that rising debt has not led to dramatic borrowing costs highlights the important role that interest rates have on the economy. Many individuals, firms, and foreign governments hold long-term (up to 30-year) Treasury bonds. During the economic crisis in the early 1980s, interest rates on 30-year Treasury bonds reached 15%, guaranteeing a bondholder a 15% annual return for 30 years.

Today, those 15% bonds from the 1980s have matured, and new 30-year bonds are paying less than 4%, resulting in tremendous savings to the government in financing the national debt. For example, an average interest rate of 2% saves the U.S. federal government $500 billion per year compared to a 5% interest rate, and saves over $1 trillion

per year compared to an 8% interest rate.

Why have long-term interest rates remained low despite the high debt and a debt downgrade in U.S. bonds? One reason is that volatility in stock markets makes U.S. debt still one of the safest investments in the world. Second, foreign governments perceive the U.S. dollar as a valuable hard currency, and thus buy our bonds as a way to build up their national reserves. For these reasons and more, the U.S. government has little trouble selling bonds at low interest rates.

Despite the current favorable conditions under which the U.S. government finances its debt, it must still focus on keeping debt in check for a number of reasons. For example, interest payments on external (foreign) holdings of U.S. debt are a leakage from our economy. Also, as interest rates rise in the future, low interest rate bonds issued today will mature and be replaced by higher interest rate bonds.

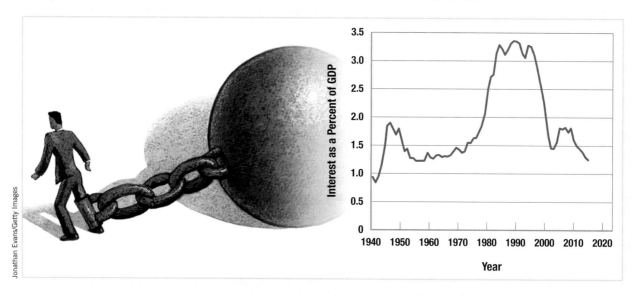

during recessions, when increased spending or lower taxes are appropriate. To some extent, balancing the budget over the business cycle happens automatically as long as fiscal policy is held constant due to the automatic stabilizers discussed earlier. However, the business cycle takes time to define (due to lags), making it difficult to enforce such a rule in practice.

Finally, some economists believe that balancing the budget should not be the primary concern of policymakers; instead, they view the government's primary macroeconomic responsibility to foster economic growth and stable prices, while keeping the economy as close as possible to full employment. This is the **functional finance** approach to the budget, where governments provide public goods and services that citizens want (such as national defense and education) and focus on policies that keep the economy growing, because rapidly growing economies do not have significant public debt or deficit issues.

In sum, balancing the budget annually or over the business cycle may be either counterproductive or difficult to do. It is not a solution to the public choice problem previously discussed of politicians' incentives to spend and not raise taxes. Budget deficits begin to look like a normal occurrence in our political system.

functional finance An approach that focuses on fostering economic growth and stable prices, while keeping the economy as close as possible to full employment.

Financing Debt and Deficits

Seeing as how deficits may be persistent, how does the government deal with its debt, and what does this imply for the economy? Government deals with debt in two ways. It can either borrow or sell assets.

Given its power to print money and collect taxes, the federal government cannot go bankrupt per se. But it does face what economists call a **government budget constraint:**

government budget constraint The government budget is limited by the fact that $G - T = \Delta M + \Delta B + \Delta A$.

$$G - T = \Delta M + \Delta B + \Delta A$$

where

G = government spending
T = tax revenues; thus, $(G - T)$ is the federal budget deficit
ΔM = the change in the money supply (selling bonds to the Federal Reserve)
ΔB = the change in bonds held by public entities, domestic and foreign
ΔA = the sales of government assets

The left side of the equation, $G - T$, represents government spending minus tax revenues. A positive $(G - T)$ value is a budget deficit, and a negative $(G - T)$ value represents a budget surplus. The right side of the equation shows how government finances its deficit. It can sell bonds to the Federal Reserve, sell bonds to the public, or sell assets. Let's look at each of these options.

- **$\Delta M > 0$:** First, the government can sell bonds to government agencies, especially the Federal Reserve, which we will study in depth in a later chapter. When the Federal Reserve buys bonds, it uses money that is created out of thin air by its power to "print" money. When the Federal Reserve pumps new money into the money supply to finance the government's debt, it is called monetizing the debt.

- **$\Delta B > 0$:** If the Federal Reserve does not purchase the bonds, they may be sold to the public, including corporations, banks, mutual funds, individuals, and foreign entities. This also has the effect of financing the government's deficit.

- **$\Delta A > 0$:** Asset sales represent only a small fraction of government finance in the United States. These sales include auctions of telecommunications spectra and offshore oil leases. Developing nations have used asset sales, or privatization, in recent years to bolster sagging government revenues and to encourage efficiency and development in the case where a government-owned industry is sold.

Thus, when the government runs a deficit, it must borrow funds from somewhere, assuming it does not sell assets. If the government borrows from the public, the quantity of publicly held bonds will rise; if it borrows from the Federal Reserve, the quantity of money in circulation will rise.

The main idea from this section is that deficits must be financed in some form, whether by the government borrowing or selling assets. As we'll see in the next section, rising levels of deficits and the corresponding interest rates raise some important issues about the ability of a country to manage its debt burden.

CHECKPOINT

FINANCING THE FEDERAL GOVERNMENT

- A deficit is the amount that government spending exceeds tax revenue in a particular year.
- The public (national) debt is the total accumulation of past deficits less surpluses.
- Approaches to financing the federal government include annually balancing the budget, balancing the budget over the business cycle, and ignoring the budget deficit and focusing on promoting full employment and stable prices.
- The federal government's debt must be financed by selling bonds to the Federal Reserve ("printing money" or "monetizing the debt"), by selling bonds to the public, or by selling government assets. This is known as the government budget constraint.

QUESTION: One reason why state governments have been more willing to pass balanced budget amendments than the federal government is the difference between mandatory and discretionary spending. What are some expenses of the federal government that are less predictable or harder to cut that make balanced budget amendments more difficult to pursue?

Answers to the Checkpoint questions can be found at the end of this chapter.

WHY IS THE PUBLIC DEBT SO IMPORTANT?

We have seen that politicians have a bias toward using expansionary fiscal policy and not contractionary fiscal policy, and also have a bias toward using debt rather than taxes to finance the ensuing deficits. This explains the persistence of federal debt. We have seen that balancing the federal budget by passing an amendment is not an ideal solution. This leads to the following questions: How big a problem is persistent deficits? Should we be worrying about this now?

Figure 9 shows the debt of mostly developed nations in 2015. Japan, Greece, and Italy had a large debt relative to their GDP, but Greece and Italy have reduced their deficit in

FIGURE 9	PUBLIC DEBT AND DEFICITS AS A PERCENT OF GDP

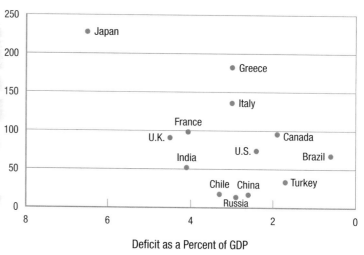

This figure shows the relationship between public debt and deficits for several nations. Countries with high deficits tend to have high debt-to-GDP ratios. An aging population in Japan contributes to its high national debt. However, the willingness of Japan's private sector to hold government bonds allows Japan's government to finance its debt at low interest rates. Still, deficit and debt remain a major problem, so much so that Japan has stopped its tradition of bestowing a commemorative silver sake dish when a citizen celebrates his or her 100th birthday.

recent years, allowing the increase in debt to slow. India has a relatively low debt ratio but has seen higher deficits recently. China, Russia, and Chile have very low debt ratios, but deficits in all three countries have risen in recent years as economic growth slowed. When an economy moves toward the upper left portion of the figure, problems begin to rise. In Japan, an aging population (fact: Japan has more people over the age of 100 than any other country in the world!) along with a shrinking working-age population has severely strained government budgets.

Politicians frequently warn that the federal government is going bankrupt, or that we are burdening future generations with our own enormous public debt. After all, U.S. public debt of nearly $14 trillion means that every baby born in the United States begins life saddled with over $42,000 in public debt. Before you start panicking, let's examine the burden of the public debt.

Is the Size of the Public Debt a Problem?

Public debt in the United States represents a little over 70% of GDP. Is this amount of debt a cause for immediate concern? It really depends on the costs of financing the debt. What is the burden of the interest rate payments on the debt?

Think about it another way. Suppose that you earn $50,000 a year and have $35,000 in student loan debt, equal to 70% of your annual income. Is this a problem? It would be if the interest rate on the student loans were 20% a year, because interest payments of $7,000 per year would take up a significant chunk (14%) of your gross salary. But if the interest rate is 3%, the debt burden from the interest ($1,050 per year) would not be as substantial, representing only about 2% of your gross salary.

For the U.S. national debt, current interest rates are relatively low due in large part to aggressive action by the Federal Reserve. Interest costs on the national debt were $223 billion in 2015, representing about 6% of the federal budget. That is not an overwhelming amount.

Wouldn't it be wise to pay the debt down or pay it off? Not necessarily. Many people today "own" some small part of the public debt in their pension plans, but many others do not. If taxes were raised across the board to pay down the debt, those who did not own any public debt would be in a worse position than those who did.

Servicing the debt requires taxing the general public to pay interest to bondholders. Most people who own part of the national debt (or who indirectly own parts of entities that hold the debt) tend to be richer than those who do not. This means that money is taken from those across the income or wealth distribution and given to those near the top. Still, the fact that taxes are mildly progressive mitigates some, and perhaps even all, of this reverse redistribution problem.

Thus, the public debt is not out of control, at least based on the economy's ability to pay the interest costs. However, rising interest rates will raise the burden of this debt. Even so, at its current size, the public debt is manageable as long as it does not experience another spike in the near term.

Another consideration is whether the debt is mostly held externally (i.e., financed by foreign governments, banks, and investors), as is the case of many developing countries. These countries have discovered that relying on foreign sources of financing has its limits.

Does It Matter If Foreigners Hold a Significant Portion of the Public Debt?

The great advantage of citizens being creditors as well as debtors with relation to the public debt is obvious. Men readily perceive that they can not be much oppressed by a debt which they owe to themselves.

—ABRAHAM LINCOLN (1864)

Consider first, as Abraham Lincoln noted in 1864, that much of the national debt held by the public is owned by American banks, corporations, mutual funds, pension plans,

TABLE 1	DISTRIBUTION OF NATIONAL DEBT, AS OF MARCH 2016 (TRILLIONS)	
	Amount	**Percent**
Held by the Federal Reserve and government agencies	$5.316	27.7%
Held by the public	13.872	72.3
Held by foreigners	6.435	33.5
Held domestically	7.437	38.8
Total national debt	19.188	100.00

Data from the U.S. Department of the Treasury.

internally held debt Public debt owned by domestic banks, corporations, mutual funds, pension plans, and individuals.

externally held debt Public debt held by foreigners, including foreign industries, banks, and governments.

and individuals. As a people, we essentially own this debt—this is **internally held debt.** Hence, the taxes collected from a wide swath of the American public to pay the interest on the debt are paid back out to yet another group of Americans. As Table 1 shows, however, foreigners own nearly half of the public debt held by the public. This is **externally held debt.**

Of the interest paid on the $19.2 trillion national debt, about 28% goes to federal agencies holding this debt—the Social Security Administration, the Federal Reserve, and other federal agencies, 39% goes to the American private sector, and 34% goes to foreigners.

The interest paid on externally held debt represents a real claim on our goods and services, and thus can be a real burden on our economy. Debt held by the public has grown, and the portion of the debt held by foreigners has expanded. Until the mid-1990s, foreigners held roughly 20% of publicly held debt.

Traditionally much of the U.S. debt is held internally, but this is changing. In just a decade, foreign holdings have doubled to nearly 50% of debt held by the public, and about 40% of this is held by China and Japan. Why such a rapid expansion of foreign holdings since the 1990s? One reason is that these countries are buying our debt to keep their currencies from rising relative to the dollar. When their currencies rise, their exports to America are more costly; as a result, sales fall, hurting their economies. It is better to accumulate U.S. debt than see their export sectors suffer.

However, the increased reliance on external financing of our debt raises some concerns. For example, the significant amount of our debt held by China makes our economy more vulnerable to policy changes by the Chinese government and/or businesses that hold our debt. On the positive side, however, creditors such as China are likely to maintain strong economic and political ties with the United States; besides, China eventually will want its money back.

Does Government Debt Crowd Out Consumption and Investment?

As we saw in the budget constraint section earlier, when the government runs a deficit, it must sell bonds to either the public or the Federal Reserve. If it sells bonds to the Federal Reserve (prints money) when the economy is near full employment, the money supply will grow and inflation will result.

crowding-out effect When deficit spending requires the government to borrow, interest rates are driven up, reducing consumer spending and business investment.

Alternatively, when the federal government spends more than tax revenues permit, it can sell bonds to the public. But doing so drives up interest rates as the demand for loanable funds (this time by the government rather than the public sector) increases. As interest rates rise, consumer spending on durable goods such as cars and appliances, often bought on credit, falls. It also reduces private business investment. Therefore, while deficit spending is usually expansionary, the consequence is that future generations will be bequeathed a smaller and potentially less productive economy, resulting in a lower standard of living. This is the **crowding-out effect** of deficit spending. However, in a severe recession when consumers and businesses are not eager to buy or invest, the crowding-out effect is less pronounced, making fiscal policy more powerful.

The crowding-out effect also can be mitigated if the funds from deficit spending are used for public investment. Improvements in the nation's transportation infrastructure, education establishment, and research facilities, for instance, are all aimed at improving the economy's future productive capacity. If the investments expand the nation's productive capacity enough, growth will be such that the debt-to-GDP ratio may fall. But if all or most of the deficit is spent on current consumption, growth in GDP may be weak and the debt-to-GDP ratio will most likely rise.

How Will the National Debt Affect Our Future? Are We Doomed?

If the federal debt is not an enormous burden now, what about in the future? Here there is a large cause for concern. Economists have argued that economic growth depends on the **fiscal sustainability** of the federal budget. For a fiscal policy to be fiscally sustainable, the present value (current dollar value) of all projected future revenues must be equal to the present value of projected future spending. If the budget is not fiscally sustainable, an intergenerational tax burden may be created, with future generations paying for the spending of the current generation.

fiscal sustainability A measure of the present value of all projected future revenues compared to the present value of projected future spending.

Clearly, some tax burden shifting is sensible. When current fiscal policy truly invests in the economy, future generations benefit, and therefore, some of the present costs may justifiably be shifted to them. Investments in infrastructure, education, research, national defense, and homeland security are good examples.

However, the federal government has immense obligations that extend over long periods that are unrelated to economic investment. Its two largest programs, Social Security and Medicare, account for over 35% of all federal spending. People who are just beginning to enter retirement can expect to live for two or three more decades. Add to this the fact that medical costs are growing at rates significantly higher than economic growth as new and more sophisticated treatments are developed and demanded.

The intergenerational impact results from the fact that Social Security and Medicare are pay-as-you-go programs. The current working generation, in other words, funds the older generation's benefits; there are no pooled funds waiting to be tapped as needed. Thus, these two programs represent huge unfunded liabilities to younger (and yet to be born) generations.

With the current national debt held by the public at nearly $14 trillion, and total future liabilities (the money that has been promised, such as for Social Security and Medicare, but have not been paid) estimated to be several times the current public debt, the implications for future budgeting are significant. In other words, without some significant change in economic or demographic growth, taxes will have to be increased dramatically at some point, or else the benefits for Social Security and Medicare will have to be drastically cut.

If these estimates of fiscal imbalance are on track, fiscal policy is headed for a train wreck as the baby boomers keep retiring. The public choice analysis discussed earlier suggests that politicians will try to keep this issue off the agenda for as long as possible, one side fighting tax increases while the other resists benefit reductions. Clearly, given the magnitudes discussed here, this problem will be difficult to solve.

We started this chapter by talking about the government's ability to address fluctuations in the business cycle by using fiscal policy to affect aggregate demand and aggregate supply. But given the government's penchant for expansionary policy, persistent budget deficits tend to result. Unlike for individuals, the federal government has the ability to incur debt for some time because of its ability to print money and borrow from the public. And while the federal government is currently able to safely manage its debt, this picture may change down the road as Social Security and Medicare liabilities continue to grow. The implication is that we are better off dealing with this future problem now rather than later.

CHECKPOINT

WHY IS THE PUBLIC DEBT SO IMPORTANT?

- Interest payments on the debt exceed 6% of the federal budget. These funds could have been spent on other programs.

- About half of the public debt held by the public is held by domestic individuals and institutions, and half is held by foreigners. The domestic half is internally held and represents transfers among individuals, but that part held by foreigners is a real claim on our resources.

- When the government pays for the deficit by selling bonds, interest rates rise, crowding out some consumption and private investment and reducing economic growth. To the extent that these funds are used for public investment and not current consumption, this effect is mitigated.

- The rising costs of Social Security and Medicare represent the biggest threat to the long-run federal budget. Either the costs of such programs eventually need to be reduced, or additional taxes will be required to cover these rising expenses.

QUESTIONS: Suppose China and Japan, the two largest external creditors of U.S. public debt, choose to diversify their asset holdings by selling some of their U.S. Treasury bonds. How will this affect the U.S. government's ability to finance its debt? What might happen to consumption and investment in the United States?

Answers to the Checkpoint questions can be found at the end of this chapter.

chapter summary

Section 1 Fiscal Policy and Aggregate Demand

21.1 **Fiscal policy** describes the use of government taxation and spending to influence the economy. Specifically, it involves three main tools: taxation, government spending on goods and services, and transfer payments.

21.2 **Contractionary fiscal policy** includes reducing government spending or transfer payments, or raising taxes. The effect is a shift of the AD curve to the left, decreasing prices and aggregate output.

Expansionary fiscal policy includes increases in government spending or transfer payments, or reducing taxes. The effect is a shift of the AD curve to the right, increasing prices and aggregate output.

21.3 The **multiplier effect** allows each dollar of government spending to expand aggregate output by a multiple of the amount spent. Changes in government spending have a larger multiplier than changes in taxes.

Kirby Hamilton/Getty Images

Unemployment benefits generally produce a high multiplier effect because recipients are likely to spend all of the money quickly.

Using expansionary fiscal policy to shift AD during a recession can reduce the time required to achieve full employment. The tradeoff of such policies is potential inflation, although the effect is small when used in a deep recession.

Section 2 Fiscal Policy and Aggregate Supply

The goal of **supply-side fiscal policy** is to shift the LRAS curve to the right. Such policies do not require a tradeoff between output and prices; however, these policies require more time to work.

Danny Lehman/Corbis

Maintaining highways such as the treacherous Trans-Alaskan Highway can increase aggregate supply if better roads increase productivity.

21.4 Common Supply-Side Policies

- **Increase Infrastructure Spending:** Improving roads and communications networks, stabilizing legal and financial systems, and improving human capital and technologies (R&D).

- **Decrease Tax Rates:** Increases aggregate supply by providing firms incentives to expand or for individuals to work more.

- **Eliminate Burdensome Regulations:** Leads to greater efficiency if the costs of regulation outweigh the benefits.

Section 3 Implementing Fiscal Policy

21.5 The economy contains **automatic stabilizers:**

When the economy is strong:

Tax receipts rise   Transfer payments fall
(both have contractionary effects to fight inflation)

When the economy is weak:

Tax receipts fall   Transfer payments rise
(both have expansionary effects to offset the recession)

21.6 Using fiscal policy involves **timing lags:**

- **Information lag:** Time required to acquire macroeconomic data
- **Recognition lag:** Time required to recognize trends in the data
- **Decision lag:** Legislative process to enact policies
- **Implementation lag:** Time required after laws are passed to set up programs

Passing new fiscal policy can take a lot of time, especially in a divided Congress.

Section 4 Financing the Federal Government

21.7 The **federal deficit** is the annual amount by which government spending exceeds tax revenues.

A **surplus** occurs when tax revenues exceed government spending. The **national debt** is the accumulation of all past deficits less surpluses. The **public debt** is the portion of the national debt that is held by the public.

How Does the Government Finance Its Deficit ($G - T$)?

- The Federal Reserve prints money to buy bonds: ΔM
- Treasury bonds held domestically and externally: ΔB
- Sales of government assets: ΔA

U.S. Savings Bonds are one form of financing government debt.

Section 5 Why Is the Public Debt So Important?

21.8 In 2015 the U.S. government paid $223 billion in interest payments on the public debt. Although this is a manageable expense, higher interest rates and rising future liabilities can make debt a more significant problem in the future.

Social Security and Medicare liabilities rise each year as Americans live longer and health care costs rise. These two components pose a big concern for future debt.

About half of U.S. public debt is held externally, by foreign governments and investors. Of this amount, about 40%, or about $2.4 trillion, is held by China and Japan.

Borrowing money to finance the debt raises interest rates, making it more expensive for individuals and businesses to borrow money. This is the **crowding-out effect.**

KEY CONCEPTS

discretionary spending, p. 558
mandatory spending, p. 558
discretionary fiscal policy, p. 558
expansionary fiscal policy, p. 561
contractionary fiscal policy, p. 562
supply-side fiscal policies, p. 563
Laffer curve, p. 565
automatic stabilizers, p. 567
information lag, p. 568

recognition lag, p. 568
decision lag, p. 568
implementation lag, p. 568
public choice theory, p. 569
deficit, p. 570
surplus, p. 570
national debt, p. 570
public debt, p. 570
annually balanced budget, p. 571

cyclically balanced budget, p. 571
functional finance, p. 573
government budget constraint, p. 573
internally held debt, p. 576
externally held debt, p. 576
crowding-out effect, p. 576
fiscal sustainability, p. 577

QUESTIONS AND PROBLEMS

Check Your Understanding

1. Explain why government spending theoretically gives a bigger boost to the economy than tax cuts.

2. Explain why increasing government purchases of goods and services is expansionary fiscal policy. Would increasing taxes or reducing transfer payments be contractionary or expansionary? Why?

3. Changes in tax rates affect both aggregate demand and aggregate supply. Explain why this is true.

4. What is one benefit to businesses when the government budget is in surplus?

5. How might interest paid on the national debt lead to greater income inequality?

6. Is the absolute size of the national debt or the national debt as a percent of GDP the best measure of its importance to our economy? Explain.

Apply the Concepts

7. One argument often heard against using fiscal policy to tame the business cycle is that the lags associated with getting a fiscal policy implemented are so long that when the program is finally passed and implemented, the business cycle has moved on to the next phase and the new program may not be necessary and may even be potentially destabilizing at that point. Does this argument seem reasonable? What counterarguments can you make in support of using fiscal policy?

8. As mandatory federal spending becomes increasingly a larger share of the budget, should we worry that the economic stabilization aspects of fiscal policy are becoming so limited as to be ineffective?

9. Our current personal income tax system is progressive: Income tax rates rise with rising incomes and are lower for low-income individuals. Some policymakers have favored a "flat tax" as a replacement for our modestly progressive income tax system. Most exemptions and deductions would be eliminated, and a single low tax rate would be applied to personal income. Would such a change in the tax laws alter the automatic stabilization characteristics of the personal income tax?

10. In 1962 in a speech before the Economic Club of New York, President Kennedy argued that "it is a paradoxical truth that taxes are too high today and tax revenues are too low—and the soundest way to raise revenues in the long run is to cut rates now." Is President Kennedy's argument consistent with supply-side economics? Why or why not?

11. A balanced budget amendment to the Constitution requiring Congress to balance the budget every year is introduced in Congress every so often. What sort of problems would the passage of such an amendment introduce for policymakers and the economy? What would be the benefit of the passage of such an amendment?

12. If the economy (gross domestic product) is growing faster than the growth of the national debt held by the public (both domestic and foreign), how does that affect the ability of the government to manage the national debt? What arguments can you make to rebut the common assertion that the national debt is bankrupting the country?

In the News

13. In recent years, a growing number of states have legalized marijuana for recreational purposes. Sales of marijuana are subject to various state sales and excise taxes that add between 25% and 44% to the price. Previously, sales of marijuana in these states took place in the informal or underground economy, where taxes are avoided and crime runs high. What are some fiscal policy justifications for legalizing marijuana?

14. In the aftermath of the 2007–2009 recession, the U.S. national debt rose to record levels as the federal government used expansionary fiscal policy to speed up the economic recovery. This led some politicians to propose a significant reduction in the size of government in order to balance the budget. Would such a policy be expansionary or contractionary in nature? What factors would determine whether or not such a policy would harm economic growth?

Solving Problems

15. Suppose a small economy has two income tax rates: 15% for all income up to $50,000 and 30% for any income earned above $50,000. Suppose that prior to the recession, the economy had five workers earning the following salaries:

Amy	$20,000
Betty	$40,000
Charlie	$60,000
Dimitry	$80,000
Evelyn	$100,000

   a. Calculate the total tax revenues paid by the five workers. What percent of total income does this represent?

   b. Now assume that a recession causes each of the five salaries to fall by 25%. Given the lower salaries, what would be the total tax revenues paid by the five workers? What percent of total income does this represent?

   c. Explain how this progressive tax structure acts as an automatic stabilizer.

WORK IT OUT   **LaunchPad** | interactive activity

16. Suppose an economy has a GDP of $40 billion and a national debt of $20 billion, and the average interest rate on this debt is currently 3%.

   a. Calculate the annual interest payments on the debt. What percentage of this economy's GDP is spent on interest payments on its debt?

   b. Suppose that next year one of two events occurs: (1) GDP and interest rates stay the same, but the economy adds $4 billion to its national debt; (2) GDP and the national debt stay the same, but interest rates increase to 4%. Which of the two events would result in a larger portion of the economy's GDP going toward interest payments on the national debt?

USING THE NUMBERS

17. According to By the Numbers, approximately what percent of total external debt is held by China? What does this suggest about the importance of U.S. relations with China?

18. According to By the Numbers, in which year between 1990 and 2016 did the United States have the biggest budget surplus and what was that value? In which year did it have the biggest budget deficit and what was that value?

ANSWERS TO QUESTIONS IN CHECKPOINTS

Checkpoint: Fiscal Policy and Aggregate Demand 563

Although the money would have hit the economy sooner, a significant portion of the proceeds would have been saved or used to pay existing bills, potentially limiting the stimulative impact of *added* spending. The other benefit of the infrastructure package is that by being spread out over several years, it won't just be a big jolt to the economy that ends as fast as it began. Thus, the impact on employment and business planning was smoother.

Checkpoint: Fiscal Policy and Aggregate Supply 567

Supply-side economics focuses on providing incentives for individuals to work and for businesses to invest, and therefore advocate lower tax rates. The reduction in the individual, corporate, and capital gains taxes would each be consistent with supply-side economics. However, if a portion of these tax savings is offset through higher consumption taxes, this would not be consistent with supply-side economics because such a tax would discourage consumption and negatively affect business and investment outlook.

Checkpoint: Implementing Fiscal Policy 569

The president would favor policies that could be implemented quickly, such as "shovel ready" infrastructure projects that have already been approved, the expansion of unemployment benefits that can take effect immediately, or tax cuts that can be applied in the current tax year. The president would not favor policies that require a new law to be passed, as such policies may take years before being implemented.

Checkpoint: Financing the Federal Government 574

The federal government must satisfy its mandatory spending requirements, including Social Security, unless it passes a law to reform such spending. Also, the federal government must pay for national defense, including wars, which are unpredictable. Also unpredictable are expenses related to natural disasters, which require action by various federal agencies. Because of the combination of various mandatory spending programs and unpredictable discretionary spending requirements, the federal government would find it difficult in practice to enforce a balanced budget amendment.

Checkpoint: Why Is the Public Debt So Important? 578

If China and Japan reduce their holdings of U.S. debt, interest rates would need to rise in order to attract other investors to purchase these bonds. Rising interest rates would adversely affect consumption and investment in the United States, potentially slowing economic growth.

22

Saving, Investment, and the Financial System

Understanding the importance of financial institutions and their role in connecting savers with borrowers

John Lund/Getty Images

Learning Objectives

22.1 Describe the functions of money.

22.2 Define the money supply according to M1 and M2.

22.3 Use the loanable funds model to show how savers and borrowers are brought together.

22.4 Describe how economic factors can lead to a change in the market for loanable funds.

22.5 Explain how financial intermediaries make it easier and less risky for people to save and borrow.

22.6 Describe the relationship between the price of bonds and interest rates.

22.7 Explain how the compounding effect makes debt and savings much larger over time.

22.8 Describe the tradeoff between risk and return, and how that influences the return on investment for bonds and stocks.

22.9 Understand how retirement savings programs function and the benefits they provide.

On August 13, 2004, the city of Athens, Greece, celebrated as the Summer Olympic Games returned to its historic homeland, the place where Olympic athletes nearly 3,000 years ago competed on the same land as athletes in the current games were about to compete.

Indeed, it was a proud moment for Greeks, and for their government, which had borrowed billions of dollars to build new stadiums, a modern transportation network, and a new airport, and to give the city a significant facelift to showcase its growing economic prosperity to a worldwide audience. Where did the government get this money? It borrowed money from banks and from the public by issuing bonds, and there was plenty of money to be borrowed. The Olympics were the ultimate showpiece of a nation on the rise.

No one could have predicted on that proud day that in less than a decade, that same city would be engulfed in financial turmoil, with large government debt, protests and riots, and a country in complete despair. What happened in Greece that led to such a dramatic reversal in fortune?

In short, it was a breakdown of financial institutions caused by a global recession along with uncontrolled government debt that caused long-term interest rates to skyrocket from 4% in 2009 to 27% in 2012. With interest rates so high, the ability to borrow, whether by the government, by businesses, or by consumers, became prohibitive, leading to a drastic decline in consumption and investment and subsequently a rise in unemployment. Clearly, Greece headed into a vicious cycle that threatened not only the country but the stability of the euro, the currency it shares with much of Europe.

Although Greece was not the only country to have undergone a financial crisis, it was one of the most difficult cases because of the challenges that affected the banks, bond market, and stock market—which form what we refer to as a country's financial system. The financial system plays an important role in the health of the macroeconomy, and when the system breaks down, as it did in Greece, the economy often goes down with it.

Up to now, we have looked at how the federal government tries to manage the macroeconomy through fiscal policy, by using government taxation and spending. We

Tim de Waele/Corbis

Alexandros Michailidis/Demotix/Corbis

586

The Financial System and Its Sheer Size and Scope

The U.S. financial system consists of commercial banks, money markets, and government institutions that issue and manage money. It is connected with the global financial system, consisting of banks and financial institutions around the world that influence one another.

Go to **LaunchPad** *to use the latest data to recreate this graph.*

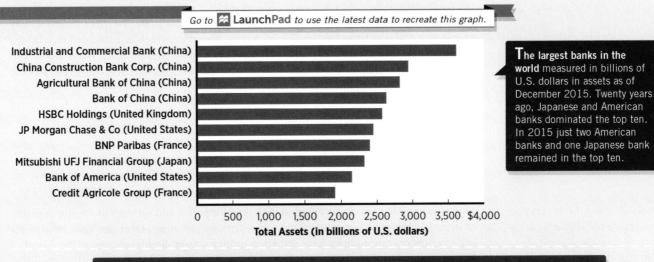

Bar chart — Total Assets (in billions of U.S. dollars):

- Industrial and Commercial Bank (China)
- China Construction Bank Corp. (China)
- Agricultural Bank of China (China)
- Bank of China (China)
- HSBC Holdings (United Kingdom)
- JP Morgan Chase & Co (United States)
- BNP Paribas (France)
- Mitsubishi UFJ Financial Group (Japan)
- Bank of America (United States)
- Credit Agricole Group (France)

X-axis: 0, 500, 1,000, 1,500, 2,000, 2,500, 3,000, 3,500, $4,000
Total Assets (in billions of U.S. dollars)

The largest banks in the world measured in billions of U.S. dollars in assets as of December 2015. Twenty years ago, Japanese and American banks dominated the top ten. In 2015 just two American banks and one Japanese bank remained in the top ten.

The eight most circulated currencies in the world. Although many currencies are widely circulated (especially in countries with large populations such as China, India, and Russia), the U.S. dollar and the euro remain by far the two largest reserve "hard" currencies held around the world (mostly in electronic form). However, in 2016, the Chinese yuan became the newest currency to be designated by the IMF as a reserve currency.

Glyn Thomas/Alamy ANDREW WALTERS/Alamy Hans-Joachim Schneider/Alamy Glyn Thomas/Alamy

Glyn Thomas/Alamy Glyn Thomas/Alamy INTERFOTO/Alamy imageBROKER/Alamy

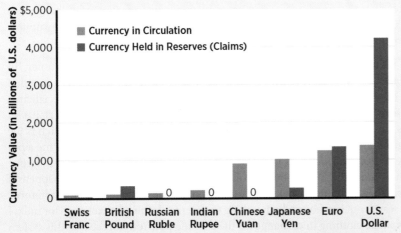

Bar chart — Currency Value (in billions of U.S. dollars):

Legend:
- Currency in Circulation
- Currency Held in Reserves (Claims)

Y-axis: 0, 1,000, 2,000, 3,000, 4,000, $5,000

Categories: Swiss Franc, British Pound, Russian Ruble, Indian Rupee, Chinese Yuan, Japanese Yen, Euro, U.S. Dollar

(0 labels shown for Russian Ruble, Indian Rupee, Chinese Yuan)

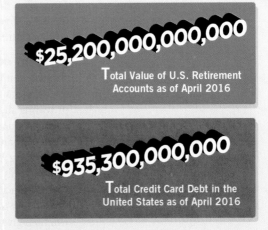

$25,200,000,000,000
Total Value of U.S. Retirement Accounts as of April 2016

$935,300,000,000
Total Credit Card Debt in the United States as of April 2016

now want to look at the government's other policy approach—monetary policy. To analyze how government uses monetary policy to influence the macroeconomy, we must first lay the foundation by examining the financial system and the role of money, which is the subject of this chapter. Building on this foundation, in the following chapters we will see how financial institutions create money and how the government enacts policies that encourage the financial system to do things that mitigate fluctuations in the macroeconomy.

We begin by looking at money: what it is and what it does. We then examine why people save and why firms borrow. We next show how the market for loanable funds brings together these two groups, and how the financial system makes this process easier and better for all. The chapter concludes with an overview of financial tools that illustrates the importance of financial literacy in our everyday lives.

WHAT IS MONEY?

Anything can serve as money, from the cowrie shells of the Maldives to the huge stone disks used on the Pacific islands of Yap. And now, it seems, in this electronic age nothing can serve as money too.
NIALL FERGUSON, THE ASCENT OF MONEY

money Anything that is accepted in exchange for goods and services or for the payment of debt.

Money is anything that is accepted in exchange for goods and services or for the payment of debt. For example, we are familiar with currency and coins. Over the ages, however, a wide variety of commodities have served as money—giant circular stones on the island of Yap, wampum (trinkets) among early Native Americans, and cigarettes in prisoner-of-war camps during World War II.

Commodity money consists of objects and materials (such as gold, silver, and trinkets) that have value in and of itself. However, commodities must meet certain criteria to be effectively used as money. First, its value must be easy to determine. Therefore, it must be easily standardized. Second, it must be divisible so that people can make change. Third, money must be durable and portable. It must be easy to carry (so much for the giant circular stones, which today are used only for ceremonial purposes in Yap.) Fourth, a commodity must be accepted by many people as money if it is to act as money. As Niall Ferguson makes clear in the quote above, today we have "virtual" money, in the sense that digital money is moved from our employer to the bank and then to the retailer for our goods and services in nothing but a series of electronic transactions. This is really the ultimate in **fiat money**: money without any intrinsic value but accepted as money because the government has made it legal tender.

fiat money Money without intrinsic value but nonetheless accepted as money because the government has decreed it to be money.

Money is so important that nearly every society has invented some form of money for its use. We begin our examination of money by looking at its functions.

The Functions of Money

Money has three primary functions in our economic system: as a medium of exchange, as a measure of value (unit of account), and as a store of value. These uses make money unique among commodities.

barter The direct exchange of goods and services for other goods and services.

Medium of Exchange Let us start with a primitive economy. There is no money. To survive, you have to produce everything yourself: food, clothing, housing. It is a fact that few of us can do all of these tasks equally well. Each one of us is better off specializing, providing those goods and services we are more efficient at supplying. Say I specialize in dairy products and you specialize in blacksmithing. We can engage in **barter,** which is the direct exchange of goods and services. I can give you gallons of milk if you make me a pot for cooking. A *double coincidence of wants* occurs if, in a barter economy, I find someone who not only has something I want, but who also wants something I have. What happens if you, the blacksmith, are willing to make the cooking pot for me but want clothing in return? Then I have to search out someone who is willing to give me clothing in exchange for milk; I will then give you the clothing in exchange for the cooking pot. You can see that this system quickly becomes complicated. This is why barter is restricted to primitive economies.

Consider what happens when money is introduced. Everyone can spend their time producing goods and services, rather than running around trying to match up exchanges. Everyone can sell their products for money, and then can use this money to buy cooking pots, clothing, or whatever else they want. Thus, money's first and most important function is as a **medium of exchange.** Without money, economies remain primitive.

Unit of Account Imagine the difficulties consumers would have in a barter economy in which every item is valued in terms of the other products offered—12 eggs are worth 1 shirt, 1 shirt equals 3 gallons of gas, and so forth. A 10-product economy of this sort, assigning every product a value for every other product, would require 45 different prices. A 100-good economy would require 4,950 prices.[1] This is another reason why only the most primitive economies use barter.

Once again, money is able to solve a problem inherent to the barter economy. It reduces the number of prices consumers need to know to the number of products on the market; a 100-good economy will have 100 prices. Thus, money is a **unit of account,** or a measure of value. Dollar prices give us a yardstick for measuring and comparing the values of a wide variety of goods and services.

Admittedly, ascribing a dollar value to some things, such as human life, love, and clean air, can be difficult. Still, courts, businesses, and government agencies manage to do so every day. For example, if someone dies and the court determines this death was due to negligence, the court tries to determine the value of the life to the person's survivors—not a pleasant task, but one that has to be undertaken. Without a monetary standard, such valuations would be not just difficult, but impossible.

Store of Value Using cherry tomatoes as a medium of exchange and unit of account might be handy, except that they have the bad habit of rotting. Money lasts, enabling people to save the money they earn today and use it to buy the goods and services they want tomorrow. Thus, money is a **store of value.** It is true that money is not unique in preserving its value. Many other commodities, including stocks, bonds, real estate, art, and jewelry, are used to store wealth for future purchases. Indeed, some of these assets may rise in value, and therefore might be preferred to money as a store of value. Why, then, use money as a store of wealth at all?

The answer is that every other type of asset must be converted into money if it is to be spent or used to pay debts. Converting other assets into cash involves transaction costs, and for some assets, these costs are significant. An asset's **liquidity** is determined by how fast, easily, and reliably it can be converted into cash.

Money is the most liquid asset because, as the medium of exchange, it requires no conversion. Stocks and bonds are also liquid, but they do require some time and often a commission fee to convert into cash. Prices in stock and bond markets fluctuate, causing the real value of these assets to be uncertain. Real estate requires considerable time to liquidate, with transaction costs that often approach 10% of a property's value.

Money differs from many other commodities in that its value does not deteriorate in the absence of inflation. When price levels do rise, however, the value of money falls: If prices double, the value of money is cut in half. In times of inflation, most people are unwilling to hold much of their wealth in money. If hyperinflation hits, money will quickly become worthless as the economy reverts to barter.

Money, then, is crucial for a well-functioning modern economy. All of its three primary functions are important: medium of exchange, unit of account, and store of value.

Defining the Money Supply

How much money is there in the U.S. economy? One of the tasks assigned to the Federal Reserve System (the Fed), the central bank of the United States, is that of measuring our money supply. The Fed has developed several different measures of monetary aggregates,

medium of exchange A function of money in which goods and services are sold for money, then the money is used to purchase other goods and services.

unit of account Money provides a yardstick for measuring and comparing the values of a wide variety of goods and services. It eliminates the problem of double coincidence of wants associated with barter.

store of value The function that enables people to save the money they earn today and use it to buy the goods and services they want tomorrow.

liquidity How quickly, easily, and reliably an asset can be converted into cash.

US Mint image

The United States has introduced $1 coins many times throughout its history, and in recent decades has included the Susan B. Anthony dollar, Sacagawea dollar, and the presidential dollar. Yet, the use of dollar coins as a medium of exchange never caught on, with the majority of dollar coins ending up in coin collections rather than in cash registers.

---

[1] The formula for determining the number of prices needed when N goods are in an economy is $[N(N − 1)]/2$. Thus, for 10 goods, the result is $[10(10 − 1)]/2 = 90/2 = 45$.

Using Plastic Money (Literally) in Australia

> How did a commemorative 1988 Australian $10 banknote made of plastic turn into a trend adopted by over 40 countries?

Kitch Bain/agefotostock

Take out a few U.S. banknotes of different denominations and notice their characteristics—they are all the same size and are made from the same cotton-and-linen-material used for over a century. Compared to banknotes in many other countries, old U.S. banknotes appear bland and worn out, and are sometimes counterfeited using advanced scanners to make realistic copies.

To minimize counterfeiting, new U.S. banknotes contain more security features such as a watermark and color-shifting ink. And since 2008, new banknotes (other than the $1 bill) contain colors different from the old green and black.

Still, other countries have transformed their banknotes in more dramatic ways. One such transformation was introduced in Australia in 1988—money made literally of plastic. How did the introduction of plastic (polymer-based) banknotes transform the way many countries produce their banknotes?

When Australia celebrated the 200th anniversary in 1988 of the first arrival of Europeans, the Australian Treasury introduced a commemorative $10 banknote made of plastic. The plastic banknote was colorful, was difficult to rip or tear, stayed crisp even after many uses, and most importantly, was nearly impossible to counterfeit. Because of the popularity of the new design and the subsequent reduction in counterfeiting, Australia changed all of its banknote denominations to polymer-based materials,

becoming the first country to do so but certainly not the last.

Today, over forty countries (including Mexico) use polymer banknotes for at least their most used denomination, while at least ten countries (including Canada) have adopted polymer banknotes for all denominations. Although polymer banknotes cost about twice as much to make as cotton-paper banknotes, they last over twice as long and dramatically reduce counterfeiting. Moreover, the rising cost of cotton in recent years has reduced the difference in cost of producing polymer banknotes.

Are Americans too wed to the paper greenback to accept polymer banknotes? Americans have mostly rejected other ideas, including attempts to eliminate the penny and to replace the $1 bill with a $1 coin. Such aversion to currency changes is ironic, considering that fewer than 25% of U.S. consumer transactions are conducted in cash and over half of Americans do not regularly carry cash at all. In fact, cash may disappear altogether in the future, which might ultimately make this debate obsolete.

GO TO **LaunchPad** TO PRACTICE THE ECONOMIC CONCEPTS IN THIS STORY

---

which it continually updates to reflect the innovative new financial instruments our financial system is constantly developing. The monetary aggregates the Fed uses most frequently are M1, the narrowest measure of money, and M2, a broader measure. An even broader measure called M3 was published until 2006 when the Fed decided the additional benefit of this measure was not worth the costs of collecting the data.

More specifically, the Fed defines M1 and M2 as follows:

M1 The narrowest definition of money that measures highly liquid instruments including currency (banknotes and coins), demand deposits (checks), and other accounts that have check-writing or debit capabilities.

M2 A broader definition of money that includes "near monies" that are not as liquid as cash, including deposits in savings accounts, money market accounts, and money market mutual fund accounts.

M1 equals:[2]
- Currency (banknotes and coins)
+ Demand deposits
+ Other checkable deposits

M2 equals:
- M1
+ Savings deposits
+ Money market deposit accounts
+ Small-denomination (less than $100,000) time deposits
+ Shares in retail money market mutual funds

[2] Traveler's checks are also officially counted as part of M1. However, the improved efficiency of international debit card and credit card transactions has made traveler's checks mostly obsolete. In 2016 traveler's checks represented less than one-tenth of 1% of M1.

Narrowly Defined Money: M1 Because money is used mainly as a medium of exchange, when defined most narrowly, it includes currency (banknotes and coins), demand deposits (checking accounts), and other accounts that have check-writing capabilities. Currency represents slightly less than half of M1, with banknotes constituting more than 90% of currency; coins form only a small part of M1. Checking accounts represent the other half of the money supply, narrowly defined. In 2016, M1 was about $3.2 trillion. It is the most liquid part of the money supply.

Checking accounts can be opened at commercial banks and at a variety of other financial institutions, including credit unions, mutual savings banks, and savings and loan associations. Also, many stock brokerage firms offer checking services on brokerage accounts.

A Broader Definition: M2 A broader definition of money, M2, includes the "near monies": money that cannot be drawn on instantaneously but that is nonetheless accessible. This includes deposits in savings accounts, money market deposit accounts, and money market mutual fund accounts. Many of these accounts have check-writing features similar to demand deposits.

Certificates of deposit (CDs) and other small-denomination time deposits can usually be cashed in at any time, although they often carry penalties for early liquidation. Thus, M2 includes the highly liquid assets in M1 and a variety of accounts that are less liquid, but still easy and inexpensive to access. This broader definition of money increased the money supply in 2016 to about $12.6 trillion.

When economists speak of "the money supply," they are usually referring to M1, the narrowest definition. Even so, the other measures are sometimes used. The index of leading economic indicators, for instance, uses M2, adjusted for inflation, to gauge the state of the economy. Economists sometimes disagree on which is the better measure of the money supply; although M1 and M2 tend to have similar trends, they have deviated significantly in certain periods. For the remainder of this book, the money supply will be considered to be M1 unless otherwise specified.

The monetary components that make up the money supply serve many purposes. But at its essence, it channels funds from savers to borrowers, an important function of the financial system that barter societies are unable to do. In the next section, we look at a simple model of loanable funds to show how savers and borrowers come together to make moneylending possible and contribute to economic growth.

CHECKPOINT

WHAT IS MONEY?

- Money is anything accepted in exchange for goods and services and for the payment of debts.
- The functions of money include: a medium of exchange, a unit of account, and a store of value.
- Liquidity refers to how fast, easily, and reliably an asset can be converted into cash.
- M1 is currency plus demand deposits plus other checkable deposits.
- M2 is equal to M1 plus savings deposits plus other savings-like deposits.

QUESTION: The U.S. penny, with Abraham Lincoln's image on the front, has been in circulation since 1909. Back then, pennies were inexpensive to produce and could be used to purchase real items. Today, a U.S. penny actually costs the government more than 1 cent to produce, and it is virtually unusable in any coin-operated machine and impractical to use in stores. How has the role of the penny changed over the past century in terms of its monetary functions (medium of exchange, unit of account, and store of value)?

Answers to the Checkpoint questions can be found at the end of this chapter.

THE MARKET FOR LOANABLE FUNDS

The market for loanable funds is a model that describes the financial market for saving and investment. Initially, we will assume that savers deal directly with investors. This simplifies our analysis. We then will bring in financial intermediaries (banks, mutual funds, and other financial institutions) to describe the benefits of a well-functioning financial system.

Supply and Demand for Loanable Funds

Why do people save? Why do they borrow? The first thought might be that people save because they *can* save. Unlike barter economies, money makes saving possible.

People supply funds to the loanable funds market because they do not spend all of their income; they save. There are many reasons why individuals save. People save "for a rainy day": They put away some of their income when times are good to take care of them when times turn bad. Saving behavior is also a cultural phenomenon: Many countries, such as China, India, and France, have savings rates far higher than those in the United States.

The reward for not spending today is the *interest* received on savings, enabling people to spend more in the future. Therefore, in the market for loanable funds shown in Figure 1, the quantity of loanable funds is measured on the horizontal axis, and the price of the funds (interest rate) is measured on the vertical axis. In this market, the supply curve represents savers, while the demand curve represents borrowers.

The supply of funds to the loanable funds market, shown as S_0, is positively related to the interest rate. Because interest rates are the price (reward) that savers receive, higher interest rates result in more saving (funds) supplied to the market. This results in an upward-sloping supply curve much like other supply curves we studied earlier, and is just another example of people reacting to incentives.

The demand for loanable funds comes from people who want to purchase goods and services, such as taking out a loan to go to college, taking out a mortgage on a house, or who, as entrepreneurs, want to start or expand a business. Firms are borrowers, too. Firms may want to invest in new plants, additional equipment, expanded warehouse facilities, or engage in additional research and development on new products. The specific investment depends on the industry. For firms in the oil industry, it might be for an offshore oil platform or refinery. For a start-up network firm that has a growing number of subscribers but limited financial capital, the loanable funds might be used for another server farm.

The demand for loanable funds, shown as D_0 in Figure 1, slopes downward because when the interest rate is high, fewer projects will have a rate of return high enough to justify

Building a new server farm requires a substantial amount of cash, often obtained by borrowing in the loanable funds market.

Martial Trezzini/Corbis

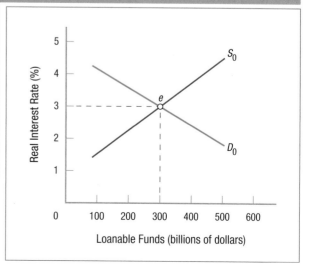

| FIGURE 1 | THE MARKET FOR LOANABLE FUNDS |

This market represents supply and demand for loanable funds. Savers spend less than they earn and supply the excess funds to the market. Borrowers (primarily businesses) have potential profit-making investment opportunities, and this leads to their demand for funds. Equilibrium is at point *e*.

the investment. A project will be undertaken only if its expected return (its benefit) is higher than the cost of funding the project. When oil prices fall, for example, an oil platform will not generate enough revenues to justify paying a high interest rate. As interest rates fall, more projects become profitable and the amount of funds demanded rises.

Keep in mind that when we refer to interest rates, we are referring to *real* interest rates (adjusted for inflation) that reflect the real cost of borrowing and the real return to savers.

The loanable funds market reaches equilibrium in Figure 1 at a 3% real interest rate and $300 billion in funds traded in the market. If for some reason the real interest rate *exceeded* 3%, savers would provide more funds to the market than investors want and interest rates would fall until the market reached point *e*. In a similar way, if interest rates were somehow *below* 3%, investors would want more funds than savers would be willing to provide. In this case, the market would push up interest rates to 3% at point *e*. Not surprisingly, this market is similar to the competitive markets for other goods and services. When compared to most markets, financial markets are typically more competitive and often reach equilibrium more quickly if something changes in the market. Let's now use this model to analyze various impacts (private and public) on the market for loanable funds.

Just as in other markets, the market for loanable funds is subject to factors that shift the supply or demand for loanable funds. When this occurs, interest rates and the level of saving and investment also change.

Shifts in the Supply of Loanable Funds

A shift in the supply curve of loanable funds occurs when a factor increases or decreases the country's willingness to save (either by private individuals or the public government) at any given interest rate. Changes in economic outlook, incentives to save, income or asset prices, and government deficits can influence savings patterns.

Economic Outlook Suppose households decide to save a larger proportion of their income because they fear job loss in a recession. If households decide to save more, the amount of funds provided to the market at all interest rates will increase, shifting the supply of loanable funds from S_0 to S_1 in Figure 2. Equilibrium will move from point *e* to point *a*, real interest rates will fall, and both saving and investment will rise from $300 billion to $400 billion. Similarly, if a recession ends and people go on a buying spree, savings will fall. In Figure 2, this would be a shift in the supply curve from S_1 to S_0.

Incentives to Save Governments and companies offer various incentives to individuals to save, such as retirement contribution plans and other tax incentives. Adjusting such incentives will change the level of savings accordingly.

FIGURE 2	CHANGES IN SUPPLY, DEMAND, AND INTEREST RATES

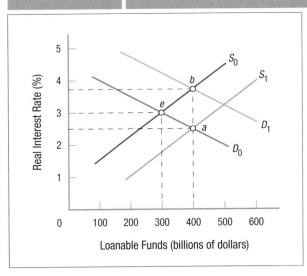

If savers decide to save more, the supply of funds will grow to S_1. At the new equilibrium, point *a*, interest rates fall and the amount of loanable funds rises. If instead there is an increase in the rate of return on investment (due to investment tax credits or increased demand for the firm's product), demand for funds will increase to D_1. At the new equilibrium, point *b*, interest rates and loanable funds rise.

Income or Asset Prices As incomes rise, people generally save a larger proportion of their income, all else equal. Asset prices, however, tend to work the other way. As home prices and stock values increase, people *feel* wealthier (without necessarily having more income) and will spend more and save less. The opposite effects occur when incomes fall or asset prices fall.

Government Deficits The supply of loanable funds includes both private and public saving. When a government runs a budget surplus, additional loanable funds are provided to the market, increasing the supply of loanable funds. However, governments often incur budget deficits, which means the government becomes a borrower instead of a saver. Governments borrow money by issuing bonds, which are then purchased by individuals and investors using their savings. Therefore, when governments borrow, they do so by reducing the amount that the private sector saves, which decreases the supply of loanable funds. Subsequently, interest rates rise, which crowds out consumption and investment, an effect discussed in the previous chapter.

Shifts in the Demand for Loanable Funds

We have seen how changes in savings can shift the supply of loanable funds. Now let's turn our attention to the demand side. Anything that changes the rate of return on potential investment will cause the demand for loanable funds to change. Let's keep saving on the initial supply curve, S_0, in Figure 2.

Investment Tax Incentives Investment tax credits effectively reduce tax payments for firms building new factories or buying new equipment. These laws give firms incentives to invest by increasing their *after-tax* rate of return, and often are created in bad economic times with the expectation of a quick jolt to investment demand.

An increase in investment demand would shift the demand for loanable funds from D_0 to D_1 in Figure 2 and results in both higher real interest rates (3.75%) and higher investment ($400 billion). An increase in business taxes would have the opposite effect on demand.

Technological Advances New technologies that increase productivity or create new products give businesses an incentive to increase production, which often results in plant expansion or the need to build an additional facility, increasing the demand for loanable funds.

Regulations Government regulations tend to influence the level of business investment. When regulations reduce corruption and instill confidence in firms and entrepreneurs, demand for investment will rise. But when regulations impose higher costs or make plant expansion difficult, the demand for investment will fall because the return on investment is reduced.

Product Demand When demand for a firm's product or service increases, the return on investment rises. This increases the demand for loanable funds. The opposite is true when product demand falls.

Business Expectations When business sentiment about the economy rises, firms will tend to increase their investment demand, which increases the demand for loanable funds. When business sentiment falls, investment demand decreases and so does demand for loanable funds.

In summary, the market for loanable funds works just like any other market where one can use the familiar tools of supply and demand analysis. The only slight difference is that the price is represented by the real interest rate on loanable funds.

We have seen that when households decide to increase saving, real interest rates fall and investment rises. When the demand by firms for investment funds rises, real interest rates rise along with expanded investment. Together, saving and investment move toward equilibrium in the market for loanable funds.

✅ CHECKPOINT

THE MARKET FOR LOANABLE FUNDS

- Households supply loanable funds to the market because they spend less than their income and because they are rewarded with interest for saving.

- Firms demand funds to invest in profitable opportunities.

- The supply curve of funds is positively sloped; higher real interest rates bring more funds into the market. The demand for loanable funds is negatively sloped, reflecting the fact that at higher real interest rates, fewer investment projects are profitable.

- Any policy that provides additional incentives for households to save will increase the supply of loanable funds, resulting in lower interest rates and greater investment.

- Anything that increases the potential profitability (rate of return) of business investments will increase the demand for loanable funds, resulting in higher interest rates and investment.

QUESTIONS: A major downturn in an economy can bring about many consequences, including a reduction in business confidence in which firms become reluctant to invest, and an increased fear of job loss among workers. How do these two events affect the supply of savings and the demand for borrowing? What happens to the supply and demand curves found in Figure 2? Once the economy recovers, what is supposed to happen to these curves?

Answers to the Checkpoint questions can be found at the end of this chapter.

THE FINANCIAL SYSTEM

The previous section discussed how savers and borrowers interact in a market such that those who demand money for various reasons are able to turn to those who have extra money to save. The interest rate is what keeps this market in equilibrium between savers and borrowers. But how does one actually go about saving or borrowing money?

Suppose you have an extra $1,000 that you want to save for the future, and a buddy from your old high school asks you to invest in a new skateboard shop he plans to open on campus. Do you lend your money to him?

That should depend on a number of factors. First, will your friend be paying you interest or a share of his profits? Second, how risky would such an investment be? Is your friend borrowing from you because he can't qualify for a small business loan elsewhere? Third, when will you expect to get your money back? Next year, or just whenever the business makes enough profit to pay you back? Or perhaps never if the shop goes bust.

These are important questions to evaluate before making financial decisions about your money. Often, the time it takes to evaluate proposals such as lending money to your buddy and to everyone else you know looking to borrow money can be significant and costly. For this reason, many individuals instead choose to save by putting money into banks, bonds, and stocks, which together represent the financial system.

Should you invest your money here?

Corbis

The Bridge Between Savers and Borrowers

The **financial system** is a complex set of institutions that, in the broadest sense, allocates scarce resources (financial capital) from savers, those who are spending less than they earn, to borrowers, those who want to use these resources to invest in potentially profitable projects. Both savers and borrowers can include households, firms, and governments, but our focus is on households as savers and firms as borrowers. As we have seen, savers expect to

financial system A complex set of institutions, including banks, bond markets, and stock markets, that allocate scarce resources (financial capital) from savers to borrowers.

earn interest on their savings and borrowers expect to pay interest on what they borrow. Households may save for a down payment on a house or a new car, and firms borrow to invest in new plants, equipment, or research and development.

Financial institutions or **financial intermediaries** are the bridge between savers and borrowers. They include, among others, commercial banks, savings and loan associations, credit unions, insurance companies, securities firms (brokerages), and pension funds. The complexity of a country's financial institutions often is a sign of economic efficiency and growth, as these financial firms take savings from savers and loan them to borrowers.

financial intermediaries Financial firms (banks, mutual funds, insurance companies, etc.) that acquire funds from savers and then lend these funds to borrowers (consumers, firms, and governments).

The Roles of Financial Institutions

Financial institutions fulfill three important roles that facilitate the flow of funds to the economy. They (1) reduce information costs, (2) reduce transaction costs, and (3) spread risk by diversifying assets.

Reducing Information Costs Information costs are the expenses associated with gathering information on individual borrowers and evaluating their creditworthiness. Savers (in this case, lenders) would have a difficult time without financial institutions. For example, when deciding whether to lend your buddy money to open his skateboard shop, you might know plenty about your friend's personality and habits, but have few ways to determine if his shop was safe to lend to or was unsound, or even just a fraud. Financial institutions reduce information costs by screening, evaluating, and monitoring firms to see that they are creditworthy and use the borrowed funds loaned in a prudent manner.

Reducing Transaction Costs Transaction costs are those associated with finding, selecting, and negotiating contracts between individual savers and borrowers. Suppose your buddy needs much more than $1,000, and asks all of his friends to lend him money. Trying to set up contracts individually between many lenders and a borrower can be time-consuming and costly, especially if every lender wants to make sure the business is a sound investment. Financial institutions reduce transaction costs by providing standardized financial products, including savings accounts, stocks, bonds, annuities, mortgages, futures, and options. In your case, you and your friends might put your money into a savings account, while your buddy applies for a loan at that bank.

Diversifying Assets to Reduce Risk Firms need funds for long-term investments, but savers want access to their money at a moment's notice and would want their funds invested in a number of diversified projects to reduce risk. In other words, you might not want to put your entire savings into one risky loan. Financial institutions accept funds from savers and pool this money into a portfolio of diversified financial instruments (stocks, bonds, etc.), reducing overall risk and at the same time permitting savers access to their funds when needed. In addition, they can also offer securities with different risk profiles to savers, from relatively safe CDs and savings accounts to more risky domestic and foreign stocks. In so doing, these institutions allow a greater flow of funds between savers and borrowers, greatly increasing the efficiency of investment in the economy.

The role of financial institutions in channeling funds from savers to investors is essential, because the people who save are often not the same people with profitable investment opportunities. Without financial institutions, investment would be a pale version of what we see today, and the economy would be a fraction of its size.

Types of Financial Assets

Savers have many options when it comes to where to put their money. The primary difference among the many types of financial assets available is the **return on investment (ROI)** one can achieve. A return on investment can be determined by the interest rate earned on savings accounts or CDs, or the capital gains, dividends, and other interest earned from investing in stocks or bonds. The ROI of an asset largely depends on the risk of the asset, with lower risk assets generally earning a lower ROI and higher risk assets earning a higher ROI.

return on investment The earnings, such as interest or capital gains, that a saver receives for making funds available to others. It is calculated as earnings divided by the amount invested.

The simplest way to save is to deposit money into a checking or savings account at your local bank. This is also the lowest risk approach to saving, because all savings up to $250,000 per account are insured by the Federal Deposit Insurance Corporation (FDIC) as long as the bank is a member. In its 85-year history, no saver's deposit insured with the FDIC has ever been lost, even when a bank has gone bankrupt.

The advantages of placing savings in banks are clear—savers have easy access to their money (high liquidity) in addition to virtually no risk. The disadvantage is that savings and checking accounts pay very low interest, and in some cases no interest at all.

Thus, in order to increase earnings on savings, savers must either (1) choose financial assets with lower liquidity, or (2) choose assets that carry a higher level of risk. One way to achieve this is to invest in bonds and stocks, to which we now turn our attention.

Savers can invest their funds *directly* in businesses by purchasing a bond or shares of stock from a firm using one of many brokerage firms easily accessible by ordinary individuals. Savers can also invest *indirectly* by providing funds to a financial institution (such as a bank or mutual fund) that channels those funds to borrowers. A share of stock represents partial ownership of a corporation, and its value is determined by the earning capacity of the firm. A bond, on the other hand, represents debt of the corporation. Bonds are typically sold in $1,000 denominations and pay a fixed amount of interest. If you own a bond, you are a creditor of the firm.

Bond Prices and Interest Rates

We examined real interest rates when we described the loanable funds market, and we described several direct and indirect financial instruments such as stocks, savings accounts, and bonds. But most of the loanable funds are in the form of corporate or government *bonds*. In 2016, the total value of loans made by U.S. commercial banks was almost $9 trillion, the total value of the U.S. bond market was about $41 trillion, and the total value of stocks traded in U.S. stock exchanges was about $25 trillion.

Because of the sheer size of the U.S. bond market, economists frequently look at financial markets from the viewpoint of the supply and demand for bonds. They often consider policy implications by their impact on the price of bonds and the quantity traded. It can be a little confusing because bond prices and interest rates are inversely related—when interest rates go up, bond prices go down, and vice versa. Let's take a quick look at the characteristics of bonds to help you see why interest rates and bond prices move in opposite directions. Understanding this will give you a better understanding of how monetary policy actually works.

To see why bond prices and interest rates are inversely related, we need to analyze bond contracts more closely. A bond is a contract between a seller (the company or government issuing the bond) and a buyer that determines the following:

- Coupon rate of the bond
- Maturity date of the bond
- Face value of the bond

The seller agrees to pay the buyer a fixed rate of interest (the coupon rate) on the face value of the bond (usually $1,000 for a corporate bond, but often much larger values for government bonds) until a future fixed date (the maturity date of the bond). For example, if XYZ Company issues a bond with a face value of $1,000 at a coupon rate of 5%, it agrees to pay the bondholder $50 per year until the maturity date of the bond. Note that this $50 payment per year is *fixed* for the life of the bond.

Once a bond is issued, it is subject to the forces of the marketplace. As economic circumstances change, people may be willing to pay more or less for a bond that originally sold for $1,000. The *yield* on a bond is the percentage return earned over the life of the bond. Yields change when bond prices change.

Assume, for instance, that when a $1,000 bond is issued, general interest rates are 5% so that the bond yields an annual interest payment of $50. For simplicity, let's assume that the bond is a perpetuity bond—that is, the bond has no maturity date. The issuer of the bond has agreed to pay $50 a year *forever* for the use of this money.

Assume that market interest rates rise to 8%. Just how much would the typical investor now be willing to pay for this bond that returns $50 a year? We can approach this intuitively. If we can buy a $1,000 bond now that pays $80 per year, why would we pay $1,000 for a similar bond that pays only $50? Would we pay more or less for the bond that pays $50? If we can get a bond that pays $80 for $1,000, we would pay *less* for a bond paying $50.

There is a simple formula we can use for perpetuity bonds:

$$\text{Yield} = \frac{\text{Interest Payment}}{\text{Price of Bond}}$$

Or rearranging terms:

$$\text{Price of Bond} = \frac{\text{Interest Payment}}{\text{Yield}}$$

The new price of the bond will be $625 ($50 ÷ 0.08 = $625). Clearly, as market interest rates went up, the price of this bond fell. Conversely, if market interest rates were to fall, say, from 5% to 3%, the price of the bond would rise to $1,666.67 ($50 ÷ 0.03 = $1,666.67).

Keep this relationship between interest rates and bond prices in mind when we focus on the tools of monetary policy in the next couple of chapters, for this approach to bond pricing is important to understanding how the government manages the money supply through the purchase and sale of bonds.

Stocks and Investment Returns

An alternative to placing savings into banks or bonds is to purchase shares of stock (also known as equity) in a company. When one buys a share of stock, this share represents one fraction (of the total shares issued) of ownership in the company, and subsequently one vote at shareholder meetings and one share of any dividends (periodic payments to shareholders).

The buying and selling of stock shares occur in stock exchanges (such as the New York Stock Exchange or NASDAQ). The price of a share of stock is determined by supply and demand just as in any other market, and for every buyer of a share of stock there must be a seller.

Compared to bonds, stocks tend to be riskier investments, because shares, representing partial ownership as opposed to a creditor of a company, become worthless when a company goes bankrupt. Bonds are generally considered safer investments because bondholders are the first to be repaid when businesses face financial trouble. However, stockholders get to share in the company's profits through dividend payments and the increase in share values, which can be substantial when a company succeeds. Both bonds and stocks are less liquid than savings and checking accounts, as both require the asset to be sold and a small commission paid in order to convert the asset into cash.

tradeoff between risk and return
The pattern of higher risk assets offering higher average annual returns on investment than lower risk assets.

Which pays more over the long run, bonds or stocks? Given their higher risk, stocks tend to reward investors with a higher average return on investment over the long run, which follows the general rule of the **tradeoff between risk and return.** Riskier assets typically offer a greater return; otherwise, investors would not choose to take such risks. With the exception of a few periods during which the stock market dropped considerably (such as the crash in technology stocks from 2000 to 2001 and the stock market crash from late 2007 to early 2009 when many companies went bankrupt or nearly bankrupt), stocks generally trend upward, providing an average return on investment higher than what can be earned through less risky bonds and the least risky savings accounts and CDs, which are FDIC insured.

The complexity of the financial system offers savers and borrowers many opportunities to conduct economic transactions quickly and efficiently. But because the financial system also can be subject to corruption, financial institutions are heavily regulated to ensure the soundness and safety of the financial system and to increase the transparency and information to investors. The agencies regulating financial markets include the Securities and Exchange Commission (SEC), the Federal Reserve System, the FDIC, and another half-dozen or so federal agencies, along with all the state agencies regulating firms in this market.

Although heavily regulated, financial markets are complex environments that are occasionally subjected to meltdowns that can lead the economy into a recession and result in huge losses for the affected firms. When meltdowns occur, the bridge that financial intermediaries bring between savers and lenders can collapse.

 CHECKPOINT

THE FINANCIAL SYSTEM

- Financial institutions are financial intermediaries that build a bridge between savers and borrowers.
- Financial institutions reduce information costs, transaction costs, and risk, making financial markets more efficient.
- Efficient financial markets foster growth because they maximize the amount of funds channeled from savers to borrowers.
- Financial assets include savings and checking accounts, certificates of deposit (CDs), bonds, stocks, and mutual funds.
- Bond prices and interest rates are inversely related.

QUESTION: In 2008 voters in California approved the construction of a high-speed rail system connecting Anaheim (near Los Angeles) and San Francisco by 2030, at a cost of over $65 billion. A portion of this cost will be financed by institutions such as Goldman Sachs, an investment banking and securities firm, while a larger portion will be financed by the issuance of bonds to investors and local governments, with the rest financed by private investors who will own shares in the rail system. Explain how financial intermediation is necessary in order to make this project a reality. Why couldn't the state government just pay for it by using tax revenues it collects this year?

Answers to the Checkpoint questions can be found at the end of this chapter.

FINANCIAL TOOLS FOR A BETTER FUTURE

Now that we have discussed the role of money, the market for loanable funds, and financial intermediaries, we should step back and ask ourselves how we can apply what we have learned to our everyday finances and our future. As a caveat, it is always best to seek financial advice from a trusted professional who has your best interests in mind. This section is meant to introduce you to the basic financial concepts encountered when borrowing and saving money.

Short-Term Borrowing

As a college student, your income is low to nonexistent as you invest (very wisely) in human capital by pursuing a college degree that will increase your earning potential during your working years. That means that in the near term, you will likely accumulate debt in the form of student loans, credit card balances, and car loans. Eventually, a home mortgage might also necessitate more borrowing.

Interest rates on personal debt vary considerably, with small differences leading to substantial payments over the long run, as we will see shortly. Student loans funded by the government typically offer low interest rates in addition to allowing you to defer payments until after you graduate. These loans often provide the lowest cost of borrowing to get you through until your income rises.

The most common short-term loan, however, comes in the form of credit card debt. Credit card companies typically charge a higher interest rate, although on occasion may provide **teaser rates**—offers of low or even zero interest for a limited time on purchases and/or balance transfers. They are called *teasers* because credit card companies hope that you actually *don't* pay off your balance at the end of the offer period. Interest rates after the

teaser rates Promotional low interest rates offered by lenders for a short period of time to attract new customers and to encourage spending.

Plastic surgery for your debt.

offer period increase considerably, and often are higher than other borrowing rates. In addition, many credit cards charge balance transfer fees of 3% to 5% of the transferred amount, which means the 0% offer that you enjoy for a limited time is not truly 0%.

Because of the high costs of holding credit card debt, it is generally advisable to:

1. Keep credit card balances to a minimum.

2. Find lower cost borrowing opportunities (such as student loans or bank loans) to keep higher interest credit card balances lower.

3. Avoid applying for too many credit cards, because fees can rack up and credit scores can be negatively affected by excessive credit applications.

4. Never miss a minimum payment, for *any amount*, even for a month. Every missed payment remains on credit reports for years, potentially raising costs for future car loans and home mortgages, and even making insurance and certain jobs harder to find.

The Power (or Danger) of Compounding Interest

compounding effect The effect of interest added to existing debt or savings leading to substantial growth in debt or savings over the long run.

Interest rates are an important factor in deciding how to go about borrowing, or saving, money. For the most part, we see interest rates as being quite low, typically less than 10%. The exceptions typically are for credit card debt or high-risk lending when the borrower has a greater likelihood of defaulting on the loan.

But even for low interest rates, the effect on long-run payments can be substantial due to the **compounding effect.** Compounding occurs when interest is calculated and added on a periodic (often daily) basis to money borrowed or saved in addition to the interest already charged or earned. Let's use annual terms for simplicity. Suppose you borrow $1,000 at a 10% interest rate. Table 1 shows how compounding interest can add up quickly. After a year, you incur $10\% \times \$1,000 = \$100$ in interest charges. Suppose you do not make any payments on the debt. The next year, you incur $10\% \times \$1,100$ (the original debt + interest already charged) = $110 in interest.

This may not seem like much. But suppose you do not make any payments on the debt for 30 years. Your original $1,000 debt will become $17,449! In fact, in year 30 alone, nearly $1,600 in interest would be added to the debt, more than the original borrowed amount. That is the danger of compounding interest on borrowed debt, and an important reason to seek low interest rates and make adequate payments. The good news, however, is that while compounding works against those with debt, it helps those who save, leading to higher future wealth.

TABLE 1	COMPOUNDING INTEREST AND DEBT		
Year	Starting Value	10% Interest	Ending Value
1	$1,000.00	$100.00	$1,100.00
2	1,100.00	110.00	1,210.00
3	1,210.00	121.00	1,331.00
4	1,331.00	133.10	1,464.10
5	1,464.10	146.41	1,610.51
...	...	...	...
28	13,109.99	1,311.00	14,420.99
29	14,420.99	1,442.10	15,863.09
30	15,863.09	1,586.31	17,449.40

Risk Assessment and Asset Allocation

As you work and accumulate savings, an important question is how to go about putting unspent money into assets that will grow over the years until you eventually need it.

The simplest and most liquid means of saving might be to keep money in cash stashed in a safe place or just letting money sit in a checking or savings account at your local bank. Although these methods give you the quickest access to your money, they are unlikely to provide much gain in value. Most checking accounts and even savings accounts pay no interest (and if they do, it's often less than 1%). With inflation, when you eventually want to use the money, the purchasing power of that money has decreased. How does one go about choosing an asset that pays higher returns?

An important consideration when choosing the type of investment is assessing your tolerance for risk. Would you be frantic if you see your savings fluctuate up and down each day? Would you instead prefer to see steady growth of your savings? Or would you be willing to accept some volatility, the fact that some investments may fall in value, in exchange for a chance of higher growth over the long term?

Risk tolerance should reflect the type of investment instruments purchased. A less risky portfolio would contain a large portion of savings in assets such as CDs and high-rated bonds, and "blue chip" stocks. A more risky portfolio would contain a greater portion of savings in growth stocks and high-return bonds.

As described in the previous section, a tradeoff between risk and return exists, where riskier assets typically offer a greater average return. This choice between risk and return not only affects one's personal investments, but also affects how one goes about saving for the future and for retirement, which we discuss next.

Saving for the Future: Employer-Based Programs

Upon graduating from college, among the exciting challenges facing the new graduate is seeking a good job and earning a salary that, hopefully, allows for a more comfortable life. But besides earning more money, decisions must be made about how to *save* for the future.

Suppose you find your dream job and begin work. Besides the Social Security (FICA) tax that is taken out of each paycheck to fund retirement benefits, you are asked whether you want to contribute to your employer's retirement program. Do you contribute, and if so, how much? 3%? 6%? More? And once you contribute to an account, in what type of assets do you invest that money? Safe or risky assets, or some combination? The tradeoff between risk and return becomes a very important factor in these decisions.

Let's begin by looking at employer-based savings programs, the most common being the 401(k) (offered by most privately held and publicly traded companies), though similar programs exist for government employees and tax-exempt organizations [such as 403(b)], and for teachers (such as TIAA-CREF).

To Contribute or Not to Contribute? Most retirement savings programs allow (or in some cases, require) employees to contribute a certain percentage of their wage earnings into a retirement account. Many companies will then offer a full or partial match of the contribution up to 3% to 4% of one's salary.

If your employer offers to match savings contributions, this is essentially "free money" that gets added to your savings, dramatically increasing your return as long as you satisfy the **vesting period,** the minimum years of employment required for the employer-paid portion to become permanent in the account, even if you leave the company.

vesting period The minimum number of years a worker must be employed before the company's contribution to a retirement account becomes permanent.

Suppose you contribute $1,000 into the savings program, and your employer matches it with another $1,000. You will have instantly earned a 100% return on your investment as long as the vesting period has been satisfied. Try finding another financial asset that offers this high a return!

Another benefit of 401(k) (or similar) programs is that contributions are tax-deferred, meaning that an employee does not pay income tax on the contributed amount until the money is eventually withdrawn. Why does this matter?

Suppose you earn $75,000 in taxable income. This means you are in the 25% tax bracket for most income earned. Suppose you increase your 401(k) contribution by $1,000. How much does your take-home pay fall? Because you normally would pay 25% in income tax on the $1,000, your take-home pay would fall by only $1,000(1 − 0.25) = $750. Essentially, you give up $750 now to add an additional $1,000 into your retirement account. That is $250 (33%) in extra savings right from the start, on top of the investment earnings on that additional amount over your life until the money is eventually withdrawn.

A downside of most retirement plans is the restriction on when you can use the savings. The minimum age for withdrawing money from most 401(k) accounts is 59.5 years. Withdrawing money before this age incurs (with few exceptions) a 10% early withdrawal penalty.

In What Assets Should One Invest? Suppose you have decided to contribute to your employer's retirement plan and to take advantage of the employer match and tax benefits. Now you are given online access to your account, where you see many options on where to invest your money.

As with all investments, risk assessment is an important consideration when it comes to managing retirement accounts. Most accounts allow you to choose a portfolio of investments ranging from safe assets (such as Treasury bills) to risky assets (such as high-growth stocks). Many financial advisors suggest that you choose a higher risk portfolio in your younger years, then gradually reduce your risk as you approach retirement. Why? Let's use the 2007–2009 stock market crash as an example.

Between October 2007 and March 2009, major stock market indexes fell by nearly 50%. Retirement accounts that were invested fully in stocks fell drastically in value. This had devastating effects on older workers who had not transitioned to safer assets as they approached retirement. However, for younger workers, stock market drops tend to have minimal effects in the long run. In fact, temporary dips in the stock market can even *improve* outcomes over time, as the Issue in this section describes.

Other Retirement Savings Tools: Social Security, Pensions, and IRAs

Besides employer-sponsored retirement contribution funds, other programs exist that allow individuals to save for their future. These include Social Security, employer-based pension programs, and individual retirement arrangement (IRA, also known as individual retirement account) programs.

Social Security Social Security is another form of retirement savings that nearly every American participates in from the time they start working as a teenager. The payroll tax (FICA) is 12.4% (of which 6.2% is paid by employees and 6.2% is paid by employers) of wage earnings up to a maximum of $118,500 in 2016. Unlike 401(k) contributions, the money you contribute to FICA is not yours, but rather is used to pay the benefits of those currently collecting Social Security benefits. Benefits are determined by a formula based on one's lifetime contributions.

The minimum age to begin collecting Social Security is 62, though if you wait until age 67, monthly benefits will be greater, and potentially will pay more overall if you live longer. Of course, if you have a family history of shorter lifespans, it might be a good idea to start collecting sooner.

Some have argued that Social Security is unfair to the poor, who generally have lower life expectancies than the rich. If the minimum age for collecting Social Security rises due to a shortfall of funds, those with lower life expectancies might not collect anything (except for a portion that can be bequeathed to a spouse or heir).

pensions A retirement program into which an employer pays a monthly amount to retired employees until they die.

Pension Plans Pensions are an alternative to 401(k)-type accounts. Pensions are monthly payments made by your employer from the day you retire until you die, based on the number of years you worked at the company. For example, a person who worked at a company 30 years might receive a pension of $3,000 per month upon retirement for the rest of his or her life, while someone who worked only 10 years might receive $1,000 per month.

ISSUE

Can a Stock Market Crash Increase Long-Term Savings?

From October 2007 to March 2009, major U.S. stock market indices (Dow, NASDAQ, and S&P 500) fell by more than 50% from their peaks. Investment savings accounts that took decades to accumulate saw their values drop in half in less than 17 months. The same was true for many retirement accounts, such as 401(k) and IRA accounts, which often are heavily invested in stocks. Indeed, this was a bleak period to follow one's retirement savings, not to mention the equally devastating loss in housing values during this period. Would the drop in stock values create long-term consequences for retirement? The answer may be surprising.

Although money invested up to October 2007 suffered a severe decline in value, most workers who continued to contribute to their retirement plans (and with matching employer additions to the new funds), saw their retirement portfolio values bounce back within a few years. How did this happen?

As new money entered retirement plans during the stock market decline, these funds were invested in assets at their new *lower* prices. When stock values recovered, old funds regained their values, while new funds saw healthy gains in value. The following example illustrates two scenarios using hypothetical numbers.

This hypothetical scenario shows that a drop in the stock market may not cause a major problem for retirement

savings over the long run *as long as* one continues to work and contribute toward retirement. And the younger the worker, the less of an impact short-term stock market corrections will have, because a smaller balance would be affected by the market drop, while new funds invested at lower prices can earn substantial gains (assuming no withdrawals or loans are made from the account). Unfortunately, some people dumped stocks after they fell, and became conservative with new money. The moral of the story: Don't panic. Slow and steady wins the race.

Sanford/Agliolo/Corbis

Scenario 1: Stocks fall 50% over the next year, then fully recover three years later.
Scenario 2: Stock market stays at the same exact level for the entire four-year period.

Description	Scenario 1	Scenario 2
Initial Account Balance:	$100,000	$100,000

Change in Value After Event:
    Scenario 1: 50% fall in stock prices
    Scenario 2: No change in stock prices
	−$50,000	−$0

Account Balance After Event:	$50,000	$100,000
New Contributions Over Four Years:	+$30,000	+$30,000

Earnings on New Contributions:
    Scenario 1: Purchased at an average of 40% below peak prices, resulting in a 67% gain
    Scenario 2: Purchased at original stock prices, with no increase in value
	+$20,000	+$0

Change in Value of Original Contributions:
    Scenario 1: Full recovery in stock prices
    Scenario 2: No change in stock prices
	+$50,000	+$0

Total Value of Account	**$150,000**	**$130,000**

Because pension benefits are difficult for companies to predict as people live longer, employers are increasingly switching to fixed-contribution plans such as a 401(k), where employer contributions are made up-front. But a few notable jobs retain comfortable pensions: The president of the United States receives a pension of over $200,000 every year after leaving office.

Finally, in addition to personal savings, investments, 401(k) and pensions plans, many individuals choose to save using individual retirement arrangements (IRAs).

Individual Retirement Arrangements (IRAs) Similar to 401(k) programs, traditional IRA programs allow one to save pretax (tax-deferred) dollars up to a certain limit, which, as discussed earlier, gives an immediate boost to savings compared to posttax dollars. Traditional IRA accounts allow one to invest in a broad range of stocks, bonds, and other assets. The minimum age to withdraw funds without penalty is 59.5 years, and taxes are paid on money withdrawn. (Note that most retirees are in lower tax brackets compared to their tax bracket during their working years.)

An alternative to a traditional IRA is a Roth IRA, which allows posttax dollars to be contributed up to a certain limit each year. Why would one contribute posttax dollars as opposed to pretax dollars? First, with a Roth IRA, money that you contribute (but not the earnings on contributions except in certain circumstances) can be withdrawn anytime without penalty. Second, Roth IRAs do not incur any taxes upon withdrawal after age 59.5, including the interest and capital gains the account accumulates over its life. Thus, while one pays taxes upfront on initial contributions, no taxes are paid on earnings, which can be very substantial with compounding.

Saving for the future is an important financial decision. Fortunately, many programs such as 401(k), Social Security, and IRAs make the process easier.

 CHECKPOINT

FINANCIAL TOOLS FOR A BETTER FUTURE

- Credit cards typically are an expensive way to finance borrowing, even with teaser rates.
- Debt and savings rise rapidly over the long run due to the compounding effect.
- A tradeoff exists between risk and return: The greater the risk, the higher the average return on investment.
- Company-sponsored retirement accounts such as a 401(k) allow employees to contribute pretax dollars and receive matching company contributions.
- Social Security is a program into which current contributors (workers) pay for benefits of the recipients (retirees) by way of a payroll tax on wages.
- Individual retirement arrangements (IRA) are similar to 401(k) programs except that they are not company sponsored and they provide greater investment choices.

QUESTIONS: Suppose Nicole is very risk averse with her money, while Jose likes to invest in riskier assets in hopes of a higher return. What type of assets would be best suited for each person? Supposing the tradeoff between risk and return holds true over the next 30 years, how would Nicole's savings compare to Jose's given the compounding effect (assuming each saves the same amount)?

Answers to the Checkpoint questions can be found at the end of this chapter.

chapter summary

Section 1 What Is Money?

Money is anything that is accepted in exchange for goods and services or for the payments of debts.

An asset's **liquidity** is determined by how fast, easily, and reliably it can be converted into cash.

22.1 Three Primary Functions of Money

1. **Medium of exchange:** Eliminates the double coincidence of wants common to barter.

2. **Unit of account:** Reduces the number of prices needed to just one per good.

3. **Store of value:** Allows people to save now and spend later.

22.2 Two Primary Money Supply Measures

M1 = currency (banknotes and coins) and demand deposits (checking accounts).

M2 = M1 + "near monies" (savings accounts, money market deposit accounts, small-denomination time deposits, and money market mutual fund accounts).

Most Liquid

Least Liquid

Jeffrey Coolidge/Getty Images Corbis
Tom Grill/Corbis
Ariel Skelley/Corbis

Section 2 The Market for Loanable Funds

22.3 The **market for loanable funds** describes the financial market for saving and investment.

Savers provide more funds to the loanable funds market as interest rates increase.

Firms demand more funds for investment opportunities as interest rates fall.

22.4 Factors affecting the willingness to save or borrow lead to a change in the market for loanable funds. For example, growing business confidence increases firms' willingness to invest, thus shifting the demand for loanable funds to the right, causing interest rates to rise.

Section 3 The Financial System

James Leynse/Corbis

Banks, savings and loans associations, credit unions, insurance companies, securities firms (brokerages), and pension funds are all types of financial intermediaries that take savings from savers and loan the funds to borrowers.

22.5 **Financial intermediaries** accept funds from savers and efficiently channel these to borrowers, reducing transaction and information costs, as well as lowering risk.

A bond is a contract between a seller (government or company) and a buyer. As a general rule, as market interest rates rise, the value of bonds (paying fixed dollars of interest) fall, and vice versa.

22.6 How to Calculate the Price of a Perpetuity Bond

Price of Bond = Annual Interest Payment ÷ Yield (%)

Example: If a bond pays $100 per year, and the yield is 6%, the price of the bond is $100 ÷ 0.06 = $1,667.

Section 4 Financial Tools for a Better Future

22.7 The **compounding effect** is powerful because it causes debt (if no payments are made) and savings to increase dramatically over time.

$10,000 in savings today invested at:

5%: equals $43,219 in 30 years

10%: equals $174,495 in 30 years

$10,000/year saved ($300,000 total over 30 years) invested at:

5%: equals $707,608 in 30 years

10%: equals $1,819,435 in 30 years

22.8 **Tradeoff Between Risk and Return:** The greater the risk involved, the higher the average annual return on investment.

Richard Cano/Getty Images

U.S. Savings Bonds and Treasury securities are among the safest assets in the world. Because of their low risk, the interest rates paid also are very low.

22.9 Programs for Retirement Savings

- Employer-sponsored programs
  - Fixed contribution plans, such as 401(k), 403(b), and TIAA-CREF, allow workers to contribute pretax dollars and employers to partially match contributions.
  - **Pensions** are monthly payments made by employers to their retired employees based on length of employment with the company.

- Government-sponsored programs
  - Social Security: Current workers pay benefits of retirees through the payroll tax on wages.

- Other retirement programs
  - Traditional IRAs use pretax dollars to fund investments; taxes are paid upon withdrawal after age 59.5.
  - Roth IRAs use after-tax dollars to fund investments. Contributed funds (but not earnings on those contributions) can be withdrawn anytime without penalty, and no taxes are paid on withdrawals (including earnings on investment) after one reaches the age of 59.5.

KEY CONCEPTS

money, p. 588
fiat money, p. 588
barter, p. 588
medium of exchange, p. 589
unit of account, p. 589
store of value, p. 589

liquidity, p. 589
M1, p. 590
M2, p. 590
financial system, p. 595
financial intermediaries, p. 596
return on investment, p. 596

tradeoff between risk and return, p. 598
teaser rates, p. 599
compounding effect, p. 600
vesting period, p. 601
pensions, p. 602

QUESTIONS AND PROBLEMS

Check Your Understanding

1. Describe the three functions of money.

2. What is a barter economy? Describe why such an approach is a difficult way for a modern economy to exist.

3. Explain the important difference between M1 and M2.

4. What gives our money its value if there is no gold or silver backing the currency?

5. What happens to savings if the real interest rate goes up? What happens to the demand for borrowing?

6. Explain why bond prices and interest rates are inversely related.

Apply the Concepts

7. List the following assets from most liquid to least liquid: a house (real estate); cash; a one-carat diamond; a savings account; 100 shares of Google stock; a Harley-Davidson motorcycle; a checking account; your old leather jacket.

8. At many game centers (such as Chuck E. Cheese's), it is common for kids to play carnival-type games to win prize tickets, which are then redeemed for a variety of prizes based on the number of tickets earned. In what ways do these prize tickets illustrate the three functions of money?

9. How do recessions affect the market for loanable funds? What happens to the supply of savings? What happens to the demand for borrowing? What is the effect on real interest rates?

10. Most individuals with average wealth choose to save their money using a financial intermediary such as a bank or a mutual fund. However, individuals with greater wealth are more likely to invest in individual stocks or directly in new or existing businesses. Explain why persons of different wealth are likely to show differences in how they save, and how financial intermediaries play a role.

11. Why would it be better to put $1,000 each year into a retirement account than to wait ten years and put in $10,000 all at once? Would it make much of a difference in the long run?

12. Why have pensions become a less common form of retirement benefit offered by companies?

In the News

13. A proposal in the government budget set forth in 2016 placed a limit on the total amount of savings that can be accumulated in tax-preferred retirement accounts to $3.4 million. The White House has argued that wealthy individuals have accumulated "tax-preferred retirement savings sufficient to finance an annual income of over $200,000 per year in retirement," and that the tax deductions from these excess savings cost the government billions each year. How do these sorts of proposals affect the market for loanable funds?

14. The U.S. stock market doubled in value between 2010 and 2016. However, a slowdown in economic growth in many countries, increased volatility in stock markets, and an anticipated rise in U.S. interest rates have led some analysts to believe bonds may outperform stocks. If more investors switch from buying stock to bonds, how might this lead to a self-fulfilling prophecy? Does this argument reflect the theory of the tradeoff between risk and return?

Solving Problems

15. Suppose a small country has the following monies in circulation:

> Cash/currency: $1 million
>
> Demand deposits: $2 million
>
> Other checkable deposits: $2 million
>
> Small-denomination time deposits: $4 million
>
> Savings deposits: $5 million
>
> Money market deposit accounts: $5 million

Calculate the value of M1 and M2 for this country.

WORK IT OUT | LaunchPad | interactive activity

16. The yield for a perpetuity bond is determined by the simple formula

$$\text{Yield} = \frac{\text{Interest Payment}}{\text{Price of Bond}}$$

a. Calculate the yield on a $1,000 perpetuity bond that pays $40 a year forever to the bondholder.

b. Suppose that actions taken by the Fed cause interest rates in the economy to fall by 2%. How will this affect the price of the bond that still pays $40 a year in interest?

c. Now suppose that one purchases a new $1,000 perpetuity bond at the lower interest rate. What will the annual interest payment be equal to?

d. If interest rates were to rise back to the original level determined in part (a), how will that affect the price of the new bond purchased in part (c)?

USING THE NUMBERS

17. According to By the Numbers, which bank had the largest amount of assets in 2015, and what was this value? How much in assets did a bank need to reach the top ten largest banks in the world in 2015?

18. According to By the Numbers, how much in U.S. dollars is currently in circulation in the world? How much in U.S. dollars is held in reserves in the world? Describe how these numbers compare to the euro and the Japanese yen.

Checkpoint: What Is Money? 591

Because the purchasing power of the penny has fallen significantly since its first introduction, its monetary role also has diminished. It still serves as a medium of exchange, though the ease of its use has become so difficult that pennies often are left in coin jars, tip jars, and charity bins, as opposed to being kept for everyday use. Its function as a unit of account remains, since most prices are still quoted to the nearest penny. And its function as a store of value remains, though a substantial jar of pennies would be needed before taking the time to bring it to a coin exchange machine or the bank.

Checkpoint: The Market for Loanable Funds 595

A fall in business confidence would reduce the demand for loanable funds, shifting the demand curve to the left in Figure 2. Meanwhile, increased insecurity about jobs will encourage people to save more, shifting the supply of savings to the right. These shifts create a huge surplus of funds at the original interest rate, and therefore interest rates would fall until a new equilibrium is reached. As the economy recovers, businesses resume their investments and consumers begin spending again, and the demand curve will shift back to the right and the supply curve would shift to the left. Interest rates would trend upward.

Checkpoint: The Financial System 599

The high-speed rail system is a multiyear, costly project that is too large to be paid for using taxes from any one year. Even if the state government pays for it using taxes over many years, it still must borrow the money first before paying it back using taxes collected in the future. Therefore, financial intermediation by banks is required. But the rail project will use more than just banks. It also relies heavily on the bond market, relying on investors willing to lend money for a relatively long period of time before being paid back with interest. Lastly, it relies on the equity markets, by selling partial ownership of the new rail system to investors willing to put up billions in hopes of a profitable return in the future once the rail line goes into service.

Checkpoint: Financial Tools for a Better Future 604

Because Nicole is more risk averse with her money, she would choose a low-risk portfolio containing safer bonds and stocks, while Jose, being more risk preferring, would invest in growth stocks and high-yield bonds. If the tradeoff between risk and return holds, Jose's savings would grow at a higher average annual rate than Nicole's. With compounding, Jose's savings over the long run will likely be substantially larger than Nicole's. One exception might be if a stock market crash occurs at the end, in which Jose's savings would fall if he didn't reduce the riskiness of his portfolio in the later years. Even so, with the power of compounding, Jose's portfolio would likely be much higher than Nicole's even if a stock market crash did occur.

23

Money Creation and the Federal Reserve

Understanding how banks play a powerful role in the economy by accepting deposits and lending money

Learning Objectives

23.1 Explain how banks create money by accepting deposits and making loans.

23.2 Define fractional reserve banking and explain why banks can lend much more than they keep in reserves.

23.3 Explain how the money multiplier works and how it makes monetary policy decisions very powerful.

23.4 Define a money leakage and explain how it affects the money multiplier.

23.5 Describe the history and structure of the Federal Reserve System.

23.6 List the important banking functions conducted by the Federal Reserve regional banks and their branches.

23.7 Describe the Federal Reserve's principal monetary tools.

23.8 Analyze the federal funds rate and how it affects all other interest rates.

23.9 Explain why the Federal Reserve's policies take time to affect the economy.

n small towns and villages throughout Central and South Asia, Africa, and Latin America, entrepreneurship is flourishing. These are not your typical high-tech start-ups or research and development centers, but rather primitive small shops selling basic goods and services. Many got their start using a microloan—a small loan (as little as $50) offered by organizations aiming to promote business enterprise among individuals who would not qualify for traditional bank loans.

These small loans and the new businesses they help create (largely by women in the poorest parts of the world) have been credited with bringing more people out of poverty in recent years than direct foreign aid has. How can a tiny loan of $50 have such a positive effect on the economy?

Quite easily, in fact. In Bangladesh, Fatima takes her $50 loan and buys cotton to make a dozen sharis. She sells the sharis at the local outdoor market for a total of $120, of which she uses $50 to pay back her microloan and $70 to buy more cotton to make even more sharis. Only this time, she is debt-free, allowing her to use all her proceeds to expand her business and provide income for her family. Meanwhile, the $50 she paid back will be loaned to another entrepreneur, allowing another small business to get its start.

When a small loan is used to create a new business, jobs are created, which allows people to spend money at other businesses (also likely started from a microloan). The collective power of new businesses, jobs, and increased spending leads to healthy economic growth in the village, and it all started from a single microloan. Now, multiply this one case by the thousands of microloans being made available throughout the developing world, and the effect on reducing poverty is staggering. This example represents a microcosm of the global economy and the money creation process in which financial intermediaries play an important role.

During the recent 2007–2009 recession and ensuing economic recovery, a very different scenario was happening in the United States. The downturn caused a steep decline in consumer and business confidence. Individuals and firms were not in a spending mood as jobs were lost and wages cut, on top of falling home and stock prices.

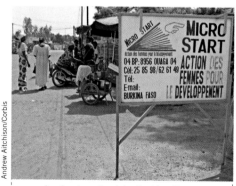

A microloan bank in Burkina Faso.

Andrew Aitchison/Corbis

Afghan women attend a village meeting to make payments on their microloans.

Shehzad Norani/Majority World

Banks and the Federal Reserve

Banks create money by accepting deposits and making loans. This process is aided by the Federal Reserve, which influences interest rates and sets reserve requirements for member banks.

Go to **LaunchPad** *to use the latest data to recreate this graph.*

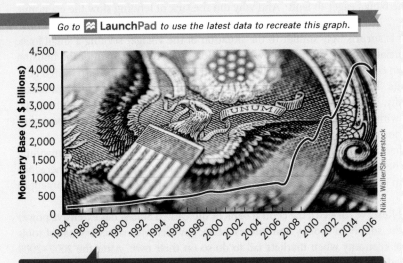

Monetary Base (in $ billions) — 0 to 4,500 — Years 1984 to 2016

Nikita Waller/Shutterstock

The monetary base is the sum of all currency in circulation and reserves held by banks. It grew steadily until the recent financial crisis, when aggressive action by the Federal Reserve caused the monetary base to skyrocket.

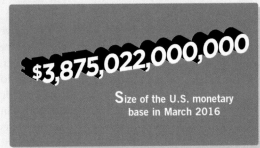

$3,875,022,000,000

Size of the U.S. monetary base in March 2016

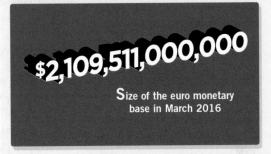

$2,109,511,000,000

Size of the euro monetary base in March 2016

Bank failures were a major problem during the Great Depression in the 1930s, during the savings and loan crisis of the 1980s, and again during the most recent financial crisis. In fact, more banks failed in 2010 and 2011 than during the 40-year period from 1940 to 1979.

Bank Failures:
- 1934–1939*: 312
- 1940–1949: 99
- 1950–1959: 28
- 1960–1969: 44
- 1970–1979: 79
- 1980–1989: 2,036
- 1990–1999: 925
- 2000–2009: 210
- 2010–2016*: 351

* bar represents a partial decade

Robert Giroux/Getty Images

In 2008 Washington Mutual became the largest bank to fail in U.S. history.

Year	FDIC Insured Limit
1934	$2,500
1935	$5,000
1950	$10,000
1966	$15,000
1969	$20,000
1974	$40,000
1980	$100,000
2008	$250,000

Zhang Jun/Corbis

Individual bank accounts are protected against bank failure by the Federal Deposit Insurance Corporation (FDIC). No FDIC insured deposit has ever been lost in its history.

The Federal Reserve intervened heavily during the 2008 financial crisis by increasing its purchases of underperforming assets from struggling banks. By doing so, the Fed altered its balance sheet in both its overall size and composition of assets.

2005
Other Assets 11%
U.S. Treasuries 89%
$847 billion

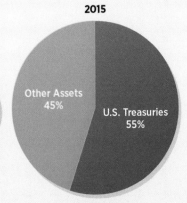

2015
Other Assets 45%
U.S. Treasuries 55%
$4,489 billion

When consumers are not eager to spend, businesses suffer. Business owners develop a much bleaker view of the economy and reduce investment. Businesses may even cut jobs, jobs that are important for economic recovery.

But this wasn't the entire story. Financial institutions during this time also lacked a willingness to lend to individuals and businesses that actually wanted to spend and invest. Why weren't the banks eager to lend? And why did the lack of lending slow the economic recovery?

The answer is surprisingly similar to the situation of the villager seeking a small loan. When the financial industry was jolted by massive losses in the aftermath of the housing and construction collapse, many banks failed while others barely survived or required government bailouts. The scare faced by banks led to a severe tightening in lending practices (which, ironically, is the type of prudent lending that might have prevented the financial crisis to begin with). The unwillingness of banks to lend money prolonged the period of time necessary for economic recovery.

In times when individuals and businesses are unwilling to spend and banks unwilling to lend, people begin to look elsewhere for help. For the small village, it was the emergence of the microloan organizations. For the U.S. economy, people turned to the government to take action.

The Federal Reserve (or Fed), the central bank of the United States, has extensive power in controlling the supply of money and interest rates, key elements in its arsenal of tools to jumpstart the economy when markets fail to do so on their own. After the 2007–2009 recession, the Fed took dramatic steps to make borrowing less expensive for consumers and homeowners, and to provide banks with more capital and the confidence to lend to qualified borrowers.

This chapter takes a detailed look at the process by which banks go about creating money, as if out of thin air, by accepting deposits by savers and channeling these funds to borrowers.

We then study in more detail the role of the Federal Reserve, the guarantor of our money and our financial system. We will look at the history of the Fed, what it does with our money, and why it is called "the lender of last resort." Lastly, we analyze the policies and tools the Fed can use to influence the money supply and interest rates.

HOW BANKS CREATE MONEY

When most people think of money being created, the typical images conjured up are of large machines at government institutions printing sheets of crisp new banknotes or a large mint hammering out shiny new coins. Although this is indeed money creation in the literal sense, in reality currency represents less than half of the money supply, as we saw in the previous chapter.

Most money that we use every day does not involve cash and coins, but rather a sophisticated system of electronic debits and credits to our bank accounts. For example, unless one works primarily for cash tips or runs a small business where most purchases are paid for in cash, most of us will receive either a physical paycheck or a direct deposit of our wages into our bank accounts. Similarly, when we make purchases, most of us might use a debit or a credit card.

Given that most transactions today do not involve cash, the idea of *creating money* takes on an additional meaning, one in which banks play a very important role in its process.

Creating Money as if Out of Thin Air

Suppose that you run a small tutoring service helping students at your school succeed in (or at least pass) their economics courses. Some of your clients pay you with a personal check at the end of their session, while others give you cash. Let's assume that this month, you received a total of $500 in checks, which you deposit into your checking account, and $500 in cash, which you keep in your safe at home. Your goal is to save as much of your tutoring earnings as possible in order to buy a new car. Aside from the potential forgone interest earnings and the temptation to spend the cash, does it really matter whether you put the cash in the bank or not?

To you, it doesn't. If you need the money, you could just as easily go to an ATM to withdraw the cash as it is to take the cash out of your safe. But for the economy, there is in fact an important difference. The $500 you hold in cash is available to you—and only you—to use. However, the $500 in checks you had deposited in your bank account is money that *others* can use until you eventually need it. How is it that other people can use your money and yet this money is still available for you to take out when you need it?

Banks hold deposits from many customers at one time, and only a small portion is withdrawn on any given day, which the banks service using the reserves they keep on hand. The rest is lent out to borrowers who pay interest to the bank, part of which is then used to pay interest on the deposits the bank holds. The deposits and lending that occur in a bank start the money creation process.

To illustrate the power of the money creation process, suppose you decide to take your $500 in cash and deposit it into your checking account. Let's analyze how the bank uses this money using a simplified balance sheet comparing a bank's assets (money the bank claims) and liabilities (money the bank owes) called a T-account. Liabilities are shown on the right side of the T-account. When you deposit money into the bank, it becomes a liability for the bank—the bank owes you this money. To balance out this liability, however, the bank now has an asset consisting of the cash from your deposit. Assets are shown on the left side of the T-account.

The following T-account shows an increase in the bank's assets by $500 (the cash that you deposit that the bank now holds). On the right side, the bank's liabilities increase by $500 because it must give back the $500 when you ask for it.

T-ACCOUNT AFTER INITIAL CASH DEPOSIT	
Assets	**Liabilities**
+$500 (cash)	+$500 (increase in your checking account balance)

It is important to note that based on this initial transaction, no new money has been created in the economy. Why? Cash and demand deposits (checking accounts) are both components of the money supply measured as M1. By taking cash and converting it into a checkable deposit, there is now $500 less cash in circulation, but $500 more in checkable deposits, for a net change in M1 of 0.

But the process is just beginning. Now that the bank has additional reserves, it can lend some of this money to someone else. Suppose another customer at the same bank, Jenna, is running low on cash and needs to take out a small loan of $300 to cover bills that are coming up at the end of the month. How would the bank handle this?

The bank would create a $300 loan for Jenna (which becomes an asset to the bank), and add $300 to Jenna's checking account for her to use when needed. The following shows the new T-account for the bank.

T-ACCOUNT AFTER LOAN TO JENNA	
Assets	**Liabilities**
+$500 (cash)	+$500 (increase in your checking account)
+$300 (loan to Jenna)	+$300 (increase in Jenna's checking account)

After the loan to Jenna is made, the total amount of checkable deposits has now increased by $800 based on the initial $500 cash deposit. In other words, the bank has *created* $300 in money, as if out of thin air, simply by making a loan to Jenna. And the process doesn't stop there. When Jenna writes a check to the vet for her cat's annual checkup, her vet deposits the check into her bank, which allows that bank to start another round of lending and money creation.

The obvious question would now be—Couldn't banks just keep making infinite amounts of loans? The answer is that the bank needs to have enough funds in place should you, Jenna, or the vet decide to make a withdrawal to pay bills or make purchases. Thus, a bank's ability to make loans is limited to a certain percentage of its total customer deposits. In other words, a bank must keep some reserves (such as cash) on hand to cover day-to-day withdrawals. The level of reserves a bank holds as a percentage of total deposits is called its **reserve ratio.** Further, the government requires that banks maintain a minimum level of reserves called the **reserve requirement.**

In our example, the reserve ratio is calculated by reserves/total deposits, which in this case is $500/($500 + $300) = 62.5%. Because most reserve requirements are much lower than this percentage, this bank is considered highly liquid, and may continue to make more loans using your initial cash deposit until the reserve ratio drops down toward its reserve requirement.

Up until now, we have assumed that all loans and deposits occurred at the same bank, but this need not be true. In fact, most money transactions in our economy take place between banks. But the way in which we analyzed loans and deposits and how that leads to money being created does not change. Our example above describes the process of a fractional reserve banking system.

Fractional Reserve Banking System

Banks loan money for consumer purchases and business investments. Assume that you deposit $1,000 into your checking account and the bank then loans this $1,000 to a local business to purchase some machinery. If you were to go to the bank the next day and ask to withdraw your funds, how would the bank pay you? The bank could not pay you if you were its only customer. Banks, however, have many customers, and the chance that all these customers would want to withdraw their money on the same day is small.

Such "runs on the bank" are rare, normally occurring only when banks or a country's currency are in trouble. In the United States, the Federal Deposit Insurance Corporation (FDIC) protects bank deposits (up to $250,000 per account) from bank failure. When a bank gets into financial trouble, the FDIC typically arranges for another (healthy) bank to take over the failing bank, resulting in virtually no interruption of services to the bank's customers. The bank takeover usually occurs late on a Friday and the bank reopens on Monday morning under a new name. Because most accounts are insured, it is business as usual on Monday.

It was the possibility of bank runs that led to the **fractional reserve banking system.** When someone deposits money into a bank account, the bank is required to hold part of this deposit in its vault as cash, or else in an account with the regional Federal Reserve Bank. We will learn more about the Federal Reserve System later in this chapter, but for the moment, let us continue to concentrate on how fractional reserve banking permits banks to create money.

The Money Creation Process Banks create money by lending some or all of their **excess reserves,** or reserves above the reserve requirement. When money is loaned out, it eventually is deposited back into the original bank or some other bank. The bank will again hold some of these new deposits as reserves, loaning out the rest. The whole process continues until the entire initial deposit is held as reserves somewhere in the banking system.

Assume that the Federal Reserve sets the reserve requirement at 20%. This means that banks must hold 20% of each deposit as reserves, whether in their vaults or in accounts with

---

reserve ratio The percentage of a bank's total deposits that are held in reserves, either as cash in the vault or as deposits at the regional Federal Reserve Bank.

reserve requirement The required ratio of funds that commercial banks and other depository institutions must hold in reserve against deposits.

fractional reserve banking system Describes a banking system in which a portion of bank deposits are held as vault cash or in an account with the regional Federal Reserve Bank, while the rest of the deposits are loaned out to generate the money creation process.

excess reserves Reserves held by banks above the legally required amount.

the regional Federal Reserve Bank. Now assume that you take $1,000 out of your personal safe at home and take it to Bank A. Bank A puts 20% of your $1,000 into its vault as reserves and loans out the rest. Its T-account balance sheet now reads:

BANK A	
Assets	**Liabilities**
Reserves +$200	Deposits +$1,000
Loans +$800	

As the balance sheet indicates, your $1,000 deposit is now a liability for Bank A. But the bank also has new assets, split between reserves and loans. In each of the transactions that follow, we assume banks become fully *loaned-up,* loaning out all they can and keeping in reserves only the amount required by law.

Assume that Bank A loans out the $800 it has in excess funds to a local gas station, and assume that this money is deposited into Bank B. Bank B's balance sheet now reads:

BANK B	
Assets	**Liabilities**
Reserves +$160	Deposits +$800
Loans +$640	

Bank B, in other words, has new deposits totaling $800. Of this, the bank must put $160 into reserves; the remaining $640 it loans out to a local winery. The winery deposits these funds into its bank, Bank C. This bank's balance sheet shows:

BANK C	
Assets	**Liabilities**
Reserves +$128	Deposits +$640
Loans +$512	

Summing up the balance sheets of the three banks shows that total reserves have grown to $488 ($200 + $160 + $128), loans have reached $1,952 ($800 + $640 + $512), and total deposits are $2,440 ($1,000 + $800 + $640). Your original $1,000 new deposit has caused the money supply to grow.

BANK A, B, C	
Assets	**Liabilities**
Reserves +$488	Deposits +$2,440
Loans +$1,952	

This process continues until the entire $1,000 of the original deposit has been placed in reserves, thus raising total reserves by $1,000. By this point, all the banks together will have loaned out a total of $4,000. A summary balance sheet for all banks reads:

ALL BANKS	
Assets	**Liabilities**
Reserves +$1,000	Deposits +$5,000
Loans +$4,000	

Notice what has happened. Keeping in mind that demand deposits form part of the money supply, your original deposit of $1,000—cash that was injected into the banking system—has turned into $5,000 in deposits, a $4,000 increase in the money supply. Bank reserves, in other words, have gone up by your initial deposit, but beyond this, an added $4,000 has been created. And this was made possible because banks were allowed to loan part of your deposit to consumers and businesses.

The ability of banks to take an initial deposit of cash and turn it into loans and deposits many times over (5 times the initial deposit in our example) demonstrates the power of the banking system to create money. Moreover, the initial deposit of cash need not come from an individual; in fact, much of the money creation that occurs in the economy begins with deposits made by the government, as we will see later in this chapter.

 CHECKPOINT

HOW BANKS CREATE MONEY

- Money is created when banks make loans to customers, because these funds are eventually deposited into other banks as checkable deposits.
- The fractional reserve system permits banks to create money through their ability to accept deposits and make loans.
- The reserve ratio is the fraction of total customer deposits held in reserves.
- The reserve requirement is the minimum reserve ratio banks must follow.
- A T-account is a simplified bank balance sheet showing assets (money banks lay claim to) and liabilities (money banks owe).

QUESTIONS: Suppose that you go to your bank and withdraw $1,000 from your checking account to spend on your Spring Break vacation to the Caribbean. If the bank has plenty of cash to pay you without falling below its reserve requirement or changing the amount of loans it has, would the money supply M1 change? Would the money supply change if the bank had planned to loan out its excess reserves?

Answers to the Checkpoint questions can be found at the end of this chapter.

THE MONEY MULTIPLIER AND ITS LEAKAGES

We have just seen how banks create new money when they make loans using the deposits of their customers. As money gets deposited and loaned out from banks over and over, an initial amount of money can generate new deposits and loans many times over. Just how much money can an initial deposit actually create? We can use the money multiplier to find out.

Bank Reserves and the Money Multiplier

In theory, money creation can be infinite if banks loaned out 100% of all money deposited, and all loaned money found its way back into another bank following their business transactions. But this is highly unlikely due to several factors, the most important being reserves held by the bank.

Because all banks are required to hold a certain percentage of their deposits as reserves in their vault or at their regional Fed bank, the maximum amount of money that can be created is limited by the reserve requirement.

Given a bank's reserve requirement, the *potential* or *maximum* amount the money supply can increase (or decrease) when a dollar of new deposits enters (exits) the system is called the **money multiplier.** The money multiplier is defined as:

$$\text{Money Multiplier} = \frac{1}{\text{Reserve Requirement}}$$

> **money multiplier** A formula that measures the *potential* or *maximum* amount the money supply can increase (or decrease) when a dollar of new deposits enters (exits) the system and is defined as 1 divided by the reserve requirement.

Thus, if the reserve requirement is 20%, as in our example in the previous section, the money multiplier is $1/0.20 = 5$. Therefore, an initial deposit of $1,000 will create an additional $4,000 in money for a total of $5,000, a five-fold increase.

The money multiplier is important to economic policy because money can be initially deposited into the banking system in two ways. The first approach, described earlier, is a cash deposit made by a bank customer. The second approach occurs when the government injects new money into the banking system through the power it has to print money.

When the government "prints money," it does not mean it is printing banknotes and spending it at the mall. Instead, the government typically adds reserves electronically to banks in exchange for bonds and other assets. This money did not exist before the Fed created it by just a stroke of a computer key. When these funds are added to bank reserves, that in itself increases the money supply (unlike a customer's cash that is already counted in the money supply). Further, the effect is compounded by the money multiplier. The government therefore possesses tremendous power in influencing the money supply through its ability to print money and via the money multiplier.

But the ability of the government to expand the money supply is subjected to various factors preventing the full money multiplier from taking place. In other words, the money multiplier formula gives us the *potential* money multiplier. The actual money multiplier will be smaller because of leakages from the banking system. How much smaller?

Money Leakages

The potential money multiplier and the actual money multiplier are rarely the same because of money **leakages.** A leakage is money that leaves the money creation process of deposits and loans due to an action taken by a bank, an individual, a business, or a foreign entity.

> **leakages** A reduction in the amount of money that is used for lending that reduces the money multiplier. It is caused by banks choosing to hold excess reserves and from individuals, businesses, and foreigners choosing to hold more cash.

Bank Leakages Banks are in the business of making loans. If they don't, they likely will not stay in business for long, especially if all they do is accept deposits and pay interest on those deposits. For any bank, profits come from the interest charged on loans made to borrowers. For this reason, it is generally presumed that banks will be *loaned-up*, or maximize the amount of loans they can make given the reserve requirement.

However, many banks choose not to be loaned-up. Instead, banks hold excess reserves, or reserves above the legally required amount. Why would a bank choose not to loan out the maximum amount of money allowed?

The lessons from the last financial crisis point to the answer. The recession caused many loan defaults and foreclosures as workers were laid off or faced wage cuts. Whenever a borrower defaults on a loan, the amount of that loan is removed (written off) from the bank's assets; however, the bank still owes the people whose deposits made those funds available. Banks absorb these losses through the profits they earn from charging interest to those who

solvency crisis A situation when a bank's liabilities exceed its assets.

pay back their loans. If a large number of borrowers default on their loans, the bank risks a **solvency crisis,** when its liabilities exceed its assets. This means that the bank owes more than what is owed to it, increasing the likelihood of bankruptcy.

Returning to our earlier example, suppose that Jenna used her $300 loan to pay off her bills (transferring money from her account to her creditor's account) but then defaults on her loan. The bank's balance sheet would now read:

Assets	Liabilities
+$500 (cash)	+$500 (increase in your checking account)
+$300 (loan to Jenna)	+$300 (increase in Jenna's creditor's account)
−$300 (Jenna's default)	−$300 (bank equity)

The difference between assets and liabilities is a bank's equity, or value that is shared by the bank's shareholders. Although equity is not a liability, it appears in the liabilities column because ultimately any gains are distributed to shareholders like a liability. When liabilities exceed assets, as in the case above, the bank has negative equity (shown as −$300 on the right-hand side of the T-account). When this occurs, the bank is insolvent; in other words, it's broke.

To reduce the risk of a solvency problem leading to bankruptcy, banks often hold excess reserves during tough economic times to ensure that they have the ability to absorb a higher rate of defaults. Further, banks also choose to be more cautious about to whom they lend money, as they did following the last financial crisis, which led to a smaller money multiplier.

When banks choose not to loan all of their excess reserves, the actual money multiplier is reduced because the reduction in loans recirculates less money back through the banking system.

As we saw in the chapter opener, the willingness of banks to lend generates a powerful effect on the economy. We now know that this is due to the money multiplier. However, the lack of lending creates the opposite effect, which makes bank leakages an extremely important obstacle to economic growth.

Leakages by Individuals and Businesses Earlier in the chapter, we saw how holding cash reduces the ability of banks to create money. Why would people choose to hold more cash?

One factor might be the interest rate the bank pays on deposits. If interest rates paid on savings and checking accounts at the bank are near 0, as they has been for much of the past decade, one might choose to hold more savings in cash out of convenience, or make fewer trips to the bank by making larger withdrawals from an ATM. Another factor might be a general rise in fear about the financial system. Despite the existence of the FDIC, when banks are in trouble, people begin to believe that their money is less safe in banks and start to hold more cash.

When individuals choose to keep money in cash rather than deposit it in a bank, a leakage in the money supply occurs because that money is not available to be loaned to someone else. The cycle of lending and saving that would be generated from that money comes to a halt, and the actual money multiplier is reduced.

Individuals are not the only ones to hold cash. Most businesses conduct a portion of their transactions using cash. Therefore, at any one time, a business will be holding a certain fraction of its money in cash rather than in a bank. The percentage of cash holdings varies by business, but regardless represents a leakage in the money supply. As businesses hold more cash, as do individuals, this diminishes their deposits, thus reducing the actual money multiplier.

Eric Chiang

Got jars of coins? Coins represent a cash leakage. Businesses such as Coinstar convert coins into banknotes or gift cards that are more likely to be spent, helping to bring money back into the banking system.

The Effect of Foreign Currency Holdings Most Americans are accustomed to using debit and credit cards for daily transactions, reducing the need to hold cash. Yet, surprisingly, the U.S. government continues to print billions of new U.S. dollars each year. If Americans generally are holding smaller amounts of cash, who then is holding all of these dollars?

The answer is foreign consumers, businesses, and governments. Because of the relative stability of the U.S. dollar, many countries hold U.S. dollars in reserves in order to provide support to their own currencies. Some countries, such as El Salvador and Ecuador, have abandoned their own currency altogether, choosing to use the U.S. dollar as their only legal form of currency. The prominent role that the U.S. dollar plays as the world's most popular reserve currency causes the majority of U.S. dollars (about two-thirds, in fact) to be held outside of the United States. Because of the sheer volume of U.S. currency being held as cash throughout the world, this has the effect of reducing the actual money multiplier relative to its potential. But keep in mind that this is not necessarily a bad thing. A popular currency allows the U.S. government to print more without worrying about a significant decrease in its value relative to other currencies.

What Is the Actual Money Multiplier in the Economy?

Given the leakages described earlier, economists have studied and estimated the actual value of the money multiplier that ultimately influences economic growth. What they have found is that leakages in the U.S. economy tend to be large, due to significant cash holdings by foreigners and banks' unwillingness to lend when the perceived risks of default are high.

To study the effect of leakages on the actual money multiplier, it is useful to modify our original money multiplier formula (1/Reserve Requirement) by adding the bank and cash leakages to the formula to create a *leakage-adjusted money multiplier*.

The Rise and Fall of the Famous (and Infamous) Swiss Bank Account

How did Switzerland become the preferred destination of the world's offshore funds and how is that changing today?

LOOK Die Bildagentur der Fotografen GmbH/Alamy

For centuries, people around the world, including the rich and famous as well as the powerful and infamous, looked to Switzerland to deposit their wealth. Swiss banks today remain the world's largest holder of offshore funds (holding about one-third of the world's total), which are deposits of money by people outside of their country of citizenship. But times are changing, as banks in other countries, especially in Hong Kong and Singapore, experience vastly higher growth rates in offshore deposits.

What made Swiss banks so popular with foreigners, and how is that changing today?

The popularity of Swiss banking derives largely from its secrecy laws, which date back several centuries. The ability of people to store money (regardless of where that money came from) without scrutiny or risk of disclosure made Swiss banks a magnet for the world's wealthy. These secrecy laws were further cemented with the Swiss Banking Act of 1934 that made it a criminal offense for banks to disclose names of account holders. It also led to the development of *numbered bank accounts* in which people accessed their accounts using code words instead of their names. Moreover, Switzerland is a centrally located, neutral nation that hasn't been invaded in centuries, adding confidence to those seeking a safe place to store money.

But times have changed. Worldwide efforts to crack down on tax evaders using Swiss bank accounts to hide profits and criminal organizations hiding stolen money led to changes in how Swiss banks do business. Although Swiss banks still have strict secrecy laws, most no longer accept hidden profits or ill-gotten gains on behalf of individuals or corporations. Moreover, Swiss banks with branches in other countries are subjected to those countries' banking laws. This has made life more difficult for the world's criminals and tax evaders.

Today, banks remain a prominent fixture in Swiss cities such as Geneva and Zurich, and an important source of economic activity for the country as a whole. But how Swiss banks operate today resembles how most banks in the world operate: by accepting deposits and making loans, and creating money in the process.

GO TO **LaunchPad** TO PRACTICE THE ECONOMIC CONCEPTS IN THIS STORY

A leakage-adjusted money multiplier takes into account the required reserve requirement along with excess reserves held by banks and cash held by individuals, businesses, and foreigners. Higher values of these components translate to greater leakages and therefore a lower actual money multiplier.

For example, suppose that the reserve requirement is 20%, but the existence of leakages doubles the percentage held in reserves and cash to 40%. These money leakages cause the money multiplier to drop from 5 (1/0.20) to 2.5 (1/0.40), a significant reduction in money creation in the economy.

Empirical data have shown that money leakages tend to increase during economic recessions, when banks are more reluctant to lend and people are more likely to hold cash. We will see in the next chapter that the resulting decrease in the money multiplier adds to the challenges of using monetary policy to pull the economy out of a recession.

During the 2007–2009 recession, the money multiplier fell precipitously from 1.7 to less than 1. A money multiplier of less than 1 means that fewer loans were being made than the new money introduced into the economy. This is very important because actions by the government to increase the money supply result in less bang for the buck when the money multiplier is smaller. Such an effect renders monetary policy much more challenging.

The fact that banks can create money by making loans represents a great deal of power. This power is mitigated by leakages and their effect on the actual money multiplier. Governments can encourage this money creation process by injecting banks with new money. But how do governments go about doing this? Once we understand how the government, meaning the Fed, creates money, we can then go on in the next chapter to discuss the short- and long-run results of this monetary policy.

The institution charged with overseeing the money supply and creating money out of thin air is the Federal Reserve System. Let us turn to a brief survey of the Federal Reserve System. Here, we consider how it is organized, what purposes it serves, and what functions it has. The next chapter takes a closer look at the Fed in action.

 CHECKPOINT

THE MONEY MULTIPLIER AND ITS LEAKAGES

- The potential money multiplier is equal to 1 divided by the reserve requirement. This is the maximum value for the multiplier.

- Money leakages are caused by banks choosing to hold excess reserves and by individuals, businesses, and foreigners holding a portion of their funds in cash rather than depositing it in a bank. Leakages reduce the money multiplier.

- The leakage-adjusted money multiplier takes leakages into account and provides a more realistic estimate of the money multiplier in the economy.

QUESTIONS: In the following table, calculate the potential money multiplier for each of the following reserve requirements if banks fully loan out all of their excess reserves. If banks were not required to hold any reserves, how big could the money multiplier potentially be? Is this a realistic money multiplier? Why or why not?

Reserve Requirement	Potential Money Multiplier
50%	
33.3%	
25%	
20%	
10%	

Answers to the Checkpoint questions can be found at the end of this chapter.

THE FEDERAL RESERVE SYSTEM

The **Federal Reserve System** is the central bank of the United States. It controls an immense power to create money in the economy.

Federal Reserve System The central bank of the United States.

Early in U.S. history, banks were private and chartered by the states. In the 1800s and early 1900s, bank panics were common. After an unusually severe banking crisis in 1907, Congress established the National Monetary Commission. This commission proposed one central bank with sweeping powers. But a powerful national bank became a political issue in the elections of 1912, and the commission's proposals gave way to a compromise that is today's Federal Reserve System.

The Federal Reserve Act of 1913 was a compromise between competing proposals for a huge central bank and for no central bank at all. The act declared that the Fed is "to provide for the establishment of Federal Reserve Banks, to furnish an elastic currency, to afford means of rediscounting commercial paper, to establish a more effective supervision of banking in the United States, and for other purposes."

Since 1913, other acts have further clarified and supplemented the original act, expanding the Fed's mission. These acts include the Employment Act of 1946, the International Banking Act of 1978, the Full Employment and Balanced Growth Act of 1978, the Depository Institutions Deregulation and Monetary Control Act of 1980, and the Federal Deposit Insurance Corporation Improvement Act of 1991.

The original Federal Reserve Act, the Employment Act of 1946, and the Full Employment and Balanced Growth Act of 1978 all mandate national economic objectives. These acts require the Fed to promote economic growth accompanied by full employment, stable prices, and moderate long-term interest rates. As we will see in the next chapter, meeting all of these objectives at once has often proved difficult.

The Federal Reserve is considered to be an independent central bank, in that its actions are not subject to executive branch control. The entire Federal Reserve System is, however, subject to oversight from Congress. The Constitution gives Congress the power to coin money and set its value, and the Federal Reserve Act delegated this power to the Fed, subject to congressional oversight. Though several presidents have disagreed with Fed policy over the years, the Fed has always managed to maintain its independence from the executive branch.

Experience in this country and abroad suggests that independent central banks are better at fighting inflation than are politically controlled banks. The main reason is that an independent central bank is less likely to be influenced by short-term political pressures to engage in excessive expansionary monetary policy to hasten a recovery.

The Structure of the Federal Reserve

The Federal Reserve Act of 1913 passed by Congress led to the establishment of *regional* banks governed by a central authority. The intent was to provide the Fed with a broad perspective on the economy, with the regional Federal Reserve Banks contributing economic analysis from all parts of the nation, while still investing a central authority with the power to carry out a national monetary policy.

The Fed is composed of a central governing agency, the Board of Governors, located in Washington, D.C., and twelve regional Federal Reserve Banks in major cities around the nation. Figure 1 shows the twelve Fed districts and their bank locations.

The Board of Governors The Fed's Board of Governors consists of seven members who are appointed by the president and confirmed by the Senate. Board members serve terms of 14 years, after which they cannot be reappointed. Appointments to the Board are staggered such that one term expires on January 31 of every even-numbered year. The Chair and the Vice Chair of the Board must already be Board members; they are appointed to their leadership positions by the president, subject to Senate confirmation, for terms of four years. The Chair and Vice Chair can be reappointed (without term limits) as long as they remain members of the Board of Governors. The Board of Governors' staff of nearly 2,000 helps the Fed carry out its responsibilities for monetary policy, and banking and consumer credit regulation.

FIGURE 1	REGIONAL FEDERAL RESERVE DISTRICTS

The twelve regional Federal Reserve districts and their bank locations.

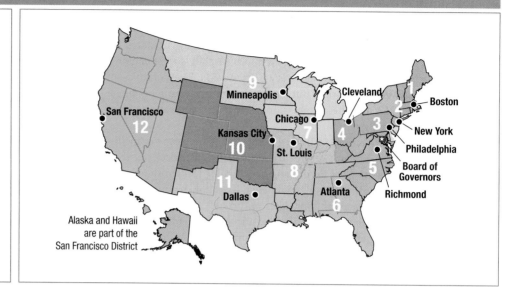

Alaska and Hawaii are part of the San Francisco District

Federal Reserve Banks Twelve Federal Reserve Banks and their branches perform a variety of functions, including providing a nationwide payments system, distributing coins and currency, regulating and supervising member banks, and serving as the banker for the U.S. Treasury. Table 1 lists all regional banks and their main locations. Each regional bank has a number and letter associated with it. If you look at your money, you will see that all U.S. currency bears the designation of the regional bank where it was first issued, as shown in Table 1.

Each regional bank also provides the Federal Reserve System and the Board of Governors with information on economic conditions in its home region. Eight times a year this information is compiled into a report—called the Beige Book—that details the economic conditions around the country. These reports are provided to the Board of Governors first,

TABLE 1	FEDERAL RESERVE REGIONAL BANKS	
Number	Bank	Letter
1	Boston	A
2	New York	B
3	Philadelphia	C
4	Cleveland	D
5	Richmond	E
6	Atlanta	F
7	Chicago	G
8	St. Louis	H
9	Minneapolis	I
10	Kansas City	J
11	Dallas	K
12	San Francisco	L

Eric Chiang

and later released to the public. The Board and the Federal Open Market Committee use the information the Beige Book contains to determine the course of the nation's monetary policy.

Federal Open Market Committee The **Federal Open Market Committee (FOMC)** oversees open market operations, the main tool of monetary policy. Open market operations involve the buying and selling of government securities. How these open market operations influence reserves available to banks and other thrift institutions will become clear shortly.

The FOMC is composed of the seven members of the Board of Governors and five of the twelve regional Federal Reserve Bank presidents. The president of the Federal Reserve Bank of New York is a permanent member because actual open market operations take place at the New York Fed. The other four members are appointed for rotating one-year terms. All regional presidents participate in FOMC deliberations, but only those serving on the committee vote. Traditionally, the Chair of the Board of Governors has also served as the Chair of the FOMC.

The Fed as Lender of Last Resort The essence of banking, as we have seen, is that banks take in short-term deposits (liabilities) and make long-term, often illiquid, loans (assets). This puts banks in the unique position of facing extraordinary withdrawals when people panic and all want their money at the same time. Banks typically do not have sufficient reserves to stem a full-fledged financial panic. They cannot turn these long-term loans into cash. During a panic, banks would be forced to dump the securities or loans onto the market at a deep discount (or "take a haircut" in modern parlance), potentially forcing them into insolvency. Lending to banks during financial panics—being a lender of last resort—is a principal reason for the existence of central banks.

The value of the Fed's ability to provide loans during a financial crisis stood out during the financial panic in late 2008. The Fed extended credit where none was available. As markets collapse during financial panics, banks become reluctant to lend out money to businesses and to other banks that need cash in an emergency. This is when the Fed steps in.

In just a few months, the Fed extended more than $2 trillion in loans to banks and other financial institutions, and by doing so changed the allocation of assets in its balance sheet in ways not seen since it was created in 1913. Specifically, instead of holding primarily government Treasury securities, the Fed began buying up large sums of risky mortgage-backed securities from banks struggling to sell them as investor confidence fell. By the end of 2008, the Fed held more bank assets than Treasury securities.

Had the Fed and its lender of last resort capability not been available, the 2007–2009 recession would have been much deeper and could possibly have resulted in another depression. The ability of the Fed to make loans and inject the banking system with new money allows the fractional banking process to work and prevents the economy from facing a much worse financial crisis.

> **Federal Open Market Committee (FOMC)** A twelve-member committee that is composed of members of the Board of Governors of the Fed and selected presidents of the regional Federal Reserve Banks. It oversees open market operations (the buying and selling of government securities), the main tool of monetary policy.

CHECKPOINT

THE FEDERAL RESERVE SYSTEM

- The Federal Reserve System is the central bank of the United States.
- The Federal Reserve is structured around twelve regional banks and a central governing agency, the Board of Governors.
- The Federal Open Market Committee (FOMC) oversees open market operations (the buying and selling of government securities) for the Federal Reserve.
- The Federal Reserve serves as the lender of last resort, stepping in to loan money to banks that are facing cash emergency shortages or other financial difficulties.

QUESTION: If a large portion of a bank's customers want their money back at the same time and other banks won't lend to it, what can the Federal Reserve do to prevent a run on the bank?

Answers to the Checkpoint questions can be found at the end of this chapter.

THE FEDERAL RESERVE AT WORK: TOOLS, TARGETS, AND POLICY LAGS

With an ability to alter the money supply, both directly and indirectly through the money multiplier, the Federal Reserve has remarkable powers to conduct monetary policy, its primary role. And because it acts independently of political parties, the Fed is able to set monetary policy with remarkable efficiency, especially compared to fiscal policy, which involves the ever common wrangling between political parties in Congress and the president. For this reason, monetary policy is often looked at as a way to provide quicker remedies to economic conditions facing the country.

But how is monetary policy actually carried out? Quite remarkably, the Federal Reserve uses just three primary tools for conducting monetary policy:

- **Reserve requirements**—The required ratio of funds that commercial banks and other depository institutions must hold in reserve against deposits.
- **The discount rate**—The interest rate the Federal Reserve charges commercial banks and other depository institutions to borrow reserves from a regional Federal Reserve Bank.
- **Open market operations**—The buying and selling on the open market of U.S. government securities, such as Treasury bills and bonds, to adjust reserves in the banking system.

Reserve Requirements

The Federal Reserve Act specifies that the Fed must establish reserve requirements for all banks and other depository institutions. As we have seen, this law gives rise to a fractional reserve system that enables banks to create new money, expanding demand deposits through loans. The potential expansion depends on the money multiplier, which in turn depends on the reserve requirement. By altering the reserve ratio, the Fed can alter reserves in the system and alter the supply of money in the economy.

Banks hold two types of reserves: required reserves and excess reserves above what they are required to hold. Roughly 15,000 depository institutions, ranging from banks to thrift institutions, are bound by the Fed's reserve requirements. Reserves are kept as vault cash or in accounts with the regional Federal Reserve Bank. These accounts not only help satisfy reserve requirements, but are also used to clear many financial transactions.

Banks are assessed a penalty if their accounts with the Fed are overdrawn at the end of the day. Given the unpredictability of the volume of transactions that may clear a bank's account on a given day, most banks choose to maintain excess reserves.

At the end of the day, banks and other depository institutions can loan one another reserves or trade reserves in the federal funds market. One bank's surplus of reserves can become loans to another institution, earning interest (the **federal funds rate**). A change in the federal funds rate reflects changes in the market demand and supply of excess reserves.

In 2008 the Fed changed its long-standing law of not paying interest on reserves. The new law allowed banks to earn interest on the reserves it deposits at the Fed. This law changed the incentives faced by banks by reducing the opportunity cost of choosing not to lend. In other words, in tough economic times, banks may choose to forgo making loans (especially risky ones) in favor of earning interest on their excess reserves deposited at the Fed. As we saw in the previous section, when banks hold more excess reserves, the money multiplier falls.

By raising or lowering the reserve requirement, the Fed can add reserves to the system or squeeze reserves from it, thereby altering the supply of money. Yet, changing the reserve requirement is almost like doing surgery with a bread knife; the impact is so massive and imprecise that the Fed rarely uses this tool.

federal funds rate The interest rate financial institutions charge each other for overnight loans used as reserves.

Discount Rate

The **discount rate** is the rate regional Federal Reserve Banks charge depository institutions for short-term loans to shore up their reserves. The discount window also serves as a backup source of liquidity for individual depository institutions.

The Fed extends discount rate credit to banks and other depository institutions typically for overnight balancing of reserves. The rate charged is roughly 0.5 percentage point higher than the FOMC's target federal funds rate. However, most banks avoid using the discount window out of fear that it might arouse suspicion by both their customers and by the Fed that they are facing financial trouble. Still, the Fed prefers that banks use the discount window when needed than to make imprudent decisions that could increase the risk of bankruptcy.

Although setting the discount rate and reserve requirement are both important tools used by the Fed, neither gives the Fed as much power to implement monetary policy as open market operations. Open market operations allow the Fed to alter the supply of money and system reserves by buying and selling government securities.

discount rate The interest rate the Federal Reserve charges commercial banks and other depository institutions to borrow reserves from a regional Federal Reserve Bank.

Open Market Operations

When one private financial institution buys a government security from another, funds are redistributed in the economy; the transaction does not change the amount of reserves in the economy. When the Fed buys a government security, however, it pays some private financial institution for this bond; therefore, it adds to aggregate reserves by putting new money into the financial system.

Open market operations are powerful because of the dollar-for-dollar change in reserves that comes from buying or selling government securities. When the FOMC buys a $100,000 bond, $100,000 of new reserves is instantly put into the banking system. These new reserves have the potential to expand the money supply as banks make loans.

Open market operations are the most important of the Fed's tools. When the Fed decides on a policy objective, the volume of bonds being traded in open market operations to achieve that objective can be staggering. With the bond market valued in the trillions, it requires billions of dollars in bond transactions in order for the FOMC to push the federal funds rate toward its target.

open market operations The buying and selling of U.S. government securities, such as Treasury bills and bonds, to adjust reserves in the banking system.

The Federal Funds Target The target federal funds rate is the Fed's primary approach to monetary policy. As we will see in the next chapter, targeting the federal funds rate through open market operations gives the Fed an ability to influence the price level and output in the economy, a very powerful effect. The FOMC meetings result in a decision on the target federal funds rate, which is announced at the end of the meeting. Keep in mind that the federal funds rate is not something that the Fed directly controls. Banks lend overnight reserves to each other in this market, and the forces of supply and demand set the interest rate.

The Fed uses open market operations to adjust reserves and thus change nominal interest rates with the goal of nudging the federal funds rate toward the Fed's target. When the Fed buys bonds, its demand raises the price of bonds, lowering nominal interest rates in the market. The opposite occurs when the Fed sells bonds and adds to the market supply of bonds for sale, lowering prices and raising the nominal interest rate. The Fed has actually been fairly good at keeping the federal funds rate near the target, as Figure 2 illustrates.

In summary, typically the Fed sets a target for the federal funds rate and then uses open market operations to manipulate reserves to alter the money supply. Changing the money supply alters market interest rates to bring the federal funds rate in line with the Fed's target. Open market purchases increase reserves, reducing the need for banks to borrow, lowering the federal funds rate, and vice versa for open market sales. The key thing to note here is that the Fed does not directly control the money supply. It proceeds indirectly, though it has been very successful in meeting its goals.

FIGURE 2	THE FEDERAL FUNDS RATE AND TARGET FEDERAL FUNDS RATE

In the last 25 years, the Fed has been very successful at hitting its federal funds target rate.

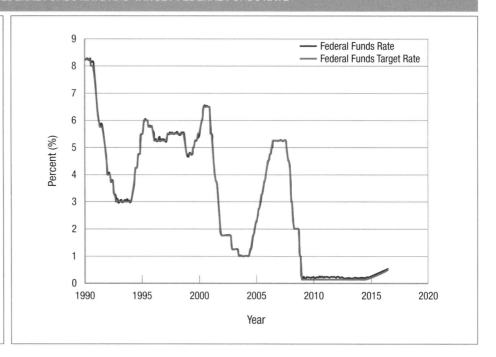

Monetary Policy Lags

Although the Fed has a remarkable ability to use tools that have important impacts on interest rates, bank reserves, and the money supply, they can still take time to have an effect on the economy. Like fiscal policy, monetary policy is subject to four major lags: information, recognition, decision, and implementation. The combination of these lags can make monetary policy difficult for the Fed. Not only does the Fed face a moving bull's-eye in terms of its economic targets, but often it can be difficult for the Fed to know when its own policies will take effect and what their effect will be.

Information Lags We discussed information lags when we discussed fiscal policy lags. Economic data are available only after a lag of one to three months. Therefore, when an economic event takes place, changes may ripple throughout the economy for up to three months before monetary authorities begin to see changes in their data. Many economic measures published by the government, moreover, are subject to future revision. It is not uncommon for these revisions to be so significant as to render the original number meaningless. Thus, it might take the Fed several quarters to identify a changing trend in prices or output clearly.

Recognition Lags Simply seeing a decline in a variable in one month or quarter does not necessarily mean that a change in policy is warranted. Data revisions upward and downward are common. In the normal course of events, for instance, unemployment rates can fluctuate by small amounts, as can GDP. A quarter-percent decline in the rate of growth of GDP does not necessarily signal the beginning of a recession, although it could. Nor does a quarter-percent increase in GDP mean that the economy has reached the bottom of a recession; double-dip recessions are always a possibility. Because of this recognition lag, policymakers are often unable to recognize problems when they first develop.

Decision Lags The Federal Reserve Board meets roughly on a monthly basis to determine broad economic policy. Therefore, once a problem is recognized, decisions are forthcoming. Decision lags for monetary policy are shorter than for fiscal policy. Once the Fed

ISSUE

What Can the Fed Do When Interest Rates Reach 0%?

At the height of the 2007–2009 recession, the Federal Reserve used aggressive expansionary policy to prevent a much more severe recession or even a depression. The Fed did so by reducing the federal funds rate target, the interest rate that influences almost all other interest rates in the economy. By December 2008 the Federal Reserve had lowered the federal funds rate target to essentially 0%. Yet, the economy was still struggling and needed additional help to prevent a deeper recession. But with interest rates already at 0%, what else could the Fed do?

The Fed developed new ways to expand the money supply without using its regular open market operations. First, it purchased poorly performing assets from banks, such as mortgage-backed securities, in an effort to remove these bad assets from bank balance sheets.

Second, the Fed reduced the difference between the federal funds target rate and the discount rate and used *term auction facilities* to encourage borrowing by banks that typically would not borrow from the Fed out of fear it would signal

that the bank was in trouble. In an effort to reduce this stigma, the Fed essentially auctioned money for banks to borrow, taking interest rate bids from banks. This tool allowed many banks to borrow money at rates lower than the discount rate, improving bank liquidity, and making it easier for banks to lend to individuals and businesses.

Then came the tool often considered to be the last resort to stimulating the economy, *quantitative easing*, or QE. With quantitative easing, the Fed purchased huge amounts of bank debt, mortgage-backed securities, and long-term Treasury notes, all with money it created electronically. Between 2008 and 2014, the Fed more than tripled the monetary base (currency in circulation plus bank reserves).

It is difficult to quantify the success of the Fed's efforts. Critics of the Fed's actions point to the fact that economic growth remained sluggish after the recession ended. But supporters of the Fed argue that had the Fed not taken these actions, the economy might have entered a depression.

In situations such as these, economists often wonder about the *counterfactual*, or what would have happened if the Fed hadn't engaged in these policies. The reality is that we may never know, because once a decision is made, it is not possible to determine what would have happened using another approach. But regardless of whether or not the Fed played a pivotal role in the economic recovery, there is no question that the Fed's power in controlling the money supply remains a very powerful tool that influences our lives in many ways.

makes a decision to, say, avert a recession, the FOMC can begin to implement that decision almost immediately. As Figure 2 illustrates, once the Fed decides on a federal funds target, nominal interest rates track that target in a hurry. In contrast, fiscal policy decisions typically require administrative proposals and then congressional action.

Implementation Lags Once the FOMC has decided on a policy, there is another lag associated with the reaction of banks and financial markets. Monetary policy affects bank reserves, interest rates, and decisions by businesses and households. As interest rates change, investment and buying decisions are altered, but often not with any great haste. Investment decisions hinge on more than just interest rate levels. Rules, regulations, permits, tax incentives, and future expectations (what Keynes called "animal spirits") all enter the decision-making process.

Economists estimate that the average lag for monetary policy is between a year and 18 months, with a range varying from a little over one quarter to slightly over two years. Using monetary policy to fine-tune the economy requires more than skill—some luck helps.

This chapter began with a discussion of how banks create money by lending excess reserves from their customer deposits or from the sale of bonds to the Federal Reserve. The power of the fractional banking system to generate money many times over allows the Fed to wield this power in several ways, mainly by targeting the federal funds rate using open market operations. The next chapter looks more deeply into how the Fed uses its monetary tools to balance its goals of keeping income growing and prices stable.

CHECKPOINT

THE FEDERAL RESERVE AT WORK: TOOLS, TARGETS, AND POLICY LAGS

- The Fed's tools include altering reserve requirements, changing the discount rate, and open market operations (the buying and selling of government securities).

- The Fed uses open market operations to keep the federal funds rate at target levels.

- The Fed's policies, as with fiscal policy, are subject to information, recognition, decision, and implementation lags. Unlike fiscal policy, the Fed's decision lags tend to be shorter because Fed policies are not subjected to lengthy legislative processes.

QUESTIONS: Of the three tools used by the Fed, open market operations are the most common. Why is the Fed more hesitant about adjusting the reserve requirement and the discount rate? What can go wrong?

Answers to the Checkpoint questions can be found at the end of this chapter.

chapter summary

Section 1 How Banks Create Money

23.1 Money is created when banks make loans that eventually get deposited back into the system, generating checkable deposits. Part of these deposits are held as new reserves while the rest is again loaned out, creating even more money as it gets deposited back into the system.

$100
$100 deposit

$90
90% loaned out

$10
10% reserve

$81
90% loaned out

$9
10% reserve

23.2 In a **fractional reserve banking system,** banks accept deposits and hold only a certain portion in reserves, loaning out the rest.

T-Accounts and Reserve Ratios

A T-account is a simple balance sheet showing a bank's assets (money the bank claims) on the left side and liabilities (money the bank owes) on the right side.

Assets	Liabilities
Cash reserves	Deposits by customers
Loans made	

A bank can continue to make loans as long as its **reserve ratio,** calculated as its reserves as a percentage of its total customer deposits, is greater than the **reserve requirement**.

Reserve Ratio = Reserves/Customer Deposits

Section 2 The Money Multiplier and Its Leakages

23.3 The **money multiplier** is the maximum amount the money supply can increase (or decrease) when a dollar of new deposits enters (or exits) the system.

Money Multiplier = 1/Reserve Requirement

Examples:
If the reserve requirement is 25%, the money multiplier = 1/0.25 = 4.

If the reserve requirement is 15%, the money multiplier = 1/0.15 = 6.67.

A **leakage-adjusted money multiplier** takes into account the excess reserves and cash holdings that reduce the loans made and therefore reduces the actual money multiplier.

23.4 The actual money multiplier found in the economy is often lower than the potential money multiplier due to **leakages** caused by:

1. Banks choosing to hold excess reserves by not lending out the maximum amount allowed.

2. Individuals and businesses holding money in cash rather than in a bank.

3. Foreign consumers, businesses, and governments holding cash in reserves or as a medium of exchange.

Stashing cash under the mattress creates a leakage in the money supply because this money cannot be loaned out to another borrower.

2/Jose Luis Pelaez/Corbis

Section 3 The Federal Reserve System

Hisham Ibrahim/Corbis

23.6 The Fed is composed of a seven-member Board of Governors and twelve regional Federal Reserve Banks. The regional banks and their branches conduct the following services:

1. Provide a nationwide payments system.
2. Distribute coins and currency.
3. Regulate and supervise member banks.
4. Serve as the banker for the U.S. Treasury.

23.5 The **Federal Reserve System** is the central bank of the United States. It was established by the Federal Reserve Act of 1913 and is required by law to promote economic growth accompanied by full employment, stable prices, and moderate long-term interest rates.

The Federal Reserve Is the Guarantor of the Financial System

Its actions are not subject to executive branch oversight, although the entire Federal Reserve System is subject to oversight by Congress.

Bank Presidents •
Boards of Directors •
Advisory Councils •
Functions •

Board of Governors

Federal Open Market Committee

Federal Reserve Banks

Member Banks

Other Depository Institutions

American People

Information from the Federal Reserve's website on 'Fed 101'.

Section 4 The Federal Reserve at Work: Tools, Targets, and Policy Lags

23.7 The Fed uses three major tools to conduct monetary policy:

1. **Reserve requirements:** Establishing the minimum level of reserves banks must hold.
2. **Discount rate:** Setting the interest rate at which banks can borrow from the Fed.
3. **Open market operations:** Buying and selling government securities to target the federal funds rate.

23.8 The Fed targets the **federal funds rate,** an interest rate that influences nearly all other interest rates. The federal funds rate was near 0% from 2008 to 2015.

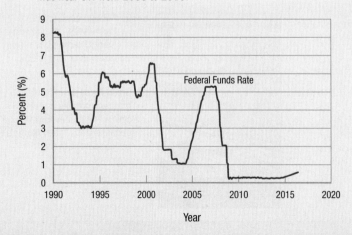

23.9 Monetary policy is subject to lags:

- **Information lag:** The time it takes for economic data to become available.
- **Recognition lag:** The time before a trend in the data is certain enough to warrant a change in policy.
- **Decision lag:** The time it takes for the Federal Reserve Board to meet and make policy decisions.
- **Implementation lag:** The time it takes for banks and financial markets to react to the policy change.

Compared to fiscal policy lags, monetary policy lags, especially decision lags, are often shorter because decisions do not require the cooperation of Congress and the president.

KEY CONCEPTS

reserve ratio, p. 616
reserve requirement, p. 616
fractional reserve banking system,
    p. 616
excess reserves, p. 616
money multiplier, p. 619

leakages, p. 619
solvency crisis, p. 620
Federal Reserve System, p. 623
Federal Open Market Committee
    (FOMC), p. 625

federal funds rate, p. 626
discount rate, p. 627
open market operations, p. 627

QUESTIONS AND PROBLEMS

Check Your Understanding

1. Describe the role required reserves play in determining how much money the banking system creates.

2. Why are checking accounts (demand deposits) considered a liability to the bank?

3. Why do leakages reduce the money multiplier from its potential?

4. What is the most common tool used by the Federal Reserve to conduct monetary policy and how does it affect interest rates?

5. For what type of borrowing do the federal funds rate and the discount rate apply? Which rate is used in more transactions in the United States?

6. Why are monetary policy lags generally shorter than fiscal policy lags?

Apply the Concepts

7. The U.S. government produces billions of dollars in banknotes and coins for use in everyday transactions. Explain why currency alone does not represent money creation.

8. During an economic boom, banks tend to increase their willingness to lend. How does this trend influence the actual money multiplier?

9. The Federal Deposit Insurance Corporation (FDIC) insures individual bank accounts up to $250,000 per account. Does the existence of this insurance eliminate the need for reserve requirements? Does it essentially prevent "runs" on banks?

10. Many central banks in the world are independent in the sense that they are partially isolated from short-run political considerations and pressures. How is this independence attained? How important is this independence to policymaking at the Federal Reserve?

11. Alan Greenspan, a former Fed Chair, noted that "the Federal Reserve has to be independent in its actions and as an institution, because if Federal Reserve independence is in any way compromised, it undercuts our capability of protecting the value of the currency in society." What is so important about protecting the value of the currency? How does Fed independence help?

12. The reserve requirement sets the required percentage of vault cash plus deposits with the regional Federal Reserve Banks that banks must keep for their deposits. Many banks have widespread branches and ATMs. Would the existence of branches and ATMs affect the level of excess reserves (above those required) that banks hold? Why or why not? What would be the effect on the actual money multiplier?

In the News

13. Eric Keetch offered an interesting anecdote in the *Financial Times* (August 12, 2009):

> *In a sleepy European holiday resort town in a depressed economy and therefore no visitors, there is great excitement when a wealthy Russian guest appears in the local hotel reception, announces that he intends to stay for an extended period and places a €100 note on the counter as surety while he demands to be shown the available rooms.*

While he is being shown the room, the hotelier takes the €100 note round to his butcher, who is pressing for payment.

The butcher in turn pays his wholesaler who, in turn, pays his farmer supplier.

The farmer takes the note round to his favorite "good time girl" to whom he owes €100 for services rendered. She, in turn, rushes round to the hotel to settle her bill for rooms provided on credit.

In the meantime, the Russian returns to the lobby, announces that no rooms are satisfactory, takes back his €100 note and leaves, never to be seen again.

No new money has been introduced into the local economy, but everyone's debts have been settled.

What's going on here? In the end, no new money was introduced into the town, but all debts were paid. Is the money multiplier infinite? How do you explain what has happened? Did local GDP increase as a result of all debts being paid?

14. Following the March 16, 2016, FOMC meeting, Fed Chair Janet Yellen announced that the federal funds rate would remain steady (around 0.5%) through the end of the year, essentially delaying the goal of raising interest rates to the long-run target of 2% to 3% for another two years. How might this announcement affect the lives of ordinary individuals, and what impact might this have on the economy?

Solving Problems

WORK IT OUT   **LaunchPad** | interactive activity

15. Assume that First Purity Bank begins with the balance sheet below and is fully loaned-up. Answer the questions that follow.

First Purity Bank	
Assets	**Liabilities**
Reserves +$700,000	Deposits +$2,000,000
Loans +$1,300,000	

a. What is the reserve requirement equal to?

b. If the bank receives a new deposit of $1 million and the bank wants to remain fully loaned-up, how much of this new deposit will the bank loan out?

c. What is the potential money multiplier equal to in this case?

d. When the new deposit to First Purity Bank works itself through the entire banking system (assume all banks keep fully loaned-up), by how much will total deposits, total loans, and total reserves increase?

16. Suppose that the leakage-adjusted money multiplier can be calculated using a modification of our money multiplier formula:

1/(Reserve Requirement + Excess Reserves + Cash Holdings)

where each component in the denominator is expressed as a percentage.

Suppose that the reserve requirement is 25%, but banks, on average, hold an additional 10% of their deposits as excess reserves. Further, assume that individuals and businesses choose to hold 15% of their borrowed funds in cash. Compare the potential money multiplier with the leakage-adjusted money multiplier. Does the existence of leakages make a significant impact on the ability to conduct monetary policy? Explain why or why not.

USING THE NUMBERS

17. According to By the Numbers, during which decade did the greatest number of U.S. banks fail? During which decade did the second most number of U.S. banks fail?

18. According to By the Numbers, about how much in U.S. Treasuries did the Federal Reserve have on its balance sheet in 2005 and 2015? (*Hint:* Use the percentages given in each pie to calculate the values.) If the amount of U.S. Treasuries held by the Fed increased over the ten years, why did the percentage drop by so much?

ANSWERS TO QUESTIONS IN CHECKPOINTS

Checkpoint: How Banks Create Money 618

The basic transaction reduces your checking account by $1,000 and adds $1,000 in cash for your trip. Therefore, M1 would stay the same because cash and checkable deposits are both part of M1. However, by withdrawing $1,000 from the bank, this is $1,000 that could be loaned out by the bank and lead to money creation. Therefore, by making the withdrawal, the money supply would drop if the bank had planned to loan out its excess reserves.

Checkpoint: The Money Multiplier and Its Leakages 622

The potential money multipliers are 2, 3, 4, 5, and 10. If banks were not required to hold any reserves, the money multiplier could theoretically be infinite if every bank loans out 100% of its deposits. This is not likely, however, due to the many leakages that occur in the banking system. Banks would still hold some reserves, just as banks currently hold excess reserves over the required limit. No bank would want to be at the mercy of a small bank run that would lead to its ruin; therefore, it would keep some currency reserves on hand. Also, individuals, businesses, and foreign entities may choose to hold a portion of their assets in cash, preventing this money from working its way through the money creation process.

Checkpoint: The Federal Reserve System 625

The Federal Reserve has the power to loan the struggling bank the money to satisfy the withdrawals. However, such withdrawals are often a sign of deeper underlying troubles at the bank. The question then becomes whether to let the bank fail and be taken over by a solvent bank, or to help it survive by purchasing bad debts and recapitalizing the bank.

Checkpoint: The Federal Reserve at Work: Tools, Targets, and Policy Lags 630

Open market operations are very effective because they influence virtually all interest rates. Reducing the reserve requirement can certainly boost lending; however, reducing it too much can put banks at risk should defaults rise. Adjusting the discount rate is generally less effective, because bank customers and investors often view borrowing from the discount window as a warning sign of the bank's deteriorating financial health. As a result, the Fed typically keeps the discount rate at a fixed level slightly above the federal funds rate.

24 Monetary Policy

Understanding how central banks alter the money supply to minimize fluctuations in the macroeconomy

Learning Objectives

24.1 Explain the importance of interest rates on the economy and how it affects our daily lives.

24.2 Explain the goals of monetary policy and how the Fed uses policies to expand or contract the economy.

24.3 Contrast classical monetary theory with Keynesian and monetarist theories.

24.4 Describe the equation of exchange and its implications for monetary policy in the long run.

24.5 Determine the effectiveness of monetary policy when demand or supply shocks occur.

24.6 Describe the debate on whether the Fed should have discretion or be governed by simple monetary rules.

24.7 Describe the federal funds target, the Taylor rule, and how they are used in modern monetary policymaking.

24.8 Explain why extraordinary powers were used in response to the financial crisis of 2008.

24.9 Discuss the monetary policy challenges faced by the European Central Bank following the financial crises affecting individual Eurozone members.

Information received since the Federal Open Market Committee met in January suggests that economic activity has been expanding at a moderate pace. . . . A range of recent indicators, including strong job gains, points to additional strengthening of the labor market. . . . However, global economic and financial developments continue to pose risks. . . . Against this backdrop, the Committee decided to maintain the target range for the federal funds rate at 1/4 to 1/2 percent. The stance of monetary policy remains accommodative, thereby supporting further improvement in labor market conditions and a return to 2 percent inflation.
—Excerpt from the FOMC Statement of March 16, 2016

At 2:00 P.M. EST on an ordinary weekday afternoon, the Federal Reserve (Fed) concludes its meeting of the Federal Open Market Committee, and just 15 minutes later, at 2:15 P.M. a meeting statement is released. To the twelve voting members of this committee, which meets about every six weeks, it's just another day on the job. But this is not your ordinary everyday job.

On Wall Street, millions of investors, physically present at a stock exchange or virtually present via their online brokerage accounts, anxiously await this Fed statement. Corporate executives, just coming back from lunch, immediately search their news app for the latest statement release.

Government policymakers in Ecuador, El Salvador, Panama, and Timor-Leste tune in to the news to hear the Fed statement because it affects their countries' interest rates and their currency, which in fact is *the U.S. dollar*. And markets in the rest of the world await the Fed statement to determine how their own economies will be affected.

Indeed, in a matter of minutes after the release of the Fed statement, the twelve members of the Federal Open Market Committee will have affected the lives of hundreds of millions of people. How do such ordinary people carry such tremendous power?

The Federal Open Market Committee is the body within the Federal Reserve that controls U.S. monetary policy. Their economic policy decisions affect not only the U.S. economy but also the entire world economy.

Although not every Fed meeting statement produces a dramatic flurry of reactions, the ability of the Fed to exert powerful policy action in times of economic fluctuation makes its meeting statement the most dissected piece of economic news in the world. Even the most slightly nuanced wording of the statement can generate mass market activity as people attempt to predict how the Fed will act not only today but also in the months and years ahead.

This chapter studies the remarkable influence the Fed has to alter the macroeconomy using the tools that form the basis of monetary policy. The Federal Reserve Act mandates that the Fed implement monetary policies that will promote economic growth accompanied by high employment, stable prices, and moderate long-term interest rates. In the

An investor awaiting the Fed statement.

Mario Tama/Getty Images

638

Monetary Policy In Action

Among the tools used by the Federal Reserve to conduct monetary policy are setting the discount rate and conducting open market operations targeting the federal funds rate. The interest rates targeted by the Fed have a profound impact on the entire economy.

Go to **LaunchPad** *to use the latest data to recreate this graph.*

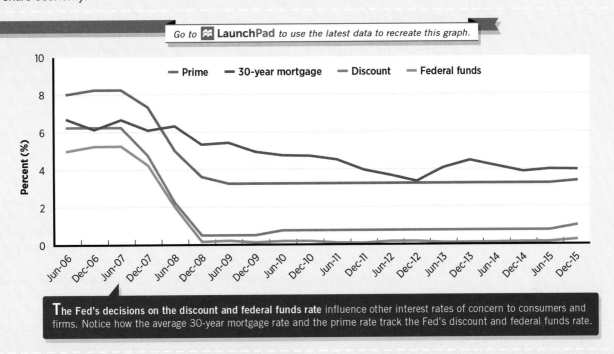

— Prime — 30-year mortgage — Discount — Federal funds

The Fed's decisions on the discount and federal funds rate influence other interest rates of concern to consumers and firms. Notice how the average 30-year mortgage rate and the prime rate track the Fed's discount and federal funds rate.

$1,380,000,000,000
Total amount of U.S. dollars and coins in circulation in April 2016

10,822,000,000
Total number of $100 bills in circulation in April 2016

One million $1 bills on display at the Money Museum in the Chicago Federal Reserve Bank

Jim West/Alamy Stock Photo

Just how much is one million $1 bills?

Weight: over 2,000 pounds
Height (one million bills stacked): 33 stories
Length (one million bills laid end-to-end): 97 miles
Cost (to produce one million $1 bills): $55,000

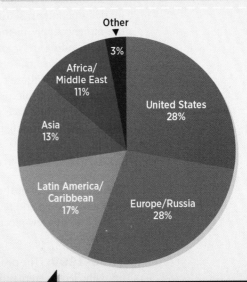

Other 3%
Africa/Middle East 11%
Asia 13%
United States 28%
Latin America/Caribbean 17%
Europe/Russia 28%

As the Fed increased the money supply, other countries have increased their holdings of U.S. dollars, mainly as reserves. Part of this is held in actual banknotes, mostly $100 bills. Where are all these $100 bills?

previous chapter, we saw how the Federal Reserve System is organized and described the three monetary policy tools the Fed uses, which are setting reserve requirements, setting the discount rate, and conducting open market operations. In this chapter, we look at what monetary policy aims to achieve and how the Fed undertakes monetary policy to deal with economic fluctuations.

The first part of this chapter describes how monetary policy is used during economic downturns and during economic booms. We then consider the question: How do changes in the money supply affect the economy? We will see that money has no effect on the economy's real growth in the long run but can have sizable effects in the short run. We examine the impact of monetary policy on controlling demand and supply shocks and how the Fed actually tries to manage the economy, a process that is considered both art and science. The chapter concludes by looking at monetary policy challenges faced by the Fed and the European Central Bank, both of which have recently dealt with financial crises not seen in generations.

WHAT IS MONETARY POLICY?

Throughout the study of macroeconomic principles, we have emphasized the effect of the business cycle in creating natural ups and downs in the economy, which often lead to inflation or unemployment. The rest of our study has dealt largely with ways to manage these fluctuations and to limit the harm from deviating too far from the long-run growth path of the economy.

One way of managing economic fluctuations is the use of fiscal policy, which we studied earlier. Fiscal policy uses the tools of taxation, government transfer payments, and government spending. The other way of managing economic fluctuations is the use of monetary policy, which deals with how the money supply is controlled to target interest rates in an economy.

The Twin Goals of Monetary Policy

The authority to control a nation's monetary policy is typically held by a country's central bank. In the United States, the central bank is the Federal Reserve, an independent organization unaffiliated with any political party. The seven members of its Board of Governors are appointed by the president for a 14-year term rather than being elected.

As discussed in the previous chapter, the Fed uses its primary tools of conducting open market operations, setting reserve requirements, and setting the discount rate to manage the money supply in the economy. By doing so, it has tremendous influence on interest rates, including those on savings accounts, money market accounts, government bonds, mortgage payments, student loans, car loans, and credit card balances.

The Fed uses these tools to promote its twin goals of economic growth with low unemployment, and stable prices with moderate long-term interest rates. When the economy enters a boom or a recession that threatens the stability of these factors, the Fed can step in to enact an appropriate policy to counteract the effect.

Examples of Monetary Policy in Action

The business cycle of the economy produces frequent ups and downs, and the Fed is kept busy anticipating and reacting to prevent major economic crises from occurring. Let's take a brief look at a few recent periods when the Fed stepped in to promote economic and price stability.

1998–1999: The peak of the Internet growth, when new "dot.com" companies sprouted up daily, led to tremendous economic growth. But along with growth came inflationary pressures, and the Fed responded by raising interest rates.

2001–2003: With the dramatic collapse in the price of technology stocks along with the short recession in 2001, the Fed lowered interest rates to stimulate employment.

2004–2006: The housing bubble led to strong growth throughout the economy and inflationary pressures crept up (especially in industries related to housing), leading the Fed to raise interest rates again.

2007–2009: When the housing bubble collapsed, unemployment rose significantly and the Fed dramatically reduced interest rates to record lows.

2010–2015: A slow economic recovery with lackluster employment growth encouraged the Fed to hold interest rates at record lows until late 2015 when the Fed began raising interest rates again.

Why Is the Interest Rate So Important to the Economy?

Examine the economic decisions you make every day, and you might discover how interest rates play a powerful role. Interest rates affect the manner in which we borrow and consume, and the way in which we save and invest.

Suppose you are looking to buy a new car, and have budgeted $2,000 for a down payment and $400 a month toward the monthly payment on a five-year loan. How much of a car can you afford with this budget?

It depends a great deal on the interest rate. Suppose the current interest rate on a car loan is 8.99%. Using the money you have, you would be able to afford a car costing up to $21,275. But now suppose that the interest rate on a car loan is 2.99%. At the lower interest rate, you would be able to afford a car costing up to $24,265, or almost $3,000 in extra spending without changing your monthly payment.

This extra $3,000 in potential spending resulting from the lower interest rate adds to the amount of consumption in the economy. Recall that aggregate demand is the sum of consumption, investment, government spending, and net exports. Just as lower interest rates make cars more affordable, they also make homes more affordable, along with equipment purchases by businesses. Therefore, a reduction in interest rates promotes greater consumption and investment, which leads to an increase in aggregate demand, shifting the aggregate demand curve to the right.

When Is It Optimal to Loosen or Tighten Monetary Policy?

By influencing interest rates, the Fed influences aggregate demand. Specifically, the Fed loosens monetary policy in times of recessionary concerns and tightens monetary policy in times of inflationary concerns.

- **Loosening monetary policy:** Reducing interest rates → increases consumption and investment → increases aggregate demand.
- **Tightening monetary policy:** Raising interest rates → decreases consumption and investment → decreases aggregate demand.

Let's explore "loosening" and "tightening" a bit more.

Expansionary Monetary Policy During times of economic downturn, the Fed will engage in **expansionary monetary policy** by conducting open market operations. By buying government bonds from banks using money it creates, the Fed puts more money into the economy, thus expanding the money supply and reducing interest rates. Lower interest rates tend to reduce the proportion of income people save and increase the amount they consume or invest, all else equal. The increase in consumption and/or investment results in an increase in aggregate demand (AD).

As interest rates are lowered, consumers and businesses find the cost of borrowing decreasing as well. For a business, this reduces the financing cost for an expansion of a factory or the building of a new restaurant or store. To a consumer, a lower interest rate on a home or car purchase can significantly reduce monthly payments, freeing up some money for other purchases. As borrowing increases to finance consumption or investment, AD again increases.

Eric Chiang

A lower interest rate allows one to afford a better car (or at least fancier rims) with the same monthly payment.

expansionary monetary policy
Fed actions designed to increase the money supply and lower interest rates to stimulate the economy (expand income and employment).

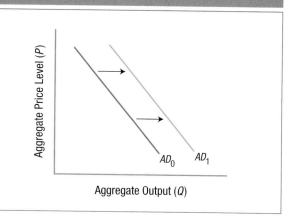

| FIGURE 1 | EXPANSIONARY MONETARY POLICY |

Expansionary monetary policies reduce interest rates, which lead to greater aggregate demand, shifting the aggregate demand curve to the right.

Further, a reduction in interest rates, in particular on Treasury securities, means that the government is spending less on financing the national debt. By spending less on financing the debt, the government is then able to spend more on other purchases, which contributes to an increase in AD.

Finally, as the interest rate falls, American bonds become less attractive to foreign investors, and this often leads to a decline in the value of the U.S. dollar in foreign exchange markets. A falling dollar makes American products cheaper relative to foreign products, which stimulates exports and reduces imports, increasing AD.

In sum, expansionary monetary policy is used when the economy faces a recessionary gap, in which output is below the level needed to reach full employment. By engaging in expansionary policy, the aggregate demand curve shifts to the right as shown in Figure 1, expanding output at every price level.

Contractionary Monetary Policy The opposite of expansionary monetary policy is **contractionary monetary policy,** which occurs when the Fed sells bonds, taking money out of the economy to reduce the money supply and raise interest rates. The Fed uses contractionary monetary policy when inflationary pressures build up. When do inflationary periods typically occur?

Inflationary pressures typically occur following a period of strong economic growth, such as during the housing bubble between 2004 and 2006. As eager consumers and investors bid up prices for homes, demand increased for related items such as furniture, appliances, and even plane tickets for those who bought second homes far away. As demand for goods and services rises, prices tend to rise as well. If prices rise too much, this would have consequences on the economy as the purchasing power of savings erodes.

To stem the growth of inflation, the Fed would reduce the money supply, thereby increasing the interest rate to slow the growth of demand. In this case, rising interest rates would lead to a fall in consumption and investment. The government would spend more financing the national debt, reducing what it can spend on other goods and services. Moreover, a rise in the value of the dollar from increased demand for higher interest bonds makes American goods more expensive, reducing net exports. Each of these effects causes the aggregate demand curve to shift to the left as shown in Figure 2, reducing output at every price level and putting downward pressure on prices.

Up until now, we have assumed that monetary policy affects the interest rate, which subsequently influences aggregate demand. But how does a simple change in the money supply influence the amount of goods and services in the real economy? The next section explores this question by analyzing how prices and output change in the short run and long run.

contractionary monetary policy
Fed actions designed to decrease the money supply and raise interest rates to shrink income and employment, usually to fight inflation.

FIGURE 2	CONTRACTIONARY MONETARY POLICY

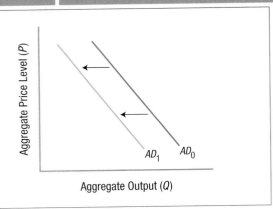

Contractionary monetary policies raise interest rates, which lead to lower aggregate demand, shifting the aggregate demand curve to the left.

 CHECKPOINT

WHAT IS MONETARY POLICY?

- Monetary policy involves the control of the money supply to target interest rates in order to stabilize fluctuations in the business cycle.
- The Federal Reserve implements monetary policy. Its goals are to promote economic growth by maintaining full employment, stable prices, and moderate long-term interest rates.
- Interest rates are crucial because they directly influence the components of aggregate demand, including consumption and investment.
- Expansionary monetary policy is used during times of recession, and involves expanding the money supply to reduce interest rates.
- Contractionary monetary policy is used during times of rising inflation, and involves reducing the money supply to raise interest rates.

QUESTION: Suppose the government passes legislation limiting the maximum interest rate that can be charged on student loans, reducing the monthly payment on your loans. How is this legislation similar to an expansionary monetary policy?

Answers to the Checkpoint questions can be found at the end of this chapter.

MONETARY THEORIES

In discussing the theories that justify the use of monetary policy, it is best to differentiate the long run from the short run. We will see that money has no effect on the real economy (such as employment and output) in the long run but can have an effect in the short run.

The Short Run Versus the Long Run: What's the Difference?

One of the important concepts covered earlier in the book is the comparison between the short-run aggregate supply curve (SRAS) and the vertical long-run aggregate supply curve (LRAS). Recall that the LRAS curve is vertical because economic output is always fixed in the long run at the full employment output when wages and prices are flexible. Only factors that increase the productivity of inputs can shift the LRAS curve. The SRAS curve, however, is upward-sloping because higher prices can cause temporary increases in output. This is due to sticky wages and prices.

We now build on the AD/AS model by explaining how changes in the money supply, which directly affect the aggregate demand curve, might change prices and output in the economy. Let's begin by looking at the long run, which is the analysis most commonly associated with the classical theory.

The Long Run: The Classical Theory

Classical economists focused on long-run adjustments in economic activity. In the long run, wages, prices, and interest rates are flexible, allowing the labor, product, and capital markets to adjust to keep the economy at full employment.

A product of the classical theory is the *quantity theory of money*, which is defined by the **equation of exchange:**

$$M \times V = P \times Q$$

equation of exchange The heart of classical monetary theory uses the equation $M \times V = P \times Q$, where M is the supply of money, V is the velocity of money (the average number of times per year a dollar is spent on goods and services, or the number of times it turns over in a year), P is the price level, and Q is the economy's real output level.

where M is the supply of money, V is the velocity of money (the average number of times per year a dollar is spent on goods and services), P is the price level, and Q is the economy's real output level. Note that the right side of the equation—the aggregate price level times the level of real output—is equal to nominal GDP.

In the long run, when the economy is at full employment, the implications for monetary policy are straightforward. Because velocity (V) is assumed to be fixed by existing monetary institutions (e.g., the amount of cash you use on a monthly basis is generally consistent), and real aggregate output (Q) is assumed to be fixed at full employment, any change in the money supply (M) will translate directly to a change in prices (P), or in other words, inflation.

Suppose you sell your grandma's old LP records on eBay. Last month you listed five records for sale and sold them at an average winning bid of $20 each. Now suppose that this month a 10% increase in the money supply causes more people to want to buy records. If you again list only five records for sale, what will likely happen? There is more money to spend on the same amount of goods. Buyers might bid up the price to, say, $22. In the end, prices rise in the exact proportion to the rise in the money supply. This is the essence of the classical theory—that increases in the money supply translate into an immediate and proportional rise in the aggregate price level with no change in real output (Q). As a result, monetary policy is ineffective.

Panel A of Figure 3 illustrates how the quantity theory works within an aggregate demand and supply model. The economy is initially in long-run equilibrium at point e with full employment output of $15 trillion and an initial money supply of $2.0 trillion. Increasing the money supply to $2.2 trillion (a 10% increase) shifts aggregate demand upward to $AD_{(\$2.2T)}$, resulting in a new equilibrium at point b where the aggregate price level increases to 110 (a 10% increase), yet real output remains constant at $15 trillion. This positive relationship between changes in the supply of money and inflation is evident in the plot

IRVING FISHER (1867–1947)

Irving Fisher was one of the ablest mathematical economists of the early 20th century. He was a staunch advocate of monetary reform, and his theories influenced economists as different as John Maynard Keynes and Milton Friedman.

Born in upstate New York in 1867, Fisher studied mathematics, science, and philosophy at Yale University. In 1905 Fisher was in a phone booth in Grand Central Terminal in New York City when someone stole his briefcase, which contained his manuscript of *The Nature of Capital and Income*, one of the first economics books about the stock market. He rewrote the book over the next year, making copies of each chapter as it was finished and always closing the doors to phone booths after that.

Monetarists owe a great debt to Fisher's next great book, *The Purchasing Power of Money*, in which he offered an "equation of exchange": $MV = PT$ (where T is the number of transactions taking place, or output). Classical economists have used variations of the formula to suggest that inflation is caused by increases in the money supply.

Fisher was prim and straight-laced, disciplined, and did not drink alcohol or coffee or tea, smoke, eat chocolate, or use pepper. His lack of humor and sometimes controversial economic beliefs (such as 100% bank reserves) led some to regard him as quite odd.

But among his many skills and interests, Fisher was a successful inventor and businessman. In 1925 he patented the "visible card index" system, an early version of the Rolodex, and earned a fortune. Unfortunately, within a few years he would lose everything in the stock market crash of 1929, an event that he famously failed to predict. His insistence of an imminent recovery during the early Depression years caused irreparable damage to a well-earned reputation as one of America's greatest economists.

Information from Robert Allen, *Irving Fisher: A Biography* (Cambridge, MA: Blackwell), 1993.

| FIGURE 3 | THE IMPACT OF A CHANGE IN THE MONEY SUPPLY IN THE LONG RUN: THEORY AND EVIDENCE |

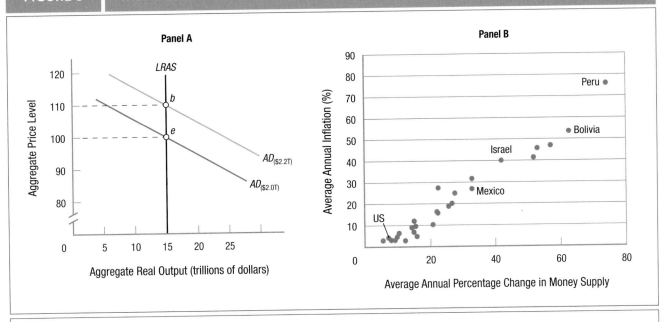

The quantity theory of money is shown using aggregate demand and aggregate supply. The economy is initially in equilibrium at point *e*. The long-run aggregate supply curve is vertical at the full employment output of $15 trillion, while the aggregate demand curve reflects a money supply of $2.0 trillion. Increasing the money supply to $2.2 trillion (a 10% increase) shifts aggregate demand upward to $AD_{(\$2.2T)}$, resulting in a new equilibrium at point *b*, where the aggregate price level rises by 10%, yet real output remains constant. The price level rise is equal to the percentage increase in the money supply. Money supply growth and inflation for thirty countries from 1975 to 2015 support this theory.

shown in panel B, which shows the strong correlation between average growth in the money supply and inflation for 30 countries from 1975 to 2015. This suggests that any central bank that wants to avoid high inflation must avoid rapid growth of its money supply.

The quantity theory of money provides a good explanation of the long-run impact of monetary growth in the larger economy. But do people really catch on so quickly to money growth? Typically not. The realization that wages and prices can be "sticky" led economists to develop theories of how prices and output can change in the short run, leading to a SRAS curve that differs from a LRAS curve. The most notable theories include the Keynesian and monetarist models.

Short-Run Effects of Monetary Policy

If the short-run effects of money supply were the same as in the long run, that would be the end of the story. In contrast to the long run, changes in the money supply can have an effect on the real economy in the short run, not just on the price level. To explain this, let's start by returning to our earlier example to show how money supply growth can affect economic output.

Money Illusion and Sticky Wages and Prices Suppose you continue to sell your grandma's records on eBay, listing five for sale each month. And every month, you notice that the average winning bids keep rising, first to $22, then to $25, then to $30, or even higher. This increase in the sales price makes you happy because you feel richer each month compared to the previous month. You think you are benefiting from the growing popularity of your grandma's good taste in music.

How would you use your additional income? Most people would spend it by going out to eat more or buying more clothes. This extra spending (by you and everyone who *feels* richer) results in a temporary increase in economic output. But then you notice that the items you typically buy each month start increasing in price, so much so that despite earning more money,

MILTON FRIEDMAN (1912–2006)

NOBEL PRIZE

Milton Friedman may be the best-known economist of the latter half of the 20th century. During the 1980s, his advocacy of free market economics and "monetarist" theories had a dramatic impact on policymakers, notably President Ronald Reagan and British Prime Minister Margaret Thatcher. His book *A Monetary History of the United States, 1867–1960,* co-authored with Anna Schwartz, is considered a modern classic of economics.

Born in 1912 in Brooklyn, New York, to poor immigrant parents, Friedman was awarded a scholarship to Rutgers University but paid for his additional expenses by waiting on tables and clerking in a store. He eventually went on to graduate school at the University of Chicago to study economics, and then to Columbia University.

In 1946 he accepted a professorship at the University of Chicago where he delved into the role of money in business cycles. In 1950 Friedman worked in Paris for the Marshall Plan, studying a precursor to the Common Market. He came to believe in the importance of flexible exchange rates between members of the European community.

Friedman's views were explicitly counter to the Keynesian belief in a range of activist government policies to stabilize the economy. Friedman emphasized the importance of monetary policy in determining the level of economic activity, and advocated a consistent policy of steady growth in the money supply to encourage stability and economic growth.

Friedman was awarded the Nobel Prize in Economics in 1976 for his work on monetary theories and also for his concept of "permanent income," the idea that people based their savings habits on the typical amount they earn instead of on increases or decreases they may view as temporary.

you end up buying about the same amount of goods as you did before. In other words, after prices caught up, you're no better off than when you made only $20 per record. What you have discovered is that grandma's records are not growing in popularity. Rather, growth in the money supply is causing an increase in all prices. You misperceived that you were wealthier when you really were not.

The example above illustrates the misperceptions in wealth that occur when the money supply grows, and is known as **money illusion**. But money illusion is not the only distinguishing factor between the short run and the long run. Another short-run effect is that wages and prices tend to react slowly to changes in the economy. Most workers' wages do not change with every paycheck; similarly, the prices of many goods and services we buy do not change every day. This delayed reaction in wages and prices to economic conditions makes them *sticky*. This is not the first time we have studied the effects of sticky wages and sticky prices—we studied them previously when explaining why the SRAS curve slopes upward. But now we look at how an upward-sloping SRAS curve can make monetary policy effective in the short run by looking at two opposing views on the effectiveness of monetary policy in the short run.

Keynesian Model Developed by John Maynard Keynes during the Great Depression of the 1930s, Keynesian analysis has had a profound effect on policymakers and economists that continues today. According to Keynesian theory, an increase in the money supply leads more people to buy interest-earning assets (bonds), causing the price of bonds to rise and the interest rate to fall. Lower interest rates should normally lead to an increase in investment that increases aggregate demand, which increases income, output, and employment.

However, Keynesians believed that this outcome occurs only when the economy is healthy. During times of recession, people become fearful and don't buy as much, leading to massive excess capacity for businesses. Reducing interest rates might not lead to greater investment, because firms are unable to sell what they were currently producing. With a decline in business expectations, firms would be reluctant to invest more.

Further, when interest rates fall to very low levels, Keynes argued that people simply hoard money because it's not worth holding bonds that pay so little interest. Keynes referred to this phenomenon as the **liquidity trap.** In a liquidity trap, an increase in the money supply does not result in a decrease in interest rates; thus, there is no change in investment, and consequently no change in income or output. Monetary policy is totally ineffective. This was one reason Keynes argued that fiscal policy, especially government spending, was needed to get the economy out of the Depression.

Monetarist Model Milton Friedman challenged the Keynesian view by arguing that government spending inherent to fiscal policy must be financed either by increased taxation and/or increased borrowing. His monetarist theory states that higher taxation means

money illusion A misperception of wealth caused by a focus on increases in nominal income but not increases in prices.

liquidity trap When interest rates are so low, people hold on to money rather than invest in bonds due to their expectations of a declining economy or an unforeseen event such as war.

consumers and firms have less money to consume and invest, while increased borrowing leads to higher interest rates, which also reduces consumption and investment. Thus, monetarists believe that the crowding out effect makes fiscal policy ineffective.

Friedman pioneered the notion that consumption is not only based on income, but also on wealth, an idea he referred to as the *permanent income hypothesis*.

With Friedman's approach, when the money supply increases, interest rates fall, and individuals rebalance their asset portfolios by exchanging money for other assets, including real estate and consumer durables such as cars and recreational equipment. Therefore, falling interest rates will lead to higher investment and/or consumption. This leads to an increase in aggregate demand and ultimately an increase in income, output, and/or the price level.

Therefore, monetarists believe that monetary policy can be effective in the short run. But, like classical economists, monetarists believe that an increase in money will ultimately increase prices in the long run. As Milton Friedman famously remarked: "Inflation is always and everywhere a monetary phenomenon."

Figure 4 illustrates the monetarist approach that a change in output will occur only in the short run. The economy is initially in long-run equilibrium at point *e*, with output at $15 trillion and a price level of 100. A 10% increase in the money supply from $2.0 trillion to $2.2 trillion shifts the aggregate demand curve from AD_0 to AD_1, initially raising output to $16 trillion and the aggregate price level to 105 (point *b*). Over time, as prices adjust, the SRAS curve will shift left to $SRAS_1$ and the economy will move back to its full employment output ($15 trillion), raising prices in the long run by 10% to 110 (point *c*).

Summary of the Effectiveness of Monetary Policy

Let's summarize the theories of the effectiveness of monetary policy.

Long Run: Changes in the money supply show up directly as increases in the price level because both velocity and output are considered fixed in the equation of exchange ($M \times V = P \times Q$). Because classical economists focused on the long run, they saw no use for monetary policy.

Short Run: Keynes believed that when the economy is well below full employment, monetary policy is ineffective because investment is more influenced by business expectations about the economy than interest rates. Further, Keynes suggested that once

---

FIGURE 4   MONETARIST THEORY ON MONEY SUPPLY

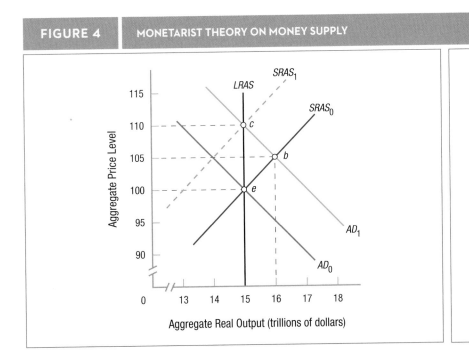

Monetarists argue that a change in output will last only for the short run; in the long run, the economy will move back to full employment. The economy begins in equilibrium at point *e*. An increase in the money supply of 10% shifts the aggregate demand curve from AD_0 to AD_1, resulting in higher short-run output, $16 trillion, and a higher price level at point *b*. Over time, the economy will move back to full employment output ($15 trillion), increasing the price level in the long run to 110 (a 10% increase) at point *c*. The long-run aggregate supply curve is vertical at the full employment output of $15 trillion.

TABLE 1	SUMMARY OF MONETARY THEORIES	
	Short Run	**Long Run**
Classical Theory	Monetary policy is ineffective. The economy always self-adjusts.	Economy self-adjusts due to flexible prices. Changes in the money supply lead only to price changes.
Keynesian Theory	Fiscal policy is effective, while monetary policy is ineffective in times of deep recession.	Economy adjusts to long-run equilibrium; increased money supply leads to higher prices.
Monetarist Theory	Fiscal policy is ineffective because government spending crowds out consumption and investment, while monetary policy is effective.	Economy adjusts to long-run equilibrium; increased money supply leads to higher prices.

interest rates get very low, monetary policy might confront a "liquidity trap," where money is just hoarded. Thus, Keynesians favor fiscal policy to move the economy toward full employment.

Monetarists, on the other hand, do see a role for monetary policy. In the short run, changes in the money supply reduce interest rates, which in turn stimulate both investment and consumption. Consumer spending is related to wealth (not just income), and changes in interest rates lead to changes in consumer spending for durable goods.

A summary of the three theories is provided in Table 1.

Monetary Policy and Economic Shocks

Our discussion thus far suggests that the Fed's approach to monetary policy should be based on both short- and long-run considerations. Low inflation represents a reasonable long-run goal, while greater income and output are more appropriate for the shorter term.

Economists generally agree that, in the long run, the Fed should focus on price stability because low rates of inflation have been shown to create the best environment for long-run economic growth.

We have seen from the equation of exchange that, in the long run, aggregate supply is vertical and fixed at full employment output. Thus, changes in the supply of money lead to changes in the price level.

But in the short run, demand and supply shocks to the economy may require differing approaches to monetary policy. The direction of monetary policy and its extent depend on whether it focuses on the price level or income and output, and whether the shock to the economy comes from the demand or the supply side.

Demand Shocks Demand shocks to the economy can come from reductions in consumer demand, investment, government spending, or exports, or from an increase in imports. For example, the economy faced a demand shock in 2008 when households, fearing unemployment after the housing bubble burst, increased saving and reduced spending. Let's consider an economy that is initially in full employment equilibrium at point *e* in panel A of Figure 5. A *demand shock* then reduces aggregate demand to AD_1. At the new equilibrium (point *a*), the price level and output both fall.

An expansionary monetary policy will increase the money supply, lower interest rates, and thereby shift aggregate demand back to AD_0, restoring employment and output to full employment levels. In this case, targeting either a stable price level (100) or the original income and output level ($15 trillion) will bring the economy back to the same point of equilibrium, point *e*, where *both* targets are reached.

FIGURE 5 | DEMAND SHOCKS, SUPPLY SHOCKS, AND MONETARY POLICY

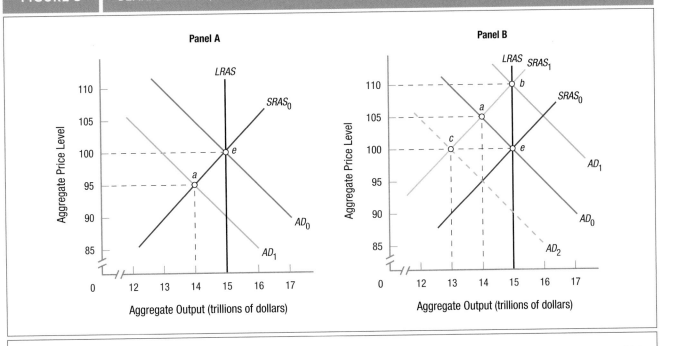

Monetary policy can be effective in counteracting a demand shock. In panel A, the economy begins in full employment equilibrium at point *e* and then a demand shock reduces aggregate demand to AD_1, resulting in a new equilibrium (point *a*). Expansionary monetary policy will shift aggregate demand back to AD_0, restoring full employment output ($15 trillion) and prices (100). Monetary policy is less effective in counteracting a supply shock. In panel B, a negative supply shock shifts $SRAS_0$ to $SRAS_1$. The new equilibrium (point *a*) is at a *higher* price level, 105, and *lower* output, $14 trillion, a doubly negative result. The Fed could use expansionary monetary policy to shift AD_0 to AD_1; this would restore the economy to full employment output (point *b*), but at an even higher price level (110). Alternatively, the Fed could focus on price level stability, using contractionary monetary policy to shift aggregate demand to AD_2, but this would further deepen the recession as output falls to $13 trillion (point *c*).

A positive demand shock produces a corresponding, though opposite, result. The positive demand shock will jolt output and the price level upward. Contractionary monetary policy will reduce both of them, restoring the economy to its original equilibrium.

For demand shocks, therefore, no conflict arises between the twin goals of monetary policy. Not only is the objective of full employment compatible with the objective of stable prices, but by the Fed targeting either one of these objectives, the other objective also will be achieved.

Supply Shocks Supply shocks can hit the economy for many reasons, including changes in resource costs such as a drought causing a rise in food prices, changes in inflationary expectations, or changes in technology. Looking at panel B of Figure 5, let us again consider an economy initially in full employment equilibrium at point *e*. Assume that a negative shock to the economy, say, a spike in crop prices, shifts short-run aggregate supply from $SRAS_0$ to $SRAS_1$. The new equilibrium (point *a*) occurs at a *higher* price level (105) and a *lower* output of $14 trillion.

This doubly negative result means that a supply shock is very difficult to counter. The Fed could use expansionary monetary policy to shift AD_0 to AD_1; this would restore the economy to full employment output of $15 trillion (point *b*), but at an even higher price level (110). Alternatively, the Fed could focus on price level stability, using contractionary monetary policy to shift aggregate demand to AD_2, but this would further deepen the recession by pushing output down to $13 trillion (point *c*).

For a negative supply shock, not only has price level stability worsened, but so has output and income. Contrast this with the situation earlier, when a demand shock worsened the economy for one of its targets, but improved it for the other. Supply shocks are difficult to counteract because of their doubly negative results.

Implications for Short-Run Monetary Policy There is general agreement among economists that monetary policy should focus on price stability in the long run, while focusing on output or income in the short run. When a demand shock strikes, following this short-run policy course has the same effect as using price stability as the goal. When a supply shock occurs, however, targeting nominal income or output is preferable, because it permits the Fed to spread the shock's impact between income and output losses and price level increases. By increasing aggregate demand, the economy will suffer some added increase in the price level, but output will rise, reducing the severity of any recession. The Fed will probably not try to push the economy back to full employment (from point *a* to point *b* in panel B of Figure 5) immediately, because this action would result in much higher inflation. Moving the economy back to full employment is typically spread over several periods.

 CHECKPOINT

MONETARY THEORIES

- The classical equation of exchange is $M \times V = P \times Q$. In the long run, velocity (V) and output (Q) are assumed to be fixed. Therefore, changes in the money supply translate directly into changes in the price level: $\Delta M = \Delta P$.

- In the short run, Keynesian monetary analysis suggests that changes in the money supply change interest rates, leading to changes in investment and aggregate demand when the economy is healthy. However, in a deep recession, changes in the money supply have no effect on the real economy.

- Monetarists suggest that in the long run, the economy functions in the way that classical economists described, but they see monetary policy affecting interest rates in the short run, which in turn affects investment *and/or* consumption.

- In the long run, the Fed targets price stability. Low rates of inflation are most conducive to long-run economic health.

- Monetary policy can offset demand shocks because the objective of full employment is compatible with the objective of stable prices.

- Supply shocks present a more challenging problem for monetary policy. A negative supply shock reduces output but increases the price level. Expansionary monetary policy to increase output further increases the price level, and contractionary policy to reduce the price level worsens the recession.

QUESTION: A common debate on dealing with rising national debt involves those who prefer a smaller government (reduced taxation with a dramatic reduction in government spending) versus those who prefer increased government spending funded by higher taxes. Which general theories described in this section best resemble the two sides of the debate?

Answers to the Checkpoint questions can be found at the end of this chapter.

easy money, quantitative easing, or accommodative monetary policy Fed actions designed to increase excess reserves and the money supply to stimulate the economy (increase income and employment). *See also* expansionary monetary policy.

tight money or restrictive monetary policy Fed actions designed to decrease excess reserves and the money supply to shrink income and employment, usually to fight inflation. *See also* contractionary monetary policy.

MODERN MONETARY POLICY

When the Fed engages in expansionary monetary policy, it is buying bonds using money it creates by adding to the existing bank reserves deposited at the Fed. Other terms used to describe this process include **easy money, quantitative easing,** and **accommodative monetary policy.** It is designed to increase excess reserves and the money supply, and ultimately reduce interest rates to stimulate the economy and expand income and employment. The opposite of an expansionary policy is contractionary monetary policy, also referred to as **tight money** or **restrictive monetary policy.** Tight money policies are designed to shrink income and employment, usually in the interest of fighting inflation. The Fed brings about tight monetary policy by selling bonds, thereby pulling reserves from the financial system.

The Federal Reserve Act gives the Board of Governors significant discretion over conducting monetary policy. It sets goals, but leaves it up to the discretion of the Board of Governors how best to reach these objectives. As we have seen, the Fed attempts to frame monetary policy to keep inflation low over the long run, but also to maintain enough flexibility to respond in the short run to demand and supply shocks.

Rules Versus Discretion

The complexities of monetary policy, especially in dealing with a supply shock, have led some economists, most notably Milton Friedman, to call for a **monetary rule** to guide monetary policymakers. Other economists argue that modern economies are too complex to be managed by a few simple rules. Constantly changing institutions, economic behaviors, and technologies means that some discretion, and perhaps even complete discretion, are essential for policymakers. Also, if policymakers could use a simple and efficient rule on which to base successful monetary policy, they would have enough incentive to adopt it voluntarily, because it would guarantee success and their job would be much easier.

Milton Friedman argued that variations in monetary growth were a major source of instability in the economy. To counter this problem, which is compounded by the long and variable lags in discretionary monetary policy, Friedman advocated the adoption of monetary growth rules. Specifically, he proposed increasing the money supply by a set percentage every year, at a level consistent with long-term price stability and economic growth.

Friedman and other monetarists, like the classical economists before them, believed the economy to be inherently stable. If a demand shock is small or temporary, a monetary growth rule will probably function well enough. But if the shock is large or persistent, as was the case during the 2007–2009 recession, a discretionary monetary policy aimed at bringing the economy back to full employment more quickly would probably be preferred.

In some cases, a monetary rule keeps policymakers from making things worse by preventing them from taking imprudent actions. Yet, the monetary rule also prevents policymakers from aiding the economy when a policy change is needed, as was the case in the 1970s when the Fed's practice of setting a fixed rate for money supply growth wasn't considered successful.

The alternative to setting money growth rules that modern monetary authorities around the world have tried is the simple rule of **inflation targeting,** which sets targets on the inflation rate, usually around 2% per year. If inflation (or the forecasted rate of inflation) exceeds the target, contractionary policy is employed; if inflation falls below the target, expansionary policy is used. Inflation targeting has the virtue of explicitly iterating that the long-run goal of monetary policy is price stability.

But while inflation targeting may work well to combat negative demand shocks, the same is not true when a negative supply shock occurs. Inflation targeting means that contractionary monetary policy should be used to reduce the inflation spiral. But contractionary policy would deepen the recession, and in reality, few monetary authorities would stick to an inflation-targeting approach in this situation. They would be more likely to stimulate the economy slightly, hoping to move it back to full employment with only a small increase in inflation. The result is that inflation targeting would be less effective in dealing with a negative supply shock.

The Federal Funds Target and the Taylor Rule

If not monetary targeting or inflation targeting, what other rule can the Fed use? We know that the Fed alters the federal funds rate as its primary monetary policy instrument. Under what circumstances will the Fed change its federal funds target? The Fed is concerned with two major factors: preventing inflation and preventing and moderating recessions. Professor John Taylor of Stanford University studied the Fed and how it makes decisions and he empirically found that the Fed tended to follow a general rule that has become known as the

monetary rule Keeps the growth of money stocks such as M1 or M2 on a steady path, following the equation of exchange (or quantity theory), to set a long-run path for the economy that keeps inflation in check.

inflation targeting The central bank sets a target on the inflation rate (usually around 2% per year) and adjusts monetary policy to keep inflation near that target.

Taylor rule A rule for the federal funds target that suggests the target is equal to 2% + Current Inflation Rate + 1/2(Inflation Gap) + 1/2(Output Gap).

Taylor rule for federal funds targeting:

$$\text{Federal Funds Target Rate} = 2 + \text{Current Inflation Rate} + 1/2(\text{Inflation Gap}) + 1/2(\text{Output Gap})$$

The Fed's inflation target is typically 2%, the inflation gap is the current inflation rate minus the Fed's inflation target, and the output gap is current GDP minus potential GDP[1]. If the Fed tries to target inflation around 2%, the current inflation rate is 4%, and output is 3% below potential GDP, then the target federal funds rate according to the Taylor rule is

$$
\begin{aligned}
FF_{\text{Target}} &= 2 + 4 + 1/2(4 - 2) + 1/2(-3) \\
&= 2 + 4 + 1/2(2) + 1/2(-3) \\
&= 2 + 4 + 1 - 1.5 \\
&= 5.5\%
\end{aligned}
$$

Notice that the high rate of inflation (4%) drives the federal funds target rate upward, while the fact that the economy is below its potential reduces the rate. If the economy were operating at its potential, the federal funds target would be 7%, because the Fed would not be worried about a recession and would be focused on controlling inflation.

Figure 6 shows how closely the Taylor rule tracks the actual federal funds rate. Some economists have blamed the large spread between the two rates during the period between 2003 and 2007 for the housing boom that precipitated the financial crisis in 2008. They argue that the extremely low interest rates fueled the housing boom.

More important, what the Taylor rule tells us is that when the Fed meets to change the federal funds target rate, the two most important factors are whether inflation is different from the Fed's target (typically 2%) and whether output varies from potential GDP. If output is below its potential, a recession threatens and the Fed will lower its target, and vice versa when output exceeds potential and inflation threatens to exceed the Fed's target.

FIGURE 6	ACTUAL FEDERAL FUNDS RATE AND THE TAYLOR RULE

The Taylor rule tracks the actual federal funds rate quite closely. Some economists have argued that the low federal funds rate during the period from 2003 to 2007 was the cause of the housing boom that precipitated the financial crisis in 2008 and the ensuing recession.

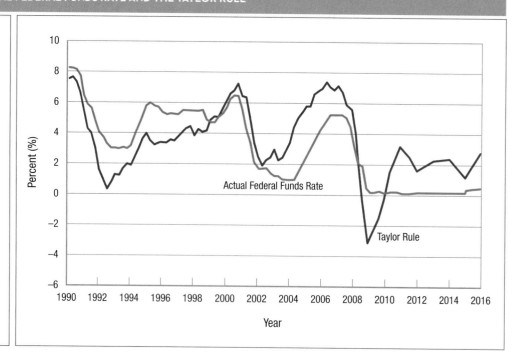

[1] The original Taylor rule used logarithms to measure the output gap. For simplicity, we use the percentage difference between current and potential GDP.

A Recap of the Fed's Policy Tools

Now is a good time to summarize the monetary policy actions that the Fed can take to achieve its twin goals of price stability and full employment.

When output exceeds potential output $(Q > Q_f)$, firms are operating above their capacities and costs will rise, adding an inflationary threat that the Fed wants to avoid. Therefore, the Fed would increase the real interest rate to cool the economy. When output is below potential $(Q < Q_f)$, the Fed's goal is to drive the economy back to its potential and avoid a recession along with the losses associated with an economy below full employment. The Fed does this by lowering the real interest rate. This reflects the Fed's desire to fight recession when output is below full employment and fight inflation when output exceeds its potential.

Today, monetary authorities set a target interest rate and then use open market operations to adjust reserves and keep the federal funds rate near this level. The Fed's interest target is the level that will keep the economy near potential GDP and/or keep inflationary pressures in check. When GDP is below its potential and a recession threatens the economy, the Fed uses expansionary policy to lower interest rates, expanding investment, consumption, and exports. When output is above potential GDP and inflation threatens, the Fed uses a higher interest rate target to slow the economy and reduce inflationary pressure.

Raising interest rates is never a politically popular act, but the Fed will be forced to balance future economic growth against rising inflationary expectations. As former Fed Chair William McChesney Martin said, "The job of a good central banker is to take away the punchbowl just as the party gets going."

Transparency and the Federal Reserve

How does the Fed convey information about its actions, and why is this important? For many years, decisions were made in secrecy, and often they were executed in secrecy. The public did not know that monetary policy was being changed. Because monetary policy affects the economy, the Fed's secrecy stimulated much speculation in financial markets about current and future Fed actions. Uncertainty often led to various counterproductive actions by people guessing incorrectly. These activities were highly inefficient.

When Alan Greenspan became head of the Fed in 1987, this policy of secrecy started to change. By 1994 the Fed released a policy statement each time it changed interest rates, and by 1998 it included a "tilt" statement forecasting what would probably happen in the next month or two. By 2000 the FOMC released a statement after each of its eight meetings per year even if policy remained the same. As the chapter opener describes, the FOMC statement is now one of the most anticipated pieces of economic news.

This new openness has come about because the Fed recognized that monetary policy is mitigated when financial actors take counterproductive actions when they are uncertain about what the Fed will do. In the words of William Poole, former president of the Federal Reserve Bank of St. Louis,

> Explaining a policy action—elucidating the considerations that led the FOMC to decide to adjust the intended funds rate, or to leave it unchanged—is worthwhile. Over time, the accumulation of such explanations helps the market, and perhaps the FOMC itself, to understand what the policy regularities are. It is also important to understand that many—perhaps most—policy actions have precedent value. . . . One of the advantages of public disclosure of the reasons for policy actions is that the required explanation forces the FOMC to think through what it is doing and why.[2]

---

[2] William Poole, "Fed Transparency: How, Not Whether," The Federal Reserve Bank of St. Louis, *Review*, November/December 2003, p. 5.

ISSUE

The Record of the Fed's Performance

Determining how to measure the impact of Federal Reserve policy on our huge, complex economy is not easy. The figure shows how three variables—unemployment, inflation, and interest rates (effective federal funds rate)—have fared during the tenure of the five* Fed Chairs over the last four decades.

Before 1980, when Arthur Burns headed the Fed, inflation was rising. An oil supply shock in 1973 was met with accommodative monetary policy and aggregate demand expanded.

The economy was hit with a second oil price shock in the late 1970s. By the early 1980s, inflation rose to double digits, peaking at over 14% in 1980. Paul Volcker, the head of the Fed at that time, tightened monetary policy to induce a recession (1981–1982) to reduce inflation. By the end of his term, inflation had been reduced to little more than 4%, a remarkable feat.

During the 1990s, the Alan Greenspan Fed alternated between encouraging output growth (mid-1990s) and fighting inflation (early and late 1990s). The Fed under Greenspan did a good job of keeping the economy near full employment. Interest rates trended down and inflation was moderate during the 1990s and early 2000s. But a housing bubble, partly the result of the extremely low interest rates from 2003 to 2007, followed by its collapse in 2008, brought on a financial panic and a deep recession.

The problems stemming from the housing collapse and financial crisis became a challenge for Fed Chair Ben Bernanke. In 2008 the Fed under Bernanke lowered the fed funds rate to almost 0%. In addition, the Bernanke Fed continued to expand the monetary base by purchasing long-term assets from banks when interest rates had already hit the floor. As the chart shows, unemployment trended down and the short period of deflation in 2009 was corrected.

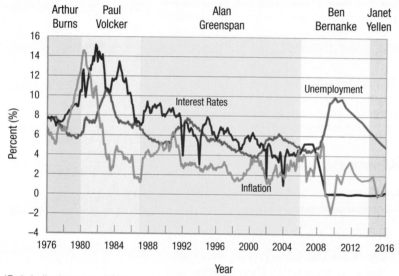

*Technically, there were six Fed Chairs over this period. However, G. William Miller's tenure lasted just over a year from 1978 to 1979, and therefore is not included in this graph.

Fed transparency helps the public understand why it is taking certain actions. This helps the market understand what the Fed does in certain circumstances, and what the Fed is likely to do in similar situations in the future. The Fed's "tilt" comment after each meeting provides a summary of the Fed's outlook on the economy and information on the target federal funds rate. Transparency helps the Fed implement its monetary policy.

Until a decade ago, the performance of monetary authorities illustrated how effective discretionary monetary policy could be. Price stability was remarkable, unemployment and output levels were near full employment levels, interest rates were kept low, and economic growth was solid.

The global financial crisis and recovery over the past decade tested the limits of central banks in preventing economic catastrophe. On the one hand, some economists such as Janet Yellen (often referred to as "doves") argue that greater Fed action is needed in times of economic hardship, while others ("hawks") warn against the inflationary effects of too much monetary policy action. The concluding section of this chapter looks at the actions of the Fed and the European Central Bank in stemming the economic effects from a crisis, and how economic "doves" have gained significant influence in the way monetary policy has been implemented.

CHECKPOINT

MODERN MONETARY POLICY

- In the past, monetary targeting was used to control the rate of growth of the money supply. Later, an alternative approach of inflation targeting, targeting the inflation rate to around 2%, became more prevalent.

- The Fed sets a target federal funds rate and then uses open market operations to adjust reserves and keep the federal funds rate near this level.

- The Taylor rule is a general rule that ties the federal funds rate target to the inflation gap and the output gap for the economy, and has done a good job in estimating the actual federal funds rate target set by the Fed.

- When inflation rises, the Fed uses contractionary monetary policy to increase the federal funds rate to slow the economy. When the economy drifts into a recession and inflationary pressures fall, the Fed does the opposite and reduces the federal funds rate, giving the economy a boost.

- Fed transparency helps us to understand why the Fed makes particular decisions and also what the Fed will probably do in similar circumstances in the future.

QUESTION: After years of quantitative easing, many worry that inflation will eventually become a problem. Why should bond investors sell when the Fed or other central bankers decide that inflation is a growing problem?

Answers to the Checkpoint questions can be found at the end of this chapter.

NEW MONETARY POLICY CHALLENGES

For much of the past century, since the Federal Reserve Act created the Federal Reserve and with it monetary policy, policies were quite predictable and the role of the Fed was seen as an ever-present but never overreaching government body. A similar sentiment was felt toward the European Central Bank (ECB), formed in 1998 in the nineteen-member (as of 2016) Eurozone.

These perceptions have changed over the past decade after both the United States and Europe experienced the worst financial crisis in nearly a century. Extraordinary times called for extraordinary efforts by the Fed and the ECB, using monetary policy beyond what is used in normal times. In the United States, the recession of 2007–2009 and the subsequent slow recovery led the Fed to take drastic actions never seen in its past. More recently, the ECB made large rescue packages for member nations that neared default on their debt, taking new drastic measures to save the euro from collapse or from members leaving the Eurozone. This section presents a brief summary of the challenges faced by the Fed and the ECB, and how both have used extraordinary powers to limit the economic impact of the crises.

The Fed: Dealing with an Economic Crisis Not Seen in 80 Years

The financial meltdown that plagued the global economy in the latter part of the last decade was caused by a perfect storm of conditions. First, a world savings glut and unusually low interest rates from 2002 to 2005 led to a housing bubble. Second, financial risk was not properly accounted for, as consumers were eager to buy homes (sometimes second homes) and banks were so eager to lend that they ignored previous lending standards. Third, investors and financial institutions (including pension funds) bought trillions of dollars of assets that depended on housing values increasing consistently in the future.

When the housing bubble collapsed, the house of cards collapsed as well. Falling home values and rising mortgage payments caused homeowners to default, leading to many foreclosures. The foreclosures caused assets dependent on housing values to plummet, resulting in trillions of dollars in losses by financial firms and investors. Banks found themselves in trouble, and the government bailed out the banks by buying up bad loans to provide capital and liquidity in order to prevent bank runs and a sharp fall in lending.

In response to the financial crisis, the Fed used its normal monetary policy tools and some that it hadn't used since the 1930s. By December 2008 the Fed had lowered its federal funds target rate, using its normal monetary policy tool, to essentially 0%. By this time, the Fed turned to extraordinary measures when it began making massive loans to banks and buying large amounts of risky mortgage-backed securities. The Fed's balance sheet ballooned in size from less than $1 trillion in 2008 to over $3 trillion in 2012, a level that well exceeds that in normal times. Further, its balance sheet allocation changed dramatically from one consisting of about 90% in safe Treasury securities to one comprising nearly half in more risky assets such as mortgage-backed securities.

The Fed was the prime mover in dealing with the financial crisis, once it recognized it. One can argue that it took too long for the Fed to recognize the problem, and the Fed may have encouraged the housing bubble by keeping interest rates very low for too long. Further, the government's response in bailing out financial institutions and other industries, along with a dramatic increase in the monetary base, led some to believe that the Fed overstepped its authority by exercising powers it did not have (such as its role in buying up troubled assets from banks) and expanding the monetary base too far, risking widespread inflation in the future.

But as former Fed Chair Ben Bernanke said, if your neighbor's house is on fire because he was smoking in bed, you deal with the fire first because if you don't, your own house can burn down. You deal with your neighbor's smoking problem later.

The U.S. economy has mostly recovered from the financial crisis, but current Fed Chair Janet Yellen has remained cautious, allowing monetary policy to remain accommodative as economic growth improves.

The Fed was not alone in taking drastic action during the financial crisis. The Fed's counterpart in Europe, the ECB, took extraordinary action as well.

The Eurozone Crisis and the Role of the European Central Bank

The Eurozone was created during a 1992 meeting in the Netherlands by twelve European nations that envisioned a single currency that would reduce transaction costs and facilitate and expand trade. The meeting resulted in the signing of the Maastricht Treaty, which set the monetary criteria that each member nation had to satisfy before joining the Eurozone. These criteria included, among others:

1. Maintaining an inflation rate no higher than 1.5% above the average of the three member countries with the lowest inflation

2. Maintaining long-term interest rates (on 10-year bonds) no higher than 2% above the average of the three member countries with the lowest interest rates

3. Maintaining annual deficits of less than 3% of GDP

4. Maintaining total debt of less than 60% of GDP

5. Having no major currency devaluation in the preceding two years

When the euro was introduced in 1999, eleven of the twelve treaty members met the monetary criteria. Greece took two extra years to satisfy the criteria and was admitted into the Eurozone in 2001.

Why were such stringent criteria needed? When a common currency is adopted, monetary policy becomes shared by all members. Therefore, a monetary crisis in one country can quickly spread to all countries. Germany, the largest and wealthiest member of the Eurozone, traditionally had maintained low inflation and a very stable economy. Although Germany had much to gain from the Eurozone, it also faced risks by integrating its monetary policy with countries whose economies were less stable. Because of Germany's fear of inflation, the Eurozone was set up in a way that prescribed austerity measures as opposed to monetary expansion as a cure for debt. However, the severity of the Eurozone crisis that would ensue a decade later changed this focus, as even Germany had to accept that extraordinary actions were needed.

Still, for much of the first decade, the euro was a success, with member nations keeping their debt under control while the ECB implemented monetary policy for the entire Eurozone. Moreover, the euro established itself as a major reserve currency, giving it significant clout among world financial institutions.

However, conditions began changing in 2007 when several member nations saw their debts rise, requiring some to sell securities (sovereign debt) on future cash revenues to keep their debt-to-GDP ratio from exceeding the Eurozone limit. However, these quick fixes worked only for a short period. A bigger crisis was brewing that would test the ability of the ECB to save the euro from collapse.

From 2008 to 2013, nearly half of the Eurozone nations faced some sort of financial crisis. In each situation, the ECB used its normal monetary policy tools in addition to extraordinary measures to lessen the economic impact of the crisis and to prevent nations from defaulting on their debt. A summary of key events faced by individual Eurozone members follows.

- **Ireland:** Ireland was one of the first member nations to face difficulties when its property bubble burst, causing all of its major banks to face insolvency in 2008. This led the Irish government to pass a law guaranteeing all bank deposits and the ECB to step in and lend billions of euros to Irish banks, an action that up to that point had never been taken on this scale.

- **Greece:** The global recession devastated Greece's shipping industry, which led to deficits and then a debt crisis in 2010. By 2012 interest rates had risen to over 25%. Further, public riots threatened Greece's ability to maintain public support for the euro and the conditions required to remain in the Eurozone. A series of bailout packages from the ECB and the International Monetary Fund (IMF) helped bring interest rates down, but unemployment remained high even in 2016. Moreover, citizens in Greece increasingly grew wary of debt-cutting measures and structural reforms that made life increasingly difficult.

- **Portugal:** The third country to receive a bailout package from the ECB in exchange for promises of budget cuts and structural reforms was Portugal, in 2011. The crisis increased unemployment, which had reached 18% by 2013. However, improved economic conditions since then allowed Portugal to exit the bailout program in 2014 and return to mostly normal times, though the effects of the crisis still linger in some parts of the country.

- **Cyprus:** In 2013 Cyprus became the fourth nation to receive a bailout package when heavy investments by investors and banks in private Greek industries went sour. It also became the first nation to borrow funds from the European Stability Mechanism (ESM), created by the ECB in September 2012 to provide loans to Eurozone members facing financial difficulties. Like Portugal, Cyprus improved its economy, allowing it to conclude its bailout program in 2016.

- **Spain:** Spain had faced an unrelenting economic crisis since 2008, as uncontrolled debt and unemployment led to many leadership changes. In 2013 the unemployment rate reached 25%, and throughout this period, the ECB bought Spanish government bonds and made extraordinary amounts of loans (around 350 billion euros) to Spanish banks, including new loans from the ESM. But unlike the countries discussed earlier, Spain never accepted a bailout, and strong economic growth in 2015 and 2016 (fueled by record tourism) has put Spain on a path to recovery.

Ireland went from being the second wealthiest member of the Eurozone (after Luxembourg) to one facing the biggest financial crisis in 2008.

bildbroker.de/Alamy

- **Italy:** Italy has long had a high debt-to-GDP ratio, even before the crisis in other countries began. It has taken many steps to reduce its debt, which has stood over 100% of its GDP for much of the past decade, though much work remains. A key obstacle facing Italy has been the lack of economic growth. While other Eurozone nations experienced economic growth following the global economic crisis, Italy remained in a recession for several more years, and today remains among the slowest growing economies in the Eurozone.

- **Slovenia:** In 2007 Slovenia became the 13th member of the Eurozone. Slovenia's economy is considerably smaller than the rest of the Eurozone, and banks were never fully privatized, resulting in political influences in banking decisions. These factors made Slovenia more prone to economic downturns, and led to its financial crisis. Fortunately, a strong rise in exports and successful reforms of state-owned companies led to healthy economic growth since 2013, setting a positive example of how good economic policy can resolve financial crises quickly.

In sum, the ECB took extraordinary actions that it had never taken in its history to prevent financial crises in individual countries from causing the collapse of the Eurozone. First, the ECB provided loans to banks and bought government debt, and created the ESM in 2012 to manage funds being disbursed. Second, the ECB negotiated deals with private

ISSUE

The Challenges of Monetary Policy with Regional Differences in Economic Performance

The Eurozone crisis of 2008–2013 led many to point to Europe as an experiment with monetary policy integration gone wrong. Members of the Eurozone were too different, not only culturally, but also economically. Prior to its formation in 1999, the richest member of the Eurozone, Luxembourg, had a GDP per capita that was more than twice the level of that of Portugal, which at the time was the poorest member of the original eleven countries, until Greece joined in 2001. In 2007 countries in Eastern Europe began joining, further spreading the difference between the richest and poorest members, which would all share the same currency and monetary policy determined by the European Central Bank (ECB).

Although each member nation would have representation in the ECB based on population, Germany and France, the two largest members, dominate decisions. The challenge faced by the ECB is formulating a common monetary policy that best fits the economic conditions faced by its members. This is not easy.

When one part of the Eurozone is booming (say, Ireland) and would benefit from contractionary monetary policy, while another is struggling with debt (Greece) and requires expansionary monetary policy, choosing a common monetary policy involves placing the priority of one country's economic concerns over another.

But is the situation in Europe the only one in which a common monetary policy needs to address wide variations in economic performance? The answer is no, and the best example of another monetary zone facing similar problems may surprise you . . . the United States.

The United States shares many similarities with the Eurozone when it comes to monetary policy. Although the United States is one country, wide variations in economic performance still exist. In 2015 Delaware's per capita income of about $72,000 was twice that of Mississippi's $36,000.

Further, U.S. monetary policy also must take into account territories that use the U.S. dollar, such as Puerto Rico, as well as countries such as Ecuador, El Salvador, and Panama, all of which have a per capita income even lower than Mississippi's. The Fed's decisions

European Central Bank in Frankfurt, Germany.

have a direct impact on all economies that use the U.S. dollar.

In sum, large monetary unions such as the Eurozone and the United States must weigh the priorities of one region against another when considering the policies they implement. Such a task makes the statement that *monetary policy is as much art as science* a realistic description facing central banks today.

Walter Bibikow/Corbis

banks and other investors to write off portions of debt and to restructure existing loans to governments. Third, it demanded that governments pass austerity measures, enact structural reforms, and be subjected to greater scrutiny. Like the Fed, the ECB's balance sheet ballooned during the crisis, from about 1 trillion euros in 2007 to over 3 trillion euros in 2012. Why was the ECB so eager to take extraordinary actions to prevent countries from defaulting on their debt?

Clearly, the number of Eurozone nations facing a financial crisis had reached a critical point by 2013. If any nation defaults and pulls out of the Eurozone, it could trigger a global loss of confidence in the euro. For example, investors might be less willing to invest in euro-denominated bonds and assets if the long-term stability of the currency came into question. Such a loss of confidence would itself reduce the stability of the euro, leading to a self-fulfilling prophecy. Imagine what would happen if a U.S. state became so much in debt that it chose to give up the U.S. dollar and create its own, much devalued, state currency. The impact could be significant.

However, the ECB used aggressive monetary policies to reduce the likelihood of a nation's exit from the Eurozone. Just as the Fed stepped in to prevent regional crises in the United States by injecting financial capital and reducing interest rates, the ECB used expansionary monetary policies to help member nations facing economic crises. This is much easier said than done, as the Issue described, when different areas of a currency zone face varying levels of economic performance.

Why Would a Country Give Up Its Monetary Policy?

> **What factors led Ecuador, El Salvador, and Panama to give up their ability to use monetary policy in favor of adopting the U.S. dollar?**

One of the first tasks when traveling abroad is to exchange currency. In most countries, this is an easy task: Just visit a foreign exchange booth or withdraw money from a local ATM. Some countries that depend on tourism, such as Jamaica and Costa Rica, readily accept U.S. dollars despite having their own national currency. But for American tourists visiting Ecuador, El Salvador, or Panama, exchanging money isn't even an option, because the official currency in these countries *is* the U.S. dollar.

Why would a country adopt the U.S. dollar as its official currency, and what effect does it have on monetary policy?

The decision for a country to use a foreign currency (in this case, the U.S.

Traveling to Ecuador? No need to exchange money. The official currency is the U.S. dollar.

dollar) as its own official currency, called dollarization, is not in any way influenced or dictated by the United States. Ecuador, El Salvador, and Panama willingly gave up their own currency to adopt the U.S. dollar. And by doing so, these countries relinquished their ability to set monetary policy, because the supply of dollars and the interest rate are managed by the U.S. Federal Reserve. Why would a country give up control of its monetary policy?

Panama adopted the U.S. dollar over a century ago to facilitate trade, given its strategic geographic location

that attracts cargo ships from around the world crossing the Panama Canal. In the case of Ecuador and El Salvador, which adopted the U.S. dollar in 2000 and 2001, respectively, their situations were different than Panama's. Prior to adopting the U.S. dollar, both countries had rampant inflation, caused by the inability of their central banks to keep money growth under control. High inflation decreases investor confidence because profits quickly lose their value. By adopting the U.S. dollar (and thereby preventing the government from adjusting the money supply), Ecuador and El Salvador sent a signal that they were serious about maintaining low inflation, which subsequently led to greater foreign direct investment.

Still, problems persist in countries that dollarize, and the lack of an independent monetary policy makes it difficult to address fluctuations in the economy, especially when they differ from those of the United States. But for these countries and others that have dollarized their economies, the potential benefits outweigh the costs.

GO TO **LaunchPad** TO PRACTICE THE ECONOMIC CONCEPTS IN THIS STORY

Still, the efforts of the ECB have not stopped European nations from voting to exit the Eurozone or the broader European Union. The European Union includes nations that do not use the euro including the United Kingdom (Britain), Sweden, Denmark, and several eastern European nations. In 2016, voters in Britain elected to leave the European Union in an unprecedented action coined Brexit, which caused uncertainty in financial markets and challenged the ability of the European Union and Eurozone to remain powerful influences in global markets.

Today, most of the Eurozone countries that faced financial crises have recovered with some countries such as Ireland and Slovenia experiencing rapid economic growth. The exception is Greece, which continued to face challenges in 2016. But overall, economic growth remains tenuous throughout the region. This is not unlike the recovery pattern experienced in the United States.

In the United States, the housing market has mostly recovered, employment growth has been strong, stock markets have set new highs, and banks have strengthened their balance sheets. Still, as in Europe, problems such as deficits and weak growth remain, which means that the Fed will continue to rely on monetary tools to prevent problems from home and abroad from engulfing the economy.

The next chapter is devoted to analyzing the major macroeconomic policy challenges involving both fiscal policy and monetary policy, allowing you to use the macroeconomic tools learned thus far to sketch out solutions.

 CHECKPOINT

NEW MONETARY POLICY CHALLENGES

- To control the financial panic of 2008, the Fed used its normal monetary policy tools and some that it hadn't used in many decades.
- The European Central Bank is the Fed's counterpart in Europe, setting the monetary policy for the nineteen-member Eurozone.
- A long and severe debt crisis occurred when several European nations neared default on their loans, requiring extraordinary actions, including bailout loans, by the ECB to keep the effects of the crisis from spreading to the entire Eurozone.

QUESTION: The collapse of the financial markets in late 2008 resulted in the Fed reducing interest rates to near 0%. Was it likely that the U.S. economy in 2009 sank into a Keynesian liquidity trap?

Answers to the Checkpoint questions can be found at the end of this chapter.

chapter summary

Section 1 What Is Monetary Policy?

 24.1 **Monetary policy** is the process by which a country's money supply is controlled to target interest rates that subsequently influences economic output and prices.

Importance of Interest Rates on the Economy

Higher interest rates affect aggregate demand by:

1. Making borrowing more expensive, forcing consumers and firms to cut spending and investing
2. Giving people more incentive to save than spend
3. Forcing the government to spend more on financing the national debt
4. Increasing the value of the U.S. dollar, making U.S. exports more expensive

24.2 **Twin Goals of Monetary Policy**

1. Economic growth and full employment
2. Stable prices and moderate long-term interest rates

Bills, bills, bills. Higher interest rates cause debt payments to take a bigger portion of each paycheck, leaving less to spend on other goods.

Expansionary Monetary Policy: More money → lower interest rates → higher C, I, G, and $(X - M)$ = increase in aggregate demand and output

Contractionary Monetary Policy: Less money → higher interest rates → lower C, I, G, and $(X - M)$ = decrease in aggregate demand and output

Section 2 Monetary Theories

 24.3 The **quantity theory of money** is a product of the classical school of thought, which concludes that the economy will tend toward equilibrium at full employment in the long run.

Classical theorists do not believe that monetary policies are effective at all.

Keynesians and monetarists believe that monetary policy can be effective in the short run, but not in the long run.

24.4 Equation of Exchange (Classical Theory)

$$M \times V = P \times Q$$
↑   ↑
Fixed   Fixed

$$\Delta M = \Delta P$$

Because velocity (V) and output (Q) are believed to be fixed in the long run, any change in the money supply (M) results in a change in prices (P).

Keynesian Money Theory

Increasing the money supply leads to greater investment when the economy is healthy. In times of severe recession, however, monetary policy is ineffective.

Fiscal policy is the preferred approach to restore the economy.

John Maynard Keynes

Monetarist Theory

Increasing the money supply reduces interest rates, which leads to greater consumption and investment. Monetary policy is therefore effective in the short run.

Fiscal policy is ineffective as it crowds out consumption and investment.

Milton Friedman

24.5 **Demand Shocks Versus Supply Shocks**

Demand shocks affect the AD curve.

- Caused by factors such as consumer confidence, business sentiment, or export demand.
- Monetary policy is more effective because targeting one goal automatically targets the other.

Supply shocks affect the SRAS curve.

- Caused by factors such as changing input prices or technological innovation.
- Monetary policy is less effective because targeting one goal makes the other target worse.

Eric Chiang

Rising food prices cause a negative supply shock that is difficult to counteract with monetary policy.

Section 3 Modern Monetary Policy

24.6 **Rules:** Money grows by a fixed amount each year, preventing monetary policy from causing too drastic an effect because the economy is inherently stable in the long run.

versus

Discretion: A flexible money approach based on current economic conditions. It is useful in severe recessions when constant money growth might not be enough.

Magictorch/Corbis

Alternative to money targeting is **inflation targeting:** implementing policy to keep inflation at about 2% to faciliate long-term economic growth.

24.7 **Taylor rule:** Used to approximate the Fed's actions on interest rates based on economic conditions:

Fed Funds Rate Target = 2 + Inflation Rate + 1/2 (Inflation Gap) + 1/2(Output Gap)

Section 4 New Monetary Policy Challenges

24.8 The U.S. financial crisis in 2008 created a major challenge to the Fed, which had lowered the federal funds rate to near 0% but still faced an economy in deep recession.

To continue expansionary monetary policy with interest rates at 0%, the Fed engaged in various **quantitative easing** strategies, including purchasing long-term assets from banks to expand the monetary base.

24.9 The nineteen member nations that form the Eurozone share a monetary policy set by the European Central Bank (ECB). In recent years, ECB has used aggressive monetary policy actions to prevent the effects of financial crises in individual nations from engulfing the entire region.

ANDY RAIN/Corbis

Protests on quantitative easing arose because people feared high potential inflation, which would reduce the value of money and savings.

KEY CONCEPTS

expansionary monetary policy, p. 641
contractionary monetary policy,
    p. 642
equation of exchange, p. 644
money illusion, p. 646

liquidity trap, p. 646
easy money, quantitative
    easing, or accommodative
    monetary policy,
        p. 650

tight money or restrictive
    monetary policy, p. 650
monetary rule, p. 651
inflation targeting, p. 651
Taylor rule, p. 652

QUESTIONS AND PROBLEMS

Check Your Understanding

1. Why is it important for the Federal Reserve Board to be independent of the executive branch of the federal government?

2. When the interest rate falls, why do people desire higher money balances?

3. Describe how open market operations alter the supply of money.

4. What does the equation of exchange, $M \times V = P \times Q$, help to explain?

5. How is the impact of expansionary monetary policy different when the economy is considerably below full employment than when it is at full employment?

6. How do sticky wages and prices make monetary policy effective in the short run?

Apply the Concepts

7. Suppose a rise in consumer confidence causes aggregate demand to increase, resulting in a short-run equilibrium that is above full employment output. What type of monetary policy might the Fed use to reduce inflationary pressures and to bring the economy back to full employment?

8. It seems that each time the Fed raises interest rates, the stock market has an awful few days. Why do higher interest rates have such an impact on the stock market?

9. If the Fed persistently pursues an easy money policy, what is the likely outcome?

10. When NASA scientists were operating the Mars rovers to get them to drive across the Martian landscape and collect and analyze rocks and crevices, the scientists complained that the 20-minute delay between when they issued a command and when the rovers responded made their job more challenging. Isn't this somewhat similar to what monetary policymakers face? How is it different?

11. Suppose a devastating drought leads to higher food prices, causing a negative supply shock to occur. What type of monetary policy should the Fed use if the goal is to maintain price stability in the economy? What are the consequences of doing so?

12. Explain how the housing bubble at the beginning of the 21st century led to the Taylor rule target exceeding the actual federal funds rate. Could increasing the federal funds rate during this time have helped to reduce the severity of the last recession?

In the News

13. *There are two forces that cause the economy to grow. One is real, the other is an illusion. The real force—entrepreneurial innovation and creativity—comes naturally as long as government policies do not drive it away. The artificial force is easy money. An increased supply of money, by creating an illusion of wealth, can increase spending in the short run, but this eventually turns into inflation. Printing money cannot possibly create wealth; if it could, counterfeiting would be legal.*[3]

    Does this quote illustrate the short-run versus the long-run aspects of monetary policy? Why or why not?

[3] Brian Wesbury, "Economic Rehab," *The Wall Street Journal*, June 7, 2006, p. A14.

14. In 2016 Greece faced another set of hurdles in its ongoing saga of managing its debt. In order for Greece to maintain its obligations under the IMF and European Central Bank bailout packages, it must continue to cut government spending, particularly pensions that have put a strain on the budget. Greece's leaders, meanwhile, have argued that the required spending cuts will push the economy back into recession. Using an AD/AS model, show what the required budget cuts might do to an economy that is still experiencing slow growth.

Solving Problems

15. Why are supply shocks so much harder than demand shocks for monetary policy to adjust? Use the grid below to show your answer to this question.

WORK IT OUT 　　　　　📖 **LaunchPad** | interactive activity

16. In 2012 U.S. inflation was 2.1% and output was 4.8% below its long-run potential. Three years later, in 2015, U.S. inflation fell to 0.4% due to falling energy prices, and output improved to 1.8% below its long-run potential.

   a. If the inflation target is 2%, what was the federal funds target in 2012 using the Taylor rule?

   b. If the actual federal funds rate was 0.1% in 2012, did the Taylor rule estimate the target accurately?

   c. Again assuming an inflation target of 2%, what was the federal funds target in 2015 using the Taylor rule?

   d. If the actual federal funds rate was 0.4% in 2015, did the Taylor rule do a better job predicting interest rates compared to 2012? Explain your answer.

#️ USING THE NUMBERS

17. According to By the Numbers, what were the approximate interest rates for the following types of loans in December 2015: federal funds rate, discount rate, prime rate, 30-year mortgage rate? Why aren't these interest rates all the same?

18. According to By the Numbers, in what region outside of the United States is the largest percentage of U.S. $100 bills in circulation held? Why is the answer not China, which holds the most U.S. debt?

Checkpoint: What Is Monetary Policy? 643

Expansionary monetary policy reduces interest rates in order to spur consumption and investment, leading to an increase in aggregate demand. A reduction in interest rates placed on student loans by the government, although technically not monetary policy, produces a similar effect. When your monthly payments are reduced due to the interest rate reduction, you now have extra money to spend on other items. This extra consumption contributes to an increase in aggregate demand, much like an expansionary monetary policy.

Checkpoint: Monetary Theories 650

Those who prefer a large government role in the economy would best resemble Keynesians who believe in fiscal policy to increase aggregate demand. Keynesians would support raising tax revenues to reduce the debt. Those who advocate for a smaller government might be considered monetarists, who believe that fiscal policy tends to crowd out consumption and investment. Monetarists would support a reduction in spending to reduce the debt. Those who do not believe in either fiscal or monetary policy interventions might resemble classical theorists who believe that the economy should be left to market forces, and that the government should be as small as possible.

Checkpoint: Modern Monetary Policy 655

When the Fed begins to view inflation as a growing problem, it usually means that some form of contractionary monetary policy is to follow. This typically means that interest rates will rise and, most important for bond investors, bond prices will *fall* and bondholders will incur capital losses.

Checkpoint: New Monetary Policy Challenges 660

Reducing interest rates to low levels to stimulate credit and the economy was probably not sufficient by itself. But as consumer spending dropped off, businesses avoided new investments as markets declined or disappeared, suggesting that the economy may have been in a liquidity trap. Keynesian analysis got the nod from policymakers with the $787 billion fiscal stimulus package passed in 2009.

25

Macroeconomic Policy: Challenges in a Global Economy

Understanding the obstacles facing our economy and the policy tools that are available to overcome them

25.1 Describe what caused the housing bubble and the financial crisis.

25.2 Describe the extraordinary steps that Congress and the Fed took to prevent the collapse of the financial system.

25.3 Explain what Phillips curves are and what relationship they postulate between inflation and unemployment.

25.4 Describe how inflationary expectations can take on a life of their own and stymie policymakers.

25.5 Contrast adaptive expectations with rational expectations and describe their implications for policymakers.

25.6 Describe the major economic issues facing the macroeconomy today and in the future.

25.7 Discuss why jobless recoveries have become the norm following recessions.

25.8 Discuss the role that globalization has in the economy and how it affects macroeconomic policy.

Between 2003 and 2007, the U.S. housing market achieved gains at a rate never before seen in its history. As soon as a house or condo was put on the market, buyers were eager to snatch it up. Banks were eager to lend to these buyers and bent over backward to accommodate them, even lowering standards if need be. If they did not, other banks were ready to jump in. The upshot: new types of loans targeted borrowers who otherwise would not have qualified for conventional loans. And the government facilitated the process by keeping interest rates low.

These factors provided incentives for individuals and firms to consume and produce. Luxury condominiums were built throughout the country, especially in popular vacation destinations such as Miami, Phoenix, and Las Vegas. New housing developments formed, each adding hundreds or thousands of homes with the expectation that buyers would come. And they did, helped by banks that became even more aggressive in their lending, advertising attractive mortgages that required no down payment, interest-only payments, and little to no credit.

Over this period, average home prices in the United States increased by 41%. In Nevada and Arizona, home prices rose by almost 80%. The growth in the housing market spurred other industries, such as home furnishings, insurance, and even automobiles. Individuals were eager to buy, developers were eager to build, banks were eager to lend, and investors were eager to put money in securities backed by the value of housing.

Unfortunately, the house of cards eventually collapsed in late 2007. The financial crisis that ensued led to a restricted lending market, a severe recession, and a long jobless recovery.

What does macroeconomics have to say about the effects of a deep economic recession and a slow economic recovery? Quite a bit, actually. We have seen in previous chapters how the Fed and the federal government intervene in markets to promote long-term economic growth and stability in employment and prices. But this is much harder than it might appear to be: There is no magic formula easily discernible to all that will correct each problem.

Before the 1930s, common wisdom was that the economy was best left alone. The Great Depression changed that, and ever since then the government's role in economic stabilization—smoothing the business cycle—expanded substantially.

This chapter studies the economic policies that address the macroeconomic issues facing the world today: slow economic growth, rising debt, long-run inflation, and persistent unemployment. One challenge is the existence of a potential tradeoff between inflation and unemployment. Another is the potential tradeoff between debt reduction and economic growth. These potential tradeoffs influence the macroeconomic policies chosen to guide the economy.

The chapter begins with a broad overview of the factors leading to the 2007–2009 Great Recession (as it is now known) and the slow recovery. The chapter then studies several theories regarding the effectiveness of macroeconomic policy, including the Phillips curve on the potential tradeoff between unemployment and inflation, the rational expectations argument about the ultimate ineffectiveness of policy, and the new Keynesian response.

The Long Road Back: The Great Recession and the Jobless Recovery

The Great Recession was caused by the collapse of the housing market, which led to reduced consumer sentiment and lower retail sales. Persistent unemployment ensued and the Fed used unprecedented monetary policy actions to speed up the economic recovery.

Go to **LaunchPad** *to use the latest data to recreate this graph.*

Median existing home prices rose significantly in the early years of the 21st century but fell quickly in the latter part of the decade. Housing prices have since risen again.

alexsl/Getty Images

Consumer sentiment fell significantly from 2007 to 2009. It took six years of economic recovery before consumer sentiment returned to its pre-recession peak.

Monthly real retail sales fell over 10% from 2007 to 2009. It took four years for real retail sales to recover and to surpass the level reached in 2007.

7,163,000 **T**otal jobs lost during the Great Recession (December 2007–June 2009)

11,033,000 **T**otal jobs created over six years of recovery (July 2009–June 2015)

Credit Application

Social Security Number

State: NY ZIP: 10036   555-39-

Tupungato/Shutterstock

The Federal Reserve undertook three rounds of quantitative easing (QE) after short-term interest rates were effectively lowered to 0%. The value of assets purchased in each round:

QE1 (December 2008–March 2010): $1,425 billion

QE2 (November 2010–June 2011): $600 billion

QE3 (September 2012–October 2014): $1,700 billion

The Fed's actions kept long-term interest rates low, encouraging consumers and businesses to borrow in order to consume and invest. Yet, banks increased their lending standards significantly after the last financial crisis, reducing the effect of low interest rates.

Finally, we discuss the economic issues that influence the future of our economy. We focus on the effects of jobless recoveries, rising debt, and globalization. We use the macroeconomic tools discussed throughout the book to analyze how economic policies affect our economy and our standard of living.

THE GREAT RECESSION AND MACROECONOMIC POLICY

The 18-month recession that lasted from December 2007 to July 2009 was dubbed the Great Recession, not because of its length, which was not much longer than the typical recession, but rather for its severity and the impact it had on so many industries and countries. Further, the economic recovery that took place after the recession was slow, requiring many years for economic indicators to return to their prerecession levels. This section presents the factors that led to the Great Recession and the macroeconomic policies used to mitigate its effects.

From the Housing Bubble to the Financial Crisis

Owning a home is a dream shared by most people. During the first few years of the 21st century, a glut in worldwide savings and the Fed's aggressive expansionary monetary policies following the 2001 recession led to low mortgage rates, helping many to achieve that dream of home ownership. Renters bought their first homes. Existing homeowners moved into larger homes or bought second homes. The resulting higher than normal demand drove up the price of housing. After a few years of rising prices, people started to think prices could only go up. This led some people to become speculators, which led to house "flipping"—purchasing a home with the intention of selling it as soon as possible for a tidy profit.

First homes, bigger homes, and second homes were the goals of many Americans during the housing bubble of the early 21st century.

Builders provide homes, but usually a third party brings the transaction to a close. A financial intermediary provides the financing for home buyers in the form of a mortgage. Traditionally, the standard is a 30-year mortgage with a fixed interest rate. The person taking out the mortgage to purchase the home made monthly payments, which consisted of interest on the loan and some payment toward the loan amount (the principal). Financial intermediaries, such as banks, usually had high standards that would-be home buyers had to meet.

This changed at the beginning of the new century, as banks eager to cash in on the lucrative housing market made loans easier to obtain. And, as long as housing prices kept rising, the borrower's collateral (the house) would protect the bank from losing money if the loan could not be repaid. Financial intermediaries encouraged home buying by offering adjustable-rate mortgages (ARMs). These mortgages offered a below-market interest rate for a short period (usually three or five years); the rate would then adjust based on the market interest rate. From a buyer's point of view, a below-market rate, at least in the short term, was an inducement to buy. From a bank's point of view, below-market rates generated business: They could expect ARM holders to seek out fixed interest rate mortgages after the initial period ended, which meant a second round of origination fees (paid whenever a mortgage is taken out).

The housing boom of 2003 to 2007 saw even more innovations in the mortgage market, as financial intermediaries felt competitive pressure from new mortgage brokers and Wall Street firms that were only too happy to meet the growing demand. Two key things happened: Mortgage credit standards fell, and the market for collateralized debt obligations (CDOs) developed.

subprime mortgage Mortgages that are given to borrowers who are a poor credit risk. These higher-risk loans charge a higher interest rate, which can be profitable to lenders if borrowers make their payments on time.

Subprime Mortgages and Collateralized Debt Obligations Subprime **mortgages** are loans made to borrowers with poor credit. These loans carried high interest rates that were profitable for the banks as long as borrowers made payments on time. Because the economy was strong, defaults were minimal. Further, many financial institutions reduced their risk by selling these loans to other investors in the form of CDOs, also known as mortgage-backed securities (which make up most CDOs).

CDOs are essentially bonds backed by a collection of mortgages: prime, subprime, home equity, and other ARMs. Banks holding mortgages found they could offset the risk of default by selling them to consolidators who put together enormous packages of CDOs, with the mortgaged homes standing as the collateral behind the security offered. Wall Street then sold off slices of these mortgage pools to investors interested in the steady income from mortgage payments. Mortgages to subprime borrowers—those with higher credit risks—could be combined with solid mortgages, a little like diluting poison in a large lake to dissipate its effects.

Banks and mortgage companies now were evaluating mortgage clients for loans that they did not intend to keep. They were simply collecting an origination fee and then immediately selling the mortgage to Wall Street. What in the past had been a long-term investment for banks and mortgage companies became nothing more than a business of advertising and selling loans quickly. Because Wall Street could package and sell as many loans as mortgage brokers could provide, banks had less incentive to keep high lending standards. Risk was being transferred elsewhere.

Trouble started in 2007 when some of the people who took on subprime mortgages started to default. These people were stretched too thin. When their ARMs reset, they faced higher payments, sometimes double or triple the original monthly payments. Worse, the spike in foreclosures as well as homeowners trying to sell their homes to escape rising mortgage payments caused the value of houses to fall, which meant that borrowers wishing to refinance their homes (to make mortgage payments affordable again) were being turned away because the amount they were seeking to borrow exceeded the value of their now lower-value home.

Compounding this, another problem arose. Risk ratings by bond rating agencies whose job it is to rate packages of mortgages turned out to be faulty. Wall Street knew the minimum requirements needed for a rating agency to assign a AAA rating to a CDO, and they manipulated the components to get that all-important rating. Also, rating firms were paid 6 times their normal fee to give the AAA rating to the mortgage packages, and were only paid *if the CDO got the AAA rating*, giving ratings agencies an incentive to lower standards. Investors wanted bonds with the security of a AAA rating, which gave the appearance of high-yield, low-risk investments. The bond packages sold well all over the world. The risk of each CDO was underestimated because of the overly rosy ratings.

Two more problems would make this a growing house of cards. Because the mortgage packages were seen as low-risk investments, many investors borrowed money at the low prevailing interest rates to purchase greater quantities. They **leveraged** their capital to earn greater returns. But with leverage comes additional risk: A small drop in prices can easily wipe out a highly leveraged account. Table 1 shows how a leveraged investment magnifies

leverage Occurs when a small amount of capital is used to support a larger amount of investment by borrowing. The risk of highly leveraged investments is that a small decrease in price can wipe out one's account.

TABLE 1	THE MAGNIFIED RISK OF LEVERAGED INVESTMENTS
Nonleveraged Investment	**Leveraged Investment**
Initial account value: $10,000	Initial account value: $10,000
Leverage ratio: 1:1	Leverage ratio: 10:1
Value of invested assets: $10,000	Value of invested assets: $100,000
($10,000 × 1)	($10,000 × 10)
Event: 10% drop in invested assets	Event: 10% drop in invested assets
Drop in value of investment: $1,000	Drop in value of investment: $10,000
($10,000 × 10%)	($100,000 × 10%)
New account value: $9,000	New account value: $0

credit default swap A financial instrument that insures against the potential default on an asset. Because of the extent of defaults in the last financial crisis, issuers of credit default swaps could not repay all of the claims, bankrupting these financial institutions.

the risk of losing money. In this case, a 10% drop in value of the security wipes out the leveraged account, while the nonleveraged account sees its value drop by just 10%. A leveraged account magnifies both gains and losses.

To protect against this risk, investors purchased **credit default swaps,** an instrument developed by the financial industry to act as an insurance policy against defaults. The biggest issuer of credit default swaps, the American International Group (AIG), sold several *trillion* dollars of these swaps with only a few *billion* dollars in capital to back them up. Here again, we see risk underestimated and therefore mispriced.

Collapsing Financial Markets This brings us to the central event that brought down the financial system. By 2007, $25 *trillion* of American CDOs were in investment portfolios of banks, pension funds, mutual funds, hedge funds, and other financial institutions worldwide. The rate of subprime mortgage defaults skyrocketed, and because investors did not know what exactly was in their CDOs, they panicked.

The collapse of the housing market forced many homeowners out of their homes and contributed to the severity of the 2007–2009 recession.

Consequently, buyers of CDOs evaporated, and prices fell as people began dumping CDOs at fire-sale prices. AIG could not cover the losses it had insured and went bankrupt. For banks, this was a catastrophe. Their CDOs were virtually worthless, and an important part of the banks' capital was wiped out. To raise capital, banks called in loans and reduced lines of credit to businesses, which reduced the money supply, contracted the economy, caused job losses, and deepened the recession.

In sum, the financial crisis was caused by a savings glut that led to low interest rates, which fueled a housing boom that led to new financial instruments and investment securities that depended on the value of housing staying high. A financial house of cards was created, and when one card at the bottom (subprime loans) lost strength, the entire edifice fell. Because all types of financial institutions worldwide were investors in CDOs, credit dried up, creating a credit crisis that precipitated a worldwide recession.

The Government's Policy Response

As long as the financial system takes on risks that it misperceives, we will have financial crises. Let's look at the government's policy response to the financial crisis:

- Bear Stearns: In July 2007 Bear Stearns, a large Wall Street investment bank, liquidated two hedge funds that invested in mortgage-backed securities as they started to collapse. By March 2008, with Bear Stearns on the verge of bankruptcy due to its holdings of mortgage-backed securities, the Fed engineered a takeover of Bear Stearns by Chase Bank. In essence, the Fed bailed out a rogue bank. This kept a lid on things for a while, but not for long.

- Lehman Brothers: Stung by criticism of its Bear Stearns bailout, the Fed let Lehman Brothers, the fourth largest commercial bank, fail on September 15, 2008. The Fed and the Treasury thought they were sending a message to the financial markets that imprudent lending behavior would result in tremendous costs to stockholders and executives. Unfortunately, this decision sent the financial markets into a tailspin, as banks lost faith in other banks, and insolvencies rose throughout the financial sector.

- AIG: The market received another shock in September when AIG announced it was bankrupt. The news of its bankruptcy turned AAA-rated CDO bonds into highly discounted junk bonds. To stem the panic, the Fed lent AIG over $100 billion.

- TARP: In October 2008 Congress responded to the crisis by passing the $700 billion Troubled Asset Relief Program (TARP), authorizing the U.S. Treasury to purchase CDOs from banks to shore up their capital. The U.S. Treasury ended up investing in banks by injecting government money for preferred equity (stock), thereby increasing bank capital and eliminating insolvency.

- Public Concerns: Policymakers were concerned about public confidence in banks and worried that depositors might begin withdrawing funds, putting banks at further risk of failure. The Federal Deposit Insurance Corporation (FDIC) increased its guarantee on deposits from $100,000 to $250,000 per account.

- The 2009 Stimulus Package: One of President Obama's initial pieces of legislation in his first term was passing the $787 billion American Recovery and Reinvestment Act, a fiscal policy aimed to boost aggregate demand following the financial crisis and recession.

- Industry Bailouts: The financial crisis had also depressed consumer demand, which led many industries to face collapse. In 2009 the government loaned significant sums of money to General Motors, Chrysler, and Ford to save the U.S. automobile industry. Today, the U.S. automobile industry is profitable and strong: In 2015 each of the three major automobile companies made substantial profits and combined earned a record profit of $19.1 billion.

- Fed's Quantitative Easing (QE) Programs: Over the next several years, the Fed would continue to buy mortgage-backed securities in order to remove these risky assets from bank balance sheets. The effort was unprecedented, with the Fed accumulating over $1.7 trillion in mortgage-backed securities by 2014 when QE ended.

These extraordinary efforts prevented the widespread bank failures that had plagued the economy during the Great Depression and during the savings and loan crisis in the 1980s. For the Fed, it was crucial to maintain public confidence and keep the recession from becoming a full-blown depression. The Fed stepped far outside of its usual role of managing the money supply, interest rates, inflation, and unemployment, and took extraordinary, lender-of-last-resort measures to prevent a financial sector meltdown.

This brief summary of the government's response during the financial crisis outlines the breadth and depth of fiscal and monetary policies designed to avert a catastrophe. They have succeeded, but the cost may not be known for a decade.

The Financial Crisis and Its Effects

The financial crisis that resulted in the 2007–2009 recession was the most serious downturn in the economy in over a generation. And the speed by which the economy deteriorated was alarming. The recession began at the end of 2007 and accelerated in 2008 until the middle of 2009. Real GDP declined by over 4% and unemployment reached 10% of the labor force.

At the onset of the financial crisis, jobs were cut as consumers reduced their spending. They tightened their belts in an effort to reduce household debt levels and hunkered down for what they perceived as a severe recession on the way. As a result, 7 million people lost their jobs during this two-year period. Job losses reduced consumer confidence, further reducing consumer spending and aggregate demand. As demand dropped, businesses reduced their production capacity through layoffs and plant closings, shifting short-run aggregate supply leftward.

Toward the end of the recession, prices began to fall as *deflation* set in for most of 2009. We have spent a considerable time in this book studying the harmful effects of inflation, yet now the economy faced deflation. Deflation can be a problem because it increases the *real* value of existing debt, making the debt more burdensome and requiring more purchasing power to make interest payments or pay off the debt. Policymakers faced the problem of preventing debt from becoming a more serious burden on households, which would further reduce aggregate demand and deepen the recession.

The tools we learned about in previous chapters helped us to understand how the government managed the last financial crisis and the accompanying recession. Let's take a further step, adding some challenges to the effective use of policy to smooth the business cycle. The next section focuses on the effectiveness of macroeconomic policy by considering the Phillips curve, which proposes a tradeoff between unemployment and inflation. If this tradeoff exists, policymaking becomes simple: Pick some rate of unemployment and face a corresponding rate of inflation. We also look at how the rational expectations model questions whether using macroeconomic policy to correct fluctuations in the business cycle can ever be effective at all.

CHECKPOINT

THE GREAT RECESSION AND MACROECONOMIC POLICY

- A world savings glut and low interest rates from 2003–2007 led to a housing price bubble. Consumers were eager to buy homes, developers were eager to build them, banks were eager to lend money to purchasers, and investors were eager to invest in CDOs.

- Financial risk was not properly accounted for in the period leading up to the financial crisis, and ratings agencies gave too many CDOs a AAA rating that wasn't deserved.

- When the housing bubble collapsed, foreclosures on subprime mortgages sent the economy into a recession.

- To control the panic, the Fed used its normal monetary policy tools and some that it hadn't used since the 1930s in its role as lender of last resort.

- Congress used fiscal policy in an attempt to nullify the drop in aggregate demand caused by the financial crisis.

QUESTION: The U.S. housing bubble in the early 21st century was caused by a number of factors that provided incentives to individuals to buy houses, to businesses to build and sell houses, and to financial institutions to loan money. In hindsight, what are some policies that the government could have implemented to mitigate this housing bubble?

Answers to the Checkpoint questions can be found at the end of this chapter.

EFFECTIVENESS OF MACROECONOMIC POLICY: PHILLIPS CURVES AND RATIONAL EXPECTATIONS

The persistent unemployment that occurred after the 2007–2009 recession in what is known as a jobless recovery had economists debating the right policy to use. Fiscal policy was undertaken to boost market activity, at the cost of rising debt. And significant monetary policy actions were taken to inject the economy with more money, at the cost of potential inflation. Questions that arise from these policies include whether the effort to reduce unemployment could result in higher inflation, or whether macroeconomic policy has any short-term effects at all. We address these issues in this section by studying two theories developed in the 1950s and 1960s: the Phillips curve and rational expectations.

With Phillips curve analysis, it first seemed that fiscal policy was easy: Pick an unemployment rate from column A and get a corresponding inflation rate from column B. Unfortunately, reality turned out to be much more complex. With rational expectations, the question was whether policy could ever be effective at all.

Unemployment and Inflation: Phillips Curves

Does a relationship exist between unemployment and inflation? In his early work, A. W. Phillips compared the rate of change in money wages to unemployment rates in Britain over the years 1861 to 1957. The negatively sloped curve shown in Figure 1 reflects his estimate of how these variables were related and has been called a **Phillips curve** in his honor. As you can see, when unemployment rises, wage rates fall.

Phillips curve The original curve posited a negative relationship between wages and unemployment, but later versions related unemployment to inflation rates.

What explains this negative relationship between wages and unemployment? Labor costs or wages are typically a firm's largest cost component. As the demand for labor rises, labor markets will tighten, making it difficult for employers to fill vacant positions. Hence, wages rise as firms bid up the price of labor to attract more workers. The opposite happens when labor demand falls: Unemployment rises and wages decline.

This relationship can be seen in specific industries that have seen spikes or downturns in employment. For example, demand for health care professionals increased in the past

FIGURE 1   THE ORIGINAL PHILLIPS CURVE FOR BRITAIN (1861–1957)

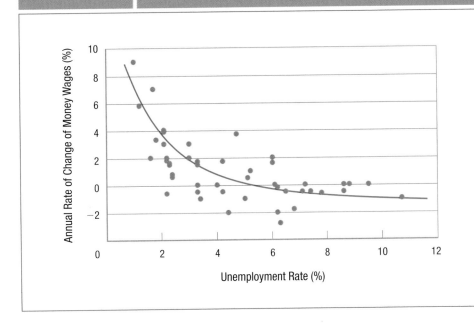

A. W. Phillips compared the rate of change in money wages to unemployment rates in Britain from 1861 to 1957. The resulting nonlinear, negatively sloped curve is the first example of a Phillips curve. When unemployment rises, wage rates fall, and vice versa. Note that some dots represent multiple years.

decade, reducing unemployment in the industry. Those who pursue a career in nursing, medicine, or other health-related fields saw their salaries increase relative to those in other careers. On the other hand, the collapse of the financial and housing sectors forced many realtors, loan specialists, and construction workers out of work. Those lucky enough to find work often made less than they did during the housing boom.

The market relationship between wages and unemployment will clearly affect prices. But worker productivity also plays an important role in determining prices.

Productivity, Prices, and Wages We might think that whenever wages rise, prices must also rise. Higher wages mean higher labor costs for employers—costs that businesses then pass along as higher prices. But this is not always the case. If worker productivity increases enough to offset the wage increase, then product prices can remain stable. The basic relationship among wages, prices, and productivity is

Inflation = Increase in Nominal Wages − Rate of Increase in Labor Productivity

For example, when wages increase by 5% and productivity increases by 3%, inflation is 2%. Given this relationship, the Phillips curve can be adapted to relate productivity to inflation and unemployment, as shown in Figure 2.

Notice that when the rates of change in productivity and wages are equal, inflation is zero (point a). This occurs at the natural rate of unemployment, the unemployment rate when inflationary pressures are nonexistent. Therefore, higher rates of productivity growth mean that for a given level of unemployment, inflation will be less (the Phillips curve would shift in toward the origin).

If policymakers want to use expansionary policy to reduce unemployment from u_n to u_1, then according to the curve shown in Figure 2, they must be willing to accept inflation of p_1. To reduce unemployment further to u_2 would raise inflation to p_2 as labor markets tightened and wages rose more rapidly.

Figure 3 shows the Phillips curve for the United States during the 1960s. Notice the nearly smooth negative relationship between the two variables, much like that in the last two figures. As unemployment fell, inflation rose. This empirical relationship led policymakers to believe that the economy presents them with a menu of choices. By accepting

FIGURE 2 | THE PHILLIPS CURVE

A rise in wages may cause a rise in prices, but if worker productivity increases sufficiently to offset the wage increase, product prices can remain stable. When the rates of change in productivity and wages are equal, inflation is zero (point a). This is the natural rate of unemployment. If policymakers want to use expansionary policy to reduce unemployment from u_n to u_1, they must be willing to accept inflation of p_1. Reducing unemployment further to u_2 would raise inflation to p_2 as labor markets tighten and wages rise more rapidly than productivity.

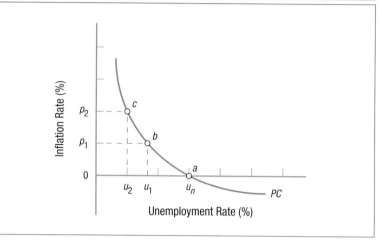

FIGURE 3 | THE PHILLIPS CURVE—1960s

The Phillips curve for the United States during the 1960s gives a negative relationship between inflation and unemployment, much like that found in the last two figures. Using this relationship, policymakers concluded that an inflation rate of 3% to 4% was required to keep unemployment below 4%.

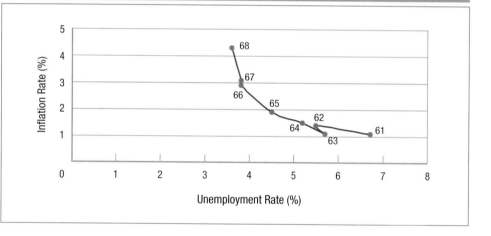

a minor rise in inflation, they could keep unemployment low. Alternatively, by accepting a rise in unemployment, they could keep inflation near zero.

But just as policymakers were getting used to the ease of making policy by accepting moderate inflation in exchange for lower unemployment rates, the economy played a big trick on them. As Figure 4 shows, the entire Phillips curve began shifting outward during the early 1970s.

What looked to be an easy tradeoff between inflation and unemployment turned ugly. Unemployment rates that, in the 1960s, had been associated with modest inflation of 2% to 3% quickly began requiring twice that rate in the early 1970s. By the late 1970s, these same unemployment rates were generating annual inflation rates approaching double digits. The reason for these shifts turned out to be the oil supply shocks of the mid-1970s and the rising inflationary expectations that followed.

The Importance of Inflationary Expectations Workers do not work for the sake of earning a specific dollar amount, or a specific nominal wage. Rather, they work for the sake of earning what those wages will buy—for real wages. Consequently, when they bargain for wage increases, workers will take their past experiences with inflation into account.

Taking **inflationary expectations** into account, wage increases can be connected to unemployment and expected inflation by adding a variable, p^e, representing inflationary

inflationary expectations The rate of inflation expected by workers for any given period. Workers do not work for a specific nominal wage but for what those wages will buy (real wages); therefore, their inflationary expectations are an important determinant of what nominal wage they are willing to work for.

FIGURE 4 | **THE PHILLIPS CURVE FROM 1961–1981: INSTABILITY AND SUPPLY SHOCKS**

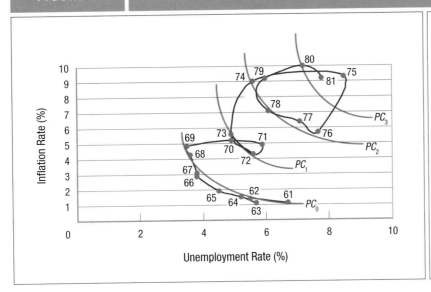

Just as policymakers were getting accustomed to accepting moderate inflation in exchange for lower unemployment rates, the economy surprised them. The entire Phillips curve began shifting outward during the early 1970s. Unemployment rates that, in the 1960s, had been associated with modest inflation of 2% to 3% quickly began requiring twice that rate. The inflation-unemployment tradeoff worsened throughout the 1970s and into the early 1980s, largely due to oil price shocks and rising inflationary expectations. Inflation and unemployment continued to rise, creating stagflation. By 1980 annual inflation was over 10%, and unemployment was over 7%.

expectations, to the inflation equation introduced earlier:

$$\text{Inflation} = \text{Increase in Nominal Wages} - \text{Rate of Increase in Labor Productivity} + P^e$$

In other words, the same tradeoff between inflation and unemployment in the short-run Phillips curve existed as we saw before, but there is a unique tradeoff for each level of inflationary expectations.

For example, suppose there are no inflationary expectations, and productivity is growing at a 3% rate when the economy's unemployment rate is 4%. In this scenario, if nominal wages increase by 5%, inflation would be 5% − 3% + 0% = 2%. However, if inflationary expectations (p^e) grow to, say, 4%, the Phillips curve will shift outward and the inflation rate now associated with 4% unemployment will be 5% − 3% + 4% = 6%.

Inflationary Expectations and the Phillips Curve Panel B of Figure 5 shows a Phillips curve augmented by inflationary expectations. The economy begins in equilibrium at full employment with zero inflation (point a in panel B). Panel A shows the aggregate demand and supply curves for this economy in equilibrium at point a. Note that the economy is producing at full employment output of Q_f, and this translates to the natural rate of unemployment, u_n, in panel B.

The Phillips curve in panel B is initially PC_0 ($p^e = 0\%$). Thus, inflation is equal to zero and so are inflationary expectations (p^e).

Now assume, however, that policymakers are unhappy with the economy's performance and want to reduce unemployment below u_n. Using expansionary policies, they shift aggregate demand in panel A from AD_0 to AD_1. This moves the economy to point b; real output and the price level rise, to Q_1 and P_1.

In panel B, meanwhile, the unemployment rate has declined to u_1 (point b), but inflation has risen to 5%. Workers had anticipated zero inflation; this *unanticipated inflation* means that real wages have fallen. Therefore, workers will begin asking for raises, and employers wanting to keep turnover at a minimum may well begin offering higher wages.

The Long-Run Phillips Curve The long-run Phillips curve (LRPC), shown in panel B of Figure 5 as the vertical line at full employment (unemployment = u_n), shows the long-term relationship between inflation and unemployment when the inflation rate and the expected inflation rate are equal. The LRPC is the Phillips curve counterpart to the vertical long-run aggregate supply curve (LRAS) in panel A.

FIGURE 5 | AGGREGATE DEMAND, AGGREGATE SUPPLY, AND THE EXPECTATIONS-AUGMENTED PHILLIPS CURVE

Panel A
Aggregate Demand and Supply

Panel B
Expectations-Augmented Phillips Curve

Panel A shows the economy's aggregate demand and supply curves, and panel B shows the economy's Phillips curve, augmented by inflationary expectations. Using expansionary policies to reduce unemployment below u_n, policymakers shift aggregate demand in panel A from AD_0 to AD_1. This moves the economy to point b, with real output and the price level rising to Q_1 and P_1. Unemployment declines to u_1 (point b in panel B), but inflation rises to something approaching 5%. If policymakers attempt to hold unemployment below the natural rate, the economy will endure accelerating inflation. The long-run Phillips curve (LRPC) in panel B shows the relationship between inflation and unemployment when the inflation rate is just equal to inflationary expectations.

stagflation Simultaneous occurrence of rising inflation and rising unemployment.

An oil crisis in the late 1970s caused inflation to spike and unemployment to rise, creating what economists call stagflation.

Accelerating Inflation As nominal wages rise, the result in panel A is that, over time, the short-run aggregate supply curve shifts leftward to $SRAS_1$, thus moving the economy back to full employment at point c. In panel B, with inflation now running at 5%, the Phillips curve shifts outward to PC_1 ($p^e = 5\%$). Workers, however, now expect 5% inflation, and the economy moves back to point c. Unemployment has moved back to its natural rate, but inflationary expectations have risen to 5%. The aggregate price level, meanwhile, has risen from P_0 to P_2, or 5%.

At this point, in order for policymakers to move the economy back to u_1 (or Q_1), they must repeat the process of expanding aggregate demand, only this time, the economy is starting from a higher Phillips curve because inflationary expectations are already elevated.

The implications of this analysis for fiscal and monetary policymakers who want to fine-tune the economy and keep unemployment below the natural rate are not pleasant. If policymakers want to keep unemployment below the natural rate, they must continually increase aggregate demand so that inflation will always exceed what is expected. Thus, policymakers must be willing to incur a permanently *accelerating* rate of inflation—hardly a popular idea.

In the late 1970s and early 1980s, oil price shocks and rising inflationary expectations caused both inflation and unemployment to rise, creating what economists call **stagflation.** Where under the original Phillips curve the conclusion was that rising unemployment would be met by *falling* inflation, the 1970s witnessed rising unemployment and *rising* inflation as the Phillips curve shifted outward. By 1980 inflation was over 10% and unemployment was over 7%.

Returning Inflation to Normal Levels To eliminate inflationary pressures when they arise, policymakers must be willing to curtail growth in aggregate demand and accept the resulting higher rates of unemployment for a certain transition period. How long it takes to reduce inflation and return to the natural rate of unemployment will depend on how rapidly the economy adjusts its inflationary expectations. Policymakers can speed this process along by ensuring their policies are credible, for instance, by issuing public announcements that are consistent with contractionary policies in both the monetary and fiscal realms.

To reduce inflationary expectations, policymakers must be willing to reduce aggregate demand and push the economy into a recession, increasing unemployment. As aggregate demand slumps, wage and price pressures will soften, reducing inflationary expectations. As these expectations decline, the Phillips curve shifts inward, back to a position with lower inflation at the natural rate of unemployment. How fast this occurs depends on the severity of the recession and the confidence the public has that policymakers are willing to stay the course.

adaptive expectations Inflationary expectations are formed from a simple extrapolation from past events.

The stagflation of the early 1980s required almost a decade to be resolved. Former Fed Chair Paul Volcker, who insisted on keeping interest rates high in the face of fierce public opposition, deserves much of the credit for this triumph over inflation.

This lesson about the importance of restraining monetary growth and focusing on stable prices was not lost on the next Fed Chair, Alan Greenspan. Throughout the 1990s, the Fed maintained a tight watch on inflation, which fell from around 4% to near 1%.

The importance of keeping inflation low has continued to influence policymaking today. As long as the threat of inflation remains low, policymakers have been willing to use expansionary policy to promote economic growth and reduce unemployment, exactly what the Phillips curve suggests would be effective. These policies assume that inflation expectations adjust with a noticeable lag, allowing some trade-off between inflation and unemployment to exist. Some economists, however, argue that consumers and businesses adapt their expectations so rapidly that their behavior tends to nullify much of policymakers' actions, which we will discuss next.

Rational Expectations and Policy Formation The use of expectations in economic analysis is nothing new. Keynes believed that expectations are driven by emotions. He suggested that investors in the stock market will jump on board trends without attempting to understand the underlying market dynamics. Milton Friedman developed his model of expectations using what are known as **adaptive expectations,** whereby people are assumed to perform a simple extrapolation from past events. Workers, for example, are assumed to expect that past rates of inflation, averaged over some time period,

ROBERT LUCAS

In the 1970s, a series of articles by Robert E. Lucas changed the course of contemporary macroeconomic theory and profoundly influenced the economic policies of governments throughout the world. His development of the rational expectations theory challenged decades of assumptions about how individuals respond to changes in fiscal and monetary policies.

Lucas was born in 1937 in Yakima, Washington. At age 17, he was awarded a scholarship to the University of Chicago, where he studied history. He then went on to the University of California, Berkeley, to pursue a Ph.D. in history, but while there he developed a keen interest in economics. Without funding from Berkeley's Economics Department, he returned to the University of Chicago, where he earned his Ph.D. in 1964. One of his professors was Milton Friedman, whose skepticism about interventionist government policies influenced a generation of economists. Lucas began his teaching career at Carnegie-Mellon University and later became a professor at the University of Chicago.

Before Lucas, economists accepted the Keynesian idea that expansionary policies could lower the unemployment rate. Lucas, however, argued that the rational expectations of individual workers and employers would adjust to the changing inflationary conditions, and unemployment rates would rise again. Lucas developed mathematical models to show that temporarily cutting taxes to increase spending was not a sound policy because individuals would base their decisions on expectations about the future, and these temporary tax cuts would find their way into savings and not added spending. In other words, individuals were rational, forward-thinking, and perfectly able to adapt to changing economic information.

When the Royal Swedish Academy of Sciences awarded Lucas the Nobel Prize in 1995, it credited Lucas with "the greatest influence on macroeconomic research since 1970."

rational expectations Rational economic agents are assumed to make the best possible use of all publicly available information, then make informed, rational judgments on what the future holds. Any errors in their forecasts will be randomly distributed.

will continue into the future. Adaptive expectations are represented by a *backward-looking* model of expectations, which contrasts with the rational expectations model.

In the **rational expectations** model developed by Robert Lucas, rational economic agents are assumed to make the best possible use of all publicly available information about what the future holds before making decisions. This does not mean that every individual's predictions about the future will be correct. Those errors that do occur will be randomly distributed, such that the expectations of large numbers of people will average out to be correct.

Assume that the economy has been in an equilibrium state for several years with low inflation (2%) and unemployment (6%). In such a stable environment, the average person would expect the inflation rate to stay right about where it is indefinitely. But now assume that the Fed announces it is going to increase the rate of growth of the money supply significantly. Basic economic theory tells us that this action will translate into higher prices, bringing about higher future inflation rates. Knowing this, households and businesses will revise their inflationary expectations upward.

As this example shows, people do not rely only on past experiences to formulate their expectations of the future, but instead use all information available to them, including current policy announcements and other information that gives them reason to believe the future might hold certain changes. If adaptive expectations are backward-looking, rational expectations are *forward-looking*.

Policy Implications of Rational Expectations Do individuals and firms really form their future expectations as the rational expectations hypothesis suggests? If so, the implications for macroeconomic policy would be enormous; indeed, it could leave macroeconomic policy ineffective.

To illustrate, let us assume that the economy depicted in Figure 6 is operating at full employment at point *a*. Short-run aggregate supply curve $SRAS_0$ ($P = 100$) reflects current inflationary expectations. Suppose the Fed announces that it intends to increase the money supply.

Expanding the money supply will shift aggregate demand from AD_0 to AD_1. This will increase the demand for labor and raise nominal wages. But what happens next?

Natural rate theorists, using adaptive expectations, would argue that workers will be fooled into thinking that the increase in money wages represents a real raise, thus driving

---

FIGURE 6   **RATIONAL EXPECTATIONS: THE POLICY INEFFECTIVENESS HYPOTHESIS**

Rational expectations theory suggests that macroeconomic policy will be ineffective, even in the short term. Assume that the economy is operating at full employment (point *a*) and short-run aggregate supply curve $SRAS_0$ ($P = 100$). Now suppose that the Fed announces that it intends to increase the money supply. Expanding the money supply will shift aggregate demand from AD_0 to AD_1, and this will increase the demand for labor and raise nominal wages. Yet, as soon as the Fed announces it is going to increase the money supply, rational economic agents will use this information immediately to raise their inflationary expectations. Thus, output will remain unchanged, though the price level rises immediately to 110.

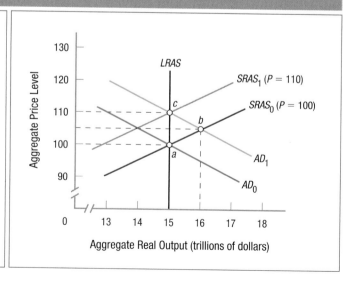

output and employment up to $16 trillion (point *b*). After a time, however, workers will realize that real wages have not risen because prices have risen by at least as much as wages. Aggregate supply will then fall to $SRAS_1$ ($P = 110$) as price expectations climb and the economy gradually moves back to full employment at a higher price level (point *c*). In this scenario, the Fed's policy succeeds in raising output and employment in the short term, but at the expense of a long-term rise in the cost of living.

Contrast this with the rational expectations model. When the Fed announces that it is going to increase the money supply, perfectly rational individuals and firms will listen to this information and immediately raise their inflationary expectations. In Figure 6, output will remain unchanged because the price level will rise immediately to 110. No one gets fooled into temporarily increasing output or employment, even though the increase in the money supply still drives up prices. Therefore, any announcement of a policy change will result in an immediate move to a new long-run equilibrium, leaving the short-term aspects of the policy change ineffective.

This suggests that if the Fed wants to use an increase in the money supply to raise output and employment in the short term, the only way it can do so is by *not* announcing its plans; it must essentially force individuals and firms to make decisions with substantially incomplete information.

A Critique of Rational Expectations To date, empirical assessments of the ineffectiveness of macroeconomic policy based on rational expectations have yielded mixed results. In general, these studies do not support the policy ineffectiveness proposition. That is, macroeconomic policies do have a real impact on the economy, and monetary policies are credited with keeping inflation low over the past three decades.

New Keynesian economists have taken a different approach to critiquing rational expectations theory. Both the adaptive and the rational expectations models assume that labor and product markets are highly competitive, with wages and prices adjusting quickly to expansionary or contractionary policies. The new Keynesians point out, however, that labor markets are often beset with imperfect information, and that efficiency wages often bring about short-term wage stickiness.

Imperfect information occurs when firms and workers do not have up-to-the-minute information on economic fluctuations due to timing lags, causing wages and prices to not react quickly. **Efficiency wage theory** disputes the notion that labor markets are like competitive commodity markets with equal prices. In other words, all labor is not equal. People need incentives to work hard, and paying workers an efficiency wage, or a wage above the market-clearing level, is one form of motivation to improve morale and productivity.

Imperfect information and efficiency wages suggest that wages and prices may be sticky because workers and firms are either unable or unwilling to make adjustments quickly to changes in the economy. This means that neither workers nor firms can react quickly to changes in monetary or fiscal policy. And this would give such policies a chance of a short-term impact.

Although the policy ineffectiveness proposition has not found significant empirical support, rational expectations as a concept has profoundly affected how economists approach macroeconomic problems. Nearly all economists agree that policy changes affect expectations, and that this affects the behavior of individuals and firms that potentially reduce the effectiveness of monetary and fiscal policy.

This section has considered two challenges to the effectiveness of macroeconomic policy. First, we looked at the Phillips curve, and showed that policies attempting to address unemployment could lead to inflation and a build-up in inflationary expectations. In other words, policymakers do not face an easy choice between rates of unemployment and rates of inflation. Second, we looked at rational expectations and showed how expectations could mitigate the effectiveness of policy.

In the next section, we now want to apply these concepts to macroeconomic issues that are important in our future: economic growth, jobs, debt, and globalization.

efficiency wage theory Employers often pay their workers wages above the market-clearing level to improve morale and productivity, reduce turnover, and create a disincentive for employees to shirk their duties.

CHECKPOINT

EFFECTIVENESS OF MACROECONOMIC POLICY: PHILLIPS CURVES AND RATIONAL EXPECTATIONS

- The Phillips curve represents the negative relationship between the unemployment rate and the inflation rate. When the unemployment rate goes up, inflation goes down, and vice versa.

- Rising inflationary expectations by the public shifts the Phillips curve to the right, worsening the tradeoff between inflation and unemployment.

- If policymakers use monetary and fiscal policy to push unemployment below the natural rate, they will face accelerating inflation. Reducing inflation requires that policymakers curtail aggregate demand and temporarily accept higher rates of unemployment.

- Adaptive expectations assume that individuals and firms extrapolate from past events; it is a *backward-looking* model. Rational expectations assume that individuals and firms make the best possible use of all publicly available information; it is a *forward-looking* model of expectations.

- Rational expectations analysis leads to the conclusion that policy changes will be ineffective; however, market imperfections and information problems are two reasons why rational expectations analysis has met with mixed results empirically.

QUESTIONS: If an economy has high unemployment but low inflation, what would the Phillips curve suggest to be an appropriate macroeconomic policy? Would your answer change if inflationary expectations rise? If we assume that all individuals and firms have excellent foreknowledge as described by the rational expectations model, would that change your answer?

Answers to the Checkpoint questions can be found at the end of this chapter.

MACROECONOMIC ISSUES THAT CONFRONT OUR FUTURE

Macroeconomic theory developed over the last 200 years, especially during the 80 years after Keynes. Until recently, economists thought they had the understanding and the tools to make depressions or deep recessions a thing of the past. For the last 30 years, a general consensus grew among economists that monetary policy should handle most of the task of keeping the economy on a steady low-inflation growth path. The recent financial crisis and subsequent recession have made the profession question that conclusion. This downturn has reinvigorated those who felt that fiscal policy should have more of a role, as well as those who believed that government should have a smaller role overall.

This section uses the theories and tools we have learned to understand the important issues that confront our economy today and in the future. Specifically, what are the pressing macroeconomic issues that will have the greatest effect on the next generation? What do macroeconomic theories tell us that policymakers can do?

If you take one idea away from this course, it should be that there is *not* one economic model or one economic policy that fits all occasions or circumstances. It often seems that one set of policymakers see "cutting taxes" as the universal cure-all, while others see "more government spending" as the only solution. Both are wrong. Different circumstances call for different approaches.

In this section, we set out the key points surrounding three important issues facing our economy today and likely in the future: (1) the existence of jobless recoveries and persistent unemployment, (2) growing debt and the threat of long-run inflation, and (3) the importance of achieving economic growth in a globalized economy. Throughout this book, we have presented different models and the circumstances in which macroeconomic policy can be effective in these situations.

Are Recoveries Becoming "Jobless Recoveries"?

Globalization, new technologies, and improved business methods are making the jobs of policymakers much more difficult and may even be changing the nature of the business cycle. The 1990–1991, 2001, and 2007–2009 recessions all deviated significantly from what has happened in past business cycles in that they were followed by jobless recoveries.

Taming the business cycle has proven to be just as much of an art as a science. Whenever economists believe they have finally gotten a handle on controlling the economy, some new event or transformation of the economy has taken place, humbling the profession. There is no doubt that between 1983 and 2007, the federal government and the Fed did a remarkable job of keeping the economy on a steady upward growth path, with only two minor recessions. The 1990–1991 and 2001 recessions were mild, but the recoveries coming out of these recessions were weak, especially for those out of work and looking for a job.

When output begins to grow after a trough in the business cycle, employment usually starts to grow. But when output begins to rise yet employment growth does not resume, the recovery is called a **jobless recovery.**

We have already seen that business cycles vary dramatically in their depth and duration. The Great Depression was the worst downturn in American history, while the 2001 recession was one of the mildest. During that recession, the unemployment rate never rose above 6% and real output (GDP) fell only one-quarter of 1% throughout the downturn. But if the recession was mild, the recovery was not as strong as in typical business cycles.

Figure 7 shows how the 2007–2009 recession compares to the two previous downturns and their recoveries. It indexes real output for all three downturns so that the most recent recession and recovery can be compared to those previous business cycles. Specifically, real GDP for each business cycle is indexed to the peak of the cycle. This involves dividing each quarter's output by output at the peak and multiplying by 100 to index the values to 100. Thus, if one quarter after the peak, output has fallen by 1%, the index would be 99 at that point. In this way we can get a graphical picture of how output is doing throughout the course of each cycle.

Notice in this figure that both the 1990–1991 and 2001 recessions lasted just under three quarters (eight months each). For the 1990–1991 recession, this is shown by the two-quarter drop in real GDP to a little below 99; then the economy resumed an upward path.

jobless recovery A phenomenon that takes place after a recession, when output begins to rise, but employment growth does not.

| FIGURE 7 | REAL GDP RELATIVE TO THE PEAK OF THE BUSINESS CYCLE |

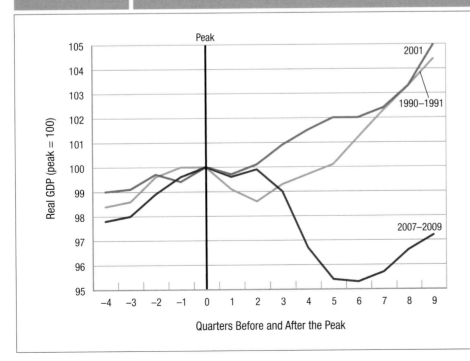

The 2007–2009 recession is compared to the previous two recessions in 1990–1991 and 2001 by indexing real output to the peak of the business cycle. The 2007–2009 downturn was deeper; in both of the previous recessions, GDP was back to the previous peak within 18 months.

Employment in the 2007–2009 recession is compared to the previous two recessions in 1990–1991 and 2001 by indexing employment to the peak of the business cycle. This downturn was deeper than the previous recessions. It took about five years before employment returned to its pre-recession peak.

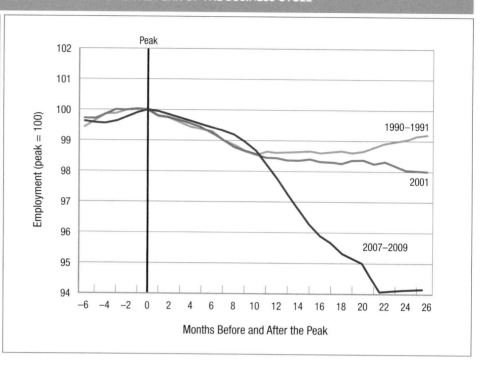

The 2001 downturn shows a slight dip in the first quarter, but then quickly rises back above 100. Clearly, both of these recessions were mild indeed.

In contrast, the 2007–2009 recession was considerably more severe than both of the previous downturns. A year and a half into this recession, real output fell by over 4% and the decline in the economy was just leveling off.

Figure 8 presents the same type of indexed graph for employment, though indexing the values monthly. Notice that for the 1990–1991 and 2001 recessions, employment had not reached its prior peak even after two years. In fact, employment took nearly three years to return to peak levels after the 1990–1991 recession, nearly four years after the 2001 recession and about five years after the 2007–2009 recession. In the past, the turnaround in employment to the previous peak was typically reached in two years.

Several factors seem to drive jobless recoveries: rapid increases in productivity, a change in employment patterns, and offshoring. Productivity increases arising from improved telecommunications and online technologies make labor far more flexible than ever before. Now when the economy contracts, employers can more easily lay off workers and shift their responsibilities to the workers who remain. As a result, output may keep growing, or at least not drop much, even though fewer workers are employed. When the market rebounds, increased productivity permits firms to adjust to their rising orders without immediately hiring more people. This gives the firm more time to evaluate the recovery to ensure that hiring permanent employees is appropriate. This is why unemployment often keeps increasing even though the economy is recovering.

Increased technology and productivity have enabled companies to use fewer workers to run their operations. In 2015 Snapchat had only 330 employees for its estimated 200 million active subscribers, a ratio of 1 employee per 600,000 users.

In addition, hiring practices have changed over the past few decades. Firms have begun substituting just-in-time hiring practices for long-term permanent employees. This includes using more temporary and part-time workers, and adding overtime shifts for permanent employees. By using temporary and part-time workers, and overtime, a firm can increase its flexibility while limiting the higher costs associated with hiring permanent employees until it has had time to evaluate the recovery and the demand for its products.

Because the past three recoveries have been slow to add jobs, economists and policymakers are concerned that jobless recoveries have become the norm following recessions. The consequence of jobless

Patrick T. Fallon/Bloomberg via Getty Images

recoveries is that reducing unemployment requires much more government action than before, especially expansionary fiscal and monetary policies. What type of fiscal and monetary policies can be used to address jobless recoveries?

Expansionary fiscal policy is most effective when government spending or tax cuts generate economic activity through the spending multiplier, which translates into jobs being created. Alternatively, fiscal policy can be used to provide incentives for employers to hire workers (such as tax incentives for hiring veterans) or employee incentives (such as increased tax deductions for low-income workers).

Alternatively, expansionary monetary policy can be used to promote employment. For example, increasing the money supply and lowering interest rates reduce the cost of financing major projects, creating jobs. The Fed's recent quantitative easing programs that bought up risky mortgage-backed assets reduced long-term interest rates, creating another boost to consumption and investment.

The VOW to Hire Heroes Act is an example of fiscal policy used to encourage employers to hire veterans returning from active duty.

Although plenty of policy options exist to address jobless recoveries, they do not come without costs. For example, a reduction in consumer or business confidence can reduce the willingness of consumers and firms to spend, diminishing the multiplier. Increased government spending can lead to greater debt and higher interest rates, which can crowd out private consumption and investment. Therefore, the intended effects of fiscal policy are mitigated. Further, increased money supply and quantitative easing programs can lead to inflation in the long run, as more money chases an economy's output. Such effects can mitigate the long-term benefits of monetary policy.

In sum, the potential consequences of using expansionary fiscal and monetary policies to reduce the unemployment rate are higher debt and potential inflation, important issues to which we turn next.

Will Rising Debt and Future Debt Obligations Lead to Inflation?

Much of the debate among policymakers in recent years has centered on rising deficits and national debt. Indeed, fiscal deficits and national debt (at least in nominal terms) have risen to levels not seen in our history. The concern over debt has changed the politics in Washington, as a bitter debate ensued regarding the use of expansionary policies (such as stimulus spending and quantitative easing) to promote economic growth versus austerity measures (cost cutting) to reduce the deficit and the burden of the debt on future generations.

Rising Future Debt Obligations: Health Care and Social Security Even if the current deficits are brought under control using a combination of government spending cuts and tax increases, the long-term debt obligations relating to Social Security payments and rising health care costs pose a bigger question about the ability to keep deficits and debt under control over the long term.

As greater numbers of baby boomers (those born in the years following the end of World War II) retire, more will begin receiving Social Security and Medicare benefits. In addition to greater numbers of beneficiaries, the cost of the benefits also rises. Social Security benefits increase based on the rate of inflation, while Medicare payments rise as the cost of health care increases.

Recent legislation has slowed the rise in health care costs, but the overall cost remains difficult to sustain in the long term. In addition, the long-term debt obligations stemming from health care and Social Security do not fully appear in current deficit statistics, because these expenses are budgeted and paid out during the year in which the costs are incurred. Therefore, if costs rise faster than revenues, deficits will persist, adding to the national debt.

The Cost of Financing Debt The cost of financing debt depends on the interest rate. Fortunately, the United States has enjoyed very low interest rates for much of the past decade. This not only helps individuals and firms looking to borrow, but also the government in financing its debt. A new 30-year Treasury bond issued in 2016 paid only about 3% per year. In 1986 a new 30-year Treasury bond paid about 8% per year. A difference of 5% in the interest rate represents a tremendous savings to the government.

Another factor in the cost of financing debt is the willingness of countries to hold U.S. debt. Part of this depends on the demand for the U.S. dollar. The U.S. dollar remains the most widely held currency in the world. When U.S. dollars are held by foreigners, this amounts to an interest-free loan to the U.S. government (also referred to as seigniorage), because no interest is paid on currency. The willingness of people around the world to use and hold dollars allows the government to print these dollars without the immediate worry of inflation.

The Effects of Debt on Inflation Addressing debt can be undertaken with fiscal policy as well as monetary policy. Fiscal policy to curb debt includes raising taxes or reducing government spending. However, neither of these policies is popular, especially the reduction of Social Security or health care benefits that make up over 50% of government spending. Further, contractionary fiscal policy can curtail economic growth, which is especially dangerous when recovering from a severe recession. For this reason, policymakers have turned to monetary policy.

monetized debt Occurs when debt is reduced by increasing the money supply, thereby making each dollar less valuable through inflation.

One of the dangers of using monetary policy to help address deficit and debt issues occurs with **monetized debt,** which is debt that is paid for by an increase in the money supply. In other words, debt is reduced by way of a lower real value of the dollar. Because U.S. Treasury securities have long been sought after as a safe investment by individuals, firms, as

---

 ISSUE

Inflating Our Way Out of Debt: Is This an Effective Approach?

In late 2012, the news media posted headlines about the possibility of the Fed authorizing the minting of a *trillion dollar coin* that would be used to pay for most of the year's fiscal deficit. By doing so, the minted coin would be sent to the U.S. Treasury to pay down the debt. Would such a strategy really work? Would there be any effects on the economy or on ordinary Americans?

Although this type of policy is highly unlikely to occur (though more than one prominent economist had endorsed the plan), what may surprise you is that the Fed has used similar types of policies for years to address our rising national debt.

When the money supply is increased, the Fed is using money that is created out of thin air to purchase treasury bonds (debt) from banks and other institutions. In other words, part of the government's debt is held by other parts of the government using money it creates through its power to print money. Does this sound like an easy solution?

Certainly, it's easier than implementing fiscal policies to combat debt, which would require the raising of taxes or the reduction of government spending, neither of which is popular, especially when much of government spending is used for our national defense or to take care of our senior citizens. Therefore, the government has relied more on monetary policy. When money is created to purchase debt instruments, this is referred to as monetizing debt.

Recall that money is neutral. When more money chases a fixed output, prices must rise. Because aggregate demand was depressed after the last recession, inflation did not immediately rise. However, as consumer and business confidence improve, all of the money sitting on the sidelines will eventually enter into the economy and drive prices higher, leading to inflation. As inflation rises, the real value of the national debt falls.

Who, then, ends up paying for this reduction in debt caused by inflation? The answer is everyone who

American Mint, LLC

holds dollar-denominated assets, such as those with a savings or retirement account, or holders of bonds including foreign investors and governments. When prices rise, the real value of savings falls. In addition, a rise in inflationary expectations causes banks to raise interest rates, and can lead to an inflation spiral, resulting in even higher prices. In sum, the costs of financing debt by way of inflation are spread among everyone. Regardless of whether fiscal or monetary policy is used, we will all feel the effect of the debt in one way or another.

well as governments around the world, the U.S. government has not had to worry about the inflationary effects of its monetary policy in recent years.

However, should world demand for U.S. Treasury securities fall as countries diversify their holdings to other assets (such as euro-denominated assets or gold-backed assets), the value of the U.S. dollar may fall. Because we purchase many goods and services from other countries, a weaker dollar increases the prices of many goods and services, leading to inflation. Therefore, although a weaker dollar and inflation both reduce the burden on the existing debt, a higher rate of inflation reduces the purchasing power of one's income and savings, thereby reducing the standard of living.

In order to stem the effects of higher inflation, contractionary monetary policy is needed once the economy has recovered enough to withstand an increase in interest rates. Such policies are not popular. In late 2015, the Fed started to raise interest rates, but very slowly to avoid scaring investors who worried about the start of another recession. Still, controlling inflation is the key to preventing more serious problems for the economy. Ultimately, a higher inflation rate may hinder productivity and economic growth.

Will Globalization Lead to Increased Obstacles to Economic Growth?

Economic growth has been the driving force in improving our standard of living. However, the world is changing, and emerging countries such as China and India have experienced higher growth rates than the United States, Japan, and countries in Europe over the past two decades. Further, smaller developing countries, such as Gabon, Ethiopia, and Vietnam, have seen stellar growth rates that have pulled millions out of poverty.

Why has economic growth spread throughout the world in this way, and what does this entail for developed nations such as the United States?

One of the most important changes to the world economy over the past generation has been the dramatic increase in international trade, international factor movements (foreign investment and immigration), offshoring (the movement of factories overseas), and international banking. The integration of the world's economies has allowed more countries to specialize and reap the gains from trade that result.

For developed countries such as the United States, Japan, and countries in Europe, increased globalization means increased competition for resources, especially talented labor, which now has many more opportunities than it did in the past. Therefore, pressures to innovate and to increase productivity have increased with globalization.

What does this mean for macroeconomic policy? Not only does fiscal and monetary policy need to be tailored to fit the problems inherent in our own country, but how these policies affect other countries becomes important as well.

Fiscal policies such as implementing trade restrictions or providing support for domestic industries tend to help one country at the expense of its trading partners. Taking these policies too far may encourage other countries to take similar actions, which would lead to fewer exports and a reduction in trade and economic growth.

Ethiopia, which experienced one of the worst famines in world history in 1985, today has an emerging economy with a high growth rate as it focuses on infrastructure, manufacturing, and trade.

Monetary policies also affect other nations through trade and the exchange rate. Expansionary monetary policy, such as reducing the interest rate, has the effect of lowering the value of one currency against others. When this occurs, the price of imports rises and the price of exports falls, helping to improve the trade balance as consumers react by purchasing more domestically produced goods than foreign-made goods. But again, such policies can lead to retaliatory actions if taken too far.

We turn our attention in the next two chapters to international trade and open economy macroeconomics. Both chapters deal with how countries interact with other countries, either through the trade of goods and services or through the exchange of currencies. Both have important implications for the ability of countries to grow and to improve their standards of living.

Life on the Autobahn: Germany's Role in European Growth and Stability

How did Germany maintain a strong economy after its reunification in 1990 and then in a Eurozone that faced many financial crises?

The autobahn has long been a symbol of Germany's quest for economic strength and prosperity. Led by its successful auto industry, Germany has achieved much economic growth over the last 50 years, and its corporate brands are among the most recognizable and respected in the world. Even more remarkable is how Germany withstood many challenges over the last 30 years that tested its ability to maintain its economic strength.

What are some major events that shaped Germany's economy over the last 30 years?

The autobahn has no speed limit in most areas, symbolizing Germany's strength in the face of many economic challenges.

One major test of Germany's resilience came with the fall of the Berlin Wall in 1989 and the reunification of West Germany with East Germany in 1990. At the time of reunification, West Germany's GDP per capita was more than twice that of East Germany. Despite vast economic differences, the reunified Germany invested heavily in capital improvements in the East where marginal returns to capital were strong, increasing labor productivity that led to rising incomes.

Another major test was the formation of the European Union, which

allowed workers and capital to move between member countries, along with the introduction of the euro, which merged the monetary policies of countries with different economic conditions. When nearly half of Eurozone members faced financial crises between 2008 and 2013, Germany led the European Central Bank's efforts to increase lending while mandating reforms to put countries back on a path to growth.

Finally, Germany played a vital role in the resettlement of refugees and migrants that began flooding into Europe in 2015 to escape war and/or poverty. In 2015 Germany accepted more than 1 million asylum seekers. Germany demonstrated its ability to show compassion to the plight of others while continuing to maintain economic growth and low inflation.

Today, Germany remains a strong economic power that embraces diversity and has become a land of opportunity for many in a time when other countries are shutting their doors. It is a symbol of globalization that has given millions a new chance at life.

GO TO **LaunchPad** TO PRACTICE THE ECONOMIC CONCEPTS IN THIS STORY

 CHECKPOINT

MACROECONOMIC ISSUES THAT CONFRONT OUR FUTURE

- No single macroeconomic model can solve all economic problems.
- Jobless recoveries are spurred by increases in labor productivity, changes in employment patterns, and increased use of offshoring. Fiscal and monetary policies provide incentives to consume and invest, leading to job growth.
- Rising deficits were caused by expansionary fiscal policies used to stem the effects of the financial crisis. Future concerns of deficits and debt center on the rising costs of Social Security and Medicare, making the use of fiscal policy to mitigate rising debt difficult.
- Rising interest rates in the future will increase borrowing costs, making it more difficult to finance debt. Increased use of expansionary monetary policy can lead to long-run inflation, reducing the debt burden but also reducing the purchasing power of savings.
- Globalization has led to economic growth throughout the world, especially in developing countries. However, increased competition from abroad has made it more challenging for developed nations to maintain high growth rates over time.

QUESTIONS: In 2009 inflation was negative (also known as deflation); average prices *fell* mostly due to a sharp decline in consumer spending and business investments from the recession. In early 2015, deflation occurred again, but this time it was caused by a sharp drop in energy prices. How does deflation affect the ability of households and businesses to manage debt? Does the cause of the deflation matter? Explain.

Answers to the Checkpoint questions can be found at the end of this chapter.

chapter summary

Section 1 The Great Recession and Macroeconomic Policy

25.1 Events Leading to the Great Recession

- A glut in worldwide savings in the early years of the 21st century reduced interest rates.
- Low interest rates and easy bank loans fueled a housing bubble.
- Risky subprime mortgages were packaged into securities that were inadequately investigated and given perfect AAA ratings.
- Loan defaults led to a reduction in home prices and the collapse of mortgage-backed securities.
- Banks lost money from poor investments, insurance companies could not cover losses, and the contagion spread to other industries and eventually to the entire economy.

philip gangler/Shutterstock

25.2 The Government's Policy Response

- Passed the $700 billion Troubled Asset Relief Program (TARP) to bail out banks nearing bankruptcy.
- Loaned over $100 billion to AIG to prevent its insolvency in insuring risky assets by financial institutions.
- Passed the $787 billion American Recovery and Reinvestment Act (stimulus package).
- Bailed out the U.S. automobile industry.
- Reduced the federal funds target rate to 0% and began a series of quantitative easing (QE) programs to purchase risky assets from banks.

Section 2 Effectiveness of Macroeconomic Policy: Phillips Curves and Rational Expectations

25.3 The **Phillips curve** shows a negative relationship between unemployment rates and inflation. As unemployment falls, firms bid up the price of labor. Greater employment increases aggregate demand, pushing prices higher.

The Phillips curve presented policymakers with a menu of choices. By accepting modest inflation, they can keep unemployment low.

Fanatic Studio/Alamy

25.4 Phillips curves are affected by **inflationary expectations.** Rising inflationary expectations by the public would be reflected in a shift in the Phillips curve to the right, worsening the tradeoff between inflation and unemployment.

If policymakers use monetary and fiscal policy to attempt to keep unemployment continually below the natural rate, they will face accelerating inflation.

Once inflation reaches a high level, the risk of **stagflation** occurs, in which high inflation is coupled with high unemployment. Reducing stagflation requires tough contractionary monetary policies to bring down inflation.

25.5 **The adaptive expectations model** assumes that people form their future expectations based on their past experiences. Therefore, it is a backward-looking model of expectations.

The rational expectations hypothesis suggests that policy-makers cannot stimulate output in the short run by raising inflation unless they keep their actions secret.

Market imperfections and information problems are two reasons why the policy ineffectiveness conclusions of rational expectations analysis have met with mixed results empirically.

The rational expectations model assumes that rational economic agents use all publicly available information in forming their expectations, and is a forward-looking model of expectations.

Lucian Milasan/Alamy

Efficiency wages are paid in many professions as a way to keep employees from shirking or leaving the company. The existence of efficiency wages brings about wage stickiness, which makes rational expectations less likely.

Section 3 Macroeconomic Issues That Confront Our Future

25.6 The use of fiscal policy or monetary policy, or both, depends on the type of issues confronting our economy. Important issues facing our country today and in the future include:

- Jobless recoveries, which are common after severe financial crises
- Rising deficits and debt
- Higher long-term inflation
- Globalization and its effect on economic growth

25.7 Jobless recoveries have become common after the last few recessions. Factors that have led to jobless recoveries include:

- Rapid increases in productivity
- Changes in employment patterns
- Offshoring

25.8 Globalization affects what we buy and what we produce, as goods and inputs move across borders.

Ilya Terentyev/iStockphoto

The growing population of seniors and the rising costs of Social Security and health care benefits are major factors affecting potential debt in the long run.

Fotosearch/agefotostock

Disney's Epcot World Showcase gives tourists a brief tour of the world. Although Epcot is located entirely in the United States, evidence of globalization abounds. Disney hires thousands of foreign workers, exports services to foreign tourists, imports millions of dollars worth of foreign-made merchandise, and invests in theme parks and companies overseas.

subprime mortgage, p. 670
leverage, p. 671
credit default swap, p. 672
Phillips curve, p. 674

inflationary expectations, p. 676
stagflation, p. 678
adaptive expectations, p. 679
rational expectations, p. 680

efficiency wage theory, p. 681
jobless recovery, p. 683
monetized debt, p. 686

QUESTIONS AND PROBLEMS

Check Your Understanding

1. Why does the Phillips curve become very steep when unemployment is low and rather shallow when unemployment is high?

2. Does the long-run Phillips curve make it difficult (if not impossible) for policymakers to increase output and employment beyond full employment in the long run?

3. Explain why inflation accelerates if policymakers use monetary and fiscal policy to keep unemployment below the natural rate.

4. Does having rational expectations mean that all economic actors act rationally and are always correct?

5. Would policymakers prefer a Phillips curve with a steep or a shallow slope? Why?

6. A negative supply shock (a huge natural disaster or significant energy price spike) would do what to the short-run Phillips curve? To the long-run Phillips curve?

Apply the Concepts

7. Why would policymakers want to drive unemployment below the natural rate, given that inflation will result?

8. Why are inflationary expectations so important for policymakers to keep under control? When a supply shock such as an oil price spike hits the economy, does it matter how fast policymakers attempt to bring the economy back to full employment?

9. How are the long-run Phillips curve (LRPC) and the long-run aggregate supply (LRAS) curve related?

10. Would the credibility of policymakers' (Congress and the Fed) commitment to keeping inflation low have an effect on inflationary expectations when the economy is beset by a supply shock?

11. Explain why those who favor the rational expectations approach to modeling the economy do not favor discretionary policymaking.

12. If efficiency wages are widespread throughout the economy but most workers feel they are significantly underpaid, will paying workers more prevent them from shirking?

In the News

13. Former Fed Chair Ben Bernanke noted that "in the 1970s the public had little confidence that the Fed would keep inflation low and stable." As a result, when oil prices rose, wages and prices quickly followed. This caused the Fed to have to increase interest rates sharply to curtail inflation. Do people have a different perspective on the Fed today than they did in the past?

14. About every year, Congress is tasked with increasing the debt ceiling that allows the government to continue borrowing. In past decades, such legislation would pass easily because it was authorizing the payment of expenses already incurred. However, in recent years, some congressional leaders took the drastic approach of opposing to raise the debt ceiling as a way to reign in government spending. If these leaders were successful in preventing the debt ceiling from being raised, what would be some benefits and costs of this action?

Solving Problems

15. The Phillips curve of the 1960s showed a negative relationship between the inflation rate and unemployment. Use the following data on inflation and unemployment to plot a Phillips curve from 2011 to 2015. Does the same relationship between inflation and unemployment hold in 2011–2015 as it did in the 1960s?

Year	Inflation Rate	Unemployment Rate
2011	3.2%	8.9%
2012	2.1%	8.1%
2013	1.5%	7.4%
2014	1.6%	6.2%
2015	0.1%	5.3%

WORK IT OUT   LaunchPad | interactive activity

16. During the recession from December 2007 to June 2009, the U.S. economy lost a total of 7,163,000 jobs. How many jobs were lost per month, on average? Suppose that a healthy economy generates an average of 200,000 jobs per month. At this rate, how long would it take the economy to gain back the number of jobs it had lost? According to data from the Bureau of Labor Statistics, the U.S. economy gained 5,485,000 jobs from June 2009 to June 2013. What was the average number of jobs per month created during the first four years of recovery? Given your answers to the previous two questions, what does this suggest about the pace of economic recovery after the 2007–2009 recession?

USING THE NUMBERS

17. About how long prior to the 2007–2009 recession did consumer sentiment peak? Why didn't the recession start immediately after the peak?

18. According to By the Numbers, what was the value of monthly real retail sales when it reached its lowest point in 2009? By what percentage did monthly real retail sales increase from 2009 to 2015?

Checkpoint: The Great Recession and Macroeconomic Policy 674

Had it been known that the collapse of the housing market bubble would have caused a severe financial crisis, the government could have implemented macroeconomic policies to slow the rise in housing prices. For example, the government could (1) use contractionary monetary policy to push interest rates higher, making it more expensive to borrow money; (2) pass regulations on financial institutions requiring greater scrutiny of potential borrowers; (3) limit the types of risky loans that could be created; and (4) eliminate tax incentives on housing market profits to limit house flipping.

Checkpoint: Effectiveness of Macroeconomic Policy: Phillips Curves and Rational Expectations 682

The Phillips curve would suggest that unemployment can be reduced by accepting a higher rate of inflation. As long as inflation is very low, a small rise in inflation would be a small cost to pay for pushing the unemployment rate down. However, if inflationary expectations rise, it would require a greater inflation rate to achieve a lower unemployment rate. Here, policymakers must be careful not to let inflation exceed a level that might cause larger problems for the economy. Finally, if individuals and firms acted according to the rational expectations model, any increase in inflation would never lead to a reduction in unemployment. In this case, macroeconomic policy is ineffective in the short run, and the best prescription would be to leave the market alone to correct itself over time.

Checkpoint: Macroeconomic Issues That Confront Our Future 688

Deflation causes the real value of debt to rise, making it more difficult to repay. Yes, it does matter how the deflation occurs. In 2009 deflation resulted from a decrease in aggregate demand (from a decline in consumption and investment), causing both prices and output to fall. In 2015 deflation resulted from an increase in the short-run aggregate supply curve (from falling input prices). This means that while the real value of debt rises, rising outcome and income make it easier to pay back debt.

26 International Trade

Understanding why trade with other countries is essential for consumers and producers

Simon Dawson/Bloomberg via Getty Images

Learning Objectives

26.1 Distinguish between absolute and comparative advantage.

26.2 Describe the benefits of free trade.

26.3 Describe the terms of trade.

26.4 Describe the economic impacts of trade on consumers and producers.

26.5 Describe how trade is restricted by tariffs and quotas.

26.6 Discuss the various arguments against free trade.

26.7 Compare the different viewpoints of how trade is believed to affect the environment.

26.8 Analyze the debate on whether foreign workers benefit from trade or are exploited as a result of trade.

Every day at the Port of Los Angeles, up to ten mega container ships arrive, each containing 10,000 to 19,000 TEU (*20-foot equivalent units, or 20 feet × 8 feet × 8.5 feet standard containers*) of goods from around the world. A standard tractor trailer can transport two TEUs, which means that up to 80,000 tractor trailers full of goods are brought into the United States each day, *at just one port*.

These cargo ships and trucks transport the goods we enjoy every day that are made in China, France, Brazil, Kenya, Australia, and the 180 other countries with which the United States has trading relations.

Take a quick look in your closet, and count how many countries contributed to your wardrobe—shirts tailored in Hong Kong, shoes made in Italy, sweaters made in Norway, jackets made in China, and the list goes on. On occasion, you might come across something made in the United States, although it is a rarity in the apparel industry. Most Americans wear foreign-made clothing, over half drive foreign cars, and even American cars contain many foreign components. Australian wines, Swiss watches, Chilean sea bass, and Brazilian coffee have become common in the United States. We also buy services from other countries, for example, when we travel to Europe and stay in hotels and use its high-speed trains. The opportunity to buy goods and services from other countries gives consumers more variety to choose from, and also provides an opportunity to buy products at lower prices.

Although the United States buys many goods from other countries, it also sells many goods to other countries—just not clothing. The "Made in USA" label is highly respected throughout the world, and the United States sells commercial airplanes, cars and trucks, tractors, high-tech machinery, and pharmaceuticals to individual consumers and businesses in other countries. It also sells agricultural goods and raw materials, such as soybeans, copper, and wood pulp. And it sells services, too, such as medical care, tourist services when foreigners visit the United States, higher education (foreign students studying at American colleges), and entertainment, including movies, software, and music.

Trade is now part of the global landscape. Worldwide foreign trade has quadrupled over the past 25 years. In the United States today, the combined value of exports and imports exceeds $5 trillion a year. Twenty-five years ago, trade represented about 20% of gross domestic product (GDP); today, it accounts for over 30% of GDP. Nearly a tenth of American workers owe their jobs to foreign consumers. Figure 1 shows the current composition of U.S. exports and imports. Note that the United States imports and exports a lot of capital goods—that is, the equipment and machinery used to produce other goods. Also, we export about 50% more services than we import, services such as education and health care. Third, exports of petroleum products are catching up to imports as the United States relies less on imports of oil as domestic oil production increases.

Does all of this world trade make consumers and producers better off? This chapter examines the effects of trade on both the importing (buying) and exporting (selling) countries, and how trade affects the prices and availability of goods and services in each country.

International Trade

Most economists would agree that trade has been a net benefit to the world. The 1947 General Agreement on Tariffs and Trade (GATT), and subsequently the formation of the World Trade Organization in 1995, lowered tariffs and led to expanded trade and higher standards of living around the world.

Go to **LaunchPad** *to use the latest data to recreate this graph.*

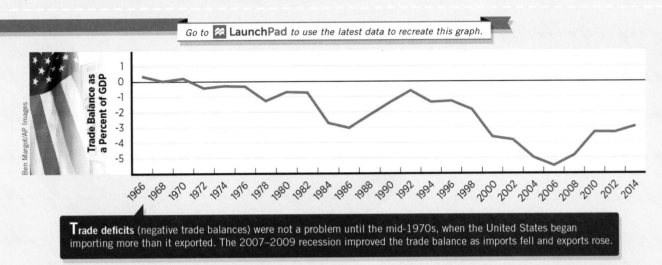

Trade Balance as a Percent of GDP

Trade deficits (negative trade balances) were not a problem until the mid-1970s, when the United States began importing more than it exported. The 2007–2009 recession improved the trade balance as imports fell and exports rose.

Tariff barriers (a tax on imports) are relatively low in most countries.

Country	Trade-Weighted Tariff (%)
India	6.8%
Brazil	6.6%
Russia	6.3%
South Korea	6.2%
Mexico	5.4%
China	3.6%
Turkey	2.8%
Australia	1.8%
Canada	1.5%
United States	1.5%
Japan	1.2%
Switzerland	0.5%
Hong Kong	0%

Medical tourism is growing because health costs are lower overseas, even including the costs of travel.

Average Cost of Various Medical Procedures

Procedure	United States	Thailand	Costa Rica
Heart Bypass	$151,533	$24,500	$40,000
Heart Valve	$186,548	$21,000	$32,000
Hip Replacement	$105,049	$14,000	$15,000
Knee Replacement	$69,214	$12,000	$12,500
Hysterectomy	$33,048	$5,000	$8,000
Spinal Fusion	$108,949	$11,000	$24,000

4,654,639 Number of American cars sold in China in 2015.

U.S. public sentiment about lowering trade barriers is mixed, and some even oppose helping displaced workers.

- Not sure 5%
- Favor lowering trade barriers but oppose helping workers who lose their job 14%
- Favor lowering trade barriers, provided there are programs to help workers who lose their job 50%
- Oppose agreements to lower trade barriers 31%

Buicks are a very popular luxury brand of cars in China, as they represent a unique American car to Chinese consumers. In 2015, over 1 million Buicks were sold in China, while only about 250,000 were sold in the United States.

FIGURE 1   U.S. TRADE BY SECTOR (2015)

This figure shows trade by sector. The United States imports and exports large amounts of capital goods, the equipment and machinery used to produce other goods. Also, nearly one-third of U.S. exports are services such as education and health care.

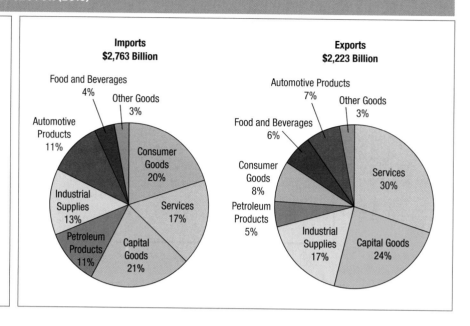

Imports
$2,763 Billion

Food and Beverages 4%
Other Goods 3%
Automotive Products 11%
Consumer Goods 20%
Industrial Supplies 13%
Services 17%
Petroleum Products 11%
Capital Goods 21%

Exports
$2,223 Billion

Automotive Products 7%
Other Goods 3%
Food and Beverages 6%
Consumer Goods 8%
Petroleum Products 5%
Services 30%
Industrial Supplies 17%
Capital Goods 24%

Improved communication and transportation technologies have worked together to promote global economic integration. In addition, most governments around the world have reduced their trade barriers in recent years.

Trade must yield significant benefits or it would not exist. After all, there are no laws requiring countries to trade, just agreements permitting trade and reducing impediments to it. This chapter begins with a discussion of why trade is beneficial. We look at the terms of trade between countries. We then look at the tariffs and quotas sometimes used to restrict trade, calculating their costs. Finally, we will consider some arguments critics have advanced against increased trade and globalization.

International trade allows consumers to buy goods (such as televisions) produced in many countries. Competition from trade allows for greater variety and lower prices.

Yuri Arcurs/age fotostock

autarky A country that does not engage in international trade, also known as a closed economy.

imports Goods and services that are purchased from abroad.

exports Goods and services that are sold abroad.

THE GAINS FROM TRADE

Economics studies voluntary exchange. People and nations do business with one another because they expect to gain through these transactions. Foreign trade is nearly as old as civilization. Centuries ago, European merchants were already sailing to the Far East to ply the spice trade. Today, people in the United States buy cars from South Korea and electronics from China, along with millions of other products from countries around the world.

Virtually all countries today engage in some form of international trade. Those that trade the least are considered *closed economies*. A country that does not trade at all is called an **autarky.** Most countries, however, are *open economies* that willingly and actively engage in trade with other countries. Trade consists of **imports,** goods and services purchased from other countries, and **exports,** goods and services sold abroad.

Many people assume that trade between nations is a zero-sum game: a game in which, for one party to gain, the other party must lose. Poker games fit this description; one person's winnings must come from another player's losses. This is not true of voluntary trade. Voluntary exchange and trade is a positive-sum game, meaning that both parties to a transaction can gain.

To understand how this works, and thus why nations trade, we need to consider the concepts of absolute and comparative advantage. Note that nations per se do not trade; individuals in specific countries do. We will refer to trade between nations but recognize that individuals, not nations, actually engage in trade.

Absolute and Comparative Advantage

Figure 2 shows hypothetical production possibilities frontiers for the United States and Canada. For simplicity, both countries are assumed to produce only beef (measured as a "side," which is half of a steer) and guitars. Given the production possibility frontiers (PPFs) in Figure 2, the United States has an absolute advantage over Canada in the production of both products. An **absolute advantage** exists when one country can produce more of a good than another country. In this case, the United States can produce twice as much beef and 5 times as many guitars as Canada. This is not to say that Canadians are inefficient in producing these goods, but rather that Canada does not have the resources to produce as many goods as the United States does (for one thing, its population is barely a tenth the size of that of the United States).

At first glance, we may wonder why the United States would be willing to trade with Canada. If the United States can produce so much more of both goods, why not just produce its own beef and guitars? The reason lies in comparative advantage.

One country enjoys a **comparative advantage** in producing some good if its opportunity costs to produce that good are lower than the other country's. In this example, Canada's comparative advantage is in producing beef. As Figure 2 shows, the opportunity cost for the United States to produce another million sides of beef is 1 million guitars; each added side of beef essentially costs 1 guitar.

absolute advantage One country can produce more of a good than another country.

comparative advantage One country has a lower opportunity cost of producing a good than another country.

FIGURE 2	**PRODUCTION POSSIBILITIES FOR THE UNITED STATES AND CANADA**

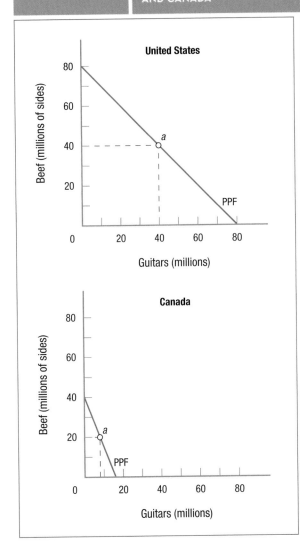

The production possibilities frontiers (PPF) shown here assume that the United States and Canada produce only beef and guitars. In this example, the United States has an absolute advantage over Canada in producing both products; the United States can produce twice as much beef and 5 times as many guitars as Canada. Canada nonetheless has a comparative advantage over the United States in producing beef.

TABLE 1	COMPARING OPPORTUNITY COSTS FOR BEEF AND GUITAR PRODUCTION		
	U.S. Opportunity Cost	Canada Opportunity Cost	Comparative Advantage
Beef production	1 guitar	0.4 guitar	Canada
Guitar production	1 side of beef	2.5 sides of beef	United States

Contrast this with the situation in Canada. For every guitar Canadian manufacturers forgo making, they can produce 2.5 more sides of beef. This means a side of beef costs only 0.4 guitar in Canada ($1/2.5 = 0.4$). Canada's comparative advantage is in producing beef, because a side of beef costs 0.4 guitar in Canada, while the same side of beef costs an entire guitar in the United States. By the same token, the United States has a comparative advantage in producing guitars: 1 guitar in the United States costs 1 side of beef, but the same guitar in Canada costs 2.5 sides of beef.

Table 1 summarizes the opportunity costs of each good in each country and shows which country has the comparative advantage for each good. These relative costs suggest that the United States should focus its resources on guitar production and that Canada should specialize in beef.

Gains from Trade

To see how specialization and trade can benefit both countries even when one has an advantage in producing more of both goods, assume that the United States and Canada at first operate at point *a* in Figure 2, producing and consuming their own beef and guitars. As we can see, the United States produces and consumes 40 million sides of beef and 40 million guitars. Canada produces and consumes 20 million sides of beef and 8 million guitars. This initial position is similarly shown as points *a* in Figure 3.

Assume now that Canada specializes in producing beef, producing all that it can—40 million sides of beef. We will assume that the two countries want to continue consuming 60 million sides of beef between them. This means that the United States needs to produce only 20 million sides of beef, because Canada is now producing 40 million. This frees up some American resources to produce guitars. Because each side of beef in the United States costs a guitar, reducing beef output by 20 million means that 20 million more guitars can now be produced.

Thus, the United States is producing 20 million sides of beef and 60 million guitars. Canada is producing 40 million sides of beef and no guitars. The combined production of beef remains the same, 60 million, but guitar production has increased by 12 million (from 48 million to 60 million).

The two countries can trade their surplus products and will be better off. This is shown in Table 2. Assuming that they agree to share the added 12 million guitars between them equally, Canada will trade 20 million sides of beef for 14 million guitars. Points *b* in Figure 3 show the resulting consumption patterns for each country. Each consumes the same quantity of beef as before trading, but each country now has 6 million more guitars: 46 million for the United States and 14 million for Canada. This is shown in the last column of the table.

One important point to remember is that even when one country has an absolute advantage over another, countries still benefit from trade. The gains are small in our example, but they will grow as the two countries approach one another in size and their comparative advantages become more pronounced.

Practical Constraints on Trade   At this point, we should take a moment to note some practical constraints on trade. First, every transaction involves costs. These include transportation, communications, and the general costs of doing business. Over the last several decades, however, transportation and communication costs have declined all over the world, resulting in growing world trade.

Second, the production possibilities frontiers for nations are not linear; rather, they are governed by increasing costs and diminishing returns. Countries find it difficult to specialize only in one product. Indeed, specializing in one product is risky because the market for

FIGURE 3	THE GAINS FROM SPECIALIZATION AND TRADE TO THE UNITED STATES AND CANADA

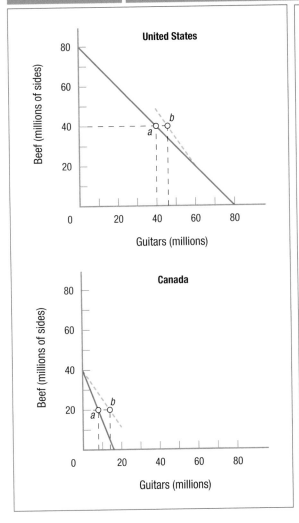

Assume Canada specializes in beef. If the two countries want to continue consuming 60 million sides of beef between them, the United States needs to produce only 20 million. This frees up resources for the United States to begin producing more guitars. Because each side of beef in the United States costs 1 guitar to produce, reducing beef output by 20 million means that 20 million more guitars can be produced. When the two countries trade their surplus products, both are better off than before.

TABLE 2	THE GAINS FROM TRADE

Country and Product	Before Specialization	After Specialization	After Trade
United States			
Beef	40 million	20 million	40 million
Guitars	40 million	60 million	46 million
Canada			
Beef	20 million	40 million	20 million
Guitars	8 million	0	14 million

the product can always decline, new technology might replace it, or its production can be disrupted by changing weather patterns. This is a perennial problem for developing countries that often build their exports and trade around one agricultural commodity.

Although it is true that trading partners benefit from trade, some individuals and groups within each country may lose. Individual workers in those industries at a comparative disadvantage are likely to lose their jobs, and thus may require retraining, relocation, or other help if they are to move smoothly into new occupations.

ISSUE

The Challenge of Measuring Imports and Exports in a Global Economy

Before the growth of globalization of manufacturing, the brand names of products would indicate their origin. For example, Sony televisions were made in Japan, Nokia telephones were made in Finland, and a Ford car would be made in the United States using American steel, engines, cloth, and, of course, American labor.

Today, a product's brand name does not tell the entire story. Production has become very complex, with parts sourced from around the world. With such complexities in trade, how then are imports and exports measured?

Do sales of Levi's jeans count as U.S. exports? Although Levi's are an American brand that has for much of its history been produced in the United States, today nearly all Levi's jeans are made in Asia. Therefore, the American-brand jeans we buy count as an *import*. On the other hand, we also consume many products that may seem foreign, but are made in the United States. The majority of Toyota

and Honda cars, for example, are assembled in American factories using American steel, glass, and other materials. The same is true to a lesser extent for luxury brands such as BMW, which produces many compact cars in South Carolina. For all but a few parts (such as the engine and transmission) that are made in Japan or Germany, these cars are as American as apple pie, and are not counted as imports.

In order to measure imports and exports accurately, the United States Bureau of Economic Analysis tabulates data from documents collected by U.S. Customs and Border Protection, which details the appraised value (price paid) for all shipments of goods into and out of the ports of entry (whether by land, air, or sea). The value of imported and exported services is more difficult to measure, and is based on a survey of monthly government and industry reports to determine the value of all services bought from and sold to foreigners.

A domestic content label of an "imported" Toyota truck.

The globalized economy has been spurred in large part by falling transportation and communication costs in the past few decades. Companies face ever greater competition, applying more pressure to reduce production costs. The expansion of the production process to a worldwide factory is just one way our economy has changed, and this trend is likely to continue into the future.

When the United States signed the North American Free Trade Agreement (NAFTA) with Canada and Mexico, many U.S. workers experienced this sort of dislocation. Some U.S. jobs went south to Mexico because of lower wages. States such as Texas and Arizona experienced greater levels of job dislocation due to their proximity to Mexico. Still, by opening up more markets for U.S. products, NAFTA has stimulated the U.S. economy. The goal is that displaced workers, newly retrained, will end up with new and better jobs, although there is no guarantee this will happen.

✓ CHECKPOINT

THE GAINS FROM TRADE

- An absolute advantage exists when one country can produce more of a good than another country.

- A comparative advantage exists when one country can produce a good at a lower opportunity cost than another country.

- Both countries gain from trade when each specializes in producing goods in which they have a comparative advantage.

- Transaction costs, diminishing returns, and the risk associated with specialization all place some practical constraints on trade.

QUESTIONS: When two individuals voluntarily engage in trade, they both benefit or the trade wouldn't occur—one party wouldn't choose to be worse off after the trade. Is the same true for nations? Is everyone in both nations better off?

Answers to the Checkpoint questions can be found at the end of this chapter.

THE TERMS OF TRADE

How much can a country charge when it sells its goods to another country? How much must it pay for imported goods? The terms of trade determine the prices of imports and exports.

To keep things simple, assume that each country has only one export and one import, priced at P_x and P_m. The ratio of the price of the exported goods to the price of the imported goods, P_x/P_m, is the terms of trade. Thus, if a country exports computers and imports coffee, with two computers trading for one ton of coffee, the price of a computer must be one-half the price of a ton of coffee.

When countries trade many commodities, the **terms of trade** are defined as the average price of exports divided by the average price of imports. This can get a bit complicated, given that the price of each import and export is quoted in its own national currency, while the exchange rate between the two currencies may be constantly changing. We will ignore these complications by translating currencies into dollars, focusing our attention on how the terms of trade are determined and the impact of trade.

terms of trade The ratio of the price of exported goods to the price of imported goods (P_x/P_m).

Determining the Terms of Trade

To get a feel for how the terms of trade are determined, let us consider the trade in golf clubs between the United States and South Korea. We will assume the United States has a comparative advantage in producing golf clubs; all prices are given in dollars.

Panel A of Figure 4 shows the supply and demand of sets of golf clubs in the United States. The upward-sloping supply curve reflects increasing opportunity costs in golf club production. As the United States continues to specialize in golf club production, resources

FIGURE 4	DETERMINING THE TERMS OF TRADE

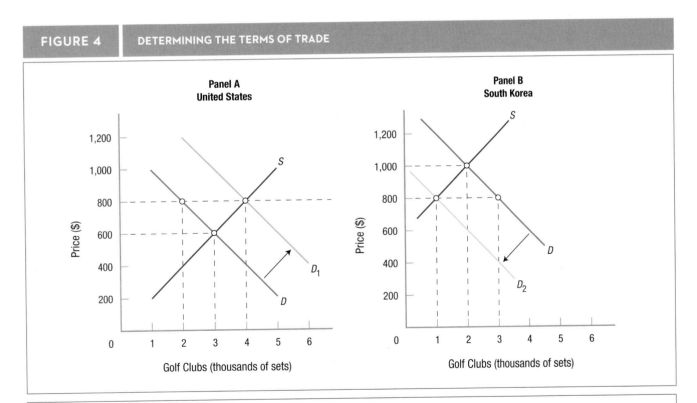

Panel A shows the supply and demand of golf clubs in the United States; the upward slope of the supply curve reflects increasing opportunity costs to produce more golf clubs. The United States begins in pretrade equilibrium at $600 and South Korea's initial equilibrium is at $1,000. With trade, Korean consumers will begin buying American golf clubs because of their lower price. American golf club makers will increase production to meet this new demand. Korean golf club firms will see sales of their golf clubs decline as prices begin to fall. Ignoring transport costs, trade will continue until prices reach $800. At this point, U.S. exports (2,000) are just equal to Korean imports (2,000).

less suited to this purpose must be employed, resulting in rising costs for golf club production. Because of this rise in costs as ever more resources are shifted to golf clubs, the United States will eventually lose its comparative advantage in golf club production. This represents one limit on specialization and trade.

Let us assume that the United States begins in pretrade equilibrium, with the price of golf club sets at $600 each. Panel B shows South Korea initially in equilibrium with a higher price of $1,000. Because prices for golf clubs from the United States are lower, when trade begins, Korean consumers will begin buying U.S. golf clubs.

American golf club makers will increase production to meet this new demand. Korean golf club firms, conversely, will see the sales of their golf clubs decline. For now, let us ignore transportation costs, such that trade continues until prices reach $800. At this point, U.S. exports (2,000 sets of golf clubs) are just equal to Korean imports. Both countries are now in equilibrium, with the price of golf clubs somewhere between the two pretrade equilibrium prices ($800 in this case).

Imagine this same process simultaneously working itself out with many other goods, including some at which the Koreans have a comparative advantage, such as interactive televisions. As each product settles into an equilibrium price, the terms of trade between these two countries are determined.

The Impact of Trade

Our examination of absolute and comparative advantage has thus far highlighted the benefits of trade. A closer look at Figure 4, however, shows that trade produces winners and losers.

Picking up on the previous example, golf club producers in the United States are happy, having watched their sales rise from 3,000 to 4,000 units. Predictably, management and workers in this industry will favor even more trade with South Korea and the rest of the world. Yet, domestic consumers of golf clubs are worse off, because after trade they purchase only 2,000 sets at the higher equilibrium price of $800.

Contrast this situation in the net exporting country, the United States, with that of the net importer, South Korea. Korean golf club producers are worse off than before because the price of golf clubs fell from $1,000 to $800, and their output was reduced to 1,000 units. Consequently, they must cut jobs, leaving workers and managers in the Korean golf club industry unhappy with its country's trade policies. Korean consumers, however, are beneficiaries of this expanded trade, because they can purchase 3,000 sets of golf clubs at a lower price of $800 each.

These results are not merely hypothetical. This is the story of free trade, which has been played out time and time again: Some sectors of the economy win, and some lose. American consumers have been happy to purchase Korean televisions such as Samsung and LG, given their high quality and low prices. American television producers (such as RCA and Zenith) have not been so pleased, nor have their employees, having watched television factories close and workers displaced as competition from abroad forced these companies out of business.

Similarly, the ranks of American textile workers have been decimated over the past three decades as domestic clothing producers have increasingly become nothing but designers and marketers of clothes, shifting their production overseas to countries in which wages are lower. American-made clothing is now essentially a thing of the past.

To be sure, American consumers have enjoyed a substantial drop in the price of clothing, because labor forms a significant part of the cost of clothing production. Still, being able to purchase inexpensive T-shirts made in China is small consolation for the unemployed textile worker in North Carolina.

The undoubted pain suffered by the losers from trade often is translated into pressure put on politicians to restrict trade in one way or another. The pain is often felt more strongly than the "happiness" felt by those who benefit from trade.

Trade allows American golf club producers to expand sales globally, while Korean golfers benefit from their availability.

Mike Flippo/Shutterstock

Robert Laberge/Getty Images

How Trade Is Restricted

Trade restrictions can range from subsidies provided to domestic firms to protect them against lower-priced imports to embargoes by which the government bans any trade with a country. Between these two extremes are more intermediate policies, such as exchange controls that limit the amount of foreign currency available to importers or citizens who travel abroad. Regulation, licensing, and government purchasing policies are all frequently used to promote or ensure the purchase of domestic products. The main reason for these trade restrictions is simple: The industry and its employees actually feel the pain and lobby extensively for protection, while the huge benefits of lower prices are diffused among millions of consumers whose benefits are each so small that fighting against a trade barrier isn't worth their time.

The most common forms of trade restrictions are tariffs and quotas, though tariffs are used more frequently than quotas. Figure 5 shows the average U.S. tariff rates since 1900. Some economists have suggested that the tariff wars that erupted in the 1920s and culminated in the passage of the Smoot-Hawley Act in 1930 were an important factor underlying the severity of the Great Depression. The high tariffs of the 1930s reduced trade, leading to a reduction in income, output, and employment, and added fuel to the worldwide depression. Since the 1930s, the United States has played a leading role in trade liberalization, with average tariff rates declining to a current rate of less than 2%.

Effects of Tariffs and Quotas

What exactly are the effects of tariffs and quotas? **Tariffs** are often *ad valorem* taxes. This means that the product is taxed by a certain percentage of its price as it crosses the border. Other tariffs are unit taxes (also known as *specific tariffs*): A fixed tax per unit of the product is assessed at the border. Tariffs are designed to generate revenues and to drive a wedge between the domestic price of a product and its price on the world market. The effects of a tariff are shown in Figure 6.

Domestic supply and demand for the product are shown in Figure 6 as *S* and *D*. Assume that the product's world price of $400 is lower than its domestic price of $600. Domestic quantity demanded (4,000 units) will consequently exceed domestic quantity supplied (2,000 units) at the world price of $400. Imports to this country will therefore be 2,000 units.

tariff A tax on imported products. When a country taxes imported products, it drives a wedge between the product's domestic price and its price on the world market.

| FIGURE 5 | AVERAGE U.S. TARIFF RATES, 1900–2015 |

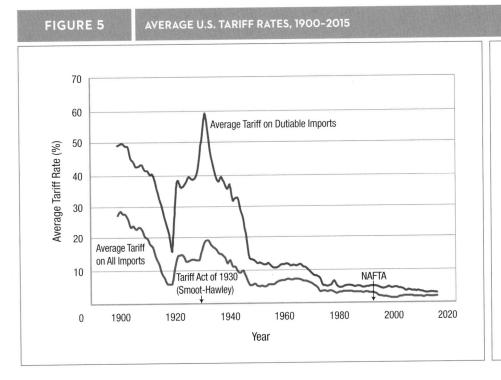

Tariffs and quotas are the most common forms of trade restrictions. Tariff rates in the United States peaked during the Great Depression. Over the last several decades, tariffs have steadily declined to an average of less than 2% today.

FIGURE 6 | EFFECTS OF A TARIFF

What are the effects of a typical tariff? Supply and demand curves *S* and *D* represent domestic supply and demand. Assume the product's world price of $400 is lower than its domestic price. Imports will therefore be 2,000 units. If the country imposes a tariff of $100 on this product, the domestic price rises to $500, and imports fall to 1,000 units. Domestic consumers now buy less of the product at higher prices. However, the domestic industry is happy because its prices and output have risen. Also, the government collects revenues equal to the shaded area.

Now assume that the firms and workers in the industry hurt by the lower world price lobby for a tariff and are successful. The country imposes a tariff of $100 per unit on this product. The results are clear. The product's price in this country rises to $500 and imports fall to 1,000 units (3,500 − 2,500). Domestic consumers buy less of the product at higher prices. Even so, the domestic industry is happy, because its prices and output have risen. The government, meanwhile, collects revenues equal to $100,000 ($100 × 1,000), the shaded area in Figure 6. These revenues can be significant: In the 1800s, tariffs were the federal government's dominant form of revenue. It is only in the last century that the federal government has come to rely more on other sources of revenue, including taxes on income, sales, and property.

Figure 7 shows the effects of a **quota.** They are similar to what we saw in Figure 6, except that the government restricts the quantity of imports into the country to 1,000 units.

quota A government-set limit on the quantity of imports into a country.

FIGURE 7 | EFFECTS OF A QUOTA

What are the effects of a quota? They are similar to the effects of a tariff, except that the government restricts the quantity of imports into the country to 1,000 units. Imports fall to the quota level, and again consumers lose as they must pay higher prices for less output. Producers and their employees gain as prices and employment in the domestic industry rise. With a quota, however, the government does not collect revenues.

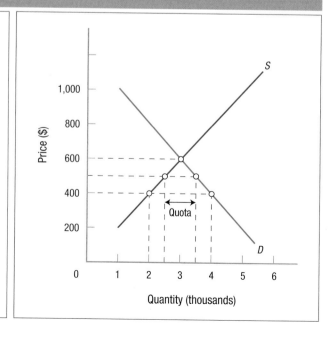

Imports fall to the quota level, and consumers again lose, because they must pay higher prices for less output. Producers and their employees gain as prices and employment in the domestic industry rise. For a quota, however, the government does not collect revenue. Then who gets this revenue? The foreign exporting company receives it in the form of higher prices for its products. This explains why governments prefer tariffs over quotas.

The United States imposed quotas on Japanese automobiles in the 1980s. The primary effect of these quotas was initially to raise the minimum standard equipment and price dramatically for some Japanese cars and ultimately to increase the number of Japanese cars made in American factories. If a firm is limited in the number of vehicles it can sell, why not sell higher-priced ones whose profit margins are higher? The Toyota Land Cruiser, for instance, was originally a bare-bones SUV selling for under $15,000. With quotas, this vehicle was transformed into a luxury behemoth that sells for over $80,000 today, with all the bells and whistles standard. Although quotas on Japanese

 ISSUE

Do Foreign Trade Zones Help or Hurt American Consumers and Workers?

Driving through the gates of the Cartago *Zona Franca* in Costa Rica, one encounters a remarkable sight in a historic Central American town: large factories adorned with the names of large American companies in industries including pharmaceuticals, semiconductors, medical supplies, and household products. What are these companies doing in Costa Rica, and why did they choose to locate within this small gated compound?

In Cartago, as well as in other cities throughout the world, clusters of multinational companies engage in manufacturing activities. These companies are taking advantage of the benefits offered by foreign trade zones, also commonly known as free trade zones or export processing zones.

A foreign trade zone is a designated area in a country where foreign companies can import inputs, without tariffs, to be used for product assembly by local workers who are often paid a fraction of what equivalent workers would be paid in the company's home country. By operating in a foreign trade zone, all inputs coming into a country are exempted from tariffs as long as the finished products (with some exceptions) are then exported from the country. Further, companies are often exempted from other taxes levied by the government.

Countries such as China, the Philippines, and Costa Rica establish foreign trade zones to attract foreign investment, which creates well-paying jobs relative to wages paid by domestic companies. Countries with high literacy rates, like Costa Rica, are especially attractive because their workers can perform semi-skilled tasks such as assembling electronic and computer products or handling customer service calls. Foreign trade zones also are prevalent along border towns, such as those in Mexico, where easy transportation to and from the United States allows inputs and products to flow rapidly.

The entrance to the free trade zone in Cartago, Costa Rica.

Although companies operating in foreign trade zones benefit from lower production costs and the host country benefits from jobs created, not everyone is in favor of foreign trade zones. Various unions in the United States view foreign trade zones as facilitating the offshoring of American jobs. Offshoring occurs when part of the production process (typically, the labor-intensive portions) is sent to countries with lower input costs.

What may be surprising, however, is that foreign trade zones and offshoring are not one-way streets. The United States has many foreign trade zones established for the same purpose: to attract foreign companies to invest in manufacturing plants. By moving production to the United States, European and Japanese companies produce goods such as cars while enjoying the same tax benefits as American companies operating abroad. In 2015 almost as many jobs were created by foreign companies in the United States as jobs lost from American companies moving production overseas.

There are both winners and losers in trade. But when all impacts are considered, including savings to consumers from lower product costs, imports of U.S. goods by foreigners, profits to U.S. affiliates, and the value of labor reemployed, the benefits tend to outweigh the costs. Clearly, those who lose their jobs suffer. But with a policy to provide training to displaced workers, the savings from offshoring can lead to greater investment and growth in the long run.

automobiles have long expired, Japanese automakers continue to produce a wide array of luxury automobiles.

One problem with tariffs and quotas is that when they are imposed, large numbers of consumers pay just a small amount more for the targeted products. Few consumers are willing to spend time and effort lobbying Congress to end or forestall these trade barriers from being introduced. Producers, however, are often few in number, and they stand to gain tremendously from such trade barriers. It is no wonder that such firms have large lobbying budgets and provide campaign contributions to political candidates.

 CHECKPOINT

THE TERMS OF TRADE

- The terms of trade are determined by the ratio of the price of exported goods to the price of imported goods.
- The terms of trade are set by the markets in each country and by exports and imports that eventually equalize the prices.
- Trade leads to winners and losers in each country and in each market.
- Trade restrictions vary from subsidies to domestic firms to government bans on the import of foreign products.
- Tariffs are taxes on imports that protect domestic producers and generate revenue for the government.
- Quotas represent restrictions on the volume of particular imports that can come into a country. Quotas do not generate revenue for governments and are infrequently used.

QUESTION: When the government imposes a quota on foreign trucks, who benefits and who loses?

Answers to the Checkpoint questions can be found at the end of this chapter.

ARGUMENTS AGAINST FREE TRADE

We have seen the benefits of trade, and have looked at how trade undoubtedly benefits some and harms others. Those who are harmed by trade often seek to restrict trade, primarily in the form of tariffs and quotas. Because trade leads to some loss, those who are harmed by trade have made arguments against free trade.

The arguments against free trade fall into two camps. Traditional economic arguments include protection for infant industries, protection against dumping, low foreign wages, and support for industries judged vital for national defense. More recent arguments focus on globalization (social and economic) concerns that embody political-economy characteristics. These include domestic employment concerns, environmental concerns, and the impact of globalization on working conditions in developing nations. In what follows, we take a critical look at each of these arguments, showing that most of these arguments do not have a solid empirical basis.

Traditional Economic Arguments

Arguments against trade are not new. Despite the huge gains from trade, distortions (subsidies and trade barriers) continue because changing current policies will hurt those dependent on subsidies and trade restrictions, and these firms and workers will show their displeasure in the voting booth. All of these traditional economic arguments against free trade seem reasonable on their face, but on closer examination, they look less attractive.

Infant Industry Argument An **infant industry,** it is argued, is one that is too underdeveloped to achieve comparative advantage or perhaps even to survive in the global market. Such an industry may be too small or undercapitalized, or its management and workers may be too inexperienced, to compete. Unless the industry's government provides it with some protection through tariffs, quotas, or subsidies, it might not survive in the face of foreign competition.

In theory, once the infant industry has been given this protection, it should be able to grow, acquiring the necessary capital and expertise needed to compete internationally. Germany and the United States used high tariffs to protect their infant manufacturing sectors in the 1800s, and Japan continued to maintain import restrictions up until the 1970s.

Although the infant industry argument sounds reasonable, it has several limitations. First, protecting an industry must be done in a way that makes the industry internationally competitive. Many countries coddle their firms, and these producers never seem to develop into "mature," internationally viable firms. Once protection is provided (typically, a protective tariff), it is difficult to remove after an industry has matured. The industry and its workers continue to convince policymakers of the need for continued protection.

Second, infant industry protection often tends to focus on capital manufacturing. Countries with huge labor supplies would do better to develop their labor-intensive industries first, letting more capital-intensive industries develop over time. Every country, after all, should seek to exploit its comparative advantages, but it is difficult to determine which industries have a chance of developing a comparative advantage in the future and should be temporarily protected.

Third, many industries seem to be able to develop without protections; therefore, countries may be wasting their resources and reducing their incomes by imposing protection measures.

Clearly, the infant industry argument is not a compelling one for advanced economies such as those of the United States, much of Europe, and Japan. The evidence for developing nations shows some benefits but is mixed for the reasons noted above.

infant industry An industry so underdeveloped that protection is needed for it to become competitive on the world stage or to ensure its survival.

Antidumping Dumping means that goods are sold at lower prices (often *below cost*) abroad than in their home market. This is typically a result of government subsidies.

In the same way that price discrimination improves profits, firms can price discriminate between their home markets and foreign markets. Let's assume that costs of production are $100 per unit for all firms (domestic and foreign). A state subsidy of $30 a unit, for example, reduces domestic costs to $70 per unit and permits the firm to sell its product in world markets at these lower prices. These state subsidies give these firms a cost advantage in foreign markets.

Firms can use dumping as a form of predatory pricing, using higher prices in their domestic markets to support unrealistically low prices in foreign markets. The goal of predatory pricing is to drive foreign competitors out of business. When this occurs, the firm doing the dumping then comes back and imposes higher prices. In the long run, these higher prices thereby offset the company's short-term losses.

Dumping violates U.S. trade laws. If the federal government determines that a foreign firm is dumping products into the United States, it can impose antidumping tariffs on the offending products. The government, however, must distinguish among dumping, legitimate price discrimination, and legitimate instances of lower-cost production arising from comparative advantage.

dumping Selling goods abroad at lower prices than in home markets, and often below cost.

Low Foreign Wages Some advocates of trade barriers maintain that domestic firms and their workers need to be protected from displacement by cheap foreign labor. Without this protection, it is argued, foreign manufacturers that pay their workers less than a dollar an hour will flood the market with low-cost products. As we have already seen, this argument has something to it: Workers in advanced economies can be displaced by low-wage foreign workers. This is what has happened in the American textile industry.

Once a handful of American clothing manufacturers began moving their production facilities overseas, thereby undercutting domestic producers, other manufacturers were forced to follow them. American consumers have benefited from lower clothing prices, but many displaced textile workers are still trying to get retrained and adapt to work in other industries. More recently, many manufacturing jobs have drifted overseas, and high-technology firms today are shifting some help desk facilities and computer programming to foreign shores.

On balance, however, the benefits of lower-priced goods considerably exceed the costs of lost employment. The federal government has resisted imposing protection measures for the sake of protecting jobs, instead funding programs that help displaced workers transition to new lines of work.

National Defense Argument In times of national crisis or war, the United States must be able to rely on key domestic industries, such as oil, steel, and defense. Some have argued that these industries may require some protection even during peacetime to ensure that they are already well established when a crisis strikes and importing key products may be impossible. Within limits, this argument is sound. Still, the United States has the capacity to produce such a wide variety of products that protections for specific industries would seem to be unjustified and unnecessary.

So what are we to make of these traditional arguments? Although they all seem reasonable, they all have deficiencies. Infant industries may be helped in the short run, but protections are often extended well beyond what is necessary, resulting in inefficient firms that are vulnerable on world markets. Dumping is clearly a potential problem, but distinguishing real cases of dumping from comparative advantage has often proven difficult in practice. Low foreign wages are often the only comparative advantage a developing nation has to offer the world economy, and typically, the benefits to consumers vastly outweigh the loss to a particular industry. Maintaining (protecting) industries for national defense has merit and may be appropriate for some countries, but for a country as huge and diversified as the United States, it is probably unnecessary.

The steel industry is one of several that are considered key domestic industries vital in times of national crisis. Therefore, industry executives frequently argue for protection against foreign competition.

Wangsong/Shutterstock

Recent Globalization Concerns

Expanded trade and globalization have provided the world's producers and consumers with many benefits. Some observers, however, have voiced concerns about globalization and its effects on domestic employment, the global environment, and working conditions in developing nations. Let's look at each one of these globalization concerns.

Trade and Domestic Employment Some critics argue that increased trade and globalization spell job losses for domestic workers. We have seen that this can be true. Some firms, unable to compete with imports, will be forced to lay off workers or even close their doors. Even so, increased trade usually allows firms that are exporters to expand their operations and hire new workers. These will be firms in industries with comparative advantages. For the United States, these industries tend to be those that require a highly skilled workforce, resulting in higher wages for American workers.

Clearly, those industries that are adding workers and those that are losing jobs are different industries. For workers who lose their jobs, switching industries can be difficult and time-consuming, and often it requires new investments in human capital. U.S. trade policy recognizes this problem, and the Trade Adjustment Assistance (TAA) program provides workers with job search assistance, job training, and some relocation allowances. In some industries sensitive to trade liberalization, including textiles and agriculture, trade policies are designed to proceed gradually, thus giving these industries and their workers some extra time to adjust.

Possible employment losses in some noncompetitive industries do not seem to provide enough justification for restricting trade. By imposing trade restrictions such as tariffs or quotas in one industry, employment opportunities in many other industries may be reduced. Open, competitive trade encourages producers to focus their production on those areas in which the country stands at a comparative advantage. Free trade puts competitive pressure on domestic firms, forcing them to be more productive and competitive, boosting the flow of information and technology across borders, and widening the availability of inputs for producers. At the end of the day, consumers benefit from these efficiencies, having more goods to choose from and enjoying a higher standard of living.

Trade and the Environment Concerns about globalization, trade, and the environment usually take one of two forms. Some people are concerned that expanded trade and globalization will lead to increased environmental degradation as companies take advantage of lax environmental laws abroad, particularly in the developing world. Others worry that attempts by the government to strengthen environmental laws will be challenged by trading partners as disguised protectionism.

Domestic environmental regulations usually target a product or process that creates pollution or other environmental problems. One concern in establishing environmental regulations, however, is that they not unfairly discriminate against the products of another country. This is usually not a serious problem. Nearly all trade agreements, including the World Trade Organization agreements and NAFTA, have provisions permitting countries to enforce measures "necessary to protect human, animal or plant life or health" or to conserve exhaustible natural resources. Nothing in our trade agreements prevents the United States from implementing environmental regulations as long as they do not unreasonably discriminate against our trading partners.

Will free trade come at the expense of the environment? Every action involves a trade-off. Clearly, there can be cases in which the benefits of trade accruing to large numbers of people result in harm to a more concentrated group. However, trade policies can also be complementary to good environmental policies. For example, increased free trade in agriculture encourages countries with fertile lands to specialize in growing crops, while discouraging countries from farming marginal lands that require the use of environmentally damaging pesticides and chemicals.

We have seen that trade raises incomes in developed and developing countries. How rising incomes affect environmental protections depends on the state of a country's development. In poor, developing countries, environmental protection will not at first be a priority. Critics of globalization argue that rich nations will exploit weaker environmental regulations with trade and foreign direct investment. Yet many studies have found that not to be the case. In fact, as countries develop and incomes rise, the demand for environmental protection rises as the issue takes on added importance even in poorer nations. The result is what economists refer to as an environmental Kuznets curve, in which economic development initially harms the environment but then improves as incomes rise. An increased emphasis on environmental issues can be seen in countries such as Costa Rica, Brazil, and even India and China, as people in these countries demand a cleaner environment as incomes rise.

Trade and Its Effect on Working Conditions in Developing Nations Some antiglobalization activists argue that trade between the United States and developing countries, where wages are low and working conditions are deplorable, exploits workers in these developing countries. Clearly, such trade does hurt American workers in low-wage, low-skilled occupations who cannot compete with the workers paid an even lower wage overseas. But it is not clear that workers in developing countries would be helped if the United States were to cut off its trade with those countries that refuse to improve wages or working conditions. For these workers, producing goods for export may be the only job opportunity they have.

Restricting trade with countries that do not raise wages to levels we think acceptable or bring working conditions up to our standards would probably do more harm than good. Low wages reflect, among other factors, small investments in human capital, low productivity, and meager living standards characteristic of developing nations. Blocking trade with these nations may deprive them of their key chance to grow and to improve in those areas in which we would like to see change.

Liberalized trade policies, economic freedom, and a legal system that respects property rights and foreign capital investment probably provide the best recipe for rapid development, economic growth, environmental protection, and improved wages and working conditions.

In summary, trade does result in job losses in some industries, but the gain for consumers and the competitive pressures that trade puts on domestic companies are beneficial to the economy as a whole. Trade raises incomes in developing nations, resulting in a growing demand for more environmentally friendly production processes. Trade is not the reason for low environmental standards in developing countries; they result from low incomes, low standards of living, and poor governmental policies. Trade brings about higher levels of income and ultimately better working conditions.

Can One Country's Festival Disrupt World Trade?

How is China's export sector so important that it can disrupt global trade during its annual Spring Festival?

Calvin Chan/Alamy

Around early to mid-February of each year (depending on the lunar calendar), one of the largest mass migrations of people begins in China—hundreds of millions of people pack onto crowded trains, airline seats sell out, and highways are jammed with cars in the world's largest auto market. Although this might sound typical of a Memorial Day or Thanksgiving weekend in the West, the sheer scale of the Spring Festival in China makes most other holidays around the world appear minuscule.

Just how big of an impact on the world does this Chinese festival have?

The 15-day Spring Festival, which coincides with the Lunar New Year and

culminates with the Lantern Festival, is so large that it actually disrupts global trade each year. Because China is the world's largest exporter of goods, consumers and producers around the world depend on Chinese exports to stock their shelves and to provide parts for manufacturing. Moreover, many companies depend on custom orders, such as custom tote bags for a large conference or custom racing medals to be handed out to runners after a marathon. Often these orders are made months in advance to allow time for production as well as shipping, usually by cargo ship.

Because nearly everyone celebrates the Spring Festival in China,

most workers take long vacations in February. Factories that employ migrants from the countryside become empty as workers leave to visit their families and friends. As a result, many factory orders are delayed or placed on hold during the festival, which can affect markets around the world as stores and customers wait for their orders to arrive.

The sheer size and influence of China's export sector can disrupt global trade when there is a halt in production. As a result, distributors anticipate delays by placing orders extra-early whenever possible around that time of year. One might wonder why factory managers do not provide incentives for workers to forgo the festival in order to fill customer orders. Most likely it's because the managers themselves are leaving to see their families! The Spring Festival is a 4,000-year-old tradition and one not to be missed, even at the cost of disrupting world trade.

GO TO **LaunchPad** TO PRACTICE THE ECONOMIC CONCEPTS IN THIS STORY

✔ CHECKPOINT

ARGUMENTS AGAINST FREE TRADE

- The infant industry argument claims that some industries are so underdeveloped that they need protection to survive in a global competitive environment.

- Dumping involves selling products at different prices in domestic and foreign markets, often with the help of subsidies from the government. This is a form of predatory pricing to gain market share in the foreign market.

- Some suggest that domestic workers need to be protected from the low wages in foreign countries. This puts the smaller aggregate loss to small groups ahead of the greater general gains from trade. Also, for many countries, a low wage is their primary comparative advantage.

- Some argue that select industries need protection to ensure that they will exist for national defense reasons.

- Globalization displaces some workers due to foreign competition, and some advocates would restrict trade on these grounds alone. But on net, trade has led to higher overall employment as exports expand and the economy grows.

- Concern about the environment is often a factor in trade negotiations. But as trade increases incomes in developing countries, environmental awareness rises.

- Some believe that trade exploits workers in developing countries; however, trade has typically resulted in higher wages for these workers.

QUESTION: Trade between the United States and China increased significantly over the last two decades. China is now the United States' second largest trading partner after Canada. Expanding trade has led to significant reductions in the price of many goods, including technology goods such as computers and tablets. However, some people have been vocal against policies that promote freer trade with China. What are some reasons why people would be against greater trade with China?

Answers to the Checkpoint questions can be found at the end of this chapter.

chapter summary

Section 1 The Gains From Trade

26.1 **Absolute advantage:** Occurs when one country can produce more of a good than another country.

Comparative advantage: Occurs when a country can produce a good at a lower opportunity cost than another country.

Fotokostic/Shutterstock

Nicholas Haig/Dreamstime.com

The United States has a comparative advantage in both soybean production (due to an abundance of fertile land) and commercial aircraft production (due to an abundance of technology and human capital).

26.2 Trade is a **positive-sum game**, which means that both countries in a trading relationship can gain compared to not trading.

Section 2 The Terms of Trade

26.3 The **terms of trade** determine the prices of imports and exports. When countries trade many commodities, the terms of trade are defined as the average price of exports divided by the average price of imports.

26.4 The Effect of Trade on Prices

Before trade, the prices charged for one good may be different in the two countries. The country with the lower price is likely to export the good; greater demand for that country's good pushes prices higher. The country with the higher price is likely to import the good; lesser demand for that country's good pushes prices lower. Market forces therefore push prices toward an equilibrium under free trade.

26.5 **Tariffs** are a tax on imports. They raise the domestic price of the good to the *world price + tariff*.

Winners: Domestic producers gain area A. Government gains area C in tariff revenues.

Losers: Domestic consumers lose areas A + B + C + D due to higher prices.

Net Loss: Areas B + D (deadweight loss from the tariff)

Quotas are an alternative to tariffs that directly restrict the quantity of imports. Quotas have a similar effect on prices as tariffs, except no tariff revenue is generated.

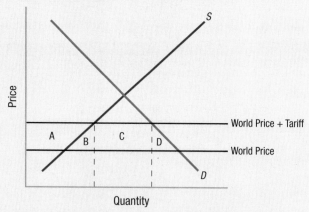

Historically, trade barriers have been high. In the 1930s, the Smoot-Hawley Act placed an average tax of 60% on most imported goods, arguably prolonging the Great Depression. Trade barriers have fallen since, and in the past three decades have fallen dramatically to nearly free trade with all countries.

Section 3 Arguments Against Free Trade

26.6 Many strong arguments against free trade exist. In each case, trade protection in the form of a tariff, quota, or subsidy is sought to protect the domestic industry.

Infant industry argument: States that a new industry requires protection to survive against established foreign competition. The problem is determining when these industries mature.

Antidumping argument: Dumping occurs when a foreign firm sells its goods below cost or at a price below what it charges in its domestic market.

Key industries argument: States that a country must be able to rely on its domestic industries for critical goods such as food, oil, steel, and defense equipment in times of conflict when trade might not be possible.

26.7 **Environmental degradation argument:** States that countries producing mass goods allow their environments to deteriorate. However, studies show that as countries develop and incomes grow, demand for environmental protection rises.

In the early 1980s, Harley-Davidson sought infant industry protection against competition from established lower-cost Japanese motorcycles, giving it time to retool its factories to become more competitive.

Protection against cheap labor argument: Argues that domestic workers need to be protected from cheap foreign labor. Most economists estimate that the benefits from lower-priced imports from free trade exceed the costs of lost employment. Further, increased trade generates jobs in export industries.

26.8 **Exploitation of foreign workers argument:** Argues that trading with developing countries where wages are low and working conditions are deplorable exploits workers in these countries. But restricting trade would probably do more harm than good. Trade may be their only chance to grow and improve their standard of living.

South Korea sustained environmental degradation during its economic development in the 1980s and 1990s. Today, it invests heavily in environmental protection and sustainable cities like Songdo outside the capital of Seoul.

Although working conditions in factories in developing countries look miserable, they often are better than working conditions before trade. In addition, trade increases demand for workers, which leads to higher wages.

KEY CONCEPTS

autarky, p. 698
imports, p. 698
exports, p. 698
absolute advantage, p. 699

comparative advantage, p. 699
terms of trade, p. 703
tariff, p. 705
quota, p. 706

infant industry, p. 709
dumping, p. 709

QUESTIONS AND PROBLEMS

Check Your Understanding

1. What is the difference between absolute and comparative advantage? Why would Lexi Thompson, who is better than you at both golf and laundry, still hire you to do her wash?

2. If the United States has a comparative advantage in the production of strawberries compared to Iceland, how might trade affect the prices of strawberries in the two countries?

3. Who are the beneficiaries from a large U.S. tariff on French and German wines? Who are the losers?

4. Why does a quota generate a larger loss to the importing country than a tariff that restricts imports to the same quantity?

5. What is the difference between an infant industry and a key industry? Why do producers in both industries desire protection against foreign imports?

6. How could free trade between the United States and China potentially lead to *more* jobs in the United States?

Apply the Concepts

7. Some American politicians claim that China's trade policies are unfair to the United States, and that a large tax (tariffs) should be placed on Chinese imports to protect American workers and industries. Why might such a policy sound better than it actually is in practice? What are the dangers of imposing large taxes on Chinese imports?

8. Expanding trade in general benefits all countries, or they would not willingly engage in trade. But we also know that consumers and society often gain while particular industries or workers lose. Because society and consumers gain, how might the government compensate the few losers for their loss?

9. Some activist groups are calling for "fair trade laws" by which other countries would be required to meet or approach our environmental standards and provide wage and working conditions approaching those of developed nations in order to be able to trade with us. Is this just another form of rent seeking by industries and unions for protection from overseas competition?

10. Why is there free trade between states in the United States but not necessarily between countries?

11. Remittances from developed countries amount to over $500 billion each year. These funds are sent to their home countries by migrants in developed nations. Is this similar to the gains from trade discussed in this chapter, or are these workers just taking jobs

that workers in developed countries would be paid more to do in the absence of the migrants?

12. Suppose Brazil developed a secret process that effectively quadrupled its output of coffee from its coffee plantations. This secret process enabled it to significantly undercut the prices of U.S. domestic producers. Would domestic producers receive a sympathetic ear to calls for protection from Brazil's lower cost coffee? How is this case different from that of protection against cheap foreign labor?

In the News

13. Much of the world's trade in goods occurs by cargo ship. Sometimes, the routes taken seem bizarre. For example, a container of goods being shipped from Shanghai to Hawaii might travel over 7,000 miles to Long Beach and then backtrack nearly 3,000 miles to Hawaii, as opposed to just traveling about 4,500 miles directly. Why would cargo companies use circuitous (and seemingly inefficient) routes to reach their destinations?

14. Since the Civil War, Hawaii had been a major producer and exporter of sugarcane. About the time Hawaii became a U.S. state in 1959, the sugar industry had already started its decline, and in 2015, the last sugar plantation in Hawaii closed. Explain how the sugar industry in Hawaii was affected by reductions in tariffs, world competition, and the opportunity costs of production relative to other states. Why does sugar continue to be produced in Florida and Louisiana but not Hawaii?

Solving Problems

 WORK IT OUT LaunchPad | interactive activity

15. This figure shows the production possibilities frontiers (PPFs) for Italy and India for their domestic production of olives and tea. Without trade, assume that each is consuming olives and tea at point *a*.

 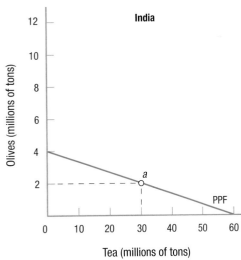

a. If Italy and India were to consider specialization and trade, what commodity would each specialize in? What is India's opportunity cost for tea and olives? What is Italy's opportunity cost for tea and olives?

b. Assume that the two countries agree to specialize entirely in one product (the one for which each country has a comparative advantage), and agree to split the total output between them. Complete the following table. Are both countries better off after trade?

Country and Product	Before Specialization	After Specialization	After Trade
Italy			
Olives	6 million tons	_____	_____
Tea	10 million tons	_____	_____
India			
Olives	2 million tons	_____	_____
Tea	30 million tons	_____	_____

16. The following figure shows the annual domestic demand and supply for 16-GB flash drives.

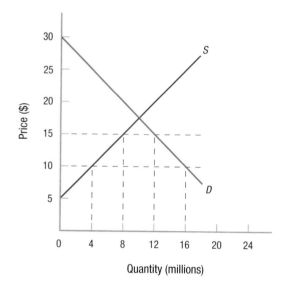

a. Assume that the worldwide price of these 16-GB flash drives is $10. What percent of United States sales would be imported?

b. Assume the U.S. government puts a $5 tariff per unit on flash drive imports. How many 16-GB flash drives would be imported into the United States?

c. Given the tariff in question (b), how much revenue would the government collect from this tariff?

d. Given the tariff in question (b), how much more sales revenue would domestic companies enjoy as a result of the tariff?

❖ USING THE NUMBERS

17. According to By the Numbers, approximately when was the last time the United States had a trade surplus? As a percentage of GDP, what was the highest trade surplus the United States has achieved in the last 50 years? What was the highest trade deficit the United States has incurred in the last 50 years?

18. According to By the Numbers, most of the developed countries (Canada, Australia, the United States, Switzerland, and Hong Kong) have relatively low tariff barriers, while much of the developing world still has high tariffs on imports. What reasons might account for why these countries continue to have high tariffs?

Checkpoint: The Gains From Trade 702

Yes, in general, nations would not trade unless they benefit. However, as we have seen, even though nations as a whole gain, specific groups—industries and their workers who do not have a comparative advantage relative to other countries—lose.

Checkpoint: The Terms of Trade 708

When a quota is imposed, the first beneficiary is the domestic industry. Foreign competition is curtailed. If the market is important enough (automobiles), foreign companies will build new plants in the United States and compete as if they are domestic firms. A second beneficiary is foreign competitors, in that they can increase the price or complexity of their products and increase their margins. Losers are consumers and, to some extent, the government, because a tariff could have accomplished the same reduction in imports and the government would have collected some revenue.

Checkpoint: Arguments Against Free Trade 713

Growth in the volume of trade with China has led to lower prices on many goods Americans enjoy. However, although trade with China has led to significant benefits to Americans, the sentiment is not always positive for a number of reasons. First, many believe that China's low prices (through its low wages as well as government efforts to keep the value of the U.S. dollar strong) forced many American factories to close or move overseas, causing job losses. Second, some believe China holds an unfair advantage due to poor working conditions and low environmental standards. Third, some believe that quality standards for Chinese products are low, leading to safety issues. These and other reasons have created a backlash against efforts to further reduce trade barriers between the two nations. However, these concerns have not diminished the benefits of low prices and the many American jobs generated through increased exports of American-made products to a growing consumer market in China.

27 Open Economy Macroeconomics

Understanding how fluctuations in exchange rates affect what we pay for goods and services in a globalized economy

Learning Objectives

27.1 Define the current account and the capital account in the balance of payments between countries.

27.2 Explain the difference between nominal and real exchange rates.

27.3 Describe the effects of currency appreciation or depreciation on imports and exports.

27.4 Describe the effects of changes in inflation rates, disposable income, and interest rates on exchange rates.

27.5 Explain the differences between fixed and flexible exchange rate systems.

27.6 Describe the implications for fiscal and monetary policies when used with fixed and flexible exchange rate systems.

You probably are aware of international finance if you have traveled abroad. To purchase goods and services in another country, you need to have an amount of that country's currency. True, you can use credit cards for major purchases, but you still need some currency for daily transactions. In Britain, you need to pay in British pounds; in France, you need euros. British and French shopkeepers and public transportation officials will not accept U.S. dollars. This means that at the beginning of your trip, whether at the airport or at a bank, you have to exchange your dollars for the currency of the country you are visiting.

This process of exchanging money applies to international trade as well. You may pay dollars for your Burberry scarf or Louis Vuitton handbag in a store in the United States, but eventually your dollars have to be converted to pounds or euros when your payments make their way back to Britain or France, respectively. And if U.S. companies export goods abroad, they will want to bring dollars back to the United States, whether the goods are paid for originally in dollars or not.

Furthermore, in today's open economies, individuals can hold domestic and foreign financial assets. Your own financial portfolio might include foreign stocks, bonds, and currency, as well as domestic stocks and bonds. Buying and selling foreign securities and goods involves the buying and selling of foreign currency, also known as foreign exchange.

We can see that foreign exchange transactions for tourism, trade, and investment would seem to be large in number and amount. In fact, foreign exchange transactions dwarf the volume of exports and imports, often by as much as 30 to 40 times, in the same way that the annual value of all stock transactions far surpasses the market value of all companies on the New York Stock Exchange. Most foreign exchange transactions are conducted not for trade but for financial or speculative purposes. The social benefit to emerge from this speculation is a highly liquid foreign exchange market that ensures the possibility of trade. The large volume of speculative trade in currencies means that there will always be a market for international trade.

Eric Chiang

BY THE NUMBERS

The Foreign Exchange Market

The foreign exchange market is the world's largest trading exchange, far surpassing the total value of all bond and stock transactions throughout the world. Currencies are traded 24 hours a day from Sunday 5 P.M. EST to Friday 5 P.M. EST in major foreign exchanges in London, Tokyo, New York, and Sydney.

The most traded currencies in the world are shown. Because each transaction involves two currencies, the percentages add up to 200%. The U.S. dollar is involved in a significant portion of all foreign exchange transactions.

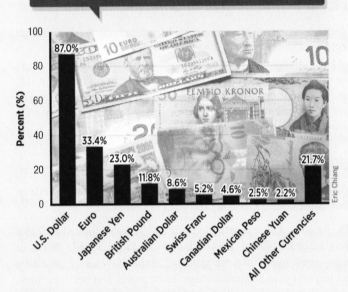

Eric Chiang

Go to **LaunchPad** *to use the latest data to recreate this graph.*

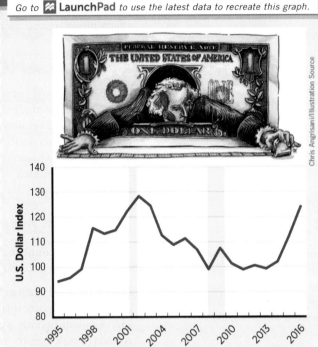

Chris Angrisani/Illustration Source

$5.3 trillion
Total value of currency traded *each day* in foreign exchange markets

90%
Percent of foreign exchange trades that are speculative (investors attempting to earn profits)

Approximately twenty nations maintain a fixed exchange rate with the U.S. dollar. The following are selected currencies pegged to the U.S. dollar.

Mark Wilson/Getty Images

Country/Region	Exchange Rate per $ (April 22, 2016)
Bahamas	1 Bahamian dollar
Djibouti	178 francs
East Caribbean	2.7 East Caribbean dollars
Hong Kong	7.8 Hong Kong dollars
Jordan	0.71 dinar
Lebanon	1,500 pounds
Qatar	3.64 riyal
Saudi Arabia	3.75 riyal
United Arab Emirates	3.67 dirham

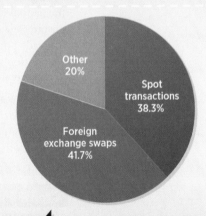

Foreign exchange swaps, or contracts to buy and sell a fixed amount of foreign currency on two different dates, are the most common type of foreign exchange transaction, followed by spot transactions, which are foreign currency trades at the current exchange rate. The remaining 20% includes other foreign exchange trades such as options and futures.

In this chapter, we want to look at foreign exchange markets to get a sense of how policymaking in the United States is affected by an open worldwide economy. We start with balance of payments accounts, which are to open economy macroeconomics what national income accounts are to an individual country's macroeconomic accounts. This accounting structure is the basis for open economy analysis. We then examine the foreign exchange market in detail, looking at both the trade and financial aspects of those common foreign currency events: currency appreciation and depreciation. Finally, we put this all together when we view fixed and flexible exchange rate systems and discuss how an open economy affects monetary and fiscal policymaking.

THE BALANCE OF PAYMENTS

All open economies have balance of payments accounts. Open financial markets permit economies to run trade surpluses and deficits.

A simplified version of the U.S. balance of payments accounts for 2015 is shown in Table 1. These accounts were compiled by the Bureau of Economic Analysis of the U.S. Department of Commerce. The balance of payments represents all payments received from foreign countries and all payments made to them. Notice that the accounts are split into two broad divisions, the current account and the capital account.

The Current Account

current account Includes payments for imports and exports of goods and services, incomes flowing into and out of the country, and net transfers of money.

The **current account** includes payments for imports and exports of goods and services, incomes flowing into and out of the country, and net transfers of money.

Imports and Exports In 2015, U.S. exports of goods and services totaled $2,223.6 billion, with imports totaling $2,763.4 billion. This exchange produced a trade deficit of $539.8 billion because we imported more than we exported. Some balance of payments accounts break exports and imports into separate categories of goods and services; here, they are combined. This component of the current account is known as the balance of trade.

TABLE 1	THE BALANCE OF PAYMENTS 2015 (BILLIONS OF U.S. DOLLARS)	
Current Account		
Exports	2,223.6	
Imports	2,763.4	
Balance of trade (exports – imports)		−539.8
Income received (inflow)	783.1	
Income payments (outflow)	591.8	
Balance on income (inflow – outflow)		191.3
Net transfers		−135.6
Current account balance		−484.1
Capital Account		
Change in foreign-owned assets in the United States	395.5	
Change in U.S.-owned assets abroad	186.3	
Net increase in foreign-owned holdings		209.2
Statistical discrepancy		274.9
Capital account		484.1

Data from Bureau of Economic Analysis.

Income Another source of foreign payments to the United States comprises income flows, which include wages, rents, interest, and profits that Americans earn abroad ($783.1 billion in 2015) minus the corresponding income foreigners earn in the United States ($591.8 billion). On balance, foreigners earned $191.3 billion less in the United States than U.S. citizens and corporations earned abroad in 2015.

Transfers Direct transfers of money also take place between the United States and other countries. These transfers include foreign aid, funds sent to such international organizations as the United Nations, and stipends paid directly to foreign students studying in the United States or U.S. students studying abroad. These transfers also include remittances, money that people working in the United States send back to their families in foreign countries. Net transfers of money for 2015 from all sources totaled −$135.6 billion.

Adding all current account categories for 2015 yields a current account deficit of $484.1 billion. In 2015, the United States paid out $484.1 billion more than it received. Therefore, the United States had to borrow $484.1 billion from the rest of the world, or the net holdings of U.S. assets by foreigners must have increased by that same amount, or some combination of the two.

The Capital Account

The **capital account** summarizes the flow of money into and out of domestic and foreign assets. This account includes investments by foreign companies in domestic plants or subsidiaries—a Toyota truck plant in Tennessee, for example. Note that the profits from such investments flow abroad, and thus they are in the income payments (outflow) category of the current account. Other foreign holdings of U.S. assets include portfolio investments such as mutual funds, stocks, bonds, and deposits in U.S. banks. American investors hold foreign financial assets in their portfolios, including foreign stocks and bonds. And American companies own plants and other assets in foreign countries.

Because the United States ran a current account deficit in 2015, it must run a capital account surplus. Net capital inflows into the United States must equal $484.1 billion to offset the current account deficit. Indeed, foreign-owned assets in the United States increased by $395.5 billion, while U.S. ownership of foreign assets increased by $186.3 billion, resulting in a net inflow of capital of $209.2 billion. Because many accounts are subjected to estimation errors, a statistical discrepancy value of $274.9 billion is added to the net inflow of capital to bring the total capital account surplus to $484.1 billion.

The key point to remember is that balance of payments accounts have to show a balance: A deficit in the current account must be offset by a corresponding surplus in the capital account, and vice versa. Keep this point in mind as we go on to look at foreign exchange and policy implications of an open economy.

The iconic Plaza Hotel in New York City, which has appeared in several dozen movies, was purchased by foreign investors in 2004. The inflow of funds to the United States used to purchase the hotel appeared in the U.S. capital account that year.

capital account Summarizes the flow of money into and out of domestic and foreign assets, including investments by foreign companies in domestic plants or subsidiaries, and other foreign holdings of U.S. assets, including mutual funds, stocks, bonds, and deposits in U.S. banks. Also included are U.S. investors' holdings of foreign financial assets, production facilities, and other assets in foreign countries.

 CHECKPOINT

THE BALANCE OF PAYMENTS

- The balance of payments represents all payments received from foreign countries and all payments made to them.
- The balance of payments is split into two categories: current and capital accounts.
- The current account includes payment for exports and imports, income flows, and net transfers of money.
- The capital account summarizes flows of money into and out of domestic and foreign assets.
- The sum of the current and capital account balances must equal zero.

QUESTIONS: China and Russia both have a high savings rate as a percent of GDP. The lack of consumption relative to domestic investment leads to substantial net exports. Would this situation lead to a current account surplus or a current account deficit? Why?

Answers to the Checkpoint questions can be found at the end of this chapter.

EXCHANGE RATES

As we saw in the chapter opening, if you wish to go abroad or to buy a product directly from a foreign firm, you need to exchange dollars for foreign currency. Today, credit cards automatically convert currencies for you, making the transaction more convenient. This conversion does not, however, alter the transaction's underlying structure.

When you decide to travel abroad, the value of the dollar compared to the currency where you are going determines how expensive your trip will be. The value of the dollar fluctuates on a daily basis against most foreign currencies that are traded in the foreign exchange market. This section looks at the issues of exchange rates and their determination.

Defining Exchange Rates

exchange rate The rate at which one currency can be exchanged for another.

The **exchange rate** is defined as the rate at which one currency, such as U.S. dollars, can be exchanged for another, such as British pounds. The exchange rate is nothing more than the price of one currency for another. Table 2 shows exchange rates for selected countries for a specific date (April 22, 2016), as found on the Web site xe.com. Exchange rates can be quoted in one of two ways: (1) the price (in domestic currency) of 1 unit of foreign currency, or (2) the number of units of a foreign currency required to purchase 1 unit of domestic currency. As Table 2 illustrates, exchange rates are often listed from both perspectives.

nominal exchange rate The price of one country's currency for another.

real exchange rate A measure of a currency's value relative to another, taking into account the price levels of both countries. It is equal to the nominal exchange rate multiplied by the ratio of the price levels of the two countries.

Nominal Exchange Rates According to Table 2, 1 British pound will buy 1.44 dollars. Equivalently, 1 dollar will purchase 0.69 pound. These numbers are reciprocal measures of each other ($1 \div 1.44 = 0.69$). A **nominal exchange rate** is the price of one country's currency for another. It is the most common way of stating exchange rates. However, nominal exchange rates do not take into account changes in prices between countries. Therefore, economists often use an alternative measure of exchange rates, called the real exchange rate, when analyzing their effects on the economy.

Real Exchange Rates The **real exchange rate** takes the price levels of both countries into account. Real exchange rates become important when inflation is an issue in one

TABLE 2	EXCHANGE RATES (APRIL 22, 2016)	
	Exchange Rates	
	U.S. Dollars	**Currency per U.S. Dollar**
Australia (dollar)	0.775	1.290
Brazil (real)	0.283	3.526
Britain (pound)	1.443	0.693
Canada (dollar)	0.787	1.271
China (yuan)	0.154	6.485
France (euro)	1.129	0.885
India (rupee)	0.015	66.528
Japan (yen)	0.010	109.989
Mexico (peso)	0.057	17.436
Russia (ruble)	0.015	66.431
Switzerland (franc)	1.026	0.974

Data from xe.com.

country. The real exchange rate between two countries is defined as

$$e_r = e_n \times (P_d/P_f),$$

where e_r is the real exchange rate, e_n is the nominal exchange rate, P_d is the domestic price level, and P_f is the foreign price level.

The real exchange rate is the nominal exchange rate multiplied by the ratio of the price levels of the two countries. In plain words, the real exchange rate tells us how many units of the foreign good can be obtained for the price of 1 unit of that good domestically. The higher this number, the cheaper the good abroad becomes. If the real exchange rate is greater than 1, prices abroad are lower than at home. In a broad sense, the real exchange rate may be viewed as a measure of the price competitiveness between the two countries. When prices rise in one country, its products are not as competitive in world markets.

Let us take British and American cars as an example. Assume that Britain suffers significant inflation, which pushes the price of Land Rovers up by 15% in Britain. The United States, meanwhile, suffers no such inflation of its price level. If the dollar-to-pound exchange rate remains constant for the moment, the price of Land Rovers in the U.S. market will climb, while domestic auto prices remain constant.

Now Land Rovers are not as competitive as before, resulting in fewer sales. Note, however, that the resulting reduction in U.S. purchases of British cars and other items will reduce the demand for British pounds. This puts downward pressure on the pound, reducing its exchange value and restoring some competitiveness. Markets do adjust! We will look at this issue in more detail later in the chapter.

Purchasing Power Parity Purchasing power parity (PPP) is the rate of exchange that allows a specific amount of currency in one country to purchase the same quantity of goods in another country. Absolute PPP would mean that nominal exchange rates equaled the same purchasing power in each country. As a result, the real exchange rate would be equal to 1. For example, PPP would exist if $4 bought a meal in the United States, and the same $4 converted to British pounds (about £2.8) bought the same meal in London.

If you have traveled abroad, you know that PPP is not absolute. Some countries, such as India and Thailand, are known as inexpensive countries, while others, such as Norway and Switzerland, can be expensive. *The Economist* provides an online interactive tool called the "Big Mac Index," a lighthearted attempt to capture the notion of PPP.

Table 3 presents some recent estimates of PPP and the Big Mac Index. It also shows the PPP implied by the relative cost of Big Macs, along with the actual exchange rate. When comparing these two, we get an approximate over- or understating of the exchange rate. Keep in mind that the cost of a McDonald's Big Mac may be influenced by many unique local factors (trade barriers on beef, customs duties, taxes, competition), and therefore it may not reflect real PPP. Also, in some countries where beef is not consumed, chicken patties are substituted; and in still other countries, fish or vegetable patties are used.

purchasing power parity The rate of exchange that allows a specific amount of currency in one country to purchase the same quantity of goods in another country.

An hour-long massage in Bangkok, Thailand, can cost as little as $10, while a quick ten-minute cab ride in Geneva, Switzerland, can run $30. Exchange rates often do not result in purchasing power parity between nations.

Eric Chiang

Prices of fast food in different nations often do not result in purchasing power parity.

TABLE 3	MEASURES OF PURCHASING POWER PARITY				
	Big Mac Prices				
	In Local Currency	**In Dollars**	**Implied PPP of the Dollar**	**Actual Dollar Exchange Rate (January 2016)**	**Under (−)/Over (+) against the Dollar (%)**
United States	US$ 4.93	4.93	1.00	—	—
Argentina	Peso 33.0	2.39	6.69	13.81	−52
Britain	Pound 2.89	4.22	0.59	0.68	−14
Canada	CAD$ 5.84	4.14	1.18	1.41	−16
China	Yuan 17.6	2.68	3.57	6.56	−46
India	Rupee 127	1.90	25.76	66.80	−61
Japan	Yen 370	3.12	75.05	118.65	−37
Mexico	Peso 49	2.81	9.94	17.44	−43
Norway	Krone 46.8	5.21	9.49	8.97	+6
Switzerland	CHF 6.5	6.44	1.32	1.01	+31
Taiwan	NT$ 69	2.08	14.00	33.23	−58
Thailand	Bhat 112	3.09	22.72	36.22	−37
Venezuela	Bolivar 132	0.66	26.77	198.70	−87

Data from the Big Mac Index interactive tool: economist.com/content/big-mac-index.

According to the Big Mac Index, in 2016 most currencies were undervalued to the U.S. dollar, with the exception of the Norwegian krone and Swiss franc. Although not perfect, changes in the Big Mac Index often are reflective of movements in true PPP, given that simultaneous changes in several of the factors that distort the index often reflect real changes in the economy.

Exchange Rate Determination

We have seen that people and institutions have two primary reasons for wanting foreign currency. The first is to purchase goods and services and conduct other transactions under the current account. The second is to purchase foreign investments under the capital account. These transactions create a demand for foreign currency and give rise to a supply of domestic currency available for foreign exchange.

A Market for Foreign Exchange Figure 1 shows a representative market for foreign exchange. The horizontal axis measures the quantity of dollars available for foreign exchange, and the vertical axis measures the exchange rate in British pounds per U.S. dollar. The demand for dollars as foreign exchange is downward-sloping; as the exchange rate falls, U.S. products become more attractive, and more dollars are desired.

Suppose, for example, that the exchange rate at first is $1 = £1 and that the U.S. game company Electronic Arts manufactures and sells its games at home and in Britain for $50 (£50). Then suppose that the dollar *depreciates* by 50%, such that $1.00 = £0.50. If the dollar price of a game remains at $50 in the United States, the pound price of games in Britain will fall to £25 because of the reduction in the exchange rate. This reduction will increase the sales of games in Britain and increase the quantity of dollars British consumers need for foreign exchange.

FIGURE 1	THE FOREIGN EXCHANGE MARKET FOR DOLLARS

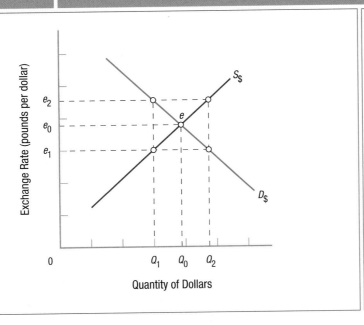

A market for foreign exchange is shown here. The horizontal axis measures the quantity of dollars available for foreign exchange, and the vertical axis measures the exchange rate in pounds per dollar. If exchange rates are fully flexible and the exchange rate is initially e_1, there is excess demand for dollars: Q_2 minus Q_1. The dollar will appreciate and the exchange rate will move to e_0. Alternatively, if the exchange rate is initially e_2, there is an excess supply of dollars. Because there are more dollars being offered than demanded, the dollar will depreciate. Eventually, the market will settle into an exchange rate of e_0, where precisely the quantity of dollars supplied is the quantity demanded.

The supply of dollars available for foreign exchange reflects the demand for pounds, because to purchase pounds, U.S. firms or individuals must supply dollars. Not surprisingly, the supply curve for dollars is positively sloped. If the dollar were to *appreciate*, say, moving to $1 = £2, British goods bought in the United States would look attractive because their dollar price would be cut in half. As Americans purchased more British goods, the demand for pounds would grow, and the quantity of dollars supplied to the foreign exchange market would increase.

Flexible Exchange Rates Assume that exchange rates are fully flexible, such that the market determines the prevailing exchange rate, and that the exchange rate in Figure 1 is initially e_1. At this exchange rate, there is an excess demand for dollars because quantity Q_2 is demanded but only Q_1 is supplied. The dollar will **appreciate,** or rise in value relative to other currencies, and the exchange rate will move in the direction of e_0 (more pounds are required to purchase a dollar). As the dollar appreciates, it becomes more expensive for British consumers, thus reducing the demand for U.S. exports. Because of the appreciating dollar, British imports are more attractive for U.S. consumers, increasing U.S. imports. These forces work to move the exchange rate to e_0, closing the gap between Q_2 and Q_1.

Alternatively, if the exchange rate begins at e_2, there will be an excess supply of dollars. Because more dollars are being offered than demanded, the value of dollars relative to British pounds will decline, or **depreciate.** American goods are now more attractive in Britain, increasing American exports and the demand for dollars, while British goods become more expensive for American consumers. Eventually, the market will settle into an exchange rate of e_0, at which precisely the quantity of dollars supplied is the quantity demanded.

appreciation (currency) When the value of a currency rises relative to other currencies.

depreciation (currency) When the value of a currency falls relative to other currencies.

Currency Appreciation and Depreciation A currency appreciates when its value rises relative to other currencies and depreciates when its value falls. This concept is clear enough in theory, but it can get confusing when we start looking at charts or tables that show exchange rates. The key is to be certain of which currency is being used to measure the value of other currencies. Does the table you are looking at show the pound price of the dollar or the dollar price of the pound?

Figure 2 shows the exchange markets for dollars and pounds. Panel A shows the market for dollars, where the price of dollars is denominated in pounds (£/$), just as in Figure 1.

FIGURE 2 | THE FOREIGN EXCHANGE MARKET

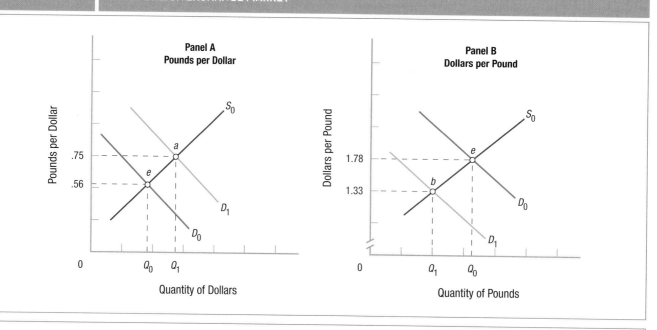

Data for dollars and pounds are graphically represented here. Panel A shows a market for dollars in which the price of dollars is denominated in pounds (£/$). In panel A, the market is in equilibrium at £0.56 per dollar (point e). Panel B shows the equivalent market for pounds in equilibrium at $1.78 per pound (again at point e). A rise in the demand for dollars means that the dollar appreciates to £0.75 per dollar (point a in panel A). Panel B shows that the corresponding decline in demand for pounds (from D_0 to D_1) leads to a depreciation

of the pound as the exchange rate falls from $1.78 to $1.33 per pound (point b).

Note that a depreciating pound in panel B indicates a decline in the exchange rate, but this simultaneously represents an appreciating dollar. Thus, graphs can be viewed as reflecting either appreciation or depreciation, depending on which currency is being used to establish the point of view.

This market is in equilibrium at £0.56 per dollar (point e). Panel B shows the equivalent market for pounds; it is in equilibrium at $1.78 per pound (again at point e). Note that $1 \div 0.56 = 1.78$; therefore, panels A and B represent the same information, just from different viewpoints.

Assume that there is a rise in the demand for dollars. In panel A, the dollar appreciates to £0.75 per dollar (point a), thus leading to a rise in the exchange rate. In panel B, the corresponding decline in demand for pounds (from D_0 to D_1) leads to a depreciation of the pound and a fall in the exchange rate from $1.78 to $1.33 per pound (point b). Notice that the pound's depreciation in panel B produces a decline in the exchange rate, but this decline simultaneously results in appreciation of the dollar. These graphs could be viewed as showing either an appreciation or a depreciation, depending on which currency represents your point of view.

For our purposes, we will try to use figures that show the exchange rate rising when the focus currency appreciates. Still, you need to be aware that exchange rates can be represented in two different ways. Exchange rate graphs are difficult and sometimes confusing; therefore, you will need to think through each graph you encounter.

Determinants of Exchange Rates What sort of conditions will cause currencies to appreciate or depreciate? First, a change in our tastes and preferences as consumers for foreign goods will result in currency appreciation or depreciation. For example, if we desire to purchase more foreign goods, this will lead to an increase in the demand for foreign currency and result in the depreciation of the dollar.

Second, if our income growth exceeds that of other countries, our demand for imports will grow faster relative to the growth of other nations. This will lead again to an increase in demand for foreign currency, resulting in the depreciation of the dollar.

Third, rising inflation in the United States relative to foreign nations makes our goods and services relatively more expensive overseas and foreign goods more attractive here at home. This results in growing imports, reduced exports, and again leads to a depreciation of the dollar.

Fourth, falling interest rates in the United States relative to foreign countries make financial investment in the United States less attractive. This reduces the demand for dollars, leading once again to a depreciation of the dollar.

Note that if we reverse these stories in each case, the dollar will appreciate.

Exchange Rates and the Current Account

As we have already seen, the current account includes payments for imports and exports. Also included are changes in income flowing into and out of the country. In this section, we focus on the effect that changes in real exchange rates have on both of these components of the current account. We will assume that import and export demands are highly elastic as prices change due to fluctuations in the exchange rate.

Changes in Inflation Rates Let's assume that inflation heats up in Britain, such that the British price level rises relative to U.S. prices. Production costs rise in Britain; therefore, British goods are more expensive. American goods appear more attractive to British consumers; therefore, exports of American goods rise, improving the U.S. current account. American consumers purchase more domestic goods and fewer British imports because of rising British prices, further improving the American current account. The opposite is true for Britain: British imports rise and exports fall, hurting the British current account.

These results are dependent on our assumption that import and export demands are highly elastic with real exchange rates. Thus, when exchange rates change, exports and imports will change proportionally more than the change in exchange rates.

Changes in Domestic Disposable Income If domestic disposable income rises, U.S. consumers will have more money to spend, and given existing exchange rates, imports will rise because some of this increased consumption will go to foreign products. As a result, the current account will worsen as imports rise. The opposite occurs when domestic income falls.

Exchange Rates and the Capital Account

The capital account summarizes flows of money or capital into and out of U.S. assets. Each day, foreign individuals, companies, and governments put billions of dollars into Treasury bonds, U.S. stocks, companies, and real estate. Today, foreign and domestic assets are available to investors. Foreign investment possibilities include direct investment in projects undertaken by multinational firms, the sale and purchase of foreign stocks and bonds, and the short-term movement of assets in foreign bank accounts.

Because these transactions all involve capital, investors must balance their risks and returns. Two factors essentially incorporate both risk and return for international assets: interest rates and expected changes in exchange rates.

Interest Rate Changes If the exchange rate is assumed to be constant, and the assets of two countries are *perfectly substitutable*, then an interest rate rise in one country will cause capital to flow into it from the other country. For example, a rise in interest rates in the United States will cause capital to flow from Britain, where interest rates have not changed, into the United States, where investors can earn a higher rate of return on their investments. Because the assets of both countries are assumed to be perfectly substitutable, this flow will continue until the interest rates (r) in Britain and the United States are equal, or

$$r_{US} = r_{UK}$$

Everything else being equal, we can expect capital to flow in the direction of the country that offers the highest interest rate, and thus, the highest return on capital. But "everything else" is rarely equal.

Expected Exchange Rate Changes Suppose that the exchange rate for U.S. currency is *expected to appreciate* ($\Delta\varepsilon > 0$). The relationship between the interest rates in the United States and Britain becomes

$$r_{US} = r_{UK} - \Delta\varepsilon$$

Investors demand a higher return in Britain to offset the expected depreciation of the British pound relative to the U.S. dollar. Unless interest rates rise in Britain, capital will flow out of Britain and into the United States until U.S. interest rates fall enough to offset the expected appreciation of the dollar.

If capital is not perfectly mobile and substitutable between two countries, a *risk premium* can be added to the relationship just described; thus,

$$r_{US} = r_{UK} - \Delta\varepsilon + x$$

where x is the risk premium. Expected exchange rate changes and risk premium changes can produce enduring interest rate differentials between two countries.

If the dollar falls relative to the yen, the euro, and the British pound, this is a sign that foreign investors were not as enthusiastic about U.S. investments. Low interest rates and high deficits may have convinced foreign investors that it was not a good time to invest in the United States. The United States is more dependent on foreign capital than ever before. Today, about half of U.S. Treasury debt held by the public is held by foreigners. Changes in inflation, interest rates, and expectations about exchange rates are important.

Exchange Rates and Aggregate Supply and Demand

How do changes in nominal exchange rates affect aggregate demand and aggregate supply? A change in nominal exchange rates will affect imports and exports. Consider what happens, for example, when the value of the dollar depreciates. The dollar is weaker, and thus the pound (or any other currency) will buy more dollars. American products become more attractive in foreign markets; therefore, American exports increase and aggregate demand expands. Yet, because some inputs into the production process may be imported (raw materials, computer programming services, or call answering services), input costs will rise, causing aggregate supply to contract.

Let us take a more detailed look at this process by considering Figure 3. Assume that the economy begins in equilibrium at point *e*, with full employment output Q_f and the price level at P_e. As the dollar depreciates, this will spur an increase in exports, thus shifting aggregate demand from AD_0 to AD_1 and raising prices to P_1 in the short run. Initially, output climbs to Q_1, but because some of the economy's inputs are imported, short-run aggregate supply will decline, mitigating this rise in output. In the short run, the economy will expand beyond Q_f, and prices will rise.

In the longer term, as domestic prices rise, workers will realize that their real wages do not purchase as much as they did before, because import prices are higher. As a result, workers will start demanding higher wages just to bring them back to where they were originally. This shifts short-run aggregate supply from $SRAS_0$ to $SRAS_1$, thereby moving the economy from point *a* in the short run to point *b* in the long run. As the economy adjusts to a higher price level, the original benefits accruing from currency depreciation will be greatly reduced.

Currency depreciation works because imports become more expensive and exports less so. When this happens, consumer income no longer goes as far, because the price of domestic goods does not change, but the cost of imports rises. In countries where imports form a substantial part of household spending, major depreciations in the national currency can produce significant declines in standards of living. Such depreciations (or devaluations) have occasioned strikes and, in some cases, even street riots; examples in recent decades include such actions in Argentina, Brazil, Mexico, and Indonesia.

FIGURE 3   EXCHANGE RATES AND AGGREGATE DEMAND AND SUPPLY

Assume that the economy initially begins in equilibrium at point *e*, with full employment output Q_f and the price level at P_e. Assume that the dollar depreciates. This will increase exports, shifting aggregate demand from AD_0 to AD_1 and raising prices to P_1 and output to Q_1 in the short run. In the long run, short-run aggregate supply will shift from $SRAS_0$ to $SRAS_1$, as workers readjust their wage demands in the long run, thus moving the economy to point *b*. As the economy adjusts to a higher price level, the benefits from currency depreciation are greatly reduced.

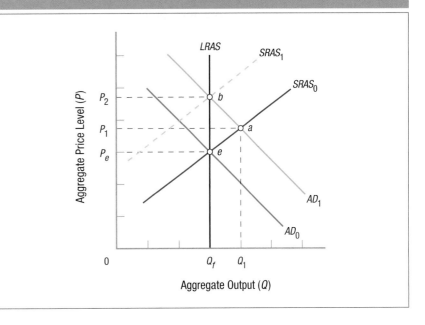

ISSUE

Would a Stronger Chinese Yuan Be Good for Americans?

Much discussion in recent years has focused on the accusation that the Chinese government manipulated the value of its currency, the yuan. What exactly did China do?

When Americans purchase goods from China (and we purchase a whole lot of goods), normally dollars must be exchanged for yuan to pay for these goods. Factories in China need to pay their workers in yuan so that their workers can pay their rent and buy groceries. When dollars are exchanged for yuan, demand for yuan increases, which raises its value. Therefore, the yuan should appreciate against the dollar.

When the yuan appreciates, it takes more dollars to obtain the same amount of yuan as before. Therefore, goods made in China, from toys you buy for your nephews and nieces to shoes, clothes, and electronics you buy for yourself, become more expensive.

To prevent the prices of China's exports from rising too much in the United States, the Chinese government

bought up many of these dollars flowing into China, preventing them from being sold on the foreign exchange market. By holding U.S. dollars, the dollar value is kept from falling. In 2016, China held over 1 trillion in U.S. dollars.

Who benefited from this policy and who lost out? The actions by the Chinese government to prevent the yuan from appreciating keeps prices of Chinese-made goods low for ordinary American consumers, especially benefiting those with limited budgets. Thanks, China, for helping the U.S. consumer.

Who lost out? China's policy made it harder for American (and other non-Chinese) companies to compete against Chinese imports.

If the winners from this policy are American consumers and the losers are American businesses and their workers, policymakers are faced with quite a dilemma. Pressuring the Chinese to let its currency appreciate might be good for American companies, though it will lead to higher prices for many

Are you ready to pay more for everyday purchases? If the Chinese yuan appreciates, you may.

goods that we buy. Are we ready to see the cost of this policy come out of our pockets? Many Americans would be reluctant to support such an outcome, because it would have a similar effect as an increase in taxes or inflation. Both reduce the purchasing power of our income and savings.

Indeed, you can see that the debate about currency manipulation goes beyond whether one side is playing by the rules. Sometimes, fairness can be a costly proposition.

What are the implications of all this for policymakers? First, a currency depreciation or devaluation can, after a period, lead to inflation. In most cases, however, the causation probably goes the other way: Macroeconomic policies or economic events force currency depreciations.

Trade balances usually improve with an exchange rate depreciation. Policymakers can get improved current account balances without inflation by pursuing devaluation first, then pursuing fiscal contraction (reducing government spending or increasing taxes), and finally moving the economy back to point *e* in Figure 3. But here again, the real long-run benefit is more stable monetary and fiscal policies.

 ## CHECKPOINT

EXCHANGE RATES

- Nominal exchange rates define the rate at which one currency can be exchanged for another.
- Real exchange rates are the nominal exchange rates multiplied by the ratio of the price levels of the two countries.
- Purchasing power parity (PPP) is a rate of exchange that permits a given level of currency to purchase the same amount of goods and services in another country.
- A currency appreciates when its value rises relative to other currencies. Currency depreciation causes a currency to lose value relative to others.
- Inflation causes depreciation of a country's currency, worsening its current account. Rising domestic income typically results in rising imports and a deteriorating current account.
- Rising interest rates cause capital to flow into the country with the higher interest rate, and expectations about a future currency appreciation or depreciation affect the capital account.
- Currency appreciation and depreciation have an effect on aggregate supply and demand. For example, currency depreciation expands aggregate demand as exports increase, but some (now higher-priced) imported inputs increase the cost of domestic production, reducing aggregate supply.

QUESTION: Cities along the U.S.–Canadian border, such as Vancouver, Niagara Falls, Detroit, and Buffalo, receive a substantial number of day visitors. For example, Americans might cross the border into Niagara Falls for a day of sightseeing, while Canadians might cross the border into Detroit to shop. Suppose that the value of the Canadian dollar appreciates against the U.S. dollar. How does this change affect tourism, businesses that depend on day-trippers, and the current account of the United States and Canada?

Answers to the Checkpoint questions can be found at the end of this chapter.

MONETARY AND FISCAL POLICY IN AN OPEN ECONOMY

How monetary and fiscal policy is affected by international trade and finance depends on the type of exchange rate system in existence. There are several ways that exchange rate systems can be organized. We will discuss the two major categories: fixed and flexible rates.

Fixed and Flexible Exchange Rate Systems

fixed exchange rate Each government determines its exchange rate, then uses macroeconomic policy to maintain the rate.

flexible or **floating exchange rate** A country's currency exchange rate is determined in international currency exchange markets.

A **fixed exchange rate** system is one in which governments determine their exchange rates, then adjust macroeconomic policies to maintain these rates. A **flexible** or **floating exchange rate** system, in contrast, relies on currency markets to determine the exchange rates consistent with macroeconomic conditions.

Before the Great Depression, most of the world economies were on the gold standard. According to Peter Temin, the gold standard was characterized by "(1) the free flow of gold between individuals and countries, (2) the maintenance of fixed values of national currencies in terms of gold and therefore each other, and (3) the absence of an international coordinating organization."[1]

Under the gold standard, each country had to maintain enough gold stocks to keep the value of its currency fixed to that of others. If a country's imports exceeded its exports, this balance of payments deficit had to come from its gold stocks. Because gold backed the national currency, the country would have to reduce the amount of money circulating in its economy, thereby reducing expenditures, output, and income. This reduction would lead to a decline in prices and wages, a rise in exports (which were getting cheaper), and a corresponding drop in imports (which were becoming more expensive). This process would continue until imports and exports were again equalized and the flow of gold ended.

In the early 1930s, the U.S. Federal Reserve pursued a contractionary monetary policy intended to cool off the overheated economy of the 1920s. This policy reduced imports and increased the flow of gold into the United States. With France pursuing a similar deflationary policy, by 1932 these two countries held more than 70% of the world's monetary gold. Other countries attempted to conserve their gold stocks by selling off assets, thereby spurring a worldwide monetary contraction. As other monetary authorities attempted to conserve their gold reserves, moreover, they reduced the liquidity available to their banks, thereby inadvertently causing bank failures. In this way, the Depression in the United States spread worldwide.

As World War II came to an end, the Allies met in Bretton Woods, New Hampshire, to design a new and less troublesome international monetary system. Exchange rates were set, and each country agreed to use its monetary authorities to buy and sell its own currency to maintain its exchange rate at fixed levels.

The Bretton Woods agreements created the International Monetary Fund to aid countries having trouble maintaining their exchange rates. In addition, the World Bank was established to loan money to countries for economic development. In the end, most countries were unwilling to make the tough adjustments required by a fixed rate system, and it collapsed in the early 1970s. Today, we operate on a flexible exchange rate system in which each currency floats in the market.

Pegging Exchange Rates Under a Flexible Exchange Rate System

Although most currencies fluctuate in value based on their relative demand and supply on the foreign exchange market, a number of countries use macroeconomic policies to peg their currency (maintain a fixed exchange rate) to another currency, most commonly the U.S. dollar or the euro.

A common reason for a country to peg its currency to another is to maintain a close trade relationship, because fixed exchange rates prevent fluctuations in prices due to changes in the exchange rate. For example, most OPEC nations peg their currencies to the U.S. dollar as a result of their dependency on oil exports, a significant portion of which goes to the United States. Many Caribbean nations that depend on tourism and trade with the United States also peg their currencies to the U.S. dollar.

Some countries do not maintain a strict fixed exchange rate with the U.S. dollar, but will intervene to control the exchange rate. For example, China has intervened in foreign exchange markets for strategic purposes, propping up the value of the U.S. dollar by holding dollars instead of exchanging them on the foreign exchange market. By keeping the U.S. dollar strong, the price of Chinese exports is kept low for American consumers, allowing China to continue expanding their export volume.

---

[1] Peter Temin, *Lessons from the Great Depression: The Lionel Robbins Lectures for 1989* (Cambridge, MA: MIT Press), 1989, p. 8.

When traveling to Panama, it is not necessary to exchange money. Panama's official currency is the U.S. dollar.

dollarization Describes the decision of a country to adopt another country's currency (most often the U.S. dollar) as its own official currency.

Another reason for maintaining a fixed exchange rate is to improve monetary stability and to attract foreign investment. For example, several countries in western Africa peg their unified currency, the CFA franc, to the euro. By maintaining a fixed exchange rate, a country is essentially giving up its ability to conduct independent monetary policy. However, some countries such as Mexico and Argentina, both of which had pegged their currencies to the U.S. dollar in the past, were forced to abandon their efforts due to high inflation, which made their products too expensive in world markets.

Finally, some countries chose to abandon their currency altogether by adopting another country's currency as their own. Panama, Ecuador, El Salvador, Timor-Leste, and others, all chose to adopt the U.S. dollar as their official currency, a process known as **dollarization.** Not only did they give up their ability to use monetary policy, they also eliminated the risk of being unable to maintain fixed exchange rates with their original currencies.

There clearly are many approaches to foreign exchange used. But how does a fixed versus a flexible exchange rate system affect each country's ability to use fiscal and monetary policy? We answer this question next.

Policies Under Fixed Exchange Rates

When the government engages in expansionary policy, aggregate demand rises, resulting in output and price increases. Figure 4 shows the result of such a policy as an increase in aggregate demand from AD_0 to AD_1, with the economy moving from equilibrium at point a to point b in the short run and the price level rising from P_0 to P_1. A rising domestic price level means that U.S. exports will decline as they become more expensive. As incomes rise, imports will rise. Combined, these forces will worsen the current account, moving it into deficit or reducing a surplus, as net exports decline.

An expansionary monetary policy, combined with a fiscal policy that is neither expansionary nor contractionary, will result in a rising money supply and falling interest rates. This causes aggregate demand to rise to AD_1 as shown in Figure 4. Lower interest rates result in capital flowing from the United States to other countries, which reduces aggregate output.

FIGURE 4   MONETARY AND FISCAL POLICY IN AN OPEN ECONOMY UNDER FIXED EXCHANGE RATES

When the government engages in expansionary policy, aggregate demand rises, resulting in output and price increases. A rising domestic price level reduces exports while rising incomes increase imports, worsening the current account.

An expansionary monetary policy (holding fiscal policy constant) increases the money supply and reduces interest rates. Lower interest rates result in capital outflow, pushing aggregate demand back toward AD_0.

An expansionary fiscal policy (holding monetary policy constant) increases interest rates, leading to capital inflow, pushing aggregate demand further to the right to AD_2.

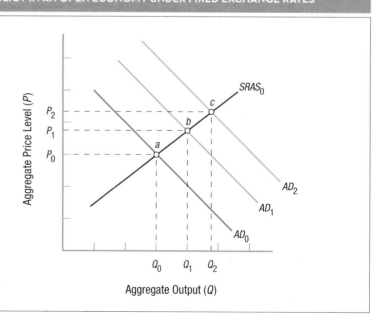

The greater the capital mobility, the more aggregate demand moves back in the direction of AD_0. With perfect capital mobility, monetary policy would be ineffective. The amount of capital leaving the United States would be just equal to the increase in the money supply to begin with, and interest rates would be returned to their original international equilibrium.

Keeping exchange rates fixed and holding the money supply constant, an expansionary fiscal policy will produce an increase in interest rates. As income rises, there will be a greater transactions demand for money, resulting in higher interest rates. Higher interest rates mean that capital will flow into the United States.

As more capital flows into U.S. capital markets, the expansionary impact of the original fiscal policy increases. Expansionary fiscal policy is reinforced by an open economy with fixed exchange rates as aggregate demand increases to AD_2.

Policies Under Flexible Exchange Rates

Expansionary monetary policy under a system of flexible exchange rates, again holding fiscal policy constant, results in a growing money supply and falling interest rates. Lower interest rates lead to a capital outflow and a balance of payments deficit, or a declining surplus. With flexible exchange rates, consumers and investors will want more foreign currency; thus, the exchange rate will depreciate. As the dollar depreciates, exports increase; U.S. exports are more attractive to foreigners as their currency buys them more. The net result is that the international market works to reinforce an expansionary policy undertaken at home.

ROBERT MUNDELL
NOBEL PRIZE

Awarded the Nobel Prize in 1999, Robert Mundell is best known for his groundbreaking work in international economics and for his contribution to the development of supply-side economic theory. Born in Canada in 1932, he attended the University of British Columbia as an undergraduate and earned his Ph.D. from the Massachusetts Institute of Technology in 1956. For a year, he served as a post-doctoral fellow at the University of Chicago, where he met the economist Arthur Laffer, his collaborator in the development of supply-side theory.

Supply-side economists advocated reductions in marginal tax rates and stabilization of the international monetary system. This approach was distinct from the two dominant schools of economic thought, Keynesianism and monetarism, although it shared some ideas with both. Mundell's work had a major influence on the economic policies of President Ronald Reagan and Federal Reserve Chair Paul Volcker, whose tight money policies helped curb inflation.

Mundell's early research focused on exchange rates and the movement of international capital. In a series of papers in the 1960s that proved to be prophetic, he speculated about the impacts of monetary and fiscal policy if exchange rates were allowed to float, emphasizing the importance of central banks acting independently of governments to promote price stability. At the time, his work may have seemed purely academic. Within 10 years, however, the Bretton Woods system of fixed exchange rates tied to the dollar broke down, exchange rates became more flexible, capital markets opened up, and Mundell's ideas were borne out.

In another feat of near prophecy, Mundell wrote about the potential benefits and disadvantages of a group of countries adopting a single currency, anticipating the development of the European currency, the euro, by many years. Since 1974, Mundell has taught at Columbia University.

Permitting exchange rates to vary and holding the money supply constant, an expansionary fiscal policy produces a rise in interest rates as rising incomes increase the transactions demand for money. Higher interest rates mean that capital will flow into the United States, generating a balance of payments surplus or a smaller deficit, causing the exchange rate to appreciate as foreigners value dollars more. As the dollar becomes more valuable, exports decline, moving aggregate demand back toward AD_0 in Figure 4. With flexible exchange rates, therefore, an open economy can hamper fiscal policy.

These movements are complex and go through several steps. Table 4 summarizes them for you. The key point to note is that under our flexible exchange rate system now, an open economy reinforces monetary policy and hampers fiscal policy. No wonder the Fed has become more important.

Several decades ago, presidents and Congress could adopt monetary and fiscal policies without much consideration of the rest of the world. Today, economies of the world are vastly more intertwined, and the macroeconomic policies of one country often have serious impacts on others. Today, open economy macroeconomics is more important, and good macroeconomic policymaking must account for changes in exchange rates and capital flows.

TABLE 4	SUMMARY OF THE EFFECTS OF AN OPEN ECONOMY ON MONETARY AND FISCAL POLICY IN A FIXED AND FLEXIBLE EXCHANGE RATE SYSTEM	
	Flexible Exchange Rate	Fixed Exchange Rate
Monetary policy (fiscal policy constant)	Reinforced	Hampered
Fiscal policy (monetary policy constant)	Hampered	Reinforced

During the financial crisis and recession of 2007–2009, the implications of monetary policy on exchange rates became important, as countries throughout the world were eager to use expansionary monetary policy to curtail the severity of the crisis. However, taking such action unilaterally can lead to adverse effects in other countries due to its effect on exchange rates, which affect trade and current accounts.

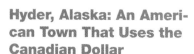

Hyder, Alaska: An American Town That Uses the Canadian Dollar

How did an American town end up using Canadian currency, utility services, and schools?

In a number of countries throughout the world, the U.S. dollar is more than just a valuable reserve currency. It's actually used as a medium of exchange. A few countries, including Panama, Ecuador, El Salvador, and Timor-Leste, have adopted the U.S. dollar as their official currency. But in many other countries, including Costa Rica, Bahamas, Cambodia, and Cuba, the U.S. dollar is accepted as legal tender as easily as their own currencies. In these countries, circumstances such as tourism and political instability encourage businesses to conduct transactions more often in U.S. dollars than in their own currency.

The 100 residents of Hyder, Alaska, live more like Canadians than Americans due to the town's isolated location.

But in one remote American town, the situation is reversed. Circumstances led its residents to conduct transactions in a foreign currency. Where is this place?

Hyder, Alaska, is a town of 100 residents in the southeastern point of Alaska. There are no airports and very few boats that come in and out of its small harbor. And there is just one road going in and out of Hyder, and that road leads to Canada. Hyder is so economically wed to its larger sister city across the border, Stewart, British

Columbia, that it relies on Canadian police, hospitals, utility services, and telecommunications (it has a Canadian area code). It also celebrates Canadian holidays because Hyder's children attend schools in Canada.

Most interestingly, Hyder adopted the Canadian dollar as its preferred currency. Although the American dollar is still legal tender in Hyder, its few businesses (with the exception of the U.S. Postal Service) conduct transactions in Canadian dollars. Much like why some countries use the U.S. dollar for convenience, businesses in Hyder use the Canadian dollar to reduce transaction costs by not having to exchange currency frequently. Because most of Hyder's product suppliers are located in Canada, conducting transactions in Canadian dollars also means that the effects of exchange rate fluctuations are minimized.

Hyder's economic ties with its Canadian neighbor exemplify the importance of strong global relations and how that can benefit individuals and businesses.

GO TO **LaunchPad** TO PRACTICE THE ECONOMIC CONCEPTS IN THIS STORY

Therefore, in October of 2008, six central banks including the Fed and the European Central Bank took a rare action of coordinated monetary policy, in which the central banks jointly announced a reduction in their target interest rates. As a result, countries engaging in a similar level of expansionary policy would prevent instability in exchange rates. As former Fed Chair Ben Bernanke put it, "The coordinated rate cut was intended to send a strong signal to the public and to markets of our resolve to act together to address global economic challenges."[2] The coordinated efforts of central banks continued over several years, especially when the Eurozone crisis intensified in 2011.

The global economy is connected not only through trade and currency exchanges. Nearly all economic decisions have effects that extend beyond our country's borders, from the types of goods that consumers purchase, to the goods firms produce and where they produce them, to how governments set policies that affect their citizens and those in other countries. As you complete your degree and prepare for your career, keep in mind the statement from Chapter 1 that has been illustrated throughout this book: *Economics is all around us.*

 CHECKPOINT

MONETARY AND FISCAL POLICY IN AN OPEN ECONOMY

- A fixed exchange rate is one in which governments determine their exchange rates and then use macroeconomic policy to maintain these rates.
- Flexible exchange rates rely on markets to determine exchange rates consistent with macroeconomic conditions.
- Some countries peg their currency to another to facilitate trade, to promote foreign investment, or to maintain monetary stability.
- Fixed exchange rate systems hinder monetary policy, but reinforce fiscal policy.
- Flexible exchange rates hamper fiscal policy, but reinforce monetary policy.

QUESTION: The United States seems to rely more on monetary policy to maintain stable prices, low interest rates, low unemployment, and healthy economic growth. Does the fact that the United States has really embraced global trade (imports and exports combined are over 30% of GDP) and has a flexible (floating) exchange rate help explain why monetary policy seems more important than fiscal policy?

Answers to the Checkpoint questions can be found at the end of this chapter.

---

[2] Ben Bernanke, *Policy Coordination Among Central Banks,* Speech at the Fifth European Central Banking Conference, The Euro at Ten: Lessons and Challenges, Frankfurt, Germany, November 14, 2008, http://www.federalreserve. gov/newsevents/speech/bernanke20081214a.htm.

chapter summary

Section 1 The Balance of Payments

27.1 The **current account** includes payments for imports and exports of goods and services, incomes flowing into and out of the country, and net transfers of money.

The **capital account** includes flows of money into and out of domestic and foreign assets.

The sum of the current account and capital account balances must equal zero.

gingercprice/Getty Images

When foreign tourists visit Miami Beach, the money that is spent adds to the U.S. current account. When a foreign tourist purchases a vacation condo, the purchase of this asset increases the U.S. capital account.

Foreign investment in the United States includes foreign ownership of domestic plants or subsidiaries; investments in mutual funds, stocks, and bonds; and deposits in U.S. banks. Similarly, U.S. investors hold foreign financial assets in their portfolios and own interests in foreign facilities and companies.

Section 2 Exchange Rates

27.2 The **exchange rate** defines the rate at which one currency can be exchanged for another.

A **nominal exchange rate** is the price of one country's currency for another.

The **real exchange rate** takes price levels into account. The real exchange rate (e_r) is the nominal exchange rate (e_n) multiplied by the ratio of the price levels of the two countries:

$$e_r = e_n \times (P_d/P_f)$$

If exchange rates are fully flexible, markets determine the prevailing exchange rate. If there is an excess demand for dollars, the dollar will appreciate, or rise in value. If there is an excess supply of dollars, the value of dollars will decline, or depreciate.

The **purchasing power parity** of a currency is the rate of exchange at which currency used to purchase an amount of goods in one country can purchase the same amount of goods in another country.

Sean Pavone/Alamy

Many services, such as playing a video game at a gaming center, are not easily traded. Therefore, price differences will exist based on the country's standard of living, and often will not reflect purchasing power parity with other countries.

27.3 It is important to keep in mind which currency is being used to measure the price of others. Graphs can be viewed as showing either an appreciation or a depreciation, depending on which currency is being considered.

In the figure, an increase in demand for U.S. dollars leads to its appreciation from 0.60 pounds per dollar to 0.75 pounds per dollar.

A shopping trip to the United States by British tourists increases demand for the dollar.

Interest rates and exchange rate expectations affect the capital account. An interest rate rise in one country will cause capital to flow into it from the other country.

27.4 Real exchange rates affect the payments for imports and exports, and also affect the current account. Inflation leads to higher prices for exports, reducing their demand and worsening the current account. And greater domestic disposable income also worsens the current account as consumers increase spending on imports.

Interest rates can differ between countries due to expected exchange rate changes ($\Delta\varepsilon$) and a risk premium (x) when capital is not perfectly substitutable between countries.

$$r_{US} = r_{UK} - \Delta\varepsilon + x$$

Section 3 Monetary and Fiscal Policy in an Open Economy

27.5 A **fixed exchange rate system** is one in which governments determine their exchange rates, then use macroeconomic adjustments to maintain these rates.

A **flexible** or **floating exchange rate system** relies on currency markets to determine the exchange rates, given macroeconomic conditions.

Some countries choose to peg their currency to another in order to facilitate trade, attract foreign investment, or promote monetary stability.

Ecuador took an extreme form of fixed exchange rate by adopting the U.S. dollar as its official currency (a process known as **dollarization**).

27.6 The ability of a country to use fiscal policy and monetary policy is affected by the type of foreign exchange system in place.

- A fixed exchange rate system hinders expansionary monetary policy because lower interest rates lead to capital outflows, which slow the economy.
- A fixed exchange rate system reinforces expansionary fiscal policy because higher interest rates lead to capital inflows, which expand the economy.
- Flexible exchange rates hamper expansionary fiscal policy because higher interest rates lead to currency appreciation, which reduces net exports.
- Flexible exchange rates reinforce expansionary monetary policy because lower interest rates lead to currency depreciation, which increases net exports.

current account, p. 724
capital account, p. 725
exchange rate, p. 726
nominal exchange rate, p. 726

real exchange rate, p. 726
purchasing power parity, p. 727
appreciation (currency), p. 729
depreciation (currency), p. 729

fixed exchange rate, p. 734
flexible or floating exchange rate, p. 734
dollarization, p. 736

Check Your Understanding

1. Describe the balance of trade. What factors contribute to our trade deficit?

2. Mexican immigrants working in the United States often send money back home (known as remittances) to help their families or to add to their savings account for the future. In 2015, these remittances surpassed $24 billion. How are these transfers recorded in the balance of payments accounts?

3. What is the important difference between the current account and the capital account, given that the sum of the two values must equal 0?

4. If the euro appreciates by 30%, what will happen to imports of Mercedes-Benz automobiles in the United States?

5. Describe the difference between fixed and flexible exchange rates.

6. Describe the difference between the nominal and real exchange rates. What does rising inflation do to a country's real exchange rate?

Apply the Concepts

7. Assume that global warming and especially high temperatures in Northern California have rendered it impossible for wine grapes in the Napa Valley (and all over California) to grow properly. Unable to get California wines, demand jumps dramatically for Australian wines. How would this affect the Australian dollar? Is this good for other Australian exports?

8. If the European economies begin having a serious bout of stagflation—high rates of both unemployment and inflation—will this affect the value of the dollar? Explain.

9. Trace through the reasoning why monetary policy is enhanced by a flexible exchange rate system.

10. Zimbabwe devalued its currency in mid-2006, essentially turning a $20,000 Zimbabwe bill into a $20 bill. People were permitted only three weeks during which to turn in their old currency for new notes; individuals were limited to $150 a day and companies were restricted to $7,000 a day. Who do you think were the losers from this devaluation, especially considering the limited turn-in period for the old currency?

11. If it costs 300 U.S. dollars to purchase an iPad in the United States and 400 Australian dollars to purchase one in Sydney, then according to purchasing power parity, the exchange rate between the Australian dollar and the U.S. dollar should be 4:3. Why might purchasing power parity be different from the exchange rate?

12. When the dollar gets stronger against major foreign currencies, does the price of French wine rise or fall in the United States? Would this be a good time to travel to Australia? What happens to U.S. exports?

In the News

13. In 2012 the worldwide musical hit *Gangnam Style* by South Korean K-pop singer Psy contributed to a boost in tourism to South Korea. Tourists from China, Japan, and even the United States wanting to see the Gangnam district in person helped South Korea's economy in 2012. How does an increase in South Korean tourism affect the foreign exchange market for the South Korean won (its currency)?

14. The Eurozone crisis has led more than one nation to consider abandoning the euro and returning to its previous currency. If a nation were to exit the Eurozone and significantly devalue its currency against the euro and other major currencies, what are some implications for trade, the current account, and the standard of living for its citizens?

Solving Problems

15. Assume that the following exchange rates prevail:

	(U.S. $ Equivalent)
Argentina (peso)	0.1904
Canada (dollar)	0.9648
Mexico (peso)	0.0812
Bahrain (dinar)	2.6525

How many Mexican pesos does it take to get 1 Bahraini dinar? If you had 20 U.S. dollars, could you take a ferry ride in Canada if it cost 25 Canadian dollars? If someone gave you 50 Argentinean pesos to settle a 150 Mexican peso bet, would it be enough?

WORK IT OUT   **LaunchPad** | interactive activity

16. Suppose that you are given an opportunity to work in Tokyo over the summer as an English tutor, and you are provided with all living expenses and a 500,000-yen cash stipend that you plan to save and bring home. If the exchange rate is 120 yen per U.S. dollar, how much is your stipend worth in dollars if you exchanged your money right away? Suppose you predict that the exchange rate will change in the next few months to 110 yen per U.S. dollar. Would you receive more dollars if you exchange the yen now or later? Show your calculations.

USING THE NUMBERS

17. According to By the Numbers, if approximately $5.3 trillion of currency is traded each day in foreign exchange markets, about how much of this is traded in U.S. dollars? Euros? Japanese yen?

18. According to By the Numbers, if you travel to Jordan to visit the archaeological site of Petra and exchange 200 U.S. dollars, about how many Jordanian dinars would you receive? If you had traveled to Petra last year, would the amount of money received for your $200 have been different?

Checkpoint: The Balance of Payments 725

When a country has a high savings rate (relative to domestic investment), it is likely that its exports will exceed imports, resulting in a trade surplus. Both China and Russia are net exporters, which shows up as a current account surplus in their balance of payments accounts.

Checkpoint: Exchange Rates 734

When the Canadian dollar appreciates against the U.S. dollar, Canadian tourists visiting the United States receive more U.S. dollars for each Canadian dollar. Therefore, purchases by Canadian tourists in the United States become cheaper. As a result, demand rises, helping American businesses that depend on Canadian tourists. Also, the increased flow of money into the United States helps improve the U.S. current account. Meanwhile, the opposite occurs for American tourists to Canada, who find it more expensive to visit Canada. Because the higher cost of travel will discourage some Americans from visiting Canada, Canadian businesses, such as those in Niagara Falls, will suffer. Also, the reduction in money being spent by Americans in Canada will hurt Canada's current account.

Checkpoint: Monetary and Fiscal Policy in an Open Economy 739

As noted in this section, monetary policy is reinforced when exchange rates are flexible, while fiscal policy is hindered. This is probably only a partial explanation, because fiscal policy today seems driven more by "events" and other priorities, and less by stabilization issues.

The deep recession a decade ago required heavy doses of both monetary and fiscal policy to keep the economy from a devastating downturn. Additional government spending, while huge, didn't seem to pack the punch many thought it would. Maybe flexible exchange rates kept it from being as effective as anticipated.

Sources for By the Numbers

Chapter 1
Data for total number of bachelor's degrees granted by major: *Digest of Education Statistics*, National Center for Education Statistics, U.S. Department of Education.

Data for technology company CEO majors: "Study Finds Most Likely Tech Sector CEO Is Dave the Ivy League Ex-Yahoo Econ Major," *Forbes*, September 28, 2012.

Fortune 100 company CEO majors: Data from Curran Career Consulting.

Percent of Fortune 500 companies founded by immigrants or their children: Data from Partnership for a New American Economy.

Average pay by major: Data from Payscale.com

Median salaries for economics jobs: Data from Payscale.com

Chapter 2
Farm productivity yields: Data from National Agricultural Statistics Service, U.S. Department of Agriculture.

U.S. trade balance: Data from United States Census Bureau, U.S. Department of Commerce.

Cost of firing workers by country: Data from World Development Indicators, The World Bank.

American attitudes on environment and economic growth: Data from Gallup.com

Chapter 3
Data for growth of Uber drivers: Hall, Jonathan and Krueger, Alan (January 2015) "An Analysis of the Labor Market for Uber's Driver-Partners in the United States." Working Paper #587; Princeton University; Industrial Relations Section.

Data for proportion of global video game revenues: Global Games Market Report; Newzoo.com

Data for total value of the worldwide online gaming market: Global Games Market Report; Newzoo.com

Total number of water bottles consumed: Data from IBWA (International Bottled Water Association) "Market Report Findings" Annual Update; www.bottledwater.org

Total sales of bottled water: Data from IBWA (International Bottled Water Association) "Market Report Findings" Annual Update; www.bottledwater.org

Data for college and university enrollment: *Digest of Education Statistics*, National Center for Education Statistics, U.S. Department of Education.

Chapter 4
Data for average in-state tuition at public universities by state: Trends in College Pricing, CollegeBoard.org

Government subsidies for renewable energy by type: Data from Direct Federal Financial Interventions and Subsidies in Energy, U.S. Energy Information Administration.

Minimum wage by state: Data from U.S. Department of Labor.

U.S. farm subsidies: Data from Farm Subsidy Database, The Environmental Working Group, farm.ewg.org

Chapter 5
Elasticity of various goods: Data compiled from numerous studies reporting estimates for price elasticity of demand.

Elasticity of food by country: Data from U.S. Department of Agriculture.

Alternative fuel vehicles in use: Data from U.S. Department of Energy Alternative Fuel Data Center, www.afdc.energy.gov/data

Data for parking alternatives: David A. Hensher and Jenny King (2011), "Parking Demand and Responsiveness to Supply, Price and Location in Sydney Central Business District," *Transportation Research* Part A, Vol. 35, No. 3, March 2011, pp. 177–196.

Average rise in public university tuition: Data from National Center for Education Statistics, U.S. Department of Education.

Average fall in international calling rates: Author calculation using data from the Federal Communications Commission.

Chapter 6
U.S. distribution of household budgets: Data from Bureau of Labor Statistics, U.S. Department of Labor.

Consumer expenditures in various categories: Data from Bureau of Labor Statistics, U.S. Department of Labor.

Total number of passenger cars: Data from U.S. Bureau of Transportation Statistics, U.S. Department of Transportation.

Charitable donations: Data from givingUSA.com

Organic foods sales: Data from 2015 Organic Industry Survey, Organic Trade Association.

Data for NBA Jerseys: www.nba.com/2015/news/04/14/nba-most-popular-jerseys-2014-15-season-lebron-james-still-reigns/

Chapter 7
The cost of industrial robots: Data from Bureau of Labor Statistics, U.S. Department of Labor.

Productivity rates: Data from Bureau of Labor Statistics, U.S. Department of Labor.

Data for size of Amazon's largest warehouse: www.wired.com/2014/06/inside-amazon-warehouse/

Number of flights into and out of Memphis by FedEx: Data from flightaware.com

Data for Apple iPad cost breakdown: Digital Manufacturing: How It's Made, www.manufacturingdigital.com/news_archive/tags/apple/apple-ipa

Online flight bookings: Data from U.S. Department of Transportation.

Online flight check-ins: Data from Airline IT Trends Survey, SITA www.sita.aero/surveys-reports/industry-surveys-reports/airline-it-trends-survey-2015

Chapter 8
Data for farm and farm-related employment by region: U.S. Department of Agriculture, maps.ers.usda.gov/mapimages/ers_reg_color.jpg

Data for top tea producers: http://www.worldatlas.com/articles/the-worlds-top-10-tea-producing-nations.html

World tea production: Data from Food and Agricultural Organization of the United Nations.

World coffee production: Data from Food and Agricultural Organization of the United Nations.

Average price of soybeans, wheat, and corn: Data from Economics Research Service, U.S. Department of Agriculture.

Chapter 9

Television viewership by championship: Data from Statista.com

Cost of a ride on Virgin Galactic: Data from Virgingalactic.com

Windows market share: Data from Netmarketshare.com

Data for most expensive drugs: Motley Fool, www.fool.com/investing/high-growth/2015/08/15/the-5-most-expensive-drugs-in-the-world-in-2015.aspx

Electricity demand: Data from U.S. Energy Information Administration, U.S. Department of Energy, www.eia.gov/electricity/data.cfm#sales

Chapter 10

Largest fast-food chains: Data from investor relations links on individual fast-food chain corporate websites.

Wireless carriers market share: Data from strategyanalytics.com

Marathon stats: Data from findmymarathon.com/statistics.php

Total number of Nike shoe models produced: Data from Solepedia.com

Most expensive private and public schools: Data from U.S. News and World Report.

Chapter 11

Data for fastest growing occupations: Bureau of Labor Statistics, U.S. Department of Labor, www.bls.gov/ooh/fastest-growing.htm

Average salary for women compared with men: Data from Bureau of Labor Statistics, U.S. Department of Labor.

Average cost of benefits as a percent of salary for full-time workers: Data from Bureau of Labor Statistics, U.S. Department of Labor.

Percent of workers with flexible work hours: Data from Bureau of Labor Statistics, U.S. Department of Labor.

Union membership as a percent of employment: Data from Bureau of Labor Statistics; U.S. Department of Labor.

Minimum wage for selected countries: Data from OECD.Stat, Organisation for Economic Co-Operation and Development.

Chapter 12

Data for percentage of high school graduates enrolling in college and percentage of college graduates pursuing postgraduate degrees: U.S. Census Bureau, www.census.gov/hhes/school/data/cps/historical/

Data for total number of patents granted in 1980 and 2015: U.S. Patent Statistics Report, U.S. Patent and Trademark Office, www.uspto.gov/web/offices/ac/ido/oeip/taf/us_stat.htm

Length of high-speed rail track by country: Data from International Union of Railways.

U.S. venture capital funds by year: Data from Dow Jones Financial Information Services; Thomson Reuters; National Venture Capital Association.

Chapter 13

Hybrid car sales by year: Data from Alternative Fuels and Advanced Vehicle Data Center; U.S. Department of Energy.

Average gasoline tax in the United States: Data from American Petroleum Institute.

Data for average gasoline tax in Britain: Fuel Duty Rates, HM Revenue & Customs.

Amount of solid waste by product (recovered and not recovered): Data from Advancing Sustainable Materials Management: Fact and Figures Report, U.S. Environmental Protection Agency.

Generation of renewable energy by source: Data from U.S. Department of Energy; www.eia.gov/electricity/monthly/epm_table_grapher.cfm?t=epmt_1_01_a

Annual savings from the use of LED bulbs: Data from Office of Energy Efficiency & Renewable Energy, U.S. Department of Energy.

Wind generation capacity by state: Data from American Wind Energy Association.

Chapter 14

Popularity of ride sharing versus taxi: Data from Certify.com

Internet penetration rates: Data from Internet World Stats, www.internetworldstats.com/stats.htm

Number of Whatsapp and Facebook users: Data from Facebook, Inc.

Number of Airbnb guests: Data from GSV Asset Management, Airbnb data: www.gsvcap.com/market-commentary/yearly-checkup, www.state.com

Data for movie streaming versus DVD revenues: www.fortune.com/2015/06/03/streaming-movies-revenue/

Chapter 15

U.S. poverty threshold: Data from U.S. Census Bureau, U.S. Department of Commerce.

U.S. minimum wage: Data from Wage and Hour Division, U.S. Department of Labor.

Poverty rates across the world: Data from *The World Factbook,* Central Intelligence Agency.

Number of Medicaid recipients: Data from Statista.com

Average monthly U.S. housing subsidy: Author calculation using budget and recipient data from the U.S. Department of Housing and Urban Development.

Percentage of Americans receiving food stamps: Data from Supplemental Nutrition Assistance Program (SNAP) Data System, Economic Research Service, U.S. Department of Agriculture.

Chapter 16

U.S. unemployment rate and real GDP growth by year: Data from Bureau of Economic Analysis, U.S. Department of Commerce; Bureau of Labor Statistics, U.S. Department of Labor.

U.S. savings rate by year: Data from Bureau of Economic Analysis, U.S. Department of Commerce.

U.S. gross domestic product: Data from Bureau of Economic Analysis, U.S. Department of Commerce.

Gross world product: Data from World Development Indicators, The World Bank.

State unemployment rates: Data from Bureau of Labor Statistics, U.S. Department of Labor.

Chapter 17

The Misery Index by year: Data from miseryindex.us

State and federal unemployment benefits: Data from Pew Analysis of Congressional Budget Office data.

Average yearly increase in Social Security benefits: Data from U.S. Social Security Administration, www.ssa.gov/news/cola/automatic-cola.htm

The social costs of unemployment: Author calculations based on available data.

Average cost of tuition at public and private universities by year and consumer price index: Data from National Center for Education Statistics, U.S. Department of Education; U.S. Bureau of Labor Statistics, U.S. Department of Labor.

U.S. Index of Housing Prices: Data from Federal Reserve Economic Data (FRED), Economic Research Division, Federal Reserve Bank of St. Louis.

Chapter 18
U.S. real GDP per capita by year: Data from *The World Factbook,* Central Intelligence Agency.

GDP and real GDP growth by country: Data from World Development Indicators, The World Bank; *The Economist.*

Real GDP per capita and average life expectancy by country: Data from World Development Indicators, The World Bank.

The tallest buildings in the world: Information compiled from various online sources.

Chapter 19
Government spending as a percentage of GDP by year: Data from Government Publishing Office: www.gpo.gov/fdsys/

Average government spending per person by country: Data from *The World Factbook,* Central Intelligence Agency.

Total U.S. private domestic investment spending: Data from Bureau of Economic Analysis, U.S. Department of Commerce.

Total U.S. spending by foreign consumers (exports): Data from Bureau of Economic Analysis, U.S. Department of Commerce.

Top categories of personal consumption expenditures: Data from Bureau of Economic Analysis, U.S. Department of Commerce.

Spending by local, state, and federal governments: Data from usgovernmentspending.com

Chapter 20
Media and entertainment revenues: Data from Statista.com

Oil consumption in the United States and China in 1985 and 2015: Data from U.S. Energy Information Administration, U.S. Department of Energy.

Total world aggregate demand: Data from *The World Factbook,* Central Intelligence Agency.

Increase in NASDAQ stock index value: Data from CNBC.com

Rates of home ownership by state: Data from U.S. Census Bureau, U.S. Department of Commerce.

Chapter 21
U.S. federal government revenues: Data from Congressional Budget Office, www.cbo.gov/about/products/budget_economic_data

U.S. federal government expenditures: Data from Congressional Budget Office, www.cbo.gov/about/products/budget_economic_data

U.S. net government expenditures by year: Data from Historical Tables, Office of Management and Budget, The White House.

U.S. external (foreign held) debt by year: Data from U.S. Department of the Treasury. Debt to the Penny (Daily History).

Top ten creditors of U.S. Treasury Debt: Data from U.S. Department of the Treasury.

Total U.S. national debt: Data from www.usdebtclock.org

Total interest paid on the U.S. national debt: Data from Federal Reserve Economic Data (FRED), Economic Research Division, Federal Reserve Bank of St. Louis.

Chapter 22
The largest banks in the world: Data from www.relbanks.com/worlds-top-banks/assets

The eight most circulated currencies and currency reserves in the world: Data from International Monetary Fund.

Total value of U.S. retirement accounts: Data from ICI Retirement Industry Report, Investment Company Institute.

Total credit card debt in the United States: Data from U.S. Federal Reserve.

Chapter 23
U.S. monetary base by year: Data from Federal Reserve Economic Data (FRED), Economic Research Division, Federal Reserve Bank of St. Louis.

Euro monetary base: Data from European Central Bank.

Number of U.S. bank failures by year: Data from Historical Statistics on Banking, Federal Deposit Insurance Corporation.

Federal Deposit Insurance Corporation insured limits: Data from Federal Deposit Insurance Corporation.

Federal Reserve balance sheet in 2005 and 2015: Data from U.S. Federal Reserve.

Chapter 24
U.S. 30-year mortgage, prime, discount, and federal funds rate: Data from Federal Reserve Economic Data (FRED), Economic Research Division, Federal Reserve Bank of St. Louis.

Total amount of U.S. dollars and coins in circulation: Data from *Treasury Bulletin,* Financial Management Service, U.S. Department of the Treasury.

Total number of $100 bills in circulation: Data from *Treasury Bulletin,* Financial Management Service, U.S. Department of the Treasury.

Facts about one million $1 bills: Data from Federal Reserve Bank of Chicago.

Holdings of U.S. $100 bills by region: Data from U.S. Federal Reserve.

Chapter 25
U.S. median existing home prices by year: Data from Federal Reserve Economic Data (FRED), Economic Research Division, Federal Reserve Bank of St. Louis.

U.S. Index of Consumer Sentiment: Data from University of Michigan: Consumer Sentiment Index.

U.S. monthly real retail sales: Data from Federal Reserve Economic Data (FRED), Economic Research Division, Federal Reserve Bank of St. Louis.

Total U.S. jobs lost during the Great Recession: Data from Bureau of Labor Statistics, U.S. Department of Labor.

Total U.S. jobs created during the economic recovery: Data from Bureau of Labor Statistics, U.S. Department of Labor.

Value of assets purchased by the Federal Reserve quantitative easing programs: Data from U.S. Federal Reserve.

Chapter 26
Trade deficit as a percent of GDP: Data from Foreign Trade Division, U.S. Census Bureau, U.S. Department of Commerce; FRED Database, Federal Reserve Bank of St. Louis.

Trade-weighted tariff barriers: Data from World Development Indicators, The World Bank.

Medical tourism services: Data from Companion Global Healthcare, Inc.

Number of American cars sold in China: Author estimate based on sales reports from Ford, Fiat Chrysler, and General Motors.

U.S. public sentiment on lower trade barriers: Data from 2014 National Survey of American Public Opinion, Chicago Council on Global Affairs.

Buick sales in China and the United States: Data from General Motors.

Chapter 27

The most traded currencies in the world: Data from 2016 Triennial Central Bank Survey, Bank of International Settlements.

U.S. Dollar Index: Data from Federal Reserve Economic Data (FRED), Economic Research Division, Federal Reserve Bank of St. Louis.

Total value of currency traded each day in foreign exchange markets: Data from 2016 Triennial Central Bank Survey, Bank of International Settlements.

Percent of foreign exchange trades that are speculative: Information compiled from various sources.

Value of currencies pegged to the U.S. dollar: Data from XE.com

Composition of foreign exchange transactions: Data from 2016 Triennial Central Bank Survey, Bank of International Settlements.

Glossary

absolute advantage One country can produce more of a good than another country.

accounting profit The difference between total revenue and explicit costs. These are the profits that are taxed by the government.

adaptive expectations Inflationary expectations are formed from a simple extrapolation from past events.

agency shop Employees are not required to join the union, but must pay dues to compensate the union for its services.

aggregate demand The output of goods and services (real GDP) demanded at different price levels.

aggregate expenditures Consist of consumer spending, business investment spending, government spending, and net foreign spending (exports minus imports): $GDP = C + I + G + (X - M)$.

aggregate supply The real GDP that firms will produce at varying price levels. The aggregate supply curve is positively sloped in the short run but vertical in the long run.

allocative efficiency The mix of goods and services produced is just what the society desires.

altruism Actions undertaken merely out of goodwill or generosity.

annually balanced budget Expenditures and taxes would have to be equal each year.

antitrust law Laws designed to maintain competition and prevent monopolies from developing.

appreciation (currency) When the value of a currency rises relative to other currencies.

asymmetric information Occurs when one party to a transaction has significantly better information than another party.

autarky A country that does not engage in international trade, also known as a closed economy.

automatic stabilizers Tax revenues and transfer payments automatically expand or contract in ways that reduce the intensity of business fluctuations without any overt action by Congress or other policymakers.

average cost pricing rule Requires a regulated monopolist to produce and sell output where price equals average total cost. This permits the regulated monopolist to earn a normal return on investment over the long term and therefore remain in business.

average fixed cost Equal to total fixed cost divided by output (FC/Q).

average product Output per worker, found by dividing total output by the number of workers employed to produce that output (Q/L).

average propensity to consume The percentage of income that is consumed ($C \div Y$).

average propensity to save The percentage of income that is saved ($S \div Y$).

average total cost Equal to total cost divided by output (TC/Q). Average total cost is also equal to $AFC + AVC$.

average variable cost Equal to total variable cost divided by output (VC/Q).

balanced budget multiplier Equal changes in government spending and taxation (a balanced budget) lead to an equal change in income (the balanced budget multiplier is equal to 1).

barriers to entry Any obstacle that makes it more difficult for a firm to enter an industry, and includes control of a key resource, prohibitive fixed costs, and government protection.

barter The direct exchange of goods and services for other goods and services.

behavioral economics The study of how human psychology enters into economic behavior as a way to explain why individuals sometimes act in predictable ways counter to economic models.

budget line A line that graphically illustrates the possible combinations of two goods that can be purchased with a given income, given the prices of both goods.

bundling A strategy of packaging several products into a single product with a single price. Bundling allows firms to capture customers of related products by making it more attractive to use the same firm's products.

business cycles Alternating increases and decreases in economic activity that are typically punctuated by periods of recession and recovery.

capital Includes manufactured products such as tractors, welding equipment, and computers that are used to produce other goods and services. The payment for capital is interest.

capital account Summarizes the flow of money into and out of domestic and foreign assets, including investments by foreign companies in domestic plants or subsidiaries, and other foreign holdings of U.S. assets, including mutual funds, stocks, bonds, and deposits in U.S. banks. Also included are U.S. investors' holdings of foreign financial assets, production facilities, and other assets in foreign countries.

capital-to-labor ratio The capital employed per worker. A higher ratio means higher labor productivity and, as a result, higher wages.

cartel An agreement between firms (or countries) in an industry to formally collude on price and output, then agree on the distribution of production.

casual user A consumer who purchases a good only after the good has matured in the market and is more sensitive to price.

catch-up effect Countries with smaller starting levels of capital experience larger benefits from increased capital, allowing these countries to grow faster than countries with abundant capital.

ceteris paribus Assumption used in economics (and other disciplines as well), that other relevant factors or variables are held constant.

change in demand Occurs when one or more of the determinants of demand changes, shown as a shift in the entire demand curve.

change in quantity demanded Occurs when the price of the product changes, shown as a movement along an existing demand curve.

change in quantity supplied Occurs when the price of the product changes, shown as a movement along an existing supply curve.

change in supply Occurs when one or more of the determinants of supply change, shown as a shift in the entire supply curve.

circular flow diagram Illustrates how households and firms interact through product and resource markets and shows that economic aggregates can be determined by examining either spending flows or income flows to households.

closed shop Workers must belong to the union before they can be hired.

Coase theorem If transaction costs are minimal (near zero), a bargain struck between beneficiaries and victims of externalities will be efficient from a resource allocation perspective. As a result, a socially optimal level of production will be reached.

collateral An asset used to secure a loan; the asset can be sold if the borrower fails to repay a loan.

command and control policies Environmental policies that set standards and issue regulations, which are then enforced by the legal and regulatory system.

comparative advantage One country has a lower opportunity cost of producing a good than another country.

complementary goods Goods that are typically consumed together. When the *price* of a complementary good rises, the *demand* for the other good declines, and vice versa.

complements Goods that are typically consumed together, such as coffee and sugar. Complements have a negative cross elasticity of demand.

compounding The ability of growth to build on previous growth. It allows variables such as income and GDP (as well as debt) to increase significantly over time.

compounding effect The effect of interest added to existing debt or savings leading to substantial growth in debt or savings over the long run.

concentration ratio The share of industry shipments or sales accounted for by the top four or eight firms.

constant cost industry An industry that, in the long run, faces roughly the same prices and costs as industry output expands. Some industries can virtually clone their operations in other areas without putting undue pressure on resource prices, resulting in constant operating costs as they expand in the long run.

constant returns to scale A range of output where average total costs are relatively constant. The expansion of fast-food restaurant franchises and movie theaters, which are essentially replications of existing franchises and theaters, reflects this.

consumer price index (CPI) An index of the average prices paid by urban consumers for a typical market basket of consumer goods and services.

consumer surplus The difference between what consumers (as individuals or the market) would be willing to pay and the market price. It is equal to the area above market price and below the demand curve.

consumption Spending by individuals and households on both durable goods (e.g., autos, appliances, and electronic equipment) and nondurable goods (e.g., food, clothing, and entertainment).

contestable markets Markets that look monopolistic, but where entry costs are low and the sheer threat of entry keeps prices low.

contractionary fiscal policy Policies that decrease aggregate demand to contract output in an economy. These include reducing government spending, reducing transfer payments, and/or raising taxes.

contractionary monetary policy Fed actions designed to decrease the money supply and raise interest rates to shrink income and employment, usually to fight inflation.

core user A consumer who has a very high willingness to pay for a new product or service and is among the first to purchase it.

corporation A business structure that has most of the legal rights of individuals, and in addition, can issue stock to raise capital. Stockholders' liability is limited to the value of their stock.

cost-benefit analysis A methodology for decision making that looks at the discounted value of the costs and benefits of a given project.

cost-push inflation Results when a supply shock hits the economy, reducing short-run aggregate supply, and thus reducing output and increasing the price level.

coupon rate A periodic fixed payment to the bondholder measured as an annual percent of the bond's face value.

credit default swap A financial instrument that insures against the potential default on an asset. Because of the extent of defaults in the last financial crisis, issuers of credit default swaps could not repay all of the claims, bankrupting these financial institutions.

cross elasticity of demand A measure of how responsive the quantity demanded of one good is to changes in the price of another good.

crowding-out effect When deficit spending requires the government to borrow, interest rates are driven up, reducing consumer spending and business investment.

current account Includes payments for imports and exports of goods and services, incomes flowing into and out of the country, and net transfers of money.

cyclical unemployment Unemployment that results from changes in the business cycle, and where public policymakers can have their greatest impact by keeping the economy on a steady, low-inflationary, solid growth path.

cyclically balanced budget Balancing the budget over the course of the business cycle by restricting spending or raising taxes when the economy is booming and using these surpluses to offset the deficits that occur during recessions.

deadweight loss The reduction in total surplus that results from the inefficiency of a market not in equilibrium.

decision lag The time it takes Congress and the administration to decide on a policy once a problem is recognized.

decreasing cost industry An industry that, in the long run, faces lower prices and costs as industry output expands. Some industries enjoy economies of scale as they expand in the long run, typically the result of technological advances.

deficit The amount by which annual government expenditures exceed tax revenues.

deflation A decline in overall prices throughout the economy. This is the opposite of inflation.

demand The maximum amount of a product that buyers are willing and able to purchase over some time period at various prices, holding all other relevant factors constant (the *ceteris paribus* condition).

demand curve A graphical illustration of the law of demand, which shows the relationship between the price of a good and the quantity demanded.

demand for labor Demand for labor is derived from the demand for the firm's product and the productivity of labor.

demand schedule A table that shows the quantity of a good a consumer purchases at each price.

demand-pull inflation Results when aggregate demand expands so much that equilibrium output exceeds full employment output and the price level rises.

depreciation (currency) When the value of a currency falls relative to other currencies.

determinants of demand Nonprice factors that affect demand, including tastes and preferences, income, prices of related goods, number of buyers, and expectations.

determinants of supply Nonprice factors that affect supply, including production technology, costs of resources, prices of related commodities, expectations, number of sellers, and taxes and subsidies.

diminishing marginal returns An additional worker adds to total output, but at a diminishing rate.

diminishing returns to capital Each additional unit of capital provides a smaller increase in output than the previous unit of capital.

discount rate The interest rate the Federal Reserve charges commercial banks and other depository institutions to borrow reserves from a regional Federal Reserve Bank.

discouraged workers Discouraged workers are the portion of marginally attached workers who have given up actively looking for work and, as a result, are not counted as unemployed.

discretionary fiscal policy Policies that involve adjusting government spending and tax policies with the express short-run goal of moving the economy toward full employment, expanding economic growth, or controlling inflation.

discretionary spending The part of the budget that works its way through the appropriations process of Congress each year and includes national defense, transportation, science, environment, and income security.

diseconomies of scale A range of output where average total costs tend to increase. Firms often become so big that management becomes bureaucratic and unable to control its operations efficiently.

disinflation A reduction in the rate of inflation. An economy experiencing disinflation still faces inflation, but at a declining rate.

dollarization Describes the decision of a country to adopt another country's currency (most often the U.S. dollar) as its own official currency.

dominant strategy Occurs when a player chooses the same strategy regardless of what his or her opponent chooses.

double-dip recession A recession that begins after only a short period of economic recovery from the previous recession.

dumping Selling goods abroad at lower prices than in home markets, and often below cost.

easy money, quantitative easing, or accommodative monetary policy Fed actions designed to increase excess reserves and the money supply to stimulate the economy (increase income and employment). *See also* expansionary monetary policy.

economic costs The sum of explicit (out-of-pocket) and implicit (opportunity) costs.

economic discrimination When workers of equal ability are paid different wages or in any other way discriminated against because of race, color, religion, gender, age, national origin, sexual orientation, or disability.

economic growth Usually measured by the annual percentage change in real GDP, reflecting an improvement in the standard of living.

economic profit Profit in excess of normal profits. These are profits in excess of both explicit and implicit costs.

economics The study of how individuals, firms, and society make decisions to allocate limited resources to many competing wants.

economies of scale As a firm's output increases, its average total cost declines. This results from specialization of labor and management, and potentially a better use of capital and complementary production techniques.

economies of scope By producing a number of products that are interdependent, firms are able to produce and market these goods at lower costs.

efficiency How well resources are used and allocated. Do people get the goods and services they want at the lowest possible resource cost? This is the chief focus of efficiency.

efficiency wage theory Employers often pay their workers wages above the market-clearing level to improve morale and productivity, reduce turnover, and create a disincentive for employees to shirk their duties.

elastic demand The percentage change in quantity demanded is greater than the percentage change in price. This results in the absolute value of the price elasticity of demand to be greater than 1. Goods with elastic demands are very responsive to changes in price.

elastic supply Price elasticity of supply is greater than 1. The percentage change in quantity supplied is greater than the percentage change in price.

elasticity of demand for labor The percentage change in the quantity of labor demanded divided by the percentage change in the wage rate.

entrepreneurs Entrepreneurs combine land, labor, and capital to produce goods and services. They absorb the risk of being in business, including the risk of bankruptcy and other liabilities associated with doing business. Entrepreneurs receive profits for their effort.

equation of exchange The heart of classical monetary theory uses the equation $M \times V = P \times Q$, where M is the supply of money, V is the velocity of money (the average number of times per year a dollar is spent on goods and services, or the number of times it turns over in a year), P is the price level, and Q is the economy's real output level.

equilibrium Market forces are in balance when the quantities demanded by consumers just equal the quantities supplied by producers.

equilibrium price The price at which the quantity demanded is just equal to quantity supplied.

equilibrium quantity The output that results when quantity demanded is just equal to quantity supplied.

equity The fairness of various issues and policies.

essential facility An input that is needed to produce a product or to allow a person to consume a product.

excess reserves Reserves held by banks above the legally required amount.

exchange rate The rate at which one currency can be exchanged for another.

expansionary fiscal policy Policies that increase aggregate demand to expand output in an economy. These include increasing government spending, increasing transfer payments, and/or decreasing taxes.

expansionary monetary policy Fed actions designed to increase the money supply and lower interest rates to stimulate the economy (expand income and employment).

explicit costs Those expenses paid directly to another economic entity, including wages, lease payments, taxes, and utilities.

exports Goods and services that are sold abroad.

externalities The impact on third parties of some transaction between others in which the third parties are not involved. An external cost (or negative externality) harms the third parties, whereas external benefits (positive externalities) result in gains to them.

externally held debt Public debt held by foreigners, including foreign industries, banks, and governments.

face value The value of a bond that is paid upon maturity. This value is fixed, and therefore not the same as the market value of a bond, which is influenced by changes in interest rates and risk.

federal funds rate The interest rate financial institutions charge each other for overnight loans used as reserves.

Federal Open Market Committee (FOMC) A twelve-member committee that is composed of members of the Board of Governors of the Fed and selected presidents of the regional Federal Reserve Banks. It oversees open market operations (the buying and selling of government securities), the main tool of monetary policy.

Federal Reserve System The central bank of the United States.

fiat money Money without intrinsic value but nonetheless accepted as money because the government has decreed it to be money.

financial capital The money required by businesses to purchase inputs for production and to run their operations.

financial intermediaries Financial firms (banks, mutual funds, insurance companies, etc.) that acquire funds from savers and then lend these funds to borrowers (consumers, firms, and governments).

financial system A complex set of institutions, including banks, bond markets, and stock markets, that allocate scarce resources (financial capital) from savers to borrowers.

firm An economic institution that transforms resources (factors of production) into outputs.

fiscal sustainability A measure of the present value of all projected future revenues compared to the present value of projected future spending.

fixed costs Costs that do not change as a firm's output expands or contracts, often called overhead.

fixed exchange rate Each government determines its exchange rate, then uses macroeconomic policy to maintain the rate.

flat tax A tax that is a constant proportion of one's income.

flexible or **floating exchange rate** A country's currency exchange rate is determined in international currency exchange markets.

fractional reserve banking system Describes a banking system in which a portion of bank deposits are held as vault cash or in an account with the regional Federal Reserve Bank, while the rest of the deposits are loaned out to generate the money creation process.

framing bias Describes when individuals are steered into making one decision over another or are convinced they are receiving a higher value for a product than what was paid for it.

free rider An individual who avoids paying for a good because he or she cannot be excluded from enjoying the good once provided.

frictional unemployment Unemployment resulting from workers who voluntarily quit their jobs to search for better positions, or are moving to new jobs but may still take several days or weeks before they can report to their new employers.

functional distribution of income The distribution of income for resources or factors of production (land, labor, capital, and entrepreneurial ability).

functional finance An approach that focuses on fostering economic growth and stable prices, while keeping the economy as close as possible to full employment.

game theory The study of how individuals and firms make strategic decisions to achieve their goals when other parties or factors can influence that outcome.

GDP deflator An index of the average prices for all goods and services in the economy, including consumer goods, investment goods, government goods and services, and exports. It is the broadest measure of inflation in the national income and product accounts (NIPA).

GDP per capita A country's GDP divided by its population. GDP per capita provides a useful measure of a country's relative standard of living.

Gini coefficient A measure of income inequality defined as the area between the Lorenz curve and the equal distribution line divided by the total area below the equal distribution line.

government budget constraint The government budget is limited by the fact that $G - T = \Delta M + \Delta B + \Delta A$.

government failure The result when the incentives of politicians and government bureaucrats do not align with the public interest.

government spending Includes the wages and salaries of government employees (federal, state, and local); the purchase of products and services from private businesses and the rest of the world; and government purchases of new structures and equipment.

gross domestic product (GDP) A measure of the economy's total output; it is the most widely reported value in the national income and product accounts (NIPA) and is equal to the total market value of all final goods and services produced by resources in a given year.

gross private domestic investment (GPDI) Investments in such things as structures (residential and nonresidential), equipment, and software, and changes in private inventories.

Herfindahl–Hirschman index (HHI) A way of measuring industry concentration, equal to the sum of the squares of market shares for all firms in the industry.

horizontal summation The process of adding the number of units of the product purchased or supplied at each price to determine market demand or supply.

hyperinflation An extremely high rate of inflation; above 100% per year.

implementation lag The time required to turn fiscal policy into law and eventually have an impact on the economy.

implicit costs The opportunity costs of using resources that belong to the firm, including depreciation, depletion of business assets, and the opportunity cost of the firm's capital employed in the business.

imports Goods and services that are purchased from abroad.

incentives The factors that motivate individuals and firms to make decisions in their best interest.

incidence of taxation Refers to who bears the economic burden of a tax. The economic entity bearing the burden of a particular tax will depend on the price elasticities of demand and supply.

income A flow measure reflecting the funds received by individuals or households over a period of time, usually a week, month, or year.

income deficit The difference between the poverty threshold and a family's income.

income effect When higher prices essentially reduce consumer income, the quantity demanded for normal goods falls. In labor markets, higher wages mean that you can maintain the same standard of living by working fewer hours.

income elasticity of demand A measure of how responsive quantity demanded is to changes in consumer income.

increasing cost industry An industry that, in the long run, faces higher prices and costs as industry output expands. Industry expansion puts upward pressure on resources (inputs), causing higher costs in the long run.

increasing marginal returns A new worker hired adds more to total output than the previous worker hired, so that both average and marginal products are rising.

indifference curve A curve that shows the combinations of two goods from which the consumer is indifferent (receives the same level of satisfaction).

indifference map An infinite set of indifference curves in which each curve represents a different level of utility or satisfaction.

industry standard A common format that is used, for example, in televisions, in digital recorders, or in software programs.

inelastic demand The percentage change in quantity demanded is less than the percentage change in price. This results in the absolute value of the price elasticity of demand to be less than 1. Goods with inelastic demands are not very responsive to changes in price.

inelastic supply Price elasticity of supply is less than 1. The percentage change in quantity supplied is less than the percentage change in price.

infant industry An industry so underdeveloped that protection is needed for it to become competitive on the world stage or to ensure its survival.

inferior goods Goods that have income elasticities that are negative. When consumer income grows, demand for inferior goods falls.

inflation A general rise in prices throughout the economy. It is a measure of changes in the cost of living.

inflation targeting The central bank sets a target on the inflation rate (usually around 2% per year) and adjusts monetary policy to keep inflation near that target.

inflationary expectations The rate of inflation expected by workers for any given period. Workers do not work for a specific nominal wage but for what those wages will buy (real wages); therefore, their inflationary expectations are an important determinant of what nominal wage they are willing to work for.

inflationary gap The spending reduction necessary (when expanded by the multiplier) to bring an overheated economy back to full employment.

informal economy Includes all transactions that are conducted but are not licensed and/or generate income that is not reported to the government (for tax collection).

information lag The time policymakers must wait for economic data to be collected, processed, and reported. Most macroeconomic data are not available until at least one quarter (three months) after the fact.

infrastructure The public capital of a nation, including transportation networks, power-generating plants and transmission facilities, public education institutions, and other intangible resources such as protection of property rights and a stable monetary environment.

injections Increments of spending, including investment, government spending, and exports.

intellectual property rights A set of exclusive rights granted to a creator of an invention or creative work, allowing the owner to earn profits over a fixed period of time. The types of protection include patents, copyrights, trademarks, and industrial designs.

interconnection The physical linking of a network to another network's essential facilities. Interconnection promotes competition by ensuring that no firm has exclusive access to a set of customers.

internally held debt Public debt owned by domestic banks, corporations, mutual funds, pension plans, and individuals.

intertemporal pricing A type of versioning in which goods are differentiated by the level of patience of consumers. Less patient consumers pay a higher price than more patient consumers.

investment Spending by businesses that adds to the productive capacity of the economy. Investment depends on factors such as its rate of return, the level of technology, and business expectations about the economy.

investment in human capital Improvements to the labor force from investments in skills, knowledge, and the overall quality of workers and their productivity.

jobless recovery A phenomenon that takes place after a recession, when output begins to rise, but employment growth does not.

Keynesian macroeconomic equilibrium The state of an economy at which all injections equal all withdrawals. There are no pressures pushing the economy to a higher or lower level of output.

kinked demand curve An oligopoly model that assumes that if a firm raises its price, competitors will not raise theirs. However, if the firm lowers its price, its competitors will lower their price to match the reduction. This leads to a kink in the demand curve and relatively stable market prices.

labor Includes the mental and physical talents of individuals who produce products and services. The payment to labor is wages.

labor force The total number of those employed and unemployed. The unemployment rate is the number of unemployed divided by the labor force, expressed as a percent.

Laffer curve A curve that shows a hypothetical relationship between income tax rates and tax revenues. As tax rates rise from zero, revenues rise, reach a maximum, then decline until revenues reach zero again at a 100% tax rate.

laissez-faire A market that is allowed to function without any government intervention.

land Includes natural resources such as mineral deposits, oil, natural gas, water, and land in the usual sense of the word. The payment for land used as a resource is rent.

law of demand Holding all other relevant factors constant, as price increases, quantity demanded falls, and as price decreases, quantity demanded rises.

law of diminishing marginal utility As we consume more of a given product, the added satisfaction we get from consuming an additional unit declines.

law of supply Holding all other relevant factors constant, as price increases, quantity supplied rises, and as price declines, quantity supplied falls.

leakages A reduction in the amount of money that is used for lending that reduces the money multiplier. It is caused by banks choosing to hold excess reserves and from individuals, businesses, and foreigners choosing to hold more cash.

leverage Occurs when a small amount of capital is used to support a larger amount of investment by borrowing. The risk of highly leveraged investments is that a small decrease in price can wipe out one's account.

liquidity How quickly, easily, and reliably an asset can be converted into cash.

liquidity trap When interest rates are so low, people hold on to money rather than invest in bonds due to their expectations of a declining economy or an unforeseen event such as war.

lock-in strategies Techniques used by firms to raise the switching costs for their customers, making it less attractive to leave the network.

long run A period of time sufficient for firms to adjust all factors of production, including plant capacity.

long-run aggregate supply (LRAS) curve The long-run aggregate supply curve is vertical at full employment because the economy has reached its capacity to produce.

long-run average total cost In the long run, firms can adjust their plant sizes so that $LRATC$ is the lowest unit cost at which any particular output can be produced in the long run.

Lorenz curve A graph showing the cumulative distribution of income or wealth. Households are measured on the horizontal axis while income or wealth is measured on the vertical axis.

lump-sum tax A fixed amount of tax regardless of income. It is a type of regressive tax.

luxury goods Goods that have income elasticities greater than 1. When consumer income grows, demand for luxury goods rises more than the rise in income.

M1 The narrowest definition of money that measures highly liquid instruments including currency (banknotes and coins), demand deposits (checks), and other accounts that have check-writing or debit capabilities.

M2 A broader definition of money that includes "near monies" that are not as liquid as cash, including deposits in savings accounts, money market accounts, and money market mutual fund accounts.

macroeconomic equilibrium Occurs at the intersection of the short-run aggregate supply and aggregate demand curves. At this output level, there are no net pressures for the economy to expand or contract.

macroeconomics The study of the broader issues in the economy such as inflation, unemployment, and national output of goods and services.

mandatory spending Spending authorized by permanent laws that does not go through the same appropriations process as discretionary spending. Mandatory spending includes Social Security, Medicare, and interest on the national debt.

marginal cost The change in total costs arising from the production of additional units of output ($\Delta TC/\Delta Q$). Because fixed costs do not change with output, marginal costs are the change in variable costs associated with additional production ($\Delta VC/\Delta Q$).

marginal cost pricing rule Regulators would prefer to have natural monopolists price where $P = MC$, but this would result in losses (long term) because $ATC > MC$.

marginal factor cost The added cost associated with hiring 1 more unit of labor. For competitive firms, it is equal to the wage; but for monopsonists, it is higher than the new wage (W) because all existing workers must be paid this higher new wage, making $MFC > W$.

marginal physical product of labor The additional output a firm receives from employing an added unit of labor ($MPP_L = \Delta Q \div \Delta L$).

marginal product The change in output that results from a change in labor ($\Delta Q \div \Delta L$).

marginal propensity to consume The change in consumption associated with a given change in income ($\Delta C \div \Delta Y$).

marginal propensity to save The change in saving associated with a given change in income ($\Delta S \div \Delta Y$).

marginal revenue The change in total revenue from selling an additional unit of output. Because competitive firms are price takers, $P = MR$ for competitive firms.

marginal revenue product The value of another worker to the firm is equal to the marginal physical product of labor (MPP_L) times marginal revenue (MR).

marginal utility The additional satisfaction received from consuming one more unit of a given product or service.

marginal utility analysis A theoretical framework underlying consumer decision making. This approach assumes that satisfaction can be measured and that consumers maximize satisfaction when the marginal utilities per dollar are equal for all products and services.

marginally attached workers Workers who were available for work and actively looked for it during the last 12 months, but not in the last 4 weeks.

market cap The market value of a firm determined by the current price per share of its stock multiplied by the total number of shares outstanding.

market failure When markets fail to provide a socially optimal level of output, and will provide output at too high or low a price.

market period The time period so short that the output and the number of firms are fixed. Agricultural products at harvest time face market periods. Products that unexpectedly become instant hits face market periods (there is a lag between when the firm realizes it has a hit on its hands and when inventory can be replaced).

market power A firm's ability to set prices for goods and services in a market.

market segmentation A strategy of making a single good in different versions to target different consumer markets with varying prices.

market structure analysis By observing a few industry characteristics such as number of firms in the industry or the level of barriers to entry, economists can use this information to predict pricing and output behavior of the firm in the industry.

market-based policies Environmental policies that use charges, taxes, subsidies, deposit-refund systems, or tradable emission permits to achieve environmental goals.

markets Institutions that bring buyers and sellers together, so they can interact and transact with each other.

maturity The date on which the face value of the bond must be repaid.

medium of exchange A function of money in which goods and services are sold for money, then the money is used to purchase other goods and services.

microeconomics The study of the decision making by individuals, businesses, and industries.

misallocation of resources Occurs when a good or service is not consumed by the person who values it the most, and typically results when a price ceiling creates an artificial shortage in the market.

monetary rule Keeps the growth of money stocks such as M1 or M2 on a steady path, following the equation of exchange (or quantity theory), to set a long-run path for the economy that keeps inflation in check.

monetized debt Occurs when debt is reduced by increasing the money supply, thereby making each dollar less valuable through inflation.

money Anything that is accepted in exchange for goods and services or for the payment of debt.

money illusion A misperception of wealth caused by a focus on increases in nominal income but not increases in prices.

money multiplier A formula that measures the *potential* or *maximum* amount the money supply can increase (or decrease) when a dollar of new deposits enters (exits) the system and is defined as 1 divided by the reserve requirement.

monopolistic competition A market structure with a large number of firms producing differentiated products. This differentiation is either real or imagined by consumers and involves innovations, advertising, location, or other ways of making one firm's product different from that of its competitors.

monopolistic exploitation of labor Occurs when workers are paid less than the value of their marginal product because the firm has monopoly power in the product market.

monopoly A one-firm industry with no close product substitutes and with substantial barriers to entry.

monopsonistic exploitation of labor Occurs when workers are paid less than the value of their marginal product because the firm is a monopsonist in the labor market.

monopsony A labor market with one employer.

multiplier Spending changes alter equilibrium income by the spending change times the multiplier. One person's spending becomes another's income, and that second person spends some (the MPC), which becomes income for another person, and so on, until income has changed by $1/(1 - MPC) = 1/MPS$. The multiplier operates in both directions.

mutual interdependence When only a few firms constitute an industry, each firm must consider the reactions of its competitors to its decisions.

Nash equilibrium An outcome that occurs when all players choose their optimal strategy in response to all other players' potential moves. At a Nash equilibrium, no player can be better off by unilaterally deviating from the noncooperative outcome.

national debt The total debt issued by the U.S. Treasury, which represents the total accumulation of past deficits less surpluses. A portion of this debt is held by other government agencies, and the rest is held by the public. It is also referred to as the gross federal debt.

national income All income, including wages, salaries and benefits, profits (for sole proprietors, partnerships, and corporations), rental income, and interest.

natural monopoly An industry exhibiting large economies of scale such that the minimum efficient scale of operations is roughly equal to market demand.

natural rate of unemployment The level of unemployment at which price and wage decisions are consistent; a level at which the actual inflation rate is equal to people's inflationary expectations and where cyclical unemployment is zero.

net exports Exports minus imports for the current period. Exports include all goods and services we sell abroad, while imports include all goods and services we buy from other countries.

network A structure that connects various entities with one another. A network can be physical, virtual, or social.

network demand curve A demand curve for a good or service that produces a network effect, causing it to slope upward at lower quantities before sloping downward once the market matures.

network effect Describes how individuals and firms incorporate the external benefit generated from network goods into their decision making, which increases the value of the good further.

network externality An external benefit generated from the consumption of a network good.

network good A good or service that requires the existence of a physical, virtual, or social network to exist.

nominal exchange rate The price of one country's currency for another.

nonexcludability Once a good or service is provided, it is not possible to exclude others from enjoying that good or service.

nonrivalry The consumption of a good or service by one person does not reduce the utility of that good or service to others.

normal goods Goods that have positive income elasticities less than 1. When consumer income grows, demand for normal goods rises, but less than the rise in income.

normal profits Equal to zero economic profits; where $P = ATC$. It is the return on capital necessary to keep investors satisfied and keep capital in the business over the long run.

normative question A question whose answer is based on societal beliefs on what should or should not take place.

oligopoly A market with just a few firms dominating the industry, where (1) each firm recognizes that it must consider its competitors' reactions when making its own decisions (mutual interdependence), and (2) there are significant barriers to entry into the market.

on-the-job training Training typically offered by employers, ranging from suggestions at work to intensive workshops and seminars.

open market operations The buying and selling of U.S. government securities, such as Treasury bills and bonds, to adjust reserves in the banking system.

opportunity cost The value of the next best alternative; what you give up to do something or purchase something. Also, it is the cost paid for a product in terms of the output of another product that must be forgone.

paradox of thrift When investment is positively related to income and households *intend* to save more, they reduce consumption. Consequently, income and output decrease, reducing investment such that savings actually end up decreasing.

partnership Similar to a sole proprietorship, but involves more than one owner who share the management of the business. Partnerships are also subject to unlimited liability.

peak-load pricing A versioning strategy of pricing a product higher during periods of higher demand, and lower during periods of lower demand.

pensions A retirement program into which an employer pays a monthly amount to retired employees until they die.

perfect competition A market structure with many relatively small buyers and sellers who take the price as given, a standardized product, full information to both buyers and sellers, and no barriers to entry or exit.

perfect (first-degree) price discrimination Charging each customer the maximum price each is willing to pay, thereby expropriating all consumer surplus.

personal consumption expenditures Goods and services purchased by residents of the United States, whether individuals or businesses; they include durable goods, nondurable goods, and services.

personal or family distribution of income The distribution of income to individuals or family groups (typically quintiles, or fifths, of the population).

Phillips curve The original curve posited a negative relationship between wages and unemployment, but later versions related unemployment to inflation rates.

physical capital All manufactured products that are used to produce goods and services.

physical network A network connected by a physical structure such as fiber optics, transportation routes, or satellites.

Pigouvian tax A tax that is placed on an activity generating negative externalities in order to achieve a socially efficient outcome.

positive question A question that can be answered using available information or facts.

poverty rate The percentage of the population living in poverty.

poverty thresholds Income levels for various household sizes, below which people are considered to be living in poverty.

present value The value of an investment (future stream of income) today. The higher the discount rate, the lower the present value today, and vice versa.

price caps Maximum price at which a regulated firm can sell its product. They are often flexible enough to allow for changing cost conditions.

price ceiling A maximum price established by government for a product or service. When the price ceiling is set below equilibrium, a shortage results.

price discrimination Charging different consumer groups different prices for the same product.

price elasticity of demand A measure of the responsiveness of quantity demanded to a change in price, equal to the percentage change in quantity demanded divided by the percentage change in price.

price elasticity of supply A measure of the responsiveness of quantity supplied to changes in price. Elastic supply has elasticity greater than 1, whereas inelastic supply has elasticity less than 1.

price floor A minimum price established by government for a product or service. When the price floor is set above equilibrium, a surplus results.

price level The absolute level of a price index, whether the consumer price index (CPI; retail prices), the producer price index (PPI; wholesale prices), or the GDP deflator (average price of all items in GDP).

price system A name given to the market economy because prices provide considerable information to both buyers and sellers.

price taker Individual firms in perfectly competitive markets determine their prices from the market because they are so small they cannot influence market price. For this reason, perfectly competitive firms can sell all the output they produce at market-determined prices.

Prisoner's Dilemma A noncooperative game in which players cannot communicate or collaborate in making their decisions, which results in inferior outcomes for both players. Many oligopoly decisions can be framed as a Prisoner's Dilemma.

producer price index (PPI) An index of the average prices received by domestic producers for their output.

producer surplus The difference between the market price and the price at which firms are willing to supply the product. It is equal to the area below market price and above the supply curve.

product differentiation One firm's product is distinguished from another's through advertising, innovation, location, and so on.

production The process of converting resources (factors of production)—land, labor, capital, and entrepreneurial ability—into goods and services.

production efficiency Goods and services are produced at their lowest resource (opportunity) cost.

production function Measures the output that is produced using various combinations of inputs and a fixed level of technology.

production possibilities frontier (PPF) Shows the combinations of two goods that are possible for a society to produce at full employment. Points on or inside the PPF are attainable, and those outside of the frontier are unattainable.

productivity How effectively inputs are converted into outputs. Labor productivity is the ratio of the output of goods and services to the labor hours devoted to the production of that output. Productivity and living standards are closely related.

profit Equal to the difference between total revenue and total cost.

profit-maximizing rule Firms maximize profit by producing output where $MR = MC$. No other level of output produces higher profits.

progressive tax A tax that rises in percentage of income as income increases.

public choice theory The economic analysis of public and political decision making, looking at issues such as voting, the impact of election incentives on politicians, the influence of special interest groups, and rent-seeking behaviors.

public debt The portion of the national debt that is held by the public, including individuals, companies, pension funds, along with foreign entities and foreign governments. This debt is also referred to as net debt or federal debt held by the public.

public goods Goods whose consumption by one person cannot diminish the benefit to others of consuming the good (i.e., nonrivalry), and once they are provided, no one person can be excluded from consuming (i.e., nonexcludability).

purchasing power parity The rate of exchange that allows a specific amount of currency in one country to purchase the same quantity of goods in another country.

quota A government-set limit on the quantity of imports into a country.

rate of return Uses the present value formula, but subtracts costs, then finds the interest rate (discount rate) at which this investment would break even.

rate of return regulation Permits product pricing that allows the firm to earn a normal return on capital invested in the firm.

ratio of income to poverty The ratio of family income to the poverty threshold. Families with ratios below 0.5 are considered severely poor, families with ratios between 0.5 and 1.0 are considered poor, and those families with ratios between 1.0 and 1.25 are considered near poor.

rational expectations Rational economic agents are assumed to make the best possible use of all publicly available information, then make informed, rational judgments on what the future holds. Any errors in their forecasts will be randomly distributed.

real exchange rate A measure of a currency's value relative to another, taking into account the price levels of both countries. It is equal to the nominal exchange rate multiplied by the ratio of the price levels of the two countries.

real GDP The total value of final goods and services produced in a country in a year measured using prices in a base year.

real GDP per capita Real GDP divided by population. Provides a rough estimate of a country's standard of living.

recessionary gap The increase in aggregate spending needed (when expanded by the multiplier) to bring a depressed economy back to full employment.

recognition lag The time it takes for policymakers to confirm that the economy is in a recession or a recovery. Short-term variations in key economic indicators are typical and sometimes represent nothing more than randomness in the data.

regressive tax A tax that falls in percentage of income as income increases.

rent The return to land as a factor of production. Sometimes called economic rent.

rent seeking Resources expended to protect a monopoly position. These are used for such activities as lobbying, extending patents, and restricting the number of licenses permitted.

reserve ratio The percentage of a bank's total deposits that are held in reserves, either as cash in the vault or as deposits at the regional Federal Reserve Bank.

reserve requirement The required ratio of funds that commercial banks and other depository institutions must hold in reserve against deposits.

resources Productive resources include land (land and natural resources), labor (mental and physical talents of people), capital (manufactured products used to produce other products), and entrepreneurial ability (the combining of the other factors to produce products and assume the risk of the business).

return on investment The earnings, such as interest or capital gains, that a saver receives for making funds available to others. It is calculated as earnings divided by the amount invested.

right-to-work laws Laws resulting from the Taft-Hartley Act that permitted states to outlaw union shops.

Rule of 70 Provides an estimate of the number of years for a value to double, and is calculated as 70 divided by the annual growth rate.

saving The difference between income and consumption; the amount of disposable income not spent.

scarcity Our unlimited wants clash with limited resources, leading to scarcity. Everyone (rich and poor) faces scarcity because, at a minimum, our time on earth is limited. Economics focuses on the allocation of scarce resources to satisfy unlimited wants as fully as possible.

screening or **signaling** The use of higher education as a way to let employers know that the prospective employee is intelligent and trainable and potentially has the discipline to be a good employee.

second-degree price discrimination Charging different customers different prices based on the quantities of the product they purchase.

segmented labor markets Labor markets split into separate parts. This leads to different wages paid to different sectors even though both markets are highly competitive.

sequential-move games Games in which players make moves one at a time, allowing players to view the progression of the game and to make decisions based on previous moves.

share of stock A unit of ownership in a business that entitles the shareholder to one vote at shareholder meetings and one share of any dividends paid.

shortage Occurs when the price is below market equilibrium, and quantity demanded exceeds quantity supplied.

short run A period of time over which at least one factor of production (resource) is fixed, or cannot be changed.

short-run aggregate supply (SRAS) curve The short-run aggregate supply curve is positively sloped because many input costs are slow to change (*sticky*) in the short run.

short-run supply curve The marginal cost curve above the minimum point on the average variable cost curve.

shutdown point When price in the short run falls below the minimum point on the *AVC* curve, the firm will minimize losses by closing its doors and stopping production. Because $P < AVC$, the firm's variable costs are not covered; therefore, by shutting the plant, losses are reduced to fixed costs only.

simultaneous-move games Games in which players' actions occur at the same time, forcing players to make decisions without knowing how the other players will act. These games are analyzed using diagrams called game tables.

social network A network that combines elements of physical and virtual networks.

sole proprietorship A type of business structure composed of a single owner who supervises and manages the business and is subject to unlimited liability.

solvency crisis A situation when a bank's liabilities exceed its assets.

stagflation Simultaneous occurrence of rising inflation and rising unemployment.

store of value The function that enables people to save the money they earn today and use it to buy the goods and services they want tomorrow.

structural unemployment Unemployment caused by changes in the structure of consumer demands or technology. It means that demand for some products declines and the skills of this industry's workers often become obsolete as well. This results in an extended bout of unemployment while new skills are developed.

subprime mortgage Mortgages that are given to borrowers who are a poor credit risk. These higher-risk loans charge a higher interest rate, which can be profitable to lenders if borrowers make their payments on time.

substitute goods Goods consumers will substitute for one another. When the *price* of one good rises, the *demand* for the other good increases, and vice versa.

substitutes Goods consumers substitute for one another depending on their relative prices, such as coffee and tea. Substitutes have a positive cross elasticity of demand.

substitution effect When the price of one good rises, consumers will substitute other goods for that good; therefore, the quantity demanded for the higher-priced good falls. In labor markets, higher wages mean that the value of work has increased, and the opportunity costs of leisure are higher; hence, work is substituted in place of leisure.

sunk cost A cost that has been paid and cannot be recovered; therefore, it should not enter into decision making affecting the present or future.

sunk cost fallacy Occurs when people make decisions based on how much was already spent, rather than how the decision might affect their current well-being.

supply The maximum amount of a product that sellers are willing and able to provide for sale over some time period at various prices, holding all other relevant factors constant (the *ceteris paribus* condition).

supply curve A graphical illustration of the law of supply, which shows the relationship between the price of a good and the quantity supplied.

supply of labor The amount of time an individual is willing to work at various wage rates.

supply-side fiscal policies Policies that focus on shifting the long-run aggregate supply curve to the right, expanding the economy without increasing inflationary pressures. Unlike policies to increase aggregate demand, supply-side policies take longer to impact the economy.

surplus Occurs when the price is above market equilibrium, and quantity supplied exceeds quantity demanded. It is also the amount by which annual tax revenues exceed government expenditures.

sustainable development The ability to meet the needs of the present without compromising the ability of future generations to meet their own needs.

switching cost A cost imposed on consumers when they change products or subscribe to a new network.

tariff A tax on imported products. When a country taxes imported products, it drives a wedge between the product's domestic price and its price on the world market.

Taylor rule A rule for the federal funds target that suggests the target is equal to 2% + Current Inflation Rate + 1/2(Inflation Gap) + 1/2(Output Gap).

teaser rates Promotional low interest rates offered by lenders for a short period of time to attract new customers and to encourage spending.

teaser strategies Attractive up-front deals used as an incentive to entice new customers into a network.

terms of trade The ratio of the price of exported goods to the price of imported goods (P_x/P_m).

third-degree price discrimination Charging different groups of people different prices based on varying elasticities of demand.

tight money or restrictive monetary policy Fed actions designed to decrease excess reserves and the money supply to shrink income and employment, usually to fight inflation. *See also* contractionary monetary policy.

tipping point (or **critical mass**) The quantity from which network effects are strong enough to support the network.

tit-for-tat strategies A trigger strategy that rewards cooperation and punishes defections. If your opponent lowers its price, you do the same. If your opponent returns to a cooperative strategy, you do the same.

total cost The sum of all costs to run a business. To an economist, this includes out-of-pocket expenses and opportunity costs.

total factor productivity The portion of output produced that is not explained by the number of inputs used in production.

total revenue Price × quantity demanded (sold). If demand is elastic and price rises, quantity demanded falls off significantly and total revenue declines, and vice versa. If demand is inelastic and price rises, quantity demanded does not decline much and total revenue rises, and vice versa.

total surplus The sum of consumer surplus and producer surplus, and a measure of the overall net benefit gained from a market transaction.

total utility The total satisfaction that a person receives from consuming a given amount of goods and services.

tradeoff between risk and return The pattern of higher risk assets offering higher average annual returns on investment than lower risk assets.

tragedy of the commons Resources that are owned by the community at large (e.g., parks, ocean fish, and the atmosphere) therefore tend to be overexploited because individuals have little incentive to use them in a sustainable fashion.

trigger strategies Action is taken contingent on your opponent's past decisions.

underemployed workers Workers who are forced to take jobs that do not fully utilize their education, background, or skills. Underemployed workers often hold part-time jobs.

union shop Nonunion hires must join the union within a specified period of time.

unit of account Money provides a yardstick for measuring and comparing the values of a wide variety of goods and services. It eliminates the problem of double coincidence of wants associated with barter.

unitary elastic demand The percentage change in quantity demanded is just equal to the percentage change in price. This results in the absolute value of the price elasticity of demand to be equal to 1.

unitary elastic supply Price elasticity of supply is equal to 1. The percentage change in quantity supplied is equal to the percentage change in price.

utility A hypothetical measure of consumer satisfaction.

utility-maximizing rule Total utility is maximized where the marginal utility per dollar is equal for all products, or $MU_a/P_a = MU_b/P_b = \cdots = MU_n/P_n$.

value of the marginal product The value of the marginal product of labor (VMP_L) is equal to marginal physical product of labor times price, or $MPP_L \times P$.

variable costs Costs that vary with output fluctuations, including expenses such as labor and material costs.

versioning A pricing strategy that involves differentiating a good by way of packaging into multiple products for people with different demands.

vesting period The minimum number of years a worker must be employed before the company's contribution to a retirement account becomes permanent.

vicious cycle When a network good does not reach its tipping point, and therefore does not increase in value enough to retain its customers, customers leave the network, thereby further diminishing the value of the good until all customers leave the network.

virtual network A network connected by groups of people using the same type or brand of good.

virtuous cycle The point at which a network good reaches its tipping point, when network effects cause demand for the good to increase on its own. As more people buy or subscribe to a good or service, it generates even more external benefits and more demand.

wealth A stock measure of an individual's or family's assets, net of liabilities, at a given point in time.

wealth effect Households usually hold some of their wealth in financial assets such as savings accounts, bonds, and cash, and a rising aggregate price level means that the purchasing power of this monetary wealth declines, reducing output demanded.

willingness-to-pay An individual's valuation of a good or service, equal to the most an individual is willing and able to pay.

withdrawals Activities that remove spending from the economy, including saving, taxes, and imports.

x-inefficiency Protected from competitive pressures, monopolies do not have to act efficiently. Examples include spending on luxury corporate jets, lavish travel, and other nonessential perks.

yield The annual return to a bond measured as the coupon payment as a percentage of the current price of a bond.

yield curve Shows the relationship between the interest rate earned on a bond (measured on the vertical axis) and the length of time until the bond's maturity date (shown on the horizontal axis).

Index

Note: Page numbers followed by f indicate figures; those followed by t indicate tables; those followed by n indicate notes.

A

ABC stores, 231, 241
Absolute advantage, 43–45, 44f, 44t, 699
ACA. *See* Affordable Care Act (ACA)
Accommodative monetary policy, 650
Accounting profit, 173
Acid rain, 359
AD. *See* Aggregate demand (AD) curve
Adaptive expectations, 679–680
AD/AS model. *See* Aggregate demand-aggregate supply (AD/AS) model
Administrative Behavior (Simon), 205
Adobe, 385
Ad valorem taxes, 705
Advertising, product differentiation and, 253
AFC. *See* Average fixed cost (*AFC*)
Affirmative action programs, 294–295
Affordable Care Act (ACA), 351, 352, 353
Africa. *See also specific countries*
    economic growth of, 480
    natural resources of, 332
AFSCME, 296
AFT, 296
Age Discrimination in Employment Act of 1967, 295
Agency shops, 297
Aggregate demand (AD) curve, 532–536, 532f
    determinants of, 533–536, 534f, 535t
    exchange rates and, 732, 733f, 734
    negative slope of, 532–533
Aggregate demand-aggregate supply (AD/AS) model, 529–549
    aggregate demand and, 532–536, 532f
    aggregate supply and, 537–541
    macroeconomic equilibrium and, 541–547, 541f
Aggregate expenditures, 501–525
    consumption and saving and, 504–508, 506t
    investment and, 508–511, 509f
    models of. *See* Full aggregate expenditures model; Simple aggregate expenditures model
    simplifying assumptions and, 504
    summing, 437
Aggregate investment schedule, 510–511, 510f
Aggregate supply curve, 537–541
    exchange rates and, 732, 733f, 734
    fiscal policy and, 563–567, 564f
    long-run, 537–538, 537f
    short-run, 538–540, 538f
Airbnb, 465
Airline industry
    competition in, 267
    as contestable market, 241
    employee perks in, 284
Air pollution. *See also* Negative externalities
    cap-and-trade and, 358, 359
Akst, Daniel, 171
Alcoa Aluminum, 222
Alibaba, 254
Allen, Robert, 644n
Allocative efficiency, 6, 34
    in competitive markets, 208, 210
AltaVista, 372
Altruism, 150–152
Amazon.com, 56, 227, 231
American Airlines, 252
American Recovery and Reinvestment Act, 673. *See also* Stimulus package
Americans with Disabilities Act of 1990, 295

Angola, oil deposits in, 488
Angry Birds, 59
Annually balanced budget, 571
Antitrust policy
    concentration ratios and, 240–241, 240t
    contestable markets and, 241
    future of, 241–242
    laws and, 238–239, 239t
    market and market power definition and, 239–241
APC. *See* Average propensity to consume (APC)
Apple Computer Inc.
    bundling strategy of, 385
    competition and, 196, 231
    growth of, 171, 321
    profits and, 12
    stock of, 324
    value of brand, 254
Apple iPad, 380
Apple iPhone, 109
Appreciation, of currencies, 729–730, 730f
APS. *See* Average propensity to save (APS)
Arctic ice caps, 340
Argentina, currency of, 736
Asia, economic growth of, 480
Assets
    allocation of, risk assessment and, 601
    choosing, for investment in, 602
    diversification of, by financial institutions, 596
    financial, types of, 596–597
    prices of, shifts in supply of loanable funds and, 594
Asymmetric information, 351
    market failure and, 92–93
ATC. *See* Average total cost (*ATC*)
Athens, Greece, Olympic Games in, 586
AT&T
    Comcast and, 382
    Verizon and, 117, 268, 372, 387
Australia
    plastic money in, 590
    saving rate in, 517
Autarky, 698
Automatic stabilizers, 567–568
Automobile industry
    bailout of, 673
    electric cars and, 168
    Japanese, quotas on exports of, 707
Autonomous investment, 510
AVC. *See* Average variable cost (*AVC*)
Average cost(s), 181–182
Average cost pricing rule, 237–238
Average fixed cost (*AFC*), 181–182, 181f
Average product, 177
Average propensity to consume (APC), 506, 506t
Average propensity to save (APS), 506, 506t
Average total cost (*ATC*), 181, 182, 182f, 183
Average variable cost (*AVC*), 181, 182, 182f

B

Bahamas, acceptance of U.S. dollar as legal tender in, 738
Balanced budget amendments, 571–573
Balanced budget multiplier, 520–521
Balance of payments, 724–725, 724t
    capital account and, 725
    current account and, 724–725
Balance transfer offers, on credit cards, 384

Balboa Island, California, 316
Bank(s), 321–322
    central. *See* European Central Bank (ECB); Federal Reserve System
    Federal Reserve, 624–625, 624t
    housing bubble and, 671
    leakages and, 619–620
    money creation by, 614–618
    reserves and. *See* Reserve(s)
    Swiss bank accounts and, 621
    World Bank, 735
Banking system, fractional reserve, 616–618
Bank of America, 322
Barbary macaques, 350
Bar charts, 22, 22f
Barriers to entry, 196, 222–224
Barter, 588
BEA. *See* Bureau of Economic Analysis (BEA)
Bear Stearns, 672
A Beautiful Mind (Nasar), 262
Becker, Gary, 291–292
Behavioral economics, 148–152
    altruism and, 150–152
    framing bias and, 149
    overconfidence and, 149–150
    overvaluing the present relative to the future and, 150
    sunk costs and, 148–149
Benefits, 2
    external, positive externalities and, 342
    of monopolies, 231
    of union membership, 296
Bentham, Jeremy, 138, 141
Bernanke, Ben, 656, 739
Bhagwati, Jagdish, 415n
Bhutan, capital-to-labor ratio in, 489
Bias, framing, 149
Big Mac Index, 727–728, 727t
Blockbuster Video, 332
Bloomekatz, Ari, 416n
BLS. *See* Bureau of Labor Statistics (BLS)
Board of Governors, 623
    rules vs. discretion and, 651
Boeing, 220
Bonds, 322–323, 323f
    prices of, interest rates and, 597–598
Booms. *See also* Business cycles
    of 1990s, 509
Borders, 268, 332
Borrowing, 321–322
    Fed as lender of last resort and, 625
    financial system and, 595–596
    government's bias toward, 568–569
    microloans and, 612, 613
    short-term, 599–600
    subprime mortgages and collateralized debt obligations and, 670–672
Bottled water industry, 54
Brand names, 254
Branson, Richard, 10, 314
Brazil
    coffee production in, 209
    economic growth of, 478, 480, 518
    GDP of, 439
    oil production in, 259
    public debt of, 574
Breit, William, 91n
Bretton Woods agreements, 735
Brexit, 660
BRIC countries. *See* Brazil; China; India; Russia
Brin, Sergey, 325

Brinkmanship, 272
Broadband Internet connections, 381
Bronco Wine Company, 73
Buchanan, James, 569
Budget
    annually balanced, 571
    cyclically balanced, 571–572
Budget constraints, government budget and, 573
Budget deficits, 570
    financing of, 573
Budget line (budget constraint), 138–139, 138f
    changes to, 139–140
Budget surpluses, 570
Bundling strategies, 385
Bureau of Economic Analysis (BEA), 480,
    702, 724
Bureau of Labor Statistics (BLS), 291
    consumer spending and inflation
        measurement by, 453–454, 455
    employment statistics and, 460
    employment surveys of, 463
Burger King, 250
Burns, Arthur, 427
Bush, George H. W., tax increase under, 559
Bush, George W.
    tax cut under, 558–559
    tax rebate under, 564
Business(es). See also Corporations; Firms
    expectations of, shifts in demand for
        loanable funds and, 594
    leakages by, 620
    structures of, 170–171
Business cycles, 426–432. See also Great
    Recession; Recession(s)
    dating of, 428–429, 431
    definition of, 427–428, 427f, 428f
    measures of, 428–429
    turning points and, 431
Busts. See Business cycles
Buyers, number of, demand and, 62

C
California, electricity crisis in, 388
Cambodia, acceptance of U.S. dollar as legal
    tender in, 738
Cameroon, oil deposits in, 488
Canada
    NAFTA and, 46, 702, 711
    Nunavut's resources and, 14
    oil production in, 259
    public debt of, 574
    saving rate in, 517
    U.S. pollution and, 359
Candy Crush Saga, 59
Canterbery, E. Ray, 43, 71n
Capacity, short- vs. long-term economic growth
    and, 484–485, 485f
Cap-and-trade, 357–358, 358f, 359
Capital, 33
    cost of, 318
    debt, 322–323, 323f
    diminishing returns to, 489
    equity, 323–324
    financial. See Financial capital
    human. See Human capital
    marginal efficiency of, 320
    physical. See Physical capital
    venture, 324–325
Capital account, 725
    exchange rates and, 731–732
Capital accumulation, economic growth and,
    39–40, 39f, 40f
Capital goods, on hand, investment demand
    and, 510

Capital investment, implicit costs and, 173
Capitalist economies, 32
Capital-to-labor ratio, increasing, economic
    growth and, 489
Carnival, 268
Cartels, 258–259, 258f
Castles, conversion into hotels, 186
Casual users, 377–378
Catch-up effect, 489
Causation, correlation vs., 28
C-CPI-U, 455
CDOs. See Collateralized debt
    obligations (CDOs)
Cell-phone providers, 372
Census Bureau, 399, 416, 460
    employment surveys of, 463, 465
    poverty measures of, 408, 412–413
Central banks. See European Central Bank
    (ECB); Federal Reserve System
CES. See Current Employment Statistics (CES)
    Survey
Ceteris paribus assumption, 6, 26–27
Changes in demand
    changes in quantity demanded vs., 62–63, 63f
    for loanable funds, 594
    move to a new equilibrium and, 72–74, 72f,
        74f, 74t
    for products, labor demand changes and, 287
Changes in quality demanded, changes in
    demand vs., 62–63, 63f
Changes in quantity supplied, changes in supply
    vs., 67, 67f, 68f
Changes in supply
    changes in quantity supplied vs., 67, 67f, 68f
    of loanable funds, 593–594
    move to a new equilibrium and, 71–72, 72f,
        73–74, 74f, 74t
Charmin, 109
Chauvet, Marcelle, 428n
Cheriton, David, 325
Chesapeake Energy, 322–323
Chevrolet, 118
Chicago Marathon, 179–182
Chicken games, 271–272, 272f
Chile
    pollution in, 441
    public debt of, 574, 575
China
    clothing production in, 704
    comparative advantage of, 47
    demand for energy in, 453
    economic growth of, 478, 480, 483, 687
    economy of, 32–33
    efforts to combat climate change in, 364
    fast food restaurants in, 256
    GDP of, 439
    greenhouse gases produced by, 362
    high-speed rail network of, 489
    intervention in foreign exchange markets,
        735
    island building by, 41
    lucky and unlucky numbers in, 152
    oil production in, 259
    public debt of, 574, 575
    saving rate in, 517
    Spring Festival in, 712
    U.S. debt held by, 576
    value of currency of, 733
China Mobile, 254
Choices
    consumer, optimal, 161, 161f
    with limited resources, 8–9
Chrysler, 673
Circuit City, 268, 332

Circular flow diagram, 433–434, 433f
Citro, Constance F., 408n
Civil Rights Act of 1964, 294
Classical theory, 424, 504, 648t
    quantity theory of money and, 644–645, 645f
Clayton Act of 1914, 239t
Clean Air Act of 1970, 358
Clean Air Act of 1990, 359
Clean Power Plan, 364
Climate change, 340, 360–362
    causes of, 360–361, 361f
    challenges of addressing, 362
    consequences of, 361–362
Clinton, Bill, tax increase under, 559
Clinton, Hillary, 261
Closed economies, 698
Closed shops, 297
Coach, 196
Coase, Ronald, 344–345
Coase theorem, 344–346
Coca-Cola Company
    brand name of, 254
    Coke recipe and, 224
    demand curve of, 109
    market value of, 220
    social responsibility of, 363
Cochran, Johnnie, 261
Coffee industry, Colombian, 209
Collateral, 322
Collateralized debt obligations (CDOs), 670–672
Collected Works (Samuelson), 91
Colombia, coffee production in, 209
Comcast, 382
Command and control environmental policy,
    355, 356, 356f. 358
Commodities, related, prices of, supply and, 66
Commodity money, 588
Common property resources, 349–351, 350f
Communist Manifesto (Marx and Engels), 309
Comparative advantage, 43–45, 44f, 44t,
    699–700, 699f, 700t
    in United States and China, 47
Competition. See also Monopolistic competition;
        Perfect competition
    lack of, market failure and, 92
    monopoly compared with, 228–232
    pricing strategies for network goods and,
        383–385
    promoting with interconnection, 386–387
    public interest and, 208, 209f, 210
Competitive labor market equilibrium,
    289, 289f
Competitive markets, government as promoter
    of, 494
Complement(s), cross elasticity of demand
    and, 117
Complementary goods, 62
Compounding
    of economic growth, 480, 481–483
    of interest, 600, 600t
    Rule of 70 and, 482–483, 482t
Compounding effect, 600, 600t
Concentration ratios, 240, 240t
Congestion charges, 92
Connally "Hot Oil" Act of 1935, 349
Connect America Fund, 381
Conniff, Richard, 359n
Constant cost industries, 211, 211f
Constant dollar value, 457
Constant returns to scale, 185, 185f
Consumer Expenditure Survey, 455
Consumer price index (CPI), 454–455
Consumers, burden of tax on, elasticity and,
    125, 125f

Consumer spending, aggregate demand and, 533–534
Consumer surplus, 86–87, 88
Consumption
    aggregate expenditures model and, 504–508, 505f, 506t
    average propensity to consume and, 506, 506t
    crowding out of, 576–577
    determinants of, 508
    marginal propensity to consume and, 506–508, 507f, 542
Containerization, 210
Contestable markets, 241
Contract(s), government enforcement of, economic growth and, 493
Contractionary fiscal policy, 562–563, 562f
Contractionary monetary policy, 642, 643f
Cooter, Robert, 344
Copyrights, market power and, 224
Core users, 377
Corn Laws (1815), 43
Corporate profits, in GDP, 438
Corporations, 171
    offshoring by, 172
    social responsibility of, 363
Correlation, causation vs., 28
Cost(s), 2
    of capital, 318
    economic, 172–173
    explicit, 172
    external, negative externalities and, 342
    implicit, 172–173
    incremental, 179
    of information. reduction by financial institutions, 596
    marginal. See Marginal cost
    of monopolies, 231
    operating, investment demand and, 510
    opportunity. See Opportunity costs
    production. See Long-run production costs; Production costs; Short-run production costs
    of resources, supply and, 66
    sunk, 148–149, 179–182
    switching, 383
    total, 171, 181, 182, 182f, 183. See also Long-run average total cost (LRATC) curve
    transaction, reduction by financial institutions, 596
    of union membership, 296
    variable, 179, 181, 182, 182f
Costa Rica
    acceptance of U.S. dollar as legal tender in, 738
    foreign trade zones in, 707
    GDP and happiness in, 441
Cost-benefit analysis, 360
Costco, 233
Cost-push inflation, 544, 545f, 546, 547f
Counterfeit money
    inflation and, 459
    preventing, 590
Coupon rate, 322
CPI. See Consumer price index (CPI)
CPI-U, 454, 455
CPI-W, 454, 455
CPS. See Current Population Survey (CPS)
Craft unions, 296
Creativity, wealth of nations, 14
Credit cards, 0% offers on, 384
Credit default swaps, 672
Critical mass, 379
Cross elasticity of demand (E_{ab}), 116–117
Crowding-out effect, 576–577

Crowe, Russell, 262
Cruise ship industry, offshoring in, 172
Cuba, acceptance of U.S. dollar as legal tender in, 738
Currencies
    appreciation and depreciation of, 729–730, 730f, 732
    Canadian, use by Hyder, Alaska, 738
    of China, value of, 733
    foreign, holdings of, leakages and, 621
    pegging of, to U.S. dollar, 735, 736
    U.S. See U.S. dollar
Current account, 724–725
    exchange rates and, 731
Current dollar value, 457
Current Employment Statistics (CES) Survey, 463
Current Population Survey (CPS), 463
Curves. See also Aggregate demand (AD) curve; Aggregate supply curve; Demand curves; Graphs; Supply curve
    shifts in, 27–28, 28f
Cyclically balanced budget, 571–572
Cyclical unemployment, 468
Cyprus, financial crisis in, 657

D
Dalton, Georgia, 317
Darby, Abraham, 34
Darwin, Charles, 196
Das Kapital (Marx and Engels), 309
Deadweight loss, 90
    monopoly and, 228–230, 229f
Dean, James, 272
Debt
    cost of financing, 685–686
    effect on inflation, 686–687
    household, consumption and saving and, 508
    monetized, 686–687
    public (net; federal), 570–571, 571f
Debt capital, 322–323, 323f
Debt obligations, future, rising, 685
Decision lags
    fiscal policy and, 568
    monetary policy and, 628–629
Decreasing cost industries, 211, 211f
Deficits, budget, 570
    financing of, 573
Deflation, 454, 673
Delta Airlines, 252
Demand, 57–63
    aggregate. See Aggregate demand (AD) curve; Aggregate demand-aggregate supply (AD/AS) model
    changes in, changes in quantity demanded vs., 62–63, 63f
    determinants of, 60–62
    elastic, 109, 110f
    inelastic, 109–110, 110f
    for investment, 509–510
    for labor. See Labor demand
    law of, 58–59
    for loanable funds, 592–593, 592f
    for products, shifts in demand for loanable funds and, 594
    for public goods, 348–349, 348f
    unitary elastic, 110, 110f
    willingness-to-pay and, 57–58, 58f
Demand curves, 59–60, 60f
    of Coca-Cola Company, 109
    deriving, 145–146, 146t, 147f, 162–163, 162f
    of firm, under monopolistic competition, 252–253, 253f
    kinked, 259–260, 260f

linear, elasticity and total revenue along, 115–116, 116f
    network. See Network demand curve
    perfectly elastic, 109, 110f
    perfectly inelastic, 109–110, 110f
Demand-pull inflation, 544–545, 544f, 545f
Demand schedule, 59
Demand shocks, monetary policy and, 648–649, 649f
Demographic changes, labor supply changes and, 284
Denmark, poverty in, 414
Department of Commerce (DOC), 432, 441
Department of Health and Human Services, 408
Deposit-refund systems, 358
Depreciation, of currencies, 729–730, 730f, 732
Depth of poverty, 410–411
Determinants of demand, 60–62
Determinants of supply, 65–67
Detroit, Michigan, 317
Dickinson, North Dakota, employment in, 466
Dillon Reservoir, 357
Diminishing marginal returns, 177
Diminishing returns effect, 181, 181f, 182
Diminishing returns to capital, 489
Discounting, 319
Discount rate, 627
Discouraged workers, 465
Discretionary fiscal policy, 558–561
Discretionary spending, 558
Discrimination. See Economic discrimination; Employment discrimination; Price discrimination
Diseconomies of scale, 185, 185f
Disinflation, 454
Disney, Walt, 254
Disruptive technologies, 210
Distribution, 32
DOC. See Department of Commerce (DOC)
Dollar
    Canadian, use by Hyder, Alaska, 738
    U.S. See U.S. dollar
Dollarization, 621, 638, 658, 659, 736, 738
Dominant strategy, 265
Domino's, 256
Double coincidence of wants, 588
Double-dip recessions, 428
Dromoland Castle, 186
Drones, in Rwanda, 375
Dual labor market hypothesis, 291–292
Dubai, diversification of economy of, 530
Dukek, Dan, 359
Dumping, as argument against free trade, 709
Dunkin' Donuts, 170

E
E_{ab}. See Cross elasticity of demand (E_{ab})
Easy money, 650
eBay, 56, 86
ECB. See European Central Bank (ECB)
Economic costs, 172–173
Economic discrimination, 291–295
    Becker's theory of, 291–292
    public policy to combat, 294–295
    segmented labor markets and, 292–294, 293f
Economic downturns. See Great Depression; Great Recession; Recession(s)
Economic freedom, government as promoter of, 494–495, 496f
Economic goals, failure to coincide, 13
Economic growth, 13, 38–42, 477–498
    compounding of, 481–483
    expanding resources and, 38, 39–40
    extreme poverty and, 483

Economic growth (*continued*)
    factors of production and, 485–487
    globalization and obstacles to, 687
    government's role in promoting, 492–496
    increasing, 414–415
    measurement of, 480–481, 481t
    production function and, 486–492
    productivity and, 488–492
    short- vs. long-term, 484–485
    technological change and, 38, 40, 41f
Economic losses, 173
Economic outlook, shifts in supply of loanable
        funds and, 593, 593f
Economic profits, 173
    monopolies and, 227, 228f
    in perfect competition, 201, 201f
Economic rent, 316
Economic shocks, monetary policy and,
        648–650, 649f
Economic slowdowns, global impact of, 424
Economic systems, 32–33
Economics
    basic questions of, 32–33
    behavioral. *See* Behavioral economics
    definition of, 4
    efficiency vs. equity and, 6–7
    in everyday life, 15
    key principles of, 8–15
    model building in, 6
    positive vs. normative questions in, 7
    reasons to study, 4–5
Economics (Samuelson), 91
The Economics of Discrimination (Becker), 291, 292
Economides, Nicholas, 376
Economies
    capitalist, 32
    closed, 698
    informal, 442
    market, 32
    market, laissez-faire, 32, 94
    open, 698
    planned, 32
Economies of scale, 184–185, 185f
    market power and, 223, 223f
    network goods and, 379
Economies of scope, 185
Economists, disagreement among, 7
Ecuador, U.S. dollar as currency of, 621, 638,
        658, 659, 736, 738
E_d. *See* Price elasticity of demand (E_d)
Edgeworth, Francis Ysidro, 138, 292
Education. *See also* Human capital
    financial aid and, 493
    as investment, 327–328, 327f
    online, 330
Edwards, Ralph, 10
Efficiency
    allocative. *See* Allocative efficiency
    of capital, marginal, 320
    equity vs., 6–7, 93
    interconnection in network industries
        and, 387
    of markets, 12–13
    in network industries, 387
    production, 6, 33–35, 34f
Efficiency wage theory, 681
E_L. *See* Elasticity of demand for labor (E_L)
Elastic demand, 109, 110f
    total revenue and, 114, 115f
Elastic supply, 119, 120f
Elasticity, 105–130
    taxes and, 125, 125f, 126f, 127–128
Elasticity of demand
    cross, 116–117

income, 117–118
    price. *See* Price elasticity of demand
    for product, elasticity of demand for labor
        and, 288
    total revenue and, 114–116, 115t, 116f
Elasticity of demand for labor (E_L), 288
Electricity crisis, in California, 388
Electronic Arts, 728
Elimination principle, 208
El Salvador, U.S. dollar as currency of, 621, 638,
        658, 659, 736, 738
Emissions taxes, 357
Employed people, 461–462
Employee compensation, in GDP, 437
Employment. *See also* Labor *entries*;
        Unemployment; Wage(s)
    domestic, free trade and, 710–711
    full, 468
    future jobs in the U.S. economy and, 300
    nonwage aspects of, labor supply changes
        and, 284
    saving programs based on, 601–602
    statistics on, 460
    trends in, 299–300, 464
    unemployment rate related to, 464
    unions and. *See* Unions
Employment discrimination
    antidiscrimination legislation and, 294–295
    against women, 292
Employment Non-Discrimination Act, 295
Engels, Friedrich, 309
Entrepreneurs, 33, 170–171
Entrepreneurship, 332
Envelope curve, 184
Environment. *See also* Climate change;
        Externalities; Pollution
    discarded plastic bottles and, 54
    free trade and, 711
Environmental Kuznets curve, 711
Environmental policy, 340, 342, 353–359
    command and control, 355, 356, 356f, 358
    intergenerational questions and,
        353–354, 354f
    market-based, 356, 357–359
    socially efficient levels of pollution and,
        354–355, 355f
Environmental quality, GDP and, 440–441
Equal Pay Act of 1963, 294
Equation of exchange, 644
Equilibrium, 69–75, 70f
    changes in supply and demand and, 71–74
    in competitive labor market, 289, 289f
    deviation from, 89–90
    macroeconomic. *See* Macroeconomic
        equilibrium
    Nash, 261, 262, 265–267, 266f, 272
    for network goods, 379–382, 380f
    tax changes and, 519–520, 520t, 521f
Equilibrium levels of human capital,
        328–329, 329f
Equilibrium price, 69
    output and, under monopoly, 225, 226f
    prices below, 90–91, 91f
    prices exceeding, 89–90, 90f
Equilibrium quantity, 69
Equity capital, 323–324
Equity (fairness), efficiency vs., 6–7, 93
Equity (financial), private, 324–325
E_s. *See* Price elasticity of supply (E_s)
Escalator clauses, 457
ESPN, 388
"An Essay on the Principle of Population as
        It Affects the Future Improvement of
        Society" (Malthus), 490

Essential facilities, 386
Ethiopia, economic growth of, 480, 687
Ethnicity, 410, 410f, 411t
European Central Bank (ECB), 655, 658
European Union
    Brexit, 660
    cartels in, 258
    poverty in, 414
Eurozone crisis, 656–660
Excess reserves, 616
Exchange rates, 726–734
    aggregate supply and demand and, 732,
        733f, 734
    capital account and, 731–732
    current account and, 731
    determinants of, 730–731
    determination of, 728–731
    expected changes in, capital account
        and, 732
    fixed. *See* Fixed exchange rates
    flexible (floating). *See* Flexible exchange rates
    nominal, 726, 726t
    purchasing power parity and, 727–728, 728t
    real, 726–727
Executive Order 11246, 294–295
Expansionary fiscal policy, 561, 561f, 562f
Expansionary monetary policy, 641–642, 642f
Expectations
    about prices, demand and, 62
    about prices, supply and, 66–67
    adaptive, 679–680
    business, shifts in demand for loanable funds
        and, 594
    consumption and saving and, 508
    demand and, 62
    inflationary. *See* Inflationary expectations
    investment demand and, 510
    rational, 679–681, 680f
    supply and, 66–67
Expenditures approach to GDP, 435–437
Explicit costs, 172
Exports, 698. *See also* International trade
    current account and, 724
    measuring, 702
    net. *See* Net exports
    prices of, aggregate demand and, 533
Express lanes, 92
External benefits and costs, market failure
        and, 93
Externalities, 342–347, 343t
    Coase theorem and, 344–346
    limitations of analysis, 346–347
    negative, 342, 343–344, 344f
    network, 374
    positive, 342–343, 346, 346f
Externally held debt, 576, 576t
E_Y. *See* Income elasticity of demand (E_Y)

F

Facebook, 9, 173
    Google and, 231, 261
    growth of, 321
    market dominance of, 271
Face value, of a bond, 322
Factors of production. *See also* Resources
    changes in prices of, labor demand changes
        and, 287–288
    control over, market power and, 222–223
    economic growth and, 485–486
    substitutability of, elasticity of demand for
        labor and, 288
Fair Labor Standards Act of 1938, 294
Family distribution of income, 399–400, 400t
Farm prices, inflation and, 453

Fast-food restaurants, 211, 256
FDIC. *See* Federal Deposit Insurance Corporation (FDIC)
Federal Communications Commission (FCC), 381
Federal debt. *See* Public debt
Federal Deposit Insurance Corporation (FDIC), 597, 673
Federal funds rate, 626
Federal funds rate target, 627, 628f, 629
    Taylor rule and, 651–652, 652f
Federal government. *See* Government
Federal Open Market Committee (FOMC), 625, 638
Federal Reserve Banks, 624–625, 624t
Federal Reserve System, 623–630
    discount rate and, 627
    federal funds rate and. *See* Federal funds rate; Federal funds rate target
    as lender of last resort, 625
    monetary policy lags and, 628–629
    open market operations and, 627
    record of performance of, 654
    reserve requirements and, 626
    structure of, 623–625, 624f
    transparency and, 653–654
Federal Trade Commission Act of 1914, 239t
Ferguson, Niall, 588
Fiat money, 588
FIFA World Cup, 566
Financial assets, types of, 596–597
Financial capital, 321–326
    banks and borrowing and, 321–322
    bonds and, 322–323, 323f
    stocks and, 323–324
    venture capital and private equity and, 324–325
Financial crisis of 2007–2009, 13. *See also* Great Recession
Financial intermediaries (institutions), 596
    roles of, 596
Financial system, 595–599. *See also* Bank(s); Borrowing; Investment; Money; Saving
    bond prices and interest rates and, 597–598
    as bridge between savers and borrowers, 595–596
    roles of financial institutions in, 596
    stability of, economic growth and, 494
    stocks and investment returns and, 598–599
    types of financial assets and, 596–597
Firms, 170. *See also* Business(es); Corporations
    business structures of, 170–171
    demand curve of, under monopolistic competition, 252–253, 253f
    extent of control of prices, 196
    market cap of, 324
    market power of, short-run aggregate supply and, 540
    number in industry, 196
    plant shutdown and, 203–205, 204f
First-degree price discrimination, 232, 233, 233f
Fiscal cliffs, 272
Fiscal policy
    aggregate demand and, 558–563
    aggregate supply and, 563–567, 564f
    automatic stabilizers and, 567–568
    contractionary, 562–563, 562f
    discretionary, 558–561, 559f
    expansionary, 561, 561f, 562f
    under fixed exchange rates, 736–737, 736f
    under flexible exchange rates, 737, 738t, 739
    following Great Recession, 556
    government's bias toward borrowing and away from taxation and, 568–569

implementation of, 567–569
    infrastructure spending and, 564
    investment expansion and, 565–566
    mandatory spending and, 558, 559f
    in open economies, 734–739
    regulation reduction and, 566
    supply-side, 563
    tax rate reduction and, 564–565, 565f
    timing lags and, 568
Fiscal sustainability, 577
Fisher, Irving, 644
Fitch, 322
Five Guys, 250
Fixed costs, 178, 179
    average, 181–182, 181f
Fixed exchange rates, 734–735
    monetary and fiscal policy under, 736–737, 736f
Flat taxes, 123, 123t, 127
Flexible exchange rates, 729, 734, 735–736
    monetary and fiscal policy under, 737, 738t, 739
    pegging exchange rates under, 735–736
Flexible pricing, 236
Floating exchange rates. *See* Flexible exchange rates
Flow, income as, 398
Flow of funds measure, income as, 398
FOMC. *See* Federal Open Market Committee (FOMC)
Ford, 117, 673
Ford, Henry, 490
Foreign currency, holdings of, leakages and, 621
Foreign exchange markets, 728–729, 729f. *See also* Exchange rates
    Chinese intervention in, 735
Foreign trade zones, 707
Foundations of Economic Analysis (Samuelson), 91
Fox River, 357
Fractional reserve banking system, 616–618
Framing bias, 149
France
    in Eurozone, 658
    fast food restaurants in, 256
    public debt of, 574
    saving rate in, 517
Franchises, government, market power and, 223
Franzia, Fred, 73
Freedom, economic, government as promoter of, 494–495, 496f
Freeman, Richard B., 416
Free riders, 347–348
Free trade, 708–712
    government as promoter of, 494
    recent globalization concerns regarding, 710–712
    traditional economic arguments against, 708–710
Frictional unemployment, 467–468
Friedman, Milton, 238, 291, 646, 679
    Fisher's influence on, 644
    monetarist model and, 646–647, 647f, 648t
    rules vs. discretion and, 651
Friendster, 372
Frisbees, market for, 87–88, 88f
Frontier Airlines, 271
Full aggregate expenditures model, 519–523
    government spending and taxes in, 519–521, 519f
    net exports in, 521, 522f
    recessionary and inflationary gaps and, 522
Full employment, 468
Functional finance, 573

Functional income distribution, 398, 399t
Future, overvaluing present relative to, 150

G
Gabon, economic growth of, 687
Gains from trade, 45–46, 45t, 46t, 698–702
    absolute and comparative advantage and, 699–700, 699f, 700t
    consumer and producer surplus and, 89–93
    practical constraints on trade and, 700–702
Game tables, 263–264, 264f
Game theory, 261–273
    applications of, 267–273
    basic game setup and assumptions and, 262
    chicken games and, 271–272, 272f
    leadership games and, 271
    Nash equilibrium and, 67, 261, 262
    repeated games and, 270–271
    sequential-move games and, 263, 263f
    simultaneous-move games and, 263–265, 264f
    simultaneous- vs. sequential-move games and, 262–263
Gaming apps market, 59–60, 60f, 64, 69–70, 70f
Gap, 254
GarageBand, 385
Gasoline
    price of, 106, 126
    taxes on, 126
GDP. *See* Gross domestic product (GDP)
GDP deflator, 456, 456f
General Motors, 673
The General Theory of Employment, Interest and Money (Keynes), 502, 513, 546
Germany
    in Eurozone, 656–657, 658
    hyperinflation in, 458–459
    innovation in, 332
    role in European growth and stability, 688
    saving rate in, 517
G.I. Bill, 493
Gibraltar, Barbary macaques in, 350
Gini coefficient, 402, 402f, 412
Global climate change. *See* Climate change
Global economy. *See also* International trade
    measuring imports and exports in, 702
Globalization
    containerization and, 210
    economic growth and, 687
    innovation and, 332–333
Gmail, 220
GNP. *See* Gross national product (GNP)
Godwin, William, 490
Gold standard, 735
Goods. *See also* Product(s)
    complementary, 62
    inferior, 61, 117–118
    luxury, 117
    net exports of, in GDP, 436
    network. *See* Network goods
    normal, 61, 117
    private, 347, 348t
    public. *See* Public goods
    related, prices of, demand and, 61–62
    substitute, 62
Google
    brand name of, 254
    Facebook and, 231, 261
    services offered by, 220, 387
    startup of, 325, 378
Gordon, Robert, 495
Gould, Jay, 239
Gould, Stephen Jay, 196

Government
    financing of, 569–574
    as promoter of free and competitive markets,
        494–496
    role in promoting economic growth,
        492–496
Government budget constraints, 573
Government failure, 353
Government franchises, market power and, 223
Government spending, 436, 436f
    aggregate demand and, 535
    in aggregate expenditures model, 519, 519f
    discretionary, 558
    discretionary fiscal policy and, 559, 560f
    mandatory, 558
    stimulus, following Great Recession, 546,
        556, 564, 568, 673
GPDI. See Gross private domestic
        investment (GPDI)
Graphs, 20–23
    bar charts, 22, 22f
    ceteris paribus assumptions and, 26–27
    information conveyed by, 22–23, 23f
    linear relationships and, 24, 25f
    models and, 23–24, 23f
    nonlinear relationships and, 25–26, 25f
    pie charts, 21, 225
    reading, 23
    scatter plots, 20, 21f
    shifts in curves and, 27–28, 28f
    of simple linear equations, 27, 27f
    time series, 20, 21f
Gratz v. Bollinger, 295
Gray, Boyden, 359
Great Depression
    consumption decline and, 505
    government role in economic stabilization
        and, 668
    Keynes on, 513, 523
    macroeconomic equilibrium and, 543, 543f
    spread of, 735
    unemployment during, 460–461, 461f
    view of government's role and, 546
Great Recession, 668, 670–674
    cause of, 424
    consequences of, 424
    consumption decline and, 505
    effects of, 673
    Federal Reserve System and, 655–656
    housing bubble and, 670–672
    macroeconomic policy response to, 672–673
    spending measures implemented during, 522
    stimulus spending and. See Stimulus package
    unemployment during, 461
Greece
    in Eurozone, 656, 658
    financial crisis in, 657
    public debt of, 574–575
Greenhouse gases, 360–361, 361f
Greenspan, Alan, 653, 679
Grim trigger, 270
Gross domestic product (GDP), 433–443
    circular flow diagram and, 433–434
    comparing across countries, 440
    environmental quality and, 440–441
    expenditures (spending) approach to,
        435–437
    happiness and, 441
    income approach to, 437–439, 438t
    nonmarket activities and informal economy
        and, 442
    per capita, population and, 440
    real. See Real GDP
Gross national product (GNP), 434

Gross private domestic investment (GPDI),
        435–436, 435t, 508
Grutter v. Bollinger, 295
Gucci, 196

H
Half.com, 56
Happiness, GDP and, 441
Hardin, Garrett, 349n
Hart-Scott-Rodino Act of 1976, 241
Health care, as public good, 351–353
Herd immunity, 352
Herfindahl-Hirschman index (HHI), 240–241
Hoffa, Jimmy, 298
Holdouts, 272
Hollister, 256
Hollywood, California, 317
Home Depot, 263–265, 267
Honda, 117, 702
Honduras, GDP per capita of, 481
Hong Kong Disneyland, 317
Horizontal summation, 60
Hospitality industry, castles converted into
        hotels and, 186
Household debt, consumption and saving
        and, 508
Housing bubble, 670–672
Housing market, in United States, 668, 670–672
HP Mini netbook, 380
Human capital, 326–331
    education and earnings and, 326, 327f
    education as investment and, 327–328, 327f
    equilibrium levels of, 328–329, 329f
    implications of human capital theory and,
        329–330
    income inequality and, 405, 405t
    increasing, economic growth and, 40
    investment in, economic growth and, 488–489
    on-the-job training and, 331
    public education and financial aid and, 493
    as screening or signaling device, 330
Human Development Index, 414
Hyperinflation, 458–459
    money as store of value and, 589

I
IBM (International Business Machines), 254
Ice caps, 340
Immunizations, 352
iMovie, 385
Imperfect price discrimination, 232,
        234–235, 235f
Implementation lags
    fiscal policy and, 568
    monetary policy and, 629
Implicit costs, 172–173
Imports, 698. See also International trade
    current account and, 724
    measuring, 702
Incentives, 5, 10–11
Incidence of taxation, 123
Income. See also Income distribution; Income
        inequality; Poverty; Wage(s)
    changes to, budget line and, 140, 140f
    current account and, 725
    definition of, 398
    demand and, 61, 61f
    domestic, changes in, current account
        and, 731
    expectations about, demand and, 62
    life cycle effects and, 398
    national, 439 . See also Gross domestic
        product (GDP); National income and
        product accounts (NIPA)

nonwage, labor supply changes and, 284
portion spent, price elasticity of demand
        and, 111
of proprietors, in GDP, 438
ratio to poverty, 411
rental, in GDP, 438
of richest 1%, 407
shifts in supply of loanable funds and, 594
Income approach to GDP, 437–439, 438t
Income deficit, 411
Income distribution, 398–407
    functional, 398, 399t
    Gini coefficient and, 402, 402f
    impact of redistribution and, 402–404,
        403f, 403t
    inequality of, causes of, 404–407, 406t
    Lorenz curves and, 400–401, 401f
    personal or family, 399–400, 400t
Income effect
    aggregate demand curve and, 532
    indifference curves and, 163–164, 164f
    labor supply and, 282–283, 283f
Income elasticity of demand (E_y), 117–118
Income inequality. See also Income distribution;
        Poverty
    causes of, 404–407, 406t
    reducing, 413–414
Income redistribution, impact of, 402–404,
        403f, 403t
Increasing cost industries, 211, 211f
Increasing marginal returns, 177
Incremental costs, 179
Index of Economic Freedom, 494
India
    demand for energy in, 453
    economic growth of, 478, 480, 483, 687
    fast food restaurants in, 256
    GDP of, 439
    public debt of, 574, 575
    purchasing power parity and, 727
    saving rate in, 517
Indifference curve(s), 138
    consumer preferences and, 159–161, 159f
    demand curve derivation and,
        162–163, 162f
    income and substitution effects and, 163–
        164, 164f
    optimal consumer choice and, 161, 161f
    properties of, 160
Indifference curve analysis, 138, 152, 159–164
Indifference maps, 160–161, 160f
Individual labor supply, 282–283
Individual mandate, 352
Individual retirement arrangements (IRAs),
        603–604
Industrial agglomeration, 317
Industrial Revolution, beginnings of, 34
Industrial unions, 296
Industries
    airline, 241, 267, 284
    automobile, 168, 707
    bottled water, 54
    concentration of, 240–241, 240t
    constant cost, 211, 211f
    cruise ship, offshoring in, 172
    decreasing cost, 211, 211f
    hospitality, castles converted into
        hotels and, 186
    increasing cost, 211, 211f
    semiconductor, 211
    telecommunications, 30
    textile, 704
    utility, 223
Industry bailouts, 673

Industry standards, 386
   network compatibility and, 387
Industry supply, long-run, 210–211, 211f
Inelastic demand, 109–110, 110f
   total revenue and, 114, 115f
Inelastic supply, 119, 120f
Infant industry argument against free trade, 709
Inferior goods, 61, 117–118
Inflation, 450, 452–460, 453t
   adjusting for, 456–457
   causes of, 453
   changes in rates of, current account and, 731
   consequences of, 457–458
   cost-push, 544, 545f, 546, 547f
   counterfeit money and, 459
   debt's effect on, 686–687
   demand-pull, 544–545, 544f, 545f
   extremely high, 458–459
   future debt obligations and, 685
   low, goal of, 13
   measurement of, 453–456
   money as store of value and, 589
   Phillips curves and. See Phillips curves
Inflation overstating, 457
Inflation targeting, 651
Inflationary expectations
   Phillips curves and, 676–677, 678f
   short-run aggregate supply and, 540
Inflationary gaps, 522
Inflationary spirals, 561–562
Infomercials, 227
Informal economy, 442
Information, asymmetric, market failure and, 92–93
Information costs, reduction by financial institutions, 596
Information lag
   fiscal policy and, 568
   monetary policy and, 628
Infrastructure
   government as contributor to, 492
   spending on, fiscal policy and, 564
Initial public offerings (IPOs), 324
Injections, 513, 514–515, 514f, 515f
Innovation
   globalization and, 332–333
   monopolies and, 230
Input prices
   changes in, labor demand changes and, 287–288
   short-run aggregate supply and, 539
Insider-outsider theory, 292
Institutions, wealth of nations and, 14
Integrated Environmental and Economic Satellite Accounts, 441
Intellectual property, 241–242, 254
Intellectual property rights, 332
Interconnection
   efficiency in network industries and, 387
   promoting network competition with, 386–387
Interest, 33
   compounding of, 482, 600, 600t
   net, in GDP, 438
Interest rates
   aggregate demand and, 533
   bond prices and, 597–598
   changes in, capital account and, 731–732
   consumption and saving and, 505
   discount rate, 627
   federal funds rate. See Federal funds rate; Federal funds rate target
   on public debt, 570–571, 572
   reasons for importance of, 641

Internally held debt, 576, 576t
Internal rate of return, 320
Internal Revenue Service (IRS), 173
International Brotherhood of Teamsters, 298
International Monetary Fund, 735
International trade, 695–716
   foreign trade zones and, 707
   free trade and. See Free trade
   gains from trade and. See Gains from trade
   practical constraints on, 700–702
   terms of trade and. See Terms of trade
   of United States, 696, 698f
Internet, markets and, 56
Intertemporal pricing, 384, 385t
Introduction to the Principles of Morals (Bentham), 141
Investment(s)
   aggregate demand and, 534–535
   aggregate expenditures model and, 508–511, 509f
   autonomous, 510
   crowding out of, 576–577
   demand for, 509–510
   expanding, 565–566
   present value approach to, 319–320
   rate of return approach to, 320–321
   return on, stocks and, 598–599
Investment in human capital, 326
   economic growth and, 488–489
Investment tax credits, shifts in demand for loanable funds and, 594
Invisible hand, 12, 84, 89, 196
IPOs. See Initial public offerings (IPOs)
IRAs. See Individual retirement arrangements (IRAs)
Ireland
   castles converted into hotels in, 186
   financial crisis in, 657
Iron, production of, 34
IRS. See Internal Revenue Service (IRS)
Israel, fast food restaurants in, 256
Italy
   financial crisis in, 658
   public debt of, 574–575
iTunes, 385
Ivory Coast, economic growth of, 480

J
Japan
   economic growth of, 687
   fast food restaurants in, 256
   innovation in, 332
   island building by, 41
   lucky and unlucky numbers in, 152
   productivity in, 488
   public debt of, 574, 575
   quotas on automobiles produced in, 707
   saving rate in, 517
   U.S. debt held by, 576
Jimenez, Luis, 280
Job crowding hypothesis, 291–292
Jobless recoveries, 428, 470–471, 683–685, 683f, 684f
Jobs. See Employment
Jobs, Steve, 171, 321, 490
Johnson, Lyndon, 294

K
Kay, John, 415n
Kazakhstan, economic growth of, 491
Kennedy, John F., 91
   tax cut under, 558–559, 564
Kershaw, Clayton, 280

Keynes, John Maynard, 71n, 424, 426, 505n
   on aggregate spending, 502
   classical perspective challenged by, 504
   development of model by, 530
   on expectations, 679
   Fisher's influence on, 644
   The General Theory of Employment, Interest and Money of, 502, 513, 546
   on Great Depression, 513, 523
   Keynesian model and, 424, 504, 646, 648t
Keynesian macroeconomic equilibrium, in simple aggregate expenditures model, 512–514
Keynesian model, 424, 504, 646, 648t. See also Aggregate expenditures; Full aggregate expenditures model; Simple aggregate expenditures model
KFC, 256
Kia Motors, 508, 509
Kinked demand curve, 259–260, 260f
Kleenex, 109
Kleiner Perkins Caufield & Byers, 325
Kokkelenberg, Edward, 432n, 441n, 442n
Korea, lucky and unlucky numbers in, 152
Kuznets, Simon, 432, 433
Kuznets curve, environmental, 711

L
Labor, 33. See also Employment; Unemployment; Wage(s)
   increasing, economic growth and, 40
   marginal physical product of, 285
   monopolistic exploitation of, 307
   monopsonistic exploitation of, 308
   ratio of capital to, economic growth and, 489
Labor demand, 285–290
   competitive labor market equilibrium and, 289, 289f
   elasticity of, 288
   factors changing, 287–288
   marginal revenue product and, 285–287, 286t, 287f
Labor force, 463
   growth of, economic growth and, 488–489
   increasing quality of, economic growth and, 488–489
Labor markets, 279–302
   factors affecting supply of labor and, 283–285
   segmented, 291, 292–294, 293f
Labor supply, 282–285
   factors changing, 283–285
   income effect and, 282–283, 283f
   individual, 282–283
   market labor supply curves and, 283, 284f
   substitution effect and, 282
Labor unions. See Unions
Laffer curve, 565, 565f
Laissez-faire market economies, 32, 94
Land, 33, 316–317, 316f
   economic growth and, 488
   reclamation of, 41
Las Vegas, Nevada, lucky and unlucky numbers in, 152
Law of demand, 58–59
Law of diminishing marginal utility, 143, 144f
Law of diminishing returns, 177
Law of supply, 64
Leadership games, 271
Leading Economic Index (LEI), 429–430
Leakages
   by banks, 619–620
   foreign currency holdings and, 621
   by individuals and businesses, 620

Learning by doing, 185
Legal disputes, Prisoner's Dilemma and, 269
Legislation
    antidiscrimination, 294–295
    antitrust, 238–239, 239t
    to curb corporate offshoring, 172
    on disabilities, 295
    employment, 294
    environmental, 358, 359
    health care, 351, 352, 353
    on mergers, 241
    price gouging, 97
    protecting common property, 349
    restricting trade, 705
    stimulus package and, 673
    on unions, 296, 297
    on veterans, 685
Lehman Brothers, 672
LEI. See Leading Economic Index (LEI)
Leveraging, 671
Levinson, Mark, 210n
Levi's, 702
LG, 704
Lily Ledbetter Fair Pay Act of 2009, 294
Limited liability, 324
Lincoln, Abraham, 575
Linear equations, simple, 27, 27f
Linear relationships, 24, 25f
Linens-N-Things, 268
Linux, 241
Liquidity, 589
Liquidity trap, 646
Live Nation, 236
Living standard, GDP and, 439–443
Loanable funds market, 318, 321, 592–595
    shifts in demand and, 594
    shifts in supply and, 593–594
    supply and demand in, 592–593, 592f
Lock-in strategies, 383
London, England, traffic congestion in, 92
Long run, 174, 199
    perfect competition in, 206–212
    price elasticity of supply in, 121–122
Long-run aggregate supply (LRAS) curve,
        537–538, 537f, 643
    determinants of, 538
Long-run average total cost (LRATC) curve, 184,
        184f, 186
    economies of scale and, 223, 223f
    price and output under monopolistic
        competition and, 254, 255f
Long-run industry supply, 210–211, 211f
Long-run macroeconomic equilibrium, 541, 541f
Long-run Phillips curve, 677
Long-run production costs, 183–186, 184f
    average total, 184, 184f
    economies and diseconomies of scale and,
        184–185, 185f
    economies of scope and, 185
    technology and, 186
Lorenz curves, 400–401, 401f
Los Alamos National Laboratory, 493
Losses
    deadweight, 90, 228–230, 229f
    economic, 173
    short-run, adjusting to, in perfect
        competition, 206–208, 207f, 208f
Loss leaders, 118
Loss minimization, 203–205, 204f
Lowe's, 263–265, 267
LRAS. See Long-run aggregate supply
        (LRAS) curve
LRATC. See Long-run average total cost
        (LRATC) curve

Lucas, Robert E., 679, 680
Lump-sum taxes, 123
Luxembourg, in Eurozone, 658
Luxuries, price elasticity of demand and, 111
Luxury goods, 117
Lynn, Michael, 151n

M
Maastricht Treaty, 656
Mac computers, 387
Macroeconomic equilibrium, 541–547, 541f
    cost-push inflation and, 545–547, 545f, 547f
    demand-pull inflation and, 544–545,
        544f, 545f
    Great Depression and, 543, 543f
    long-run, 541, 541f
    short-run, 541, 541f
    in simple aggregate expenditures model,
        512–514
    spending multiplier and, 542–543, 542f
Macroeconomic policy, 667–690. See also Fiscal
        policy; Monetary policy
    future issues faced by, 682–688
    globalization and obstacles to economic
        growth and, 687
    Great Recession and, 670–674
    jobless recoveries and, 683–685, 683f, 684f
    Phillips curves and rational expectations
        and, 674–682, 675f
    rising debt and future debt obligation and,
        685–687
Macroeconomics, 5
Macroeconomy, markets and institutions in,
        426, 426f
Madawaska, Maine, paper mill in, 502
Major League Baseball, 280
Major League Baseball Players Association, 282
Malthus, Thomas, 43, 490
Mandatory spending, 558
"Manhattan Project," 493
Marginal analysis, 11
Marginal cost(s), 180, 180t, 182f, 183
    network goods and, 379
Marginal cost pricing rule, 237
Marginal efficiency of capital, 320
Marginal factor cost (MFC), 307–308, 308f
Marginally attached workers, 465
Marginal physical product of labor (MPP_L), 285
Marginal private cost (MPC) of production,
        343, 344f
Marginal product, 177
Marginal productivity, 177
Marginal propensity to consume (MPC),
        506–508, 507f
    macroeconomic equilibrium and, 542
Marginal propensity to save (MPS),
        506–508, 507f
    macroeconomic equilibrium and, 542
Marginal returns, diminishing and increasing, 177
Marginal revenue (MR)
    monopoly pricing and output decisions and,
        224–225, 224f
    in perfect competition, 199–200
Marginal revenue product (MRP_L), 285–287,
        286t, 287f, 317
Marginal social cost (MSC) of production,
        343–344, 344f
Marginal utility, 142, 142t
    diminishing, law of, 143, 144f
Marginal utility analysis, 141–148
    demand curve derivation and, 145–146,
        146t, 147f
    limitations of, 146–147
    preferences and, 141–145

Market(s), 56–57
    barriers to entry and, 196, 222–224
    competitive, government as promoter of, 494
    contestable, 241
    efficiency of, 12–13
    for foreign exchange. See Foreign exchange
        markets
    for Frisbees, 87–88, 88f
    for gaming apps, 59–60, 60f, 64, 69–70, 70f
    labor. See Labor markets
    laissez-faire, 32, 94
    for loanable funds. See Loanable funds
        market
    monopoly, 222–228
    for pet products, 56
    price system and, 57
    product, monopoly power in, 306–307, 306f
    for sushi, 84
    tax effects on, 124, 124f
Marketable permits, 357–358, 358f
Market-based environmental policy, 356,
        357–359
Market cap, 324
Market-clearing price. See Equilibrium price
Market economies, 32
Market equilibrium. See Equilibrium
Market failure, 92–93, 343
Market labor supply curves, 283, 284f
Market period, price elasticity of supply and,
        120–121, 121f
Market power, 222–224
    of firms, short-run aggregate supply and, 540
    measuring, 239–241
    of OPEC, 295
    in product markets, 306–307, 306f
    sources of, 222–224
Market segmentation, to maximize profits,
        383–385, 385f, 385t
Market structure(s), 197, 272–273. See also
        Monopolistic competition; Monopoly;
        Oligopoly; Perfect competition
Market structure analysis, 196–199
Market supply curve, 65, 65f
Marshall, Alfred, 71
Marshall, Howard, 13n, 43, 490n
Martin, William McChesney, 651–652, 652f
Marx, Karl, 309, 513
Massive open online courses (MOOCs), 330
Maturity date of a bond, 322
Maximin principle, 415
McDonald's, 170, 220, 250, 256
Measles, 352
Medicaid, 402
    mandatory spending for, 558
Medicare, 402
    mandatory spending for, 558
    national debt and, 577
    rising future debt obligations and, 685
Medium of exchange, money as, 588–589
Metcalfe's law, 381
Mexico
    currency of, 736
    GDP per capita of, 481
    NAFTA and, 46, 702, 711
    oil production in, 259
MFC. See Marginal factor cost (MFC)
Michael, Robert T., 408n
Micklethwait, 171n
Microeconomics, 5
Microloans, 612, 613
Microsoft, 241, 254
Microsoft Excel, 387
Midpoint method, for computing elasticity,
        112–113

Mill, John Stuart, 43
Millward Brown, 254
Misallocation of resources, 95
Mitchell, Wesley, 427
Model(s)
    aggregate expenditures. *See* Full aggregate
        expenditures model; Simple aggregate
        expenditures model
    classical. *See* Classical theory
    graphs and, 23–24, 23f
    Keynesian, 106, 186, 328, 330t
    monetarist, 646–647, 647f, 648, 648t
Model building, 6
Monday Night Football (TV Show), 388
Monetarist model, 646–647, 647f, 648t
A Monetary History of the United States
        (Friedman), 646
Monetary policy, 637–662
    accommodative, 650
    contractionary, 642, 643f
    economic shocks and, 648–650
    effectiveness of, 647–648, 648t
    Eurozone crisis and European Central Bank
        and, 656–660
    examples of, 640–641
    expansionary, 641–642, 642f
    federal funds target and Taylor rule and,
        651–652, 652f
    under fixed exchange rates, 736–737, 736f
    under flexible exchange rates, 737, 738t, 739
    Great Recession and, 641, 655–656
    long-run effects of, 643–645, 645f
    in open economies, 734–739
    policy tools of, 653
    with regional differences in economic
        performance, 658
    restrictive, 650
    rules vs. discretion and, 651
    short-run effects of, 643, 645–647, 650
    timing lags and, 628–629
    transparency and Federal Reserve System
        and, 653–654
    twin goals of, 640
Monetary rule, 651
Monetized debt, 686–687
Money, 588–591
    commodity, 588
    counterfeit, 459, 590
    creation by banks, 614–618
    easy, 650
    fiat, 588
    functions of, 588–589
    leakages and, 619–621
    plastic, in Australia, 590
    quantity theory of, 644–645, 645f
    supply of. *See* Money supply
    tight, 650
Money illusion, 645–646
Money multiplier, 619
Money supply, 589–591
    M1, 590, 591
    M2, 590, 591
Monopolistic competition, 197, 252–257
    perfect competition compared with, 256
    price and output under, 254, 255f
    product differentiation and firm's demand
        curve and, 252–253, 253f
Monopolistic exploitation of labor, 307
Monopoly, 197, 219–244
    antitrust policy and. *See* Antitrust policy
    benefits vs. costs of, 231
    competition compared with, 228–232
    contestable markets and, 241
    innovation and, 230

    marginal revenue for, 224–225, 224f
    market power and. *See* Market power
    natural, 223
    price discrimination under, 232–236
    pricing and output decisions in, 224–227
    regulation of, 236–238, 237f
    rent seeking and, 230
Monopoly power. *See* Market power
Monopsonistic exploitation of labor, 308
Monopsony, 306, 307–309, 307f, 308f
Monopsony power, 306
MOOCs. *See* Massive open online
        courses (MOOCs)
Moody's, 322
Mortgages, subprime, 670–672
MPC. *See* Marginal private cost (MPC) of
        production; Marginal propensity to
        consume (MPC)
MPP_L. *See* Marginal physical product of
        labor (MPP_L)
MPS. *See* Marginal propensity to save (MPS)
MR. *See* Marginal revenue (*MR*)
MRP_L. *See* Marginal revenue product (MRP_L)
MSC. *See* Marginal social cost (MSC) of
        production
Multinational companies, foreign trade zones
        and, 707
Multiplier
    balanced budget, 520–521
    injections and withdrawals and, 514–515,
        514f, 515f
    money, 619
    spending, macroeconomic equilibrium and,
        542–543, 542f
Mutual interdependence, 257
Myanmar
    economic growth of, 480
    increase in aggregate demand and, 536
Myspace, 372

N
NAFTA. *See* North American Free Trade
        Agreement (NAFTA)
NAIRU. *See* Nonaccelerating inflation rate of
        unemployment (NAIRU)
Nalebuff, Barry, 266
NASA. *See* National Aeronautics and Space
        Administration (NASA)
Nasar, Sylvia, 261
Nash, John, 261, 262
Nash equilibrium, 261, 262, 265–267, 266f, 272
National Activity Index, 429, 429f
National Aeronautics and Space Administration
        (NASA), 493
National Bureau of Economic Research
        (NBER), dating of business cycles by,
        428–429, 431
National debt, 570
National defense argument, against free
        trade, 710
National Federation of Coffee Growers, 209
National Football League (NFL), 223
National income, 439. *See also* Gross domestic
        product (GDP); National income and
        product accounts (NIPA)
National income and product accounts (NIPA),
        432–439, 442–443
    circular flow diagram and, 433–434, 433f
    GDP and. *See* Gross domestic product (GDP)
National Institutes of Health, 493, 565–566
National Labor Relations Act (NLRA), 296, 297
National Labor Relations Board (NLRB), 296
National Oceanic and Atmospheric
        Administration (NOAA), 493

National Science Foundation (NSF), 493
National Venture Capital Association
        (NVCA), 325
Natural monopolies, 223, 237
    regulation of, 237–238, 237f
Natural rate of unemployment, 468–469
Natural resources, 33
    economic growth and, 488
The Nature of Capital and Income (Fisher), 644
NBA, 222
NBER. *See* National Bureau of Economic
        Research (NBER)
Necessities, 111
Negative externalities, 342, 343–344, 344f
Negative returns, 175
Nepal, Sherpas in, 290
Net debt. *See* Public debt
Net exports
    aggregate demand and, 535
    in aggregate expenditures model, 521, 522f
    in GDP, 436
Net interest, in GDP, 438
Net present value (NPV), 320
Netscape, 372
Network(s), 374
Network compatibility, industry standards
        and, 387
Network demand curve, 376–378
    fixed capacity network goods and,
        376–377, 377f
    for full network, 377–378, 378f
    network demand curve pricing examples
        and, 378
Network effects, 374
Network externalities, 374
Network goods, 371–391
    competition and pricing strategies for,
        383–385
    demand curve for, 376–379
    demand curve pricing examples for. *See*
        Network demand curve
    market equilibrium for, 379–382
    network effects and, 374, 375f, 376
    regulation of, 386–388
    types of, 374
New York City
    focal points in, 266
    rent controls in, 94
    taxi medallions in, 230
New York Stock Exchange, 56
NFL. *See* National Football League (NFL)
NHL, 272
Nicaragua, GDP per capita of, 481
Nike, 254
Nintendo Wii, 382
NIPA. *See* National income and product
        accounts (NIPA)
NLRA. *See* National Labor Relations Act
        (NLRA)
NLRB. *See* National Labor Relations Board
        (NLRB)
NOAA. *See* National Oceanic and Atmospheric
        Administration (NOAA)
Nominal exchange rate, 726, 726t
Nominal values, real values vs., 457
Nonaccelerating inflation rate of unemployment
        (NAIRU), 469–470, 469f
Nonexcludability, of public goods, 347, 348t
Nonlinear relationships, 25–26, 25f
Nonmoney perks, labor supply changes
        and, 284
Nonrivalry, of public goods, 347, 348t
Nordhaus, William, 432n, 441n, 442n
Normal goods, 61, 117

Normal profits, 173
    in perfect competition, 202–203, 203f
Normative questions, 7
Norris-LaGuardia Act of 1932, 296
North American Free Trade Agreement
        (NAFTA), 46, 702, 711
Norway
    gasoline tax in, 126
    Gini coefficient in, 412
    purchasing power parity and, 727
Nozick, Robert, 415–416
NPV. *See* Net present value (NPV)
NSF. *See* National Science Foundation (NSF)
Numbered bank accounts, 621
NVCA. *See* National Venture Capital
        Association (NVCA)

O

Obama, Barack, 261, 522
    stimulus package under, 522, 546, 556, 564,
        568, 673
Ocean thermal energy conversion, 41
OECD. *See* Organisation for Economic Co-
        operation and Development (OECD)
Office Depot, 267
Offshoring, 172
Oil prices, 106
    employment and, 466
    inflation and, 453
    OPEC's power to raise, 540
Oil production, OPEC's share of, 259
Oligopoly, 197, 257–260
    cartels and, 258–259, 258f
    definition of, 257
    kinked demand curve model and stability of,
        259–260, 260f
Olympic Games, 586
Online education, 330
On-the-job training, 331
OPEC. *See* Organization of Petroleum Exporting
        Countries (OPEC)
Open economies, 698
    monetary and fiscal policy in, 734–739
Open market operations, 627
Open shops, 297
Operating costs, investment demand and, 510
Opportunity costs, 9
    comparative advantage and, 43–45, 44t,
        699–700, 699f, 700t
    production possibilities frontier and, 36–38,
        37f, 43–44, 44f, 699, 699f
Organisation for Economic Co-operation and
        Development (OECD), 414
Organization of Petroleum Exporting Countries
        (OPEC), 258, 259
    market power of, 540
    pegging of currencies by, 735
Origin of Species (Darwin), 196
Orshansky, Mollie, 408
Ostrom, Elinor, 362
Output
    under monopolistic competition, 254–255, 255f
    monopoly pricing and output decisions and,
        224–227
    profit-maximizing, in perfect competition,
        200–201, 200f
Outsourcing. *See* Offshoring
Overconfidence, 149–150
Overhead, 178, 179

P

Page, Larry, 325
Panama, U.S. dollar as currency of, 638, 658,
        659, 736, 738

Paradox of thrift, 516–517, 516f
Parker, Trey, 224
Partnerships, 171
Passell, Peter, 292n, 344n
PATCO, 296
Patents, market power and, 224
Patrinos, H., 328n
Peak(s), in business cycle, 427
Peak-load pricing, 384–385, 385f
Ped Egg, 227
Pegging, of exchange rates, 735–736
Pell Grants, 493
Pensions, 602–603
    unions and, 297
PepsiCo, 363
Perfect competition, 197–212
    definition of, 197–198, 198f
    long-run adjustments in, 206–212
    marginal revenue, 199–200
    monopolistic competition compared with, 256
    public interest and, 208, 209f, 210
    short-run decisions in, 199–206
Perfectly elastic demand curve, 109, 110f
Perfect price discrimination, 232, 233, 233f
Permanent income hypothesis, 647
Personal consumption expenditures, 435
Personal distribution of income, 399–400, 400t
Pet-related products market, 56
Phillips, A. W., 674
Phillips curves, 674–682, 675f
    accelerating inflation and, 678
    inflationary expectations and, 676–677, 678f
    long-run, 677
    productivity, prices, and wages, 675–676,
        676f, 677f
    rational expectations and, 679–681, 680f
    returning inflation to normal levels and, 679
Physical capital, 317–318, 318f
    government as contributor to, 492
Physical networks, 374
Pie charts, 21, 225
Piger, Jeremy, 428n
Pigou, Arthur, 357
Pigouvian taxes, 357
Planned economies, 32
Plant shutdown, 203–205, 204f
Plaza Hotel, 725
Point-of-Purchase Survey, 455
Political campaigns, Prisoner's Dilemma
        and, 269
Political Justice (Godwin), 490
Pollution
    climate change and, 360–361, 361f
    environmental policy and. *See*
        Environmental policy
    as government failure, 353
    as negative externality, 342, 343–344, 344f
    socially efficient levels of, 354–355, 355f
Poole, William, 653
Portugal
    in Eurozone, 658
    financial crisis in, 657
Positive externalities, 342–343, 346, 346f
Positive questions, 7
Posner, Richard A., 242
Poverty, 408–417
    causes of, 413
    depth of, 410–411
    eliminating, 413–416
    extreme, economic growth and, 483
    incidence of, 409–410, 409f, 410f, 411t
    measurement of, 408–409, 409t, 411–413
    ratio of income to, 411
    in South Africa, 412

Poverty rate, 409–410, 410f, 411t
Poverty thresholds, 408–409, 409t, 414
PPF. *See* Production possibilities frontier (PPF)
PPI. *See* Producer price index (PPI)
PPP. *See* Purchasing power parity (PPP)
Preference(s)
    demand and, 61
    indifference curves and, 159–161, 159f
    utility and, 142–145
Preference maps, 160–161, 160f
Present, overvaluing relative to the future, 150
Present value, 319–320
Pressman, Steven, 43
Price(s)
    of assets, shifts in supply of loanable funds
        and, 594
    below equilibrium, 90–91, 91f
    of bonds, interest rates and, 597–598
    changes to, budget line and, 139–140, 139f
    consumer. *See* Consumer price index (CPI)
    control by individual firms, 196
    equilibrium (market-clearing), 69
    exceeding equilibrium, 89–90, 90f
    expectations about, demand and, 62
    expectations about, supply and, 66–67
    of exports, aggregate demand and, 533
    extent of control of firms overprices, 196
    of factors of production, changes in, labor
        demand and, 287–288
    of gasoline, 106, 126
    of inputs. *See* Input prices
    under monopolistic competition,
        254–255, 255f
    of oil. *See* Oil prices
    Phillips curves and, 675–676, 676f, 677f
    of related commodities, supply and, 66
    of related goods, demand and, 61–62
    sticky, 646
Price cap(s), 238
Price cap regulation, 238
Price ceilings, 94–96, 94f
Price discrimination, 232–236
    perfect (first-degree), 232, 233, 233f
    second-degree, 232, 233–234, 234f
    third-degree (imperfect), 232, 234–235, 235f
Price elasticity of demand (E_d), 108–113
    as absolute value, 108–109
    computing, 112–113, 112f
    determinants of, 110–111
    measuring with percentages, 109
    selected estimates of, 111, 111t
Price elasticity of supply (E_s), 119–122, 120f
    time and, 120–122
Price floors, 96–98, 96f
Price gouging laws, 97
Price level, 454
Price makers, 222. *See also* Monopoly
Price system, 57
Price takers, 198. *See also* Perfect competition
Pricing. *See also* Price(s)
    average cost pricing rule and, 237–238
    of electricity, 388
    intertemporal, 384, 385t
    marginal cost pricing rule and, 237
    monopoly pricing and output decisions and,
        224–227
    network demand curve, examples of, 378
    of network goods, 383–385
    peak-load, 384–385, 385f
PrimeTime (TV show), 266
Principles of Economics (Marshall), 71
Prisoner's Dilemma, 267–270, 268f
    classic, 268–269, 269f
    resolving, 269–270

Private equity, 324–325
Private Equity Growth Capital Council, 325
Private goods, 347, 348t
"The Problem of Social Cost" (Coase), 344, 345
Procter & Gamble, 185, 186
Producer(s), burden of tax on, elasticity and, 125, 126f, 127–128
Producer price index (PPI), 454, 455–456
Producer surplus, 86, 88
Product(s). *See also* Goods
    average, 177
    expectations about availability of, demand and, 62
    marginal, 177
    nature of, 196
    proportion of income spent on, price elasticity of demand and, 111
    total, 175, 176f, 176t
Product differentiation, under monopolistic competition, 252–253, 253f
Production
    average product and, 177
    costs of. *See* Production costs
    efficiency and, 6, 33–35, 34f
    increasing and diminishing marginal returns and, 177
    marginal product and, 177
    resources and, 33
    in short run, 175–178
    total product and, 175, 176f, 176t
Production costs, 178–186
    labor's share of, elasticity of demand for labor and, 288
    long-run. *See* Long-run production costs
    private, marginal, 343, 344f
    short-run. *See* Short-run production costs
    social, marginal, 343–344, 344f
Production efficiency, 6, 33–35, 34f
Production function, economic growth and, 486–487
Production possibilities frontier (PPF), 35–38, 36f
    absolute and comparative advantage and, 43, 44f
    opportunity costs and, 36–38, 37f, 43–44, 44f, 699, 699f
Production technology, supply and, 65–66, 66f
Productive efficiency, in competitive markets, 208
Productivity
    changes in, labor demand changes and, 287
    economic growth and, 488–492
    marginal, 177
    Phillips curves and, 675–676, 676f, 677f
    short-run aggregate supply and, 539–540, 539f
    total factor, 490–491
Profit(s), 33, 171–172
    accounting, 173
    corporate, in GDP, 438
    economic. *See* Economic profits
    normal. *See* Normal profits
    short-run, adjusting to, in perfect competition, 206–208, 207f, 208f
Profit maximization
    market segmentation for, 383–385, 385f, 385t
    steps to, 201–202, 202f, 225, 226f, 227
Profit-maximizing output, in perfect competition, 200–201, 200f
Profit-maximizing rule, 201
Progressive taxes, 123, 123t
Property rights, economic growth and, 493–494
Proprietors' income, in GDP, 438
Psacharopoulos, G., 328n

Public choice theory, 569
Public confidence, policy response to financial crisis and, 672–673
Public debt, 570–571, 571f, 574–578, 574f
    crowding out of consumption and investment by, 576–577
    financing of, 573
    future problems due to, 577
    interest rates on, 570–571, 572
    portion held by foreigners, 575–576, 576t
    size of, 575
Public goods, 347–353
    common property resources as, 349–351, 350f
    demand for, 348–349, 348f
    health care as, 351–353
    market failure and, 93
    optimal provision of, 349
Public interest, competition and, 208, 209f, 210
Public policy. *See* Antitrust policy; Environmental policy; Legislation; Regulation
Public utilities, regulation of, 238
Puerto Rico, U.S. dollar as currency of, 658
The Purchasing Power of Money (Fisher), 644
Purchasing power parity (PPP), 727–728, 727t
    GDP adjusted by, 440

Q
Qatar, FIFA World Cup in, 566
QE. *See* Quantitative easing (QE)
Quantitative easing (QE), 629, 650
Quantity, equilibrium, 69
Quantity demanded, changes in, changes in demand and, 62–63, 63f
Quantity theory of money, 644–645, 645f
Quilted Northern, 109
Quotas, import, 706–708, 706f

R
Race
    affirmative action programs and, 294–295
    poverty rates and, 410, 410f, 411t
Rate of return, internal, 320
Rate of return regulation, 238
Rational expectations, 679–681, 680f
Ratio of income to poverty, 411
Rawls, John, 415
RCA, 704
Reagan, Ronald, 646
    tax cut under, 558–559
Real, 385
Real exchange rate, 726–727
Real GDP, 440, 480–481, 481t
    per capita, 480
Real values, nominal values vs., 457
Rebel Without a Cause (film), 272
Recession(s), 427
    double-dip, 428
    jobless recoveries from, 428, 470–471, 683–685, 683f, 684f
    length of, saving rate and, 517
    of 2007–2009. *See* Great Recession
    unemployment during, 428
Recessionary gaps, 522
Recognition lags
    fiscal policy and, 568
    monetary policy and, 628
Reddy, Sundeep, 513
Regressive taxes, 123, 123t, 127
Regulation(s)
    of inputs, short-run aggregate supply and, 540
    of natural monopolies, 237–238, 237f

of network goods, 386–388
of public utilities, 238
rate of return (price cap), 238
reducing, 566
shifts in demand for loanable funds and, 594
Rent, 33, 316
Rental income, in GDP, 438
Rent controls, 94
Rent seeking, 230
Repeated games, 270–271
Reserve(s)
    excess, 616
    money multiplier and, 619
    requirements for, 616–617, 626
    reserve ratio and, 616
Reserve ratios, 616
Reserve requirements, 616–617, 626
Resources
    common property, 349–351, 350f
    costs of, supply and, 66
    expanding, economic growth and, 39–40
    limited, 8–9
    misallocation of, 95
    natural. *See* Natural resources
    production and, 33
    scarcity of, 14
    user-managed, 362
Restrictive monetary policy, 650
Retail stores, 211
Return(s)
    internal rate of, 320
    marginal, increasing and diminishing, 177
Return on investment (ROI), 596
    tradeoff between risk and, 598
Revenue. *See* Marginal revenue (MR); Total revenue (TR)
Ricardo, David, 43
Right-to-work laws, 297
The Rise and Fall of American Growth (Gordon), 495
Risk
    assessment of, asset allocation and, 601
    assessment of, choosing assets to invest in and, 602
    tradeoff between return and, 598
Robber barons, 239
Rockefeller, John D., 239
ROI. *See* Return on investment (ROI)
Roosevelt, Franklin D., 513, 523
Ross, Ian, 13n
Roth IRAs, 604
Royal Caribbean, 268
Rule of 70, 482–483, 482t
Russia
    economic growth of, 478, 480
    oil production in, 259
    public debt of, 574, 575
Rwanda, drones in, 375

S
Safari, 385
Sales taxes, 127
Sam's Club, 233
Samsung, 254, 704
Samuel, Graeme, 258
Samuelson, Paul A., 91, 238
Sandia National Laboratories, 493
Saudi Arabia, fuel prices in, 126
Saving
    aggregate expenditures model and, 504–508, 505f, 506t
    average propensity to save and, 506, 506t
    determinants of, 508
    employer-based programs for, 601–602

Saving (*continued*)
  financial system and, 595–596
  incentives for, shifts in supply of loanable
    funds and, 593
  long-term, stock market crashes and, 603
  marginal propensity to save and, 506–508,
    507f, 542
  rates of, length of recessions and, 517
Scale economies. *See* Economies of scale
Scarcity, 4
Scatter plots, 20, 21f
Schools, financial aid and, 493
Scope economies. *See* Economies of scope
Scott, 109
Screening device, human capital as, 330
Sea-Land, 210
Search engine market, 220
Second-degree price discrimination, 232,
    233–234, 234f
Sega Genesis, 372
Segmented labor markets, 291, 292–294, 293f
Sellers, number of, supply and, 67
Semiconductor industry, 211
Sequential-move analysis, to model repeated
    games, 271, 271f
Sequential-move games, 263, 263f
  simultaneous-move games vs., 262–263
Sequoia Capital, 325
Services, net exports of, in GDP, 436
Shares of stock, 323
Sharper Image, 268
Shaw, George Bernard, 513
Sherman Act, 239t, 241
Sherpas, 290
Shortages, 70
Short run, 174, 199
  adjusting to profits and losses in, in perfect
    competition, 206–208, 207f, 208f
  price elasticity of supply in, 121
  production in, 175–178
Short-run aggregate supply (SRAS) curve,
    538–540, 538f, 643
  determinants of, 538–540
Short-run macroeconomic equilibrium,
    541, 541f
Short-run production costs, 178–183
  average, 181–182
  fixed (overhead), 178, 179
  incremental, 179
  marginal, 180, 180t
  short-run cost curves for profit-maximizing
    decisions and, 182–183, 182f
  sunk, 179–182
  variable, 179
Short-run supply curve, in perfect competition,
    205–206, 205f
Short-term borrowing, 599–600
Shutdown point, 204, 204f
Signaling device, human capital as, 330
Silicon Valley, 317
Simon, Herbert, 205
Simple aggregate expenditures model,
    511–518, 512f
  macroeconomic equilibrium in, 512–514
  multiplier and, 514–517, 514f–516f
Simpson, O. J., 261
Simultaneous-move games, 262–265,
    263–265, 264f
  sequential-move games vs., 262–263
Singapore
  island building by, 41
  traffic jams in, 92
Skidelsky, Robert, 71n
Ski Dubai, 333

Skype, 381
Slope
  of linear line, computing, 24, 25f
  of nonlinear curve, computing, 26, 26f
Slovenia, financial crisis in, 658
Smartphones, economic growth and, 38
Smith, Adam, 12, 13, 71, 84, 89, 513, 569
  The Wealth of Nations of, 43, 196
Smith, Stephen, 292n
Smoot-Hawley Act of 1930, 705
SNAP (Supplementary Nutrition Assistance
    Program), mandatory spending for, 558
Socialism, 33
Social networks, 374
Social responsibility
  corporate, 363
  individual, 363–364
Social Security, 402
  benefits under, 602
  mandatory spending for, 558
  national debt and, 577, 685
Sole proprietorships, 170–171
Solvency crises, 620
Sony, 231
Sony PlayStation 3, 382
South Africa, income inequality and poverty
    reduction in, 412
South Korea, saving rate in, 517
South Park (TV show), 224
Soviet Union, former, economy of, 32–33
S&P. *See* Standard & Poor's (S&P)
Spaceport America, 10
SpaceX, 263
Spain, financial crisis in, 657
Specialization, 10
Specific tariffs, 705
Spencer, Roger, 91n
Spending. *See* Aggregate expenditures;
    Consumer spending; Government
    spending; Stimulus package
Spending approach to GDP, 435–437
Spending multiplier, macroeconomic
    equilibrium and, 542–543, 542f
Spillovers. *See* Externalities
Spreading effect, 181, 181f, 182
SRAS. *See* Short-run aggregate supply
    (SRAS) curve
Stagflation, 678
Standard of living, GDP and, 439–443
Standard Oil, 239
Standard & Poor's (S&P), 322, 556
Stanford Digital Library Project, 325
Staples, 267
Starbucks, 117, 254, 317
Star Island, Florida, 316
Sticky wages and prices, 646
Stigler, George, 238, 345
Stimulus package, 522, 556, 564, 568, 673
  failure to lead to inflation, 546
  tax credits in, 564
Stock(s), 323–324
  investment returns and, 598–599
Stock exchanges, 324
  wealth as, 398
Stock market crashes, long-term savings and, 603
Stone, Matt, 224
Stop Tax Haven Abuse Act, 172
Store of value, money as, 589
Strathern, Paul, 13n, 490n
Structural unemployment, 468
Subprime mortgages, 670–672
Subsidies
  as environmental policy, 358
  supply and, 67

Substitutability
  of inputs, elasticity of demand for labor
    and, 288
  price elasticity of demand and, 111
Substitute(s), cross elasticity of demand
    and, 117
Substitute goods, 62
Substitution effect
  aggregate demand curve and, 532
  indifference curves and, 163–164, 164f
  labor supply and, 282
Sunk cost(s), 148–149, 179–182
Sunk cost fallacy, 149
Sun Microsystems, 325
Superstitions, effect on economic decisions, 152
Supplementary Nutrition Assistance Program
    (SNAP), mandatory spending for, 558
Supply, 64–69
  aggregate. *See* Aggregate demand-supply
    (AD/AS) model; Aggregate supply curve
  changes in, changes in quantity supplied vs.,
    67, 67f, 68f
  determinants of, 65–67
  elastic, 119, 120f
  industry, long-run, 210–211, 211f
  inelastic, 119, 120f
  of labor. *See* Labor supply
  law of, 64
  of loanable funds, 592–593, 592f
  of money. *See* Money supply
  price elasticity of, 119–122, 120f
  unitary elastic, 119, 120f
Supply curve, 64–65
  market, 65, 65f
  short-run, in perfect competition,
    205–206, 205f
Supply shocks, monetary policy and, 649
Supply-side fiscal policy, 563
Surpluses, 69–70
  budget, 570
  consumer, 86–87, 88
  producer, 86, 88
  total, 89
Sushi, market for, 84
Sustainable development, 360, 363–364
  corporate social responsibility and, 363
  individual social responsibility and,
    363–364
  promoting, 363
Sustainable energy resources, 168
Sweden
  innovation in, 332
  saving rate in, 517
Swiss bank accounts, 621
Switching costs, 383
Switzerland
  purchasing power parity and, 727
  saving rate in, 517
Sycamore, Illinois, parking meters in, 453

T
TAA. *See* Trade Adjustment Assistance (TAA)
    program
Taft-Hartley Act, 297
Taiwan, lucky and unlucky numbers in, 152
TANF (Temporary Assistance to Needy
    Families), mandatory spending for, 558
Target, Walmart and, 268
Tariffs, 705–706, 705f, 706f
Tar-Pimlico River, 357
TARP (Troubled Asset Relief Program), 672
Tastes. *See* Preference(s)
Taxation, government's bias away from,
    568–569

Taxes
   ad valorem, 705
   in aggregate expenditures model,
     519–521, 519f
   changes in, equilibrium and, 519–520,
     520t, 521f
   consumption and saving and, 508
   cuts in, 558–559
   discretionary fiscal policy and, 559–560
   effect on market, 124, 124f
   elasticity and, 125, 125f, 126f, 127–128
   flat, 123, 123t, 127
   on gasoline, 126
   incidence of taxation and, 123
   on income sources, 123, 123t
   of inputs, short-run aggregate supply
     and, 540
   lump-sum, 123
   progressive, 123, 123t
   regressive, 123, 123t, 127
   sales, 127
   on spending, 123
   supply and, 67
Taxi and Limousine Commission, 230
Taxi medallions, 230
Tax rates, reducing, fiscal policy and,
   564–565, 565f
Taylor rule, federal funds targeting and, 651–
   652, 652f
T-bills, 570
Teamsters, 296
Teaser strategies, 383
Technological change
   economic growth and, 38, 40, 41f, 490
   investment demand and, 510
   shifts in demand for loanable funds and, 594
Technology(ies)
   disruptive, 210
   government R&D and grants for, 493
   long-run production costs and, 186
   production, supply and, 65–66, 66f
Telecommunications industry, 30
Temin, Peter, 735
Temporary Assistance to Needy Families
   (TANF), mandatory spending for, 558
Tencent, 254
Term auction facilities, 629
Terms of trade, 703–708
   determining, 703–704, 703f
   impact of trade and, 704
   tariffs and quotas and, 705–707, 705f, 706f
Tesla, 168
Textile industry, 704
Thailand, purchasing power parity and, 727
Thatcher, Margaret, 646
Third-degree price discrimination, 232, 234–
   235, 235f
Ticketmaster, 236
Tight money, 650
Tilly, Chris, 416
Timberlake, Justin, 378
Time. *See also* Long run; Short run
   consequences of climate change and,
     361–362
   overvaluing the present relative to the future
     and, 150
   price elasticity of demand and, 111, 111t
   price elasticity of supply and, 120–122
Time periods, 111
Time series graphs, 20, 21f
Timing lags
   fiscal policy and, 568
   monetary policy and, 628–629
Timor-Leste, U.S. dollar as currency of, 736, 738

Tipping, 151
Tipping point, 379
Tit-for-tat strategy, 270–271
Tokyo Disneyland, 75
Total cost, 171
   average, 181, 182, 182f, 183
Total factor productivity, 490–491
Total product, 175, 176f, 176t
Total revenue (*TR*), 171
   elasticity and, 114–116, 115t, 116f
   loss leaders to generate, 118
   in perfect competition, 200
Total surplus, 89
Total utility, 142, 142t
Toyota, 117, 168, 702, 707
Toyota Prius, 109
TR. See Total revenue (*TR*)
Tradable permits, 357–358, 358f, 359
Trade. *See also* Exports; Imports; International
   trade; Net exports; Terms of trade
   free. *See* Free trade
   gains from, 45–46, 45t, 46t
   practical constraints on, 46
Trade Adjustment Assistance (TAA) program, 710
Trade disputes, Prisoner's Dilemma and, 269
Tradeoffs, 2
   between risk and return, 598
Trade restriction, 705–707, 705f, 706f
Trader Joe's, 73
Traffic congestion, congestion charges and, 92
Tragedy of the commons, 349–351, 350f
Transaction costs, reduction by financial
   institutions, 596
Transfer payments, 402
   current account and, 725
   discretionary fiscal policy and, 560–561
Transparency, Federal Reserve System and,
   653–654
Traveler's checks, 590n
Treasury bills, 570
Treasury notes, 570
A Treatise on the Family (Becker), 291
Trembling hand trigger, 270
Trigger strategies, 270–271
Troubled Asset Relief Program (TARP), 672
True Religion, 256
Truman, Harry S., 7
Trusts, 238–239
Truth or Consequences, New Mexico, 10
Tsukiji fish market, 84
Turkey, public debt of, 574
Turkmenistan, economic growth of, 480
The 20/20 Experience (album), 378
Two-Buck Chuck, 73

U

UAW, 296
Uber, 465
Underemployed workers, 465
Underwater cities, 41
Unemployed people, 462–463
Unemployment, 450, 460–471
   cyclical, 468
   definition and measurement of, 461–463
   employment trends and, 464
   frictional, 467–468
   historical record of, 460–461, 461f, 462t
   jobless recoveries and, 428, 470–471,
     683–685, 683f, 684f
   low, goal of, 13
   monthly employment surveys and, 463
   Phillips curves and. *See* Phillips curves
   problems with statistics and, 464–466
   structural, 468

Unemployment Insurance Weekly Claims
   Report, 464
Unemployment rate, 450, 452
   changes in, 469–470, 469f
   differences in, 471
   employment related to, 464
   natural, 468–470, 469f
Unions, 295–299
   benefits and costs of membership in, 296
   history of, 296–298
   pensions and, 297
   types of, 296
   union vs. nonunion wage differentials and,
     298–299, 298f
   wage differentials and, 298–299, 298f
Unitary elastic demand, 110, 110f
   total revenue and, 114–115, 115f
Unitary elastic supply, 119, 120f
United Airlines, 252, 271
United Arab Emirates
   island building by, 41
   ski resort in, 333
United Kingdom
   public debt of, 574
   saving rate in, 517
United Nations Climate Change Conference, 364
United States
   automobile industry of, 673
   balance of payments of, 724–725, 724t
   capital-to-labor ratio in, 489
   cartels in, 258
   comparative advantage of, 47
   currency of. *See* U.S. dollar
   debt rating of, 556
   economic growth of, 480, 687
   efforts to combat climate change in, 364
   exports and imports of, 696, 698f
   express lanes in, 92
   Gini coefficient in, 412
   greenhouse gases produced by, 362
   housing market in, 668, 670–672
   hyperinflation during Revolutionary War
     and, 458
   inflation in, 450, 452, 544, 545f, 546, 547f
   NAFTA and, 46, 702, 711
   oil production in, 259
   public debt of, 574
   public education in, 493
   quotas on Japanese automobile
     imports of, 707
   saving rate in, 517
   tariffs of, 705, 705f
   textile industry in, 704
   unemployment in, 450, 452, 471
U.S. dollar
   as currency of other countries, 621, 638, 658,
     659, 736, 738
   dollar coins and, 589
   pegging of OPEC nations' currencies to, 735
United States Postal Service, 223, 231
Unit of account, money as, 589
Universal Studios, 71
Universities, financial aid and, 493
University of Michigan, 295
University of Michigan Panel Study of Income
   Dynamics, 416
Unpaid family workers, 462
User-managed resources, 362
Utility, 142–145
   marginal. *See* Marginal utility; Marginal
     utility analysis
   maximizing, 143, 144t, 145
   preferences and, 142–145
   total, 142, 142t

Utility industries, as natural monopolists, 223
Utility-maximizing rule, 145
Utility theory (utilitarianism), 138, 141, 142–145

V

Vaccinations, 352
Valdez, Juan, 209
Value of the marginal product (VMP_L), 286, 287f
Variable costs, 179
    average, 181, 182, 182f
Vazquez, José, 330
Venezuela, fuel prices in, 126
Venture capital, 324–325
Verizon, 117, 268, 372, 387
Versioning, 384
Vesting period, 601
Vicious cycle, 380, 381
Vietnam
    economic growth of, 687
    lucky and unlucky numbers in, 152
Virgin Galactic, 10, 263, 314
Virgin Group, 314
Virtual networks, 374
Virtuous cycle, 379, 381
Visa, 254
VMP_L. *See* Value of the marginal product (VMP_L)
Volcker, Paul, 679
Von Bechtolsheim, Andreas (Andy), 325
VOW to Hire Heroes Act, 685

W

Wage(s), 33
    in alternative jobs, labor supply changes and, 284
    efficiency wage theory and, 681
    foreign, low, as argument against free trade, 709–710
    Phillips curves and, 675–676, 676f, 677f
    sticky, 646
Wage differentials, union vs. nonunion, 298–299, 298f
Wagner Act, 296, 297
Walgreens, 227
Walmart, 12, 186, 211, 220
    Target and, 268
Warsh, David, 91n
Waze, 220
Wealth, 398
    consumption and saving and, 508
    of nations, explanation for, 14
Wealth effect, aggregate demand and, 533
The Wealth of Nations (Smith), 43, 196
Weekly Jobs Report, 464
Welfare programs, 402
Wendy's, 250
West Point, Georgia, Kia Motors in, 508, 509
Whooping cough, 352
Wilkinson, Nick, 271n
Willingness-to-pay (WTP), 57–58, 58f
    consumer and producer surplus and, 87
Willingness-to-sell (WTS), consumer and producer surplus and, 87

Winch, Donald, 490n
Withdrawals, 513–515, 514f, 515f
Withrow, Chris, 280
WNBA, 222
Women, employment discrimination against, 292
Wooldridge, Adrian, 171n
WordPerfect, 372
Words with Friends, 59
World Bank, 735
World Trade Organization agreements, 711
Wozniak, Steve, 171, 321
Wrangler, 256
WTP. *See* Willingness-to-pay (WTP)
WTS. *See* Willingness-to-sell (WTS)
Wynn, Steve, 152

X

X-inefficiency, 230

Y

Yahoo!, 220
Yellow dog contracts, 296
Yergin, Daniel, 349n
Yield, of a bond, 322
Yield curve, 430, 430f
YouTube, 220

Z

Zenith, 704
Zimbabwe, hyperinflation in, 458
Zuckerberg, Mark, 9, 173, 261, 321